Mr. WILLIAM

SHAKESPEARES

COMEDIES,
HISTORIES, &
TRAGEDIES.

Published according to the True Originall Copies.

Martin Droeshout sculpsit London.

LONDON

Printed by Isaac Iaggard, and Ed. Blount. 1623.

Frontispiece to the First Folio (1623). By permission of the Folger Shakespeare Library.

ISSN 0883-9123

3 1705 00357 8835

Volume 10

shakespearean criticism

Excerpts from the Criticism of
William Shakespeare's Plays and Poetry,
from the First Published Appraisals
to Current Evaluations

James E. Person, Jr
Sandra L. Williamson
Editors

Lawrence J. Trudeau
Associate Editor

Gale Research Inc.

DETROIT • NEW YORK • FORT LAUDERDALE • LONDON

Contents

Preface

The works of William Shakespeare have delighted audiences and inspired scholars for nearly four hundred years. Shakespeare's appeal is universal, for his work evokes a timeless insight into the human condition.

The vast amount of Shakespearean criticism is a testament to his enduring popularity. Critics of each epoch have contributed to this legacy, responding to the comments of earlier essayists, bringing the moral and intellectual atmosphere of their own era to the works, and suggesting interpretations that continue to inspire critics today.

Scope of the Work

Shakespearean Criticism (SC) serves as an introduction for the student of Shakespeare to his plays and non-dramatic poems and to the most significant commentators on these works. Since the criticism of Shakespeare's canon spans four centuries and is larger in size and scope than that of any other author, an extraordinary amount of critical material confronts the student. For that reason, *SC* presents significant passages from the most important published criticism to aid students in their study of Shakespeare. Typically, each volume of *SC* contains essays from more than thirty-five periodicals and 130 books, many of which are not widely available or are no longer in print. The need for *SC* was suggested by the usefulness of Gale's companion literary series: *Contemporary Literary Criticism (CLC), Twentieth-Century Literary Criticism (TCLC), Nineteenth-Century Literature Criticism (NCLC), Literature Criticism from 1400 to 1800 (LC),* and *Classical and Medieval Literature Criticism (CMLC).*

Nine volumes of the series are devoted to aesthetic criticism of the plays. Performance criticism will be treated in separate volumes. Other special volumes will be devoted to such topics as the authorship controversy, the apocrypha, and such general subjects as Shakespeare's language, religious and philosophical thought, and characterization. The first nine volumes contain criticism on three to six plays, with a mixture of genres and balance of plays based on their critical importance. Volume 10 contains criticism on the non-dramatic poems: *The Phoenix and Turtle, The Rape of Lucrece,* the Sonnets, and *Venus and Adonis.*

The length of each entry represents the amount of critical attention the play or poem has received from critics writing in English and from foreign criticism in translation. Each entry represents a historical overview of the critical response to the play or poem. Early criticism is presented to indicate initial responses and later selections represent significant trends in the history of criticism of that work. Seminal essays on each play or poem by the most important Shakespearean critics are identified and excerpted. The series is directed to secondary school, undergraduate, and graduate students. *SC* is not a work for the specialist, but a survey of the critical commentary on Shakespeare's works for both the novice and the advanced student.

Organization of the Book

Each entry consists of the following elements: an introduction, excerpts of criticism (each followed by a full bibliographical citation), and an additional bibliography for further reading.

The *introduction* begins with a discussion of the date, text, and sources of the work under review. This section is followed by a critical history, which outlines the major critical trends and identifies the prominent commentators on the play or poem.

Criticism is arranged chronologically within each entry to provide a perspective on the changes in evaluation over the years. For purposes of easier identification, the critic's name and the date of the essay are given at the beginning of each piece. For an unsigned essay whose authorship can be determined, the critic's name appears in brackets at the beginning of the excerpt and in the bibliographical citation. Within the text of the criticism, some parenthetical information (such as publisher names, journal titles, footnotes, or page references) has been deleted to provide smoother reading of the text. Also, whenever necessary, act, scene, and line designations have been changed to conform to *The Riverside Shakespeare,* published by Houghton Mifflin Company, which is a standard text used in many high school and college English classes.

All of the individual essays are preceded by *explanatory notes* as an additional aid to students using *SC.* The explanatory notes provide several types of useful information, including the importance of the critics in literary history, the critical schools with which they are identified, and the importance of their comments on Shakespeare and the work discussed. The explanatory notes also summarize the commentary and furnish previous publication information, such as original title and date, for reprinted and translated publications.

A complete *bibliographical citation* designed to facilitate the location of the original essay or book follows each piece of criticism.

Within each entry are *illustrations,* such as facsimiles of title pages taken from the quarto, First Folio, and other editions of the plays and poems, as well as pictures drawn from such sources as early editions of the collected works and artists' renderings of some of the famous scenes and characters. The captions following each illustration indicate act, scene, characters, and the artist and date, if known.

The *additional bibliography* appearing at the end of each entry suggests further reading on the play or poem. This section includes references to the major discussions of the date, the text, and the sources of each work. The principal arguments of each essay listed here are summarized in annotations.

Additional Features

A *list of plays and poems* covered in the series follows the Preface. This listing indicates which works are treated in existing or future volumes.

To help students locate essays by specific commentators, *SC* includes a *cumulative index to critics.* Under each critic's name are listed the plays and non-dramatic poems on which the critic has written and the volume and page where the commentary begins.

SC also provides a *cumulative index to topics.* This feature identifies the principal topics of debate in the criticism of each work. The topics are arranged alphabetically, and the initial page number is indicated for each excerpt that offers innovative or substantial commentary on that topic.

As an additional aid to students, *SC* offers a *glossary* of terms relating to date, text, and source information frequently mentioned by critics and used throughout the introductions to the play or poem entries. The glossed terms and source names are identified by small capital letters when they first appear in the introductions.

An *acknowledgments* section listing the sources from which material in the volume is reprinted follows the list of plays and poems. This section does not, however, record every book or periodical consulted for the volume.

Suggestions Are Welcome

The editors encourage comments and suggestions from readers to expand the coverage and enhance the usefulness of the series. In response to various recommendations, several features have been added to *SC* since the series began, including the list of plays and poems covered in each volume, the glossary, and the topic index. Readers are cordially invited to write the editors or call our toll-free number: 1-800-347-GALE.

Acknowledgments

The editors wish to thank the copyright holders of the excerpted criticism included in this volume, the permissions managers of many book and magazine publishing companies for assisting us in securing reprint rights, and Anthony Bogucki for assistance with copyright research. We are also grateful to the staffs of the Detroit Public Library, the Library of Congress, the University of Detroit Library, the University of Michigan Library, and the Wayne State University Library for making their resources available to us. Following is a list of the copyright holders who have granted us permission to reprint material in this volume of *SC*. Every effort has been made to trace copyright, but if omissions have been made, please let us know.

List of Plays and Poems Covered in *SC*

[The year or years in parentheses indicate the composition date of the
work as determined by G. Blakemore Evans in *The Riverside Shakespeare*]

Volume 1

The Comedy of Errors (1592-94)
Hamlet (1600-01)
1 and *2 Henry IV* (1596-98)
Timon of Athens (1607-08)
Twelfth Night (1601-02)

Volume 2

Henry VIII (1612-13)
King Lear (1605)
Love's Labour's Lost (1594-95)
Measure for Measure (1604)
Pericles (1607-08)

Volume 3

1, 2, and *3 Henry VI* (1589-91)
Macbeth (1606)
A Midsummer Night's Dream (1595-96)
Troilus and Cressida (1601-02)

Volume 4

Cymbeline (1609-10)
The Merchant of Venice (1596-97)
Othello (1604)
Titus Andronicus (1593-94)

Volume 5

As You Like It (1599)
Henry V (1599)
The Merry Wives of Windsor (1597)
Romeo and Juliet (1595-96)

Volume 6

Antony and Cleopatra (1606-07)
Richard II (1595)
The Two Gentlemen of Verona (1594)

Volume 7

All's Well That Ends Well (1602-03)
Julius Caesar (1599)
The Winter's Tale (1610-11)

Volume 8

Much Ado about Nothing (1598-99)
Richard III (1592-93)
The Tempest (1611)

Volume 9

Coriolanus (1607-08)
King John (1594-96)
The Taming of the Shrew (1593-94)
The Two Noble Kinsmen (1613)

Volume 10

The Phoenix and Turtle (1601)
The Rape of Lucrece (1593-94)
Sonnets (1593-99)
Venus and Adonis (1592-93)

Forthcoming

Plays in Performance
Volume 11: *King Lear*
Othello
Romeo and Juliet

The Phoenix and Turtle

DATE: In 1601, a poem dedicated to a patron of the arts, Sir John Salusbury, and entitled *Love's Martyr, or Rosalin's Complaint: Allegorically Shadowing the Truth of Love in the Constant Fate of the Phoenix and Turtle* by Robert Chester, was published in a volume that also included poems signed by Ben Jonson, George Chapman, John Marston, and William Shakespeare. According to the editor of the New Variorum edition of Shakespeare's poems, Hyder Rollins (see Additional Bibliography), the "majority of scholars" believe Shakespeare's contribution to the volume, *The Phoenix and Turtle,* was composed for this occasion in 1600 or 1601. More recently, M. C. Bradbrook (see her first entry in the Additional Bibliography) and F. T. Prince, the editor of the new Arden Shakespeare, cited only 1601 in connection with the poem, which would imply that they agree the publication and composition dates more or less coincide. In addition, many twentieth-century critics—including John Middleton Murry, Daniel Seltzer, Ronald Bates, Heinrich Straumann, K. T. S. Campbell, and Murray Copland—have drawn parallels between elements in the poem and aspects of the mature tragedies, suggesting that *The Phoenix and Turtle* immediately preceded such works as *Hamlet* (1601).

Critics who diverge from this consensus typically cite internal evidence to support their assertions. In 1893 the German critic Alfred von Mauntz dated the poem 1595-1596, and later he suggested 1593; however, Rollins found his reasons "purely fanciful." Frederick Boas posited no specific composition date, but his remarks linking the poem with Shakespeare's "early lyrical manner" imply a composition date before 1600. Some twentieth-century commentators have also proposed that the *The Phoenix and Turtle* was written prior to 1600. For example, Kenneth Muir and Sean O'Loughlin argued that Chester composed *Love's Martyr* sometime in the mid-1590s in celebration of Sir John Salusbury's marriage; however, they were ambiguous about similarly ascribing an earlier composition date to Shakespeare's poem. William Empson argued that Chester's entire volume must have been ready for publication prior to the War of the Theaters in 1599-1602, a time during which many of the contributing authors were feuding and unlikely to have cooperated in this venture. Thus, Empson claimed 1598 or early 1599 as a likely composition date (see Additional Bibliography). Most recently, in accord with his allegorical interpretation of *The Phoenix and Turtle,* William Matchett theorized that Shakespeare wrote the poem when it became clear there was no hope of a reconciliation between Queen Elizabeth and the Earl of Essex (the presumed allegorical correspondences to the Phoenix and Turtle). Although Matchett conceded that he could only speculate about a date, perhaps 1599, when Shakespeare became aware of Essex's likely fate, he contended that this realization precipitated the composition of *The Phoenix and Turtle* (see Additional Bibliography).

TEXT: Robert Chester's *Love's Martyr,* with appended poems signed by the authors, was published in London by Edward Blount in 1601. Ten years later, the original sheets of Chester's volume were reissued by a new publisher, Mat-

LOVES MARTYR:
OR,
ROSALINS COMPLAINT.

Allegorically shadowing the truth of Loue,
in the constant Fate of the Phœnix
and Turtle.

A Poeme enterlaced with much varietie and raritie;
now first translated out of the venerable Italian Torquato
Cæliano, by Robert Chester.

With the true legend of famous King *Arthur,* the last of the nine
Worthies, being the first *Essay* of a new *Brytish* Poet: collected
out of diuerse Authenticall Records.

*To these are added some new compositions, of seuerall moderne Writers
whose names are subscribed to their seuerall workes, vpon the
first subiect: viz. the* Phœnix and
Turtle.

Mar: — Mutare dominum non potest liber notus.

LONDON
Imprinted for E. B.
1601.

Quasifacsimile title page of the 1601 edition of Loves Martyr.

thew Lownes, with a revised title page. The text of 1601 is generally accepted as the sole authority for *The Phoenix and Turtle.* The poem, originally untitled, appeared throughout the seventeenth, eighteenth, and nineteenth centuries in various editions of Shakespeare's verse. It did not receive a heading until 1807, when two editions published in Boston titled it *The Phoenix and the Turtle.* One of the most influential of the early editors, Edmund Malone, included the poem in the collection known as *The Passionate Pilgrim* and referred to it by number: XX in his 1790 edition and XVIII in his edition of 1821. Subsequent editors have either followed Malone's precedent or adopted the title proposed by the Boston editors, sometimes omitting the second article and sometimes eliding both.

In general, scholars accept the authenticity of *The Phoenix and Turtle.* However, in its first phase of prolonged critical attention during the late nineteenth and early twentieth centuries, there were a handful of skeptics. In 1877, F. J. Furnivall declared that the poem was "no doubt spurious" (see Additional Bibliography) and Edward Dowden called Shakespeare's authorship "in high degree doubtful." Both critics were later reported as having recanted their doubts. Sidney Lee, in his *A Life of William Shakespeare* (1898), referred to *The Phoenix and Turtle* as Shakespeare's "alleged contribution" to Chester's volume. In 1931, Ranjee Shahani praised *The Phoenix and Turtle* at length in a monograph entitled *Towards the Stars*. Although in this work he attributed the poem to John Fletcher, he later abandoned this position in favor of Shakespearean authorship. A few years later, Bernard Newdigate expressed the reaction of many scholars when they first encounter *The Phoenix and Turtle:* "The lines on the Phoenix and Turtle which are printed over Shakespeare's name . . . seem so remote in sentiment, language and manner from nearly everything else that he wrote that they would have been rejected from the Shakespeare canon were it not for the evidence of authenticity presented by the book in which they were printed" (see Additional Bibliography). The poem's diction, style, and emotional intensity appear at first entirely foreign and without precedent in Shakespeare's work. However, the external evidence of authenticity, the author's signature below the printed text of the poem in the first edition, is usually considered utterly persuasive if not irrefutable. Although the question of authorship continues to be raised by a few critics, in the past fifty years the vast majority of scholars have granted the poem's authenticity.

SOURCES: Identifying literary sources for a particular poem is an infinite process that often sparks critical contention. *The Phoenix and Turtle* is no exception to this principle. Its allusions, style, themes, diction, and conceits have prompted scholars to enumerate a wide range of literary antecedents from the classical through the Renaissance and Elizabethan ages. Although a few critics have proposed their candidates as definite sources, most have more tentatively suggested certain works as possible parallels to or influences on Shakespeare's poem.

W. F. Wigston, writing in 1884, was apparently the earliest commentator to note the influence of Plato's philosophy on *The Phoenix and Turtle*'s central paradox regarding the spiritual union of lovers. Many subsequent critics including Arthur H. R. Fairchild, J. V. Cunningham, Murray Copland, Vincent F. Petronella, John Arthos, and Richard Wilbur (see Additional Bibliography), have also discussed the poem's Platonic and Neoplatonic elements. In 1893, the German critic Alfred von Mauntz was the first to suggest a parallel with OVID, specifically citing the Roman poet's parrot elegy. Later in that decade, Sidney Lee suggested that the poem may derive from Matthew Roydon's elegy on Sir Philip Sidney, first printed in a poetical miscellany *The Phoenix Nest* (1593). Many scholars have adopted and elaborated on Lee's suggestion. For example, in 1937 Muir and O'Loughlin also cited Roydon's elegy as a possible source. In addition, they suggested that "An excellent Dialogue between Constancie and Inconstancie," from the same collection, is another possible source, noting similarities in language and conceits between this poem and Shakespeare's and calling particular attention to a line in the earlier work: "Love hath reason, Reason none." In the 1960s, Robert Ellrodt cited Roydon's elegy as a potential influence (see Additional Bibliography), and Matchett applied the Roydon theory to the third section of *The Phoenix and Turtle,* the Threnos, which, he noted, is rarely discussed in terms of literary precedents.

Another literary antecedent was identified by Fairchild, who asserted that *The Phoenix and Turtle* "belongs to that class of poems connected with the institution (real or otherwise)

known as the Court of Love. It has a two-fold source, stanzas (I-V) especially being suggested by Chaucer's poem *The Parlement of Foules;* the remaining stanzas (VI-XVIII) being adapted to these from the emblem literature and conceptions of Shakespeare's period." Many critics, including Carleton Brown (see Additional Bibliography) and M. C. Bradbrook, also have discerned an allusion to Chaucer and an emulation of Court of Love poetry in Shakespeare's poem.

The identification of Shakespeare's source for the phoenix myth has provoked considerable scholarly debate. Various writers have speculated whether Shakespeare drew his Phoenix from Pliny's depiction in the *Natural History*. In contrast, Osbert Sitwell (see Additional Bibliography) suggested that Shakespeare's knowledge of the phoenix legend and "the sole Arabian tree" (1.2) derived from the *Travels of Marco Polo,* first translated into English in 1579 by John Frampton; his suggestion, however, has garnered no adherents. T. W. Baldwin, on the other hand, proposed that Shakespeare's chief sources for the Phoenix were Erasmus's translations of Ovid and Lactantius (see Additional Bibliography). Ellrodt conducted a comprehensive study of the phoenix legend as a literary conceit from the classical period, through the Renaissance, and up to the Elizabethan age. He discovered many possible influences on Shakespeare's poem, including Roydon's elegy and Donne's *The First Anniversary* (1611), as well as Lactantius, Claudianus, Michelangelo, Drayton, Petrarch, Edward Dyer, William Smith, Thomas Lodge, and Giles Fletcher. Ultimately, however, Ellrodt's study showed that the phoenix legend was common knowledge and Shakespeare needed no special access or literary antecedent to assist him in his own depiction. Ellrodt concluded that Shakespeare's principal source was Chester's *Love's Martyr,* although even here, he noted, Shakespeare's treatment of the phoenix myth is unique.

Several commentators have called attention to parallels between *The Phoenix and Turtle* and John Donne's metaphysical verse. In 1923, Joseph Quincy Adams remarked that Shakespeare's poem is "a graceful funeral song . . . in the metaphysical style of John Donne." The comparison first proposed by Adams became a point of contention for later critics. Among those who accepted the parallel with Donne are Cleanth Brooks—who cited Donne's *Canonization* (1635)—G. Wilson Knight (see his first entry in the Additional Bibliography), Seltzer, Copland, and Empson. Empson, however, attenuated the link, stating that the poem "depends on the same ideas as Donne's *First Anniversary* [1611], but gets very different feelings out of them." Some critics have pointed out important distinctions between the two poets or even rejected the comparison entirely. For example, C. S. Lewis judged that Shakespeare "is not writing 'metaphysical poetry' in the technical sense critics give to that term, but he is writing in the true sense, a metaphysical poem." Similarly, A. Alvarez asserted that the poem attains the very metaphysical heights that other so-called "Metaphysical poetry" proposes but fails to reach. Prince wholly rejected the comparison, declaring that "Nothing could in fact be further from the methods of Donne's love-poetry than the method of this poem." Prince, in fact, denied there were any explicit external sources other than the most proximate, that is, Chester's *Love's Martyr* itself.

The stream of source theories has also yielded a number of less obvious parallels and influences. To the list of contemporary poets whose work is analogous to or possibly a source of *The Phoenix and Turtle,* Matchett added one other: Nicholas Breton and his *Britton's Bowre of Delights* (1591). In 1979, Brian Green proposed that the language of alchemy infused *The Phoenix and Turtle* and that the alchemical process itself served as the model for the poem's structure (see Additional Bibliography). Recently, Alur Janakiram discerned a resemblance between *The Phoenix and Turtle* and the Italian philosopher Leone Ebreo's *Dialoghi d'amore* (1535) (see Additional Bibliography). And finally, in 1981, Roy Eriksen attempted to show the influence of the Italian poet-philosopher Giordano Bruno, specifically his *De gli eroici furori* (1585), on Shakespeare's poem (see Additional Bibliography).

CRITICAL HISTORY: Critical reaction to Shakespeare's *The Phoenix and Turtle* has ranged from disdain to effusive admiration and praise. In his ten-volume edition of the works of Shakespeare published in 1899-1904, the respected English scholar and critic Charles H. Herford dismissed the poem as "a trifle thrown off at the urgency of a resolute Album-maker." In contrast, in 1922, the eminent Shakespearean scholar John Middleton Murry categorically asserted that *The Phoenix and Turtle* was "the most perfect short poem in any language." The majority of scholars have sided with Murry and his more favorable appraisal. However, the diversity of critical opinion attests to the complexity of ideas in the poem and reflects the multifaceted nature of *The Phoenix and Turtle.* As Heinrich Straumann first observed in his *Phönix und Taube; zur Interpretation von Shakespeare's Gedankenwelt* (1953), critical theories regarding the poem can be divided into roughly three categories or approaches: positivist, formalist, and idealist. The positivist approach includes those theories that provide an allegorical interpretation for the poem. According to adherents of this method, the key to the poem will be found through biographical and historical investigation. Proponents of the formalist approach interpret the poem within the context of its presumed genre and investigate the literary traditions and conventions that may have influenced Shakespeare's composition. The idealist category represents those critics who either address the poem in terms of its own themes, without consideration of any literary or historical context, or within the thematic context of Shakespeare's dramatic works. This is not to suggest that individual commentators have confined themselves to a single approach. On the contrary, many scholars necessarily move between categories, another indication, perhaps, of the poem's complexity. Within this critical framework, scholars have also frequently alluded to two questions: whether the Phoenix in Shakespeare's poem is immortal (as tradition holds) or dies leaving no issue; and whether by virtue of its metaphysical nature this work is comparable to the poetry of John Donne.

The earliest critical interpretations of *The Phoenix and Turtle* appeared in the last quarter of the nineteenth century. In 1875, one of the most prominent literary figures of the time, Ralph Waldo Emerson, issued a challenge to fellow poets and critics to explicate *The Phoenix and Turtle.* Emerson sought critical attention to help illuminate the "frame and allusions" of Shakespeare's poem, intimating that historical and biographical research would assist in interpretation. He not only rescued *The Phoenix and Turtle* from obscurity, but through his praise of the poem's technical merits inspired scholars of diverse critical philosophies to study Shakespeare's long-forgotten poem.

The first critic to answer Emerson's challenge was Alexander B. Grosart (see Additional Bibliography), who proceeded from the suggestion proposed by Emerson that the poem's "frame and allusions," if discovered, would provide the key to understanding *The Phoenix and Turtle.* Thus he analyzed the poem in its original context as one of the verses appended to Robert Chester's *Love's Martyr or Rosalin's Complaint.* In Grosart's estimation, to pierce the veil of personal allegory that hung over *The Phoenix and Turtle,* one must return to Chester's poem, a self-professed allegory, and assume that the correspondences there would pertain to all the poems collected in the volume. Grosart attempted to resolve several questions, including: Who was Robert Chester? Who was Sir John Salusbury? Whom did the Phoenix and Turtle allegorically represent? What is the "message or motif" of these poems? What is the relation between *Love's Martyr* and the other poems, including *The Phoenix and Turtle*? Are these good poems? Over time, many of Grosart's resolutions have been refuted, modified, or more elaborately detailed; however, his work is important as a departure point for subsequent criticism, as critics invariably chose one or more of these very questions as the focal point of their own studies.

Grosart identified Robert Chester as a knight and patron of the arts who was a "follower not to say partizan of Essex," once a political ally and possibly a lover of Queen Elizabeth, who turned rebel and was beheaded. Grosart further contended that the country squire and patron of the arts, Sir John Salusbury, to whom *Love's Martyr* was dedicated, was actually a dependent in the service of Sir Robert Chester. To support his allegorical interpretation, Grosart pointed to the explicitness of the subtitle of Chester's poem: *Allegorically shadowing the truth of love in the constant fate of the Phoenix and Turtle.* He also argued that the language and imagery that Chester employed to describe the Phoenix was common parlance in discussions of Elizabeth and that it would be both improper and imprudent to speak of any other woman in such a manner as long as the Queen lived. As for the identification of the Turtle, Grosart relied principally on the internal evidence of *Love's Martyr* and the appended poems to show that Chester had in mind the Earl of Essex. Having established the allegorical references, Grosart presented the "message" of Chester's poem. In essence, he claimed that in this work Chester mourns the failure of the relationship between Elizabeth and Essex, and the critic joined the poet in chiding the Queen for executing her rebellious lover. In response to the question of the relationship between Shakespeare's *The Phoenix and Turtle* and the other poems in Chester's volume, Grosart contended that Shakespeare was a member of the chorus of Essex loyalists. He further proposed that the allegorical references he established for *Love's Martyr* apply equally to *The Phoenix and Turtle.* "Let the reader take with him the golden key that by the 'Phoenix' Shakespeare intended Elizabeth, and by the 'Dove' Essex, and the 'Phoenix and Turtle,' hitherto regarded as a mere enigmatical epicedial lay . . . will be recognized as of rarest interest."

Although very little of Grosart's allegorical interpretation has endured, he helped draw critical attention to Shakespeare's long-overlooked poem, and deeply influenced the path that criticism of *The Phoenix and Turtle* would take over the next century. However, in 1879, F. J. Furnivall unequivocally rejected Grosart's theory on the grounds that it distorts historical chronology to maintain the allegory (see Additional Bibliography). Furnivall asked scholars "to be cautious in accepting the theory, as at present develort, that the Phoenix and Turtle are Elizabeth and Essex, for it may lead them into the mixture of the man who next week went last month to find a mare's nest." Although Grosart's Eliza-beth-Essex allegorical theory attracted little praise and con-siderable ridicule, critical suspicions that interpretation of *The Phoenix and Turtle* relied on allegorical revelation did not subside. In 1898, Sidney Lee expressed the frustration that many late nineteenth-century critics experienced when they confronted *The Phoenix and Turtle:* he questioned the authenticity of the poem and raised a series of possible inter-pretations based on allegory and historical events that ap-peared hopelessly irretrievable. Carleton Brown, in his 1913 introduction to the *Poems by Sir John Salusbury and Robert Chester* (see Additional Bibliography), revived the allegorical debate and refuted Grosart's references, arguing that Grosart misidentified Chester and erroneously conferred the title of knight on this modest Welsh poet. Whereas Grosart had pos-ited that Salusbury was Chester's dependent, Brown showed that Salusbury was Chester's patron. Further, Brown identi-fied Salusbury, to whom *Love's Martyr* is dedicated, as a po-litical opponent of the Essex faction and reasoned that Gro-sart's claim that *Love's Martyr* was dedicated to one of these figures and yet allegorically celebrated the virtues of the other is dubious at best. Brown instead proposed that Chester's poem symbolically represents the marriage of Sir John to Lady Ursula Stanley and that the new Phoenix was their daughter, born in 1586. Although Shakespeare observed Chester's allegory, the critic maintained, "he chose to devel-op his theme along a widely divergent line." Brown admired the poem's "ingenuity and its epigrammatic brilliance," but he also discerned a "frigid and perfunctory tone" indicating that Shakespeare's poem was composed as "a matter of cour-teous compliance rather than a tribute to a personal friend." Brown's allegorical theory went unchallenged until 1936, when Bernard Newdigate proposed a new group of allegori-cal references (see Additional Bibliography). In research for his own introduction to the phoenix poems, Newdigate dis-covered a manuscript version of Ben Jonson's contributory poem to Chester's volume that included an inscription: "To:L:C:off:B." Newdigate claimed this inscription referred to Lucy Countess of Bedford, and the critic deduced that if Jonson dedicated his poem to Lucy Bedford, then so did Shakespeare. Newdigate posited that the poems in Chester's collection address the childless union of the Bedfords six years following their wedding.

After Newdigate, scholars seemed less inclined to apply the allegorical approach; however, subsequent critics occasional-ly offered some biographical or historical material intended to corroborate the allegorical theories already proposed. G. Bonnard, for example, employed a biographical/historical approach to illuminate the circumstances behind the origin of Chester's *Love's Martyr* and the contributions of Shake-speare and the other poets to the volume. The critic argued that Shakespeare and his fellow poets, encumbered with a prescribed theme and Chester's awkward, if not ludicrous, al-legorical apparatus and central conceit—the use of the phoe-nix myth and the depiction of a funeral to celebrate a mar-riage—rebelled and wrote with tongue in cheek; Shakespeare, in particular, he speculated, could not resist making a joke of the logical conclusion of Chester's allegory. In a 1941 essay, Sir Gurney Benham reconsidered the allegorical theo-ries in circulation and concluded that the Phoenix probably stands for Elizabeth in Chester's *Love's Martyr,* but he was dubious about the Essex-Turtle correspondence (see Addi-tional Bibliography). Elizabeth, he pointed out, was thirty-four years older than Essex and, given the proximity of Essex's execution and the publication of *Love's Martyr,* "it

would have been unsafe to represent [Essex] as Love's martyr or any other kind of martyr."

After a hiatus of almost twenty-five years, the positivist ap-proach resurfaced, first in William Matchett's 1965 study of Chester's and Shakespeare's poems, and subsequently in es-says by William Empson, Walter Oakeshott, and Marie Axton. Matchett claimed to have purged himself of the im-pulse to embrace allegorical assumptions; nevertheless he en-dorsed Grosart's Elizabeth-Essex theory of correspondence (see Additional Bibliography), agreeing that *The Phoenix and Turtle* reflects Shakespeare's admiration for the Earl of Essex and his grief over the failure of their alliance. Empson sought a reconciliation of the competing allegorical theories, espe-cially Brown's and Newdigate's, and offered his own recon-struction of the facts and the chronology (see Additional Bib-liography). To account for the Jonson manuscript with the inscription dedicated to the Countess of Bedford, Empson suggested that Jonson may have simply given her an auto-graph copy of the poem he wrote for Salusbury. Oakeshott attempted yet another variation of Grosart's theory, focusing primarily on Chester's *Love's Martyr,* but also discussing the appended poems (see Additional Bibliography). According to Oakeshott, Shakespeare invoked Chester's allegorical ap-paratus not to exalt Elizabeth, as called for by convention, but to honor her association with Essex, who, the critic as-serted, "symbolized, for the writer of the 'Phoenix and Tur-tle,' the embodiment of an age of liberality, artistic brilliance and political triumph." Finally, in 1977, Axton maintained that Shakespeare's verse was "a politically philosophical oc-casional poem" composed in anticipation of "an historical moment of transition," the succession of Elizabeth I (see Ad-ditional Bibliography). Axton argued that Shakespeare adopted the iconography and myths of Elizabethan succes-sion drama, specifically the phoenix, to expound his own thoughts on political theory. In essence, according to Axton, *The Phoenix and Turtle* symbolizes the relationship between monarch and subject, and, perhaps, represents the poet's own view of Elizabeth.

As with Grosart and the allegorists, the formalist approach to *The Phoenix and Turtle* emerged principally from a single, seminal essay—this one published in 1904 by Arthur Fair-child. Before Fairchild, however, J. O. Halliwell-Phillipps and W. F. Wigston alluded to the poem's literary context and antecedents. In his remarks on *The Phoenix and Turtle* in 1882, Halliwell-Phillipps showed little interest in allegorical references, but rather marveled that Shakespeare adopted "for the first and only time" the guise of "a philosophical writer." Two years later, Wigston defined Shakespeare's "philosophical" style as "applied Platonism." In addition to elaborating on the philosophical context of the poem, Wig-ston was the first critic to term *The Phoenix and Turtle* a "metaphysical" poem. Fairchild, however, was the earliest critic to examine a specific literary context or source for Shakespeare's poem. According to Fairchild, *The Phoenix and Turtle* derives principally from two sources, Chaucer's *Parlement of Foules* and from a body of works produced by the fashionable emblem writers, and conforms to a Renais-sance literary vogue known as the Court of Love. The critic discerned no personal or biographical element in the poem, but rather characterized it as a formal exercise, a convention-al rendering of popular Platonic conceptions of love, devoid of ingenuity or wit, and perhaps intended as a valentine poem for Sir John Salusbury.

Subsequent critics who employed the formalist approach to *The Phoenix and Turtle* include Joseph Quincy Adams, J. V. Cunningham, A. Alvarez, Robert Ellrodt, Murry Copland, Peter Dronke, and Vincent Petronella. Although he was not the first critic to comment on the metaphysical style of *The Phoenix and Turtle,* in 1923 Joseph Quincy Adams was the first to compare it with the metaphysical poetry of John Donne. Adams did not specify a particular poem of Donne's as an overt source, but he intimated that Shakespeare and his fellow poets, including Jonson, Marston, and Chapman, adopted the obscure metaphysical language and conceits in order to mock Chester's own obscure and pretentious poem. In 1952, Cunningham observed that the language of *The Phoenix and Turtle* is replete with terms appropriated from Scholastic theology and deduced that Shakespeare superimposed Neoplatonic notions over the material he had borrowed from courtly love poetry. The critic argued that Shakespeare relied on the Scholastic doctrine of love to formulate the central paradox of the poem: the mystical union of the two lovers, whereby two become one to the consternation of Reason. Although this mystical notion of unification through divine love evolved from classical and medieval sources into Christian dogma and the Trinitarian Doctrine, Cunningham asserted that Shakespeare's use of Scholastic terms in their technical sense suggests that the poet's sources for these Neoplatonic ideas were such Christian texts as St. Thomas Aquinas's *Summa Theologica.* According to Cunningham's interpretation of the poem and its central conceit, the Scholastic doctrine of the Trinity underlies the poem's diction and structure and illuminates the mystical union between Phoenix and Turtle. Three years later, Alvarez also discussed Shakespeare's use of Scholastic terminology, balancing the poem's Christian context and its tragic elements. Alvarez argued that Shakespeare employs the logic and language of a formal proof as he pursues "the inner mystery of Love," yet ultimately, as Reason discovers, the highest mysteries of Love are impervious to logic, and can only be approached through "their own metaphysic, religion, logic and their own poetic ritual." In 1962, Robert Ellrodt offered a comprehensive survey of Renaissance and Elizabethan conceptions of the phoenix in order to assess Shakespeare's adaptation of that legend (see Additional Bibliography). Although Ellrodt adopted the formalist approach, he concluded that Shakespeare's use of the phoenix myth was not derivative, but in fact unique: "a modification of the Phoenix myth which implied disbelief in, or at least disregard for, the time-honoured legend." Focusing on another literary context, Murray Copland argued that *The Phoenix and Turtle* represents Shakespeare's "contribution to the fashion of which Donne was the acknowledged leader." The critic called attention to the Platonic theories of love that were current around 1600 and declared that Shakespeare was not only engaging in the metaphysical rhetoric currently in vogue, but even seeking to "outdo all the others in sheer transcendence of transcendentalism." Even the startling image of the Phoenix dead in its nest can be reconciled within the metaphysical tradition of the shock conceit, he pointed out. As did Ellrodt, Dronke sought an interpretation of the poem based on a study of conventional Elizabethan literary thought (see Additional Bibliography). In Dronke's view, the poem is a meditation on the notion of love through a careful, balanced consideration of ideas and paradoxes imported from the realms of literary convention, Neoplatonism, metaphysics, and medieval theology. Although he acknowledged the import of "their tragic scene" (l. 52), the critic argued that a sense of immortality or transcendence survives

the death of the Phoenix and the Turtle, because the poem celebrates the eternal quality of love. In 1975, Petronella asserted that structurally *The Phoenix and Turtle* resembles the procession-rapture-recession triad of the Neoplatonists and reflects the "Orphic tradition of poetic theology" which typically encompassed both serious and lighthearted tones. Thus, he declared, although the poem engages philosophical issues and presents a vision of the apocalypse, it does so with a measure of wit and irony. According to Petronella, *The Phoenix and Turtle* follows in the literary and intellectual fashion of the Elizabethan era; even the dead Phoenix, which some critics cite as Shakespeare's invention, has precedents in Petrarch, Marot, and Spenser, he noted.

The last of the three principal approaches to *The Phoenix and Turtle*—the idealist—stresses the poem's themes and often addresses those motifs within the context of Shakespeare's dramatic works. Idealist interpretations were first advanced in the late nineteenth and early twentieth centuries, often by critics who were poets themselves. In 1879, Sidney Lanier, a distinguished, American poet, called attention to the poem's unusual compression of "complex ideas" and its unique tone of personal withdrawal and intimacy. W. F. Wigston, mentioned above in connection with the early formalist critics, asserted that *The Phoenix and Turtle* is about "Learning, Beauty and Truth," the Ideal that informs all of Shakespeare's art. He further described it as a symbolic rendering of the artist's endeavor: to overcome the duality, the chasm that separates subject and object, the real and ideal, through artistic synthesis. Similarly, in 1902, Charles Downing argued that the Phoenix and the Turtle symbolize, respectively, the ideal (Shakespeare's) and the idealist (the poet himself) (see Additional Bibliography). Downing also pointed out the threefold ideal represented in the poem, "Beauty, Truth and Rarity, Grace in all simplicity" (ll. 53-4), judging it emblematic of the human spirit and noting that this ideal recurs in the Sonnets as well as in Shakespeare's dramatic works. In 1911, the English poet John Masefield interpreted *The Phoenix and Turtle* as a lyrical rendering of spiritual ecstasy, an evocation of thought "too subtle and too intense" for conventional expression. Masefield argued that Shakespeare's intention was to grasp within the constraints of language and dictates of communication the very essence of such abstract notions as truth and beauty. Similarly, John Middleton Murry, in a lecture given in 1922, argued that in *The Phoenix and Turtle,* Shakespeare was trying to express the inexpressible, to translate into symbolic and necessarily abstract and obscure language, the poet's own mystical experience: his vision of "perfect and celestial love." In his tragedies, the critic maintained, Shakespeare sought to convey an other-worldly vision in terms of temporal events and characters. That impulse, according to Murry, underlies *The Phoenix and Turtle,* but Shakespeare was later thwarted and "torn asunder by the effort to express a perception which is not of this world in terms of events and characters which are." The critic proposed that the poem and the tragedies represent a demarcation point between the earlier optimism of the comedies and the deceptive serenity of the romances. In this poem, Murry contended, Shakespeare made no compromises to ensure intelligibility as he strove to express a mystical experience. In this sense, he concluded, *The Phoenix and Turtle* constitutes a rare example of "pure poetry."

Following Murry, the idealist approach gained popularity among such critics as Kenneth Muir and Sean O'Loughlin, C. S. Lewis, Rangee Shahani, Cleanth Brooks, Walter Ong, and K. T. S. Campbell. In 1937, Muir and O'Loughlin, viewing *The Phoenix and Turtle* in relation to Shakespeare's other works, argued that it represents a pivotal point in Shakespeare's art and foreshadows the tragic phase in his drama. Like Murry and others, these critics contended that the poem symbolizes a mystical experience; yet, in contrast to Murry, who argued that Shakespeare emerged from the experience frustrated by the gulf between art and reality, Muir and O'Loughlin asserted that the poet here rekindles his lost faith in love. Following his break with Southampton, the friend of the Sonnets, Shakespeare lost faith in such absolutes as beauty, truth, and goodness, they postulated; but even though his love was betrayed, the fact that it existed once sufficed to establish the miracle of love. Thus, according to the critics, Shakespeare reaffirmed his faith in love as an eternally redemptive power and recorded this recovery of faith in *The Phoenix and Turtle*. In his remarks on Shakespeare's poem in 1944, Lewis adopted an idealist approach, denying the significance and presence of allegory and arguing instead that "Shakespeare uses his poem to expound a philosophy of love." According to Lewis, the poem is metaphysical not by design, but through the effect of such rhetorical devices as the rigid, hypnotic metrical pattern, the "oracular" style, and the "supreme invention" of Reason as an advocate for the supremacy of love. All of these help create, he declared, "the illusion that we have been in another world and heard the voices of gods." In 1946, Shahani became the first critic to offer a comprehensive, line-by-line interpretation of *The Phoenix and Turtle*. Perhaps most notably, he was the earliest to identify the poem's Scholastic terminology, although he denied a Christian subtext, positing instead that the poem was suffused with pagan thought and reflected the universal doctrine of "sympathetic communion." Cleanth Brooks, one of the pioneers of New Criticism, turned his attention to *The Phoenix and Turtle* in 1947 and, like earlier idealist critics, read the poem as a statement concerning the very nature of poetry and artistic creation (see Additional Bibliography). He argued that the poem celebrates the unifying power of creative imagination—the achievement of metaphor as a kind of paradox that can accommodate conflicting or contradictory entities. In 1955, writing along similar lines, Walter Ong proposed that the structure and theme of *The Phoenix and Turtle* revolve around the concept of metaphor, so that, in effect, the poem becomes "a metaphor of metaphor itself." Ong held that the universal desire to find unity in a divided world leads the creative imagination to accommodate disparate ideas or meanings within a single image or symbol. In this instance, he noted, Shakespeare used the archetypal symbols of the phoenix and turtle, each capable of a variety of interpretations, to depict the essence of metaphor. In a lecture delivered in 1969, K. T. S. Campbell also examined the role of poetic expression in *The Phoenix and Turtle*. He maintained that the work deals "with the essence and with the fate of poetry itself," and he called the poem "a metaphoric crystallization" of the nihilism inherent in the idea that a poem has no signification beyond its own universe. According to Campbell, the process of forming poetical concepts by uniting distinct entities into a new conceptual identity is an attempt to represent reality; ultimately, however, it is a destructive process that violates the integrity of each independent element. Shakespeare's realization of this triggered a crisis, the critic speculated, that he was only able to avert by erecting an image of the process—as in the central metaphors of *The Phoenix and Turtle*—and then sublimating the image through an act of poetic wit and logic: by denying its reality. Campbell claimed

that this self-conscious poetic device constitutes Shakespeare's theory of poetry; it is manifest in every aspect of his plays, the critic asserted, but appears most prominently in *Hamlet* and *King Lear*.

Other idealist interpretations include those of I. A. Richards, F. T. Prince, Daniel Seltzer, and Heinrich Straumann. Writing in 1958, Richards rejected the notion that a knowledge of the historical or literary context, or of any allegorical reference, is necessary to appreciate the poem (see Additional Bibliography). A few years later, Prince echoed Murry's classification of the work as "pure poetry," but also discerned an element of "conscious self-caricature" at work in the poem that reveals Shakespeare indulging in a burlesque of Chester's *Love's Martyr*. Nevertheless, Prince argued, Shakespeare was fascinated by Chester's fantastic conceit and produced, in *The Phoenix and Turtle*, an evocation of all the poet's "feeling for pure passion and loyalty in human love." In 1961, Seltzer provided a comprehensive examination of the relationship between *The Phoenix and Turtle* and Shakespeare's dramatic works, claiming that the poem resembled the plot of a play, specifically a love-tragedy. The many parallels between this poem and his plays—especially in diction and theme, form and tone, content and sentiment—suggested to Seltzer that the poem is "a lyric statement of truths which the tragedies set forth dramatically." Finally, Heinrich Straumann argued that *The Phoenix and Turtle* represents a "turning point both in poetic expression and in the abstract of Shakespeare's existential concept of the possible union of beauty and truth." He noted that in the plays Shakespeare wrote prior to 1601, beauty and truth, emblems of the highest aesthetic and moral values, co-existed in Shakespeare's heroines. In 1601, however, in *Hamlet* and *The Phoenix and Turtle*, Shakespeare abandoned this idealized, heroic depiction of women. After 1601, Straumann remarked, the qualities of "beauty, truth, love, constancy" recur, but they are seldom found together in a single female character. The romances appear to offer a return to the idealized depiction of women, he averred, but the heroines in these plays achieve their successes only through magic or miracle. Thus Straumann, like many other critics who adopted the idealist approach, identified *The Phoenix and Turtle* as a poem that captures the poet-dramatist in a moment of intense passion and irrevocable transition. Although he maintained that all three approaches, positivist, formalist, and idealist, were valid, Straumann favored the idealist for yielding the most illuminating conclusions.

Thus the critical history of *The Phoenix and Turtle* follows the poem from near obscurity as late as 1875 to critical acclaim just a century later, as scholars have come to equate this sixty-seven line work with Shakespeare's epic tragedies. The three levels of meaning identified by Straumann and the parallel critical approaches continue to spawn diverse reaction to the poem; however, the general trend of twentieth-century scholarship has been to recuperate the poem within the context of the Shakespearean canon. Although the concise, metaphysical, abstract, and, to some degree, allegorical style of *The Phoenix and Turtle* appears unique in relation to Shakespeare's dramatic works, commentators continue to identify links between them, for example in themes and ideals. As Sidney Lanier remarked in 1879, just four years after Ralph Waldo Emerson called for critical examination of Shakespeare's overlooked poem, "it has more complex ideas in it, for the number of words, than perhaps any other poem in our language." A review of the diverse commentary on *The*

Phoenix and Turtle will corroborate Lee's assertion.

RALPH WALDO EMERSON (essay date 1875)

[*Emerson was one of the most influential literary figures of the nineteenth century. An American essayist and poet, he founded the Transcendental movement and shaped a distinctly American philosophy which embraces optimism, individuality, and mysticism. His philosophy stresses the presence of ongoing creation and revelation by a god apparent in everything and everyone, as well as the essential unity of all thoughts, persons, and things in the divine world. In the excerpt below, Emerson cites the technical merits of* The Phoenix and Turtle, *but he also challenges critics to illuminate its "frame and allusions." Although this is apparently a poem for poets, he declares, research into its historical and allegorical elements might make it accessible to general readers. Despite their brevity, Emerson's remarks on* The Phoenix and Turtle *established the agenda for many subsequent studies of the poem, as reflected by the number of critics of all approaches who refer to them in their own analyses.*]

I should like to have the Academy of Letters propose a prize for an essay on Shakespeare's poem, "*Let the bird of loudest lay*" [l.1], and the "*Threnos*" with which it closes; the aim of the essay being to explain, by a historical research into the poetic myths and tendencies of the age in which it was written, the frame and allusions of the poem. I have not seen Chester's "*Love's Martyr*," and "the Additional Poems" (1601), in which it appeared. Perhaps that book will suggest all the explanation this poem requires. To unassisted readers, it would appear to be a lament on the death of a poet, and of his poetic mistress. But the poem is so quaint, and charming in diction, tone, and allusions, and in its perfect metre and harmony, that I would gladly have the fullest illustration yet attainable. I consider this piece a good example of the rule, that there is a poetry for bards proper, as well as a poetry for the world of readers. This poem, if published for the first time, and without a known author's name, would find no general reception. Only the poets would save it. (pp. v-vi)

> *Ralph Waldo Emerson, in a preface to* Parnassus, *edited by Ralph Waldo Emerson, James R. Osgood and Company, 1875, pp. iii-xi.*

SIDNEY LANIER (lecture date 1879-80)

[*Lanier, a distinguished nineteenth-century American Romantic poet, espoused a controversial literary theory that sought to unite poetry and music. His remarks on* The Phoenix and Turtle *excerpted below were originally presented in a lecture delivered in the winter of 1879-80. Lanier calls attention to the unusual compression of "complex ideas" in* The Phoenix and Turtle *and to its unique tone of personal withdrawal and tenderness.*]

Permit me now to close this lecture with Shakspere's singular threnody of *The Phoenix and the Dove,* or Turtle, where the Phoenix represents constancy—I suppose from its ever returning after death to its "sun-bright seats" (as the old Anglo-Saxon poet calls them)—and the Turtle-dove represents true love. I do not in the least present this as a poem for reading aloud: it has more complex ideas in it, for the number of words, than perhaps any other poem in our language, and it takes some diligence of mind, with the poem before your eyes, to make out all its meaning. But if I can

only call your attention to it—for I don't think it is much read—I am satisfied. For a certain far-withdrawn and heart-conquering tenderness, we have not another poem like it. (pp. 94-5)

> *Sidney Lanier, "Some Birds of English Poetry: 'The Phoenix' of Cynewulf and of Shakspere, and 'The Twa Dows'," in his* Shakspere and His Forerunners: Studies in Elizabethan Poetry and Its Development from Early English, Vol. 1, *Doubleday, Page & Co., 1902, pp. 74-97.*

J. O. HALLIWELL-PHILLIPPS (essay date 1882)

[*A nineteenth-century English bibliophile and scholar, Halliwell-Phillipps originally concentrated on textual criticism in his study of Shakespeare's works. However, later in his career he shifted his interest from textual and critical problems to those of historical background. In doing so, he became the first scholar to make extensive use of town records from Stratford in the study of Shakespeare's life and work. Halliwell-Phillipps is the earliest critic to suggest that in* The Phoenix and Turtle *Shakespeare was consciously adopting, "for the first and only time," the role of "a philosophical writer." Additionally, the critic declares that while Robert Chester may have intended his* Love's Martyr *as "a personal allegory," there is no evidence that Shakespeare had a similar purpose in composing his poem.*]

It was towards the close of . . . 1600, or at some time in the following [year], that Shakespeare, for the first and only time, came forward in the avowed character of a philosophical writer. One Robert Chester was the author of a long allegorical poem, which was issued in 1601, under the title of,— "Love's Martyr or Rosalins Complaint, allegorically shadowing the truth of Love in the constant fate of the Phoenix and Turtle," and "To these are added some new compositions of severall moderne writers whose names are subscribed to their severall workes, upon the first subject; viz., the Phoenix and Turtle." The latter were stated, in a separate title-page, to have been "done by the best and chiefest of our moderne writers, with their names subscribed to their particular workes: neuer before extant; and now first consecrated by them all generally, to the loue and merite of the true-noble Knight, Sir Iohn Salisburie",—the names of Shakespeare, Marston, Chapman, and Jonson being attached to the recognized pieces of this latter series. The contribution of the great dramatist is a remarkable poem in which he makes a notice of the obsequies of the phoenix and turtle-dove subservient to the delineation of spiritual union. It is generally thought that Chester himself intended a personal allegory, but, if that be the case, there is nothing to indicate that Shakespeare participated in the design, nor even that he had endured the punishment of reading Love's Martyr. (pp. 125-26)

> *J. O. Halliwell-Phillipps, in an excerpt in his* Outlines of the Life of Shakespeare, *second edition, Longmans, Green, and Co., 1882, pp. 125-26.*

W. F. WIGSTON (essay date 1884)

[*Wigston, a nineteenth-century anti-Shakespearean scholar, devoted his critical career to proving that the plays and poems of Shakespeare were actually the work of a secret society of Rosicrucians under the direction of Francis Bacon. He is the first critic to attempt to explicate* The Phoenix and Turtle *in terms of its philosophical content, focusing on Shakespeare's use of Neoplatonism and "the paradox of a dual unity" inherent in nature. According to Wigston, Shakespeare employs the conceit of two lovers becoming one through love to symbolically resolve this paradox and to represent his own artistic endeavor, here and throughout his works, to synthesize "subject and object, mind and matter, the real and the ideal." Ironically, this Baconian critic insists on the poem's authenticity and celebrates Shakespeare's achievement. In portions of his essay not excerpted here, Wigston argues that the apparent obscurity of the poem's diction is evidence of a secret, Platonic language developed by a brotherhood of Renaissance poets.*]

There have been critics who have denied [*The Phoenix and the Turtle*] to be Shakespeare's. We are not of their number. It was published during the poet's lifetime, and bears his signature. Such a forgery is comprehensible after death, not before. Before all things, however, the style is Shakespeare's. It bears in the most supreme manner the imprint of that condensed, pithy, and profound strength of workmanship, and is as surely the poet's, as anything he ever penned. (p. 162)

The one significant fact of this poem is the paradox of a dual unity. This dual unity constitutes "two distincts, division none" [l. 27]. *We are told that:—*

> Reason in itself confounded,
> Saw division grow together;
> To themselves yet, either neither,
> Simple were so well compounded.
>
> [ll. 41-4]

Now we maintain that this refers to the paradox of *Participation* viz., the synthesis of mind and matter viewed from the point of unity established by Plato. But it bears equally upon creative art with even greater force, for the unity of symbolic art is apparent to the commonest intellect. And if Shakespeare has imitated Nature in this double sense of applied Platonism, then the mystery of this poem begins to lighten. Let us mark the first line, which significantly tells us Reason became confounded in itself. But how?—By its participation with art in the full Platonic sense of creation through Love. And what is Love?—The begetting of truth (Reason), upon the body of beauty for the sake of perpetual offspring or immortality. Now we are told that—

> *Reason* in itself confounded,
> Saw *division* grow together.

This seems to us very significant of that process of creative art, when a conscious artist embodies his creative ideal, idea, or logos, through Love upon the body of the Beautiful. How Platonic this is, the following verse proves:—

> That it cried' how true a twain,
> Seemeth this concordant one!
> Love hath reason, reason none,
> If what parts can so remain.
>
> [ll. 45-8]

Here again is the presentation of this paradox of a duo-uno something that is *"twain,"* viz., *two separate* things, yet "concordant one," or unity. What these two are the poem repeatedly tells us. They are as the above verse declares,—*Love and reason*. Now Plato *identifies* love and reason. . . . Love with Plato, is simply creation itself. Love *fuses together* subject and object, mind and matter, the ideal and the real. . . . In the Platonic philosophy he who knew Love, knew all things, for he understood creation. Love with Plato is closely bound up with the theory of the Beautiful. And it is here again that Art finds its closest point of contact with Plato's doctrine of creation through Love. In love there is intimate union. This

union is existence,—for it is the union of mind and matter, of the ideal and the real. Love therefore is dual, since it binds two things together. Those two things are invisible thought or spirit, and visible phenomena. All this is laid down in the *Banquet* of Plato. It is for this reason that Love is creative. Now love in human art corresponds to the passionate idea that unites in itself idea and form,—in short, it is Art unity; for it corresponds to the ideal world. In this sense therefore we may understand the significance Shakespeare intends, in the poem we are discussing, to attach to this word. Love as reason, constitutes, we suggest, the rational element of his creative art,—separate in thought (when revealed), inseparate as participating in unity with his outer art unrevealed. These "two distincts division none," are simply the synthesis of an art imitative of the paradox of Nature. Reason, or the logos of this art is joined with such profundity to creation that it is confounded or lost in the union which is indivisible in one sense yet separate in another. There is no other paradox so complete as the one we are discussing. It is the secret of existence and of all art that imitates existence. And it seems to us most clear that this dualism that is at once unity, and combines reason and love in one essence, is Shakespeare's own art, the nature of which he thus finally and obscurely reveals. (pp. 164-66)

W. F. Wigston, " 'The Phoenix and the Turtle'," in his A New Study of Shakespeare: An Inquiry into the Connection of the Plays and Poems, *Trübner and Co., 1884, pp. 161-201.*

FREDERICK S. BOAS (essay date 1896)

[*Boas was a specialist in Elizabethan and Tudor drama who combined the biographical interest prevalent in the late nineteenth century with the historical approach that developed in the first decades of the twentieth. His commentary thus reflects the important transition that occurred in Shakespearean criticism during this period. In his brief remarks on* The Phoenix and Turtle, *Boas tentatively acknowledges that the poem contains "an allegorical, possibly a personal, reference," but he also asserts that exact correspondences cannot be determined. On another matter, he suggests that the poem's style, reminiscent of Shakespeare's "early lyrical manner," is evidence of its authenticity.*]

The Phoenix and the Turtle appeared in Chester's *Love's Martyr* or *Rosalin's Complaint,* 1601, and is there attributed to Shakspere. It would seem to have an allegorical, possibly a personal, reference, which cannot now be solved, but the fine verses describing the 'mutual flame' of the two birds,

> Two distincts: division none:
> Number there in love was slain,
>
> [ll. 27-8]

with their ingenious antitheses and conceits are quite in Shakspere's early lyrical manner. (pp. 162-63)

Frederick S. Boas, "Shakspere's Poems: The Early Period of Comedy," in his Shakspere and His Predecessors, *J. Murray, 1896, pp. 158-96.*

SIDNEY LEE (essay date 1898)

[*Lee was an English biographer, Elizabethan scholar, and editor of* The Dictionary of National Biography. *His works on Shakespeare include* Stratford-on-Avon from the Earliest Times to the Death of Shakespeare (*1885); the highly success-*

ful Life of William Shakespeare (*1898*)*; a facsimile edition of the First Folio* (*1905*)*; Shakespeare and the Modern Stage* (*1906*)*; and* Shakespeare in the Italian Renaissance (*1915*)*. In the excerpt below, Lee questions the authenticity of* The Phoenix and Turtle *and speculates that it may be no more than a "play of fancy." If topical allusions exist in the poem, they remain elusive, the critic concludes. Lee also affirms the poem's uniqueness in the Shakespearean canon.*]

In 1601 Shakespeare's . . . name was appended to 'a poetical essaie on the Phoenix and the Turtle,' which was published by Edward Blount in an appendix to Robert Chester's 'Love's Martyr, or Rosalins complaint, allegorically shadowing the Truth of Love in the Constant Fate of the Phoenix and Turtle.' . . . Shakespeare's alleged contribution consists of thirteen four-lined stanzas in trochaics, each line being of seven syllables, with the rhymes disposed as in Tennyson's 'In Memoriam.' The concluding 'threnos' is in five three-lined stanzas, also in trochaics, each stanza having a single rhyme. The poet describes in enigmatic language the obsequies of the Phoenix and the Turtle-dove, who had been united in life by the ties of a purely spiritual love. The poem may be a mere play of fancy without recondite intention, or it may be of allegorical import; but whether it bear relation to pending ecclesiastical, political, or metaphysical controversy, or whether it interpret popular grief for the death of some leaders of contemporary society, is not easily determined. Happily Shakespeare wrote nothing else of like character. (pp. 183-84)

Sidney Lee, *"The Development of Dramatic Power," in his* A Life of William Shakespeare, *Smith, Elder & Co., 1898, pp. 161-84.*

EDWARD DOWDEN   (essay date 1903)

[*Dowden was an Irish critic and biographer whose* Shakspere: A Critical Study of His Mind and Art, *first published in 1875 and revised in 1881, was the leading example of the biographical criticism popular in the English-speaking world near the end of the nineteenth century. Biographical critics sought a record of Shakespeare's personal development in the plays and poems. As that approach gave way in the twentieth century to aesthetic theories with greater emphasis on the constructed, formal nature of literary works, the biographical analysis of Dowden and other critics came to be regarded as limited and often misleading. Dowden's comments on* The Phoenix and Turtle *excerpted below first appeared in the introduction to his 1903 edition of* The Poems and Sonnets of Shakspere. *He states that although Chester's poem was allegorical, no evidence exists to supply the exact correspondences or even to show that Shakespeare and his colleagues adopted Chester's allegorical framework. In fact, Dowden maintains, Shakespeare diverges from the "prescribed theme" in his depiction of the phoenix as mortal and without progeny. When Dowden first formally addressed* The Phoenix and Turtle *in his* Shakspere (*1877*)*, he disputed Shakespeare's authorship, but in this 1922 work, it is evident that he has come to accept the poem's authenticity.*]

The Phoenix and the Turtle, taken out of its original environment, seems hardly intelligible, but studied *in situ,* the general significance becomes clear. *Love's Martyr: or Rosalins Complaint,* a long, an incoherent, and a dull poem, professedly, but not really, a translation from the Italian, . . . tells of the chaste love of a phoenix, who represents a woman, and a turtle, who represents a man; they are consumed in the flames of the Arabian pyre, and from their ashes arises a new phoenix—perfect Love. The theme was proposed, perhaps by Chester, to several poets of eminence, Marston, Chapman,

Ben Jonson, Shakspere, and they were willing, if not for hire (which one writer repudiates) yet in honour of Sir John Salisbury, . . . to make their several contributions to this strange volume. The hypothesis of Dr. Grosart [see Additional Bibliography], that the phoenix is Elizabeth, and the turtle Essex, seems to me to be without the slenderest foundation. Shakspere, like his fellow-poets, endeavours to do justice to the prescribed theme; his general intention is to celebrate the decease of two chaste lovers, who were perfectly united in an ideal passion; but he omits one motive of which Marston makes much—the birth of the new phoenix, ideal Love, from the ashes of the chaste and impassioned birds. If actual persons were allegorized, it must not be assumed that the fiery transmutation typifies death in the literal sense of the word. (pp. 1159-60)

Edward Dowden, *" 'The Phoenix and the Turtle': Introduction," in* The Histories and Poems of Shakespeare, *edited by W. J. Craig, Oxford University Press, London, 1922, pp. 1157-60.*

ARTHUR H. R. FAIRCHILD   (essay date 1904)

[*Fairchild's critical and historical interpretation of* The Phoenix and Turtle *represents the first effort to examine possible literary sources of the poem and to link it with a specific genre. According to Fairchild, the poem derives principally from two*

Second title page of Love's Martyr *(1601).*

sources: Chaucer's Parlement of Foules *and the emblem litera-*
ture that flourished in Shakespeare's time. The critic asserts
that in composing The Phoenix and Turtle *Shakespeare was*
conforming to a Renaissance literary vogue known as the Court
of Love. No positive evidence exists to show the occasion for the
poem, the critic avers, although it might have been written "as
a Valentine-poem (without explicit reference) to Sir John Salis-
bury." Fairchild concludes that the poem contains no bio-
graphical elements and lacks both ingenuity and sustained ar-
gument.]

The Phoenix and Turtle has long been regarded as one of the
cruces of Shakespearian study. Published in 1601 by Edward
Blount, in a volume containing Robert Chester's *Loves Mar-*
tyr and companion pieces by Jonson, Chapman, Marston,
and some unknown writer, this poem stands as yet without
satisfactory interpretation of either an historical or her-
meneutic character. The absolute failure to obtain anything
convincing and conclusive in the former case has generally
and, we might say, justly been regarded as properly restricting the latitude of expository or allegorical interpretation,
which the poem might otherwise permit. Critics and biographers, accordingly, have almost uniformly considered the
question of interpretation a closed one. A few regard the
poem as of doubtful authorship. Others, who openly or tacitly acknowledge its authenticity, simply repeat the notes of
one or two previous discerning editors, and in several cases
reveal their misapprehension of the poem by additions which
are either manifestly absurd or easily confuted by historical
evidence. (p. 337)

This poem is, in an unusual sense, unique. It is unparalleled
in the remainder of Shakespeare's work, and, as it would
seem, in the work of any other author; it stands apparently
independent of all accessible historical evidence by which it
might be explained; and, finally, it is tantalizingly noncom-
mittal in the character of its internal evidence. Small wonder,
then, that critics and biographers alike have failed in their interpretations, and that the poem has consistently forced from
even the most astute a confession of its difficulty and obscurity. (p. 338)

Dr. Grosart has reproduced the contents of the volume containing Chester's *Loves Martyr,* in *The New Shakspere Society*
publications [see Additional Bibliography]. On the basis of
evidence which may there be examined in detail, he maintains
that in the poem *The Phoenix and Turtle,* the phoenix was
intended by Shakespeare as the allegorical representative of
Queen Elizabeth, and that the turtle-dove represented "the
brilliant but impetuous, the greatly dowered but rash, the illustrious but unhappy Robert Devereux, second Earl of
Essex". The numerous adjectives and vigorous exhortations
by which Dr. Grosart endeavored to win acceptance for his
theory were, however, without much avail. From the time of
its introduction it was regarded as unsatisfactory; . . . and
this theory is now generally regarded as an exploded one. Dr.
Furnivall, indeed, has successfully controverted Dr. Grosart's statements [see Additional Bibliography]. But even he
presented only a portion of the evidence which may be
brought against the principal arguments; and it will presently
become apparent upon other grounds that Dr. Grosart's theory is based upon an entirely inadequate body of evidence.

The other attempt at an historical interpretation, which is
also the most recent and most ambitious, is that made by A.
von Mauntz in a volume entitled *Heraldik in diensten der*
Shakespeare-forschung (Berlin 1903). This writer . . . has endeavored to show that the poem is a lament over the death

of Marlowe and especially over the loss of his blank verse.
The various birds, accordingly, are identified with members
of the literary coterie of the day, such as Harvey, Spenser,
Shakespeare himself, and Nash. This theory, however, aside
from numerous other considerations, is impossible on its own
ground for, in order to establish the chief premise upon which
it rests, certain lines are forced into an interpretation which
it is manifestly quite impossible for them to bear. The theory,
indeed, is barely worthy of serious consideration. (pp. 343-
44)

Of those interpretations which make no reference to historical data, the most important is probably that made by Halliwell-Phillipps [see excerpt above, 1882]. "It was towards the
close of the present year, 1600," he writes in his *Outlines,* "or
at some time in the following one, that Shakespeare for the
first and only time, came forward in the avowed character of
a philosophical writer." And then, referring to Chester's production, and to the names of those whose poems also appear
in the volume, he continues: "The contribution of the great
dramatist is a remarkable poem in which he makes a notice
of the obsequies of the phoenix and turtle-dove subservient
to the delineation of spiritual union. It is generally thought
that, in his own work, Chester meditated a personal allegory,
but, if that be the case, there is nothing to indicate that Shakespeare participated in the design." Professor Dowden, in his
introduction to Phin's recent Cyclopaedia, intimates his acceptance of practically the same interpretation. "The sole
Arabian bird," he says, "alights for a moment on many a
bough in the forest of Elizabethan poetry. At the close of
Robert Chester's strange poem of 1601, 'Love's Martyr',
some of the most eminent of Shakespeare's fellows, and
Shakespeare himself with them, unite in celebrating ideal love
under the allegory of the phoenix and the turtle." Lanier
also, in his recently published lectures, accepts a somewhat
similar interpretation. "The Phoenix," he says, "represents
constancy . . . I suppose from its ever returning after death
to its 'sun-bright seats' (as the old Anglo Saxon poet calls
them) . . . and the Turtle-dove represents true love" [see excerpt above, 1879].

None of these latter interpretations, however, is grounded
upon historical evidence, or even upon a detailed explanation
of the lines themselves. Each is as slight as the source of its
suggestion is apparent. . . . That which, first above all, is
here demanded is historical evidence affording a *rationale* for
the writing of this poem. Then and only then should we draw
our conclusions concerning its inner meaning and its possible
allegorical references. These latter writers, indeed, make no
special pretensions to originality in their literal acceptance of
the statement contained in the descriptive title. Excepting
Halliwell-Phillipps' assertion of his belief that Shakespeare
here became a philosophical writer, they venture little more,
in addition to the information conveyed by the descriptive
title, than an admission of this poem as belonging to Shakespeare, and as having a possible determinative significance
and import in the greater volume of the poet's work.

An examination of all these interpretations, therefore, reveals
at once their unsatisfactory character. The historical interpretations may possibly be regarded as somewhat interestingly original or ingenious. But if the other interpretations are
felt to be founded on insufficient data, these fail entirely to
carry with them any convincing quality or even an air of
probability. They ignore the fact that, *prima facie,* general
conceptions of Shakespeare argue alike against the probabili-

ty of this poem containing either a compendium of personal philosophy or possible historical references. (pp. 344-46)

What we have, then, is a poem (1) which is extensively regarded as genuinely Shakespeare's (for the few who call the authorship into question present no positive evidence to support their statements); (2) which has no light directly thrown upon it by the poems in conjunction with which it was published; (3) which is without known historical connections; and (4) for which existing interpretations are entirely inadequate and unsatisfactory. And yet the difficulties involved in each one of these points can be considerably enlightened, if not absolutely settled. (p. 346)

Our thesis in brief is this: *The Phoenix and Turtle* belongs to that class of poems connected with the institution (real or otherwise) known as the Court of Love. It has a twofold source, stanzas (I–V) especially being suggested by Chaucer's poem *The Parlement of Foules,* part IV (ll. 323 to end); the remaining stanzas (VI–XVIII) being adapted to these from the emblem literature and conceptions of Shakespeare's period. (pp. 346-47)

[The Court of Love] began, it is said, in the songs sung at the festivals of May by the peasant girls of Poitou and Limousin. The natural place of love-songs among themes ranging from love of liberty and the joy of living to all forms of wantonness will readily be perceived. The glorifying of love became a central subject. Poets vied and competed in their productions. Beauty became the object of an absurdly extravagant worship, the statement of which, coupled with the passionate pleadings for response to, unrequited love, taxed language to the limits of its expressive power. Words soon passed into deeds, for they could no longer adequately indicate the fervor of a lover's devotion. The transference, however, effected no reduction in the wooer's ardor. Self-imposed tests of physical endurance were as readily undergone as words had been previously uttered, and even death seems to have been sought as an ultimate manifestation of this over-powering love. "To check such excesses as these, and likewise to regulate the conduct of ladies, whose harshness and severity brought their knights to such a pass, Courts of Love arose in various places, the object of which was to legislate on all questions of the affections, to arrange disputes between lovers, to pass sentence on any lover who was in the wrong, and generally to establish a system of jurisprudence, which should be useful in determining any vexed questions which might arise between lovers themselves, and so to render unnecessary any appeal to the courts, except as a last resource" [John F. Rowbotham, in his *The Troubadours and Courts of Love*].

As opposed to any such historical account of the Court of Love as is here suggested it is maintained by many that no such institution ever existed. With the dispute itself we are not specially concerned. Incontrovertible evidence exists to show that a certain literary fashion prevailed in Provençal, French, Italian, Middle-High German, and English literature which, from the accounts of the Court of Love itself, might reasonably be regarded as its literary outgrowth. However that may be, or however real the Court of Love as an institution may or may not have been, it is at least certain that a number of conceptions, said to have been connected with it, gradually became conventionalized and were eventually formulated and codified. These conceptions, commonly called the "laws of love" were presented in a variety of forms and in a number of books, "the most important of which is the *Roman de la Rose,* 'où l'art d'amour est tout enclose' "

[where the art of love is all contained]. This great representative poem itself indicates that the embodiment of the laws was sometimes artistic, sometimes not. Its double authorship is in this respect significant. It indicates the two types of allegory cultivated in the middle-ages and usually distinguishable also on the basis of artistic merit. One was distinctly religious and moralistic in character, and rose to something of excellence later in the adopted personifications of the moralities. The other type was the more artistic and romantic allegory, devoted especially to the God of Love, and productive eventually of the greater Renaissance literature.

It was through Chaucer that this latter type found its way into England. *The Parlement of Foules* is, of course, the one poem in which we are particularly interested. It embodies many prominent features of the Court of Love literature. So extensively, indeed, are these characteristics found in Chaucer's work, especially in that of his French and Italian periods, that the English *Court of Love* was attributed to him by his uncritical followers. From Chaucer the art passed through Lydgate, Gawain Douglas and others to its highest artistic perfection in Spenser's *Faery Queen.* The dramatists in common also inherited certain traditions concerning the subtleties of love. We might mention as illustrative, Jonson's *Masque at Lord Hadington's Marriage,* Middleton's *The Triumphs of Love and Antiquity,* Marston's *Parasitaster,* or *The Fawn,* etc. Shakespeare reveals his acquaintance with the Court of Love conventions especially in *Love's Labour's Lost, Romeo and Juliet,* and *The Two Gentlemen of Verona.* There is nothing surprising, therefore, in finding that Shakespeare, in writing *The Phoenix and Turtle,* simply conformed to a literary practice in dealing with a subject in which, when vitalized into the concrete realities of life, he had an indomitable interest both by heritage and by preference.

Shakespeare's poem, however, represents the extreme of modification incident upon the decadent stages of all original Court of Love traditions. It is even difficult to determine precisely what these traditions were. [In his *The Origins and Sources of the Court of Love*] Neilson mentions the following as among the chief ones: "the abundance of flowers and birds and their use as erotic symbols; the Courts of Venus, Minerva, and Fortune with the allegorical figures and the shades of departed lovers in attendance; the palace of crystal and the meadow watered by a river; the instructions to the true lover, and the binding together of the whole by the thread of the hero's love story." In the later stages especially of its development a number of these features were lost. *The Parlement of Foules,* while unquestionably belonging to the Court of Love literature, departs in several respects from the set traditions. The prominence of birds "as erotic symbols" is especially noticeable. The Court of Love commonly closed with a service sung by birds in honor of the God of Love, and this feature seems to have been selected as a prolific source for poetic material. It is that which affords the central situation in *The Phoenix and Turtle.* The popular belief that birds mated on St. Valentine's Day may account also for the presumable transference of this feature to a great list of Valentine poems. The Valentine tradition is found in Chaucer and Lydgate, and becomes prolific in Turberville, Drayton, Herrick, Gay and others. The possibilities of placing *The Phoenix and Turtle* in this subclass will presently be considered, but the prominence of birds and the nature of the subject itself leave little doubt that this poem is properly placed in the Court of Love literature in its later development. Let us next briefly consider emblems. (pp. 347-50)

Shakespeare lived just in the period of the most fertile production of emblem literature. About the middle of the sixteenth century an eminent jurisconsult of Milan, Andrea Alciati, compiled a volume of emblems written in Latin verse. They met with distinct and immediate approbation, and the volume was forthwith translated into the Italian, French, and German languages. "Thus established, as an elegant and useful method of inculcating, both by word and eye-pictures, the virtues of civil-life; men of learning, poets, and statesmen, in France, Holland, Germany, Spain, and England, vied with each other, as it were, throughout the seventeenth century, in the cultivation of this branch of composition, insomuch that it had become a favourite and admired medium for the diffusion of religious, social, and political maxims, and maintained that position in public favour up to the end of the eighteenth century" [Jacob Cats and Robert Farlie, in their *Moral Emblems with Aphorisms, Adages, and Proverbs, of All Ages and Nations*]. (pp. 351-52)

A more exact conception of an emblem is worth attempting. Quarles says it is "but a silent Parable". Bacon's definition [in his *Advancement of Learning*] is that it "deduceth conceits intellectual to images sensible, which strike the memory more". [Henry] Green says [in his *Shakespeare and the Emblem Writers*]: "We shall form a sufficiently correct notion on this subject if we conclude that any figure engraven, embossed, or drawn . . . any moulding or picture, the implied meaning of which is something additional to what the actual delineation represents, is an emblem. Some thought or fancy, some sentiment or saying, is portrayed, and the portraiture constitutes an emblem . . . Naturally and easily the term emblem became applicable to any painting, drawing, or print that was representative of an action, of a quality of mind, or of any peculiarity or attribute of character". (pp. 352-53)

The eminent suitability of animal and bird life as affording illustrative material for emblems will be apparent. There was a host of traditional beliefs, inherited chiefly from the earlier days of folk-lore, which were associated with animals and birds, and which naturally adapted themselves to the most varied and extensive cultivation. To these were added the conceptions gathered from classical literature. The field in which the artist's fancy might play, therefore, was almost unbounded; and it is perhaps fortunate that our present interests are confined to but a few examples of its activity. In the interpretation of *The Phoenix and Turtle* the beliefs attached to the several birds will be incidentally referred to. The peculiar relations in which the phoenix and turtle-dove stand, however, demand a more detailed examination of their associations in Shakespeare's day.

Turning first to the turtle-dove, we may dismiss it with but a few references. Whether due in part to biblical influence or not, the general conceptions concerning this bird have been, throughout the ages, most interestingly uniform. Shakespeare, therefore, came to a tradition concerning the dove which he used just as those who lived centuries before had employed it. It was "the time-honoured emblem of tenderness and conjugal love" [Alfred Newton, in his *Dictionary of Birds*]. Consider the following:

> so turtles pair
> That never mean to part.
> [*The Winter's Tale*, IV. iv. 153-54]

> As true as steel, as plantage to the moon,
> As sun to day, as turtle to her mate.
> [*Troilus and Cressida*, III. ii. 177-78]

> Like to a pair of loving turtle-doves
> That could not live asunder day or night.
> [*1 Henry VI*, II. ii. 30-1]

It was the common belief that "when one of a couple died, the survivor would take no new mate, but remain the rest of his or her life in a condition of single-blessedness". This belief is referred to by Shakespeare in *The Winter's Tale* in that sweetly-pathetic scene where Paulina says:

> Go together,
> You precious winners all: your exultation
> Partake to everyone. I, an old turtle,
> Will wing me to some wither'd bough and there
> My mate, that's never to be found again,
> Lament till I am lost.
>
> [V. iii. 130-35]
> (pp. 354-55)

The phoenix is not so easily disposed of. The origin of the well-known tradition concerning this fabulous bird seems to be lost in obscurity. It appears to have been current even before historic times; and the references to it in classical, mediaeval, and, to a considerable extent, in modern literature, are exceedingly numerous. The literature, too, in connection with it is quite voluminous. It may be possible, as Dr. Grosart maintains with respect to the Elizabethan age, "to multiply contemporary and funereal 'flatteries' " of Elizabeth under the 'Phoenix', but the references are very far from being confined to her. Indeed, . . . the word 'phoenix' had become a descriptive term which was applied to any person or thing regarded as possessing unique excellence; it was a synonym for 'paragon', 'distinguished', or 'wonderful'. (pp. 355-56)

Shakespeare has a number of references to the phoenix. Several of them refer to it simply as a bird, yet one of great rarity. For example, in *The Tempest,* Sebastian remarks, after seeing the banquet brought in by the spirits:

> Now I will believe
> That there are unicorns; that in Arabia
> There is one tree, the phoenix' throne; one phoenix
> At this hour reigning there.
>
> [III. iii. 21-4]

Other references concerning the phoenix are to men and women. Both Antony and Imogen [in *Cymbeline*] are called the "Arabian bird", and Timon "flashes now a phoenix" [*Timon of Athens*, II. i. 32]. In the *Comedy of Errors* there are three references to an *inn* called the *Phoenix*. Still another reference [in *Twelfth Night*] is to a vessel called the *Phoenix*, and there is one even [in *A Lover's Complaint*] to a "phoenix-beard". (pp. 357-58)

[This] word, in and about Shakespeare's day, was applied indifferently to persons, things, and conceptions simply as a distinguishing mark. . . . [It] was applied to either a man or woman of excellence, distinction, or striking eccentricity; to a theatre, a badge, an inn, and a sign. It was employed as the symbol of Christ, Chastity, Constancy, Hope, Immortality, Resurrection; it was an emblem of new-birth, of duration, loneliness and of "oneliness". It is evident, therefore, that though the phoenix might refer to almost everything it was not pre-eminently the symbol of any one person or thing. Dr. Grosart, therefore, manifestly based his conclusions upon insufficient evidence when he endeavored to identify Elizabethan allusions to the phoenix with that queen. The phoenix was one of the most popular and extensively employed of all emblems. It had a correspondingly remarkable applicability, but possessed, nevertheless, a distinct uniformity in its central conception. This conception, as already intimated, signified distinction or excellence. Unless, therefore, there is direct identification of the symbol, it is hazardous to make dogmatic statements and positive interpretations wherever it is employed as a central figure. (p. 358)

All conjectures concerning the occasion of *The Phoenix and Turtle* must, in the lack of specific reference or identification of the symbols employed, be based upon the general historical data already presented and upon . . . a minute and detailed interpretation of the poem. . . . Confirmation of any theory based upon the historical matter would naturally be looked for in the explanation of references contained within the poem itself. The result is perhaps disappointing. There is no positive evidence affording an indisputable conclusion concerning the occasion of this poem. Not only so, but the demand for *some* occasion has itself arisen artificially. The absence of definite historical explanation and the peculiar metaphysical character of the poem have afforded almost the sole basis for the conjecture of reference to the personal life of Shakespeare or to that of some friend. (pp. 373-74)

Two theories, which really have a common substratum, present themselves as affording possible and reasonable explanations [of the poem's occasion]. The first of these is that *The Phoenix and Turtle* is a *Valentine-poem,* addressed, possibly, to Sir John Salisbury. The second is that it belongs essentially to The Court of Love literature, containing important adaptations from the emblem literature of the period; and that in the writing of it Shakespeare was simply bending in a conformity (elsewhere paralleled) to a literary vogue not only prevalent but extensively cultivated in his day.

The Valentine-poem was one of the most extensively cultivated literary forms of Shakespeare's period. Certain characteristic marks indicate an inseparable connection with the Court of Love, but the immediate process by which it arose, like the origin of the beliefs concerning St. Valentine himself, are doubtless effectually clouded in mystery. The belief had arisen that birds paired on that Saint's day. Valentine-poems, accordingly, employed birds very extensively as symbols, and in the usage evinced an adoption and acceptance of the peculiar beliefs attached to various birds and traditionally established in the Court of Love. (pp. 374-75)

In support of the Valentine-theory, therefore, we have to note 1) the general similarity of subject to that of *The Phoenix and Turtle;* 2) the dedication to Salisbury of the poems contained in Chester's volume; 3) the extensive employment of birds under dominant figurative conceptions; and 4) the fact that Chaucer (regarding the *Parlement* as source, in part) makes St. Valentine's Day the occasion of his assembly. As opposed to these points we should observe the following: 1) the fact that Shakespeare's poem celebrates a funeral differentiates it almost fundamentally from Valentine-poems, which celebrate existing love and marriage; 2) the dedication of the "new compositions" was "by them all generally", and is too indefinite to bear specific reference to the content of any one poem; 3) Valentine's Day is not (so far as we recall) mentioned in Chester's volume, in which the poem appeared; 4) Shakespeare's references to this day are extraordinarily few, considering the prevalence of the conception; and, finally, 5) according to our apprehension of the matter, Valentine-

poems are to be regarded, in any case, as a special development of the Court of Love.

This last point practically constitutes the second theory and is also the basis of the blending referred to. The central conceptions of Valentine-poems and the Court of Love are too closely allied and related to fail to suggest identification of the two forms. Even though *The Phoenix and Turtle* be placed in the sub-class, therefore, it would seem ultimately to belong to the Court of Love also. It is, of course, much easier to identify it with the latter, which is less specialized. The features which specially characterize the Court of Love were sufficiently reviewed in our consideration of its historical aspect to make it apparent now, in the light of our interpretation, that this poem falls readily into this class. This is because the symbols employed in it, the peculiar manner of their arrangement, the subject itself, and the method of treatment, all harmonize with the dominant conceptions of the class as seen in their later development.

This theory, moreover, affords a most inviting field for conjecture, which is not entirely unsupported by historical evidence. Courtly love is said by [Lewis F.] Mott [in his *The System of Courtly Love*] to have been declared incompatible with marriage. That something of the conception came to Shakespeare as a lingering heritage, which was finally vitalized by the great preceptors of love, is not, perhaps, an altogether baseless supposition. Indeed, the peculiar nature of some of the poet's earlier subjects, such as those of the early poems, *Love's Labour's Lost,* and the positive conceptions of the sonnets, serve to support it. May not he who, of all the great poets, is regarded in *The Century of Praise* as the greatest authority on love, have rebelled against the hollow conceptions and subversive teachings of his predecessors? (pp. 375-76)

Sidney Lee observes that, even with important omissions, there were nearly twelve hundred sonnets "of the amorous kind" printed between 1591 and 1597. Indeed, when we consider Watson's *Centurie of Love* (1582), Sidney's *Astrophel and Stella* (1591), Daniel's *Delia* (1592), Lodge's *Phillis* (1593), Barnes's *Parthenophil and Parthenophe:* Sonnets, Madrigals, Elegies, and Odes (1593), and numerous other publications in which we find amorous sonnets, elegies, and odes, there can be little doubt about the conclusions at which we must arrive. These are practically two in number. In the first place there can be no doubt as to Shakespeare's familiarity with this class of literature. . . . The second conclusion at which we arrive, concerning this class of literature, is that Court of Love poems, and sonnets, odes, etc., were employed alike to give expression to similar, if not identical, prevalent conceptions, though derived beyond question from different original sources.

But this amorous literature, especially as it found expression in the sonnets, was confessedly artificial. It contained, as Sir Philip Sidney confessed, "no inward note", in many instances; and, for that reason, it was subjected to the most incisive criticism from opposing contemporaries. The possibility that Shakespeare responded to this trenchant criticism, and the acknowledged truth of the relations which he portrayed in all his productions, constitute the argument which may be brought to support the conjecture which is based on Mott's statement, above referred to, concerning Courtly Love and marriage. It might, therefore, be plausibly argued that Shakespeare did revolt against the hollow conceptions of love. On the basis of such evidence, accordingly, some might be disposed to urge acceptance of the hypothesis, that *The Phoenix* and Turtle expresses a subjective phase of the poet's mind. The internal character of the poem, however, in no way supports such a theory, and external evidence even argues against it. Mr. Sidney Lee holds that Shakespeare's sonnets contain but the slightest autobiographical element. It is the safer position to assume. When Shakespeare's work has been identified with a literary vogue, and the characteristics of that vogue have been established, we have proceeded as far as the sustained dramatic quality and the universal imaginative range of the poet's mind will allow us to advance, however deep may be inexplicable impressions to the contrary.

The one indisputable fact, then, which emerges clear and untrammeled from this somewhat bulky and involved mass of evidence, is that *The Phoenix and Turtle* is a poem of a common class and that that class is the Court of Love. Viewed in the light of this fact and of the evidence generally which has been presented, the logical *inference* is that Shakespeare, in company with Jonson, Chapman, Marston, and some unknown writer, contributed verses for a volume all of which were upon a conventional Court of Love subject, though not all written in precisely the same conventional manner.

In the light of the evidence adduced, therefore, and of the prevalence of certain dominant conceptions, and of the common use of phrases and of such words as "constancy", "rarity", "wonder", "urne", etc., found in the companion poems, we conclude that *The Phoenix and Turtle* was written, possibly as a Valentine-poem (without explicit reference) to Sir John Salisbury, but most probably simply in compliance (such as is adequately paralleled) with a prevalent literary vogue, which encouraged the writing of Court of Love poems of a modified character; that it has no recondite meaning beyond that involved in the historic conditions of its production; that it contains no allusions either to the poet's own life or to that of another; and, finally, that it contains the confession of metaphysical conceptions only to the extent to which they would be implied by an emotional interest in a peculiar form of poetical activity, devoid, however, of any explicit intellectual formulation. (pp. 380-82)

> *Arthur H. R. Fairchild, " 'The Phoenix and Turtle':*
> *A Critical and Historical Interpretation," in* Englis-
> che Studien, *Vol. 33, 1904, pp. 337-84.*

JOHN MASEFIELD   (essay date 1911)

[*Masefield was an English poet, dramatist, and novelist who was appointed poet laureate in 1930. Although not a scholar, he wrote* William Shakespeare (*1911*), *an introductory overview of the entire canon intended to stimulate the study of Shakespeare by the general public. In his 1924 lecture entitled "Shakespeare and the Spiritual Life," Masefield was one of the earliest commentators to address the issue of symbolism in Shakespearean drama. In the following excerpt on* The Phoenix and Turtle, *Masefield claims that the key to the poem is "spiritual ecstasy," an evocation of a thought "too subtle and too intense" for conventional expression. The critic suggests that Shakespeare's treatment of the prescribed subject is an attempt to grasp within the constraints of language the very essence of "the passing of truth and beauty."*]

The Phoenix and The Turtle.—This strange, very beautiful poem was published in 1601 in an appendix to Robert Chester's *Love's Martyr, or Rosalin's Complaint,* to which several famous poets contributed. In dark and noble verse it describes a spiritual marriage, suddenly ended by death. It is too strange to be the fruit of a human sorrow. It is the work

of a great mind trying to express in unusual symbols a thought too subtle and too intense to be expressed in any other way. Spiritual ecstasy is the only key to work of this kind. To the reader without that key it can only be so many strange words set in a noble rhythm for no apparent cause.

Poetry moves in many ways. It may glorify and make spiritual some action of man, or it may give to thoughts such life as thoughts can have, an intenser and stranger life than man knows, with forms that are not human and a speech unintelligible to normal human moods. This poem gives to a flock of thoughts about the passing of truth and beauty the mystery and vitality of birds, who come from a far country, to fill the mind with their crying. (pp. 249-50)

> *John Masefield, " 'The Phoenix and the Turtle'," in*
> his William Shakespeare, *Williams and Norgate,*
> *1911, pp. 249-50.*

JOHN MIDDLETON MURRY   (lecture date 1922)

[*A twentieth-century English editor and critic, Murry has been called the most "level-headed" of Shakespeare's major biographical critics. Unlike other proponents of the biographical approach, such as Frank Harris and Edward Dowden, Murry refused to attribute to Shakespeare a definite personality or creative neurosis which determined all of his work, but regarded the poet as a man of powerful insights rather than character, an individual possessing Keats's negative capability, in the sense that he was able to withstand "uncertainties, mysteries, doubts, without any irritable reaching after fact and reason." What Murry considered Shakespeare's greatest gift was his ability to uncover the true spirit of Elizabethan England, to fuse "not merely the poet and dramatist in himself," but to establish "a unique creative relation between himself, his dramatic material, his audience, and his actors." In the excerpt below, Murry lauds* The Phoenix and Turtle *as "the most perfect short poem in any language," a rare example of "pure poetry" that grants no compromise for the sake of communication or intelligibility. He argues that Shakespeare is trying to express the inexpressible: to translate into symbolic and necessarily abstract and obscure language his own mystical vision of "perfect and celestial love." In the plays that immediately followed* The Phoenix and Turtle, *Murry suggests, Shakespeare sought to convey this otherworldly vision in terms of temporal events and characters. According to Murry, Shakespeare was "torn asunder by the effort to express a perception which is not of this world in terms of events and characters which are," yet eventually he came to accept the impossibility of creating a dramatic "imitation of emotions and actions" that would fully express his perception of reality. Murry's remarks on* The Phoenix and Turtle *were originally presented in a lecture in 1922.*]

It would not be easy to say with confidence what *The Phoenix and the Turtle* is *about.* On the face of it, it is a requiem over the death of a phoenix and a turtle-dove, who are the symbols of a love made perfect by refinement from all earthly passion and become virginal. There is surely no more astonishing description of the highest attainable by human love.

> Hearts remote, yet not asunder;
> Distance, and no space was seen
> 'Twixt the turtle and his queen.
> But in them, it were a wonder.
>
> [ll. 29-32]

But the poem floats high above the plane of intellectual apprehension: what we understand is only a poor simulacrum of what we feel—feel with some element of our being which chafes in silence against the bars of sense. And in the poet's own imagination it is Reason itself which makes and chants the dirge, Reason baffled by the sight of perfect individuality in perfect union.

> Reason, in itself confounded,
> Saw division grow together,
> To themselves yet either neither,
> Simple were so well compounded. . . .
>
> [ll. 41-4]

> Truth may seem, but cannot be;
> Beauty brag, but 'tis not she;
> Truth and beauty buried be.

> To this urn let those repair
> That are either true or fair;
> For these dead birds sigh a prayer.
>
> [ll. 62-7]

And we feel, in some inexplicable sense, that the poet's claim that Reason bows its head in this poem is a true one. There is an absolute harmony in *The Phoenix and the Turtle* which can easily appear to our heightened awareness as the necessary gesture of Reason's deliberate homage to a higher power. Through it we have a glimpse of a mode of experience wholly beyond our own, and touch the finality of a consummation. This veritably, we might say if we had the courage of our imaginations, *is* the music of the spheres; this is indeed the hymn of that celestial love which "moves the sun and the other stars."

For reasons which evade expression in ordinary speech, *The Phoenix and the Turtle* is the most perfect short poem in any language. It is *pure* poetry in the loftiest and most abstract meaning of the words: that is to say, it gives us the highest experience which it is possible for poetry to give, and it gives it without intermission. Here for once, it seems, Shakespeare had direct command over an essential source of inspiration; here he surrendered himself completely to a kind of experience, and to the task of communicating a kind of experience, which elsewhere he conveys to us only through "the shadows of things"; for a moment he reveals himself as an inhabitant of a strange kingdom wherein he moves serene and with mastery. (pp. 23-6)

What . . . if we were to . . . suppose that Shakespeare had access to a plane of experience beyond our own, and that he had apprehended as realities a truth, a harmony and a love—apprehended them as one and not as three—which are not to be found on earth, and are not to be fully expressed in terms of earthly happenings? This apprehension in all its purity we should regard as fixed in *The Phoenix and the Turtle,* where it appears (for causes which we may look for, if we will, in what little we know of Shakespeare's life) as a symbolic vision of perfect and celestial love, through which "the white radiance of eternity" shines without spot. By what stress of soul Shakespeare attained to this experience we do not know: we can only guess. But after this experience, which was valid only so long as it lasted, he was bewildered. Having seen something beyond the world, he was bewildered in the world. We can explain the preoccupation with death which entered into his work with the plays of the *Hamlet* period—*Hamlet* and *Measure for Measure* followed immediately after *The Phoenix and the Turtle*—and we can explain the apparent cynicism with which they are pervaded by appealing to the actual experience which is recorded in the Sonnets: what we cannot explain in such terms is the strange quality of this preoccupation with death, the sudden extension of his poetic

range, and his production of effects which we most naturally describe as superhuman: his command, let us say, of a new majestic and unearthly music. From this time onward Shakespeare rejects life; and he never accepts it again. It is true that there is something which is often described as "serenity" in his latest romantic plays, culminating in *The Tempest,* but to insist on this quality, indeed to describe it by such a word, is to exaggerate it and to distort the total effect of Shakespeare's work. For the "serenity" of the final period is not of the same order as the tumult and despair of the great tragedies. The acceptance that is in them is not an acceptance of life; it is something quite different, it is an acceptance of his own rejection of life. He is no longer rebellious against the discrepancy, the utter hostility between the thing he knows and the thing which is. He has tried to reconcile them. Shakespeare's tragedies are essentially nothing but the repeated attempt to express his knowledge in terms of this world; that is why they are terrible and moving as no other tragedies, not even the greatest, have been. We feel within them an overstraining of the human soul. Not for nothing does madness and hallucination count for so much in their structure. Shakespeare is torn asunder by the effort to express a perception which is not of this world in terms of events and characters which are. They derive their mysterious potency from the double tragedy of which they are the record: the tragedy of the characters, and the tragedy of Shakespeare who invented them in vain—in vain, not for our purposes, but for his own intentions. And, in spite of the magnificent triumphs he was to achieve, in spite of the incomparable victory which is represented by *King Lear* and *Antony and Cleopatra* in the kingdom of art, Shakespeare's great tragic period ends in failure for himself. He has attempted the impossible; he has come nearer to achieving it than any other human being we know. But the impossible remains the impossible, and Shakespeare fails. (pp. 32-4)

[Precisely] because Shakespeare was the greatest of all poets, he accepted his own essential and inevitable failure. Because his intuition into reality was deepest, his was the deepest consciousness of the impossibility of ever fully and truly manifesting it through "the imitation of emotions and actions" [Aristotle, in his *Poetics*]. No man has ever done that; if ever it can be done, the world and the human mind will be changed. And this, and nothing else, I believe, is what Shakespeare is saying when he has given up the struggle with the impossible. His Perdita [in *The Winter's Tale*], his Miranda [in *The Tempest*], his Marina [in *Pericles*], these new-born creatures who look on the world with a new vision and cry, like Miranda,

> O brave new world
> That has such creatures in it!
>
> [*The Tempest,* V. i. 183-84]

are merely the form of speech with which the great poet utters the truth of the great prophet: "Except ye be born again ye can in no wise enter into the Kingdom of Heaven" [John 3:3]. And, further, I believe that it was because Shakespeare also had, by his own way, attained to that knowledge that he cared not at all what happened to his great work, and it was left to the pious offices of two fellow actors to save the most magnificent poetry of the world from oblivion.

Poetry is relative; but the intuition and the knowledge from which poetry is born is absolute. And there is no reconciling them; the greatest poetry is a compromise. And Shakespeare had reached a point where compromise and the effort of compromise had no more interest for him. He was, in a sense, the ideal poet, and he reached an ideal conclusion: the more we understand him, the more we can understand the essential laws of poetic genius, and the nature of poetry itself.

Poetry, I have said, is relative: in order to be universal and comprehensible it must be. But there is a poetry that may almost be called absolute. *The Phoenix and the Turtle* belongs to this kind of poetry. It is the direct embodiment, through symbols which are necessarily dark, of a pure, comprehensive and self-satisfying experience, which we may call, if we please, an immediate intuition into the hidden nature of things. It is inevitable that such poetry should be obscure, mystical, and strictly unintelligible: it is too abstract for our comprehension, too essential, too little mediated. There is not much poetry of this kind; because it is too personal and too esoteric to gain the general ear. And it necessarily hovers between the condition of being the highest poetry of all and not being poetry at all. But, wherever in the scale we place it, it gives us a clue to the nature of poetry itself. For relative poetry—which is practically the whole of what we call poetry—is born of the adjustment of the human soul to the knowledge and memory of such an experience. It comes of the effort to communicate this knowledge through a world of symbols; and the highest among this relative poetry is that in which the symbols chosen from the world of our human experience are most completely saturated with the quality of this intuition. (pp. 41-3)

> John Middleton Murry, "The Nature of Poetry," in his Discoveries: Essays in Literary Criticism, W. Collins Sons & Co. Ltd., 1924, pp. 11-44.

C. H. HERFORD (essay date 1922)

[*A distinguished English scholar and critic, Herford published commentary on Renaissance and nineteenth-century English literature and also championed the works of such European writers as Goethe, Ibsen, and Pushkin. His works include a ten-volume edition of the plays and poems of Shakespeare (1899-1904), Shakespeare's Treatment of Love and Marriage (1921), A Sketch of Recent Shakespearean Investigation, 1893-1923 (1923), and A Sketch of the History of Shakespeare's Influence on the Continent (1925). The following excerpt is taken from an essay originally written for a revised edition (1922) of* The Henry Irving Shakespeare. *Herford commends the allegorical interpretation of* The Phoenix and the Turtle *posited by Carleton Brown (see Additional Bibliography) and accepts the poem's authenticity. Nevertheless, he appears to rate Shakespeare's poem and its companions in Chester's volume as mere occasional pieces composed on demand, but in "good-natured spirit," to flatter Sir John Salisbury.*]

Fresh light has been thrown . . . on the curious piece of allegory and symbolism which mystifies many readers on the closing page of the Globe and other modern editions—*The Phoenix and the Turtle*. The poem, which is unlike any other verse of Shakespeare's, was published with his full name in 1601, and there is no reason to doubt its authenticity. It was contributed, as is commonly believed, to a collection of verse tributes presented by Robert Chester to his patron Sir John Salisbury, under the general title, *Love's Martyr*. Several other well-known writers contributed, in particular Marston, Chapman, and Jonson; but the persons of Salisbury and Chester themselves were hitherto obscure. In one of the *Bryn Mawr College Monographs* (No. 14, 1913), Mr. Carleton Brown [see Additional Bibliography] has collected many poems by Chester and Salisbury, preserved in MS. at Christ

Church, Oxford, and elsewhere, and thus indirectly helped us to take the measure of the literary proclivities of these amiable but not distinguished minds, and to understand the good-natured spirit in which illustrious men of letters paid indulgent compliments to the Welsh knight. (pp. 24-5)

> C. H. Herford, "The Publication of Shakespeare's Works: The Stage and the Press," in his A Sketch of Recent Shakespearean Investigation: 1893-1923, Blackie & Son Limited, 1923, pp. 8-25.

JOSEPH QUINCY ADAMS (essay date 1923)

[*Adams was an American scholar and general editor of the New Variorum Shakespeare. He also authored* Shakespearean Playhouses (1917) *and the* Life of William Shakespeare (1923) *and edited* The First Quarto of Titus Andronicus (1936) *and* The Passionate Pilgrim (1939). *He also served as director of the Folger Shakespeare Library from 1931-46. In the excerpt below, Adams is the first critic to compare* The Phoenix and Turtle *with the metaphysical poetry of John Donne. He suggests that Shakespeare neglected to read far enough into Chester's "tedious poem" to unravel its "cryptic meaning," which would account for his divergent treatment of the phoenix myth. Adams also intimates that in following Chester's use of metaphysical language and conceits, Shakespeare and his fellow poets appear to be mocking Chester's own obscure and pretentious poem.*]

In the latter months of 1601 there appeared a volume by an obscure provincial writer, Robert Chester, entitled *Love's Martyr: or Rosalin's Complaint. Allegorically shadowing the truth of Love, in the constant Fate of the Phoenix and Turtle*, at the end of which Shakespeare affixed a poem—the only time he is known to have contributed to the published work of another author.

Chester in all probability was a domestic retainer—a chaplain or a tutor—in the household of a wealthy country gentleman, John Salisbury, Esq., of Lleweni, County Denbigh, Wales. . . . *Love's Martyr* was dedicated to Salisbury, and solely designed to celebrate him, and . . . Shakespeare contributed his poem not as a compliment to Chester, or to Chester's work, but as an expression of his personal esteem for Salisbury. . . . (p. 335)

The verses Shakespeare contributed, though ostensibly on the theme of the Phoenix and the Turtle, are not closely related to that theme as Chester had developed it. Indeed Shakespeare seems not to have read Chester's tedious poem far enough to have unraveled its cryptic meaning, or to have discovered that from the ashes of the dead birds, whose death was merely an allegorical representation of matrimony, there came noble offspring. Accordingly, in his haste jumping to the conclusion that the two birds died in reality "leaving no posterity" [l. 59], he wrote a graceful funeral song, in which, in the metaphysical style of John Donne, he played with the ideas that marriage makes two into one and that "one is no number." The concluding lines of the *"Threnos"* may be slyly humorous when the poet calls upon his readers to repair to the urn and—

> For these dead birds sigh a prayer.
>
> [l. 67]

The whole undertaking on the part of these distinguished London poets reminds one, at least in a way, of the commendatory poems which many writers contributed to Coryat's *Crudities*. Jonson begins jocularly: "We must sing too?" and all the poets seem to try in a sly way to be as obscure as Chester himself. But, of course, the contributors restrained themselves in order rightly "to gratulate an honorable friend."

The episode may be taken as illustrating Shakespeare's good nature in humoring the vanity of a country knight who had been a generous friend to the theatres and the London playwrights. (pp. 341-42)

> *Joseph Quincy Adams, " 'The Passionate Pilgrim' and 'Love's Martyr',* " in his A Life of William Shakespeare, *Houghton Mifflin Company, 1923, pp. 332-42.*

G. BONNARD   (essay date 1937)

[*Bonnard regards* The Phoenix and Turtle *and the other poems that constitute the "poeticall Essaies" appended to* Love's Martyr *as satires not only of Chester's poem, but of the author himself. Encumbered with a prescribed theme and Chester's clumsy, if not illogical, allegorical apparatus and central conceit, Shakespeare and his fellow poets rebelled, but prudently "concealed their mockery under a pretense of high seriousness." Shakespeare, in particular, Bonnard argues, could not resist making a joke of the logical conclusion of Chester's allegory and conceit; his poem is not at all difficult to understand, the critic claims, once one sees the indelicate joke written into it. Bonnard's interpretation has won few adherents, although many critics concur on the presence of humorous elements in these poems.*]

The rather unusual circumstances of the publication of *Love's Martyr* are well-known. As, however, they must be kept in mind if the true meaning of Shakespeare's little poem is to be grasped, I must be suffered to relate them once again.

Among Shakespeare's friends in London there was a wealthy country gentleman, John Salisbury, who, leaving his Welsh estate, came to London with his family in 1595 and spent the greater part of the next ten years in the metropolis. His wealth, his birth and his marriage made it easy for him to mix in the most aristocratic society: he had royal blood in his veins, descending from an illegitimate son of King Henry VIII, and his wife was the illegitimate daughter of the Earl of Derby. He won the favour of the Queen, who made him one of her esquires and knighted him in 1601. Before settling in London, the worthy squire had been conspicuous in Wales as a patron of letters and a protector of local poets. In London he continued to show the deepest interest in literature, in the theatre in particular, and was soon the friend of the best-known playwrights of the day. In 1601, one of the poets he had encouraged in Wales determined to have a volume of his own verse published in London, in the hope thus to achieve the renown he thought he fully deserved. Chester—for that was the name of this pretentious person—collected all the verse he had been writing on all sorts of subjects for the last ten years, arranged it into what purposed to be a single composition, the avowed intent of which was to celebrate the marriage of Salisbury in 1587. This he naturally dedicated to his former Patron. Out of mere foolish vanity, or perhaps out of kindness, Salisbury not only accepted the dedication, but determined to do all he could to prevent the volume of his Welsh protégé sinking into immediate oblivion, as it plainly deserved to do. He appears to have called upon some of his literary friends in London, all well-known poets, begging them to honour the volume with poems of their own. This they agreed to do. But, instead of composing, according to custom, complimentary pieces on the author and his work,

they all penned verses celebrating Sir John himself, their generous friend and patron, and penned them with their tongues in their cheeks. They had read enough of the Welshman's poem to discover how very absurd a production it was, how little it deserved the honour Sir John wanted them to pay to it. But they resolved to humour him by pretending to celebrate his merits while taking their own pleasure. He was sure to be mightily pleased at being celebrated by such eminent poets, and his vanity or his obtuseness would keep him from seeing that he was being made a fool of.

Chester had sung the marriage of his patron under an allegorical disguise: a turtle—the turtle of course typifies constancy in love—impersonated Salisbury and a phoenix—symbol of love and beauty—stood for his wife. Their marriage was most strangely represented by the death of the phoenix: married life, this I imagine was Chester's sensible but rather unflattering meaning, effectively destroys a woman's beauty. Out of the ashes of the wonderful bird, however, there rises a new phoenix, as beautiful as her mother was; which was meant as a compliment to Sir John's daughter, a girl of fourteen in 1601. . . . After Chester's long rambling poem, the reader of *Love's Martyr* comes on a new title-page: *Hereafter follow diuerse poeticall Essaies on the former subject, viz. the Turtle and Phoenix. Done by the best and chiefest of our modern writers, with their names subscribed to their particular works: never before extant: And now first consecrated by them all generally to the love and merit of the true-noble Knight, Sir John Salisburie. Dignum laude virum Musa vetat mori* [A man worthy of praise will not allow the muse to die]. *MDCI.* In which title-page, I need hardly point out, the mocking intent is evident. All the poems that follow, by Shakespeare, Marston, Chapman, Jonson and another poet who signs 'Ignoto', refer, in accordance with the title, to the subject of the Turtle and the Phoenix: to their marriage, that is to the death of the Phoenix, to their constancy in love, and to their reward in a new little phoenix their daughter.

Shakespeare, possibly because he was the foremost poet of the group, was entrusted with the task of celebrating the death of the Phoenix. Chapman undertook to praise the constancy of the Turtle, Sir John. Jonson, besides expatiating on the same theme, added the necessary explanation in the form of an encomium on the Phoenix and her 'illustre brightness'

> O, so divine a creature,
> Who could be false to?

Lastly Marston sang the perfections of the new phoenix, Sir John's young daughter. They all wrote in a spirit of rollicking fun, apparently enjoying the joke to the full. But prudently—they did not want to hurt their devoted friend—they concealed their mockery under a pretense of high seriousness calculated to lead him astray. In this they were so successful that they have led astray not Sir John alone, but all the critics so far as I know. The amount of nonsense which has been written and published on their little sequence, and on Shakespeare's contribution in particular, is really staggering.

As a matter of fact, Shakespeare's poem is not difficult to understand, provided one sees the joke. "These are 'country matters'; from which, thank Heaven, we are never far away in Shakespeare", as Middleton Murry says [in his *Shakespeare*]. And if the reader is afraid of being shocked, let him stop here. The joke is indelicate. But I'll do what I can to explain it delicately.

Chester had allegorized the marriage of Salisbury and his

wife as the death of the Phoenix. This absurd idea tickled Shakespeare's fancy who, in view I suppose of the Turtle's constancy, would not have it that the Phoenix died alone; the Turtle must die with her; they both must die together. This being settled, he determined to celebrate their death, that is the marriage, by means of a funeral song. So, remembering a famous nursery rhyme, the poet calls on different birds to attend the funeral in various capacities suited to their character or plumage: the nightingale will act as 'herald sad', the eagle will be present to see to it that everything is done as it should be, to keep 'the obsequy so strict' [l. 12], the swan will be the 'priest in surplice white' [l. 13], and the crow one of the mourners. When all the birds have assembled, an anthem is sung, the purpose of which is to explain the circumstances of the 'tragic scene' of the two lovers' death: at the very moment when their love was to be consummated, when, as the poet says, from two they were growing to one, and

> no space was seen
> 'Twixt the turtle and his queen.
>
> [ll. 30-1]

when reason was being puzzled how two could be one though remaining two, they were both and together consumed in the mutual flame of their love. . . . To complete the obsequies, there only remains to sing the threnody or funeral lamentation. And here Shakespeare's own explanation of what was to be understood by the lovers' death comes out quite plainly, and his motive is apparent: he wishes to make fun of Chester's preposterous idea of representing Sir John's daughter as rising out of the ashes of her dead mother. So her birth was a miracle! Poor Sir John had nothing to do with it! Very well! He and his bride must be made to die then before anything has happened:

> Death is now the phoenix' nest;
> And the turtle's loyal breast
> To eternity doth rest,
>
> Leaving no posterity;
> 'Twas not their infirmity,
> It was married chastity.
>
> [ll. 56-61]

Thus, Shakespeare's contribution to the second part of Chester's volume was a joke, and one which was not in the best of tastes. But the creator of Juliet's Nurse was not overdelicate. Like most men, like all full-blooded young men at any rate, Shakespeare had a particular relish for what is called obscene jests. Not to admit it, would be absurd. Here the grossness is carefully concealed, but so it is in many of Mercutio's [in *Romeo and Juliet*], or Hamlet's jokes. And just as most editors either do not see or pretend not to see the worst kind of indecencies in the plays, so critics have not realized or pretend not to have grasped the true signification of this little piece of verse. (pp. 66-8)

> *G. Bonnard, "Shakespeare's Contribution to R. Chester's 'Love's Martyr': 'The Phoenix and the Turtle'," in* English Studies, *Netherlands, Vol. XIX, No. 1, February, 1937, pp. 66-9.*

KENNETH MUIR AND SEAN O'LOUGHLIN (essay date 1937)

[*In the excerpt below, Muir and O'Loughlin offer an interpretation of* The Phoenix and Turtle *based on biographical and contextual studies, claiming that the poem represents a pivotal*

Threnos.

Beautie, Truth, and Raritie,
Grace in all simplicitie,
Here enclosde, in cinders lie.

Death is now the *Phœnix* nest,
And the *Turtles* loyall brest,
To eternitie doth rest.

Leauing no posteritie,
Twas not their infirmitie,
It was married Chastitie.

Truth may seeme, but cannot be,
Beautie bragge, but tis not she,
Truth and Beautie buried be.

To this vrne let those repaire,
That are either true or faire,
For these dead Birds, sigh a prayer.

William Shake-speare.

Last page of the 1601 edition of The Phoenix and Turtle.

point in Shakespeare's art and foreshadows the subsequent tragic phase in his drama. The critics contend that following the break with Southampton, the friend of the Sonnets, Shakespeare lost faith in such absolutes as beauty, truth, and reason; but even though his love was betrayed, the fact that it existed once sufficed to establish the miracle of love. With this new vision, the critics argue, Shakespeare reaffirmed his faith in love as an eternal absolute and recorded this restoration of faith in The Phoenix and Turtle. *Muir and O'Loughlin also discover in this poem intimations of "a belief in constancy and faithfulness" that would find its fullest expression in Shakespeare's mature tragedies and romances.*]

The idea of death was naturally associated in [Shakespeare's] mind with the irreparable ravages of time, and in the *Sonnets,* especially, he declared that there were two ways of conquering death and time, by marriage and breed, or by the immortalizing power of art. . . . [In] the last years of the century, he had lost his faith in the absolutes in which he had once believed, beauty, truth and goodness. Silvia, in *The Two Gentlemen of Verona,* was holy, fair and wise in the eyes of love, and it is love which converts these absolutes from abstractions into realities. That . . . was the significance of the imagery of *Romeo and Juliet.* When he wrote that play, love was Shakespeare's religion. It is also the religion expressed in the *Sonnets.* When, therefore, in the profound pessimism of *2*

Henry IV, Shakespeare revealed his loss of faith in life, it was because he was losing or had already lost his faith in love.

Either he must recover his lost faith, or he will continue to write bad imitations of his early work, all the more barren because they exhibit a more dexterous technique. The plays that followed were his three finest comedies, and *Julius Caesar,* the first of the great tragedies. We must infer, therefore, that by some means, by some experience, he had achieved a new faith in life. He must have undergone some mystical experience which transformed him from the best of the Elizabethans to the Shakespeare we all know. If we had no evidence to go upon, we could safely infer that this experience was concerned with the conquest of death and time, and with the reaffirmation of his belief in love. If we had no record, so much would be certain. The record we have, in *The Phoenix and the Turtle,* a poem which has suffered at the hands of most Shakespearean critics a strange neglect. Doubtless the obscurity of its language has contributed very largely to this, and Professor Carleton Brown expressed accepted opinion when he said: 'Shakespere's brief poem in itself presents a hopeless enigma' [see Additional Bibliography]. But the impression still remains that the poem is heavily charged with meaning, and it is our purpose to attempt a solution by means of the clues that Shakespeare has so freely dispersed throughout the rest of his work. (pp. 127-28)

The Phoenix and the Turtle came not long after [Shakespeare's] final break with Southampton. It must be emphasized that this break is not to be confused with the estrangement mentioned in the *Sonnets* themselves, but was a deeper and more disturbing one, which came after the last sonnet had been written. Despite this, the poem is not one of despair, but of quiet assurance. 'Hope creates From its own wreck the thing it contemplates' [Shelley, *Prometheus Unbound*]. Therein lies its significance. Southampton had destroyed the love for which the poet had been willing to sacrifice everything. 'Take all my loues, my loue, yea take them all' [*Sonnet 40*], and Shakespeare now proclaims that though their mutual love is ended in the actual world, it exists for ever in eternity. This may be thought a poor consolation, a sentimental brooding over what might have been; but this is to misunderstand the poem's significance. Though love has been betrayed brutally, even sordidly, the fact that it once existed is sufficient assurance to the poet that 'Loue hath Reason' [l. 47], that is to say is an absolute. He will not admit, as he afterwards did in a moment of bitterness, that love's betrayal is a proof that it never existed. Here, he re-enunciates the testament he wrote when he suspected that Southampton's affection was cooling:

> Loue is not loue
> Which alters when it alteration findes,
> Or bends with the remouer to remoue.
> O no, it is an euer fixed marke
> That lookes on tempests and is neuer shaken;
> It is the star to euery wandring barke,
> Whose worths vnknowne, although his higth be
>   taken.
> Loue's not Times foole, though rosie lips and
>   cheeks
> Within his bending sickles compasse come,
> Loue alters not with his breefe houres and weekes,
> But beares it out euen to the edge of doome.
>
> [*Sonnet 116*]

Though 'Loue and Constancie is dead' [l. 22], the miracle of perfect love exists in eternity,

> *Phoenix* and the *Turtle* fled,
> In a mutuall flame from hence,
>
> [ll. 23-4]

so great was their love on earth.

We come now to the more metaphysical parts of the poem, where the problems are of a different order. Let us take the stanzas that express the unity in disunity of the two birds:

> So they loued as loue in twaine,
> Had the essence but in one,
> Two distincts, Diuision none,
> Number there in loue was slaine.
>
> Hearts remote, yet not asunder;
> Distance and no space was seene,
> Twixt this *Turtle* and his Queene;
> But in them it were a wonder.
>
> [ll. 25-32]

Shakespeare had already expressed this view of his love in *Sonnet 36,* addressed to Southampton:

> Let me confesse that we two must be twaine,
> Although our vndeuided loues are one.
>
> [ll. 1-2]

It was this feeling of the unity of the spirit that enabled Shakespeare to preserve an ultimate faith in love and beauty, even in the Inferno through which he was to pass. Cordelia would be impossible without the emotional conviction expressed in *The Phoenix and the Turtle.* (pp. 131-33)

By reason of the mutual disaster which is to engulf them, Lear and Cordelia are lifted up into the condition of *The Phoenix and the Turtle.* Lear's very words: 'We two will sing alone like birds i' the cage' [V. iii. 9], contain a trembling mortal echo of their song, and Reason might chant over Cordelia the dirge it chanted over them.

Julius Caesar is the first of the tragedies to be 'illuminated by the splendour of the vision', and this brief poem, written during the same period, is the first expression of that vision. In it, the seed of all Shakespeare's later development is contained. Professor Wilson Knight, in his essay, *The Shakespearian Aviary* [see Additional Bibliography], has attempted to show that the symbolism of the first six stanzas can be referred to a particular play. But this is to consider too curiously for our purpose. All we would claim is that the mourners at the obsequies are 'heraulds sad' of the 'tragique scene' on to which the poet was about to enter, and that the essence of Shakespearean tragedy is the conflict between the vision and life as we know it. It is clear that when the poem was written, Shakespeare had a prophetic understanding of the experience he must undergo. Shakespearean tragedy is, in a very real sense, the tragedy of Shakespeare himself.

As we can gather from the *Sonnets,* for example, the idea of sex was tarnished for the poet, and he still clung to the ideal of the marriage of true minds, chaste, and therefore

> Leauing no posteritie,
> Twas not their infirmitie,
> It was married Chastitie.
>
> [ll. 59-61]

The poem is a recognition that this love, divorced from its original object, is the motive force behind all his poetry ('So oft haue I inuok'd thee for my Muse'—*Sonnet 78*); and it

marks the transformation of the lovely boy into the spirit of
Ariel. The validity of this love is next established:

> Truth may seeme, but cannot be,
> Beautie bragge, but tis not she.
>
> [ll. 62-3]

It was not Truth, for Truth had been betrayed. It was not
Beauty, for the Beauty he had worshipped played him false.
The answer comes in a brief couplet:

> Loue hath Reason, Reason none,
> If what parts, can so remaine.
>
> [ll. 47-8]

Love, it was, to which the others were subsumed, that inspired Shakespeare's plays, a love that would be eventually
extended to embrace the whole world. He had not reached
that state, but already his prophetic soul looked forward to
the ultimate synthesis, the emotional serenity of *The Tempest.* He looked forward to the time when even Reason would
recognize that Love was above Reason. As Arviragus in
Cymbeline says:

> I know not why
> I loue this youth, and I haue heard you say,
> Loue's reason's, without reason.
>
> [IV. ii. 20-2]

Though 'in itself confounded' [l. 41], it was Reason that made
the threne in honour of the co-supremes and stars of love.
(pp. 134-36)

Truth and Beauty had been set side by side by the poet in *Sonnet 14.* Addressing the lovely boy, he had said, 'Thy end is
Truthes and Beauties doome and date', and so now

> Truth may seeme, but cannot be,
> Beautie bragge, but tis not she,
> Truth and Beautie buried be.

This must not be taken to imply physical death so much as
the admission of the power of Death which faithlessness
brings in its train, just as fidelity, by its very existence, conquers Death.

This consideration brings us to the problem of why Shakespeare chose the symbolism of the Phoenix to express this determining experience of his life. The Phoenix has been, from
time immemorial, a symbol of immortality and resurrection,
and Shakespeare's aching desire to overcome the iniquity of
oblivion, so manifest in the *Sonnets,* here finds relief:

> Deuouring time blunt thou the Lyons pawes,
> And make the earth deuoure her owne sweet brood,
> Plucke the keene teeth from the fierce Tygers
>   yawes,
> And burne the long liu'd Phænix in her blood.
>
> [*Sonnet 19*]

The immortal Phoenix must make this concession to Time.
She must burn in a flame of love, and hence, the bird is a love
symbol. . . . Shakespeare doubtless took the idea of the turtle as the devoted mate of the Phoenix from Chester's own
poem, *Love's Martyr,* the turtle being, of course, the Paphian
dove of Venus.

The Phoenix, finally, is a symbol not only of immortality, but
also of death, and the emphasis on death and mourning is a
parallel to the thoughts of death in *Julius Caesar* and *Hamlet.*
Shakespeare, at the turn of the century, stood on the thresh-

old of the tragic period. The experience which finds expression in the poem enabled him to endure to the end. Love was
the star that enabled his 'wandring barke' to survive the 'tempest'. In the plays that follow upon this new attitude, notably
Antony and Cleopatra and *King Lear,* his concept of order in
the Universe is expressed as a belief in constancy and faithfulness, a constancy and faithfulness that, in the tragedies, receives death as its reward, and is the antithesis of the betrayal
that compassed the death of Caesar. Years later, Imogen,
'alone the Arabian bird' [*Cymbeline,* I. vi. 17], escaped the
normal penalty for constancy, though she had a funeral, and,
in *The Tempest,* Prospero's enemies are compelled to admit
that

> In *Arabia*
> There is one Tree, the Phoenix throne, one Phoenix
> At this houre reigning there.
>
> [III. iii. 22-4]

When the validity of the vision of *The Phoenix and the Turtle*
had been acknowledged, the poet's task was done. (pp. 136-
38)

> *Kenneth Muir and Sean O'Loughlin, "Journey to
> the Phoenix," in their* The Voyage to Illyria: A New
> Study of Shakespeare, *1937. Reprint by Barnes &
> Noble, Inc., 1970, pp. 115-40.*

C. S. LEWIS   (lecture date 1944)

[*An English literary critic and novelist, Lewis was also a distinguished Renaissance scholar whose writing was strongly influenced by his Christian beliefs. As a Shakespearean critic, he argued that commentators who pay too much attention to character analysis are apt to overlook the intention of the plays, particularly their moral and ethical impact. Instead, Lewis suggested
that the critic should surrender him or herself to "the poetry
and situation" in all of Shakespeare's dramas. His remarks on
* The Phoenix and Turtle *were first delivered in a lecture at
Trinity College, Cambridge, in 1944. Lewis adopts an idealistic
approach, asserting that "Shakespeare uses his poem to expound a philosophy of love" and to celebrate "the exchanged
death, and life, of a fully mutual love." According to Lewis,
the poem is metaphysical not by design, but through the effect
of such devices as the rigid, hypnotic metrical pattern, the
"oracular" style, and Shakespeare's "supreme invention" of
Reason as a spokesman for the supremacy of love. The critic
declares that these elements together create "the illusion that
we have been in another world and heard the voices of gods."*]

In 1601 there came out *Love's Martyr* by Robert Chester, a
long, mysterious allegory about a male Turtle-dove and a female Phoenix, halting in metre, defective in rhyme, and almost to be classed with Copley's *Fig for Fortune* as Late Medieval. To this are appended 'diverse poeticall Essaies' on the
same subject, signed by *Vatum Chorus, Ignoto,* William
Shakespeare, John Marston, George Chapman, and Ben Jonson. Shakespeare's piece is, of course, what we call 'The
Phoenix and the Turtle', though it appears without title.
Whatever the external occasion may have been, Shakespeare
uses his poem to expound a philosophy of love; the last word,
presumably, that he has given us in his own person on that
subject. Its doctrine consummates that of the *Sonnets.* In
them the 'naughting' had been one sided. He had lost himself
in another but that other had not lost himself in Shakespeare.
Now Shakespeare celebrates the exchanged death, and life, of
a fully mutual love. He is not writing 'metaphysical poetry'
in the technical sense critics give to that term, but he is writ-

ing in the true sense, a metaphysical poem. Such a task leads some poets . . . into a loose form and a style *sermoni proprior* [more appropriate to conversation]. Shakespeare, on the other hand, gives us formality within formality, the *threnos* within the funeral poem, the conduct of his work ritualistic, his metres rigid, deliberately, hypnotically, monotonous. His supreme invention was the introduction of Reason as the principal speaker. The words which sum up Shakespeare's doctrine, 'Love hath reason, reason none' [l. 47] owe all their importance to the fact that it is Reason who utters them. In the mouth of a passionate lover or a passionate mourner they would be the stalest claptrap; one more expression of 'will' revolting against 'wit', one more confirmation of the assumption, traditional since Chrétien, that Love and Reason are adversaries. But it is Reason who here exalts love above reason. It is Reason who has seen rational categories overthrown: 'distincts' becoming indivisible, propriety (*proprium*) 'appalled' by the discovery that the self-same is yet not the same (for of course *the self* in [l. 38] does not mean 'the ego'), and something brought into existence which cannot be called two or one. It is Reason who confesses that neither truth (which is Reason's natural goal) nor beauty is the highest good. For beauty is only a brag or a bravery, a sign or hint, of the true good: and truth 'cannot be', it is not being, but only 'about' being. Reason, in fact, rationally recognizes what is beyond reason. We could not have guessed, I think, from internal evidence that this poem was by Shakespeare. As an anonymous work it would command our highest admiration. The oracular, which of all styles is most contemptible when it fails, is here completely successful; the illusion that we have been in another world and heard the voices of gods is achieved. Approached, as we usually approach it, after long familiarity with the plays, 'The Phoenix and the Turtle' has, in addition, another interest. We feel that we have been admitted to the *natura naturans* from which the *natura naturata* of the plays proceeded: as though we had reached the garden of Adonis and seen where Imogens [in *Cymbeline*] and Cordelias [in *King Lear*] are made. (pp. 508-09)

C. S. Lewis, "Verse in the 'Golden' Period," in his English Literature in the Sixteenth Century, Excluding Drama, *Oxford at the Clarendon Press, 1954, pp. 464-535.*

RANJEE G. SHAHANI (essay date 1946)

[*When the Indian critic Shahani first addressed* The Phoenix and Turtle, *in his* Towards the Stars *(1931), he lavished great praise on this "brave" poem for its "divine optimism" and "fearless uncompromising assurance," but he also disputed its authenticity, claiming it was written by John Fletcher. The essay from which the excerpt below is taken is essentially a recapitulation and refinement of his previous views, although here he acknowledges Shakespeare's authorship of the poem. Arguing that previous approaches have proven unproductive, Shahani provides a close, stanza-by-stanza reading and raises, for the first time, several issues of significance in subsequent criticism. Most notably, Shahani draws attention to Shakespeare's use of such scholastic terms as "essence," as well as his apparent allusion to the Trinitarian Doctrine. Yet the critic denies a Christian subtext, positing instead that the poem is suffused with pagan thought and the universal doctrine of "sympathetic communion." Additionally, Shahani is the first commentator to describe the poem in terms of Hegel's dialectic, observing a kinship between Hegelian contradictions and the series of paradoxes in* The Phoenix and Turtle. *Shahani also* calls attention to Shakespeare's borrowings from the alchemist's vocabulary and to ideas associated with Neoplatonism.*]

'The Phoenix and the Turtle' is unique in European literature. It is like a tropical bird descried in an English woodland. Yet critics have paid but scant attention to it. The exotic character of its beauty has caused them to misapprehend its real significance and to dismiss it as a pretty trifle. (p. 99)

Emerson was the first writer to recognise the strange beauty of this poem. He has left us, in the preface to his 'Parnassus' [see excerpt above, 1875], a suggestive and welcome piece of criticism:

> I should like to have the Academy of Letters propose a prize for an essay on Shakespeare's poem, *Let the bird of loudest lay,* and the *Threnos* with which it closes, the aim of the essay being to explain by historical research into the poetical myths and tendencies of the age in which it was written, the frame and allusions of the poem. . . .

Alexander B. Grosart was the first in order of time to take up Emerson's challenge [see Additional Bibliography]. He remarks as follows, in his introduction to Chester's 'Love's Martyr':

> . . . Let the reader take with him the golden key that by the "Phoenix" Shakespeare intended Elizabeth, and by the "Dove" Essex, and the "Phoenix and Turtle," hitherto regarded as a mere enigmatical epecedial lay . . . will be recognised as of rarest interest.
>
> (p. 100)

We feel grateful to Dr. Grosart for his penetration into the greatness of this poem, but the penetration we thank him for is into the mystical greatness. His application to the reigning queen leaves us unsatisfied: it does not fill the needs of the case. The lyrical note is too poignant. Our poem breathes something more than personal heartache—rather something of the cosmic tragedy of love. It is from this high altitude that the poem appeals to us, and this is the secret of its appeal. Allegories and the mere scaffolding of thought and feeling have done their duty, and we are concerned only with the stark facing of reality that we mean by intuition. The poet had come in touch with the Eternal. But Grosart's commentary ties us down to sadly mundane levels. Emerson's challenge still remains open; for almost all European critics . . . have given up the poem as incomprehensible. J. M. Robertson even called it, along with Chapman's 'The Shadow of Night,' "palpable darkness." In 1936 Mr. Pearsall Smith, writing in the *Nation and Athenaeum,* said:

> . . . and even more extraordinary is the way he (Shakespeare) imitates Mallarmé and our modern non-sense poets in "The Phoenix and the Turtle"— that conscious and deliberate construction of a merely musical pattern of words:
>
> Let the priest in surplice white,
> That defunctive music can,
> Be the death-divining swan,
> Lest the requiem lack his right.
>
> [ll. 13-16]

Can Valéry or T. S. Eliot beat the beautiful meaninglessness of this?

Criticism of this kind leads us nowhere: it only makes confusion worse confounded. . . . [It] is surprising that so many good judges of literature should have failed to understand the gracious import of 'The Phoenix and the Turtle.' To us—and we say this in all humility—the poem is self-interpreting, and we read it as follows. (pp. 100-01)

The main intention of the piece is surely fairly obvious. It is essentially an offering of divine honours to the mutual loyalty of married souls:

> So they loved, as love in twain
> Had the essence but in one;
> Two distincts, division none;
> Number there in love was slain
>
> [ll. 25-8]

This contact of twin souls is the leitmotiv of the poem. But what sort of contact do we sense? First and last and before all, a loyalty transcending all expression:

> Love and constancy is dead;
> Phoenix and the turtle fled
> In a mutual flame from hence.
>
> [ll. 22-4]

A dauntless defiance of whatever fate may have in store—a divine optimism:

> Reason in itself confounded
> Saw division grow together,
> To themselves yet either neither,
> Simple were so well compounded;
>
> That it cried, How true a twain
> Seemeth this concordant one!
> Love hath reason, reason none,
> If what parts can so remain.
>
> [ll. 41-8]

Two hearts that beat as one is the consummation the poet demands, despite gods or men:

> Hearts remote, yet not asunder;
> Distance, and no space was seen
> 'Twixt the turtle and his queen:
> But in them it were a wonder.
>
> So between them love did shine,
> That the turtle saw his right
> Flaming in the phoenix' sight;
> Either was the other's mine.
>
> [ll. 29-36]

To the poet this *is* the finality—nothing else matters. *Amor vincit omnia* [Love conquers all].

There is no trace of Christian theology in the poem, but a lovely saturation with pagan thought. The very title suggests the sex duality. It is a sex poem, albeit in a very special sense. There is, however, no slightest suggestion of lower levels: it is all pure ether.

The poem is clearly divisible into three sections: the requiem, the anthem, and the threne. We will take stanza by stanza in elaborating our thesis.

> Let the bird of loudest lay
> On the sole Arabian tree,
> Herald sad and trumpet be,
> To whose sound chaste wings obey.
>
> [ll. 1-4]

The poet himself is the chief mourner, but it requires a herald or choragus among the birds (the nightingale) to support him and to summon the blessed ones among his kind to join in the solemn function.

> But thou shrieking harbinger,
> Foul precurrer of the fiend,
> Augur of the fever's end,
> To this troop come thou not near!
>
> [ll. 5-8]

But the poet excludes and warns off some particular bird (the owl) as unworthy to approach the sacred obsequies.

> From this session interdict
> Every fowl of tyrant wing,
> Save the eagle, feather'd king:
> Keep the obsequy so strict.
>
> [ll. 9-12]

From this consultation are banished all birds only "great" through physical strength. But the eagle is not one of these. He has his regal rights apart from mere physical prowess. The eagle was the bird of Jove, adding dignity to every occasion.

> Let the priest in surplice white,
> That defunctive music can,
> Be the death-divining swan,
> Lest the requiem lack his right.
>
> [ll. 13-16]

Here the intention of the "session" is clearly indicated. It is the perfection of the requiem. The priest shall be the swan in its snowy plumage—fitting in such a celebrant. (pp. 120-21)

> Here the anthem doth commence:
> Love and constancy is dead;
> Phoenix and the turtle fled
> In a mutual flame from hence.
>
> [ll. 21-4]

Now we face our problem—our threnody—our ode of lamentation. The divinity of love and constancy has passed beyond our ken for their rightful place far above the futilities of speech and sorrow. They have sought the judgment of the Eternal. But it is not two who have gone—it is *one,* and this is a sacrifice that the gods must receive at the hands of Fate.

> And thou treble-dated crow,
> That thy sable gender makest
> With the breath thou givest and takest,
> 'Mongst our mourners shalt thou go.
>
> [ll. 17-20]

And the long-lived crow (a reference to the black plumage of the bird, always an emblem of mourning) shall be an apt companion among the mourners.

The difficulty of interpretation really begins with the stanza I am about to quote, not because it is obscure in meaning, but because the words of the poet are marvellously well chosen, and we must realise their hidden flavour.

> So they loved, as love in twain
> Had the essence but in one;
> Two distincts, division none;
> Number there in love was slain.
>
> [ll. 25-8]

The word "essence" is used in a special sense here. General

literature borrowed it from Scholasticism. It means "spring of existence." Again, the words "distinct" and "division" in their antithesis are a feature of Scholastic thought. Like object and shadow they suggest thoroughgoing dependence: one can't be without the other. Finally, the last line shows kinship in thought with the dialect of Trinitarian Doctrine. It means: duality transcended into unity.

> Hearts remote, yet not asunder;
> Distance, and no space was seen
> 'Twixt the turtle and his queen:
> But in them it were a wonder.
>
> [ll. 29-32]

At first, this stanza seems very obscure, but when the doctrine that lies behind it is perceived, it looks uncommonly simple. The reference here is to *sympathetic communion*. This is a doctrine that is universal, though of course implicit, among all primitive peoples—a belief that things that have been intimately associated are mystically bound together even after separation and far removal. The fates of the two parts are interlinked. So distance and space do not enter into the question. It is this that our poet has in mind. He says it was miraculous to see this perfection of the two birds.

> So between them love did shine,
> That the turtle saw his right
> Flaming in the phoenix' sight;
> Either was the other's mine.
>
> [ll. 33-6]

The word "shine" is used in its original sense here (A.-S., Scinan; Goth., Skeinan; Ger., Sceinan). It means "appear." The epithet "right" conveys the sense of "justification of existence"; and the line "Flaming in the phoenix' sight" indicates: "in the appreciation with which the phoenix regarded him." The last line suggests that each was the *alter ego* of the other.

> Property was thus appalled,
> That the self was not the same;
> Single nature's double name
> Neither two nor one was called.
>
> [ll. 37-40]

"Property" is a severely technical word. It suggests the scholastic doctrine which moderns might describe as a doctrine about quality. In strictness of subtle thought it is nothing of the kind. It had to do with existence in its metaphysical aspect. We are reminded of the medieval stream of thought that proceeded from the 'Isagoge' of Porphyry (fourth century A.D.?). Very likely there is an allusion here to the doctrine of the categories. This betrays acquaintance with the mode of thought—conventionalised Aristotelianism—then current in Europe. So the words "Property was thus appalled" mean that there was a logical conflict with the very concept of "proprium." Existence in its metaphysical aspect was scandalised at this impossible condition.

The paradoxes in our poem not only corelate with the subtleties of Scholastic thought but also with the stranger dreams of Hegelian speculation.

> Reason, in itself confounded,
> Saw division grow together,
> To themselves, yet either neither,
> Simple were so well compounded.
>
> [ll. 41-4]

Reason here means human intellect. The words "simple" and "compounded" are taken from alchemy. Now what does the stanza mean? Human intellect was perplexed by the paradox, $1 + 1 = 1$. (This is so when the units are globules of mercury.) They were so conjoined that neither could distinguish itself from the other. (This is something like the case of identical twins.) They were two things but so mingled that distinction of parts was impossible. (All this is the language of the alchemists: the terms indicate acquaintance with the conceptions of physiology and alchemy.)

> That it cried, How true a twain
> Seemeth this concordant one!
> Love hath reason, reason none,
> If what parts can so remain.
>
> [ll. 45-7]

Love has a logic of its own, if it should ever deign to mechanise its miracles into a technique. The principle of contradiction has no place in its deliverances. Even Hegel saw the truth of this on the tortuous level of mere intellectualism—a level that love will have none of. For love speaks the language of the gods; and we are assured on good authority that the gods never reason. They despise the dialect of dialectics.

> Thereupon it made this threne
> To the phoenix and the dove,
> Co-supremes and stars of love,
> As chorus to their tragic scene.
>
> [ll. 49-52]

Reason, unable to understand the great paradox, makes a song of lamentation to honour the tragic memory of the perfect pair.

> Beauty, truth, and rarity,
> Grace in all simplicity,
> Here enclosed in cinders lie.
>
> [ll. 53-5]

All that we have loved and reverenced is a mere packet of ashes. This is the general sense of the stanza, but the words "enclosed" and "cinders" may conceal a subtle allusion to some theory of the relation between a combustible body and the ashes (cinis). This is quite possible in a period when alchemical research was rampant.

> Death is now the phoenix' nest;
> And the turtle's loyal breast
> To eternity doth rest.
>
> [ll. 56-8]

The phoenix's nest is now only a memory of death, and the turtle's loyal breast is in charge of the gods. "Se réfugier dans la mort" [To find refuge in death].

> Leaving no posterity:
> 'Twas not their infirmity,
> It was married chastity.
>
> [ll. 59-61]

To us the stanza is perfectly clear, but directly an attempt is made to translate it into the dialect of thought called common-sense, all meaning vanishes. The poet has expressed his idea simply and perfectly.

We may, however, mention that many of the early Christian saints are credited with the same virtue of married chastity. It is a union of souls that the poet describes. Marriage to him is a sacrament.

> Truth may seem, but cannot be;

Beauty brag, but 'tis not she;
Truth and beauty buried be.

[ll. 62-4]

These lines concentrate in one perfect crystal the mellow wisdom of a lifetime. The obvious scepticism of the poet is not untouched by a fitting reverence for the verities. He decries the futile identification of appearance with reality. Let us cease, he seems to say, from our impertinent scrutinies and affectations of knowledge. It is nothing less than an insult to truth and reality to make believe that they are known. Let them pass into silence.

To this urn let those repair
That are either true or fair;
For these dead birds sigh a prayer.

[ll. 65-7]

Let those who are either true or fair make a pilgrimage to this altar of loyalty, and then depart in fitting reverence and silence. For this is all that they can either give or get.

A grand finale! *Ave atque vale.*

There is no finer appreciation of this poem than Mr. Middleton Murry's essay on "The Nature of Poetry" in his 'Discoveries' [see excerpt above, 1922]. Although he confesses that he does not know what the poem is about, he has lovingly sought out its beauties, and his work is before the world. Yet there are some features of "The Phoenix and the Turtle" that seem to demand fuller notice. These we would seek to indicate.

The first thing that impresses us about the poem is its fearless, uncompromising assurance. It is a *brave* poem. There is nothing quite like it in all English literature. Let us make two comparisons.

The year's at the spring,
The day's at the morn;
Morning's at seven;
The hill-side's dew-pearled;
The lark's on the wing;
The snail's on the thorn;
God's in his heaven—
All's right with the world.
[Robert Browning, 'Pippa Passes.']

The words are breezy, but surely they are words of humble trust—not of flaming assertion.

We have but faith: we cannot know;
For knowledge is of things we see;
And yet we trust it comes from thee,
A beam in darkness; let it grow.
[Alfred, Lord Tennyson, 'In Memoriam,' Proem.]

This too is the language of faith, diffident faith—not the faith that moves mountains.

But our poem in its entirety, though not in dissected fragments, strikes a note that rives all clouds of doubt.

The mist that shrouds the meaning is illumined by an inner fire—like the mystic fire in the heart of the opal. In what other poem in the whole of English literature do we find this effect? The reader may be challenged to name it. (pp. 121-23)

Ranjee G. Shahani, " 'The Phoenix and the Turtle','" in Notes and Queries, *Vol. 191, Nos. 5 and 6, September 7 and 21, 1946, pp. 99-101; 120-23.*

J. V. CUNNINGHAM (essay date 1952)

[*Cunningham points out that the language of* The Phoenix and Turtle *is replete with terms borrowed from Scholastic theology, including "essence," "distincts," "division," and "property," and he deduces that in this poem Shakespeare has superimposed Neoplatonic notions onto material he borrowed from courtly love poetry. Shakespeare relied on the Scholastic doctrine of love, the critic asserts, to formulate the central paradox of the poem: the mystical union of the two lovers, whereby two become one to the consternation of Reason. According to Cunningham, the mystery shrouding the union between the Phoenix and Turtle is readily dispelled when one discovers that the Scholastic doctrine of the Trinity underlies the poem's diction as well as its structure. Although the mystical notion of unification through divine love evolved from classical sources, the critic notes, Shakespeare's use of scholastic terms in their technical sense suggests that such Christian texts as Aquinas's* Summa Theologica *comprised the poet's source for these Neoplatonic ideas.*]

I am concerned in this essay with one of the principles of order that determine the structure and detail of a poem. The particular kind of principle I have in mind here consists in the use of some field or system of ideas in the writer's tradition which serves as a scheme or paradigm by which material of another order is apprehended and expounded. I shall show how the material of courtly love in Shakespeare's *Phoenix and Turtle* is treated in terms of scholastic theology. But since the relevance of scholastic thought to this poem is not generally recognized I shall proceed by a close and extended examination of the ideas and the text.

The characteristic feature of scholasticism for our purpose is its terminology. The whole system, in fact, may be said to be implicit in the definition of its terms, as in our own times the systems of clinical psychology are implicit in such terms as "regression," "libido," "flight from reality," and "inferiority complex." Consequently, if we find that Shakespeare uses such a scholastic term as "essence" in its technical sense and in a technical context we may presume not only that he was acquainted with scholastic notions but also that he was capable of thinking and feeling in those terms.

"Essence" occurs three times in Shakespeare. It appears in a well-known passage in *Measure for Measure:*

Merciful heaven,
Thou rather with thy sharp and sulphurous bolt
Split'st the unwedgeable and gnarled oak
Than the soft myrtle. But man, proud man,
Drest in a little brief authority,
Most ignorant of what he's most assur'd
(His glassy essence), like an angry ape,
Plays such fantastic tricks before high heaven
As make the angels weep. . . .

[II. ii. 114-22]

This is the scholastic notion in a scholastic context: man's essence is his intellectual soul, which is an image of God, and hence is *glassy* for it mirrors God. (pp. 265-66)

Essence is also used technically in Valentine's speech about Silvia in the *Two Gentlemen of Verona:*

And why not death rather than living torment?
To die is to be banish'd from myself;
And Silvia is myself. Banish'd from her
Is self from self—a deadly banishment!
What light is light, if Silvia be not seen?
What joy is joy, if Silvia be not by?
Unless it be to think that she is by

And feed upon the shadow of perfection.
Except I be by Silvia in the night,
There is no music in the nightingale.
Unless I look on Silvia in the day,
There is no day for me to look upon.
She is my essence, and I leave to be
If I be not by her fair influence
Foster'd, illumin'd, cherish'd, kept alive.

[III. i. 170-85]

The speech begins on a relatively human level, for the assertion that Silvia is myself and the question, "What light is
light, if Silvia be not seen?" may both be taken sufficiently
metaphorically. Nevertheless, Silvia is designated as perfection, for to imagine her present when she is absent is to feed
upon the shadow, the image, of perfection. If she were here
one would be in the presence of perfection. However, when
a Christian of Elizabeth's time comes right down to it, there
is only one true perfection, God, and only one set of terms
in which to discuss it, the theological language of the Schools.
And it is precisely in these terms that Valentine speaks. (pp.
266-67)

Silvia, consequently, is regarded as perfection, as Love in the
absolute sense, as the ultimate principle of the lover's being,
as that by which he is fostered, illumined, cherished, sustained. She is God. She is immanent and transcendent, and
the lover's relation to her is that of scholastic creature to
scholastic Creator. Apart from the blasphemy involved, there
is only one difficulty in the passage: this resides in the proposition, *She is my essence*. The proposition is technically incorrect with regard to the relation of creature and Creator in the
scholastic system, for it it manifestly false to say that the soul
is of the substance of God. Although the soul is a simple form
in its essence, it is not its own being but is a being by participation. Therefore, it is not pure act like God [Thomas Aquinas, in his *Summa Theologica*]. For man is made to the image
and likeness of God, but "the preposition *to* signifies only a
certain approach, as of something at a distance [Thomas].

Valentine's relation to Silvia, it is true, conforms in general
to the centuries-old scheme of courtly love: the lover is to the
beloved as vassal to lord, or if the scheme be construed in
Neo-Platonic terms, as it often was, as shadow to substance
or as image to archetype. But the commonest and most available source of Neo-Platonic ideas in the sixteenth century
was the scholastic doctrine of the Christian God, who is only
protected from utter Neo-Platonism by an unceasing vigilance in qualification. If one abandons the qualification, locates the infinite Idea in the finite beloved, maintains the
theological language of the Schools regarding God's imma-
nence and ceaseless providence and yet ascribes all reality to
the Idea to the extent that the lover's essence is the Idea, he
arrives at this passage. It is wordly Neo-Platonism, precipitated out of the latent Neo-Platonism of Christian dogma.
However, there remain two difficulties for anyone familiar
with these schemes of thought: 1) the analogical relationship
of the derived and Underived is contradicted by the predica-
tion of identity of essence, and 2) the identity of essence takes
the special form that the essence of the derived *is* the Underived.

The difficulties can be understood and their source located in
the light of a poem of Shakespeare's that has puzzled generations of scholars. This is the *Phoenix and Turtle,* which first
appeared as one of a series of poems on the subject indicated
by the title in Chester's *Love's Martyr,* 1601. The poem begins

with a kind of parliament of fowls gathered to perform a memorial service for the Turtle and the Phoenix, the lover and
the beloved. It continues:

Here the anthem doth commence:
Love and constancy is dead,
Phoenix and the turtle fled
In a mutual flame from hence.

So they lov'd as love in twain
Had the essence but in one;
Two distincts, division none:
Number there in love was slain.

Hearts remote, yet not asunder;
Distance, and no space was seen
'Twixt this turtle and his queen;
But in them it were a wonder.

So between them love did shine
That the turtle saw his right
Flaming in the phoenix' sight:
Either was the other's mine.

Property was thus appalled,
That the self was not the same;
Single nature's double name
Neither two nor one was called.

Reason, in itself confounded,
Saw division grow together,
To themselves yet either neither,
Simple were so well compounded;

That it cried, 'How true a twain
Seemeth this concordant one!
Love hath reason, reason none,
If what parts can so remain.

[ll. 21-48]

The poem concludes with a threne over the urn where their
cinders lie, to the effect that Beauty and Truth (that is, Love
and Constancy) are now dead, for these were their ideal
forms, the substances of which any subsequent appearances
are shadows.

The central part of the poem quoted above refines in exact,
technical, scholastic language the relationship of the lovers.
They are Love and Constancy, Beauty and Truth, Phoenix
and Turtle. The nature of their love was such that love in
each had the essence (the defining principle by which anything that is, is what it is) only in one. Obviously, then, the
effect of their love was unitive. But in terms of what scheme
of ideas is this union conceived? It is not unlike, of course,
the Neo-Platonic union, in which the soul, being reduced to
the trace of the One which constitutes its resemblance to it,
is absorbed, submerged, and lost in the presence of the One.
There is no more distance, no doubleness, the two fuse in one.

But the language here is Latin and has passed, as had the doctrine of Plotinus, through the disputations of the Schoolmen:
*essence, distincts, division, property, single nature's double
name, simple, compounded.* Furthermore, the chief point of
Shakespeare's poem is lost in the Plotinan formulation: for
the central part of the poem consists wholly in the reiteration—line after line as if the poet would have you understand
even to exhaustion—of the paradox that though identical the
two are distinct; they are both truly one and truly two. Thus,
for example, in the Plotinan union there is no interval between the two—*And no space was seen*—but the contrary element of the paradox—*distance*—is lacking.

The language and the ideas of the poem are technical and scholastic. But is this the scholastic doctrine of love? Is the scheme of thought here of the same order as the material of the poem? The doctrine of Thomas Aquinas on this point is sufficiently representative of the scholastic position. Love, he tells us (he is quoting the Neo-Platonist, the Pseudo-Dionysius) is a unitive force. The manner of this union, the way in which the beloved can be said to be in the lover, can be comprehended by an analogy. For just as when someone understands something there is a certain notion of the thing in the man who understands, so when someone loves something there is a certain impress, so to speak, of what is loved in the feeling of the lover, and with reference to this one can say that what is loved is in the lover as what is understood is in him who understands. But union in this sense by no means amounts to absolute identification; it is not possible to say according to this account that she is my essence.

Thomas in another place distinguishes a three-fold sense in which union is related to love. There is the union which is the cause of love, and this is a genuine and substantial union with respect to one's love of himself; it is a union based on similitude with respect to one's love of others. Secondly, there is that union which is essentially love itself, and which involves a certain conformation of feeling toward the object. If this is the love of friendship, the nature of the relationship is similar to the substantial union spoken of above, for the lover loves the other as himself; if it is the love of desire, he loves the other as something that belongs to him. There is, finally, a third kind of union which is an effect of love, and that is that union of the parties involved which the lover seeks of the loved. This union is in accordance with the demands of love, for, as Aristotle says in the *Politics,* "Aristophanes said that lovers desire from being two to become one," but since "the result of this would be to destroy either one of them or both," they seek a suitable and proper union, namely to live and speak together and to be joined in other ways of this nature [Thomas].

From this much it is clear how carefully Thomas distinguishes and how painstakingly he points out that the effect of union in love, together with those other related effects which he goes on to discuss—a mutual inherence of one in the other, an ecstatic going out of oneself, and a zealousness in appropriating the good which one loves—only take place in a certain sense. The love of desire, it is true, does not rest with attaining any external or surface enjoyment of what it loves, but seeks to possess it absolutely, penetrating as if to the very heart of the beloved. But it is only *as if.* For human love admits of no real identification. Though we desire it, if it were attained, one or both would be destroyed.

In Shakespeare's poem, however, the lover is identified with the beloved; the beloved in his essence; they become one and yet neither is annihilated. The lovers are of course destroyed in that they have passed in a mutual flame from this life, but clearly they have only passed into the real life of Ideas from the unreal life of materiality.

It might be suspected, looking back on the passage in the *Two Gentlemen of Verona,* that the relation implied here is that of the Beatific Vision, in which our love of God and God's love for us finds its ultimate fulfilment. If this were so it would certainly offer us what we are looking for. It would offer us a model or paradigm by means of which the relationship of the lovers in this poem is constructed and construed. But though the doctrine of the Beatific Vision be thorny and difficult to understand, nevertheless one thing is clear: even in that last eternal embrace, in which, no longer through a glass darkly, we see the essence of God face to face . . . , there is no absolute identification of essence. (pp. 268-72)

But anything is forgiven a lover, the reader may exclaim at this point, even the grossest hyperbole: love is only foolery, and one falls in love only to fool and be fooled. Perhaps this is so; our present business, however, is simply with interpreting a text. Now, if anything be clear in the history of the lyric, it is that *The Phoenix and Turtle,* whatever its merits, is not a gracious and charming trifle, and could not have been intended as such. One half of the poem consists of a grimly reiterated paradox, stated with the minimum of decoration and the maximum of technical exactitude. The inference is that the poet was trying to say something precisely, and this lays on us the obligation, if we wish to read the poem at all, of trying to find out precisely what he was saying.

The doctrine of the poem is not sanctioned by the scholastic doctrine of human love, nor indeed, so far as I know, by the facts of nature. It is not sanctioned by the doctrine of the Beatific Vision. Is there a source in the tradition from which is derived the structure of thought and the technical terms by which it is displayed? There is, in fact, only one model in the tradition for the notion that distinct persons may have only one essence, and that is the doctrine of the Trinity. Not, of course, the Incarnation, for the two Natures (or Essences) of Christ are distinct. The relation of lover and beloved in Shakespeare's poem is that of the Persons of the Trinity, and the technical language employed is that of scholastic discussion on the subject. With this clue, all the difficulties of the expository part of the poem are resolved, and if it still remains difficult to understand, it is no more difficult than the Trinity.

The principal point of the doctrine of the Trinity in this connection is summed up in Hooker's *Laws of Ecclesiastical Polity:*

> The Persons of the Godhead, by reason of the unity of their substance, do as necessarily remain one within another, as they are of necessity to be distinguished one from another . . . And sith they all are but one God in number, one indivisible essence or substance, their distinction cannot possibly admit separation . . . Again, sith all things accordingly love their offspring as themselves are more or less contained in it, he which is thus the only-begotten, must needs be in this degree the only-beloved of the Father. He therefore which is in the Father by eternal derivation of being and life from him, must needs be in him through an eternal affection of love.

The Father and Son are distinct persons, yet one essence. Furthermore, as the learned Doctors tell us, the Son proceeds from the Father by way of the intellect in that he is the Father's understanding of Himself; and the Holy Ghost proceeds from both by way of the will in that He is the mutual love of both. But when anyone understands and loves himself, he is in himself not only through the identity of the subject, but also in the way in which what is understood is in the one who understands, and what is loved is in the lover. Thus the Holy Ghost, who proceeds from the reciprocal relation of the Father and Son, is a distinct person, but is at the same time the bond between Them, inasmuch as He is Love:

> So they lov'd as love in twain
> Had the essence but in one . . .

[ll. 25-6]

In the next line—*Two distincts, division none*—the terminology is obviously scholastic, and its context is the doctrine of the Trinity. "To avoid the Arian heresy," Thomas says, "we must avoid the terms *diversity* and *difference* so as not to take away the unity of essence; we can, however, use the term *distinction* . . . So also to avoid taking away the simplicity of the divine essence we must avoid the terms *separation* and *division,* which apply to parts of a whole . . .".

Number there in love was slain, for plurality is always the consequence of a division, as Thomas points out; but the division of a continuum from which springs number, which is a species of quantity, is found only in material things. But number in this sense cannot be applied to God. When numerical terms are used they signify only the things of which they are said, and so we may say one essence, signifying only the essence undivided, and many persons, signifying only those persons and the undividedness of each. *Hearts remote, yet not asunder* repeats the central paradox. *Distance, and no space was seen;* the Son is co-eternal with the Father in order of time and hence in order of space. *But in them* (and in God!) it were a wonder.

The next stanzas are based on the scholastic distinction of *proprium* and *alienum:* what is proper is what belongs to the one, but not to the other; what is alien is what belongs to the other, but not to the one. The terms are contraries, and exclude each other. But in the Trinity the relations which constitute the three Persons are their several Properties. Though property is the same as person, yet in the Father and the Son, as there is one essence in the two persons, so also there is one property in the two persons. So also in the Phoenix and Turtle: love so shone between them (and Love is the relationship of the Father and the Son in the Holy Ghost) that the one saw what belonged to him ("his right": *suum proprium*) in the sight of the other; but the other's sight was the instrument by which the second saw reciprocally what belonged to him in the sight of the first. Each was the other's "mine": *meum.* No wonder *Property was thus appalled:* for *property* is the personification of *propuium.*

Single nature's double name: Each of the Persons of the Trinity has His proper name, yet they are all of one nature, one essence, and the name *God* stands of itself for the common nature—hence, *Neither two nor one was called.*

Reason, in itself confounded,—for reason is the principle of distinction and its method is division—*Saw division grow together;* each of the two was distinct (*To themselves*), yet neither one of them was one or the other (*yet either neither*). And the last line of this stanza repeats again the same paradox, and again by one of the common scholastic dichotomies: *Simple were so well compounded.* Any separated substance is simple; thus the Phoenix and the Turtle are simples, but are so compounded as to form a simple. Hence, at the final recapitulation of the paradox, Reason confesses its inadequacy to deal with the mystery of love: *Love has reason, reason none / If what parts* can remain unparted (*can so remain*).

The relation of the Phoenix to the Turtle is now clear. It is conceived and expressed in terms of the scholastic doctrine of the Trinity, which forms in this sense the principle of order of the poem. The Phoenix and Turtle are distinct persons, yet one in love, on the analogy of the Father and the Son in the Holy Ghost. If the reader does not immediately understand this mystery, the point of the poem is that it is a mystery at

which Reason is confounded and confesses that true Reason is above it and is Love. (pp. 273-76)

> *J. V. Cunningham, " 'Essence' and the 'Phoenix and Turtle',' in* ELH, *Vol. 19, No. 4, December, 1952, pp. 265-76.*

RONALD BATES (essay date 1955)

[*Bates detects and describes an ambiguous, "strange and unique tone" in* The Phoenix and Turtle, *characterized by the intrusion of comic notes into a "profoundly serious" atmosphere. To account for this mixed tone, he analyzes the poem within the context of Shakespeare's plays, principally* Hamlet, *and discovers not only verbal links between the two works, but also the author's preoccupation with "inconstancy, unchastity, and lust" bordering on a "repugnance to the relation between the sexes." In support of his claim that a comic element exists in the poem (especially in stanza 16, which depicts, according to Bates, the comic failure to consummate and produce offspring), the critic points out that Shakespeare employed a metrical pattern and rhyme scheme typically reserved in the plays for "comic and the magical or proverbial" situations. He concludes that the poem itself is a highly compressed, "skeletal form" of tragi-comic drama that evokes bathos as well as pathos.*]

There are few English poems more enigmatic than Shakespeare's "The Phoenix and Turtle". This fact, obvious from a single reading, is further emphasized by the relative paucity of studies devoted to its elucidation. Moreover, a good deal of the criticism has been concentrated on the more external aspects; the occasion of the work and the actual persons symbolized by Phoenix and Turtle have so taken up scholarly interest as to leave the poem itself a relative mystery. Yet, even if it could be proved beyond a doubt that the Phoenix was meant to "shadow forth", say, Lady Bedford, this historical fact would not in any aesthetically satisfactory way elucidate the main problem: the particular poem by Shakespeare and its particular effect on the reader. In this essay I do not claim to have completely solved the problem, but by a closer attention to the poem, in relation to Shakespeare's work as a whole, I have attempted to . . . indicate certain relations with his other works that may help us understand to some degree Shakespeare's strange and unique tone in "The Phoenix and Turtle". (p. 19)

If we consider the proximity in time of the composition of *Hamlet* and "The Phoenix and Turtle" it is not irrelevant to examine the grave-side scenes that are presented in the two works. Are there any similarities, other than what could be expected in a treatment of the particular situation, between Ophelia's funeral and that of our birds?

What first struck me in reading "The Phoenix and Turtle" and gave me the impulse to attempt this study, was the line referring to the swan-priest: "Lest the requiem lack his right" [l. 16]. This seems, for some reason, a more weighted idea than the poem alone demands. The fact that the structural order in stanza four (let priest be swan) is the reverse of the other stanzas (e.g. let bird be herald) seems to draw attention to this. At this point, Ophelia's burial came to mind, for in it there was a danger of the funeral lacking sacerdotal sanctification, because of the suspicion of suicide.

> *Hamlet.* The queen, the courtiers: who is that they follow?
> And with such maimed rites? . . .

Queen Elizabeth. Engraving by Crispin van de Passe the elder, after a drawing by Isaac Oliver.

Laertes.   What ceremony else?
Priest. Her obsequies have been as far enlarg'd
        As we have warrantise: her death was
        doubtful;
        And, but that great command o'ersways
        the order,
        She should in ground unsanctified have
        lodg'd
        Till the last trumpet; for charitable
        prayers,
        Shards, flints, and pebbles, should be
        thrown on her,
        Yet here she is allow'd her virgin rites,
        Her maiden strewments, and the bringing
        home
        Of bell and burial.
Laertes.   Must there no more be done?
Priest.   No more be done?
        We should profane the service of the dead
        To sing a *requiem,* and such rest to her
        As to peace-parted souls.
                        [*Hamlet,* V. i. 218-19, 225-38]

One notices at once that Ophelia's "virgin rites" lack a "requiem". There are other verbal links, besides "requiem" (which is used by Shakespeare only these two times)— "obsequy" and "trumpet".

I hasten to add that I do not claim that the Phoenix *is* Ophelia, though I feel that almost as good a case could be made for her as for Lady Bedford or Lady Salisbury. What I do say, however, is that the verbal links between the poem and the play, particularly if we also consider the "trumpet" link with the Ghost scene in Act I, can scarcely be pure accident, though they may not necessarily indicate such a formal equivalence as: Phoenix = Ophelia, Turtle = Hamlet (?) or Laertes (?), "fowl of tyrant wing" = Claudius (cf. Hamlet's remark, ". . . . and now reigns here / A very, very—pajock" [III. ii. 283-84]), and so on. The relationship is not fortuitous because the two works were written at approximately the same time, and both, moreover, are much concerned with "constancy" and "chastity".

Most of the critics have seemingly been aware of something peculiar about "The Phoenix and Turtle" as a whole, something in its tone that is puzzling. . . . B. H. Newdigate, for instance, says, "The lines on the Phoenix and Turtle . . . present one of the most difficult problems to be found in his works" [see his first entry in the Additional Bibliography], and Ranjee G. Shahani notes that "As a composition 'The Phoenix and Turtle' is unique in European literature" [see excerpt above, 1946]. Newdigate then, however, concentrates on the possible external references of Phoenix and Turtle; Shahani, and Cunningham [see excerpt above, 1952], discuss the metaphysical ideas contained in the scholastic terminology of the anthem. None of the critics, with the exception of Bonnard [see excerpt above, 1937], come at all near what seems to me the central problem, the strange way in which Shakespeare handles his subject and the ambiguous tone which results.

The point of Bonnard's article is that Shakespeare, along with Marston, Chapman, Jonson, and "Ignoto", annoyed at having to appear in print in Chester's rather turgid company, wrote their contributions tongue in cheek. I am concerned with this suggestion only insofar as it indicates that Bonnard sensed a mocking or comic tone in "The Phoenix and Tur-

tle". He enlarges on what he considers Shakespeare's rather obscene joke, seeing in the whole poem nothing more than this. So eager is he to prove that all the other critics have been fooled in seeing anything serious in what is only a "leg-pull", that he overplays his hand. The intrusion of the comic must be examined, but an inability to see anything more than that in the poem seems a fault of taste. Nonetheless, there is more than a suggestion of the ridiculous in "The Phoenix and Turtle", particularly in the threnos.

The threnos begins with a simple and moving stanza:

        Beauty, truth, and rarity,
        Grace in all simplicity,
        Here enclos'd in cinders lie.

                                    [ll. 53-5]

This is followed by a less emotional and more mythologically pictorial stanza:

        Death is now the phoenix' nest;
        And the turtle's loyal breast
        To eternity doth rest,

                                    [ll. 56-8]

which moves, with a bump, on into the third stanza, which has almost a ludicrous tone to it:

        Leaving no posterity:—
        'Twas not their infirmity,
        It was married chastity.

                                    [ll. 59-61]

The last two lines, particularly, sound almost like a Falstaffian quip at some over fanatic Puritan pair. The double-rhyme, extended for three lines, could scarcely help hovering on the verge of comic verse. An examination of the other uses Shakespeare makes of this kind of rhyme effect only confirms this.

Fifteen other times, the rhyming of three consecutive lines or more occurs in the plays. Once it is in a song sung by an at least slightly intoxicated comic character:

        Do nothing but eat, and make good cheer,
        And praise heaven for the merry year;
        When flesh is cheap, and females dear.
                    [*2 Henry IV,* V. iii. 17-19]

Twice it is used by Lear's fool to convey a prophetic, almost magical, message, e.g.:

        Have more than thou showest,
        Speak less than thou knowest,
        Lend less than thou owest.
                    [*King Lear,* I. iv. 118-20]

Three times it is used in spells, e.g.:

        Flower of this purple dye,
        Hit with Cupid's archery,
        Sink in apple of his eye.
                    [*A Midsummer Night's Dream,* III. ii. 102-04]

Four times it is used in connection with Portia's casket riddle, e.g.:

        All that glisters is not gold,—
        Often have you heard that told;
        Many a man his life hath sold.
                    [*The Merchant of Venice,* II. vii. 65-7]

And, finally, it is used five times for definite comic effect:

Thine own true knight,
By day or night,
Or any kind of light.
        [*The Merry Wives of Windsor,* II. i. 14-16]

The raging rocks,
With shivering shocks,
Shall break the locks.
        [*A Midsummer Night's Dream,* I. ii. 31-4]

I trust to taste of truest Thisby's sight.
        But stay;—O spite!
        But mark,—poor knight.
        [*A Midsummer Night's Dream,* V. i. 275-77]

From the east to the western Ind,
No jewel is like Rosalind.
Her worth being mounted on the wind.
        [*As You Like It,* III. ii. 88-90]

On which Touchstone comments, "This is the very false gallop of verses. . ." [*As You Like It,* III. ii. 113].

        For us, and for our tragedy,
        Here stooping to your clemency,
        We beg your hearing patiently.
                [*Hamlet,* III. ii. 149-51]

Hamlet's remark on this is most scornful. "Is this a prologue, or the posy of a ring?" [III. ii. 152].

This kind of rhyme-scheme, then, has very definite associations in Shakespeare's work. Two general elements can be recognized—the comic, and the magical or proverbial. The second element, which is closely connected with some of the earliest types of poetry—for example, Old English riddle poems and Finnish *runot*—has a serious poetic function in the threnos, giving it some of the objective, eternal qualities of an actual epitaph carved on the funeral urn. However, we cannot ignore the third stanza of the threnos, nor avoid putting it alongside the three lines from *Hamlet.* When we do so, we are constrained to say, with Hamlet, "Is this a prologue [or a threnos], or the posy of a ring?" The final and most important question is obvious: "Why this curious mixture of the profoundly serious and the ludicrous?" "The Phoenix and Turtle" is not a five-act tragedy which could assimilate comic relief. The comic here is anything but relief; it is intrusive, if not disruptive.

I suggest the reason for this is an irreconcilable clash between the attitude expressed in Chester's poem [*Love's Martyr*] to the subject of constancy, chastity, and love (which the other poets were presumably expected to adopt) and the particular attitude to constancy, chastity, and love which we find in *Hamlet* or *Troilus and Cressida.* Bonnard says, "All the poems that follow, by Shakespeare, Marston, Chapman, Jonson, and another poet who signs "Ignoto", refer, in accordance with the title, to the subject of the Turtle and the Phoenix: to their marriage, that is to the death of the Phoenix, to their constancy in love, and to their reward in a new little phoenix their daughter." The point is, of course, that this, as regards Shakespeare's contribution, is wrong. The threnos says explicitly, "Leaving no posterity". There can be no doubt of this: Shakespeare on this point contradicts Chester and the others.

Chester's subject is quite clear, despite his mediocre and long-winded presentation. Employing the Phoenix myth, he celebrates the union of a human pair. The phoenix, of course, symbolizes "enchanting beautie", "wits raritie", and "vir-

tue", the turtle symbolizes "love and chastitie", and "constancie" [*Love's Martyr*]. The phoenix's fiery consummation has its obvious physical meaning, and its resurrection is natural, too, in the form of the child born of that union. This, then, is the subject Shakespeare must write on, too. But how do we find him treating these matters in *Hamlet,* or in *Troilus and Cressida?*

Not only are the plays of this period concerned with inconstancy, unchastity, and lust, but the treatment itself indicates a deep and, as critics have pointed out, almost unbalanced repugnance to the relation between the sexes. Not even the truly innocent escape, as Hamlet shows when he says to Ophelia:

        If thou dost marry, I'll give thee this plague for thy
        dowry,—be thou as chaste as ice, as pure as snow,
        thou shalt not escape calumny.
                [*Hamlet,* III. i. 134-36]

At this point in Shakespeare's career there is no place for a simple eulogizing of marital faith and love, particularly if the physical aspect of the relationship is considered. When [Laertes] consigns "Conscience and grace to the profoundest pit" [*Hamlet,* IV. v. 133], he is thinking of a very different kind of fire from that which produced the "cinders" in which lie "Grace in all simplicity". The poet does what he can with the subject by concentrating on the death itself, and treating the situation, which for Chester is essentially epithalamic, by a threnody. Not only is posterity refused the Phoenix and the Turtle; the sexual act itself is as good as denied: "It was married chastity". It seems significant that the one place where the whole problem of the divergent attitudes is most obvious, the stanza where the two most important aspects of Chester's allegory—the consummation and the child—are denied, should also be the place where the ludicrous element intrudes.

One final point about the poem as a whole may be considered. . . . [Its] structure is tripartite: the funeral party, the anthem, and the threnos. The progression of "speakers" of the poem follows this division. The funeral party is listed in objective imperatives: "Let the bird of loudest lay", "From this session interdict" [ll. 1, 9]. The anthem, which is announced in the same detached, objective manner—"Here the anthem doth commence"[l. 21]—is, presumably, spoken or sung by the funeral party as a whole, or by the priest-swan alone. Judging from its scholastic terminology, perhaps the latter is indicated. Reason, who appears in the anthem, then speaks the threnos, "Whereupon it [Reason] made this threne" [l. 49]. Now, the manner in which these sections are spoken is dramatic, in a skeletal form. In a way, "The Phoenix and Turtle" is the outline of a drama, or rather, perhaps, what is left when all action has been reduced to narrative or removed. The first five stanzas are part of a dramatis personae, the anthem gives the substance of the drama in a highly intellectualized and compressed form, while the threnos is the epilogue. That something of all this is in Shakespeare's mind is obvious, for Reason "made this threne . . . As chorus to their tragic scene" [l. 52]. It is scarcely surprising that the artist, who at the time is putting all his powers into the dramatic form, should make of a short poem, like "The Phoenix and Turtle", almost a tragedy—in the form of a posy of a ring. (pp. 26-30)

Ronald Bates, "Shakespeare's 'The Phoenix and Turtle'," in *Shakespeare Quarterly, Vol. VI, No. 1, Winter, 1955, pp. 19-30.*

WALTER J. ONG   (essay date 1955)

[Ong argues that the concept of metaphor governs the design of The Phoenix and Turtle *and that the poem's theme becomes "a metaphor of metaphor itself." Human reason is so constituted, the critic believes, that our perception is binary, and thus an eternal frustration to the soul yearning for the simplicity of a unified reality. This quest for unity leads the poetic imagination to metaphor, a linguistic device that readily accommodates disparate ideas or meanings within a single symbol or image. According to Ong, Shakespeare employs the archetypal symbols of the phoenix and turtle, each susceptible to varied interpretations, to depict the essence of metaphor: a psychological desire to recover unity, at least intellectually, in a divided world.]*

The Phoenix and the Turtle has long seemed to me a poem in which metaphor rules with particular insistence. The economy of the poem comes so far under the control of metaphor that, in a twinkling, by a simple flick of attention, the theme of the poem converts into a metaphor of metaphor itself. The cardinal metaphors at work can be discerned at once. The phoenix, as suggesting change which is both death and birth, and the turtle, symbol of devotedness moved by love, can be considered each as a metaphor with a particularly wide range of applicability—as potentially multiple metaphors. Like the archetypal symbols of Jung, these are capable of engaging reality at all sorts of levels simultaneously and indeterminately. . . . The exact reference of the phoenix and the turtle will depend on where you choose to pull them up for the moment by arresting your attention momentarily. They can be metaphorical terms for persons, for philosophical abstractions such as love and death, for mind and body, for Christ and the Church.

We cannot go into the means by which these and all the other possibilities are kept in agitation within this poem in a way such possibilities seldom enough are. We must note only the fact that the possibilities *are* kept alive, are not killed off by the disasters which can overtake a poem less well managed than this. Here the reader is not distracted by irrelevancies but encouraged to let the metaphor grow and extend its range of applicability without particular limit.

It is while letting the metaphor grow that we may suddenly become aware that the phoenix and the turtle can fly off as symbols into a still further dimension and become a metaphor of metaphor itself, for the union of these two divergent terms—the "mutual flame" in which they are united—lends itself with surprising readiness to being taken as a symbol of the union of two terms which is the precise thing that metaphor realizes.

> So they loved, as love in twain
> Had the essence but in one;
> Two distincts, division none;
> Number there in love was slain.
>
> Hearts remote, yet not asunder;
> Distance, and no space was seen.
>
> [ll. 25-30]

The way the symbolism accommodates itself here to metaphor should be no surprise, for . . . the union of the two meanings in one term, the unity of the twinned vision, is as intimately and deeply involved in the meshes of being as are the kind of symbols here operating.

Metaphor, in its strange double focus, brings us quickly to the quest for unity with which the phoenix and the turtle are pre-

occupied and which conditions their appearance in this poem—the quest for unity set in motion by the mysterious structure of a composite being, man, nostalgic for a simplicity which he cannot find within his own consciousness, resentful of everything short of this simplicity, ultimately discontent with his grasp of truth in statements, which are poor divided things like man himself, bearing the mark of their own destruction within themselves. Even when they contain no margin of error, when everything they assert is absolutely true, our statements have a way of leaving us unsatisfied by not meaning so much as we had thought ourselves on the point of uttering. (pp. 199-201)

The difficulty goes deep, for it lodges in the structure of human cognition itself. Hence it is not surprising that among the elemental, archetypal symbols he is operating with, Shakespeare encounters human reason itself, nonplussed by the divided unities and the united divisions with which it must deal:

> Reason, in itself confounded,
> Saw division grow together,
> To themselves yet either neither,
> Simple were so well compounded
>
> That it cried, How true a twain
> Seemeth this concordant one!
>
> [ll. 41-6]

Although more explicitly focused on something else, this last phrase hits off the metaphorical situation to perfection, because it touches the depths of the human situation out of which the need for metaphor grows. (p. 201)

> *Walter J. Ong, "Metaphor and the Twinned Vision," in* The Sewanee Review, *Vol. LXIII, No. 2, Spring, 1955, pp. 193-201.*

A. ALVAREZ   (essay date 1955)

[Alvarez proposes that The Phoenix and Turtle *requires "a total reading," that is, one with an appreciation of the following elements: its poetic technique, philosophical terminology, Christian symbolism, and its description of human love. He devotes considerable attention to the many technical terms that Shakespeare borrowed from the metaphysics of his time and discerns in the poem the logic and language of a formal proof, arguing that Shakespeare works through "metaphor, accurate perception, ambiguity, and word-play" to reach "the inner mystery of Love." In essence, Alvarez declares, the poet seeks his own or love's own metaphysic, which, "like all valid systems . . . must be proved," yet the point of the poem and Shakespeare's paradox, according to the critic, is that Love transcends Reason. The critic asserts that the poem shows how the highest mysteries of Love can only be approached through "their own metaphysic, religion, logic and their own poetic ritual." These elements, Alvarez contends, are not only interwoven in the poem, they also converge in the final mystery or paradox of "married chastitie," leaving the reader poised between a sense of tragedy and Christian reassurance.]*

The *Phoenix and Turtle* is a difficult poem, but it is knowingly so. The complications are intentional, witty and precise. They are carried off with such confidence, such buoyancy, and yet for no obvious purpose. The poem seems so self-contained that it is impregnable. Certainly, no simple approach will do on its own. Of the four ways into the poem, each is relevant, each by itself inadequate.

The usual line is to treat the poem as a wittily complicated effusion which reworks what was, even then, the well-nigh exhausted conceit of the two lovers making one flesh. This yields one level of meaning and emphasizes what is too easily overlooked: the human situation involved. Although the poem is not a direct love poem to a mistress, it is at least a description, a definition of perfect love. But approached in this way the introduction becomes a mere ornament, the sixfold repetition of the conceit a tedious exaggeration, and the Threnos . . . a separate poem.

If this reading fails to take the poem seriously enough, to interpret it exclusively through its religious symbolism is a sin of overseriousness. No doubt the Phoenix *was* a mediaeval symbol for Christ, and the Dove might well be an unmarried lady devoted to piety and good works. But the mystical marriage in Christ is not the only purity. The chastity of human love—the love, say, of a Perdita and Florizel [in *The Winter's Tale*]—is equally rare and as worthy of celebration. And perhaps it is more able to assume on its own terms and without irreverence, the poem's aimed wit and buoyancy.

The third approach is the 'poetic'. It is best summed up by Emerson's enigmatic statement in the preface to *Parnassus:*

> I consider this piece to be a good example of the
> rule that there is a poetry for bards proper, as well
> as a poetry for the world of readers. This poem, if
> published for the first time, and without a known
> author's name, would have no general reception.
> Only the poets would save it [see excerpt above,
> 1875].

Clearly, we are to make what we can of this. I will take it at its face value: the poem can be read as a copy-book example of technique; of how to take the abiding themes of love poetry—Love, Death and the Absolutes—and give them a perfect aesthetic order. It is a limited approach but a necessary one.

Finally, there is the approach by way of knowledge. The poem is genuinely difficult, not because it complicates metaphysical conceit upon conceit, nor because it presumes a hidden, a historical depth of religious symbolism, but because we too often fail to understand the terms it employs. It is metaphysical in a more obviously intellectual way than most 'Metaphysical' poetry. It states its problems precisely and consistently in the philosophical language of the time, with a rigorous clarity which even Donne or Herbert of Cherbury hardly attained. One move towards understanding the poem, then, is to define some of its terms.

In a total reading of the poem these four ways of approach merge and clarify each other. I will start with the heavy work, the bulldozing needed in the latter two. Once the ground is cleared there will be room enough to assume and judge the others.

My chief quarrel with symbolic interpretation is that, in more or less covert ways, it constantly poses the question, 'What does this poem mean?' It is a mistake of emphasis. A poem does not *mean* in any simple way. It does not stand for something else. . . . To criticize a poem closely is to understand and then to describe. It is an act of imaginative sympathy. On this the relevance and accuracy of the criticism rests. The elements of a poem—and its symbolic 'meaning' is one—are like traits of character; they can be isolated for convenience and clarity, but they exist only as parts of the whole.

The interdependence of the parts is particularly to the point in the *Phoenix and Turtle*. Take, for instance, the language.

Shakespeare was never so obviously 'knowing' with his metaphors as Donne. On the other hand, he rarely used them as sparingly as here. Increasingly throughout the poem concrete is evaporated into abstract—'*Death* is now the Phoenix *nest*' [l. 56]—or even into the flatly grammatical; for instance, in one of the few ambiguities, 'mine' in stanza 9, the choice lies between a concrete metaphor and a grammatical tool. Where the language is associational it leads to the realm of speculation, not of human particularity. This rarity of diction gives the poem the generalizable quality of philosophical discourse and it strictly limits your conception of the sort of love described. . . . At the same time, this bareness of language concentrates your attention on the poetic procedures themselves, and allows it little chance to be dispersed in local complexity. Puzzled, you say, 'I don't follow', not 'I don't see'.

The mechanics of the thing are important, complex and formally perfect. You are moved from an invitation to 'the bird of lowdest lay' [l.1] to a command to 'sigh a prayer' [l. 6]; from a tragic cry to a sigh of reconciled acceptance; it is the momentum of a catharsis, which unifies the actors of the three stages of the poem—the birds, the abstracts 'Love and Constancie' [l. 22], and the other lovers who are 'true or faire' [l. 66]—and makes them all part of the same coherent dramatic movement.

As the purity of the love echoes through the purified language, so the poem too, section by section, refines and withdraws itself. The structure is precise and coherent: the invocation gives the setting and announces the theme; in the antheme is the descriptive argumentation; the bare statements of the Threnos are the climax and conclusion. The topics of the poem stretch out towards abstraction, from the 'chaste wings', through the abstract concepts of the world of Reason, to the transcendentals of the world of Love. At the same time the poem withdraws steadily into its own poetic elements. The antheme is sung by the invoked birds, themselves part of a literary tradition; the Threnos, in turn, is composed by Reason, an abstract quality within the song sung by these characters, and composed, moreover, 'As *Chorus* to their Tragique Scene' [l. 52]—a further distancing by theatrical metaphor. Although the N.E.D. will not allow theatrical overtones to 'Troupe' and 'Session' we are still left with a song within a song within a formal literary setting.

I have suggested that the chastity of the language at once qualifies the subject and emphasizes the poetic logic by which the work unfolds. Any unfolding, however intensely linguistic, is a series of actions, and the action of language is expressed clearest through the moods of the verbs used. In the opening section all these are imperatives. The authority of tone sets the poem in motion and creates a fitting atmosphere.

Let the bird of lowdest lay

The heavily stressed imperative and alliterating superlative give the poem a great push forward into a rhythmical buoyancy which it never loses. It is this that gives the confidence which guides the poem through the badly mapped country of speculation, and helps the sureness of its final affirmations. But the imperatives also include a number of words of command, 'obay', 'keepe', 'interdict'. Deliberately and ceremoniously a setting is being invoked. Again it is a matter of purity. The birds are summoned to a 'requiem' mass from which 'tyrants', 'the fiend' and his 'precurrer' are exorcised. They are provided with a full array of religious trappings: 'obsequie', 'Priest in Surples white' [l. 13], 'defunctive Musicke', 'the Requiem', 'his (the priest's or the requiem's) right' (also rite), the 'mourners'. Then there is the heraldic pomp of royalty: the 'herauld', 'trumpet' and 'feth'red King'. And above all this there is the essential purity of the birds themselves, 'chaste', 'strict', 'white', and the 'crow' who gains his place less for his mourning colour or his 'voys of care', as in Chaucer, than for his quaintly pure way of propagation, 'With the breath thou giu'st and tak'st' [l. 19].

But then the birds, for all the vitality of Shakespeare's writing, appear with the accumulations, the wit and familiarity, that is, of at least some two centuries of literary life. They are straight from the widely known and, to the Elizabethans, easily recognizable convention of the *Parlement of Fowles*. Scholars have accepted this for fifty years, together with the probability that Shakespeare was working directly from Chaucer. Whether he was or not is beside my immediate point. The parallels are there, but their importance is negative. The conventional treatment was to follow Chaucer and let each bird come forward and say something in character. Shakespeare does not make them so crudely self-explanatory. They are less symbols than literary properties. Certainly they are given considerable literary power; a power not of substance and detail but of verbal grandeur. The traditional make-believe (it has come down to us in the nursery-rhyme *Who Killed Cock Robin?*) is dignified by slow-paced and deeply serious language:

> Let the Priest in Surples white,
> That defunctive Musicke can,
> Be the death-deuining Swan,
> Lest the *Requiem* lacke his right.
>
> [ll. 13-16]

Much depends on the solemnity of the language to set the tone and qualify the subject. It makes the setting, like the love of the Phoenix and Turtle, chaste, regal and holy. It helps the poem to its grand manner, to make it so purposeful, detached and moving.

There is a difference between poetic rarity and difficulty, between the deliberate withdrawal of the invocation and the complications of the antheme. To us the birds are unfamiliar, and Shakespeare puts in details from literary and popular traditions which make them stranger yet. But this is a short-winded obscurity that takes us no further than the footnotes of a competent editor: for example, all those details about the crow. The antheme, on the other hand, presents real intellectual difficulties. It uses vocabulary which is indeed obscure, and uses it to shift and balance round metaphysical precipices with a bewildering skill.

While the invocation prepared us for their purity by literary device, the antheme insists logically on the *absolute* perfection of the lovers. In most love poems (and this includes Shakespeare's plays) actions and attitudes are judged against *implicit* moral standards. Celebration affirms them, lament and disgust deny. In this poem the lovers themselves are *explicitly* these standards:

> Love and Constancie is dead,
> *Phoenix* and the *Turtle* fled . . . ;
>
> [ll. 22-3]

elsewhere they are incarnations of Platonic and Christian ideals, 'Beautie, Truth and Grace'. By these terms the Christian symbolist would throw a shaft of light on to the subject, which, for all its accuracy, does not illuminate the whole bulk and humanity of the love. The theme of the poem is the transcendence of Reason by Love. The great theological paradoxes are used—often, indeed, stated in specifically theological terms—because religion *also* rests on faith. This does not necessarily limit the subject of the poem; it only qualifies it.

The very difficulty of the antheme is that it will not rest in the power of faith to transcend Reason (and this makes me suspicious of a purely Christian interpretation); it sets out poetically and logically to *prove* its case. It uses the traditional means, the paradox, accommodated to a stringent logic; for if the poet is to go convincingly beyond Reason he must also include it. The simple paradox is not enough. It asserts only its own ingenuity and gives a temporary, unqualified perception. To prove its point, to outreason Reason, the paradox must be rationally accurate and sustained.

Even the simplest insurance of accuracy is used: Shakespeare develops the argument in juxtaposition with numbers, the most precise, least misinterpretable words. 'Twaine', 'none', 'one' are used as a set of rhymes twice in six stanzas, and two of the most difficult lines of the poem are circumscribed in the same way:

> *Single* Natures *double* name,
> Neither *two* nor *one* was called.
>
> [ll. 39-40]

(My italics.) The numbers are an assurance that the situation can be spoken of rationally, worked out, almost, on paper—provided, of course, you understand the basic conceit.

Much of the difficulty of the antheme lies in its accuracy. The paradoxes are more than a literary device supporting the weight of a questionable argumentation; they balance and juggle technical terms from the metaphysics of Shakespeare's time, quite regardless of the pull of philosophical gravity. Relentlessly, the constants of Reason are stated and then destroyed in exactly the language in which the philosophers would have upheld them. The terminology is rational, its application flatly anti-rational.

The technical complexity stands in its own right. The position is stated immediately, fully, accurately, and thereafter only briefly restated in terms of the constants so briskly to be destroyed. The whole argument moves from the lines:

> So they loued as loue in twaine,
> Had the essence but in one,
>
> [ll. 25-6]

It is important to keep the original punctuation: 'they', rather than 'loue', is the subject of 'had'. The poem is about these particular lovers, their embodiment, not their assumptions of ideal love. Roughly you could paraphrase it: 'They loved as though they were two separate people, or as though love resided in each of them apart; but in essence they were one.' 'So', in a minor way, is ambiguous: it has a logical force, making the stanza follow from the 'mutuall flame' of the last; at the same time it expresses the degree of their love: 'Their love was so great it had the strength of two, but their soul was one.' The important word is 'essence'. It is a metaphysical term, *essentia*, for substance or absolute being. Theologians used it to denote, as the N.E.D. says, 'that in respect of which the three persons of the Trinity were one'. More loosely, it was the soul, the 'glassy essence', joining man to God. Like Donne's *Ecstacie*, the poem turns on the grace of love, the paradox which makes the spiritual reality belie the material appearance.

But Shakespeare's objective, for the moment, is the logical re-sults of this unity *in essentia,* and he moves towards it with a brisk rationality, stepping out in full scholastical array.

Two distincts, Division none.

[l. 27]

'Definition, Division, Methodus', says Miss Tuve, with her usual monumental authority, '. . . were cant terms; not only every budding Schoolman but every youth of parts found himself constrained to learn how to define and divide' [in her *Elizabethan and Metaphysical Imagery*]. The point, then, for the Elizabethans was obvious and pedantic. A contemporary handbook of logic makes the paradox clearer: 'As a definition doth declare what a thing is, so a devision sheweth how many things are contained in the same' [Thomas Wilson, in his *The Rule of Reason*]. Although the definition 'loue in twaine' would show 'two distincts', the next step, 'Division', is impos-sible because of the common 'essence'. Yet it is logically im-possible not to be able to divide when you can distinguish. The basic tools and presumptions of Reason are rendered useless. The argument is pushed forward. 'Division' is a mathematical as well as a logical process:

Number there in loue was slaine.

[l. 28]

The range of the logic is wide, for by 'number' Shakespeare seems to mean both a rational skill, arithmetic, and an ab-stract concept, mathematics; for the force of the overthrow may be augmented by a mathematical dictum, 'One is no number'.

The logic, in short, is teased out with more pertinacity than is usual, even in Donne. For Shakespeare argues formally and in the abstract, from a single literary trope, the paradox. Donne, on the other hand, for all his logical 'business', usual-ly starts from an alogical hypothesis; he begins with an analo-gy and argues two parallel cases at once on the understanding that they are at most points convertible. Shakespeare, in this poem at least, is the more honest logician and not at all the Metaphysical poet.

Appearance, however, *is* important to his paradox, though before this can emerge, the related rational abstracts, 'Dis-tance' and 'Space', are in turn overwhelmed by the continu-ing force of the logic. This done, stanza 9 reveals the source of the paradox; it is accurate description. Effortlessly and without exaggeration the paradox holds for the particular act of love the poem celebrates, the Phoenix's consuming fire. Not only is the love of God for man infinitely divisible yet al-ways one, so too is the 'mutuall flame' in which the birds burn to their consummation. . . . This is why there is so much stress on visual description: 'shine', 'saw', 'flaming', 'sight'. Underlying all the logic is the certainty of accurate percep-tion.

The last line [of stanza 9] works in two directions at once. It continues the description of the lovers' fire; a 'mine' is a place in which treasure is found. The lovers are their own riches, gems glinting only to each others' sight in the surrounding darkness of the ordinary world. At the same time, the sense moves forward to 'Propertie' in the next stanza: when two are one, 'yours' and 'mine' are no longer meaningful distinctions; the flat grammatical tool, like the scholastic quiddities, be-comes inaccurate and useless.

So far the difficulties have been resolved, for the most part,

by definition. You have only to make the words precise and, simply, the meaning follows, the direction of the poem be-comes plain. Stanza 10 is more complicated. If you tug at the word 'Propertie' three skeins of abstraction emerge, instead of one. And they are all knotted, for strength, in that most intricate of terms, 'Nature'. The logic of the work embraces them all; no one seems more important than the others, for the purpose of Shakespeare's paradox is to undercut the whole world of Reason.

In its simplest sense 'Propertie' refers back to the line before: it is the power of ownership personified (it becomes 'ap-palled'). Concrete 'Propertie', the things you own, is appro-priated under people's 'names', and so there is something le-galistic in the attempts that follow to distinguish between the 'double name' of the 'single Nature' (here, perhaps, simply a person or body which might be discussed in a court of law). There is no withholding in Love; it is beyond greed and own-ership.

But then 'Propertie' refers back more clearly to the earlier stanzas if taken to be one of the five Predicables of Aristote-lian logic. It is the quality common to a class, what makes that class individual and separate. . . . Nature . . . is the principle of individuation, as in the definition in Thomas Spencer's *The Art of Logick,* 1628: 'Properties are necessary emanations from the principle of nature.' This reading makes the stanza another attack on the abstract principles of defini-tion and distinction. Love is a shared uniqueness.

But 'Propertie' has still another meaning: the proper use of language, what we now call 'propriety'. Hence Mr. Ridley's paraphrase in his notes to the *New Temple Shakespeare.* He overstates the case, perhaps, but neatly: 'In Shakespearian idiom "self" and "same" are almost always identical. The phrase means, I think, that the sense of the proper use of lan-guage is outraged by the discovery that a synonym is not a synonym.' The lines, then, carry on the implications of the grammatical paradox, 'Either was the others mine'; carries them, that is, through 'Single Natures double name', where the important word is 'name', and through yet another re-phrasing where the stressed rhyme-word is 'called'. Even if you do not believe Mr. Ridley that 'selfe' and 'same' were synonymous, the language difficulties are no less real, al-though perhaps a little more human. The point is that words, even words as precise as numbers, will not fit these lovers. Propriety is 'appalled' because what one lover calls himself is not in fact him; a 'single nature' ('essence' of stanza 7) has two distinct names. Language is a rational convention. It will not do for the mysteries of love. The quibbling with numbers only drives home the impossibility.

All this is footnoting. The critical point is a simple one. In none of these stanzas are the complications there for their own sakes. Metaphor, accurate perception, ambiguity, word-play, in short, all the associative energies of Shake-speare's verse have rarified into this abstract allusiveness, by which . . . he feels towards the inner mystery of love. For this he builds up his own—or love's own—metaphysic. Like all valid systems, it must be proved.

With 'Reason confounded' in its own terms, the proof is well-nigh complete. In the best rhetorical fashion stanza 11 re-peats the main stages of the argument. 'Division grows to-gether', as it did in stanza 7; the lovers grow 'to themselves' (partly *towards*), hence 'Distance and no space'; 'either nei-ther' echoes the grammatical contortions. A final antithesis rounds off the whole affair. 'Simple' and 'compound' were technical terms of alchemy, also used in theology to describe the paradoxical nature of God. Another science is stated, contradicted, resolved in mystery. The original punctuation, with commas at the end of each line, emphasizes the step by step recapitulation. (pp. 3-13)

Reason pursues itself to an *O altitudo* [plea to the heavens] when confronted with the overwhelming proofs of Love:

> Loue hath Reason, Reason none,
> If what parts, can so remaine.
>
> [ll. 47-8]

Note that 'If '. The rational habit dies hard, and in the end expires only before rational proof. But the paradox of pure and perfect love is at last substantiated. Reason, an abstract quality within the already withdrawn and purified setting of the Bird Parliament, having acknowledged its own worthlessness, sings the praises of the lovers.

If the love Shakespeare is celebrating were merely the usual courtly Platonic passion, the perception the usual paradox of the Two-in-One, if Reason were merely transcended by Love as the poets would usually have it, then the poem deals with topics far too slight to support the weight of all that logical complication and literary device. The conclusions of the Threnos must be less commonplace to justify their difficulty. Yet at first they seem a little obvious, almost thin. It is all so detached. The poem is an artifact, something carefully made. It is also a logical construction, something clearly argued. But it is impersonal in a way Shakespeare is nowhere else. This is why it can bear, perhaps, the niggling, factual analysis I have subjected it to. There is little personal tone to violate. Its uniqueness is in its detached conviction. It handles obscurities for a purpose.

The detachment is seen in the poem's climax, the Threnos. It is largely made up of a series of powerful but bare assertions of abstract qualities. You can see it, as in the antheme, in the verbs. Again and again rhyme and rhythm force plain, dogmatic indicative statements on your attention: 'lie', 'is now', 'doth rest', 'Twas not', 'It was', 'cannot be', 'tis not', 'buried be'. Indeed, 'be'/'she'/'be' might seem to be slipshod writing without the purposeful air the Threnos exudes. The assertiveness is increased, moreover, by changing the already buoyant rhythm of the quatrains into triplets, their jauntiness exaggerated by the use of only three rhymes in fifteen lines. It begins to seem that so much vitality might be disproportionate to the abstraction and solemnity of the subject.

But I said earlier that this is a poem of proof, of articulate, aimed structure. For this reason, if for no other, the absolutes of Love are needed logically: they are the criteria by which Reason has been refuted and which Reason finally acknowledges. But the poem is *not* a celebration of Love in its generality, nor yet of Love in the dubious particularity of a myth. In homage to the Phoenix and his Turtle Shakespeare changes even the myth and the simple attributes of Love are themselves left behind. Look again at the verbs and you will see that nearly every assertion contains its own denial: 'in cinders lie', 'Death is now', 'To eternitie doth rest. Leaving no posteritie' [ll. 58-9], 'cannot be', 'tis not', 'buried be'. Neither the Phoenix nor the Dove, neither 'Love' nor 'Constancie', 'Beautie' nor 'Truth' will do by themselves. They are all simplicities, all units you can name, all, in a way, aspects of that same rationality the antheme has destroyed. The perfect achievement of love is union, complex in itself, but trans-

formed by the purity of the birds into a deeper, a stranger complexity, resolvable only in death.

Their final mystery, to which all the rest of the poem leads and which the bare statements of the Threnos bleakly assert, is the transcendence of even the simple values of Love in a last tragic paradox of purity:

> It was married Chastitie.
>
> [l. 61]

It is the only paradox in the Threnos, the only positive value, positively and unequivocally affirmed. For the moment the myth of the Phoenix is changed to emphasize the single force of the revelation, the *raison d'être* for all the preceding theologizing. The detail, the logic, the aesthetic distancing are all necessary steps to this final inner core of purity.

From the full moment of knowledge in the 'Tragique Scene' the catastrophe follows inevitably, driven home by repetition and heavy alliteration:

> *Truth* may seeme, *but* cannot *be*,
> *Beautie b*ragge, *but* tis not she,
> *Truth* and *Beautie b*uried *be*.
>
> [ll. 62-4]

(My italics.) But this tragedy is not final. It involves too much. The Phoenix and Turtle are more than lovers; they are all the values of Love as well. Their vitality, like their purity and their sacrifice, continues beyond them. The four approaches to the poem at last merge as the tragedy is played off against the background of Christian assurance and poetic wit. The religion is clear enough. The birds rest 'to eternitie', in a final resolution of chastity and theology. Their virtues, dignified by celebration, substantiated by logic and gaining power by the associations of their mystical paradoxes, are consummated in the act of chaste love and remain. From this energy of faith the poetic myth reasserts itself as the 'true' and 'faire' rise again from the ashes of 'Truth' and 'Beautie'. The wit keeps control. The new generation may only be the bragging semblances of the old, but they are no less true and fair for that. And the old, in whom all the transcendental qualities of Love have so passionately existed, are seen, in turn, to be only a pair of 'dead birds', not totally different from the other birds whose sighs end the poem as their laments had begun it. They are all, for all their pomp and style, a little pathetic.

What does it all add up to? A way, I think, of showing that the highest mysteries of Love demand their own metaphysic, religion and logic, and their own poetic ritual to give them at once grandeur and detachment. In the end Christianity, wit, metaphysics and poetic device are assimilated into the mystery of 'married Chastitie'; they all rest in the calm of a delicately, but logically and passionately attained sense of proportion. (pp. 14-16)

> *A. Alvarez, "Shakespeare: 'The Phoenix and the Turtle'," in* Interpretations: Essays on Twelve English Poems, *edited by John Wain, Routledge and Kegan Paul, 1955, pp. 1-16.*

F. T. PRINCE (essay date 1960)

[*Prince cites* The Phoenix and Turtle *as an example of "Shakespeare's capacity for 'pure' poetry," yet he also perceives an element of "conscious self-caricature" at work in the poem.*

Robert Devereux, Earl of Essex.

Although on one level Shakespeare participated with the other poets in developing the conceit in which martyrdom symbolizes marriage, he also responded with "a sudden intensity of emotion" that precipitated the "expression of his deepest compulsions." Prince notes that the beauty of the poem "consists in a marriage between intense emotion and almost unintelligible fantasy," and he remarks that as "pure" lyric The Phoenix and Turtle *is a foreshadowing of English Romantic poetry— indeed closer in form and spirit to that movement than to metaphysical poetry in the manner of John Donne.* The Phoenix and Turtle *reflects Shakespeare's powers of incantation, the critic concludes, and expresses in pure and concentrated form "all his feeling for pure passion and loyalty in human love."*]

The Phoenix and Turtle, slight as it is, is a priceless addition to Shakespeare's lyrics. The magic of many of the songs in the plays is beyond praise, but we are fortunate in having here a somewhat longer, and independent, example of his powers of incantation.

But even the most potent of incantations must sometimes fail: indeed, the fact that they are ineffective at certain times, or with certain temperaments, or in some states of mind, is itself an indication of their nature, telling us that they rely upon factors which are not often or easily brought together, or brought to bear with such purpose. All poetry is vulnerable to changes of thought, taste, and language, or to mere indifference, dullness, and spiritual deafness; this kind of poetry, because it is pure and concentrated, is more obviously vulnerable than most—unless we choose to say that it is the least vulnerable of any, because it is the least concerned to succeed or fail, or to offer anything but itself.

Shakespeare took the notion of the Phoenix and the Turtle from *Loves Martyr* and treated it as he might have treated a dramatic subject, projecting himself into it and giving what he saw. His poem falls into three divisions. It is an elegiac poem on the death of the two birds, and begins by summoning the other birds to a funeral pageant. This calling together of the birds passes into an 'Antheme' which they are to sing, describing the mutual love of the Phoenix and the Turtle. The anthem passes into a 'Threne', the final lyrical celebration of their identity in love and death. The poem shows unsurpassed musical imagination, in its passage from the quatrains of the first section to the tercets of the *Threnos;* as the mood is evoked and rises to its full intensity, the verse follows it, seems to climb and soar in flight.

The assembly of the birds, though it is but indirectly conveyed and takes up no more than twenty lines, is a wonderfully effective opening. Shakespeare did not need to think of [Chaucer's] *Parlement of Foules,* though that poem is an evocation of a kindred image. The kingdom of the birds, their divisions and occupations, was a theme deeply rooted in European and Oriental folk-lore. The natural poetry of these fancies was bound to leave its mark on literature, as it had become involved with pagan religion and with popular superstition. John Masefield has said, in the idiom of his time:

> This poem gives to a flock of thoughts about the passing of truth and beauty the mystery and vitality of birds, who come from a far country, to fill the mind with their crying [see excerpt above, 1911].

And among the innumerable associations of Shakespeare's verses there is indeed to be found this ancient folk memory of the significance of birds, their suggestions of myth; a homeliness like that of the burial of Cock-Robin is fused with apprehensions of the mystery of death and the migration of the soul.

The identity in love of the two dead birds is celebrated with a display of scholastic terms which gives a vague impression that the poem is 'metaphysical' in the manner of Donne. Nothing could in fact be further from the methods of Donne's love-poetry than the method of this poem. Shakespeare's use of analytic terminology here is free and rhapsodic, a kind of ethereal frenzy; in using it so lavishly, he may well have been influenced by fashion, and by the manner of his fellow-poets writing on this theme, which evidently to them suggested abstract sublimities and verbiage. Donne's analytic procedures are indeed not his personal property, coming to him as they do from Italy and France, and coming to many other learned poets of his generation; but they are distinguished by the concentration and deliberation with which he applies them to sexual experience, and this quality is certainly not paralleled in *The Phoenix and Turtle.*

In this curious poem, sprung from as curious a set of circumstances, we see the imaginative power which charges one after another of Shakespeare's mature plays with inexhaustible suggestions of meaning. Nowhere else, however, have we an opportunity to see this power at work in isolation and in so small a compass. What we see in effect is Shakespeare's capacity for 'pure' poetry; and the poem must be placed in what may seem an ill-assorted company, which includes Poe's *Ulalume* and Mallarmé's *Prose pour des Esseintes.* It is only in the nineteenth century, and particularly in France, that we find the conscious attempt to cultivate poetry in a 'pure' state. But the theories of Baudelaire and Mallarmé derived from

Poe, and it is in the English Romantic school that we find the first glimpses of a poetry that is 'pure' in this sense. *Kubla Khan,* some of Keats's Odes, some of Tennyson's lyrics, provide more familiar examples than Poe or Mallarmé, whose work is for different reasons unlikely to fit into our current scale of poetic appreciation. Yet perhaps the suggestions of self-caricature in Poe, the rigorous self-consciousness and irony of Mallarmé, may also help us to approach *The Phoenix and Turtle.* For this element of irony, hyperbole, and high fantasy is generally missing in the Romantic and Victorian poets, unless we include in our survey the nonsense of Edward Lear and Lewis Carroll: and it is precisely this element which gives the point of departure for Shakespeare's poem, and the convention which supports it throughout.

For after all, the beauty of the poem consists in a marriage between intense emotion and almost unintelligible fantasy. It is inexhaustible because it is inexplicable; and it is inexplicable because it is deliberately unreasonable, beyond and contrary to both reason and nature. When Middleton Murry wrote that 'the poem floats high above the plane of intellectual apprehension [see excerpt above, 1922] (and yet proceeded to gloss its significance with surprising success), he nevertheless failed to indicate the presence of this conscious self-caricature, and its use of a language 'bouffonne et égarée au possible' [clownish and disoriented to the extreme].

Yet Murry's account perhaps gives the 'feel' of the poem in as adequate terms as modern critical equipment has yet found:

> There is surely no more astonishing description of the highest attainable by human love . . . It is the direct embodiment, through symbols which are necessarily dark, of a pure, comprehensive and self-satisfying experience, which we may call, if we please, an immediate intuition into the nature of things. It is inevitable that such poetry should be obscure, mystical, and strictly unintelligible: it is too abstract for our comprehension, too little mediated . . . And it necessarily hovers between the condition of being the highest poetry of all and not being poetry at all. But, wherever in the scale we place it, it gives us a clue to the nature of poetry itself.

In *The Mutual Flame* Mr Wilson Knight goes further [see Additional Bibliography], and tries to relate the poem, on the one hand, to the experience of passionate friendship recorded in the *Sonnets,* and, on the other hand, to the total pattern of the dramas, which he imagines to spring out of that uniquely intense experience, as a kind of expansion and objectification of it. Nothing could be more convincing, as far as it goes, than Mr Wilson Knight's exposition of the *Sonnets:* he grasps the living emotional realities which run through them, and shows Shakespeare's miraculous poetic gift at work to dominate and transform those realities. But he is less successful in trying to tie *The Phoenix and Turtle* closely to his main theme. Much special pleading is required to prove that *Loves Martyr* and its appended poems are inspired by 'sexual confusions and abnormalities', even if we agree that *The Phoenix and Turtle* itself is 'in celebration of a mystical love-union beyond sex, as we understand it, and all biological categories'. Not that one would deny that this wonderful poem is an expression of the same sensibility, the same play of passion and thought, that led Shakespeare through the *Sonnets;* or that Shakespeare has here put into smaller compass the faith in disinterested love, the admiration, the fer-

vour, the irrational hope, which he had struggled to win and to express. But these are things, as Mr Wilson Knight would admit, which Shakespeare could not but put into almost every serious poem he wrote. They may be in *The Phoenix and Turtle* because the poet had quite accidentally found a theme which drew them to itself. Such a possibility is suggested by Mr Wilson Knight himself, in discussing Shelley's *Epipsychidion;* he defines Emilia Viviani as a 'release-mechanism', and maintains that the ideals of love Shelley poured into the poem go far beyond the immediate realities of his situation.

So it probably was with *The Phoenix and Turtle.* A chance conjunction of images precipitates a sudden intensity of emotion in the poet: thoughts and rhythms become the mysterious yet transparent expression of his deepest compulsions. The 'pure' poem is born, marked above all by its apparent remoteness from everyday experience. Many will always feel of such poetry that it is 'not poetry at all', or that, if it is, it is a minor variety, cut off from common life and thought. All one need reply is that a great poet may well allow himself to make an occasional dazzling excursion in this direction. Into *The Phoenix and Turtle,* fantastic as it is, Shakespeare has compressed all his feeling for pure passion and loyalty in human love. (pp. xlii-xlvi)

> *F. T. Prince, in an introduction to* The Arden Shakespeare: The Poems, *edited by F. T. Prince, Methuen, 1960, pp. xi-xlvi.*

DANIEL SELTZER　(essay date 1961)

[*Seltzer examines the relationship, and in many ways the strong affinity, between* The Phoenix and Turtle *and Shakespeare's dramatic works. He points out that the poem's movement resembles the plot of a love-tragedy and that the use of such theatrical words as "chorus" and "tragic scene" are indicative of the poet's design in endowing abstractions with human qualities. According to Seltzer, the Threnos parallels many of the concluding speeches in the tragedies, for it attempts, as they do, to clarify rather than attenuate the impact of the tragic action. The many parallels between* The Phoenix and Turtle *and Shakespeare's dramatic works suggest to Seltzer that the poem states truths dramatized in the tragedies and is "constructed so as to reveal not only the inevitable doom of the sovereignty of nature when it achieves the pure essence of love but also to describe in some measure the emotional effects of such action."*]

Juliet's "What's in a name?" [*Romeo and Juliet,* II. ii. 43] is an expression of one of Shakespeare's most persistent poetic interests: that of describing a person, quality, or emotion by suggesting that the powers of ordinary communication are not sufficient to the task. Her apostrophe functions dramatically in the scene, of course, for Juliet does not know that Romeo can hear her; but the speech draws attention to an aspect of literary composition which obviously intrigued Shakespeare throughout his career. (p. 91)

Shakespeare's interest in the vocabulary of definition was general and in no way systematic. Such definition may serve characterization or over-all theme; but . . . sometimes it appears simply as a protest of the difficulty or unreliability of descriptive definition (although this, in turn, may be highly important thematically). Occasionally, a character expresses a desire to analyze the mystery of human composition, and the articulate expression of inability to understand renders more powerful such speeches as Lear's "Let us anatomize

Regan. See what breeds about her heart" [III. vi. 76-7]. Not infrequently, however, this expression becomes more complicated, for a character will tell us, to his joy or despair, not only that identifying properties are hard to verbalize and trust, but that property itself can actually change—to paraphrase a line from "The Phoenix and Turtle", that the *self* will not be the *same*. For example, Brabantio's fears that Desdemona is the victim of black magic are specifically fears that wizardry has changed her nature:

> Is there not charms
> By which the *property* of youth and maidhood
> May be abus'd?
>
> [*Othello,* I. i. 171-73]

Scroop informs Richard that many of his friends have made peace with Bolingbroke, and after the king's hysterical rage, observes that "sweet love . . . changing his property, / Turns to the sourest and most deadly hate" [*Richard II,* III. ii. 135-36]. Claudius repeats the thought in a different context:

> I know love is begun by time,
> And . . . I see, in passages of proof,
> Time qualifies the spark and fire of it.
> There lives within the very flame of love
> A kind of wick or snuff that will abate it;
> And nothing is at a like goodness still;
> For goodness, growing to a plurisy,
> Dies in his own too-much.
>
> [*Hamlet,* IV. vii. 111-19]

In contrast is Oliver's joyous:

> 'Twas I. But 'tis not I! I do not shame
> To tell you what I was, since my conversion
> So sweetly tastes, being the thing I am.
>
> [*As You Like It,* IV. iii. 135-37]

We know that the necessary abatement of love and the plurisy of goodness must be Claudius' sentiments and not Shakespeare's, for whom "Love is not love / Which alters when it alteration finds. . . . But bears it out even to the edge of doom" (Sonnet CXVI). The sonnet states the ideal, however. Shakespeare's most powerful irony, pervading his tragedies of love—that the purity of love, while stronger than any other human achievement, cannot survive in the reasonable world—does not enter the last plays, where the power of love to cure folly is efficacious within the literary frame of the tragi-comic romance; but especially in *Romeo and Juliet, Othello,* and *Antony and Cleopatra* the irony is played out until "Beauty, truth, and rarity" [*The Phoenix and Turtle,* l. 53] may be admired only in death, with "nothing left remarkable / Beneath the visiting moon" [*Antony and Cleopatra,* IV. xv. 67-8]. Goodness may be born of evil when the decorum of the plot requires reformation, but it must have been one of Shakespeare's firmest beliefs that the constancy or metamorphosis of a human quality ultimately represented the power or frailty of man's will.

Shakespeare's use of such terms as "essence", "distincts", "division", "number", "simple", and "property", in "The Phoenix and Turtle", is not unique in his works. Because the poem is so concise, such vocabulary is immediately noticeable, but neither the words themselves nor the poetic and moral interests behind them are different from the statement of such interests in the plays. I do not think this similarity has been generally observed, although Shakespeare's treatment of the nature of "property" in the plays invites the comparison.

It may help for a moment to ignore the poem's reputation for difficulty and obscurity, and to assume that its meaning is more often than not explicit. "Difficult" it is, to be sure; but the linguistic probing to which it has been occasionally subjected may not be absolutely necessary. "The Phoenix and Turtle" is a hard poem because it compresses into succinct statement ideas remarkable in scope—ideas which, on the other hand, may appear commonplace when removed from the dramatic and poetic context in which we are accustomed to find them in the plays. The statement of the poem is unusually suggestive; but there is no insurmountable difficulty of allusion except as the work as a whole "alludes" to a way of thinking which is large in the grandeur of simplicity.

Shakespeare obviously took great pains to express himself with precision and clarity, if with equally great compactness, for the subject matter was most important to him. The effect of obscurity he could not consciously have desired, and the work is not, as Emerson suggested, a poem only for poets [see excerpt above, 1875]. The language seems obscure because while it is curiously unadorned imagistically, the poem as a whole, as Walter J. Ong observes, has the qualities of a metaphor [see excerpt above, 1955]. . . . Furthermore, the merging of the lovers may itself be considered as "a metaphor of a metaphor", and the poem as a whole, therefore, approached as a kind of treatise on this literary device. Ong's approach is an instructive one, but we must remember as well that the story in the poem is set forth concretely and explicitly. It is charged with action which keeps not only the birds but also the abstracted qualities of constancy, truth, and beauty as discrete agents (actors might be the better word), which build, gradually, the total meaning. In this sense the whole movement of the poem, much as the plot of a play, is a metaphor; and the movement is clear on a literal level, no matter how pregnant it may be with larger implication.

One of Shakespeare's favorite observations—the potential metamorphosis of an "identifying" property—is instrumental in establishing criteria for tragedy, and these are defined, and the "tragic scene" effected, by the energetic action which runs through the poem. The way in which "The Phoenix and Turtle" states the wonder of love is similar to that way in which the emotions of some of Shakespeare's tragic characters are played off against each other in the course of the plays. J. V. Cunningham suggests in a valuable essay that "the relation of the lover and beloved in Shakespeare's poem is that of the Persons of the Trinity, and the technical language employed is that of scholastic discussion on the subject" [see excerpt above, 1952]. (pp. 93-5)

One cannot disagree with Cunningham's basic premise that it is the obligation of the critic to try "to find out precisely what [Shakespeare] was saying", but because of the strictness with which he adheres to scholastic sources, he illuminates the author's vocabulary, but does not fully make use of it. For example, the reiteration of such paradoxes as "Two distincts, division none" [l. 27] indicates that Shakespeare wished to emphasize previous separateness as much as the "present" union in which plurality of number is excluded ("Hearts remote, yet not asunder" [l. 29]; "Number there in love was slain" [l. 40]). If the references in Aquinas would seem to elucidate "no space", they do not say why Shakespeare tells us in the same line [l. 30] that "Distance" between the lovers was "seen" too. Shakespeare's terms are somehow *active,* as the courting, joining, and death of lovers in drama would be active. The scholastic doctrine of the union of the Persons of the Trinity, whether or not it was in the back of Shakespeare's mind, is a description after the fact, and is therefore as dramatically static as it may be, indeed, potentially poetic. All St. Thomas says about the Persons of the Trinity is that They co-exist in a certain relationship; in the poem, a coming together previous to union is emphasized as much as the wonder of the joining: "Hearts remote, yet not asunder", and

> So between them love did shine
> That the turtle saw his right
> Flaming in the phoenix' sight:
> Either was the other's mine.
>
> [ll. 33-6]

While the miracle which is "seen" and described—"but in them it were a wonder" [l. 32]—may be also (or be *like*) the wonder of God, it seems in Shakespeare's poem primarily the result of the attraction of qualities which one might observe, almost as one would observe actors on a stage, moving toward death, their paths determined by the potential for metamorphosis within the fixed properties of love and constancy themselves. This is not to say that the metaphor of the poem is not like the relationship within the Trinity, but we must remember that Shakespeare's use of scholastic doctrine, and the way the poem re-vivifies it, may be as different from his "source" as is his use of the myth of the Phoenix. Cunningham tells us that the lovers "become one and yet neither is annihilated. [They] are of course destroyed in that they have passed in a mutual flame from this life, but clearly they have only passed into the real life of Ideas from the unreal life of materiality". I find nothing like this so "clearly" stated in the poem. Within its dramatic context, the paradoxical union, the mutual *death,* and the command to admire wonderingly are what Shakespeare stresses, and there is no mention or strong implication of an afterlife, platonic or Christian. The poem is about the tragic event and its observation, and a suggestion of whatever afterlife may exist "from hence", or whatever the "eternity" may be to which "the turtle's loyal breast" [l. 57] rests, if it is not oblivion, seems strongly negated by the "cinders" in which "Beauty, truth, and rarity" are now "enclos'd" [ll. 53, 55], just as the new Phoenix of the myth is absent in the "now" of "Death is now the phoenix' nest" [l. 56]. Since the vocabulary of the poem is powerfully suggestive, Cunningham's study is of great interest. Perhaps, however, the source and reason for its vitality are closer to home, deriving from the sense of action implicit in the poem's concrete "plot"—as much from the "distance" between the lovers as from their "essence but in one" [l. 26], and from the way in which the observing voice of Reason—the voice of a worldly "audience"—is introduced.

A movement in the poem, actually born within individual words, and a specifically arranged "scene" which may be observed by Reason (and the reasonable reader), are characteristics of a work in which the "images (tropes, concretions, metaphorical epithets, descriptive definitions) are 'arguments' " [Rosamond Tuve, in her *Elizabethan and Metaphysical Imagery*]. I have quoted Miss Tuve's descriptive summary of the influential Ramist concept which led to "the dialectical toughness of the Metaphysical poem", with its "substitution of intellectual probing for rhetorical persuasion." At first glance, it would seem that "The Phoenix and Turtle" is a poem greatly dependent on "rhetorical persuasion", but in fact its rhetoric is poetry of pure and unadorned statement. As Miss Tuve points out, it was an old notion that the poet should move from the specific to the general; but Ramist theory explicitly stated that ordinary poetic tropes could be ar-

guments in themselves. This may help us understand Shakespeare's method. (I do not suggest that Ramist theories of any sort were actually in Shakespeare's mind when he wrote the poem.) "The Phoenix and Turtle" seems to state the general in the first place, concretely, and without the "help of earthly images", until we realize that the actors of the poem, including the "abstractions" of love, constancy, and reason, are treated *as though they were earthly realities,* and that we have, as readers, followed them outwards to the generalities of nature, allowing them to lead us, in fact, as "arguments" of intellectual debate. Shakespeare does not "*add* to what we see", but amplifies through the intense purity of his vocabulary and by the repetition of the paradoxes of single two-ness. These suggest larger application to explicitly stated action, and Shakespeare uses them for this purpose instead of precisely detailed categories of imagistic allusion.

Although a poet may describe the "tragic scene", he cannot ultimately reduce the tragic effect to the vocabulary of logic; the reasonable audience, left behind, celebrates and admires it, but it is beyond common emotional experience. This is why "The Phoenix and Turtle" is a Metaphysical poem *par excellence.* To use Fraunce's fine phrase [in his *The Arcadian Rhetorike*], "the motion of the mind" which encompasses Shakespeare's description of perfect (and, frequently, therefore, in his view, necessarily tragic) love, occurs within the very terminology which Cunningham calls—and which may be—scholastic in origin. The details of Trinitarian doctrine do not really enlarge the paradoxes of the poem for us as much as they themselves have the power to do.

"The Phoenix and Turtle" carefully states the nature of love to remain always itself, with a power stronger than the power of two identifiable ("propertied") individuals to remain separate and discrete quantities. There is great capacity for moral statement in describing emotions and qualities as distinct abstractions capable of action. We may compare Ulysses' powerful definition of ungoverned will become appetite, which "must make perforce an universal prey, / And last eat up himself " [*Troilus and Cressida*, I. iii. 123-24], with Claudius' view of the "too-much" of goodness, inevitably metamorphosed into less than itself; but both examples may be contrasted with the "Two distincts, division none" of the Phoenix and the turtle-dove, uniting in love, admitting no impediments to the marriage of true minds. The lack of importance in the name "Romeo", as a verbal tag to identify Juliet's lover, emphasizes, so far as the lack of importance is discussed in the play, the constancy of his "single nature", definable only as their love is a "double name". Speaking quantitatively, the pure strains of the love of Troilus for Cressida and of Antony for Cleopatra are the same, but a tragedy can be made of Antony's because his love finds the miracle of beauty as felicitous as he is constant. "Property", in *Troilus and Cressida,* cannot be "appalled" by "simple . . . so well compounded" [l. 44]; no marriage of "Truth and Beauty" deserves in this play the repose of death.

To achieve the stature of tragedy, the individual lover must remain a "distinct", even in the unification of love. This is why the emphasis on distance and distinction in "The Phoenix and Turtle" is as strong as that on the merging—indeed, the maintaining of discrete actors causes the hyperbole of paradox in the anthem (stanzas 7-10). (pp. 95-7)

Shakespeare describes the positive achievement of such love as very great, and the fact of death, of course, does not negate it. One might almost say, in over-generalization, that death occurs when the "sovereignty of nature" is pure *enough,* when no other action in the material world can be worthy of the hero. [In his *The Mutual Flame*] Wilson Knight argues that "The Phoenix and Turtle" describes "a maximum of ardour with a minimum of possible accomplishment", and that whatever spiritual values the poem suggests, it cannot refer "in general [to] any ordinary marriage" since, participating in the doctrines of courtly love, it denies sexual consummation [see Additional Bibliography]. The stanza in question is the sixteenth, the third of the Threnos:

> Leaving no posterity:
> 'Twas not their infirmity,
> It was married chastity.

> [ll. 59-61]

It is always possible that these lines refer specifically to the real persons celebrated by the poem, but in our ignorance of them . . . , we need not consider the lines senseless in a larger context. The main trouble, of course, is "married chastity", but this means neither virginity nor total restraint from sexual activity. The common modern meaning of "chaste" (= celibate, virgin) occurs frequently in Shakespeare, but no more so than the equally acceptable meaning of complete fidelity within marriage. (p. 98)

Miss Bradbrook, in a comment on Ronald Bates's article on the poem, in which he considers this stanza as possibly "a suggestion of the ridiculous" [see Additional Bibliography], correctly states that "the associations of 'married chastity' for an Elizabethan would not be either with impotence or with abstinence" [see her second entry in the Additional Bibliography]. However, she explains the lines literally: "the Phoenix and Turtle could not mate, for they were not of a species . . . the only level on which the poem can be read in a physical sense *is* in terms of birds. That is perhaps why it is about birds and not about human beings. The idea of the human pair is behind the image: but the image of a human union is excluded. It is irrelevant to think in terms of Romeo and Juliet." I agree that in the poem "chastity" need not mean "abstinence", but that the reason for "no posterity" is the inability of a Phoenix and a dove to mate, does not ring true. "Leaving no posterity" may refer to the uniqueness of the love; as Miss Bradbrook puts it, "Truth and Beauty do not make more than a fugitive appearance on earth." The other stanzas of the Threnos reinforce this, especially

> Truth may seem, but cannot be;
> Beauty brag, but 'tis not she:
> Truth and Beauty buried be.

> [ll. 62-4]

What may still give confusion is "married chastity" as a *reason* for "no posterity". But if the phrase means the state of married fidelity so complete and constant that lust is no part of it, a sexual level . . . is not excluded. In Shakespeare's poem there is "no posterity" because no issue could possibly equal the lovers. "To think in terms of Romeo and Juliet"— and of Antony and Cleopatra—is, I believe, entirely relevant. The addition of the dove to the Phoenix-legend, as well as Shakespeare's general attitude throughout his plays, and particularly in the comedies, indicates that he would have agreed with Robert Greene, who observed [in his *Mammilia*] that "there is nothing more faire the*n* the Phoenix, yet nothing lesse necessary, because she is single."

The merging of the lovers in "The Phoenix and Turtle" actively defines love, for without the paradoxical union of con-

stancy and beauty there is nothing for Reason to observe which cannot be described in the ordinary words of the material world. The relation of the "tragic scene" in the poem to the conclusions of some of Shakespeare's tragedies is fairly clear. Whatever one's opinion may be concerning an afterlife for his tragic heroes, it is still true that the predominant effects of the last scenes of these plays are, as Cunningham says [in his *Woe or Wonder*], in Horatio's words, "woe and wonder" [*Hamlet,* V. ii. 363]. Reason's Threnos in "The Phoenix and Turtle" emphasizes these emotions as well, with its insistence upon the death of the lovers and with its command to admire. We are told that Reason composes "this threne. . . . As chorus to their tragic scene" [ll. 49, 52]. Although no definition of tragedy precisely applicable to Shakespeare's plays had been formulated, it is doubtful, in a poem so deliberately planned and so carefully written, that Shakespeare would have used loosely the theatrical words "Chorus" and "tragic", although they might well have come to mind automatically. . . . We must remember that not only is the "tragic scene" in the poem meant to be "sad", but that the "scene" itself includes the action of the consummation as well as the passing away of the lovers "in a mutual flame" [l. 24]. We know this because we are told that Reason sees it, and because we sense action in the paradoxes of the anthem.

It may be that Shakespeare was attracted to the Phoenix legend . . . as a vehicle for describing the "events" of love-tragedy. (pp. 98-100)

"The Phoenix and Turtle" is a lyric statement of truths which the tragedies set forth dramatically, constructed so as to reveal not only the inevitable doom of "the sovereignty of nature" when it achieves the pure essence of love, but also to describe in some measure the emotional effects of such action. Shakespeare invites an ideal audience, and, although it may appear a quibble, we may observe that Reason is moved. The content of the Threnos acknowledges "to these still figures we have pitied . . . the gift of feeling pity" [Alfred Harbage, in his introduction to *King Lear*], and its effect is similar to the concluding speeches of Fortinbras [in *Hamlet*], Albany [in *King Lear*], Malcolm [in *Macbeth*], Lodovico [in *Othello*], and Octavius Caesar [in *Antony and Cleopatra*], which clear the air of confusion, but are not meant to remove the memory of death and sorrow. Perhaps most of all they command admiration, and none more than Caesar, the observing voice of Reason in Egypt: "Come, Dolabella, see / High order in this great solemnity" [*Antony and Cleopatra,* V. ii. 365-66]. (p. 101)

Daniel Seltzer, " 'Their Tragic Scene': 'The Phoenix and Turtle' and Shakespeare's Love Tragedies," in Shakespeare Quarterly, *Vol. XII, No. 2, Spring, 1961, pp. 91-101.*

MURRAY COPLAND   (essay date 1965)

[*Copland discerns a half-humorous, half-serious treatment of the idea of human love in* The Phoenix and Turtle. *Yet ultimately, he asserts, this is "a poem of mourning, a meditation on the hard fact of mortality." Platonic theories of love were fashionable during the Elizabethan age, the critic points out, and in this context Shakespeare composed a poem that not only engages in the popular metaphysical rhetoric, but even seeks to "outdo all the others in sheer transcendence of transcendentalism." However, Copland remarks, Shakespeare transmuted Chester's conceit of a mated phoenix, portraying it as lifeless in its nest at the conclusion of the poem. This "twist" is in line with the convention of the metaphysical shock conceit, Copland notes; but, further, it is reminiscent of a dramatic analogue: the hanging of Cordelia in* King Lear. *On another issue, Copland chides critics who give the poem's title as* The Phoenix and the Turtle; *this violates the sense of Platonic unity, he claims, the idea of two-in-one that Shakespeare wishes to express in the poem.*]

The Phoenix was a striking bird on three counts: (a) its beauty, (b) its uniqueness, and (c) its self-resurrecting habit.

In Shakespeare's poem *The Phoenix and Turtle* the attribute (a) is prominently present:

> Truth and Beautie buried be.
>
> [l. 64]

Here Truth = the Turtle, and Beautie = the Phoenix.

As for (b), Robert Chester, whose *Love's Martyr* prescribed the bare postulates for the poem, had introduced a personal variation of a certain imaginative power. The usual Phoenix is complete in itself; Chester's requires a mate, and finds that mate in a true Turtle. This is not necessarily a muddling idea. If the Phoenix is seen as a poetic hyperbole for the summit of female attainment in beauty, accomplishment and virtue—the vision of a lady who might be complimented on such freedom from flaw as to seem virtually superhuman, so that one might expect her, by some divine dispensation, to be raised above the embarrassing necessities of normal human procreation—then the Turtle becomes, equally, a hyperbolical compliment to a man refined enough to deserve her. I do not claim that Chester's own intention was as simple as this; but it does seem to me that it is on much these straightforward terms that Shakespeare elects to understand Chester's brace of birds.

Countless writers, even Wilson Knight among them [see Additional Bibliography], have committed the howler—for surely it is that—of referring to Shakespeare's poem as 'The Phoenix and the Turtle'. If, in Platonic terms, the Phoenix represents the 'idea' of female beauty and the Turtle the 'idea' of fidelity, mated they have grown into a third 'idea' which by virtue of its ideality will necessarily have to include these two. This is, of course, the 'idea' of human love—human love in its barely imaginable perfection. Now I take it that an 'idea' cannot be a duality; it must be a unity. Shakespeare appears to have called his poem *The Phoenix and Turtle*. That is, the subject is *one* thing, not two.

In the line

> *Phoenix* and the *Turtle* fled,
>
> [l. 23]

they *are* presented as separate creatures, but only in aid of the next antithetical line wherein they are all the more strikingly fused:

> In a mutuall flame from hence.
>
> [l. 24]

Here *Phoenix* needs no article, precisely because of the bird's uniqueness: whereas *Turtle* needs its 'the' to establish (for this is the first mention of the dead protagonists) that this is not any old turtle (as, in fact, is the case in *Love's Martyr*) but itself a type, an ideal, and therefore unique, just as much as its mate.

It is immaterial whether Shakespeare had two actual dead lovers in mind. But I do not think the poem is being properly read if the reader does not realise that human love is under discussion; he should appreciate that behind the birds an eminently desirable human possibility is being mooted. If such a man and woman could exist and love like this, then *The Phoenix and Turtle* would be their fitting elegy.

It may be clear by now that I am against overmuch mystifying of this poem, which critics have tended to etherealise out of existence.

Is it so very crude to see in Shakespeare's acceptance of Chester's bright idea of a mated Phoenix a rather original, compellingly beautiful, but nonetheless natural and likely enough conceit to come upon in a late-Elizabethan Platonizing poem? (pp. 279-80)

The Elizabethans, sexually, must have been on the whole a happily proficient, promiscuous, and uninhibited race. We can assume this from the fascinated glee with which they pounced upon the newly unearthed Platonic version of love and made it all the fashionable rage. . . . It is their sense of the wild eccentricity of the notion which causes these poets to place such stress on the abstention from physical intercourse. The exaggerated contempt in which they place bodily pleasure has little to do with Plato, who notably conveys an appreciation of its charms.

The Shakespeare stanza about 'married Chastitie' comes as a shock because Shakespeare meant it to do so. Poems in the 'metaphysical' mode characteristically proceed by shock tactics, both of style and of thought. *The Phoenix and Turtle* is very obviously a single, somewhat haughtily restrained demonstration on Shakespeare's part that if 'everyone was doing it, doing it, doing it' he was very well competent to do it too; and, by a natural enough impulse under the circumstances, there is perhaps present a certain willingness to outdo all the others in sheer transcendence of transcendentalism.

Can it be doubted that this is, consciously, Shakespeare's contribution to the fashion of which Donne was the acknowledged leader—a fashion which I fancy the contemporary bright young men took with a certain seriousness as a discussion of the problem 'What should love be like'? Think how Lord Herbert's *Ode upon a Question moved, whether Love should continue for ever?* takes exception to Sidney's *In a Grove most rich of Shade* (in *Astrophil and Stella*) and Donne's *The Ecstasy* cocks a snook at both. Shakespeare's poem is clearly at home in this context. Place stanzas 7-12 of *The Phoenix and Turtle* beside stanzas 32-33 of Lord Herbert's *Ode* and stanzas 9-12 of *The Ecstasy* and the community of ambition to be brilliantly intellectual and ineffably Platonic shines out. (p. 281)

But there is no need to see Shakespeare as *merely* following a fashion. More than one critic has sensed that Shakespeare was aware of the quaintness and artificiality of the form he had chosen. Chester had landed him not only with 'metaphysics' but with birds. And not only the bird-obsequies idea, but also the curious Chinese-nest-of-boxes development whereby the birds gather to chant an anthem to the dead lovers in which Reason is alleged to have composed an elegy on the same dead lovers, seems to be Shakespeare's half-humorous, half-affectionate pastiche-tribute to the odd charm and elusive structure of the mediaeval dream-allegory form. (pp. 282-83)

[What] for brevity's sake we may call the Chaucerian element in conceit and structure allows Shakespeare to wear his 'metaphysics' with a difference—as any dandy will want to bring his own touch to the prevailing fashion, to preserve his self-respect. Nonetheless, it *is* a modish poem; but that also entails making a perfectly sober contribution to the contemporary inter-poets debate which aimed at evaluating the new ideas of love that were in the air.

This brings me at last to the third of the Phoenix's traditional attributes, the most distinctive of all, its immortality.

Most commentators have assumed that, since the Phoenix was traditionally an immortal bird, Shakespeare's poem must be 'about' some kind of immortality. (pp. 283-84)

I cannot, however, admit that the poem is about immortality in any sense whatsoever, unless perhaps it was conceived as an *attack on* the belief in immortality.

When a poet in the Donne vogue condescends to use a traditional image, he plumes himself on his ingenuity in giving it a new twist—see what Donne does with the Phoenix itself in . . . his Epithalamion. Shakespeare's most original and imaginative stroke in *The Phoenix and Turtle* is to assert that the unique, peerlessly beautiful bird is fully and finally *dead*. Only this can account for the combination of such depth and gravity of mourning with a certain mischievousness brought in by the Cock Robin framework, of which, after so much ineffability, we are somewhat bluntly reminded in the last line:

> For *these dead Birds,* sigh a prayer.
> [l. 67]

In the words I have italicised pathetic simplicity is not incompatible with a certain smile.

The Dead Phoenix is *the* 'metaphysical' shock conceit on which the whole poem depends.

> Death is now the *Phoenix* nest
> [l. 56]

represents poetic inversion for the sake of emphasis. A nest is not only 'a symbol of rebirth', as Richards claims [see Additional Bibliography], but also a symbol of the home, the family, security, warmth, and snuggling down to sleep. Previous Phoenixes, homing to their welcoming *hearth* (sacrificial altar), folded their wings to sleep, only to wake the next 'day', to rise again. But the Phoenix is now laid asleep for ever. Its bed is, simply and baldly, the final bed of death.

> And the *Turtles* loyall brest,
> To eternitie doth rest.
> [ll. 57-8]

The 'And' links, as it should, two equalities. Nothing else would be decent in a poem which has put the Phoenix and the Turtle so absolutely on the same level (co-supremes).

The muted ending of '*sigh* a prayer' (my italics) is analogous, although on a different scale, to the drained, stunned close of *King Lear.* And, indeed, need we be surprised that a poet should wish to shock us with a mortal Phoenix who also confronted us inexorably with a hanged Cordelia? *The Phoenix and Turtle* is genuinely a poem of mourning, a meditation on the hard fact of mortality. It is thus centrally, not peripherally, Shakespearian.

In the world of *King Lear* there is no revealed God, no saving Christ sent in from outside. If human beings want the amelioration of the Christ-function, they can have it only in so far

as they are prepared to shoulder the burden themselves and *become* Christ to the extent that a human being is capable of doing this. Only human beings can 'show the heavens more just' [*King Lear,* III. iv. 36], by enacting heaven in their own behaviour. The saintly, Christlike imagery which clusters around Cordelia in the later part of the play indicates that she is the summit of human success in this direction. But she remains mortal for all that: no woman is so much of a Phoenix that she cannot be killed. All of Christ that the world can have can be murdered any day in the death of one person. This is why the death of one such person can reasonably affect us as if all the Christlike potentialities of the world had been snatched away from us for ever at one fell swoop. (pp. 285-6)

If *The Phoenix and Turtle* does not, after all, impress us as a work loomingly tragic in the manner of *King Lear,* that is partly because of the poem's most subtle paradox, slipped gently into the last two stanzas (in which I trust I may be allowed to assume that 'faire' is a straightforward synonym for 'beautiful'):

> Truth may seeme, but cannot be,
> Beautie bragge, but tis not she,
> Truth and Beautie buried be.
>
> To this urne let those repaire,
> That are either true or faire,
> For these dead Birds, sigh a prayer.
> [ll. 62-7]

If, as we are told, Truth and Beautie are irrecoverably buried, who are these surviving 'true and beautiful' mourners who are invited to sigh a prayer—'bragging', 'seeming' impostors? Obviously not. Human beings (or birds) may still be born who may be called true or beautiful, but we cannot believe, in this moment of particular grieving, that we shall ever want to revere them as the embodied 'ideas' of Truth and Beautie (notice where we do and do not find capital letters in these stanzas). I sense a touch of affectionate humour in 'dead Birds' in that Shakespeare is not, characteristically, concerned about the forms in the heavenly warehouse; the sigh is a wistful one; the poem is rather addressed (how Chaucerian this is!) to the uncapitalised 'yonge, fresshe folkes, he or she' of the penultimate line—it is an admonition to them, in view of their certain mortality, to be as true and beautiful (yes, and as *chaste*) as it lies in their power to be, but not to be too humourless about it. 'Ideas' are strange birds; and, poor birds, they're dead.

Humorous or not, the paradox of these last stanzas is paralleled in the paradoxical closing lines of *King Lear:*

> The oldest hath borne most, we that are yong,
> Shall never see so much, nor live so long.
> [V. iii. 326-27]

Mystical readings of *The Phoenix and Turtle* debase it. The poem is as sad, searching, tender, human, and humane, as we should expect from the author of the tragedies. (p. 287)

Murray Copland, "The Dead Phoenix," in Essays in Criticism, *Vol. XV, No. 3, July, 1965, pp. 279-87.*

K. T. S. CAMPBELL (lecture date 1969)

[The following excerpt is from a lecture presented to the Fifth Annual Conference of The British Society of Aesthetics in 1969. Campbell asserts that The Phoenix and Turtle *"has something*

Phoenix in flames. By Geffrey Whitney (1586).

fundamentally to do with the essence and with the fate of poetry itself" and represents "a metaphoric crystallization" of the nihilism inherent in the idea that poetry has no meaning beyond its own universe. According to Campbell, the process of formulating poetical concepts by uniting previously disparate entities into a new conceptual identity is an attempt to apprehend reality, understood as appearance; ultimately, however, this is a destructive process that violates the integrity of each independent agent. Thus poetry, he argues, faces a crisis; the very act of artistic creation, of "making the unspeaking speak," is itself a tragic act. A self-conscious artist, as Shakespeare most certainly was, must either succumb to the "shattering of every symbol," as many twentieth-century poets and writers have done, or, as Shakespeare chose, sublimate "the real destruction of the poetic symbol understood abstractly into a concrete image of destruction, into tragedy, in fact." The crisis encountered by the poet at the moment of self-awareness, when art appears destined for annihilation, is averted, paradoxically, by poetic wit: that is, through the construction of an image whose mortality seems preordained, but which "by the very logic of the self-conscious must necessarily be unreal." Campbell claims this self-conscious poetic device constitutes Shakespeare's theory of poetry; while it is manifest in every aspect of his dramatic works, the critic contends, it assumes central stage in Hamlet *and* King Lear.]

[*The Phoenix and the Turtle*] is a curious, almost uncanny poem. Its origins are wrapped in mystery; I believe that it is by Shakespeare; if any proof is needed in addition to the fact that it appeared over his name in 1601 (something which has not always convinced critics), there is the very similar phraseology of Troilus's speech in the last act of *Troilus and Cressida:* 'If beautie have a soule, this is not she' [V. ii. 138], and so on. There is also the fact that, as Alvarez puts it, 'increasingly throughout the poem concrete is evaporated into abstract' [see excerpt above, 1955]—and this is very characteristic of Shakespeare's mature style. Finally, Wilson Knight has discovered that stanzas 2-6 in particular are 'made of leading Shakespearian themes and symbols' and that the entire poem 'might be said to constitute a brief summing up of Shakespeare's total work' [see his second entry in the Additional Bibliography].

This insight brings us to the as yet unsettled question of the

meaning of the poem. It has been, for instance, connected with the Essex scandal of the last years of Queen Elizabeth; alternatively, it has been suggested that the poem is representative of the union of Christ and the Church. It is obvious, of course, that the conceit of two lovers becoming one flesh plays an important part in the poem, but I think that this is an element of surface pattern and not a final meaning. I agree with Alvarez when he describes the lover-conceit as being, even in 1601, 'well-nigh exhausted'. Good poems have, of course, continued to be written on this theme, but this poem in particular is *too* good, too much of a major poem—too vigorous, too serious and too well done—to have this trifling conceit as its true centre. It would be like stealing Promethean fire to light a cigarette. As for the Christ-and-Church theory, again I agree with Alvarez that this is 'a sin of overseriousness': although *The Phoenix and the Turtle* is not what I should describe as a secular poem, I think that a poem of comparable weight that had even one strand of religious signification, for instance at the anagogical level of Dante's scheme of interpretation, would leave you in much less doubt as to its real function. If this poem refers to a love, it is rarified above the particularly human level, but not in a specifically heavenly direction. I do not say that it cannot refer to a love. But in any case it is obvious that the heart of the matter lies in a riddle, which, since it is an abstract riddle, may also be expressed in simplified terms: what is simultaneously simple and complex, and in this way contains and reveals the fact of its own nothingness?

In pondering this riddle, we may remember the words of the rhetorician John Hoskins, written in 1599: 'besides, a metaphor is pleasant because it enricheth our knowledge with two things at once, with the truth and with similitude' [in his *Directions for Speech and Style*]. Now if, for the sake of argument, we agree provisionally that the truth is always complex and that similitude is always simple, then we may begin to feel that Shakespeare's *The Phoenix and the Turtle* has something fundamentally to do with the essence and with the fate of poetry itself. (pp. 169-70)

[In] our own time we have become familiar with art turning back on itself, questioning itself and seeking to know what lies beyond the surface of artistic images; some of us think of this as a characteristically modern phenomenon. I, however, do not believe that this is an exclusively twentieth-century phenomenon and I do not believe, as some of our twentieth-century practitioners appear to do, that the coming of art to an awareness of itself necessarily implies the destruction or shattering of every artistic symbol. I believe that Shakespeare chose another way. And in this connexion I refer to the essentially *tragic* form of *The Phoenix and the Turtle* which, I think, is a metaphoric crystallization of the forces which Shakespeare in 1601 (the year of *Hamlet*) felt burgeoning within him.

If *The Phoenix and the Turtle* is Shakespeare's emblematic representation of his self-conscious understanding of poetry, then this understanding has two stages: the first is that of the paradox . . . in which 'Division grows together' [l. 42] and 'Simple is so well compounded' [l. 44]; the second is that of the 'mutuall flame' in which Phoenix and Turtle flee away together and in which we understand that

> Death is now the *Phoenix* nest,
> And the *Turtles* loyall brest,
> To eternitie doth rest.

[ll. 56-8]

Within the poem itself this can be fairly clearly understood as a logical consequence of the paradox; division that no longer divides and simplicity revealed as complexity may be said to have extinguished each other's vital principles by mutual invasion. But has it a further significance? May we understand this first as a prevision of the development of poetry, and second as a controlling theme or figure by which the poem may be linked to Shakespeare's own subsequent development?

With regard to the first question, . . . I believe that the development of poetry is linked to the development of self-conscious understanding generally in the poetic field of culture. Perhaps 'self-conscious' is not the best term, carrying overtones of awkwardness and egoism; what I mean is the stage of development reached in any given field, such as poetry, when—as Ernst Cassirer says [in his *The Philosophy of Symbolic Form*]—'man ceases merely to live in and with reality and demands a knowledge of this reality'. One of the first functions of such a critical understanding is to divide appearance from reality, or to penetrate to reality beyond appearance. Thus even in myth the primitive undifferentiated miracles which flood the mind with supernatural power give place to the perception of the all-embracing universality of a High God interpreted through dogma; in cognition the concrete images of Nature give way to a reality of abstract law represented in them and through them. But in poetry what happens? In poetry appearance *is* reality; the aesthetic image does not pretend to be or to represent another reality more real than image function itself. Appearance here is its own reality and has its own laws—the laws of sheer appearance, as Suzanne Langer rightly termed it [in her *Feeling and Form*]. It stands for nothing outside itself. And thus when, as Jacques Maritain says [in his "Concerning Poetic Knowledge"], poetry 'takes cognisance of itself as poetry', it speedily 'transfigures' the 'function' and 'exigency' of the creation of a poetic object into the necessity of the creation of a totally independent 'world'. Maritain says: 'the poem will by itself be a self-sufficient universe, without the need of signifying anything but itself'.

Already in this formulation, therefore, a choice may be seen to emerge for the self-conscious poet. To some modern poets the only way in which a poem may mean nothing beyond itself and in which they may create a self-sufficient, blind universe is the way of Ezra Pound or James Joyce, in which the artist takes the radical course of actively wrecking the meaning-structure of poetry itself and thus not allowing a single shred of real meaning to escape into the outer world. . . . Thus in the advanced phase of poetry on the one hand the complexity of the poetic self-conscious reveals meaninglessness, and in fact *nothing* through the simplicity of the poetic surface, and conversely, this same meaningless surface appearance of course destroys rational complexity—thus fulfilling the fatal augury of *The Phoenix and the Turtle* in a manner approaching the literal death of poetry. But, on the other hand, there is another path open perhaps to those poets who, like Yeats, have such a strong current of mature vigour in their verse already that they can overcome and sublimate the nihilistic tendency to destroy the substance of their own work. We can after all construe Maritain's reference to 'a self-sufficient universe, without the need of signifying anything but itself' in another sense, one that will revive and deepen poetry rather than destroy it. Poets of intelligence and skill

can make poetry that attains greater depths than ever before because it covertly represents nothing but poetry itself in its doom-tending progress. Shakespeare, in other words, exorcises the demon of annihilation which he knew to be stirring within himself in 1601 by making an image of that demon—of inevitable, fate-impelled death, of *tragedy*—an image which by the very logic of the self-conscious must necessarily be unreal, a mere matter of the 'dead birds' of the last stanza of *The Phoenix and the Turtle,* in which I believe he crystallizes in prevision the themes which were to occupy him in the years after 1601 in his great tragedies. For if the image represents nothing—why, then, the image shall represent nothing; nothing will come of nothing, as King Lear remarks to his daughter. Hence, indeed, Shakespeare's 'Reason in itself confounded' [l. 41] acts as Chorus to the most awe-inspiring Tragique Scene that the English-speaking world of poetry and drama has ever witnessed:

> Truth may seem, but cannot be,
> Beauty bragge, but tis not she,
> Truth and Beauty buried be.
>
> [ll. 62-4]

And in 1601, simultaneously with *The Phoenix and the Turtle,* we have *Hamlet.*

Horatio's advice in the first scene is to tell Hamlet of the ghost,

> for upon my life,
> This spirit, dumbe to us, will speake to him.
>
> [I. i. 170-71]

And so indeed it turns out, for Hamlet, Reason incarnate, makes the unspeaking speak—an act of as tragic significance as King Lear's division of the indivisible—his kingdom. The very act of artistic creation—what else is art but to make the unspeaking speak?—is invested with fatal import. Horatio's foreboding is immediately fulfilled—

> What if it tempt you toward the Floude my Lord?
> Or to the dreadful Summit of the Cliffe,
> That beetles o'er his base into the Sea,
> And there assumes some other horrible forme,
> Which might deprive your Sovereignty of Reason,
> And draw you into madnesse. . .?
>
> [I. iv. 69-74]

The Ghost's ominous utterance makes Hamlet, that complex man, simple:

> Remember thee?
> I, thou poore Ghost, while memory holds a seate
> In this distracted Globe: Remember thee?
> Yea, from the Table of my Memory,
> Ile wipe away all triviall fond Records,
> All sawes of Bookes, all formes, all presures past,
> That youth and observation coppied there;
> And thy Commandment all alone shall live
> Within the Booke and Volume of my Braine,
> Unmixt with baser matter.
>
> [I. v. 95-104]

And so he becomes, disputable, mad—that is, not quite mad; for the Reason that is in it selfe confounded is still sane enough to behold with an anguished eye Division grow together—Gertrude and Claudius who, by the laws of God and man are to themselves yet either neither and, becoming one flesh, are simple yet so well compounded.

If I may remark other resemblances, the suggestive word

'slaine' in 'Number there in loue was slaine' [l. 28] recalls to us the death of old King Hamlet, whose love for his wife proclaimed the seemingly irrevocable twoness of Gertrude and Claudius. If 'Propertie was thus appalled that the selfe was not the same' [ll. 37-8], at least two of the three meanings for Propertie that Alvarez distinguishes are confirmed—Propertie in the sense of things owned, like a wife by her husband, and Propertie in the sense of Propriety, recalling Hamlet's horror at the fact that Gertrude, formerly one with Old Hamlet, is now united with Claudius.

The conclusion is clear: Wolfgang Clemen has noted [in his *The Development of Shakespeare's Imagery*], with especial emphasis on the transfiguration of Shakespeare's style hereby implied, that the special Hamlet imagery reveals a power to penetrate beyond the façades of other men and mere earthly appearance: but what does Hamlet see with this superb intellect? Nothing but falsehood, insincerity, folly, corruption and death.

> This most excellent Canopy the Ayre, look you, this brave ore-hanging firmament, this Maiesticall Roofe, fretted with golden fire: why, it appears no other thing to mee, then a foule and pestilent congregation of vapours. What a piece of worke is a man! How Noble in Reason? how infinite in faculty? in forme and moving how expresse and admirable? in Action, how like an Angel? in apprehension, how like a God? the beauty of the world, the Parragon of Animals; and yet to me, what is this Quintessence of Dust?
>
> [II. ii. 299-308]

The play *Hamlet,* I dare say, is as near as anything this side of Samuel Beckett to a *non-play,* with the whole course of action composed out of false starts, hesitations, errors and the inertia of sheer negative reaction; and in the end all the characters are destroyed. But also in the end Shakespeare, the master ironist, turns the tables on what might have been his own destiny. As Alvarez points out in his penetrating critique of *The Phoenix and the Turtle,* the poetic myth reasserts itself as 'the "true" and "faire" rise again from the ashes of "Truth" and "Beautie". The wit keeps control.' After all, Gertrude and Claudius, as well as the Phoenix and the Turtle, are 'only a pair of "dead birds" '; Shakespeare transforms the death of an image into the image of death. He does not obey—does not need to obey—the savage and suicidal commandment of Verlaine: 'Prends l'éloquence et tords-lui son cou!' [Take eloquence and wring its neck!]

If we can return to the basic riddle of *The Phoenix and the Turtle*—What is simple and complex and contains within itself the fact of its own nothingness?—it seems to me that the great tragedies in particular are not only the dramatic expression of but the answer to this riddle—and that they represent successive reworkings of the general theme indicated by this set of paradoxes, with *Hamlet* nearest to the matrix of *The Phoenix and the Turtle* and *King Lear* perhaps the most perfected example. (pp. 173-78)

I suggest that Shakespeare's titanic tragedies are evidence (a) that Shakespeare knew in himself the destructive crisis of identity and purpose in which, paradoxically, the poetry of our own time lives; (b) that he was able to choose to avoid the radical resolution of this crisis adopted by many of our present-day poets in their fragmentation and destruction of the poetic symbol itself; and (c) that by means of his unequalled ability to conceive in and through poetic images, his

choice involved the sublimation of the real destruction of the poetic symbol, understood abstractly, into a concrete image of destruction, into tragedy, in fact. (p. 178)

> K. T. S. Campbell, " 'The Phoenix and the Turtle' as a Signpost of Shakespeare's Development," in The British Journal of Aesthetics, *Vol. 10, 1970, pp. 169-79.*

VINCENT F. PETRONELLA   (essay date 1975)

[*Petronella suggests that in both style and content,* The Phoenix and Turtle *conveys the sense of a failed attempt to reach a state of mystical ecstasy. The poem's lyricism, he points out, is expressed through "musical-aural imagery" and an insistent metrical pattern that imparts the same sense of intensity and urgency associated with poetic and divine madness. Petronella notes, however, that the music is "defunctive"; instead of the achievement of ecstatic fulfillment, reason steps forth to present a dirge. He further argues that the poem's structure resembles the procession-rapture-recession triad of the Neoplatonic pastoral and reflects the "Orphic tradition of poetic theology" which typically encompassed both a serious and a light-hearted or playful tone. Thus, although the poem engages philosophical issues and presents a vision of apocalypse, it does so with a measure of wit and irony.* The Phoenix and Turtle *captures Shakespeare's spirit of quasi-mystical humanism, according to Petronella, and follows the literary and intellectual fashion of the Elizabethan era; even the dead phoenix, which some critics cite as Shakespeare's invention, has precedents in Petrarch, Marot, and Spenser.*]

I should make it clear at the outset that I believe [*The Phoenix and the Turtle*] is not to be restricted to any one explanation. Its highly suggestive imagery and its sometimes intriguing genesis do not allow for rigid critiques of origin, meaning, and structure. Straumann's emphasis upon the principle of *Mehrdeutigkeit,* or "layers of meaning," as it concerns *The Phoenix and the Turtle* is a perfectly sound one [see excerpt below, 1976], as is Muriel Bradbrook's reminder [in her " 'The Phoenix and the Turtle' "] that "negative capability, or the power to refrain from specific associations is not out of place in the reading of poetry" [see Additional Bibliography]. At the outset, then, I can say that my study of *The Phoenix and the Turtle* will be a critical conflation—hopefully, one that leads to a greater awareness and comprehension of the intricacies of the poem at hand—rather than strictly a refutation of what has already been said by others.

If we look first at Shakespeare's image of the unrevived Phoenix, we see before us a symbol of death—a symbol of a supposedly immortal force rendered mortal. The call is out for "defunctive music" for a defunctive pair of birds, one of which has in some mysterious way lost the legendary function of self-regeneration. This depiction of the Phoenix should not be loosely referred to as an original detail, for it is unlikely that the dead, unrevived Phoenix in Shakespeare's poem would have come as a shock to the well-read Renaissance Englishman, primarily because prior to the composition of *The Phoenix and the Turtle* three important writers had already dealt with the same idea. Petrarch, Marot, and Spenser are names that do not crop up often enough in discussions of sources and analogues for *The Phoenix and the Turtle,* and one wonders why this is so, for in Petrarch's *Canzoniere* 323 . . . lurks the unrevived Phoenix that remains just as unrevived in Marot's *Des Visions de Petrarque* and Spenser's *Visions of Petrarch.* (pp. 315-16)

Shakespeare in *The Phoenix and the Turtle* uses not only the image of the unrevived Phoenix but also another ingredient found in the Petrarch-Marot-Spenser poems and referred to in Marot's and Spenser's titles: the wondrous visionary experience. To see the Phoenix is marvelous enough, but to see the Phoenix die and fail to regain its own life is a nightmare vision almost beyond words. Shakespeare's *The Phoenix and the Turtle* is similarly a vision of an overwhelming disaster—the destruction of those values linked with the Phoenix and the Turtle-Dove. Love—spiritual and erotic—is central to Shakespeare's poem but is dealt with as part of a mystical or magical perception of the obliteration of love and truth symbolized by the Turtle-Dove and the Phoenix. The poem is apocalyptic. It is a "Jacobean" insight into what could and what might indeed happen in the lives of individual men or in the world in general. What makes the poem's vision powerful is the pulsation of *energia* [vigor of style] and *enargia* [vivid description] generated by an intense, ecstatic music. Or, to put it another way, *The Phoenix and the Turtle* is a work dealing with the music of ecstasy. But the ecstasy does not succeed in doing what it is traditionally supposed to do, although the poetry achieves a power of expression that compels our sensory faculties to respond fully. To put it still another way, we may say that the music and the ecstasy are "defunctive"—that is, no longer capable of functioning to bring about a hopeful and enduring vision of truth and love. In brief, *The Phoenix and the Turtle* is about "defunctive" ecstasy, mystical ecstasy that does not work.

To understand why mystical ecstasy is ineffectual in *The Phoenix and the Turtle,* we should review briefly the tradition of ecstasy and the very close association between music and spiritual rapture, always bearing in mind that ecstasy and music are present in Shakespeare's poem not only as subjects but also as principles governing the poem's style. (pp. 317-18)

"Mystic ecstasy in the Christian sense," says the *Oxford Dictionary of the Christian Church,* "is one of the normal stages of the mystic life. . . . The chief characteristic of the ecstatic state is the alienation of the senses, caused by the violence of the Divine action on the soul." In his edition of Donne's poetry, John T. Shawcross tells us that Christian mystics used the term "ecstasy" to describe "a state of extreme and abnormal awareness"—an awareness "derived from the detachment of the soul from the body, the soul standing outside the body contemplating their [i.e., body's and soul's] unity and relationship." To these statements we may add Theodore Redpath's explanation [in his edition of *The Songs and Sonnets of John Donne*] that "ecstasy" is the "mystical state in which a soul, liberated from the body, contemplates divine truths." If we let the one word *ecstasy* stand for a cluster of related words, Robert Petersson advises us [in his *The Art of Ecstasy: Teresa, Bernini, and Crashaw*], it refers to "the state in which man is farthest removed from his normal human condition, the state in which prayer perfectly attains its ideals"; it is a term inseparable from closely related experiences such as vision, trance, transport, rapture, and union itself. Such is the nature of spiritual ecstasy. But what of sensual ecstasy? A commonplace similarity exists between spiritual ecstasy and sensual ecstasy despite the emphasis that the first places on the soul and the second on the body. It is not necessary to argue here about the similarity. Only the naïve or the strictly puritanical would fail to respond to the erotic element in St. Teresa's spiritual ecstasy and the spiritual power of the earthly lovers' experience in *The Extasie* of Donne. Love theorists from Plato through Ficino, Bruno and Leone Ebreo have said

much about the role of "divine madness" (i.e., "frenzy," "furor," "enthusiasm," or "ecstasy") in the life of the lover. In his *Commentary on Plato's "Symposium,"* Ficino writes: ". . . there are four kinds of divine madness. The first is the poetic madness, the second is that of the mysteries, the third is that of prophecy, and the fourth is that of love." Ecstasy, we are to understand, occurs over a wide range of categories; it is not limited solely to a world of disembodied creatures.

The Phoenix and the Turtle reflects the Ficinian analysis of the *furores* [forms of madness], but whether Shakespeare was consciously using Ficino's work or that of any other Renaissance writer in composing this poem is impossible to determine finally. Standing within a rich intellectual tradition as it does, Shakespeare's poem is a reflector of developments in the history of thought. And the relationship between poetic text and the intellectual tradition strikes me as shedding more light on this poem than any theory of biographical or political associations. What I am suggesting is that the Neoplatonic discussions of "divine madness" (or what Shakespeare calls "fine frenzy" in *A Midsummer Night's Dream* [V. i. 12]), with the religious mystical vestiges that the term carries, are deeply involved in the thematic and stylistic constitution of *The Phoenix and the Turtle.*

Consider first "poetic madness": this is heard and felt by virtue of the poem's heightened incantatory quality. The poetry is intense, marked sometimes by what apparently is a sense of total abandon. Its lyrical intensity is achieved by a hard-driving, basically trochaic, meter that energetically presses all sixty-seven lines of the poem to get somewhere without hesitation. No caesural rest-stops here—Shakespeare's libretto affords no timeless fermatas. To complement this rhythmical urgency, the poem is structured so that prior to the Threnos, several stanzas, although rhyming *abba,* very often become four lines ending not only in rhymed words but also in words related through assonance:

> Let the bird of loudest lay,
> . . . tree,
> . . . be,
> . . . obey.
>
> [ll. 1-4]

> Here the anthem doth commence;
> . . . dead;
> . . . fled
> . . . hence.
>
> [ll. 21-4]

> So between them love did shine
> . . . right
> . . . sight:
> . . . mine.
>
> [ll. 33-6]

Or the line endings may be related through consonance—assisted by one instance of a partial repetition of end words (stanzas 9 and 12):

> So they lov'd, as love in twain
> . . . one;
> . . . none:
> . . . slain.
>
> [ll. 25-8]

> Hearts remote, yet not asunder;
> . . . seen
> . . . queen;
> . . . wonder.
>
> [ll. 29-32]

That it cried, How true a twain
   . . . one!
   . . . none,
   . . . remain.

[ll. 45-8]

And at least one stanza has a touch of both assonance and consonance:

But thou shrieking harbinger,
   . . . fiend,
   . . . end,
   . . . near.

[ll. 5-8]

This handling of the line endings, together with the rhymed triplets of the Threnos and the quick-paced rhythm of the lines throughout the poem, creates a lyrical intensity that flickers occasionally to permit, as it were, an almost Skeltonic flippancy to flash through. But Shakespeare is not writing meaningless doggerel or a *jeu d'esprit*. The intense lyricism he develops is an attempt to capture a poetic ecstasy commensurate with the vision that the poem offers us. This is done neither with grim solemnity nor tongue-in-cheek; on the contrary, Shakespeare executes it with a metaphysical mixture of levity and seriousness.

Never mellifluous, yet melodic (even to a frenetic degree), the lyricism of *The Phoenix and the Turtle* is bolstered by several musical-aural images: "loudest lay," "trumpet," "sound," "shrieking," "defunctive music," "requiem," "anthem," "Threne," "Chorus." Several of the words in the poem have a double function, one of which is submerged musical metaphor: "treble," "division" (occurring twice, once at [l. 27] and again at [l. 42], "number," "concordant," "parts," and perhaps "confounded" [l. 41]. In addition to the individual words and phrases with musical-aural values, the poem has as its conclusion a funeral song. That the poem becomes a piece of music is a result of the sound it makes combined with its many musical-aural references. In this way *The Phoenix and the Turtle* is poetic and musical at the same time that it speaks about poetry and music; and as the style is in keeping with the idea of "defunctive music," so the subject matter is defunction—the lack of function and the lack of effective power to prevent defunction. G. Wilson Knight [in his *The Christian Renaissance*] maintains that in *The Phoenix and the Turtle* tempest (usually associated with tragedy) becomes music (symbolically linked with love and union in Shakespeare) and that "the tempest-music distinction is resolved."

It is true that love and union do occur in *The Phoenix and the Turtle,* but what does not occur is the regeneration of love and union. The magic does not work. The music here would not succeed in reviving a broken Coriolanus. If the music of *The Phoenix and the Turtle* can in any way be thought of as a kind of Orphic incantation, with its traditionally magic power to influence the astrological powers above in order to achieve a revival of spirit, the incantation fails.

Incantation, magic-song, ecstasy, furor are all terms that apply to the style and subject matter of *The Phoenix and the Turtle.* But if ecstasy is supposed to be the state in which a literal separation of soul from body takes place, then why talk of union of Phoenix (soul) and Turtle-Dove (body), as if this were the end toward which the poem's central characters are supposed ultimately to be headed? Ideally the ecstatic state would find soul released from body. But in *The Phoenix and the Turtle* the ecstasy is never brought off, and this is the reason why Shakespeare speaks of "division none" and the "mutual flame" of death. The problem here is that body and soul are consumed together, mutually. Never does the soul become separated in order to enjoy observing the body from a distance as it would do if true spiritual ecstasy took place. If any separation were to occur (either explicitly or implicitly) in Shakespeare's poem, it would become the kind of separation of body and soul that is in fact death. But rather than dramatizing the soul's standing off from the body, the poem confronts us with the death of both body and soul. Immortality, then, is out of the picture, no less than ecstatic fulfillment. Tragic tempest does not become comic or unifying music here, as Knight argues; instead, the enthusiastic music of ecstasy falls on the deaf ears of stony mortality, which in turn means that music gives way to a brewing tempest, the tempest suggestive not of tragedy but of pathetic calamity. One's awareness of what Shakespeare is doing is greatly increased if one understands that the sound of music in *The Phoenix and the Turtle* is also the sound of ominous, far-off thunder.

The monitory and oracular quality of *The Phoenix and the Turtle* links it with those two other *furores* discussed in the Platonic tradition: the madness of prophecy and the madness of mystery (religious rite). The bird imagery of the poem asks us to recall the commonplace use of winged creatures in discerning omens or prophecies. Furthermore, the personification Reason singing the Threnos is symbolically apt in that it suggests the clear-mindedness and hence the clear-sightedness rather than simply the frenzy of prophecy. In this way Shakespeare concludes his poem. Earlier, Reason has been puzzled, stumped—its dilemma reinforcing the "madness" element in the poem:

> Reason, in itself confounded,
> Saw division grow together,
> To themselves yet either neither,
> Simple were so well compounded:
>
> That it cried, How true a twain
> Seemeth this concordant one!
> Love hath reason, reason none,
> If what parts, can so remain.

[ll. 41-8]

At this point it appears that ecstasy or "enthusiasm" has prevailed, for Reason is at sixes and sevens. But Reason has the last word in *The Phoenix and the Turtle,* and what Reason is talking about to us is death as the finality of being—what is described in *Macbeth* as "the be-all and the end-all—here" [I. vii. 5].

Reason makes its recovery in the third section of the poem's tripartite structure. It is this framework that organizes the ritualistic movement, the first notable indication of which is the formal gathering of the different birds who are asked to "keep the obsequy so strict" [l. 12], particularly the swan, who will bring to the requiem his "right" (i.e., "his due" with a pun on "rite"). Prophecy and religious rite are traditionally interconnected, and in Shakespeare's poem the themes of prophecy and mystery-rite, although not presented in any clearly sectarian way, work together to heighten the ecstatic pulse of the poetry. Instead of working toward the level of divine understanding, however, *The Phoenix and the Turtle* takes us in the direction of a rational, rather than a nonrational or "enthusiastic," vision. Shakespeare is using ecstatic style and content for strictly terrestrial ends. . . . (pp. 318-23)

All of the *furores* involve emotional intensity and are in this way related to one another, but central to *The Phoenix and the Turtle* is the all-important love-madness, which, as Ficino tells us, turns the head of the charioteer in man's soul "toward the head of all things." The poem's tripartite structure, a feature recognized by many . . . commentators . . . , acts as a vehicle for the theme of love-madness. Commentary on the poem's structure, however, has not touched upon the similarity between the stylistic mode of *The Phoenix and the Turtle* and that of the Orphic pastoral. A consideration of the similarity is illuminating. Richard Cody, commenting on the *Orfeo* of Poliziano as part of a discussion that eventually focuses on Shakespearean drama, analyzes the basic rhythm of Neoplatonic pastoral in terms of three phases: *Emanatio* (procession), *Raptio* (rapture or ecstasy), and *Remeatio* (return or recession) [in his *The Landscape of the Mind*]. Poliziano, like Pico della Mirandola and Ficino, envisions the Orpheus myth as an allegory of the death and the new life of the Rational Soul, "lost and found again in the flames of intellectual love"; the *Orfeo,* moreover, portrays the death of Orpheus as a gift of Love (Eros) to the Rational Soul. This is not to say that Shakespeare's poem is about Orpheus or that it is a Neoplatonic pastoral. It does manifest, however, pastoral elements and a handling of the mystery of love-in-death. But *The Phoenix and the Turtle* is more than a quasi-pastoral depiction of birds in a forest or meadow, and it is more than a poem expressing Neoplatonic values. It is, in fact, a richly metaphorical portrait of an attitude, a frame of mind. And I contend that the intellectual attitude is made concrete not only by suggestive symbols but also by structural rhythm. The first twenty lines constitute the *Emanatio* of Shakespeare's poem: in comes a procession made up of "the bird of loudest lay," the "shrieking harbinger" (i.e., screech owl), the eagle, the swan, and the crow. We then move into the anthem and its attempt to analyze the mystery of love-madness and the love-death of Phoenix and Turtle-Dove; this is the poem's *Raptio,* and rapturous it is. Union is spiritual and physical for Phoenix and Turtle-Dove; their mutual consummation, given one of the meanings of dying in Shakespeare's time, is highly erotic as well as hopefully regenerative. But although the erotic ecstasy takes place, the spiritual ecstasy never reaches its special kind of climax. Reason, as I have already indicated, is perplexed at this point: only momentarily do Apollonian values surrender to Dionysian ones. It is as if the *furores* (poetry, prophecy, and religious rite) combine to drive the love-ecstasy into divine clarification, a clarification that hopefully will endure forever. But, alas, with the *Remeatio* (the Threnos in this case) the poem's movement recedes, and Reason leads the way. Phoenix and Turtle-Dove have not attained the divine level through ecstasy; instead, they become the subject of Reason's dirge on the grim fact that truth and beauty have been destroyed beyond the point of revival. If the poem is a frame of mind, it portrays the Jacobean intellectual landscape.

Poetry, ritual, prophecy, and love are the enticing ingredients in an artistic *olla podrida;* they blend and become the overall tone and meaning of *The Phoenix and the Turtle.* To say that the tone of *The Phoenix and the Turtle* is a mixture of seriousness and playfulness is to get closer to what the poem means. With its tripartite structure reflecting the *Emanatio-Raptio-Remeatio* triad of the Neoplatonists, *The Phoenix and the Turtle* to some extent partakes of the Orphic tradition of poetic theology, which always implies *serio ludere,* that is, jesting in earnest, playfulness combined with learned diligence. This helps us to understand why the verse technique dis-

cussed earlier has a flippant air about it and why levity works hand in hand with seriousness. The poem exhibits a metaphysical wit as it deals with "serious" metaphysical issues. Seen this way, the poem is simultaneously a metaphysical poem (in the literary sense) and a metaphysical poem (in the philosophical sense). We are asked to take its vision seriously, but we are also permitted to enjoy the wit and the irony of the vision. Ecstasy is ultimately defunctive in the world of *The Phoenix and the Turtle,* but ecstasy also governs the pulse of the poem until the voice of Reason enumerates the ontological details of life and especially those of death. (pp. 323-25)

Vincent F. Petronella, "Shakespeare's 'The Phoenix and the Turtle' and the Defunctive Music of Ecstasy," in Shakespeare Studies: An Annual Gathering of Research, Criticism, and Reviews, *Vol. VIII, 1975, pp. 311-31.*

HEINRICH STRAUMANN   (lecture date 1976)

[*Straumann proposes a multi-level approach to* The Phoenix and Turtle, *dividing previous critical studies of the poem into three categories: those which underscore the primacy of personal allegorical elements; those which emphasize the use of literary conventions and investigate possible classical and contemporary literary antecedents or sources; and those which stress thematic issues, especially the symbolization of spiritual values, and often place the poem in the context of Shakespeare's dramatic work. Straumann focuses on the third approach, arguing that* The Phoenix and Turtle *represents a "turning point both in poetic expression and in the abstract of Shakespeare's existential concept of the possible union of beauty and truth." Through a survey of the plays, he shows that prior to 1601, the composition date generally attributed to* The Phoenix and Turtle, *beauty and truth, emblems of the highest aesthetic and moral values, co-existed in Shakespeare's heroines. In 1601, however, in* Hamlet *and* The Phoenix and Turtle, *Shakespeare abandoned this idealized, heroic depiction of women, notes Straumann. After 1601, he points out, the qualities of "beauty, truth, love, constancy" recur, but rarely are they united in a single female character; where this does occur, the union is "destroyed by hostile forces." Straumann acknowledges that the romances appear to offer a return to the idealized depiction of women, but he remarks that the heroines in these plays achieve their successes only through magic or miracle. Straumann's commentary on* The Phoenix and Turtle *excerpted here was first presented in a lecture at Stratford-upon-Avon in 1976.*]

Scholars and critics seem, on the whole, agreed on the opinion that at the turn of the 16th to the 17th century Shakespeare must have undergone some vital changes, if not a crisis, in his views about man and the basic values he had accepted before that time. And even those who are sceptical of interpretations along such lines will readily admit that the tone of his works is clearly no longer the same after 1601. Whatever conflicting views on 'The Phoenix and the Turtle' may exist, there can be no doubt about the poem being published just at the time when that change had taken place or was still taking place. Incidentally Professor Kenneth Muir was one of the first to point out that aspect [see excerpt above, 1937]. The difficulties begin with the interpretation of its basic meaning and its possible significance for the understanding of that change. . . . I can only briefly—as a sort of reminder—refer to some of the main aspects of the well over one hundred different viewpoints, theories and interpretations that have been set forth in the last fifty years or so before we get to the main point, that is the significance of the poem in the context of the plays.

One can roughly distinguish three different trends in the various approaches. First there are those who are above all interested in what they consider to be the personal allegory of the poem. (pp. 494-95)

The second group of interpreters try to approach the poem by putting it in the context of the traditions and conventions of that genre. (p. 495)

Finally there is a third group of critics whom for lack of a better term we may refer to as idealists. The idealists stress the intellectual and thematic aspect of the poem, i.e. for them the theme of the poem is the miracle of fulfilled love, the fusion of the feminine and the masculine principles in bisexual love, the union of two different entities beyond the world of human realities, beyond life and death and therefore beyond any rational understanding, partly in the sense of scholastic philosophy (especially according to J. V. Cunningham) . . . [see excerpt above, 1952]. In view of all the possibilities represented by the three groups of interpretations one may well have one's doubts about any definite solution of the problem. But I think there *is* a way out—as I tried to show as early as 1953 [in *Phoenix und Taube: Zur Interpretation von Shakespeares Gedankenwelt*]—and this lies in the principle of interleaved levels of meaning, i.e. in the fact that the poem was composed with an inherent multiple appeal, so that it could be read first as a personal allegory (now lost), secondly as a brilliant display of a number of literary conventions and fashionable topics, and thirdly as the expression of a highly complex idea about the union of two values fatally exposed to destruction and yet continuing in their existence. To this may be added a hidden quasi magical element appearing in the use of trochaic tetrameters otherwise rather rare in Shakespeare but used by the poet for songs approaching that character in the plays, e.g.

> Pardon, goddess of the night . . .
>> [*Much Ado about Nothing,* V. iii. 12]
> Fie on sinful fantasy . . .
>> [*The Merry Wives of Windsor,* V. v. 93]
> Be thy mouth or black or white . . .
>> [*King Lear,* III. vi. 66]

Whatever part the scholastic element in the poem may have played at that time—one thing is certain and it must have struck the contemporary reader as well as it strikes the modern one: the couple of the phoenix and the turtle dove are referred to by Shakespeare as 'co-supremes and stars of love' [l. 51], that is as two ultimate values associated with beauty and truth and further connected with qualities such as grace, simplicity, rarity, loyalty, and love.

Now beauty and truth are united in love—but this union is not permanent: the two co-supremes disappear in a mutual flame, they are enclosed in the cinders of an urn and do not, together, exist any more in reality. Real truth and real beauty have gone from this world, because as realities they only exist in a union through love, and love and constancy are dead. Or, in a more abstract paraphrase: a synthesis of a highest aesthetic value with a highest moral value is only possible as an idea—but not as a real thing, or at the utmost as a very short-

lived phenomenon. And yet the last three lines of the poem seem to contradict this:

> To this urn let those repair
> That are either true or fair
> For these dead birds sigh a prayer.
>> [ll. 65-7]

This can only mean that there *are* still true and fair human beings—but one is *either* true *or* fair, i.e., one cannot be both at the same time, and with reference to the other three lines immediately preceding them and expressing the idea that there is only apparent truth and apparent beauty, one may add that even those who may be considered as bearers of these attributes do not really possess them—because the attributes can only be real in the aforementioned shortlived union through love. We may pray for the synthesis but we cannot achieve it as a permanent entity.

Now the question is: does this concept occur elsewhere in Shakespeare, and if so in what context? There is no other passage in which the phoenix and the turtle dove appear together directly in a combined metaphor. On the other hand there are a number of passages where at least attitudes similar to the one expressed in our poem can be found—especially the sonnets, where the question of truth or constancy and beauty existing together in one person is repeatedly brought up, for instance in sonnets 14, 53, 105. In the latter the final couplet clearly says that the attributes 'fair, kind and true' have so far never existed in one person together:

> Fair, kind and true, have often lived alone
> Which three till now never kept seat in one.
>> [ll. 13-14]

In the plays, too, the theme plays its special part. (pp. 496-98)

A well known example is the passage in *Cymbeline,* where Iachimo on first meeting Imogen begins to doubt whether he will win his wager about the faithlessness of woman and of Imogen especially:

> If she be furnished with a mind so rare
> She is alone the *Arabian* bird
>> [I. vi. 16-17]

Iachimo does not believe in the miracle of the absolute constancy of a beautiful woman's love, and he tries everything to prove his point, but the miracle though seriously threatened with destruction continues to the end. Beauty and truth, love and constancy remain victorious.

Cymbeline is a late play, and it is obvious that in the plays of our period (that is shortly before and after 1601) the situation is different. In the following plays normally considered to have been composed before 1600 the question of truth and beauty appearing together in one and the same person is clearly put: in *The Two Gentlemen of Verona* it is the girls Julia and Silvia whose constancy in love and belief in their lovers is put to a test which they pass successfully though not without difficulties. Similarly Helena and Hermia in *A Midsummer Night's Dream,* although their love and their lovers are threatened with deception finally manage to get through their trials and hardships unscathed.

In *Romeo and Juliet* love and constancy triumph but it is a short-lived triumph and yet the catastrophy that overtakes the lovers makes them as Capulet says:

> Poor sacrifices of our enmity.
>> [V. iii. 304]

That is through their death they create goodwill and peace between the hitherto hostile families, not forgetting Montague's final word about '. . . true and faithful Juliet' [V. iii. 302], as he says.

A remarkable though not yet vital change in this syndrome of values is to be found with the women characters in *The Merchant of Venice, Much Ado About Nothing, Twelfth Night* and *As You Like It,* that is the four plays which according to Chambers were produced between 1597 and 1600, or if one prefers to follow Peter Alexander somewhat earlier, but definitely before 1600. The change in no way affects the attractiveness of the women characters—on the contrary critics generally seem to agree that they are definitely more mature, more differentiated and therefore more human and more 'real' than the earlier ones; they are equally devoted in their love and constancy—but in order to get united with their lovers they are willing or obliged to resort to all sorts of tactics, ruses and mystifications to achieve their ends. [In *The Merchant of Venice*] Portia cheats a little when arranging the test of the caskets for Bassanio; Nerissa joins Portia in feigning disbelief about her ring; Jessica on eloping with Lorenzo takes part of Shylock's treasure with her. [In *Twelfth Night*] Viola cleverly conceals her identity and yet manages to express her true feelings in her cryptic remarks to Orsino. [In *As You Like It*] Rosalind risks, or pretends to risk making fun of the sonneteering Orlando although or rather because she loves him deeply. In all these plays the union of love, constancy and beauty remains intact, but truth has to be kept secret—at least temporarily.

This theme borders on the tragic in *Much Ado About Nothing* where through a diabolical intrigue the 'maiden truth' of the heroine seems to be so utterly defiled that her lover can only speak of her in the contradictory terms of 'most foul, most fair' and will henceforth 'turn all beauty into thoughts of harm' [IV. i. 103, 107]—i.e. even there the negative statement is enhanced by its juxtaposition with the principle of beauty. Here, too, truth and the person embodying both truth and beauty have to be carefully hidden in order to survive until the veils and the masks can be dropped and love be restored. This, on a level of wit and bantering also applies to Beatrice and Benedick. Whatever the impediments, the trinity of love, beauty and truth in these plays finally remains undisputed.

All these plays were written before the publication of our poem. In the plays composed after 1601 the situation is entirely different. In *Hamlet* the physical beauty of Ophelia is repeatedly referred to and never questioned but in her dependence on her father she betrays her qualities of honesty and truth towards her lover. In the nunnery scene Hamlet himself puts the problem in a nutshell:

> . . . the power of beauty will sooner transform
> honesty from what it is to a bawd than the force of
> honesty can translate beauty into his likeness: this
> was sometime a paradox, but now the time gives it
> proof. I did love thee once.
>
> [III. i. 110-14]

That is: Hamlet once believed in the union of beauty and honesty in human beings, especially in Ophelia and possibly also in his mother—but through what has happened at court and particularly through Ophelia's conduct at this moment his belief in that union has totally collapsed. Ophelia perishes.

In *Troilus and Cressida* the theme of the infidelity of an attractive woman was and has remained a classic. In *All's Well That Ends Well* Helena is forced to take refuge in deceit in order to achieve her end. In *Measure for Measure* the problem is somewhat different, but here, too, Isabella's virtue can only be saved at the price of the bed trick, i.e. through carefully prepared deceit.

In Desdemona [in *Othello*] we see absolute truth, devotion, love and constancy united—but she becomes a victim of the terrible blindness and delusion of her husband and is killed. For Cordelia [in *King Lear*], to whom the term 'grace in all simplicity' [l. 54] seems to be specially applicable truthfulness towards her father and her devotion for him assume absolute priority—she is not allowed to live. In *Antony and Cleopatra* Shakespeare chose a subject that corresponded exactly to the new concept: the race towards catastrophe of a couple ensnared in uncontrolled passion but unable to believe in mutual loyalty except in a moment of violent death. In short the attributes of beauty, truth, love, constancy etc. still appear in all these plays, but their union in one and the same person does not occur anymore or if it does, it will be destroyed by hostile forces—bodily strangled as in the case of Desdemona and Cordelia.

Only in the very last plays, the romances, is the existence of a woman character embodying both beauty and truth and finding fulfillment in love again made possible—but Imogen and Hermione, as well as Perdita [both in *The Winter's Tale*] and Miranda [in *The Tempest*] owe this to almost incredible luck or else to magic.

From all this I for one can only draw one conclusion. As in no other work and in the smallest possible space the *Phoenix and the Turtle* represents a clearly defined turning point both in poetic expression and in the abstract of Shakespeare's existential concept of the possible union of beauty and truth i.e. of two highest values, through love in a woman character. Before 1601 this union is seen as possible and it can even be permanent. After 1601 the union, if it occurs at all, is only very short-lived and is bound to end in death through violence. Only in the last plays can the union be found again—but by then it is nothing short of a miracle. (pp. 498-500)

Heinrich Straumann, "'The Phoenix and the Turtle' in Its Dramatic Context," in English Studies, Netherlands, *Vol. 58, No. 6, December, 1977, pp. 494-500.*

JOHN ARTHOS   (essay date 1977)

[*Arthos argues that in* The Phoenix and Turtle, *Shakespeare strives to conjure a sense of the authority and atmosphere of a dream in order to appeal to his readers' subconscious notions of the infinite and eternal. Dream features inform both the style and structure of the poem, according to Arthos, and convey the mesmerizing convergence of fantastic images and truth. The critic maintains that the power of the poem derives partly from the variety of poetic conventions that Shakespeare uses: ancient symbols; the medieval parliament of fowls and the bird-mass; the language of courtly love and romantic poetry; and metaphysical issues and paradoxes. Through these diverse means, Arthos claims, the poem achieves a fantastic or preposterous note that underscores the failure of reason and language to apprehend the miraculous nature of love.*]

The first words of *The Phoenix and Turtle,* announcing a call of birds to a requiem mass, are strange, archaic, and even om-

Phoenix upon a flaming pyre. By Geffrey Whitney (1586).

inous. But as those who are to come are called by name and others are debarred we learn the ceremony is to be in honor of everything that is excellent, love and beauty and truth—the note of the strange and the forbidding is all but silenced in invoking what most graces humans. A succession of abstract words, virtues as it were embodied, brings into the account of a rite to be performed by birds the suggestion of human presences, and when one such, Reason, at the end is heard chanting, asking for a prayer for the dead, we realize that what has been wild and fantastic in it all is an index to the dread and hope humans know in contemplating the loss of life. Through the strangeness and the fear and then in notes of exultation we come to feel a power in the poem as astonishing as the range and depth of the thought it draws on. (p. 17)

Shakespeare's poem owes its power in part to the richness and variety of the poetic conventions fused in a form representing the preparation of a funeral: the medieval conceits of the bird-mass and of parliaments of fowls; hyperboles from the poetry of courtly and romantic love; symbols from ancient legends; suggestions of the ancient and medieval 'complaints of nature' assimilated to the manner of liturgy. But the power as the beauty depend almost equally on the skill with which, through the barest of language and deceptively bald statements, metaphysical issues are raised and resolved.

We learn from the beginning verses, at first indirectly, that two birds have died, their love for each other in some sense the instrument of their deaths, for it was this that consumed them in 'a mutuall flame'. The air of celebration appropriate to the rite suggests that love was not so much the cause of the deaths of bodies as of the freeing and transformation of souls.

Certain birds are invited by name to join in the rite, others are enjoined from appearing. After the summoning and the invocation there is an anthem in which the nature of the love that bound these two is represented, chiefly expressed in the language of philosophy and theology, the assertions so flatly made they must be accepted as precisely meant. In the concluding Threnos a figure identified as Reason confesses its incapacity to comprehend what is happening, although it supposes Love is able to. Reason nevertheless sings a dirge, ex-

plaining, as it had not been explained before, the nature of the life and death of the two the requiem is honoring, and ends in bidding those present, and all who would join them, to pray for the dead:

> To this urne let those repaire,
> That are either true or faire,
> For these dead Birds, sigh a prayer.
>
> [ll. 65-7]

A succession of assertions and paradoxes has told us that in their loves and in their deaths each of the two has at once lost and preserved his individual being. In the steadily increasing complexity of the ideas sustaining these claims the images of birds consumed with fire and of their ashes and of the urn dissolve as we try to conceive of a union of selves that transcends the limits reason and the senses place on our imagining. We are left in the end rapt by the appeal of the conception, invited to share in the hopes of those who remain in life, not only such birds who are the fit symbols and sponsors of devotion, but all humans as well who in the dignity of faithfulness and beauty wish a like end for themselves, praying before a monument to the power rewarding love with rest.

Reducing the substance of the poem to so limited a summary we see plainly how much the paradoxical and the preposterous require of metaphysics if the sense of seriousness with which all is being uttered is to be justified. And metaphysics employed responsibly as we are told that a certain attachment in love attests to a miraculous power.

The initial circumstance is the key one—it is humans, not birds, we are learning of, persons so joined in sympathy we may not think of them as ever to be separated. They inhabited two bodies, and yet, in death as in life, it seems, they remain united. Each looked upon the other and into the other's eyes—

> So betweene them Love did shine.
>
> [l. 33]

Seeing love each saw itself. The words that say this are at once flat assertions and oracular. There is in them something of the manner of occult speech, for the reader is left to figure for himself the stages through which what has happened has taken place.

Each sees, we judge, what it recognizes as itself loving and being loved, at one and the same timeless instant disappearing and finding itself in the minglings of sight, an unceasing and as it were a growing exchange. Intent with love, sight ceases to be sight and becomes love, and in this transformation, this splendor and illumination, the lovers lose the sense of themselves, they feel the loss of self as it would seem to be if annihilated by fire, yet in fact there is no loss for not even what one might call solitary in the self is destroyed since it rediscovers itself in the other:

> So betweene them Love did shine,
> That the *Turtle* saw his right,
> Flaming in the *Phoenix* sight;
> Either was the others mine.
>
> [ll. 33-6]

There is continuous, exultant gain, each forever discovering new wealth.

The Turtle, seeing himself possessed by what he knows as love, has no care for himself any longer, nor does the Phoenix care to remain only herself, to survive alone. In some sense each ceases to be its own and yet each is now another self—the language of paradox is inescapable—neither owns itself nor, on the other hand, is owned by the other for each is being preserved even as it is being destroyed. Although reason would say that the bodies were separated yet the sense of even that separation is lost in the sense of gain. Both reason and language acknowledge their shortcomings in affirming the miraculous.

A single assertion is not enough so the summoner to the rite and the Anthem continue with still others that bring into the conception more and more extensive meaning:

> Propertie was thus appalled,
> That the selfe was not the same:
> Single Natures double name,
> Neither two nor one was called.
>
> [ll. 37-40]

A personification, an allusion to philosophic doctrine, a paradox, ring changes upon the same idea in order to lead feeling into such sympathy with thought that we shall be led to agree that love can indeed escape the confinements of time and space and come into another order of existence.

The suggestion of astonishment, the sense of wordlessness in 'appalled', signifies that philosophy will be tested to the limit to account for this, and so we are prepared to be brought into the almost innumerable paths of speculation philosophy and theology have prepared. In the end, however, it will be the ghost-like images, the movement of the verse, the half-plaintive half-exultant tone, the continuous evocation of wonder in the face of what is so curiously explained, that will support the thought with conviction. The images that are only on the verge of taking shape, the almost monotone chant with its rising pitch, the rhythms so dominant they recall 'the blessed mutter of the mass' [Robert Browning, "The Bishop Orders His Tomb"]—all this to carry us along into an acceptance of the preposterous in every sense. The meaning almost breaks free from the words but the intricacies of the reasoning as much as the strangeness of the circumstances hold us so intently and yet as it were confusedly that we all but overlook Reason's calling attention to itself. The illusion that images are about to take form, the limit set to the harmonies, the narrow range of the pitch, hold us so strangely we are persuaded to take nonsense for sense, contradiction as resolution, wordlessness as the testimony for wonder, the laboring of reason as its own disqualification—the whole justifying the faith. The apprehension of another in loving, this is the reality. The verse will re-create the state, the thought will accentuate it. The but partly seen figuring, the efforts of logic, the suggestion of incantation, are succeeding in doing what they do for Plato—as in the allegory of the cave, all that is elusive or obscure is emphasized in order to help us know about light: 'La nuit de la contradiction est en effet plus libératrice que toutes les évidences positives' [The night of contradiction is more liberating than all the positive proofs]. Antithesis, contradiction, paradox, even, perhaps, the *coincidentia oppositorum* [coincidence of opposites].

The repetitions, but no more than the variations, like the sounding of changes suggest endless enumeration, and the wealth of them emphasizes the irony in the preposterousness of paying such honor to the ashes of birds. And that irony in turn leads into the sense that is anything but preposterous or susceptible of exaggeration—the purity at the heart of love.

There is a sense in which the state of the lovers is to be spoken of as ecstasy. The poem is not, however, the expression of the lovers themselves but of someone, knowing the state of these two, who is giving witness to it. . . . [The] techniques of irony are counted on to achieve by indirection what ecstatic utterance would tell if it could. And there is irony . . . in the technical terminology used not to describe but to communicate the sense of the state it was invented only to describe. Thus by all such devices, but above all by the treatment of the relationship of the Phoenix and Turtle as of that nature that reason cannot comprehend, the poem works to show that the idea of infinite satisfaction is justified.

The poem will hardly let us put it down. It achieves its success through such almost unintelligible means that it requires to be pored over. There are puzzles to be solved but there are also other demands—we need to know why the paradoxes follow in their particular succession, why there should be a breaking-off where there is, and why a figure called Reason should be brought in to take over—

> Reason in it selfe confounded,
> Saw Division grow together.
>
> [ll. 41-2]

And so we, similarly at a loss, yet as persuaded as Reason of what it saw increasing, persuaded that the contradictions express truths, are held so intently we recognize in our very attention a power like that ascribed to love, the power to free the spirit from constraint.

The figures that at first seemed hardly more than artifice and calculation—

> Number there in love was slaine—
>
> [l. 28]

the language of love talking to itself, are presenting us with a universe conceived to be without dimension, a realm of being thought is able to conceive of although imagination cannot. The abstract words, the contradictions and oppositions, speak with perfect assurance in denying what our senses as well as reason tell us. Statement after statement points to a conception of the ground and substance of reality, of what underlies appearances. . . . So there is the recourse to paradox and to abstractions as bodiless as may be to acquaint us with a sense of the very quality of what is alone real, of Being.

The paradoxes have their own logic, they open up into a metaphysics reason is able to entertain, or believes it is. At every step we are being reminded that our idea of what is limited depends upon an idea of the limitless, our ideas of number and of space to that which is without quantity and dimension. All, in short, provokes us with our capacity to entertain the thought of the infinite and eternal. (pp. 27-32)

We knew from the beginning—really in the mere sound of the first words—we should be meeting with the mysterious and even with confusion, but as the poem went on this never tempered the almost unearthly lucidity that seemed always on the verge of breaking through. The confusion we first recognized when we learned some birds were being invited to the rite and others were excluded, for some of the reasons were hidden from us. Then, bare assertion imposed itself upon the outrageous, outfacing contradiction, in paradox after paradox, the language apparently simple but in fact occult. Yet the sense of the unexceptionable survived so assuredly, the suggestion of lucidity was so persistent, we could only think we were treating with truth.

A call to a requiem is followed by statements defining in abstract terms the state of the lovers in their sympathy and harmony. There then comes the concluding eulogy. But with the very last words the scene of the worship shifts, the congregation is enlarged to take in those attending to the re-enactment of the celebration. And now not only those invited to the mass but we ourselves, the readers, are instructed to pray. Yet the strangeness of it all and the impersonality persist, and in words that might have been expected to utter grief most openly, even to soliciting the participation of strangers, we are compelled to draw back—

> For these dead *Birds,* sigh a prayer.
> [l. 67]

We know this is no mere breaking off, for although we as readers and also as ones included in the summoning, have had very little guidance on what to expect as the poem commenced: we had only been able to recognize the form it was taking as the parts were joined, but at the end we know enough to recognize that what had been undertaken was completed. The poem had commenced abruptly . . . for we were compelled to divine what occasioned this first injunction to a bird obscurely if at all identified—'the bird of lowdest lay' [l. 1]. We then followed along with the few uncertain directions while the burden of meaning grew. And then in the final lament, when the words were at once the most solemn and joyful, we found ourselves returned to the world in which we might be mourning our own friends. (pp. 61-3)

Two individuals have died. There is awe and grief at their passing because they were who they were, and because their love was of a superlative kind. The nature of that love and its effects are explained—were it not that we learn this from what is called an anthem we would hardly know a liturgical rite was in process.

We see nothing happening until a hitherto unknown celebrant, Reason, enters to chant the dirge, and this gives us a deeper understanding of the purpose of the ceremony and of the marvel of the loves of these two. This accomplished, we are asked to pray, and with the words that we take to be addressed also to us, the readers, who are now for the first time acknowledged to be in the audience—we become privy to what the verses have been giving form to. We get to know this in some such way as a dreamer in awakening becomes privy to what he has been thinking in his dream, believing we perceive a method in the procession of images and thoughts in this vaguely indicated rite. We notice, too, as with many poems telling of dreams and visions, that the form is completed with the exhaustion of the questions the dream feeds on, not with the supplying of answers. The abruptness of the ending is in fact the sign the burden of the dream has been defined as, for example, we recognize in that abruptness with which Milton ended his poem—'I waked, she fled, and day brought back my night' ["On His Deceased Wife"].

Seeing how it was that our thoughts were led on we begin to understand that the hold the poem has had upon us is indeed of the kind we know in dreams and visions. And the more we credit the beauty and power in this re-creation of a fancy, the more we begin to think that the language treating of ideas of essence and participation and the eternal present harmonizes with the picturing of the preparations for a fantastic rite.

And now we find ourselves looking at the dream-like succession in still another way.

A dreamer is re-living a dream in which he himself is speaking. Two of his friends are dead and in the dream he seemed to be arranging their funeral rite. His friends had become birds and he was summoning other birds to the mass. In life his friends had embodied the perfection of love and constancy, and it seems there could have been no thought of their perishing. Because the legend of the phoenix is understood to tell something about the nature of love, and of immortality attained through sacrifice and resurrection, in the dream one of his friends appeared as a phoenix, the turtle as her mate, and their death through love became the means of entry into eternal life.

But the dream is wilder still, as if in the dreamer's thoughts there was a turbulence of equal strangenesses—not only humans become birds, and birds passing through fire into life, but such strangeness in attempting to hold on to what this referred to in actuality, ideas took such glory as eye could not hear, nor ear see. There were the drilled-in formulas of philosophers and churchmen, curiously distorted or expressed straightforwardly, that two may become one, that the heart has its reasons, that duration may be swallowed up in eternity, that nature in being born would also be nature perfected. All these strangenesses, these preposterous verities, seemed to be harmonious. For one matter was constantly impelling, the sense of the unimaginable, the reality of the sleep out of which all this was coming to birth. The preposterousness no more than the authentic particulars misrepresented the reality of that abyss. Reality was what might swallow up beauty and truth and constancy in the dark of the urn, obliterate all good, all that humans as much as the figures in the strange sequences of dreams were so curiously holding to. The preposterousness signified the possibility of endurance. And so, passing through the tragic scene, as thoughts succeeding each other in dreams, the two birds came into a place where there was company and light—the Supreme itself.

Most of the other poems in *Loves Martyr* embodied reflections on the passage from death into another life in largely philosophic expoundings. Chester's was the most elaborately imaginative, drawing upon a number of medieval poetic conventions—visions, the ascents into heaven, even the romantic epic. In using the symbol and legend of the phoenix Chester set the theme for the others to follow, and established the tone not only of the fanciful and mysterious but of the allegorical.

By its nature any such undertaking tempts ridicule. Private ritual, eulogy, particular philosophies risk seeming trivial by contrast with time-sanctioned funeral rites, and the glory of language equal to the faith of centuries. But the demand here as always was inescapable, the challenge was accepted, the risk taken, contempt defied.

Shakespeare's poem avoided every abuse. It is offered as a dream, and thereby, by definition, it escapes the most damaging pretentiousness. Such authority as dreams may claim to is shared with an at least equally mysterious image in one of the strangest of legends. Referring to the fantastic notion of a mass participated in by birds the dream calls attention to what it dare not call itself, a true rite. Developing the most intricate reasoning it insists upon limits to reason. By such means it honors what is barely if at all conceivable, leading through images and thought to the praise of what is beyond thought. (pp. 63-5)

> *John Arthos, "The Dream and the Vision," in his*
> Shakespeare's Use of Dream and Vision, *Rowman*
> *and Littlefield, 1977, pp. 15-84.*

ADDITIONAL BIBLIOGRAPHY

Axton, Marie. "Miraculous Succession: *The Phoenix and the Turtle* 1601." In her *The Queen's Two Bodies: Drama and the Elizabethan Succession,* pp. 116-30. London: Royal Historical Society, 1977.

Asserts that *The Phoenix and Turtle* "was a politically philosophical occasional poem" composed in anticipation of "an historical moment of transition," the succession of Elizabeth I. Axton argues that Shakespeare adopted the iconography and myths of Elizabethan succession drama, specifically the phoenix, to render his own thoughts on political theory; kingship; love and duty; and the monarch-subject relationship. According to Axton, the poem represents Shakespeare's confession of personal faith in Elizabeth; it simultaneously exhorts and invites the reader, as loyal subject, to assist in the phoenix-like miracle of succession, she concludes.

Baldwin, T. W. "Letter to the Editor." *The Times Literary Supplement,* no. 2054 (14 June 1941): 287.

Discusses several possible sources of *The Phoenix and Turtle,* including Pliny, Erasmus, Ovid, and Lactantius. "It is clear," Baldwin declares, "that the *Incerti Auctoris Phoenix* to be found in contemporary editions of Lactantius is Shakespeare's ultimate and probably proximate chief source" for the Phoenix.

——. "The Literary Genetics of *The Phoenix and the Turtle.*" In his *On The Literary Genetics of Shakespeare's Poems & Sonnets,* pp. 363-84. Urbana: University of Illinois Press, 1950.

Argues that for *The Phoenix and Turtle* Shakespeare borrowed elements from such classical writers as Ovid and Lactantius and placed these within the context of a conventional Elizabethan funeral. Baldwin claims that Shakespeare turned to Ovid for his Turtle and Lactantius for his Phoenix, and he also traces each of the birds identified in the poem back to either of these two classical sources.

Benham, Sir Gurney. "*The Phoenix and the Turtle.*" *The Times Literary Supplement,* nos. 2059 and 2060 (19 and 26 July 1941): 352, 354.

Contends that although the Phoenix probably stands for Elizabeth in Robert Chester's *Love's Martyr,* there is less assurance about the Essex-Turtle correspondence. In his analysis of Shakespeare's *The Phoenix and Turtle,* Benham explicates many of the ornithological references, intimates that Shakespeare might have employed obfuscation to indicate that he was attempting to express the inexpressible, and ventures that the poem may be taken as mocking the fashion of euphuism prescribed by Chester and emulated by the other poets in Chester's volume.

Bilton, Peter. "Graves on Lovers, and Shakespeare at a Lovers' Funeral." *Shakespeare Survey* 36 (1983): 39-42.

Suggests that twentieth-century poet Robert Graves's *The Thieves* is "a response to" *The Phoenix and Turtle.* Bilton reveals similarities between the two poems in terms of music and rhythm; meter and rhyme; expression of ideas; and the transposition of pronouns. Ultimately, however, Bilton argues that Graves consciously echoed Shakespeare, first, in the tradition of the "dedicated poet" who pays homage to his predecessors by borrowing their vocabulary and conceits, and second, in

order to refute Shakespeare's conception of a transcendent union: "Graves, in *The Thieves* at least, claims that the concept of such a perfect union deludes us."

Bonaventure, Sister Mary. "The Phoenix Renewed." *Ball State Teachers College Forum* V, No. 3 (Autumn 1964): 72-6.

Dismisses tragic readings of *The Phoenix and Turtle* and denies that there is any irony or satire in Shakespeare's tone, discerning instead an optimistic voice of "triumph and universal hope." According to Bonaventure, the paradox of two-in-one encountered by Reason is readily explained by the "Christian concept of grace fundamental in Elizabethan thought." This concept of grace, by which one is unified with Christ without surrendering individuality, rescues Reason from the apparent negation of the self in death.

Bradbrook, M. C. "The Artifice of Eternity: Court Poetry of Elizabeth's Reign." In her *Shakespeare and Elizabethan Poetry: A Study of his Earlier Work in Relation to the Poetry of the Time,* pp. 18-34. London: Chatto and Windus, 1951.

Offers a brief look at *The Phoenix and the Turtle,* "the one poem which [Shakespeare] wrote in a courtly kind." Bradbrook views the poem in accord with the "great tradition" of court poetry, as Shakespeare's one work in the Platonic mode, and a paragon of "concentration and simplicity."

——. " 'The Phoenix and the Turtle'." *Shakespeare Quarterly* VI, No. 3 (Summer 1955): 356-58.

Responds directly to Ronald Bates (see excerpt above, 1955), disputing his identification of comic or ironic elements in *The Phoenix and Turtle.* Bradbrook contends that Bates is mistaken in his assumption that the Phoenix and Turtle have human referents. While she concedes that "the idea of the human pair is behind the image," the figures in the poem are indeed birds; thus the image of human union is precluded and the allegations of impropriety dispelled. Bates is misled by modern connotations of certain terms, such as "married chastity" and "infirmity," she believes; these have assumed a suggestion of physicality or deficiency that an Elizabethan, according to Bradbrook, would not recognize.

Brooks, Cleanth. "The Language of Paradox." In his *The Well Wrought Urn,* pp. 3-20. New York: Harcourt, Brace and Co., 1947.

Suggests that *The Phoenix and Turtle* celebrates the unifying power of creative imagination and, in particular, the paradoxical capacity of metaphor to accommodate conflicting or contradictory entities. The poem pivots around such a paradox, to the confusion of Reason, Brooks notes, but Reason "recovers to admit its own bankruptcy" and is privileged to express the concluding Threnos. Lastly, Brooks intimates that the funerary urn represents the poem itself: a receptacle for transcendent ideals and phoenix-ashes that will remain lifeless unless they are liberated by imagination.

Brown, Carleton, ed. Introduction to *Poems by Sir John Salusbury and Robert Chester,* pp. ix-lxxiv. London: Kegan Paul, Trench, Trübner & Co., 1914.

Refutes Grosart's theory that the Phoenix and Turtle allegorically refer to Queen Elizabeth and the Earl of Essex (see entry below). Brown's historical analysis leads him to conclude that Chester's *Love's Martyr* symbolically celebrates the union of his patrons, Sir John and Lady Ursula Stanley. With respect to *The Phoenix and Turtle,* Brown argues that although Shakespeare adopted Chester's allegory, "he chose to develop his theme along a widely divergent line." The poem's "perfunctory tone" suggests to Brown that Shakespeare composed it as "a matter of courteous compliance rather than a tribute to a personal friend."

Buxton, John. "Two Dead Birds: A Note on *The Phoenix and Turtle.*" In *English Renaissance Studies: Presented to Dame Helen Gardner in honour of her Seventieth Birthday,* edited by John Carey, pp. 44-55. Oxford: At the Clarendon Press, 1980.

Discerns an ironic tone in *The Phoenix and Turtle*'s "extravagantly sophisticated diction," which may be interpreted as Shakespeare's subtle satire of Chester's "clownish original," *Love's Martyr.* Buxton contends that Shakespeare's mastery of meter and diction, his fusing of scholastic and Platonic terms, and his handling of the phoenix conceit far exceed Chester's poetic technique. The critic also discusses the historical context of *Love's Martyr.*

Cooper, Margaret. "Letter to the Editor." *The Times Literary Supplement,* no. 2051 (24 May 1941): 251.

Proposes that *The Phoenix and Turtle*'s "thinly veiled" evocation of "an intensely intimate and vital experience" suggests that "the sole Arabian tree" of the first stanza represents the Tree of the Knowledge of Good and Evil.

Downing, Charles. *"The Phoenix and Turtle." The Shrine* I, No. 1 (May, June, July 1902): 34-45.

Maintains that the Phoenix and the Turtle symbolize, respectively, the ideal (Shakespeare's) and the idealist (the poet himself). Downing contends that this three-fold ideal, embracing "Beauty, Truth and Rarity, Grace in all simplicity" (ll. 53-4), is emblematic of the human spirit and is symbolically represented throughout Shakespeare's works. The "Phoenix, or Perfect Ideal, is that dominant element in Shakespeare," the critic asserts, and the poet assumes in this work a "pseudo-identity," a feeling of rapture that links his soul with his ideal. *The Phoenix and Turtle,* according to Downing, simultaneously evokes a sense of cold, personal detachment in its technical precision and conceits, and intense spiritual identity with the overarching ideal.

Dronke, Peter. *"The Phoenix and the Turtle." Orbis Litterarum* XXIII (1968): 199-220.

Interprets *The Phoenix and Turtle* on the basis of conventional Elizabethan literary thought. Although Dronke concludes that "the poet's dominant concern is with 'the truth of love,'" he also emphasizes that the Phoenix and Turtle are "complex figurae in the best medieval fashion" and warns that "to limit their meaning rigidly would be arbitrary." Despite "their tragic scene" (l. 52), Dronke argues, the tone of the poem is "exhilarating" in its dramatic and emotional portrait of human love and "serene" in its depiction of the transcendent, eternal quality of divine love.

Ellrodt, Robert. "An Anatomy of 'The Phoenix and the Turtle'." *Shakespeare Survey* 15 (1962): 99-110.

Surveys Renaissance and Elizabethan conceptions of the phoenix in order to assess Shakespeare's adaptation of this myth. Ellrodt concludes that Shakespeare's approach was unique and represented "a modification of the phoenix myth which implied disbelief in, or at least disregard for, the time-honoured legend." Ellrodt rejects an allegorical interpretation of the poem and instead affirms that "the poet is genuinely concerned with ultimates."

Empson, William. *"The Phoenix and the Turtle." Essays in Criticism* XVI, No. 2 (April 1966): 147-53.

Examines the historical context and allegorical references of Chester's *Love's Martyr* and proposes an earlier composition date—1599—for Shakespeare's poem. According to Empson, this "exquisite but baffling poem," written in "his only consistent use of the Metaphysical style," is best illuminated by its occasion and context.

Eriksen, Roy T. " 'Un certo amoroso martire': Shakespeare's 'The Phoenix and the Turtle' and Giordano Bruno's *De gli eroici furori."* *Spenser Studies: A Renaissance Poetry Annual* II (1981): 193-215.

Attempts to show that Shakespeare's choice of imagery, development of the phoenix conceit, grammatical invention, funerary symbolism, and oracular tone of voice all reflect the influence of Giordano Bruno, a sixteenth-century Italian poet-philosopher. Eriksen asserts that much of the material in *The Phoenix and Turtle* derives from Bruno's *De gli eroici furori* (1585), in which Bruno "employed a male turtle and a female

phoenix to expound his philosophy of love according to which the death of the turtle in the phoenix's flames symbolizes the union between the furioso and the vessel of the deity."

Furnivall, F. J. "On Chester's *Love's Martyr:* Essex is not the Turtle-Dove of Shakspere's *Phoenix and Turtle." The New Shakspere Society's Transactions* I, No. 7 (1879): 451-55.

Rejects Grosart's allegorical interpretation of *Love's Martyr* and of the other poems in Chester's collection (see entry below). Furnivall cites historical evidence to refute Grosart's theory linking Queen Elizabeth with the Phoenix and the Earl of Essex with the Turtledove.

Green, Brian. "Shakespeare's Heroic Elixir: A New Context for *The Phoenix and Turtle." Studia Neophilologica,* LI, No. 2 (1979): 215-23.

Examines Shakespeare's use of the language of alchemy as an "imaginative context" for *The Phoenix and Turtle.* Green argues that the tripartite structure of the poem mirrors the three stage alchemical process in the production of elixir: *separatio, divisio,* and *putrefactio.* In addition, he shows that the Summons, Anthem, and Threnos correspond to the doctrine of the three primary substances: 1) sulphur, symbol of the soul (anima) represented by fire, 2) mercury, symbol of the spirit (spiritus) represented by fumes, and 3) salt, symbol of the body (corpus) represented by ash.

————. " 'Single Natures double name': An Exegesis of *The Phoenix and Turtle." In Generous Converse: English Essays in Memory of Edward Davis,* edited by Brian Green, pp. 44-54. Cape Town: Oxford University Press, 1980.

Labels *The Phoenix and Turtle* a paradigm of Shakespearian love-tragedy. Green claims that each of the three divisions of the poem, Summons, Anthem, and Threnos, corresponds to a specific attitude toward love—noble versus vulgar, chaste, and sublime—and reflects three philosophical contexts: Neoplatonic, Elizabethan, and Petrarchan. The "interaction between [these] three attitudes to sexual love," he contends, is the basis of Shakespearean love-tragedy.

Grosart, Alexander B. *Robert Chester's "Love's Martyr or Rosalin's Complaint" with its supplement "Diverse Poeticall Essaies" on the Turtle and Phoenix by Shakspere, Ben Jonson, George Chapman, John Marston, Etc.,* edited by Alexander B. Grosart. London: N. Trübner & Co., 1878, 254 p.

Proposes an allegorical interpretation for Chester's *Love's Martyr* wherein the Phoenix represents Queen Elizabeth and the Turtle refers to the Earl of Essex. Grosart argues that Shakespeare and his fellow poets were political partisans of Essex and that they adopted Chester's poetical scheme of personal allegory to delicately rebuke the Queen for ending her alliance with the brash, young noble. Grosart's introduction represents the earliest sustained analysis of Shakespeare's poem. His republication of Chester's volume and his commentary mark the beginning of scholarly debate on *The Phoenix and Turtle.*

Hume, Anthea. " 'Love's Martyr', 'The Phoenix and the Turtle', and the aftermath of the Essex Rebellion." *The Review of English Studies* XL, No. 157 (February 1989): 48-71.

Elaborates on the allegorical interpretation of *The Phoenix and Turtle* proposed by Marie Axton (see entry above) in which the Phoenix represents Queen Elizabeth and the Turtle stands for her subjects. Hume claims that in *Love's Martyr,* Chester sought to portray Elizabeth's emotions following the Essex rebellion and to assuage her envy of the loyalty of Essex's partisans by celebrating the mutual love encompassed in the monarch-subject relationship. Shakespeare adopted a similar theme in *The Phoenix and Turtle,* according to Hume, using this occasion "to write a political variation on the sonnet-theme" of mutual love.

Janakiram, Alur. "Leone Ebreo and Shakespeare: Love and Reason in *Dialoghi D'Amore* and 'The Phoenix and the Turtle'." *English Studies* 61, No. 3 (June 1980): 224-35.

Discerns a resemblance between Shakespeare's treatment of the paradoxical union and the love-reason relationship central to *The Phoenix and Turtle* and Leone Ebreo's restatement of the Neoplatonic theory of love in his *Dialogues.* Janakiram asserts that two levels of reason operate within Shakespeare's poem: 1) logic or common-sense reason, which is thwarted by the two-in-one paradox, and 2) an intuitive reason, which comprehends the union. He finds in Ebreo and Shakespeare a parity between this intuitive notion of reason and love and suggests that Ebreo should be recognized as "one of the intellectual contexts for the metaphysic of love underlying Shakespeare's masterpiece."

Knight, G. Wilson. "The Shakespearian Aviary." In his *The Shakespearian Tempest,* pp. 293-325. London: Oxford University Press, 1932.

Examines Shakespeare's use of bird imagery throughout the plays to illuminate the bird references in *The Phoenix and Turtle.* Knight argues that Shakespeare regularly uses bird imagery "to suggest the finer harmonies of human aspiration" and to connote the love-tragedy themes, "the blending of duality in unity, of life and death in love's immortality." The critic perceives a particularly close thematic kinship between *The Phoenix and Turtle* and *Antony and Cleopatra.*

———. *The Mutual Flame: on Shakespeare's Sonnets and The Phoenix and the Turtle.* New York: Barnes & Noble, 1955, 233 p.

Reviews a vast range of critical study of *The Phoenix and Turtle* and the Elizabethan period in order to explicate the poem's symbolism. Knight proposes that the Phoenix is a complex, multi-faceted figure connoting the transcendent and the physical; human and divine; royalty; love; and "a difficult, tragic and yet victorious experience." He equates the Turtle with the female element in Shakespeare's bisexuality and speculates that Shakespeare consciously strove to confuse his readers regarding the sexual identification and relation of the Phoenix and Turtle to evoke a sense of their "mystical love-union beyond sex and all normal biological categories."

Matchett, William H. *The Phoenix and the Turtle: Shakespeare's Poem and Chester's Loues Martyr.* The Hague: Mouton & Co., 1965, 213 p.

Argues that assumptions about allegorical references and literary antecedents inevitably color interpretations of *The Phoenix and Turtle* and, thus, opts for a close textual analysis of the poem itself. Matchett finds separate approaches to the death of the Phoenix and Turtle in each of the poem's three divisions: "that of the poet, who would naturally arrange a properly symbolic ceremony, that of the 'chaste wings,' who would naturally offer praise, and that of Reason, who would naturally attempt to understand." Although many critics maintain that Shakespeare makes conventional use of the metaphysical two-in-one paradox, wherein love vanquishes reason, Matchett claims that reason is here not defeated but merely confused. Matchett also offers a reading of Chester's *Love's Martyr* and returns to *The Phoenix and Turtle* within this context, convinced that Shakespeare's poem refers to Elizabeth and Essex. In this second, biographical reading, Matchett suggests several possible sources and concludes that Shakespeare's poem reflects concern for Elizabeth's succession and dismay over the failure of the Elizabeth-Essex alliance.

Newdigate, Bernard H. " 'The Phoenix and Turtle': Was Lady Bedford the Phoenix?" *The Times Literary Supplement,* no. 1812 (24 March 1936): 862.

Theorizes that the poems in Chester's volume allegorically refer to the childless union of the Earl and Countess of Bedford. Newdigate cites external and internal evidence to refute Alexander Grosart's and Carleton Brown's allegorical interpretations (see entries above) and to bolster his own reading.

———. Introduction to *The Phoenix and Turtle: by William Shakespeare, John Marston, George Chapman, Ben Jonson and Others,* edited by Bernard Newdigate, pp. xv-xxiv. Oxford: Shakespeare Head Press, 1937.

Asserts that the poems in Chester's collection address the childless union of the Earl and Countess of Bedford six years after their wedding. Thus, in Newdigate's reading, Shakespeare's poem is "a song of requiem and of mourning for the sacrifice and death of the two birds." Shakespeare's unorthodox use of the phoenix legend underscores the tragedy: "There is a sense of entombment but not a resurrection."

Oakeshott, Walter. *"Loves Martyr." The Huntington Library Quarterly* XXXIX, No. 1 (November 1975): 29-49.

Attempts, through extensive historical research, to strengthen the case that Chester's *Love's Martyr* is an allegory in which the Phoenix refers to Elizabeth and the Turtle refers to Essex. Oakeshott asserts that Shakespeare invoked Chester's allegorical apparatus not to exalt the Queen, as called for by convention, but to honor her association with Essex, who, Oakeshott asserts, "symbolized, for the writer of the 'Phoenix and Turtle,' the embodiment of an age of liberality, artistic brilliance and political triumph."

Richards, I. A. "The Sense of Poetry: Shakespeare's 'The Phoenix and the Turtle'." *Daedalus* 87, No. 3 (Summer 1958): 86-94.

Offers a line-by-line, literal interpretation of *The Phoenix and Turtle,* together with an introduction to its themes and ideas. Richards intimates that a knowledge of the poem's historical or literary context, as well as an understanding of any possible allegorical references, is not necessary to follow the movement of the poem from the temporal to the ethereal, from the ephemeral to the transcendent, to the very brink of the "mystery of being."

Rollins, Hyder E., ed. Appendix to *The Poems,* by William Shakespeare, pp. 559-83. A New Variorum Edition of Shakespeare, edited by Joseph Q. Adams. Philadelphia: J. B. Lippincott Co., 1938.

Provides an informative introduction to *The Phoenix and Turtle.* Rollins addresses, with many critical references, such topics as textual issues; date of composition; criticism; interpretation; and metrical pattern.

Schwartz, Elias. "Shakespeare's Dead Phoenix." *English Language Notes* VII, No. I (September 1969): 25-32.

Asserts that *The Phoenix and Turtle* is a funeral elegy for two dead lovers, not a philosophical or metaphysical love poem. Schwartz argues that Christian interpretations of the poem are inconsistent with Shakespeare's depiction of a mortal phoenix; the deaths of the Phoenix and Turtle, he contends, represent the logical consequence of the idealized, transcendent love described in the Antheme. The mood of the poem parallels the disillusionment expressed in *Hamlet, Troilus and Cressida,* and *Othello,* according to Schwartz, and does not portend "the triumphant vision of human love—the quasi-mystical humanism—of Shakespeare's late plays."

Sitwell, Osbert. " 'The Sole Arabian Tree'." *The Times Literary Supplement,* no. 2047 (26 April 1941): 199, 206.

Speculates that Shakespeare's knowledge of the phoenix legend and the "sole Arabian tree" (l. 2) was derived from the *Travels of Marco Polo,* first translated into English in 1579 by John Frampton. Sitwell also suggests that the poem itself allegorically celebrates the "effect of this book upon the poet as the magic union of Phoenix and Turtle."

Underwood, Richard A. *Shakespeare's "The Phoenix and Turtle": A Survey of Scholarship.* Salzburg: Universitat Salzburg, 1974, 336 p.

Presents a critical review of the scholarship on *The Phoenix and Turtle,* with extensive quotations from the sources. Underwood divides critical study of the poem into three groups: "the poem as allegory," "classical and source studies," and "critical and 'dramatic' interpretations." In addition, he discusses critical assessments of the poem's texts, authenticity, and date of composition.

Wilbur, Richard. "Shakespeare's Poems." In his *Responses: Prose*

Pieces, 1953-1976, pp. 78-90. New York: Harcourt Brace
Jovanovich, 1966.

Presents a concise, orthodox interpretation of Shakespeare's
"strange and masterly metaphysical poem." Wilbur contends
that although Shakespeare, in the tradition of good poets, re-
vises somewhat the mythology and conventional symbolism of
the phoenix, he retains the "spirit of renewal" through the creature's association with the idea of rebirth. The critic also speculates that Shakespeare was influenced by Plato's *Phaedrus* in
forming his poetic conception of ideal lovers.

The Rape of Lucrece

DATE: On May 9, 1594, Shakespeare's *The Rape of Lucrece* was entered for copyright in the STATIONERS' REGISTER. The first edition was printed in QUARTO form that same year with the inscription "Lucrece. London. Printed by Richard Field, for John Harrison, and are to be sold at the signe of the White Greyhound in Paules Churchyard. 1594." Critical consensus assigns the poem a composition date of 1593-94, following the publication of *Venus and Adonis* in 1593. In the signed dedication prefacing *Venus,* Shakespeare writes to Southampton, "If your Honour seeme but pleased, I . . . vowe to take advantage of all idle houres, till I have honoured you with some graver labour." Beginning with F. J. Furnivall in 1877 (see Additional Bibliography), many commentators—including Sidney Lee, T. W. Baldwin (see Additional Bibliography), Geoffrey Bullough (see Additional Bibliography), and A. C. Hamilton (see Additional Bibliography)—have routinely identified that "graver labour" as *The Rape of Lucrece.*

Scholars have also offered external evidence to support a 1593-94 composition date. For example, in 1790 Edmond Malone observed that the applause bestowed on Samuel Daniel's complaint poem *Rosamond* (1592) may have influenced Shakespeare to write *Lucrece.* Such twentieth-century critics as J. C. Maxwell (see Additional Bibliography) and F. T. Prince have contended that the closing of the London theaters from August 1592 to April 1594 because of the plague further substantiates a 1593-94 composition date, for during this crisis Shakespeare and other dramatists were forced to seek private patrons. Prince remarked, "If *Venus,* and *Lucrece* a year later, are taken to be a result of the enforced idleness of the London players in 1592-93, their motives being to compensate in part for the disastrous financial losses at that time, we have an explanation . . . of why the rising young dramatist turned to 'narrative' verse."

Two nineteenth-century scholars offered other views, however. G. G. Gervinus argued that *Lucrece* and *Venus* were composed about 1587, before the young Shakespeare left Stratford for London. Although "both poems were certainly revised at publication," he claimed, "everything betrays that they were written in the first passion of youth." Similarly, T. S. Baynes wrote, "They are wonderful poems to have been produced by an English youth writing in the country between the years 1580 and 1586-7. . . . The marvel is that [these] poems . . . should have been produced by a 'prentice hand' in a small provincial town" (see Additional Bibliography). The suppositions of Gervinus and Baynes have not been endorsed by twentieth-century scholars.

TEXT: Many scholars believe the narrative poems are unique in the Shakespearean canon in that the printing of these works may have been supervised by the author himself. The first edition of *The Rape of Lucrece* (1594) was apparently set from Shakespeare's FAIR COPY, and thus most critics accept this as an authoritative text. For example, in 1938, Rollins asserted that "most commentators believe that the type was set directly from Shakespeare's manuscript and that Shake-

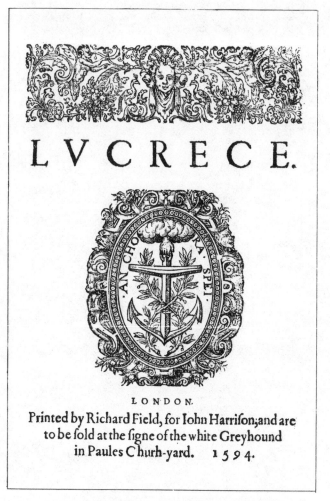

Title page of The Rape of Lucrece *(1594).*

speare read the proofs." Earlier, Sidney Lee offered a dissenting opinion: "It is improbable that the author supervised the production of the first edition," he claimed. Lee agreed, however, that "greater care was taken in its typography than in the case of any other of Shakespeare's works—not excepting *Venus and Adonis*"—and that the first edition of 1594 is "the sole authentic source of the text of the poem." Despite the careful preparation of this edition, some typographical errors eluded the proofreader. Malone, who in 1790 produced the first and most influential critical edition of *The Rape of Lucrece,* remarked: "Though the first quarto seems to have been printed under our author's inspection, we are not therefore to conclude that it is entirely free from typographical faults. Shakespeare was probably not a very diligent corrector of his sheets; and however attentive he might have been . . . some errors will happen at the press." Rollins deemed the first printing "excellent," although he too acknowledged the presence of "a few" undetected errors.

The 1594 title-page gives the poem's title as "Lucrece." "The Rape of Lucrece" appears as the running caption on every text page, however, "presumably following the title given in the poet's manuscript," according to Rollins. In the 1616 edition, the full title, *The Rape of Lucrece,* was used, and this is the one most twentieth-century editors have adopted.

The poem enjoyed considerable popularity during Shakespeare's lifetime, running through eight editions by 1632. The ninth edition of *The Rape of Lucrece* appeared in 1655, after which the poem lapsed into relative obscurity for more than a hundred years. Although it was reprinted in various collections during the eighteenth century by such editors as George Sewell and Charles Gildon, these texts were based on later quartos and were heavily emendated and "corrected." It was not until 1790, when Malone issued his edition of *The Rape of Lucrece,* that the first quarto was again used as a copy text.

Although Shakespeare's name does not appear on the title-page of the first edition, it is printed on the second page following the dedication to Southampton. With rare exception, the poem's authenticity has gone unchallenged. Contemporary allusions link Shakespeare with *Lucrece* as early as 1595, as evidenced by John Weever's poem, "Ad Gulielmum Shakespeare." In addition, between 1598 and 1601, Francis Meres, Richard Barnfield, and Gabriel Harvey also alluded to Shakespeare's *Lucrece.* Nevertheless, in 1936, G. W. Phillips disputed Shakespeare's authorship and contended that he was merely the dedicator (see Additional Bibliography). Phillips asserted that *The Rape of Lucrece,* as well as *Venus and Adonis,* were anonymous poems, possibly composed by several writers. In 1950, James Tolbert speculated that the Argument prefacing *The Rape of Lucrece* was hastily added to the manuscript as an afterthought by a "friend or hack" (see Additional Bibliography). Tolbert did not, however, contest Shakespeare's authorship of the poem itself, and modern critics continue to affirm Shakespeare's authorship of *Lucrece.*

SOURCES: The story of Lucrece's rape captured the imagination of many prominent artists from the classical, medieval, and Renaissance periods. Beginning with Roman poets and historians, most notably OVID and Livy, her grievous tale was interpreted in verse, in prose, on canvas, and in marble. The proliferation of portraits makes it difficult to pinpoint with certainty the ultimate origin of Shakespeare's Lucrece. Virtually every discussion of Shakespeare's models cites Ovid, who is generally acknowledged as the principal source; however, nearly every critic has also offered various secondary influences.

As noted by Rollins, Malone's remarks in his 1780 edition of the poems represent the first attempt to establish Shakespeare's sources, and Ovid is among Malone's list of potential influences. Baynes, who undertook an investigation of "What Shakespeare learnt at school," named Ovid's *Fasti,* Book II, as the chief source (see Additional Bibliography). Subsequent critics who have cited Ovid include Lee; Edward Dowden; E. P. Kuhl (see Additional Bibliography); Baldwin, who concluded that Shakespeare relied most heavily "on a copy of Ovid with the notes [Latin annotations] of [Paulus Marsus]"; M. C. Bradbrook, who cited Ovid's *Metamorphoses* as well as the *Fasti;* the editor of the Cambridge edition of the poems, J. C. Maxwell; and the Penguin editor, J. Lever. Despite the disparity in size—Ovid's 73 lines compared to Shakespeare's 1,855—there are significant similarities in plot, characterization, diction and phrasing. As Geoffrey Bullough commented (see Additional Bibliography): "We see then that Shake-

speare used Ovid's terse and clear-cut tale as a series of suggestions for a full-scale exercise in lyrical and descriptive dilation."

Certain elements of style and plot details in Shakespeare's *Lucrece* have incited critics to perceive further classical allusions. Malone noted that the Lucrece story was also related by Livy in his *Ab Urbe Condita* (*History of Rome*). Baynes dismissed the influence of Livy's version, although many textual scholars have supported the connection, including Lee, Dowden, Kuhl, Bullough, Maxwell, and Baldwin. In his early eighteenth-century edition of *Lucrece,* Charles Gildon asserted the influence of Virgil on Shakespeare: "There is . . . in this Poem I think a Proof of his knowing Virgil, for he has painted Sinon, as Virgil has done before him." Baynes cited Shakespeare's debt to Virgil's *Aeneid* for the scene depicting the fall of Troy. The inclusive critic, Lee, also acknowledged Virgil, as did Bradbrook, Lever, and John Velz, who argued that Shakespeare relied on a passage from Plutarch, as well as Virgil's *Aeneid,* to formulate his portrait of the fall of Troy. In an article published in 1953, James M. Tolbert proposed that Shakespeare's *Lucrece* shows the influence of the translations of Seneca in grammar school texts, specifically the *Illustrium Poetarum Flores,* "a book of passages from the ancient poets collected and codified early in the sixteenth century by Octavianus Mirandula" (see Additional Bibliography). Similarly, Esther Cloudman Dunn commented on the resemblance between Lucrece's oratory and Senecan declamation; Bradbrook, however, rejected any connection with the Roman statesman and writer. Kuhl detected the influence of Cicero, "at least indirectly." Also among Malone's list of classical writers who related the Lucrece story are Dionysius Halicarnassensis, Diodorus Siculus, and Dion Cassius. Finally, in 1978, the discussion of aesthetics in the ecphrasis of *Lucrece* prompted S. Clark Hulse to infer Shakespeare's familiarity with classical aesthetic theorists, such as Philostratus, Quintilian, and Hermogenes; Hulse also mentions Homer as a possible influence.

Critics have also investigated the field of medieval and Elizabethan English literature for possible sources of *Lucrece.* In *The Legend of Good Women* (c.1386), Geoffrey Chaucer retold the Lucrece story, and several critics, among them Lee, Dowden, Bradbrook, Maxwell, and Lever, identified this work as a precursor of Shakespeare's *Lucrece.* Once again, Malone, in his 1790 edition of the poems, set a critical precedent by implying that Samuel Daniel's *Rosamond's Complaint* (1592) influenced Shakespeare. Lee asserted that Shakespeare follows *Rosamond* closely in creating his own work in the fashionable complaint genre. Subsequently, Bradbrook and Lever cited Daniel as the source of Lucrece's lament, as did Rolf Soellner (see Additional Bibliography) who, in 1982, proposed that Shakespeare might have been influenced by three Neoclassical closet tragedies written by Robert Garnier and Daniel. Several critics, including Lee, Bradbrook, and Lever, referred to the general influence of the complaint genre as developed in John Lydgate's *Fall of Princes* (1431-38)—which is a translation of a French version of Boccaccio's *De Casibus Virorum Illustrium*)—and in the *Mirror for Magistrates* (1559). However, at least two critics, C. S. Lewis and Baldwin, dismissed the parallel between the complaint form and *Lucrece.* Baldwin discovered no evidence that Shakespeare composed with a copy at his side of any English versions of the Lucrece story. Nevertheless, critics have identified several other possible sources among English authors. According to Baynes, William Painter's *Palace of Plea-*

sure (1566) "is indeed little more than a paraphrase of Livy's brief account of the tragedy," and unconvincing as a source for *Lucrece;* Lee and Dowden, however, included Painter as a possible influence, and Baldwin stated that Shakespeare used, in addition to classical sources, Painter's translation. Dowden rejected John Gower's Lucrece legend in his *Confession Amantis* (c.1390), yet Maxwell later added Gower to his source list. Lewis and Bradbrook recalled Thomas Kyd, an Elizabethan dramatist, and his *Spanish Tragedy* (1592). Bradbrook also cited Sir Philip Sidney's *Astrophel and Stella* (c.1582). To this catalog of influences, Lee added two English poets, Giles Fletcher and Thomas Watson, Lever contributed Spenser's *Faerie Queen* (c. 1590), and G. K. Hunter proposed a translation by Barnaby Googe of *The proverbes of the noble and woorthy Souldier Sir John Lopez de Mendoza.*

CRITICAL HISTORY: The record of scholarly assessment of *The Rape of Lucrece* reflects three stages. During the first half of the seventeenth century, Shakespeare's narrative poems reached the high point of their popularity, eclipsing, in this respect, the majority of his plays. This period was followed, however, by more than a century of relative obscurity, during which critics focused almost exclusively on the plays and many editors omitted the poems from their collections of Shakespeare's works. The first quarter of the nineteenth century saw the beginnings of renewed interest as critics sought to reconcile the universally acclaimed plays with the often disregarded narrative works and to compare *Lucrece* with epic and complaint poems by other authors. Much twentieth-century criticism of *Lucrece* has diverged from this formalist or genre approach and explored a variety of topics from a wide range of perspectives, analyzing its tragic and dramatic elements, language and imagery, aspects of political allegory, and religious elements. Recently, commentators have also examined the poem's perspective on aesthetic ideas and cultural definitions of gender relations.

In the Elizabethan age, an aspiring writer who wished to establish a literary reputation had to demonstrate his or her skill in the composition of verse. Thus, Shakespeare's stature as a man of letters depended on the critical reception of his poems, *The Rape of Lucrece, Venus and Adonis,* and *The Phoenix and Turtle,* apparently the only works published in his lifetime with his consent. Shakespeare's concern that the narrative poems impress his audience is reflected in the care he took in personally supervising the printing of *Lucrece* and *Venus and Adonis* (see TEXT section above). His artistry and his diligence at the printing shop were well-rewarded, for six editions of *The Rape of Lucrece* were published in his lifetime. According to John Munro's *Shakspere Allusion Book,* only *Hamlet, Venus and Adonis, Romeo and Juliet,* and *Henry IV* surpass *Lucrece* in the number of references each received prior to 1650. Among these allusions are Francis Meres's famous 1598 tribute to the "mellifluous and honytongued Shakespeare," and Gabriel Harvey's contemporaneous remark linking *Lucrece* and *Hamlet.*

After 1655, the plays began to overshadow the poems in both popularity and critical reputation. According to Hyder Edward Rollins (see Additional Bibliography), only one edition of *The Rape of Lucrece* was published between 1655 and 1710. In 1710, Charles Gildon reprinted the 1640 edition and praised the poem's subject, its "fine similes," and classical allusions. But Lucrece's verbosity and conduct offended the critic's Neoclassical standards. Alexander Pope had such scant regard for the poems that he omitted them from his

1725 edition of Shakespeare's works, as did George Steevens in 1793. Edmond Malone, one of the most influential Shakespearean editors, reprinted *The Rape of Lucrece* in his 1790 collection of the poems, using the first edition of 1594 as textual authority. In his critical remarks, Malone set the precedent for many subsequent commentators by noting that in crafting a garrulous Lucrece, Shakespeare was merely following contemporary poetic fashion. Ultimately the poem reveals, according to Malone, that Shakespeare was more inclined toward drama than poetry; however, the command of imagery and language characteristic of the plays is at least nascent in this work, he claimed. In addition, in his critical annotations, Malone was the first to make explicit and extensive references to the plays.

Many nineteenth-century critics followed Malone's example, attempting to resolve the apparent artistic discrepancy between the poems and the plays by attributing flaws in the former to Shakespeare's youthfulness and noting certain elements that presage the achievement of his dramatic works. Samuel Taylor Coleridge, in his 1811-12 lecture series, affirmed that *Lucrece* has "impetuous vigour and activity," "profound reflection, and a perfect dominion over the whole of our language—but nothing deeply pathetic." In 1817, William Hazlitt echoed Malone's assertion that Shakespeare's artistry was inhibited by rigid poetic forms but liberated by drama; in his estimation, even the best parts of the poems are inferior to anything in the plays. Shakespeare's genius, according to Hazlitt, lay in his ability to identify with a character, to adopt a dramatic mask, rather than in more direct self-expression. James Boswell, who collaborated with Malone on the third variorum edition of Shakespeare's works (1821), preferred *Lucrece* to *Venus,* and detected in the former "upon some occasions an energy both of expression and sentiment which we shall not easily find surpassed by any poet of any age." Like others before him, the German critic G. G. Gervinus, writing in 1849-50, argued that Shakespeare's talents were confined by the conventions of fashionable conceit poetry—a form he emulated as a young poet but repudiated, according to Gervinus, as a mature dramatist. Edward Dowden viewed *The Rape of Lucrece* as the product of a youthful poet compensating for his lack of self-confidence by exhaustively addressing his chosen subject as a formal artistic exercise. Although Shakespeare here maintains a distance between himself and his subject, and subordinates narrative action and dramatic potential to prolonged description, Dowden contended, the epic poems "show us the materials laid out in detail from which dramatic poetry originates." Fifteen years later, in 1896, Frederick S. Boas uttered virtually identical sentiments, calling attention to stylistic elements in *Lucrece* that reappear in the poet's later work.

This slow process of recuperating critical attention and esteem continued into the early twentieth century as scholars such as Sidney Lee and Walter Raleigh attributed the flaws of *The Rape of Lucrece* to artistic immaturity and the particular excesses of fashionable Elizabethan poetry. But they also found redeeming glimpses of Shakespeare's future dramatic development in this poem. Lee discerned amid the rambling rhetorical digressions of *Lucrece* a keen intellect willing to grapple with moral complexities. Writing in 1907, Raleigh argued that in this work Shakespeare reveals his youthful devotion to beauty and an impulse to demonstrate his wit; these, more than a concern for truth or the need for self-expression, represent the impetus behind the poem. In 1909, two critics, J. M. Robertson and Algernon Charles Swinburne, diverged from the trend toward reconciling Shakespeare's narrative and dramatic works. Robertson found nothing of poetical worth to redeem the uninspired and tedious *Lucrece,* and he concluded that the poem was "manufactured" to gratify the particular literary tastes of Shakespeare's general audience. Swinburne dismissed both *Venus and Adonis* and *Lucrece,* declaring that they do not portend the author's dramas.

Critics have continued to evaluate *The Rape of Lucrece* in the context of all of Shakespeare's works—by which standard the poem invariably looks youthful and flawed—and in the context of contemporary literary vogue—in which light *Lucrece* compares favorably to and perhaps outshines the work of other Elizabethan poets. Barrett Wendell, writing in 1895, is an apt example of this pervasive critical view (see Additional Bibliography). Wendell instructed his readers to consider Shakespeare's narrative poems as "little else than elaborate feats of phrase-making," in accord with literary fashion. However, he also noted that Shakespeare distinguished himself from his literary rivals by his occasional use of "the concrete phrase, more true to nature," that is a hallmark of his plays. Although this formalist or genre approach prevailed primarily during the nineteenth and early twentieth centuries, a few later critics were also attracted to it. In 1944, C. S. Lewis deemed the "emotional and intellectual content" of *Lucrece* weak, and he criticized the cumbersome and unimaginative medieval narrative technique. Nevertheless, Lewis conceded that Shakespeare's poem is engaging, in spite of its many digressions. Richard Wilbur, commenting in 1966, believed that in this piece Shakespeare intentionally subordinated ideas and content to form and the conscious display of rhetorical prowess; however, *Lucrece* is only redeemed by a few admirable passages, he asserted (see Additional Bibliography).

Two early twentieth-century critics, Esther Cloudman Dunn and George H. W. Rylands, characterized *Lucrece* as a transitional work that employs both narrative and dramatic devices. Dunn argued that the late sixteenth century was an era dominated by literary experimentation. *Lucrece,* with its alternation of narrative and dramatic modes, often in a declamatory style reminiscent of Senecan plays, exemplifies the hybrid form typical of this period: a dramatic poem. Rylands's comparison of the verse of *Lucrece* with the dramatic style of several early Shakespearean plays revealed many similarities, especially in terms of language and imagery. However, the critic declared, in both cases, Shakespeare's impulse to dramatize his source material often competes with a literary style solidly grounded in narrative techniques; the end result is the creation of verse that "is to be read, not spoken." Rylands was the first critic since Malone to extensively examine parallels between Shakespeare's dramas and *Lucrece,* helping to open a new vein of critical study. Many mid-twentieth-century critics have investigated dramatic parallels and specifically tragic elements in *The Rape of Lucrece.* Although she discussed many other aspects of the poem in her influential 1951 essay, M. C. Bradbrook stressed that *Lucrece* represents Shakespeare's earliest expression of his idea of tragedy, and she noted, as did Rylands and several others, the resemblance between Tarquin and Macbeth. Harold C. Goddard analyzed at length the numerous dramatic parallels between *Lucrece* and *The Taming of the Shrew, Cymbeline, Troilus and Cressida, Macbeth, Hamlet, Othello,* and *King Lear;* he also discovered in this poem "the germs of half-a-dozen other plays" (see Additional Bibliography). In 1959, Sam Hynes argued that the real moral focus of *Lucrece* is Tarquin and

that the tragic vision evident in the poem is more in line with the "Christian tragedies," *Othello* and *Macbeth,* than with the ostensibly similar Roman plays. According to Hynes, the crucial rape in the poem is the defilement of Tarquin's soul by his own passions, an act resulting from the impulse toward self-destruction that is characteristic of Shakespeare's tragic heroes. The critic remarked that like Desdemona and Cordelia, the pure Lucrece symbolizes a "spiritual quality" or moral goodness that is latent in the male protagonist. In the following year, F. T. Prince described *Lucrece* as an expression of Shakespeare's youthful conception of tragedy. He found much in the poem to dispraise, foremost the meandering digressions that, he asserted, undermine a sympathetic portrayal of the heroine. Yet the poem is worth attention, he declared, because it reveals Shakespeare's fascination with "morbidity" and "physical and moral violence" and demonstrates the conflict between "vile evil and ideal virtue" which, at this early stage, constitutes the poet's notion of tragedy. In addition, Prince explained, this dichotomy also reflects Shakespeare's "divided consciousness," a distinctive feature which led him to identify with his dramatic personae and helped him create such vivid characters. In 1961, Harold R. Walley wrote a frequently cited essay in which he asserted that *Lucrece* represents a pivotal point in Shakespeare's development as a dramatist. According to Walley, *Lucrece* "establish[es] the matrix of the later great tragedies," in that it encompasses both Shakespeare's conception of tragedy and "a rationale for tragedy" itself. Two editors of *Lucrece,* Edward Hubler, in 1959, and J. C. Maxwell, in 1966, called attention to the poem as, in Hubler's words, "Shakespeare's first statement of the conception of tragedy he was later to realize in *Hamlet* and *Othello*" (see Additional Bibliography). Similarly, in his 1974 book-length study of *Lucrece,* R. Thomas Simone contended that Shakespeare here "state[s] for the first time his theory of tragedy" (see Additional Bibliography).

Several twentieth-century scholars have interpreted *Lucrece,* at least in some aspects, as political allegory. They have viewed *Lucrece* as providing Shakespeare with the opportunity to address conditions in Elizabethan England within the context of a Roman setting. In an essay written in 1941, E. P. Kuhl proposed that Shakespeare chose the time-proven Lucrece story to serve as a vehicle for examining contemporary issues and advancing his own political agenda, invoking the conventional analogy between Rome and England so as not to violate decorum (see Additional Bibliography). Bickford Sylvester, writing in 1965, commented on what he perceived as an element of allegory operating in the poem; Tarquin's violence, he claimed, is equated with the tyranny of the Tarquin dynasty and Lucrece's passivity represents the Roman citizens' acquiescence in their subjugation. One year later, Franklin Dickey described *Lucrece* as an example of "moralized history" intended to portray the debilitating effect of lust in princes and the danger they pose to the state. Dickey interpreted the poem as Shakespeare's first expression, somewhat awkwardly and didactically presented, of moral and political philosophy. In his evaluation of *Lucrece,* the prominent critic William Empson discussed, among other things, Elizabethan censorship and Shakespeare's need to allegorize so that such potentially subversive thoughts as republicanism could be safely incorporated within the poem. In 1975, Michael Platt elaborated on Empson's interpretation, contending that the reality of censorship dictated that Shakespeare adopt an epic "style of compactness," indirect and oblique, in order to examine, although not necessarily advocate, republicanism and the overthrow of tyranny.

Two critics, D. C. Allen in 1962 and Roy Battenhouse in 1969, offered interpretations of *Lucrece* based on the proposition that the poem exhibits a Christian subtext. Allen did not dispute that Shakespeare provides a sympathetic portrayal of Lucrece, but he also pointed out that the medieval trend, beginning with Augustine, to evaluate Lucrece's motives and actions according to Christian tenets and to question their propriety renders her depiction problematic. Whereas in Allen's view the Christian perspective intruded unintentionally, according to Battenhouse, Shakespeare consciously employs a double perspective that comments ironically on the classical treatment of the Lucrece story. This embedded Christian view portrays Lucrece as narcissistically seeking her own martyrdom. Thus, the critic judged, Shakespeare's Lucrece is at least partially culpable for her fate. In 1982, Ian Donaldson found *Lucrece* morally ambiguous because, in his view, it vacillates between Roman and Christian viewpoints: between sympathy for Lucrece and condemnation of her suicide (see Additional Bibliography). To account for this confusion, Donaldson contended that Shakespeare, respecting Augustine's objections, began to "Christianize the old story," but mysteriously stopped, "content to allow the story to drift down its traditional narrative course."

The apparently self-reflexive scene in *Lucrece* which depicts the heroine before the painted rendering of the fall of Troy has led several twentieth-century critics to investigate the role of art in the poem and the degree to which classical and Renaissance aesthetic theories inform its composition. Hyder Edward Rollins was apparently the first to employ the term "ecphrasis" in regard to this scene. The term is borrowed from aesthetic theory and denotes an extended description of something, often in the form of one mode of art mimicking another. The term also conjures up the centuries-old rivalry between poesy and painting, verse and visual representation. A. C. Hamilton was one of the earliest commentators to examine the role of art, specifically painting, in *Lucrece* and the relation of the two art forms, painting and poetry, in this work (see Additional Bibliography). He also claimed that Lucrece is portrayed as an emblem or "speaking picture." In his 1978 essay, Clark Hulse argued that Shakespeare adheres to classical aesthetic theories in creating his own "proper epic ecphrasis." Within the realm of poetry, Lucrece is empowered and rhetorically persuasive; thus, in this sense, she is an artistic success. However, Hulse asserts, in the public realm, Lucrece is denied heroic stature. Instead, she must surrender the stage to the pragmatic Brutus, who emerges to extol her—and, implicitly, the artist who created her—and to incite Collatine and the others to seek revenge. According to David Rosand's 1980 analysis of the function of the ecphrasis, Shakespeare is seeking to instruct his readers in "the proper reading of images": "to look with our ears" (see Additional Bibliography). Although the eyes were typically regarded, according to Renaissance aesthetic theory, as the "paragone of the senses," poetry could attain the same emotional effect as painting through a rhetoric of mimesis or "pictorial vocabulary," which, Rosand argued, Shakespeare employs in *Lucrece*. In 1983, Judith Dundas also examined the ecphrasis and asserted that here Shakespeare "gives his most explicit account of how art works." As demonstrated in the poem, art, itself an illusion like the "well-painted piece," functions paradoxically as a mirror to illuminate Tarquin's deception and Lucrece's predicament. All of these critics

maintained that even at this early period of his development, Shakespeare was a highly self-conscious artist, concerned about the limitations of art but also an advocate of its mimetic function.

Shakespeare's masterful and inventive use of language and imagery is a critical commonplace, and several commentators in the last forty years have argued that, in this regard, *Lucrece* is no exception to his other works. Bradbrook, in line with the formalist critics of the nineteenth and early twentieth centuries, proposed that Shakespeare attempted in this work to emulate the "high style" of accepted classical and contemporary models. However, Bradbrook demonstrated, his use of language and imagery derived principally from the medieval tradition of "moral heraldry," in which characters are emblematic of various vices and virtues. Subsequent students of Shakespeare's style and his use of rhetorical conventions—including those borrowed from moral heraldry—have debated whether the author of *Lucrece* endorses the values implicit in these terms or whether he invokes these stylized images in order to undermine them or comment ironically on their traditional usage. In his discussion of how metaphor operates in the poem and influences our perception of reality, Goddard described Shakespeare's depiction of Lucrece's rape in terms of war: "Rape is miniature war is what the poem says in so many words." In 1964, Robert Griffin analyzed *Lucrece*'s substructure of motifs, images, extended metaphors, antitheses, and oxymorons. He concluded that these tropes did cohere and achieve a formal unity (see Additional Bibliography). Similarly, Jerome Kramer and Judith Kaminsky asserted that the poem, paradoxically, attains a sense of unity through Shakespeare's use of "contraries," such as antitheses, dichotomies, and irony in the development of theme and characterization (see Additional Bibliography). In addition, they cited several examples of image patterns throughout *Lucrece* that underscore the series of oppositions in the poem. Richard Lanham, writing in 1976, argued that the actions of the two protagonists, Tarquin and Lucrece, are determined by "motives of eloquence" or impulses toward self-dramatization. Tarquin and Lucrece are, in effect, prisoners of the chivalric metaphors through which they have constructed their own identities. According to Lanham, both characters have fallen in love with these terms—Tarquin with feudal rhetoric and Lucrece with the language of feeling—and tragically destroy themselves rather than relinquish their roles. In 1985, Nancy Vickers proposed that Shakespeare adopts the rhetoric of moral heraldry to simultaneously display his artistic talent and mastery of conventional forms and, paradoxically, to subvert the very conventions upon which this descriptive mode rests. In the following year, Katherine Maus perceived, as Lanham had earlier, an "intimacy between the characters' metaphors and their decisions and between their language and their psychological states" (see Additional Bibliography). She argued that both Tarquin and Lucrece come to understand the metaphors they use to figuratively describe themselves as "literal representations, conceptions of their state," which they in turn use to rationalize their actions. In this poem, Maus contended, Shakespeare reveals the violence latent in conventional, figurative terms and indicates that he himself is troubled by the problematic and potentially harmful nature of figurative language.

Recently, three feminist critics, beginning in 1976 with Coppélia Kahn, have brought their critical perspectives to studies of *Lucrece*. Kahn approached the text as a treatise on the institution of marriage and the role of women in marriage. Lucrece's predicament, her moral innocence and physical stain, symbolizes women's position in such patriarchal societies as Rome and Elizabethan England. She represents the paradigmatic patriarchal woman because she accepts her role as her husband's possession and perceives her stain as an irrevocable material fact that threatens the institution of marriage, private property—the foundation of that society—and her husband's honor. According to Kahn, Lucrece has "no sense of herself as an independent moral being apart from this role in marriage" and she realizes that she must sacrifice herself to protect the patriarchal system. In 1980, Catharine Stimpson examined Shakespeare's conception of rape as developed in several of his works, including *Lucrece* (see Additional Bibliography). She concluded that although Shakespeare portrays rape victims and other abused women sympathetically and castigates rapists, he does not challenge the patriarchal order that governs sexual identity and relationships. In Stimpson's judgment, Shakespeare is interested not in eradicating the "confinements" imposed by society, but in protesting "assaults upon them," such as Tarquin's act, which denies Collatine's exclusive right to Lucrece. In Vickers's discussion of the rhetoric of moral heraldry mentioned above, she stressed its function as an exclusively male dialogue that displays or advertises the objectified female, in this case Lucrece, and renders her vulnerable to male violence. It is unclear, according to Vickers, if Shakespeare shares complicity for objectifying Lucrece in his art in order to prove his rhetorical skills, or whether he merely adapts the conventions of moral heraldry in order to undermine them.

As we have seen, within the last twenty-five years, many critics of *Lucrece* have abandoned the formal or structural criteria adopted by previous commentators and have chosen instead a materialist approach. A. Robin Bowers, however, writing in 1981, sought to recover the literary context of the poem (see Additional Bibliography). *Lucrece*, Bowers argued, derives from the "popular medieval debate literature" and portrays "medieval ways of explaining the corruption of the mind"; to import classical or contemporary dramatic standards into an assessment of the poem is to violate the literary foundation of the work, the critic contended. In 1986, Heather Dubrow proposed that Shakespeare has provided in *Lucrece* a treatise on various Renaissance modes of reading and writing history. Depicting the protagonists as representatives of the rival styles, the poem illuminates the limitations of each style by tracing the flaws of the characters who advocate these methods of interpreting history and refusing to privilege one mode above another. However, the critic averred, the mere act of identifying the limitations of historiography and, in the broader context, language itself, suggests that a sounder method, or discourse, exists and is worth pursuing.

The Rape of Lucrece has never recovered the popularity it enjoyed during Shakespeare's lifetime; however, in the twentieth century it has risen from relative obscurity, attracting considerable attention and provoking diverse interpretations. Although some recent critics have analyzed the poem in terms of its own merits and independent of the plays, the majority of commentators seem attracted to *Lucrece* because it is one of Shakespeare's earliest literary efforts. Although commentators have typically disparaged *Lucrece*'s relentless moralizing and her ironically self-defeating lament, they also have recalled *Lucrece*'s Elizabethan literary context, in which, they have maintained, the poem is clearly noteworthy, even meritorious. As a precursor of Shakespearean drama,

Lucrece attains even more value in the eyes of students and commentators. The desire to resolve the apparent artistic disparity between Shakespeare's narrative poems and the plays of his middle and late periods has led recent critics to employ materialist or historicist approaches to the poem that reveal a wealth of complex issues in *Lucrece*. Lately, scholars have also shown a greater willingness to accept or raise the question of Shakespeare's use of irony and to consider the possibility that by adopting poetic conventions and conforming to literary fashion, he may be undermining or transmuting those very forms. Thus, despite the frequent cataloging of the poem's flaws, especially in characterization and style, a parallel movement aimed at recuperation has emerged. At this point, it is far from clear whether *Lucrece* will ever recapture its initial stature as a peer of Shakespeare's dramatic works. Ambivalence has thus far proven to be the prevailing critical reaction to the poem.

FRANCIS MERES   (essay date 1598)

[*Meres was an English schoolmaster, critic, and clergyman. The following excerpt is taken from his* Palladis Tamia, Wit's Treasury *(1598), a compendium of observations and commentary on a wide range of topics that has played a valuable role in determining the dates of several of Shakespeare's plays and poems. Meres's allusion to* The Rape of Lucrece, *in which he likens the author to the great Roman poet, Ovid, represents one of the most important early appraisals of Shakespeare's poem.*]

As the soule of *Euphòrbus* was thought to liue in *Pythagoras:* so the sweete wittie soule of *Ouid* liues in mellifluous & honytongued *Shakespeare,* witnes his *Venus* and *Adonis,* his *Lucrece,* his sugred Sonnets among his priuate friends, &c. (pp. 281-82)

> *Francis Meres, "A Comparative Discourse of Our English Poets with the Greeke, Latine, and Italian Poets," in his* Palladis Tamia: Wits Treasury, *1598. Reprint by Garland Publishing, Inc., 1973, pp. 279-87.*

GABRIEL HARVEY   (essay date 1598?)

[*Harvey was an English poet, critic and satirist, as well as a Latin scholar and close friend of Edmund Spenser. He is perhaps best known for his bitter literary feud with Robert Green and Thomas Nashe, involving a prolonged exchange of acrimonious pamphlets. Harvey's allusion to Shakespeare's epic poems, excerpted below, appeared in the margin of his copy of Thomas Speght's biography of Chaucer, published in 1598. Another marginal note refers, in the present tense, to the Earl of Essex, who was executed in 1601, which would place the date of these comments sometime between 1598 and 1601. Harvey's remark comparing* The Rape of Lucrece *with* Hamlet *and* Venus and Adonis *are frequently cited by critics to describe contemporary assessment of Shakespeare's epics.*]

The younger sort takes much delight in Shakespeares *Venus, & Adonis:* but his *Lucrece,* & his tragedie of *Hamlet, Prince of Denmarke,* haue it in them, to please the wiser sort. (p. 232)

> *Gabriel Harvey, "Marginalia in Speght's 'Chaucer'," in* Gabriel Harvey's Marginalia, *edited by G. C. Moore Smith, Shakespeare Head Press, 1913, pp. 225-34.*

CHARLES GILDON (essay date 1710)

[*Gildon was the first critic to write an extended commentary on the entire Shakespearean dramatic canon. Like many other Neoclassicists, he regarded Shakespeare as an imaginative playwright who nevertheless frequently violated the dramatic "rules" necessary for correct writing. In the excerpt below, Gildon praises* The Rape of Lucrece *for its subject, its "fine similes," and its classical allusions. However, the critic objects to the heroine's verbosity and excessive contemplation of her condition; this strikes Gildon as unrealistic behavior for someone in Lucrece's circumstances.*]

This Poem [*Lucrece*] in my Opinion is much inferiour to the former, tho' a much better Subject for a Poem. *Lucrece* is too talkative and of too wanton a Fancy for one in her Condition and of her Temper, yet there are many good Lines, some very good Topics, tho' a little too far spread as those of *Night, Opportunity,* and *Time.*

> *Oh! Comfort-killing Night! Image of Hell*
> *Dim Register and Notary of Shame.*
> [ll. 764-65]

> *Oh! Opportunity thy Guilt is great!*
> *'Tis thou, that execut'st the Traitor's Treason.*
> [ll. 876-77]

> *Mishapen Time, Copesmate of ugly Night*
> *Swift subtle Post, Carrier of grisly Care.*
> [ll. 925-26]

These tho' they express a great many Properties and Effects of the *Topics,* are yet too curious and too long to entertain a Lady in so desperate a Condition as *Lucrece* was; and the same will hold good of several things before she gives herself the fatal Wound.

There are some other common Places in this Poem worth minding as [that] of the Avaritious, tho' brought in by Way of Simile

> *Those that much covet are of Gain so fond*
> *That oft they have not that which they possess.*
> [ll. 134-35]

Which is the Sense of this Latin Saying, *Tam deest Avaro quod habet, quam quod non habet* [A miser lacks what he has as much as he lacks what he doesn't have]. And of the same Subject:

> *The aged Man that coffers up his Gold.*
> [l. 855]

[Ll. 615-16] are two Verses very like this of *Claudian.*

> *Regis ad Exemplum totus componitur Orbis.* [The entire world is composed following the example of the kings.]

> *For Princes are the Glass, the School, the Book*
> *Where Subjects Eyes do learn, do read do look.*

I urge not this to charge him with *Plagiarism,* but only to shew, that if the Similitude of Thought may be a Proof of his having read the Classics, as well as the finding no such, an Argument that he had not, these and various other Instances, which I might give from both his Poems and Plays wou'd prove that he was not so unacquainted with them, as some Gentleman wou'd perswade us. There are in this Poem as well as in the former a great many fine Similes. (pp. 456-57)

Charles Gildon, "Remarks on the Poems of Shakespear," in The Works of Mr. William Shakespear, *Vol. 7, 1710. Reprint by AMS Press, Inc., 1967, pp. 445-64.*

EDMOND MALONE (essay date 1790)

[*An eighteenth-century Irish literary scholar and editor, Malone was the first critic to establish a chronology of Shakespeare's plays. He was also the first scholar to prepare a critical edition of Shakespeare's sonnets and the first to write a comprehensive history of the English stage based on extensive research into original sources. As the major Shakespearean editor of the eighteenth century, Malone collaborated with George Steevens on Steevens's second and third editions of Shakespeare's plays and issued his own edition in 1790. His importance resides not so much in textual emendation as in his unrivaled knowledge of primary sources. In the following excerpt, Malone points out that the prolixity of* The Rape of Lucrece *is typical of contemporary poetic fashion. Nevertheless, the poem contains the seeds of much of the imagery and poetic language developed in the plays.*]

[In examining *The Rape of Lucrece* and *Venus and Adonis*] we should do Shakspeare injustice, were we to try them by a comparison with more modern and polished productions, or with our present idea of poetical excellence.

It has been observed, that few authours rise much above the age in which they live. If their performances reach the standard of perfecton established in their own time, or surpass somewhat the productions of their contemporaries, they seldom aim further; for if their readers are satisfied, it is not probable that they should be discontented. The poems of *Venus and Adonis,* and *The Rape of Lucrece,* whatever opinion may be now entertained of them, were certainly much admired in Shakspeare's life-time. In thirteen years after their first appearance, six impressions of each of them were printed, while in nearly the same period his *Romeo and Juliet* (one of his most popular plays) passed only twice through the press. They appear to me superior to any pieces of the same kind produced by Daniel or Drayton, the most celebrated writers in this species of narrative poetry that were then known. The applause bestowed on the *Rosamond* of the former authour, which was published in 1592, gave birth, I imagine, to [*Lucrece*]. The stanza is the same in both. (p. 186)

If it should be asked, how comes it to pass that Shakspeare in his dramatick productions also, did not content himself with only doing as well as those play-wrights who had gone before him, or somewhat surpassing them; how it happened, that whilst his contemporaries on the stage crept in the most groveling and contemptible prose, or stalked in ridiculous and bombastick blank verse, he has penetrated the inmost recesses of the human mind, and, not contented with ranging through the wide field of nature, has with equal boldness and felicity often expatiated *extra flammantia moenia mundi* [beyond the fiery walls of the world (Lucretius, *De Rerum Natura*)], the answer, I believe, must be that his disposition was more inclined to the drama than to the other kinds of poetry; that his genius for the one appears to have been almost a gift from heaven, his abilities for the other, of a less splendid and transcendent kind, and approaching nearer to those of other mortals.

Of these two poems *Venus and Adonis* appears to me entitled to superior praise. Their great defect is, the wearisome circumlocution with which the tale in each of them is told, particularly in . . . [*Lucrece*]. When the reader thinks himself almost at his journey's end, he is led through many an intricate path, and after travelling for some hours, finds his inn at a distance: nor are his wanderings always repaid, or his labour alleviated, by the fertility of the country through which he passes; by grotesqueness of scenery or variety of prospect.

Let us, however, never forget the state of poetry when these pieces appeared; and after perusing the productions of the contemporary and preceding writers, Shakspeare will have little to fear from the unprejudiced decision of his judges. . . . [Almost] every stanza of these poems [is] fraught with images and expressions that occur also in his plays. To the liquid lapse of his numbers, in his *Venus and Adonis,* his *Lucrece,* his *Sonnets,* his *Lovers Complaint,* and in all the songs which are introduced in his dramas, I wish particularly to call the attention of the reader. In this respect he leaves all his contemporaries many paces behind him.— Even the length of his two principal poems will be pardoned, when the practice of his age is adverted to. Like some advocates at the Bar, our elder poets seem to have thought it impossible to say too much on any subject. (p. 187)

> Edmond Malone, "Rape of Lucrece," in The Plays and Poems of William Shakspeare, Vol. 10, *edited by Edmond Malone, 1790. Reprint by AMS Press, 1968, pp. 186-87.*

WILLIAM HAZLITT   (essay date 1817)

[*Hazlitt is considered a leading Shakespearean critic of the English Romantic movement. A prolific essayist and commentator on a wide range of subjects, Hazlitt remarked in the preface to his* Characters of Shakespear's Plays, *first published in 1817, that he was inspired by the German critic August Wilhelm Schlegel and was determined to supplant what he considered the pernicious influence of Samuel Johnson's Shakespearean criticism. Hazlitt's commentary is typically Romantic in its emphasis on character studies. His experience as a drama critic was an important factor in shaping his descriptive, as opposed to analytical, interpretation of Shakespeare. In the following excerpt from the work cited above, Hazlitt argues that Shakespeare's narrative poetry is generally inferior to his drama because, while the mask of his dramatic characters allows him free expression, in his poetry he submerges himself and his thoughts in an impersonal, fashionable display of technique and rhetoric. What is a strength in the plays, according to Hazlitt—Shakespeare's gift of description and characterization—is in the epic poems a cumbersome, self-conscious, and ultimately unrealistic depiction of human nature and reality.*]

Our idolatry of Shakespear (not to say our admiration) ceases with his plays. In his other productions, he was a mere author, though not a common author. It was only by representing others, that he became himself. He could go out of himself, and express the soul of Cleopatra; but in his own person, he appeared to be always waiting for the prompter's cue. In expressing the thoughts of others, he seemed inspired; in expressing his own, he was a mechanic. The licence of an assumed character was necessary to restore his genius to the privileges of nature, and to give him courage to break through the tyranny of fashion, the trammels of custom. In his plays, he was "as broad and casing as the general air" [*Macbeth,* III. iv. 22]: in his poems, on the contrary, he appears to be "cooped and cabined in" by all the technicalities of art, by all the petty intricacies of thought and language, which poetry had learned from the controversial jargon of the schools, where words had been made a substitute for things. There

was, if we mistake not, something of modesty, and a painful sense of personal propriety at the bottom of this. Shakespear's imagination, by identifying itself with the strongest characters in the most trying circumstances, grappled at once with nature, and trampled the littleness of art under his feet: the rapid changes of situation, the wide range of the universe, gave him life and spirit, and afforded full scope to his genius; but returned into his closet again, and having assumed the badge of his profession, he could only labour in his vocation, and conform himself to existing models. The thoughts, the passions, the words which the poet's pen, "glancing from heaven to earth, from earth to heaven" [*A Midsummer Night's Dream,* V. i. 13], lent to others, shook off the fetters of pedantry and affectation; while his own thoughts and feelings, standing by themselves, were seized upon as lawful prey, and tortured to death according to the established rules and practice of the day. In a word, we do not like Shakespear's poems, because we like his plays: the one, in all their excellencies, are just the reverse of the other. It has been the fashion of late to cry up our author's poems, as equal to his plays: this is the desperate cant of modern criticism. We would ask, was there the slightest comparison between Shakespear, and either Chaucer or Spenser, as mere poets? Not any.—The two poems of *Venus and Adonis* and of *Tarquin and Lucrece* appear to us like a couple of ice-houses. They are about as hard, as glittering, and as cold. The author seems all the time to be thinking of his verses, and not of his subject,—not of what his characters would feel, but of what he shall say; and as it must happen in all such cases, he always puts into their mouths those things which they would be the last to think of, and which it shews the greatest ingenuity in him to find out. The whole is laboured, up-hill work. The poet is perpetually singling out the difficulties of the art to make an exhibition of his strength and skill in wrestling with them. He is making perpetual trials of them as if his mastery over them were doubted. The images, which are often striking, are generally applied to things which they are the least like: so that they do not blend with the poem, but seem stuck upon it, like splendid patch-work, or remain quite distinct from it, like detached substances, painted and varnished over. A beautiful thought is sure to be lost in an endless commentary upon it. The speakers are like persons who have both leisure and inclination to make riddles on their own situation, and to twist and turn every object or incident into acrostics and anagrams. Every thing is spun out into allegory; and a digression is always preferred to the main story. Sentiment is built up upon plays of words; the hero or heroine feels, not from the impulse of passion, but from the force of dialectics. There is besides a strange attempt to substitute the language of painting for that of poetry, to make us *see* their feelings in the faces of the persons; and again, consistently with this, in the description of the picture in *Tarquin and Lucrece,* those circumstances are chiefly insisted on, which it would be impossible to convey except by words. The invocation to opportunity in the *Tarquin and Lucrece* is full of thoughts and images, but at the same time it is over-loaded by them. The concluding stanza expresses all our objections to this kind of poetry:—

> "Oh! idle words, servants to shallow
> fools;
> Unprofitable sounds, weak arbitrators;
> Busy yourselves in skill-contending schools;
> Debate when leisure serves with dull debaters;
> To trembling clients be their mediators:
> For me I force not argument a straw,

Since that my case is past all help of law."

[ll. 1016-22]

The description of the horse in *Venus and Adonis* has been particularly admired, and not without reason:—

> Round hoof'd, short jointed, fetlocks shag and
>   long,
> Broad breast, full eyes, small head, and nostril
>   wide,
> High crest, short ears, strait legs, and passing
>   strong,
> Thin mane, thick tail, broad buttock, tender hide,
> Look what a horse should have, he did not lack,
> Save a proud rider on so proud a back.

[ll. 295-300]

Now this inventory of perfections shews great knowledge of the horse; and is good matter-of-fact poetry. Let the reader but compare it with a speech in the *Midsummer Night's Dream* where Theseus describes his hounds—

> "And their heads are hung
> With ears that sweep away the morning dew"—

[IV. i. 120-01]

and he will perceive at once what we mean by the difference between Shakespear's own poetry, and that of his plays. (pp. 211-14)

> *William Hazlitt, "Poems and Sonnets," in his* Characters of Shakespear's Plays & Lectures on the English Poets, *The Macmillan Company, 1903, pp. 211-15.*

G. G. GERVINUS (essay date 1849–50)

[*One of the most widely read Shakespearean critics of the latter half of the nineteenth century, the German critic Gervinus was praised by such eminent contemporaries as Edward Dowden, F. J. Furnivall, and James Russell Lowell; however, he is little known in the English-speaking world today. Like his predecessor Hermann Ulrici, Gervinus wrote in the tradition of the "philosophical criticism" developed in Germany in the mid-nineteenth century. Under the influence of August Wilhelm Schlegel's literary theory and Georg Wilhelm Friedrich Hegel's philosophy, such German critics as Gervinus tended to focus their analyses around a search for the literary work's organic unity and ethical import. Gervinus believed that Shakespeare's work contained a rational ethical system independent of any religion—in contrast to Ulrici, for whom Shakespeare's morality was basically Christian. The following excerpt is reprinted from an English translation of his* Shakespeare Commentaries, *first published in German in 1849-50. Gervinus maintains that in* The Rape of Lucrece *Shakespeare indulges in the conceit poetry of the Italian school to an "extravagant excess." This amatory style is replete with fashionable conceits, artificial wit, sophistry, and "profound thoughts lavished on shallow subjects," he notes. Writers in this mode generally ignored the dramatic potential of situations, favored verbose, rhetorical description over the concise, concrete image (the hallmark of Shakespearean drama), and produced caricatures rather than psychologically profound protagonists. According to Gervinus, Shakespeare's portrayal of Lucrece "suffers from an inner lack of truth," except in passages with her maid and groom.*]

Of the two narrative or rather descriptive poems which we possess of Shakespeare, the one (*Venus and Adonis*) was first printed in the year 1593, the other (*Lucrece*) in 1594. Both are dedicated to the Earl of Southampton. The poet himself, in his dedication, calls *Venus and Adonis* his first work, but *Lucrece* belongs indisputably to the same period. Both poems

TO THE RIGHT
HONOVRABLE, HENRY
VVriothefley, Earle of Southhampton,
and Baron of Titchfield.

HE loue I dedicate to your Lordfhip is without end:wherof this Pamphlet without beginning is but a fuperfluous Moity. The warrant I haue of your Honourable difpofition, not the worth of my vntutord Lines makes it affured of acceptance. VVhat I haue done is yours, what I haue to doe is yours, being part in all I haue, deuoted yours. VVere my worth greater, my duety would fhew greater, meane time, as it is, it is bound to your Lordfhip; To whom I wifh long life ftill lengthned with all happineffe.

Your Lordfhips in all duety.

William Shakefpeare.

A 2

Shakespeare's dedication of The Rape of Lucrece *to the Earl of Southampton.*

were certainly revised at publication. Their first conception may place them at a period previous to Shakespeare's settlement in London. Everything betrays that they were written in the first passion of youth.

We at once perceive how completely in matter and treatment they are interwoven with the youthful circumstances and moods of the poet. . . . The subject of *Venus and Adonis* is the goddess of love wooing the cold yet insensible boy, and her laments upon his sudden death. . . . Like Goethe's 'Werther,' it was proverbially held as the model of a love-poem; it was frequently reprinted, and called forth a series of imitations; and poets praised it as 'the quintessence of love,' as a talisman and pattern for lovers, from which might be learned the art of successful wooing.

Glowing as are the colours with which Shakespeare has portrayed this passion, his delight in the subject of his picture has never betrayed him into exclusive sensuality. He knows that he is sketching, not the image of human love in which mind and soul have their ennobling share, but the image of a purely sensual desire, which, purely animal, like 'an empty eagle [l. 55], feeds on its prey. In the passage where he depicts the wooing of Adonis' horse which had broken loose from its rein, his intention is evidently to compare the animal passion in the episode with that of the goddess, not in opposition but in juxtaposition. Rebukingly Adonis tells the loving goddess that she should not call that love, which even he, the poet, names careless lust, 'beating reason back, forgetting shame's pure blush, and honour's wrack' [ll. 557-58]. This purer thought, which more than once occurs in the poem, is yet, it must be admitted, half concealed by the grace of the style and by the poet's lingering on sensual descriptions.

In *Lucrece,* on the contrary, this purer thought lies in the subject itself, which seems intentionally to be selected as a counterpart to the first poem; in opposition to the blindly idolised passion, the poet places the chastity of the matron, in whom strength of will and morality triumph in a tragic form over the conquest of lust. The delineation of the seduction scene in *Lucrece* is neither more modest nor more cold; it might even appear that in the colouring of the chaste beauty there lay still more alluring warmth than in any passage of *Venus and Adonis.* Yet the repentance and atonement of the heroine, the vengeance of her unstained soul, and her death; all these are treated in a totally different manner, in a more elevated tone and with corresponding emphasis. The poet indeed significantly leaves the narrower limits of the description of a single scene, and gives the situation of the heroine a great historical background. The solitary Lucrece, whilst she contemplates suicide, stands in meditation before a picture of the destruction of Troy, and the reader is led to observe the similar fate which the fall of Lucrece brought upon the Tarquinians and the rape of Helen upon the family of Priam. If the poet in *Venus and Adonis,* led on by the tender heart of Ovid, was absorbed in presenting a merely voluptuous picture which would have been a fitter subject for the painter, we see him here assuming a higher standard of morality, and, evidently incited by Virgil, casting a glance towards that field of great and important actions in which he afterwards became so eminent. To exhibit such contrasts was a necessity of Shakespeare's versatile mind; they are a characteristic of his nature and his poetry; they appear here in the first beginnings of his art, and recur incessantly throughout all his dramatic works. Our own Goethe delighted in the repetition of one favourite form of character, which he reproduced only slightly changed in 'Weisslingen' and 'Werther,' in 'Clavigo,' 'Ferdinand,' and 'Egmont;' this would have been impossible with Shakespeare. It lay in his nature to work out a given subject to that degree of perfection and completeness which renders a recurrence to it difficult, and rather invites to a path with a directly opposite aim.

To those who only know Shakespeare through his dramas, these two poems present in their structure a totally foreign aspect. Whilst in the dramas, with their conversational form, everything tends to action, in the narrative form of these poems everything lies in words. Even where an opportunity occurs, all action is avoided; in *Venus and Adonis* not even the boar's hunt is recounted; in *Lucrece* the eventful cause and consequence of the one described scene is scarcely mentioned; in the description of the situation itself all is lost in rhetoric. *Before* his deed, Tarquin in a lengthy reflection holds 'disputation' tween frozen conscience and hot burning will' [ll. 246-47]; *after it,* Lucrece in endless soliloquy inveighs against Tarquin, night, opportunity, and time, and loses herself in vague reflections as to her suicide. Measured by the standard of nature that marks the other works of the poet, this would be the height of unnaturalness in a woman of modest retirement and cold will. That which in Shakespeare's dramas so wonderfully distinguishes his soliloquies,

namely the art of expressing infinite feelings by a few grand touches, is not here exhibited. Only two small indications of it do we meet with in Lucrece, the places where she questions the maid upon Tarquin's departure, and asks for 'paper, ink, and pen' [l. 1289], although they are near her; and where she sends away the groom, who blushes from bashfulness—but, as *she* believes—'to see her shame' [l. 1344]; in these passages the psychological poet, such as we know him, glances forth. Everywhere, besides, in this more important of the two poems, his representation of Lucrece suffers from an inner lack of truth, and shares the faulty structure of the Italian pastoral poetry. Its distinctive characteristic are those so-called conceits, strange and startling ideas and images, profound thoughts lavished on shallow subjects, sophistry and artificial wit in the place of poetry, imagination directed to logical contrasts, acute distinctions, and epigrammatic points. The poet here works after a pattern which he surpasses in redundancy; he takes a false track with his accustomed superiority; he tries an artistic mannerism, and carries it beyond its originators. He carries it to a height at which he himself, as it were, becomes conscious of the extravagant excess, of the strange alternation of sublimity and flatness, which is peculiar to this style. This impression is made by the passage in which Lucrece writes the letter to her husband and passes her criticisms upon it:

> This is too curious-good, this blunt and ill:
> Much like a press of people at a door
> Throng her inventions, which shall go before.
>
> [ll. 1300-02]

In one of his earliest comedies, *Love's Labour's Lost,* Shakespeare repudiates this kind of style. There, in the person of Biron, while he designates most excellently the peculiarities of this kind of poetry, he bids farewell to the

> Taffata phrases, silken terms precise,
> Three pil'd hyperboles, spruce affection,
> Figures pedantical: these summer-flies
> Have blown me full of maggot ostentation.
>
> [V. ii. 406-09]

And, indeed, it was just in the amatory style, to which these peculiarities especially belonged, that Shakespeare first and for ever discarded them; and whilst no poetry was ever so decidedly conventional as this conceit-poetry of the Italian school, none is more opposed to this conventionality than that of Shakespeare's dramas. In many passages of his works, something of the false glitter of the art yet remains; in many parts he used it purposely for some definite aim. In his tragic pathos especially, he has been reproached with degenerating into pomposity and bombast. And it is certain that he sincerely delighted in the grandiloquence of Seneca and in the glowing style of Virgil. The admiration of the account of Pyrrhus' death, which he places in the lips of such a judge as Hamlet, leaves us no doubt of it. *Lucrece* bears the same character of diction in many parts. No German can read this poem without being reminded of Schiller's attempt to translate Virgil into stanzas. The delight of young students in the Roman master was similar, and proceeded from similar causes: youth receives a greater impression of the heroic from the grandiloquent than from the simple grandeur of Homer; the Latin type of epic art is more readily received than the Greek; thus Goethe cherished a preference for Virgil, until he had read Homer with greater ease in German. It is for this reason that Shakespeare was a Virgilian even in his sympathies; as in *Lucrece* in the freshness of early impressions, so at a later period he is always on the side of the Trojans in all allusions to the great Homeric myth. We must remember that, according to tradition, the ancient Britons are descended from the Trojans, and that this illustrious pedigree was held in remembrance in dramatic poems; and in one of Shakespeare's last works, *Troilus and Cressida,* we must keep clearly before us these early youthful feelings, if we would understand the poem. (pp. 36-40)

G. G. Gervinus, "Shakespeare's Descriptive Poems," in his Shakespeare Commentaries, *translated by F. E. Bunnètt, revised edition, 1877. Reprint by AMS Press, Inc., 1971, pp. 36-44.*

EDWARD DOWDEN   (essay date 1881)

[*Dowden was an Irish critic and biographer whose* Shakspere: A Critical Study of His Mind and Art, *first published in 1875 and revised in 1881, was the leading example of the biographical criticism popular in the English-speaking world near the end of the nineteenth century. Biographical critics sought a record of Shakespeare's personal development in the plays and poems. As that approach gave way in the twentieth century to aesthetic theories with greater emphasis on the constructed, formal nature of literary works, the biographical analysis of Dowden and other critics came to be regarded as limited and often misleading. In the excerpt below, Dowden argues that* The Rape of Lucrece *is the product of a youthful poet who compensates for his lack of self-confidence by exhaustively and formally addressing his chosen subject as an artistic study to develop his skills. According to Dowden, Shakespeare is following models closely learning his craft until "he can trust himself to draw from memory." Although Shakespeare maintains a distance between himself and his subject, and subordinates narrative action and dramatic potential to prolonged description, Dowden contends, his epic poems do "show us the materials laid out in detail from which dramatic poetry originates."*]

The specialty of these poems [*Venus and Adonis* and *The Rape of Lucrece*] as portions of Shakspere's art has perhaps not been sufficiently observed. Each is an artistic *study;* and they form . . . companion studies—one of female lust and boyish coldness, the other of male lust and womanly chastity. Coleridge [in his *Biographia Literaria*] noticed "the utter aloofness of the poet's own feelings from those of which he is at once the painter and the analyist;" but it can hardly be admitted that this aloofness of the poet's own feelings proceeds from a dramatic abandonment of self. The subjects of these two poems did not call and choose their poet; they did not possess him and compel him to render them into art. Rather the poet expressly made choice of the subjects, and deliberately set himself down before each to accomplish an exhaustive study of it. (pp. 43-4)

In *Lucrece* the action is delayed and delayed, that every minute particular may be described, every minor incident recorded. In the newness of her suffering and shame, Lucrece finds time for an elaborate *tirade* appropriate to the theme "Night," another to that of "Time," another to that of "Opportunity." Each topic is exhausted. Then, studiously, a new incident is introduced, and its significance for the emotions is drained to the last drop in a new tirade. We nowhere else discover Shakspere so evidently engaged upon his work. Afterwards he puts a stress upon his verses to compel them to contain the hidden wealth of his thought and imagination. Here he displays at large such wealth as he possesses; he will have none of it half seen. The descriptions and declamations are undramatic, but they show us the materials laid out in de-

tail from which dramatic poetry originates. Having drawn so carefully from models, the time comes when he can trust himself to draw from memory, and he possesses marvellous freedom of hand, because his previous studies have been so laborious. (p. 45)

When these poems were written, Shakspere was cautiously feeling his way. Large, slow-growing natures, gifted with a sense of concrete fact and with humor, ordinarily possess no great self-confidence in youth. An idealist, like Milton, may resolve in early manhood that he will achieve a great epic poem, and in old age may turn into fact the ideas of his youth. An idealist, like Marlowe, may begin his career with a splendid youthful audacity, a stupendous "Tamburlaine." A man of the kind to which Shakspere belonged, although very resolute, and determined, if possible, to succeed, requires the evidence of objective facts to give him self-confidence. His special virtue lies in a peculiarly pregnant and rich relation with the actual world, and such relation commonly establishes itself by a gradual process. Accordingly, instead of flinging abroad into the world while still a stripling some unprecedented creation, as Marlowe did, or as Victor Hugo did, and securing thereby the position of a leader of an insurgent school, Shakspere began, if not timidly, at least cautiously and tentatively. He undertakes work of any and every description, and tries and tests himself upon all. (pp. 46-7)

Edward Dowden, "The Growth of Shakspere's Mind and Art," in his Shakspere: A Critical Study of His Mind and Art, *third edition, Harper & Brothers Publishers, 1881, pp. 37-83.*

FREDERICK S. BOAS   (essay date 1896)

[*Boas was a specialist in Elizabethan and Tudor drama who combined the biographical interest prevalent in the late nineteenth century with the historical approach that developed in the first decades of the twentieth. His commentary thus reflects the important transition that occurred in Shakespearean criticism during this period. In the excerpt below, Boas argues that* The Rape of Lucrece *demonstrates Shakespeare's artistic development in the year since he composed* Venus and Adonis. *Although he believes both poems suffer when subjected to the standards for drama, Boas admires certain aspects of Shakespeare's characterization of Lucrece and Tarquin and notes that some elements in* Lucrece *are reworked in Shakespeare's subsequent writing.*]

The *Lucrece* is probably the 'graver labour' with which Shakspere, in his dedication to *Venus and Adonis,* had promised to honour Southampton. It is longer than the earlier poem by just above a third, and is written, not in a six-lined stanza, but in the more complicated 'rhyme-royal.' In the choice of theme and in its handling there are further signs of a 'graver' temper and a maturing art. The exact source upon which Shakspere drew cannot be determined, but the story of Lucretia had already been told by Livy and Ovid in Latin, and by Chaucer, Gower, Lydgate, and Painter in English. It doubtless attracted the poet as offering the materials for a companion study to *Venus and Adonis.* The picture of woman's lust and man's chastity needed for its foil the contrasted picture of woman's chastity and man's lust. Thus the two poems naturally present many similar characteristics. *Lucrece* repeats the balanced and often paradoxical antitheses of *Venus and Adonis,* and, like it, subordinates action almost entirely to pictorial effect, and to declamation. Nothing could be dramatically more inappropriate than the long-drawn rhetoric of the heroine upon the themes of Night, Opportunity, and Time, while she is yet in the first agony of her hideous wrong, and the detailed description of the painting 'made for Priam's Troy' [l. 1367] stops the movement of the main story for a couple of hundred lines. Yet *Lucrece* shows unmistakable signs of advance upon its predecessor. The ethical tone is more consistent, and there is far greater reserve in dealing with the physical details of passion: even the somewhat overheated picture of the charms of the sleeping Lucrece is tempered by touches of sweet and fresh fancy:

> Without the bed her other fair hand was,
> On the green coverlet: whose perfect white
> Show'd like an April daisy on the grass
> With pearly sweat, resembling dew of night.
> Her eyes, like marigolds, had sheathed their light,
> And canopied in darkness sweetly lay,
> Till they might open to adorn the day.
>
> [ll. 393-99]

The character of Lucrece is drawn in firm and vigorous outline. Her perfect loyalty to her lord, and unsuspicious courtesy to the guest who is alike his friend and king, her appeal to Tarquin not to dishonour his princely name by outrage, and her resolve to die by her own hand, and so 'bail' her soul from its 'polluted prison' [l. 1726], all combine to form the type of the ideal Roman matron, and show the early cunning of the hand that was hereafter to create Brutus' Portia [in *Julius Caesar*] and Volumnia [in *Coriolanus*]. Tarquin also is forcibly conceived, struggling for a time between conscience and desire, then hardening his heart as a millstone, and finally, after the accomplishment of his fell purpose, jaded and self-loathing with the horrible recoil of surfeited passion. The stanzas that tell of his torturing remorse, of the bitter cry of 'the spotted princess' [l. 721], his soul, are the most powerful in the poem and strikingly anticipate some of the Sonnets of the second series. Interesting in a different way is the account of the picture of Troy besieged by the Greeks. Though introduced somewhat inaptly, it is the most detailed study of a painting that Shakspere has left us, the most elaborate attempt to translate into words 'pencilled pensiveness and coloured sorrow' [l. 1497], and it proves that the young poet had already been attracted by the incidents which were to form the basis of his *Troilus and Cressida,* and of the first player's recitation in *Hamlet.* (pp. 160-62)

> *Frederick S. Boas, "Shakspere's Poems: The Early Period of Comedy, " in his* Shakspere and His Predecessors, *1896. Reprint by Charles Scribner's Sons, 1902, pp. 158-96.*

ALGERNON CHARLES SWINBURNE   (essay date 1905)

[*Swinburne was an English poet, dramatist, and critic who devoted much of his literary career to the study of Elizabethan writers. His three books on Shakespeare—* A Study of Shakespeare *(1880),* Shakespeare *(1909), and* Three Plays of Shakespeare *(1909)—all demonstrate his keen interest in the dramatist's poetic talents and, especially, his major tragedies. In the excerpt below, written four years before its first publication, Swinburne declares that* Venus and Adonis *and* The Rape of Lucrece *are undistinguished poems that do not foreshadow Shakespeare's ascent to literary preeminence.*]

It cannot, or rather it must not, be denied that no promise of so great a future was given or was suggested by the first two booklets which presented to the world of readers the name of the greatest among all the writers of all time. There

are touches of inspiration and streaks of beauty in 'Venus and Adonis': there are fits of power and freaks of poetry in the 'Rape of Lucrece': but good poems they are not: indeed they are hardly above the level of the imitations which followed the fashion set by them, from the emulous hands of such minor through genuine poets as Lodge and Barksted.

> *Algernon Charles Swinburne, in an excerpt in his* Shakespeare, *Henry Frowde, 1909, p. 7.*

SIDNEY LEE   (essay date 1905)

[*Lee was an English biographer, Elizabethan scholar, and editor of* The Dictionary of National Biography. *His works on Shakespeare include* Stratford-on-Avon from the Earliest Times to the Death of Shakespeare *(1885), the highly successful* Life of William Shakespeare *(1898), a facsimile edition of the First Folio (1905),* Shakespeare and the Modern Stage *(1906), and* Shakespeare in the Italian Renaissance *(1915). With regard to* The Rape of Lucrece, *Lee remarks that the poem reflects the author's great intellectual enthusiasm and willingness to grapple with moral complexities. However, he claims, Shakespeare also indulges in the excessively rhetorical style that he subsequently repudiates in Sonnet 82.*]

When dedicating his first narrative poem, *Venus and Adonis,* to his patron, the Earl of Southampton, Shakespeare wrote: 'If your Honour seem but pleased, I account myself highly praised, and vow to take advantage of all idle hours till I have honoured you with some graver labour.' There is no reason to doubt that Shakespeare's poem of *Lucrece* was the fulfilment of this vow. *Lucrece* was ready for the press in May, 1594, thirteen months after *Venus and Adonis.* During those thirteen months his labour as dramatist had occupied most of his time. In the interval he had probably been at work on as many as four plays, on *Richard III, Richard II, King John,* and *Titus Andronicus.* Consequently *Lucrece* was, as he had foretold, the fruit, not of what he deemed his serious employment, but of 'all idle hours'. At the same time the increased gravity in subject and treatment which characterizes the second poem of *Lucrece* as compared with *Venus and Adonis,* its predecessor, showed that Shakespeare had faithfully carried into effect the promise that he had given to his patron of offering him 'some graver labour'.

Lucrece with its 1855 lines is more than half as long again as *Venus and Adonis* with its 1194 lines. It is written with a flowing pen and shows few signs of careful planning or revision. The most interesting feature of the poem lies in the moral reflections which the poet scatters with a free hand about the narrative. They bear witness to great fertility of mind, to wide reading, and to meditation on life's complexities. The heroine's allegorical addresses [ll. 869-1001] to Opportunity, Time's servant, and to Time, the lackey of Eternity, turn to poetic account philosophic ideas of pith and moment.

In general design and execution, *Lucrece,* despite its superior gravity of tone and topic, exaggerates many of the defects of its forerunner. The digressions are ampler. The longest of them, which describes with spirit the siege of Troy, reaches a total of 217 lines, nearly one-ninth of the whole poem, and, although it is deserving of the critic's close attention, it delays the progress of the story beyond all artistic law. The conceits are more extravagant and the luxuriant imagery is a thought less fresh and less sharply pointed than in *Venus and Adonis.* Throughout, there is a lack of directness and a tendency to grandiose language where simplicity would prove more effective. Haste may account for some bombastic periphrases. But Shakespeare often seems to fall a passing victim to the faults of which he accuses contemporary poets in his *Sonnets*. Ingenuity was wasted in devising 'what strained touches rhetoric could lend' [Sonnet 82] to episodes capable of narration in plain words. There is much in the poem which might be condemned in the poet's own terminology as the 'helpless smoke of words' [*Lucrece*, l. 1027]. (pp. 7-9)

> Sidney Lee, in an introduction to Shakespeare's Lucrece, *Oxford at the Clarendon Press, 1905, pp. 7-56.*

WALTER RALEIGH   (essay date 1907)

[*Raleigh was a professor of English literature at Oxford and an essayist, literary critic, and biographer who employed a humanistic approach in his work. In addition to biographies of Milton, Wordsworth, Robert Louis Stevenson, and Shakespeare, he published several works on Samuel Johnson and on the English novel. In the following excerpt, Raleigh argues that Shakespeare's epic poems are "poetic exercises by one who has set himself to prove his craftsmanship upon a given subject." According to the critic, Shakespeare's youthful devotion to beauty and "the exercise of wit," rather than similitude, didactics, or self-expression, constitute the aesthetic guidelines that shape the poem.*]

Venus and Adonis and *The Rape of Lucrece,* which were published in 1593 and the following year, are, first of all, works of art. They are poetic exercises by one who has set himself to prove his craftsmanship upon a given subject. If traces of the prentice hand are visible, it is not in any uncertainty of execution, nor in any failure to achieve an absolute beauty, but rather in the very ostentation of artistic skill. There is no remission, at any point, from the sense of conscious art. The poems are as delicate as carved ivory, and as bright as burnished silver. They deal with disappointment, crime, passion, and tragedy, yet are destitute of feeling for the human situation, and are, in effect, painless. This painlessness, which made Hazlitt compare them to a couple of ice-houses [see excerpt above, 1817], is due not to insensibility in the poet, but to his preoccupation with his art. He handles life from a distance, at two removes, and all the emotions awakened by the poems are emotions felt in the presence of art, not those suggested by life. The arts of painting and rhetoric are called upon to lend to poetry their subjects and their methods. From many passages in the plays it may be inferred that Shakespeare loved painting, and was familiar with a whole gallery of Renaissance pictures. Portia's elaborate comparison of Bassanio [in *The Merchant of Venice*] to

> young Alcides, when he did redeem
> The virgin tribute paid by howling Troy
> To the sea-monster.
>
> [III. ii. 55-7]

is only one of many allusions which can be nothing but reminiscences of pictures; and in the Induction to *The Taming of the Shrew* the servants submit to Christopher Sly a catalogue which is the best possible commentary on Shakespeare's early poems:

> We will fetch thee straight
> Adonis painted by a running brook,
> And Cytherea all in sedges hid,
> Which seem to move and wanton with her breath,
> Even as the waving sedges play with wind.
>   We'll show thee Io as she was a maid,

> And how she was beguiled and surpris'd,
> As lively painted as the deed was done:
>   Or Daphne roaming through a thorny wood,
> Scratching her legs, that one shall swear she bleeds;
> And at that sight shall sad Apollo weep,
> So workmanly the blood and tears are drawn.
>
> [Induction ii. 49-60]

Here is the very theme of *Venus and Adonis,* and another theme closely akin to *The Rape of Lucrece.* It would not be rash to say outright that both the poems were suggested by pictures, and must be read and appreciated in the light of that fact. But the truth for criticism remains the same if they took their sole origin from the series of pictures painted in words by the master-hand of Ovid. "So workmanly the blood and tears are drawn."

The rhetorical art of the poems is no less manifest. The tirades and laments of both poems, on Love and Lust, on Night, and Time, and Opportunity, are exquisitely modulated rhetorical diversions; they express rage, sorrow, melancholy, despair; and it is all equally soothing and pleasant, like listening to a dreamy sonata. Lucrece, at the tragic crisis of her history, decorates her speech with far-fetched illustrations and the arabesques of a pensive fancy. And as if her own disputation of her case were not enough, the poet pursues her with "sentences," conveying appropriate moral reflections. She is sadder than ever when she hears the birds sing; and he is ready with the poetical statutes that apply to her case:

> 'Tis double death to drown in ken of shore;
> He ten times pines that pines beholding food;
> To see the salve doth make the wound ache more;
> Great grief grieves most at that would do it good.
>
> [ll. 1114-17]

There is no morality in the general scheme of these poems; the morality is all inlaid, making of the poem a rich mosaic. The plays have to do with a world too real to be included in a simple moral scheme; the poems with a world too artificial to be brought into any vital relation with morality. The main motive prompting the poet is the love of beauty for beauty's sake, and of wit for the exercise of wit. (pp. 80-3)

> Walter Raleigh, "Books and Poetry," in his Shakespeare, *Macmillan and Co., Limited, 1907, pp. 63-93.*

JOHN M. ROBERTSON   (essay date 1909)

[*Robertson was an English scholar and politician and a proponent of the disintegration theory of Shakespeare's texts. This theory, based on statistical analysis of Shakespeare's verse, attempted to show that metrical irregularities were the result of multiple authorship of Shakespeare's plays. Robertson developed this theory over many years and in several books culminating in* The Shakespeare Canon *(1922-1930), in which he closely examined each play and attributed certain passages and works to Christopher Marlowe and George Chapman. Verse analysis and the disintegration theory enjoyed considerable popularity around the turn of the century; however, most twentieth-century scholars have come to reject this method and its conclusions. In the excerpt below, Robertson finds nothing of poetical worth to redeem the uninspired and tedious* Venus and Adonis *and* The Rape of Lucrece. *He declares that both poems were "manufactured" according to reigning literary fashion.*]

The tasks which the greatest of our poets set himself when near the age of thirty, and to which he presumably brought

all the powers of which he was then conscious, were the uninspired and pitilessly prolix poems of VENUS AND ADONIS
and THE RAPE OF LUCRECE, the first consisting of some 1200
lines and the second of more than 1800; one a calculated picture of female concupiscence and the other a still more calculated picture of female chastity: the two alike abnormally fluent, yet external, unimpassioned, endlessly descriptive, elaborately unimpressive. Save for the sexual attraction of the
subjects, on the current vogue of which the poet had obviously reckoned in choosing them, these performances could have
no unstudious readers in our day and few warm admirers in
their own, so little sign do they give of any high poetic faculty
save the two which singly occur so often without any determining superiority of mind—inexhaustible flow of words and
endless observation of concrete detail. Of the countless thrill-
ing felicities of phrase and feeling for which Shakespeare is
renowned above all English poets, not one, I think, is to be
found in those three thousand fluently-scanned and smooth-
ly-worded lines: on the contrary, the fatiguing succession of
stanzas, stretching the themes immeasurably beyond all natural fitness and all narrative interest, might seem to signalise
such a lack of artistic judgment as must preclude all great
performance; while the apparent plan of producing an effect
by mere multiplication of words, mere extension of description without intension of idea, might seem to prove a lack of
capacity for any real depth of passion. Above all, by the admission of the most devoted of Shakespeareans, they are devoid of dramatic quality. They were simply manufactured
poems, consciously constructed for the market, the first designed at the same time to secure the patronage of the Maece-
nas of the hour, Lord Southampton, to whom it was dedicated, and the second produced and similarly dedicated on the
strength of the success of the first. The point here to be noted
is that they gained the poet's ends. They succeeded as saleable
literature, and they gained the Earl's favour. (pp. 144-46)

> *John M. Robertson, "Shakespeare's Culture-*
> *Evolution," in his* Montaigne and Shakespeare, and
> Other Essays on Cognate Questions, *second edition,*
> *Adam and Charles Black, 1909, pp. 139-60.*

GEORGE H. W. RYLANDS   (essay date 1928)

[*Rylands compares the verse of* The Rape of Lucrece *with the
dramatic style of several of Shakespeare's early plays and finds
many similarities. According to the critic, the diction and description of this work, like those of the first history plays, are
often cluttered with excessive paradoxes, proverbs, and euphuisms that impede dramatic development. Despite the dramatic
qualities evident in* Lucrece, *Rylands argues the poem's versification "is to be read, not spoken."*]

Morton Luce finds the *Lucrece* far inferior to the *Venus and
Adonis.* "We have less nature, less melody, less beauty, less
poetry than in the earlier poem" [in his *Handbook to the
Works of William Shakespeare*]. The answer is that we have
more Shakespeare, more of the dramatic poet. He himself
promises in his dedication of the first poem that the second
is to be "some graver labour". (p. 135)

Lucrece is dramatic. Shakespeare is striving to realise the sensations of the two protagonists. There is a conflict in Tarquin
before the rape, similar to that in the heart of Macbeth—

> But as he is my kinsman, my dear friend,
> The shame and fault finds no excuse or end.
> > [*Lucrece,* ll. 237-38]

He's here in double trust;
First, as I am his kinsman and his subject;
> [*Macbeth,* I. vii. 12-13]

and to Brutus's "insurrection in the state of man" [*Julius
Caesar,* II. i. 67, 69]—

> Between the acting of a dreadful thing
> And the first motion
> > [*Julius Caesar,* II. i. 63-4]

Again when Tarquin prays that the heavens may countenance his sin, he starts reflecting—

> The powers to whom I pray abhor this fact,
> How can they then assist me in the act?
> > [*Lucrece,* ll. 349-50]

and he is in the same position as Claudius—

> O what form of prayer
> Can serve my turn?
> > [*Hamlet,* III. iii. 51-2]

Dramatically imaginative is the meeting between Lucrece
and her maid; even more so her misinterpretation of the
"homely villein's" bashful blushes as consciousness of her
shame.

In this piece poetry gives place to rhetoric, simile to metaphor, description to soliloquy, Spenserian imagery to euphuistic, antithetical conceits. The metaphors are pursued laboriously and at length in a way which is very characteristic of
Shakespeare's early manner; for although *Lucrece* is more
dramatic, the plays, especially (and naturally so) the chronicle plays, suffer stylistically from their narrative qualities.

Here the metaphorical idea of an army setting siege to a city,
which is found elsewhere in Shakespeare and the Elizabethans, for example—

> She will not stay the siege of loving terms
> Nor bide the encounter of assailing eyes.
> > [*Romeo and Juliet,* I. i. 12-13]

is elaborated over eight stanzas [ll. 427-83]. Here also the familiar conceits upon "windy sighs", "the ocean of tears beating on the rocky heart" [l. 590], which are to be found even
in the final plays. *Lucrece,* weighty, prest, obstructive, contains most of the material, the superstitions, saws, fables and
unnatural history, out of which *Henry VI., Richard III.* and
II., and *Romeo and Juliet* are composed.

> Nor read the subtle-shining secrecies
> Writ in the glassy margents of such books.
> > [*Lucrece,* ll. 101-02]

And what obscured in this fair volume lies
Find written in the margent of his eyes.
> [*Romeo and Juliet,* I. iii. 85-6]

Mud not the fountain that gave drink to thee.
> [*Lucrece,* l. 577]

The purest spring is not so free from mud
As I am clear from treason to my sovereign.
> [*2 Henry VI,* III. i. 101-02]

Roses have thorns and silver fountains mud.
> [*Sonnet* 35]

Thou sheer, immaculate and silver fountain,
From whence the stream through muddy passages
Hath held his current and defiled himself.
> [*Richard II*, V. iii. 61-3]

The proverbial instance is elaborated, as often.

And now this pale swan in her watery nest
Begins the sad dirge of her certain ending.
> [*Lucrece*, ll. 1611-12]

I am the cygnet to this pale faint swan,
Who chants a doleful hymn to his own death.
> [*King John*, V. vii. 21-2]

The face, that map which deep impression bears
Of hard misfortune.
> [*Lucrece*, ll. 1711-12]

I see as in a map the end of all.
> [*Richard III*, II. iv. 54]

In thy face I see
The map of honour, truth and loyalty.
> [*2 Henry VI*, III. i. 202-03]

Thus is his cheek the map of days outworn.
> [*Sonnet* 68]

Poor broken glass, I often did behold
In thy sweet semblance my old age new born.
> [*Lucrece*, ll. 1758-59]

Thou art thy mother's glass and she in thee
Calls back the lovely April of her prime.
> [*Sonnet* 3]

Lucrece has the seeds of the history plays—the few examples above could be multiplied. The style is dense and cumbersome, a cloak worn without grace, whereas the style of the tragedies, no less compact and closely woven, falls gracefully from the shoulder and does not cramp the movement.

Movement: there lies the weakness of the early plays: there are no *gestures,* as it were, and little variety of speed. Paradoxes, proverbs and euphuisms litter one's path.

Smooth runs the water where the brook is deep.
> [*2 Henry VI*, III. i. 53]

The smallest worm will turn being trodden on.
> [*3 Henry VI*, II. ii. 17]

Seems he a dove? His feathers are but borrowed,
For he's disposed as is the hateful raven.
Is he a lamb? His skin is surely lent him,
For he's inclined as is the ravenous wolf.
> [*2 Henry VI*, III. i. 75-8]

Or as the snake rolled in the flowering bank.
> [*2 Henry VI*, III. i. 228]

Even in *Romeo and Juliet* the diction sometimes impedes the pace:

O serpent heart hid with a flowering face,
Did ever dragon keep so fair a cave?
Dove-feathered raven! Wolfish-ravening lamb!
> [III. ii. 73-4, 76]

All the animals in and out of Aesop are herded together with the heroes of Greece and Rome. The similes are careful and lengthy. Here are two from *Henry VI.,* Pt. 3:

Look, as I blow this feather from my face,
And as the air blows it to me again,
Obeying with my wind when I do blow,
And yielding to another when it blows,
Commanded always by the greater gust:
Such is the lightness of you common men.
> [III. i. 84-9]

Why then I do but dream on sovereignty;
Like one that stands upon a promontory,
And spies a far-off shore where he would tread,
Wishing his feet were equal with his eye,
And chides the sea that sunders him from hence,
Saying, he'll lade it dry to have his way.
> [III. ii. 134-39]

These are straightforward, excellent in their way; but it is the narrative, not the dramatic way, the way of [Matthew Arnold's] *Sohrab and Rustum*. There is a natural pause at the end of each line and the lines are piled one upon the other. This form of versification which is so common in all his work previous to 1600 is the versification of poetry which is to be read, not spoken. It is the versification of Spenser, of *Venus and Adonis* and *Lucrece,* and it was some time before Shakespeare grew out of it. (pp. 135-40)

George H. W. Rylands, "The Early Shakespearian Manner," in his Words and Poetry, *Payson & Clarke Ltd., 1928, pp. 135-43*

THE RAPE OF
LVCRECE.

FRom the besieged Ardea all in post,
Borne by the trustlesse wings of false desire,
   Lust-breathed TARQVIN, leaues the Roman host,
And to Colatium beares the lightlesse fire,
VVhich in pale embers hid, lurkes to aspire,
   And girdle with embracing flames, the wast
   Of COLATINES fair loue, LVCRECE the chast.

Hap'ly that name of chast, vnhap'ly set
This batelesse edge on his keene appetite:
VVhen COLATINE vnwisely did not let,
To praise the cleare vnmatched red and white,
VVhich triumpht in that skie of his delight:
   VVhere mortal stars as bright as heaues Beauties,
   VVith pure aspects did him peculiar dueties.

B

First text page of The Rape of Lucrece *(1594).*

DOUGLAS BUSH (essay date 1932)

[*Bush argues that "Shakespeare, in trying to be both serious and decorative" in* The Rape of Lucrece, *achieves neither. In his view, although the poem is more ambitious than* Venus and Adonis, *it is equally "soulless" and even more "wearisome."* Lucrece *reflects Shakespeare's penchant for rhetorical display, as well as an artistic self-consciousness, both of which contribute to the defeat of dramatic realism. Bush concludes that "one discerns in this baffling tissue of ingenuities only a clever brain, not a quickened pulse."*]

Having produced an erotic poem much to the taste of Southampton and the emancipated in general, Shakespeare, with easy nonchalance, paid his debt to morality and the non-emancipated by celebrating, in the following year, the most famous of all martyrs of chastity. Although *Lucrece* contains few indications of intense feeling in the author, when he comes later to conjure up the sinister specters of night no image is more vivid in his memory than that of Tarquin's ravishing stride. However, the poem seems to be quite as deliberate a literary exercise as *Venus and Adonis,* and the reversal of the theme and the graver style need not imply anything in the way of apology. Almost any Elizabethan could write a sensuous mythological poem once; he could hardly do it twice. *Lucrece* is not a sensuous mythological poem, and, if less attractive than its predecessor, it is in some respects much more ambitious. (pp. 149-50)

Lucrece differs from *Venus and Adonis* in attempting to deal dramatically and realistically with a tragic situation involving two "historical" persons. The versions of the story that Shakespeare knew are very brief compared with his eighteen hundred and fifty-five lines, and, while the action is spun out as much as possible, the great additions are the long passages of dramatic or rhetorical moralizing. He does try to enter into the feelings of the characters, though his love of rhetoric runs away with his sense of drama. The conflict in Tarquin's mind when he sets out for Lucrece's room occupies nearly two hundred lines of soliloquy and description; like the villains of the plays he leaves nothing unsaid in the way of self-condemnation. Lucrece, when awakened, marshals orderly arguments in about eighty lines. Later, after a few hundred lines of rhetoric, she exclaims, with justice:

> In vain I rail at Opportunity,
> At Time, at Tarquin, and uncheerful Night . . .
>
> [ll. 1023-24]

Declamation roars while passion sleeps. The description of the Trojan scenes and Lucrece's reflections thereupon involve a further smoke of words, to the extent of about two hundred lines.

Dramatic realism is likewise defeated by the incessant conceits. Shakespeare does not, as Spenser sometimes does, treat rape as a decorative theme, but his handling, in trying to be both serious and decorative, falls between two stools. When Tarquin arrives on his evil errand, three stanzas are given up to the "silent war of lilies and of roses" [l. 71] in the face of his hostess:

> This heraldry in Lucrece' face was seen,
> Argu'd by beauty's red and virtue's white:
> Of either's colour was the other queen,

> Proving from world's minority their right:
> Yet their ambition makes them still to fight;
> The sovereignty of either being so great,
> That oft they interchange each other's seat.
>
> [ll. 64-70]

Granting of course that the conceited style was instinctive with most Elizabethans as it cannot be with us, one discerns in this baffling tissue of ingenuities only a clever brain, not a quickened pulse. So too when Tarquin gazes at his prospective victim we have such a conceit as this, in Marlowe's worst vein:

> Her lily hand her rosy cheek lies under,
> Cozening the pillow of a lawful kiss;
> Who, therefore angry, seems to part in sunder,
> Swelling on either side to want his bliss.
>
> [ll. 386-89]

As often in the early plays, the author has quite forgotten the situation; he is holding the subject at arm's length, turning it round, saying as much as he can about every side of it.

Almost every line gives evidence of a self-conscious pride in rhetorical skill. . . . A Tarquin who "justly thus controls his thoughts unjust" [l. 189] is too cool, his creator too epigrammatic, for the matter in hand; one thinks of the equally strained phrase of Tennyson, "And faith unfaithful kept him falsely true" [*Idylls of the King*].

In addition to the usual gnomic lines we have an extraordinary profusion of proverbs, singly and in series, after the style of the euphuists in verse and prose. *Venus and Adonis* had its heaped-up illustrations, but the quantity of them in *Lucrece* helps to give the poem an old-fashioned air. Says Tarquin to Lucrece, in words feverish with desire:

> I see what crosses my attempt will bring;
> I know what thorns the growing rose defends;
> I think the honey guarded with a sting . . .
>
> [ll. 491-93]

And, justly controlling her just thoughts, Lucrece replies:

> Mud not the fountain that gave drink to thee;
> Mar not the thing that cannot be amended;
> End thy ill aim before thy shoot be ended;
> He is no woodman that doth bend his bow
> To strike a poor unseasonable doe.
>
> [ll. 577-81]

Accompanied by such antiphonal wisdom vice loses half its evil by losing all its grossness.

The mere bulk of Lucrece's declamation after the event demands that something be said of it. Having tried his hand at oratory in *Venus and Adonis,* Shakespeare liked it well enough to provide Lucrece with a whole series of apostrophes. They have undeniable force, but the effect is like that of Senecan declamation, like an explosion in a vacuum. The apostrophe to Time may have been inspired by contemporary poets, but it has a literary pedigree that goes back to Ovid's *Tristia.* The apostrophe to Night is likewise conventional in style and subject matter, but it bears a special resemblance to a speech that Spenser puts in the mouth of Arthur. Sir Sidney Lee remarked that Lucrece's address to Opportunity "seems an original device of Shakespeare" [see excerpt above, 1905]. The matter at least is proverbial; in fact most of it is contained or suggested in the comment on *Nosce tempus* in [Richard] Taverner's *Proverbes or Adagies, gathered out of the Chiliades of Erasmus.* This trick of apostrophe, inherited from the more rhetorical Roman writers, was one of the most important devices of rhetoric in the Middle Ages, and Lucrece's declamations are of obvious medieval flavor.

In technique *Lucrece* is nearer to Chaucer's *Troilus* than to Ovid, though it has nothing of Chaucer's irony, emotion, and depth. With all its Renaissance trappings it is thoroughly in the medieval tradition. On the other hand, with its undramatic drama, its endless rhetorical digressions, it reads at times like an unconscious burlesque of Elizabethan plays. There are a few really dramatic touches, such as parts of Tarquin's behavior, and especially the sympathetic maid and the "sourfac'd groom." This "homely villein," who, summoned to act as Lucrece's messenger, "curtsies to her low" [l. 1338], receives only a few phrases, but he is almost as real a person as either of the principals. These various bits are slighter and paler than the pictures of the lark and the hare in *Venus and Adonis,* but they are similarly out of key. They introduce an air of truth and actuality into a would-be dramatic but quite bookish poem, and they are too few to do more than heighten the artificial unreality of all the rest. For all its seriousness of theme and intention *Lucrece* is as soulless as the earlier poem, and much more wearisome. (pp. 152-55)

> *Douglas Bush, "Shakespeare: 'Venus and Adonis' and 'The Rape of Lucrece',"* in his *Mythology and the Renaissance Tradition in English Poetry, 1932. Reprint by Pageant Book Company, 1957, pp. 139-55.*

ESTHER CLOUDMAN DUNN   (essay date 1936)

[*Dunn characterizes* The Rape of Lucrece *as a transition piece between narrative poetry and drama. According to Dunn, the late sixteenth century was an era dominated by experimentation and flux in literary fashion. Shakespeare's* Lucrece *is typical of the period in that it employs various narrative and dramatic techniques, elements of morality plays, and the declamatory style reminiscent of Senecan drama. Through the use of these diverse conventional methods of story-telling, Shakespeare creates a hybrid: a dramatic poem that verges on poetic drama.*]

Elizabethan poetry of the [1590s] is at once imitative and original. It has the enthusiasm of amateurishness and experiment. One no sooner defines a type of poem, as for instance the long narrative poem on Greek mythology or English history, than the type alters into something else. The sonnets of the first years of the Nineties have become something quite different by 1600. Everything is in flux. New combinations, new re-workings of new combinations, daring innovation make this decade in English poetry one of the most various and spirited in the whole span of English literature.

It is one of the most difficult, too, to classify and describe. Obviously one must not lean too heavily upon classification or description. One must live through the actual poetry. Also one must keep an eye on the year when a poem was composed, for in the passage of a single year the poetical fashion may alter. One must not have preconceived ideas about the category to which a poem belongs. The understanding of Shakespeare's long poem, *The Rape of Lucrece,* may depend more upon comparing it to a Senecan stage play than to another poem which is superficially like it in type. A good deal of what is said generally about the sonnet in the Nineties is not applicable to the greatest sonnet cycle of that decade,

Shakespeare's. Again the standard in Shakespeare's sonnets will not fit Donne's, or Ralegh's or even Drayton's later ones. The only thing in fact which is constant in this mass of divergence is the spirit, the energy of poetic feeling and the will to express it, no matter how unconventionally. With this warning, let us look at two long narrative poems by Shakespeare which have been much misunderstood and little read. They are *Venus and Adonis* and *The Rape of Lucrece.* They were written in 1593 and 1594, in the very heart of this difficult decade.

The modern reader must not be deceived by the word "poem" as applied to these two pieces of work. The word may betray him into looking for something different from what is there. Neither of them is a "poem" in the narrow sense of that word. (pp. 37-8)

The Rape of Lucrece in some 1850 lines tells a story as old as Ovid and Livy, handled too by Shakespeare's great forebear, Chaucer. Shakespeare in his dedication to the Earl of Southampton calls it a "pamphlet." This is a sufficiently nondescript category. For the modern reader it is useful to think of it as a narrative poem, very closely approaching the form of dramatic poems which Seneca, nearly sixteen centuries earlier, had the temerity to call plays, when they were declaimed for his master, Nero. Or, coming to Shakespeare's own time, it is not unlike, in general technique, Marlowe's early lyrical drama, *Tamburlaine.* To say this is, of course, to overstate the case. *The Rape of Lucrece* is not a play. Yet it hovers on the borderline between the narrative and the dramatic method of telling a story. Because it is such a borderline piece, it is peculiarly helpful to the modern reader. It furnishes a concrete instance of the fact that ancient and famous stories altered their contours or deformed them in the Elizabethan Age so that they could be put upon the stage.

With just a slight effort, Shakespeare could have pushed *The Rape of Lucrece* into a "lamentable tragedy of a chaste Roman lady, with the revenge of Collatine upon the wicked Tarquin." It is significant that just at the time he produced this "pamphlet" he was working on the revision of a play on Roman history, full of rage and brutality and revenge. That play, *Titus Andronicus,* is hardly more of a play from the modern point of view than *Lucrece.* Both pieces of work carry the burden of a violent story. Tucked into the interstices of these stories are rhetorical passages of incitement to violence and reflection upon it. Such passages bulk large. In the "pamphlet" Shakespeare puts the preliminary stages of the action in a prose "Argument" of twenty-six lines. There is in this "Argument" the stuff of some excellent stage scenes. How effectively Shakespeare might have dramatised the following sentence:

> The principal men of the army meeting one evening at the tent of Sextus Tarquinius . . . in their discourse after supper everyone commended the virtues of his own wife.

Because Shakespeare is creating a dramatic poem and not a poetic drama, he passes this material over. He opens his story at the point where Tarquin, already having seen the beautiful Lucrece and having listened to her husband extolling her faithfulness and chastity, suddenly is possessed to visit her alone and win her.

> From the besieged Ardea all in post,
> Borne by the trustless wings of false desire,
> Lust-breathed Tarquin leaves the Roman host

And to Collatium bears the lightless fire.

[ll. 1-4]

Shakespeare plunges *in medias res* as relentlessly as all the great story-tellers, Homer, Vergil and the rest.

Once within the confines of his story, he uses the double facilities of narrative and dramatic technique. At first Tarquin and Lucrece are opposed with the sharp simplicity of a symbolic morality play. They are types of good and evil, about to engage in mortal strife:

This earthly saint, adored by this devil.

[l. 85]

But after supper when, as decorous-seeming guest, Tarquin has gone to bed for the night, he debates with himself in the privacy of his room. He subtly weighs motives and analyses emotion in speeches packed with rhetoric. This debate reveals a living person, not a typical villain. He is, in fact, a potential subject for a moving play around a conflict in character. He debates with himself the meaning of honour, as Falstaff is to do with such dramatic effectiveness on the battlefield of Shrewsbury [*I Henry IV*, V. iv]. He reflects in witty rhetoric upon the complexity of his position:

And for himself himself he must forsake.

[l. 157]

At the hour of midnight when Tarquin is about to set forth for Lucrece's bed-chamber, Shakespeare creates by poetry the same kind of frightening atmosphere which the blank boards and hard daylight of the Elizabethan stage forced him to use in place of lighting or setting in *Hamlet* or *Macbeth*.

No comfortable star did lend his light
No noise but owls and wolves' death-boding cries.

[ll. 164-65]

This sort of thing is conventional. But as Tarquin sets forth along the dark, drafty passages of the palace, the setting gets more realistic:

As each unwilling portal yields him way
Through little vents and crannies of the place
The wind wars with his torch to make him stay,
And blows the smoke of it into his face.

[ll. 309-12]

Whether the method is story or play, little things have a symbolic significance at dreadful moments. For example, to light his torch for the journey from his room to hers,

His falchion on a flint he softly smiteth
That from the cold stone sparks of fire do fly
Whereat a waxen torch forthwith he lighteth
Which must be lode-star to his lustful eye;
'As from this cold flint I enforced this fire
So Lucrece must I force to my desire.'

[ll. 176-81]

On his way to her chamber he finds a glove of Lucrece's which has been dropped with a needle in it. He picks it up from the rushes on the floor and the needle pricks him as a kind of warning. It seems to say:

. . . . . This glove to wanton
tricks
Is not inured; return again in haste;
Thou see'st our mistress' ornaments are chaste.

[ll. 320-22]

In the plays, too, this kind of symbolic implication from little events at great moments, is made again and again. It is one way in which the universal meaning of the particular story is enforced. In *Lucrece* Shakespeare does it awkwardly with prentice skill and conscious effort. Yet sometimes even in *Lucrece* the device is effective. The reason for noticing it at all lies in the fact that it is a device common to the dramatic rendering of events, whether in "poem" or "play."

So too the debate which features the struggle between good and evil in Tarquin's soul is not different in kind though different in intensity from the soliloquies which portray character in the plays. The same kind of thing occurs in *Richard III, Richard II, Henry IV, Hamlet, Macbeth, Antony and Cleopatra, The Tempest*. The débat which presents both sides of an issue is as old as story. Ovid used it. The mediaeval story-tellers in lays, ballads and romances used it. It was useful, too, in the dramatic poems of Seneca. This practice, therefore, was there in his sources ready for Shakespeare when as a dramatist he undertook to transfer secular story to the stage. Because this rhetorical debating of motives had so long been familiar in story form, it was undoubtedly less awkward on the stage for the Elizabethan audience than for the modern. At any rate it turns up in *Lucrece,* longer, more consciously rhetorical perhaps but fundamentally not different from the soliloquies upon the stage.

There is also a good deal of dialogue in this "pamphlet." Lucrece pleading with Tarquin speaks (uninterruptedly, to be sure) for ten stanzas. He replies in one. She continues for two when he interrupts her again. Her conversation with her maid the next morning is much more broken up and nearer to stage dialogue. Speeches of two characters in conversation sometimes exist within a single stanza. Another element in the poem which belongs equally to drama is the description of gestures and behaviour. Shakespeare visualises the action that would accompany the words and offers potential "stage business" and "stage direction." Lucrece hesitating about how to begin the note which shall summon her husband home, is mentally seen by Shakespeare doing her part upon the stage:

Her maid is gone and she prepares to write,
First hovering o'er the paper with her quill:
Conceit and grief an eager combat fight;
What wit sets down is blotted straight with will.

[ll. 1296-99]

The groom who is to bear the letter to her husband, has no lines but there is enough "business" suggested to give him upon the stage a spirited minor part:

The homely villain court'sies to her low,
And, blushing on her, with a steadfast eye
Receives the scroll without a yea or no,
And forth with bashful innocence doth hie.
But they whose guilt within their bosoms lie
Imagine every eye beholds their blame;
For Lucrece thought he blush'd to see her
shame.

[ll. 1338-44]

The situation, innocent on his side, significant and terrible on hers, is prolonged for two more stanzas of description. On the stage it would make a moving scene. It is the germ of such a scene as Juliet's with her nurse, or Hamlet's with the grave-diggers, or Cleopatra's with the countryman. Lucrece's groom of course is not humourous. Yet he is awkward and lumbering, and would need only a slight push to be made the humourous point to a pathetic moment.

The motivation of Tarquin's character is clumsy. In the first third of the poem he is too sensitive a fellow, too deeply enamoured. Then suddenly for the sake of the story he becomes the crude, scheming villain. This kind of inconsistent motivation is found in the plays, too, whenever story is stronger than probability or whenever a sensational scene is needed. Another point in common between *Lucrece* and the plays is the way in which individualised characterisation alternates with characterisation of type. After a highly individualised scene between Lucrece and Tarquin, Shakespeare shifts and makes them like two figures in a tapestry:

> He thence departs a heavy convertite;
> She there remains a hopeless castaway.
>
> [ll. 743-44]

For the modern reader this abrupt change is ludicrous. Yet one must believe that both methods of characterisation held pleasure for the Elizabethan.

The end of the poem like the end of many Elizabethan plays carries the story beyond what the modern audiences would call "the final curtain." After Lucrece has confessed, charged her husband to revenge her upon Tarquin, after the embroidered grief in the speeches by her father and Collatine, we should cry for an end. But Shakespeare carries the story on. Neither he nor his public could forego the tidying up of the events. This fact, at least from the modern point of view, ruins the end of many of his plays.

The part of the "pamphlet" which is essentially "poetry" and not even potential drama comes in Lucrece's twenty-seven stanzas of lament with which she greets the day after the departure of Tarquin. Yet even here one remembers the apostrophe of Juliet to her wedding night; thirty-one lines of conventional wedding song by Juliet alone on the stage at the opening of II, ii. There is, too, the lyric duet to the dawn by Juliet and Romeo in III, v. The feelings in *Romeo and Juliet* and in *Lucrece* are entirely different. Yet the emotional need for self-expression in rhetoric is common to both. Even in the play Shakespeare halts the action while Juliet apostrophises night:

> Come, gentle night, come, loving, black-browed
>   night
> Give me my Romeo and when he shall die
> Take him and cut him out in little stars
> And he will make the face of heaven so fine
> That all the world will be in love with night.
>
> [III. ii. 20-4]

The play is stopped again later while Juliet and Romeo in antiphonal lines fear and cajole the dawn that will separate them. What this means is that the rhetoric of apostrophe, of set invocation for set occasions, though essentially not dramatic material, is used with equal assurance in a poem like *Lucrece* and a play like *Romeo and Juliet*.

Lucrece's apostrophes to Night, to Opportunity, to Time (that cruel Time that let Tarquin into her bedchamber) occupy the centre of the poem. The rhetoric in these apostrophes is sometimes merely dexterous, not moving. Take the following. Time's glory is, among other things,

> To fill with wormholes stately monuments,

> To feed oblivion with decay of things,
> To blot old books and alter their contents,
> To pluck the quills from ancient ravens' wings,
> To dry the old oak's sap and cherish spring.
>
> [ll. 946-50]

The figures here are good enough but not notable. Yet a few lines further on, Lucrece's apostrophe to Time as

> Thou ceaseless lackey to eternity,
>
> [l. 967]

is Shakespeare, the poet, at his best.

In these passages, the reader moves from the presentation of factual life in figures to the presentation of ideas behind factual experience. "Thou ceaseless lackey to eternity" is not different in kind from the figures that precede and follow it. In the idea it evokes, however, it is at the other pole. It is a brief abstract from living; it gives the meaning of a whole phase of life. Yet it comes in here in the poem with no trumpets. It is not even the climax of the poetical discussion of Time. Did Shakespeare know it was better than the rest? Is he, half consciously, beginning to appropriate to his highly personal uses the rhetoric which his literary world offered him ready-made? He seems here to be equally content, as in the earlier plays, either with merely ingenious figures of speech or with this other creative use of figures which belongs to poetry of the first order. When Lucrece and her maid stand weeping, he likens their tear-stained faces to

> . . . conduits coral cisterns filling
>
> [l. 1234]

The image is forced and obscure. But when Lucrece, sad and in black, meets her husband after all that has passed, the figure Shakespeare uses to describe them is exquisite:

> Both stood, like old acquaintance in a trance
> Met far from home, wondering each other's
>   chance.
>
> [ll. 1595-96]

In twenty-five stanzas Lucrece beguiles the time between her note to Collatine and his return by studying a "well-painted piece" of the Fall of Troy. The form of painting whether tapestry or painted cloth and the possible identification of the actual piece of work, have been the subject of much inquiry. Also critics have wondered whether it might be possible to gather from the description whether Shakespeare knew something about the art of painting. Nothing very definite or satisfactory has come of these inquiries. In the many stanzas of description, Shakespeare's repeated point is that the presentation is life-like. It is full of "pencill'd pensiveness" and "colour'd sorrow." Ever since the days of Achilles' shield and the carved bowl of Theocritus' shepherd, the meticulous description of a curiously wrought object has been a *tour de force* of the poet's art. Daniel's *Rosamond* describes a casket on which are wrought scenes from Greek mythology appropriate to persuade Rosamond to yield to Henry II. Shakespeare is giving the same kind of performance in the description of the painting of Troy. He makes it pertinent to Lucrece's situation. She finds Hecuba's face as full of grief as her own and Simon as plausible a villain as Tarquin who ruined her:

> . . . as Priam him did cherish,
> So did I Tarquin: so my Troy did perish.
>
> [ll. 1546-47]

With such diversions and digressions this amphibious creature, *Lucrece,* creeps to its end. In the course of its 1850 lines, Shakespeare has met all the requirements he contracted for. He has told a story drawn from the enchanted land of Roman mythical history. He has provided the appropriate accompaniments of rhetoric, débat, descriptions of wall paintings, apostrophe and lament. While he has been telling it, however, he has added to the story an element not called for in the specifications. The skeleton for a Senecan play has appeared with the curses and invocations to revenge. Because the potential dramatist here is Shakespeare, the dramatic formula has taken on life. At times both Tarquin and Lucrece give promise of the tragic figures of the great period yet to come. At times the narrative stanzas yield dialogue and stage setting. To be sure the story falls half-way between a tale in a book and an action on the stage. But this indecision between these two habitations did not worry the Elizabethans. They themselves hardly thought beyond the great simple category "story"; though they were coming to have a decided preference for the fashion of telling it by way of the stage. (pp. 53-64)

> Esther Cloudman Dunn, *"Poetry in the Nineties,"*
> *in her* The Literature of Shakespeare's England,
> *Charles Scribner's Sons, 1936, pp. 36-96.*

C. S. LEWIS   (essay date 1944)

[*An English literary critic and novelist, Lewis was also a distinguished Renaissance scholar whose writing was strongly influenced by his Christian beliefs. As a Shakespearean critic, he argued that those commentators who pay too much attention to character analysis are apt to overlook the intention of the plays, particularly their moral and ethical impact. Instead, Lewis suggested that the critic should surrender him- or herself to "the poetry and the situation" in all of Shakespeare's dramas. His remarks on* The Rape of Lucrece *were first delivered in a lecture at Trinity College, Cambridge, in 1944. In the excerpt below, Lewis comments that* The Rape of Lucrece *exemplifies the relative artistic immaturity of its author. He declares that the medieval narrative technique employed in the poem, with its emphasis on "theme and variations," is cumbersome, unimaginative, and "plagued by many digressions;" further, its "emotional and intellectual content" is "weak." However, Lewis concedes that the poem is often metrically pleasing, and, in addition to some "formal beauties," the narrative is engrossing.*]

Venus and Adonis, if it were [Shakespeare's] only work, might not now be highly praised; but his next poem might stand higher if it stood alone and were compared solely with other Elizabethan products, not with his own masterpieces. *The Rape of Lucrece* (1594) presumably discharges the promise made in the Epistle to *Venus and Adonis* of 'some graver labour'. It is heroic poetry as the heroic was understood before Virgil had been sufficiently distinguished from Lucan and Ovid; and it differs from its predecessor in merit as much as in kind. The theme would at that time have tempted almost any other poet to one more 'tragedy' modelled on the *Mirror for Magistrates,* and only those who have read many such 'tragedies' can adequately thank Shakespeare for rejecting that form. It is, however, very much a work of its own age. It contains prettinesses and puerilities which the later Shakespeare would have seen to be unsuitable to his heart-rending subject. The conceit which makes Lucrece's pillow 'angrie' at [l. 388] would have been tolerable in [Marlowe's] *Hero and Leander* but is here repellent; and so is the aetiological myth at [l. 1747], or the competitive laments of the husband and

the father at Lucrece's death. There is some of Kyd's fustian in the apostrophe to Night [ll. 764-77]. It is hard not to smile when Lucrece invites the nightingale to use her hair as a grove [l. 1129], but Edward Lear may be partly to blame. The passage in which she becomes preoccupied, like Troilus or a lover in [Sannazar's] *Arcadia,* about the style of her letter to her husband is more difficult to judge: perhaps it is not impossible that a woman of the nineties, brought up by a humanist tutor, might, even at such a moment, have remembered the claims of *eloquentia.* These are merely local imperfections. But there is also, whether we reckon it an imperfection or not, something in the structure of the whole poem which is not quite congenial to our taste. It starts indeed with twenty-one lines of purposeful narration, not rivalled in that age outside [Spenser's] *Faerie Queene:* then our sails flap in three stanzas of digression. And we must be prepared for this throughout. Shakespeare's version of the story is about twelve times as long as Ovid's in the *Fasti* and, even so, omits the earlier stages. Much of this length is accounted for by digression [ll. 131-54 or ll. 1237-53], *exclamatio* [ll. 701-14], *sententiae* [ll. 131-54], and *descriptio* [ll. 1366-1526]. The technique is in fact that of the medieval rhetoricians. Even in those passages which, taken as a whole, are narrative, a great deal of gnomic amplification is brought in. We have 'theme and variations'. Thus at [l. 211] ('What win I if I gain the thing I seek?') Tarquin states the theme of the game not being worth the candle in two lines: it is then varied for five. At [l. 1002] Lucrece states her theme (*noblesse oblige*) in two lines and then varies it for twelve. At [l. 1107] we have theme in two lines and again twelve lines of variation. Minor instances occur throughout. We must not put this down too exclusively to the Age, for Shakespeare was in fact fonder of amplification than many other Elizabethans and used it, sometimes rather grossly, in his earlier plays. There is nothing in *Lucrece* quite so crude as Gaunt's successive variations on the theme 'His rash fierce blaze of riot cannot last' in *Richard II* [ll. i. 33 et seq.]. There is a free use of simple one-for-one parallelism, as in the Psalms;

> The shame that from them no device can take,
> The blemish that will never be forgot,
>
>   [ll. 535-36]

or

> Bearing away the wound that nothing healeth,
> The scarre that will despite of cure remaine.
>
>   [ll. 731-32]

Whether the method shall prove tedious or delightful depends on style, in the narrowest sense of the word: that is, on the volubility of phrase which makes the variant seem effortless, and on phonetic qualities. Thus in *shame, device,* and *blemish* we have long monosyllable, disyllable in rising rhythm, disyllable in falling rhythm. In the second example we have the alliteration of *away* and *wound* and the very subtle consonantal pattern of *scarre, despite,* and *cure.* The first consonant group (*sk*) is not repeated, but one of its elements recurs in *-spite* and the other in *cure.*

Another example is:

> To stamp the seal of time in aged things.
>
>   [l. 941]

No one reads such a line without pleasure. Yet its emotional content is weak and its intellectual weaker still: to say that time stamps the seal of time on things that have existed a long time is near tautology. The charm depends partly, as before, on the distribution of a consonant group between the simple consonants of two later words (*st, s, t*), and partly on the fact that all the stressed syllables are long and all have different vowels.

But *Lucrece* has more than formal beauties to offer us. If not continuously, yet again and again, our sympathies are fully engaged. The rape itself, from the moment at which Tarquin strikes his falchion on the flint to the moment when he 'creeps sadly thence' [l. 736] is presented with a terror and horror unequalled in Elizabethan narrative verse. And here, certainly, the digression on 'drunken desire' before and after its 'vomit' [l. 703] is fully justified. 'The spotted princess' (Tarquin's soul) [l. 721] is admirable: still a princess, unable to abdicate, and there's the tragedy. Lucrece, too rhetorical in her agonies, is not quite so good as Tarquin, but she has her great moments: 'I sue for exil'd majestie's repeal', pleading 'in a wilderness where are no laws' [ll. 640, 544]. And of all the good things that Shakespeare said about Time he puts perhaps the best into her mouth:

> Why work'st thou mischief in thy pilgrimage
> Unless thou couldst returne to make amendes?
>
> [ll. 960-61]

She should not have gone on (good though the line is) to add 'Thou ceaslesse lackeye to eternitie' [l. 967]. It matters nothing that the historical Lucretia would have known neither Plato nor Boethius: the Elizabethan Lucrece ought not to have displayed her learning at that moment. For of course the characters are to be judged as Elizabethans throughout: even Christianity creeps in at [ll. 624 and 1156-58]. (pp. 499-501)

Shakespeare would be a considerable non-dramatic poet if he had written only the *Lucrece:* but it sinks almost to nothing in comparison with his sonnets. (p. 502)

> C. S. Lewis, "Verse in the 'Golden' Period," in his English Literature in the Sixteenth Century, Excluding Drama, *Oxford at the Clarendon Press, 1954, pp. 464-535.*

M. C. BRADBROOK   (essay date 1951)

[*Bradbrook is an English scholar noted especially for her commentary on the development of Elizabethan drama and poetry. In her Shakespearean criticism, she combines both biographical and historical research, paying particular attention to the stage conventions of Elizabethan and earlier periods. Her* Shakespeare and Elizabethan Poetry (1951) *is a comprehensive work relating Shakespeare's poetry to that of George Chapman, Christopher Marlowe, Edmund Spenser, and Philip Sydney, and describing the evolution of Shakespeare's verse. In the excerpt below, Bradbrook contends that* The Rape of Lucrece *represents Shakespeare's earliest expression of his conception of tragedy. In this poem, the critic argues, Shakespeare is trying to convey "the blind senseless horror of purely physical outrage, which constituted for the moment his idea of tragedy." Bradbrook notes that as a precursor of later Shakespearean tragic figures, Tarquin resembles Macbeth. In addition, Shakespeare's use of language and imagery derives from the medieval tradition of "moral heraldry," according to Bradbrook, in which characters are emblematic of various vices and virtues. In tandem, the shock of evil's violation of virtue and the descriptive use of moral heraldry "allowed Shakespeare to leave a blank at the centre of the picture." On another issue, Bradbrook claims that Shakespeare sought in* Lucrece *to emulate the "high style" of accepted models from classical and contemporary sources, in particular the late medieval nondramatic complaint.*]

Titus Andronicus and *The Rape of Lucrece,* Shakespeare's two 'tragical discourses' were in their time extremely well thought on. We have Ben Jonson's word that the public enjoyed *Titus,* and Gabriel Harvey's that the judicious read *Lucrece* [see excerpt above, 1598]. They are now among the least studied of his work, and *Titus* has often been rejected from the canon, though its many echoes of *The Rape of Lucrece* should alone be enough to retain it.

In these two works, where Shakespeare was trying his hand in the high style, he models from accepted designs. Early Elizabethan tragedy was closely connected with the nondramatic Complaint: *Lucrece* is comparable with Daniel's *Rosamund's Complaint,* and *Titus* is largely a dramatic lament. The Complaint was a late medieval form: in *The Mirror for Magistrates,* the medieval tradition was transmitted to the Elizabethans. The Vergilian journey to the underworld, the allegorical figures and wailing ghosts, the imagery of hell and judgment and the demonstration of the turn of Fortune's wheel as Chaucer described it:

> Tragedy is to seyn a certeyn storie . . .
> Of hym that stood in greet prosperitee
> And is yfallen out of high degree
> Into myserie and endeth wrecchedly—

are all transferred to the stage in the early revenge play, the other parent-stock from which *Titus Andronicus* derives. Kyd's *Spanish Tragedy* provided the dramatic model: Ovid's *Metamorphoses,* part of the story, which is based on the Rape of Philomel. Shakespeare was drawing on as many good authorities as he could: but the Senecan influence is now generally disallowed.

There is an emblematic or heraldic quality about all the characters of *Titus Andronicus.* (pp. 104-05)

The Rape of Lucrece is even more heraldic than *Titus Andronicus.* The combat between Lucrece and Tarquin, saint and devil (as they are called) is introduced by a passage in which the heraldry of Lucrece's face is set forth in a manner derived from the thirteenth sonnet of *Astrophel and Stella* [by Sir Philip Sidney], where Cupid wins the contest of arms from Jove and Mars:

> . . . on his crest there lies
> Stella's faire haire, her face he makes his shield,
> Where roses gules are borne in silver field.

In Lucrece's face there is a contest between the red and white of beauty and virtue:

> But Beautie in that white entituled,
> From Venus doves doth challenge that faire field,
> Then Vertue claimes from Beautie, Beauties red,
> Which Vertue gave the golden age, to guild
> Their silver cheekes, and calld it then their shield:
> Teaching them thus to use it in the fight,
> When shame assaild, the red should fence the white.
>
> [ll. 57-63]

Tarquin, caught between these two armies, yields himself as many a Petrarchan lover had done. He sees clearly the result of his action: 'O shame to knighthood and to shining Armes' [l. 197]. The heralds will contrive some mark of abatement for his coat, but

Affection is my Captaine and he leadeth
And when his gaudie banner is displaide,
The coward fights, and will not be dismaide.

[ll. 271-73]

The long account of Tarquin's assault goes into minute detail of his 'drumming heart', his 'Burning eye', Lucrece's 'ranks of blew vains' which run pale when his hand like a 'Rude Ram' batters the 'Ivorie wall' of the 'sweet Citty' [ll. 435, 440, 464, 469]. Later his soul is compared with a 'sacked temple' and her body at the end to a 'late-sacked island' [ll. 1172, 1740]. Her shame is an abatement on Collatine's arms.

O unfelt sore, crest-wounding, private scare!
Reproch is stampt in Collatinus' face,
And Tarquin's eye maie read the mot a farre.

[ll. 828-30]

All this imagery is centred in the great lament of Lucrece before the tapestry depicting the Sack of Troy, in which she sees an emblem of her own state. In the figure of Hecuba she sees a mirror image of her grief and in the deceitful Sinon a mirror of Tarquin. The whole passage—it begins by describing the 'life' of the piece which seemed to 'scorn nature'—embodies the violence of war, and confirms the theme implicit in the metaphors describing Tarquin and Lucrece. The lament of the bereaved, the dignity of the commanders, the terror of cowards, are all depicted in little, and what is not depicted is implied by 'conceit deceitful, so compact, so kind' that a part was left to represent the whole which was 'left unseen, save to the eye of mind' [ll. 1423, 1426]. This insistence upon natural representation, within an artificial tapestry, set as an illustration to an artificially-devised poem has a strange recessional effect, comparable in some ways to the play-within-the-play.

The main body of the poem consists of the speeches of Tarquin and of Lucrece: his debate with himself, the debate between them both, the lament, testament and final speech of Lucrece. More than a third of the whole poem consists of her complaints, in which she 'rails' at Time, Night and Opportunity, the authors of her woe. Tarquin's debate with himself is more dramatic, since there is a conflict in his mind between conscience and will. As *Titus* in a simplified and distorted form presents some of the elements of *King Lear,* so the soliloquies of Tarquin are like a first cartoon for the study of *Macbeth.* Here, too, there is an expense of spirit in a waste of shame, a figure of conscious guilt calling in night and the creatures of night for aid, an act of physical violence followed by as quick a repentance. Tarquin, like Macbeth, tries to pray in the very act of committing the act and is startled to find he cannot do it. The atmosphere of Rome is that of Inverness:

Now stole uppon the time the dead of night,
When heavie sleep had closd up mortall eyes,
No comfortable starre did lend his light,
No noise but Owles and wolves' death-boding cries
Now serves the season that they may surprise
The sillie Lambes, pure thoughts are dead and still,
While Lust and Murder wakes to staine and kill.

[ll. 162-68]

Now o'er the one half world
Nature seems dead and wicked dreams abuse
The curtain'd sleep: Witchcraft celebrates
Pale Hecate's offerings; and withered Murther,
Alarum'd by his sentinel, the Wolf,
Whose howl's his watch thus with his stealthy pace,

With Tarquin's ravishing strides, towards his designs
Moves like a ghost.

[*Macbeth,* II. i. 49-56]

This figure of 'a creeping creature with a flaming light' [l. 1627] remained with Shakespeare as late as *Cymbeline* where Iachimo, stealing towards the sleeping Imogen, says

Our Tarquin thus
Did softly press the rushes ere he wakened
The chastity he wounded.

[II. ii. 12-14]

Imogen had been reading the tale of Tereus: Lucrece compares herself, as Lavinia [in *Titus Andronicus*] had so often done, to Philomel, and the Ovidian story was evidently at the back of Shakespeare's mind on all three occasions. It may indeed have inspired the expository use of the tapestry of Troy.

Unlike Macbeth, however, Tarquin knows the emptiness of his satisfaction before he ventures on his act of violence, whereas Macbeth does not fully understand it till afterwards. Tarquin's debate with himself is carried out with a clear sense of the issues; too clear to be dramatically plausible. His comments none the less would apply exactly to the later story.

Those that much covet are with gaine so fond,
That what they have not, that which they possesse
They scatter and unloose it from their bond,
And so by hoping more, they have but lesse. . . .
So that in ventring ill, we leave to be
The things we are, for that which we expect:
And this ambitious foule infirmitie,
In having much torments us with defect
Of that we have: so then we doe neglect
The thing we have, and all for want of wit,
Make something nothing, by augmenting it.

[ll. 134-37, 148-55]

Sententious and explicit posing of the moral question is continued in the laments of Lucrece, in which she indicts the agents of her wrongs: first the allegorical 'Causes' and then the criminal person. Her formal and highly patterned apostrophes are the most artificial part of the poem. 'The well-tuned warble of her nightly sorrow' [l. 1080] is copied in [Thomas Middleton's] *Ghost of Lucrece,* a pure Complaint:

O comfort-killing night, image of Hell,
Dim register, and notarie of shame,
Blacke stage for tragedies and murthers fell,
Vast sin-concealing Chaos, nourse of blame,
Blinde muffled bawd, dark harber for defame
Grim cave of death, whispring conspirator,
With close-tongd treason and the ravisher:

This recalls at once the laments over Juliet, and the absurd Pyramus:

O grim-lookt night, O night with hue so blacke,
O night, which ever art when day is not:
O night, O night, alacke, alacke, alacke,
I fear my Thisby's promise is forgot.

[*A Midsummer Night's Dream,* V. i. 170-74]

but even such parody cannot be taken as guarantee that by the time he wrote it, Shakespeare had rejected the style of *Lucrece.* Her long apostrophe to Time looks forward to the soliloquy of Richard II in his prison cell: the mental confusion and bewilderment which in the midst of all their speeches can strike the characters dumb prefigure those more dramatic moments when Romeo and Juliet see their hope destroyed.

> Well, thou hast comforted me marvailous much.
>   [III. v. 230]

> Is it even so? then I defie you, starres.
>   [V. i. 24]

On the other hand *Romeo and Juliet* is not without those set pictures or icons of the older fashion, such as the description of Lucrece as she lies in her bed, or the description of how she and her maid weep together:

> A prettie while these prettie creatures stand,
> Like Ivorie conduites corall cisterns filling.
>   [ll. 1233-34]

These deliberate similes help to give Lucrece her emblematic character of Chastity personified. The Elizabethans saw her as a kind of pagan saint: in [John Fletcher's] *Bonduca* the Queen speaks scornfully to the Romans of 'your great saint Lucrece':

> Tarquin tupped her well,
> And mad she could not hold him, bled.

This blasphemy—for as such it is intended—is a measure of Lucrece's significance. The particular crime was so shocking that it allowed Shakespeare to leave a blank at the centre of the picture. In this poem and *Titus Andronicus* he seems to be trying to indicate the blind senseless horror of purely physical outrage, which constituted for the moment his idea of tragedy. Some atrocity that stuns its victim falls upon Lavinia, Titus, Lucrece, and also on the victims of Richard III. They come up against a stone. Titus kneels and pleads with the stones, Lucrece pleads with the 'remorseless' Tarquin, in *Romeo and Juliet* the lovers are literally brought up against a stone wall: that of the orchard, and that of the grave. Tragedy is something that slaps you in the face: it is tragedy in the newspaper sense. Lucrece

>   the picture of pure pietie,
> Like a white Hinde under the grypes sharpe clawes,
> Pleades in a wildernesse where are no lawes.
>   [ll. 542-44]

Violence inexplicable and shattering overwhelms her.

The Rape of Lucrece is an ambitious poem. It is more than a third as long again as *Venus and Adonis,* and while *Venus and Adonis* was put out in an unimpressive little quarto, *The Rape of Lucrece* is a handsome and much more costly piece of book-production. It has altogether the air of being more studied and deliberate: yet in the very centre of the poem there is a link with the most personal of the sonnets. The description of Tarquin's revulsion after his crime [ll. 693-714] is an expansion of Sonnet CXXIX. The self-knowledge which Tarquin had is also present there:

> All this the world well knows: yet none knows well
> To shun the heaven that leads men to this hell.
>   (pp. 110-16)

> *M. C. Bradbrook, "Moral Heraldry," in her* Shakespeare and Elizabethan Poetry: A Study of His Earlier Work in Relation to the Poetry of the Time, *Chatto and Windus, 1951, pp. 104-22.*

Tarquin and Lucrece. Frontispiece to the Rowe edition of The Rape of Lucrece *(1714).*

SAM HYNES   (essay date 1959)

[*Hynes asserts that Tarquin's internal siege, the rape of his soul, is ultimately the moral focus of* Lucrece *and the element which aligns the poem with the "Christian tragedies,"* Othello *and* Macbeth. *Rejecting the notion that Lucrece's view of the world as a "wilderness where are no laws" (l. 544) constitutes the moral vision of the poem, Hynes argues that there is an implicit moral order in the judgment of Tarquin and his self-destruction. Further, as a precursor of Desdemona and Cordelia, the pure Lucrece symbolizes Tarquin's "spiritual quality" or latent moral goodness, which succumbs to his evil or violent nature. In Hynes's estimation, the weakness of* Lucrece *is the early departure of Tarquin: the poem's most interesting character and an early model for subsequent Shakespearean tragic figures.*]

Most readers of *The Rape of Lucrece* would probably agree that the principal structural element in the poem is the emblematic imagery centered in the tapestry of the fall of Troy. Not only does the description of this tapestry occupy some 200 lines of an 1800-line poem; it also provides the dominant trope by which the rape itself is described, and thus lends the emotional weight of the classic betrayal to the action of the poem. The siege-rape analogy is drawn again and again, most overtly by Lucrece when she says:

. . . as Priam him [Sinon] did cherish,
So did I Tarquin; so my Troy did perish.
                              [ll. 1546-47]

Elsewhere Lucrece is the city, her breasts the walls, her blood
the defending troops, while Tarquin is the besieging army, his
hand the battering ram, his tongue a trumpet, and so on in
a detailed emblematic figure.

The analogy is ingeniously and extensively developed; too
much so, perhaps, for it has not generally pleased Shakespeare's critics. Douglas Bush complains of the "incessant
conceits" of the poem [see excerpt above, 1932], and George
Rylands observes: "The metaphors are pursued laboriously
and at length in a way which is very characteristic of Shakespeare's early manner . . . the metaphorical idea of an army
setting siege to a city . . . is elaborated over eight
stanzas . . . [see excerpt above, 1928]. The implication is that
such elaboration is unnecessary, tiresome, and redundant.

In fact, this is not the case. The metaphor, in all its elaborate-
ness, is a careful preparation for the one place in the poem
where it does not work as one would expect it to. This passage, describing Tarquin, occurs just after the rape scene.

> So fares it with this faultful lord of Rome,
> Who this accomplishment so hotly chas'd;
> For now against himself he sounds this doom,
> That through the length of times he stands dis-
>   grac'd;
> Besides, his soul's fair temple is defac'd;
>   To whose weak ruins muster troops of cares,
>   To ask the spotted princess how she fares.
>
> She says, her subjects with foul insurrection
> Have batter'd down her consecrated wall,
> And by their mortal fault brought in subjection
> Her immortality, and made her thrall
> To living death and pain perpetual:
>   Which in her prescience she controlled still,
>   But her foresight could not forestall their will.
>   [ll. 715-28]

Here expectation is reversed, the besieger becomes the besieged. Such a reversal is, to be sure, typical of the conceited
style of the poem. In this case, however, the reversal is with
a difference, and that difference constitutes the moral core of
the poem. Lucrece was assaulted, in the siege metaphor, by
an external enemy, a "foul usurper"; the attack on Tarquin's
soul comes from within. Tarquin's state of man, like Brutus'
[in *Julius Caesar*], suffers the nature of an insurrection; the
attackers are his own passions. Earlier, in the rape scene,
those passions had been mutinous, "obdurate vassals"; now
the mutiny is accomplished, the consecrated walls of Grace
lie in ruins, and Tarquin faces the consequences.

Those consequences are of two kinds, one mortal, the other
immortal. In the first stanza above Tarquin condemns himself to disgrace "through the length of times", that is
throughout history. This is the doom of Cressida and Pandarus [in *Troilus and Cressida*], and an idea common to the
Roman plays; man, by his actions, determines his "fame".
But the second stanza is very un-Roman; in it the soul, the
"spotted princess", accepts her eternal damnation. This is the
doom of Macbeth and Othello, an idea out of the Christian
tragedies.

A further resemblance to the Christian tragedies stems from
the way in which Tarquin's soul becomes identified, in this

passage, with Lucrece. This identification is most apparent in
the transference of imagery heretofore characteristically Lucrece's to Tarquin; but it is strengthened and extended by the
"plot line" of the passage quoted, which closely parallels Lucrece's actions later in the poem: the spotted princess is asked
how she fares, as Lucrece's maid asks to know Lucrece's
heaviness, and Collatine wishes, but "hath no power to ask
her how she fares" [l. 1594]. She replies with a metaphorical
account of her ravishment, and accepts her stain as absolute
and eternal, while yet asserting her inability to forestall it.
Thus Lucrece becomes a symbol of the spiritual quality in
Tarquin which his deed violates. This use of the pure woman
as a symbol of a protagonist's ultimate moral possibilities is
characteristic of the Christian tragedies, and is absent from
the Roman plays with which one might expect to place *Lucrece*. Lucrece, in her relation to Tarquin, belongs with Desdemona [in *Othello*] and Cordelia [in *King Lear*] rather than
with Roman matrons like Virgilia [in *Coriolanus*] and Brutus'
Portia.

The stanzas I have quoted occur at the moment of Tarquin's
withdrawal from the poem. He bears away with him "the
burden of a guilty mind" [l. 735], and we should not be distracted by Lucrece's subsequent apostrophizing from recognizing the importance of his state. For in Tarquin (and particularly through these two stanzas) Shakespeare has created a
prototype of his later tragic moralities, particularly *Macbeth*
(this parallel has often been remarked though, as M. C. Bradbrook points out [see excerpt above, 1951], more often by *Lucrece* editors than by *Macbeth* editors). Tarquin's conflict is
internal—"Desire doth fight with Grace" [l. 712]. He chooses
wrongly, against his own moral sense, and it is this free choice
which damns him, and which makes the poem more than a
windy statement of chastity outraged. The significant rape is
the rape of Tarquin's soul, and in this sense the poem is closer
to the mature tragedies than either *Titus* or *Romeo and Juliet*
is.

It is an obvious weakness of the poem from this point of view
that the subsequent suffering of Tarquin is ignored, that he
leaves the action just at the point where he begins to interest
us—it is as if we saw the last of Macbeth at his Act II exit.
Nevertheless, the sack of Tarquin's soul offers a strong contradiction to Miss Bradbrook's argument that the moral vision of the poem is summed up in Lucrece's "wilderness
where are no laws" [l. 544] speech. Perhaps the morality is
inconsistent, or incompletely worked out, and perhaps for
this reason (among others) the poem is not completely successful. But the judgment of Tarquin implies a moral order,
though Lucrece cannot see it. And in this judgment we may
see Shakespeare's moral sense already powerfully at work.
(pp. 451-53)

Sam Hynes, "The Rape of Tarquin," in Shakespeare Quarterly, *Vol. X, No. 3, Summer, 1959, pp.
451-53.*

F. T. PRINCE (essay date 1960)

[Prince argues that ultimately The Rape of Lucrece *is a failure, not because Shakespeare lacks a gift for language, but because the vivid descriptions and poetic digressions, while independently remarkable, do not cohere, but rather detract from
the tragic subject. The dramatization of Lucrece's grief, her
self-expression and her "remorseless eloquence," undermine
Shakespeare's sympathetic portrayal, whereas those moments
in which she reveals her despair in silence or gestures are most*

poignant. Despite the artistic "miscalculation," the poem is still worthy of interest, according to Prince, because it expresses Shakespeare's youthful conception of tragedy: his fascination with morbidity and "physical and moral violence." The struggle between "vile evil and ideal virtue" strikes the critic as sensational and vulgar; however, it reflects the poet's "divided consciousness" which allows him to identify with the lustful Tarquin as well as the virtuous Lucrece.]

'In Shakespeare's *poems,*' wrote Coleridge [in his *Biographia Literaria*], 'the creative power and the intellectual energy wrestle as in a war embrace. Each in its excess of strength seems to threaten the extinction of the other. At length in the DRAMA they were reconciled, and fought each with its shield before the breast of the other.' Fervid imagery increases the real difficulty offered by Coleridge's thought; yet his criticism of *Venus and Adonis* and *Lucrece* nevertheless first provided the point of view from which it is most profitable to examine these poems. His appreciation of *Venus and Adonis* shows indeed that he fully felt its intrinsic beauty; but he was wise to make his criticism serve the larger purpose of illuminating Shakespeare the dramatist. Nothing else was likely then, or is likely even now, to win an attentive reading of these poems. For one thing, their eroticism is hardly more acceptable than it was in Coleridge's day; few English or American readers nowadays will respond to such happily wanton fancies as *Venus and Adonis.* The guilty and tormented passions of *Lucrece* are perhaps more to the taste of our time; but the poem is in itself much less readable than its predecessor. Moreover, both poems must compete with a body of dramatic work which is immensely superior in poetic achievement, and which offers endless opportunities, or temptations, for research and speculation.

The two narrative poems have nevertheless a unique distinction: they were the only works Shakespeare published in which he claims the status of a professional poet. The poems are given signed dedications to a noble patron, and presented with as much care as Spenser gave to his books. It is ironical that these works, so put forward by their young author, should be among those of his productions which have been least valued by posterity. But their later fortunes cannot detract from their value as evidence: evidence both of Shakespeare's ambition (no doubt transient) to be taken for a 'real' poet, and of the powers he could in fact bring to non-dramatic poetry. (pp. xxiv-xxv)

Despite the presentation of *Venus and Adonis* and *Lucrece* as the works of a conscious artist, Shakespeare probably sat down to write them in the hope that they would bring him some immediate practical reward. It has sometimes been suggested that *Venus* was written in the 1580's, perhaps before Shakespeare came to London. However, its appearance in 1593, and that of *Lucrece* in the following year, coincided with a difficult period for the London theatres: they were closed in August 1592, when the plague broke out with violence, and remained closed throughout 1593. Shakespeare's own description of the poem as the 'first heir' of his 'invention' offers an apparent difficulty, since he had already begun to make his name as a playwright; but Lord Southampton would not have been flattered, and might even have been annoyed, by a reference to the vulgar dramatic successes of the young writer: such works were not considered to fall into the category of literature. If *Venus,* and *Lucrece* a year later, are taken to be a result of the enforced idleness of the London players in 1592-3, their motives being to compensate in part for the disastrous financial losses of that time, we have an ex-

planation both of why the rising young dramatist turned to 'narrative' verse, and of why he chose first such a subject as that of *Venus and Adonis.*

The theme was wanton, and was to be made witty. That Shakespeare gauged the taste of his readers as successfully as he had been gauging that of his audiences is proved by the many editions of the poem in his own time and by frequent allusions to its somewhat disreputable popularity. But wantonness and wit were to be found elsewhere. The finer interest of the poem lies in its demonstration that for Shakespeare these are only manifestations of an intenser activity: they become the adjuncts of an almost intoxicating poetic vision. Verse and language, though of wonderful beauty, may be compared to their disadvantage with Marlowe's style in *Hero and Leander,* and with Shakespeare's own unequalled later achievements; but no other Elizabethan, not even Spenser, had yet shown such a gift for poetic eloquence. In its general quality, above all in its capacity for both opulent delicacy and fresh, blunt, colloquial statement, the language of the poem is characteristically Elizabethan; but the range may be seen very clearly here because here it corresponds to Shakespeare's rejuvenation of his theme, the sensual mythological tale of the youth and the goddess being suffused with the familiar freshness of English landscape, and the savour and the harshness of country sports. (pp. xxvi-xxvii)

All that has been said of Shakespeare's gift for language as it appears in *Venus and Adonis* is confirmed by the style of *Lucrece.* Here are many passages which are quite different in mood and content, yet which in richness and power of expression equal or surpass anything in the previous poem. The best sustained passages of this kind are Lucrece's long tirade against Opportunity and Time [ll. 876-994], and the description of the pictures of the siege and fall of Troy [ll. 1366-1561]. Everywhere there stand out ingenious fancies, dexterous thoughts and phrases, vividly felt emotions and actions and images; and an unfailing rhythmic power throbs through the verse. Yet it is only too obvious that the poem, as a whole, is a failure. Shakespeare's skill of expression is self-defeating. 'From end to end of the poem,' says [Emile] Legouis, 'the reader is exasperated by the poet's very talent, his fancy and eloquence' [in his *History of English Literature,* 1924]. To account for this failure, rather than to linger over the more obvious beauties of the poem, would seem to be the most rewarding task offered by *Lucrece* to the literary critic.

It is generally accepted that *Lucrece* is the 'graver labour' which Shakespeare promised Southampton when he dedicated *Venus and Adonis* to him. The kinship between the two poems is as plain as the contrast. *Venus and Adonis* treats sexual desire in the spirit of romantic comedy; *Lucrece* does so in the spirit of tragedy. *Venus and Adonis* had no serious moral purpose—rather did it delight in its release from such restraints; *Lucrece* is therefore to have a positively obsessive moral purpose, to present an example of 'lust in action' and enforce a terrible lesson.

Lucrece, narrative in form, is in substance a tragedy. And the comparison with its serio-comic predecessor bears out what Dr Johnson says [in his *Preface to Shakespeare,* 1765], concerning Shakespeare's aptitude for these two modes of writing: 'His disposition, as *Rhymer* has remarked, led him to comedy. In tragedy he often writes with great appearance of toil and study, what is written at last with little felicity; but in his comick scenes, he seems to produce without labour, what no labour can improve. In tragedy he is always struggling after some occasion to be comick, but in comedy he seems to repose, or to luxuriate, as in a mode of thinking congenial to his nature. In his tragick scenes there is always something wanting, but his comedy often surpasses expectation or desire. His comedy pleases by the thoughts and the language, and his tragedy for the greater part by incident and action. His tragedy seems to be skill, his comedy to be instinct.'

Johnson shrank from Shakespearian tragedy even at its most magnificent, and we cannot acquiesce in his view of the great tragedies; but what he says of the poet's natural bent carries conviction. It is a critical summary which easily sweeps *Lucrece* into its scope, pointing to its faults, and enabling us to look at them in the light of the poet's other achievements. For if *Lucrece* is a tragedy, it is of course a tragedy by the author of *Titus Andronicus,* and not by the author of *Lear* or *Othello.* We think of the failure of the poem most readily in terms of its treatment, for its excesses of rhetoric are glaringly obvious. But the true weakness lies in the subject, as it does in *Titus Andronicus:* there is 'an original sin' in it, as Hazlitt said of *Measure for Measure,* and this reveals itself ever more disastrously as the poem proceeds.

In spite of its length and over-elaboration, its apparent excess, there is indeed 'something wanting' in *Lucrece.* We remember from it images such as the 'pale swan in her watery nest' [l. 1611], or Collatine's suppressed grief compared to the tide rushing through the arch of a bridge. Various living pictures are imprinted on our minds: Tarquin creeping through the dark house; Lucrece weeping with her maid or blushing in the presence of her groom; her reddened eyes surrounded by 'blue circles'; and the 'watery rigol' which separates itself from her 'black blood'. Typical of such nightmarish impressions is the image of Tarquin's hot hand, 'smoking with pride' [l. 438], placed upon his victim's naked breast:

> Whose ranks of blue veins, as his hand did scale,
> Left their round turrets destitute and pale.
>
> [ll. 440-41]

But these and many other powerful effects are isolated from one another by long passages which may be coherent and magnificent in themselves, like the picture of the fall of Troy, or full of brilliant or tormented force, like Tarquin's deliberations before the crime or Lucrece's endless tirades after it; but which confuse the total impression. It is remarkable that, while the digressions in *Venus and Adonis* strengthen the whole, those in *Lucrece* consistently weaken it. In *Venus and Adonis* the episode of the lustful stallion, and the description of the hunted hare, bring movement and perspective, give a sense of air and freedom, add a strong fresh savour of natural appetites and physical energy; Shakespeare's 'instinct' for comedy never served him better. But in *Lucrece* all his 'skill' cannot achieve a corresponding balance, though the digression into the 'matter of Troy' comes nearer to it than anything else in the poem.

Success in a poem constructed with such wanton exuberance must always no doubt be a matter of 'touch and go'; but there are several possible reasons for Shakespeare's failure here. In the first place, the poem offers, in turn, two centres of interest. Until the crime is committed, Tarquin is the focus of our attention, and convinces us that he is a tragically complex character. After the deed, Lucrece becomes the tragic heroine; but we are never wholly convinced that she deserves the part, and the more we ponder the more clearly we can see why she does

not. Not only is she a less *interesting* character than Tarquin: she is forced to express herself in a way which dissipates the real pathos of her situation.

The tragedy of Lucrece is in fact unsuited to direct 'dramatic' presentation; it should be related in the true narrative manner of Ovid or Chaucer, not in the semi-dramatic, semi-rhetorical manner of Shakespeare's poem. If the story is treated at length, and above all if the heroine is given great powers of self-expression, her sufferings become sensational and not tragic. Her part is not wholly passive, since it ends in a heroic act of self-sacrifice. But this final positive action, which alone can give significance to her fate, should be presented with as few preliminaries as possible. It should come as a startling revelation of the final dimension of her character, the depth of her feeling, and the strength of her determination. The greatest weakness of Shakespeare's Lucrece is therefore her remorseless eloquence. In Ovid Lucrece does not even plead with Tarquin; but Shakespeare makes her start an argument which might have continued indefinitely, if the ravisher had not cut it short. After her violation, Lucrece loses our sympathy exactly in proportion as she gives tongue.

The most moving passages are those in which she is silent, or nearly so: the interviews with the maid and with the groom. Here we are shown her grief momentarily from without, or indirectly, checked by social circumstance. These scenes are, like much in *Venus and Adonis,* a true equivalent in narrative form of Shakespeare's dramatic vision, a fusion of dialogue, action, and description. Lucrece's lengthy self-expression in other passages is *apparently* dramatic, but the conditions of the stage would soon have revealed its absurdity.

When we look at the poem in this way we may be inclined to think that Shakespeare had a clear vision neither of his subject nor of the treatment which would have fitted it. We may further doubt whether *any* tragic theme could have been treated successfully in the fashion of these 'narrative' poems; and the end of all our analysis may be that the whole thing was simply an artistic miscalculation, a misuse of remarkable, yet immature, talents.

Yet there is another way of looking at *Lucrece,* and measuring its value to our interpretation of Shakespeare. Does the poem not convey after all, fully and unmistakably, the poet's vision of his subject? From this point of view the artistic effect may be the same, but the critical interest is much enhanced. We may still be irritated by the poem's faults of taste and wearied by its length and emphasis; but if we look upon it all as Shakespeare's projection of his own immature spirit, it has much to tell us. This is a young man's idea of tragedy, and the imagination of the young man in question is a curious blend of health and morbidity, a bundle of self-contradictory impulses. The youthful idea of tragedy reveals itself in the physical and moral violence of the theme: the contrast between vile evil and ideal virtue, the presentation of a sexual crime, accompanied by physical force and cruelty, and resulting in the bloody death of the victim. The subject is less nightmarish than *Titus Andronicus* only because its horrors are less elaborately redoubled and drawn out, and because drama is necessarily more violent in effect than narrative. In both works there is the fascinated contemplation of lust and bloodshed and violated virtue. This is indeed a conception of tragedy which is not only youthful, but vulgar; it is crude in its craving for sensation, and vulgar because the physical suffering is over-emphasized.

The subject sufficiently accounts for the painful, half-real and half-unreal, oppressiveness of the poem; since the poet's vision is itself nightmarish, he has perhaps found a true equivalent for it in the clotted fancies, the agonizingly insistent cleverness of the long 'metaphysical' tirades. There is madness in Shakespeare's method, but it is a madness appropriate to something which lurks in Tarquin's lust and Lucrece's wounded chastity. It is not enough to judge, with Dr Johnson, that the young poet is forcing himself to feel and write in a self-consciously tragic manner, and that we are made aware of the strain by his lapses and faults of judgement. We must go further, and see the whole imaginative process as a phase in Shakespeare's vision of reality, something that was later to be transformed into the vision of the great tragedies.

In *Venus and Adonis* and *Lucrece* Shakespeare both identifies himself with the various characters and remains detached from them. He identifies himself in imagination with both the uncontrollable physical desire of Venus and the coldness of Adonis, both with her persuasions to love and with his condemnation of lust. In *Lucrece* he is similarly divided between a sense of the irresistible force of Tarquin's desires and of the beauty of virtue in Lucrece. This double or divided consciousness is indeed the secret of poetic genius; but to have it in the intense degree in which Shakespeare had it is to come close, at times, to delirium or mental instability. Comedy was the easier, safer, form for Shakespeare, because he could there remain at a certain distance from reality, moving in a familiar range between laughter, wit, sensuality, and pathos. In tragedy he was compelled to come closer to the seamy side of things, and to try to grasp the full reality of human crimes and passions. The instability latent in his genius then led him into strange aberrations: *Titus Andronicus* and *Lucrece* are there to show what dangers lay in wait for this youthful imagination, more rashly responsive both to physical desire and physical horror than it would be a few years later.

The morbidity of *Lucrece,* however, is but an earlier manifestation of that tragic disgust and revulsion which appear in various forms in *Hamlet, Lear,* and *Timon,* and underlie so much of Shakespeare's later work. An amazing process of development lies between the early poem and the plays of even only a few years later; and yet there are constant elements in this poetic growth. The murk of *Macbeth* is not without its reminiscence of Tarquin stalking his prey, and in *Cymbeline* Iachimo's penetration of Imogen's bedchamber becomes almost a deliberate allusion to the early work. These are incidental and external parallels, but they indicate the deeper continuity of Shakespeare's sensibility, concerning which *Lucrece* has more to tell us than many more pleasing pieces of work. (pp. xxxiii-xxxviii)

F. T. Prince, in an introduction to The Poems *by William Shakespeare, edited by F. T. Prince, Methuen, 1960, pp. xi-xlvi.*

HAROLD R. WALLEY   (essay date 1961)

[*Walley asserts that* The Rape of Lucrece *represents a pivotal point in Shakespeare's development as a writer in that the poem "establish[es] the matrix of the later great tragedies." The poem encompasses both Shakespeare's conception of tragedy and "a rationale for tragedy," he declares. Although the technique of* Lucrece *is primarily "analytic and discursive," rather than intentionally theatrical, Shakespeare reveals a tendency, according to Walley, to "approach his materials in terms of dramatic problems"; in this sense, the poem affords the first*

glimpse of Shakespeare's dramatic method in operation. Despite the presence of dramatic elements, the critic maintains, Lucrece *is an "analysis of tragedy" devoted to a systematic "exposition of ideas" in which narrative and drama are purposely subdued.*]

Since its initial vogue during the lifetime of Shakespeare *The Rape of Lucrece* has received short shrift from the general public and little more attention from critics and scholars. This relative neglect has done much to obscure the actual importance of the poem; for, quite apart from its intrinsic merits as poetry, *The Rape of Lucrece* constitutes one of the most explicit and illuminating documents which bear upon Shakespeare's development, and especially upon his coming of age as an artist. Written almost certainly during the year immediately preceding its registration on 9 May 1594, and hence in the interval between Shakespeare's apprentice experiments in the theater and his mature dramatic achievements with the Lord Chamberlain's Men, the poem provides unique information about Shakespeare at a crucial point in his career. Frankly advertised, moreover, as a serious poem on a serious theme, it bears every evidence of having been undertaken by its author as a premeditated and highly self-conscious bid for recognition as a serious literary artist. Indeed, in the deliberate thoughtfulness of its conception and the conscientious care of its execution *The Rape of Lucrece* is one of the most laborious and studied works of art that Shakespeare ever produced. And as such, it affords a revealing index to the kind of thinking imposed on its creator at the time, and by the process, of its creation.

Although ostensibly a narrative poem, *Lucrece* exhibits close affiliations with Shakespeare's dramatic work. At every turn both its technique and its predominant concerns betray the hand of a poet whose preoccupations are basically those of a dramatist. Its methods of presentation abound in passages of dialogue and debate, in analytical soliloquies, in symbolic acts and incidents, and in descriptions of action conceived dramatically. More significantly, the poem conceives of its narrative in terms of a sequence of situations to be exploited for their dramatic qualities, and describes actions which are visualized as scenes to be staged, with a vivid awareness of their theatrical values, and which are designed to create their artistic effect by the same direct means as stage business in the theater. Yet, in spite of these dramatic features, the final effect of the poem is actually no more dramatic than it is properly narrative. Its focus is not on the overt conflict of dramatic action, but on the human context of conflict and on an exploration of the conditions, causes, and connotations of action. In fact, the actual incidents of the story occupy less than a third of the total poem. The bulk of its attention is concentrated, not on the drama itself, but rather on the deliberation which precedes and lies back on drama. The truth is that, essentially, *Lucrece* is analytic and discursive. What its treatment reflects is not so much a dramatic intention on the part of the poet as the thinking of a poet who approaches his materials in terms of dramatic problems.

The artistic scheme of *Lucrece* is designed to bring home to men's business and bosoms the broad significance of certain historical events. To this end, the historical facts in the case are set forth in a preliminary Argument, and the purpose of the poem itself is to make clear their general human purport. Now, substantially, this correlation between poem and argument forms a paradigm of Shakespeare's regular dramatic procedure. Although the process is fundamental to all his dramatic work, the most obvious parallel with *Lucrece* oc-

84

curs in his history plays, where the artistic purpose is a similar transformation of given historical facts into significant human realities. In the plays, of course, one encounters only the end result of this interpretative process, the explicit manifestation of an implicit rationale. What is unique about the discursive *Lucrece* is its presentation of the rationale itself, the explicated pattern of thought which validates the dramatic representation. In this respect it records Shakespeare's first overt endeavor to work out systematically the implications of what became his characteristic dramatic method.

Besides being historical, however, the situation with which *Lucrece* deals is also tragic; and any attempt to provide a satisfactory rationale of the tragic necessarily presupposes some coherent philosophy of its nature and human purport. In its frank recognition of this fact, and in its conscientious endeavor to come to terms with this larger question, *Lucrece* lays the foundation for Shakespeare's whole subsequent treatment of tragedy. That, in dealing with *Lucrece,* Shakespeare was consciously working toward a permanent organization of his thinking about tragedy is indicated by the many anticipations of later dramatic work with which the poem fairly bristles. By the same token, the constant echoes of *Lucrece* in the later tragedies suggest the basic importance which he attached to its pattern of thought. For these anticipations and echoes are a matter not so much of simple parallels in phraseology or recurring images as of persisting interests, ideas, and turns of thought.

A few of the more superficial instances will serve to illustrate the extent and variety of these correspondences. For example, the picture in *Lucrece* of Hecuba as an embodiment of sorrowing devotion,

> Staring on Priams wounds with her old eyes,
> Which bleeding under Pirrhvs proud foot lies,
>
> [ll. 1448-49]

supplies the theme for the player's declamation in *Hamlet* [II. ii. 474 f]. The lament of Lucrece, "Priam why art thou old, and yet not wise?" [l. 1550] portends the tragic irony of *Lear,* a play which is again suggested by her comments on the bitter disillusionment of a father destined to see his heirs abuse their heritage [ll. 855-68], and on the divergent attitudes adopted by men toward the same faults in others and in themselves [ll. 631-37]. Lucrece's appeal for mercy in the mighty [ll. 583-95] reappears in the more familiar pleas of Portia in *The Merchant of Venice* [IV. i. 184-205] and Isabella in *Measure for Measure* [II. ii. 72 ff]. Her despairing cry,

> And that deepe torture may be cal'd a Hell,
> When more is felt than one hath power to tell,
>
> [ll. 1287-88]

finds an echo in Hamlet's "But break, my heart; for I must hold my tongue" [I. ii. 159]. And even such a passing trifle as the comment on her maid's "soft slow-tongue, true marke of modestie" [ll. 1220] is repeated in Lear's recollection of Cordelia:

> Her voice was ever soft,
> Gentle, and low, an excellent thing in woman.
>
> [V. iii. 273-74]

On the problem of evil the correspondences are especially striking. The poem's stress on the deceptive appearance of evil, "Whose inward ill no outward harme exprest" [l. 91]; is a basic premise of Shakespeare's plays explicitly stated in Antonio's "O, what a goodly outside falsehood hath" (*Merchant of Venice,* I. iii. 102); its portrayal of Tarquin's disarming hypocrisy [ll. 106-19] forms a preliminary sketch for Iago [in *Othello*]; and its epitomizing of evil in the cynical guile of Sinon [ll. 1513-19] prepares not only for the unctuous treachery of Iago and Edmund [in *King Lear*], but for Hamlet's discovery that "one may smile, and smile, and be a villain" [I. v. 108]. The observation that great good can be nullified by one small defect [ll. 197-210] becomes a central idea of Shakespeare's tragedy, which is pointed up by Hamlet's speech on "the dram of eale" [I. iv. 23-38]. The shame of martial valor enslaved by "soft fancies" [ll. 200-03] provides a major theme for *Antony and Cleopatra.* The confusion of Tarquin's grotesque prayer for divine aid in iniquity, together with his recognition of its incongruity [ll. 342-50], is repeated by Claudius in *Hamlet* [III. iii. 36-72, 97-98]. The contrasting argument in behalf of personal integrity, with its corollary, "Then where is truth if there be no selfe-trust?" [ll. 148-58, 596-644] has double issue in Polonius' "This above all: to thine own self be true" [I. iii. 78], and in the disrupting effect of Hamlet's own loss of self-confidence. And the corresponding emphasis on the importance of maintaining an honored name [ll. 204-10] is echoed in both Iago's "Who steals my purse steals trash" [*Othello,* III. iii. 155-61] and Hamlet's

> O God! Horatio, what a wounded name,
> Things standing thus unknown, shall live behind
> me!
>
> [V. ii. 344-45]

Much more important, however, than such incidental resemblances, which are more impressive in their bulk than in their individual significance, is the preoccupation of the poem with concerns of a more fundamental bearing on Shakespeare's tragedy. For the first time in his known career, *Lucrece* explicitly poses the essential problems of tragedy as Shakespeare conceived of it, reveals his thinking about them, and works out the conclusions concerning their purport to which he adhered from then on. In considerable detail it examines the nature of tragedy as a fact of human experience and identifies the distinctive features of what becomes Shakespeare's characteristic tragic situation. It analyzes the psychological factors which account for both susceptibility to tragedy and the immedicable suffering produced. Turning to the moral issues necessarily involved, it explores the nature, operation, and effects of evil, and the quality of a human existence which makes possible such occurrences. Finally, it arrives at an attitude toward experiences of this sort which permeates the whole pattern of Shakespeare's mature tragic philosophy. In effect, the poem affords a unique entry into the workshop of Shakespeare's dramatic development; and the results of this intensive exercise in dramatic thinking not only differentiate such plays as *Richard II* and *Romeo and Juliet* from *Richard III* and *Titus Andronicus* but establish the matrix of the later great tragedies.

The structural organization of *Lucrece* is designed to give effect to this deliberate and systematic elucidation of tragedy. The poem is divided into three major sections, punctuated by the events of the story which give occasion for expository discussion, and arranged in the logical order of the tragic problems which they raise. The first of these sections, culminating in the act of rape, occupies some 693 lines, or a little more than a third of the poem. Its attention is concentrated on two fundamental problems with which any satisfactory exposition of tragedy is obliged to deal at the outset. The one is to clarify precisely what is involved in the commission of an act like that of Tarquin. The other is to explain, in the light of these considerations, how it comes about that such an act is ever committed.

The initial 161 lines of this section set the stage for Tarquin's crime. In doing so, they direct attention to certain inherent paradoxes of life, which lie at the root of tragedy and account for its ironic tincture. The constitution of life, they point out, is such that there is a wide discrepancy between appearance and reality, and there is no such thing as an unequivocal good. Between beauty and virtue there is no necessary alliance, only an uneasy tension; for beauty is quite as likely to incite lust as to inspire virtue. Both beauty and goodness invite envy and theft as much as they do admiration. Indeed, virtue itself incurs an even more serious liability; for innocence of mind and purity of spirit can by their very integrity leave their possessors defenseless against the unsuspected guile of evil. With corresponding inconsistency, the natural desire of man to promote his welfare and happiness neither insures an adequate understanding of what is requisite for their achievement nor precludes actions which militate against it. No more does the actual possession of riches, power, and honor guarantee any lasting satisfaction. The fact is that the more one possesses, the more one is inclined to dwell on what one lacks, with the ironic result that

> hauing much torments vs with defect
> Of that we haue: so then we doe neglect
> The thing we haue, and all for want of wit,
> Make something nothing, by augmenting it.
>
> [ll. 151-54]

The effect of this paradoxical situation is a perverse tendency in human life to confuse ends and means, to sacrifice the ultimate to the immediate, to subordinate the greater to the less, and to risk existing good for phantom prospects.

Against this general background of life the remaining 532 lines take up the specific issues inherent in Tarquin's act. Although in large measure couched in the form of a soliloquy by Tarquin with commentary by the author, and of a subsequent dialogue between Tarquin and Lucrece, their obvious purpose is not dramatic but expository. And since at this point in the poem the chief tragic problem is to account for the occurrence of evil, they quite properly concentrate their attention upon Tarquin as its immediate agent. Their point of departure is the self-defeating folly of his whole enterprise. What he proposes is an act so dangerous and rash that it can scarcely qualify as a calculated risk: its consequences are as virtually certain as they are potentially disastrous. Considered as a bargain, its cost is equally out of all proportion to the possible gain; for in order to obtain what at best can be no more than a momentary gratification, Tarquin is obliged to exchange not only all that combines to give him excellence as an individual, but everything which alone can give value to life itself. On every count, his evil impulse is completely irrational; it flies in the face of human intelligence and sets at defiance the very logic of nature.

The moral issue which it raises is first presented in purely personal terms. Tarquin has no illusions about the degrading nature of his "lothsome enterprise" [l. 184], an "impious act including all foule harmes" [l. 199]. It is a stain on knighthood, a blot on manly valor, a treason to honor and friendship, a dishonor to lineage, and an enduring shame to posterity [ll. 197-210, 232-38]. To make it worse, it has no extenuating excuse [ll. 225 ff.] Against these deterrents Tarquin can oppose only his naked desire. To clothe it with some semblance of

sanction, his sole recourse is, like that of Lady Macbeth decrying her husband's scruples, to impugn the validity of normal moral standards and to confuse the issue with sophistical arguments about courage and the power of beauty. "All Orators are dumbe when Beautie pleadeth" [l. 268], and

> Who feares a sentence or an old mans saw,
> Shall by a painted cloth be kept in awe.
>
> [ll. 244-45]

The result is a frank abandonment to the demands of appetite [ll. 491-504]—"Desire my Pilot is, Beautie my prise" [l. 279]—which forsakes reason and righteousness to let "Loue and Fortune be my Gods" [l. 351], reduces the whole issue to a bald question of success or failure [ll. 295 ff.], and ends in such moral confusion that Tarquin finds himself praying "the Heavens should countenance his sin" [l. 343].

The broader aspects of moral responsibility are considered in the following debate between Tarquin and Lucrece. On Tarquin's part, the approach is now entirely pragmatic, but it exhibits all the treacherous rationalization which, for Shakespeare, makes evil insidious. He urges Lucrece to be realistic and accept life as it is. Contending that transgression can be erased by concealment, he argues that actually a little evil may be the means of accomplishing much good, or at least be mitigated by such good intentions. He threatens that the only alternative to submission is death and the very scandal which she seeks to avert. Finally, he pleads that, since there is no escape from her fate, for the good of all concerned she simply relax and be reasonable about it, which rather reminds one of Iago's advice to Othello on being philosophical about cuckoldry.

For Lucrece, on the contrary, Tarquin's proposed act cannot be isolated as a merely incidental vagary. Indicting its treason to all the demands of chivalry, gentle blood, and friendship, its violation of sacred wedlock, law, and common honesty, its infamy in repaying generous hospitality with wanton ill, and its shame in taking advantage of the weak and helpless, she points out that it vitiates not only his personal honor but his whole obligation as a human being to foster what is conducive to human welfare [ll. 568-602]. Even more, it subverts his responsibility as a prince and public figure to maintain a proper precedent for general behavior, and thus nullifies his prime function in the common weal.

> This deede will make thee only lou'd for feare,
> But happie Monarchs still are feard for loue:
> With fowle offendors thou perforce must beare,
> When they in thee the like offences proue;
> If but for feare of this, thy will remoue.
>   For Princes are the glasse, the schoole, the
>   booke,
>   Where subiects eies do learn, do read, do looke.
>
> [ll. 610-16]

The power to govern must be exercised for good, and this exercise must begin in rule of oneself. Although "Mens faults do seldome to themselues appeare" [l. 633], to an objective view truth has another estimate. While, like the sea, the ruler must receive into himself all influences, it is vital that he maintain his sovereign virtue and hold all in their due proportion; for without this observance of order and degree the inevitable result is anarchy. In short, as the first indictment by Lucrece itemizes the personal iniquities which recur to haunt Macbeth, this later lecture on the whole duty of the ruler provides a succinct preview of the themes which form the substance of Shakespeare's history plays.

Tarquin's refusal to be deterred by either practical or moral considerations inevitably poses the problem of accounting for his irrational behavior. Concurrent with his examination of the moral issues, therefore, Shakespeare takes appropriate opportunity to explain the psychology of evil. This explanation, which consistently underlies all susceptibility to evil in his tragedies, whether on the part of agent or victim, follows a familiar renaissance pattern. Beginning with the inherent faculty of the desirable to generate desire, it points out how, physiologically, the eye of sense and its surrogate, the imagination, influence the heart until its instrument, the will, can be infected by inflamed appetite. As the senses excite the emotions, reason becomes gradually paralyzed by the power of passion. And from this subversion of the superior by the inferior ensues the ultimate overthrow of all rational order by the anarchy of unleashed impulse. The specific human reactions which mark this psychological process conform with Shakespeare's customary portrayal of villainy. As in the case of Macbeth, there is an initial revulsion from evil. The transition from this to a temporizing with evil is induced by a highly characteristic lapse into specious rationalization. Its concomitant is a descent from moral inhibitions to a pragmatic fear of consequences, coupled with a fatal hope for concealment of wrongdoing and escape from it unscathed. Eventually hesitation is overwhelmed by imperious desire, and the final stage is a degeneracy into ruthless savagery and brute force.

The tragedy of Lucrece. Artist unknown (1469).

Most comprehensively exemplified in Macbeth, this is the basic psychological pattern which also governs the delineation of such other figures of evil as Claudius, Edmund, Goneril, Regan [in *King Lear*], and Iago. Its larger implications and inevitable impact on human life receive perhaps their most overt dramatic exposition in *Troilus and Cressida,* with its controlling themes of will perverted by appetite, justice overthrown by self-interest, right supplanted by might, and rational order collapsing into anarchy. Not only is the action of the play an extended illustration of the pattern in operation, with choric comments by Thersites to point the moral; but the principles involved in its fatal logic are explicitly stated by Ulysses in his famous speech on degree.

> The heavens themselves, the planets and this centre
> Observe degree, priority and place,
> Insisture, course, proportion, season, form,
> Office and custom, in all line of order; . . .
> Take but degree away, untune that string,
> And hark, what discord follows! . . .
> Force should be right; or rather, right and wrong,
> Between whose endless jar justice resides,
> Should lose their names, and so should justice too.
> Then every thing includes itself in power,
> Power into will, will into appetite;
> And appetite, an universal wolf,
> So doubly seconded with will and power,
> Must make perforce an universal prey,
> And last eat up himself. Great Agamemnon,
> This chaos, when degree is suffocate,
> Follows the choking.
>
> [I. iii. 85-8, 109-10, 116-26]

The account of the rape, which concludes this section, is brutal but brief. From its summary treatment it is evident that, in Shakespeare's scheme of the poem, the rape itself is less important as an act than as a fact which has antecedents and consequences. What is involved before and after is his main concern. Succinct as the treatment is, however, it provides an opportunity for Shakespeare to single out what he continues to emphasize as the three fatal characteristics of a tragic act: that it seriously disrupts the basic order of life; that it is irrevocable; and that it automatically sets up dangerous repercussions which can be neither controlled nor evaded. With this transition, the second, and longest, section of the poem addresses its 889 lines to the supreme fact of tragedy, the impact on those involved.

First it takes up the immediate effects on the two principals. With the pressure of desire released by satiation, Tarquin abruptly reverts to sanity. The result is a sickening revulsion from both the deed and its provocation, which resembles that of Macbeth and his wife after the murder of Duncan. Too late Tarquin appreciates the appalling nature of the barter to which he is committed and discovers, like Claudius and Macbeth, the weary burden of a "scarre that will dispight of Cure remaine" [l. 732]. Slinking from the shambles of his lust, he is driven by a single impulse—vain flight from a pursuit which, as he recognizes, comes finally from within himself. As for Lucrece, her reactions to evil in many respects anticipate those of Ophelia [in *Hamlet*], Desdemona [in *Othello*], Hamlet, and Lear in comparable situations. Benumbed by the shock of an incredible outrage without reason or remedy, and by the blight of an intolerable pollution, like Tarquin she can think only of flight, into a secrecy which she lacks the guile to maintain, and from a fouled body of which she would be rid. Worst of all, upon both Lucrece and Tarquin there descends, along with the sense of contamination and irretrievable loss, the horrified despair of a fatal commitment which they can neither cancel nor escape.

Having disposed of these immediate effects, as well as of the tragic agent, who has now served his purpose, the poem then proceeds to concentrate on the central interest of tragedy, the plight of the victim. Quite properly it also concentrates on the major fact of tragic experience, the suffering which is induced. As a mode of expression most appropriate to the subject, the bulk of this section is cast in the form of lyrical lamentation. Despite the form of expression, however, the purpose behind it is again expository. Enthusiastically as Lucrece subscribes to the doctrine of the Duchess of York in *Richard III,* "be copious in exclaims" [IV. iv. 135], her lamentations do not simply give voluble tongue to anguish; they raise vital questions which demand, and precipitate, answers. How can it be that such things come to pass? What is the nature of a life which enables them to exist? Has right no intrinsic advantage over wrong? Why is good will so fallible in effect? What solace or redress is there for violated virtue? They are the inevitable questions posed by every tragedy.

The answers to these questions are expounded in the three formal expostulations which Lucrece directs against Night, Opportunity, and Time. That against Night reverts to the theme with which Shakespeare opens the poem, the essential ambivalence of life. The fact is that life presents two aspects: the day of unobscured reality and of open dealing which will sustain the scrutiny of light; and the night which with its cloak of concealment breeds the spawn of darkness. In effect, it embraces an alternation of contradictory principles, which interact and often countermand each other. Hence there is in life no absolute potential, no perfect day without enveloping shadows:

> . . . no perfection is so absolute,
> That some impuritie doth not pollute.
>
> [ll. 853-54]

The inevitable consequence is a condition of mutability in which

> The sweets we wish for, turne to lothed sowrs,
> Euen in the moment that we call them ours,
>
> [ll. 867-68]

and only too often "What Vertue breedes iniquity deuours" [l. 872]. On the other hand, and with equal peril, it also follows that in life there is no utter night without the threat of dawn. Day, in its turn, as Lucrece and Tarquin recognize with dread, "nights scapes doth open lay" [l. 747].

It is the bawd Opportunity that couples the potential with the actual and thus propagates specific progeny. Theoretically, its operation should be at least neutral. The irony is, however, that Opportunity, whether because of its own capacity for deception or because of native human instinct, seems to exert its force predominantly for the fostering of evil. The forty-eight lines of violent invective with which Lucrece denounces this propensity [ll. 876-924] not only run the gamut of human iniquity but virtually itemize the roster of transgressions which complicate Shakespeare's later histories and tragedies.

> Guilty thou art of murther, and of
> theft,
> Guilty of periurie, and subornation,
> Guilty of treason, forgerie, and shift,
> Guilty of incest that abhomination,
> An accessarie by thine inclination,
> To all sinnes past and all that are to come,

> From the creation to the generall doome.
>
> [ll. 918-24]

The bitter accusation that, although "The poore, lame, blind, hault, creepe, cry out for thee" [l. 902],

> The patient dies while the Phisitian sleepes,
> The Orphane pines while the oppressor feedes.
> Iustice is feasting while the widow weepes.
> Aduise is sporting while infection breeds
>
> [ll. 904-07]

finds an echo in Lear's indictment, "A man may see how this world goes . . ." [IV. vi. 150-73]. Similarly, the fraudulent promise of Opportunity, whereby "Thy honie turnes to gall, thy ioy to greefe,"

> Thy secret pleasure turnes to open shame,
> Thy priuate feasting to a publicke fast,
> Thy smoothing titles to a ragged name,
> Thy sugred tongue to bitter wormwood tast,
>
> [ll. 889-93]

provides a text for the history of tragic evil in Shakespeare to its culminating "tale told by an idiot" of *Macbeth* [V. v. 26-7].

Yet, finally, Opportunity is but the agent and creature of Time, which creates the conditions of all human existence. And Time is flux and perpetual change, the mutability of day and night, the nurse and destroyer of all that is. Ideally, its function should be to bring good to fruition, to correct errors, and to redress wrongs; and this is the function which it does perform in the idealized world of Shakespeare's romantic comedies. Actually, its operation reflects the impartiality of life itself, of which it is the integument. Nevertheless, this very impartiality, with its process of mutation and decay, carries with it an important corollary: in the revolutions of time it must eventually bring ills to light and destroy evil as it does good. Here is the crux of Shakespeare's whole treatment of evil; whatever other damage evil may do, its destructive force inevitably ends in self-destruction. Otherwise, in this instability of Time only one thing is certain, that it cannot be turned back. This is the wheel of fire on which are tortured Hamlet, Othello, and Lear, to say nothing of Macbeth. Could one re-approach time past with the knowledge of hindsight,

> One poore retyring minute in an age
> Would purchase thee a thousand thousand friends.
>
> [ll. 962-63]

But what is done cannot be undone. The sole recourse is to cooperate with time by taking action for the future [ll. 1016-27].

Recognizing this fact, Lucrece abandons futile lament for what cannot be retracted, and in doing so shifts the attention of the poem from the conditions of tragic life to the expedients which they call for. As day with its exigent realities replaces the shameful secrecy of night, Lucrece confronts the problem of necessary action [ll. 1016-78]. Her first reaction is a feeling of nightmare estrangement from all normal activity [ll. 1084-1113], like that of Macbeth as he comes from the murder of Duncan [II. ii. 15-74]. Like Hamlet in his "To be or not to be" soliloquy [III. i. 55-87],

> . . . with her selfe is shee in mutinie,
> To liue or die which of the twaine were better,
> When life is sham'd and death reproaches detter.
>
> [ll. 1153-55]

She would like to seclude herself from the world in some un-
inhabited wilderness [ll. 1144-48], as Lear covets a similar
flight to prison with Cordelia [V. iii. 8-19]. The difficulty,
however, as she quickly perceives, is that her personal disaster cannot be isolated or confined. Lucrece is not an island
entire of itself; the stain which she has suffered extends to others—to her husband, to her family, and indirectly to the
whole of society. Here one approaches the crucial dilemma
of Shakespeare's tragedy. To conceal or disregard the evil,
even if it were possible, would be but to spread the compost
on the weeds; for the ignorance of the innocent does not cancel the knowledge of the guilty, nor does secrecy suspend the
working of evil once set in motion [ll. 1065-66]. To expose it,
on the other hand, unfortunately solves none of the basic
problems.

In the first place, the situation in which Lucrece finds herself
is an ambiguous one, which readily lends itself to misconstruction. Although she herself may be blameless and publicly exonerated from wrongdoing, the actual facts in the case
are by no means self-evident or proof against suspicion. And
even if they were, they still could afford a precedent for more
dubious falls from grace. This ambiguity of her position leads
to a second and more disquieting problem, her actual freedom from guilt. To be sure, she was overcome by surprise and
force, by the fear which paralyzed her resistance, and by the
dread of additional shame which Tarquin threatened. Besides, she was handicapped by the innate weakness and plas-
ticity of womankind. At the same time Lucrece cannot close
her eyes to the fact that, regardless of intentions or excuses,
she has been a party to evil: that "Tarquin wronged me, I
Colatine" [l. 819] in a deed which "Will couple my reproach
to Tarquin's shame" [l. 816]. And thereby hangs a serious
question. Does innocence, or weakness, or confusion, in point
of fact, absolve the victim from responsibility for disaster? It
is a question at the core of every tragedy that Shakespeare
wrote, with a particular bearing on the familiar "tragic flaw."
Even if her technical innocence be conceded, however, Lucrece still confronts the final and most devastating problem
of tragedy, the actual condition with which she is forced to
live.

> Her house is sackt, her quiet interrupted,
> Her mansion batterd by the enemie,
> Her sacred temple spotted, spoild, corrupted,
> Groslie ingirt with daring infamie.
>
> [ll. 1170-73]

No amount of palliative or recrimination or solace can eliminate or alter this ugly reality. Whatever the circumstances or
the extenuations, for Lucrece the fact still remains that,
whereas once "I was a loyall wife" [l. 1048], now and forever
"Of that true tipe hath Tarquin rifled me" [l. 1050].

For Lucrece the situation is intolerable, yet it is also inescapable. It is a diabolical trap which leaves the victim alive but
in torment and without hope of release. From its insupport-
able pressure the only issue can be the protracted suffering
of futile agony. This is the invariable pattern of Shakespeare's
tragic situation. For the tragic protagonist it is a dilemma
with no possible resolution in satisfactory human terms; its
only surcease is the merciful *coup de grace* of death. As for
the evil which destroys him, it also engenders its own destiny.
Fatal to its victims, it must contend with the no less fatal
nemesis of Time. These are the conclusions to which Lucrece
is finally brought; and it is in accordance with them that she

determines the actions called for. For herself there is but one
choice:

> The remedie indeede to do me good,
> Is to let forth my fowle defiled blood.
>
> [ll. 1028-29]

Before embracing this personal consummation devoutly to be
wished, however, she also recognizes the need to discharge
a broader responsibility. Since "sparing Iustice feeds iniqui-
tie" [l. 1687], she has a moral obligation not to leave evil unchallenged. In fulfillment of this obligation, Lucrece therefore summons her husband and friends, reveals the crime to
them, and exacts from them a pledge of vengeance upon the
guilty. In other words, she provides for their commitment as
active agents of Time to implement its retribution.

With this long second section of the poem Shakespeare concludes his analysis of tragedy. The last section merely displays its ultimate results as presented in the dénouement of
the story. Although actually this final part of the poem contains most of the action connected with the story, Shakespeare discharges its function swiftly in 273 lines. Not only
is his treatment of the material brief, but in his presentation
of it, for the first time, he shifts the prevailing emphasis from
exposition to a narrative and descriptive account of what is
substantially a dramatic situation. From this relative distribution of space and emphasis, therefore, it is evident where
his real interest lies. Minimizing the opportunities for narrative and drama, he devotes the bulk of his poem to the exposition of ideas. Essentially, *Lucrece* is an examination of what
constitutes tragedy and an explanation of how it operates. It
is a rationale of tragedy which is both comprehensive and
complete. What is more, it is also the very rationale which
underlies the whole of Shakespearean tragedy.

Perhaps the most significant feature of this rationale is the
fact that it is set forth for the first time explicitly in *Lucrece*.
Indeed, the ambitious aims of the poem, its calculated bid for
literary recognition, and its conscientious effort to be intellectually impressive argue strongly that its composition was the
express occasion for Shakespeare's systematic organization of
his thinking about the subjects involved. For these reasons
The Rape of Lucrece is a key document in the record of
Shakespeare's coming of age as an artist. It provides a unique
and overt account of his mind in action on dramatic problems
of prime importance at a crucial, and datable, point in his career. In fact, it constitutes the one systematic and authoritative declaration extant of the dramatic thinking upon which
Shakespeare based his whole tragic practice. (pp. 480-87)

> *Harold R. Walley, "'The Rape of Lucrece' and
> Shakespearean Tragedy," in PMLA, Vol. LXXVI,
> No. 5, December, 1961, pp. 480-87.*

D. C. ALLEN (essay date 1962)

[*Allen claims that Shakespeare's obvious sympathy for Lucrece
is tempered by medieval and Renaissance readings of the Lucrece story that imposed Christian perspectives on her actions.
Although Allen stops short of calling the poem an "overt allegory," he asserts that it "has certain sub-literal possibilities"
which may lead to a more judgmental view of the Roman matron and the nobility of her suicide and may even implicate her
as an accessory to Tarquin's rape. In the Roman context, Lucrece's self-sacrifice is "rare and wonderful," for it precipitated
the banishment of the Tarquins and the establishment of the
republic. In the Christian context, however, it appears that Lu-*

crece's decision to subordinate Christian virtue to pagan honor is "morally improper."]

Lucrece, the heroine of Shakespeare's second brief epic and the human opposite of his foolish and frustrated Venus, had long been for men, and hence for their wives, a gracious yet tragic example of married love. During most of the Middle Ages, she was placed on the short-list of wives and widows celebrated for their chastity and faith; sometimes she was bracketed with the patriotic Judith, whose established purity helped to disestablish a tyrant. (p. 89)

But there was another reason why men remembered Lucrece and why her tragedy attracted the attention of the young poet; she was not only a Roman heroine but also the centre of a Christian controversy. (p. 90)

To stern Tertullian and austere Jerome, Lucrece was a splendid example of pagan domestic virtue, a woman whose actions might well be countenanced by Christian ladies possessed of the inner light. With the views of these mighty predecessors, St. Augustine, who was inclined to condemn even the worthiest heathen when he was making a case against the spiritually unredeemed, heartily disagreed. In the *City of God* he attacks the conduct of Collatine's poor wife. 'This case is caught between both sides to such a degree that if suicide is extenuated, adultery is proved; if adultery is denied, the conviction is for suicide.' There is no way, he thinks, to resolve the problem. 'If she was adulterous, why is she praised? If she was chaste, why was she killed?' If she had been a Christian, she would have eschewed 'Roman pride in glory' and found another way 'to reveal her conscience to men'.

For the sixteenth century the tragedy of Lucrece was a kind of casuistic problem, a matter of legal gamesmanship for canon lawyers. From controversy of this nature the case got into the writings of the humanists, and we find Speroni remarking [in his "Orazione contra le Cortigiane"] that Lucrece was of 'imperfect chastity' or she would have held fort against the assaults of Tarquin. A truly chaste woman, he assures us, would have died before surrender; but Lucrece abandoned her virtue just as a distressed ship jettisons its cargo. Her compliance with the desires of Tarquin was, in fact, an act midway between the forced and the voluntary. With this view the French humanist, Henri Estienne [in his *Apologie pour Hérodote,*] agrees: 'poore *Lucretia* did not judge aright of herselfe and her own estate'. Suicide is no revenge. 'Be it that her death were Vindicative, yet it were but a revenge of the injury done to the defiled body, and not of the wrong done to the undefiled mind, which is the seate of chastitie.' The story of Lucrece was, I expect, made important for Shakespeare by this ancient yet current controversy; and without the benefit of this knowledge, we are nonplussed by the tenor of certain areas of his poem.

One may comprehend Shakespeare's consideration of the great argument by watching his Lucrece after the departure of Tarquin. She recites arias on Time, Night, and Occasion; then, looking at her sharp-nailed fingers, she blames them for not defending their 'loyal dame'. A few stanzas later [ll. 1149-76] the notion of suicide crosses her mind, and she recalls what Augustine has said, or, in a historical sense, is going to say: ' "To kill myself," quoth she, "alack, what were it, But with my body my poor soul's pollution?" ' [ll. 1156-57]. The moral dilemma is made almost emblematic when Lucrece—almost her own symbol—lies dead in 'rigols' of pure and corrupt blood [ll. 1737-50]; the Christian rather than the Roman

lesson is to be read in this stylized *cul-de-lampe.* The living nature of the questions about Lucrece's action is also italicized when Brutus, who fails to speak the lines of the historians, says to the hysterical husband:

> Is it revenge to give thyself a blow
> For his foul act by whom thy fair wife bleeds?
> Such childish humour from weak minds proceeds:
> Thy wretched wife mistook the matter so,
> To slay herself, that should have slain her foe.
>
> [ll. 1823-27]

We must, I think, face the fact that Shakespeare read the story of Lucrece in its Christian context. There was no question in his mind about its tragic import, but he felt that it must be glossed in terms of Christian options. Lucrece should have defended herself to the death, or, having been forced, lived free of blame with a guiltless conscience. Her action was rare and wonderful, but a little beyond forgiveness.

Shakespeare's recognition of the double understanding of the Lucrece story explains, I think, the symbolic mileposts that guide us through this poem as they lead us through Spenser's *Faerie Queen.* His successors cling to the literal, and as a result Heywood's *The Rape of Lucrece* is simply a jolly exercise in dramatic bad taste, whereas Middleton's (?) *The Ghost of Lucrece,* while clinging to Shakespeare's text and superficially appearing to recognize the problem, fails to understand the ultimate lesson of Shakespeare's poem. . . . But if Shakespeare's poem cannot be interpreted in terms of its English successors, it can only be partially understood when read under the light of its predecessor *Venus and Adonis.*

The conventional statements about the relation of these two poems need not be rehearsed; it is almost enough to say that they are no more in opposition with each other than are 'L'Allegro' and 'Il Penseroso' with which they are sometimes compared. Milton's poems, I think, represent a progressive course of thinking about the preparation of the poet-prophet; Shakespeare's poems are a similar sequence of discourses on the nature of human love. The poems are continuations rather than contradictions. In *Venus and Adonis* love, though veiled by courtly compliment, is discussed mainly on the basis of animal heat and placed outside the limits of a proper definition of the reasonable life. The animal theme returns in *Lucrece,* but in this second poem (a rougher Venus taking one part) the opposition comes from a different aspect of love: the devotion of a wife to her fleshly honour. The problem, as in subsequent plays, has something to do with *honour,* but it is also concerned with a total estimate of chastity on a higher level.

In *Venus and Adonis* the animal metaphors that point towards the ultimate theme depend to a degree on the hunter and the hunted; the same type of metaphor controls the first third of *The Rape of Lucrece,* but here the hunt is less equal than in the other poem. Tarquin is not a proper hunter pitted against an equal quarry. He enters in the night when only owls and wolves are heard because he is the 'night owle' that will catch the sleeping dove. In due course, he is compared to a serpent, a 'grim Lion', a 'faulcon towring', a 'Cockeatrice', a 'rough beast', a 'night waking Cat', a vulture, and a wolf. After his crime is done, he changes into a 'full-fed Hound, or gorged Hawke', and then slips away like a 'theevish dog'. Lucrece is naturally an innocent thing of nature: a 'white Hind', a mouse, a doe, a lamb, but more commonly a dove, a 'new-kild bird', a lesser fowl crouching under the shadow of the hawk's wings. She continues conscious of her metaphoric identity and eventually compares herself with the birds and with her mythological similar, Philomele. In the end, a 'pale swan', she sings before she dies.

These comparisons are plain enough and certainly to be expected, but whereas in *Venus and Adonis* there are several real animals—a stallion, a jennet, a hare, and a boar—in the cast of characters, *Lucrece* has only one. As Tarquin creeps to the bed of Lucrece bearing the 'lightless fire', 'Night-wandering weasels fright him, yet he still pursues his fear' [ll. 307-08]. We know from the annotations on this passage that 'especially among the British' it is inauspicious to meet a weasel, but the British were not alone in this superstition which was widely held . . . in the sixteenth century. . . . But the weasel was more than a warning; it was a sign 'of evil to those whose houses they infest' [A. Alciata, in his *Emblemata*, 1593]. The literal weasel not only warns Tarquin, but foretells the evil that awaits Lucrece. But the literal weasel is more than a weasel. The poet who was going to make us see the spider Iago without saying 'spider' can make us see who the weasel, well-known as a bird-nester, is. . . . (pp. 90-2)

Tarquin, who is evil on the animal level, sins against his creed when he attains human shape. Long before he commits his rape, he denounces himself: 'O shame to knighthood, and to shining Armes' [l. 197]. He is a warrior in arms but not in love, because he carries over the violence of battle to the tents of Love. The animal metaphors which bring Shakespeare's two poems momently together change when Tarquin crosses the threshold of Lucrece's bed-chamber; and, as befits a poem laid against a background of war and siege, love and battle make the terms of the analogues. 'Love', says the quiet poet George Herbert, 'is a man of war', and Shakespeare knew this trope only too well. He may have learned it from the *Aeneid* (XI, 736-7), or from the Latin elegiac poets; but his probable master was Ovid, who gave him in the *Fasti* the basic material of his poem, and whose great pattern poem, 'Militat omnis amans et habet sua castra Cupido', is in the first of the *Amores*. From this book of the heart we learn that lovers and soldiers are the same except that the comrades of 'Frater Amor' are never demobbed. The wars that they fight under the erotic banners are, however, seldom bitter and never violent.

From the texts of the Roman poets the troubadours, the goliards, the stilnovists, and the only begetters of Renaissance French and Italian poetry took their lessons. As a consequence of this long tradition, Shakespeare cannot avoid these comparisons when he writes about soldiers and their women. Tarquin says that 'Affection is my captain' [l. 271] and follows the metaphor through three stanzas as he follows the passageway to Lucrece's chamber. His lusts obey their 'Captain', too; and as he stands beside the sleeping young woman, his pulsing veins are 'like straggling slaves for pillage fighting' [l. 428]. But these figures are all ironic when applied to Tarquin. He is not a soldier of love fencing with his dear enemy or sharing her field-bed as an amorous companion; even when the metaphors turn to those of siege and assault, they are improperly in his company and exhibit him for what he is. (pp. 92-3)

In the age of chivalry, when the taking of fortified places was a high military science, the metaphor of the capture of love's castle is fairly common. . . . It is . . . in this classical-medieval tradition that ardent Tarquin gallops from the siege of Ardea to the ravishing of Lucrece, but there is no indication that he has read its literature rightly. (p. 93)

The 'false lord' Tarquin runs furiously like an enraged captain at the breaching of a wall; and, as Shakespeare sees him charge, 'Honour and beauty, in the owner's arms Are weakly fortress'd from a world of harms' [ll. 27-8]. Lucrece's husband is likewise unaware that 'This siege . . . hath engirt his marriage' [l. 221]. The unknightly ravisher—his heart beating like a drum—lets his hands 'scale' the 'round turrets' of the lady's breasts, and by this action informs her that she 'is dreadfully beset'.

> His hand, that yet remains upon her breast,—
> Rude ram, to batter such an ivory wall!—
> May feel her heart—poor citizen!—distress'd,
> Wounding itself to death, rise up and fall,
> Beating her bulk, that his hand shakes withal.
> This moves in him more rage and lesser pity,
> To make the breach and enter this sweet city.
>
> [ll. 463-69]

In keeping with the traditional tropes, Tarquin sounds 'a parley', and the pale face of Lucrece appearing over the turret of her white sheets seems a flag of surrender. 'Under that colour I am come to scale Thy never-conquer'd fort' [ll. 481-82]. Lucrece, like a damsel of the romances, defends herself with words, but the situation is once again ironic. She is no coy and half-persuaded girl refuting the kindly arguments of her decent lover. She cannot prevail, and the fortress of her chastity is overcome not by favour but through force and duress. But though the castle of her virtue falls to an exterior force, the walls of Tarquin's soul are also demolished by interior revolt. 'Her subjects with foul insurrection Have batter'd down her consecrated wall' [ll. 722-23]. One of the central paradoxes of *Venus and Adonis* is that of the hunter hunted; in this part of *The Rape of Lucrece* the ruiner is ruined.

Tarquin goes off with his spotted soul, bearing Lucrece's honour as his 'prisoner', and leaving the girl behind 'like a late-sacked island' [l. 1740]; then Lucrece writes her series of poems to Night, to Opportunity, and to her mythological predecessor, Philomele. A modern reader could object that all this rhetoric is hardly in keeping with the events, but he must remember that these early poems are barns in which the young poet is storing up themes and metaphors for the future. They are virtuoso performances in which Shakespeare like a good musician is demonstrating both his repertoire and his skill with his instrument. The Troy cloth which follows them and occupies such a large section of the poem is possibly in the same tradition, but it may also have a deeper meaning.

The painted spectacle of the war before Troy that Lucrece studies and that Shakespeare describes has struck many critics as simply another rhetorical description that slows the movement of the poem until Collatine arrives and that gives the reader a chance to meditate on the tragedy. There have been various comments on whether or not Shakespeare had a real picture in mind; and if he did, the Italian painter, Giulio Romano, who painted Troy scenes, has been nominated as the most likely artist. The ecphrastic poetry of ancient and modern poets has been brought forward to account for Shakespeare's lines, and it has even been asserted that Shakespeare is attempting in this episode to distinguish in an aesthetic fashion between the task and skill of the artist in paint and verse. All of these observations have been helpful in their ways, but the main questions are why the idea occurred to Shakespeare and what would a sixteenth-century reader see in the picture.

T. W. Baldwin has pointed to the commentaries of Marsus

and Constantius on the Lucrece story in Ovid's *Fasti* as the text that carried Shakespeare from Rome to Troy [see Additional Bibliography]. In these commentaries, Lucrece is not only defended against the charges of St Augustine, but Tarquin is compared obliquely, by a quotation from the *Aeneid*, to Sinon, the betrayer of Troy. One hardly knows how a poet's imagination works, and Baldwin may be completely right; however, a few other matters might have brought this idea into Shakespeare's mind. Lucrece was, of course, a Trojan by ancestry, and the destruction of Troy was the greatest tragedy that she knew. She was also regularly associated in lists of noble women with Hecuba, that other faithful and suffering wife. There is finally the fact that the Renaissance attributed, until Goldast [in his *Erotica et Amatoria Opusculi*] argued otherwise, a poem on Philomela and a *De Excidio Trojae* to Ovid and that Shakespeare could have found these now rejected poems in the *Opera*. But we shall probably never know exactly how Shakespeare got from the rape of Lucrece, that fallen fortress of chastity, to the destruction of Troy.

Though we cannot explain the turns and halts of Shakespeare's imagination, we most certainly know that the Trojan episode in *The Rape of Lucrece* came from the first two books of the *Aeneid*: the 'pictura inanis' from the first book, the fall of the city from the second. If we now think in terms of the Renaissance Vergil, we may be able to read a meaning into this section that may not be Shakespeare's but that suits the moral trend of his poem and may represent what a certain type of Renaissance reader saw in it. To introduce this last point, we must simply remember that the sixteenth century regarded Vergil as a superb moral poet and his hero as a man of high human perfection. In this regard they had, as we know, no quarrel with the Middle Ages; but even with this knowledge, we sometimes forget that a man of the Renaissance could read with the help of the experts the great allegory of the career of Aeneas. It is, then, not so much a question of how the Troy painting got into *Lucrece* or why it is there as what consonant meaning a man of the Renaissance might find in it.

Petrarch is always a good figure to stand at the door of any study of Renaissance intellectual attitudes, and in one of his letters he informs Frederico Aretino that the city of Troy is a symbol of the human body deep in sleep. Its gates are opened by sins that kill the defenders of the soul on the threshold. . . . Now all this tumult, this ruin, this destruction in which the voluptuous city, victim of its own passions, struggles between the fires kindled by libidinousness and the sword of anger occurs fitly at night to denote the darkness of human error and the blackness in which our life, buried in sleep and drenched in wine, is ignorantly and drunkenly immersed.' This is the tone of Petrarch's reading and he continues to match the poetry to the moral. The great horse is made by the evils of youth; and Laocoön or reason being overthrown, the 'infausta machina' is admitted conveying into the town Odysseus or 'wicked cunning', Neoptolemus or 'pride and vindictive ardour', and Menelaus or 'revenge'.

Boccaccio, Petrarch's friend, always looked under 'the fitting veil of the fable for hidden truth' [in his *Della Geneologia*, 1585], . . . and in his *Genealogy of the Gods*, he illustrates what he finds under this covering with a moral reading of the story of Perseus. He would obviously have approved of the letter to Aretino because, as he informs us, he looked into 'the core or literal sense' for the other allegorical significances. The apparently medieval practices of both these poets were

also followed by the humanist Colluccio Salutati, who insisted on searching for 'the allegorical meanings in the traditional stories of the poets' [R. H. Green in *Critical Approaches to Medieval Literature*, 1960]. A century later, the Florentine humanists, Ficino and Pico della Mirandola, both recommend that the classical poets be read in terms of the four-fold exegesis of the twelfth-century theologians; and a member of their society, Landino, took it upon himself to provide such a reading of the *Aeneid*, a poem in which 'Vergil hid the most profound knowledge'. His *In Virgilii Opera Allegoria* was printed either in the *Quaestiones Camaldulenses* or as an appendix to the *Aeneid* at least twenty times between 1480 and 1596.

For Landino, Troy is the youthful life of man when reason slumbers and the senses rule; it is what philosophers call the 'natural state' and in this state the body reigns among fleshly pleasures. But some men discover, as they near maturity, that there is a road leading to the right which they must follow. To make plainer this notion of the divided way, Landino states that both Aeneas and Paris lived in Troy but followed separate courses. Paris preferred pleasure to virtue and perished with Troy; Aeneas, impelled by his mother, the higher Venus, left Troy to seek the truth and came eventually to Italy or divine sapience. One may object, Landino acknowledges, that Aeneas fought for Troy, but one must also admit that even though the night of passions surrounded him, he foresaw the fall of the city. For Aeneas was son of flesh (Anchises), but he also had a soul (Venus), and it is the death of his father as well as the wisdom of his mother that brings him in the end to perfection.

We have only to remember Spenser's allegorical presentation of portions of the Troy story or Chapman's remarks on the Homeric allegory in the epistle to the *Odyssey*, to realize that Landino's formal symbolic reading is not a unique medieval retention. This impression of a strong sense of allegory in the Renaissance's interpretation of classical poets (aided, perhaps, by the discovery of some of the ancient moral and physical glosses on Homer) is given further emphasis by Fabrini's edition of the *Aeneid* in 1588. In this edition the Latin text is surrounded by the usual morass of an *apparatus criticus*, but the editor adds to the customary comments on syntax, history and so forth a separate 'allegorical exposition' that draws heavily on Landino's method and results. When, for instance, Venus pays her son a nocturnal visit (II, 489-504), Fabrini observes that this is the celestial Venus described by Plato, Pythagoras, Empedocles, and St. Paul. She comes, he writes, to lead Aeneas away from Troy, the body of man besieged by pleasures and passions, in order that he may follow a divine course. Anchises (the flesh) naturally refuses to leave because he would rather die than give up his sensual desires, and so he must be carried off by force on the shoulders of the soul. Fabrini's moral commentary omits much that is in Landino's, but what it accepts is elaborately annotated, and its basic conclusion is the same. Troy is the body which must be destroyed and abandoned so that the ideal man can gain the profits of a higher life.

Now there is absolutely no reason to believe that Shakespeare had any of Spenser's liking for overt allegory, but it is quite probable that he could allude to matters that had intrinsic allegorical values for his readers. The garden scene in *Richard II* connects symbolically with John of Gaunt's 'This other Eden' [II. i. 42]; and Falstaff, the 'old white-bearded Satan' [*1 Henry* IV, II. iv. 463], takes us promptly to the Pauline 'homo vetus'. Neither of these suggestions are allegorical in the strict sense; but granted the intellectual inclinations of the audience, one cannot feel that corn was being sown on stony ground. I am moved to suppose, considering the nature of the central discussion and the symbolic signposts, that *The Rape of Lucrece* (although it is not an allegory in the same sense as Spenser's 'Muiopotomos') has certain sub-literal possibilities.

I cannot assume that Shakespeare knew the moral readings of Landino and Fabrini, but Lucrece, who compares the ravishment of her body with the fall of Troy, 'so my Troy did fall' [l. 1547], seems to have intimations of this nature. Like the allegorizers of the *Aeneid* and, of course, in keeping with her historical utterances, she makes a careful distinction between her flesh and her soul:

> My body or my soul which was the dearer,
> When the one pure, the other made divine?
> Whose love of either to my self was nearer,
> When both were kept for heaven and Collatine?
>
> [ll. 1163-66]

But the house of her soul is 'sackt', her mansion 'batter'd', her temple 'corrupted'. There is but one thing left to do: she must leave. 'If in this blemisht fort I make some hole, Through which I may convay this troubled soule' [ll. 1175-76].

In the allegories, Aeneas' Troy is equally ravaged by sins and sensations from without; and so on the advice of his mother, he departs to find divine wisdom. Lucrece's decision is similar, but, like Tarquin's amorous soldiership, morally improper. Her Troy is ruined by Tarquin-Sinon, and she believes that it must be annihilated to preserve the purity of her mind. Unfortunately she does not aspire to divine sapience but to pagan honour. Unled by the celestial Venus, her maculate body appears to control her decision more than her immaculate soul, which, according to her own statement, only endures in 'her poyson'd closet' [l. 1659]. So while Brutus seems to have the last word in the pagan sense, it is really St Augustine (whose words fitted to Lucrece's tongue have earlier taken their place in the poem) who wins, in spite of Shakespeare's obvious sympathy for the lady, the debate between the classical and the Christian worlds. (pp. 93-7)

> D. C. Allen, "Some Observations on 'The Rape of Lucrece'," in Shakespeare Survey: An Annual Survey of Shakespearian Study and Production, *Vol. 15, 1962, pp. 89-98.*

BICKFORD SYLVESTER   (essay date 1965)

[*Sylvester suggests that both the structure and imagery of* The Rape of Lucrece *are designed to develop the central theme of natural mutability or "the inconstancy of the world." The underlying precept of the poem, according to the critic, is expressed through Lucrece's heroic actions: the necessity to impose order on the forces of violence and egotism in nature and humanity. Sylvester maintains that Tarquin and Lucrece both vacillate between irresponsible impulses and ethical ideals; but whereas Tarquin succumbs to his lust, creating Lucrece's tragic dilemma, she overcomes her "self-pitying dependence," thus enhancing our appreciation of her achievement. In addition, Sylvester comments on aspects of political allegory in the poem, contending that Tarquin's violence is equated with the tyranny of his family's dynasty and Lucrece's passivity represents the Roman citizens' acquiescence. In further defence of Lucrece's actions, Sylvester notes that according to medieval medical be-*

Tarquin and Lucrece. By Titian.

lief, Lucrece's stain was not just figurative, but literal. Thus, as a "physical microcosm of the intolerably ambiguous natural world," "half-pure and half-corrupted," she can, by killing herself, "re-affirm the system of orderly absolutes necessary to man, and exemplify the human responsibility upon which it stands."]

Perhaps one reason why *Lucrece* is infrequently found in the classroom is that readers have traditionally written the poem off as a tedious, if sometimes brilliant, rhetorical exercise, lacking the formal unity useful to teachers of literature courses. But I want to point out patterns in the imagery and in the structure of *Lucrece,* patterns running through the digressions and apostrophes and coalescing in a coherent scheme. An awakening recognition of the poem's formal possibilities has been reflected in two notable articles within the last four years [by Harold R. Walley (see excerpt above, 1961), and by Robert J. Griffin (see Additional Bibliography)]. There is one much earlier attempt to expose a unifying rationale in *Lucrece,* however—that of the German critic, E. W. Sievers, written in 1866 and condensed in translation by Rollins in his New Variorum edition of the poem [see Additional Bibliography]. Sievers' discussion has been neglected, probably because of his preoccupation with theological issues outside the poem. But his approach is suggestive, I think, and I shall use it as a point of departure in my own examination of *Lucrece* as a poetic construction.

For Sievers, the poem is Shakespeare's "first great theodicy, a justification of God in relation to the existence of evil in the world." Shakespeare presents a universe in which weakness and beauty are ever subject to the encroachments of evil. He reconciles us to this terrifying view of reality, however, by creating a "picture of world order" in which individuals may be "supported by the whole and by the supporters of the whole." Tragic disorder has been created by the irresponsibility of Lucrece's husband and that of Tarquin himself who, as the son of the king, is ironically most responsible for the safety of all citizens. For safety and salvation lie only in man's "consciousness of his own moral responsibility, the ability in reason, his exclusive possession, and will-power." With the digression on the fall of Troy, a comparison is demanded between the "characterless good nature" of Collatine and that of Priam, so that we see the public, as well as the private disaster that follows upon individual irresponsibility. But order is restored by the manner of Lucrece's death. Her insistence upon controlling her destiny after her helpless submission is an example of the human responsibility required by God.

Certainly the poem's language emphasizes the imperfection and mutability of the natural world within which the human action takes place. As early as the fourth stanza we are told that happiness is "as soon decay'd and done / As is the morning's silver melting dew" [ll. 23-4]. From then on the ubiquitous animal imagery centers about the imminent destruction which menaces beauty and gentleness, but which must be accepted as integral to nature. In a striking series of figures, Tarquin and Lucrece are compared to a predator and its prey: "The dove sleeps fast that this night-owl will catch" [l. 360]; "As the grim lion fawneth o'er his prey . . . So o'er this sleeping soul doth Tarquin stay" [ll. 421, 423]; "Like to a new-kill'd bird she trembling lies" [l. 457]; "The wolf hath seized his prey, the poor lamb cries" [l. 677]; "This said, he shakes aloft his Roman blade, / Which, like a falcon towering in the skies, / Coucheth the fowl below with his wings' shade, / Whose crooked beak threats if he mount he dies" [ll. 505-08]; "Yet, foul night-waking cat, he doth but dally, / While in his hold-fast foot the weak mouse panteth" [ll. 554-55]; "Here with a cockatrice' dead-killing eye / He rouseth up himself and makes a pause; / While she, the picture of pure piety . . . Pleads, in a wilderness where are no laws" [ll. 540-42, 544].

And after the lawless wilderness has overwhelmed her body, Lucrece's apostrophes to Time and Opportunity function—organically rather than as mere ornament—by developing this motif of natural mutability into an explicit theme. "O Opportunity, thy guilt is great" [l. 876], and "O Time, thou tutor both to good and bad" [l. 995], cries Lucrece reproachfully. From lines 846 to 1015 her words remind us that as "the worm" intrudes "the maiden bud" [l. 848], "what virtue breeds iniquity devours" [l. 872].

The poem's color imagery calls further attention to the bewildering inconstancy of the world. Red, which represents beauty, is also the color of Tarquin's lust, and after the rape the red which in Lucrece's cheek had marked her beauty and the flush of her modesty moves to her eyes, "red and raw" with sorrow [l. 1592]. And there are many shades of white [ll. 56, 407, 420]; for, as Lucrece says, "no perfection is so absolute, / That some impurity doth not pollute" [ll. 853-54].

Accordingly, Lucrece's lament after her violation turns upon her bitter recognition that "The sweets we wish for turn to loathed sours / Even in the moment that we call them ours" [ll. 867-68]. These lines prompt us to reflect that the entire action of *Lucrece* takes place in a fallen world precisely like that prophecied by Venus at the end of *Venus and Adonis*. Indeed, I think we may well read *Lucrece* as Shakespeare's attempt to portray the paradox inherent in the experience of love at the end of *Venus and Adonis* as extended to encompass all of human experience. The focus of the second poem, then, is on man's struggle to maintain his equilibrium in an ambiguous and shifting world. This, indeed, would make *Lucrece* qualify as that "graver labour" with which, in dedicating *Venus and Adonis* a year earlier, Shakespeare had promised soon to honor his patron. Just as in *Venus and Adonis* the willful and artificial separation of beauty from love causes a permanent state of paradox to prevail in nature, so in *Lucrece* whatever order may exist against this imperfect field must in turn be artificially forged and maintained by man's vigilance and by his exercise of will. And I suggest that both the texture and the structure of the poem emphasize man's responsibility to control the forces of selfishness and violence which, within himself and in external nature, are constantly straining to overwhelm beauty and gentleness. For "honor and Beauty, in the owner's arms, / Are weakly fortress'd from a world of harms" [ll. 27-8].

Tarquin's father has made the family name synonymous with the overbearing selfishness that facilitates a surrender to the senses. The first sentence of Shakespeare's argument before the poem refers to the elder Tarquin who "for his excessive pride surnamed Superbus, after he had caused his own father-in-law Servius Tullius to be cruelly murdered, and, contrary to the Roman laws and customs, not requiring or staying for the people's suffrages, had possessed himself of the kingdom." And the young Tarquin yields to the family weakness. Unleashed by his arrogant resentment "that meaner men should vaunt / That golden hap which their superiors want" [ll. 41-2], his lust transforms him from friend to the worst kind of foe—one who comes, like "subtle Sinon" in the Trojan tapestry, "armed to beguild / With outward honesty, but yet defil'd / With inward vice" [ll. 1544-46]. Once its members irresponsibly abandon the conscious control upon which it depends, society's fragile order topples, and things revert to the state of paradox ruling nature. Appropriately, then, after violence has invaded the fair Lucrece, she clings to the night [l. 806], virtue fears the day [ll. 771-78], and as I have pointed out, the red bloom of beauty becomes associated with sorrow. That this condition has come to dominate society around Lucrece is also emphasized by the apostrophes, which contain examples of paradox about equally drawn from the realms of nature and of man. If "hateful cockoos hatch in sparrows' nests," or "toads infect fair founts with venom mud," a "tyrant folly lurks in gentle breasts" and kings are "breakers of their own behests" [ll. 849-52]. If "unruly blasts wait on the tender spring," it is also true that "the patient dies while the physician sleeps" [ll. 869, 904].

Man cannot endure "where are no laws," however. He requires a one-for-one system of absolutes in which black equals evil and white equals good; where "light and lust are deadly enemies" [l. 674], and things are what they seem. Such stability must be manufactured, of course, in the changing world of the poem. And it is affirmatively associated with man by the equation of permanence and fabrication in the descriptions of Lucrece—and of Tarquin when he is sympathetically viewed. Her breasts are ivory walls [l. 464] and "round turrets" [l. 441]; her body is a "never-conquer'd fort" [l. 482]. And both protagonists are described in terms of civil institutions—man-made by definition: her heart is a "poor citizen" inhabiting the "sweet city" of her body [ll. 465, 469], and his soul is a "spotted princess" whose "fair temple" is "defaced" by his sinful act [ll. 721, 719]. The language is conventionally Petrarchan, of course. But we can appreciate its fortunate appropriateness here only if we perceive its relevance to the conflict in the poem between natural fluidity and man-made order. If we do not, the choice of brick and mortar associations to describe human beings in this solemn context disturbs us, and must seem an excess of "Renaissance exuberance."

But there is order in Shakespeare's extravagance. Indeed, the poem's structure, like its texture, is built around man's responsibility in the face of natural flux to create for himself the stability which his psychology requires. There is a neat parallel between Tarquin's entry of Lucrece's body and her suicidal act: "Then let it not be call'd impiety," she implores, "if in this blemish'd fort I make some hole / Through which I may convey this troubled soul" [ll. 1174-76]. She must right aggression by aggression: "Faint not, faint heart, but stoutly say 'So be it': / Yield to my hand; my hand shall conquer thee" [ll. 1209-10]. Significantly, precisely at the culmination of her apostrophes to Opportunity and Time, just as she finishes bewailing the sway of chance over all living things, she says: "In vain I rail at Opportunity, / At time, at Tarquin, and uncheerful Night; / In vain I cavil with mine infamy, / In vain I spurn at my confirm'd despite . . . For me, I am the mistress of my fate, / And with my trespass never will dispense, / Till life to death acquit my forced offence" [ll. 1023-26, 1069-71]. Recognizing the futility of a passive stance she chooses, by a certain kind of death, to restore the small portion of human order which is her personal responsibility. With sudden resolution she adopts aggressive measures to restore the balance that has been upset by her enforced acquiescence during Tarquin's visit.

A further structural nicety is that the rape itself, at the near center of the poem, at once begins Lucrece's eventual triumph over nature, and culminates Tarquin's surrender to the same force. His spiritual defeat is her physical defeat so that neither entirely escapes the encroaching flood. Yet the victory of her will over feminine passivity in the last part of the poem is in effective contrast to his earlier surrender to masculine pride and sensuality during the complication. The parallel struggles emphasize the theme of human responsibility, then, in that each protagonist has before him a clearly-perceived ethical ideal which engages in a running debate with his fleshly weakness. And Tarquin's loss to his passion creates the tragic dilemma resolved by Lucrece's victory over her self-pitying dependency.

Thus the similarity between the plights of the protagonists increases our appreciation of Lucrece's achievement. And it also serves to heighten the poignancy of her position. For Tarquin is as clearly self-damned as she is victimized. The "uncontrolled tide" of his blood [l. 615] sweeps over the beleagured princess of his own soul [l. 721] before it engulfs Lucrece. He stalks toward Lucrece, fully aware of his folly: "What win I, if I gain the thing I seek . . . Who buys a minute's mirth to wail a week? / Or sells eternity to get a toy?" [ll. 211, 213-14]. And as he stands over her, he admits, "I see what crosses my attempt will bring . . . But will is deaf and hears no heedful friends . . . I know repentant tears ensue the deed . . . Yet strive I to embrace mine infamy" [ll. 491, 495, 502, 504]. During his march through the house he has had to force a series of doors, in symbolic prelude to his sexual entry. Each one has been a reminder that he might still turn back; yet at each he has succumbed to craven and absurd rationalizations [ll. 344-57] and pushed ahead, to open the door of Lucrece's chamber with an arrogant thrust of his knee [l. 359]. "Hast thou command?" she asks him at last. "By him

that gave it thee, / From a pure heart command thy rebel will" [ll. 624-25]. But this general is not the commander of his fate as the housewife is to become of hers, and the poem's structure calls our attention to the irony.

For Lucrece must struggle not only against a condition forced on her by another, but against the proper limitations of her nature. Like the hind and the dove, she is innately passive: "For men have marble, women waxen, minds, / And therefore are they form'd as marble will" [ll. 1240-41]. Yet Lucrece triumphs—by aggression—over the violence which has overwhelmed the lusty Tarquin. Herein is the crux of her tragedy, then, as it reflects the full complexity of the poem's meaning. It is through the delinquency of the men that an inverted state exists in the realm of man: a legacy of aggression has been entrusted to a submissive creature and order can only be restored by her carrying out a mode of behavior as foreign to her psychology as it is destructive to her body. When Lucrece first resolves to end her futile lamentations ("This helpless smoke of words doth me no right" [l. 1027]), she reverts almost immediately ("Thus cavils she with every thing she sees" [l. 1093]). When she later confronts Collatine she accurately remembers, "Mine enemy was strong, my poor self weak, / And far the weaker with so strong a fear" [ll. 1646-47], so that we are reminded of what it costs her now to plead, "O teach me how to make mine own excuse" [l. 1653]. And we notice finally her "many accents and delays, / Untimely breathings, sick and short assays" [ll. 1719-20] just before she stabs herself. Precisely because the role she takes upon herself is not one that she bears easily, or even well, her acceptance of its strictures is all the more moving.

And significantly, her personal responsibility has consequences beyond her intention, consequences which imply the ultimate rectitude of her mode of behavior. In maneuvering her suicide so that it obliges the men to retaliate, she not only returns responsibility to its proper source—she turns her knife upon all the Tarquins and what they represent. Indeed, she provides Brutus with the very weapon he has not been able to forge for himself. As he siezes upon her body as a political bludgeon with which to destroy the tyrant king, he is indebted to Lucrece for a means of delivering the Roman people from long and ignominious passivity. It is hardly Lucrece's fault that her blubbering husband has momentarily forgotten her charge that he act and leave the weeping to her [ll. 1679-83]. In fact, Brutus' graceless disparagement of what he calls Lucrece's "childish humour" [l. 1825] can be taken as a shrewd taunt to the flagging masculinity of Collatine and Lucretius. At any rate, Brutus' exhortation is, appropriately, a continuation of the ritual initiated by Lucrece. As he kisses the fatal knife and bids the men swear around him, he merely extends the return of salutary responsibility from Collatine's private domain to the Roman empire. As the argument specifies, "the state government" will change "from kings to consuls"; participation will replace dependency.

Natural violence, which through the irresponsibility of the Tarquins and the passivity of the Roman citizenry had overwhelmed the body politic before the opening action, has within the narrative caused young Tarquin's veins to mutiny [ll. 426-27] against the princess of his soul and has "unpeopled" the "late-sack'd island" of Lucrece's body [ll. 1740-41]. But this is to be a final conquest by the "wilderness." For thanks to the ironic courage of a woman, the men of Rome will accept their responsibility to reconstruct and maintain a fortress of order at the center of a fallen world. The structure is complete.

Shakespeare thus provides artistic justification for the self-slaughter demanded by his sources, an act for which Lucrece had been held up by St. Augustine as a model of cowardice rather than of nobility. Further justification can be found in Elizabethan medical history, which also helps to solve another critical problem presented by the poem—that of Lucrece's confessed guilt. If "not that devour'd but that which doth devour, / Is worthy blame" [ll. 1256-57], why does Lucrece stress her continued involvement in Tarquin's act, as well as her responsibility to atone for it? Does her refusal to accept the men's assurance that "her body's stain her mind untainted clears" [l. 1710] reveal a morbid concern for the outward forms of virtue, or a shallow inability to withstand the suspicions of the community—or does it perhaps betray a repressed memory of pleasure in Tarquin's arms? Shakespeare's readers, at any rate, very probably took "her body's stain" as a literal, rather than a figurative reality, considering her soul to be sheathed in a literally "polluted prison" [l. 1726]. It is likely that they believed the act of intercourse permanently to change a woman's physiology, and that they therefore applauded her destruction of a body forever joined with that of a man other than her husband as an act prompted by courageous acceptance of physical fact.

As William Harvey observed, even in 1651 doctors assumed that the male seminal fluid mixed in the uterus with a corresponding female seminal fluid which was thought to exist. Now Harvey himself had declared earlier that "the veins, by means of their orifices, absorb some of the things that are applied externally and carry this inwards with the blood." How much more likely, then, that a foreign fluid already intermixed with a fluid in the uterus should be thought to enter a woman's bloodstream. This gives point, of course, to Lucrece's concern for her "gross blood" [l. 1655] and to the line in which she compares herself to a poison'd fountain [l. 1707]. Indeed, Harvey's discussions bear directly upon the scholarly speculation as to whether Shakespeare's description of Lucrece's blood as separating into a pure, red portion and a black, "corrupted" portion "that false Tarquin stained" [ll. 1743, 1748] was "merely poetic" or reflected Elizabethan medical belief. We find a solution to the problem, I suggest, in Harvey's reference to a passage in Aristotle still seriously considered in the seventeenth century: "For the blood, if it be entire, is of a red colour and sweet taste; but if vitiated either by nature or disease, it is blacker." And as Rollins notices, Harvey himself attributed the coagulation of the blood to corruption, as does the poem.

It is because Lucrece thinks herself physically divided that she sees herself as a living rebuke to her husband; thus her private vow to Collatine: "Myself, thy friend, will kill myself, thy foe" [l. 1196]. This oath, for Elizabethan readers, must have reflected a classically tragic dilemma, to which they could freely respond.

And looking through their eyes will help us to see frankness rather than hysteria in Lucrece's declaration later: "Suppose thou dost defend me / From what is past: the help that thou shalt lend me / Comes all too late" [ll. 1684-86]. An irremediable condition has been created by the widespread complacency of those around Lucrece. She cannot exist half-pure and half-corrupted, a physical microcosm of the intolerably ambiguous natural world. But in destroying herself she can at once reaffirm the system of orderly absolutes necessary to

man, and exemplify the human responsibility upon which it depends. (pp. 505-11)

Bickford Sylvester, "Natural Mutability and Human Responsibility: Form in Shakespeare's Lucrece," in College English, *Vol. 26, No. 7, April, 1965, pp. 505-11.*

WILLIAM EMPSON   (essay date 1968)

[*An English poet, critic, and scholar, Empson is considered one of the most influential theorists of modern criticism. In his two important studies,* Seven Types of Ambiguity *(1930) and* The Structure of Complex Words *(1951), Empson adapted the ideas of I. A. Richards, the English critic and forerunner of New Criticism, and argued that the value of poetic discourse resides not in any ultimate critical evaluation, but in the correspondences and contradictions of the creative structure itself. In short, Empson was more interested in the manner in which poetic elements work together in a literary piece than in assessing the final value of a creative work as a whole. As a Shakespearean critic, he focused mainly on the emotive and connotative aspects of Shakespeare's language, as well as on the ambiguity present in much of the playwright's verse. Although many critics have attacked his methods and questioned the practicality of his theories, Empson contributed significantly to the development of New Criticism in the twentieth century. The essay from which the following excerpt is taken was first published in* Shakespeare's Narrative Poems *(1968), edited by William Burto. Empson calls* The Rape of Lucrece *a "Myth of Origin" concerning the genesis of the Roman republic, with possible Elizabethan implications as political allegory. Elizabethan censorship necessitated the submersion of any republican sentiments, and the critic suggests that the "static" nature of the poem may be a means of encoding these potentially subversive thoughts without disrupting the poem's "decorum." In addition, Empson discusses Shakespeare's ambiguous treatment of Lucrece's actions and culpability, proclaiming that "she took an involuntary pleasure in the rape, though she would have resisted it in any way possible." Despite the Christian condemnation of Lucrece, Empson suggests, Shakespeare was aware that her actions would also inspire admiration because of their political consequences.*]

[*The Rape of Lucrece*] is a Myth of Origin; to insist upon it, the death of Lucrece causes an absurd change in human blood [l. 1750]. A hero did not need to be a god before such things could happen; one could easily have a historical Myth of Origin (for example, *Macbeth* is about how the Scots, thanks to the Stuarts, took to civilised hereditary rule instead of tribal warfare). The story of Lucrece was an exciting and dangerous example because it explained how Rome threw off her kings and thus acquired an almost superhuman virtue; though somewhat obscurely, this gave its justifying importance to the heroine's choice of suicide. Both the Bible (I Sam. 12:12-25) and the classics (in practice, Plutarch) disapproved of royalty; the institution could only be defended as a necessity for our fallen natures. Also Brutus had a mysterious importance for a patriot and a dramatist. No other great period of drama, anywhere in the world, had so much interest in madmen as the Elizabethan one. This apparently derived from the Hamlet of Kyd, whose story came from a twelfth-century historian of Denmark, "the Saxon who knew Latin". But the story had classical authority from Livy's brief remarks on Lucius Junius Brutus, who pretended imbecility in order to be safe till he could take revenge; indeed, Saxo has been suspected of imitating Livy to provide elegance for his savage material, so that Hamlet, whose basic trouble in the fairy tale was that he could not tell a lie, was truthful as ever when he said "I am more an antique Roman than a Dane" [V. ii. 341]. The Brutus who killed Caesar was his bastard, as Shakespeare remarks in *Henry VI, Part Two* (IV. i), though he kept it out of *Caesar*; and a more antique Brutus, a parricide as usual, had been the first to civilise Britain; hence the name. Now, it was Brutus who plucked the dagger from Lucrece's body and championed the expulsion of the kings. He had pretended imbecility up to that very moment . . .

> Burying in Lucrece' wound his folly's show.
> He with the Romans was esteemed so
> As seely jeering idiots are with kings,
> For sportive words and utt'ring foolish things;
> But now he lays that shallow habit by
> Wherein deep policy did him disguise . . .
>
> [ll. 1810-15]

The Romans take an oath, and the last line of the poem says that the Tarquins were banished forever.

J. C. Maxwell says in his note [in the Cambridge edition of *The Rape of Lucrece*]:

> It is curious that Shakespeare makes no mention here (though the Argument concludes with it) of the historical importance of this, as involving the abolition of the monarchy (unless "everlasting" glances at it); this tells heavily against the view . . . that the popularity of the poem owed much to its bearing on political issues.

It is curious that the scholars of our age, though geared up as never before, are unable to imagine living under a censorship or making an effort to avoid trouble with Thought Police; these unpleasant features of current experience were also familiar in most historical periods, so that the disability must regularly prevent scholars from understanding what they read.

Southampton, who seemed fated to irritate the Queen, might well be inclined to cool thoughts about royalty; and Shakespeare would be wise to hesitate as to how far one might go. Though never very republican, you would think, he was certainly interested in Brutus; he had already, in *Titus Andronicus,* written better than any other Elizabethan the part of the half-genuine madman. Yet both themes are subdued to the decorum of his poem.

The resulting work is hard to read straight through, but one should realise that Shakespeare has made it static by deliberate choice. Francis Berry pointed out in *The Shakespeare Inset* that, although both these poems contain a high proportion of dialogue, the reader does not remember them so, because all the harangues might just as well be soliloquies. Indeed the silent colloquy between Lucrece and the low-class messenger, blushing together at cross-purposes [l. 1339], stands out because it is as near as we get to any contact between two minds. In a play the audience wants the story to go forward, but here the Bard could practise rhetoric like five-finger exercises on the piano. Also, the rhetoric works mainly by calling up parallel cases, so that here again the figure of myth becomes a sort of generalisation. Even this perhaps hardly excuses the long stretch of looking at tapestries of the Fall of Troy, which one may suspect was written later as a substitute for dangerous thoughts about royalty; Lucrece when appealing to Tarquin flatters his assumptions by recalling the virtues of royalty, and the highly formal structure of the work demands that she should recognize the inadequacy of such ideals after her appeal has failed. It would be sensible

to have an unpublished version suited to the patron, who contributed a great deal more than the buyers would; and besides, it would give the welcome feeling of conspiracy. But anyhow the poem needs here a feeling of grim delay—she has already decided upon suicide, but has to wait for the arrival of the proper witnesses.

Whether she was right to kill herself has long been discussed, and Shakespeare was probably not so absurd as we think to let her review the Christian objection to suicide—its origins are hard to trace. St Augustine [in his *City of God*], caddish as usual, had written "if adulterous, why praised? if chaste, why killed?"; and one might suspect that the romantic rhetoric of Shakespeare is used only to evade this old dilemma. But he is interested in the details of the case, and probably had in mind a solution, though he did not care to express it grossly. Livy already has Tarquin force her by an inherently social threat; if she rejects him, he will stab both her and a male servant in the same bed and claim afterwards that he had been righteously indignant at finding them there [l. 670]. It is assumed that her reputation has a political importance for her aristocratic family, which she puts before everything else; he gags her with her bedclothes, but not because she is expected to resist. Immediately after the rape, and till her death, she speaks of herself as guilty, and Shakespeare concurs. However, just before she stabs herself the assembled lords protest that she is still innocent, and she does not deny this, but brushes it aside as unimportant beside a social consequence:

> "No, no!" quoth she, "no dame hereafter living
> By my excuse shall claim excuse's giving."
>
> [ll. 1714-15]

Coleridge in a famous passage derided Beaumont and Fletcher because the ladies in their plays regard chastity as a costly trinket which they are liable to mislay, and it is not obvious why Shakespeare is different here. When Tarquin slinks from her bed, he says, "She bears the load of lust he left behind"; "She desperate with her nails her flesh doth tear"; she "there remains a hopeless castaway" [ll. 734, 739, 744]. Perhaps, he reflects, the instability of women is an excuse for her: they have "waxen minds . . . Then call them not the authors of their ill" [ll. 1240-44]. Just before killing herself, she speaks to her husband and the assembled lords of her "gross blood" and its "accessory yieldings" [ll. 1655, 1658]; one could hardly ask her to be much plainer. She was no virgin, having several children; and it is a basic fact about the young Shakespeare that he considers young men in general overwhelmingly desirable to women, let alone brave young lords. Thus she took an involuntary pleasure in the rape, though she would have resisted it in any way possible; that is why she felt guilty, and why some of her blood turned black, making a precedent for all future corrupted blood [l. 1750]. The reader perhaps is also guilty, having taken a sexual pleasure in these descriptions of sexual wrong—as much at least as the "homely villain" who wondered how she was making him blush. But we are not told that she would have killed herself for this private shame; she considers the suicide useful for public reasons. St Augustine would conclude that she deserved death for enjoying the rape and Hell for her suicide afterwards; but the dramatist is sure that all her reactions, in this tricky situation, do her the greatest credit and are enough to explain the permanent majesty of Rome. (pp. 8-11)

William Empson, "The Narrative Poems," in his Essays on Shakespeare, *edited by David B. Pirie, Cambridge University Press, 1986, pp. 1-28.*

ROY W. BATTENHOUSE   (essay date 1969)

[*Battenhouse is well known for his studies on religion and literature and for his theory that Shakespeare's works embody a specifically Christian world view. In the excerpt below, he argues that Shakespeare employed a double perspective in his treatment of the classical Lucrece story to comment ironically, from a Christian viewpoint, on the conventionally tragic reading of the story. This embedded Christian perspective, derived perhaps from Augustine and the Bible, portrays Lucrece as self-deluded and egotistically seeking her own martyrdom, akin to Richard II and Hamlet, according to Battenhouse. Thus, the critic finds Lucrece at least partially culpable for her own demise, and reasons that if she really desired to be rescued from Tarquin, she would have called for help. Battenhouse suggests that "her pleas have an underside of intimated invitation to sexual play," and her suicide, contrived to secure her own fame, "is a kind of masturbatory self-rape." In essence, Lucrece's actions parallel Tarquin's; both protagonists present themselves as victims and yet, ultimately, both are seducers, Battenhouse argues. As Lucrece seeks to convince her audience that revenge, a Christian sin, can be noble in defence of honor, a pagan virtue, she renders the Romans complicit in her evil.*]

At the age of thirty—after having written *Richard III* and before completing *Romeo and Juliet*—Shakespeare published his *Rape of Lucrece* (1594). This tragic story in narrative verse was immediately and for a generation afterwards very well received, going into six further editions. (p. 3)

Today's historians of literature see in the poem's tuneful rhetoric the tradition of Ovid. But only rarely does anyone sense, besides this, a sophisticated psychology of tragedy—perhaps as intricate as that of Chaucer's *Troilus,* whose rime-royal stanza Shakespeare is here using. Probably because *Lucrece,* unlike Chaucer's *Troilus,* depicts a love which is consummated in violence and then plunges the heroine into a nightmare of grief, almost all readers since Dr. Johnson's era have misliked this work of Shakespeare's. Johnson himself (a moralist with scant understanding of tragedy) found lapses of judgment in it, which condescendingly he attributed to Shakespeare's straining as a young poet to write in a self-consciously tragic manner.

Using Johnson's view as a springboard, the editor of the new Arden text (1960) has outspokenly voiced his own more bitter distaste. *Lucrece* is a young man's idea of tragedy, F. T. Prince believes, "and the imagination of the young man in question is a curious blend of health and morbidity, a bundle of self-contradictory impulses" [see excerpt above, 1960]. Lured by a "craving for sensation," says this critic, the poet has misused his talents, and as a result it is "only too obvious that the poem, as a whole, is a failure." (pp. 3-4)

Toward a rehabilitation of the artistic greatness of *Lucrece,* there has appeared a more recent essay by Harold R. Walley [see excerpt above, 1961]. Here the poem is defended as a work carefully structured and designed to give a "systematic elucidation of tragedy." In Walley's view, it "lays the foundation of Shakespeare's whole subsequent treatment of tragedy" and fairly bristles with anticipations of his later dramatic work. (pp. 4-5)

I consider Walley's main contention valid, and his supporting analysis correct, as far as it goes. Yet it falls short, in various ways, of a fully adequate focus on the causes of tragedy. Tarquin's motive has not been quite grasped in its deepest dimensions, and Lucrece's responsibility has been seen only as she herself envisions it. Omitted in this picture are her own self-deception and its causes, and her husband's significant folly,

and in the background the tragedy of Roman civilization as a whole. Lucrece's tragedy, in its implications, needs to be seen as that of all Rome. It rests, as I shall be showing, on a tragic flaw that is distinctively Roman yet typically human. Precisely what this flaw is, Walley has not perceived, simply because like most other readers he has overlooked the story's persistent ironies. Yet these ironies are available to us through innumerable verbal clues. And when pondered they bring to the classical story a special perspective, the product of a heritage of Christian interpretation.

Modern-day lack of enthusiasm for *Lucrece* (Walley excepted) goes back, as I have indicated, to the limited perspective which emerged with English neoclassicism. Viewed from within such limits, the purpose of the poem's rhetoric seemed merely ornamental. (pp. 5-6)

Are . . . critics justified in thinking the rhetoric nonfunctional to plot and characterization? Shakespeare in his dedication of the earlier *Venus and Adonis* had promised Southampton a forthcoming "graver labour." Did he mean by this a labor of merely ornamental engraving, a show of his skill in grammar-book exercises? Surely something more, I believe: the retelling of an ancient tragedy in a seriously revelatory way— or, as Walley says, designing it "to bring home to men's business and bosoms the broad significance of certain historical events."

But where was the "broad significance" of those events to be found? Could it be truly found in the 132 lines on Lucrece in Ovid's *Fasti*? Or in Ovid's text when supplemented by the slightly more detailed account given in Livy's history (and translated into English prose by Painter in 1566)? These were Shakespeare's chief sources in the opinion of critics, and all told they are scant ones. Their substance is adequately conveyed in the brief prose Argument with which Shakespeare prefaces his poem. Let me suggest, however, that this Argument sums up the legend as the Romans understood it, whereas Shakespeare's own profounder understanding is embedded in the poem which follows. That is, theirs can be an outward "cover" for his version, now to be offered within such a husk.

The inner story, we immediately discover, not only expands into 1855 lines but, astonishingly, achieves this huge enlargement while completely omitting the first episode of the Roman legend. The noblemen's visit to Rome for a testing of their wives, and finding that only Lucrece vindicates her husband's commendation, is told in the Argument but is absent from the poem itself. We enter on the story as if *in medias res.* A lust-breathing Tarquin is on his way, alone, to Lucrece's house. Even more significantly, his lust has arisen without his ever having seen Lucrece. (pp. 6-7)

"It seems to be unlikely," remarks one modern editor of *The Rape of Lucrece,* "that Tarquin should desire Lucrece before he sees her" [Charlotte Porter, in an introduction to her edition (1912) of *The Rape of Lucrece*]; this "mechanical" improvement "loses more than it gains." But is Shakespeare's alteration merely a mechanical one? It does indeed lose something—namely, the basic assumption of the Ovid-Livy tale, that Tarquin's lust has as its cause his earlier sight of a chaste Lucrece, modestly engaged in spinning a war-cloak for her husband, and saying tearfully to her maids as she directs the work: "Whenever I picture him to myself in the midst of battle, I tremble, I feel ready to die, sudden cold strikes at my heart" (Ovid, as translated by Charlotte Porter). It loses this important assumption, that an idyllically pious wife, whose one concern is her husband's safety, has by her very sanctity aroused a sexual lust in her husband's friend, through his witnessing her at work and then beholding her beauty as she rises to embrace lovingly her returned husband. What Shakespeare's revised beginning gains, instead, is a quite different cause for the tragedy—an untested boast of a chaste Lucrece on the part of her husband. On this more problematic base Shakespeare has set his version. It permits, in turn, a significantly variant psychology and a deeper rationale for the whole story. I would suggest, indeed, that all of Shakespeare's subsequent rhetorical inventions—including such major ones as Tarquin's internal debate, Lucrece's sermon when under threat, her long aftermath of complaint, and even the Troy tapestry introduced for her contemplation—function as a development of this new rationale.

In other words, Shakespeare is dilating the classical legend not simply with rhetoric, but rather *through rhetoric* with a truth hidden from the Romans and their story-tellers. Unlike his tragic heroine Lucrece, who cannot read "the subtle-shining secrecies / Writ in the glassy margents" of Tarquin's "parling lookes" [ll. 100-01], Shakespeare can read these secrecies and can trace them to their complex source. Furthermore, he can read certain subtle shinings on the glassy margins of Lucrece's own face, since (as he has her say significantly in line 1253) "Poor women's faces are their own faults' books." That is, there are facts in her face which covertly contribute to the tragedy, and which can be imaginatively indicated through the parleyings Shakespeare invents for her in the course of Tarquin's visit. As narrator of the encounter he can provide a kind of perspective glass—like that described by Bushy in *Richard II* [II. ii. 18-20] (written around 1594). In a perspective glass, the griefs of human beings "show nothing but confusion" when gazed on directly, yet reveal significant "form" when "eyed awry." Shapes of grief, says Bushy in that important passage, are "naught but shadows / Of what is not" [II. ii. 23-4]. Only by eyeing these shadowy shapes *awry* will we discover that they are but the vision of "false sorrow's eye" [II. ii. 26].

The metaphor of a perspective glass suggests a concept common in medieval art—the distinction between a work's surface of "beautiful lie" and a truth hidden under this fiction, the kernel beneath its husk, its fruit amid the chaff. All such metaphors involve the notion of a double perspective, through which a covert meaning is discoverable inside an overt one. In *Lucrece,* therefore, may not Shakespeare be giving us, on the surface of his poem, the grief of "false sorrow's eye," and at the same time inviting us to eye awry this surface that we may thereby discover what is being falsified? If we will but "attend each line" (as Shakespeare invites us to do in line 818), I think we will find easily enough this double perspective. The tragic tale requires, for its surface movement, a rhetoric of woe; yet built into that rhetoric are hidden "forms" for a wry reading of the tragedy. In this respect Shakespeare has restyled, and gone quite beyond, Ovid and Livy.

But where could Shakespeare have found sources for the marginal vision I have just defined and postulated? Might he have found a source in Chaucer's tale of Lucrece in *The Legend of Good Women?* Various critics have surmised that the *Legend* was possibly or probably known to Shakespeare, but most seem to feel, as Kittredge does [in his 1936 edition of *The Complete Works of Shakespeare*], that Shakespeare's *Lu-*

crece "owes nothing to Chaucer." Those scholars who have compared most closely Shakespeare's story details with Ovid's and Livy's have seen in Chaucer's version so little additional to the Roman version that they think him either an uncertain influence on Shakespeare, as Ewig does, or a "negligible one," as Baldwin [see Additional Bibliography] does. What they have overlooked, however, is Chaucer's irony in the *Legend.* Such oversight is understandable, since most of our specialists in the study of Chaucer have likewise failed to see this irony. . . . Chaucer's irony in celebrating the "goodness" of Lucrece is exactly the point at which Shakespeare could have learned from him.

Yet Chaucer's way of telling the Lucrece story is not quite Shakespeare's. Chaucer, I think, was covertly making a farce of Ovid's martyrology, while on the surface keeping his own version studiously deferential to Ovid, almost as brief, and seemingly in accord with the order of episodes as given by Ovid. Shakespeare, on the other hand, was transubstantiating Ovid into the magnitude required for serious tragedy, while reformulating Ovid's episodes to support an intricately incremental tragedy on the theme of "ambitious foul infirmity" [l. 150]. Nevertheless, what Chaucer and Shakespeare have in common is double perspective. Both bring to the Roman tale a wry underside of perception which evaluates the classical world view moving at the surface. The "source" for which we should inquire, in both these authors, is the source which makes possible their marginal perception. In Chaucer's case, we have our clue to such a source when he casually fumbles a reference to Augustine at the beginning, and then at the very end bungles a reference to the Bible. These two Christian sources are, surreptitiously, the basis for the true meaning of Chaucer's tale. Likewise they are so for Shakespeare's tale, even though Shakespeare does not openly name either one. A moral vision whose source is St. Augustine (especially his chapter on Lucrece in *City of God* I. 19), and behind him the Bible, ultimately accounts for the art with which Shakespeare has thoroughly reformulated classical story.

To show how this is so, let us now examine the rich texture of Shakespeare's *Lucrece.* (pp. 7-10)

First let us note how, at the poem's very outset, Shakespeare focuses on the unwise boasting of Lucrece's husband, Collatine. In Tarquin's presence, Collatine has praised Lucrece "at such high-proud rate" [l. 19], that kings might be "espoused to more fame" [l. 20] but never to so peerless a dame as his. In fact, Collatine thinks of Lucrece as his highest heaven—a view which Shakespeare as narrator criticizes indirectly, by commenting on the transitoriness of all happiness that is centered on the gifts a man possesses. Moreover, the poet remarks that Collatine's boast, perchance, was what tainted Tarquin's heart with envy, thus stirring up in him the fires of lust. With a delicacy of touch the poem is intimating that what was referred to in the Argument as simply the "pleasant humor" of the Roman noblemen is tainted, actually, with passions which any reader of Genesis would recognize— pride followed by envy. These make of Tarquin "this devil." He has become a "false worshipper" of an "earthly saint," Lucrece. But note the word *earthly.* It hints at a mistaken worship, quite antecedent to Tarquin's false dealings. The worshipping of an earthly beauty implies idolatry, which is one kind of falsity; it can issue in another kind, treachery.

Next, the poem tells us of Lucrece's two conspicuous endowments: virtue and beauty. But the white of the one and the red of the other are located, in Shakespeare's description, in her "face" simply. There they make show of themselves—not at peace but in a constant combat to outdo each other. Very prettily, Shakespeare describes how the two colors oscillate in vanquishing each other:

> When virtue bragged, beauty would blush for
>   shame;
> When beauty boasted blushes, in despite
> Virtue would stain that o'er with silver white.
>
>   [ll. 54-6]

Behind the prettiness of this warfare, there are moral implications. Note that virtue's only activity here is to brag, or alternately to stain, while beauty's is to blush shamefacedly, or alternately to boast blushingly. What Shakespeare calls "this heraldry in Lucrece' face" [l. 64] hints at a nature dialectically ruled by two ambitious forces, each guided by no purpose other than (as he says) to "underprop" the "fame" of Lucrece. It is this fame which has attracted Tarquin, who in order to vindicate his own fame now feels he must vanquish Lucrece's fame, and who himself is inwardly at war between affection for beauty and his virtuous conscience. In him, as our story will reveal, a bloody lust vanquishes his pale virtue, and then in response Lucrece's pallid virtue dominates over her own red blood. (Meanwhile Shakespeare suggests indirectly, in [ll. 1511-12], that blushing-red is a sign of guilt, and paleness of cheek a sign of "the fear that false hearts have.") Thus nature's strife between red and white becomes, as I read it, an emblem of a dialectic which encompasses the story's whole action, enslaving man and woman alike to a tragic love of fame, protean in its mutability.

Thirdly, let us observe that early in the poem, soon after Shakespeare has brought Tarquin and Lucrece under the same roof, he pauses for three stanzas (20-22) to moralize on covetousness and its effects. To covet honor, wealth, or ease, he says, is to engage in a "thwarting strife," in which we gain only bankruptcy and death. Stanza 22, in particular, sums up the metaphysics of this paradox:

>   in venturing ill we leave to be
> The things we are for that which we expect.
> And this ambitious foul infirmity,
> In having much, torments us with defect
> Of that we have. So then we do neglect
>   The thing we have, and, all for want of wit,
>   Make something nothing by augmenting it.
>
>   [ll. 148-54]

This explanation of evil is the traditionally Christian one, and here it is being offered us as a vantage point from which to assess the more limited understanding possessed by the characters within the tragedy. If we apply the narrator's moralizing to a judging of Tarquin only—as we may be tempted to do by the fact that it is applied immediately to "doting Tarquin"—we will be falling into a moral myopia, like that of Lucrece and her Roman admirers. Although Shakespeare is permitting such a trap for unwary readers, if they yield to it they will be indulging superficial emotions which the poem as a whole, when rightly pondered, can purge. Actually the narrator's theme applies universally to the full range of events to come within the total story. Covetousness will figure later, for instance, in the poet's comment that Tarquin's "greedy eyeballs" treasonously mislead his heart [ll. 368-69]. But also it will crop up in Lucrece's moralizing—through which unwittingly she describes herself—when she speaks of "The aged man that coffers up his gold . . . And useless barns the harvest of his wits" [ll. 855-59]. Here the word "barns," inci-

dentally, carries an allusion by Shakespeare to the parable of the covetous rich man in Luke 12.

If I may now recall two of St. Augustine's most famous passages, it will become evident that covetousness can take either of two closely allied forms: one, an abandoning of personal honor in the blind pursuit of a fleshly good; or secondly, an abandoning of fleshly good in the blind pursuit of a personal honor. A paradigm of the first, I suggest, is Augustine's story in *The Confessions* (II. 9-18) of his youthful pear-stealing; and a paradigm of the second is his story in *The City of God* (I. 19) of the suicide of Lucrece. In polar ways, these may have a pertinence to the two major sections of Shakespeare's narrative. Let us therefore digress to take a look, first, at the pear-stealing episode in *The Confessions*.

Augustine there describes himself as running headlong into shamelessness. What compelled the theft, he says, was not a famished poverty, but rather a delight in the theft itself because it would be misliked. "Fair were the pears, but not them did my wretched soul desire; . . . I gathered only that I might steal." Once gained, the pears were scarcely tasted before he flung them away. Hence it can be inferred that what he chiefly loved was the audacity of his act, and the fact that it was foul. Yet, on more final analysis, Augustine concludes that he loved not the villainy itself, but rather a kind of "maimed liberty," which was but a darkened shadow of Divine omnipotency. He sees a likeness between this boyish act of his and the adult tyrannies of Catiline—of whom it was said that he was cruel lest through idleness his hand or heart should grow inactive. All such savageries, in Augustine's view, are but a mimicking of God's freedom; they have their root in a coveting of sovereignty.

Does not the behavior of Shakespeare's Tarquin parallel Augustine's explanation? Note that although Tarquin professes Lucrece's beauty as his prize, he nevertheless discards her after the rape, having barely tasted her body. Moreover, in advance of the rape he acknowledges that his desire is mere dotage, against both law and duty; "Yet strive I," he says, "to embrace mine infamy" [l. 504]. Infamy has become for him a perverse form of fame-seeking. Basically what he loves is his own resoluteness, and the illusion of power which his fearlessness of consequences gives him, and in particular the satisfying sense of activity he gets from striking his falchion against flint, or in setting his foot upon the light. It is utterly futile, therefore, for Lucrece to emphasize in her pleas the dishonor and ruin Tarquin is bringing on himself. He already knows that, but is subconsciously enjoying his own capacity to dare such a doom. From the outset of his enterprise, the very blameworthiness of his design has excited his will. Actual physical sight of Lucrece, in Shakespeare's reading, has not been the initial cause. Later, in the bedroom scene, when at last Tarquin has full opportunity to survey her beauty as she lies sleeping "like a virtuous monument," Shakespeare's five stanzas of anatomical description [ll. 386-420] conclude with a sixth telling us that such gazing actually "qualified" and "slacked" Tarquin's rage of lust, until his eye began to tempt his veins. Plainly, what he chiefly covets is a proof of his audacity.

And what triggers his final enacting of a conquest is Lucrece's offering opposition by lecturing him on its forbiddenness. Her negatives, as Tarquin himself comments, are a "let" (a word meaning "hindrance" but suggesting also "permission"), which turns not the tide of his uncontrolled passion, but rather "swells [it] the higher" [l. 646]. This is true, also, of other negatives he encounters. The fact that his conscience opposes his crime in a long internal debate becomes to Tarquin a reason for overriding reason in order to show his own bravery. Likewise when he faces ominous external warnings—the frightening cries of weasels, the smoke blown from a torch onto his face, the needle in Lucrece's glove which pricks his finger—he "in the worst sense" construes their denial. They are but "lets," he says, which "attend the time" [l. 330]. That is, they help make his adventure an exciting pastime.

Walley has claimed rightly, I believe, that the psychological pattern in Tarquin is basically that of Shakespearean characters such as Macbeth. In a character of this type there is an open acceptance of what is known to be a crime, a deliberate flouting of the moral sense. But what about another type of tragic hero—the type represented in Hamlet, Brutus, or Othello? Does not Shakespeare more often, and more typically, choose for his tragic hero some self-deluded champion of virtue, rather than a conscious villain? Should we not in the present instance, therefore, look to Lucrece rather than to Tarquin as our model for highest tragedy? Our present poem, as a matter of fact, is named after Lucrece. Perhaps hers is the tragedy in which Shakespeare has summed up his most subtle insights into evil.

But this second type of tragedy, as I have already suggested, has also its paradigm in the pages of St. Augustine. Whereas Augustine associates his pear-stealing with what he calls a Babylonian mire and with Catiline, Rome's worst, on the other hand he associates Lucrece with Rome's boasted best, yet with Rome's most characteristic fault, an inordinate love of glory. To Augustine, Lucrece's obsessive fear of scandal and her ultimate suicide illustrate the moral contradictions inherent in a misplaced idealism. He brings up her story as a capital instance of pagan heroism at its alleged noblest, then shows such nobleness to be self-deceptive and illogical, the product of a superficial and distorted notion of virtue. Later, in Book V of *The City of God,* he rates ambition for glory as "nearer to virtue" than crude avarice, but underscores for his readers the pitiableness of those Roman heroes who sacrificed wealth, and even life itself, simply that men might think well of them. Theirs is the sad story of "splendid vices." In coveting praise, Rome has gained only an empty and tragic eminence. (pp. 10-14)

Shakespeare's treatment of Lucrece . . . accounts for her fate in terms of a Roman love of fame, and there are occasional hints of kinship to Eve's vanity in Genesis. By a close reading we can sense these factors from the very beginning of Lucrece's encounter with Tarquin. Why does she blush in giving "reverent welcome" to her visitor when he stares at her with "still gazing eyes"? Why is she unsuspicious of his "wanton sight"? The narrator says she "little suspecteth" and is impressed by his shows of honor, his "plaits of majesty." When he avoids speaking of the purpose of his coming and makes excuses, why is she still unalarmed? The poem's clue is in the fact that he "decks with praises Collatine's high name" and "stories to her ears her husband's fame" [ll. 108, 106]. He praises Collatine's "*bruised* arms and *wreaths* of victory" [l. 110]—an equivocal kind of chivalry, we might say. Lucrece responds "with heaved-up hand" to express her joy, and "wordless so greets heaven" [ll. 111-12]. But is she saluting heaven—or, rather, Tarquin for his story-telling? (Some five hundred lines later, we find her heaving up *both* her hands to Tarquin, a gesture that could represent ambiguously either

plea or surrender.) She stayed "after supper long" [l. 122], we are told, in conversation devoted to his questionings.

On retiring to bed Tarquin has memories of how, holding his hand, she "gazed for tidings in my eager eyes" [l. 254], while in her face her color rose to deep red, then blanched to white; and how, with her hand "locked" in his, she both trembled and smiled. Tarquin innocently attributes these actions to her "loyal fear," but Shakespeare may be suggesting that the fear thus displayed is less loyal to Collatine than this parleying couple realizes. In any case, we have here a broad spectrum of compromising detail—all of it by way of marginal addition to Ovid and Livy. Ovid has only four lines, in which he tells us simply that the good woman, thinking no evil of her visiting kinsman, gave him welcome and a supper at her table, after which "came the hour for slumber," presumably right after supper. Chaucer impishly, I think, omits the prefatory supper. He has Tarquin enter the house late at night, as a thief, through a window—thus implying, for the surface reader, Lucrece's utter lack of any opportunity to suspect evil, but giving the alert reader a hint as to her knack for leaving windows open, through a negligence due perhaps to subconscious motive. A subconscious preparation in Shakespeare's Lucrece seems indicated by a detail given of her bedroom sleeping. When the intruding Tarquin draws the curtains of her bed, he sees a "pearly sweat" on the hand that is lying outside the coverlet.

Lucrece. By Titian.

In all versions Lucrece awakens to find Tarquin in her bed-room. But in Shakespeare's version Tarquin's threat, that if she denies him he will not merely slay her but devise scandalous circumstances to blacken her reputation, moves Lucrece to plead—after a lengthy silence, and then with sighs prefacing her eloquence—not for life but for reputation. She preaches a long sermon on lust's dishonor, by which actually she increases its fascination. Why does Shakespeare have her react in this way? Is he not contriving to show, in anticipation of the second half of his poem, that a concern for self-justification on her part is leading her even now, not to avoid ruin but to tempt it? "If thou deny," Tarquin warns her, "then force must work my way" [l. 513]. So, deny she does—as if subconsciously she wished force to work his way, but only after she has had time to excuse herself from responsibility. "Tears *harden* lust," says Shakespeare [l. 560]—and then shows us Lucrece aiding such hardening in Tarquin by her own tearful looks. (Like Shakespeare's later heroes, Richard II and Hamlet, she seems covertly to desire some "plight" that will facilitate a self-pitying and self-vindicating role.)

Surely if Lucrece really wished rescue, she has plenty of time to cry out for it; for Shakespeare, in contrast to Ovid, makes much of Tarquin's long dallying. And surely there are servants in the house to answer calls for help; for Tarquin's own threat mentions a household "slave," and the Argument has mentioned housemaids. (One of them comes "fleet-winged" at Lucrece's call the next morning; and a hint that this maid was awake to goings-on the night before is given in her statement that she was "stirring ere the break of day" [l. 1280]. Shakespeare is but giving his reader time to realize that actually Lucrece's resort to complaints is her way of escaping from calling for help, and that her spinning out a lecture to Tarquin is a way of pulling her own wool over her sheepish eyes. Indeed, her pleas have an underside of intimated invitation to sexual play, as for instance in the lines:

> Thou look'st not like deceit; do not deceive me.
> My sighs, like whirlwinds, labor hence to heave
>   thee.
>   If ever man were moved with woman's moans,
>   Be moved with my tears, my sighs, my groans.
>
> [ll. 585-88]

This is whip-saw moralizing: no and yes in the same breath. It gives special irony to her rhetorical question: "And wilt *thou* be the school where Lust shall learn?" [l. 617]; and then to her rhetorical answer, "Thou back'st *reproach* against long-living *laud*" [l. 622]. This epitomizes what, blindly, she is herself doing.

In her steadfast determination to upbraid *his* sin, Lucrece is being completely successful in failing to see how her preachings apply to herself:

> Men's faults do seldom to themselves appear.
> Their own transgressions partially they smother.
> This guilt would seem death-worthy in thy brother.
>   Oh, how are they wrapped in with infamies
>   That from their own misdeeds askance their eyes!
>
> [ll. 633-37]

Here her surface woe is fabricating a denunciation of man, which Shakespeare's context is universalizing to include woman. Any reader less self-deluded than Lucrece cannot fail to be reminded of the biblical sermon: "Why beholdest thou not the mote that is in thine own eye? . . . Can the blind lead the blind? Shall they not both fall into the ditch?" [Mat-

thew 15:14]. Into the ditch, inevitably, they both do fall. (pp. 15-17)

After the rape we see Lucrece obsessed by feelings of shame and disgrace. She thinks now only of the burden of "offense" put upon her. In Shakespeare's words, she "bids her eyes hereafter still be blind," while she beats her breast and "prays she never may behold the day" [ll. 758, 746]. Here the poet is hinting at the real measure of Lucrece's fault—her desire to shut her eyes against daylight examination of her action and, instead, treasure her own fancies of truth. No wonder she is unable to recognize (as Augustine so carefully does) that a rifling of the body involves no true dishonor unless the will consents to such an act. It would be fatal to her fancy of herself if she were to search into the meaning of "consent."

Fearing for loss of social status, Lucrece now luxuriates in grief, virtually wrapping herself in a cocoon of it. She breaks out in self-pitying expostulations against Night, Opportunity, and Time—as if these were gods determining her destiny, rather than means which she has misused and could better use in another way. She inconsistently both blames them and invokes their aid. And we hear her call on smoky Night to let not Day behold the face of Lucrece, which "Immodestly lies martyred with disgrace" [l. 802]. In this phrase she unwittingly confesses her own "immodesty" and hints at the "lie" her martyrdom presents in being devoted to disgrace, not grace. Such are Shakespeare's subtle ironies of diction. A stanza later he lets her complain that

> The light will show, charactered in my brow,
> The story of sweet chastity's decay
>
> [ll. 807-08]

—a statement true certainly of Lucrece's chastity, although she is wriggling for some way to disprove it. Essentially her chastity is even now decadent, and thus makes her sour-faced rather than sweet.

Four stanzas later she introduces a beautiful simile. She complains that she is like a drone bee, her honey lost, stolen from her by a "wandering wasp" that has crept into her "weak hive" and sucked the honey which as a chaste bee she kept. Figuratively this is truer than its speaker realizes. Her chastity has indeed been weakly guarded—by buzzing complaints as impotent as any drone's, both now and from the moment she first used them against Tarquin. Moreover, the wandering wasp which has sucked her honey may figure, not solely Tarquin (as she supposes), but her own waspish dawdling, which has emptied her chastity of all its substance, and is even now distracting her from the final end of beeing (metaphorically the proper end of every human "being"), the producing of honey.

A similar irony attends her complaints against Opportunity. Bitterly she accuses Opportunity of failing to be "the humble suppliant's friend" [l. 897] of never showing her presence to the lame and the blind. Hence,

> The patient dies while the physician sleeps;
> The orphan pines while the oppressor feeds;
> Justice is feasting while the widow weeps;
> Advice is sporting while infection breeds.
> Thou grant'st no time for charitable deeds.
>
> [ll. 904-08]

But surely the "thou" who here grants no time for charitable deeds is actually Lucrece herself, who instead of seeking to be a physician is sporting herself in advice-giving, while infection breeds within *her*. It is she who is neglecting the "patient" in herself and feeding on oppression, while weeping lamely like a widow—although she has in fact a husband. The multiple ironies of human self-delusion are here Shakespeare's tragic theme. "Why work'st thou mischief in thy pilgrimage?" [l. 960] Lucrece asks of Time, but never thinks to ask of herself. In her view, Time is the enemy, injurious and irresponsible Time. If only Time would grant her now the return of one past hour, she sighs, she herself could prevent this night's dread storm and its wrack! But with her next breath she is using the *present* moment to stir up and fan in herself a tempest of hate toward Tarquin, for whom she begs Time to devise "extremes beyond extremity."

> Stone him with hardened hearts, harder than
> stones,
> And let mild women to him lose their mildness,
> Wilder to him than tigers in their wildness.
>
> [ll. 978-80]

Here she is making herself into the very tiger she invokes. (pp. 17-19)

Lucrece's expostulations to Night, Opportunity, and Time have alternated between blaming and begging. Weaving her feelings through a maze of contradictions—which Shakespeare is letting us see as the vanity of reasonings motivated by vanity—Lucrece regards these cosmic powers as irresponsible yet somehow responsible for her infamy. They are in her view detestable traitors, to whom she nevertheless calls for divine aid in establishing justice. Time, for example, she rails at as being a murderer [l. 929], yet ends by asking that Time teach her how to curse the thief (Tarquin? or herself?) with a madness of self-murder [l. 996]. Such a madness is precisely what *we* can see she has been taking time to teach herself.

Having touched on suicide, she breaks off her harangue. Deploring what she calls "this helpless smoke of words," she resolves on a "remedy indeed to do me good" [ll. 1027-28]. Since in Shakespeare's art the "smoke of words" has been the very means by which she has been making herself helpless, what kind of "good" may we expect? Appropriately, that of a forged martyrdom. But there is the further irony that Lucrece's proposal now to "let forth my foul defiled blood" [l. 1029] is actually a remedy analogous to Tarquin's: he, merely in a different way, had let forth his foul blood (the lust of his defiled nobility). Shakespeare has already told us that Tarquin's act "defaced" his "soul's fair temple," leaving as legacy a "spotted princess" [ll. 719-21]. Now this spotted princess can be seen in Lucrece, intent on razing her own soul's temple, her body of flesh and blood.

"My honor I'll bequeath unto the knife" [l. 1184], she vows, recalling thus the knife Tarquin had cowed her with, and through which now illogically she hopes for remedy. "So of shame's ashes shall my fame be bred" [l. 1188]. (A latter-day reader can hardly avoid thinking here of the similar heroism of Shakespeare's later Romans—Brutus, Antony, and Cleopatra.) But before Lucrece can pitch herself to such an action, she must first justify herself—not quite as Tarquin did, by deliberately overriding conscience, but (like Brutus in *Julius Caesar*) by a shifting and self-contradictory conscience. Her mad reasonings weave, in Shakespeare's telling, a tapestry of beautiful ironies. There is her argument, for instance, that since what she sought to live for is gone, she can now "clear this spot" by death, which will cover "slander's livery" with a "badge of fame" [ll. 1053-54]. The illogic here is in propos-

ing death as a remedy for what is already dead, and fame as a remedy for slander. "I am the mistress of my fate" [l. 1069], she boasts in another stanza,

> And with my trespass never will dispense,
> Till life to death acquit my forced offence.
>
> [ll. 1070-71]

But if indeed "mistress" of her fate, how did she become the victim of any "forced" offence? Or why cannot the trespass be now dispensed by forgiveness? "Mistress of my fate" is a claim that here makes no sense unless, ironically, it means mistress of her trespass, which she is forcing herself to find indispensable to her life. That is, she would rather die than give it up.

The height of Lucrece's nonsense, perhaps, comes with her boast that "in my death I murder shameful scorn" [l. 1189]. Actually, will not her death merely illustrate a shameful scorn, Lucrece's own scorn of life? Scorn (as readers of Matthew 5:22 know) is not murder's victim but murder's motive. Lucrece's logic is topsy-turvy. Yet Shakespeare, by the doleful tone of his verses, keeps the irony subdued. He is writing tragedy, not satire, and hence must avoid overt mockery, must keep pathos uppermost.

Shakespeare maintains this delicate balance by spinning out Lucrece's anguish long enough that it can become for us an object of contemplation. And to further distance it, he shows Lucrece catching at mirrors of herself in classical story. One such digression is her turning to the nightingale, Philomel, to join in a singing of ravishment and languishment. . . . "Make thy sad grove in my disheveled hair," begs Lucrece, so that "While thou on Tereus descant'st, / I'll hum on Tarquin" [ll. 1129, 1133-34]. But note that Shakespeare has placed this request against an early morning setting, in which birds of day are singing mirthful melody. Against these Lucrece wilfully shuts her ears, to hearken instead to this one bird of night. She calls day's birds "mocking birds" and bids them be mute. "A woeful hostess brooks not merry guests" [l. 1125], she says. But Shakespeare-as-narrator has tucked in the comment: "Great grief grieves most at that would do it good" [l. 1117]. Self-pity, he goes on to imply, is a prelude to lawless behavior: "Grief dallied with nor law nor limit knows" [l. 1120]. Can any reader of this scene doubt the poet's maturity as moralist and psychologist?

Observe, further, how skilfully he has integrated the Philomela motif into his larger story. He shows Lucrece fascinated with the "thorn" at Philomela's breast. He shows her resolving to keep Philomela's "woes waking" by fixing "a sharp knife" to her own heart, that she may imitate "well" the wretched nightingale. Significantly, Lucrece does not altogether lack an awareness of the wrongness of such action:

> "To kill myself," quoth she, "alack, what were it,
> But with my body my poor soul's pollution?"
>
> [ll. 1156-57]

Moreover, it would be "a merciless conclusion," she admits, for any mother to slay her second baby because the first had died. But these glimmerings of truth are evaded by immediately burying them under a maze of contrary reasoning—that by making "some hole" in her "blemished fort" she can provide escape for her troubled soul; that by spending her blood she can ensure revenge on Tarquin; that by bequeathing her honor to the knife "fame" shall be bred; and that by leaving to Collatine this example of her "resolution" she can "boast" herself his true friend.

As we listen to such argument, are we not reminded, perhaps, of similar make-believe persuasions on the part of Shakespeare's suicides in his later *Julius Caesar* or *Antony and Cleopatra*? There is some resemblance, also, to the logic by which Hector, in *Troilus and Cressida* (II. ii), is shown arriving at his "resolution" to disregard the moral laws of nature: affection for the "fame" which in time to come may "canonize" him overwhelms all else. But this desire for worldly canonization proved to be Hector's ruin, and Troy's with him. It may be significant, therefore, that in the present poem Troy's dismal story is the theme of a tapestry on which Lucrece next fixes her attention. It furnishes her a major mirror for self-study, and chiefly fills up the hours while she is awaiting the delivery of her letter to her husband.

Surely Shakespeare has not introduced this long digression, as some critics seem to think, merely to exercise his rhetoric on a set piece. More likely he is seizing an opportunity to project Lucrece's Roman plight against the larger canvas of Greek story—and also, in accordance with his general understanding of tragedy, to show her (like Hamlet) seizing on this opportunity to work herself up emotionally for a later "let go" release into self-dramatization. Even though the digression takes 217 lines, one-ninth of the poem, we need not suppose with Sir Sidney Lee that this "delays the progress of the story beyond all artistic law" [see excerpt above, 1905]. Rather, it belongs to Shakespeare's artistic purpose to affiliate new Troy's developing tragedy to old Troy's, and to show how the imagined past helps precipitate Lucrece's latent revenge motive. Lucrece herself may be blind to various of the figurative Troy-Rome parallels, or distort the ones she does seize on. Yet the poem's reader may grasp them, if he will, and thereby gain perspective on Lucrece. We are to be shown how Lucrece reads Troy's prototypal tragedy for clues to her personal tragedy. And while she reads we can ask: With how much self-understanding is she capable of reading? Her shallowness as an explicator of great art can then become for us both amusingly pathetic and a caveat for explicators like ourselves.

Lucrece identifies herself, we observe, first (at line 1447) with the despairing Hecuba, in whose face "all distress is stelled" [l. 1444], and then finally (at line 1546) with credulous Priam, who was beguiled by the "outward honesty" of subtle Sinon. How appropriate for Lucrece is either one of these self-identifications? Putting her own feelings into Hecuba's mouth, she rails on Pyrrhus. Comparing herself with Priam, she declares Tarquin to be the Sinon through whom "my Troy" perished, and again vents her revenge feelings. But all the while she is raging against the violence and guile of the Greeks, she seems wholly unaware that their motive for such actions was basically the same as the motive she herself now cherishes, namely, glory for oneself by avenging a rape. Is not she herself about to incite her own husband to become a Pyrrhus-like destroyer of Rome's royal family? And will she not go about her revenge with quite as much "saintlike" show as Sinon used in beguiling Priam? There is Shakespearean irony, therefore, in her lament that Sinon's "borrowed tears" were but a hellish means for burning Troy with water:

> Priam, why art thou old and yet not wise?
> For every tear he falls a Trojan bleeds.
> His eye drops fire, no water thence proceeds.
>   Those round clear pearls of his that move thy
>   pity

> Are balls of quenchless fire to burn thy city.
>
> [ll. 1550-54]

Lucrece's own pearl-like tears presently will hide a fire that will burn new Troy's institution of kingship; and many a Roman will bleed for every tear she sheds, betrayed to this ruin by pity for her.

Lucrece, of course, is blind to this deeper analogy between Troy's tragedy and her own Roman situation. Self-pity prevents her from seeing that her own tears are more like Sinon's than like Hecuba's; and, further, that if she is seeking in the Troy legend for some woman with whom to identify herself, a truer parallel would be the beautiful young Helen rather than motherly old Hecuba. Lucrece's outcry against Helen thus carries a special irony:

> Show me the strumpet that began this stir,
> That with my nails her beauty I may tear.
>
> [ll. 1471-72]

The strumpet whose beauty Lucrece here clamors to tear can be found, equivalently, in the present situation, in Lucrece's own hidden self. Shakespeare so hints by placing the "me" of the first line in a position of latent iambic stress. What the speaker pleads to be "shown," she is shown to be.

We turn next to the climactic scene of Lucrece's self-immolation. She has been preparing for this moment of public show while awaiting the gathering of an audience. When writing her summoning letter, we are told, she was but *hoarding* her passion (note this motif of covetousness in line 1318), in order to spend it when her husband would be at hand to hear her sighs and groans. These, she hopes,

> may *grace the fashion*
> *Of her disgrace,* the better so to clear her
> From that suspicion which the world might bear
> her.
>
> (Italics mine) [ll. 1319-21]

Shakespeare, I think, understands Lucrece's staged suicide as paganism's dark substitute for the Christian Passion story. That is, her "My blood shall wash the slander of mine ill" [l. 1207] parodies the Christian hope of being washed in the blood of the Lamb. Lucrece as lamb will enact a "martyrdom" formally similar to, but morally the opposite of, a true atonement. To convey this implication, he lets her ritualize her "show" with details suggestive of a priestess in some Roman cult. When her congregation arrives, they find her "clad in mourning black" and with blue circles streaming "like rainbows" round about her eyes. . . . Moreover, her look reflects such "deadly cares" that Collatine can only stare "as in a trance" for a long while. Then, as he is able at last to make loving inquiry, his phrases (through Shakespeare's diction) carry an ambiguous import:

> Sweet love, what *spite* hath thy fair color spent?
> Why art thou thus attired in *discontent*?
>   *Unmask,* dear dear, this moody heaviness . . .
>
> (Italics mine) [ll. 1600-02]

Lucrece's response at this point is to "sigh" three times to give her sorrows "fire"—probably Shakespeare's parody of a preacher invoking the Trinity before beginning his sermon. Then she addresses herself to speaking, and beginning with a promise of "Few words," launches into seven uninterrupted stanzas of "sad dirge" on the theme of "foul enforcement." Superficially her manner may be construed as simple embarrassment; but the artistry of it suggests a deliberateness, if only subconscious on her part, yet given significant form by Shakespeare. The prefatory three signs, followed by a seven-fold organization of message, hint analogy to Christian ritual, but on a theme the utter opposite of Christian "good news." Following a five-line preface, the story of the rape is set forth in 42 lines (a number symbolic of evil) and organized with great neatness—first a one-stanza statement of theme, then a three-stanza account of the rape, concluded by two stanzas of meditation on its tragedy. (pp. 25-6)

[The] climactic stanza, by reason of its crucial position in the story, warrants our keenest attention:

> Here with a sigh, as if her heart would break,
> She throws forth Tarquin's name: "He, he," she
>   says,
> But more than "he" her poor tongue could not
>   speak
> Till after many accents and delays,
>   Untimely breathing, sick and short assays,
>   She utters this: "He, he, fair lords, 'tis he,
>   That guides this hand to give this wound to me."
>
> [ll. 1716-22]

There are unmistakable hints of orgy in these lines. Not only the "sighs" and "delays," but especially the untimely breathing, "sick and short assays," suggest an analogy to sexual climax. Besides, there is an obvious undertone of glee in the reiterated "he, he." . . . May we not imagine Lucrece, as she reaches the end of this penultimate line, pausing momentarily in a suspended "tizzy" of elation? Then, with stress on *That*, she guides the knife downward into her bosom. Emblematically, we have been shown martyrdom in an obscene mode, a religious "dying" which Shakespeare hints, figuratively, is a kind of masturbatory self-rape. (pp. 27-8)

What Shakespeare's reconstructed scene further implies is that Lucrece, through her mode of publishing Tarquin's guilt, has reembodied in her own actions Tarquin's spirit. In a polar but analogous way, she has figuratively repeated his devilish triumph. Indeed, her method of vindication parallels, although in telescoped form, the stages by which in the earlier bedroom scene her visitor had seduced her. Tarquin, let us recall, had begun his suit by pleading in excuse his own helplessness, "ensnared" by the beauty in her face (specifically its color of blushing-red and pale-white anger). So, likewise, Lucrece pleads to her husband in self-excuse (but now with tear-red eyes and pallid trembling) the helplessness of her own "poor weak self" [l. 1646], entrapped by fear of Tarquin's visage (specifically his "scarlet lust" and ghastly threats). In both cases there is the heraldry of red in league with white. In both cases the pleading becomes a disowning of responsibility, with the speaker self-pictured as mere victim of fatal forces. And in each case the effect on the hearer is to encourage a further fatalism. Thus, in the bedroom scene Lucrece's response was first some broken sighs, then a tide of moralizing complaint undercut by signs of acquiescence. In the public scene Collatine's response to Lucrece is figuratively parallel: first a voice "damn'd up with woe" [l. 1661] that drinks up its own breath; then a "violent roaring tide" [l. 1667] of sighs and sorrows, which (although in this case not verbalized) are described as making "a saw" (equivalent to Lucrece's earlier resort to moral saws) that both pushes back and draws on grief. In the bedroom scene the dallying was ended when Tarquin, sensing Lucrece's sympathetic passion, cried: "Yield to my love" [l. 668] or else suffer the consequences of being slain and afterwards disgraced by scandal.

In the later public scene it is ended when Lucrece, sensing her husband's "frenzy," cries in effect: Yield to my revenge or else suffer the consequences of drowning in woe and being reputed no knightly champion. It is this threat that hypnotizes.

In this second instance, of course, the wiles of feminine insinuation cloak the naked threat. Lucrece's demand, "Be suddenly revenged," is beguilingly preceded by the clause "for my sake, when I might charm thee so" [ll. 1683, 1681]. But the implication that a stigma of dishonor will result if compliance should be refused is made clear—first by associating "honorable faiths" with the merit of "revengeful arms," and then by adding that "Knights, by their oaths, should right poor ladies harms" [l. 1694]. Thus Lucrece seduces her audience. The absurdity of righting harms by revenge is overlooked. "Each present lord," we are told, promises aid, "As bound in Knighthood to her imposition" [ll. 1696-97]. So subtly have they been *imposed* on, they remain unaware of how *benighted* is the *bondage* they are accepting. The wiping away of what Lucrece calls her "forced stain" seems to them a noble obligation. The ironic truth, however, is that Lucrece's stain at Tarquin's hands was actually no more "forced" than is now the general public's unwitting stain on its own honor in yielding to Lucrece's lust for revenge. In reversible ways, both the "victimized" Lucrece and now (through her) the victimized public have been drawn into complicity with evil because of a shallow notion of honor, a dread of loss of fame. Lucrece's rape has ramified into a "rapturing" of all Rome. (pp. 29-30)

Shakespeare's poem is profoundly moral, but by now it should be evident that its moral is no simple one. We are invited to grasp it, in fact, at no less than three levels of meaning. The poet announces these, very craftily, in a stanza near the mid-point of his work, immediately after Lucrece's six stanzas of expostulation to Night. As she turns next to imagining the dreadful fate which "telltale Day" may have in store for her, she cries out:

> *The nurse,* to still her child, will tell my story,
> And fright her crying babe with Tarquin's name;
> *The orator,* to deck his oratory,
> Will couple my reproach to Tarquin's shame;
> *Feast-finding minstrels,* tuning my defame,
>   Will tie the hearers to *attend each line,*
>   How Tarquin wronged me, I Collatine.
>
> (italics mine) [ll. 813-19]

Indirectly Shakespeare is here telling us, I would say, that the Lucrece legend in the future may take any one, or more, of three possible versions. The simplest of these will focus on Tarquin and his frightful villainy, thereby making the story's emotional impact, and its moral, turn about the ruin caused by a big bad wolf. Or secondly, the story can take on an added "deck," the result of a binocular vision. The focus then will be that of an orator, weighing judicially Lucrece as well as Tarquin, and finding blame in both parties. Thirdly, the story can be *sung* within a three-dimensional perspective, in which the background figure of Collatine is considered, and the tragedy is then so tuned as to reveal the wrong committed against family welfare, the defaming of the husband-wife relationship.

The nursemaid's version, the orator's version, and the feast-finding minstrel's version are thus three successive levels of understanding, related to each other like a nest of spheres or the layers of an onion. The nursemaid's version, Shakespeare implies, is superficial, good enough only for frightening infants. The orator's version, however, is for adult minds, for a public interested in the complex apologetics of a case, and prepared jury-like to size up its moral aspects. The minstrel's version, finally, is for royal listeners at a feast—for seasoned minds eager to be entertained with comprehensive insight, and alert therefore to watch for it in every well-tuned line. In distinguishing these three levels, did Shakespeare perhaps have in mind, respectively, Ovid's version, Augustine's version, and his own version? Certainly Ovid's brief poem, while smooth and picturesque, is ethically superficial. Augustine's oratorical treatment by comparison is ethically profound, yet yields dialectic rather than poetry. Shakespeare as minstrel seems to have absorbed and reorchestrated these predecessors. (pp. 35-6)

Around Augustine's interpretation Shakespeare could develop his own more expanded reading. For with love-of-glory clearly posited as the root cause of Lucrece's act of suicide, the tragedy could be truly unified, since this same motive could be posited for Tarquin's act of rape as a more basic motive for it than mere sexual desire. The two crimes then interrelate by a fascinating polarity. Behind Tarquin's adultery can be shown his self-murdering of his reason, while behind Lucrece's self-murder can be shown her prior sin of adulterating human love. But to give this story its proper social frame, the role of Collatine too must be developed, a role left unexamined by Augustine, although by implication Collatine was included by Augustine with those Romans who unreasonably extol Lucrece out of their love of human glory. The full tragic cause comprises the ethos of a whole civilization.

Unlike Augustine, however, Shakespeare is a poet rather than an orator. That means that for him the art of mimesis must circumscribe and use the art of rhetoric. As a narrator of tragic psychology, Shakespeare has the task, not of resolving the ethical dilemma which Augustine had so ironically set forth, but of showing dramatically how the Romans could reason themselves into it, and how hero and heroine alike could sink themselves in its mazes. Having learned the causes of tragedy from Augustine, and the rudiments of story-telling from Ovid, Shakespeare was trying for the more complex role of Feast-finding minstrel.

Minstrels will say, says Lucrece, that I wronged Collatine. She means: wronged him by the scandal of her rape. But Shakespeare means, additionally: wronged him by serving, not his welfare, but his reputation; by speaking up, not for his sake, but for her own fame; and finally by sacrificing herself, not to bring him happiness, but to bind him and all Rome in a covenant of revenge and death. Moreover, Shakespeare can show how Collatine, too, through his own love of glory, has neglected to protect his wife, and even has stood idly by while she slays herself. There is irony, therefore, when Lucrece tells Collatine of Tarquin's threat that unless she took all "patiently" her shame would rest "on record" as "the adulterate death of Lucrece and her *groom*" [l. 1645]. Who is this groom? In one sense, he is the base houseboy whom Tarquin had in mind to place murdered in her bed. But in a deeper sense does not this lackey figuratively denote Collatine? When Collatine was away at war, did not Lucrece value him as lackeying to her own love of glory? And after the rape, did she not impatiently override his efforts to console, exploiting these for her own ends? Thus she has treated her husband like a base groom; and ironically he himself has accepted this role. In this respect, both have prostituted the husband-wife relationship. In them, family life has become tragically disor-

dered by a mutual addiction to fame. But the community life of Rome as a whole reflects this same disorder.

Within such a Roman background Shakespeare can place the balancing tragedies of his two principals, Tarquin and Lucrece, reciprocal versions of tragic shame and waste. For if rape shames by its wastefulness, revenge wastes by its shamefulness. The two major sections of the poem may thus be said to display, in summary, two successive but interdependent phases of evil. Tarquin's quest shows us how things rank and gross in nature can grow in an unweeded garden. Lucrece's reaction, balancing this, shows us in what sense "lilies that fester" [Sonnet 94] can smell far worse than weeds. An "expense of spirit in a waste of shame" [Sonnet 129] is common to both, although in polar ways. Their polarity can be further understood if we will recall, from Shakespeare's later *Measure for Measure* [I. i. 29-31], the two sides of Duke Vincentio's warning: against, on the one hand, wasting one's self on one's virtues; on the other hand, wasting one's virtues on one's self. On these twin counts, the protagonists of *The Rape of Lucrece* prove wasteful. Hence, morally there are no "fine issues" to their story. But esthetically the art form of simple tragedy thus achieves its distinctive beauty. It mirrors faithfully the defective actions of noble persons and the sad consequences which coherently ensue. (pp. 38-9)

Roy W. Battenhouse, "Shakespeare's Re-Vision of Lucrece," in his Shakespearean Tragedy: Its Art and Its Christian Premises, *Indiana University Press, 1969, pp. 3-41.*

G. W. MAJORS (essay date 1974)

[*Majors suggests that the often neglected character Brutus is ultimately the norm by which the other figures in* The Rape of Lucrece *are to be measured. In contrast to Lucrece, with her moral idealism and gullibility, Brutus emerges as a pragmatist, willing to manipulate appearances to serve his own ends. Brutus transforms the knife Lucrece uses to commit suicide—a meaningless act from Brutus's realistic perspective—into the weapon that will depose the Tarquin dynasty and enable him to become first consul in the new republic. According to Majors, Brutus's motivations, whether selfless or self-interested, are intentionally ambiguous; nevertheless, his appearance in an "extradramatic role" underscores Lucrece's partial responsibility for her own fate.*]

Moral ambiguities scarcely abound in *The Rape of Lucrece*. For all the attention given their "psychological aspects," Tarquin and Lucrece are characters no more elusive, ethically, than Lust and Chastity in a morality play. They are humanized, to be sure, racked by doubt, and possessed of a self-scrutiny totally foreign to their allegorical forebears. But their aching hearts still beat in clean sight. However searching the analysis, the essential goodness of Shakespeare's heroine remains invulnerable to argument. Nor can the evil embodied in the rapist be extenuated, either by his awareness of pain or by our awareness of Freud.

If there is a moral enigma in the poem, it waits in the last seven stanzas, those dominated by L. Junius Brutus. Coming where it does, Brutus's share of the poem would seem to court notice, and his character appears mysterious enough to warrant this attempt to pluck it out. Admittedly, the conclusion always excites more attention as source evidence than as poetry. It concerns the major characters only incidentally and exhibits none of the self-conscious artfulness manifest in the passages most remembered and discussed. Hasty, derivative, these uninspired stanzas have evoked almost nothing from critics, save an occasional remark about Shakespeare's desire to tie up loose ends before concluding. Of the few who have bothered to comment, Esther C. Dunn is typically sketchy:

> The end of the poem like the end of many Elizabethan plays carries the story beyond what the modern audiences would call "the final curtain." After Lucrece has confessed, charged her husband to revenge her upon Tarquin, after the embroidered grief in the speeches by her father and Collatine, we should cry for an end. But Shakespeare carries the story on. Neither he nor his public could forego the tidying up of the events [see excerpt above, 1936].

She does right to assume that the Brutus segment, anticlimactic, invites apology in view of its apparent superfluousness. But to pretend that the purpose of these verses lies in "the tidying up of the events" requires exception of all but the final stanza. Taken as they stand, the last forty-nine lines argue strongly to the contrary. Shakespeare, whatever his purposes, was not content to put a hem on the work until he had spun a final thread—one which dangles in the reader's face long before it is used in stitching the poem to a tidy conclusion.

Probably I am not the only reader who has been puzzled by the intrusive stanza that cuts us off from the lamentations of Collatine and Lucretius. With slight regard for continuity, the poet shifts our attention to a character who has been named [l. 1734] but hardly noticed:

> Brutus, who pluck'd the knife from Lucrece' side,
> Seeing such emulation in their woe,
> Began to clothe his wit in state and pride,
> Burying in Lucrece' wound his folly's show.
>   He with the Romans was esteemed so
>   As silly jeering idiots are with kings,
>   For sportive words and utt'ring foolish things.
>
>   [ll. 1807-13]

Here, *Lucrece* having already run more than ninety-seven per cent of its lengthy course, we suddenly encounter the only ethically indistinct figure in the poem. To the reader uninitiated in Roman legendary history, the lines at first suggest another villain in our midst. The reader will soon change his mind, however; and by the end of the poem, unless he is more chary than most, he will err again by supposing Brutus a right champion of unambiguous virtue. L. Junius Brutus doubtless belongs with the innocent inasmuch as he opposes the wicked. Yet to view Shakespeare's Roman hero with so easy an eye is to misunderstand both the character and his function in the poem.

From the outset it is evident that Brutus is not the simple instrument we find, for example, in Chaucer's version of the story. An avenger still, and a means for concluding, Shakespeare's handy vindicator nevertheless raises as many problems as he solves. When he "throws that shallow habit by, / Wherein deep policy did him disguise" [ll. 1844-45], Brutus tempts us to fancy that he reveals nothing less than naked heroism. As it happens, we have already been told of *another* garment which will replace the shallow habit of foolery, this one woven of "state and pride" [l. 1809] and the rich connotations that attend them. Hero or none, Brutus has put off one role only to put on another. And the rightness of his cause should not blind us to the chance that he may be pursuing his "deep policy" still.

After this metaphorical change of costume, Brutus sets about to persuade Collatine to stop sobbing and join with him in seeking revenge—revenge not against the rapist alone, but against Tarquin's father the King, against the whole government (cf. Lucrece's insistence [ll. 1478-84] that private sins ought to be punished without public consequences). For in Lucrece's rape, Brutus casually alleges, " 'Rome herself . . . doth stand disgraced' " [l. 1833]. This point made, he can now tender his dramatic pledge of revenge:

>   "Now by that Capitol that we
>   adore,
> And by this chaste blood so unjustly stained,
> By heaven's fair sun that breeds the fat earth's
>   store,
> By all our country rights in Rome maintained,
> And by chaste Lucrece' soul that late complained
>   Her wrongs to us, and by this bloody knife,
>   We will revenge the death of this true wife."
>
>   [ll. 1835-41]

Even allowing for the rhetorical flavor of the entire poem, Brutus's sumptuous avowal smacks vaguely of humbug, especially when we are told [ll. 1847-48] that he will recite the whole thing over again for those who agree to join him. More striking than the oratory is the curiously indecorous gesture that follows: "This said, he strook his hand upon his breast, / And kiss'd the fatal knife to end his vow" [ll. 1842-43]. Probably not since Judas's was a kiss so sticky with ambiguity. Even Seneca's revengers had taste enough to avoid this kind of grotesquerie, so we cannot help remarking the incongruousness of the gesture. Though we seek in Brutus such selflessness as befits a proper champion, we are obliged to concede the possibility that his kiss conveys a note of private thanks. The same knife which destroyed Lucrece will, after all, serve as the weapon with which this shrewd republican deposes his enemies and becomes first consul of Rome. Nor is it impertinent to recall Brutus's political rise. The story being a popular one, Shakespeare likely assumes his audience will know the result of Brutus's conquest, just as he earlier found it unnecessary to tell us *why* Brutus had been posing as a fool. He can assume that the educated reader will be familiar with at least the broad outline of the "history" he recounts.

Now, before confessing that I have overvalued the argument against Brutus, I should put the case in its simplest form. The poem ends with the banishment of the offender, a direct result of Brutus and his pledgers' having paraded the martyred Lucrece from spot to spot. "To show her bleeding body thorough Rome, / And so to publish Tarquin's foul offence" [ll. 1851-52]. Careful readers at this point will think back to Brutus's abrupt transformation and ask a question which seemed only secondary at the time: what exactly was it that moved him to put aside his show of folly for the sobriety of a determined avenger? From convenience and romantic impulses, we want to reply that it was simple indignation born of the pitiful spectacle he had just witnessed. But Shakespeare tells us only that it was because Brutus saw "such emulation" [l. 1808] in the plaints of Collatine and Lucretius. We are invited to wonder, then, whether Brutus aims to assuage their woe or to *capitalize* on it. Although a case could be made both ways, surely the final stanza italicizes the less Christly objective. Earlier, in one of several dozen gnomic precepts contained in the poem, Shakespeare teaches a theatrical lesson now implicit in the conclusion: "To see sad sights moves more than hear them told" [l. 1324]. Pointedly commonsensical, this Horatian dictum might just as well have come from an ambitious Machiavel when he spied, in the blood-spattered Lucrece, a "sad sight" that could move the people to join in supplanting a regime which he hated and feared. (pp. 339-43)

To readers like Machiavelli or Shakespeare, heroes—even Roman ones—were made of human stuff. Certain questions were bound to arise. Machiavelli could not read Livy's account [of the Lucrece story] without probing for unspoken motives behind Brutus's dissemblance. As to his shedding of the disguise at a crucial moment later on, Machiavelli confidently assumes that Brutus seized upon Lucrece's affliction as a political pretext, else why should he have been the one to pull the dagger from Lucrece's wound in the presence of her relatives and to exact from bystanders a pledge to abolish monarchy (in his *Discourses,* I, 464)? In *Lucrece* the same assumption is writ, if not large, at least legibly in the space between the lines. Like other Elizabethans, Shakespeare grew up with the Lucrece story and probably read it or heard it in a dozen versions. But unlike so many of his contemporaries, he was enough a realist to recognize and publicize the fact that the men who slay dragons are as often bounty hunters as chevaliers. To what extent might Brutus's famous commitment proceed from compassion or moral outrage, and to what extent from plain opportunism, whether patriotic or self-seeking? With a few deft touches, Shakespeare hints at this motivational riddle in the last forty-nine lines of *Lucrece.* He asks us to be bothered by the same questions that Ovid and Livy seemingly contrived to suppress.

Editors are right when they tell us that Shakespeare followed his sources closely in the poem's final stanzas. Indeed, he followed so closely that he stepped on them. Then he moved ahead, unemphatically, without breaking stride. He did not alter the course taken by his Latin references; he merely went farther than they did. He went farther by insisting on the equivocality that was always there. In the broad outline of the event, and in a number of grammatical and incidental particulars, the last stanzas of *Lucrece* correspond to the probable sources. But more essential to the total effect are the bits and pieces the Elizabethan poet added on his own. Brutus's kissing of the bloody knife, the clothing of his wit in "state and pride," the explicit contradiction between his and Lucrece's notions of private justice in a political world—these and other such nagging details appear, so far as I am aware, in no previous treatment of the story. (pp. 345-46)

In a poem dominated by two characters not perplexing but perplexed, Brutus comes as a disturbing antithesis. Ethically unfixed, this slippery character nearly slides off the page. The poem that has relied so largely on painstaking exploration of motive, and on the assumption of a normative ethic, can only barely accommodate him. But precisely this difficulty accounts for Brutus's important, extradramatic role in the poem. His true moral worth matters nothing. Shakespeare encourages us to ask unanswerable questions about Brutus's intentions and then to recognize that whatever his real motives and whatever his ethical stature, Brutus is self-contained, passionless, unerring. . . . As such, he stands out like a marginal gloss when set beside the other figures in the story.

Structurally, he looks the part of an epilogue. He occupies center stage in the last seven stanzas, outside the boundaries of the main action. From this vantage point Brutus oversees the conclusion while offering an informal review of the other characters. Of course, only three characters really count in the poem: Tarquin, Lucrece, and Collatine. Their vices and virtues have been studied throughout, but their means and strategies remain secondary, their practical failings largely untallied, until the coming of Brutus. In the anticlimactic last stanzas dedicated to a sturdy realist, efficiency supplants morality as the prevailing standard. Here, in other words, Shakespeare finally provides the norm by which to measure his characters on an other than ethical basis.

First consider Lucrece, whose tragedy comes in two parts. Responsibility for the rape rests, as always, most immediately with the rapist. But the poet has implied—and now, I would suggest, demonstrates—that the innocent victim owns a share of the blame. Open and unsuspicious, Lucrece flounders for lack of the same skills by which Brutus succeeds. She is beguiled by Tarquin because she trusts appearances [ll. 89-91, 99-105] and because her public sensibility makes her overly dainty about etiquette [ll. 841-44]. The suspiciousness that might prompt *faux pas* she avoids by a gullibility that prompts deadly missteps. The tracks of these missteps show up tellingly when the disguised Brutus shows up at the end. His mere appearance reminds us that Lucrece's tragedy was avoidable, that not everybody plays gull to a dissembling tyrant. For here, more inscrutable than ever, comes the famous

> Roman Brutus,
> Covering discretion with a coat of folly;
> As gardeners do with ordure hide those roots
> That shall first spring and be most delicate.
>
> [*Henry V,* II. iv. 37-40]

Lucrece misses such discretion and such a covering. Her trustfulness and openhanded hospitality reflect proper social conduct, but not the conduct needed to survive in a world inhabited by the likes of Tarquin.

Lucrece's suicide is another matter. Hers alone is the burden of direct responsibility, yet she seems to have the not too reluctant admiration of Shakespeare (and of most readers) when she makes her fatal decision—a decision which, as Hallett Smith has remarked [in his *Elizabethan Poetry*], "is a heroically simple one." With the entrance of Brutus, however, the scene shifts to the real world. In this setting passion wants splendor, and heroic virtues appear absurd. With a single stroke, the cool realist would destroy our illusions about the beauty and aptness of Lucrece's tragic end: " 'Thy wretched wife mistook the matter so, / To slay herself that should have slain her foe' " [ll. 1826-27]. He is right. Seen outside a romantic context (and not in Battenhouse's Christian one [see excerpt above, 1969]), Lucrece's self-destruction reflects only the fact that she "mistook the matter," since it neither restored what she lost nor punished the thief who took it. Brutus is a practical man urging practical action. In his Rome goodness and heroism, when they prove ineffectual, translate as folly.

Lucrece's needless suicide issues from a motive to which Brutus, once again, provides the potent counterstatement. Although shame weighs immoderately on such saints, the decisive factor in Lucrece's tragic choice is not that she herself doubts her innocence:

> "Though my gross blood be stain'd with this abuse,
> Immaculate and spotless is my mind;
> That was not forc'd, that never was inclin'd
>   To accessory yieldings, but still pure
>   Doth in her poison'd closet yet endure."
>
> [ll. 1655-59]

Instead, it is her fear of what *others* will think [ll. 810-19, 1314-23]. That the wiser, self-contained Brutus pays tiny regard to such rumor appears plain enough by his willingness to act the public fool in order to further his private strategy. Simply because she makes inexpedient ado about her public standing, Lucrece is obliged to destroy both the "poison'd closet" and the pure mind that hurts within it, rather than risk that the world infer the guilt of the one from the outward shame of the other. Her tragedy, in one important respect, is that no matter how convinced of her indwelling taintlessness, she knows she cannot hide from her countenance the shame that would argue guilt. Unhappily, she lacks Brutus's aptitude for making outward appearance subject to inner command. While he is among those who, lords and owners of their faces, do not do the thing they most do show, Lucrece desponds untutored in such ways of the wise: " 'And my true eyes have never practis'd how / To cloak offences with a cunning brow' ' [ll. 748-49]. All considered, Lucrece perishes because she is too good, too trusting, too idealistic, too artless for survival in a post-Saturnian world. And that is exactly what Brutus tells us—with his disguise, his actions, his words—when he makes his belated appearance, a realist epilogue in an idealistic fable.

Brutus's commentary on Lucrece's husband and on Tarquin can be more speedily summarized. Shakespeare has told us that Collatine's boasting was the spark that ignited lustful flames in Tarquin's heart. The didactic poet advises, along the way, that some treasures are best kept hidden, that the beauty and virtue of Lucrece ought to have remained the secret blessing of the one man fortunate enough to enjoy them [ll. 33-5]. And now, in the closing section of the poem, he introduces a character more studious than Collatine of this prudent individualism. By maintaining his show of folly, Brutus has managed to keep his own dearest possession "long-hid" [l. 1816] and thus safe from the envy of tyrants. Far from boasting, as Collatine did, Brutus committed himself to the most self-deprecatory course available. Pretending idiocy and subjecting himself to the reputation that goes with it, the "unsounded" tactician was satisfied to be thought capable of nothing more than "sportive words and utt'ring foolish things" [l. 1813]. He belongs with those who husband nature's riches from expense, just as Collatine joins the lesser group, those but stewards of their excellence.

Shakespeare makes his enigmatic revenger the most efficient character in *Lucrece,* not just for the ways he contrasts with Collatine and his virtuous lady, but also for his superiority over the creature on the other end of the moral spectrum. As already noticed, Brutus shares with his enemy the ability to pretend to be other than he is. In design and execution, however, he reverses the pattern established by Tarquin. When he arrived at Lucrece's, Tarquin succeeded in masking his "inward ill" by feigning dignity and propriety:

> For that he colour'd with his high estate,
> Hiding base sin in pleats of majesty.
> That nothing in him seem'd inordinate.
>
> [ll. 92-4]

Now, when we meet Brutus in the final section of the poem, has he not been turning the same trick in another direction—coloring his true worth with his low estate, hiding his natural majesty in pleats of baseness, so that all about him (since he was playing the fool) seemed more than a little inordinate?

Brutus is every bit as furtive as Tarquin, else he had not managed to survive. The signal distinction, with or without the moral overtones, is that the dissimulation in the one springs from wit, in the other from mindless passion. Tarquin makes a somewhat palliative confession in this regard: " 'My will is strong past reason's weak removing' " [l. 243]. *Palliative,* that is, because the weakness he attributes to "reason" belongs, more particularly, elsewhere. Although Brutus's later words are directed against a very different outburst of passion, his commentary, granted the choric privilege it deserves, pronounces judgment on Tarquin as well: " 'Such childish humour from weak minds proceeds' " [l. 1825].

Whether victim or villain, those who err suffer exposure beside the mysterious pragmatist who gets the last word and the last seven stanzas. More than a narrative expedient, Shakespeare's Brutus earns significance as a community foil. In his role in the poem, however late and slight, he behaves in such a way as to provide a practical assessment of the main characters. Hence, if he comes from Shakespeare's pen a more blotched and problematic figure than before, he does so to a purpose. The moralizing poet supplies neat ethical determinations but stops short, cannily, when he reaches the last stanzas. Relieved of obligation to the idealistic schema, Brutus affords the means for understanding this sentimental, moral tale on a basis unsentimental and unmoral. (pp. 347-51)

G. W. Majors, "Shakespeare's First Brutus: His Role in 'Lucrece'," in Modern Language Quarterly, Vol. 35, No. 4, December, 1974, pp. 339-51.

COPPÉLIA KAHN   (essay date 1976)

[*Kahn argues that Shakespeare's interest in exploring the moral stigma of rape led him to the Lucrece story and an examination of the institution of marriage and the role of women in marriage. In essence, according to Kahn, Lucrece's dilemma, her moral innocence and physical stain, reflects woman's position in a patriarchal society, whether Elizabethan England or classical Rome. The critic views Lucrece as "the perfect patriarchal woman," because she accepts her stain as an irrevocable material fact that threatens the institution of marriage and destroys Collatine's honor, and because she has "no sense of herself as an independent moral being apart from this role in marriage." Kahn suggests that in this poem, Shakespeare portrays the injustice of degrading women to the status of property and the imprudence of "making property the basis of human relationships." In a patriarchy, she points out, Tarquin's crime is not rape, but theft, and the victim is not Lucrece, but Collatine.*]

The central problem in Shakespeare's *Lucrece* is rape—a moral, social, and psychological problem which Shakespeare sets before us in all its ambiguities and contradictions, but which criticism has so far failed to confront, for several reasons. In *Venus and Adonis,* traditional sex roles are reversed, with humorous effect; in *Lucrece,* they are taken with deadly seriousness and carried to a logical and bitter extreme, which makes it painful to confront the poem squarely. Furthermore, the rhetorical display-pieces invite critical attention for their own sake, offering readers a happy escape from the poem's insistent concern with the relationship between sex and power. That relationship is established by the terms of marriage in a patriarchal society. The rape is ultimately a means by which Shakespeare can explore the nature of marriage in such a society and the role of women in marriage. Therefore, the poem must be understood in a psycho-social context

Tragedy of Lucrece. By Sandro Botticelli.

which takes account of sex roles and cultural attitudes toward sexuality.

In this context, the terms "patriarchal" and "sex role," rather than being modern impositions on a Renaissance sensibility, accurately reflect both the Elizabethan and the Roman reality. Because Shakespeare's own society was patriarchal in the means by which it maintained degree as the basis of the social order, it would be surprising if he had not sensed a strong kinship between Rome and England. As M. W. MacCallum states [in his *Shakespeare's Roman Plays and Their Background*],

> Thus Shakespeare in his picture of Rome and Romans, does not give the notes that mark off Roman from every other civilization, but rather those that it possessed in common with the rest, and especially with his own.

It is a critical commonplace that Elizabethans regarded Rome as a political mirror of their own times finding in it a series of lessons about the fall of princes, the dangers of mob rule, the horrors of rebellion—lessons which they considered to have more than theoretical value. The story of Lucrece as Shakespeare found it in his Latin sources is also a mirror—a mirror of the patriarchal marriage system obtaining in England, in which matches were arranged so as to insure, through the provision of legitimate male heirs, the proper continuance of wealth and status. In marriage as the propertied classes of the sixteenth century knew it, women were to serve the interests of their fathers' and their husbands' family lines; only in that way could they acquire their own rights and privileges. (pp. 45-6)

Shakespeare's interest in rape lies in the consequences of the crime for the victim, rather than in the act of committing the crime; hence the poem's original title is simply *Lucrece; The Rape of Lucrece* was an addition by the editor of the 1616 quarto. Shakespeare focuses our attention on the curious fact that Lucrece acquires a moral stigma from *being* raped. Though innocent of the crime, she finds herself disgraced, ru-

ined, an object of shame to herself and the world. In the language of the poem, she is morally "stained" and sexually "tainted." Why should Tarquin's crime pollute Lucrece? Why should she bear, in more than the physical sense, the "load of shame" which he "leaves behind"? (p. 46)

The central metaphor in the poem is that of a stain, which is repeatedly and forcefully attached to Lucrece. The words "stain" or "stained" are mentioned eighteen times in the poem's 1855 lines, and synonyms such as blot, spot, blur, blemish, attaint, scar, and pollution are frequently used. Other words denoting either moral error, social disgrace, or both occur with great frequency: shame, blame, infamy, offence, disgrace, sin, guilt, crime, trespass, defame, fault, and corruption. Tarquin introduces the metaphor as he is contemplating the rape, using it to characterize the effect of the act on her:

> Fair torch, burn out thy light, and lend it not
> To darken her whose light excelleth thine;
> And die, unhallow'd thought, before you blot
> With your uncleanness that which is divine;
> Offer pure incense to so pure a shrine.
>   Let fair humanity abhor the deed
>   That spots and stains love's modest snow-white
>   weed.
>
> [ll. 190-96]

He again employs it to describe the disgrace which will follow her death if she resists him:

> Then for thy husband and thy children's sake,
> Tender my suit; bequeath not to their lot
> The shame that from them no device can take,
> The blemish that will never be forgot,
> Worse than a slavish wipe or birth-hour's blot.
>
> [ll. 533-37]

After the rape, the idea that she is "stained" becomes the leitmotif of all her laments and the motivation for her suicide.

The poem's major concern is expressed through the metaphor of the stain, but it is expressed ironically. Whatever the stain is, Lucrece believes it to be indelibly hers and tragically lives out the implications of her belief. But Shakespeare has molded the poem so as to examine and question her belief from many angles, as I shall show. First of all, the simple moral facts of the rape impel us to doubt Lucrece's self-indictment. In the poem, as in its sources, Lucrece is wholly innocent of any provocation or complicity in the crime, therefore, the stain cannot indicate her guilt. In fact, it is hard to find any single term or moral category which encompasses Lucrece's conception of how the rape has stained her, as this passage, one of several similar passages, shows:

> He in his speed looks for the morning light,
> She prays she never may behold the day:
> "For day," quoth she, "night's scapes doth open lay,
> And my true eyes have never practis'd how
> To cloak offenses with a cunning brow.
>
> They think not but that every eye can see
> The same disgrace which they themselves behold;
> And therefore would they still in darkness be,
> To have their unseen sin remain untold.
> For they their guilt with weeping will unfold,
> And grave like water that doth eat in steel,
> Upon my cheeks, what helpless shame I feel."
>
> [ll. 745-56]

On the one hand, she mourns her "disgrace" and "helpless shame," terms which might indicate a fear of social disapproval or loss of prestige but do not necessarily imply that she has done anything to deserve such moral judgments. On the other hand, she refers to "sin" and "guilt" which must, in the rhetorical context, be hers, the result of her own moral failing. To complicate the matter further, she reviles Tarquin as the one who committed the crime but declares herself equally guilty of a crime against Collatine:

> Feast-finding minstrels tuning my defame,
> Will tie the hearers to attend each line,
> How Tarquin wronged me, I Collatine.
>
> [ll. 817-19]

Our difficulties in comprehending the basis on which Lucrece judges herself guilty of such a crime arise from her conception of herself as a woman in a patriarchal society, a conception which renders irrelevant for her the questions of moral responsibility and guilt in rape. Though Lucrece uses moral terms such as sin and guilt, she actually condemns herself according to primitive, nonmoral standards of pollution and uncleanness, in which only the material circumstances of an act determine its goodness or evil. In doing so, she embodies the attitudes toward female sexuality underlying Roman marriage. Shakespeare poises these attitudes against another standard of judgment, radically different from Lucrece's but more familiar to us. He weaves through the narrator's comments and through the heroine's speeches suggestions of a Christian ethic which disregards material circumstances and judges an act wholly according to the motives and disposition of the agent. His point of view, as a result, is a blend of ironic distance from Lucrece's materialistic conception of chastity and compassionate respect for her integrity in adhering to chastity as the only value which gives meaning to her as a Roman wife. What the poem conveys above all is the tragic cost Lucrece pays for her exquisite awareness of her Roman duty. She upholds the social order by accepting her stain and dying for the sake of marriage as an institution.

The poem deals with the rape of a *married* woman. Lucrece's chastity is emphatically that of the wife who has dedicated her body to her husband. This dedication has so rarified and sanctified her sexuality that she seems virginal or even unsexual. She is imbued with a modesty so profound as to make us wonder, perhaps, what sexual satisfactions the marriage bed could hold for Collatine. The vocabulary of purity and holiness surrounds her like a halo throughout the poem. In the second stanza, she is

> that sky of his [Collatine's] delight;
> Where mortal stars as bright as heaven's beauties,
> With pure aspects did him peculiar duties.
>
> [ll. 12-14]

She is called "This earthly saint" [l. 85], a "heavenly image" [l. 288], "the picture of pure piety" [l. 542]. In a stanza already quoted, she is "divine," "so pure a shrine," and her chastity is "love's modest snow-white weed" [ll. 190-96]. (pp. 47-9)

It is precisely such virginal qualities which make Lucrece the paragon of wives. The sexual act in marriage has not altered the perfect innocence which presumably characterized her before she married, and it has hallowed in Collatine the desire which is evil in Tarquin. The marriage bed which Lucrece shares with Collatine is, before the rape, "clear" [l. 382] and "pure" [l. 684]—free of any carnal sin, and her breasts are "maiden worlds" [l. 408], a phrase which strikingly expresses the anomaly of this conception of woman in marriage. Though she is supposedly her husband's sexual partner, she is also untouched, unchanged by her participation in the sexual act. Marriage has invested sex with a prelapsarian sinlessness, and herein lies its psychological value for man. It is his defense against sexual desire with its risks, perils, and humiliations, and Lucrece is the embodiment of that defense. In her, woman made wife, desire is legitimized; it is made a habit and a right instead of an adventure into the illicit. No longer taboo, desire now is shrouded in the pieties of domestic life. (p. 50)

The two descriptions of Lucrece's person in the poem, both remarkably nonerotic, elaborate a paradoxical desire to desexualize the woman who, by virtue of her status as wife, is entitled to be sexually possessed. . . . The first is the narrator's account of the heroine greeting Tarquin on his arrival at her house in Rome [ll. 150-84]. This description is so heavily encrusted with heraldic terminology and so burdened with the conceit of a chivalric contest between the lady's beauty and her virtue that nothing of a plausible female face or body survives. Shakespeare is trying to convey the impression that she is surpassingly beautiful without admitting any suggestion that she might be physically desirable—a difficult task. In order to accomplish it, he has recourse to chivalric conventions and to allegory, the battle between red and white representing the parity of beauty and virtue in Lucrece. The result is confusion, in physical reference (is the red and white her habitual complexion, or a succession of blushes?) and in syntax (especially in [ll. 57-63]). But if this contest tells us nothing about Lucrece physically, it does hint at the tension between two conceptions of her, as sexual object and as sexually taboo, that is shortly to explode. It is interesting that she is characterized in terms of two qualities, beauty and virtue, that are necessarily opposed in this context. Insofar as she is beautiful, it is inevitable that men should desire her; but insofar as she is a virtuous wife, she belongs to Collatine and no other man may have her. (p. 51)

Shakespeare begins the poem by announcing in the first stanza that Tarquin

> lurks to aspire
> And girdle with embracing flames the waist
> Of *Collatine's fair love, Lucrece the chaste.*
>
> [ll. 5-7; italics mine]

In the next stanza he suggests that Collatine's praise of his wife's "unmatched red and white" [l. 11] has inspired Tarquin's lust. But it is not only the fact that Lucrece is both beautiful and unavailable which arouses Tarquin; it is the fact that Collatine's proprietorship over Lucrece *makes* her unavailable.

Notice how heavily Shakespeare emphasizes the husband's private possession of his wife:

> For he the night before, in Tarquin's tent
> Unlock'd the treasure of his happy state:
> What priceless wealth the heavens had him lent,
> In the possession of his beauteous mate;
> Reck'ning his fortune at such high proud rate
> That kings might be espoused to more fame,
> But king nor peer to such a peerless dame.
>
> [ll. 15-21]

The strong similarity, in image and in situation, between this boasting contest and that in *Cymbeline,* written some sixteen years later, attests to Shakespeare's enduring perception of the chaste wife as an aspect of her husband's status amongst male rivals. . . . In both works, the chaste wife is seen as a precious jewel which tempts the thief; in both works, the husband's boasts initiate the temptation, in effect challenging his peers to take that jewel.

The conventional metaphor of jewels, treasure, or wealth to represent the value of the lady to her lover has an additional meaning in *Lucrece.* The frequent references throughout the poem to Lucrece as "treasure," "prize," and "spoil," and the comparison of Tarquin to a thief [ll. 134-40, 710-11, to cite two of many examples] constitute a running metaphorical commentary on marriage as ownership of women. As the elegiac stanza lamenting the destruction of Collatine's marital happiness tells us,

> Honour and beauty in the *owner's* arms
> Are weakly fortress'd from a world of harms.
>
> [ll. 27-8; italics mine]

Marriage is no fortress against the greedy lust of Tarquin, just as the rich man's coffers cannot prevent his gold from being robbed. If Collatine even speaks of Lucrece to another man, he invites competition for possession of her; Lucrece is "that rich jewel he should keep unknown / From thievish ears, because it is his own" [ll. 34-5].

For the husband, his wife's sexuality is both neutralized and protected by marriage; for other men, it is heightened in value because another man, a potential rival, possesses it. When Tarquin considers "his loathsome enterprise" [l. 184] before departing for Lucrece's chamber, he devotes only one stanza to abstract moral arguments against the contemplated rape . . . , as an act that would unjustifiably harm the good, as embodied in Lucrece. Otherwise, he thinks of the act as a social disgrace to himself as a nobleman and to his family [ll. 196-210], and as one which would place him in a morally disadvantageous position vis-á-vis Collatine:

> If Collatine dream of my intent,

> Will he not wake, and in a desp'rate rage
> Post hither, this vile purpose to prevent?—
> . . . .
> O what excuse can my invention make
> When thou shalt charge me with so black a deed?
>
> [ll. 218-20; 225-26]

He then considers hypothetical circumstances which would have justified the deed and made it honorable:

> Had Collatinus kill'd my son or sire,
> Or lain in ambush to betray my life;
> Or were he not my dear friend.
>
> [ll. 232-34]

That is, he is primarily concerned, not with the absolute moral quality of the rape nor with the harm it will do to Lucrece specifically, but with the possible damage it may cause to his status as a nobleman of honorable reputation. This status, of course, is relative to Collatine's power to accuse him of a dishonorable act and shame him thereby. Tarquin regards Collatine as ultimately the judge of his (Tarquin's) acts, and the only real obstacle to his desire:

> Within his thought her heavenly image sits,
> And in the self-same seat sits Collatine.
> That eye which looks on her confounds his wits;
> That eye which him beholds, as more divine,
> Unto a view so false will not incline. . . .
>
> [ll. 288-92]

Basically, Tarquin considers the rape a violation not of Lucrece's chastity but of Collatine's honor. It is an affair between men, as the ending of the poem will reveal.

The competition between these two men for possession of Lucrece is exacerbated by the difference in their status, for Tarquin is the king's son and Collatine is merely of a noble family [ll. 39-42]. But Livy relates that Tarquin's father seized the throne unlawfully, brutally murdering his father-in-law and simply naming himself king without observing the custom of calling on the senate for their approval. *Tel père, tel fils* [like father, like son]; both men display a kingly disregard for the legitimate sanction of power, and take power into their own hands. Tarquin's private conduct in seizing his friend's wife is parallel to his father's public conduct in seizing the throne; both actions are inimical to a just and ordered society. Another parallel between the realms of sex and politics is notable; the structure of both is patriarchal, with authority over subordinates designated to certain individual men. But authority cannot withstand the strains exerted against it by rivalry between the men and breaks down in violence and disorder. The rape of Lucrece not only parallels the abuse of kingship in Rome but also precipitates its end. Thus the revenge against Tarquin with which the poem concludes involves (as an educated Elizabethan familiar with Livy would know) not only his banishment but the exile of all the Tarquins, the end of monarchy, and the election of Collatine and his fellow-avenger Brutus as the first consuls of the new republic. (pp. 52-5)

The second description of Lucrece raises similar issues concerning marriage and the competition for ownership and power between men. Unlike the first, it portrays Lucrece's body directly, viewed as Tarquin sees her sleeping in her chamber [ll. 386-420], but again, it fends off erotic suggestiveness. Since the heroine is being described through Tarquin's lustful eyes, we might expect the titillating detail which the poet handles so deftly in *Venus and Adonis.* Instead, he portrays her as "a virtuous monument" [l. 391] or gravestone effigy, her head "entombed" in her pillow, with a hand like an April daisy and eyes like marigolds, "Showing life's triumph in the map of death, / And death's dim look in life's mortality" [ll. 402-03]. Even her breasts convey no impression of soft and inviting womanly flesh. They are depicted in legal and political terms, as venerable emblems of her status as Collatine's wife:

> Her breasts like ivory globes circled with blue,
> A pair of maiden worlds unconquered;
> Save of their lord, no bearing yoke they knew,
> And him by oath they truly honoured.
> These worlds in Tarquin new ambition bred;
>   Who like a foul usurper went about,
>   From this fair throne to heave the owner out.
>
>   [ll. 407-13]

But the whole stanza disturbingly portrays Lucrece's sexuality politically, as the colonization of her very flesh by the men who would "lay claim" to her. As at the beginning of the poem, here it is Collatine's proprietorship which provokes Tarquin's desire to rape Lucrece. The last three lines depict his desire in political language; the sight of her naked bosom breeds not new lust but "new ambition." The heroine becomes an image for two fields of political conquest, the expanding Roman empire and the New World . . . , and Tarquin, correspondingly, is a rival power who would snatch the newly won territory from its rightful possessor. In lines 3 and 4, the marriage of Lucrece and Collatine is metaphorically a feudal contract in which she swears fealty to him as her lord. Its awesome legality is sharply contrasted to the lawless "usurpation" of Tarquin's rapine. But both forms of conquest over woman, legal and illegal, involve force. Notice the "bearing yoke" of marriage, an allusion both to the husband's right to subjugate his wife and command, by force if necessary, that she serve him, and to childbearing, the wife's duty to her husband.

In the action of the poem, force is a primary element in both the sexual and political realms, and Tarquin is the primary embodiment of it. . . . From the beginning he can conceive of taking Lucrece only by force; because of her undoubted chastity and because Collatine would never voluntarily surrender his rights, seduction or persuasion never figure as alternatives. . . . He forces open all the locked doors between his chambers and hers [ll. 301-02], and when he places his hand on her breast, it is compared to the invasion of a conquering army [ll. 435-39], "a rude ram, to batter such an ivory wall!" [l. 464]. He announces his purpose to Lucrece in the language of feudal conquest, saying "Under that colour am I come to scale / Thy never-conquer'd fort" [ll. 480-81], a common figure in Renaissance love poetry which regains its martial undertones in this context. He concludes his announcement by shaking "his Roman blade" over the defenseless Lucrece [ll. 505-06], a familiar gesture of military victory. . . . Needless to say, in this context the sword symbolizes phallic as well as military power.

In the end, of course, his victory is hollow, and the "Roman lord" who marched to Lucrece's bed creeps away guiltily, "A captive victor that hath lost in gain" [l. 730]. He is vanquished, as he knew from the beginning that he would be, by his own conscience. But in political terms, he is destroyed by Lucrece's avenging guardians. After she kills herself, Brutus ritually legitimizes counter-violence against Tarquin by asking the assembled nobles to swear, by the bloody knife she used, vengeance against Tarquin. On this level, woman is but a pawn in the struggle of the state to maintain its laws (represented by marriage) against the arrogant individual who would seize what he wants in scorn of the law.

Ironically, Tarquin is driven to risk all for Lucrece *because* the law makes her taboo to anyone but her husband. Officially, as a chaste wife, she is desexualized, but to one who desires her despite the law, because she is forbidden she acquires a high erotic potency totally extraneous to her sense of herself as Collatine's wife. Thus the poem suggests that the rape represents in part the failure of marriage as a means of establishing sexual ownership of women. That marriage does not succeed in eradicating illicit desire is conveyed forcefully in Tarquin's tortured debates with himself as he approaches Lucrece's bed. Scrupulously, he enumerates the perils of robbing another man's treasure, then recklessly denies them in frenzied rationalizations [ll. 127-441]. Honor, piety, reason, and self-respect melt before his desire and bear witness to the destructiveness of this woman's erotic power over him, of which she is wholly unaware.

Tarquin, however, can wield a far greater power over Lucrece and does so with great cunning. This power rests not in his "Roman blade" but in the nature of his threat against her, which derives its coercive strength from the conditions of Roman marriage, conditions implied in the threat itself. If she refuses to submit to his lust, he will force her and then kill her. But even worse, he will slander her posthumously by killing a slave, placing him in Lucrece's arms, and claiming that he killed them both for their sexual trespass. This slander will do irreparable damage to Lucrece's reputation as a chaste wife, but that is not its cutting edge. What matters to Lucrece, as Tarquin knows well, is that it will destroy Collatine's honor and his family's:

> So thy surviving husband shall remain,
> The scornful mark of every open eye;
> Thy kinsmen hang their heads at this disdain,
> Thy issue blurr'd with nameless bastardy.
>
>   [ll. 519-22]

In conformity with the patriarchal idea of woman, Lucrece has perfectly identified herself with her husband and sees herself as the seal of his honor. Therefore she cannot forcibly resist Tarquin (though she pleads with him), not because it would result in her death, but because it would dishonor Collatine and all his kin. On the other hand, if she submits to Tarquin, he will say nothing and Collatine's honor will remain unblemished. Neither alternative allows her to remain chaste, if chastity is considered a physical state. The first means death but, more importantly, public dishonor. The second allows her to live, presumably with the secret knowledge of dishonor.

Lucrece's pleas are useless, and she does not struggle when at last the rape occurs. Tacitly, she has chosen the second alternative of not resisting Tarquin and could now simply keep her secret. But because chastity for Lucrece is not merely a matter of social appearance but is a physical reality, she cannot pretend to be the exemplary wife once she is no longer technically chaste. Her extended apostrophe to Night, usually criticized on aesthetic grounds as undramatic and cumbrously rhetorical, has firm psychological justification as an illustration of her profound sense of the reality of chastity and of its loss. She begs Night to conceal her from "the tell-tale day" [l. 806], contending that in the light all would see the evidence of rape [ll. 746-56; 806-09]. Of course they would not; the topos is only intended to convey her belief in the stain; *she* knows it is there and assumes that everyone else could see it. As she dilates upon her grief, it becomes evident that she thinks of the rape as comprising two crimes, that which Tarquin committed against her and that which she committed against Collatine:

> The nurse to still her child will tell my story,
> And fright her crying babe with Tarquin's name.
> The orator to deck his oratory
> Will couple my reproach to Tarquin's shame.
> Feast-finding minstrels tuning my defame,
>   Will tie the hearers to attend each line,
>   *How Tarquin wronged me, I Collatine.*
>
> Let my good name, that senseless reputation,
> For Collatine's dear love be kept unspotted.
> If that be made a theme for disputation,
> The branches of another root are rotted,
>   *And undeserv'd reproach to him allotted*
>   *That is as clear from this attaint of mine*
>   As I ere this was pure to Collatine.
>
>   [ll. 813-26; italics mine]

Whatever Lucrece believes that she has done to her husband, terms such as "offense" or "crime" do not exactly fit it. Her word "attaint" and the prevailing metaphor of the stain come much closer to describing it. Marriage makes sex, and woman as sexual object, clean; outside of marriage sex is unclean. Once the pure, unsexual wife is brought into contact with sexuality outside of marriage, though it be beyond her powers to avoid that contact, she is a polluted object. According to the anthropologist Mary Dougles [in her *Purity and Danger: An Analysis of Concepts of Pollution and Taboo*], "Pollution rules are unequivocal, [and] do not depend on intention or on rights and duties. The only material question is whether a forbidden contact has taken place or not." "A forbidden contact" is exactly what has taken place, and it is understandable that Lucrece sees it as such and does not take into account what for us would be paramount: the moral questions of intention and responsibility. She is the perfect patriarchal woman, content to be but an accessory to the passage of property and family honor from father to son; she has no sense of herself as an independent moral being apart from this role in marriage. Thus she views her chastity as a material thing, not as a moral attitude transcending circumstances.

(pp. 56-60)

Only Lucrece, of all the characters in the poem, fully understands her importance to the Roman social system, possessing an insight which transcends that of an ordinary wife and makes her "a singular patterne of chastity, both to hir tyme, and to all ages following" [Thomas Cooper, in his *Thesaurus Lingae Romance and Britannicae*]. Lucrece's "singularity" is most marked when, after revealing the rape to her kinsmen, she rejects the forgiveness they hasten to offer and plunges the knife into her breast, on the grounds that

>   no dame hereafter living
> Shall claim excuses by my excuse's giving.
>   [ll. 1714-15]

They are persuaded by her narration of the particular circumstances surrounding the rape that she is innocent, but she sees herself as a "patterne," a paradigm for all ages of the meaning of female chastity in a patriarchy. In the terms of that paradigm, when a chaste wife is polluted by sexual contact outside

of marriage, no matter what the circumstances, she is forced across the line between sexuality and innocence which marriage has drawn for her and becomes a marginal and dangerous person. Furthermore, given Lucrece's total identification with this paradigm, no alternative identity is possible for her once she can no longer call herself a chaste wife. The tragedy of Lucrece is that only by dying is she able to escape from marginality and regain her social and personal identity as a chaste wife.

The suicide of Lucrece was a nexus of controversy long before Shakespeare wrote his poem. In Book I of *The City of God*, Augustine questions Livy's presentation of her suicide as the proof of her virtue. His way of articulating the problem is relevant to Shakespeare's Lucrece in two ways. First, the poet has woven suggestions of the Augustinian viewpoint into his heroine's speech and into the narrative commentary. Second, these suggestions form a contrast to Lucrece's attitude, distinguishing it sharply and enabling us to understand its peculiarities. Augustine's discussion touches some of the same points of contrast, which fall under the broad headings of patriarchal versus moral, or pagan versus Christian attitudes toward chastity.

Augustine's conception of chastity is built on the dichotomy of mind and body: "In the first place, then, let the principle be stated and affirmed that the virtue whereby a good life is lived controls the members of the body from its seat in the mind, and that the body becomes holy through the exercise of a holy will, and while such a will remains unshaken and steadfast, no matter what anyone else does with the body or in the body that a person has no power to avoid without sin on his own part, no blame attaches to the one who suffers it." Nothing could be further from the view of chastity represented by Lucrece herself, for whom the only important consideration is material: what Tarquin did with her body. For Augustine, the only important consideration is spiritual: whether Lucrece's will remained steadfast in mental opposition to the rape, or whether she consented to it. If she remained steadfast, then as far as Augustine is concerned, her chastity is intact, and she had no defensible reason for committing suicide. If she inwardly consented to the rape, presumably because she took carnal pleasure in it, then she sinned and added to her guilt by the sin of self-murder. Augustine is not convinced that Lucrece did not consent, but assuming for the sake of the argument that she did not, he concludes that her death was motivated "not by her love of chastity, but her irresolute shame. For she was ashamed of another's foul crime committed on her person, even though not committed with her . . ." [I. xix, p. 89] and declares that she was "a Roman lady, too greedy of praise [who] feared that if she remained alive, she would be thought to have enjoyed suffering the violence that she had suffered while alive" [I. xix, p. 89]. The shame and love of praise that he sees in her are in his eyes mere worldliness, for he dwells in the city of God and she in the city of Rome. He regards her as a moral agent whose will is free and whose will determines all; she finds herself trapped by the obligations of her marital role, a role crucially important to the social order. Roman she certainly is, but Augustine is wrong in calling her "too greedy of praise," for she dies not to save her honor but to save Collatine's. Indeed, her honor *is* Collatine's. . . . Though, generally speaking, Shakespeare distrusts honor as a social ideal which is easily perverted, becoming an excuse for political expediency, blind egotism, or vicious rivalry (some of the many forms it takes in the Roman plays), his realistic tolerance impels him to distinguish between the quality of personal commitment to the ideal and the ideal as shaped by a social milieu. In *Lucrece,* he may deplore the social order which requires dishonored women to martyr themselves or be despised, but he sees in Lucrece's suicide a brilliantly successful attempt to re-create Collatine's honor by symbolically restoring to herself the sexual purity on which it depends.

Lucrece stage-manages her death so as to maximize its social effectiveness for this purpose. She summons her husband cryptically by letter, hinting at some disaster connected with herself but not mentioning the rape [ll. 1314-23]. First, to tell Collatine she was raped is to risk or invite public knowledge of that fact before she can rally her public to Collatine's cause. Second, she fears that even Collatine would suspect *her* of "gross abuse" were she to tell him plainly that she had been raped. Even to relate the extenuating circumstances, she feels, would be a "stain'd excuse"—stained, perhaps, by his suspicion that she protests too much to cover up her own possible guilt [ll. 1314-16]. She therefore plans to delay her revelation until she can counteract the social prejudice against her by a histrionic demonstration in which the stain of her rape will be obscured by the stain of her blood in suicide.

When she first resolves on suicide, it is evident that Lucrece understands the blood she will shed as the literal equivalent of the stain which she so laments; she is determined to "let forth my foul defiled blood" [l. 1029]. (pp. 61-4)

It is significant, though, that the heroine's blood is not *wholly* corrupted, as she believes it to be. The division of her blood into two streams is a detail not found in Livy, Ovid, or any other possible source for the poem. Through it Shakespeare symbolizes a tragic duality in Lucrece which she does not perceive. While she regards herself merely as a polluted object, he sees her as a moral agent whose mind remains pure, whose courage and integrity in taking her own life testify to that purity and make her death tragically ironic. In the final scene Lucrece does distinguish firmly between the staining of her blood, that is, her body consecrated to Collatine, and the purity of her mind:

> Though my gross blood be stain'd with this abuse,
> Immaculate and spotless is my mind;
> That was not forc'd, that never was inclin'd
>   To accessory yieldings, but still pure
>   Doth in her poison'd closet yet endure.
>
>   [ll. 1655-59]

But for her it is a purely intellectual distinction, irrelevant to her vision of herself as a "singular patterne of chastity," whose value does, therefore, reside in her body.

The shedding of Lucrece's "defiled blood" is based on a clearly worked out social rationale. When she submitted to Tarquin instead of resisting, she thereby saved her husband from public disgrace, but only by incurring her private stain. This stain brought upon her an existential crisis in that it deprived her of her raison d'être: being a truly chaste wife. Integrity to the ideal of married chastity prevents her from continuing to be Collatine's loyal wife in name only; thus the sole course of action for her is to renounce her role and die. The problem then facing her is how to accomplish this renunciation, which necessarily involves confessing the rape, without bringing disgrace on him and on their families. This problem she solves by contriving her death in such a manner that she symbolically restores her body to its previous sexual purity by the purga-

tion of shedding her blood, thus removing the stain which would dishonor Collatine.

She also wrests from the degradation of rape a considerable moral triumph for herself. Addressing the hand which will wield the dagger, she declares, "For if I die, my honor lives in thee, / But if I live, thou liv'st in my defame" [ll. 1032-33], and later adds,

> O that is gone for which I sought to live,
> And therefore now I need not fear to die!
> To clear this spot by death, at least I give
> A badge of fame to slander's livery,
> A dying life to living infamy.
>
>   [ll. 1051-55]

The paradoxes of life and death, honor and "defame," slander and fame indicate Lucrece's imaginative understanding of the potential in her situation. She sees that the death made necessary by the rape can be the means of recreating that ideal self which the rape destroyed and of restoring Collatine's honor (implied in "badge" and "livery" in the above lines), which becomes the theme of the following three stanzas [ll. 1058-78].

On a larger scale, the social rationale for the heroine's death is that she must sacrifice herself for the survival of marriage as the strongest bulwark against lust. This aspect of her death is revealed in the last scene, when Shakespeare makes her step out of character in reversing her previous attitude toward the stain. After describing the circumstances of the rape, she declares that she will reveal her assailant's name only if the assembled lords swear to avenge her. They do so, and then she pauses melodramatically to ask:

> "How may this forced stain be wip'd from me?
>
> What is the quality of my offence,
> Being constrain'd with dreadful circumstance?
> May my pure mind with the foul act dispense,
> My low-declined honour to advance?
> May any terms acquit me from this chance?
>   The poisoned fountain clears itself again,
>   And why not I from this compelled stain?"
>
>   [ll. 1701-08]

Her questions are predicated on the Christian idea, voiced by Augustine, that the "Pure mind" can rule the body and transcend "dreadful circumstance." For nearly a thousand lines previously, Lucrece has seemed unaware of such a distinction. Furthermore, in referring to the stain as "forced" and "compelled," she deviates from her previous, amply elaborated belief that it is the inevitable consequence of the rape for her and her appropriate moral burden. Here Shakespeare simply forsakes consistency of characterization, as he often does, to clarify an idea which the character represents. This dramatic last-minute appeal to a moral justice untainted by sexual prejudice is only the rhetorical prelude, however, to Lucrece's final enactment of her selflessly patriarchal conception of the role of woman in marriage.

Not trusting the easy forgiveness of her audience, which immediately follows the above lines, she declares, "No dame hereafter living / By my excuse shall claim excuse's giving" [ll. 1714-15]. She hereby rejects any attempt to make married chastity for woman conformable with rational moral standards which take into account the intention of the accused and the circumstances in which the crime occurred. There is simply no excuse for a raped wife, because the social order depends upon pure descent as a mark of status, legitimate heirs as a means of insuring property rights, and the control of male sexual rivalry through the ownership of sexual rights to women in marriage. In addition, as I have argued, marriage enables man to cope with his ambivalence toward his sexual desire by dividing women into two classes, clean and unclean sexual objects. It could be argued that all of these goals, while beneficial to men in particular, are also beneficial to society as a whole. But they all require women to sacrifice themselves, to live or die for the sake of marriage. Lucrece's last words charge Tarquin with guilt for her death as well as for the rape, but her last action, plunging the knife into her breast, indicates her final acceptance of the ultimate female responsibility: to keep herself sexually pure for the sake of her husband and of Rome. (pp. 64-7)

> Coppélia Kahn, *"The Rape in Shakespeare's 'Lucrece',"* in Shakespeare Studies: An Annual Gathering of Research, Criticism, and Reviews, *Vol. IX, 1976, pp. 45-72.*

RICHARD A. LANHAM   (essay date 1976)

[*Lanham explores Shakespeare's depiction of "dramatic motive" and human identity in Tarquin and Lucrece, each of whom displays, according to the critic, a "natural impulse" toward self-dramatization and excessive eloquence that threatens selfhood and "clarity." Tarquin's chivalric identity and love of feudal rhetoric compel him to rape Lucrece, Lanham argues; he is the pawn of his own feudal metaphors and perceives her not as an object of lust, but as a city to be sacked. In her grief, the critic claims, Lucrece becomes enamored with the language of feeling and reveals that her former sense of identity derived from an entirely rhetorical, constructed self—a role which Tarquin's rape destroyed. This rhetorical or dramatic identity*

Tarquin and Lucrece. By Jacobo Robusti Tintoretto.

leads Lucrece to an action that is ultimately self-defeating: her suicide, or, in Lanham's words, her "narcissistic stab." According to Lanham, Brutus exemplifies the "new kind of personality" needed for governance now that the age of feudalism has ended; in his ability to adopt roles and manipulate appearances to his own advantage, he foreshadows the successful monarchs of Shakespeare's history plays.]

The Rape of Lucrece seems the "graver labor" promised Southampton in the dedication to *Venus and Adonis.* It appeared a year later (1594) at any rate, and no one has ever questioned its gravity. The two poems ask to be grouped together: Shakespeare's only narratives, his only "dedicated" polite poems, both seen through the press with care, both Ovidian *epyllia,* show-off diploma pieces short on action but long on speeches, intensely rhetorical in their verbal polish, both dealing with sexual passion and beauty in compulsively antithetical ways, both preoccupied with two central figures, unified in time (one takes a day, the second a night), both gestures of social courtship toward an aristocratic patron, both products—if really written during the plague years—of the only leisure Shakespeare was to know until retirement, and both directed to an aristocratic audience habituated to such leisure. In some respects they seem complementary; one a mythical subject and one historical; woman as sexual aggressor (mock-rape) in one and man (real rape) in the other. But finally more important are the antithetical tones of the two. The problem *Venus and Adonis* presents is how take it, in what spirit to read. There is nothing like this in *Lucrece;* no bawdy punning, no sex, a pitilessly serious tone, plenty of moral platitudes. The question here is why the world master of double plotting pitched his tent on such solemn ground. As in the earlier poem, nothing happens except the focal incidents. Preparing for these and following them comes a great deal of heavy speechifying about motive. It seems logical to conclude that *Lucrece* explores the motives for these two ultimately serious acts. Let us assume as a premise: a poem about serious motive, also a poetic and rhetorical masterpiece, however cloying to the modern palate. Manifestly an act of courtship, *Lucrece* may also preface the plays somehow. What does it say about motive? What magisterial poetic powers does it demonstrate? What gesture of courtship does it embody? And what, if any, relation does it bear to the plays to follow? Or toward its Ovidian twin sister?

The prose argument, which represents a reasonable conflation of Ovid's version with Livy's, does not reflect the Shakespearean version it prefaces. This has puzzled commentators into obelizing it as non-Shakespearean or at least betraying Shakespeare's impatience with detail. But neither *Venus and Adonis* nor *Lucrece* betrays signs of haste. Just the opposite. Maybe the discrepancies form part of the poem, an intended juxtaposition between the received version of the story and the version Shakespeare chooses to tell. The prose argument does not skimp the poem's argument. It is, if anything, fuller. But a page of argument and eighteen hundred lines of poem; does this not indicate a Shakespeare less interested in event than in motivation for event, in exploding an historical moment for analytic purposes? The first difference between argument and poem concerns Tarquin's motive. The story has him falling for Lucrece when he and his messmates post home to check on their wives and he *sees* her. "Forma placet," Ovid tells us, "niueusque color flauique capilli" [pleasing figure with snowy golden hair] (*Fasti* 2.763). Livy adds her chastity as an attraction ("cum forma tum spectata castitas incitat" [with a figure that also inspires chastity] [1.57]), a detail Shakespeare borrows for the poem but not for the argument. But in Shakespeare's pamphlet "without begin-ning," as the dedication calls it, Tarquin falls in love from re-port only. The husbands' quick trip home is left out. Not beauty but *envy* stimulates Tarquin to ultimate rashness. The poem's opening strategy drives the point home. The first stan-za surprises Tarquin in full cry: "From the besiegèd Ardea all in post, / Borne by the trustless wings of false desire, / Lust-breathèd Tarquin leaves the Roman host . . ." [ll. 1-3]. Having set a rapist malignity thus loose on the world, the nar-rator in the second stanza starts guessing at what motivates him: "Haply that name of 'chaste' unhap'ly set / This bate-less edge on his keen appetite . . ." [ll. 8-9]. Livy's secondary motive becomes primary. Collatine had, most unwisely in our moralizing narrator's eye, been bragging about his good for-tune, "the possession of his beauteous mate" [l. 18]. Tarquin, that is, does not fall in love. He comes to envy a possession. The narrator asks, "What needeth then apologies be made / To set forth that which is so singular?" [ll. 31-2]. Not so oti-ose a question as it seems. We come to learn that in this poem unpublished things don't exist. But here the question interro-gates the prose argument. What kind of man bets on his wife's virtue, makes a public trial of it? In one of the abrupt discon-tinuities this poem depends on, the narrator goes on to an-swer, not this question, but the previous one, Tarquin's mo-tive: "Perchance his boast of Lucrece' sov'reignty / Suggest-ed this proud issue of a king; / For by our ears our hearts oft tainted be" [ll. 36-8]. The OED first listing for "sov'reignty" as "Supremacy or pre-eminence in respect of excellence or ef-ficacy" is for 1340, and the last 1610. This slightly antique sense calls attention to itself. Tarquin is stimulated, we are asked to speculate, by an entirely symbolic, indeed *ludic,* mo-tivation. He wants to rape Lucrece *because* she is preeminent in virtuous womanhood. Debauching here must be the es-sence of rape. The narrator hastens from this sick motive to one slightly less despicable: "Perchance that envy of so rich a thing / Braving compare, disdainfully did sting / His high-pitched thoughts" [ll. 39-41]. Envy and jealousy of rank, if less vile, are still bloodless motives, entirely symbolic. They have nothing to do with sex. They are the best the narrator can do, however, since Shakespeare has so pointedly removed the obvious motive—sight of the beloved. The narrator, as third guess, just gives up: "But some untimely thought did instigate / His all too timeless speed, if none of those" [ll. 43-4]. When Tarquin arrives at Collatium, we might expect a little flesh-and-blood feeling. Not at all. An allegorical background is described:

> But Beauty, in that white entitulèd,
> From Venus' doves doth challenge that fair field.
> Then Virtue claims from Beauty Beauty's red,
> Which Virtue gave the Golden Age to gild
> Their silver cheeks, and called it then their shield,
>   Teaching them thus to use it in the fight,
>   When shame assailed, the red should fence the
>   white.
>
> [ll. 57-63]

The sense is deliberately hard to follow. We must stop and puzzle it out: red and white, when he looks at her, change to gold and silver. Red and white stand halfway between flesh tone and symbolic value, and his gaze moves them entirely into symbol. The next stanza admits to the poem's surface what we had already privately acknowledged (another habit of this poem). Tarquin sees in Lucrece's face a *heraldic crest:* "This heraldry in Lucrece' face was seen, / Argued by Beau-ty's red and Virtue's white" [ll. 64-5]. If this poem were really

about passion, we should be by now knee-deep in feudal met-aphor, Lucrece's face lit up like an allegorical light show:

> This silent war of lilies and of roses
> Which Tarquin viewed in her fair face's field,
> In their pure ranks his traitor eye encloses;
> Where, lest between them both it should be killed,
> The coward captive vanquishèd doth yield
>   To those two armies that would let him go
>   Rather than triumph in so false a foe.
>
> [ll. 71-7]

Again the sense is hard to follow, the imagery not. Tarquin sees the same complex of motives the narrator had just guessed at. We don't see Lucrece at all. We see her beauty and virtue translated into their feudal equivalents. We see a mind which thinks in heraldic pageants. Tarquin's "lust" has nothing to do with sex and, finally, nothing to do with Lu-crece. It is entirely narcissistic, made up wholly of self, and this self is built up of clustered feudal images, images so fre-quent in the first half of the poem as to seem less excessive than obsessive.

While Tarquin lies thinking on the great treasure yet to gain, the narrator treats us to a digression on greed and envy less relevant to sexual passion even than Tarquin's revolving thought.

> Those that much covet are with gain so fond
> That what they have not, that which they possess,
> They scatter and unloose it from their bond,
> And so, by hoping more, they have but less;
> Or, gaining more, the profit of excess
>   Is but to surfeit, and such griefs sustain
>   That they prove bankrout in this poor rich gain.
>
> The aim of all is but to nurse the life
> With honor, wealth, and ease in waning age;
> And in this aim there is such thwarting strife
> That one for all, or all for one we gage:
> As life for honor in fell battle's rage;
>   Honor for wealth; and oft that wealth doth cost
>   The death of all, and all together lost;
>
> So that in vent'ring ill we leave to be
> The things we are for that which we expect;
> And this ambitious foul infirmity,
> In having much, torments us with defect
> Of that we have: so then we do neglect
>   The thing we have; and, all for want of wit,
>   Make something nothing by augmenting it.
>
> [ll. 134-54]

The meditation bears less on the vanity of human wishes than on the ironies of possession. It is not that we fail but that suc-cess, and the striving for it, destroy the self. "We leave to be / The things we are." Not the things we *have* but the things we *are*. The something we make nothing is our *self*. We spend our youth preparing for a waning age of honor, wealth, and ease which will be spent looking back on a youth spent look-ing forward to the time when we will look back. Honor, wealth, and ease add up to a definition of aristocratic *otium* [leisure], and Shakespeare points out the inevitable internal contradictions such a definition contains. But what has this to do with Tarquin?

> Such hazard now must doting Tarquin make,
> Pawning his honor to obtain his lust;
> And for himself himself he must forsake.
> Then where is truth, if there be no self-trust?
> When shall he think to find a stranger just

When he himself himself confounds, betrays
To sland'rous tongues and wretched hateful
   days?

[ll. 155-61]

The connection is a self which splits apart like those favorite lines in *Venus and Adonis* and *Lucrece* and the sonnets which divide in half, "And for himself himself he must forsake." His "honor," however, *is* his "lust." The poem's imagery has worked hard to conflate honor, wealth, and ease. Thus Tarquin's motive is at the same time narcissistic and self-dividing, suicidal. The final culprit is "want of wit," our naive slavery to symbols and the words which carry them. By this point in the poem Tarquin has come to be a study of symbolic motive. Shakespeare has inquired into the most serious motive and found it the most rhetorical. Tarquin cannot see outside his own universe of feudal metaphors. He betrays his imprisonment fittingly enough in a pre-rape apostrophe to the torch which will light him to Lucrece's chamber:

Fair torch, burn out thy light, and lend it not
To darken her whose light excelleth thine;
And die, unhallowed thoughts, before you blot
With your uncleanness that which is divine.
Offer pure incense to so pure a shrine.
   Let fair humanity abhor the deed
   That spots and stains love's modest snow-white
      weed.

O shame to knighthood and to shining arms!
O foul dishonor to my household's grave!
O impious act including all foul harms!
A martial man to be soft fancy's slave!
True valor still a true respect should have;
   Then my digression is so vile, so base,
   That it will live engraven in my face.

Yea, though I die, the scandal will survive
And be an eyesore in my golden coat.
Some loathsome dash the herald will contrive
To cipher me how fondly I did dote;
That my posterity, shamed with the note,
   Shall curse my bones, and hold it for no sin
   To wish that I their father had not been.

[ll. 190-210]

He must inflate Lucrece into a saint so as to add resonance to his desire. His regrets, of course, have nothing to do with the rape or with Lucrece. They focus on *him,* his chivalric, martial, feudal identity, past, present, and future. His impious act, symbolic of all motive, including all foul harms, is "to be soft fancy's slave." It means one thing to him. He thinks he is in love with Lucrece. It means something else to us. He is a slave to fancy indeed, to metaphor, to the golden coat of arms on which he is ciphered, to symbolic motive.

Shakespeare has denied Tarquin the motive that fiction—and life—usually awards, sight of the lady, to concentrate not simply on another motive but another kind of motive, a motiveless malignity which turns out to be the self-generating malignancy of the imagination. Tarquin has *no* "real" motive for the rape, no hunger for revenge ("Had Collatinus killed my son or sire" [l. 232]), and both friendship and kinship urge against it ("But as he is my kinsman, my dear friend" [l. 237]). He stands to lose everything, to gain only "a dream, a breath, a froth of fleeting joy" [l. 212]. An imagery of treasons, leagues, and maps accompanies him to Lucrece's chamber and what he sees when he arrives is, again, not Lucrece but a miasma of feudal value-symbols, worlds unconquered, himself a foul usurper, Lucrece first a rich statue [ll. 419-20]

and then, and in overpowering detail, a castle which he, as diabolic hero, must storm, possess, sack:

His drumming heart cheers up his burning eye,
His eye commends the leading to his hand;
His hand, as proud of such a dignity,
Smoking with pride, marched on to make his stand
On her bare breast, the heart of all her land;
   Whose ranks of blue veins, as his hand did scale,
   Left their round turrets destitute and pale.

[ll. 435-41]

If we think the poem about sexual passion, we shall again collapse into laughter at the absurd language. Tarquin puts his hand on Lucrece's breast much as Napoleon must have pointed to Russia on the map. The language makes sense only if rhetoric, and more especially feudal rhetoric, is the subject of the poem. Tarquin finally tells Lucrece that because "nothing can affection's course control" he must "embrace mine infamy" [ll. 500, 504]. The force *we* have seen in the poem is not affection but language, and he is doomed to embrace his own infamy because it has been within him all the time.

The poem has become, by this point, clearly a study in dramatic motive. It should not surprise us, therefore, that Tarquin's attempt to persuade Lucrece, and her reply, are both developed within a rhetorical reality. He argues, "The fault unknown is as a thought unacted" [l. 527]. A feudal threat again, nameless bastardy: "Bequeath not to their lot / The shame that from them no device can take" [ll. 534-35]. It is the heraldic term he thinks of—"device." Lucrece replies that he has changed roles: "In Tarquin's likeness I did entertain thee. / Hast thou put on his shape to do him shame?" [ll. 596-97]. He is not acting the king, she tells him at length, concluding again with a theatrical metaphor: "Think but how vile a spectacle it were / To view thy present trespass in another" [ll. 631-32]. And, after only a few dozen lines more, he steps on the torch and, between lines 686 and 687, does the deed. The poem never describes it. Shakespeare stresses again that his subject is motive, not sexual passion, not an act but the psychic superstructure built upon it. Tarquin then slinks off in shame, the narrator comparing, in a complex figure [l. 715 ff.], *his hero*'s state of mind to a besieged temple, his soul the doyenne thereof.

Compare Tarquin's "desire" with Venus's in *Venus and Adonis,* and you see how complex a portrait Tarquin's is and how utterly asexual his passion. He falls in love with a feudal rhetoric, not a woman; falls, in an odd but real way, in love with himself. His "lust" springs from his imagination as spontaneously as evil from the brain of Iago and for much the same reasons. Shakespeare begins with an undeniably serious motive and finds it, on analysis, more rhetorical even than Venus's substantial hunger.

The original title page of the poem, which read simply *Lucrece,* suggests that the poem explores less the rape than the Lucrece her rape reveals. She begins her self-revelation in a curious image: "She wakes her heart by beating on her breast" [l. 759], the first in a series of images which suggests self-exacerbated sorrow. Not one to "cloak offenses with a cunning brow" [l. 749], she wants night to stay forever. Then she excoriates it in a full-dress apostrophe, "O comfort-killing Night" [l. 763 ff.], which reveals the voice of outraged virtue resonating in a chamber of ego. Space and time must be annihilated to cover her disgrace: "O hateful, vaporous, and foggy Night, / . . . Make war against proportioned course of time" [ll. 771, 774]. The moon and stars must be ravished to keep her company: "Were Tarquin Night, as he is but Night's child, / The silver-shining queen he would distain; / Her twinkling handmaids too, by him defiled, / . . . So should I have co-partners in my pain" [ll. 785-87, 789]. She again thinks of her face as a mask, her predicament as a story:

> Make me not object to the telltale Day.
> The light will show, charactered in my brow,
> The story of sweet chastity's decay,
> The impious breach of holy wedlock vow.
> Yea, the illiterate, that know not how
>   To cipher what is writ in learnèd books,
>   Will quote my loathsome trespass in my looks.
>
> The nurse, to still her child, will tell my story
> And fright her crying babe with Tarquin's name.
> The orator, to deck his oratory,
> Will couple my reproach to Tarquin's shame.
> Feast-finding minstrels, tuning my defame,
>   Will tie the hearers to attend each line,
>   How Tarquin wrongèd me, I Collatine.
>
>   [ll. 806-19]

We step back not simply from her echoing ego but from what she says. How has she wronged Collatine? She puts the problem in terms of feudal possession: "O unseen shame, invisible disgrace! / O unfelt sore, crest-wounding private scar!" [ll. 827-28]. The excursus on the instability of possessions [l. 855 ff.] intensifies the question. Is sexual chastity, or honor, adequately described by the feudal cluster of metaphors? They describe a surface, a crest. And she is again vexed that her predicament is not *social*. To make the sin real, she has to confess it. This poem grows from a *demande*, of course, but as with Tarquin, the emphasis shifts: not, "Should she have given in?" but "Should she confess or shut up?" Lucrece herself cannot pose the problem so clearly. Carried away by her own eloquence, she bursts into an apostrophe to Opportunity. Absurd enough applied to Tarquin, as she does—he has *seized* his opportunity—it finds its real relevance applied to her, seizing the occasion to enjoy a good rant. The compulsive anaphora—one stanza begins uniformly with *Thou,* the next with *Thy* [l. 883 ff.], seventeen lines in three stanzas [l. 940 ff.] with *To*—tips the rhetorical explosion into something like comedy. She so obviously *enjoys* unpacking her heart with words. The poem acknowledges our suspicions openly at the end of the rant. She explodes with "Out, idle words, servants to shallow fools" [l. 1016], and the reader returns a prompt "Just so."

Shakespeare then increases the comic distance by making language yet more self-consciously the subject: "Unprofitable sounds, weak arbitrators! / Busy yourselves in skill-contending schools; / Debate where leisure serves with full debaters; / . . . For me, I force not argument a straw" [ll. 1017-19, 1021]. This is ridiculous and meant to seem so. And gets more so. After forcing the argument yet further, she plunges back into—*anaphora!*

> In vain I rail at Opportunity,
> At Time, at Tarquin, and uncheerful Night;
> In vain I cavil with mine infamy;
> In vain I spurn at my confirmed despite:
> This helpless smoke of words doth me no right.
>   The remedy indeed to do me good
>   Is to let forth my foul defilèd blood.
>
>   [ll. 1023-29]

The non sequitur of the couplet is magnificent: "Words fail

me. I'll kill myself!" She vows "in vain" some more because . . . at the crucial moment she can't find a knife. The language here is meant to be entirely opaque. The point depends on it—what use in fact she is putting words to, the process by which vanity translates sorrow into pleasure. She is confused. She has lost her role. "Of that true type hath Tarquin rifled me" [l. 1050]. She is hammering out a new one—martyr of chastity. The logic of such a role is laughable but the language doesn't speak as the voice of logic, it speaks as the voice of ego, of identity trying to reconstitute itself.

We are meant to see a woman carried away as much by the language of feeling as by feeling itself. In the process, she exposes her former selfhood. It was entirely rhetorical. She was only a role; that gone, she is as good as dead: "O, that is gone for which I sought to live, / And therefore now I need not fear to die" [ll. 1051-52]. She must kill herself, she thinks, to prove she did not betray that role. She must die, that is, to prove that she had lived, that the role was genuine. We are now as far from sincerity and serious identity as can be. Shakespeare makes the point clear: the force of dramatic identity is stronger than life itself. Lucrece's alternative to suicide does not seem so dreadful to us. Let her learn a little hypocrisy. Let her learn to balance two roles at once, develop a self in some way independent of circumstance, recognize that she possesses such. But she must find this alternative the real fate worse than death *just because she has been conceived as a study in rhetorical, dramatic personality.* Her suicide makes sense only on such a premise. If her "honor" were a *means* to preserve the family, if it were the tool of personality, not identical with it, then she could continue, as best she might, to uphold the family. But the point of life is to play the role. The role comes first, its use second.

Lucrece's "virtue" comes to mean, just as does Isabella's in *Measure for Measure,* the dramatic pleasure and assurance of playing a role. In creating Lucrece as in creating Tarquin, Shakespeare began by equipping them with the most serious of motives, only to find, as the fundamental reality of his portraits, a rhetorical self. In both cases, the analysis is carried out through feudal imagery. Surely this is part of his point. He anatomizes the feudal, aristocratic conception of identity. It is egotistical: Lucrece sees herself everywhere she looks, just as Tarquin does. It is dramatic, not complex. And, as Lucrece's behavior goes on to illustrate at length, it is sentimental. It generates feeling for the sake of feeling. And the more sentimental she becomes, the further back Shakespeare stands from the opaque rhetoric.

Day comes and Lucrece, who had spent on Night's damnation an outrush of breath Shakespeare compares to Mount Aetna erupting [l. 1040 ff.], now damns the coming of day. Again the poem voices our reflection: "Thus cavils she with everything she sees" [l. 1093]. Is it "true" grief which follows? If so, all grief, not only Lucrece's, is at heart sentimental, demands and resolutely creates a full, satisfactory dramatic equivalent. Grief must be public to be true. So Lucrece disputes with all she sees, "to herself all sorrow doth compare; / No object but her passion's strength renews" [ll. 1102-03]. She must keep sorrow fresh and biting, stave off even the assuagement time and exhaustion bring. She enshrines this in a telling figure, compares herself to Philomela:

> And whiles against a thorn thou bear'st thy part
> To keep thy sharp woes waking, wretched I,
> To imitate thee well, against my heart
> Will fix a sharp knife to affright mine eye;

Who, if it wink, shall thereon fall and die.
These means, as frets upon an instrument,
Shall tune our heartstrings to true languishment.
[ll. 1135-41]

"True languishment" here begins to sound false.

Lucrece shows herself increasingly in love with her own virtue: "My body or my soul, which was the dearer / When the one, pure, the other made divine? / Whose love of either to myself was nearer / When both were kept for heaven and Collatine?" [ll. 1163-66]. Heaven and Collatine seem valuable largely as the occasion for Lucrece's virtue. She begins her posthumous life in other men's minds with a will-and-testament topos [l. 1181 ff.], then cries a little, joined by a maid who cries to keep her company [l. 1236]. The poem takes pains to voice our own thoughts again [l. 1254 ff.] that Lucrece is not to blame, before it returns to her sentimental grief. It is not real unless fully and oft expressed: "that deep torture may be called a hell / When more is felt than one hath power to tell. / Go get me hither paper, ink, and pen" [ll. 1287-89]. When she writes to Collatine, the muse does not fail her: "First hovering o'er the paper with her quill. / Conceit and grief an eager combat fight; / What wit sets down is blotted straight with will. / This is too curious good, this blunt and ill" [ll. 1297-1300]. Yet the note she finally writes is plainness itself. What's going on? Shakespeare seems to describe eloquence as a natural impulse, primary, one which has to be *suppressed* in favor of clarity. The muse shares the "true grief," in some sense creates it.

Lucrece now becomes an actress admitted: "the life and feeling of her passion / She hoards, to spend when he is by to hear her, / When sighs and groans and tears may grace the fashion / Of her disgrace" [ll. 1317-20]. The poem pursues this theme relentlessly. Even the groom who takes the letter [l. 1345 ff.] is reproached for being a bad actor.

Lucrece finally wearies of grieving and looks around, "pausing for means to mourn some newer way" [l. 1365]. She hits upon a sentimentalist's dream, "a piece / Of skillful painting, made for Priam's Troy" [ll. 1366-67]. A perfect choice—rape, siege, huge, dramatic, artificial, flat, as conceited as the poem itself. Lucrece pounces on it with delight. The painting is full of faces, of masks, and Lucrece searches among them "to find a face where all distress is stelled" [l. 1444]. Only the mask is real. She pities Hecuba; the painter had heaped woes upon her but given her no mouth to speak. She has it. *She'll play Hecuba.* "'Poor instrument,' quoth she, 'without a sound: / I'll tune thy woes with my lamenting tongue'" [ll. 1464-65]. Shakespeare's poem at this point veers toward his own craft, toward the uses of drama. What's Hecuba to her, she to Hecuba? Her rehearsal declares: "Why should the private pleasure of some one / Become the public plague of many moe? / Let sin, alone committed, light alone / Upon his head that hath transgressèd so" [ll. 1478-81]. Lucrece, not Helen, wears the mantle of this argument. She takes it on herself to reenact the whole poem: "So Lucrece, set awork, sad tales doth tell / To pencilled pensiveness and colored sorrow: / She lends them words, and she their looks doth borrow" [ll. 1496-98]. She plays the siege of Troy. She plays *all* the parts, we come to see, because she sees herself not as Helen but as *Troy!* As Priam trusted Sinon, "So did I Tarquin; so my Troy did perish." She has found a role big enough even for her elephantine ego.

She has now practiced enough and begins readying her last big scene. She knows that timing is everything:

Here with a sigh as if her heart would break
She throws forth Tarquin's name: "He, he!" she says,
But more than "he" her poor tongue could not speak,
Till after many accents and delays,
Untimely breathings, sick and short assays,
She utters this: "He, he! fair lords, 'tis he
That guides this hand to give this wound to me."
[ll. 1716-22]

Even Jung might Freudianize that culminating narcissistic stab. She makes love to herself for the last time.

To make *Lucrece* a poem beyond doubt about dramatic identity, an exploration of rhetorical life, Shakespeare ends it with two displays depending neither on Tarquin nor Lucrece. Lucretius expresses a grief as dramatic and self-centered as his daughter's: "'Daughter, dear daughter!' old Lucretius cries / 'That life was mine which thou hast here deprivèd. / If in the child the father's image lies, / Where shall I live now Lucrece is unlivèd?'" [ll. 1751-54]. Collatine bathes in Lucrece's blood and "counterfeits to die with her a space" [l. 1776]. Then, no longer to be kept from "heart-easing words," he "begins to talk" [ll. 1782-83]. The two mourners next proceed to a grief contest: "'O,' quoth Lucretius, 'I did give that life / Which she too early and too late hath spilled.' / 'Woe, woe!' quoth Collatine. 'She was my wife, / I owed her, and 'tis mine that she hath killed'" [ll. 1800-03]. Brutus, thinking this grief contest as silly as we do, decides it is time to resume his sanity, "clothe his wit in state and pride, / Burying in Lucrece' wound his folly's show" [ll. 1809-10]. Brutus's late appearance has puzzled scholiasts but it could scarcely be clearer. He represents the kind of personality Lucrece could not adjust to, the complex self that uses a role without becoming it. Through his mouth πράγματα not δόγματα [actions not opinions] finally speak:

Why, Collatine, is woe the cure for woe?
Do wounds help wounds, or grief help grievous deeds?
Is it revenge to give thyself a blow
For his foul act by whom thy fair wife bleeds?
Such childish humor from weak minds proceeds.
Thy wretched wife mistook the matter so,
To slay herself that should have slain her foe.
[ll. 1821-27]

The sentimentalism ends just as the sentimental rhetoric does, and Brutus provides the control for both. He is not out of place, his appearance sudden. He is inevitable.

It is usually neither sensible nor legitimate to read one poem as rehearsal for another. But a masterpiece invites such prophetic attention and rewards it. *Lucrece* does not, let me hasten to add, present itself as a rough draft of anything. Shakespeare's two masterpieces are both *polished,* diabolically so. But *Lucrece* does prophesy things to come. Shakespeare reflects on the nature of an historical event, on the feudal aristocracy the poem courts; he reflects on the uses of art; he sets out above all the range of styles and attitudes toward style his kind of poetry will require. It is this last point, the kind of stylistic attention he solicits, which *Lucrece* especially strives to make. Let me deal with these topics in order.

Tarquin's rape and Lucrece's suicide changed the nature of

Roman government, got rid of the kings. Shakespeare examines the crucial event and finds, at its base, δόγματα not πράαγματα, not circumstances but attitudes, narcissism, romantic pleasure. Both Tarquin and Lucrece live in the future and tread the present as a stage. Shakespeare concludes from this that the present is intrinsically dramatic, that the dramatist, in staging history, need not fret about destroying its verisimilitude. *Lucrece* teaches that history happens on a stage to begin with. Just this reflection lies behind the history plays, and prompts . . . the choruses in *Henry V*. It is a theory of history Shakespeare shared with Cervantes. And the Ovidian exposure of Rome's theatricality was to premise the Roman plays. In history so construed, of course, speeches offer not less verisimilitude than narrative but more.

The gesture of courtship embodied in *Lucrece* strikes the modern reader as ambiguous. The poem abounds in feudal language and in acceptable aristocratic sentiments: subject high, style polished, proverbial wisdom unremitting. *Lucrece* has presented a surface sufficiently conventional and sufficiently reflective of critical naivete to masquerade for a long time as suitable for noble dedication. But it ends far from the political banalities that float on its surface. Shakespeare is not least Ovidian in his political statement. Naive feudal role playing, he warns, is no longer adequate. Nor is the naive feudal self. It has become suicidal, as Lucrece so amply demonstrates. A new *kind* of personality is needed for governance, the integrated personality Brutus symbolizes. Rhetorical display may be needed as mask but is no longer tolerable as indulgence. A governor must be self-aware and self-conscious about language. And so Prince Hal is put through his rhetorical education at the hands of the master sophist Falstaff. The governor needs a sense of theatre but he cannot, like Richard, be stagestruck. Shakespeare teaches these lessons as both dramatist and bourgeois. And, like that other bourgeois expert in courtship, Geoffrey Chaucer, he teaches through a poetry which can be read as totally conventional or totally the opposite. Both Tarquin's act and Lucrece's stem from a *demande,* an aristocratic pastime. But motive also comes from event, from commonsense behavior, from the dog that does not bark. Its absence in *Lucrece* warns that the aristocratic view omits this half of motive at its peril. Lucrece's response is very aristocratic and very silly. Shakespeare makes both points.

Lucrece as art critic need not detain us. She uses the painting as reflection from her own thoughts, holds the mirror up to Lucrece. Shakespeare staked out the opposite, critical detachment, as the goal of our poetic paideia. His readers would run from narcissistic absorption to Ovidian detachment. His own poem was designed as a mirror and has worked beautifully as one. But his plays work this way too, offer simplistic morals for those who need them. A generic verdict seems manifest: a reflective surface forms part of any work of literature, shows how it fits into its own time, comes to terms with expectation. It is part of the ingratiation of Shakespeare's address that he supplies a narcissistic stimulus with such willing ease, refrains politely from overt challenge. Such may have been the manner of the age. The strategy of surplus moralizing occurs again and again in Renaissance literature, and, just as frequently, an answering critical simplicity. The people in Renaissance poems often fool themselves too, as here. Modern thinking about language thinks it a prison. Shakespeare dwells concomitantly on its rich resources of illusion, on our ability like Lucrece to make a new self from a painting and The Method. *Lucrece* seems to conclude that art is not in es-

sence different from life. They inhabit the same spectrum of symbolic behavior. Shakespeare did not anticipate an audience of disinterested, disengaged critics. At least not many of them. People use poetry in all kinds of ways. Part of *Lucrece*'s gesture as masterpiece is to stake out the theoretical extremes. (pp. 94-110)

> *Richard A. Lanham, "The Ovidian Shakespeare: 'Venus and Adonis' and 'Lucrece'," in his* The Motives of Eloquence: Literary Rhetoric in the Renaissance, *Yale University Press, 1976, pp. 82-110.*

CLARK HULSE   (essay date 1978)

[*Hulse contends that in* The Rape of Lucrece *Shakespeare adheres to classical aesthetic theories in creating his own "proper epic ecphrasis," an extended description that mimics other art forms. He concludes that whereas* Lucrece *succeeds as an artistic creation, she fails in heroic terms, reflecting, according to the critic, Shakespeare's "ambivalence" toward the epic tradition and his assertion of the powerlessness of women. In Hulse's view,* Lucrece *possesses the same powers of rhetorical persuasion as the artist, and, assisted by the painted Troy piece, she attains a moment of self-revelation that reveals her lack of complicity in the rape; however, because "her body is soiled," she cannot escape the appearance of guilt. "Her mistake," according to Hulse, "is that she is a woman, blocked from full heroic action in the public realm, condemned instead to constantly proving her sexual honor." Ultimately,* Lucrece *must defer heroics to the pragmatic Brutus, who emerges to extol Lucrece and incite the men to seek revenge.*]

In 1593, Shakespeare promised Southampton 'some graver labour' to follow *Venus and Adonis*. Indeed, Muriel Bradbrook has persuasively argued that *Venus* itself was an attempt by Shakespeare to silence the slanders uttered by Greene in 1592 and establish himself as a respectable poet. In the elaborate description of a tapestry or painting of Troy which takes up over two hundred lines in *Lucrece,* Shakespeare draws on Virgil and Classical art theorists to create for his poem a proper epic *ecphrasis,* comparable to the shield of Achilles, to the bronze doors at Carthage where Aeneas sees written the fate of his people, or to the 'clothes of *Arras* and of *Toure*' which decorate Malacasta's castle in [Spenser's] *Faerie Queene*. When he describes the painter's wondrous skill, Shakespeare invokes the ancient *paragone* of poet and painter, asserting his own mastery of his craft and equality to the ancient masters of the arts. When he describes the response of Lucrece to the 'well-painted piece' [l. 1443], Shakespeare defines her stature as a woman and as the hero of his poem.

Shakespeare's *Lucrece* may be called a 'minor' epic in the sense that Ariosto or Spenser are epic, concerned with 'Knights and Ladies gentle deeds, . . . Fierce warres and faithfull loves' [*Faerie Queene*]. In the progress from *Venus and Adonis* to *Lucrece,* Shakespeare travels the Virgilian path, beginning in a middle style akin to sonnet, pastoral and comedy, and ending in the regions of epic and tragedy. The erotic and the heroic are mingled in Tarquin's siege of the fort of Lucrece's chastity, until the moment when he is able 'To make the breach and enter this sweet city' [l. 469]. When Lucrece calls to mind the 'well-painted piece', the extended comparison between bedroom and battlefield is completed in images of the fall of Troy:

> 'For even as subtle Sinon here is painted,
> So sober sad, so weary and so mild,—

As if with grief or travail he had fainted,—
To me came Tarquin armed to beguild
With outward honesty, but yet defil'd
    With inward vice. As Priam him did cherish,
    So did I Tarquin,—so my Troy did perish.'

[ll. 1541-47]

The Troy passage is set into the poem as an extended simile or *icon*. Originally the term *icon* meant 'statue' or 'image', before becoming a technical term of rhetoric. The *Rhetorica ad Herennium* defines it as a comparison between two things, used either for praise or blame. Aristotle notes that *icon* is best suited to poetry, and Erasmus praises it for vividness. . . . I shall stay with the . . . usage of Classical and Renaissance rhetoricians, who call any vivid, sensuous image *iconic;* define *ecphrasis* as an extended description of something, such as a person, place, battle or work of art; and use *prosopopoeia* for the lending of voice to an inanimate object. (pp. 13-14)

Shakespeare's *icon* sums up a comparison which has been carefully developed from the opening line of the poem. 'From the besieged Ardea all in post' [Argument] comes Tarquin, from battle to bed, and, one may wonder, from Ardea to ardor. In a system of 'moral heraldry', as Bradbrook calls it [see excerpt above, 1951], Shakespeare transforms the faces of both protagonists into the shields of opposing warriors. In Tarquin's face and coat of arms are written the signs of his dishonor:

'Then my digression is so vile, so base,
That it will live engraven in my face.

'Yea, though I die the scandal will survive
And be an eye-sore in my golden coat;
Some loathsome dash the herald will contrive,
To cipher me how fondly I did dote.'

[ll. 202-07]

While the foul intent of Tarquin is immediately visible to Shakespeare, to the reader and to Tarquin himself, it is hidden from Lucrece, who

Could pick no meaning from their parling looks,
Nor read the subtle shining secrecies
Writ in the glassy margents of such books.

[ll. 100-02]

For all her simplicity, the face of Lucrece is painted with equal subtlety:

When beauty boasted blushes, in despite
Virtue would stain that o'er with silver white.

But beauty in that white entituled
From Venus' doves, doth challenge that fair field;
Then virtue claims from beauty beauty's red,
Which virtue gave the golden age to gild
Their silver cheeks, and call'd it then their shield;
    Teaching them thus to use it in the fight,
    When shame assail'd, the red should fence the
    white.

This heraldry in Lucrece' face was seen,
Argu'd by beauty's red and virtue's white;
Of either's colour was the other queen.

[ll. 55-66]

First virtue is white and beauty blushing red; then beauty is white, like Venus's doves, and virtue red by association with the golden age. The very slipperiness of the image suggests there is an ambiguity about moral heraldry. It is hard to tell

from the crest just what is under the visor. If Lucrece had trouble reading Tarquin's face, her own features, however clear and honest, are no less a puzzle for the poet, and in that puzzle is something of an ambivalence toward the epic tradition. Tarquin is decidedly villainous, a perfect anti-hero, whose own soul is desecrated by his crime. But Lucrece, as his opponent, is not at first clearly heroic, either in understanding or in action.

Is she, after all, sufficiently noble to be the heroine of a little epic? As Saint Augustine asked [in his *City of God*], if she was chaste, why did she kill herself, and if guilty, why worthy of praise? The question has been repeated at some length by two modern Augustinians, Don Cameron Allen and Roy Battenhouse [see excerpts above, 1962 and 1969]. We might—should—be tempted to dismiss this out of hand as shallow misogyny, confusing the victim with the criminal, except that Lucrece repeatedly asks the same question of herself. In her first words after the rape she speaks of her 'offences', 'disgrace', 'unseen sin', 'guilt', and 'shame' [ll. 747-56]. The misogyny is enough part of the poem that we must deal with it.

Livy and Ovid clearly say that Lucrece consented to her rape under duress. Chaucer [in his *The Legend of Good Women*] is evasive. He takes Ovid's verb 'succubuit,', 'she yielded', to mean that she sank away or fainted, eliminating the nagging question of her state of mind:

She loste bothe at ones wit and breth,
And in a swogh she lay, and wex so ded,
Men myghte smyten of hire arm or hed;
She feleth no thyng, neyther foul ne fayr.

Shakespeare takes a third way, having Tarquin use force throughout. Even so, Lucrece spends the night examining herself and the other potential culprits, Night, Opportunity, Time, and, incidentally, Tarquin. So the unstable identity of the opening lines is still unfixed as she comes to the 'well-painted piece'. Its function as *comparatio* [showing similarities between persons or things] is all the more important for this reason. In viewing the work, Lucrece may be able to view herself, to successfully 'read' it and her own character, as neither she nor Shakespeare could do at the outset.

In seeing how Lucrece 'reads' the Troy-piece, we may first ask just what it is she is looking at. Shakespeare describes at least six different scenes: the Greek army arrayed before the walls; Nestor addressing the troops; Hector issuing forth from the gates; the battle on 'Simois' reedy banks' [l. 1437]; the final sack of the citadel; and (out of chronological order) Sinon deluding Priam. He praises the painter's realism and his 'art of physiognomy' [ll. 1394-95], which is not the description of features, but the rendering of the emotions in each face. What could depict so many scenes, with such a technique? Is it a tapestry or a painting? Even to think about Elizabethan painting is to encounter next to nothing which could evoke such a description. Sidney Colvin, convinced by the detail of the passage that Shakespeare had an actual work in mind, suggested a tapestry of fifteenth-century France [in *A Book of Homage to Shakespeare,* ed. by I. Gollancz]. Margaret Thorp in 1931 thought it was a panel painting [in her essay "Shakespeare and the Fine Arts"]. A. H. R. Fairchild suggested that Shakespeare was combining the composition of fifteenth-century French tapestries with the 'physiognomy' of sixteenth-century works [in his *Shakespeare and the Arts of Design*].

Personally, I vote for a tapestry. The only real objection to a tapestry is the term 'painted', which, as Fairchild points out, Elizabethans, and Shakespeare, used with great looseness as a synonym for 'colored' or 'portrayed'. . . . The passage really tells us less about the actual object than about the illusion it creates. It is sufficiently incomplete that we may see what we please as long as we see *something*. (pp. 14-16)

Shakespeare's *ecphrasis* begins with praise for the perfect imitation of the visible [ll. 1366-86], then praise for the perfect rendering of expression [ll. 1387-1407], and finally praise for the artist's ability to suggest the parts of the figure invisible to the eye [ll. 1408-28]. These are the criteria by which Pliny [in his *Historia Naturalis*] measures the perfection of painting. . . . If Shakespeare had any intention of constructing a proper Roman decoration for Lucrece's house, Pliny would have been the likely place to start.

The adherence of Shakespeare's *ecphrasis* to Classical aesthetics is underscored by a parallel, first noted by E. H. Gombrich [in his *Eikones*], between Shakespeare's description of Nestor haranguing the troops with the account by Philostratus [in his *Art and Illusion*], of a painting of the siege of Thebes. It is worth quoting in full. 'Some are seen in full figure, others with the legs hidden, others from the waist up, then only the busts of some, heads only, helmets only, and finally just spear-points. This, my boy, is perspective; since the problem is to deceive the eyes as they travel back along with the proper receding planes of the picture.'

> For much imaginary work was there,—
> Conceit deceitful, so compact, so kind,
> That for Achilles' image stood his spear
> Gripp'd in an armed hand; himself behind
> Was left unseen, save to the eye of mind:
> A hand, a foot, a face, a leg, a head
> Stood for the whole to be imagined.
>
> [ll. 1422-28]

Even in translation, the parallel strikes me as sufficiently full and detailed to be an actual borrowing. Both stress the painter's cheating skill, and linger over the spear. If Shakespeare's 'lesse Greeke' were inadequate to the task, he could have read Philostratus in any of the five Latin editions between 1517 and 1550, or in the 1578 French translation of Blaise de Vigenere.

Whether we accept Philostratus as a source or not, his *ecphrasis* establishes a rhetorical pattern for describing a visual artifact which was so widely diffused that it would have been virtually impossible for any serious poet to be ignorant of it. Philostratus does not so much describe as suggest, concentrating not on the object itself, but on how it would appear to a viewer. In a sense he practises, as does Shakespeare, exactly the kind of rhetoric and the kind of art to which Plato objected. The representation, either in word, paint or marble, is not true to life, much less to an objective ideal. It is distorted to accommodate the process of perception, and those very distortions are Shakespeare's main interest.

The remainder of the passage, describing the fall of Troy, is largely modeled on two *ecphrases* in the *Aeneid:* the description of the bronze doors of the temple of Venus at Carthage in Book I, and Aeneas's account of the battle in Book II. (pp. 16-17)

The pattern Shakespeare is following, established by Virgil, Philostratus, Quintilian, and of course Homer, was codified in the *Progymnasmata* of Hermogenes, the rhetorician of the second sophistic. *Ecphrasis* he defines as:

> an account in detail, visible, as they say, bringing before one's eyes what is to be shown . . . Ecphrasis of actions will proceed from what went before, from what happened at that time, and from what followed. Thus if we make an ecphrasis on war, first we shall tell what happened before the war, the levy, the expenditures, the fears; then the engagements, the slaughter, the deaths; then the monument of victory; then the paeans of the victors and, of the others, the tears, the slavery.

The poet, departing from the literal limits of the scene to what came before and after, strives to make it as vivid as possible for the audience by rendering the emotions of the participants. To Quintilian this was the highest of all oratorical achievement, though not the most difficult to attain.

The achievement of this vividness is a common goal for both poetry and painting in the ecphrastic tradition. Plutarch [in his *Moralia*], after quoting the aphorism of Simonides that painting is silent poetry and poetry is a speaking picture, observes that the two arts differ only in the materials by which they seek the same end. As the humanist theorists of each art dwelt on that material difference, they defined the limits of each art by the capacities of the other. Castelvetro, for example, says that painting can only show bodies, not the soul, while poetry can never equal the visual immediacy of painting. So Shakespeare concludes in Sonnet 24 that his eyes, like painters, 'draw but what they see, know not the heart'.

The highest form of skill, then, is to surpass the limits of your material and achieve the perfection of the rival art. (pp. 17-18)

Shakespeare perfectly fulfills the goal of the *paragone* in his Troy-piece, with the variety of its action and vividness of emotion. He stresses how the painter has shown the things impossible to depict—the concealed parts of the body, the sounds of the scenes, the feelings of the participants. Since this impossible painting is so perfect, he may well praise the artist for rivalling nature. Since it is possible only in the medium of poetry, and is measured by the standard of Virgil, he is also subtly praising himself.

The Virgilian model defines not just the task of the artist, but also the response of the audience to the artist's skill. Virgil lingers over Aeneas's reaction to the scene of Troy:

> constitit et lacrimans, 'quis iam locus,' inquit, 'Achate,
> quae regio in terris nostri non plena laboris?
> en Priamus! sunt hic etiam sua praemia laudi,
> sunt lacrimae rerum et mentem mortalia tangunt.'
>
> [He stopped and weeping cried: "What land, Achates, what tract on earth is now not full of our sorrow? Lo, Priam! Here, too, virtue has its due rewards; here, too, are tears for misfortune and mortal sorrows touch the heart"]

His close identification with the emotions portrayed move Aeneas to a fresh lament over his own fate. Lucrece, too, overcome with the sorrow of Hecuba, laments that the painter gave her 'so much grief, and not a tongue':

> 'Poor instrument,' quoth she, 'without a sound,
> I'll tune thy woes with my lamenting tongue,
> And drop sweet balm in Priam's painted wound,

Lucrece. By Marcantonio Raimondi.

And rail on Pyrrhus that hath done him wrong,
And with my tears quench Troy that burns so long,
    And with my knife scratch out the angry eyes
    Of all the Greeks that are thine enemies.'

[ll. 1464-70]

As she moves through the tapestry, naming and sorrowing with each figure, she comes finally to Sinon, whose smooth face conceals his inner treachery. Confronting him, she must finally penetrate surfaces, and in doing so, recognize just how similar her own story is:

'It cannot be,' quoth she, 'that so much guile,'—
She would have said,—'can lurk in such a look.'
But Tarquin's shape came in her mind the while,
And from her tongue 'can lurk' from 'cannot' took.

[ll. 1534-37]

Shakespeare's one violation of chronological order, leaving Sinon for last, is thus dictated by his rhetorical order, moving from the tapestry itself, to Lucrece's vocal response, to her recognition of the similarity to her own fate: from *ecphrasis* to *prosopopoeia* to *icon*.

We may think of Shakespeare as recapitulating the instructions for looking at a painting which Philostratus gave in sections 1-4 of the *Eikones* (concluding with the siege of Thebes). First, he tells us, the mere physical illusion of the paint creates wonder, but to interpret it properly, we must look away from the painting to the events which are depicted. As we enter the illusion, we expand the scene with our own imagination, hearing its sounds, seeing what is only suggested, until our identification with it is so close that we are actors

in it: 'Let us catch the blood, my boy, holding under it a fold of our garments.' This expressive view of aesthetic experience was shared as well by Renaissance art theorists. Dependent on Philostratus, Pliny and the poets for their knowledge of Classical painting, they were influenced by *ecphrasis* perhaps as deeply as their literary colleagues. Alberti [in his *On Painting*] echoes Horace to explain how we look at paintings: 'We weep with the weeping, laugh with the laughing, and grieve with the grieving.' Lucrece's response is exactly to seek out the 'face where all distress is stell'd' [l. 1444] as the analogue to her own grief. (pp. 18-19)

Lucrece does not empathize equally with all the figures in the painting. She must penetrate the appearance of each to weigh properly the gullibility of Priam with the duplicity of Sinon. It is in looking at the painting, in examining by comparison the woes of Hecuba, that Lucrece is finally able to face the full diabolism of Tarquin and her own lack of responsibility for what has occurred. This is no easy lesson, for Hamlet needed supernatural prompting to discover that 'one may smile, and smile, and be a villain' [I. v. 108]. In that moment of recognition, Lucrece reaches her fullest heroic stature.

I have claimed at this point that Lucrece bears no responsibility for what has happened. Why, then, does she kill herself? The reasoning for the final act returns us to Shakespeare's misogyny, for while Lucrece is not to blame, she is clearly guilty. As Shakespeare says in [l. 80] and Collatine and Lucretius in [ll. 1709-10], her mind is pure though her body is soiled. Lucrece is dwelling with the most severe mind-body split conceivable, and only by suicide can she make this fully clear, so that others can read her as she has read the Troy tapestry, and revenge her, as she has sought to revenge Hecuba by tearing at Sinon with her nails.

For Lucrece has herself become an emblem, and she fears the interpretations which others may make of her. Immediately after her apostrophe to Night, she laments:

'Yea, the illiterate that know not how
    To cipher what is writ in learned books,
    Will quote my loathsome trespass in my looks.'

[ll. 810-12]

She fears that she and Collatine have become an example of cuckoldry, 'And Tarquin's eye may read the mot afar' [l. 830], she adds in the technical language of devices. Yet the inability of others to interpret this way suggests that Lucrece at first misunderstands her own symbolism. When Lucrece's maid enters, she weeps at the sight of the face of her mistress without knowing the reason. She has empathy without judgment. When the groom enters to receive the message to Collatine, he blushes from sheer nervousness, which Lucrece takes to mean that he has seen her shame.

The blushing servants, who are the first audience of the ravished Lucrece, are imperfect prototypes for her own response to Hecuba. Indeed, the maid's response, like that of Lucrece to the tapestry, is one of like to like. As Lucrece will be 'impressed' by the emotions of the tapestry, so the maid is 'impressed' by the countenance of her mistress:

For men have marble, women waxen, minds,
And therefore are they form'd as marble will;
The weak oppress'd, th'impression of strange kinds
Is form'd in them by force, by fraud, or skill.
Then call them not the authors of their ill,
    No more than wax shall be accounted evil,
    Wherein is stamp'd the semblance of a devil.

[ll. 1240-46]

'By force, by fraud, or skill': Tarquin, Sinon and the painter. The metaphor of wax has undergone an interesting displacement, beginning as an explanation of the behavior of the maid, but ending with what men do to women. Is it too much to speculate that the process of 'impressing' which is worked out in Lucrece's initial reaction to the Troy-piece can be a model for the rape itself: that is, that Tarquin, who is elsewhere called a devil, stamps his evil in the wax that is Lucrece?

Though Lucrece will desperately claim that 'I am the mistress of my fate' [l. 1069], she is at the outset pliant and without anything that might be called a free will. Isabella will say to Angelo in *Measure for Measure:*

> For we are soft as our complexions are,
> And credulous to false prints.
>
> [II. iv. 129-30]

Shakespeare indeed stresses the point in *Lucrece* by likening the moral condition of women to the beautiful but passive flower:

> No man inveigh against the withered flower,
> But chide rough winter that the flower hath kill'd;
> Not that devour'd, but that which doth devour
> Is worthy blame; O let it not be hild
> Poor women's faults, that they are so fulfill'd
> With men's abuses! those proud lords to blame
> Make weak-made women tenants to their shame.
>
> [ll. 1254-60]

Her inability to control her own body limits the actions of the heroic self which Lucrece defines while standing before the Troy-piece. Only at the end of the passage does she rise beyond external impressions to judge, define and act. And even then she is, paradoxically, Hecuba the sufferer, not Aeneas the rebuilder. In Hecuba,

> the painter had anatomiz'd
> Time's ruin, beauty's wrack, and grim care's reign.
>
> [ll. 1450-51]

Lucrece bears

> The face, that map which deep impression bears
> Of hard misfortune, carv'd in it with tears.
>
> [ll. 1712-13]

The world crowds in on her, shaping her body and mind, while she has little scope to push back and control events. If she were a man, she could of course avenge herself. 'O God, that I were a man!' cries Beatrice in *Much Ado*, 'I would eat his heart in the marketplace' [IV. i. 306-07]. But they are women, and must employ men to wield their swords. The only women in Shakespeare's plays who successfully use weapons on stage are the villains: La Pucelle, Queen Margaret [both in *Henry VI*], and Regan [in *King Lear*]. There are no Jaels and no Judiths.

The only power left to Lucrece is in the realm of art. As audience, she can enter into the epic action of Troy. As artist, she can move her own audience by the vivid portrayal of the significance of her figures. Immediately after the rape, Lucrece was plagued with misreadings, seeing herself as Adultery, an image which her servants found unintelligible. After her confrontation with the Troy-piece, she is prepared to present herself as the image of woe and suffering, and to demand from

Collatine and Lucretius the revenge she offered to Hecuba. Her suicide is nothing more or less than the *energeia,* or forcibleness, which gives the tableau its impact. It releases her blood, which separates into two rivers, one of pure red, the other black and foul. She shows what could not be seen, the inner self which signifies visually what all have insisted verbally:

> 'Though my gross blood be stain'd with this abuse,
> Immaculate and spotless is my mind.'
>
> [ll. 1655-56]

The *ecphrasis* or detailed description of the blood is followed by *apostrophe,* in which Lucretius and Collatine each address Lucrece, pour out their sorrows, and proclaim their own impending deaths. Only Brutus seems fully to understand her meaning, and chides the others:

> 'Why Collatine, is woe the cure for woe?
> Do wounds help wounds, or grief help grievous
>   deeds?
> Is it revenge to give thyself a blow
> For his foul act by whom thy fair wife bleeds?
> Such childish humour from weak minds proceeds;
>   Thy wretched wife mistook the matter so,
>   To slay herself that should have slain her foe.'
>
> [ll. 1821-27]

Is this really a condemnation of her suicide? I do not think so. What Brutus scorns is the mere empathy of answering woe with woe; he is calling for the men to perform the same vengeance on Tarquin which Lucrece herself sought to inflict on Sinon. He reprimands the men for considering suicide, calls them childish, and speaks of 'weak minds', much like the phrases Shakespeare has earlier used for all women. Her mistake, then, is that she is a woman, blocked from full heroic action in the public realm, condemned instead to constantly proving her sexual honor.

Brutus stands as a marker for the ultimate failure of Lucrece in heroic terms, but her success in artistic terms. We may compare him to that figure which Alberti recommended that the artist place at the margin of the picture:

> In an *istoria* I like to see someone who admonishes and points out to us what is happening there; or beckons with his hand to see; or menaces with an angry face and with flashing eyes, so that no one should come near; or shows some danger or marvellous thing there; or invites us to weep or to laugh together with them.

It is Brutus who directs the response of the audience to the story of Lucrece, pointing out to the Romans their proper course of action, and pointing out to Southampton the artistry of his servant Shakespeare. (pp. 19-22)

Clark Hulse, " 'A Piece of Skilful Painting' in Shakespeare's 'Lucrece'," in Shakespeare Survey: An Annual Survey of Shakespearian Study and Production, *Vol. 31, 1978, pp. 13-22.*

DONALD CHENEY (essay date 1982)

[Cheney examines the influence of Virgil, Livy, and Plutarch on Shakespeare's themes, imagery, and vocabulary in The Rape of Lucrece. Shakespeare's concept of Rome, which, according to the critic, informs many of the English history plays as well, derives principally from the Virgilian political myth that depicts the subordination of human desire to historic ne-

cessity and "the human cost of political stability." From this perspective, the tragic stories of Lucrece and Tarquin "are of secondary importance compared to the heroic emergence of Brutus." Cheney points out that in the "great Shakespearean microcosmic metaphor" relating individual victims to besieged cities or households, the aggressors are ultimately as powerless as their victims in the face of historical destiny. In portions of his essay not excerpted here, the critic evaluates evidence of similar themes and imagery in Romeo and Juliet.]

Both overtly and more cryptically as well, references to the protagonists and incidents of Roman history appear throughout Shakespeare's works, becoming essential elements of his dramatic vocabulary. This essay proposes to look at the imagery of two early works, *The Rape of Lucrece* and *Romeo and Juliet,* in the context of Shakespeare's Roman sources and his own later Roman plays, and to consider how his vision of Rome may have figured in the evolution of his language. These earlier works begin to elaborate the great Shakespearean microcosmic metaphor whereby an individual is seen as besieged city or household, darkly sharing and conspiring with the enemy forces that seek to ravish and enthrall it. In ways that reason rejects (and the language of the young Shakespeare cannot always accommodate), tyrants and victims alike move from obsession to compulsion, knowing that they are participating in their self-destruction while remaining powerless to escape what seems the fulfillment of time's promise.

In the case of *Lucrece,* the operation of this microcosmic metaphor is relatively obvious, for the same reason that modern readers may find it distasteful: attorneys for the Tarquins of this world have traditionally relied on more or less blatant forms of it. Thus it is suggested that both Collatine and his wife share some responsibility for the rape, the former as "publisher / Of that rich jewel" [ll. 33-4] of his wife's chastity, and the latter as possessor of a chaste beauty which "itself doth of itself persuade / The eyes of men without an orator" [ll. 29-30]. Like Troy itself, Lucrece 's mere existence is an invitation to destruction; she is perhaps unlike Troy in that her destruction is simultaneously the tragedy of her ravisher. (p. 111)

Thematic discussion of Shakespeare's Rome normally and usefully starts from his Roman plays, especially perhaps those two plays most frequently performed and most immediately concerned with the emergence of Rome's imperial identity. *Julius Caesar* and *Antony* demonstrate a pattern of historical necessity that might be called Vergilian in its sense of the human cost of political stability; it is this pattern, doubtless, that most critics think of when speaking of Shakespeare's myth of Rome. The Rome of these plays is both an invincible political machine and a state of the spirit in which the demands of heroic self-denial have created, or come to symbolize, grave psychic imbalance. One thinks of Portia [in *Julius Caesar*], the daughter of Cato, swallowing fire when Brutus avoids her bed and her counsel; or of the bachelor party on Pompey's galley [in *Antony and Cleopatra*] as contrasted with the coeducational dormitories of Egypt. A similar sense of men without women and women without their womanliness, of a virile society denying its *anima,* is at least as conspicuous in the other Roman plays: in the early Rome of *Coriolanus,* where little Marcius is praised for tearing a butterfly to pieces, and in that legendary but surely late imperial Rome of *The Most Lamentable Romaine Tragedie of Titus Andronicus,* where Roman *devotio* is measured in hewn limbs and the dominant image of family cohesiveness is the

tomb of the Andronici. It seems undeniable that one of Shakespeare's principal ideas of Rome was this Vergilian theme of grandeur purchased at great price, a cautionary mirror for Elizabethans in their own most high and palmy state.

I have called this theme Vergilian, since readers today tend to view Augustan Rome largely through Vergil's eyes. But of course Shakespeare obtained his knowledge of Rome from other sources as well, two of which are important not only for the incidents they describe but also for the imaginative context they establish: a context that must have inspired or at least confirmed a major tendency in Shakespeare's poetic. That he was a careful reader of Plutarch is apparent from the adroitness and assiduousness with which he moves among the various lives in adapting episodes and hints of character. What is harder to demonstrate, but no less obvious, is his debt to Plutarch's fundamental method in writing parallel lives. Perhaps the most direct piece of evidence here is a somewhat negative one, Fluellen's parody of Plutarch when he compares the triumphant Hal to Alexander the Pig:

> I warrant you sall find, in the comparisons between Macedon and Monmouth, that the situations, look you, is both alike. There is a river in Macedon, and there is also moreover a river at Monmouth. . . . If you mark Alexander's life well, Harry of Monmouth's life is come after it indifferent well, for there is figures in all things.
>
> [*Henry V*, IV. vii. 24-33]

Although Fluellen may be limited, in his reading of such figures, to noting that there are salmons in both rivers, the reader of the *Henriad* may observe other, more instructive parallels. After taking the crown from Richard [II], Henry Bolingbroke has scrutinized the behavior of two younger Henrys for auguries of his own undoing. Though he may dream of exchanging sons with Northumberland, in order to have one "who is the theme of honor's tongue" [*1 Henry IV*, I. i. 81], in fact, it is Hotspur who is the usurper and Hal who will prove himself the loyal and rightful heir to the throne. Plutarch had compared Alexander to Julius Caesar; Fluellen compares Alexander to a British king who has imitated Junius Brutus in spending his youth in pretended foolishness, lest he be taken for a later Brutus with regicidal, indeed parricidal tendencies, or for a would-be Caesar with designs on the center of political power. By the time Fluellen speaks, Hotspur's time has had an abrupt stop, and the elder Henry's has flowed to its natural end in the Jerusalem Chamber; Hal is a conquering Caesar with a dream of imperial union with France. Shakespeare's audience will be reminded by the epilogue that Henry VI will lose all that Henry V gains; and they may feel in this present passage that Fluellen's attempt to contrast Alexander's drunken killing of his friend Cleitus with Hal's sober repudiation of Falstaff raises some awkward questions about the morality, or psychic integrity, of the new king; but it is clear, at least, that the method of the *Parallel Lives* is alive and functioning in the history plays.

The other principal source for Shakespeare's complex of Roman myths is Livy's history "From the Founding of the City," *ab urbe condita,* the first book of which provides the material for his poem on Lucrece. And since the fall of Lucrece coincides with the rise of Junius Brutus, Livy's story of the primitive origins of Rome must have figured in Shakespeare's continuing fascination with this early Roman hero, an archetype of the Hamlets and Hals and Edgars [in *King Lear*] who survive by means of play-acting. Livy's narrative stresses a number of elements which are not made explicit in Shakespeare's *Lucrece* but help to explain some of that poem's brooding intensity as well as its anticipations of the imagery of the later plays. One such element is the omnipresence of Tarquins in this early, claustrophobic Rome. Not only is Lucrece's rapist a Tarquin, Sextus Tarquinius, son of the usurping King Tarquin the Proud; but also her husband is Lucius Tarquinius Collatinus, and Junius Brutus himself, savior of Rome when he banishes the Tarquins, is a son of the king's sister Tarquinia. So there is a fine irony to the piece of theatre with which the story of poor Lucrece concludes: "The Romans plausibly did give consent / To Tarquin's everlasting banishment" [ll. 1854-55]. This moment of Rome's liberation, effected by the eloquent funeral oration of Brutus over the body of Lucrece, may have occasioned applause from Romans then and in times to come; but the idea that this could represent a definitive banishment of Tarquins seems less plausible when one notes that the new consuls of Republican Rome, Brutus and Collatinus, are themselves members of the detested family.

Another element in Livy's story of Lucrece and Brutus seems strikingly pertinent to Shakespeare's evolution of his microcosmic metaphor. When he is exiled from Rome, Sextus Tarquinius unaccountably and suicidally decides to return to a city, Gabii, which he had previously betrayed to his father. There, not surprisingly, he is put to death—like Coriolanus in Corioli, whose story appears in the next book of Livy's history. In these and other respects, Livy's story of civil or inter-familial strife turns out on closer examination to be essentially intrafamilial, even to the extent of being intrapersonal, at times virtually a psychomachia. Shakespeare sets his poem in a period of Roman history when the nation's further evolution seems mired in its leaders' inability to move beyond the first marriage of Trojan and native Italian stock that Vergil had celebrated at the conclusion of his epic. The marriage of reason and passion has collapsed, so to speak, and become a battleground for renewed struggle between patriarchal and matriarchal forces; political ambition and sexual passion are seen turning inwards once again, infesting the royal household and appearing bewilderingly even in the names of people and places. Lucrece herself seems yet another of these curiously subjective pieces of the Roman landscape, for she is wed to a collateral Tarquin whose name, Collatinus, and residence at Collatium, echo the sense of latency, of "lurking to aspire" as Tarquin's lust for her is characterized, that is implicit in the name of Latium itself, the region in which this Rome is located.

Shakespeare's opening stanza, with its abrupt motion and difficult epithets, introduces the reader to this psychological landscape:

> From the besieged Ardea all in post,
> Borne by the trustless wings of false desire,
> Lust-breathed Tarquin leaves the Roman host,
> And to Collatium bears the lightless fire,
> Which in pale embers hid, lurks to aspire,
>   And girdle with embracing flames the waist
>   Of Collatine's fair love, Lucrece the chaste.
>
> [ll. 1-7]

Tarquin is turning from the protracted siege of one city to a more active assault on another, Lucrece. The name of the first city, Ardea, with its suggestion of burning, ardor, gives point to the image of bearing "lightless fire" to Collatium; that Tarquin is "lust-breathed" suggests not so much that he

breathes out lust as a dragon breathes fire, as that he is inspired by lust, has breathed it in at his earlier view of Lucrece, and also perhaps confuses it with his parallel lust for the city of Ardea.

Driven by "trustless wings of false desire" [l. 2], Tarquin is shown in a self-destructive frenzy which is essentially irreversible once he is admitted to Lucrece's presence, or for that matter once he has left Ardea with his burden (or gift) of fire. . . . Obviously, from Lucrece's viewpoint there is a world of difference between rape and self-mutilation, but Tarquin does not seem to see it. . . . Tarquin is consumed by self-loathing, and as he proceeds to his victim's bedchamber he broods despairingly on his inevitable disgrace: "He doth despise / His naked armour of still slaughter'd lust" [ll. 185-86]. Since it is clearly his naked "weapon" or phallus which is the object of his concern, it is noteworthy that Tarquin seems to see it as both the instrument and the *object* of his destructive will. Presumably this embodiment of his lust is characterized as "still slaughter'd" in that it repeatedly "dies" but springs back to new life.

Much of Tarquin's protracted debate with himself elaborates the inherent confusion he seems to feel over the meaning of his act. In his view, the warrior enters the city as the male enters the female, with a desire to possess the other and a fear of being possessed by it in turn:

> I know repentant tears ensue the deed,
> Reproach, disdain and deadly enmity,
> Yet strive I to embrace mine infamy.
>
> [ll. 502-04]

This seems much the same image as that of lightless fire at the beginning of the poem, seeking to girdle its victim's waist; the difference is that by now it is clear that Tarquin is concerned less with subverting or corrupting Lucrece than with encompassing his own destruction.

Lucrece, meanwhile, is as vulnerable to envy as the city of Ardea had been—or as Eden. In Shakespeare's companion poem, Adonis succeeds in resisting Venus's attempted rape and is rewarded with a flowery metamorphosis which fulfills his desire "to grow unto himself" [l. 1180]. But Lucrece lives in the harsh world of Roman history, and is not subsumed into an Ovidian metaphor of fertility at the end of her story. Instead, she finds an infinitely divided image of herself, when she scans a painting of Troy's destruction to find an apt image of her own condition. She can compare Tarquin to Sinon with some ease, and feel that "as Priam him did cherish, / So did I Tarquin—so my Troy did perish" [ll. 1546-47]. Or she can identify with Hecuba as a grieving matron; but she cannot overlook the fact that the fall of Troy resulted from another kind of rape, that of Helen. She can only grieve with Hecuba by tearing at the beauty of the strumpet who was the object of Paris's lust.

At length she realizes that she cannot exhaust her vengeance on painted images, or on partial reflections of herself; she must let out the pure blood along with the corrupt. Similarly, with both her father and her husband competing in their lamentation at having lost the claim that each had in her, it remains for Brutus to turn their energies away from narcissistic, self-destructive complaint, and toward the less "childish" or effeminate arena of political action. To do so is to reverse the pattern seen at the opening of the story. By publishing Lucrece's virtue, Collatine had diverted energy from war to lust; now it is for Brutus to publish her virtue in such a way as to provoke Tarquin's banishment and his own accession to power in Rome. Such publication makes Brutus a playwright of sorts, a rhetorician who knows how to show Lucrece to best advantage and win the applause of the people; but language is being used in the service of political rather than purely artistic, sentimental goals: history is being written, or revised.

Finally, then, both Sextus Tarquinius and Lucrece are shown to be tragic victims whose stories are of secondary importance compared to the heroic emergence of Junius Brutus. Like Turnus and Dido in the *Aeneid,* they stand in the way of historical process and are destroyed by flames of misdirected energy. I would suggest that the imagery of Shakespeare's poem owes much to Vergil as well as to Livy. Lucrece's painting (or tapestry) of Troy seems borrowed from Dido's similar representation described in book 1, which had shown Aeneas that in Carthage there was sympathy for human suffering; and from the tale of Troy's destruction that Aeneas subsequently relates. The entire story of Dido is framed in fire, from the first stirrings of the old flames which she had denied herself since her husband's death, to the flames of her funeral pyre which prefigure the destruction of Carthage itself in later times. Even Augustine's question of the legitimacy of Lucrece's suicide is anticipated by this Vergilian model: it takes a special act of pity on Juno's part to release Dido's soul for death before her allotted time. But Sextus Tarquinius is no Aeneas, capable of escaping the flames; like Coriolanus and other victims of matriarchal nemesis, he is swallowed up and destroyed by the cities he has subverted, by Gabii if not by Lucrece. (pp. 112-16)

Donald Cheney, "Tarquin, Juliet, and Other 'Romei'," in Spenser Studies: A Renaissance Poetry Annual, *Vol. III, 1982, pp. 111-24.*

JUDITH DUNDAS (essay date 1983)

[*Dundas describes Shakespeare's manipulation of illusion and reality in* The Rape of Lucrece *to show how artifice, specifically the "well-painted piece," actually serves to illuminate Tarquin's deception and Lucrece's predicament: "illusion in fact comes to act as a mirror in which the truth may be read." In this ecphrasis, Dundas contends, Shakespeare "gives his most explicit account of how art works." The critic demonstrates that in extracting the best elements of painting and poetry to create* Lucrece, *Shakespeare self-reflexively draws attention to the illusion or artifice inherent in representational art and contrasts the harmless or educative effects of art with Tarquin's malevolent deception. On another issue, Dundas rejects the notion that Brutus, the "voice of reason," represents Shakespeare's views: as an exemplum for history and an object of art,* Lucrece *transcends Brutus's pragmatic criteria for heroic or tragic action.*]

The eyes of Lucrece are like stars: in her face, "that sky" of her husband's delight, shone "mortal stars, as bright as heaven's beauties" [ll. 12-14]. In this seemingly conventional analogy lies the key to Shakespeare's poem on her tragedy. From every page of it eyes look out at us, reflecting the souls and emotions of characters in the story, as well as of those in the wall-painting of Troy. The rape itself is enacted first through the eyes of Tarquin, as we are shown his ominous progress from the "silent wonder of still gazing eyes" to "burning eye" and "greedy eyeballs," until finally, it is the "cockatrice's dead killing eye" which shows him transformed from admiring spectator to rapacious possessor [ll. 84, 435, 368, 540].

For Lucrece, her sorrow is most signally expressed by the blue circles around her eyes, "like rainbows in the sky" [l. 1587]. But when she turns to the wall-painting to occupy herself until her husband's return, her eyes become the instrument for understanding what has happened to her. Throughout the poem the soul not only speaks but listens through the eyes; yet Shakespeare as poet is far from unaware that his own art is meant only for "the eye of mind" [l. 1426].

When he refers to the wall-painting of his poem as a "well-painted piece" [l. 1443], this might be taken as a connoisseur's straightforward praise. But there are ironies in the very word "painted," as Lucrece's lament for herself indicates: "My sable ground of sin I will not paint. / To hide the truth of this false night's abuses" [ll. 1074-75]. The word "painted," with its implications of deception, provides one of the links between her tragedy and the mural which she views in her distress. As Shakespeare was to make clear in *Timon of Athens,* the deceptions of art are harmless because they do not pretend to be the thing itself but are, rather, "Even such as they give out" [I. i.160]. The only work of art in his plays that oversteps the bounds of artistic illusion and appears to be the reality is the statue in *The Winter's Tale,* which of course proves not to be a statue at all but a living woman. For the rest, the deception practiced by artists is treated as a harmless mocking of the mind, in contrast with the deceptions practiced by such a villain as Tarquin.

But there is another, less obvious, irony in the phrase "well-painted piece." As the distraught Lucrece studies the wall-painting of Troy, we must be aware that for all the suffering it depicts, it has less claim upon our feelings than the suffering of the heroine with whom we are concerned. We forget—so convincing is Shakespeare's narrative—that Lucrece and her tragedy are just as illusory as the painting of Troy. There are degrees of reality within Shakespeare's works, and paintings or statues by definition are less real than his own dramatic characters. He can represent a play within a play with the same separation of art from life, a difference underlined when Hamlet, witnessing a piece of tragic acting, asks, "What's Hecuba to him, or he to Hecuba, / That he should weep for her?" [II. ii. 559-60]. But the mocking of man by visual art is the mockery implicit in the way art, itself cold and unfeeling, can arouse so much feeling in the living, breathing spectator. Leontes' [in *The Winter's Tale*] complaint against the supposed statue of his wife is that it is cold; its very lifelikeness makes the gulf between art and life seem the more impassable and poignant. In *Lucrece* there is a similar irony in the contrast between the heroine's own life-and-death situation and the "well-painted piece," which can be admired as artifact, regardless of the suffering portrayed.

Lucrece's story, on the other hand, is presented less as art than as history. Although Shakespeare has created a work of art, we are not invited to comment upon his skill as we are made to see the skill of the craftsman who painted the fall of Troy. In responding to this painting, Lucrece herself turns it back into history, into affecting narrative, so that for her it in effect becomes reality. In the same way we must "weep with the weeping," as we become lost in the illusion. It is only by detaching ourselves from the illusion that we can assess the poem as art.

Despite Lucrece's awareness of herself as potential *exemplum,* she does not, cannot, see herself as art. Her dagger pointed at her heart was in later times to become her attribute, the ultimate sign of her chastity and valor. But in

Shakespeare's poem she is not yet symbol but suffering human being, one who has been so wounded in her heart's core that she can only manifest her truth through suicide. Once she has made her decision, we can no more question its rightness than we can question a martyr's willingness to die for his faith. Because Lucrece's suicide is a "given" of the story, Shakespeare makes it seem both tragic and stoically right within the realm of Lucrece's own being. Brutus's final words to Collatine, Lucrece's husband, move from this realm into that of political action, but they cannot be taken as the final judgment that Shakespeare passes on Lucrece:

> Thy wretched wife mistook the matter so,
> To slay herself, that should have slain her foe.
>
> [ll. 1826-27]

This comment is made from the outside, by the voice of reason, and it marks the return to the daylight world of normal life; but it is not for this message that Shakespeare has taken us so slowly on a journey through Lucrece's mind.

If we would learn how to read her story, she herself sets an example in the way she responds to the wall-painting described in such detail. Here, in Shakespeare's most developed ekphrasis, he gives his most explicit account of how art works. As art, this painting is praised in the highest terms, for the poet must try to justify Lucrece's impassioned address to it by somehow conveying the expressiveness with which the artist has endowed it. But he need not confine himself exclusively to what she might have observed; it is rather what is needed to put the painting before the eyes of the reader. Thus he comments on the transformation of the medium into something that seems to possess life and motion:

> Many a dry drop seem'd a weeping tear,
> Shed for the slaught'red husband by the wife;
> The red blood reek'd, to show the painter's strife,
> And dying eyes gleam'd forth their ashy lights,
> Like dying coals burnt out in tedious nights.
>
> [ll. 1375-79]

It may seem indeed that Shakespeare was doing no more than following the ekphrastic tradition in describing a painting in all its narrative detail, giving, as it were, a voice to the "dumb poesy." Such descriptions as those of Philostratus, or Achilles Tatius, or later, Vasari, exemplify the model he was following.

But there is a difference between ekphrasis which is an end in itself and ekphrasis which is dramatically part of a story and symbolically the essence of it. As Lucrece pauses in her lament, seeking "for means to mourn some newer way" [l. 1365], she recalls "the piece / Of skillful painting" [ll. 1366-67] depicting the fall of Troy. Gazing at it, she comes to realize that she herself is Troy, the city betrayed. But set off from the narrative proper as the description of the mural is, it both concentrates and amplifies the significance of the story. We are able to see that a principle has been violated: not simply Lucrece as an individual but the whole principle of truth; that through perjury and guile, virtue has been trampled on.

Illusion in fact comes to act as a mirror in which the truth may be read. What might be purely conventional in another context thus becomes charged with new significance. The usual ekphrastic praise for the artist's skill in overcoming the limitations of his medium—paint turned into tears and blood, for example—shows art acting as an echo for the real tears and real blood shed by Lucrece. She in turn echoes the figures in the painting: "She lends them words, and she their looks doth borrow" [l. 1498]. It might even be said that the poem as a whole shows imitation to be a law of the universe: in the painting the waves of the river Simois sought to imitate the battle "with swelling ridges" [l. 1439], while in real life Lucrece's maid and her groom reflect her expressions of grief. A sympathetic echo seems to govern all things, including man in his relationship both to art and to life. Not for nothing did Leonardo da Vinci compare the painter's imitation of nature to images seen in a mirror.

At the center of the painter's art is his knowledge of physiognomy. Shakespeare introduces his allusion to this skill almost casually, as part of the ekphrastic tradition although its deeper significance will soon become apparent:

> In Ajax and Ulysses, O what art
> Of physiognomy might one behold!
> The face of either cipher'd either's heart,
> Their face their manners most expressly told.
>
> [ll. 1394-97]

But all faces, as Lucrece has yet to learn, do not tell the story of their owner's manners. At this point in the description, the narrator is still giving an objective account of the painting. Only when Lucrece's response takes over does a subjective view prevail. She addresses the figures in the painting, looking first for a face "where all distress is stelled" [l. 1444]; then for Helen, whose unchastity—represented by a very different sort of rape—she believes to be the vice most opposed to her own virtue. At last, when she has seen the sufferings of the Trojans, she comes by chance, it seems, upon Sinon, painted so as to show the plausible face of falsehood. Identifying him with Tarquin, whose face also concealed his wickedness, she tears the painted visage "with her nails" [l. 739]. The cardinal sin is deception more than unchastity, and this is something that art, using its own means of deception, now reveals to Lucrece. At first she "chid the painter for his wondrous skill / Saying some shape in Sinon was abus'd: / So fair a form lodg'd not a mind so ill" [ll. 1528-30]. But at last she remembers that Tarquin came to her in just such a guise of "outward honesty, but defil'd with inward vice" [ll. 1545-46]. Through the deceptions of art, she comes to understand the real nature of vice. We in turn are shown how imagination can take the artistic illusion and learn from it. The dialectical role of this ekphrasis makes it very different in effect from those that are detachable, meant to adorn, or simply to provide a thematic counterpoint to a narrative.

Ordinarily in ekphrases of this kind the narrative success of the work overrides attention to the methods used. But underlying Shakespeare's references to the means of illusion lies his fascination with what man's imagination contributes to his sense perceptions. Methods of suggesting depth on the two-dimensional wall surface are mentioned, not solely for the sake of praising the artist's technique, but for what they reveal about man's capacity to see what is not there: "The scalps of many almost hid behind / To jump up higher seem'd, to mock the mind" [ll. 1413-14]. Here he refers briefly to the device of overlap—a few lines later, it is explained more fully—and he also refers, apparently, to the so-called terraced form, by which heads are arranged in tiers, to suggest a crowd. But above all, he believed that he was describing the best in classical art, as he had learned of it from ancient ekphrases. Somehow, too, he had picked up the notion that perspective is "best painter's art," and regardless of the sort of perspective he is describing, he is fully convinced of its illusionistic value.

One of the most interesting of his references to the means of creating a three-dimensional effect on the wall surface is the passage in which he reflects on the artist's use of overlap:

> For much imaginary work was there,
> conceit deceitful, so compact, so kind,
> That for Achilles' image stood his spear,
> Grip'd in an armed hand; himself behind
> Was left unseen, save to the eye of mind;
>   A hand, a foot, a face, a leg, a head
>   Stood for the whole to be imagined.
>
> [ll. 1422-28]

As [E. H.] Gombrich was the first to observe [in his *Art and Illusion*], this is remarkably similar to a passage in Philostratus's description of the siege at Thebes (in his *Imagines,* trans. by A. Fairbanks]:

> The clever artifice of the painter is delightful. Encompassing the walls with armed men, he depicts them so that some are seen in full figure, others with the legs hidden, others from the waist up, then only the busts of some, heads only, helmets only, and finally just spearpoints. This, my boy, is perspective; since the problem is to deceive the eyes as they travel back along with the proper receding planes of the picture.

But, assuming this to be Shakespeare's source, the question still arises: why should this passage have made such an impression on him that he found room for it in his poem? The clue lies, I think, in his phrase "left unseen, save to the eye of mind," because what interests him is precisely what is not represented, what has to be imagined. It is here that he finds the meeting-point of poetry and painting, just as Philostratus the Younger did when he said that "the art of painting has a certain kinship with poetry, and . . . an element of imagination is common to both."

Significantly, Shakespeare's predecessors in descriptions of wall-paintings do not comment on the role of the imagination in the creation of illusion. If we look for example at the description of the Fall of Troy that supplied the model for Shakespeare, Virgil's account of the murals on the Temple of Juno which Aeneas sees on his arrival in Carthage, we find only the briefest identification of personages and their activities. All that really concerns Virgil is Aeneas's elegiac response to a portrayal of the fall of his city:

> At this point Aenas uttered a deep groan
> To see the spoils, the chariot, the actual body of
> His friend, and Priam's defenceless hands stretched
>   out to Achilles.

There is no reference to the artist's method of depiction or comment on the art as art, unless we except Virgil's remark, that Aeneas "fed his soul on those insubstantial figures." This picture explains itself in purely emotional terms. Perhaps with the same topos in mind, Plutarch [in his "Marcus Brutus"] has Portia recognize herself in a painting showing the farewell of Andromache to Hector. She weeps, "likening herself to be in the same case . . . and coming thither oftentimes in a day to see it, she wept still."

A similar recognition governs Lucrece's response to Hecuba in the painting of Shakespeare's poem, but he makes her something of a critic of art, as well as a responder. She mar-

vels that the painter could depict Hecuba so well and not give her cries and "bitter words." To this familiar ekphrastic topos Shakespeare adds a proverbial expression: "The painter was no god to lend her those" [l. 1461]. But it is really the poet who is godlike in being able both to paint figures and make them speak; so Lucrece will speak for Hecuba, as well as for herself: "I'll tune thy woes with my lamenting tongue" [l. 1465]. However conventional this reference to the *paragone*, the rivalry between poetry and painting, for Shakespeare it has a special interest: inevitably, it brings to the fore the whole nature of illusion, whereby the senses, with the help of imagination, are beguiled into perceiving what is not there.

But if the deceptions of art are harmless, those of real life are not. Shakespeare comes closest to making explicit his analogy between these two kinds of deception when he describes the painter's skill exercised upon Sinon: "In him the painter labour'd with his skill / To hide deceit and give the harmless show . . ." [ll. 1506-07]. It is a measure of the painter's success that Lucrece at first rejects this as a portrayal of the traitor; she must relearn the lesson this night has taught her, but this time through the artistic experience. In suggesting how the deceptions of art can actually be illuminating to the observer, Shakespeare may have in mind Plutarch's remark in the essay "How a Young Man Ought to Hear Poems": "And Gorgias used to call tragical poems cheats, wherein he that did cheat was juster than he that did not cheat, and he that was cheated was wiser than he that was not cheated." No such lesson is implied in the artist's depiction of Sinon either in Virgil's wall-painting or in Chaucer's in *The House of Fame.* None of Shakespeare's play with paradox informs his predecessors' lines; rather they allude to Sinon as the type of betrayer, without saying exactly how the painter would represent him. The real details belong to Virgil's account in Book II of *The Aeneid,* in which they have a purely narrative function, and it is left to Shakespeare to put them into a picture, in order to make a little discourse on the way art works.

Complete as the illusion is which momentarily distracts Lucrece from her own terrible situation, she declares she will with her knife "scratch out the angry eyes" [l. 1469] of all the Greeks that are the enemies of Hecuba. In the end she "tears the senseless Sinon with her nails" [l. 1564], reserving the knife for herself when it is time for art to give way to reality. Then she "smilingly gives o'er" [l. 1567], deriding herself for being so foolish as to be taken in by the truthfulness of art. But the mocking by art has not been in vain: what she has learned is that she is not the first to suffer at the hands of the guilty. Her eyes have seen as in a mirror all the other eyes which the painter has depicted, from "dying eyes," to the "very eyes of men through loop-holes thrust," to the eyes of Ajax and Ulysses, and finally to the "old eyes" of Hecuba, staring at Priam's wounds, and "On this sad shadow Lucrece spends her eyes" [ll. 1378, 1383, 1448, 1457]. As she "throws her eyes" around the painting, she at last finds Sinon with his "eyes wailing still," while Priam "wets his eyes" to see the borrowed tears of Sinon [ll. 1499, 1508, 1548]; her moment of revelation is expressed through the crucial image of Sinon's deceptive eyes as she addresses Priam: "His eye drops fire, no water thence proceeds: / Those round clear pearls of his that move thy pity / Are balls of quenchless fire to burn thy city" [ll. 1552-54]. Lucrece's eyes, on the other hand, have wept copious tears, becoming red and raw, even as her face grows paler. All the frigid conceits of red and white, fire and water, take on new meaning when translated into the veracity of this tragic drama.

But eyes do not only express emotion; they are, as well, receptors for experience. If Lucrece was deluded by the message her eyes received from Tarquin, so was he by the domination of his reason through the lustful response of his eyes to the sight of Lucrece. She had tried to persuade him to be true to his princely office:

> I sue for exil'd majesty's repeal,
> Let him return, and flatt'ring thoughts retire;
> His true respect will prison false desire,
> And wipe the dim mist from thy doting eye,
> That thou shalt see thy state, and pity mine.
>
> [ll. 640-44]

Tarquin's fall through the eyes is, of course, beyond redemption, but Lucrece's own blindness will be purged by the wall-painting of Troy, which teaches her how little safety there is in the world for trusting innocence, and how much a part of the universal scheme of things her own fate is. She had tried to make Tarquin follow the path of virtue by alluding to the judgment of history upon him; her own suicide is motivated by a concern for the same judgment. No unchaste wives shall draw comfort from her.

So conscious is Lucrece of herself as mirror or model that it is as though Shakespeare were trying to reconstruct a Lucrece who foresees her subsequent reputation in literature and art. She plays a certain role, including her conventional diatribe against Night, Time, and Opportunity, because she sees herself before the court of history. Not being an ordinary woman, she mourns ritually as well as naturally.

In one vital sense her father is mistaken when he addresses the dead body thus:

> Poor broken glass, I often did behold
> In thy sweet semblance my old age new-born;
> But now that fair, fresh mirror, dim, and old,
> Shows me a bare-bon'd death by time outworn,
> O from thy cheeks my image thou has torn;
> And shiver'd all the beauty of my glass,
> That no more can see what once I was!
>
> [ll. 1758-64]

He is mistaken, for she will live on as a mirror or model for succeeding ages in the perfection of her virtue. Troy too seemed a broken mirror when it was destroyed by Sinon's words, which

> . . . like wildfire burnt the shining
> glory
> Of rich built Illion, that the skies were sorry,
> And little stars shot from their fixed places,
> When their glass fell, wherein they view'd their
> faces.
>
> [ll. 1523-26]

Like the stars—those emblems of virtue—Lucrece found herself mirrored in Troy, and despite the destruction of both city and woman by the forces of evil, they live on in the imaginations of men.

In Shakespeare's poem Troy, in the form of a wall-painting, appears almost literally as mirror. Its illusionistic qualities support the usual Renaissance view that good painting resembles images seen in a mirror. Although the art of Elizabethan England was inadequate to such a task of lifelike and complete narration, the literary tradition of ekphrasis requires no particular visual models. It simply requires a poet's imagination to speak to "the eye of mind," even as Shake-

speare believed that the true painter would speak too. More than an academic doctrine, *ut pictura poesis,* the analogy between painting and poetry, implied not only the mimetic function of poetry, but its power to move the reader, as picture directly touches the heart of the viewer. Gazing at this lifelike painting, Lucrece finds herself absorbing what has happened to her, and, in the depths of her heart, prepares for her end. In this way the mural fulfills its role as art; that is to say, it educates the spirit. The time Lucrece spends with the painting is an important and necessary interlude between the violence she has suffered and the further deliberate violence against herself to which she is compelled by Tarquin's deed: "He, he! fair lords, 'tis he / That guides this hand to give this wound to me" [ll. 1721-22].

The whole poem reads like an ekphrasis of the sort of painting Sir Philip Sidney describes [in his *An Apology for Poetry*] when he wishes to compare "right poets" to "the more excellent" kind of painters, "who having no law but wit, bestow that in colours upon you which is fittest for the eye to see: as the constant though lamenting look of Lucretia when she punished in herself another's fault; wherein he painteth not Lucretia whom he never saw, but painteth the outward beauty of such a virtue." Just so, Shakespeare, "having no law but wit," paints the "outward beauty of such a virtue;" but on his own ground as poet, he also paints the inward beauty. At their best, however, artists of both kinds excel by borrowing what is strongest in the other, and this is the real significance of the *paragone.* Shakespeare's only rivals in his portrayal of Lucrece are Titian, Tintoretto, and Rembrandt, themselves poets of the highest order. (pp. 13-22)

> *Judith Dundas, "Mocking the Mind: The Role of Art in Shakespeare's 'Rape of Lucrece'," in The Sixteenth Century Journal, Vol. XIV, No. 1, March, 1983, pp. 13-22.*

NANCY J. VICKERS (essay date 1985)

[*Vickers argues that in* The Rape of Lucrece *Shakespeare adopts the rhetoric of moral heraldry in order both to demonstrate his artistic talent and to reveal the injustice of the patriar-*]

Lucrece. By Lorenzo Lotto.

chal conventions upon which this descriptive mode rests. According to the critic, the poem essentially depicts a "male battle" instigated by "male oratory" in which Lucrece is merely the displayed object, or battlefield. Vickers claims that the rape and Lucrece's suicide have their origin in the male boasting contest and Collatine's "rhetoric of display": "rape is the price Lucrece pays for having been described." While Collatine's praise of his wife is really praise of himself, it also establishes the value of his possession, inspiring envy and jealousy: "and jealousy, once inspired, may be carried to its logical conclusion—theft." The poem concludes as it began, Vickers points out, with a scene in which "men rhetorically compete with each other over Lucrece's body" in an oratorical contest of grief and blame. In an unexcerpted portion of her essay, Vickers raises the question of unintentional irony; at least in one sense, she notes, Shakespeare recapitulates Collatine's crime by appropriating Lucrece's story to establish his own reputation.]

> "But, good lieutenant, is your general wiv'd?"
>
> "Most fortunately: he hath achiev'd a maid
> That paragons description and wild fame;
> One that excels the quirks of blazoning pens,
> And in th' essential vesture of creation
> Does tire the ingener."

> [*Othello*, II. i. 60-5]

The brief exchange between a governor and a lieutenant that figures as epigraph to this essay is curiously about the limits of description. As they stand in the stormy port of the "warlike isle" of Cyprus [II. i. 43] awaiting the "warlike Moor Othello" [II. i. 27], Montano and Cassio digress from appropriately warlike concerns to evoke Othello's exquisite and doomed bride, Desdemona. Cassio comments that she is so beautiful as to be beyond description: her charms surpass all praise that the rhetorician can muster; they cannot effectively be listed ("blazoned") or captured in rhetorical conceits ("quirks"); indeed, even the most ingenious of poets ("the ingener") would exhaust himself in attempting to do them justice. Cassio thus recites not only the strengths of Desdemona but also the weaknesses of a poetic tradition that, from the classics to the Renaissance moderns, had celebrated the beauties of woman's body.

Like Shakespeare's warlike exchange, that tradition was, in large part, the product of men talking to men about women. The canonical legacy of description is a legacy shaped predominantly by the male imagination for the male imagination. This is not, of course, to deny the possibility of the flattery poem; praising a woman to her face might well be intended as a preamble to seduction, as a maneuver for advantage. But in this essay, I will focus on those occasions in which men praise beautiful women among men, on the rhetorical strategies such occasions generate, and finally on some logical consequences of being matter for male oratory. Indeed, I will argue that occasion, rhetoric, and result are all informed by, and thus inscribe, a battle between men that is figuratively fought out on the fields of woman's "celebrated" body.

When, in "The Laugh of the Medusa," Hélène Cixous maintains "that there is such a thing as *marked* writing" she alludes to those literary codes that reinforce "a libidinal and cultural—hence political, typically masculine—economy" and thus constitute "a locus where the repression of women has been perpetuated." "By writing her self," Cixous continues, "woman will return to the body which has been more than confiscated from her, which has been turned into the uncanny stranger on display." This essay scrutinizes one manifestation of that "uncanny stranger" in an attempt to define

both the motives for and the strategies of "display"; it examines a telling example of description through comparison—a fundamental tactic of rhetorical invention—by pressuring a single, canonical metaphor as it appears in Shakespeare's narrative poem *Lucrece* (1594). For here the poet transforms the repetition of convention into its subversion; he simultaneously masters and undermines the descriptive mode he employs.

The warlike metaphor in question—the beautiful woman's face is (is like) a shield—informs descriptions of Shakespeare's heroine throughout the poem. By the late sixteenth century, gunpowder had, of course, seriously diminished the defensive usefulness of shields. Less and less the practical gear of the warrior, they remained, however, his emblem; they were used in nostalgically chivalric court entertainments; in pageants, tilts, and tourneys; and in a variety of decorative contexts where they displayed symbolic figurations of gentlemanly pedigree. Aristocratic Elizabethans were fascinated by the "colorful paraphernalia of heraldry" which "tended to proliferate as the practical function of knighthood disappeared" [A. Ferguson, in his *The Indian Summer of English Chivalry: Studies in the Decline and Transformation of Chivalric Idealism*]. That interest was related, Lawrence Stone has argued [in his *The Crisis of Aristocracy 1558-1641*], to the "extreme development" of patriarchal family structure that characterized the period: " . . . it was the male line whose ancestry was traced so diligently by the genealogists and heralds, and in almost all cases via the male line that titles were inherited". *Lucrece* both reflects and reinforces that fascination; from beginning to end, Shakespeare expands his imagistic network by exploiting the highly codified vocabulary of heraldic convention. (pp. 171-73)

Lucrece opens with a contest. Its initial focus is on "lust-breathed Tarquin" [1. 3] as he speeds away from the Roman camp, but within the space of one stanza that focus shifts to present a flashback revealing the origins of his uncontrollable desire:

> Haply that name of "chaste" unhapp'ly set
> This bateless edge on his keen appetite,
> When Collatine unwisely did not let
> To praise the clear unmatched red and white
> Which triumph'd in that sky of his delight;
>   Where mortal stars as bright as heaven's beauties,
>   With pure aspects did him peculiar duties.
>
> For he the night before, in Tarquin's tent
> Unlock'd the treasure of his happy state:
> What priceless wealth the heavens had him lent,
> In the possession of his beauteous mate;
> Reck'ning his fortune at such high proud rate
>   That kings might be espoused to more fame,
>   But king nor peer to such a peerless dame.
>
> Beauty itself doth of itself persuade
> The eyes of men without an orator;
> What needeth then apologies be made,
> To set forth that which is so singular?
> Or why is Collatine the publisher
>   Of that rich jewel he should keep unknown
>   From thievish ears, because it is his own?
>
> Perchance his boast of Lucrece' sov'reignty
> Suggested this proud issue of a king;
> For by our ears our hearts oft tainted be.
> Perchance that envy of so rich a thing,
> Braving compare, disdainfully did sting
>   His high-pitch'd thoughts, that meaner men

should vaunt
That golden hap which their superiors want.

[11. 8-21, 29-42]

Shakespeare locates the ultimate cause of Tarquin's crime, and Lucrece's subsequent suicide, in an evening's entertainment. The prose argument that precedes the poem adds further clarification: "In their discourses after supper everyone commended the virtues of his own wife; among them Collatinus extolled the incomparable chastity of his wife Lucretia." The prose next narrates an event that Shakespeare significantly writes out of the poetry: the competitors ride from Ardea to Rome to test their wives and, with the exception of Lucrece, all are "found dancing and revelling, or in several disports." It is for this reason that "the noblemen yielded Collatinus the victory, and his wife the fame." The argument, in contrast to the poem, then, remains faithful to Shakespeare's two principal sources, Ovid and Livy.

Young Tarquin entertained his comrades with feast and wine: . . . Each praised his wife: in their eagerness dispute ran high, and every tongue and heart grew hot with deep draughts of wine. Then up and spake the man who from Collatia took his famous name: No need of words! Trust deeds!

[Ovid, *Fasti,* II. 725-26, 731-34]

The young princes for their part passed their idle hours together at dinners and drinking bouts. It chanced, as they were drinking . . . that the subject of wives came up. Every man fell to praising his own wife with enthusiasm, and, as their rivalry grew hot, Collatinus said that there was no need to talk about it, for it was in their power to know . . . how far the rest were excelled by his own Lucretia.

[Livy, *From the Founding of the City,* I. lvii. 5-7]

Rereading Shakespeare's classical models reveals the radical nature of his transformation of them. The descriptive occasion remains the same—the lighthearted boasting contest—but the all important test, ironically proposed by Collatine in both Ovid and Livy, has been eliminated. In *Lucrece* Collatine becomes a foolish orator, not an enemy of words but their champion. He who stops the descriptive speeches is now blamed for not knowing when to stop: "When Collatine unwisely did not let / To praise. . . ." [11. 10-11]. Moreover, in both Latin subtexts the sight of Lucrece inflames Tarquin's passion; in *Lucrece* he sets off for Collatia without having seen her. The result, then, of this rewriting is a heightened insistence on the power of description, on the dangers inherent in descriptive occasions. Here, Collatine's rhetoric, not Lucrece's behavior, wins over his companions; Collatine's rhetoric, not Lucrece's beauty, prompts Tarquin's departure.

What transpires in Tarquin's tent, then, is an after-dinner conversation during which, in a "pleasant humor" ("Argument"), his warlike guests amuse each other through a contest of epideictic oratory—oratory intended to persuade, in this case, through hyperbolic praise of its female subject. Shakespeare's soldiers present "discourses" ("Argument"), and his narrator characterizes them as orators [l. 30]. Collatine is labeled a "publisher" of his possession [l. 33], his descriptive speech is called a "boast" [l. 36], and his rhetoric, thus, is specifically in the mode of "blazon." The verb "to blazon," "to describe in proper heraldic language, to paint or depict in colors, to inscribe with arms . . . in some ornamental way, to describe fitly, to publish vauntingly or boastfully, to proclaim" [*Oxford English Dictionary*], first appears in En-

glish in the sixteenth century. Although French in origin, from *blasonner,* it is related to and reacts upon the earlier English verb "to blaze," "to proclaim as with a trumpet, to publish, to divulge, to make known; and, by extension, to defame or celebrate, to depict, to portray." In France, *blasonner* was so commonly used that it signified little more than "to describe," but its usage was rooted in two specific descriptive traditions, one heraldic and the other poetic. A *blason* was, first, a codified heraldic description of a shield, and, second, a codified poetic description of an object praised or blamed by a rhetorician-poet. The most celebrated examples of French poetic blazon were the *Blasons anatomiques du corps fémenin* (1543), a collective work in which each poem praised a separate part of the female body. The metaphor, "woman's face (or body) is a shield," literalizes this double extension of the term "blazon"—text describing a shield and text describing a body. Collatine's boastful publication of Lucrece's virtue and beauty, then, inscribes itself within a specific mode of rhetorical praise, a mode grounded in and thus generative of metaphors of heraldic display.

A question of purpose imposes itself: to what end does Collatine blazon Lucrece? Why is he not content to enjoy his "treasure" [1. 16], his "priceless wealth" [1. 17], his "fortune" [1. 19], in silence? Within the economy of competition, of course, wealth is not wealth unless flaunted, unless inspiring envy, unless affirming superiority. Tarquin's family has recently assumed power and is thus "espoused to more fame" [1. 20], but it is Collatine who owns the "peerless dame" [1. 21]. In the play of power between Tarquin and Collatine, at least for the privileged duration of this after-dinner sport, Collatine has carried the day—or rather, the evening. Description within a like context clearly serves the describer and not the described. Praise of Lucrece is more precisely praise of Collatine, be it as proud possessor or as proud rhetorician. But more important, Collatine's descriptive gesture entails a risk inherent in the gesture itself: he generates description, he opens Lucrece up for display, *in order to* inspire jealousy; and jealousy, once inspired, may be carried to its logical conclusion—theft. The cause of the rape ("the act of taking anything by force, violent seizure (of goods), robbery, and, after 1481, violation of a woman") is precisely that Collatine's self-serving oratory has fallen on "thievish" rather than passive, but none the less envious, ears. As Catharine Stimpson points out, "men rape what other men possess" [see Additional Bibliography]. The rapist is indeed the villain of the piece, but the instigation of this particular villainy is more correctly located along the fine line walked by the boaster. Rape is the price Lucrece pays for having been described.

The matter for Collatine's rhetoric, the argument suggests, is Lucrece's chastity; the poem, however, progressively shifts its reader's perspective. Although virtue is always at issue, it soon competes with beauty for the distinction of being Lucrece's most appreciable quality. Beauty, the narrative voice insists, does not need the embellishments of an orator: "Beauty itself doth of itself persuade" [1. 29]. It "excels the quirks of blazoning pens," and is sufficiently persuasive "in th' essential vesture of creation" [*Othello,* II. i. 63-4]. And still, in Tarquin's tent it seems that Collatine called upon all of the conceits of descriptive convention to outdo his comrades at arms. Shakespeare's narrator succinctly re-presents Collatine's speech:

When Collatine unwisely did not let
To praise the clear unmatched red and white
Which triumph'd in that sky of his delight;

Where mortal stars as bright as heaven's beauties,
With pure aspects did him peculiar duties.

[11. 10-14]

Less important than the conventional nature of the language—red and white complexion; face like a clear sky; eyes bright as stars—is the choice of detail that figures in the narrator's description of Collatine's description. The body Collatine praised, we are told, is a partial body, a face; its distinctive features are the colors of its flesh and the brightness of its eyes. Color and brightness define Lucrece. By the time the reader, like Tarquin, first "sees" Lucrece, the stage has been set for a repeat performance of a now familiar rhetorical portrait:

> When at Collatium this false lord [Tarquin] arrived,
> Well was he welcom'd by the Roman dame [Lucrece],
> Within whose face beauty and virtue strived
> Which of them both should underprop her fame.
> When virtue bragg'd, beauty would blush for shame;
>   When beauty boasted blushes, in despite
>   Virtue would stain that o'er with silver white.
>
> But beauty in that white entituled
> From Venus' doves, doth challenge that fair field;
> Then virtue claims from beauty beauty's red,
> Which virtue gave the golden age to gild
> Their silver cheeks, and call'd it then their shield
>   Teaching them thus to use it in the fight,
>   When shame assail'd, the red should fence the white.
>
> This heraldry in Lucrece' face was seen,
> Argu'd by beauty's red and virtue's white;
> Of either colour was the other queen,
> Proving the world's minority their right.
> Yet their ambition makes them still to fight;
>   The sov'reignty of either being so great,
>   That oft they interchange each other's seat. . . .
>
> Now thinks he that her husband's shallow tongue,—
> That niggard prodigal that prais'd her so,—
> In that high task hath done her beauty wrong,
> Which far exceeds his barren skill to show.
> Therefore that praise which Collatine doth owe
>   Enchanted Tarquin answers with surmise,
>   In silent wonder of still-gazing eyes.

[11. 50-70, 78-84]

In the presence of the "silent war of lilies and of roses" [1. 71], in Lucrece's "fair face's field" [1. 72], Tarquin stands awestruck, frozen. And yet, his mind is filled with Collatine's evening oratory; before a real, as opposed to a rhetorical, beauty his thoughts tellingly return to an assessment of the paradoxes inherent in Collatine's speech. Tarquin mentally characterizes the previous blazon of Lucrece as an expression of both a prideful need to possess and a foolish propensity to squander. But more important, when the reader "sees" what Tarquin sees, that spectacle proves to be little more than a heraldic amplification of one element of Collatine's description, an amplification operated through the introduction of a conceit that literalizes the rivalry already prefigured in the narrator's synopsis—her "unmatched red and white . . . triumph'd" [11. 11-12]. Lucrece's face becomes an animated shield colored in alternating red and white. Collatine's original praise was "unwise" to dilate or expand upon that coloration, and yet here her milky complexion and rosy blush fill

four stanzas. Shakespeare's narrator, it appears, would outdo Collatine in rhetorical *copia* [abundance].

The form the expansion assumes, moreover, makes plain the implications of the heraldic metaphor upon which it depends: here metaphor re-enacts the descriptive scene the narrative has just recounted. What we read in Lucrece's face is the story of a competition that, although between allegorical queens, is entirely cast in the vocabulary of gentlemanly combat: first, beauty and virtue strive for predominance, "virtue bragg'd" [1. 54], and "beauty boasted" [1. 55]; then, moving to territorially figured counterclaims for the right to display the other's colors, they shift ground to a field where the "red should fence the white" [1. 63]; and, finally, skirmish becomes serious as two ambitious warriors confront each other, "The sov'reignty of either being so great, / That oft they interchange each other's seat" [11. 69-70]. The warlike tale inscribed in Lucrece's face is, then, the tale of *Lucrece:* it proceeds from a boasting match—as in Tarquin's tent; to a claim for the opponent's "field" and "colors"—as we will see in the rape; to an exchange of sovereignty—as will follow the action of the poem.

Lucrece is fully blazoned only when Tarquin approaches her bed. He draws back the curtain, and his eyes begin "to wink, being blinded with a greater light" [1. 375]: the beauty of Lucrece "dazzleth" [1. 377] her spectator into a state of suspended contemplation. The narrator describes Lucrece's body part by part, metaphorically identifying it with a city or country to be conquered. Although his description introduces new colors, it opens and closes with variations on Collatine's "red and white." Tarquin's initial assault, in the form of a touch, awakens Lucrece, and he tellingly explains his presence by evoking not what he has just seen with his eyes (her hands, her hair, her breasts) but rather what he had previously "seen" with his ears:

> First like a trumpet doth his tongue begin
> To sound a parley to his heartless foe, . . .
>
> But she with vehement prayers urgeth still
> Under what colour he commits this ill.
>
> Thus he replies: "The colour in thy face,
> That even for anger makes the lily pale
> And the red rose blush at her own disgrace,
> Shall plead for me and tell my loving tale.
> Under that colour am I come to scale
>   Thy never-conquer'd fort: the fault is thine,
>   For those thine eyes betray thee unto mine.

[11. 470-71, 475-83]

Tarquin would persuade Lucrece with flattery. Indeed, taken out of the context of a rape, his language is that conventional to "loving tales": he celebrates her complexion; he represents her as a virtuously unassailable fortress; he praises the irresistible beauty of her eyes.

Tarquin goes on to define two moments in which Lucrece's beauty has acted upon him: first, the moment in which her described beauty destined her to be raped; and second, the moment, after his period of self-examination, in which her perceived beauty reinforced his conviction. It is clear, however, that the determining moment is the first: in *Lucrece* vision is shaped by description. The rapist returns obsessively to the narrator's five-line synopsis of Collatine's winning blazon; he locates motive in that initial fragmentary portrait; he speaks to his victim only of the bright eyes that "charge" and of the red and white that "color" her shield. Although Tarquin assigns responsibility to Lucrece, "the fault is thine" [1. 482], his rhetoric of praise reveals its agonistic subtext. Indeed, his descriptive strategies literally repeat those of Collatine: he moves from Lucrece's complexion to her eyes; his final line, "For those thine eyes betray thee unto mine" [1. 483], usurps the "peculiar duties" [1. 14] of Collatine's conclusion.

In addition, Tarquin's pun on the word "color"—a word that appears more often in *Lucrece* than in any other Shakespearean text—signals the rhetorical origins of the crime. Lucrece asks under what "colour" [pretext] he "commits this ill" [1. 476], and he responds that the color in her face will serve as orator to justify his action, that under that color he rapes her. This word play is not new to Tarquin; he has already used it in his self-vindicating soliloquy:

> O how her fear did make her colour rise!
>   First red as roses that on lawn we lay,
>   Then white as lawn, the roses took away. . . .
>
> Why hunt I then for colour or excuses?
> All orators are dumb when beauty pleadeth.
>   [11. 257-59, 267-68]

Semantic play here depends upon the sixteenth-century possibilities of the term "color": the "colors" of Lucrece's flesh—the red and white of her face—are indistinguishable from the "colors" of heraldry—the symbolic colors on the shield that is her face—which, in turn, are indistinguishable from the "colors" of Collatine's rhetoric—the embellishing figures that fatally represent that face. Here body, shield, and rhetoric become one.

After the rape, the "heraldry in Lucrece' face" is transformed: she perceives herself as marked or tainted; her face wears "sorrow's livery" [1. 1222]. When Collatine arrives, he stares "amazedly" at "her sad face" [1. 1591], at "her lively colour kill'd with deadly cares" [1. 1593], and asks "what spite hath [her] fair colour spent" [1. 1600]. As the color pours out of Lucrece's body, her father and her husband compete for possession of the corpse: "Then one doth call her his, the other his, / Yet neither may possess the claim they lay" [11. 1793-94]. Her father laments the loss of that "fair fresh mirror" that revealed in its complexion—its red and white—the blush of his youth: "O from thy cheeks my image thou hast torn" [1. 1762]. Her husband "bathes the pale fear in his face"—white—[1. 1775], in Lucrece's "bleeding stream"—red, now tainted with black—[1. 1774], and then, significantly, fails to make rhetoric of his experience:

> The deep vexation of his inward soul
> Hath serv'd a dumb arrest upon his tongue;
> Who, mad that sorrow should his use control
> Or keep him from heart-easing words so long,
> Begins to talk; but through his lips do throng
>   Weak words, so thick come in his poor heart's aid
> That no man could distinguish what he said.
>   [11. 1779-85]

Shakespeare's poem closes as it opened, as men rhetorically compete with each other over Lucrece's body. Now that the victorious orator has been rendered incomprehensible, another takes over with a call to revenge. The events that begin in a playful rhetoric of praise end in a serious rhetoric of blame. *Lucrece,* then, is clearly "about the rhetoric of display, about the motives of eloquence" [see excerpt above by Richard A. Lanham, 1976], but what is "displayed" at each privileged moment is the woman's body raped at the poem's center. (pp. 173-80)

Nancy J. Vickers, "This Heraldry in Lucrece' Face," in Poetics Today, *Vol. 6, No. 1-2, 1985, pp. 171-84.*

HEATHER DUBROW (essay date 1986)

[*Dubrow maintains that Renaissance theories of historiography as well as Shakespeare's own experience in interpreting and writing history inform his composition of* The Rape of Lucrece, *and that, indeed, "each of the principal characters is associated with—and characterized by—a distinctive approach to history." Lucrece exemplifies the complaint genre's vision of history, fatalistic and passive, while Brutus represents the epic or heroic mode which emphasizes the possibility of shaping historical events in order to carry out providential destiny. Shakespeare shows, according to Dubrow, that all history writing, even the austerely prosaic Argument, involves style and the process of authorial choice; thus, no one mode is more objective than any other form of story-telling. Ultimately, each mode of history, of reading and writing, has its own advantages and limitations, although recognition of the problems inherent in history-writing and in language itself is an important step in evaluating history, and, Dubrow claims, a lesson of the poem.*]

As she stares intently at the depiction of Troy, Shakespeare's Lucrece provides an emblem for a central preoccupation of the poem in which she figures: the problem of reading and writing history. Composed in a period that witnessed intensive and extensive debates on that issue, *The Rape of Lucrece* implicitly comments on several of the Renaissance controversies about Clio; it explores not only history but also historiography. In so doing, Shakespeare's narrative also illuminates broader questions about the nature of language. *The Rape of Lucrece* is often dismissed as "a gorgeous gallery of gallant inventions," a literary sampler that is crammed with tropes and schemes at the expense of sustained and serious inquiry into intellectual or psychological concerns. The subtle investigations of history that inform the whole poem suggest that it deserves more attention—and more respect—than we generally bestow on it.

Although historiography came to encompass a wide range of issues during the Renaissance, the trustworthiness of historical accounts is perhaps the most recurrent. Following the example set by their classical predecessors, Renaissance historians frequently stress the reliability of such narratives; [Jacques] Amyot, for instance, confidently declares that history "helpeth not itself with any other thing than with the plaine truth" [in his introduction to *Plutarch's Lives of the Noble Grecians and Romans Englished by Thomas North*], and [William] Camden observes [in his *Britain*], that the historian can "recall home Veritie." But this enthusiasm does not go unchallenged; the very texts that celebrate history with an assurance that anticipates Ranke's historicism may in other passages undermine the praises they are bestowing on Clio. Sir Walter Ralegh's confidence about history, for example, is undercut by his enumeration of the reasons it can be difficult to know the truth: "Informations are often false, records not alwaies true, and notorious actions commonly insufficient to discouer the passions, which did set them first on foote" [in his *The History of the World*]. (pp. 425-26)

A further reason Renaissance historians are prone to distrust their field is that they realize how frequently their colleagues prostitute Clio in the course of pandering to their employers; Polydore Vergil, for instance, was widely known to have been more interested in pleasing Henry VIII than in telling the truth. Finally, several historians acknowledge the difficulty of writing dispassionately, yet another issue on which contemporary historical thought echoes that of the Renaissance. [Jean] Bodin discusses this problem at several points [in his *Method for the Easy Comprehension of History*], while Ralegh admits the problems of recording the historical events of one's own time.

Another controversial issue in Renaissance historiography is the nature of causality. Historians typically accept the conventional wisdom about providentiality, even going as far as to see a new star as a commemoration of the St. Bartholomew's Day massacre. Thus Ralegh, whose *History of the World* is crammed with allusions to the wonder-working providence of God, declares that history allows us to know "for what vertue and piety GOD made prosperous; and for what vice and deformity he made wretched." But writers are, of course, notoriously unwilling to ease the task of intellectual historians by holding consistently to the opinions customarily ascribed to them, and the providential interpretation of history is no exception. It is evidently challenged by a Machiavellian notion of political process. . . . (pp. 426-27)

Also central to historiography during the Renaissance are discussions of the difference between history and poesy. These debates were to culminate in the seventeenth century in a widespread insistence on separating the two fields, an insistence aptly symbolized by Daniel's abandonment of his role as historian. Another related issue, however, is more relevant to *The Rape of Lucrece*: most historians assert that texts in their field have no style, being unencumbered by rhetorical devices and principles. Holinshed announces in his dedicatory epistle [to his *Chronicles*], "I neuer made any choise of stile, or words . . . thinking it sufficient, truelie and plainelie to set forth such things as I minded to intreat of, rather than with vaine affection of eloquence to paint out a rotten sepulchre." . . . And in his *Britain* Camden takes pride in the fact that he has neglected the very issues that concern poets: "neither have I waied every word in Goldsmithes scales . . . neither purposed to picke flowres out of the gardens of Eloquence," he writes in "To the Reader," quoting Cicero in support of his approach to historical prose.

The Rape of Lucrece is shaped not only by these Renaissance debates but also by its author's own experiences writing history. Indeed, these influences are as interwined as the fates of Tarquin and his victim: Shakespeare's experiments in his history plays no doubt intensified his interest in the very issues contemporary historians were disputing. Thus the process of comparing his sources repeatedly reminded him how much accounts of the same event can differ from each other—a concern that emerges in *Richard III*, say, when the title character carefully plants reports of putative historical events like his wife's illness to further his own ends. Both the act of excerpting stories from the longer accounts he found in the chronicles and that of shaping several plays into his first tetralogy directed Shakespeare's attention to one reason historical accounts differ so much: where narrators open a story and where they close it in no small measure influence how the occurrences in between are viewed. Even if one does not wholly accept the providential view of history, the events of the reign of Henry VI seem very different when one acknowledges that they culminate in the rise of Richard III. Similarly, selecting historical details from among the multitude in his sources must have made Shakespeare reflect on how what one omits affects a story. He was later to make this concern explicit in the Epilogue to *Henry V*, where the admission that the drama

is "mangling by starts [i.e., omissions]" [l. 4] the deeds of the heroes is not only a tribute to their glorious feats but also an acknowledgement of the difficulty of writing a play about those or any other historical happenings. Finally, in the early years of his career Shakespeare doubtless analyzed the differences between the genres in which history can be told. Certainly he must have mused on the distinctions between how the same stories are variously handled in the chronicles, in the *Mirror for Magistrates,* and in a play; and, like modern critics, he must have speculated on the distinctions between a tragedy and a history play about, say, Richard III.

Moreover, it is evident that the process of writing *The Rape of Lucrece* raised these very issues for its author. Like Lucrece standing before the rendition of Troy, he studied others' accounts of historical events; unlike Lucrece, he confronted a number of different and even contradictory accounts. Thus Ovid and Livy disagree not only in their handling of a few minor facts but also in their tone: Ovid's account is more emotional, offering more details about the characters' feelings and expressing more sympathy for them. And the notes in the most popular Renaissance editions of Ovid draw attention repeatedly to how much the various retellings of Lucrece's story differ from each other. In addition, a comparison of Livy's version with Ovid's foregrounds the issues about openings and closure that, as I have suggested, Shakespeare no doubt debated even before writing this poem. For Livy's account places Lucrece's tragedy in the broader historical context of the previous misdeeds of Tarquin's father and the subsequent political changes in Rome, while Ovid focuses more on Lucrece herself, referring only briefly to the historical events that frame the story. Finally, one suspects that comparing the prose historical narratives composed by Livy and Ovid with his own account (and with that of Chaucer, if he did indeed draw from that well of English undefiled) intensified Shakespeare's interest in how historical genres differ from each other. In any event, he was to incorporate this issue, like so many of the other historiographical questions we have examined, in the text of *The Rape of Lucrece*.

If, as Robert Ornstein among others has shown [in his *A Kingdom for a Stage; The Achievement of Shakespeare's History Plays*], Shakespeare continues to experiment with history-writing throughout his career, construing it in radically different ways each time he returns to it, that same process of vision and revision is enacted synchronically within *The Rape of Lucrece*. Playing different methods of interpreting history against each other, the poem explores the very problems that were debated by contemporary historians and posed by Shakespeare's own engagement with Clio. Each of the principal characters is associated with—and characterized by—a distinctive approach to history; by linking these approaches to particular genres, Shakespeare reminds us of the connections between psychological styles of behavior and formal styles of writing. In addition, the poem juxtaposes the mode of history-writing represented by its Argument with that of the text itself.

The complaint is significant not only as a generic model for the narrative but also as one of the historical visions within it: the type of complaint that is found in the *Mirror for Magistrates* as well as in later imitations of that poem and employed by Tarquin's victim herself becomes a metaphor for Lucrece's characteristic approach to history. Such complaints are rooted in the events of the past, not those of the present or future. This temporal perspective reflects the role in history frequently assumed by those who deliver such poems: unlike their counterparts in the *Heroides,* the suffering (and often insufferable) protagonists of Elizabethan complaints generally cannot affect the present and future, except very indirectly, through their roles as moral exempla. The fact that most of the figures delivering such poems are ghosts not only explains but also symbolizes this powerlessness: however potent they once have been, at the point when they appear before us they are as insubstantial politically as they are physically.

Furthermore, by their very nature complaints focus on the suffering of their protagonists, referring only in passing to the larger historical backdrop. Thus [Michael] Drayton's "Peirs Gaveston," unlike Marlowe's play in which that unlovely lover figures, concentrates primarily on the title character's own relationship to Edward II; the other problems of Edward's reign command comparatively brief attention. Similarly, though the complaints of women pursued by monarchs do raise important issues about the nature of tyranny, these poems devote less space to such problems than, say, a prose tract or a historical drama might do.

It is evident, then, that the complaint typifies Lucrece's own approach to history. Unable to redeem or reshape the horrors of the past by achieving revenge in the present, unable to envision the long-term political results of the rape, she must depend on others to punish Tarquin. The way she interprets the incidents of the Trojan war also exemplifies what I have termed the complaint's vision of history. Rather than observing the events that hint that the suffering of Troy will be redeemed, she devotes most of her attention to Hecuba's grief. In doing so, she demonstrates a concern with the horrors of the past rather than the hopes of the future and with the needs of the individual rather than with the broader historical and social issues of his or her culture.

In associating Lucrece with the complaint, then, Shakespeare is providing an image for the role of women in history. This is not to say, of course, that he presents the complaint as an exclusively female version of history: no reader of the *Mirror,* which included only male ghosts in its early editions, would be tempted to invoke the genre for that purpose. Shakespeare is, however, reminding us that the passivity of the complaint can aptly represent the role women typically assume in history: bemoaning events thay cannot influence. His Lucrece takes her place among the wailing women in *Richard III.*

While bodying forth one vision of history in the person of Lucrece, Shakespeare also offers us a contrasting vision, the epic or heroic mode of reading and writing history. Brutus condenses many implications of this mode when he exhorts Collatine,

> Courageous Roman, do not steep thy heart
> In such relenting dew of lamentations;
> But kneel with me and help to bear thy part
> To rouse our Roman gods with invocations,
> That they will suffer these abominations,—
>   Since Rome herself in them doth stand disgraced,—
>   By our strong arms from forth her fair streets
>   chased.

[ll. 1828-34]

The epic approach to Clio involves the sublimation or mitigation of suffering through "strong arms" [l. 1834] rather than the expression of it in a "dew of lamentations" [l. 1829]. And

it involves aggressively shaping historical happenings rather than passively being shaped by them, acting in the present and future rather than reacting to the past. Brutus plays Bolingbroke to Lucrece's Richard II.

The proponents of the epic viewpoint on history characteristically interpret causality providentially—and sometimes, as in the case of Brutus, conveniently see themselves as the agents of providence. Notice, for example, that he adheres to the most conservative notion of how tyrants fall (and in so doing defuses the explosive issues about rebellion latent in the poem): he claims that in banishing Tarquin he will merely be an agent of the gods.

The epic perspective is in fact best represented by a character who is very important in *The Rape of Lucrece* even though it nowhere refers to him specifically: *pius* Aeneas. It is possible that some of Shakespeare's readers were aware of the legend from *Metamorphoses* XIV to which the notes in many Renaissance editions of the *Fasti* refer: Aeneas, like Tarquin himself, is said to have attacked the city of Ardea. But whether or not they recalled this story, they would surely have realized that Lucrece's responses to the depiction of Troy mirror—and invite us to compare—Aeneas' reactions when he views the story of Troy on Dido's temple doors. Throughout the *Aeneid* Aeneas dedicates himself, though at the cost of Dido and her values, to achievement. Thus, carrying his father and all that parent symbolizes on his back, he sets out to found a brave new world. Like Brutus, he is committed to the belief that the suffering of the past may be reshaped to yield a glorious future.

Unlike Brutus, however, he attempts to reshape it not only by committing glorious deeds but also by reading and recounting historical events so that they conform to the epic pattern: if his behavior before Dido's doors establishes him as an historian's audience, his performance at her feast, where he tells the story of Troy, establishes him as an historian. Hence Aeneas' approach to history, so implicitly but so importantly present in *The Rape of Lucrece,* suggests the contours of an epic vision of Lucrece's story. To read or write history from this perspective, we come to realize, is to stress long-term gains rather than short-term griefs. This is especially evident when the hero of the *Aeneid* reads the temple doors. While Lucrece found only sorrow in the fall of Troy, Aeneas finds *salus* (*Aeneid* I. 451, 463). (By using that noun twice in the passage, Vergil encourages us to reflect on its varied meanings, from "physical safety" to "well-being" in a more general sense.) And Aeneas implicitly reminds us, too, that an heroic version of the rape of Lucrece would effect closure considerably after her suffering or death, encompassing the attempts to unseat the Tarquins and found a better society.

In addition to contrasting the historiography of the complaint with that of epic poetry, *The Rape of Lucrece* plays its Argument against the succeeding text. Although these versions are strikingly different from each other, most critics have ignored the distinctions between them. One reason for this neglect is the common tendency to overlook prefatory material. But the relationship between the Induction of *The Taming of the Shrew* and the play itself should conclusively give the lie to that habit. Another reason Shakespeareans have neglected the differences between the Argument of *The Rape of Lucrece* and the poetic text is that they assume that the divergences between the two are inevitable and hence insignificant; any Argument, so this case goes, necessarily ab-

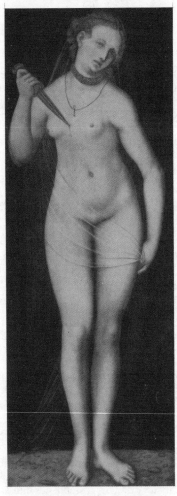

Lucrece. By Lucas Cranach.

breviates the succeeding story, and hence the resulting changes are not worthy of critical attention. But these assumptions ignore the complexities of a reader's reactions: knowing that such alterations have to occur often limits the intensity of our responses to them, but they may stimulate responses and reflections nonetheless and hence function as an important part of our experience of the work. Moreover, a writer may heighten our reactions by emphasizing and, in particular, rendering thematic the inevitable distinctions between prefatory material and what ensues, as Shakespeare does when he weights the Prologue to *Troilus and Cressida* with polysyllabic, Latinate diction. Similarly, the fact that Coleridge explores interpretive acts throughout "The Rime of the Ancient Mariner" draws our attention to the disparities between the glosses and the text.

In the case of *The Rape of Lucrece,* the concern for different interpretations of history that we find throughout the narrative activates the potential significance of the contrasts between the Argument and the rest of the poem. But we are prepared for the significance of those differences even earlier in our experience of reading Shakespeare's narrative; the contrast between the formal rhetoric of the dedication and the simpler prose of the Argument makes us think more about the language of both of them. Compare

The love I dedicate to your Lordship is without end; whereof this pamphlet without beginning is but a superfluous moiety. The warrant I have of your Honourable disposition, not the worth of my untutored lines, makes it assured of acceptance. What I have done is yours, what I have to do is yours, being part in all I have, devoted yours

and

Lucius Tarquinius (for his excessive pride surnamed Superbus), after he had caused his own father-in-law Servius Tullius to be cruelly murdered, and, contrary to the Roman laws and customs, not requiring or staying for the people's suffrages, had possessed himself of the kingdom, went, accompanied with his sons and other noblemen of Rome, to besiege Ardea.

Shakespeare crams instances of antithesis, alliteration, polyptoton, and epiphora into his dedication, as into the poem itself, while the clumsily long opening sentence of the Argument is bare of such devices. This is not to say, however, that the Argument—or any prose selection—lacks a style. In fact, its many Latinate constructions (such as the ablative absolute "Which done") encourage us to associate this passage with the work of the great Latin historians. As we will see, it is in fact linked to their writings in content as well as in style. And, recognizing the stylistic differences between the Argument and what precedes and follows it, we may begin to anticipate substantive differences as well between the poem and the Argument that purports simply to summarize it.

When, responding to such hints, we compare the Argument with the text itself, what we discover is a contrast quite as striking as that between the Prologue of *Troilus and Cressida* and the play. First of all, the time span of the Argument differs from that of the poem even more than the chronological boundaries of complaint and epic differ. As well as grounding Tarquin's actions in earlier ones by his father, the Argument devotes proportionately more space to the downfall of the Tarquins: in the poem the concluding allusion to the banishment of Lucrece's attacker seems very abrupt, while in contrast about one-fifth of the Argument discusses the events in question. Comparing these two accounts reminds us, then, that the nature of our historical tracts depends in part on the questions they are attempting to answer: the time span of the Argument reflects the fact that it implicitly responds to the query, "Why were the Tarquins banished?" while the inquiry behind the poem might be phrased as, "What happened to Lucrece?" In short, the concerns of the Argument are more political, those of the poem itself more personal.

These differing approaches to temporality reflect—and help to generate—differing approaches to historical causality. By playing up the tyranny of Tarquin's father, which is so clearly related to the son's sexual tyranny, and by stressing that the entire family is banished, the Argument hints at the providential view of history: the fall of the Tarquins is a just punishment for their misdeeds. In contrast, the abrupt opening and conclusion of the body of the poem mime on the narrative level the arbitrariness that characterizes Lucrece's own view of causality. We have less sense of the appropriateness of Tarquin's punishment, less sense of order being restored. At the same time, however, by linking the characters' behavior to the values of their society, the text suggests motivations more subtle than any indicated by the Argument: causality is traced to a network of human drives and assumptions and to the culture that breeds them. In a way, indeed, the differences between the Argument and the poem correspond to that between traditional political history and contemporary studies of *mentalite*: the Argument traces historical change to the public actions of characters, such as besieging Ardea, while the poem uncovers the unspoken and even unconscious attitudes behind those actions, such as beliefs about chastity.

But the most striking difference between the Argument and the poem that succeeds it lies in the way they treat emotion. First of all, the poem devotes considerably more attention to the feelings of its characters, while the Argument contents itself with obvious observations like "Lucrece, in this lamentable plight." In this respect the distinction between the two parallels that between the accounts of Ovid and Livy. Similarly, the poetic version appeals to its readers' emotions, not only describing but also evoking *lacrimae rerum* [the tears of things], while the Argument is in more senses than one very dry. The prose account of the events teaches us by appealing to our reason; as assured in its didacticism as the *Mirror for Magistrates,* it clearly demonstrates that tyrannous actions breed their own downfall. The succeeding poem, in contrast, performs its didactic function in no small part by engaging—and often confounding—our feelings.

As its detached tone would suggest, the Argument at first strikes us as an unimpeachable account: unswayed by the subtle political and moral judgements that lead the narrator of the poem to, say, apply the judgmental verb "clothe" [l. 1809] to Brutus' secretive behavior, the speaker in the Argument appears to be giving us, as it were, all the truth that's fit to print. But this initial confidence in his trustworthiness in fact heightens our dismay when we discover the significance of what the Argument omits (leaving out both Brutus' earlier deceptions and his manipulations of his listeners, for example, casts a more positive light on his rise to power, avoiding the very facts that render the transition to republicanism morally problematical). Hence as we contrast the Argument with the text, our confidence in that prefatory passage falters a little. We ourselves experience the loss of trust in seemingly objective sources that characterizes Renaissance historians.

If competition is a central moral problem in *The Rape of Lucrece* (Tarquin competes with Collatine in pursuing Lucrece, Collatine with Lucretius in mourning her), it is also a central structural device. For, as we have just observed, the poem repeatedly plays competing interpretations of the same historical incident against each other. Shakespeare, like the modern historian Hayden White [in his *Metahistory*], is intensely conscious of the varying genres through which historical events can be told. But whereas his concern with those genres may anticipate many of the stylistic questions that White and other twentieth-century historians have been debating, it also contributes to the Renaissance discussion of history that we examined earlier.

As my analysis of its conflicting genres would suggest, one of the principal truths Shakespeare's narrative offers us is that even historical accounts that seem totally reliable may exemplify the errors that Bodin charts. If the omissions in the Argument hint at this point, the rest of the poem helps us to understand why history is so often unreliable. We witness both Lucrece and Brutus reshaping history, and we are reminded, too, of the ways Aeneas does so. Citing the instance of a general who attempts to report a battle which he has led, the modern historian Marc Bloch demonstrates [in his *The Historian's Craft*] the propensity for distortion inherent even in

eyewitness reportage. No literary work supports his observations more cogently than *The Rape of Lucrece.*

Shakespeare's narrative also implicitly participates in sixteenth-century discussions of historical causality. On one level, the story suggests itself as an exemplum of the providential interpretation. Tyrants are, conveniently enough, banished when and because that tyranny becomes manifest in a rape. We need not even worry about the unfairness of visiting the sins of the fathers on the sons, an issue that often troubles proponents of the providential view: in a sense here the sins of the son are visited on the father, but in fact both are guilty of the same type of wrongdoing. Yet, as I began to indicate earlier, the poem itself undercuts the providential viewpoint implicit in its Argument. The abrupt conclusion leaves us uneasy, conscious that providence may have chosen a morally dubious agent in the person of Brutus. Moreover, by focusing so much attention on Lucrece's pain, *The Rape of Lucrece* allows to surface what is often a troubling undercurrent in providential interpretations: the good must suffer so that the evil may be punished. For if Lucrece's rape is the necessary precondition to the change to republicanism, then she is being used by history much as she has been used by Tarquin and Brutus. Many have been able to accept that God's ways are mysterious, but we are hardly comfortable with the idea that they are also malicious. These problems, like so many others in the poem, are never resolved: they remain a disturbing reminder of the difficulties of interpreting history. This early in his career Shakespeare may have found it easier to ponder such issues in relation to a culture other than his own, although he was to raise the same troubled and troubling questions about providentiality in his later English history plays, most notably in *Henry VIII.*

But the most original contributions to Renaissance historiography in *The Rape of Lucrece* concern those sibling rivals history and poesy. Unlike Sidney, Shakespeare does not wholly discount the advantages of the former; the broader historical sweep of the Argument provides a perspective on the story that is clearly lacking in the poem itself. But as we read *The Rape of Lucrece* we are very aware that in omitting the subtle and shifting emotions of the actors in history, the Argument neglects a central component in their motivations. And in leaving out the moral questions that we discern in the poem, the Argument ignores the ethical complexities that complicate seemingly straightforward events like Brutus' rise to power.

No doubt many of Shakespeare's contemporaries would have seconded his points about the advantages and limitations of these two modes of presenting the story. More original and more controversial is his implicit reminder that historical writing does indeed have a style. We have already observed that the contrast with the mellifluous rhetoric of the dedication draws attention to what is Latinate in the syntax of the Argument. Similarly, the contrast with the time span of the poem demonstrates that where the Argument opens and where it concludes are the result not of insignificant or arbitrary decisions but rather of a kind of artistic shaping that inevitably affects the whole meaning of the passage. Hence the historian too is inevitably, if at times unwittingly, a Second Maker. Shakespeare would agree with the modern historian J. H. Hexter when he observes [in his *Doing History*], "Rhetoric is ordinarily deemed icing on the cake of history, but . . . it is mixed right into the batter." For the differences between the Argument and the rest of *The Rape of Lucrece* do not reside in the fact that the former is more reliable because it is free of the colors of rhetoric; rather, each employs its own distinctive form of rhetoric.

If the commentary on history in *The Rape of Lucrece* operates centrifugally, directing our attention to contemporary discussions of historiography, at the same time it also works centripetally, emphasizing issues within the poem itself. Thus the narrative focuses on one question that renders our interpretation of history especially problematical: our decisions about where to begin a story and where to end it inevitably color our reactions to the events in between those points. Established by the contrast between competing views of history, this issue is echoed elsewhere in *The Rape of Lucrece* as well. In a sense Lucrece's suicide is an attempt to effect closure, as are Brutus' political actions. Moreover, the *rime royal* stanza enacts on the prosodic level the points Shakespeare is making about closure in history. For this stanzaic form incorporates three possible resting-places within its seven-line structure of *ababbcc*: we may experience at least some sense of closure after line four, line five, and of course, at the end of the stanza. In some verses enjambment undermines the potential closure after line four, or more often, line five, but in others the tension between the various places we could stop provides an analogue to the tension between the various places an historian could terminate Lucrece's story itself:

> By this, starts Collatine as from a dream,
> And bids Lucretius give his sorrow place;
> And then in key-cold Lucrece' bleeding stream
> He falls, and bathes the pale fear in his face,
> And counterfeits to die with her a space;
>   Till manly shame bids him possess his breath,
>   And live to be revenged on her death.
>
> [ll. 1772-78]

Both the syntax and the rhyme tempt us to pause where Collatine does, at the end of line five; the fact that the stanza does not end there but resumes to report his revenge mirrors the fact that Collatine himself rises up. Or, to put it another way, in lines one to five we find the response to history and the type of closure represented by the complaint, while the concluding lines move into the epic mode.

Above all, however, the preoccupation with history-writing in *The Rape of Lucrece* is part of a broader concern with the nature of language itself. The poem opens and closes on references to publishing: Collatine is, we are informed at the outset, the unfortunate "publisher" [l. 33] of his wife's fame, while at the conclusion of the narrative the Romans agree to "publish" [l. 1852] Tarquin's infamy. And the narrative is packed with other allusions to language: the characters praise and slander each other, they refer to delivering declamations and orations, they swear oaths, they curse, they name and misname. Moreover, *The Rape of Lucrece,* like *Venus and Adonis,* repeatedly mentions various types of storytelling. Shortly after meeting Lucrece, Tarquin "*stories* to her ears" ([l. 106]; my italics) her husband's deeds, reminding us how easily storytelling may be conscripted into the service of flattery. Sinon offers his credulous listeners an "enchanting *story*" ([l. 1520]; my italics). Lucrece fears she will feature in ballads and nursery tales. Hence we are invited to compare history-writing with other forms of story-telling.

But Shakespeare, like many of the Renaissance humanists, is interested in language less as an abstract system of symbols than as one component in the process of interpretation and misinterpretation. Thus the image of Lucrece reading the

tapestry of Troy participates in a series of other references to reading. *Legere* and *intellegere* [To read and to understand], like so many other aspects of the Roman world evoked by this poem, are more often enemies than allies. During their initial encounter, Lucrece misreads Tarquin's face. Shortly afterwards, he misconstrues the portents warning him against the rape:

> But all these poor forbiddings could not stay him;
> He in the worst sense consters their denial.
> The doors, the wind, the glove, that did delay him,
> He takes for accidental things of trial.
>
> [ll. 323-26]

Attempting to explain his behavior, Lucrece claims he is not viewing the situation clearly: "And wipe the dim mist from thy doting eyne, / That thou shalt see thy state, and pity mine" [ll. 643-44]. She in turn misreads the expression on the groom's face. And the description of the rendition of Troy repeatedly draws attention to the act of viewing it: "There might you see" [l. 1380], "That one might see" [l. 1386], "You might behold" [l. 1388], "That one would swear he saw them quake and tremble" [l. 1393], "might one behold!" [l. 1395]. Throughout the poem, too, Lucrece believes that Tarquin's deed can be read on her face; she fearfully predicts, for instance, that,

> Yea, the illiterate that know not how
> To cipher what is writ in learned books,
> Will quote my loathsome trespass in my looks.
>
> [ll. 810-12]

Hence one sign of her attempt to become "mistress of [her] fate" [l. 1069] is her new-found belief that her face can serve a different function than it has previously assumed, becoming a text that will punish, not merely publish, Tarquin's deed: "How Tarquin must be us'd, *read* it in me" [l. 1195]; my italics). Notice that even at this point she innocently maintains that the text will be read correctly. We, however, have come to distrust both books and their interpreters.

If Lucrece herself repeatedly reads texts, we are engaged in reading, or perhaps at times misreading, the text that is merely called *"Lucrece"* on its 1594 title page. The final act in *Troilus and Cressida* includes a scene in which the audience watches Thersites watching Troilus and Ulysses watching Cressida and Diomedes. Similarly, in *The Rape of Lucrece* the audience reads the story of Lucrece reading the story of Hecuba. That reflexive process is heightened by references that again find an analogue in *Troilus and Cressida,* as well as in *Julius Caesar* and *Antony and Cleopatra:* the poem frequently alludes to the fact that later authors will tell the story of Lucrece. On one level, of course, such allusions playfully assert that what we are encountering is not one of those versions but rather the actual, unfolding events. At the same time, on another level we are reminded that what we are reading is indeed an instance of those fictive accounts whose popularity Lucrece so accurately predicts. In other words, such references function very like a phenomenon in the visual arts: a border or frame on which the painting itself intrudes, or from which it extrudes. The fact that the work will not be confined to its border implies that it has a reality beyond that of art—while at the same time we are all the more conscious of that border and hence all the more aware that this is in fact a work of art.

In short, then, Shakespeare's analysis of history and historiography extends and complicates his scrutiny of language and the process of interpretation. Having denied that the straightforward historical accounts represented by the Argument are privileged, having undercut the conventional wisdom that the absence of style guarantees the presence of truth, the poem questions the trustworthiness of any form of history, whether it is expressed as a prose narrative or a type of poesy. It asks, in other words, whether all history-writing is but another example of the unreliability of narratives, like the flattering stories, the slanderous rumors, and the hypocritical lies with which the poem is so concerned. And it asks if we are fated to misread historical accounts. We may at first be tempted to answer these questions in the affirmative. *The Rape of Lucrece* alludes to no single instance of an historical mode we can trust. If Lucrece, like Renaissance historians, warns us that time will "blot old books and alter their contents" [l. 948], newer history books—and their audiences—may prove no more reliable. On another level, however, Shakespeare's is not a counsel of despair. For the poem as a whole is evidently an attempt to write history more accurately than any of the accounts within it. And not the least of the skills *The Rape of Lucrece* teaches its readers is the ability to evaluate history and its sources better than the characters within the narrative are able to do. We come to acknowledge the limitations in both the complaint's and the epic's approach to history; we come to recognize the complex motivations of its actors. If Clio herself is raped by some of the characters in the poem and menaced by even the speaker in its Argument, its readers learn to treat her with more respect. (pp. 427-41)

> Heather Dubrow, "The Rape of Clio: Attitudes to History in Shakespeare's 'Lucrece'," in English Literary Renaissance, Vol. 16, No. 3, Autumn, 1986, pp. 425-41.

ADDITIONAL BIBLIOGRAPHY

Adams, Joseph Quincy. "Period of Non-Dramatic Composition." In his *A Life of William Shakespeare*, pp. 145-83. Boston: Houghton Mifflin Co., 1923.

Characterizes the Elizabethan reception of *The Rape of Lucrece* by citing contemporary reviews, references, and allusions to Shakespeare's popular poem.

Bailey, John. "The Poems." In his *Shakespeare*, pp. 44-65. London: Longmans, Green and Co., 1929.

States that "the art of 'Lucrece' is rather young" and more closely resembles a formal exercise based on a set theme than an inspired work, such as the later Shakespearean tragedies. Nevertheless, Bailey contends, the poem merits attention because "Shakespeare the dramatist makes his first tentative appearance" in his realistic rendering of the two protagonists.

Baldwin, T. W. "The Literary Genetics of 'Lucrece'." In his *On the Literary Genetics of Shakspere's Poems and Sonnets*, pp. 97-153. Urbana: University of Illinois Press, 1950.

Offers a detailed study of the classical and contemporary sources that Shakespeare likely relied upon in composing *The Rape of Lucrece*. After a close, phrase-by-phrase comparison of Shakespeare's text and classical versions of the story, Baldwin concludes that Shakespeare's principal sources were Ovid and Livy, and secondarily the English author and translator William Painter.

Baynes, Thomas Spencer. "What Shakespeare Learnt at School." In his *Shakespeare Studies and Essay on English Dictionaries*, pp. 147-249. London: Longmans, Green and Co., 1894.

Compares Shakespeare's text with Ovid's, acknowledges his debt to Virgil, and argues that the poet's knowledge of Latin was sufficient to obviate a reliance on such contemporary English versions of the Lucrece story as William Painter's. On another issue, Baynes ascribes an earlier composition date than is traditionally argued, placing it somewhere between 1580 and 1587, prior to Shakespeare's arrival in London.

Bowers, A. Robin. "Iconography and Rhetoric in Shakespeare's 'Lucrece'." *Shakespeare Studies* XIV (1981): 1-21.

Argues that *The Rape of Lucrece* is based on an "essentially forensic structure" typical of "popular medieval debate literature" and thus deserves to be assessed according to Renaissance psychological and literary theory, rather than by the dramatic standards that many critics impose. Although the debates or interior monologues engaged in by the two protagonists appear to violate the decorum observed by many modern dramatists and critics, the characters' portrayal conforms to the "traditional, medieval ways of explaining the corruption of the mind."

Braunmuller, A. R. "Early Shakespearian Tragedy and Its Contemporary Context: Cause and Emotion in 'Titus Andronicus', 'Richard III' and 'The Rape of Lucrece'." In *Shakespearian Tragedy*, edited by Malcolm Bradbury and David Palmer, pp. 97-128. London: Edward Arnold, 1984.

Characterizes *The Rape of Lucrece* as a transition piece poised between narrative poetry and drama, a status which accords the author certain liberties and constraints. Despite the formal disputations and other narrative conventions, Braunmuller observes, there is a tendency to invoke dialogue and other dramatic devices, resulting in "an affective theory of drama and a small demonstration" of stagecraft.

Bromley, Laura G. "Lucrece's Re-Creation." *Shakespeare Quarterly* XXXIV, No. 2 (Summer 1983): 200-11.

Views Lucrece not as a pawn of fate, but as a heroic figure who endures a moral struggle, undergoes a transformation, and emerges as an integrated self empowered to transcend her own defilement and restore order to her similarly corrupted society. The critic argues that Lucrece's suicide is neither an act of "self-promotion" nor "self-destruction," but, paradoxically, a heroic "self-creative" act.

Bullough, Geoffrey, ed. " 'The Rape of Lucrece'." In his *Narrative and Dramatic Sources of Shakespeare: "Early Comedies," "Poems," " 'Romeo and Juliet',"* pp. 179-201. New York: Columbia University Press, 1957.

Addresses the literary sources employed by Shakespeare—principally Ovid, but also Livy, Virgil, and William Painter—in the composition of *The Rape of Lucrece*.

Dickey, Franklin M. "Attitudes toward Love in 'Venus and Adonis' and 'The Rape of Lucrece'." In his *Not Wisely But Too Well: Shakespeare's Love Tragedies*, pp. 46-62. San Marino, Calif.: The Huntington Library, 1966.

Argues that *The Rape of Lucrece* is an example of "moralized history" intended to portray the debilitating effect of lust in princes and the danger such conduct poses to the state. Dickey views the poem as the youthful Shakespeare's often awkward, didactic expression of moral and political philosophy, similar to the sentiments he would state more elegantly in the mature tragedies.

Donaldson, Ian. " 'A Theme for Disputation': Shakespeare's Lucrece." In his *The Rapes of Lucretia: A Myth and Its Transformations*, pp. 40-56. Oxford: Clarendon Press, 1982.

Contends that Shakespeare's depiction of the Lucrece story is morally ambiguous because it vacillates between Roman and Christian viewpoints, alternately sympathizing with and condemning Lucrece. "In so vividly dramatizing Tarquin's and Lucrece's moral uncertainties," the critic avers, "Shakespeare in-

troduces a fatal element of moral uncertainty into the poem itself." Donaldson posits that Shakespeare, swayed by the Augustinian argument critical of Lucrece's motivations and actions, began to "Christianize the old story," but unaccountably
stopped, "content to allow the story to drift down its traditional
narrative course."

Dowden, Edward. Introduction to *The Rape of Lucrece,* by William
Shakespeare, pp. 987-92. In *The Histories and Poems of Shakespeare,*
edited by W. J. Craig. London: Oxford University Press, 1932.

Claims the artistry of *The Rape of Lucrece* is hindered by the
conflict between the poet's narrative and dramatic modes of
presentation. Dowden blames the poem's faults partly on the
contemporary literary fashion that valued wit and rhetoric
above inspiration, and partly on the poet's own immaturity.
Nevertheless, the critic asserts, flashes of brilliance in the poem
portend Shakespeare's mature works.

Dubrow, Heather. "A Mirror for Complaints: Shakespeare's 'Lucrece' and Generic Tradition." In *Renaissance Genres: Essays on
Theory, History and Interpretation,* edited by Barbara K. Lewalski,
pp. 399-417. Cambridge, Mass.: Harvard University Press, 1986.

Describes the popularity of the complaint genre—in which a
woman protagonist defends her chastity against a politically
powerful man—in the 1590s. In *The Rape of Lucrece,* Dubrow
argues, Shakespeare was writing "not merely within the complaint form but against it . . . rendering many of its assumptions very prominent and very problematical." In contrast to
complaint poems by Daniel, Churchyard, Lodge, and Drayton,
Shakespeare's poem probes psychological issues and challenges
conventional views of guilt and chastity.

El-Gabalawy, Saad. "The Ethical Question of Lucrece: A Case of
Rape." *Mosaic* XII, No. 4 (Summer 1979): 75-86.

Explores three approaches to the Lucrece legend. These constitute: 1) the Augustinian, Christian point of view harshly critical
of her motives and suicide; 2) a more sympathetic attitude, held
by Chaucer and Shakespeare, depicting Lucrece as an exemplum of "fidelity, chastity and self-sacrifice"; 3) the perspective
of "libertines," such as Pierto Aretino, who denounced conventional ideas and values and castigated Lucrece for defending her
chastity.

Frye, Roland M. "Shakespeare's Composition of 'Lucrece': New Evidence." *Shakespeare Quarterly* XVI, No. 4 (Autumn 1965): 289-96.

Reveals new material to support the theory that Shakespeare
originally composed *The Rape of Lucrece,* or at least part of it,
in sesta rima form rather than rhyme royal. Frye postulates that
the poet inserted the additional line after completing his first
version. The critic further suggests that in a large number of
stanzas, the fifth line could be omitted without substantially altering the meaning.

Furnivall, F. J. Introduction to *The Rape of Lucrece,* by William
Shakespeare, pp. xxxiii-xxxv. In *The Leopold Shakspere.* London:
Cassell Petter and Galpin, 1877.

Briefly introduces the poem with commentary on possible classical and contemporary sources. Furnivall calls attention to the
animal imagery, reminiscent of that found in *Henry VI;* the
"verbal-thematic links" with *Coriolanus* and *Troilus and Cressida;* and Lucrece's stature: "a figure fit to stand by Brutus's Portia [in *Julius Caesar*], by Volumnia [in *Coriolanus*], of Shakspere's greatest time."

Gibian, George. "Pushkin's Parody on 'The Rape of Lucrece'."
Shakespeare Quarterly I, No. 4 (October 1950): 264-66.

Identifies the Russian author Pushkin's play "Count Nulin"
(1825) as a parody of *The Rape of Lucrece* and, thus, "one of
the few comments on Shakespeare's nondramatic works by a
major Continental figure." Gibian quotes Pushkin: "Reading
Lucrece, a rather weak poem of Shakespeare's, I thought—what
if it had occurred to Lucrece to slap Tarquin?"

Goddard, Harold C. "The Integrity of Shakespeare." In his *The*

Meaning of Shakespeare, pp. 15-24. Chicago: University of Chicago
Press, 1951.

Discusses the numerous dramatic parallels between *The Rape
of Lucrece* and Shakespearean plays, and the allegorical or metaphorical dimension of the poem according to which terms of
war are used to describe the rape. "Rape is miniature war is
what the poem says in so many words," declares Goddard.

Griffin, Robert J. "'These Contraries Such Unity Do Hold': Patterned Imagery in Shakespeare's Narrative Poems." *Studies in English Literature 1500-1900* IV, No. 1 (Winter 1964): 43-55.

Examines the substructure of motifs, images, extended metaphors, antitheses, and oxymorons in the narrative poems.
Through these elements, Griffin contends, the poems cohere
and achieve a formal unity and effectiveness characteristic of
poetic genius.

Hamilton, A. C. "The Poems: 'Lucrece'." In his *The Early Shakespeare,* pp. 167-85. San Marino, Calif.: The Huntington Library,
1967.

Asserts that Shakespeare's poem, relative to prior accounts,
represents "the first time the story of Lucrece is told comprehensively and in all its complexity." According to Hamilton,
the poem presents three moral states: Tarquin's self-conscious
confrontation with lust; Lucrece's sense of private guilt for what
is Tarquin's sin; and the public shame Lucrece fears and hopes
to avert through suicide. In addition, the critic examines the
function of painting in the poem and the relation between painting and poetry, views Lucrece as a "speaking picture" and as
an emblem, and relates the poem to *Titus Andronicus.*

Hubler, Edward, ed. Introduction to *Shakespeare's Songs and
Poems,* pp. xi-1v. New York: McGraw-Hill Co., 1959.

Provides introductory material and commentary on publication
history, the title, texts, sources, and metrical pattern for *The
Rape of Lucrece.* Despite the poem's excesses and formal faults,
the critic argues, *Lucrece* represents "Shakespeare's first statement of the conception of tragedy he was later to realize in
Hamlet and *Othello,* and, so considered, the poem gains in dignity and power." Hubler rejects the notion that *Lucrece* was intended as a companion poem for *Venus and Adonis.*

Hunter, G. K. "A Source for Shakespeare's 'Lucrece'?" *Notes and
Queries* CXCVII (2 February 1952): 46.

Notes that none of the traditional sources given for *The Rape
of Lucrece* can account for the scene change from Collatium to
Rome. The critic proposes another source for consideration:
Barnaby Googe's translation of *The proverbes of the noble and
woorthy souldier Sir John Lopez de Mendoza . . . with the Paraphrase of D. Peter Diaz* (1579). Hunter argues that although this
translation closely follows Livy's version of the Lucrece story,
it also incorporates the same scene change found in Shakespeare's *Lucrece.*

Janakiram, A. "Chastity and Unreason in Shakespeare's 'The Rape
of Lucrece'." *Triveni* 49, No. 2 (July-September 1980): 21-30.

Analyzes *The Rape of Lucrece* in terms of themes, language,
and imagery, and concludes that Shakespeare sought a sympathetic portrayal of the heroine and envisioned her as an "emblem of Roman honour and fidelity." The critic asserts that
even by Elizabethan standards, Lucrece's suicide is a noble gesture. In addition, Janakiram remarks that the poem examines
two concepts of love: 1) the lust exemplified by Tarquin wherein
reason succumbs to passion, and 2) the rational manifestation
of love in marriage characterized by chastity and fidelity.

Kerrigan, John. "Keats and 'Lucrece'." *Shakespeare Survey* 41
(1989): 103-18.

Examines John Keats's marked-up copy of Shakespeare's *Poeti-
cal Works* and argues, after a comparison of the two poets, that
The Rape of Lucrece is "the missing source of [Keats's] 'Saint
Agnes' Eve'." In regard to *Lucrece,* Kerrigan argues that
Shakespeare did not exploit all the dramatic potential of the Lu-
crece story; in fact, the critic asserts, Shakespeare chose to be

"untheatrical." The poet's dominant concern, he avers, is "to show in *Lucrece* an initiation by violence into reading."

Kramer, Jerome A. and Kaminsky, Judith. " 'These Contraries Such Unity Do Hold': Structure in 'The Rape of Lucrece'." *Mosaic* X, No. 4 (Summer 1977): 143-55.

Attempts to show that, paradoxically, Shakespeare's use of "contraries"—including antitheses, dichotomies, and irony—in developing theme and characterization provides a sense of formal unity. The critics review a range of scholarship devoted to demonstrating that *The Rape of Lucrece* fails artistically because it lacks a unified structure. In contrast, Kramer and Kaminsky argue that several image patterns, particularly those of animals, vegetation, and the elements, are evident throughout the poem and are recurrently invoked to develop such oppositions as the one between saint and devil.

Kuhl, E. P. "Shakespeare's 'Rape of Lucrece'." *Philological Quarterly* XX, No. 3 (July 1941): 352-60.

Seeks to reconcile modern critical disdain of *The Rape of Lucrece* with the poem's public popularity during Shakespeare's time by recuperating the work's socio-political context. Kuhl argues that Shakespeare chose the time-proven Lucrece story to serve as a vehicle for addressing contemporary issues and for advancing his own political agenda and views of kingship, tyranny, lust, and justice. Contemporary writers and pamphleteers often drew an analogy between Rome's era of civil wars and England's own domestic struggles, according to Kuhl, and *Lucrece* engages that tradition.

Lanham, Richard A. "The Politics of 'Lucrece'." *The Hebrew University Studies in Literature*, VIII, No. 1 (Spring 1980): 66-76.

Argues that in *The Rape of Lucrece* Shakespeare depicts "the change from a naive sense of self, role and society," governed by the chivalric ideal, to a "radically dramatic" or politicized kind of self and society. In order to render this transformation, Lanham maintains, *Lucrece* looks both backward to its classical antecedents, Ovid and Livy, as a "declaration of poetic mastery," and forward to Shakespeare's mature drama as allegory and "a political lesson for princes," specifically Southampton. By showing the causal relationship between the rape of Lucrece and the founding of the republic, the poem allegorically depicts the historical moment when private acts become political gestures.

Lever, J. W., ed. Introduction to *The Rape of Lucrece,* by William Shakespeare, pp. 7-28. Middlesex, England: Penguin Books, 1971.

Assesses the strengths and weaknesses of *The Rape of Lucrece.* Lever divides the poem in two parts and finds the first half, the third-person narrative recounting Tarquin's "exploit," more artistically accomplished, except for Tarquin's apparent lack of motive for his crime. In the second half, Lucrece's first-person lament is too verbose, "too explicitly moralizing," and, ironically, the heroine's eloquence is ultimately "self-defeating." Lever argues that Shakespeare was hampered by his choice of the declamatory style common in sixteenth-century narrative verse. Given the poet's vast imagination, the "narrowly moralistic mold" in which Lucrece is cast is unable to sustain the moral complexities and ambiguities which Shakespeare wishes to explore; it also prevents him from endowing his protagonists (especially Lucrece) with a credible psychology. Nevertheless, Lever maintains, the poem's achievements are noteworthy within the Elizabethan context and adumbrate the poet's eventual progress from narrative to drama.

Levin, Richard. "The Ironic Reading of 'The Rape of Lucrece' and the Problem of External Evidence." *Shakespeare Survey* 34 (1981): 85-92.

Responds to those critics, especially D. C. Allen and Roy W. Battenhouse (see excerpts above, 1962 and 1969) who find a "covert, inner ironic" subtext critical of the poem's overtly sympathetic portrayal of Lucrece. Charging that the ironists' stance is ahistorical, Levin gives several examples of Elizabe-

than writers who exhibited sympathy for Lucrece. In addition, he points out that Shakespeare's references to Lucrece in other works undermine the ironic reading, for these describe her either as "a model of chastity or an innocent victim."

Maus, Katharine E. "Taking Tropes Seriously: Language and Violence in Shakespeare's 'Rape of Lucrece'." *Shakespeare Quarterly* XXXVII, No. 1 (Spring 1986): 66-82.

Explores the relationship between figurative language and characterization in *The Rape of Lucrece,* discerning an "intimacy between the characters' metaphors and their decisions and between their language and their psychological states." Maus argues that both Tarquin and Lucrece come to understand the metaphors they use to figuratively describe themselves as "literal representations, conceptions of their state," which they in turn use to rationalize their choice of action. Thus, both characters become, in a sense, prisoners of their own metaphors and suffer the destructive effects of the violence latent in conventional, figurative terms, particularly the "language of desire." The critic suggests that Shakespeare is struck by the "obtrusiveness and unreliability of language" and by the problematic nature of metaphor; the poet reveals, she believes, a "profoundly uneasy self-consciousness about poetic technique and resources."

Maxwell, J. C., ed. Introduction to *The Poems,* by William Shakespeare, pp. ix-xxxvi. Cambridge: At the University Press, 1966.

Provides commentary on sources, the complaint genre, and a range of critical views of *The Rape of Lucrece.* Maxwell regards Shakespeare's characterization of Tarquin as particularly noteworthy in that it foreshadows later Shakespearean tragedy. Shakespeare's portrayal of Lucrece is problematic, the critic contends: the poet's moral ambiguity renders Augustinian objections inevitable.

Miola, Robert S. " 'The Rape of Lucrece': Rome and Romans." In his *Shakespeare's Rome,* pp. 18-41. Cambridge: Cambridge University Press, 1983.

Evaluates *The Rape of Lucrece* within the context of Shakespeare's conception of Rome and Romans as developed in *Titus Andronicus, Julius Caesar, Antony and Cleopatra, Coriolanus,* and *Cymbeline.* Although these works all concern the relationship between private and public virtue, the predominantly narrative form of *Lucrece* suffers by comparison with the dramatic presentations of this theme: "What is self-conscious and external in the poem will become subtle and integral in the plays."

Montgomery, Robert L. "Shakespeare's Gaudy: The Method of 'The Rape of Lucrece'." In *Studies in Honor of Dewitt T. Starnes,* edited by Thomas P. Harrison, Archibald A. Hill, Ernest C. Mossner, and James Sledd, pp. 25-36. Austin: University of Texas, 1967.

Defends Shakespeare from the common critique that *The Rape of Lucrece* is too verbose on the grounds that the poet is employing a rhetorical technique designed to "shift perspective, create mood, explore psychology, moralize and suggest a broad philosophical atmosphere." The critic asserts that it was not the poet's intention to gather all these effects into an "ideologically coherent whole." According to Montgomery, the disruptions in narrative action, such as Lucrece's apostrophes, are attempts to translate movement into "motivation and sensation."

Muir, Kenneth and O'Loughlin, Sean. "Tutelage." In their *The Voyage to Illyria: A New Study of Shakespeare,* pp. 31-80. New York: Barnes & Noble, 1937.

Examines the imagery in *The Rape of Lucrece* and finds, in contrast to the nature imagery of *Venus and Adonis,* that most of Shakespeare's figurative language here derives from "his reading and the intercourse of civilized life." The critics also discern a "deeper power and a greater sense of drama" in *Lucrece* than in the earlier work, and they conclude that the poem's form and content anticipates much of Shakespeare's dramatic development.

Phillips, G. W. "A Discussion of the Authenticity of 'Venus' and

'Lucrece'." In his *Lord Burghley in Shakespeare: Falstaff, Sly and Others,* pp. 199-200. London: Thornton Butterworth, 1936.

Postulates that Shakespeare was not the author of *The Rape of Lucrece* but merely the dedicator and that *Lucrece* and *Venus and Adonis* are both anonymous poems, possibly composed by many writers. Phillips argues that the narrative poems differ from Shakespeare's other work in moral tone, poetic value, style, and diction. The critic also cites Sonnet 76 wherein Shakespeare appears to deny that he has composed the kind of polished, rhetorical verse more frequently associated with the university wits but prevalent in *Lucrece.*

Platt, Michael. " 'The Rape of Lucrece' and the Republic for Which It Stands." *The Centennial Review* XIX, No. 2 (Spring 1975): 59-79.

Argues that *The Rape of Lucrece* constitutes an "abbreviation" of epics in addressing both the fall of Troy and the founding of Rome. However, Platt remarks, in contrast to the epics of Homer and Virgil, Shakespeare's poem equates the founding of Rome not with Aeneas but with the founding of the republic by Lucrece, Collatine, and Brutus. Thus, according to Platt, Shakespeare shifts the focus away from the legacy of tyranny as represented by Tarquin and indirectly seeks to mobilize popular support for such republican values as honor and self-sacrifice, exemplified by Lucrece.

Rollins, Hyder Edward, ed. Appendix to *The Poems,* by William Shakespeare, pp. 406-523. A New Variorum Edition of Shakespeare, edited by Joseph Q. Adams. Philadelphia: J. B. Lippincott Co., 1938.

Offers an informative introduction to *The Rape of Lucrece.* With many critical references, Rollins addresses such topics as the texts, date of composition, sources, criticism, literary fashion, and popularity of *Lucrece.*

Rosand, David. " 'Troyes Painted Woes': Shakespeare and the Pictorial Imagination." *The Hebrew University Studies in Literature* VIII, No. 1 (Spring 1980): 77-97.

Analyzes the function of the ecphrasis, Shakespeare's description of the "painted piece" depicting the fall of Troy, in *The Rape of Lucrece.* In the Renaissance tradition, according to the critic, although the eyes were typically revered as the "paragone of the senses," aesthetic theory held that poetry could achieve the same emotional effect as painting, through a rhetoric of mimesis, a "pictorial vocabulary" capable of recreating visual images through language. Rosand argues that Shakespeare skillfully employs this rhetoric of mimesis in order to instruct his readers in "the proper reading of images": "to look with our ears."

Simone, R. Thomas. *Shakespeare and 'Lucrece': A Study of the Poem and Its Relation to the Plays.* Salzburg: Universitat Salzburg, 1974, 228 p.

Proposes that *The Rape of Lucrece* is characterized by "thematic exploration through digression and expansion" in which Shakespeare employs a range of styles to state for the first time his theory of tragedy—of damnation and of innocence. In addition, the critic discusses previous versions of the Lucrece story and relates Shakespeare's poem to his other works and artistic development. In an epilogue, Simone surveys scholarly evaluations of *Lucrece.*

Soellner, Rolf. "Shakespeare's 'Lucrece' and the Garnier-Pembroke Connection." *Shakespeare Studies* XV (1982): 1-20.

Investigates the possibility that Shakespeare, in composing *The Rape of Lucrece,* was influenced by three Neoclassical closet tragedies written by Robert Garnier and Samuel Daniel and published under the patronage of Mary Herbert, Countess of Pembroke. Soellner argues that Shakespeare adopted the pattern established by these "heroine tragedies," although his superior treatment widens the scope of the form. Additionally, the critic suggests that Shakespeare's "fervent" dedication of *Lucrece* to Southampton was intended to reassure his patron that the poet would not abandon him for the Countess of Pembroke, "a more refined and prestigious competitor."

Stimpson, Catharine R. "Shakespeare and the Soil of Rape." In *The Woman's Part: Feminist Criticism of Shakespeare,* edited by Carolyn Ruth Swift Lenz, Gayle Greene, and Carol Thomas Neely, pp. 56-64. Urbana: University of Illinois Press, 1980.

Explores Shakespeare's conception of rape in *The Rape of Lucrece* and in *Titus Andronicus, Measure for Measure, Coriolanus,* and *Cymbeline.* Stimpson concludes that Shakespeare aptly and sympathetically portrays rape victims and other abused women and chastises rapists; however, the patriarchal order that governs sexual identity and relationships remains unchallenged. Shakespeare's protest, Stimpson argues, is not directed at the "confinements" imposed by society, in which female identity is equated with sexual identity, "but against assaults upon" those confinements.

Tolbert, James M. "The Argument of Shakespeare's 'Lucrece': Its Sources and Authorship." *Texas Studies in English* XXIX (1950): 77-90.

Asserts that the Argument prefacing *The Rape of Lucrece* was not written by Shakespeare but was hastily added by "a friend or hack" as an afterthought, perhaps on commission of the publisher. Tolbert suggests that the Argument was compiled from three sources: the Tarquinius Superbus entry in Thomas Cooper's thesaurus; a passage from Livy; and Thomas Lanquet's version of the Lucrece story in *Cooper's Chronicle* (1549).

Velz, John W. " 'Nothing Undervalued to Cato's Daughter': Plutarch's Porcia in the Shakespeare Canon." In *Comparative Drama* II, No. 4 (Winter 1977-78): 303-15.

Proposes that the idea for the passage in *The Rape of Lucrece* in which Lucrece empathizes with the figure of Hecuba in the painting of Troy derived from a similar episode told by Plutarch. According to Velz, Shakespeare combined Plutarch's story of Porcia mourning before the painting of Andromache with Virgil's two accounts of the fall of Troy to form his portrait of Lucrece.

Wendell, Barrett. " 'Venus and Adonis' and 'The Rape of Lucrece'." In his *William Shakspere: A Study in Elizabethan Literature,* pp. 51-65. New York: Charles Scribner's Sons, 1895.

Maintains that literary fashion at the time *The Rape of Lucrece* was written subordinated ideas to verbal ingenuity. Elizabethan phrase-makers frequently retold classic tales in ornate, inventive, and contemporary terms, the critic notes. Although Wendell instructs readers to consider Shakespeare's narrative poems as "little else than elaborate feats of phrase-making," he argues that Shakespeare distinguished himself from his literary rivals in his occasional use of "the concrete phrase, more true to nature."

Wilbur, Richard. Introduction to *The Narrative Poems and Poems of Doubtful Authenticity,* edited by Richard Wilbur and Alfred Harbage, pp. 8-21. Baltimore: Penguin Books, 1974.

Contends that style, rather than content, is paramount in *The Rape of Lucrece;* even the appearance of psychological probing that sometimes gives the illusion of depth of characterization results, Wilbur declares, from the poet's desire for more elements to be "balanced and elaborated," and from his impulse to exhibit his rhetorical prowess. Wilbur also comments on literary influences and sources and on a few "passages to admire," including "Lucrece's contemplation of the painting of Troy."

Wilson, R. Rawdon. "Shakespearean Narrative: 'The Rape of Lucrece' Reconsidered." *Studies in English Literature 1500-1900* 28, No. 1 (Winter 1988): 39-59.

Declares that *"The Rape of Lucrece* is a compendium of the conventions that constitute the embedded narratives, many and frequent, of the plays." Stage action in the plays is often interrupted by characters who deliver narratives that are apparently unrelated or superfluous in terms of dramatic development; these occurrences reflect the emphasis on narrative in the author's Renaissance education. In *Lucrece,* according to Wilson, two examples of Shakespeare's narrative method are evident in his modification of the Lucrece legend: elaboration and allusions to previous versions to underscore their shortcomings.

Sonnets

DATE: Attempts to date Shakespeare's sonnets have proved extremely problematic. There is no solid evidence indicating when Shakespeare began writing the poems, when he completed them, or how long he was occupied with their composition. All that can be said with certainty is that the sonnets as we know them were completed no later than 1609, the year of their first publication. Certain historical and circumstantial evidence, however, suggests possible composition dates for the poems. Most often cited in this regard is FRANCIS MERES's reference in his *Palladis Tamia: Wit's Treasury* (1598) to Shakespeare's "sugred Sonnets" circulated "among his private friends." Whether any of the verses noted by Meres were later included in the 1609 QUARTO edition of the sonnets cannot be determined. Concrete evidence that Shakespeare had written at least two of the sonnets included in the Quarto before the turn of the century exists in William Jaggard's miscellany *The Passionate Pilgrim,* published in 1599. This work contains twenty poems, five of which are known to be by Shakespeare: Sonnets 138 and 144, marked by a number of variants from the 1609 Quarto, and three poems from *Love's Labour's Lost.* It is generally acknowledged that Jaggard's text of Sonnets 138 and 144 is corrupt and unrevised. This suggests, critics have maintained, that the poems were taken from a manuscript or manuscripts in circulation and that Shakespeare himself had no hand in preparing the two sonnets for the press.

On the basis of the evidence of Meres and Jaggard, it would appear that a number of the sonnets were written, or at least drafted, by 1598 or 1599. Earlier and later dates have been proposed, however, for many of the poems. Commentators have pursued five principal methods of inquiry in their attempts to date the sonnets. The first approach involves identifying the person or persons to whom one or more of the sonnets is addressed. Arguing that Shakespeare addressed Sonnet 145 to Anne Hathaway before she became his wife, Andrew Gurr proposed 1582 as the composition date of the poem. While Gurr's dating of Sonnet 145 has won acceptance among some scholars, others doubt that Shakespeare began writing his sonnets at the age of seventeen or eighteen. Even if Gurr's dating is correct, it applies to one sonnet only, not to the entire Quarto sequence or even a sustained portion of it. The year 1588 has also been proposed as the date for some of the sonnets in the 1609 Quarto. This determination, offered by Leslie Hotson (see Additional Bibliography), assumes that Shakespeare addressed at least some of the sonnets to William Hatcliffe of Lincolnshire. Other commentators have proposed Henry Wriothesley, third Earl of Southampton, as the recipient of Sonnets 1-126. If this view is correct, most of the sonnets, including the Dark Lady poems, were written in the early 1590s. Commentators have also pointed to William Herbert, third Earl of Pembroke, as the young man addressed in Sonnets 1-126. In the event that Herbert is indeed the addressee, the poems must date from 1596 or later. A second method of inquiry involves the identification of the Rival Poet referred to in Sonnets 79, 80, 83, and 86. The man most often nominated in this respect is Christopher Marlowe, whose death in 1593 apparently renders im-

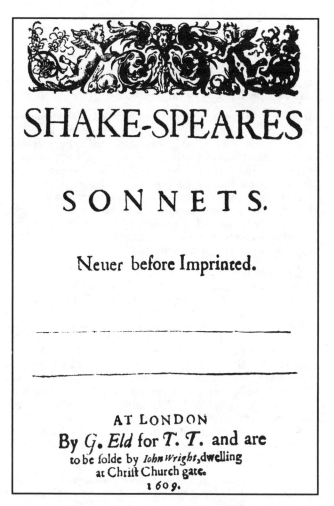

SHAKE-SPEARES

SONNETS.

Neuer before Imprinted.

AT LONDON
By *G. Eld* for *T. T.* and are
to be folde by *Iohn Wright,* dwelling
at Chrift Church gate.
1609.

Title page of the 1609 edition of Shakespeare's Sonnets.

possible a post-1593 dating of these poems. George Chapman has also been named as the rival; if indeed he is the competitor alluded to, the relevant sonnets likely date from the mid-1590s. Many critics are unwilling to date the sonnets on evidence of the rival's identity alone. Of greater value, they believe, are topical references in the poems. Citing an apparent reference to the Spanish Armada in Sonnet 107, Hotson argued that the poem was composed in 1588. Hotson's view, which hinges upon the sense of "mortal moon" in line 5 of the poem, has been endorsed by some critics. Altogether, nearly a dozen dates have been proposed, solely on topical evidence, for this particular sonnet. The most frequently suggested dates are 1596, when Elizabeth I survived a critical illness; 1601, when Elizabeth put down the Essex rebellion; and 1603, the year of James I's succession. A fourth method of dating the sonnets is to locate parallels between the poems and Shakespeare's other works. By far the greatest number of parallels are with *The Rape of Lucrece, Venus and Adonis,*

Love's Labour's Lost, and *Romeo and Juliet,* all of which were probably written between 1592 and 1596. Commentators have cautioned, however, that these parallels may be due as much to a coincidence of content and theme as to any truly meaningful congruities of language, diction, meter, or poetic style. Furthermore, other works of the 1592-96 period, most notably *Titus Andronicus, The Taming of the Shrew,* and *Richard II,* offer few or no meaningful parallels with the sonnets. The fifth principal method of dating the sonnets involves discerning resemblances between Shakespeare's sonnets and the works of his contemporaries. This method, which forms the basis of several studies, generally points to the years 1591-92 and 1594-95 as the most likely composition dates for the majority of the poems.

It is by no means certain that any of these methods may be relied upon for accurately dating Shakespeare's sonnets. Nor is it clear that one method should be adopted to the exclusion of all others. Commentators therefore generally acknowledge the value of using a combination of methods to date the sequence. While the preponderance of evidence points to the early to mid-1590s for most of the sonnets, strong arguments have been made for dates well outside this range. Ultimately, critics concur, no well-grounded hypothesis should be ignored or discounted, for any reasonable argument may hold the key to the date of the sonnets.

TEXT: The sonnets were entered in the STATIONERS' REGISTER in 1609 in these words: "20 maii. Thomas Thorpe entred for his copie vnder th[e] [h]andes of master Wilson and master Lownes warden, a Booke called Shakespeare's *sonnettes.*" In the same year, the first edition appeared: "SHAKE-SPEARES SONNETS. Neuer before Imprinted. AT LONDON. By G. Eld for T. T., and are to be solde by *William Aspley.* 1609." Instead of "William Aspley," seven of the eleven known copies with intact title pages bear the following imprint: "*Iohn Wright,* dwelling at Christ church gate. 1609." This text, commonly known as the 1609 Quarto, or "Q," is the only witness for nearly all of Shakespeare's sonnets and is the basis for all modern editions of the poems. It is also the only authoritative text of *A Lover's Complaint,* which was printed at the end of the sonnets.

Scholars have differed widely in their estimates of the merits of the Quarto. There is no evidence that the 1609 text was printed from Shakespeare's own manuscript. Nor is it known who provided "T. T."—the publisher Thomas Thorpe—with the copy he used for his edition. These uncertainties, combined with the possibility that the sonnets manuscript may have been repointed in the printing house, make it impossible to tell how much of the Quarto's punctuation and spelling is authorial. Nor is it clear whether publication of the sonnets was authorized by Shakespeare himself. Many scholars believe, however, that given the "private" nature of the sonnets, the lack of a dedication by the poet himself, and the strong likelihood that the author did not correct proofs of the text, Shakespeare had no hand in bringing the poems into print.

A number of other texts diverge from that of the Quarto. As noted above (see *DATE* section), Sonnets 138 and 144 were printed in 1599 in *The Passionate Pilgrim,* with a number of variants from the 1609 text. Nearly all critics agree that the versions printed in *The Passionate Pilgrim* are corrupt and unrevised. Several seventeenth-century manuscript miscellanies and verse anthologies contain further variant texts. Most of these are derivative and therefore of little interest textually. Post-Quarto editions of the sonnets have no independent tex-

tual authority, although one printing has attracted considerable commentary. The volume, bearing the date 1640, was published by John Benson in 1639. The title page reads: "POEMS: WRITTEN BY WIL. SHAKE-SPEARE. Gent. Printed at *London* by *Tho. Cotes,* and are to be sold by *Iohn Benson,* dwelling in *St. Dunstans* Church-yard. 1640." Benson's publication of the sonnets was piratical. With the exception of Sonnets 138 and 144, taken from the 1612 edition of *The Passionate Pilgrim,* all the poems are reprinted from the Quarto. Benson reordered the poems, and sometimes changed masculine pronouns and adjectives into their feminine counterparts. He also interpolated other poems from *The Passionate Pilgrim* as well as from the works of Ben Jonson and John Milton in his arrangement. Benson included both *A Lover's Complaint* and Shakespeare's *The Phoenix and Turtle* in this volume. In spite of its manifold weaknesses, Benson's text was the one best known by critics for the next 150 years. Not until 1780, when Edmond Malone offered the first critical edition of the sonnets, was the textual superiority of the 1609 edition meaningfully demonstrated.

SOURCES: There is no solid evidence that Shakespeare drew directly on any single known work for the precise form or content of one or more of his sonnets. He was, however, following a tradition of sonnet writing that dates back to the fourteenth-century *Rime* of the Italian poet Petrarch. The first English sonneteer of note was Sir Thomas Wyatt, who translated a number of Petrarch's sonnets into English and wrote original compositions closely modeled on Italian antecedents. Along with his friend Henry Howard, Earl of Surrey, Wyatt is credited with introducing a vogue for sonnet-writing in England that lasted until the end of the sixteenth century. English sonnets first saw print in 1557 in *Songes and Sonettes, Written by the Ryght Honorable Lorde Henry Haward Late Earle of Surrey, and other.* This collection, which was published by Richard Tottel and contains sonnets by both Surrey and Wyatt, is now commonly called *Tottel's Miscellany.* Surrey's contribution to this work is especially significant in one important respect: he always ended his sonnets with a rhymed couplet. This practice, which was followed by most Elizabethan sonneteers, became Shakespeare's own.

In the two and one-half decades following the publication of *Tottel's Miscellany,* few new English sonnets made their way into print. In 1582, however, with the publication of Thomas Watson's *The Hecatompathia,* the writing of sonnets became a decidedly Elizabethan literary exercise. Watson's work consists of one hundred eighteen-line poems in English, each made up of three six-line stanzas. The next major sonnet collection to be published was Sir Philip Sidney's *Astrophel and Stella,* which appeared posthumously in a corrupt version in 1591. This work, which circulated in manuscript long before publication, was probably written around the time that Watson's *Hecatompathia* was published. Here, Sidney offered a carefully wrought sequence of fourteen-line sonnets rhyming ABBAABBACDCDEE. As a group, the poems chronicle the speaker's love for his beloved. Critics concur that in aspects of subject matter, tone, and form, they anticipate Shakespeare's own sonnets. Sidney's work had many imitators, including Henry Constable, Thomas Lodge, Barnebe Barnes, and Michael Drayton. These are just a few of the poets who apparently took inspiration from *Astrophel and Stella.* One work of the early 1590s is made up entirely of linked sonnets: *The Tears of Fancie; or, Love Disdained* (1593). This publication, which is signed "T. W.," is often attributed to Thomas Watson. Many critics have argued that the sequential arrangement of *Astrophel and Stella* and the sustained linked sonnets of *The Tears of Fancie* significantly influenced Shakespeare's Sonnet writing.

Aside from the sonneteers already mentioned, two others are notable as contemporaries of Shakespeare. In 1592, Samuel Daniel published the first version of his *Delia; An Ode; The Complaint of Rosamond.* Critics have noted that the theme of many of Daniel's sonnets, the transitory, ephemeral quality of physical beauty, is prominent in Shakespeare's own sequence. Edmund Spenser's *Amoretti* (1595) is the remaining major sonnet collection of the Elizabethan Age. This sequence is highly regarded for its artistry, but its connection, if any, with Shakespeare's sonnets is not judged to be especially strong or meaningful. More significant are similarities between the contents and arrangement of the 1609 Quarto and earlier sonnet collections. The Quarto, with its inclusion of *A Lover's Complaint* following the sonnets, mirrors the framework of Daniel's *Delia* and Lodge's *Phillis,* both of which contain longer poems in addition to sonnets. This has led critics to inquire whether Shakespeare may have been following a tradition involving complementary, mutually illuminating poetic statements when he composed *A Lover's Complaint.*

A few critics have attempted to demonstrate Shakespeare's use of sources for specific themes and images in his sonnets. Yet according to Hyder Edward Rollins, editor of the New Variorum edition of the poems, such attempts are generally unsuccessful (see Additional Bibliography). "[Many] of the alleged sources," Rollins contended, "turn out to be analogs or even mere commonplaces." Katharine M. Wilson, in her 1974 study *Shakespeare's Sugared Sonnets* (see Additional Bibliography), maintained that many of Shakespeare's sonnets were written as parodies of the verse of other sonnet writers. Her argument, while admired by some commentators for its ingenuity, has not been widely accepted. In *Themes and Variations in Shakespeare's Sonnets,* J. B. Leishman (see Additional Bibliography) cited affinities between Shakespeare's sonnets and those of his predecessors. Leishman concluded that evidence for direct borrowing in Shakespeare is generally so scant, so uncertain, that it tends to prove Shakespeare's distinctive originality. A few commentators have deduced borrowings from Constable, Sidney, Nicholas Breton, and Bartholomew Griffin, but the evidence has been seriously questioned in light of the conventional themes treated by all of these authors. Plato, Ovid, Horace, and Erasmus have also been named as significant influences upon the themes of Shakespeare's sonnets, but again no direct borrowings have been proved to the satisfaction of most commentators.

Authorities generally agree that in evaluating possible sources for Shakespeare's sonnets, the numerous differences are far more significant than the similarities. This suggests, they argue, that in his sonnets Shakespeare was highly original—more so than in any other of his works. Yet, critics note, Shakespeare was following a well-established English tradition of sonnet-writing. His special contribution to the vogue for sonnets, critics have concluded, therefore lies chiefly in his sustained poetic artistry.

CRITICAL HISTORY: Critical approaches to the sonnets have varied through nearly four centuries of interpretation, yet a relatively small number of issues have predominated. Prominent among them are the identity of the young man or

"Friend" addressed in Sonnets 1-126, the possible autobiographical basis of the poems, and the artistic merit of these verses. Throughout the nineteenth century and the first decades of the twentieth, commentators devoted a great deal of attention to identifying the Friend and determining whether the sonnets are autobiographical. From the 1930s to the present, however, critics have been more concerned with such issues as language, imagery, tone, and structure. Twentieth-century scholars have also explored Shakespeare's treatment of the motifs of time and love in the sonnets. And from 1950 to the present, they have analyzed the poet's representation of the relationship between the Friend and the speaker, with little attention to questions of personal biography. Additionally, a number of secondary concerns have persisted throughout the critical history of the sonnets, including the poems addressed to the Dark Lady, the arrangement of the 1609 Quarto, and the significance of the sonnets alluding to a Rival Poet.

The first mention of sonnets by Shakespeare was by Francis Meres in 1598. His reference to the poet's "sugred Sonnets" is considered highly important in the dating of these verses. The next reference to the sonnets is the dedication in the Quarto itself. Signed "T. T." for Thomas Thorpe, the dedication names a "Mr. W. H." as "the onlie begetter of these insuing sonnets." The identity of "Mr. W. H.," as well as the exact sense in which Thorpe considered him "the onlie begetter" of the sonnets, has given rise to extensive commentary and conjecture. It was not until 1640 that the sonnets were next given public notice, and then it was in Benson's pirated, highly corrupt edition. In his preface to the reader, Benson referred to the poems he was publishing as "*Seren,* cleere and eligantly plaine, such gentle straines as shall recreate and not perplexe your braine, no intricate or cloudy stuffs to puzzell intellect, but perfect eloquence."

In the eighteenth century, commentators offered their opinions on a variety of issues, including the identity of the persons addressed in the sonnets, whether the verses are licentious, and the literary merit of these poems. Two critics, Charles Gildon in 1710 and George Sewell in 1725, were concerned with the authenticity of the sonnets; both believed them to be genuine works of Shakespeare. Gildon also claimed to discern an unfavorable effect of the works of Petrarch on Shakespeare's treatment of love. And Sewell alluded to the object of Shakespeare's desires in the sonnets as "a Mistress," noting the poet's indebtedness to Edmund Spenser for the conceit of "a real or an imaginary Lady." Shakespeare's sonnets received little further attention from critics until the fourth quarter of the eighteenth century, when one of the earliest textual critics of Shakespeare's works, Edmond Malone, helped spur a renewed interest in Shakespeare's nondramatic poetry. In notes to the 1780 edition of Shakespeare's plays and poems, Malone and George Steevens offered their judgments of the sonnets. Malone described as "not . . . improbable" a theory proposed by Thomas Tyrwhitt that "Mr. W. H." in the Quarto dedication stands for W. Hughes, an actor in Shakespeare's company. Malone also discussed the artistic merits of the poems, maintaining that their "great defects" are neither their "affectation" nor their many conceits, but their "want of variety, and the majority of them not being directed to a female." Steevens generally dispraised the sonnet form as quaint and artificial, claiming that this "species of composition" had "reduced the most exalted poets to a level with the meanest rhimers." Ten years later, in his own edition of Shakespeare's works, Malone returned to the question of the gender of the person addressed in the sonnets. Responding to a disparaging footnote in Steevens's 1780 edition of Shakespeare's works in which the critic expressed his "disgust and indignation" at the thought of the poet addressing a man as "the master-mistress of my passions" (Sonnet 20), Malone asserted that although this kind of expression "cannot but appear strange to a modern reader," "such addresses to men were common in Shakespeare's time, and were not thought indecorous." Subsequently, in a note in his fifteen-volume edition of Shakespeare's plays (1793), Steevens informed readers of his collection that he has not included the sonnets because "the strongest act of Parliament . . . would fail to compel readers into their service."

Steevens's negative view of Shakespeare's sonnets was shared by other eighteenth-century critics. For example, in 1785, the Irish essayist John Monck Mason referred to the sonnets as "miserable," made up of "a dozen insipid lines" that "serve as an introduction to an epigram of two, which generally turns upon some forced conceit." Mason added that only Shakespeare's "violent attachment" to the Italian poets who originated the sonnet could have induced him to compose in such a form. Alexander Chalmers, a Scottish historical critic, contended that the sonnets, "as a whole poem . . . have two of the worst faults, that can degrade any writing": tediousness and obscurity. He also was concerned with the question of the identity of the person addressed in these verses, maintaining that all of Shakespeare's sonnets are addressed to Elizabeth I. He emphasized the queen's passion for flattery, noted that poets and ministers of her court gained preferment by eulogizing her, and asserted that many Elizabethan writers conventionally praised the youthful beauty of the queen and referred to her in masculine terms.

From 1800 to 1850, commentators focused on such questions as the artistic merit of the sonnets, their possible autobiographical nature, and the identities of the persons the poet is addressing. In 1800, Nathan Drake averred that the sonnets are "buried beneath a load of obscurity and quaintness," and he commended Steevens for not including the sonnets in his 1793 edition of Shakespeare's works. Seventeen years later, however, in a significant departure from his earlier view, Drake argued that although these verses have been "rendered hard and repulsive by the peculiarities of the period of their production," one need only "search beneath, in order to discover a rich ore of thought, imagery, and sentiment." In this 1817 essay, Drake also commented on the identities of "W. H." and the Dark Lady. He surmised that the "W. H." referred to by Thorpe in the dedication as the "begetter" was the "obtainer" of the sonnets manuscript, and therefore should not be confused with the Friend addressed in Sonnets 1-126—whom Drake identified as Henry Wriothesley, Earl of Southampton. Drake further maintained that because no poet would "publish such an open confession of his own culpability," the Dark Lady sonnets "were solely intended to express, aloof from all individual application, the contrarieties, the inconsistencies, and the miseries of illicit love." Other critics of the period also considered the identity of the Dark Lady and the Friend. Writing in 1832, James Boaden disputed Chalmers's claim that Sonnets 1-126 are addressed to Elizabeth I, suggesting instead that they were written in honor of William Herbert, Earl of Pembroke. D. L. Richardson responded to Boaden's contentions in 1835. Like Drake, he proposed that the "onlie begetter" mentioned in the dedication refers to the obtainer of the sonnets, not their object or inspirer. The sonnets "are addressed," Richardson claimed,

"to several different individuals, male and female, in some cases real and in others imaginary."

Commentators of the period also strongly emphasized psychological and autobiographical issues in their remarks on the Friend and the Dark Lady. In an 1803 note, Samuel Taylor Coleridge proposed that Shakespeare's love for his male friend was "pure" and free from sexual desire. Later, in 1833, he further declared that although it is possible for one man to love another, the passion depicted in the sonnets "could only have come from a man deeply in love, and in love with a woman." In 1821, James Boswell questioned the assumption behind critical attempts to identify the Friend and the Dark Lady of Shakespeare's sonnets, denying that these verses are autobiographical. He asserted that while little is known of Shakespeare's life, what is known does not coincide with the apparent character of the sonnets. In contrast, in 1827, William Wordsworth suggested that the sonnets are the "key" with which Shakespeare "unlocked his heart." Wordsworth's remark, touching as it does on the personal motivation of the sonnets, is one of the best-known statements concerning the possible autobiographical basis of the poems. Two years after Wordsworth's claim, Anna Brownell Jameson viewed the sonnets similarly, regarding these poems as the only writings of Shakespeare which reveal "his personal feelings and affections." She also believed that Sonnets 1-55 are addressed to Southampton, others to Elizabeth Vernon on Southampton's behalf, and still others to an unknown woman whom the poet found irresistably fascinating. A decade later, the English historian Henry Hallam contended that the sonnets are directed to a real person and that they express sincere and intense emotions of the heart. He added that the poems "relate to one definite period of the poet's life," when an attachment to a woman was disrupted by a passionate friendship with a young man.

Several early nineteenth-century critics addressed the issue of the artistry of the sonnets. In an undated marginal note, Wordsworth labeled Sonnets 127-54 "abominably harsh, obscure, and worthless," adding that the preceding ones are generally much superior. In 1815, however, Wordsworth praised the "exquisite feelings felicitously expressed" in Shakespeare's sonnets. Writing in 1803 in direct response to Wordsworth's undated note, Coleridge declared that the sonnets are "rich in metre [and] full of thought and exquisite diction." Coleridge spoke favorably of the sonnets again in 1833, describing them as "characterized by boundless fertility and laboured condensation of thought." In 1817, the Romantic poet and critic John Keats also praised the sonnets, stating that they "seem to be full of fine things said unintentionally" and quoting part of Sonnet 12 as an example of such inadvertent beauties. In the same year, William Hazlitt similarly maintained that many of the sonnets "are highly beautiful in themselves," noting also the interest they have as mirrors of Shakespeare's personal feelings. Walter Savage Landor, however, offered qualified praise of these poems, declaring that while "not a single one is very admirable," only a "few sink very low."

At least two new critical approaches to the sonnets emerged during the first half of the nineteenth century: the first involved identifying the Rival Poet; the second determining the proper arrangement, or sequence, of the poems. The principal commentator on the first topic was Boaden, who theorized that the rival is Samuel Daniel. Boaden noted that Shakespeare had motive for regarding Daniel as a competitor because Daniel dedicated his *Defence of Ryme* (1603) to "W. H." At least two critics commented on the arrangement of the poems in the Quarto. Writing in 1838, Charles Armitage Brown asserted that although the Quarto is legitimate, the sonnets should be arranged into six "poems" consisting of twenty-two to twenty-six "stanzas" each. Each of these "poems," Brown maintained, is unified by such dominant concerns as urging the Friend to marry or reproaching him for his faults and susceptibility to flattery. Eleven years after Brown, Charles Knight argued that the sonnets should not be read as one continuous poem describing a significant experience in the writer's life. He maintained that although the arrangement of the Quarto gives the impression that all the verses trace actual events in Shakespeare's life, many of the sonnets are dramatic and convey imaginary characters and feelings.

Much was contributed to the study of the sonnets by nineteenth-century German critics. In 1811, August Wilhelm Schlegel proposed that the sonnets are rich sources for Shakespeare's biography. According to Schlegel, the sonnets provide important information about Shakespeare's sentiments, passions, and "youthful errors." The critic's younger brother, Friedrich Schlegel, also viewed the sonnets as valuable historical documents. He argued that the poems are indispensable to a proper understanding of their author, because in his plays Shakespeare seldom reveals his thoughts and emotions. In 1839, Hermann Ulrici contended that the sonnets underscore the fact that Shakespeare is "pre-eminently a *dramatic* poet," for these poems reveal "not merely [his] own individual personality . . . but still more the character of the personalities (whether real or feigned) whom he is addressing." The critic also emphasized the epigrammatic nature of the sonnets, claiming that they are argumentative and, as such, "more like speeches than lyrical songs." Ten years later, G. G. Gervinus stressed the autobiographical character of Sonnets 1-126. He divided these into eight groups that trace, in sequence, the poet's growing relationship with his Friend, their falling out and separation, and, ultimately, the poet's serene acceptance of the course of events. Gervinus called attention to the progressively more serious tone of Sonnets 62-95 and remarked on the violent jealousy, even "tragic despondency," in Sonnets 78-95. During the second half of the century, other German critics took up already well-established issues. D. Barnstorff, for example, averred that the subject of the sonnets is the poet's "own *self*" and speculated that the poems in the Quarto were intentionally made to appear as if Shakespeare himself had not published them. The poet orchestrated this deception, Barnstorff added, to veil the true nature of his sonnets from his contemporaries.

The second half of the nineteenth century witnessed refinements of established positions, as well as the introduction of new issues in criticism of the sonnets. The question of the autobiographical basis of the poems continued to attract a great deal of interest. Alluding to Wordsworth's 1827 remark that the sonnets provide the "key" to Shakespeare's heart, English poet and playwright Robert Browning declared in 1876 that if the verses were truly self-revealing, "the less Shakespeare he!" A year later, F. J. Furnivall asserted that the sonnets are indeed autobiographical. He further argued that while accepting this view means that we recognize sensual errors on the poet's part, this does not undermine Shakespeare's genius. Furnivall's analysis was echoed in 1881 by Edward Dowden, who declared that although the sonnets may demonstrate that Shakespeare was not free from moral faults,

they nevertheless show him to be a man whose errors are traceable to his sensitive, imaginative nature. Several late nineteenth-century critics strongly disputed such autobiographical or personal views of the sonnets. Gerald Massey, for example, writing in 1864, declared that in most of the sonnets Shakespeare is simply the spokesman in a dramatic monologue. Similarly, James Orchard Halliwell-Phillipps, exploring what he termed the "personal application of the sonnets," concluded that there are "abundant difficulties" connected with any autobiographical theory, most notably that "the victim of spiritual emotions that involve criminatory reflections does not usually protrude them voluntarily on the consideration of society." Sidney Lee disputed the notion that the poems are autobiographical, arguing that they are decidedly conventional. According to Lee, Shakespeare was concerned not with conveying personal experiences, but with adapting the sonnet form to his own talents. Lee did claim, however, that Sonnets 40, 41, 42, 133, 134, and 144—those dealing with the speaker's loss of his mistress to his young friend—treat an unconventional theme and appear autobiographical in emotional intensity.

Several studies concerning the identities of the young friend, the mistress, and the Rival Poet appeared toward the end of the nineteenth century. In 1884, W. A. Harrison argued that the Dark Lady is probably Queen Elizabeth's maid of honor, Mary Fitton, who is known to have had connections with the LORD CHAMBERLAIN'S MEN, Shakespeare's acting company. Harrison's hypothesis was supported by Thomas Tyler, who noted correspondences between historical evidence concerning Fitton's physical appearance and Shakespeare's description of the Dark Lady in Sonnets 127-52. On the basis of apparent correspondences between recorded events and allusions in the sonnets, Tyler also endorsed the case for Pembroke as the Friend of Sonnets 1-126. The best-known attempt to identify the Friend is Oscar Wilde's "The Portrait of Mr. W. H." (1889). Wilde suggested, by way of a fictional sketch, that "W. H." is William Hughes, a boy-actor in Shakespeare's company. Wilde proposed that Hughes's youth, beauty, and compelling acting ability made him a source of inspiration for Shakespeare and an embodiment of the poet's dramatic ideals. Although the correlation of "W. H." with William Hughes had been suggested as early as 1780 by Edmond Malone, critics have noted that Wilde was the first to propose that the Friend was a boy-actor and to interpret many of the sonnets in light of this possibility.

From 1850 to 1890, commentators also examined Platonic elements in the sonnets, stylistic issues, and the arrangement of these poems in the Quarto. In 1862, John A. Heraud contended that the sonnets are directed to Shakespeare's "interior individuality," and he proposed that the poems are unified by a Platonic philosophy. The subject and the object of the sonnets are the same, Heraud maintained: the human ideal, which is both male and female, a part of the poet but separate from him. Heraud's study of the sonnets was followed six years later by another Platonic reading of the poems. In 1868, Richard Simpson contended that a Platonic philosophy of love and beauty, modified by Italian and English Renaissance sonneteers, informs and unifies Shakespeare's sonnets. He identified six levels of love—from the lowest of passion and awareness of beauty based solely on physical perception to the highest founded on the lover's recognition of truth in the beloved—in Sonnets 1-126. Although little aesthetic commentary on the sonnets was offered by late-nineenth century critics, several scholars noted in passing high points in the poetry. What commentary there was was largely favorable—a confirmation of Shakespeare's eminence as a sonneteer that contrasts markedly with the numerous negative appraisals of the previous century. One late nineteenth-century critic, however, is often cited for his decisive contribution to aesthetic evaluation: James Ashcroft Noble, who described the development of the English sonnet in an important essay published in 1880. Noble contended that the principal merit of Shakespeare's sonnets is "their pervading Shakespearianism," a quality the critic defined as "an unmistakable amplitude of treatment, a large utterance, [and] a more impressive spiritual present." Noble also modified Coleridge's claim that the sonnets display a "condensation of thought," asserting that "the thing which gives to them their specific gravity is not what is usually understood by thought, but what may rather be described as intellectualized emotion."

Both Thomas Tyler and George Wyndham addressed the question of sonnet arrangement in the Quarto. Tyler judged it to be legitimate, because it provides thematic integrity among groups of poems. In this respect, he added, the burden of proof lies on those who would discredit the Quarto arrangement of the sonnets. Wyndham argued that Sonnets 1-126 can be broken down into "seven main groups, each with its own principal theme" and set off "by gaps of silence from the sonnets that succeed them." Among the themes that Wyndham identified are absence, infidelity, immortality, and "Beauty and Delay."

In the twentieth century, there has been a significant movement away from biographical criticism of the sonnets, with increasing emphasis on elements of poetic style. This tendency is especially noticeable in commentary written after 1950. Even in the first half of this century, however, such critics as L. C. Knights, George Rylands, William Empson, John Crowe Ransom, and Arthur Mizener contributed noteworthy assessments of the artistry of Shakespeare's sonnets. In 1934, Knights disparaged the biographical approach to the sonnets, asserting that the "most profitable" analysis is one which evaluates the technical elements and considers them in relation to Shakespeare's developing artistry. The critic judged that although the language and imagery in the sonnets are not as complex or encompassing as in Shakespeare's later plays, they demonstrate a significant advance from the decorative verse of his earlier works. According to Knights, the language of the sonnets plays a crucial part in conveying the meaning of the poems; the vocabulary, imagery, and diction are not merely ornamental, but rather are inseparable from the various themes within each poem. Writing in the same year as Knights, Rylands remarked on the diversity of natural imagery in the sonnets and commented on the function of the concluding couplet of the Shakespearean sonnet. He claimed that it is "employed sometimes as climax, sometimes as comment, sometimes as a dying fall," and occasionally, "it must be confessed—as a lame and impotent conclusion." In 1935, Empson assessed the emotive and connotative aspects of the language of the sonnets, emphasizing the multiple, ironic meanings of Sonnet 94. He maintained that the poet here presents the young friend as at once coldly hard but sensitive, vulnerable and impulsive, egotistic and inscrutable. These qualities, Empson declared, are the sources of the highly suggestive linking of the youth with flowers and flower imagery, a linking that gives Shakespeare a way of extolling the young man in spite of his essential egotism. A few years later, in a highly controversial essay, John Crowe Ransom contended that the majority of the sonnets are written in a ro-

mantic or associationist vein—that is, a style in which "pretty words have pleasing if indefinite associations" and whose only precision stems from the metrical pattern itself. He added that many of the remaining sonnets represent an attempt to develop a poem from a single figure of speech instead of a range of associations. In Ransom's judgment, Shakespeare's imagination was unequal to the kind of "peculiar and systematic exercises" required to compose superlative metaphysical poetry. Ransom also charged that Shakespeare frequently fails to meet the requirements of the English sonnet form in terms of logic and coherence. In 1940, Mizener disputed Ranson's contention that many of the sonnets are metaphysical. He pointed out that Shakespeare's finest sonnets are characterized by a richness, complexity, and inclusiveness of poetic language that is in sharp contrast to metaphysical poetry. Mizener offered a detailed reading of Sonnet 124, calling attention to the many possible implications of its imagery and to the recurring metaphors for the destructive power of time.

During the 1950s, such critics as G. K. Hunter, C. S. Lewis, G. Wilson Knight, and M. M. Mahood contributed significantly to the growing body of commentary on the artistry of Shakespeare's sonnets. Hunter examined the techniques the poet uses to transform the conventional themes and tones of Petrarchan sonneteers and to create verse so dramatic and expressive it evokes in readers "an overwhelmingly biographical reaction." Shakespeare conveys individual emotional states within the context of brilliantly vivid language, Hunter demonstrated, and with a minimum of characterization he leads us to believe we have become involved with real personalities. Lewis offered an assessment of the sonnets' language and metrics, calling attention to such elements as rhythm, vocabulary, alliteration, and rhetorical patterns of "theme and variations" within several of these verses. Knight's focus was on Shakespeare's use of poetic symbolism in the sonnets. He declared that the principal associations the poet uses are, "on the natural plane, flowers, especially the rose; on the human plane, kingship, with gold; on the universal, the Sun, with gold; on the spiritual, jewels." Mahood evaluated the wordplay in a selection of the sonnets, contending that Shakespeare's verbal wit is most effective when he is writing "at a satisfying dramatic distance" from "the experience behind the poem," and when he is able to link the wordplay directly to the sonnet's structure. Mahood judged the sonnets about the Rival Poet and those addressed to the Dark Lady much more "formally satisfying" than those addressed to the Friend. In these two groups of poems, she contended, the irony is fully developed and, through subtle use of wordplay, Shakespeare carefully controls the counter-movement of thought from the quatrains to the final couplet.

The 1960s is a particularly important decade in the critical history of Shakespeare's sonnets. During this period, a great many commentators offered judgments on the poetic artistry of these verses. C. L. Barber, for example, demonstrated that within each sonnet, the momentum from one quatrain to the next is sustained not by the imagery—which frequently changes several times from beginning to end—but by "the patterned movement of discourse." He also remarked that in the absence of a consistent metaphorical scheme, seemingly unconnected "strains of meaning" are frequently held together by the interplay of sound and rhythm. R. P. Blackmur proposed that the sonnets represent Shakespeare's transformation of the theme of infatuation into a discourse on the principles of poetic composition. The collection "gives to infatuation a theoretic form," he asserted, and depicts "its initiation, cultivation, and history, together with its peaks of triumph and devastation." Blackmur noted that the sonnets illuminate the process through which an artist may contend with reality by creating another truth to rival it. W. H. Auden offered an assessment of the Shakespearean sonnet form, with particular attention to the concluding couplet. He also declared that melodiousness and "a mastery of every possible rhetorical device" are the most striking stylistic features of these poems. David Parker focused on verbal forms in Shakespeare's sonnets, contending that although the imperative mood predominates, it is generally disguised in other forms. At the heart of Shakespeare's eloquence, Parker judged, is the intent to persuade—either himself or another. Stephen Booth's exploration of what he termed the "paradoxical style" of Sonnet 53 has been frequently cited by later critics. Booth called attention to the conflicts between syntactical and logical patterns, remarking that nonparallel constructions help achieve a style aptly suited to the essential contrariness of the poem. Patterns of rhyme scheme, phonetics, and syntax coexist within the formal pattern of the poem, he noted, and these patterns reinforce the paradox evident in, for example, the nonparallel construction of the Adonis/Helen quatrain. Thus, Booth contended, unity and division exist simultaneously in both the sonnet's theme and structure.

Since 1970, critics have continued to offer assessments of stylistic elements in Shakespeare's sonnets. In 1970, Thomas P. Roche emphasized the logical patterns of these poems; the meaning of these verses, he contended, can best be determined by careful analysis of their logic and structure. Roche offered extended evaluations of the "intellectual abstraction" of Sonnet 94 and "the intricate balance between structure and imagery" in Sonnet 73. Later in the decade, William Bowman Piper traced what he termed "a process of poetic shift and change" in the syntax, diction, grammatical construction, and metrical organization of the sonnets. In an extensive analysis of Sonnet 104, Piper drew attention to the instability of the rhetorical and metrical patterns throughout the poem, to the change of discourse from descriptive to figurative in the third quatrain, and, especially, to the couplet, with its abrupt and shocking shift in viewpoint. In the 1980s, Heather Dubrow and Janette Dillon have offered new perspectives on the artistry of Shakespeare's sonnets. Dubrow analyzed the lyrical mode in these poems, noting how this mode heightens our emotional response to the speaker. Our identification is further intensified, she contended, by the lack of specificity about the persons, situations, and circumstances alluded to in the sonnets. Dubrow further pointed out that just as the speaker frequently searches for simplistic answers to moral chaos, so we reach out for explanations that will resolve the uncertainties and ambiguities evoked so vividly in these poems. Dillon called attention to the images of mirrors, windows, and shadows in the sonnets. In her judgment, Shakespeare employs these images in order to emphasize the young man's narcissism and underscore "the weakness, instability, and delusion" of self-love.

Shakespeare's representation of love in the sonnets has been evaluated by several critics from 1950 to the present. C. S. Lewis suggested that the poet's depiction of love in these verses resists easy classification. It moves from particularity in the early sonnets, he noted, to universality in the later ones, ultimately encompassing "all loves whether erotic, parental, filial, amicable, or feudal." G. Wilson Knight commented on the way in which symbolic language enhances the theme of love in the sonnets to the Friend. He determined that it is the idealized Friend, "the distilled truth of the boy, the eternal 'idea,' in Plato's sense," whom the poet loves, "rather than the boy himself." C. L. Barber also examined Shakespeare's expression of love for the Friend, arguing that by writing verses praising the young man's beauty and worth, the poet is able to realize and fulfill the relationship and to experience "a lover's sense of triumphing over time." In 1962, Northrop Frye outlined the antecedents of Renaissance courtly love poetry and showed that within this genre, the theme of love is variously depicted in "high" and "low" phases. Shakespeare's Sonnets 1 through 126 represent "a 'high' story of devotion," according to Frye, while the Dark Lady verses focus on desire and "the 'low' dialectic of bondage and freedom." Frye further pointed out that pairs of male friends recur throughout the development of the genre in which Shakespeare is writing and such relationships are traditionally depicted as a "high" form of courtly love. W. H. Auden proposed that the principal experience out of which Sonnets 1-126 arose was a mystical "Vision of Eros," a quasi-religious episode in which the beloved is revealed "as being of infinite sacred importance." Auden declared that the sonnets depict Shakespeare's tortured endeavor to preserve this vision. In 1986, John Kerrigan examined Shakespeare's depiction of love in the Dark Lady poems. The woman, he claimed, is generally identified with debased love: an infertile, sexually enshrined "hell" that contrasts markedly with the Friend's amplitude. Yet, Kerrigan concluded, even the young friend is not immune from the same effects of time that worked ill upon the Dark Lady, for in the sonnets, "at the last, Time circumscribes the natural world and the very springs of life."

The themes of time and mutability had been examined by several twentieth-century critics before Kerrigan. J. L. Broadbent, in a 1964 study, discussed the themes of mutability, corruption, and "undivided but separable love" in Shakespeare's sonnets. Throughout the sequence, he claimed, a "general mutability of things is observed and enacted," but an antidote is also presented: the procreation of children or art, which preserves intact the substance of beauty or the essence of love. As mentioned above, William Bowman Piper assessed the theme of time in the sonnets and called attention to the conclusion of Sonnet 104. Through most of that poem the speaker appears confident that the young man's beauty will survive the attacks of time, yet in the couplet, Piper remarked, that assurance is abruptly withdrawn. In 1985, Judith Kegan Gardiner proposed that the inexorability of time is one of the principal concerns of Shakespeare's sonnets. These poems reveal, she maintained, Shakespeare's conviction that "a committed and unified love" is the only means of transcending time.

In addition to the motifs of love and time, twentieth-century commentators have identified other thematic issues in Shakespeare's sonnets. As noted above, J. L. Broadbent pointed out the significance of the theme of procreation in these verses. In 1985, Thomas M. Greene argued that Sonnets 1-126 provide evidence of a failure to give substance to the axiom of Sonnet 1: "From fairest creatures we desire increase." In Sonnets 1-17, the critic declared, procreation is the central focus, although the Friend's refusal to marry and have children gives rise to a "terrible fear of cosmic destitution." Murray Krieger, writing in 1964, identified the motifs of state, property, and the "politics of reason" in a selection of the sonnets. These poems demonstrate, he claimed, that to destroy the hold of the "loveless political world," one must stand outside politics, fortune, and worldliness, and acknowledge "love's sovereign aloneness." In her 1981 study, Janette Dillon explored the implications of the repetition of the word "self" in the sonnets, remarking that inwardness and singleness are powerful, controlling concepts throughout the poems addressed to the Friend. Dillon argued that the poet becomes increasingly aware of the existence in himself of the very qualities of solitude, self-division, and withdrawal he has disparaged in the young man. The moral perspectives of both men, she contended, are compromised by virtue of their withdrawal from the judgments of the world into "the prison of the inward self."

Although critics from the 1930s to the present have tended to emphasize thematic and stylistic issues in their discussions of the sonnets, many early twentieth-century commentators dealt with the questions of autobiographical elements and the persons described in these poems. In 1904, A. C. Bradley declared that the sonnets are autobiographical and provide clear impressions of Shakespeare's personality. He asserted that these verses demonstrate that the poet was especially sensitive to the charms of physical beauty and had a forgiving nature. Shakespeare was "probably incapable of fierce or prolonged resentment," Bradley speculated, particularly toward someone, like his young friend, of whom he was so enamored. A few years later, Frank Harris argued that although Shakespeare revealed his nature more fully in his plays than in his lyrics, the sonnets are indeed autobiographical, conveying "the whole terrible, sinful, magical story of Shakespeare's passion." The shift away from this point of view can be seen in L. C. Knights's 1934 essay. Even if we could prove that Shakespeare's sonnets are autobiographical, Knights maintained, "the only importance they could have for us would be as poetry, as something *made out of* experience." Yet some critics continued to find intimations of the poet himself in his sonnets. C. L. Barber, for example, writing in 1960, discovered in these verses a "complex, resonant personality." Shakespeare seemingly possessed an "almost unbearable openness to desire and to life," Barber suggested, as well as an over-eagerness that repeatedly betrayed him into acting out "unworthy parts." Northrop Frye, however, recommended that Shakespeare's sonnets be read not as "transcripts of experience," but as poetry written within the framework of a particular literary convention. He declared that notwithstanding all the speculation and research that has gone into the effort to discover what these verses may tell us about Shakespeare, "our knowledge of what in the sonnets is direct biographical allegory remains precisely zero." In 1968, James Winny discerned "two distinct characters" in the narrator of Shakespeare's sonnets, but he denied that either one of them represents a self-portrait. In the sonnets on time, he remarked, the narrator is superbly self-assured, but generally the speaker presents himself as a minor poet who has enjoyed only mild success. Winny maintained that following Sonnet 112, the narrator relinquishes his habitual self-effacement and demonstrates his growing appreciation of "man's divided nature." In this respect, the critic declared, although the sonnets yield nothing about the circumstances of Shakespeare's life, they do provide an account of the development of their author's moral perspective.

The sonnets addressed to the Dark Lady and those alluding to a Rival Poet have attracted a measure of critical interest in the twentieth century. In 1956, J. W. Lever closely examined Sonnets 127 to 152, arguing that this series is governed by satire. The satire, he demonstrated, moves in a "vicious descending spiral," beginning with parodies of pseudo-Petrarchan versifiers, but soon turning to cynicism, nihilism, and even "deliberate obscenity," as the poet struggles to extricate himself from the "emotional dilemma" of loving a woman who has neither virtue nor beauty. Although Lever viewed these poems as a "fierce diatribe against sexual infatuation," he noted that they describe only one aspect of Shakespeare's estimation of human nature. To achieve a complete perspective on the poet's attitude toward love, he argued, we must be aware of the "dual interpretation" that operates throughout the entire sonnet sequence. In his 1957 overview of Sonnets 127-52, Ivor Brown stated that the Dark Lady "has not been certainly identified, and perhaps never will be" (see Additional Bibliography). Although he determined that the Dark Lady must be left as "Mistress Anonyma," Brown conceded that he favors the candidacy of Mary Fitton above all others. In 1968, Philip Edwards assessed the Dark Lady sonnets as a coherent, highly self-conscious portrayal not only of the degradations of sexual desire, but also of "the driving need of the poet to use his art . . . to make sense of his condition." Sonnets 127-54, he maintained, attempt to show how lust impels a man to self-betrayal, but ultimately, he asserted, these verses are merely descriptive rather than explanatory. A. L. Rowse, in an essay published in 1984, identified the Dark Lady as Emilia Lanier, a woman at once "promiscuous and notorious . . . a strong personality, mercurial and fascinating." According to Rowse, the Dark Lady sonnets constitute Shakespeare's retrospective thoughts about their affair, which ended when she grew tired of his attentions. Recently, Samuel Schoenbaum offered a survey of the allegorical possibilities (see Additional Bibliography). He considered the evidence for several candidates and concluded—as have many commentators—that the identity of this woman may never be known. One important contribution to criticism of the Rival Poet sonnets was made by John Dover Wilson in 1966. He suggested that these poems constitute a satire on the youthful writings of George Chapman. Although Chapman's early work is abstruse and pedantic, his later efforts received the approbation of Shakespeare's friend and patron, the Earl of Southampton, the critic noted.

From the 1950s to the present, critics have shown less interest in identifying any historical personage who may be the Friend of Sonnets 1-126 and greater curiosity about the relationship between the speaker and the youth represented in these poems. In 1952, Edward Hubler discussed the evolution of Shakespeare's attitude toward his young friend throughout the sequence. He argued that although the opening sonnets celebrate the young man's physical beauty, subsequent ones hint at his lack of integrity and constancy. Noting the poet's reproofs of the young man in the later sonnets, the critic claimed that these rebukes suggest "a certain arrogance in the young man . . . and tell of his growing self-importance." A decade later, Northrop Frye remarked on the archetypal characterization of the young friend. The relation between the poet and the youth, he maintained, had no element of sexual interest. In 1985, Judith Kegan Gardiner, Thomas M. Greene, and Joseph Pequigney offered assessments of the relationship between the Friend and the speaker of Sonnets 1-126. These poems, Gardiner asserted, deal with the impossibility of legitimizing male friendship through marriage. She pointed out that the poet seeks to assimilate the "anomalous emotions" he experiences in the relationship with his young friend and patron by treating them in terms of the conventions of marriage and the law. Nevertheless, she suggested, Shakespeare's attempts to discover in male friendship "the 'ever-fixed mark' of spiritual 'marriage' " are generally un-successful, thus accounting for "the brooding introspection" of these sonnets. Greene proposed that Sonnets 1-126 repeat-edly question the Friend's worth and suggest that the young man's value "may reside after all in the poet's fancy." In Son-net 125, he remarked, it becomes evident that writing poetry is as costly as loving, and neither expense is ever truly recov-ered. "The increase we desire from fairest creatures", he ar-gued, "never materializes." Pequigney judged that Sonnet 20 is pivotal in the sequence, claiming that it clearly demon-strates the poet is sexually attracted to the Friend. The person depicted in this sonnet, he declared, is "the classic figure of homoerotic poetry": a young man who resembles a woman and displays such "feminine" attributes as shyness, modesty, and naiveté. Pequigney maintained, however, that there is no "seductive intent" in Sonnet 20. Indeed, he argued, the poet acknowledges that the young man has been formed by Nature to gratify women.

In the past fifty years, a growing number of commentators on Shakespeare's sonnets have proposed that attempts to deter-mine autobiographical elements or personal allegory are un-likely to increase our appreciation or understanding of these poems. Instead, they have suggested, the sonnets should be approached as a purely literary effort. From 1950 to the pres-ent, critics have thus placed greater emphasis on such formal elements as language and imagery, structural design, and the motifs of beauty, love, and time. Most recently, there has been an increasing interest in Shakespeare's depiction of the relationship between the Friend and the speaker of the son-nets, with critics evaluating these figures as they would char-acters in Shakespeare's plays. Very little is certain about these verses, and scholars continue to differ over such issues as po-etic merit and the coherence of the sonnet sequence. Recent commentators generally acknowledge the rich complexities of Shakespeare's sonnets, however, and they are more likely to regard them as challenges to critical interpretation than to accept Wordsworth's confident assertion that they are the "key" to Shakespeare's heart.

FRANCIS MERES   (essay date 1598)

[*Meres was an English schoolmaster, critic, and clergyman. The following excerpt is taken from his* Palladis Tamia, Wit's Treasury *(1598), a compendium of observations and commen-tary on a wide range of topics that has played a valuable role in determining the dates of several of Shakespeare's plays and poems. Meres's specific reference here to the "sugred Sonnets" of Shakespeare is considered highly important in the dating of these poems.*]

As the soule of *Euphorbus* was thought to live in *Pythagoras:* so the sweete wittie soule of *Ovid* lives in mellifluous & hony-tongued *Shakespeare,* witnes his *Venus* and *Adonis,* his *Lu-crece,* his sugred Sonnets among his private friends, &c. (pp. 281-82)

> *Francis Meres, "A Comparative Discourse of Our English Poets with the Greeke, Latine, and Italian Poets," in his* Palladis Tamia: Wits Treasury, *1598. Reprint by Garland Publishing, Inc., 1973, pp. 279-87.*

THOMAS THORPE   (poem date 1609)

[*Thorpe was the publisher of the 1609 Quarto edition of Shake-speare's sonnets. In the following title-page dedication of this edition, he identifies a "Mr. W. H." as "the onlie begetter of these insving sonnets."*]

TO.THE.ONLIE.BEGETTER.OF.
THESE.INSVING.SONNETS.
Mr.W.H.ALL.HAPPINESSE.
AND.THAT.ETERNITIE.
PROMISED.
BY.
OVR. EVER-LIVING.POET.
WISHETH.
THE.WELL-WISHING.
ADVENTVRER.IN.
SETTING.
FORTH.

T. T.

> *Thomas Thorpe, in an excerpt in* The Shakspere Al-lusion-Book: A Collection of Allusions to Shak-spere from 1591 to 1700, Vol. I, *edited by John Munro, revised edition, 1932. Reprint by Books for Libraries Press, 1970, p. 206.*

JOHN BENSON   (essay date 1640)

[*In the following address to the reader prefacing his 1640 pi-rated and corrupt edition of the sonnets, Benson refers to the poems and sonnets of Shakespeare as "Seren, cleere and eli-gantly plaine . . . , no intricate or cloudy stuffe to puzzell in-tellect, but perfect eloquence."*]

I here presume (under favour) to present to your view, some excellent and sweetely composed Poems, of Master *William Shakespeare,* Which in themselves appear of the same puri-ty, the Authour himselfe then living avouched; they had not the fortune by reason of their Infancie in his death, to have the due accommodatiō of proportionable glory, with the rest of his everliving Workes, yet the lines of themselves will af-ford you a more authentick approbation than my assurance any way can, to invite your allowance, in your perusall you shall finde them *Seren,* cleere and eligantly plaine, such gentle straines as shall recreate and not perplexe your braine, no in-tricate or cloudy stuffe to puzzell intellect, but perfect elo-quence; such as will raise your admiration to his praise: this assurance I know will not differ from your acknowledgement. And certaine I am, my opinion will be seconded by the suffi-ciency of these ensuing Lines; I have been some what solicitus to bring this forth to the perfect view of all men; and in so doing, glad to be serviceable for the continuance of glory to the deserved Author in these his Poems.

> *John Benson, in an extract in* The Shakspere Allu-sion-Book: A Collection of Allusions to Shakspere from 1591 to 1700, Vol. I, *edited by John Munro, revised edition, 1932. Reprint by Books for Libraries Press, 1970, p. 454.*

CHARLES GILDON   (essay date 1710)

[*Gildon was the first critic to write an extended commentary on the entire Shakespearean dramatic canon. Like many other Neoclassicists, he regarded Shakespeare as an imaginative playwright who nevertheless frequently violated the dramatic "rules" necessary for correct writing. In the following excerpt, he argues that Shakespeare is indeed the author of the sonnets*] *attributed to him, claiming: "there is not one of them, that does not carry its Author's Mark, and Stamp upon it." Gildon acknowledges as well the unfavorable effect of the works of Petrarch on Shakespeare's treatment of love in his poetry.*]

I come now to *Shakespear*'s Poems the Publication of which in one Volume, and of a Piece with the rest of the Works, gave Occasion to my Perusal of his other Writings, with so much Attention, that I cou'd not easily be impos'd on by any spurious Copy of that Poet. 'Tis true there may perhaps be a *Michael Angelo* found, who may copy the Antique so admirably, as to puzzle the greatest Masters, but then, the very Copy must have the Beauty, and Merit of an Original. Thus I am confident, that tho' the Poems this Volume contains are extreamly distinguish'd in their Excellence, and Value, yet there is not one of them, that does not carry its Author's Mark, and Stamp upon it. Not only the same Manner of Thinking, the same Turn of Thought, but even the same Mode of Dress and Expression, the Decompounds, his peculiar sort of Epithets, which distinguishes his from the Verses of all his Contempories or Successors. . . . (p. 445)

But some, perhaps, who are for undervaluing what they have no Share in may say, that granting them to be *Shakespears,* yet they are not valuable enough to be reprinted, as was plain by the first Editors of his Works who wou'd otherwise have join'd them altogether.

To this I answer—That the Assertion is false, or were it not it is more, than the Objector knows by his own Judgment, and Understanding, but to prove it false we need only consider, that they are much less imperfect in their Kind, than ev'n the best of his Plays . . . ; in the next Place the first Editors were Players, who had nothing to do with any thing but the Dramatic Part, which yet they publish'd full of gross Mistakes, most of which remain to this Day; nor were they by any means Judges of the Goodness or Badness of, the Beauties or Defects of either Plays or Poems.

There is next an Objection, that if these Poems had been Genuine, they had been publish'd in the Life time of the Author and by himself, but coming out almost thirty Years after his Death there is great Reason to suspect that they are not Genuine.

To this I answer, that if nothing was to be thought his but what was publish'd in his Life time, much the greater Number of his Plays wou'd be as lyable to this Objection as his Poems. . . . No, no, there is a Likeness in one Man's Children generally, which extends not beyond the Family, and in the Children of the Brain it is always so, when they are begot by a Genius indeed. Besides these Poems being most to his Mistress it is not at all unlikely, that she kept them by her till they fell into her Executors Hands or some Friend, who would not let them be any longer conceal'd. (pp. 446-47)

This leads me to a Book lately publish'd containing only some few of his Poems confusedly put together; for what is there call'd *The Passionate Pilgrim* is no more than a medly of *Shakespear*'s thrown into a Heap without any Distinction, tho' they are on several and different Subjects. . . . The first *Stanza,* in these Poems, is call'd *The false Relief.* The next *Stanza* is call'd *The Temptation* and on quite another Subject tho' incorporated into one under that general Title of the *Passionate Pilgrim.* The next *Stanza* is call'd *Fast and Loose* and still of another Subject; the next *Stanza* tho' join'd as the Rest as Part of the same Poem is on a Subject vastly different from that of the former *Stanza* and is call'd the *Sweet Provocation,*

the same holds good of the next which is call'd *The Constant Vow.*

I might go on with the Rest, which confounds the Reader, and very much injures the Poet, by palming on his Memory such absurd Incoherences, as none but such a wise Editor cou'd ever have stumbled on. (p. 449)

Tho' Love and its Effects are often happily enough touch'd in many of these Poems, yet I must confess that it is but too visible, that *Petrarch* had a little infected his way of thinking on that Subject, yet who ever can admire Mr *Cowley*'s Mistress, has a thousand Times more Cause of Admiration of our *Shakespear* in his Love Verses, because he has sometimes such touches of Nature as will make Amends for those Points, those *Epigrammatic Acumina,* which are not or ever can be the Product of a Soul truly touch'd with the Passion of Love. (p. 450)

Charles Gildon, "Remarks on the Poems of Shakespear," in The Works of Mr. William Shakespear, Vol. 7, *edited by Charles Gildon, 1710. Reprint by AMS Press, Inc., 1967, pp. 445-64.*

GEORGE SEWELL   (essay date 1725)

[*Sewell was an eighteenth-century English critic and man of letters. The excerpt below is taken from the preface to "Volume Seven" of Pope's 1725 edition of the works of Shakespeare. After briefly concurring with Gildon on the genuineness of Shakespere's poems, he alludes to the object of Shakespeare's desires in the sonnets, whom he refers to as "a Mistress." He also notes the dramatist's indebtedness to Edmund Spenser for the conceit of "a real or an imaginary Lady," though he wrongly attributes to Shakespeare an acknowledgment of this debt in one of his sonnets. Indeed, the poem Sewell mentions was one of those in* The Passionate Pilgrim *(Sonnet 8) written not by Shakespeare but by Richard Barnfield.*]

[Mr. Gildon] republish'd [Shakespeare's] Poems from an old Impression in the Year 1710 [see excerpt above, 1710], at the same time with Mr. *Rowe*'s Publication of his Plays. He uses many Arguments to prove them genuine, but the best is the Style, Spirit, and Fancy of SHAKESPEARE, which are not to be mistaken by any tolerable Judge in these Matters. *Venus and Adonis, The Rape of Lucrece,* are out of Dispute, they being put to the Press, and dedicated by the Author himself to the Earl of *Southampton* his great Patron. So that Mr. *Rowe* is evidently mistaken when he says, *That his* Venus and Adonis *was the only Piece of Poetry he publish'd himself;* there being the same Authority for his *Rape of Lucrece,* as for the other.

IF we allow the rest of these Poems to be genuine (as I think Mr. *Gildon* has prov'd them) the Occasional ones [sonnets] will appear to be the first of his Works. A young Muse must have a Mistress to play off the beginnings of Fancy, nothing being so apt to raise and elevate the Soul to a pitch of Poetry as the Passion of Love. We find, to wander no farther, that *Spenser, Cowley,* and many others paid their First-fruits of Poetry to a real or an imaginary Lady. Upon this occasion I conjecture that SHAKESPEARE took fire on reading our admirable *Spenser,* who went but just before him in the Line of Life, and was in all probability the Poet most in Vogue at that time. To make this Argument the stronger, *Spenser* is taken notice of in one of these little Pieces as a Favourite of our Author's. He alludes certainly to the *Faery Queen* when he mentions his *Deep Conceit,* that Poem being entirely Allegorical.

It has been remark'd that more Poets have sprung from *Spenser* than all our other *English* Writers; to which let me add an Observation of the late Dr. *Garth,* that most of our late ones have been spoil'd by too early an Admiration of *Milton.* Be it to *Spenser* then that we owe SHAKESPEARE! (pp. 420-21)

George Sewell, *in an extract in* Shakespeare, the Critical Heritage: 1693-1733, Vol. 2, *edited by Brian Vickers, Routledge & Kegan Paul, 1974, pp. 419-23.*

EDMOND MALONE   (essay date 1780)

[*An eighteenth-century Irish literary scholar and editor, Malone was the first critic to establish a chronology of Shakespeare's plays. He was also the first scholar to prepare a critical edition of Shakespeare's sonnets and the first to write a comprehensive history of the English stage based on extensive research into original sources. As the major Shakespearean editor of the eighteenth century, Malone collaborated with George Steevens on Steevens's second and third editions of Shakespeare's plays and issued his own edition in 1790. His importance resides not so much in textual emendation as in his unrivaled knowledge of primary sources. The excerpt below contains Malone's famous reference to the opinions of Richard Farmer and Thomas Tyrwhitt concerning the identity of the Friend addressed in Shakespeare's sonnets. Malone disputes Farmer's claim that this person is Shakespeare's nephew William Harte, noting that in 1598, when some if not all of the sonnets were in circulation, Harte would have only been twelve years old. Malone does, however, describe as "not . . . improbable" Tyrwhitt's theory that "W. H." in the dedication of the 1609 Quarto stands for W. Hughes, an actor in Shakespeare's company.*]

Dr. Farmer supposes that many of [Shakspeare's] Sonnets are addressed to our author's nephew Mr. William Harte. But this, I think, may be doubted. Shakspeare's sister, *Joan Harte,* was born in April, 1569. Supposing her to have married at so early an age as sixteen, her eldest son William could not have been more than twelve years old in 1598, at which time these Sonnets were composed, though not published for several years afterwards. Many of them are written to show the propriety of marriage; and therefore cannot well be supposed to be addressed to a school-boy.

Mr. Tyrwhitt has pointed out to me a line in the twentieth Sonnet, which inclines me to think that the initials W. H. stand for W. Hughes. Speaking of this person, the poet says he is—

A man in *hew* all *Hews* in his controlling—

so the line is exhibited in the old copy [Thomas Thorpe's 1609 Quarto]. When it is considered that one of these Sonnets is formed entirely on a play on our author's Christian name, this conjecture will not appear improbable.—To this person, whoever he was, one hundred and twenty [six] of the following poems are addressed; the remaining twenty-eight are addressed to a lady. (p. 579)

Edmond Malone, "Sonnets," *in* Supplement to the Edition of Shakespeare's Plays Published in 1778 by Samuel Johnson and George Steevens, Vol. I, *edited by E. Malone; C. Bathurst and others, 1780.*

GEORGE STEEVENS   (essay date 1780)

[*Steevens was an English scholar who collaborated with Samuel Johnson on a ten-volume edition of Shakespeare's dramatic works in 1773. The subsequent revision of this collection, along with Steevens's own edition of 1793, formed the textual basis for the first two variorum editions of Shakespeare's plays. In the following excerpt Steevens generally dispraises the sonnet form as quaint and artificial, claiming that this "species of composition" has "reduced the most exalted poets to a level with the meanest rhimers." Thus, he suggests that the sonnets add nothing to Shakespeare's stature as an artist.*]

Of the Sonnets before us, one hundred and twenty-six are inscribed (as Mr. Malone observes [see excerpt above, 1780]) to a friend: the remaining twenty-eight (a small proportion out of so many) are devoted to a mistress. Yet if our author's Ferdinand and Romeo had not expressed themselves in terms more familiar to human understanding, I believe few readers would have rejoiced in the happiness of the one, or sympathized with the sorrows of the other. Perhaps, indeed, quaintness, obscurity, and tautology, are to be regarded as the constituent parts of this exotick species of composition. But, in whatever the excellence of it may consist, I profess I am one of those who should have wished it to have expired in the country where it was born. (p. 682)

In the mean time, let inferiour writers be warned against a species of composition which has reduced the most exalted poets to a level with the meanest rhimers; has almost cut down Milton and Shakspeare to the standards of Pomfret and—but the name of Pomfret is perhaps the lowest in the scale of English versifiers. As for Mr. Malone, whose animadversions are to follow mine [see excerpt below, 1780], "Now is he for the numbers that Petrarch flowed in" [*Romeo and Juliet,* II. iv. 38-9]. Let me however borrow somewhat in my own favour from the same speech of Mercutio, by observing that "Laura had a better love to be-rhyme her" [*Romeo and Juliet,* II. iv. 40-1]. Let me adopt also the sentiment which Shakspeare himself, on his amended judgment, has put into the mouth of his favourite character in *Love's Labour's lost:*

"Tut! none but minstrels like of *Sonneting.*"
                                   [IV. iii. 156] (p. 684)

George Steevens, "Sonnets," *in* Supplement to the Edition of Shakspeare's Plays Published in 1778 by Samuel Johnson and George Steevens, Vol. I, *edited by E. Malone; C. Bathurst and others, 1780.*

EDMOND MALONE   (essay date 1780)

[*In the following excerpt, Malone discusses the artistic merit of Shakespeare's sonnets, maintaining that their "great defects" are neither their "affectation" nor their many conceits (which Malone finds equally prevalent in the plays), but their "want of variety, and the majority of them not being directed to a female."*]

I do not feel any great propensity to stand forth as the champion of these compositions. However, as it appears to me that they have been somewhat under-rated, I think it incumbent on me to do them that justice to which they seem entitled. (p. 684)

When they are described as a mass of affectation, pedantry, circumlocution, and nonsense, the picture appears to me overcharged. Their great defects seem to be a want of variety, and the majority of them not being directed to a female, to whom alone such ardent expressions of esteem could with propriety be addressed. It cannot be denied too that they contain some far-fetched conceits; but are our author's plays entirely free from them? Many of the thoughts that occur in his dramatick productions, are found here likewise. . . . Had they therefore no other merit, they are entitled to our attention, as often illustrating obscure passages in his plays.

I do not perceive that the versification of these pieces is less smooth and harmonious than that of Shakspeare's other compositions. Though many of them are not so simple and clear as they ought to be, yet some of them are written with perspicuity and energy. . . . [And] many beautiful lines, scattered through these poems, will, it is supposed, strike every reader who is not determined to allow no praise to any species of poetry except blank verse or heroick couplets. (pp. 684-85)

> *Edmond Malone, "Sonnets," in* Supplement to the Edition of Shakespeare's Plays Published in 1778 by Samuel Johnson and George Steevens, Vol. I, *edited by E. Malone; C. Bathurst and others, 1780.*

JOHN MONCK MASON   (essay date 1785)

[*Mason was an Irish essayist, editor, and Shakespeare commentator. In the following excerpt from his* Comments on the Last Edition of Shakespeare's Plays *(1785), he refers to the sonnets as "miserable," made up of "a dozen insipid lines" that "serve as an introduction to an epigram of two, which generally turns upon some forced conceit." Mason states that only Shakespeare's "violent attachment" to the Italian poets who originated the sonnet form could have induced him to compose such "species of composition."*]

It was much the fashion in Shakespeare's days to study and imitate the Italian poets, and he has proved his particular admiration of them by a collection of no less than 154 very miserable sonnets, a quaint and languid kind of poem of Italian origin, in which a dozen insipid lines are to serve as an introduction to an epigram of two, which generally turns upon some forced conceit. Nothing but a violent attachment to those poets could have induced Shakespeare to deal so largely in a species of composition but ill adapted either to the English language or the taste of his countrymen. . . . (p. 406)

> *John Monck Mason, in an extract in* Shakespeare, the Critical Heritage: 1774-1801, Vol. 6, *edited by Brian Vickers, Routledge & Kegan Paul, 1981, pp. 403-07.*

EDMOND MALONE   (essay date 1790)

[*In a footnote to Malone and Steevens's 1780 edition of Shakespeare's works, the latter expressed his "disgust and indignation" at the thought of the poet addressing a man as "the master-mistress of my passions" (Sonnet 20). In the following excerpt, Malone responds to Steevens's disapproving remark, asserting that although this kind of expression "cannot but appear strange to a modern reader," "such addresses to men were common in Shakspeare's time, and were not thought indecorous." Malone adds that the Elizabethan Age was apparently "very indelicate and gross."*]

The numerous expressions of this kind in these Sonnets, as well as the general tenour of the greater part of them, cannot but appear strange to a modern reader. In justice therefore to our authour it is proper to observe, that such addresses to men were common in Shakspeare's time, and were not thought indecorous. That age seems to have been very indelicate and gross in many other particulars beside this, but they certainly did not think themselves so. Nothing can prove more strongly the different notions which they entertained on subjects of decorum from those which prevail at present, than the elogiums which were pronounced on Fletcher's plays for the *chastity* of their language; those very plays, which are now banished from the stage for their *licentiousness* and *obscenity.* (pp. 219-20)

> *Edmond Malone, in a footnote in* The Plays and Poems of William Shakspeare, Vol. 10, *edited by Edmond Malone 1790. Reprint by AMS Press, 1968, pp. 219-20.*

GEORGE STEEVENS   (essay date 1793)

[*In the following preface to his fifteen-volume 1793 edition of Shakespeare's plays, Steevens informs readers of his collection that he has not included the sonnets, for "the strongest act of Parliament . . . would fail to compel readers into their service." According to the critic, "had Shakespeare produced no other works than these," he would be as little celebrated as Thomas Watson, "an older and much more elegant sonnetteer."*]

We have not reprinted the *Sonnets,* &c. of Shakespeare, because the strongest act of Parliament that could be framed would fail to compel readers into their service; notwithstanding these miscellaneous Poems have derived every possible advantage from the literature and judgement of their only intelligent editor, Mr. Malone [see excerpt above, 1780], whose implements of criticism, like the ivory rake and golden spade in Prudentius, are on this occasion disgraced by the objects of their culture.—Had Shakespeare produced no other works than these, his name would have reached us with as little celebrity as time has conferred on that of Thomas Watson, an older and much more elegant sonnetteer. (p. 577)

> *George Steevens, in an extract in* Shakespeare, the Critical Heritage: 1774-1801, Vol. 6, *edited by Brian Vickers, Routledge & Kegan Paul, 1981, pp. 576-605.*

GEORGE CHALMERS   (essay date 1797)

[*A Scottish antiquarian, lawyer, and essayist, Chalmers practiced law in the colonial courts of Maryland from 1763 to 1775. At the outbreak of the American Revolution he returned to England, where he published numerous biographical, historical, and political tracts and essays. One of many scholars duped by the Shakespeare forgeries of William Henry Ireland, Chalmers published two works in defense of his position:* An Apology for the Believers in the Shakspeare-Papers *(1797) and* A Supplemental Apology for the Believers in the Shakspeare-Papers *(1799). Although these works are mainly an attack against Edmond Malone's scholarship concerning the Ireland forgeries, the historical facts upon which Chalmers based his arguments were an important contribution to Shakespearean studies. In the following excerpt, Chalmers maintains that Shakespeare's sonnets are all addressed to Queen Elizabeth. In support of his hypothesis, which has been frequently ridiculed by subsequent critics, Chalmers emphasizes the queen's "passion" for flattery and notes that many poets and ministers of her court gained preferment by eulogizing her. The critic also argues that neither the obvious youthfulness of the person addressed in the sonnets nor the allusions to this person as a male may be considered barriers against his theory. Many Elizabe-*]

than writers, Chalmers asserts, conventionally praised the youthful beauty of the queen and referred to her in masculine terms.]

[The] SONNETS of Shakspeare were addressed, by him, to [Queen] Elizabeth. . . . In order to see this curious point, in its true light, it will be necessary to advert, with discriminative eye, to the character of Elizabeth, and to the situation of Shakspeare.

Elizabeth was born in 1533; and was, of course, one-and-thirty years older than Shakspeare. Being bred in the school of adversity, she acquired early habits of personal address; being called on to play a part, during critical times, she learned the cunning, which the necessity of circumspection, in *political* revolutions, always teaches; and being, in her early age, without hopes of future greatness, she indulged in the natural propensities of meaner mortals. She was from constitution amorous; but, without the power of enjoyment. She was led thus to cultivate all the arts, and to acquire all the accomplishments, which make women irresistible, when they preserve the modesty of their nature, and study the mild graces of their sex. With the understanding of a man, and the knowledge of a scholar, she indulged the vanity of the weakest woman, and carried her passion for praise, even in the extremity of age, beyond the limits, which are scarcely allowed in girls: And, by exposing this weakness to the world, she became the dupe of her own servants, of her subjects, and also of foreigners, who all knew how to gain their several objects, by gratifying her prevailing passion. . . . Most of her courtiers, therefore, feigned affection, and desire towards her; addressing her in the usual style of gallantry. By such artifices, Leicester, and Essex, Raleigh, and Hatton rose to favour, and acquired estates. (pp. 42-5)

Shakspeare entered the world, with little but his love to make him happy, and little but his genius to prevent the intrusion of misery. An increasing family, and pressing wants, obliged him to look, beyond the limits of Stratford, for subsistence, and for fame. He felt, doubtless, emotions of genius, and he saw, certainly, persons who had not better pretensions, than his own, rising to eminence in a higher scene. By these motives was he probably induced to remove to London, in the period, between the years 1585, and 1588. . . . He may have received, perhaps, an introduction to the theatre from Robert Green, his kinsman, an actor, of whom "*none were of greater grace at the court,* or of more general love in the city;" and Shakspeare, certainly, enjoyed the patronage of Lord Southampton, to whom was dedicated "the first heir of his invention."

Shakspeare, however, soon became sensible of the *impression,* "which vulgar scandal stamp'd upon his brow" [Sonnet 112]. His gentle nature was ere long subdued. He perceived, with regret that, from his *occupation, his name had received a brand.* . . . [In] this *bitterness* of misery, he adopted the resolution, wherein he was, no doubt, confirmed by Green, his townsman, and relation, to address his *prettye verses* to Elizabeth.

It may be pertinently asked, was Elizabeth a princess, who was likely to receive such verses; was Shakspeare a poet, who was likely to write such verses? I answer both these questions, positively, in the affirmative. We have seen her natural voluptuousness; we have beheld her passion for praises; we have observed her great ministers, offering her the grossest flattery, which she received, as her accustomed due. . . . Shak-

speare knew, perfectly, the real character of Elizabeth, which made her the dupe of daily solicitation; he saw how many men of less genius, and fewer pretensions, than his own, had gained their objects, and risen to greatness, by gratifying her domineering passion: And, thus was he induced to send her, by the Lord Chamberlain, no doubt, his *sugr'd sonnets,* composed in *filed phrase,* which no other woman, than Elizabeth, would have been pleased to receive, and no other poet, than Shakspeare, could easily have written. (pp. 47-50)

[Mr. Malone] is positive that, of the whole number of one hundred and fifty-four [sonnets], there were addressed to a man one hundred and twenty, and twenty-eight to a lady; to *show her the propriety of marriage* [see excerpt above, 1780]. Now; Shakspeare, who knew his own purpose, expressly says:—

> Let not my love be call'd idolatry;
> Nor my beloved, as an idol show;
> Since all alike my songs, and praises, be,
> To ONE, of ONE, still such, and ever so.
>
> [Sonnet 105]

Thus, in the arithmetic of Mr. Malone *one* is, by a ready operation, multiplied into *two:* He can *divide, split hairs,* and *still divide,* it seems. The fact is, that Shakspeare had not leisure to write one hundred and twenty such sonnets to any *man;* being wholly occupied in *providing for the day, which was passing over him;* that the poet had no *love,* but a teeming wife, to whom he was strongly attached, by early ties; and for whom he could hardly provide, by any means: Add to these circumstances, that in another sonnet, Shakespeare maintains the *unity* of his *object,* by saying to *his* idol, Elizabeth:

> For, to *no other pass, my verses tend,*
> Than of *your graces,* and *your gifts,* to tell;
> And more, much more, than in my verse can fit,
> Your own glass shows you, when you look in it.
>
> [Sonnet 103]

Yet, Mr. Malone is not convinced: He still objects, that many more of the sonnets are addressed to a male, than to a female. His objection proves, that he did not know, that Elizabeth was often considered as a man:—In poetry; Drant hails her as a *Prince;* Spenser paints her as a *Prince:* In prose; Ascham celebrates her as a *Prince;* Bacon describes her as a *Prince,* unparalleled among women. Add to this, that there was much darkness, and confusion, introduced into writing, in the days of Shakspeare, by the frequent use of the masculine pronoun *his* instead of the neuter demonstrative, *it.* . . . [Thus] I maintain my great position, that the *sugr'd sonnets* were addressed by Shakspeare to Elizabeth, whom the greatest philologists, and philosophers, of her reign, addressed both as a male, and female.

Knowing the passions of Elizabeth and willing to gratify them, Shakspeare opens his purposes, in his first sonnet, by a direct address to the great object of his flattery:

> Thou, that art now the world's fresh ornament,
> And *only herald* to the *gaudy spring.*
>
> [Sonnet 1]

Whatever may have been the beauty, or celebrity, of the Warwickshire lasses, in that age, I doubt, whether the prettiest of them could properly be called *the world's fresh ornament, and only herald to the gaudy spring.* Our panegyrist goes on, in his second sonnet, to praise his love, as the heir of perpetual youth; as the object of universal admiration. . . . (pp. 50-4)

Queen Elizabeth was certainly forty, in the year 1573; and was probably more than fifty, at the epoch of this panegyric: But, this objection, in the present case, does not strike with the same force, as when applied to other women of inferior rank, and of less affectation, in their daily habits. At the age of sixty, Elizabeth was commonly addressed by ministers, and ambassadors, as an *Angel*, as a *Goddess*. . . . (pp. 54-5)

[In] his ninety-sixth sonnet, Shakspeare calmly describes Elizabeth, in such explicit terms, as to remove even the doubts of scepticism:

> Some say thy fault is youth, some wantonness;
> Some say thy grace is youth, and gentle sport;
> Both grace, and faults, are lov'd of more and less:
> Thou makst faults graces, that to thee resort;
> As on *the finger of a throned queen*
> The *basest jewel will be well esteem'd;*
> So are *those errors,* that in thee are seen,
> To *truths translated,* and for true things deem'd.
> How many gazers mightst thou lead away,
> If *thou should'st use the strength of all thy state.*
>
> (pp. 58-9)

One hundred and twenty of [his] sonnets are supposed, though without sufficient proof, to be addressed to a friend; and are reprobated, though without adequate cause, as professing too much love to be addressed to a man. When the admirers of Shakspeare come to perceive, that his sonnets were addressed to Elizabeth, they will be happy to find, that the poet was incapable of such grossness. The fact is, that Shakspeare, knowing the voracity of Elizabeth, determined to gorge her with praise. . . . Ought we to wonder that, in performing this great operation, he should confound the sexes? Let us appeal to *the truth,* which is always the best justification: He knew the mighty object of his adoration to be of a very *mixed staple:* and he addressed her, as Spenser, Raleigh, and Bacon had addressed her before, both as a princess, and a prince; as a heroine, and a hero; as an angel, and a goddess; as Adonis, and Helen. Knowing her patience, while listening to panegyric, Shakspeare determined, with the resolution of his own Dogberry [in *Much Ado about Nothing*], to bestow his *whole tediousness upon her,* if he were as tedious as a king. (pp. 60-2)

I have now closed the proofs, which have convinced me, that the sonnets of Shakspeare were addressed by him to Elizabeth. The strong presumption, which is set up by those proofs, cannot be destroyed, but by proofs of greater weight, that would carry with them a contrary persuasion. (p. 66)

> *George Chalmers, in his* An Apology for the Believers in the Shakspeare-Papers, *Thomas Egerton, 1797, 628 p.*

GEORGE CHALMERS   (essay date 1799)

[*In the following excerpt from* A Supplemental Apology *(1799), Chalmers contends that Shakespeare's sonnets, "as a whole poem, . . . have two of the worst faults, that can degrade any writing": tediousness and obscurity. He compares Shakespeare's sonnets with those of Edmund Spenser, noting the superiority of the latter but adding that the dramatist "shows sometimes a manifest superiority in imagination over Spenser."*]

Of . . . [Shakspeare's Sonnets], it may be truly said, that as a whole poem, which is often tied together by a very slight ligature, they have two of the worst faults, that can degrade any writing; they are obscure; and they are tedious. Spenser,

who furnished the model of them, has his obscurities, and tediousness; but he has withal, more distinctness, in his topicks, and more facility, in his style. Shakspeare plainly endeavoured to go beyond the mark of his rivalry; but, in affecting the sublime, he sunk, by a natural cadence, into the unintelligible. Spenser having no rival, and only a single object, caught at such topicks of praise, as he thought would please the most, and adopted such a style, as he could most easily manage. Of such a poet, as Shakspeare, it may easily be conceived, that he has many happy phrases, and elegant lines, though they are generally darkened by conceit, and marred by affectation; with as many happy phrases, and elegant lines, Spenser has fewer conceits and less affectation; having from inheritance, as fruitful a garden of images, which he watered from a deeper fountain of learning. Shakspeare 'fancy's sweetest child', shows sometimes a manifest superiority in *imagination* over Spenser, when this wonderful poet is forming the same images. By an effort of his creative powers, Shakspeare appears to have carried away the palm, in this great quality of a true poet, from his illustrious rival, even when Spenser put forth his whole strength, in cultivating the same field.

> *George Chalmers, in an extract in* Shakespeare, "The Sonnets". A Casebook, *edited by Peter Jones, The Macmillan Press Ltd., 1977, p. 38.*

NATHAN DRAKE   (essay date 1800)

[*Drake was a physician, poet, and essayist. In 1817 he produced* Shakspeare and His Times, *a two-volume study of the dramatist's life and the "Manners, Customs, and Amusements, Superstitions, Poetry, and Elegant Literature of His Age." In the following excerpt from the second edition (1800) of* Literary Hours; or, Sketches Critical and Narrative, *he avers that "the sonnets of Shakespeare are buried beneath a load of obscurity and quaintness." He also commends Steevens for not including these poems in his 1793 edition of Shakespeare's works, for, Drake rhetorically asks, "where is the utility of propagating compositions which no one can endure to read?"*]

> La brevità del sonetto non comporta, che una sola parola sia vana, ed il vero subietto e materia del sonetto debbe essere qualche acuta e gentile sentenza, narrata attamente, ed in pochi versi ristretta, e fuggendo la oscurità e durezza.
>
> [The brevity of the sonnet does not permit a single empty or unnecessary word. The true subject matter of the sonnet should be some sharp and refined thought, suitably related, limited to a few verses, and avoiding all obscurity and harshness.]

Lorenzo de Medici has thus, in few words, accurately defined the true character of the Sonnet, a species of composition which has lately been cultivated with considerable success in England. Italy, however, may boast the honour of giving birth to this elegant and elaborate little poem, which, confined as it is to a frequent return of rhyme, and limited to a certain number of lines, imposes no small difficulty on the poet. (p. 103)

One of the best and earliest attempts in England to naturalize the sonnet, is to be found in the pages of the gallant Surrey, whose compositions in this department, making due allowance for the imperfect state of the language in which he wrote, have a simplicity and chastity in their style and thought which merit every encomium. Our romantic Spenser, likewise, has endeavoured to transfuse the ease and amenity of the Petrarchian stanza. It is scarcely necessary to say that he has completely failed. In his long series of sonnets, the critic will recognise many of the trifling conceits of the Italian, but find little to recompense the trouble of research.

These Opuscula of the gentle poet of the *Fairy Queen* are, however, far superior to the attempts of the mighty Father of the English Drama. The sonnets of Shakspeare are buried beneath a load of obscurity and quaintness; nor does there issue a single ray of light to quicken, or to warm the heavy mass. Mr. Malone has once more given them to the press, but his last Editor has, I think, acted with greater judgment in forbearing to obtrude such crude efforts upon the public eye [see excerpt above by George Steevens, 1793]; for where is the utility of propagating compositions which no one can endure to read. (pp. 107-08)

> Nathan Drake, "On Sonnet-Writing. Four Sonnets," in his Literary Hours, or Sketches Critical and Narrative, Vol. I, *second edition, 1800. Reprint by Garland Publishing, Inc., 1970, pp. 103-18.*

WILLIAM WORDSWORTH   (essay date 1803?)

[*Wordsworth is considered by many scholars to be the greatest and most influential English Romantic poet. His literary criticism reflects his beliefs that neither the language nor the content of poetry should be stylized or elaborate and that the poet should feel and express the relation between man and nature. The following excerpt is taken from an undated marginal note in a volume of Robert Anderson's* Poets of Great Britain (1793-1807). *Wordsworth labels Sonnets 127-54 "abominably harsh, obscure, and worthless." He adds, however, that the preceding ones are generally much superior. Wordsworth's remarks must have been inscribed by 1803, for Samuel Taylor Coleridge commented on them in his own, dated note in this volume (see excerpt below, 1803).*]

[Shakespeare's] sonnets beginning at CXXVII to his mistress, are worse than a puzzle-peg. They are abominably harsh, obscure, and worthless. The others are for the most part much better, have many fine lines . . . and passages. They are also in many places warm with passion. Their chief faults—and heavy ones they are—are sameness, tediousness, quaintness, and elaborate obscurity.

> William Wordsworth, in an extract in Shakespeare, "The Sonnets". A Casebook, *edited by Peter Jones, The Macmillan Press Ltd., 1977, p. 41.*

SAMUEL TAYLOR COLERIDGE   (essay date 1803)

[*Coleridge's lectures and writings on Shakespeare constitute a major chapter in the history of English Shakespearean criticism. As an advocate for the critical ideas of the German Romantics and as an original interpreter of Shakespeare in the new spirit of Romanticism, Coleridge played a strategic role in overthrowing the Neoclassical approach to Shakespeare and in establishing the modern view of the dramatist as a conscious artist and masterful portrayer of human character. Coleridge's remarks on Shakespeare survive largely as fragmentary notes, marginalia, and reports by auditors of lectures he delivered. The following excerpt is taken from a marginal note dated November 2, 1803—the day his eldest son Hartley was christened—and inscribed in the volume containing the remarks by William Wordsworth excerpted above (1803). Coleridge considers the artistic merit of the sonnets and comments on the question of Shakespeare's sexual nature. He disagrees with*]

Wordsworth's statement that the sonnets are quaint and obscure; on the contrary, he declares, they are "rich in metre [and] full of thought and exquisitest diction." Coleridge also instructs his son on how to "understand" the apparently homosexual relationship depicted in Sonnets 1-126, urging him to recognize that Shakespeare's love for his male friend is "pure" and free from sexual desire.]

I can by no means subscribe to the above pencil mark of W. Wordsworth [see excerpt above, 1803]; which, however, it is my wish should never be erased. It is *his:* and grievously am I mistaken, and deplorably will Englishmen have degenerated if the being *his* will not in times to come give it a value, as of a little reverential relic. . . . My sweet Hartley! if thou livest, thou wilt not part with this book [Shakespeare's sonnets] without sad necessity and a pang at heart. Oh, be never weary of reperusing the first four volumes of this collection, my eldest born! . . . These sonnets thou, I trust, if God preserve thy life, Hartley! thou wilt read with a deep interest, having learnt to love the plays of Shakespeare, co-ordinate with Milton, and subordinate only to thy Bible. To thee, I trust, they will help to explain the mind of Shakespeare, and if thou wouldst understand these sonnets, thou must read the chapter in Potter's *Antiquities* on the Greek lovers—of whom were that Theban band of brothers over whom Philip, their victor, stood weeping; and surveying their dead bodies, each with his shield over the body of his friend, all dead in the place where they fought, solemnly cursed those whose base, fleshly, and most calumnious fancies had suspected their love of desires against nature. This pure love Shakespeare appears to have felt—to have been in no way ashamed of—or even to have suspected that others could have suspected it. Yet at the same time he knew that so strong a love would have been made more completely a thing of permanence and reality, and have been blessed more by nature and taken under her more especial protection, if this object of his love had been at the same time a possible object of desire—for nature is not soul only. In this feeling he must have written the twentieth sonnet; but its possibility seems never to have entered even his imagination. It is noticeable that not even an allusion to that very worst of all possible vices (for it is wise to think of the disposition, as a *vice,* not of the absurd and despicable act, as a *crime*) not even any allusion to it [occurs] in all his numerous plays—whereas Jonson, Beaumont and Fletcher, and Massinger are full of them. O my son! I pray fervently that thou may'st know inwardly how impossible it was for a Shakespeare not to have been in his heart's heart chaste. I see no elaborate obscurity and very little quaintness—nor do I know any sonnets that will bear such frequent reperusal; so rich in metre, so full of thought and *exquisitest* diction. (pp. 41-2)

> Samuel Taylor Coleridge, in an extract in Shakespeare, "The Sonnets". A Casebook, *edited by Peter Jones, The Macmillan Press Ltd., 1977, pp. 41-2.*

AUGUST WILHELM SCHLEGEL   (essay date 1811)

[*A prominent German Romantic critic, Schlegel holds a key place in the history of Shakespeare's reputation in European criticism. His translations of sixteen of the plays are still considered the best German editions of Shakespeare. Schlegel was also a leading spokesman for the Romantic movement, which permanently overthrew the Neoclassical contention that Shakespeare was a child of nature whose plays lacked artistic form. In the excerpt below, originally published in German in his* Über dramatische Kunst und Literatur *(1811). Schlegel finds*] *it telling that "none" of the Shakespeare commentators "have ever thought of availing themselves of his sonnets for tracing the circumstances of his life." According to Schlegel, these verses provide important information about Shakespeare's sentiments, passions, and "youthful errors."]*

It betrays more than ordinary deficiency of critical acumen in Shakspeare's commentators, that none of them, so far as we know, have ever thought of availing themselves of his sonnets for tracing the circumstances of his life. These sonnets paint most unequivocally the actual situation and sentiments of the poet; they make us acquainted with the passions of the man; they even contain remarkable confessions of his youthful errors. (p. 352)

> *August Wilhelm Schlegel, "Lecture XXII," in his* A Course of Lectures on Dramatic Art and Literature, *edited by Rev. A. J. W. Morrison, translated by John Black, revised edition, 1846. Reprint by AMS Press, Inc., 1965, pp. 338-53.*

FREDERICK SCHLEGEL   (lecture date 1812)

[A German essayist, critic, orientalist, and poet, Schlegel was the younger brother of writer and critic August Wilhelm Schlegel. One of the founders of German Romanticism, Frederick is perhaps best remembered for his many works of historical criticism. In the following excerpt from an 1812 lecture, Schlegel argues that Shakespeare's sonnets are "indispensable" to a proper understanding of their author, for in his dramatic works, he seldom revealed his thoughts and feelings. According to Schlegel, the sonnets indicate that Shakespeare possessed a "deep tenderness of soul."]

Shakspere evidently regarded the stage of which he was so distinguished a master, only as a prosaic application of his art, a faithful sketch of life for the multitude, at the best a condescension of his powers. How little he who sounded all the depths of varied passion, who drew human nature as it is, and with his magic pencil fixed each expression of its changing lineaments, the noblest and the coarsest, was himself rude or savage, is testified by the extreme tenderness that breathes over those idyllic effusions [his sonnets]. Small is the number of those who are touched by this mild softness, just because it is so exquisite and so deep; but to a just comprehension of his dramas these lyrics are indispensable. They shew us that, in his dramatic works, he seldom represents the reflection of himself, of what he felt and was, but the world as it stood clearly before him, though separated by a wide interval from himself and his deep tenderness of soul. Accordingly, the images presented to our view are thoroughly faithful, devoid of flattery or embellishment. (p. 274)

> *Frederick Schlegel, "Lecture XII," in his* Lectures on the History of Literature: Ancient and Modern, *translated by Henry G. Bohn, 1859. Reprint by George Bell and Sons, 1896, pp. 258-85.*

WILLIAM WORDSWORTH   (essay date 1815)

[In the following excerpt from "Essay, Supplementary to the Preface" to Lyrical Ballads *(1815) Wordsworth notes the "exquisite feelings felicitously expressed" in Shakespeare's sonnets.]*

There is extant a small Volume of miscellaneous Poems in which Shakespeare expresses his own feelings in his own Person. It is not difficult to conceive that the Editor, George Stevens, should have been insensible to the beauties of one por-

tion of that Volume, the Sonnets [see excerpt above, 1793]; though there is not a part of the writings of this Poet where is found in an equal compass a greater number of exquisite feelings felicitously expressed. But, from regard to the Critic's own credit, he would not have ventured to talk of an act of parliament not being strong enough to compel the perusal of these, or any production of Shakespeare, if he had not known that the people of England were ignorant of the treasures contained in those little pieces; and if he had not, moreover, shared the too common propensity of human nature to exult over a supposed fall into the mire of a genius whom he had been compelled to regard with admiration, as an inmate of the celestial regions,—"there sitting where he durst not soar." (p. 168)

> *William Wordsworth, "Essay, Supplementary to the Preface," in* Literary Criticism of William Wordsworth, *edited by Paul M. Zall, University of Nebraska Press, 1966, pp. 158-87.*

JOHN KEATS   (letter date 1817)

[Keats is considered a key figure in the English Romantic movement and one of the major poets in the English language. Critics note that although his creative career spanned only four years, he achieved remarkable intellectual and artistic development. His poems, notably those contained in the collection Lamia, Isabella, The Eve of St. Agnes, and Other Poems *(1820), are valued not only for their sensuous imagery, simplicity, and passionate tone, but also for the insight they provide into aesthetic and human concerns, particularly the conflict between art and life. In the following excerpt from an 1817 letter to John Hamilton Reynolds, Keats mentions that Shakespeare's sonnets "seem to be full of fine things said unintentionally," and he quotes part of Sonnet 12 as an example of such inadvertent beauties.]*

I neer found so many beauties in [Shakespear's] Sonnets—they seem to be full of fine things said unintentionally—in the intensity of working out conceits. Is this to be borne? Hark ye!

> When lofty trees I see barren of leaves
>   Which erst from heat did canopy the herd,
> And Summer's green all girded up in sheaves,
>   Borne on the bier with white and bristly beard.
>   [Sonnet 12]

> *John Keats, in an extract from a letter to John Hamilton Reynolds on November 22, 1817, in* The Letters of John Keats, *edited by Maurice Buxton Forman, second edition, Oxford University Press, 1935, p. 65.*

WILLIAM HAZLITT   (essay date 1817)

[Hazlitt is considered a leading Shakespearean critic of the English Romantic movement. A prolific essayist and commentator on a wide range of subjects, he remarked in the preface to his Characters of Shakespear's Plays, *first published in 1817, that he was inspired by the German critic August Wilhelm Schlegel and was determined to supplant what he considered the pernicious influence of Samuel Johnson's Shakespearean criticism. Hazlitt's commentary is typically Romantic in its emphasis on character studies. His experience as a drama critic was an important factor in shaping his descriptive, as opposed to analytical, interpretations of Shakespeare. In the following excerpt from the work cited above, he discusses Shakespeare's nondramatic works in general, maintaining that the playwright's*

feelings only become manifest through the "licence of an assumed character." Regarding the sonnets specifically, Hazlitt states that "many of them are highly beautiful in themselves" and interesting in what they reveal about Shakespeare's personal thoughts.]

Our idolatry of Shakespear (not to say our admiration) ceases with his plays. In his other productions, he was a mere author, though not a common author. It was only by representing others, that he became himself. He could go out of himself, and express the soul of Cleopatra; but in his own person, he appeared to be always waiting for the prompter's cue. In expressing the thoughts of others, he seemed inspired; in expressing his own, he was a mechanic. The licence of an assumed character was necessary to restore his genius to the privileges of nature, and to give him courage to break through the tyranny of fashion, the trammels of custom. In his plays, he was "as broad and casing as the general air:" in his poems, on the contrary, he appears to be "cooped and cabined in" [*Macbeth,* III. iv. 22-3] by all the technicalities of art, by all the petty intricacies of thought and language, which poetry had learned from the controversial jargon of the schools, where words had been made a substitute for things. There was, if we mistake not, something of modesty, and a painful sense of personal propriety at the bottom of this. Shakespear's imagination, by identifying itself with the strongest characters in the most trying circumstances, grappled at once with nature, and trampled the littleness of art under his feet: the rapid changes of situation, the wide range of the universe, gave him life and spirit, and afforded full scope to his genius; but returned into his closet again, and having assumed the badge of his profession, he could only labour in his vocation, and conform himself to existing models. The thoughts, the passions, the words which the poet's pen, "glancing from heaven to earth, from earth to heaven" [*A Midsummer Night's Dream,* V. i. 13], lent to others, shook off the fetters of pedantry and affectation; while his own thoughts and feelings, standing by themselves, were seized upon as lawful prey, and tortured to death according to the established rules and practice of the day. (pp. 211-12)

Of the Sonnets we do not well know what to say. The subject of them seems to be somewhat equivocal; but many of them are highly beautiful in themselves, and interesting as they relate to the state of the personal feelings of the author. (p. 214)

> *William Hazlitt, "Poems and Sonnets," in his* Characters of Shakespear's Plays & Lectures on the English Poets, *The Macmillan Company, 1903, pp. 211-15.*

NATHAN DRAKE   (essay date 1817)

[*In the following excerpt from* Shakspeare and His Times, *Drake comments on three topics concerning the sonnets: the identity of "W. H.," the identity of the Dark Lady, and the poems' artistic merit. Drake claims that the "Mr. W. H." referred to by Thomas Thorpe (see excerpt above, 1609) is the "begetter" of the sonnets in the sense of the "obtainer," and thus not to be confused with the Friend addressed in Sonnets 1-126. This person the critic identifies as Henry Wriothesley, Earl of Southampton, basing his claim on the similarities in wording between the dedication to Southampton in* The Rape of Lucrece *and Sonnet 26 as well as on connections between events in the earl's life and Sonnets 1-17. On the second topic, Drake maintains that no poet would "publish such an open confession of his own culpability." He suggests that the Dark Lady sonnets "were solely intended to express, aloof from all*

individual application, the contrarieties, the inconsistencies, and the miseries of illicit love." Lastly, Drake disputes Steevens's negative assessments of the sonnets (see excerpts above, 1780 and 1793). In a departure from his earlier view (see excerpt above, 1800), Drake argues that although these verses have been "rendered hard and repulsive by the peculiarities of the period of their production, we have only to search beneath, in order to discover a rich ore of thought, imagery, and sentiment."]

When Thomas Thorpe published [Shakspeare's] sonnets in 1609, he accompanied them with the following mysterious dedication [see excerpt above, 1609]:—

> To the Only Begetter
> Of These Ensuing Sonnets,
> Mr. W. H.
> All Happiness
> And That Eternity Promised
> By Our Ever-Living Poet
> Wisheth The
> Well-Wishing Adventurer
> In Setting Forth,
>
>   T. T.

On the first perusal of this address, the import would seem to be, that Mr. W. H. had been the sole object of Shakspeare's poetry, and of the eternity promised by the bard. But a little attention to the language of the times in which it was written, will induce us to correct this conclusion; for as a part of our author's sonnets is most certainly addressed to a female, it is evident that W. H. could not be the only begetter of them in the sense which primarily suggests itself. For the true meaning of the word we are indebted to Mr. Chalmers, who observes, on the authority of Minsheu's Dictionary of 1616, that one sense of the verb to beget is there given to bring forth. (p. 376)

We must infer, therefore, from this explanation of the word, that Mr. W. H. had influence enough to obtain the manuscript from the poet, and that he lodged it in Thorpe's hands for the purpose of publication, a favour which the bookseller returned, by wishing him all happiness, and that eternity which had been promised by the bard, in such glowing colours, to another, namely, to one of the immediate subjects of his sonnets.

That this is the only rational meaning which can be annexed to the word "promised," will appear, when we reflect that for Thorpe to have wished W. H. the eternity which had been promised him by an ever-living poet, would have been not only superfluous, but downright nonsense: the eternity of an ever-living poet must necessarily ensue, and was a proper subject of congratulation, but not of wishing or of hope.

It appears also that this dedication was understood in the same light by some of the earlier editors of the sonnets. . . . [When] Gildon re-printed them in 1710, he gives it as his opinion that they were "all of them in praise of his mistress" [see excerpt above, 1710]: and Dr. Sewell, when he edited them in [1725], had embraced a similar idea, for he tells us, in reference to our author's example, that "A young muse must have *a mistress,* to play off the beginning of fancy; nothing being so apt to elevate the soul to a pitch of poetry, as the passion of love" [see excerpt above, 1725].

The conclusion of these editors remained undisputed for more than half a century, when Mr. Malone, in 1780, published his Supplement to the Edition of Shakspeare's Plays of 1778, which includes the Sonnets of the poet, accompanied by his own notes [see excerpt above, 1780], and those of his friends. Here, beside the opinion which he has himself avowed, he has given the conjectures of Dr. Farmer, and Mr. Tyrwhitt, and the decision of Mr. Steevens.

All these gentlemen concur in believing, that more than one hundred of our author's sonnets are addressed to a male object. Dr. Farmer, influenced by the initials in the dedication, supposes, that Mr. William Harte, the poet's nephew, was the object in question [see excerpt above, 1780] but a reference to the Stratford Register completely overturns this hypothesis, for it there appears, that William, eldest son of William Harte, who married Shakspeare's Sister Joan, was baptized August 28th, 1600, and consequently could not be even in existence when the greater part of these compositions were written.

Mr. Tyrwhitt, founding his conjecture on a line in the twentieth sonnet, which is thus printed in the old copy,

A man in *hew* all *Hews* in his controlling,

conceives that the letters W. H. were intended to imply William Hughes. If we recollect, however, our bard's uncontrollable passion for playing upon words; that hew frequently meant, in the usage of his time, mien and appearance, as well as tint, and that Daniel, who was probably his archetype in these pieces, has spelt it in the same way, and once, if not oftener, for the sake of emphasis, with a capital, we shall not feel inclined to place such reliance on this supposition.

When Mr. Steevens, in 1766, annexed a reprint of the sonnets to Shakspeare's plays, from the quarto editions, he hazarded no observations on their scope or origin; but in Malone's Supplement, he ventured, in a note on the twentieth sonnet, to declare his conviction that it was addressed to a male object.

Lastly, Mr. Malone, in the Supplement just mentioned, after specifying his concurrence in the conjecture of Mr. Tyrwhitt, adds—"To this person, whoever he was, one hundred and twenty of the following poems are addressed; the remaining twenty-eight are addressed to a lady."

Thus the matter rested on the decision of these four celebrated commentators, who were uniform in asserting their belief, that Shakspeare had addressed the greater part of his sonnets to a man. . . . (pp. 376-77)

The question then returns upon us, To whom are these sonnets addressed? We agree with Farmer, Tyrwhitt, Steevens, and Malone, in thinking the object of the greater part of the sonnets to have been of the male sex; but, for the reasons already assigned, we cannot concede that either Harte or Hughes was the individual.

If we may be allowed, in our turn, to conjecture, we would fix upon Lord Southampton as the subject of Shakspeare's sonnets, from the first to the hundredth and twenty-sixth, inclusive.

Before we enter, however, on the quotation of such passages as are calculated to give probability to our conclusion, it will be necessary to show that, in the age of Shakspeare, the language of love and friendship was mutually convertible. The terms lover and love, indeed, were as often applied to those of the same sex who had an esteem for each other, as they are now exclusively directed to express the love of the male for the female. Thus, for instance, Ben Johnson subscribes himself the lover of Camden, and tells Dr. Donne, at the close

of a letter to him, that he is his "ever true lover;" and with the same import, Drayton, in a letter to Drummond of Hawthornden, informs him, that Mr. Joseph Davis is in *love* with him. Shakspeare, in his Dramas, frequently adopts the same phraseology in expressing the relations of friendship . . . , but it is to his poems that we must refer for a complete and extensive proof of this perplexing ambiguity of diction, which will gradually unfold itself as we proceed to quote instances in support of Lord Southampton's being the subject of his muse.

That Shakspeare was, at the same time, attached by friendship, and by love; that, according to the fashion of his age, he employed the same epithet for both, though, in one instance, at least, he has accurately distinguished the sexes, positively appears from the opening stanza of a sonnet in the *Passionate Pilgrim* of 1599:—

> Two *loves* I have of comfort and despair,
> Which like two spirits do suggest me still;
> The *better angel* is a *man* right fair,
> The worser spirit a *woman*, colour'd ill.
>
> [Sonnet 144]

That this better angel was Lord Southampton, and that to him was addressed the number of sonnets mentioned above, we shall now endeavour to substantiate.

Perhaps one of the most striking proofs of this position, is the hitherto unnoticed fact, that the language of the Dedication to the *Rape of Lucrece*, and that of part of the twenty-sixth sonnet, are almost precisely the same.

The Dedication runs thus:—"The love I dedicate to your Lordship is without end;—The warrant I have of your honourable disposition, not the worth of my untutored lines, makes it assured of acceptance. What I have done is yours, what I have to do is yours; being part in all I have devoted yours. Were my worth greater, my duty would shew greater."

The sonnet is as follows:

> *Lord of my love*, to whom in vassalage
> Thy merit hath my duty strongly knit,
> To thee I send this written embassage,
> To witness duty, not to show my wit,
> Duty so great, which wit so poor as mine
> May make seem bare, in wanting words to show it.
>
> [Sonnet 26]

Here, in the first place, it may be observed, that in his prose, as well as in his verse, our author uses the same amatory language; for he opens the dedication to His Lordship with the assurance that "his love for him is without end." In correspondence with this declaration, the sonnet commences with this remarkable expression,—"Lord of my love;" while the residue tells us, in exact conformity with the prose address, his high sense of His Lordship's merit and his own unworthiness.

That no doubt may remain of the meaning and direction of this phraseology, we shall bring forward a few lines from the 110th sonnet, which uniting the language of both the passages just quoted, most incontrovertibly designate the sex, and, at the same time, we think, the individual to whom they are addressed:—

> My best of love,
> Now all is done, save what shall have no end:
> Mine appetite I never more will grind

On newer proof, to try an older friend,
A God in love, to whom I am confin'd.

Before we proceed any further, however, it may be necessary
to obviate an objection to our hypothesis which must immediately suggest itself. It will be said, that the first *seventeen* sonnets are written for the sole purpose of persuading their object to marry, and how could this exhortation be applicable
to Lord Southampton, who, from the year 1594 to the year
1599, was the devoted admirer of the fair Mrs. Vernon?

To remove this apparent incongruity, we have only to recollect, that His Lordship's attachment to his mistress met with
the most decided and relentless opposition from the Queen;
and there is every reason to infer, from the voluntary absences of the Earl in the years 1597 and 1598, and the extreme
distress of his mistress on these occasions, that the connection
had been twice given up, on his part, in deference to the will
of his capricious sovereign.

Shakspeare, when his friend at the age of twenty-one was first
smitten with the charms of Elizabeth Vernon, was high in His
Lordship's confidence and favour, as the dedication of his *Lucrece,* at this period, fully evinces. We also know, that the
Earl was very indignant at the interference of the Queen; that
he very reluctantly submitted for some years to her cruel re-
strictions in this affair; and if, in conformity with his constitutional irritability of temper, and the natural impulse of passion on such a subject, we merely admit, his having declared
what every lover would be tempted to utter on the occasion,
that if he could not marry the object of his choice, he would
die single, a complete key will be given to what has hitherto
proved inexplicable.

It immediately, indeed, and most satisfactorily accounts for
four circumstances, not to be explained on any other plan. It
affords, in the first place, an easy and natural clue to the
poet's expostulatory language, who, being ardently attached
to his patron, wished, of course, to see him happy either in
the possession of his first choice or in the arms of a second,
and, therefore, reprobates, in strong terms, such a premature
vow of celibacy: it gives in the second place, an adequate solution of the question, why so few as only seventeen sonnets,
and these the earliest in the collection, are employed to enforce the argument? for when His Lordship, on his return to
London from the Continent in 1598, embraced the resolution
of marrying his mistress, notwithstanding the continued opposition of the Queen, all ground for further expostulation
was instantly withdrawn. These seventeen sonnets, therefore,
were written between the years 1594 and 1598, and were consequently among those noticed by Meres in 1598, as in private circulation [see excerpt above, 1598]: in the third place,
it assigns a sufficient motive for withholding from public
view, until after the death of the Queen, a collection of which
part was written to counteract her known wishes, by exciting
the Earl to form an early and independent choice: and in the
fourth place, it furnishes a cogent reason why Jaggard, in his
surreptitious edition of the *Passionate Pilgrim* in 1599, did
not dare to publish any of these sonnets, at a time when
Southampton and his lady were imprisoned by the enraged
Elizabeth, as a punishment for their clandestine union.

Having thus, satisfactorily as we think, not only removed the
objection but strikingly corroborated the argument through
the medium of our defence, we shall select a few passages
from these initiatory sonnets in order still further to show the

TO.THE.ONLIE.BEGETTER.OF.
THESE.INSVING.SONNETS.
Mr.W. H. ALL.HAPPINESSE.
AND.THAT.ETERNITIE.
PROMISED.

BY.

OVR.EVER-LIVING.POET.

WISHETH.

THE.WELL-WISHING.
ADVENTVRER.IN.
SETTING.
FORTH.

T. T.

Dedication page of the 1609 edition of Shakespeare's Sonnets.

masculine nature of their object, and to give a specimen of the
poet's expostulatory freedom:—

   —Where is *she so fair,* whose *un-ear'd womb*
   Disdains the *tillage of thy husbandry?*
   Or who is *he* so fond, will be the tomb
   Of *his* self-love, to stop posterity.

                          [Sonnet 3]

   —thou . . .
   Unlook'd on diest, unless thou *get a son.*

                          [Sonnet 7]

The world will be *thy widow* and still weep—
No love toward others in that bosom sits,
That on *himself* such murderous shame commits.

                          [Sonnet 9]

   . . . Dear my love, you know,
   You had a *father; let your son say so.*

                          [Sonnet 13]

Now stand you on the top of happy hours;
And many *maiden* garlands yet unset,
With virtuous wish *would bear you living flowers.*

                          [Sonnet 16]
                         (pp. 378-80)

The subsequent sonnets, likewise, as far as the hundred and
twenty-seventh, which appear to have been written at various
periods anterior to 1609, not only bear the strongest additional testimony to the masculity of the person addressed, but

in several instances clearly evince the nature of the affection borne to him, which without any doubt consisted solely of ardent friendship and intellectual adoration. Two entire sonnets (the 31st and the 74th), indeed, are dedicated to the expression of these sentiments, in the first of which he tells his noble patron, that he had absorbed in his own person all the friendship which he (Shakspeare) had ever borne to the living or the dead, and he finely terms this attachment "religious love."

That Shakspeare looked up to his friend not only with admiration and gratitude, but with reverence and homage and, consequently, that neither William Harte nor William Hughes, nor any person of his own rank in society could be the subject of his verse, must be evident from the passages already adduced, and will be still more so, when we weigh the import of the following extracts.

We are told, in the seventy-eighth sonnet, what, indeed, we might have supposed from the Earl's well-known munificence to literary men, that he was the theme of every muse; and it is added, that his patronage gave dignity to learning, and majesty to grace.

In his ninety-first sonnet the poet informs us, that he values the affection of his friend more than riches, birth, or splendour, finishing his eulogium by asserting that he was not his peculiar boast, but the pride of all men:

> Thy love is better than high birth to me,
> Richer than wealth, prouder than garment's cost,
> Of more delight than hawks or horses be,
> And having thee, of all men's pride I boast.

But in terms the most emphatic and explicit does he point to his object, in the Sonnet 101, distinctly marking the sex, the dignity, the rank, and moral virtue of his friend: to whom can this sonnet, or indeed all the passages which we have cited apply, if not to Lord Southampton, the bosom-friend, the munificent patron of Shakspeare, the noble, the elegant, the brave, the protector of literature and the theme of many a song. And let it be remembered, that if the hundredth and first sonnet be justly ascribed to Lord Southampton, or if any one of the passages which we have adduced, be fairly applicable to him, the whole of the hundred and twenty-six sonnets must necessarily apply to the same individual, for the poet has more than once affirmed this to have been his plan and object. . . . (pp. 380-81)

It may be objected, that the opening and closing sonnet of the collection which we conceive to be exclusively devoted to Lord Southampton, admit neither of reconcilement with each other, nor with the hypothesis which we wish to establish. This discrepancy, however, will altogether vanish, if we compare the import of these sonnets with that of two others of the same series.

It will be allowed that the expressions, "the world's fresh ornament," the "only herald to the gaudy spring," and the epithets "tender churl," in the first sonnet, may with great propriety be applied to a young nobleman of twenty-one, just entering on a public and splendid career; but, if it be true, that these sonnets were written at various times, between the years 1594 and 1609, how comes it, that in the hundred and twenty-sixth, the last addressed to his patron, he still uses an equally youthful designation; and terms him "my lovely boy," an appellation certainly not then adapted to His Lordship, who, in 1609, was in his thirty-sixth year? (p. 381)

The mystery arising from the use of the juvenile epithets, he completely clears up in his hundred and eighth sonnet, where he says, that having exhausted every figure to express his patron's merit and his own affection, he is compelled to say the same things over again; that he is determined to consider him as young as when "he first hallowed his fair name;" that friendship, in fact, weighs not the advance of life, but adheres to its first conception, when youth and beauty clothed the object of its regard. In pursuance of this determination, he calls him, in this very sonnet, "sweet boy."

In conformity with this resolution of considering his friend as endowed whilst he lives with perpetual youth, he closes his sonnets to him, not only with the repetition of the juvenile epithet "boy," but he positively assures him that he has "time in his power," that "he grows by waning," and that "nature, as he goes onward, still plucks him back, in order to disgrace time." The conceit is somewhat puerile, though clearly explanatory of the systematic intention of the poet:—

> O thou, my lovely boy, who in thy power
> Dost hold *time's* fickle glass, his fickle hour;
> Who hast by *waning grown,* and therein show'st
> Thy lovers withering, as thy sweet self grow'st;
> If *nature,* sovereign mistress over wrack,
> *As thou goest onwards, still will pluck thee back,*
> She keeps thee to this purpose, that her skill
> *May time disgrace,* and wretched minutes kill.
>
> [Sonnet 126]

He terminates this sonnet, however, and his series of poetical addresses to Lord Southampton, with a powerful corrective of all flattery, in reminding him that although nature "may detain," she cannot "keep her treasure," and that he must ultimately yield to death.

We must also observe, that the poet has marked the termination of these sonnets to his friend, not only by the solemn nature of the concluding sentiment, but by a striking deviation from the customary form of his composition in these pieces; the closing poem not being constructed with alternate rhymes, but consisting of six couplets! (pp. 381-82)

[It] is not true, as Mr. Malone has asserted, that [Sonnets 127-54] are *all* addressed to a female. Two, at least, have not the slightest reference to any individual; the hundred and twenty-ninth sonnet being a general and moral declamation on the misery resulting from sensual love, and the hundred and forty-sixth, an address to his own soul of a somewhat severe and religious cast.

Of the residue, four have no very determinate application, and to whom the twenty-two are dedicated, is not now to be ascertained, and, if it were, not worth the enquiry; for, a more worthless character, or described as such in stronger terms, no poet ever drew. We much wish, indeed, these sonnets had never been published, or that their subject could be proved to have been perfectly ideal. We are the more willing to consider them in this light, since, if we dismiss these confessional sonnets, not the slightest moral stain can rest on the character of Shakspeare. . . . It is very improbable, also, that any poet should publish such an open confession of his own culpability.

Of the grossly meretricious conduct of his mistress, of whose personal charms and accomplishments we know nothing more than that she had black eyes, black hair, and could play on the virginal, Sonnets 137, 142, and 144, bear the most indubitable evidence. Well, therefore, might the poet term her his "false plague," his "worser spirit," his "female evil," and his "bad angel;" well might he tell her, notwithstanding the colour of her eyes and hair,

> Thy black is fairest in my judgment's place;
> In nothing art thou black, save in thy deeds.
>
> [Sonnet 131]

> For I have sworn thee fair, and thought thee bright,
> Who art as black as hell, as dark as night.
>
> [Sonnet 147]

Well might he blame his pliability of temper, his insufficiency of judgment and resolution, well might he call himself "past cure," and "frantic-mad," when, addressing this profligate woman, he exclaims,

> Whence hast thou this becoming of things ill,
> That in the very refuse of thy deeds
> There is such strength and warrantise of skill,
> That in my mind, thy worst all best exceeds?
> Who taught thee how to make me love thee more,
> The more I hear and see just cause of hate?
> O, though I love what others do abhor,
> With others thou should'st not abhor my state;
>   If thy unworthiness rais'd love in me,
>   More worthy I to be belov'd by thee.
>
> [Sonnet 150]

Now, weighing, what almost every other personal event in our author's life establishes, the general and moral beauty of his character, and reflecting, at the same time, that he was at this period a husband, and the father of a family, we cannot but feel the most entire conviction, that these sonnets were never directed to a real object: but that, notwithstanding they were written in his own person, and two of them, indeed (Sonnets 135 and 136), a perpetual pun on his Christian name, they were solely intended to express, aloof from all individual application, the contrarieties, the inconsistencies, and the miseries of illicit love. Credulity itself, we think, cannot suppose otherwise, and, at the same time, believe that the poet was privy to their publication.

To this discussion of a subject clogged with so many difficulties, we shall now subjoin some remarks on the poetical merits and demerits of our author's sonnets; and here, we are irresistibly induced to notice the absurd charge against, and the inadequate defence of, sonnet-writing, brought forward by Messrs. Steevens and Malone, in the Supplement of the latter gentleman.

The antipathy of Mr. Steevens to this species of lyric poetry, seems to have amounted to the highest pitch of extravagance. . . . [He] informs us that the sonnet is "a species of composition which has reduced the most exalted poets to a level with the meanest rhymers; has almost cut down Milton and Shakspeare to the standards of Pomfret and—, but the name of Pomfret is perhaps the lowest in the scale of English versifiers." Nothing can exceed the futility and bad taste of this remark, and yet Mr. Malone has advanced no other defence of the "exalted poets" of Italy than that, "he is slow to believe that Petrarch is without merit;" and for Milton he offers this strange apology,—"that he generally failed when he attempted rhyme, whether his verses assumed the shape of a sonnet, or any other form."

When we recollect, that the noblest poets of Italy, from Dante to Alfieri, have employed their talents in the construction of the sonnet, and that many of their most popular and beautiful passages have been derived through this medium; when we recollect, that the first bards of our own country, from Surrey to Southey, have followed their example with an emulation which has conferred immortality on their efforts; when we further call to mind the exquisite specimens of rhymed poetry which Milton has given us in his *L'Allegro* and *Il Penseroso;* and when, above all, we retrace the dignity, the simplicity, the moral sublimity of many of his sonnets, perhaps not surpassed by any other part of his works, we stand amazed at the unqualified censure on the one hand, and at the impotency of the defence on the other.

If such be the fate, then, between these commentators, of the general question, and of the one more peculiarly relative to Milton, it cannot be expected that Shakspeare should meet with milder treatment. In fact, Mr. Steevens has asserted, that his sonnets are "composed in the highest strain of affectation, pedantry, circumlocution, and nonsense;" a picture which Mr. Malone endeavours to soften, by telling us that "it appears to him overcharged:" that similar defects occur in his dramas, and that the sonnets, "if they have no other merit, are entitled to our attention, as often illustrating obscure passages in his plays."

It is true that in the next paragraph he ventures to declare, that he cannot perceive that their versification is less smooth than that of Shakspeare's other compositions, and that he can perceive perspicuity and energy in some of them; but well might Mr. Steevens reply, that "the case of these sonnets is certainly bad, when so little can be advanced in support of them."

Let us try, therefore, if we cannot, and that also with great ease, prove that these sonnets have been not only miserably criticised, but unmercifully abused; and that, in point of poetical merit, they are superior to all those which preceded the era of Drummond.

In the first place, then, we altogether deny that either affectation or pedantry can, in the proper sense of the terms, be applied to the sonnets of Shakspeare. Were any modern, indeed, of the nineteenth century to adopt their language and style, he might justly be taxed with both; but in Sidney and Shakspeare it was habit, indissoluble habit, and not affectation; it was the diction in which they had been practised from early youth to clothe their sentiments and feelings; it was identified with all their associations and intellectual operations; it was the language, in fact, the mode of expression, in a greater or less degree, of all their contemporaries; and to have stripped their thoughts of a dress, which to us appears quaint and artificial, would have been to them a painful and more elaborate task. When once, indeed, we can attribute this artificial, though often emphatic style, as we ought to do, to the universally defective taste of the age in which it sprang, and not to individual usage, we shall be prepared to do justice to injured genius, and to confess, that frequently beneath this laboured phraseology are to be found sentiments simple, natural, and touching. We may also very safely affirm of Shakspeare's sonnets, that, if their style be compared with that of his predecessors and contemporaries, in the same department of poetry, a manifest superiority must often be awarded him, on the score of force, dignity, and simplicity of expression. . . . (pp. 382-84)

To a certain extent, we must admit the charge of circumlocution, not as applied to individual sonnets, but to the subject on which the whole series is written. The obscurities of this species of poem have almost uniformly arisen from density and compression of style, nor are the compositions of Shakspeare more than usually free from this source of defect; but when it is considered that our author has written one hundred and twenty-six sonnets for the sole purpose of expressing his attachment to his patron, it must necessarily follow, that a subject so continually reiterated, would display no small share of circumlocution. Great ingenuity has been exhibited by the poet in varying his phraseology and ideas; but no effort could possibly obviate the monotony, as the result of such a task.

We shall not condescend to a refutation of the fourth epithet, which, if at all applicable to any portion of Shakspeare's minor poems, can alone apply to Sonnets 135 and 136, which are a continued pun upon his Christian name, a species of trifling which was the peculiar vice of our author's age.

That an attempt to exhaust the subject of friendship; to say all that could be collected on the topic, would almost certainly lead, in the days of Shakspeare, to abstractions too subtle and metaphysical, and to a cast of diction sometimes too artificial and scholastic for modern taste, no person well acquainted with the progress of our literature can deny; but candour will, at the same time, admit, that the expression and versification of his sonnets are often natural, spirited, and harmonious, and that where the surface has been rendered hard and repulsive by the peculiarities of the period of their production, we have only to search beneath, in order to discover a rich ore of thought, imagery, and sentiment. (pp. 384-85)

> *Nathan Drake, in an excerpt in his* Shakspeare and His Times, *1817. Reprint by Burt Franklin, 1969, pp. 352-88.*

JAMES BOSWELL (essay date 1821)

[*The second surviving son of the celebrated biographer of Samuel Johnson, Boswell edited the twenty-one volume third variorum edition of Shakespeare's works,* The Plays and Poems of William Shakespeare, with the Corrections and Illustrations of Various Commentators, Comprehending a Life of the Poet, and an Enlarged History of the Stage, *by the Late Edmond Malone (1821). In the following excerpt from Volume XX of this work, Boswell questions the assumption behind critical attempts to identify the Friend and Dark Lady of Shakespeare's sonnets, denying that these verses are autobiographical. He asserts that although we have little knowledge of Shakespeare's life, what we do know does not coincide with the apparent character of the speaker in the sonnets. Noting that all evidence suggests that Shakespeare was a gentle, honest man, Boswell claims that the sonnets "were merely the effusions of [the poet's] fancy, written upon various topicks for the amusement of a private circle."*]

There are few topicks connected with Shakspeare upon which the ingenuity and research of his criticks have been more fruitlessly exercised, than upon the questions which have arisen with regard to the [Sonnets], the individual to whom they were principally addressed, and the circumstances under which they were written. Dr. Farmer's conjecture, we find, has been decisively overthrown by the Stratford Register; and Mr. Tyrwhitt's, even if we should admit it to be well-founded, would furnish us with no very satisfactory information [see excerpt above by Edmond Malone, 1780]. We shall have made but a slight advancement in knowledge by barely having ascertained that some person of the name of Hughes, but

of whose character and history we are wholly ignorant, was the object of the poet's encomiums. . . . Mr. Chalmers some years ago made a singular attempt to unravel this question, and contrived to persuade himself that the "lovely boy," whom Shakspeare addressed, was no less a person than our *maiden queen* Elizabeth [see excerpt above, 1797]. As I cannot permit myself to doubt that Mr. Chalmers (if he ever was serious) must now himself look back to the recollection of this whimsical fancy with a smile, I shall dismiss it without further observation. (p. 218)

But whoever the person might be to whom the greater part of these Sonnets was addressed, it seems to have been generally admitted that the poet speaks in his own person; and some of his criticks have attempted, by inferences drawn from them, to eke out the scanty memorials, which have come down to us, of the incidents of his life. . . . Mr. Malone, in a note on the 111th Sonnet, has observed, that "the author seems to lament his being reduced to the necessity of appearing on the stage, or writing for the theatre." The passage alluded to is as follows:

> O! for my sake, do you with fortune chide,
> The guilty goddess of my harmful deeds,
> That did not better for my life provide,
> *Than publick means, which publick manners breeds.*

But is there any thing in these words which, read without a preconceived hypothesis, would particularly apply to the publick profession of a player or writer for the stage? The troubles and dangers which attend upon publick life in general, and the happiness and virtue of retirement, are among the tritest common places of poetry. Nor was such querulous language likely to have proceeded from Shakspeare. Ben Jonson, who was frequently obliged to exhibit before audiences who were incapable of appreciating the depth of his knowledge, the accuracy of his judgment, or the dignity of his moral, might at one time be desirous of quitting "the loathed stage," or Massinger might have murmured at a calling which scarcely procured him a subsistence; but our poet appears, from the commencement to the close of his dramatick career, to have met with uninterrupted success, and would scarcely indulge in such bitter complaints against a profession which was rapidly conducting him to fortune as well as to fame. . . . If Shakspeare was speaking of himself in this passage, it would follow that he is equally pointed at upon other occasions. We must then suppose him to have written them when he was *old;* for such is the language of many of these poems. Yet, if they were composed before Meres's publication [see excerpt above, 1598], he could not have been at a more advanced age than thirty-four; and even if we were to adopt the theory of Dr. Drake, and suppose that most of them were produced at a subsequent period, and fix upon the latest possible year, 1609 [see excerpt above, 1817], yet still the description of decrepitude, which is found in the 73d Sonnet, could scarcely, without violent exaggeration, be applicable to a man of forty-five. But he must not only have been old, he must also have been grossly and notoriously profligate. To say nothing of the criminal connection, (for criminal in a high degree it would certainly have been in a married man,) which is frequently alluded to in those Sonnets which are said to be addressed by him in his own character to a female; we find him, in a passage already quoted, speaking in terms of shame and remorse of his "harmful deeds," of something from which his "name had received a brand;" and of "the impression which vulgar scandal had stamped upon his brow" [Sonnets 111 and 112]. I trust it will not require much argument to show that this picture could not be put for gentle Shakspeare. We may lament that we know so little of his history; but this, at least, may be asserted with confidence, that at no time was the slightest imputation cast upon his moral character; and that, in an age abounding, as Mr. Steevens has observed, with illiberal private abuse and peevish satire, the concurring testimony of his contemporaries will confirm the declaration of honest Chettle, that "his demeanour was no less civil, than he excellent in the quality he professed."

Upon the whole, I am satisfied that these compositions had neither the poet himself nor any individual in view; but were merely the effusions of his fancy, written upon various topics for the amusement of a private circle, as indeed the words of Meres point out: "Witness—his sugred Sonnets among his private friends." The Sonnet was at that time a popular species of poetry, and was a favourite mode of expressing either the writer's own sentiments, or of embellishing a work of fiction. The novels of Lodge and Greene, and their contemporaries, are full of them; and something, which in the lax language of that day may be classed under the same title, is even to be found in the early dramatick productions of our author. . . . It has been observed, indeed, as a proof of these poems having some man of high rank as their object, that Shakspeare, upon several occasions, has declared that one person alone is the object of his praise, and that the language which he employs could only be applicable to a peculiarly dignified individual; but such, I apprehend, is the constant strain of amatory or encomiastick poetry. (pp. 219-21)

> *James Boswell, "Preliminary Remarks," in* The Plays and Poems of William Shakspeare, *Vol. XX by Edmond Malone, edited by James Boswell, 1821. Reprint by AMS Press, Inc., 1966, pp. 217-22.*

WILLIAM WORDSWORTH (poem date 1827)

[*In the following brief passage from his 1827 poem "Scorn Not the Sonnet," often referred to by critics addressing the autobiographical basis of Shakespeare's sonnets, Wordsworth praises the verse form that "unlocked" Shakespeare's heart.*]

> Scorn not the Sonnet; Critic, you have
> 　　　　frowned,
> Mindless of its just honours; with this key
> Shakspeare unlocked his heart. . . .

> *William Wordsworth, " 'Scorn Not the Sonnet' " in his* The Complete Poetical Works of William Wordsworth, *Houghton Mifflin Company, 1904, p. 650.*

WALTER SAVAGE LANDOR (essay date 1828)

[*Landor was an English poet, essayist, critic, and dialogue writer. He is best known as the author of* Imaginary Conversations of Literary Men and Statesmen *(1824-29), in which he presented hypothetical dialogues on literary, political, and other subjects. In the following brief passage from an "imaginary conversation" between himself and the English poet Robert Southey, Landor comments, in his own person, on the artistry of Shakespeare's sonnets. He states that while "not a single one is very admirable" and "few sink very low," they are yet more appealing to him than the verse of his own contemporaries.*]

Among all Shakspeare's [sonnets], not a single one is very admirable, and few sink very low. They are hot and pothery:

there is much condensation, little delicacy; like raspberry jam without cream, without crust, without bread, to break its viscidity. But I would rather sit down to one of them again than to a string of such musty sausages as are exposed in our streets at the present dull season. (p. 285)

> *Walter Savage Landor, "Southey and Landor (second conversation)," in his* Imaginary Conversations, *Vol. 4, edited by Charles G. Crump, J. M. Dent & Co., 1891, pp. 246-302.*

ANNA BROWNELL JAMESON (essay date 1829)

[*Jameson was a well-known nineteenth-century essayist. Her essays and criticism span the end of the Romantic age and the beginning of Victorian realism, reflecting elements from both periods. She is best remembered for her study* Characteristics of Women: Moral, Poetical, and Historical, *originally published in 1832 but revised one year later. This work demonstrates both her historical interests and her sympathetic appreciation of Shakespeare's female characters. In the following excerpt from a work originally published under the title* The Loves of the Poets *(1829), she probes the sonnets for evidence of Shakespeare's personal views concerning love, premising her commentary on the belief that they are the only writings of Shakespeare "through which we can trace any thing of his personal feelings and affections." Maintaining that Numbers 1-55 are addressed to Southampton while some of the others are addressed "in Southampton's name" to Elizabeth Vernon, Jameson senses in the remaining poems a writer "certainly under the full and irresistable influence of female fascination." This accounts, she notes, for "the very soul of profound tenderness and melancholy feeling" in Sonnet 71. Nevertheless, the critic continues, the identity of the woman addressed in some of the most heart-inspired sonnets remains unknown. Jameson also touches on the composition dates of the sonnets, which she sees connected with a time when Shakespeare "was living a wild and irregular life, between the court and the theatre, after his flight from Stratford."*]

Shakspeare—I approach the subject with reverence, and even with fear,—is the only poet I am acquainted with and able to appreciate, who appears to have been really heaven-inspired: the workings of his wondrous and all-embracing mind were directed by a higher influence than ever was exercised by woman, even in the plenitude of her power and her charms. Shakspeare's genius waited not on Love and Beauty, but Love and Beauty ministered to *him;* he perceived like a spirit; he was created, to create; his own individuality is lost in the splendor, the reality, and the variety of his own conceptions. When I think what those are, I feel how needless, how vain it were to swell the universal voice with one so weak as mine. Who would care for it that knows and feels Shakspeare? Who would listen to it that does not, if there be such?

It is not Shakspeare as a great power bearing a great name,—but Shakspeare in his less divine and less known character,—as a lover and a man, who finds a place here. The only writings he has left, through which we can trace any thing of his personal feelings and affections, are his Sonnets. Every one who reads them, who has tenderness or taste, will echo Wordsworth's denunciation against the "flippant insensibility" of some of his commentators, who talked of an Act of Parliament not being strong enough to compel their perusal [see excerpt above by George Steevens, 1793]; and will agree in his opinion, that they are full of the most exquisite feelings, most felicitously expressed [see excerpt above, 1815]; but as to the object to whom they were addressed, a difference of opinion prevails. From a reference, however, to all that is known of Shakspeare's life and fortunes, compared with the internal presumptive evidence contained in the Sonnets, it appears that some of them are addressed to his amiable friend, Lord Southampton: and others, I think, are addressed in Southampton's name, to that beautiful Elizabeth Vernon, to whom the Earl was so long and ardently attached. The Queen, who did not encourage matrimony among her courtiers, absolutely refused her consent to their union. She treated him as she did Raleigh in the affair of Elizabeth Throckmorton; and Southampton, after four years' impatient submission and still increasing love, as tenderly returned by his mistress, married without the Queen's knowledge, lost her favor forever, and nearly lost his head.

That Lord Southampton is the subject of the first fifty-five Sonnets is sufficiently clear; and some of these are perfectly beautiful,—as the 30th, 32d, 41st, 54th. There are others scattered through the rest of the volume, on the same subject; but there are many which admit of no such interpretation, and are without doubt inspired by the real object of a real passion, of whom nothing can be discovered, but that she was dark-eyed and dark-haired, that she excelled in music, and that she was one of a class of females who do not always, in losing all right to our respect, lose also their claim to the admiration of the sex who wronged them, or the compassion of the gentler part of their own, who have rejected them. This is so clear from various passages, that unhappily there can be no doubt of it. He has flung over her, designedly it should seem, a veil of immortal texture and fadeless hues, "branched and embroidered like the painted Spring," but almost impenetrable even to our imagination. There are few allusions to her personal beauty, which can in any way individualize her, but bursts of deep and passionate feeling, and eloquent reproach, and contending emotions, which show, that if she could awaken as much love and impart as much happiness as woman ever inspired or bestowed, he endured on her account all the pangs of agony, and shame, and jealousy;—that our Shakspeare—he, who, in the omnipotence of genius, wielded the two worlds of reality and imagination in either hand, who was in conception and in act scarce less than a GOD, was in passion and suffering not more than a MAN.

Instead of any elaborate description of her person, we have, in the only Sonnet which sets forth her charms, the rich materials for a picture, rather than the picture itself.

> The forward violet thus did I chide:
> Sweet thief, whence didst thou steal thy sweet that
>   smells,
> If not from my Love's breath? The purple pride
> Which on thy soft cheek for complexion dwells,
> In my Love's veins thou hast too grossly dy'd.
> The lily I condemned for thy hand,
> And buds of marjoram had stolen thy hair:
> The roses fearfully on thorns did stand,
> One blushing shame, another white despair;
> A third, nor red nor white, had stolen of both,
> And to his robbery had annex'd thy breath;
> But for his theft, in pride of all his growth
> A vengeful canker eat him up to death.
> More flowers I noted, yet I none could see,
> But sweet, or color, it had stolen from thee.
>
> [Sonnet 99]

He intimates that he found a rival in one of his own most intimate friends, who was also a poet. He laments her absence in this exquisite strain;—

> How like a winter hath my absence been

> From thee, the pleasure of the fleeting year!
> What freezings have I felt, what dark days seen,
> What old December's bareness everywhere!
> * * * * *
> For Summer and his pleasure wait on thee,
> And thou away, the very birds are mute!
>
> [Sonnet 97]

He dwells with complacency on her supposed truth and tenderness, her bounty like Juliet's, "boundless as the sea, her love as deep" [*Romeo and Juliet,* II. ii. 133].

> Kind is my love to-day, to-morrow kind,
> Still constant in a wondrous excellence.
>
> [Sonnet 105]

Then, as if conscious upon how unstable a foundation he had built his love, he expresses his fear lest he should be betrayed, yet remain unconscious of the wrong.

> For there can live no hatred in thine eye,
>   Therefore in that I cannot know thy change!
> In many's looks, the false heart's history
>   Is writ in moods and frowns, and wrinkles
>   strange.
> But heaven in thy creation did decree,
>   That in thy face sweet love should ever dwell.
>
> [Sonnet 93]

He bitterly reproaches her with her levity and falsehood, and himself that he can be thus unworthily enslaved,—

> What potions have I drunk of Syren tears, &c.
>
> [Sonnet 119]

Then, with lover-like inconsistency, excuses her.—

> As on the finger of a throned queen
>   The basest jewel will be well esteemed;
> So are those errors that in thee are seen
>   To truths translated, and for true things deem'd.
>
> [Sonnet 96]

And the following are powerfully and painfully expressive:—

> How sweet and lovely dost thou make the shame,
>   Which, like a canker in the fragrant rose,
> Doth spot the beauty of thy budding name!
>   Oh, in what sweets dost thou thy sins enclose!
>
> O, what a mansion have those vices got,
>   Which for their habitation chose out thee,
> Where Beauty's veil doth cover every blot,
>   And all things turn to fair that eyes can see!
>
> [Sonnet 95]

"Who taught thee," he says in another Sonnet,

>   —to make me love thee more
> The more I hear, and see just cause for hate?
>
> [Sonnet 150]

He who wrote these and similar passages was certainly under the full and irresistible influence of female fascination. But who it was that thus ruled the universal heart and mighty spirit of our Shakspeare, we know not. She stands behind him a veiled and a nameless phantom. Neither dare we call in Fancy to penetrate that veil; for who would presume to trace even the faintest outline of such a being as Shakspeare could have loved?

* * * * *

I think it doubtful to whom were addressed those exquisite lines,

> Then hate me when thou wilt, if ever, now! &c.
>
> [Sonnet 90]

but probably to this very person.

The Sonnets in which he alludes to his profession as an actor; where he speaks of the brand, "which vulgar scandal stamped upon his brow" [Sonnet 112], and of having made himself "a motley to men's view" [Sonnet 110], are undoubtedly addressed to Lord Southampton.

> O, for my sake, do you with Fortune chide,
>   The guilty goddess of my harmful deeds,
> That did not better for my life provide,
>   Than public means, which public manners breeds;
> Thence comes it that my name receives a brand,
>   And almost thence my nature is subdu'd
> To what it works in, like the dyer's hand.
>   Pity me then, and wish I were renew'd.
>
> [Sonnet 111]

The last I shall remark, perhaps the finest of all, and breathing the very soul of profound tenderness and melancholy feeling, must, I think, have been addressed to a female.

> No longer mourn for me when I am dead
>   Than you shall hear the surly sullen bell
> Give warning to the world that I am fled
>   From this vile earth, with vilest worms to dwell:
> Nay, if you read this line, remember not
>   The hand that writ it; for I love you so,
> That I in your sweet thoughts would be forgot,
>   If thinking on me then should make you woe.
> O if (I say) you look upon this verse,
>   When I perhaps compounded am with clay
> Do not so much as my poor name rehearse:
>   But let your love ev'n with my life decay:
> Lest the wise world should look into your moan,
> And mock you with me after I am gone.
>
> [Sonnet 71]

The period assigned to the composition of these Sonnets, and the attachment which inspired them, is the time when Shakspeare was living a wild and irregular life, between the court and the theatre, after his flight from Stratford. He had previously married, at the age of seventeen, Judith Hathaway, who was eight or ten years older than himself: he returned to his native town, after having sounded all depths of life, of nature, of passion, and ended his days as the respected father of a family, in calm, unostentatious privacy.

One thing I will confess:—It is natural to feel an intense and insatiable curiosity relative to great men, a curiosity and interest for which nothing can be too minute, too personal.— And yet when I had ransacked all that had ever been written, discovered, or surmised, relative to Shakspeare's private life, for the purpose of throwing some light upon his Sonnets, I felt no gratification, no thankfulness to those whose industry had raked up the very few particulars which can be known. It is too much, and it is not enough: it disappoints us in one point of view—it is superfluous in another: what need to surround with common-place, trivial associations, registers of wills and genealogies, and I know not what,—the mighty spirit who in dying left behind him not merely a name and fame, but a perpetual being, a presence and a power, identified with our nature, diffused through all time, and ruling the heart and the fancy with an uncontrollable and universal sway!

I rejoice that the name of no one woman is popularly identified with that of Shakspeare. He belongs to us all!—the creator of Desdemona, and Juliet, and Ophelia, and Imogen, and Viola, and Constance, and Cordelia, and Rosalind, and Portia, was not the poet of one woman, but the POET OF WOMANKIND.(pp. 182-90)

> *Anna Brownell Jameson, "On the Love of Shakspeare," in her* Memoirs of the Loves of the Poets, *1831. Reprint by Houghton Mifflin and Company, 1892, pp. 182-90.*

JAMES BOADEN   (essay date 1832)

[*Boaden was an English biographer, dramatist, and journalist. In the following excerpt, he professes that he has deciphered the identity of W. H., the Friend, and the Rival Poet. Boaden declares that the dedicatee and the object of Shakespeare's admiration in Sonnets 1-126 are selfsame: William Herbert, Earl of Pembroke. All the specifics of the relationship between the Friend and the sonneteer apply easily to the association of Pembroke and Shakespeare, Boaden claims, and there are also a host of correspondences between events in Pembroke's life and elements in the sonnets. Concerning the identity of the Rival Poet, the critic theorizes that this "better spirit" is Samuel Daniel; he notes that Ben Jonson considered Daniel the equal of Edmund Spenser. Boaden adds that Shakespeare's jealousy arose from Daniel's dedication of his* Defence of Rhyme *(1601) to William Herbert. Much of Boaden's commentary here was originally published, in a shorter form, in the* Gentleman's Magazine *(September-October, 1832). B. Heywood Bright claimed (in the* Gentleman's Magazine, *October 1832) that he, not Boaden, was the first to construct the theory that W. H. is William Herbert; Bright averred that he had formulated his argument in 1819, but did not publish his findings.*]

The Sonnets of Shakespeare were first printed in the year 1609, by Thomas Thorpe. . . . They make a thin quarto, neither carelessly nor inelegantly set forth, and are inscribed by the publisher, under initials, to the person addressed by the poet. It will be proper to bring this dedication immediately forward, because, *prima facie,* no one can be a competitor for the eternity promised in the verses, whose name does not display the initials given to us as a clue by the dedicator.

The inscription is arranged monumentally, in short lines, with full points after every word.

> To. The. onlie. begetter. of.
> These. insuing. Sonnets.
> Mr. W. H. all. Happinesse.
> And.that.eternitie.
> Promised.
> By.
> Our. ever-living. Poet.
> Wisheth.
> The. well-wishing.
> Adventurer. in.
> Setting.
> Forth.
>
> T. T.

That the words "only begetter" mean the person addressed by the poet, cannot, I should think, be reasonably questioned—they imply him who, as a *cause,* excited these verses as effects in the grateful mind of Shakespeare. Indeed, for a long time, it seemed to be the only notion that was entertained; and accordingly WILLIAM HART, the poet's relation, was mentioned, without examining whether his age was suitable, or himself, either in person or fortunes, corresponding with what is stated in the sonnets. A moment's reflection would have rendered it *certain,* that the child of very humble parents was not the *lofty patrician* commemorated in these compositions:

> Thou, that art now the world's fresh ornament,
> And only herauld to the gaudy spring.
>
> > [Sonnet 1]
> > (pp.1-3)

[Shakespeare is here plainly] imitating the sonnet of Spenser to the great courtier Sir Walter Raleigh, published in 1590, with the first three books of the *Faerie Queene:*

> To thee that art the Sommer's nightingale,
> Thy soveraine Goddesses most deare delight.

Indeed the parallel is strikingly made out in the course of the poet's addresses to this beloved patron, whom he places in a station of such dignity and gravity, that he might not be able from prudential motives to honour him with kindness in *public,* unless by suffering in the general estimation for his familiarity with a player:

> Against that time, if ever that time come,
> When I shall see thee frown on my defects,
> When as thy love hath cast his utmost sum,
> Call'd to that audit by *advis'd respects;*
> Against that time, when thou shalt strangely pass,
> And scarcely greet me with that sun, thine eye;
> When love converted from the thing it was,
> Shall reasons find of *settled gravity.*
>
> > [Sonnet 49]

We may therefore dismiss Mr. William Hart, notwithstanding his initial pretensions, and pass . . . for some other candidate.

The initials W. H. do not appear to have formerly suggested one suitable ascription; and at length it was thought advisable to review the obnoxious Dedication, and try whether the language might not *bend* a little to the necessity of the case. If the "only begetter," for instance, could be interpreted to signify *procuring* a copy of the sonnets for the Publisher, the field of conjecture as to the Patron was expanded ad libitum. W. H. then got his "promised eternity" for merely bringing out the papers; and the person addressed might be any great amiable patron of poetry, who was a male—and even a *female* in the fantastical conception of one great Shakespearean. The reasoning was formal—whoever begets, they said, *obtains* something:—whoever obtains these papers, therefore, is their *sole begetter.* Mr. W. H. therefore embarrasses no longer; and the late Mr. George Chalmers settled that the person addressed by Shakespeare was, and could be, no other human being than Queen Elizabeth [see excerpt above, 1797]. Common sense stood aghast, as it had frequently done, at the monstrous absurdity of the critic's speculation; and respectfully enquired how he could reconcile it to the everlasting allusions to the *male* sex, which are found throughout these poems? Shakespeare calls him every where the *Lord* of his love. One instance however shall here suffice:

> Lord of my love, to whom in vassalage
> Thy merit hath my duty strongly knit.
>
> > [Sonnet 26]

And in the 3d Sonnet, when he incites him to marry, and

leave an image behind him of his own perfections, he thus pointedly marks the sex of the person addressed:

> For where is she so fair, whose un-eard womb
> Disdains the *tillage* of thy *husbandry?*
>
> > (pp. 3-5)

On the present occasion [Mr. Chalmers] was led into his absurdity by another equally great, namely, that SPENSER addressed his *Amoretti,* a collection of Sonnets, to the great Queen; and that Shakespeare, from a feeling of *jealousy,* would needs pay the same compliment to her beauties. This inference was drawn from an expression in his 80th Sonnet.

> O how I faint when I of you do write,
> Knowing a BETTER SPIRIT doth use your name,
> And in the praise thereof spends all his might,
> To make me tongue-tied, speaking of your fame!

I shall show . . . who the *better spirit* really was, and his connection with the *subject* of Shakespeare's Sonnets. But could our Poet here have really referred to Spenser, no *Sonnets* would have crossed his mind, and alarmed his jealousy. Shakespeare had too deep a feeling of poetry, and too much modesty, not to know and declare, that the *Faery Queene* did more to illustrate Elizabeth, than could all the Sonnets in the universe, whoever were the writers. (pp. 16-17)

It may be proper to concede to Dr. Drake, that he has shown the absolute certainty that 126 of the Sonnets in question were addressed to a *male* friend and patron of Shakespeare; and he thinks that friend was Lord Southampton [see excerpt above, 1817]. The reasons must be strong indeed that overturn so natural an ascription.

The *first* which I shall adduce, in my opinion, has force sufficient to set his Lordship aside. It is the Dedication of Thorpe the publisher, which is printed at the outset of this essay, who wishes Mr. W. H., as the only begetter of the Sonnets, *"all happiness,* and that *Eternity promised* by our ever-living Poet." Now it is proper to look at this promised eternity in the Poet's own language, that we may be quite sure of its application to the person addressed by him, and to no other; because it will then follow that no friend or patron can be he, whose name is not figured truly by those initials. Thus he writes in the 81st Sonnet:

> Your name from hence immortal life shall have,
> Though I once gone to all the world must die;
> The earth can yield me but a common grave,
> When you entombed in men's eyes shall lie.
> Your monument shall be my gentle verse,
> Which eyes not yet created shall o'er read;
> And tongues to be, your being shall rehearse,
> When all the breathers of the world are dead;
> You still shall live (such virtue hath my pen,)
> Where breath most breathes—even in the mouths
>   of men.

Now the initials do not apply to Lord Southampton, who was named Henry Wriothesly; and who, ten years before Shakespeare became known to him, was Earl of Southampton and Baron of Tichfield. I state this firmly, because in 1593, when the Poet dedicated his *Venus and Adonis,* it was at a distance that implied no acquaintance; for the very dedication was *without permission,* and he says, "I know not how I shall offend in dedicating my unpolished lines to your Lordship." *Tarquin and Lucrece,* in 1594, shows that his former offering had been well received. If we suppose him therefore to have begun these Sonnets as soon as his latter poem had done its work, how did the relative *ages* stand of the Poet and the Patron? In 1594 Lord Southampton was 21, being born in 1573; and Shakespeare exactly 30, being born in 1564. The disparity is nothing; yet, in the poems, one of the parties is stated to be in the *spring* of life, and the other in the *autumn.*—One "the *sweet boy,*" "the world's fresh ornament" [Sonnet 1], the other "crush'd and o'erworn by the injurious hand of Time" [Sonnet 63]. . . . Southampton therefore could not be the object addressed in the Sonnets. Take the very *last* of them, and we find him still saluted "O thou, my lovely boy" [Sonnet 126]. Dr. Drake thinks the uniformity of the affection borne may justify the iteration of the term at any part of the intimacy. I think, as to Southampton, it was unjustifiable in *any one* year of it.

But out of respect to an hypothesis advocated by Dr. Drake, let us wave this decorous objection. Yet surely we may reasonably ask, why the Sonnets were restricted to the *personal beauty* of Southampton, (which he does not seem to have had, if his portrait resembled him), and a *devoted attachment* on the Poet's side, which never seemed to sympathize with the actual circumstances of that nobleman's *life?* Did [Southampton's] achievements in 1596 and 1597, as a great Captain, at Cadiz and in the Azores, yield nothing? In 1598 he went with his friend Essex to Ireland. On his marriage in 1596 with Miss Vernon being known, he was thrown into prison; had Shakespeare alone been indifferent to these occurrences—the latter amatorial, and quite in his line of compliment, his success with the fair? How did the Poet feel upon his rash daring with Essex? had he no soothing balm to shed upon the agonies of his trial, sentence, and imprisonment? and finally, when James had restored him to his liberty and his honours, could his eulogist find no call upon him for *secure* congratulation? but, amid combats by sea and land, secret attachment and marriage, irritation of his Royal Mistress, rebellion against her authority, sentence to an ignominious death, release from a captivity bitter as death,—could, I say, this most loving and fertile of all poets "set down in the tables," which his friend had given to him (as the Sonnets inform us), nothing but one cuckoo note upon a theme which that friend, unless he never matured, must have long dismissed from his attention, I mean his personal beauty? I answer, I cannot conceive it. If these Sonnets were *periodically* sent to a man so circumstanced as we find Lord Southampton to have been, he must have nauseated their uniformity. If they were *not* so dispatched to him, the Poet would chuse his topics out of the passing events, and reserve the series for a time when they might be transmitted without danger. But we should expect a Shakespeare to tell him in a masterly tone—that calamity was the nurse of great spirits;—that his afflictions had been the sources of his best fame;—that mankind never could have known the resources of his mighty mind, if he had not been summoned to endure disgrace, and to gaze undaunted upon the menacing preparations of death itself. Nothing of this kind is hinted at, and therefore the Sonnets *cannot* apply to Lord Southampton. (pp. 21-5)

The difficulty is, to select a person who, from his youth and station, called for no other topics than the Sonnets afford; who was beautiful enough to be considered "the world's fresh ornament;" interesting enough that the Poet should wish his *straying youth* removed from temptation; great enough to be courted, as willing and able to patronize a condition that could not exist without it, and who actually became the patron of Shakespeare; one moreover whom, as the Sonnets tell us, rival poets were courting, with all the arts, and more than

the *charms* of verse. Such a person I shall proceed to point out. (p. 27)

It is obvious that the Patron of Shakespeare was a person of rank superior to himself: that he was in the may-morn of life: that his personal beauty was remarkable: that he was much addicted to pleasure, courted by the women, and guilty of some breaches of friendship in consequence: that his counsellor and poet, fully aware of his tendency to dissipation, exhorted him to marry, and bequeath to the world a copy of himself. It is also clear that, during the time of writing these compositions, their object had not coveted public business, he was something more than the mere 'child of state,' and by shunning its perilous honours, might be said, almost alone, to be 'hugely politic.'

He is announced in the first Sonnet in the tone of Spenser's address to Raleigh, as I have before observed,

> Thou that art now the world's fresh ornament,
> And only herauld to the gaudy spring.

This is unquestionably said of a youth of distinction, who had just then offered himself to the public gaze and towards whom every eye was turned, from the circumstances of his descent, and the graces with which he seemed personally accomplished.

If we were told that the nephew of Sir Philip Sydney, soon after he quitted Oxford in 1594, had been allowed by his father the Earl of Pembroke, to come to London, in his *fifteenth* year;—that with the *beauty* of his mother the Countess, and the taste for *poetry* of her and Sir Philip, he had addicted himself to the stage, and among the professors of dramatic art had distinguished Shakespeare, and entertained an ardent *affection* for so great a master; we should receive such an anecdote as one at all events highly probable. If we were subsequently to learn that persons who well knew the poet and his connections, had left their intimacy upon record, it would excite, it is true, no surprise, though it might lead us to expect that the poet himself had also publicly expressed his sense of so honourable a distinction.

Now Messieurs Heminges and Condell, when publishing the folio edition of Shakespeare's Plays in the year 1623, in their dedication to William then Earl of Pembroke, and Philip Earl of Montgomery his brother, testify to this friendly connexion, and, as it appears certain that Ben Jonson held the pen for them, the facts stated acquire *his* full knowledge, in corroboration of the assertion made by the actual dedicators. Jonson himself knew these noblemen well. Thus he writes for the dedicators, as to the plays now collected:

> But since your Lordshippes have beene pleas'd to thinke these trifles some-thing heereto-fore; and have prosequuted both them, *and their authour living, with so much favour:* we hope that (they outliving him, and he not having the fate, common with some, to be exequutor to his owne writings,) you will use the like indulgence towards them, *you have done unto their parent.*
>
> (pp. 31-3)

It is my opinion, then, that Shakespeare addressed 126 of these Sonnets to Mr. WILLIAM HERBERT, subsequently third Earl of Pembroke, and that a variety of circumstances alluded to in these Sonnets, as well as the initials, apply fully, personally, and unequivocally to the said young nobleman; and that the other Sonnets, though not addressed, were sent to him, as alluding to matters mentioned in the 126; and that it is probable the Earl sanctioned their publication in 1609 under his untitled initials. There will appear an obvious propriety in thus restricting Thorpe to his designation when they were written, if we consider that the Earl in 1609 had become a statesman, and, as his poet had predicted, attentive to his own dignity and importance at court. To justify me in the hypothesis just laid down, every circumstance in the 126 Sonnets addressed to one person, should apply to an intercourse between Shakespeare and Mr. William Herbert, and apply moreover easily. There should be no straining of words, no wringing of a poor phrase to torture it into a lame supporter of an hypothesis. As I have already proved that, without such torture, these productions cannot be applied to other candidates, so I shall now in detail proceed to show, that they do strictly, fairly, and undeniably apply to the young nobleman I have named. (pp. 34-5)

[Clarendon's famous biography of Mr. William Herbert] has one feature, which biographers of the present day are careful to omit. It speaks fearlessly of the "exorbitant proportion of his infirmities," and yet shows him to have been one of the most amiable of the race of men. One of these infirmities is pointed at in the Sonnets, and the great poet himself seems implicated with him. Dr. Drake wishes that 22 of the Sonnets had never been published—"because if we dismiss these confessional Sonnets, not the slightest moral stain can rest on the character of Shakespeare." But why should he be so anxious, in the case of Shakespeare, to exhibit "a faultless monster which the world ne'er saw?"—a being transcending us so immeasurably in the powers of the mind, and not evincing his kindred by the slightest error in his personal conduct! Surely, as *repented* error excites no imitation, it is better to keep down our arrogance, by showing the *greatest* of us not entirely spotless. (pp. 41-2)

[When] Mr. William Herbert came up to town from college, he was in the vernal blossom of existence; and all that the Sonnets express as to the beauty of his person may be credited upon a sight of Vandyke's picture of him in his maturity. . . . Even the particular temper of our youth, who was addicted, says Rowland Whyte, to *melancholy,* is marked by Shakespeare in the 8th Sonnet.

> Musick to hear, why hear'st thou musick *sadly?*
> Why lov'st thou that, which thou receiv'st not gladly?

There are many passages in these Sonnets, which, as they infer the superior condition of his young friend, express also the fear that reasons of *rank* and *state* might separate them: that an intimacy with the Player might sully the future Peer, and that it would be incumbent on the latter to "hold his honour at a wary distance." This reflection induces the poet to lament his degraded condition, which made him "*a motley to the view*" of an unworthy crowd [Sonnet 110]. A few such complaints shall follow.

> Let me confess, that we two must be twain.
> In our two loves there is but one respect,
> Though in our lives a separable spight.
> I may not evermore acknowledge thee,
> Lest my bewailed guilt should do thee shame;
> Nor thou with *publick kindness* honour me,
> Unless thou take that honour from thy name.
>
> [Sonnet 36]

> Against that time, if ever that time come,

When I shall see thee frown on my defects,
When as thy love hath cast his utmost sum,
Call'd to that audit by *advis'd respects?*
Against that time, when thou shalt strangely pass,
And scarcely greet me with that sun, thine eye;
When love, converted from the thing it was,
Shall reasons find of *settled gravity.*

> [Sonnet 49]

I reasoned upon the latter passage in the opening, without pointing to the particular person addressed; it is here repeated to establish my hypothesis. (pp. 42-4)

How Shakespeare conceived himself *degraded* by the profession to which he owes his immortality, it is worth while to show fully. . . .

> O, for my sake do you with Fortune chide,
> The guilty goddess of my harmful deeds,
> That did not better for my life provide
> Than *publick means,* which publick manners breeds.
> Thence comes it that my NAME receives a *brand;*
> And almost thence my nature is subdu'd
> To what it *works in,* like the dyer's hand.
>
> [Sonnet 111]

One more struggle of the Poet to bear himself above the reach of illiberal obloquy, by the shield which his Patron's favour threw before him.

> Your love and pity doth the impression *fill,*
> Which vulgar scandal stamp'd upon my brow;
> For what care I who calls me well or ill,
> So YOU o'er-green my bad, my good allow?
> You are my *all-the-world,* and I must strive
> To know my *shames* and *praises* from your tongue.
> In so profound abysm I throw all care
> Of others' voices, that my adder's sense
> To *critick* and to *flatterer* stopped are.
>
> [Sonnet 112]

That Shakespeare's sensibility would be shocked by the usual treatment of his profession, may be obvious from the language even of King James's licence to his own company acting at the Globe. That monarch wills and commands all Justices, Mayors, Sheriffs, Constables, Headboroughs, and other officers, to allow them to act throughout his dominions, "without any letts, hindrances, or molestations: and not only so, but to be aiding or assisting to them, if any *wrong* be to them offered; and to allow them such former *courtesies* as hath been given to men of *their* place and quality."

As Lord Pembroke received the garter in the first year of the new reign, there is every reason for thinking that his friendship for our Poet procured the above licence from King James.

The 80th, 82nd, 85th, and 86th Sonnets contain references to the *better spirit,* who studiously celebrated the same object with Shakespeare. . . .

> O, how I faint when I of YOU do write,
> Knowing a *better spirit* doth use your name,
> And in the praise thereof spends all his might,
> To make me tongue-tied, speaking of your fame!
>
> [Sonnet 80]

The modern reader would be apt to think that Shakespeare could only regard Spenser as his superior—but this is to be unacquainted with the estimates of poetry in the age of Elizabeth. Acknowledged learning greatly predominated over genius. The modern stage had not drawn aside the veneration for the classic drama, and the *scholar* still indulged his followers with plays upon the ancient model. He thought the best of modern plays but *gross* and *barbarous;* and, in imitation of Sir Philip Sidney, called upon scholars like himself, to resist the barbarian of the north, who threatened with oblivion their more classical productions. . . . I have no doubt that Shakespeare actually vailed his bonnet, not only to Spenser, but to Daniel and Chapman, to Harrington, and to Fairefax. We see *them* invariably "pass him by," not deigning to consider him of their fraternity; and a modern worshipper of our Poet, after toiling through names with which he is little acquainted, wonders by what strange blindness that Jupiter was *ever* unobserved, to whom the rest have become merely satellites, invisible to the common eye, and only known to exist from the telescopic discoveries of the antiquary.

But that Spenser was not so absolute a sovereign in the period to which I have referred, is proved by Ben Jonson, who points out *that* poet's *rival* and his *own,* in his delightful comedy of *Epicoene, or the Silent Woman.* It is one of the topics chosen by Truewit, to deter Morose from marriage; whose lady, he tells him, will not care how his acres melt, "so as she may bee a stateswoman, know all the news, what was done at *Salisbury,* what at the *Bath,* what at Court, what in Progresse; or, so she may censure *Poets,* and authors, and stiles, and compare them, DANIEL with SPENCER, Jonson with the *tother youth,* and so foorth."

This leads me easily to my decision, that Daniel was the *better spirit* alluded to. He was in fact brought up at Wilton, the seat of the Pembrokes, and in 1601, inscribed his *Defence of Ryme* to William Herbert. (pp. 45-8)

Therefore, when Shakespeare wrote the 82nd Sonnet, he hints at the actual ground of his jealousy—Daniel had *dedicated* to William Herbert.

> I grant thou wert not married to my muse,
> And therefore may'st without attaint o'erlook
> The *dedicated words,* which writers use
> Of their fair subject, blessing every book.

Spenser, let me add, did not live to *dedicate* to William Herbert, though it is admitted he eulogized his parents. This establishes Daniel firmly. (pp. 48-9)

[When] a point is clearly established, enough has been done. The enquiry, now brought to its close, will I think be found to have proved:—

That in the bookseller's dedication of the Sonnets to Mr. W. H., the *object* of them, and not their *bringer forth,* is certainly intended.

That the person to whom the initials were first applied [William Harte], could *not* be the object of them, either as to age or rank.

That it is *impossible* Queen Elizabeth could ever have been the object of Shakespeare's Sonnets, even though Spenser *had* addressed his *Amoretti* to her. (pp. 57-8)

That Shakespeare's Sonnets do not at all apply to Lord Southampton—either as to his age, character, or the bustle and activity of a life distinguished by distant and hazardous services—to some of which they must have alluded, had *he* been their object.

That they were really addressed to Mr. William Herbert, in his youth, to whom the initials *do* apply; and that he *was* a patron and friend of Shakespeare. (p. 58)

So that it is conceived, from these united proofs, the question to whom Shakespeare's Sonnets were addressed, is now decided, and that in future, W. H. as William Herbert, subsequently Earl of Pembroke, will be deemed, as Mr. Thorpe says, fully entitled to

> THE ETERNITY PROMISED BY OUR EVER-LIVING
> POET.

(p. 59)

James Boaden, in his On the Sonnets of Shakespeare, *1837. Reprint by AMS Press, Inc., 1972, 62 p.*

SAMUEL TAYLOR COLERIDGE [as reported by H. N. COLERIDGE] (conversation date 1833)

[*From 1822 until Coleridge's death in 1834, his nephew and son-in-law, H. N. Coleridge, recorded the critic's remarks on a wide variety of subjects; he later published portions of these accounts in* Specimens of the Table Talk of the Late Samuel Taylor Coleridge *(1835). In the excerpt below, from a conversation which took place in 1833, Coleridge comments on the identity of the person addressed in Shakespeare's sonnets. Although he initially acknowledges that it is possible for one man to feel love for another and that such relationships between men were common in Shakespeare's age, he insists that the passion depicted in the sonnets "could only have come from a man deeply in love, and in love with a woman." Coleridge argues that Shakespeare would not have found it necessary to veil his emotions if he were addressing Pembroke, but because the object of his passion was a woman, he had to conceal the identity of his beloved. Coleridge also remarks on the artistry of the sonnets, noting in a famous quotation that the sonnets "are characterized by boundless fertility and laboured condensation of thought."*]

I believe it possible that a man may, under certain states of the moral feeling, entertain something deserving the name of love towards a male object—an affection beyond friendship, and wholly aloof from appetite. In Elizabeth's and James's time it seems to have been almost fashionable to cherish such a feeling; and perhaps we may account in some measure for it by considering how very inferior the women of that age, taken generally, were in education and accomplishment of mind to the men. . . . I mention this with reference to Shakespeare's sonnets, which have been supposed, by some, to be addressed to William Herbert, Earl of Pembroke, whom Clarendon calls the most beloved man of his age, though his licentiousness was equal to his virtues. I doubt this. I do not think that Shakespeare, merely because he was an actor, would have thought it necessary to veil his emotions towards Pembroke under a disguise, though he might probably have done so if the real object had perchance been a Laura or a Leonora. It seems to me that the sonnets could only have come from a man deeply in love, and in love with a woman; and there is one sonnet which, from its incongruity, I take to be a purposed blind. These extraordinary sonnets form, in fact, a poem of so many stanzas of fourteen lines each; and, like the passion which inspired them, the sonnets are always the same, with a variety of expression,—continuous, if you regard the lover's soul—distinct, if you listen to him, as he heaves them sigh after sigh.

These sonnets, like the *Venus and Adonis,* and the *Rape of Lucrece,* are characterised by boundless fertility and laboured condensation of thought, with perfection of sweetness in rhythm and metre. These are the essentials in the budding of a great poet. (pp. 71-2)

> *Samuel Taylor Coleridge, "On Shakespeare as Poet," in his* Coleridge's Writings on Shakespeare, *edited by Terence Hawkes, Capricorn Books, 1959, pp. 55-72.*

D. L. RICHARDSON   (essay date 1835)

[*Richardson was a nineteenth-century English poet and essayist. In the following excerpt, he declares that Shakespeare's sonnets "are addressed to several different individuals, male and female, in some cases real and in others imaginary," and that "perhaps some two or three of them" are spurious. Richardson further contends that Shakespeare did not authorize the 1609 Quarto edition of these poems and that the "onlie begetter" mentioned by Thomas Thorpe in the troublesome dedication refers to the "obtainer," not the object or inspirer. Critics have noted that Richardson is the first to claim that the persons addressed in some of the sonnets are imaginary.*]

Dr. Drake has entered into a very elaborate and certainly a very ingenious and plausible disquisition, to prove that the first one hundred and twenty-six of [Shakspeare's] sonnets are addressed to Lord Southampton [see excerpt above, 1817]. I think, however, that I have discovered various reasonable objections to this hypothesis. The first seventeen sonnets, which so strongly urge the Poet's friend to marry, could scarcely have been addressed to Lord Southampton, because that nobleman, then not quite 22 years of age, assiduously courted Mrs. Vernon in 1595 (about 14 years before the Sonnets were published, and three years before they were alluded to by Meres as being in private circulation amongst the poet's friends), and he married her (his marriage having been delayed by the interference of Queen Elizabeth) in 1599. In the next place, almost the only praise bestowed on these Sonnets, is that of extraordinary beauty, and I do not recollect that Lord Southampton has been celebrated for the wonderful perfection of his face or person. . . . His wit and learning were, however, indisputable, and were warmly eulogized by Chapman, Brathwaite, Nash, and other contemporary writers; but throughout the 126 Sonnets, supposed to be dedicated to his merits, it is remarkable that there are but two allusions to any mental qualities. (p. 365)

If the object of the Sonnets was intellectually gifted, and it was thought desirable to please and compliment him, it would seem that mental endowments must have been of very minor importance in the poet's estimation, and beauty every thing, even in a man. . . . [In] only two places in 126 sonnets, or 1764 lines, supposed to be devoted to eulogiums on a single male character, is there any allusion to his mind, while almost every line conveys some compliment to his exterior charms. Had he been distinguished for any other qualification than his pretty looks, we think Shakspeare was not the man to have done injustice to his merit. Even his moral character appears as doubtful as his intellectual. In Sonnet 33 he says, that as "full many a glorious morning" has permitted

> The basest clouds to ride
> With ugly rack on his celestial face,
> And from the forlorn world his visage hide,
> Stealing unseen to west with his disgrace:
> E'en so my sun one early morn did shine,
> With all triumphant splendour on his brow;
> But out! alack! he was but one hour mine,

The region cloud hath mask'd him from me now.
Yet him for this my love no whit disdaineth;
Suns of the world may stain, when heaven's sun
  staineth.

This surely implies something infamous in his conduct. But the subject is continued in the ensuing lines:

> 'Tis not enough that through the cloud thou break,
> To dry the rain on my storm-beaten face,
> For no man well of such a salve can speak,
> That heals the wound, and cures not the disgrace;
> Nor can thy shame give physick to my grief.
>
> [Sonnet 34]
> (p. 366)

Is this the style in which Shakspeare would have addressed his distinguished patron?

It affords another very strong presumption against the notion that Lord Southampton was the object of so many of these sonnets by the greatest of our English poets, that his remarkable personal bravery, his gallant action at sea, in which he sunk a Spanish frigate, and was wounded in the arm, his many and strange duels, the personal and public assault on him by Lord Grey, his imprisonment in the Tower by Elizabeth, and his restoration to liberty and honour by King James, are in no instance in the slightest degree alluded to, though we should think that they must naturally have occurred to the mind of his friend and admirer, when collecting topics of sympathy or eulogium. It is to be observed also, that between the ages of Shakspeare and Southampton, there was only a difference of nine years, and yet the Poet alludes to the autumn of his own life, and the spring of the object of the Sonnets. The last Sonnet in the number supposed to be addressed to a male, speaks of him as a "lovely boy."

I find myself in some respects partly forestalled in these objections to Dr. Drake's hypothesis, by a writer in the *Gentleman's Magazine* for September and October, 1832 [see excerpt above by James Boaden, 1832]. . . . [This contributor] has endeavoured to prove, in a very shrewd and able paper, that Lord Southampton is not the person addressed in the first 126 sonnets, and that the real object of them is Mr. William Herbert, subsequently third Earl of Pembroke. (pp. 366-67)

I admire his sagacity and acuteness, and I admit that many of his illustrations tell with great effect; but yet I am by no means satisfied that he has solved the riddle which has perplexed and puzzled so many learned heads. (p. 367)

I shall state my reasons for still remaining sceptical on this intricate question. The Earl of Pembroke, though certainly a patron of Shakspeare, was not so generally known as such, as Lord Southampton was, and the Sonnets frequently allude to the "publick kindness shown to the poet." Lord Southampton is said to have presented him with the munificent gift of a thousand pounds, a sum at that period equal to five thousand pounds in the present day. This large donation is supposed to have been bestowed on Shakspeare in the decline of his life, to enable him to purchase "New Place," at Stafford, when he was about to retire from public life. . . . Is it likely that his noble patron, who appears to have favoured him with such warm friendship and generous assistance from the commencement of the Poet's career to its close, should have been thus indirectly slighted or insulted, as he must have been if the Sonnets, which are often expressive of such exclusive friendship, gratitude, and duty, were addressed to William Herbert?

In the account by the Oxford historian A. à Wood, of the life and character of the Earl of Pembroke, he is described as "learned and endowed to admiration with a poetical genius, as by those amorous and not inelegant airs and poems of his composition doth evidently appear; some of which had musical notes set to them by Henry Lawes." Can it be supposed that Shakspeare would have dedicated 126 sonnets to the praise of a poet whose pieces had been set to music by a popular composer, without a single allusion to his poetical genius? Shakspeare knew too well the nature of the commendation which a poet most dearly covets, to be guilty of so offensive an omission. I would draw another argument against Dr. Drake and the Magazine writer who signs himself J. B. (I believe John Boaden) from the inconsistent and contradictory character of the dedication. The more I think of it, the more I am convinced that Shakspeare had nothing to do with the publication of the Sonnets. It is clear as the sun at noon-day that some of the Sonnets are addressed to a male object and others to a female. But the dedication is addressed to a single individual, who is described as the "only begetter" of them. There has been a great deal of quibbling upon the word "begetter;" some critics insisting that it means the "obtainer," and others the object or inspirer. For my own part I think it means the obtainer, for this seems the most easy and natural interpretation, and is attended with the fewest difficulties, though it partly nullifies much of the ingenious conjectural criticism of both Dr. Drake and J. B. The Sonnets having been some years in circulation amongst the author's friends, we ought not to be surprised that they should at last have found their way into print without his sanction. The assertion that the person who gave or sold them to the bookseller is the only obtainer of them, is a bookseller's boast, *precisely in the style of a modern fashionable publisher.*

If Shakspeare had had any thing to do with the superintendance of the publication, he would hardly have allowed himself to be styled "our ever living poet;" or supposing that the practice of the age might have carried off the appearance of any peculiar impropriety in such a puff direct from his own bookseller, it is not to be credited for a moment that he would have left it to a mere trader to dedicate his work to either of his high and noble patrons. Shakspeare did not bring out his two first poems in this way. They were openly inscribed to his great patron, not giving him the sneaking and disrespectful address of Mr. W. H., but his full rank, the Right Honourable Henry Wriothesley, Earl of Southampton and Baron of Titchfield.

That the whole of the 154 Sonnets cannot have been exclusively addressed to one individual, will admit of no reasonable doubt; and yet if we are to believe that the dedication was addressed to Mr. W. H., as the sole object of the Sonnets, the dedicator committed an egregious blunder. Is it likely that such a blunder would have been passed over by the eye of Shakspeare? The bookseller's application of the term 'adventurer' to himself, seems an additional indication that the risk and responsibility of the speculation were exclusively his own. (pp. 367-68)

The bookseller, in his eagerness and ignorance, perhaps misunderstood the "begetter" or obtainer, and attributed the whole series to him, instead, perhaps, of some half a dozen. He accordingly mingled them all together under one head, and occasioned that inextricable confusion which has since

been the cause of so much painful and despairing research. If Shakspeare had had anything to do with the edition, I think he would have dedicated the work in an open manner to his faithful friend and munificent patron (his earliest and latest) Lord Southampton, and that he would have taken care so to divide and arrange the Sonnets, and to indicate the subjects, as to have made them intelligible to the reader. As they now stand, abstracting their poetical merit, they are nothing but a painful puzzle. (pp. 368-69)

Shakspeare himself had a high opinion of his own Sonnets, which he appears to have thought would secure to himself and the several objects of them an immortal fame. And this is another reason why it is improbable that he had any concern in their publication; for, as it is clear that he intended to immortalize his friends, he would never have arranged the Sonnets in so obscure a style as to leave the objects of them to be guessed at. . . .

To end at once this . . . article, the following are the conclusions I have arrived at. The Sonnets are incorrectly arranged by an ignorant bookseller; they are addressed to several different individuals, male and female, in some cases real and in others imaginary; some of them are possibly written in the character of Lord Southampton to the "faire Mrs. Vernon" (afterwards his wife), and some in the character of that lady to her lover; some are written in the poet's own character; and perhaps some two or three of them are the production of an inferior pen. (p. 369)

> *D. L. Richardson, "On the Sonnets of Shakspeare,"* in The Gentleman's Magazine, *n.s. Vol. IV, October, 1835, pp. 361-69.*

HENRY HALLAM (essay date 1837-39)

[*Hallam was a nineteenth-century English historian, best known for his* Constitutional History of England *(1827). The following excerpt is from his* Introduction to the Literature of Europe, *a four-volume work first published between 1837 and 1839. With respect to the autobiographical basis of the sonnets, Hallam asserts that they "relate to one definite, though obscure, period of the poet's life" when an attachment to a woman was disrupted by a passionate friendship with a young man. He adds that the identification of this individual with William Herbert, although not "strictly proved," is probably correct. Lastly, Hallam considers the artistry of the sonnets, averring that they demonstrate the "weakness and folly" characteristic of "all excessive and misplaced affection." In his opinion, the faults are "not redeemed by the touches of noble sentiments" that appear repeatedly throughout these verses.*]

The sonnets of Shakspeare . . . were published in 1609, in a manner as mysterious as their subject and contents. They are dedicated by an editor (Thomas Thorpe, a bookseller) "to Mr. W. H., the only begetter of these sonnets." No one, as far as I remember, has ever doubted their genuineness; no one can doubt that they express not only real but intense emotions of the heart: but when they were written, who was the W. H. quaintly called their begetter, by which we can only understand the cause of their being written, and to what persons or circumstances they allude, has of late years been the subject of much curiosity. These sonnets were long overlooked: Steevens spoke of them with the utmost scorn, as productions which no one could read [see excerpt above, 1793]: but a very different suffrage is generally given by the lovers of poetry; and perhaps there is now a tendency, especially among young men of poetical tempers, to exaggerate the beauties of these remarkable productions. They rise, indeed, in estimation, as we attentively read and reflect upon them; for I do not think that at first they give us much pleasure. No one ever entered more fully than Shakspeare into the character of this species of poetry, which admits of no expletive imagery, no merely ornamental line. But, though each sonnet has generally its proper unity, the sense, I do not mean the grammatical construction, will sometimes be found to spread from one to another, independently of that repetition of the leading idea, like variations of an air, which a series of them frequently exhibits, and on account of which they have latterly been reckoned by some rather an integral poem than a collection of sonnets. But this is not uncommon among the Italians, and belongs, in fact, to those of Petrarch himself. They may easily be resolved into several series, according to their subjects: but, when read attentively, we find them relate to one definite, though obscure, period of the poet's life; in which an attachment to some female, which seems to have touched neither his heart nor his fancy very sensibly, was over-powered, without entirely ceasing, by one to a friend; and this last is of such an enthusiastic character, and so extravagant in the phrases that the author uses, as to have thrown an unaccountable mystery over the whole work. It is true, that in the poetry as well as in the fictions of early ages we find a more ardent tone of affection in the language of friendship than has since been usual; and yet no instance has been adduced of such rapturous devotedness, such an idolatry of admiring love as one of the greatest beings whom nature ever produced in the human form pours forth to some unknown youth in the majority of these sonnets.

The notion that a woman was their general object is totally untenable, and it is strange that Coleridge should have entertained it [see excerpt above, 1833]. Those that were evidently addressed to a woman . . . are by much the smaller part of the whole,—but twenty-eight out of one hundred and fifty-four. And this mysterious Mr. W. H. must be presumed to be the idolized friend of Shakspeare. But who could he be? No one recorded as such in literary history or anecdote answers the description. But if we seize a clew which innumerable passages give us, and suppose that they allude to a youth of high rank as well as personal beauty and accomplishment, in whose favor and intimacy, according to the base prejudices of the world, a player and a poet, though he were the author of *Macbeth,* might be thought honored, something of the strangeness, as it appears to us, of Shakspeare's humiliation in addressing him as a being before whose feet he crouched, whose frown he feared, whose injuries, and those of the most insulting kind,—the seduction of the mistress to whom we have alluded,—he felt and bewailed without resenting; something, I say, of the strangeness of this humiliation, and at best it is but little, may be lightened, and in a certain sense rendered intelligible. And it has been ingeniously conjectured within a few years, by inquirers independent of each other, that William Herbert, Earl of Pembroke, born in 1580, and afterwards a man of noble and gallant character, though always of a licentious life, was shadowed under the initials of Mr. W. H. This hypothesis is not strictly proved, but sufficiently so, in my opinion, to demand our assent. (pp. 253-55)

[It] is impossible not to wish that Shakspeare had never written [his sonnets]. There is a weakness and folly in all excessive and misplaced affection, which is not redeemed by the touches of nobler sentiments that abound in this long series of sonnets: But there are also faults of a merely critical nature. The obscurity is often such as only conjecture can penetrate; the

strain of tenderness and adoration would be too monotonous, were it less unpleasing; and so many frigid conceits are scattered around, that we might almost fancy the poet to have written without genuine emotion, did not such a host of other passages attest the contrary. (p. 256)

Henry Hallam, "History of Poetry from 1600 to 1650," in his Introduction to the Literature of Europe in the Fifteenth, Sixteenth, and Seventeenth Centuries, Vols. III and IV, *A. C. Armstrong and Son, 1891, pp. 221-70.*

CHARLES ARMITAGE BROWN (essay date 1838)

[*In the excerpt below from one of the earliest full-length studies of the autobiographical character of Shakespeare's sonnets, Brown deals principally with the arrangement of the 1609 Quarto. He asserts that Thorpe's edition is legitimate but that the sonnets should be arranged into six "poems" consisting of twenty-two to twenty-six "stanzas" each. Applying the term "stanza" rather than sonnet (for he claims that only three in the entire collection can be called sonnets). Brown thus divides the Quarto as follows: first poem, 1-26; second poem, 27-55; third poem, 56-77; fourth poem, 78-101; fifth poem, 102-26; and sixth poem, 127-52. Each of these "poems" is unified by a dominant concern, the critic argues, such as urging the friend to marry or reproaching him for his faults and susceptibility to flattery. Brown also contends that the first five poems are addressed to William Herbert, Earl of Pembroke; that these sonnets are sincere, not flattery, written as a testament to the nobleman's "truth" and "personal beauty"; and that the whole collection is autobiographical, providing a "pure uninterrupted biography" of Shakespeare's life. Brown regards the sixth poem, or Sonnets 127-52, as a bitter denunciation of his mistress' infidelity as well as a vivid portrayal of the suffering "caused by an almost overwhelming passion for a worthless object."*]

[Shakespeare's] *Sonnets* are not, properly speaking, sonnets. A sonnet is one entire poem contained in fourteen heroic lines, of which there are but three in the collection; the two last, and one near the last, which will be explained. The two last intruders, utterly foreign to every thing preceding them, contain nothing else but repetitions of the same thought,— the stealing of Cupid's brand by a nymph of Diana. The remainder of the sonnets, so miscalled, are POEMS in the *sonnet-stanza*. These poems are six in number; the first five are addressed to his friend, and the sixth to his mistress. This key, simple as it may appear, unlocks every difficulty, and we have nothing but pure uninterrupted biography.

Owing to their having been always called sonnets, a reader, accustomed to consider a sonnet as a poem complete within itself, is perplexed at finding them connected with each other. If this difficulty is so far overcome as to induce him to read right onward, he is again baffled at the sudden contrariety of subject and feeling, owing to the want of division in the work. He then, it may be, returns to his first idea of a legitimate sonnet, and endeavours to understand them separately; till, finding that mode of reading impracticable, he hurries on in confusion, lamenting that a total disregard to chronological order should have rendered them incomprehensible. In no other way can I account for the wild notions that have been published respecting them. It seems never to have crossed the mind of any one, editor or critic, that they are divisible poems in the sonnet-stanza; though so great a poet as Spenser had, only a few years previously, written his *Visions of Petrarch,*

Visions of Bellay, Visions of the World's Vanity, and *The Ruines of Rome,* all precisely in the same sonnet-stanza.

About ten years have passed since I sat down with a determination to understand these *Sonnets* fully. At the time I was offended, and indeed indignant, at meeting with some unworthy strictures on them by an anonymous writer. In common with others, he spoke of them throughout as detached sonnets. As I never had regarded them in any other light than as, for the most part, connected sonnets, I endeavoured to discover if the whole could not, without violence, be divided into separate poems, so that I might arrive at their sense without confusion. To my surprise, while I read them with that intention, they, as it were, divided themselves, and, still more extraordinary, each poem concluding with an appropriate *Envoy,* to mark their bounds distinctly, and beyond a doubt.

The excitement at finding a long hidden treasure has passed away,—for a treasure it was, by which I purchased a knowledge of the intention of every sonnet, or rather of every stanza, (I refuse to call them *sonnets* for the future,) delighting myself the more in the poetry, the more I was enabled to comprehend the theme. Now that many years are gone by, I cannot imagine a possible reason for disturbing the divisions I then made, which were as follows:—

FIRST POEM. Stanzas 1 to 26. *To his friend, persuading him to marry.*

SECOND POEM. Stanzas 27 to 55. *To his friend, who had robbed the poet of his mistress, forgiving him.*

THIRD POEM. Stanzas 56 to 77. *To his friend, complaining of his coldness, and warning him of life's decay.*

FOURTH POEM. Stanzas 78 to 101. *To his friend, complaining that he prefers another poet's praises, and reproving him for faults that may injure his character.*

FIFTH POEM. Stanzas 102 to 126. *To his friend, excusing himself for having been some time silent, and disclaiming the charge of inconstancy.*

SIXTH POEM. Stanzas 127 to 152. *To his mistress, on her infidelity.*

Such should have been (had the printers in 1609 received efficient directions, and had they done their duty) the order and manner of these poems. The attentive reader will be convinced that these divisions are neither arbitrary nor fanciful, but inevitable. An unsought-for recommendation is that they are thus formed into poems tolerably equal in length, varying from twenty-two to twenty-six stanzas each. (pp. 44-7)

Before we proceed farther, it is necessary to interpret some particular expressions he has used. In his time the language of love or of friendship was the same. His contemporaries spoke of a friendship between those of the same sex by the term of *love;* and the usual address to a friend, as may be seen in their letters, was *lover.* . . . This, has been already explained by Malone, Dr. Drake and others [see excerpts above, 1790 and 1817]. Not only did friendship, in poetical and prosaic addresses, adopt the language of love; but, to express its utmost sincerity, it breathed of tenderness. On the other hand, love, eager to free itself from the imputation of transient desire, strove to be assimilated to a pure friendship. Thus the language of love and friendship became confounded; till fashion, or something worse, endeavoured to separate their terms.

There is another phrase, used by our ancestors, sounding strange to modern ears, which is *sweet,* when applied to a friend. We are accustomed to it among the poetical personages of Shakespeare's plays. Prince Hal calls Poins "*sweet Ned*" [in *I Henry IV*]; Antonio begins his letter to his friend with "*sweet* Bassanio" [in *The Merchant of Venice*]; and the two gentle youths of Verona call each other "*sweet,*" and "*sweet* Valentine," and "*sweet* Proteus" [in *The Two Gentlemen of Verona*]; yet many may wonder to find that our poet writes of Master William Herbert's "*sweet* respect," of his "*sweet* thoughts," his "*sweet* beloved name," his "*sweet* graces," and that he even calls him "*sweet love;*" though this last expression was but equivalent to *dear,* or *kind friend,* of the present day; and there was nothing wonderful in any of them at the time it was written. Language is for ever changing, and the language of familiar discourse more than any other. (pp. 48-9)

I had nearly forgotten another change in which Shakespeare is concerned. In these days we talk of the beauty of a woman, a child, a flower, or a painting,—nay, of the beauty of a horse, or a dog, and that continually; but, though we by no means deny there is such a thing as manly beauty, we talk of it under a different name, choosing rather to say of a man that he has a handsome face, or a handsome person,—"Sir, he is the handsomest man in all England." Yet this word *handsome,* in Shakespeare's time, had rarely any other meaning than *suitable, dexterous, clever;* and therefore he, and all his contemporaries, spoke of the good looks of a man under the name of *beauty.*

With these hints of explanation I proceed.

FIRST POEM.

STANZAS I TO XXVI.

TO HIS FRIEND, PERSUADING HIM TO MARRY.

The arguments used, to this effect, entirely occupy the first sixteen stanzas; then, from stanza 17th to 25th, with the same arguments still introduced, the poet resolves, in case his friend will not consent to perpetuate the beauty of his youth in his offspring, to make him live for ever young in verse. Stanza 26th, and last, is what Spenser would have designated *L'Envoy.*

This poem, it will be seen, is entire and indivisible; every stanza is connected with the foregoing, and every line is in the same feeling.

The chief argument made use of to induce his friend to marry, is like Viola's address to Olivia:

> Lady, you are the cruel'st she alive,
> If you would lead these graces to the grave,
> And leave the world no copy.
> > [*Twelfth Night,* I. v. 241-43]
> > (pp. 50-1)

Those who from experience know how important it is to attend to the breed of cattle, sheep, horses, or dogs; and who are aware in their own persons (others may be excused) that the human race is superior to the bestial, must highly appreciate this part of Shakespeare's philosophy.

The poem gives its theme in the two first lines,—

> From fairest creatures we desire increase,
> That thereby beauty's rose might never die,
> > [Sonnet 1]

and it is followed up by a great variety of compliment and reasoning, particularly that of the honourable pride of being a father.

Some persons, reading thus far, will be apt to regret that the arguments were not urged to some Olivia, instead of to his friend. An answer to this is, and ought to be conclusive, that the Earl of Pembroke's son happened not to be a woman. Women, in their extreme beauty, might lay claim to all our praise, did they not themselves acknowledge manly beauty. As men, in their imagination, formed a Venus, so women formed an Apollo; and when these deities were embodied by the sculptor's art, all equally acknowledged that both were beautiful. It comes to this: either sex has beauty; but neither has a charm except towards the other. The word *charm* settles the question. We all, men and women, acknowledge and admire the beauty of men, women, and children, together with every thing that nature has given excellent in form and feature; but when the charm—the love charm—the charm of sympathy between the sexes—is wanting, it is merely acknowledged and admired. These poems afford us a case in point. Throughout the first five the tenour is,—I delight in you, my friend, therefore I rejoice that you have beauty of person; and I will immortalize that beauty in my verse. Compare this with the sixth poem, addressed to his mistress, and then we understand the charm. There the whole tenour, is,—I delight in your beauty, not in you, for you have deceived me. Besides, we soon get entangled amidst lips, palms, and kisses. (pp. 51-2)

But, it may be asked, did Shakespeare meanly stoop to flatter an earl's son for personal beauty? Did he seek to make a profit out of the youth, at the expense of turning him into a coxcomb? Not so; public encomiums of this sort were not rare in his days. Nevertheless, it must be owned, he has eulogized the beauty of one of his own sex beyond any other poet; and, doubtless, what he did may be justified. Not content with bestowing common praise, he insists upon it that all the descriptions of "lovely knights," in ancient chronicles, were but prophecies of Master William Herbert; that he has—

> A woman's face with Nature's own hand painted;
>
>   [Sonnet 20]

and that Nature first intended him for a woman; but being herself a woman, she "fell a doting on her own work, and made a man of him" [Sonnet 20] much to Shakespeare's displeasure. . . . Nothing is put on a par with his beauty, unless it be his truth; while, throughout the poems, he contends that he speaks nothing but what is freely acknowledged by all the world, without a thought of flattery. (p. 53)

Then, again, was [Shakespeare] to trumpet forth his [friend's] accomplishments, his talents, his wealth, his birth? No; many others might be equal, many superior to him on all these points. . . . In order, therefore, to place him with truth above his fellows, to make him deservedly eminent, he celebrated him for the beauty of his person, which he contended no one could gainsay. The lovers of Shakespeare may safely conclude that whatever he did on principle was, and ever will be, worthy of imitation. According to his existing portrait, that Earl of Pembroke must have been, in his youth, remarkably beautiful; and Shakespeare, swayed by grateful feelings, regarded him as more beautiful than any one who had been, or would hereafter be. In this spirit he wrote; and however much the ugly may shake their heads, the claim of personal

First text page of Shakespeare's Sonnets *(1609).*

beauty will be ever allowed: it is beyond all other gifts; it necessarily includes health and strength; nobility, riches, and sometimes talents, are trifles compared to its influence; it enforces respect; it commands attention; it is the natural and therefore the best recommendation to the love of women; and to be possessed of it is the earnest desire of men, whatever they may pretend to the contrary, as well as of women. There was no flattery in telling the earl's son that he surpassed all others in form and feature, while it was an acknowledged truth; and there was no flattery in attempting to immortalize in verse his beauty more than in a Raffaelle or a Titian, when they give us the youth of both sexes glowing in their best looks on the canvas. There was only the error in hoping that poetry could represent a face like painting. Shakespeare, indeed, does no more than attempt the task; he sees how impossible it is to describe form by words, and contents himself with assuring posterity that his friend was, beyond all other men, excellent in beauty. (pp. 55-6)

SECOND POEM.

STANZAS XXVII TO LV.

TO HIS FRIEND—WHO HAD ROBBED THE POET OF HIS MISTRESS—FORGIVING HIM.

Here is a curious change of subject. While these high compliments were paid in verse to manly beauty, the poet's mistress added a still higher one. She allured the youth into an approval of her inconstancy; and, what was worse, into a forgetfulness of his own ties of friendship. The wiles and cheats of love, when we are not the sufferers, generally provoke our laughter; possibly because we are more apt to sympathize with the winners than the losers. With a spice of malice it would be easy to draw a picture of this intrigue, so as to throw a large portion of ridicule on Shakespeare; but I am withheld, as I observe not only the acuteness of suffering in the loser, but also in one of the winners.

We can scarcely imagine Shakespeare in a fit of rage; such, however, was the fact. He was stung to the quick; and his resentment, though we are ignorant of the manner in which it was shown, appears to have been ungovernable. He alludes to it in this poem with deep regret:

> I may not evermore acknowledge thee,
>   Lest my bewailed guilt should do thee shame.
>   [Sonnet 36]

These lines, no doubt, were intended to be vague. I could merely offer a guess at their meaning, were it not that the quarrel is referred to in the fifth poem, where the interpretation of *"bewailed guilt,"* is complete.

> O benefit of ill! now I find true
>   That better is by evil still made better;
> And ruin'd love, when it is built anew,
>   Grows fairer than at first, more strong, far great-
>   er.
> So I return rebuked to my content,
> And gain by ill, thrice more than I have spent.
>   [Sonnet 119]

> That you were once unkind befriends me now,
>   And for that sorrow, which I then did feel,
> Needs must I *under my transgression* bow,
>   Unless my nerves were brass or hammer'd steel;
> For if you were *by my unkindness shaken*
>   As I by your's, you've passed a hell of time;
> And I, a tyrant, have no leisure taken
>   To weigh how once I suffer'd in your crime.
> O that our night of woe might have remember'd
>   My deepest sense, how hard true sorrow hits!
> And soon to you, as you to me, then tender'd
>   The humble salve which wounded bosom fits!
> But that your trespass now becomes a fee;
> *Mine ransoms yours,* and your's must ransom me.
>   [Sonnet 120]

"And soon to you, as you to me," &c. inform us also, that it was not long before a reconciliation took place. Taking the words exactly in their order, they imply that Shakespeare was the first to write; but this second poem seems to have been written in answer to his friend, who had expressed sorrow for the fault he had committed, even, as we read in stanza 34, to tears. This sorrow instantly disarmed Shakespeare of his anger.

Throughout his works, it may be observed, there is ever a ready pardon for those who, tempted by opportunity, or swayed by prejudice, become criminals from a want of strength of mind, provided they are sensible of their faults, and lament them. . . . There is a case in point in the *Two Gentlemen of Verona,* one of his earliest plays, if not his first: Proteus attempts, by treachery and mean artifices, to deprive Valentine of his mistress; yet when his "shame and guilt confound" him, when he entreats forgiveness, and expresses his

hearty sorrow, the generous Valentine, without a moment's pause, exclaims,

> Then I am paid,
> And once again I do receive thee honest.
> Who by repentance is not satisfied,
> Is nor of heaven, nor earth; for these are pleased;
> By penitence the Eternal's wrath appeased.
>   [*The Two Gentlemen of Verona,* V. iv. 77-81]
>   (pp. 62-5)

It is delightful, in this "rarer action," so hard of attainment, to discover that an author has practised what he taught. There was, it is true, a reasonable inducement to his forgiveness, if rage can hearken to reason. He had discovered that his mistress was the more to blame of the two; that she had solicited the youth . . . , and therefore his guilt was less than it might have been. In one respect, the poet surpasses his own Valentine in generosity; for no sooner is his heart at peace with his friend, than he reproaches himself for the bitter resentment he had shown. Whatever it was, he reflects on it with anguish, and almost thinks it a sufficient ground for their lasting separation. Judging from his expressions, we are led to conjecture that his resentment had been public.

Continually has it been lamented that we know almost nothing of our poet's life; yet here we have an event in it, on which we can rely, described by his own hand, with many attending circumstances, every one of which exemplifies his character; and together they form a tale of interest, the like of which, among the biographies of other great men, poets or not, we may seek in vain. This is fresh from the well-spring of truth in his own bosom. To learn how any man, whose genius we reverence, might have acted in his trying situation, would excite that species of curiosity which is commendable;—a desire to be more intimately acquainted with his mind and his character, by a knowledge of the working of his passions. Here, at the first glance, we find the deeply philosophic poet giving loose to a storm of anger, like one of the common herd, as if philosophy were vain indeed. But this proceeded from the animal portion of his being,—no more. Nor is this conduct wanting in useful speculation. His usual epithet, given by his personal friends, was the *gentle;* and we must believe he was rarely otherwise, never except under a stinging provocation; and it may tend to prove that strong passions, however subdued, will be found among the hidden attributes of genius. On the other hand, let us view him, soon as his "nobler reason" had overcome the animal within him, acting up to the dictates, or beyond them, of his own philosophy; not simply and coldly forgiving—a most virtuous effort in the estimation of many,—but kind, affectionate, seeking excuses for the wrong he had endured, and heart-struck at the recollection of his resentment. (pp. 65-7)

THIRD POEM.

STANZAS LVI TO LXXVII.

TO HIS FRIEND, COMPLAINING OF HIS COLDNESS, AND
WARNING HIM OF LIFE'S DECAY.

Such a friendship as this between the Earl's son and Shakespeare, was not, according to Bacon, uncommon in his time. "There is," he tells us in his *Essays,* "little friendship in the world, and least of all between equals, which was wont to be magnified. That that is, is between superior and inferior, whose fortunes may comprehend the one the other." We now consider an approach to equality in rank and fortune as necessary to the union of minds; and this poem, together with the two succeeding ones, tends to confirm the modern doctrine, and, according to Bacon, that of more ancient times.

Soon after the reconciliation, the youth evinced a coldness towards his friend. It may be that he could not forgive himself so frankly as he had been forgiven; and that therefore the sight of a man, whom he had injured, was painful, perhaps humbling. But it seems more probable, without going to history for his character, he was of a good and generous nature, though, at his age, of a volatile disposition; and, highly situated as he was by birth, in danger of being spoiled by the flattery of the world.

In the three first stanzas Shakespeare complains of this coldness. . . . Reproach is conveyed more forcibly, and, at the same time, with more kindness, in their strained humility, than it would have been by direct expostulation.

> Being your slave, what should I do but tend
>   Upon the hours and times of your desire?
> I have no precious time at all to spend,
>   Nor services to do, till you require.
> Nor dare I chide the world-without-end hour,
>   Whilst I, my sovereign, watch the clock for you,
> Nor think the bitterness of absence sour,
>   When you have bid your servant once adieu;
> Nor dare I question with my jealous thought,
>   Where you may be, or your affairs suppose,
> But, like a sad slave, stay and think of nought,
>   Save, where you are how happy you make those:
> So true a fool is love, that in your will
> (Though you do anything) he thinks no ill.
>
>   [Sonnet 57]

> That God forbid, that made me first your slave,
>   I should in thought controul your times of plea-
>   sure,
> Or at your hand the account of hours to crave,
>   Being your vassal, bound to stay your leisure!
> Oh, let me suffer, (being at your beck,)
>   The imprison'd absence of your liberty,
> And patient, tame to sufferance, bide each check,
>   Without accusing you of injury.
> Be where you list, your charter is so strong,
>   That you yourself may privilege your time;
> Do what you will, to you it doth belong,
>   Yourself to pardon of self-doing crime;
> I am to wait, though waiting so be hell,
> Not blame your pleasure, be it ill or well.
>
>   [Sonnet 58]

After this complaint of his seeming indifference, it is only once more referred to. . . .

> From me far off, with others all too near.
>
>   [Sonnet 61]

And the remainder of the poem is filled with compliments, and assurances of unaltered affection, mixed with warnings of the fleeting nature of youth,—exemplified in the poet himself, now passed his best days, and looking forward to age and death.

                                       (pp. 72-4)

FOURTH POEM.

STANZAS LXXVIII TO CI.

TO HIS FRIEND, COMPLAINING THAT HE PREFERS ANOTHER POET'S PRAISES, AND REPROVING HIM FOR FAULTS THAT MAY INJURE HIS CHARACTER.

Who this rival poet was is beyond my conjecture; nor does it matter. We perceive many intimations that he owed his preferment to flattery. Accordingly Shakespeare, in this poem particularly, disclaims such unworthiness; asserting that he praises his friend for nothing but what all men, friends and foes, freely acknowledged. His personal beauty, which the newly favoured poet was also celebrating, he had ever made the chief subject of eulogy, as none could contradict it. Even when it became, at the time of his mistress's falling in love with it, a curse to himself, he still continued to do it justice, and, in his magnanimity, paid it equal or greater compliments while suffering from its influence. Farther, to point out how different he is from a servile poet, and to prove his honesty, he now blames the youth for his faults, excusing himself for interference by reminding him that a stain on his character affects a friend. The faults he notices are those of licentious conversation, and fickleness in his friendship. (p. 79)

FIFTH POEM.

STANZAS CII TO CXXVI.

TO HIS FRIEND, EXCUSING HIMSELF FOR HAVING BEEN SOME TIME SILENT, AND DISCLAIMING THE CHARGE OF INCONSTANCY.

In the three first poems we see tenderness and integrity expressed, for the most part, in monotonous lines; the sentiment often disguised in conceits. The fourth is far less objectionable; but the fifth is full of varied, rich, and energetic poetry. As we know that three years had elapsed between the first and the fifth, it is highly interesting to observe his improvement in rhymed versification, and his gradual abandonment of the fashion of the day. Few will differ from me when I say it is to be regretted that he ever departed from blank verse in his plays. He himself was doubtless of this opinion, for he seldom penned even a couplet in his latest plays. Ease, harmony, strength, and pregnancy of meaning, all so wonderfully his attributes, often seemed to forsake him when he wrote in rhyme, at least in the heroic measure.

He opens this poem with an elegant apology for his silence. The stanza is one of the best he has written.

> My love is strengthen'd, though more weak in
>   seeming;
>   I love not less, though less the show appear;
> That love is merchandised, whose rich esteeming
>   The owner's tongue doth publish every where.
> Our love was new, and then but in the spring,
>   When I was wont to greet it with my lays;
> As Philomel in summer's front doth sing,
>   And stops her pipe in growth of riper days:
> Not that the summer is less pleasant now
>   Than when her mournful hymns did hush
>   the night,
> But that wild music burthens every bough,
>   And sweets, grown common, lose their dear de-
>   light.
> Therefore, like her, I sometimes hold my tongue,
> Because I would not dull you with my song.
>
>   [Sonnet 102]

As he had been accused, in addition to his silence, of giving a preference to new acquaintances, he exults in these evidences of the youth's friendship, repeatedly calling him "fair, kind, and true," and declaring his own sincerity. He talks more than usual of himself, as if he were assured of the youth's being interested in him, and even calls to mind their old quarrel as a matter of triumph to both parties.

For some time I was baffled in discovering the meaning of stanza 121; the only real difficulty I have encountered in these poems. He there mentions he had been accused of something "vile;" complains that on his "frailities" there have been "frailer spies," and strenuously rebuts the charge. The word *frailities* naturally sent my thoughts on his mistress, but as he says, speaking of his calumniators:

> Which in their wills count bad what I think *good,*
> [Sonnet 121]

of course he had not her in his mind, as, in other passages, he condemns himself for having had any acquaintanceship with her. It follows then it must have been something else which was esteemed "vile;" and, connecting the stanza with the preceding and following ones, we find he had been pronounced guilty of the *vileness of frailty in friendship,*—a phrase used in the same sense also in stanza 109. His reasoning on this subject is likewise obscure, and might be mistaken to his discredit:

> 'Tis better to be vile, than vile esteem'd:
> When not to be receives reproach of being;
> And the just pleasure lost, which is so deem'd,
> Not by our feeling, but by others' seeing.
> [Sonnet 121]

My interpretation will be seen. He owns he had been long absent, that he had "frequent been with unknown minds," and that he had "forgot upon his dearest love (friend) to call" [Sonnet 117], but still contends he was heartily attached to him. After reminding him of the cordiality of their reconciliation in times past, he utterly denies that he had been so "vile" as to be fickle in friendship. Immediately after this stanza, he acknowledges having given his present of a memorandum book, "thy gift, thy tables" [Sonnet 122], to another, (which, we may suppose, was ranked among his offences) and handsomely excuses himself for having parted with it. Then he exclaims:

> No! Time, thou shalt not boast that I do change!
> [Sonnet 123]

and continues in the same strain to the end of the poem. (pp. 85-8)

As he had given in this poem a reason for not addressing more verses to his young friend, the *Envoy,* without actually bidding him farewell, seems to take a poetical leave of him; and, to mark it the more, it is written, not in the sonnet-stanza, but in half-a-dozen couplets. (p. 89)

I am far from believing that every person will precisely coincide in all the interpretations I have given. Better readings, though unimportant to the whole, may be made of some of the passages. It would be strange if no one disagreed with me on so many minor disputable points. But allowing every objection of that nature, I contend that the main points must remain undisturbed, which are these:

First; The *Sonnets,* as they have hitherto been called, up to the 126th inclusive, evidently ought to form five distinct poems in the sonnet-stanza.

Secondly; Each poem terminates at the place I have indicated, with its proper *Envoy.*

Thirdly; Each stanza is connected with the preceding and the following ones, so as to produce consecutive sense and feeling

throughout, as much, or more, as will be usually found in any poetical, or even any prose epistle.

Fourthly; They are all addressed to one person; and that person must have been very young, and of high rank; if not Master William Herbert, some other of his age in 1597 or 8, and of his condition.

Fifthly; Each poem is entitled to the description or argument prefixed to it.

Our poet's lovers, once convinced on these several points, which is my aim, will readily understand and enjoy this neglected portion of his works. While proceeding in the explanation, my endeavour has been, far as the nature of the poems permitted, to make them a comment on the author's character. In doing this, however, I have omitted to notice numerous touches, because they must be observable to every attentive reader.

Taking a general view of the poems, the predominant peculiarity is in the variety, ingenuity, and almost ideal painting displayed in their lengthened strain of elegant compliment; and this question inevitably intrudes itself,—is it probable that he wrote all, as he asserts, in the spirit of honest truth? Granting that this high-born youth was eminently beautiful, as well as kind-hearted and true, at least in Shakespeare's belief, with one exception, which was forgiven, at the commencement of their friendship, we shall find that, amidst all this continued praise, he is not endowed by the poet with any quality beyond beauty, kindness, and truth,—"fair, kind, and true," being the burthen of the song throughout. No prophecy of the future excellence of his mind is admitted; his birth and wealth are scarcely mentioned, never celebrated; the hopes of the nation are faintly and indirectly hinted at, not assured; all these have ever been the common themes for flattery of the great, and were very common in those days: Shakespeare avoids them all. It may be argued that so much praise of personal beauty, whether merited or not, amounts to flattery; and the answer may be,—if merited, there was no flattery, as I have already endeavoured to prove. But the question ought to resolve itself into this consideration; either the youth is to be regarded simply as a friend, or as a patron. If as a friend, we cannot find fault with him for celebrating the most worthy qualities he perceived; first, truth, and, next to that, personal beauty. If as a patron, the poet was assuredly a wretched courtier, openly reproving the noble youth for having committed the "crime," such is the plain term, of treachery to his friend; for having been addicted to licentious conversation; and for having delighted in the "gross painting" of another poet, in preference to honest praise. . . . (pp. 93-5)

It must follow that, if Shakespeare, with all his knowledge of the human heart, intended to flatter a patron, he betrayed more ignorance of the means to accomplish his end than the dullest slave. Such a conclusion is an absurdity.

SIXTH POEM.

STANZAS CXXVII TO CLII.

TO HIS MISTRESS, ON HER INFIDELITY.

All the stanzas in the preceding poems are retained in their original order; the printers, without disturbing the links, having done no worse than the joining together of five chains into one. But I suspect the same attention has not been paid to this address to his mistress. Indeed I farther suspect that some stanzas, irrelevant to the subject, have been introduced into the body of it. For instance, stanzas 135th and 136th, containing a string of puns upon his own name, Will, may very well have been addressed to his mistress prior to her infidelity, but they are contradictory to his resolution to leave her for ever. If it be urged that he is constantly, as in these stanzas, confessing his love for her in spite of her infidelity, I answer that it is no more than the confession, by no means in a playful mood, of an acknowledged weakness, which he is resolute to overcome. . . . However he may waver, and, for the moment, seem to return to his former thraldom, indignation at her faithlessness, and at her having been, through treachery, the cause of his estrangement from a friend, at the last completely conquers his "sinful loving." In the concluding stanza he leaves her in the bitterest language that could be framed for the occasion. On this account, the stanzas containing the puns on his name, appear to me out of keeping with the rest, being altogether of too playful a character.

Stanza 145th strangely comes upon us in the octosyllabic measure; and stanza 146th is an address to his own soul, the solemn nature of which cannot be regarded as congruous with the rest. These two stanzas should be expunged from the poem. It is remarkable that they are placed exactly where there seems to have been a pause or division; the first part being written in doubt and jealousy, and the after part in certainty of the woman's infidelity. Another division of the same kind may indeed be pointed out; and both, or the three parts, taken together, may be well likened to the struggles and love, each overcoming the other by turns, till finally such love is utterly destroyed as worthless. But the octosyllabic stanza, and the address to his soul which follows, can, neither of them, for different reasons, belong to the poem.

Allowing these exceptions, the poem may be read with a tolerable continuity of feeling, possibly as much as the subject will admit. It is a stormy feeling, buffeted to and fro, and presents an admirable picture of pain and distraction, caused by an almost overwhelming passion for a worthless object. (pp. 95-7)

I fear some readers may be surprised that I have not yet noticed a certain fault in Shakespeare, a glaring one,—his having a mistress, while he had a wife of his own, perhaps, at Stratford. May no persons be inclined, on this account, to condemn him with a bitterness equal to their own virtue! For myself, I confess I have not the heart to blame him at all,—purely because he so keenly reproaches himself for his own sin and folly. Fascinated as he was, he did not, like other poets similarly guilty, directly or by implication, obtrude his own passions on the world as reasonable laws. Had such been the case, he might have merited our censure, possibly our contempt. On the contrary, he condemned and subdued his fault, and may therefore be cited as a good rather than as a bad example. Should it be contended that he seems to have quitted his mistress more on account of her unworthiness than from conscientious feelings, I have nothing to answer beyond this: I will not join in seeking after questionable motives for good actions, well knowing, by experience, that when intruded on me, they have been nothing but a nuisance to my better thoughts. (pp. 98-9)

Charles Armitage Brown, in his Shakespeare's Autobiographical Poems, Being His Sonnets Clearly Developed, *James Bohn, 1838, 306 p.*

HERMANN ULRICI (essay date 1839)

[*A German scholar, Ulrici was a professor of philosophy and the author of works on Greek poetry and Shakespeare. The following excerpt is from an English translation of his* Über Shakespeares dramatische Kunst, und sein Verhaltniss zu Calderon und Gothe, *a work first published in 1839. This study exemplifies the "philosophical criticism" developed in Germany during the nineteenth century. The immediate sources for Ulrici's critical approach appear to be August Wilhelm Schlegel's conception of the play as an organic, interconnected whole and Georg Wilhelm Friedrich Hegel's view of drama as an embodiment of the conflict of historical forces and ideas. Unlike his fellow German Shakespearean critic G. G. Gervinus, Ulrici sought to develop a specifically Christian aesthetics, but one which, as he carefully points out in the introduction to the work mentioned above, in no way intrudes on "that unity of idea, which preeminently constitutes a work of art a living creation in the world of beauty." In the following excerpt from the work cited above, he contends that the sonnets underscore the fact that Shakespeare is "pre-eminently a dramatic poet," for these poems reveal "not merely [the playwright's] own individual personality, . . . but still more the character of the personalities (whether real or feigned) whom he is addressing." Ulrici also emphasizes the epigrammatic nature of the sonnets, claiming that they are argumentative and, as such, "more like speeches than lyrical songs."*]

Shakspeare is pre-eminently a *dramatic* poet; this is sufficiently proved by such works of his as we possess, which are not directly of a dramatic character. In his lyrical pieces—the 154 Sonnets, and the collection entitled "The Passionate Pilgrim,"—he reveals not merely his own individual personality, he depicts not only the emotions of his own soul, his own experience and views, but still more the character of the personages (whether real or feigned) whom he is addressing, and it is only in the interwoven description of his *own* connexion with them that his individual feelings are allowed to transpire. These pieces, moreover, are chiefly of an epigrammatic turn, full of verbal play and antithesis, replete with wit and acuteness, and distinguished not so much by the free, poetic flow of feeling, or by the unbroken and harmonious echo of external life in the poet's rich and exquisite sensibility—wherein, in truth, the subject-matter of lyrical poetry consists—as rather by the depth and fulness of the thoughts and reflections. They argue far too much; they are more like speeches than lyrical songs; indeed, we might justly describe them as dialogical, in so far as the reasons and objections, the principles and views, as well as the whole personal character of the persons to whom they are addressed, find distinct utterance in them. It is on this account that they can only be rightly understood in the order which Shakspeare himself has given to them, and that taken singly they are for the most part extremely obscure. (p. 129)

Hermann Ulrici, "Shakspeare's Dramatic Style and Poetical View of Things in General," in his Shakspeare's Dramatic Art: And His Relation to Calderon and Goethe, *translated by Rev. A. J. W. Morrison, Chapman, Brothers, 1846, pp. 128-68.*

CHARLES KNIGHT (essay date 1849)

[*Knight, an English educator and publisher, wrote numerous books and periodicals intended to educate the Victorian working class. Among these were his highly popular illustrated edition of Shakespeare's plays and a complementary illustrated biography of Shakespeare. In addition, Knight also produced a book of critical commentary on the plays,* Studies in Shak-

spere (1849), and was a founder of the first Shakespeare Society. In the following excerpt, he argues that the 1609 Quarto is spurious, that Shakespeare had no hand in its publication. This being the case, he asserts, the notion that the sonnets (at least, the first 126) present one continuous poem on a significant experience in the poet's life is erroneous. Knight maintains instead that whereas some of the poems are personal or autobiographical, others are dramatic, conveying imaginary characters and feelings. In portions of his essay not excerpted here, Knight regroups the sonnets according to their various motifs or themes and their imaginary or autobiographical foundations.]

Upon the question of the *continuity* of [Shakspere's] Sonnets depend many important considerations with reference to the life and personal character of the poet; and it is necessary, therefore, to examine that question with proportionate care.

The Sonnets of Shakspere are distinguished from the general character of that class of poems by the continuity manifestly existing in many successive stanzas, which form, as it were, a group of flowers of the same hue and fragrance. Mr. Hallam has justly explained this peculiarity:—

> No one ever entered more fully than Shakspeare into the character of this species of poetry, which admits of no expletive imagery, no merely ornamental line. But though each Sonnet has generally its proper unity, the sense—I do not mean the grammatical construction—will sometimes be found to spread from one to another, independently of that repetition of the leading idea, like variations of an air, which a series of them frequently exhibits, and on account of which they have latterly been reckoned by some rather an integral poem than a collection of Sonnets. But this is not uncommon among the Italians, and belongs, in fact, to those of Petrarch himself [see excerpt above, 1837-39].

But, although a series may frequently exhibit a "repetition of the leading idea, like variations of an air," it by no means follows that they are to be therefore considered "rather an integral poem than a collection of Sonnets." In [John Benson's] edition of 1640 the "variations" were arbitrarily separated, in many cases, from the "air;" but, on the other hand, it is scarcely conceivable that in the earlier edition of 1609 these verses were intended to be presented as "an integral poem." Before we examine this matter, let us inquire into some of the circumstances connected with the original publication.

The first seventeen Sonnets contain a "leading idea" under every form of "variation." They are an exhortation to a friend, a male friend, to marry. Who this friend was has been the subject of infinite discussion. Chalmers maintains that it was Queen Elizabeth [see excerpt above, 1797], and that there was no impropriety in Shakspere addressing the queen by the masculine pronoun, because a queen is a prince; as we still say in the Liturgy, "our queen and *governor.*" The reasoning of Chalmers on this subject . . . is one of the most amusing pieces of learned and ingenious nonsense that ever met our view. We believe that we must very summarily dismiss Queen Elizabeth. But Chalmers with more reason threw over the idea that the dedication of the bookseller to the edition of 1609 implied the person to whom the Sonnets were addressed. T. T., who dedicates, is . . . Thomas Thorpe, the publisher. W. H., to whom the dedication is addressed, was, according to the earlier critics, an humble person. He was either William Harte, the poet's nephew, or William Hews, some unknown individual; but Drake said, and said truly, that the person addressed in some of the Sonnets themselves

was one of rank [see excerpt above, 1817], and he maintained that it was Lord Southampton. "W. H.," he said, ought to have been H. W.—Henry Wriothesley. But Mr. Boaden and Mr. Brown have subsequently affirmed that "W. H." is William Herbert, Earl of Pembroke, who, in his youth and his rank, exactly corresponded with the person addressed by the poet [see excerpts above, 1832 and 1838]. The words "begetter of these Sonnets," in the dedication, must mean, it is maintained, the person who was the immediate cause of their being written—to whom they were addressed. But *he* was "the *only* begetter of these Sonnets." The latter portion of the Sonnets are unquestionably addressed to a female, which at once disposes of the assertion that he was the *only* begetter, assuming the "begetter" to be used in the sense of *inspirer.* Chalmers disposes of this meaning of the word very cleverly:—"W. H. was the bringer forth of the Sonnets. *Beget* is derived by Skinner from the Anglo-Saxon *begettan,* obtinere. Johnson adopts this derivation and sense: so that *begetter,* in the quaint language of Thorpe the bookseller, Pistol the ancient, and such affected persons, signified the *obtainer:* as to *get* and *getter,* in the present day, mean *obtain* and *obtainer,* or to procure and the procurer." But then, on the other hand, it is held that, when the bookseller wishes Mr. W. H. "that eternity promised by our ever-living poet," he means promised *him.* This inference we must think is somewhat strained. Be this as it may, the material question to examine is this— are the greater portion of the Sonnets, putting aside those which manifestly apply to a female, or females, addressed to *one* male friend? Or are these the "sugared Sonnets" scattered among *many* "private friends?" When Meres printed his 'Palladis Tamia,' in 1598 [see excerpt above], there can be no doubt that Shakspere's Sonnets, then existing only in manuscript, had obtained a reputation in the literary and courtly circles of that time. Probably the notoriety which Meres had given to the "sugared Sonnets" excited a publisher, in 1599, to produce something which should gratify the general curiosity. In that year appeared a collection of poems bearing the name of Shakspere, and published by W. Jaggard, entitled 'The Passionate Pilgrim.' This little collection contains two Sonnets which are also given in the larger collection of 1609. They are those numbered 138 and 144 in that collection. In the modern reprints of 'The Passionate Pilgrim' it is usual to omit these two Sonnets without explanation, because they have been previously given in the larger collection of Sonnets. But it is essential to bear in mind the fact that in 1599 two of the Sonnets of the hundred and fifty-four published in 1609 were printed; and that one of them especially, the one numbered 144, has been held to form an important part of the supposed "integral poem." We may therefore conclude that the other Sonnets which appear to relate to the same persons as are referred to in the 144th Sonnet were also in existence. Further, the publication of these Sonnets in 1599 tends to remove the impression that might be derived from the tone of some of those in the larger collection of 1609,—that they were written when Shakspere had passed the middle period of life. For example, in the 73rd Sonnet the poet refers to the autumn of his years, the twilight of his day, the ashes of his youth. In the 138th, printed in 1599, he describes himself as "past the best"—as "old." He was then thirty-five. Dante was exactly this age when he described himself in "the midway of this our mortal life." In these remarkable particulars, therefore,—the mention of two persons real or fictitious, who occupy an important position in the larger collection, and in the notice of the poet's age,—the two Sonnets of 'The Passionate Pilgrim' are strictly connected with those published in 1609, of which they also form a part; and they lead to the conclusion that they were obtained for publication out of the scattered leaves floating about amongst "private friends." The publication of 'The Passionate Pilgrim' was unquestionably unauthorized and piratical. The publisher got all he could which existed in manuscript; and he took two poems out of 'Love's Labour's Lost,' which was printed only the year before. In 1609, we have no hesitation in believing that the same process was repeated; that without the consent of the writer the hundred and fifty-four Sonnets—some forming a continuous poem, or poems; others isolated, in the subjects to which they relate, and the persons to whom they were addressed—were collected together without any key to their arrangement, and given to the public. Believing as we do that "W. H.," be he who he may, who put these poems in the hands of "T. T.," the publisher, arranged them in the most arbitrary manner (of which there are many proofs), we believe that the assumption of continuity, however ingeniously it may be maintained, is altogether fallacious. Where is the difficulty of imagining, with regard to poems of which each separate poem, sonnet, or stanza, is either a "leading idea," or its "variation," that, picked up as we think they were from many quarters, the supposed connexion must be in many respects fanciful, in some a result of chance, mixing what the poet wrote in his own person, either in moments of elation or depression, with other apparently continuous stanzas that painted an imaginary character, indulging in all the warmth of an exaggerated friendship, in the complaints of an abused confidence, in the pictures of an unhallowed and unhappy love; sometimes speaking with the real earnestness of true friendship and a modest estimation of his own merits; sometimes employing the language of an extravagant eulogy, and a more extravagant estimation of the powers of the man who was writing that eulogy? Suppose, for example, that in the leisure hours, we will say, of William Herbert, Earl of Pembroke, and William Shakspere, the poet should have undertaken to address to the youth an argument why he should marry. Without believing the Earl to be the W. H. of the Dedication, we know that he was a friend of Shakspere. There is nothing in the first seventeen Sonnets which might not have been written in the artificial tone of the Italian poetry, in the working out of this scheme. Suppose, again, that in other Sonnets the poet, in the same artificial spirit, complains that the friend has robbed him of his mistress, and avows that he forgives the falsehood. There is nothing in all this which might not have been written essentially as a work of fiction,—received as a work of fiction,—handed about amongst "private friends" without the slightest apprehension that it would be regarded as an exposition of the private relations of two persons separated in rank as they probably were in their habitual intimacies,—of very different ages,—the one an avowedly profligate boy, the other a matured man. But this supposition does not exclude the idea that the poet had also, at various times, composed, in the same measure, other poems, truly expressing his personal feelings,—with nothing inflated in their tone, perfectly simple and natural, offering praise, expressing love to his actual friends (in the language of the time "lovers"), showing regret in separation, dreading unkindness, hopeful of continued affection. These are also circulated amongst "private friends." Some "W. H." collects them together, ten, or twelve, or fifteen years after they have been written; and a publisher, of course, is found to give to the world any productions of a man so eminent as Shakspere. But who arranged them? Certainly not the poet himself: for those who believe in their continuity must admit that there are portions which it is impossible to regard as continuous. In the same volume with these Sonnets was published a most exquisite narrative poem, 'A Lover's Complaint.' The form of it entirely prevents any attempts to consider it autobiographical. The Sonnets, on the contrary, are personal in their form; but it is not therefore to be assumed that they are *all* personal in their relation to the author. It is impossible to be assumed that they could have been printed with the consent of the author as they now stand. If he had meant in all of them to express his actual feelings and position, the very slightest labour on his part—a few words of introduction either in prose or verse—would have taken those parts which he would have naturally desired to appear like fiction, and which to us even now look like fiction, out of the possible range of reality. The same slight labour would, on the other hand, have classed amongst the real, apart from the artificial, those Sonnets which he would have desired to stand apart, and which appear to us to stand apart, as the result of genuine moods of the poet's own mind. (pp. 458-60)

[In many of these Sonnets, Shakspere] displays his art in a style accordant with the existing fashion and the example of other poets. The theme is the personal beauty of a wonderful youth, and the strong affection of a poet. Beauty is to be perpetuated by marriage, and to be immortalized in the poet's verses. Beauty is gradually to fade before Time, but is to be still immortalized. Beauty is to yield to Death, as the poet himself yields, but its memory is to endure in "eternal lines." [But if we separate] from this somewhat monotonous theme those portions of a hundred and fifty-four Sonnets which do not appear essentially to belong to it, we separate, as we believe, more or less, what has a personal interest in these compositions from what is meant to be dramatic—the real from the fictitious. Our theory, we well know, is liable to many objections; but it is based upon the unquestionable fact that these one hundred and fifty-four Sonnets cannot be received as a continuous poem upon any other principle than that the author had written them continuously. If there are some parts which are acknowledged interpolations, may there not be other parts that are open to the same belief? If there are parts entirely different in their tone from the bulk of these Sonnets, may we not consider that one portion was meant to be artificial and another real,—that the poet sometimes spoke in an assumed character, sometimes in a natural one? This theory we know could not hold if the poet had himself arranged the sequence of these verses; but as it is manifest that two stanzas have been introduced from a poem printed ten years earlier,—that others are acknowledged to be out of order, and others positively dragged in without the slightest connexion,—may we not carry the separation still further, and, believing that the "begetter"—the *getter-up*—of these Sonnets had levied contributions upon all Shakspere's "private friends,"—assume that he was indifferent to any arrangement which might make each portion of the poem tell its own history? There is one decided advantage in the separation which we have proposed—the idea with which the series opens, and which is carried, *here and there,* in the original, through the first hundred and twenty-six Sonnets, does not now over-ride the whole of the series. The separate parts may be read with more pleasure when they are relieved from this strained and exaggerated association. (pp. 497-98)

Charles Knight, "The Sonnets," in his Studies of Shakspere, *Charles Knight, 1849, pp. 457-504.*

G. G. GERVINUS (essay date 1849-50)

[*One of the most widely read Shakespearean critics of the latter half of the nineteenth century, the German critic Gervinus was praised by such eminent contemporaries as Edward Dowden, F. J. Furnivall, and James Russell Lowell; however, he is little known in the English-speaking world today. Like his predecessor Hermann Ulrici, Gervinus wrote in the tradition of the "philosophical criticism" developed in Germany in the mid-nineteenth century. Under the influence of August Wilhelm Schlegel's literary theory and Georg Wilhelm Friedrich Hegel's philosophy, such German critics as Gervinus tended to focus their analyses around a search for the literary work's organic unity and ethical import. Gervinus believed that Shakespeare's work contained a rational ethical system independent of any religion—in contrast to Ulrici, for whom Shakespeare's morality was basically Christian. The following excerpt is reprinted from an English translation of his* Shakespeare Commentaries, *first published in German in 1849-50. Gervinus emphasizes the autobiographical character of Sonnets 1-126, contending that these poems "form together a single whole, a history of the poet's inner life." He divides them into eight internally cohesive groups that trace, in sequence, the poet's growing relationship with his Friend, their falling out and separation, and, ultimately, the poet's serene acceptance of the course of events. Perhaps most significantly, Gervinus calls attention to the progressively more serious tone of Sonnets 62-95, and he remarks on the violent jealousy, even "tragic despondency," in Sonnets 78-95. On other matters, the critic claims that the Young Friend and W. H. are identical: Henry Wriothesley, Earl of Southampton. The use of initials was necessary, he suggests, because of the unusual nature of the relationship treated in the sonnets. Finally, Gervinus alludes briefly to Sonnets 127-54, stressing the physical unattractiveness of the Dark Lady as presented by the poet and characterizing their relationship as "sinful affection."*]

It was to Nicholas Rowe, who in 1709 wrote a life of [Shakespeare] that the actor Betterton related the oft-told anecdote of Shakespeare's deer-stealing, which he had heard at Stratford. He had fallen, so the story goes, into bad company, and had taken part in some deer-stealing at Charlcote, the property of Sir Thomas Lucy; he had been prosecuted by Sir Thomas, and had revenged himself with a satirical ballad, a stanza of which is still extant; this had redoubled the persecution against him to such a degree, that he was obliged to leave Stratford and go to London. Country people near Stratford to this day point out indeed to strangers a statue of Diana with the hind, which they exhibit as the poacher Shakespeare; and if Betterton's authority were of this kind, the anecdote would certainly be very suspicious.

The anecdote, however, carries with it decided marks of a most characteristic trait. . . . His deer-stealing may easily have been the most innocent part of his life. . . . There are . . . other and as it seems indisputable testimonies existing, which prove the young Shakespeare to have been also addicted to dissolute habits of a different character.

We might indeed already infer these habits from a series of Shakespeare's poems, at the close of his collection of sonnets; poems which, with just as much unvarnished morality as candour, declare the poet's connection with a married woman, who shared a faithless love between him and one of his friends. (pp. 28-30)

The poet depicts in those sonnets (127-152) the singular woman with whom he exchanged a sinful affection; he describes her as ugly, black in complexion, hair, and eyes, considered beautiful by none, and with no charm for any physical sense. That which drew her to him was her music, her intel-

lectual grace, and an aptness which clothed the ugly with beauty and raised in his eyes 'the worst in her above all best.' In vain he struggled against this passion, in vain he called to aid his reason, and even his hate. For she ensnared his much-loved young friend, whom the remaining sonnets extol; but even this perfidy he forgave her, which seems to have been rather an act of wantonness, for the passion was not returned; so that it must be admitted we are looking upon a flippant and thus upon no tender intercourse between two lovers. . . . (p. 33)

Shakespeare's sonnets are occasional poems, which were not originally intended for publication. . . . They appeared at the same time with the supplementary poem of 'The Lover's Complaint,' 1609, under the title: 'Shakespeare's Sonnets. Never before imprinted.' A mysterious obscurity surrounds even now this manifestly legitimate edition. It has the appearance of not being published by the poet himself. Contrary to all custom, the publisher T. T. (Thomas Thorpe) wrote a dedication to them, and this indeed to an unknown individual, designated only by the initials Mr. W. H., whom he styles 'the onlie begetter of these sonnets,' and to whom he wishes 'all happinesse and that eternitie promised by our ever-living poet' [see excerpt above, 1609].

The sonnets of Shakespeare, from the mystery in which they were veiled with respect to this 'begetter,' and from the obscurity of their whole purport, have ever been a perplexity to the interpreter and biographer; and in the only clear and distinct part of this purport, they have been a perplexity to the admirers of the poet. The first 126 sonnets in the collection are addressed to a friend; the last 28, the contents of which we have before characterised, bespeak that intercourse with a lightminded woman which was an outrage to all who wished to see no defect in the poet. But even the greater part, it was here and there believed, must be interpreted to the disadvantage of the poet. . . . When at length it was established (a fact at the outset impossible to be mistaken) that the sonnets were written to a young friend, the enthusiastic and amorous style awakened a severe suspicion, from which even other poets of the time were not free. It belonged to the superabundant style of this Italian school of poetry, as it did to the complimentary character of the age, that an unmeasured expression of flattery and tenderness distinguished all writers of that day, and all clients of noble art-patrons from Naples to London. Shakespeare, in the dedication of his 'Lucrece' to the Earl of Southampton, speaks of 'the love without end' which he devoted to him. . . . This was in harmony with the style of the age, although the age itself did not always thus regard it. Barnfield, in his 'Passionate Shepherd' (1595), bewails in a series of sonnets his love for a beautiful youth; it was an innocent imitation of one of Virgil's Eclogues; but the same construction was put upon it as upon Shakespeare's sonnets. On closer consideration this revealed itself. But uncertainty still prevailed as to the youth who won from Shakespeare such extraordinarily deep affection or such shallow pompous flattery. It was of no use for interpreters to suggest that the sonnets should be regarded as if they were merely addressed to a creature of the imagination, as if they were fictions of the fancy, and as if they had been written in the name of other friends; they must indeed have had scarcely a presentiment of the nature of this realistic poet seriously to believe that he had used his pen thus dipped in his own heart's blood in the hire of another, or that he could ever with his free choice have suffered his art to depict so strange a fiction as that most strange connection delineated in these sonnets. For where the subjects are distinct, where profound reflections and feelings occupy the poet, what in all the world could have induced him to utter these emotions of his soul in the form of amorous outpourings to a friend, if such a friend were not truly and bodily at his side, sharing his inner life? We are too much accustomed to see this form of sonnet only employed in the idle play of forced fancy among spiritualistic poets. But if the Shakespeare sonnets are really to be distinguished above others, they are so only because a warm life lies within them, because actual circumstances of life appear even under the pale colouring of this form of poetry, and because the full pulsation of a deeply excited heart penetrates the thick veil of poetic formalism.

It is clear that the sonnets are addressed only to one and the same youth; even the last twenty-eight sonnets to a woman relate from their purport to the one connection between Shakespeare and his young friend. . . . The sonnettist says himself that he is continually expressing one old love in a new form. The same caressing tone ever returns, even after it has been interrupted by more serious subjects of discussion; the 'sweet boy' is the poet's bud and rose to the last. If we must even admit, as has been often the case, that the sonnets originated at great intervals of time, the poet has himself told us why he continues even at a later period to ascribe in poetic fiction the bloom of youth to his friend; he would, he says in Sonnet 108, 'like prayers divine, each day say over the very same, counting no old thing old;' his 'eternal love' weighed not 'the dust and injury of age.' To this ever-loved one Shakespeare assigns beauty, birth, learning, and riches; from the most superficial reading it is evident that he was a young man of high rank in society, whose distance from the poet rendered it necessary that their mutual relation should be concealed from the world. It was evidently on account of this outward incongruity that the sonnets, when they appeared, were neither dedicated by Shakespeare himself, nor was the name of the 'only begetter' designated by the publisher; indeed, we may admit with certainty that the initials Mr. W. H. were intended to mislead. The begetter, that is the person to whom the sonnets were addressed, was evidently not of the middle class. [Some critics], indeed, have understood by the 'begetter' only the *procurer* who collected the sonnets for the publisher, but the publisher himself in the dedication plainly designates that 'begetter' as the very man to whom Shakespeare in the sonnets promised immortality through his verse. (pp. 441-44)

That the man to whom the sonnets in the edition of 1609 are dedicated is therefore the man to whom they were addressed is quite indubitable. We shall scarcely guess his name, however, from the initials Mr. W. H., by which the dedication designates him, as they were evidently intended to deceive. . . . [The] doubtful begetter might even bear a name to which the initials W. H. had no reference. If the darling of Shakespeare were, according to Drake's supposition [see excerpt above, 1817], Henry Wriothesley, Earl of Southampton, we might believe that the initials W. H. concealed and betrayed just as much of the truth as was intended by the dedication. . . . Nathan Drake's supposition that the Earl of Southampton was Shakespeare's youthful friend, the object of such hearty affection and reverence, rests . . . upon such sure grounds, that we must regard all hypothesis in the light of a sin, if we do not adhere to this one. The caution of the critic does not require that we should repudiate a supposition so extraordinarily probable; it requires alone that we should not obstinately insist upon it and set it up as an established certainty, but that

we should lend a willing ear to better and surer knowledge whenever it is offered.

The Earl of Southampton was born in the year 1573, and from 1590 he resided in London. His mother's second husband was the Lord Treasurer Sir Thomas Heneage, whose office brought him into connection with the theatre; this may have given his step-son opportunity of gaining a taste for the works of the stage and inclination to afford them protection. He was early a patron and a passionate friend of the drama. . . . [The] excellent Chapman calls him in his 'Iliad' 'the choice of all our country's noblest spirits;' Nash, in speaking of him, says: 'Incomprehensible is the height of his spirit, both in heroical resolution and matters of conceit.' Beaumont asks, who lives on England's stage and knows him not? All poets and writers vied with each other in dedicating their works to him. . . . Shakespeare himself, in 1593, dedicated to him his 'Venus and Adonis,' in a style of humble distance; in the following year his 'Lucrece' appeared with a bolder dedication, which speaks already of the 'love without end' which he devotes to him, on account of which the poet feels himself assured of a good reception for his little work, not from the worth of his 'untutored lines,' but from 'the warrant' which he has of the Earl's honourable disposition. . . . In this same year, 1594-5, which might easily be the date of the commencement of the sonnets, judging from the intimate connection between Southampton and Shakespeare which the dedication of 'Lucrece' betrays, the earl paid his addresses to Elizabeth Vernon, a cousin of his friend the Earl of Essex. The queen did not desire this union, and subsequently, when in 1598 or 1599 they married without her knowledge, she ordered both to be placed in confinement; this seems indeed to indicate a position in which such an impressive admonition as that which Shakespeare repeats in those first seventeen sonnets would not be out of place. At that time Southampton was scarcely twenty-two years old, an age young enough to admit of Shakespeare's caressing expressions, 'sweet boy' and others, and advanced enough to allow of exhortations to marry. With respect to this connection between the earl and Shakespeare, a notice is preserved which, if it were fully proved, would testify the unusual nature of this union between two men of unequal birth, and this in such a manner as to explain to us the entire devotion of our poet towards the youth. Rowe relates in his life of Shakespeare, as a matter which would have been incredible to him had it not rested on the authority of Sir William Davenant, who was well acquainted with Shakespeare's affairs, that Southampton once gave Shakespeare the sum of a thousand pounds, a sum that according to the present value of money we may estimate at five times as much, in order to enable him 'to go through with a purchase which he heard he had a mind to.' It was customary to reward dedications with gifts, but not with gifts of such importance. It was at the very time of Shakespeare's two dedications that the Blackfriars company began to build the Globe on the Bankside. In consideration of the interest which the earl took in all that concerned the stage, and in consideration also of those dedications and of this undertaking of his favourite company, [it is] . . . not improbable that Southampton might have given this sum, partly to reward Shakespeare, and partly to enable him to take a share in the new building. . . . At all events the connection which these relations between the two parties indicate was a most unusual one, and in those days especially was quite out of rule; both Shakespeare's personal contact with Southampton, as well as the connection to which the sonnets refer. That Shakespeare should have made several such uncommon alliances is certainly hard to believe. And it has, therefore, always appeared to me incomprehensible why in England the identity of the object of these sonnets with the Earl of Southampton should be an idea so much opposed. For if ever a supposition bordered on certainty, it is this. (pp. 444-48)

We will now endeavour to follow the inner thread which binds together the sonnets of Shakespeare. In so doing we shall not suffer ourselves to be misled by the adversaries to this mode of explanation, some of whom must have read these poems without any attention or imagination, and who have in consequence interpreted this interpretation as if the sonnets were regarded as an originally connected whole, as a rhyming chronicle intentionally delineating a section of the poet's life. Others already have perceived before us (Armitage Brown, 'Shakespeare's Autobiographical Poems,' 1838 [see excerpt above]) that these poems are divided into different groups, each of which touches on a distinct subject; but in the separation and characterisation of these groups we do not wholly coincide with Brown's views. All these groups form together a single whole, a history of the poet's inner life, following an exact psychological course full of nature and truth; the sonnets are chronologically arranged in order to unroll this course before us. What renders the distinction between these groups difficult, and may easily mislead the reader into denying a distinction at all, is the interruption of the sonnets relating to stated circumstances by some of an entirely general character, which proclaim with great uniformity the praise of the friend. These vague songs of praise are scattered throughout the whole collection, veiling the real purport of the rest, that is of the true occasional poems. The sonnets were of course written singly, and the greater part would naturally belong to those universal poems of homage which expressed the constant relation between the friends, and which, from their purport, did not belong to any fixed condition or period. The poet, in arranging them for the press, would hardly accurately observe to what time they belonged; he could not place them monotonously together; he would be obliged to distribute them among the groups which exhibit the touching history of the connection. If we do not suffer ourselves to be disturbed by the insertion of these insignificant pieces, we shall find the history of that inner life distinct and expressive. (p. 451)

We are of opinion . . . that the sonnets of our poet, aesthetically considered, have been overestimated. With respect to their psychological tenor, they appear to us, with the total lack of all other sources for the history of Shakespeare's inner life, to be of inestimable value. They exhibit the poet to us just in the most interesting period of his mental development, when he passed from dependent to independent art, from foreign to national taste, from subserviency and distress to prosperity and happiness; aye, even from loose morality to inner reformation. And in addition to the gigantic, scarcely comprehensible picture of his mental development, which is presented to us in his dramas of this period, we here receive a small intelligible painting of his inner life, which brings us more closely to the poet himself. We live with him throughout an intercourse which was probably one of the greatest events in the calm routine of his existence; we read the touching story of a full, feeling, and warm heart, a story that no one can contemplate without deep emotion; we perceive the gentle undulation and the stronger current of an aspiring passion ebbing and flowing, the psychological story of which we can follow in all its depth. We [know] that Shakespeare was not happy in his married life. The void which would thus be

left in his heart seemed to be entirely filled when he received the love of the noble youth, who from his high position extended his helpful hand to him in his lowliness and poverty, and perhaps first cast a higher intellectual light into an outwardly joyless existence. Truly the development of this connection of the poet with his 'fair friend' is the detail of a strong passion, violent even to suffering, such as a man generally feels only for a woman. In England no one until now has felt any sympathy in this history of the poet's heart. Great care has been taken to discover, from a hundred scattered notices, how much the poet was 'worth' at the different periods of his life, but no one, with true devotion has studied these sources connected with the history of his heart. Perhaps for this a more youthful people is required, a people such as the German, whose hearts are not yet hardened by exclusive attention to politics and common interests. Nay, the whole secret of our deep interest in Shakespeare seems to rest in this— that the degree of development and culture of our nation at the present day is nearly the same as that of England in Shakespeare's time, and that advantageously for us this great poet has not come upon us unawares, as was the case with England, but that since the period of his appearance, by the nurture of poetry through two hundred years, the soil with us has been slowly and thoroughly prepared for him.

We will now pass . . . to the analysis of the separate groups of our sonnet series, and following the given arrangement of the poems, we will relate the history of the connection between the two friends.

Sonnets 1-17. The first seventeen sonnets urge upon the 'tender churl' in a forcible and even importunate manner to marry; they call him 'the world's fresh ornament,' the 'only herald to the gaudy spring' [Sonnet 1], on whom it is enjoined as a duty to leave behind a new impress of the beautiful seal, carved by nature as a copy; and in this series we may admire the rich invention of images with which the poet varies a theme so simple. From the 14th sonnet the subject passes gradually into the more general praise of the beauty and truth of his young friend; yet in Sonnet 17 he says, in pursuance of his former theme,

> Who will believe my verse in time to come,
> If it were fill'd with your most high deserts?
> But were some child of yours alive that time,
> You should live twice; in it, and in my rhyme.

Nevertheless, continues Sonnet 18, abandoning this theme, 'thy eternal summer shall not fade.' The praise of his friend was carried to a great height in these first sonnets; further on the poet recollects, as it were, that he will not continue in this exaggerated style. . . . In fact, in the following group, the elaborate form of the first series is interrupted by the expression of the most lively sentiments, while their theme is no longer of so superficial a character as that of the earlier ones, but is drawn from the soul of the poet.

Sonnets 18-40. The subject which links together the second series is the inequality of the position of the two friends. The history of their close connection begins here, for the first seventeen sonnets might have been written from a distance. We here plainly perceive the devotion with which the young nobleman surrendered himself to the poet so superior in mind, and with which the poet returns this condescending friendship, by turns exhibiting modesty and self-confidence, reserve and familiarity. He must confess [Sonnet 36] that

> we two must be twain,

Although our undivided loves are one:
So shall those blots that do with me remain,
Without thy help by me be borne alone.
In our two loves there is but one respect,
Though in our lives a separable spite,
Which though it alter not love's sole effect,
Yet doth it steal sweet hours from love's delight.

He may not evermore acknowledge his friend, nor may he with public kindness honour him, lest he take from his name that honour which he would give to his friend. . . . Thus subsequently he desires that his friend [Sonnet 71] should not mourn for him when he is dead, but let his love decay even with his life, lest, as he says,

The wise world should look into your moan,
And mock you with me after I am gone.

The poet has many departed friends to deplore, but the one new friend compensates for all. Yet the sense of the cleft which separates them both torments him throughout, and his humility suffers him not to continue in his self-reliance. If in one place, elevated by the honouring friendship, he declares his readiness to resign all dignities of rank, elsewhere he longs after a more honourable position that he may be more worthy of his friend. The contentment expressed in Sonnet 25, where he willingly renounces honour and title for the place where he 'may not remove, nor be removed,' is at variance with his desire elsewhere [Sonnet 26] for a favourable star, which 'puts apparel on his tattered loving, to show him worthy,' that he may dare to boast how he loves his friend; till then he will not show his head where he may be proved. This double condition of feeling is expressed by the 29th sonnet in the most poetic and deeply affecting manner. . . . (pp. 452-55)

Sonnets 40-42. The three following sonnets, in which the poet complains of the robbery of his love, have been already anticipated by Sonnets 33-35; in the former group the connection is introduced and defended in a roundabout way, which the poet himself designates as a fault. The Sonnets 40-42 gently reproach the young friend for his robbery of a beloved one, for whom, according to the whole tone, the poet cares but little; whom his friend on his side also, as it seems, despises, and apparently withdraws from only in wanton raillery. The Sonnets 133 and 134 make it clear that the same woman is here intended as the one to whom the last group of sonnets . . . was addressed. This group ought to have been introduced here as an episode, although it was certainly expedient to remove it, in order not to interrupt the development of the connection between the two friends. The wantonness which is alluded to indicates, in a new and no very edifying manner, how closely the two friends were now united. The rich man takes from the poor friend his one lamb, blemished as it might be; he forgives it in his compliant position, he finds that in the 'lascivious grace' of the youth, 'all ill well shows,' and that these 'pretty wrongs' befit his years, which are ever exposed to temptation.

Sonnets 43-61. The following series, as far as the 61st sonnet, were written during the absence of his young friend; they were temporarily separated; a 'sad interim' is bewailed, though it does not 'kill the spirit of love with a perpetual dulness' [Sonnet 56]. Even when the single poems do not speak plainly of this theme, they yet have reference to it. It is begun in Sonnets 43-45; in Sonnet 46 it seems to be lost sight of, but the 47th sonnet refers both poems again to the principal theme. Thus subsequently the Sonnets 53-55 appear to deviate, but the 56th sonnet unites the little series again to the main subject, the absence of the friend. The whole tone of these poems expresses longing after the absent one; the friendship is strangely mingled with a jealousy which throughout gives it a painful sting; it is as if the poet strove more earnestly in the separation to preserve the favour of his friend. How natural it is that just in this time of absence the thought should torment him, whether the man of high position, accustomed from early youth to the happy principles of equality, might not some day wholly alienate himself from him. In this presentiment of a bare possibility, a timid half-expressed self-reliance on his own desert struggles with the devotion of the moment while he yet possesses his friend. The 49th sonnet is in this respect full of expression. . . . (pp. 455-57)

Sonnets 62-77. The serious mood, which has before overcome the poet, gains still more ground. The formerly often playful tone ceases; another period begins; events seem to lie between this and the earlier parts. The poet speaks much and often of his age, thoughts of decay and of the frailty of all things occupy his mind, and the glance he casts upon the eternity of his poetry seems but little to divert him. In Sonnet 73, the presentiment of an early death appears; even the idea of his favourite's future age now torments him. A longing after death seizes him when he looks upon the evils of society generally, or upon those more closely connected with himself—evils that abound in the republic of letters. A disgust, which he often expresses in his dramas, takes possession of him when he observes the falsehood of the world, borrowing beauty from paint and plaited hair. . . . As years advance he sees this abhorred world entered by his young friend, whom for a delicious moment he had alone possessed; he sees him fallen into bad company; they slander the beauty of his mind according to the outward appearance; to his fair flower they add 'the rank smell of weeds' [Sonnet 69]. Whilst he protects him from every suspicion, he blames him gently, because this contradiction between his true desert and its 'show' is his own fault, as he does 'common grow.' The dawning jealousy of the favourite, whom now other society also claims, conceals itself under the veil of moral carefulness. It lies in the nature of this passion, that where it once has taken root it is difficult to eradicate it. (pp. 457-58)

A greater austerity, it must be admitted, appears in these later sonnets, and in such a manner as allows us to infer a change of mind in the poet; yet we hear in them still more plainly the voice of jealousy, which grudges to the world and its judgment both his friend's virtues and faults. Now he wishes that the world could once see his pleasure, and then he counts it best to be alone with his friend; now he is 'proud as an enjoyer,' and anon doubting 'the filching age will steal his treasure' [Sonnet 75]. We feel throughout that the social relations of the young nobleman change and expand, that he steps beyond the exclusive possession of the poet. The way is prepared for the following group, in which the noble patron of art appears more decidedly surrounded by other poets and literary clients.

Sonnets 78-86. There was a time when our poet alone called upon the aid of the kind patron, and when his verse alone 'had all his gentle grace;' but now he laments that his 'gracious numbers are decayed,' and that his 'sick muse doth give another place' [Sonnet 79]. Alien pens had got his use, and under his patron's name dispersed their poesy. . . . Yet he commends to him his simple, 'true, plain words' [Sonnet 82], which would retain their value by the side of the strained rhetoric of the other. Nay, he arms himself with his proudest self-reliance, and tells his friend,

> Your monument shall be my gentle verse,
> Which eyes not yet created shall o'er-read;
> And tongues to be your being shall rehearse
> When all the breathers of this world are dead.
>
> [Sonnet 71]

But this self-reliance endures not the jealous emotions in the poet's heart; there is no passion which so completely casts down proud self-confidence as a jealousy not entirely hopeless, and springing from true love. As he says in the 80th sonnet,

> O, how I faint when I of you do write,
> Knowing a *better spirit* doth use your name,
> And in the praise thereof spends all his might,
> To make me tongue-tied, speaking of your fame!
>
> (pp. 458-59)

Sonnets 87-95. That feeling of estrangement, which in this increasing jealousy we have seen taking possession of the poet's heart, appears consummated in the next epoch of the development of this union of the friends, and is coupled with the deepest, most touching grief. Still the value of this love stands to him high above everything, but the fear that his darling may suddenly wholly withdraw from him has grown to a certainty. The remembrance of the difference of his friend's rank rises again in the poet's soul with a bitter warning. Once, when he had described this union with his friend, it had been with joyful confidence, even when concealed under elegiac laments; now it is with tragic despondency. He had once expressed [Sonnet 49] that he had no ground, no right, no claim upon his love, but he did this so calmly, because himself incredulous; he had exhibited only as a poetic fancy the case which now is at hand as a reality. Notwithstanding, he is so kind, so ready for resignation, that he permits his friend to add to his self-known unworthiness even invented faults, which can justify him in forsaking him. . . . In the 87th sonnet he writes him as it were a parting letter:—

> Farewell! thou art too dear for my possessing,
> And like enough thou know'st thy estimate:
> The charter of thy worth gives thee releasing;
> My bonds in thee are all determinate.
> For how do I hold thee but by thy granting?
> And for that riches where is my deserving?
> The cause of this fair gift in me is wanting,
> And so my patent back again is swerving.
> Thyself thou gavest, thy own worth then not knowing,
> Or me, to whom thou gavest it, else mistaking;
> So thy great gift, upon misprision growing,
> Comes home again, on better judgment making.
>   Thus have I had thee, as a dream doth flatter,
>   In sleep a king, but waking, no such matter.

However resolute this letter of renunciation sounds, it was not so seriously intended. The strength of fidelity or the weakness of love leads him ever back again to the object, who rises above the power of his resignation and stifles every feeling of self-reliance. He wallows deeper in the painful thoughts of this separation, and tears his wounds wider and wider asunder, nevertheless without being able to bleed to death. (pp. 459-60)

Even this degree of pain at wounded affection and self-love is not the worst. He fears even that his love may be false, and he, the lover, know it not. His looks may be with him, his

heart in another place. He seems in Sonnet 94 to doubt whether he shall reckon him among those dangerous superior natures 'that do not do the thing they most do show,' who misuse the privilege they possess to cover every blot with beauty's veil; who are lords and owners of their faces; who move others, while they are themselves as stone, unmoved, cold, and slow to temptation. He fears that he might have lavished his heart laden with rich treasure upon cold superficial vanity, and no more painful experience could have befallen the man who had staked so much pure love and fidelity upon this one friend.

Sonnets 100-126. But a happier destiny spared our poet this bitter experience. It had certainly come to this—that a neglect on the part of the noble friend was followed by a corresponding neglect on the part of the poet; that a cooling of the first love, an estrangement between the two had arisen; that a shadow had fallen on the union which had begun with so much promise. But these shadows dispersed, and the equal fault of both counterbalanced and neutralised each other. The 120th sonnet clearly sets forth the circumstances which the whole of the last group allows us to conjecture. It 'befriends' the poet that his friend was once unkind; for now, when the sky is again serene above them, every word in this last series of sonnets proclaims that their union now for the first time stands above the reach of caprice, that full contentment has returned, that

> ruined love, when it is built anew,
> Grows fairer than at first, more strong, far greater.
>
> [Sonnet 119]

The poet now accuses himself, that he had alienated himself from his friend, that he had neglected his 'dear purchased right' [Sonnet 117], and had for a time slumbered in his love. He looks back upon the three years past, when their love was new, and he celebrated its spring:—

> Then I was wont to greet it with my lays,
> As Philomel in summer's front doth sing
> And stops her pipe in growth of riper days:
> Not that the summer is less pleasant now
> Than when her mournful hymns did hush the
>   night,
> But that wild music burdens every bough
> And sweets grown common lose their dear delight.
>   Therefore like her I sometime hold my tongue,
>   Because I would not dull you with my song.
>
> [Sonnet 102]

His silence and his absence thus began with that song of the new favourite's, with the divided favour of his friend, with the jealousy which disburdened itself in those outbursts of inward pain, when the poet looked backward to the old times, and forward to the day when he should see his darling completely separated from him. He now pathetically calls upon his muse to begin anew the interrupted song, to celebrate again the old idolatrous worship of his love. . . . His song goes on with the old praise upon the excellence of his friend, and extols the poet's love as 'strengthened, though more weak in seeming' [Sonnet 102]. He triumphs that neither his own fears, nor the prophetic soul of the wide world, could control the lease of his true love. The moon has endured her eclipse, the sad augurs mock their own presage, and peace proclaims olives of endless age; with the drops of this most balmy time his love looks fresh. . . . Once more he casts a glance upon the stigma 'which vulgar scandal stamped upon his brow' [Sonnet 112], but he feels now for ever assured that his friend's love and pity will efface the impression. Even this last matter which depressed him he seems to cast aside with lighter heart, in new confidence in the duration of their friendship. 'What care I,' he says in the 112th sonnet,

> who calls me well or ill,
> So you o'ergreen my bad, my good allow?
> You are my all-the-world, and I must strive
> To know my shames and praises from your tongue;
> None else to me, nor I to none alive,
> That my steel'd sense or changes, right or wrong.
> In so profound abysm I throw all care
> Of others' voices, that my adder's sense
> To critic and to flatterer stopped are.

This, then, is the history of the origin and growth of this union of soul as we read it in Shakespeare's sonnets. It is a connection in itself of no great importance; nay, in the way in which it is poetically expressed, it is not without distortion. But it testifies to a strength of feeling and passion in our poet, to a childlike nature and a candid mind, to a simple ingenuousness, to a perfect inability to veil his thoughts or to dissemble, to an innate capacity for allowing circumstances to act upon his mind in all their force and for re-acting upon them—in a word, it testifies to a nature as truthful, genuine, and straightforward as we imagine the poet from his dramatic works to have possessed. (pp. 461-63)

> G. G. Gervinus, "Shakespeare at Stratford" and "Shakespeare's Sonnets," in his Shakespeare Commentaries, translated by F. E. Bunnètt, revised edition, 1877. Reprint by AMS Press, Inc., 1971, pp. 23-35, 441-74.

D. BARNSTORFF   (essay date 1860)

[In the following excerpt from his Key to Shakespeare's Sonnets, originally published in German in 1860 as Schüssel zu Shakspeares Sonnetten, Barnstorff avers that the subjects of Shakespeare's sonnets are "his genius, and the drama, and his own self." The critic theorizes that the collection is an elaborate allegory in which the mortal man addresses an appeal to his immortal genius (Sonnets 1-126) and the playwright offers us his "innermost thoughts" on dramatic art (Sonnets 127-54). Barnstorff also speculates that the initials W. H. in the dedication of the 1609 Quarto refer to "William and Himself."]

How could a doubt prevail in the literary world upon the subject of Shakespeare's Sonnets! How could a vulgar superficial reading of this work so cloud the intellects of thinking men, that they should remain satisfied with interpretations and assumptions, not only unreliable, but which tend to drag the name of the poet in the dirt of the earth.—It has been well said, that when we meet with a passage in any work of a Shakespeare's, that at the first reading appears strange and incomprehensible, we are to ponder over and criticize it with a settled conviction of our own intellectual inferiority,—of our utter insignificance compared with him. We echo this opinion; yet who, unless a mere blind admirer, on reading the sonnets, under the impression that they were addressed to a patron, a friend, or a mistress could help condemning these apparently overstrained and long-drawn verses as devoid of taste, and true feeling;—altogether unmanly, and opposed to all elevation of soul? But Shakespeare, the Great Dramatist, was their author, and we have to read carefully and judge timidly. Shakespeare is distinguished for sound sense, discretion, and discrimination. His detestation of bombast and mouthing is plainly shewn in the play of Hamlet. Now is it

conceivable that he should have been so false to himself in these sonnets, as Laertes-like to prate, and whine, and rant of love,—or that he should waste his genius, and that Time upon which he sets so great a value in fawning, adulatory effusions dedicated to a young man of rank, to a friend, or to a mistress? This struck us as so utterly improbable, that we resolved to fling aside the vulgar acceptation and seek whether some other object more worthy of such an expenditure of time and talent might not be latent in the sonnets. Modestly and almost without the hope of obtaining a satisfactory result, we bent to our task; and discovered—what? darkness? confusion? No! light and order. Every word and every symbol displayed convincingly that the poet had been misunderstood.

We could now hardly comprehend the fact, that men of high attainments should have disputed about the corporeal beings to whom the poet was supposed to have dedicated these poetic emanations. We could still less familiarize ourselves with the flattering circumstance, that it should be reserved for us to perceive and draw aside the veil of allegory with which the poet had so cunningly hid himself. That we should discover in this literary stumbling block against which so many commentators have broken their shins, a literary gem of purest ray serene was more than we could possibly anticipate. Yet such was . . . the result of our study.

We scarcely know where to commence in proof of that which really requires no proof. . . . It is indeed altogether a work of supererogation to attempt to render Shakespeare's language plainer than it is of itself. The mists of indifference, the surmises of presumptuous commentators which have hitherto surrounded the sonnets will not endure for a moment the steady penetrating gaze of independent analysis. We need indeed spend no words to prove that which a modest confidence in the poet's genius and good sense, and a careful unbiassed study of his work will render self evident. Nevertheless, experience teaches,—the fate of the sonnets teaches, how hard it is for the most of us to forsake an adopted, or rather imposed error, and disentangle ourselves from the meshes of misconception, and prejudice.

It is always difficult to disassociate ourselves from our environments, and transpose ourselves into the individuality of him we seek to understand. And the fact, that Hamlet, whom we had moving in flesh and blood so to speak before us, proved for a couple of centuries an enigma, may serve as an excuse for the universal misconception regarding a poetic effusion which has its source in regions of the purest abstractness.

The subjects of the poet's muse, in these sonnets is no Earl of Southampton, no Earl of Pembroke, no Queen Elizabeth, no Mrs. Varnon—no corporeal friend, no corporeal mistress, but Genius and the Drama. Shakespeare, in these sonnets, holding before his own individuality a mask of allegory, presents to those who will stop to scrutinize, a picture of his innerself. He describes the secret thoughts of his heart;—Firstly in the form of an appeal addressed by his mortal to his immortal man,—his prescribed, external individuality to his innerself,—his intellectual power, his intellectuality,—his genius (Sonnets I—CXXVI). Secondly by the symbol of a mistress, an outward, mundane love, whose womb his genius is to fructify, he gives us his innermost thoughts upon the Drama or his Art (Sonnets CXXVII—CLII). William Shakespeare, the actor, the lowly, disregarded, uncomprehended man of the age in which he lived, dedicates these verses to his *genius.* Upon this latter is imposed the love-task of raising the former to undying honour and fame among mankind. His genius must triumph over the unfavourable circumstances of birth and fortune, or, failing to do so, sink like his body into earth and oblivion.

Considered from this point of view, little that is dark or doubtful will be found in the sonnets, and that little may hereafter be proved attributable to the mutilations of superficial and presumptuous critics. In these verses we think may be discovered that which imparted to his works their peculiar originality, their innate logic, and wonderful combination of natural simplicity and poetic beauty. We may also comprehend why he never wasted his time and powers in the invention of the mere plot or fiction, which was to receive the inspirations of his genius. Further, it may be seen in what light he viewed his art and how he expected it would be comprehended by posterity. All this and much more we have here revealed to the mind's eye in a manner most cunningly devised, and in the only possible form that would afford him perfect freedom of expression and, at the same time, effectually screen him from any uncharitable criticism on the part of his cotemporaries or even succeeding commentators. (pp. 11-15)

Shakespeare's dramas are, even in their outward show,—even in their very scenery, the embodiment of psychological truths. . . . [If] we view the most minute, as well as the most striking details, as the offspring of his innerself, begotten through the already prepared plot, or fable;—if we conceive the original story, historical or fictitious, which he selected for the reception of his intellectual images as the feminine attribute, the mistress:—if we can adopt this simple and natural symbol, we may easily comprehend, that for the poet to reveal his mind, it was necessary to divide his two existences,—his intellectual and physical. No allegory could be more apt and convenient than that by which he revealed his most recondite thoughts, and, at the same time shielded his outward self.

In the first half of sonnet XXXIX the poet says this in words sufficiently plain and unequivocal:

> O! how thy worth with manners may I sing
> *When thou art all the better part of me?*
> What can *mine own praise* to *mine own self* bring?
> And what is't but mine own, when I praise thee?
> Even for this let us *divided* live,
> And our dear love lose name of single one,
> That *by this separation* I may give
> That due to thee which thou deserv'st alone.

Although we base our arguments as to the object and sense of the sonnets upon internal evidence, yet we may express our conviction that all the circumstances connected with their origin and publication must appear to every unbiassed mind as favourable to our interpretation. Though what we . . . advance is a mere *supposition,* still it is the most plausible, and indeed the only supposition that has internal and external grounds to support it.

The sonnets are dedicated to a person whose initials were W. H. We venture now to declare that it seems to us very probable, looking at sonnets CXXXV—CXXXVI that these letters stand for the words *William* and *Himself.* As already observed, we have no proof for this, and throw it out simply as a guess. We set no value on it, as far as it relates to our interpretation; for, although offering a certain coincidence, it does not affect it, either one way or the other. It is observable that

the dedication in question seems to have been written by the publisher, which we think is contrary to all custom. The publisher terms the unmentioned personage "the only begetter of the ensuing sonnets," and wishes him all the happiness and that *eternity* promised to him therein. In a work containing no name, and consequently giving no fame to any one but the writer himself, there would be no sense in such a dedication, unless it referred to the author, or his genius. The first legitimate edition of the sonnets was published under circumstances of great mystery. It was made to appear as if the poet himself had not published them. This was, in our opinion, but natural in sending forth a work intended only for posterity,—a work which, if the key to it had been found, would have exposed the author to the taunts of his cotemporaries.

We have only to repeat, in conclusion, that nothing is required but simply to direct attention to the fact, that in these sonnets the poet is occupied, not with beings of flesh and blood, but with his *genius,* the *drama,* and his own *self.* . . . (pp. 15-17)

> *D. Barnstorff, in his* A Key to Shakespeare's Sonnets, *translated by T. J. Graham, 1862. Reprint by AMS Press Inc., 1975, 215 p.*

JOHN A. HERAUD (essay date 1862)

[*In the excerpt below, Heraud disputes the theory that "Mr. W. H." in the dedication of the 1609 Quarto edition of the sonnets means "William Himself" and that the poems "are directed to [Shakespeare's] interior individuality." Heraud argues that this problematic collection is unified not by such a subjective philosophy, but by a Platonic one. According to Heraud, the subject and object of the sonnets are the same: the human ideal, which is both male and female, a part of the poet but separate from him. The critic traces the progression from the particular to the universal in Sonnets 1-126 and emphasizes the theological significance of the themes of love and beauty. Living in a period of religious conflicts, "Shakespeare found himself between two loves," Heraud contends. The sonnets demonstrate, he concludes, that the poet aligned himself with the Protestant belief in the moderation of "natural appetites" rather than the Mariolotry and "impossible abstinence" of Catholicism.*]

A German writer [D. Barnstorff] has recently projected a new theory in regard to the vexed question of Shakespeare's Sonnets [see excerpt above, 1860]. The theory is very characteristic of the national mind, carried, however, to an extreme, so as to be almost an example of the *reductio ad absurdum.* His notion is, that the poet's dedication "To W. H." means to *William Himself,* and that all the personal apostrophes are directed to his interior Individuality. This, as I have suggested, is too German. Yet I can see clearly how it is that the critic has found the hypothesis help him in understanding this mysterious series of poems. The ordinary notion, in fact, that because the poems are dedicated to W. H. they are necessarily addressed to the dedicatee, is about as absurd as the merely subjective notion of the Teutonic critic. After a careful reperusal, I have come to the conclusion that there is not a single sonnet which is addressed to any individual at all; and that there is an obvious point of view, in which not only the general drift and design of all the sonnets, as a connected whole, become apparent enough, but the details also abundantly intelligible. I proceed to show the grounds of my position, and to add such illustrations as it may require. (p. 53)

The German's notion of the sonnets being purely subjective is refuted by the impossibility of the thing. A purely subjective philosophy did not then exist, and an objective poet like Shakespeare was not likely to be its initiator. Undoubtedly there is subjective matter in all Shakespeare's works; but he had formed no exclusive theory of the sort, if any theory at all. That Shakespeare's philosophy is identical with Bacon's is sufficiently proved by Delia Bacon, though she has of course failed in attempting to prove that he is not the author of his own plays. The manner in which she has applied the Negative Instances of the Baconian philosophy, and the marvellous results she brings out by the process, are perfectly convincing on this point. Now Bacon's induction combines both the subjective and objective in one common method; the Shakesperian drama does the same. We can scarcely, therefore, err in applying the Baconian method of induction to an examination of the sonnets.

I begin, and shall, indeed, altogether conduct the inquiry with and by inferences. The first seventeen sonnets, I find, are all pervaded with the same theme—a declaration against celibacy. In this we find Shakespeare expressing the Protestant feeling of the time, and moving with the age. That Shakespeare, notwithstanding that in his dramatic capacity he appears to hold the balance pretty even between the claims of the two Churches, was thoroughly Protestant, even to an extreme, is abundantly evident. . . . [How] true he was to the principles of the Reformation is manifest in his dramas of *Measure for Measure, Love's Labour's Lost, &c.,* where Angelo doubtless represents the Pontiff, and the state he rules over allegorises the Church; and where the declaration against celibacy is repeated with humoristic force, and corroborated with philosophic argument. Nature is thoroughly vindicated. The vice that Angelo would suppress is declared to be of "a great kindred; it is well allied; but it is *impossible* to extirp it quite, friar, till eating and drinking be put down" [*Measure for Measure,* III. ii. 101-03]. Ecclesiastical authority had included marriage and license in the same category; and no man could claim to be a saint who was not also a celibate, or rather esteemed to be so, for the *impossibility* of all being sincere in this assumption made many to be hypocrites. Against this monstrous injustice the sonneteer utters his protest in the first seventeen sonnets. Each has but one moral, repeated sixteen times. Why this iteration and reiteration, but to enforce a truth with which time was teeming, and which was already destined to inaugurate a new and better age?

We must trace the course of the poet's argument. In introducing it, he apostrophises a supposed individual who has resolved on celibacy,—one who was selfishly "contracted to his own bright eyes,"—who would make a famine where there was abundance,—who "within his own bud would bury his content" [Sonnet 1],—and finally, by his absurd conduct and example, hasten on the end of the world. In these topics the whole of the proposed argument is well-nigh involved; but the poet is intent on enlarging on each and all. He reminds the ideal celibate that at the age of forty his brow will become wrinkled, and that, not having a child to image his former beauty, he will have no living evidence of its existence. In the next place, he urges that celibacy is unjust to the individual, to the world, and to the opposite sex. It is also contrary to nature. (pp. 53-4)

The poet, in the fifth sonnet, proceeds to point out that there is progress in nature and in the seasons. Winter will come at last, and annihilation would ensue, but that nature provides for the same succession another year. In the sixth sonnet, the celibate is called on to make a like provision; the poet justly

urging that the use of the gift of reproduction is not invalidated by the abuse of it, and that the fact of such reproduction is man's conquest over Death. The point is enforced with an earnestness almost sublime:

> Then, what could Death do if thou shouldst depart,
>   Leaving thee living in posterity?
> Be not self-willed, for thou art much too fair
> To be Death's conquest, and make worms thine
>   heir.
>   . . .
>
>   [Sonnet 6]

The eighth sonnet also illustrates the same argument, by a simile taken from harmony in music, and by a picture in which "sire, and child, and happy mother" are all engaged in "singing one pleasing note." The poet then becomes ironical, and supposes for a moment that the celibate chooses a "single life" out of "fear to wet a widow's eye." But he urges that, if he dies childless, the world will be his widow, and himself be guilty of a "murderous shame," a suicide who loves others as little as he really loves himself. (p. 55)

[Here] we may suitably advert to a remark of Coleridge's, namely, that Shakespeare's minor poems suggest all the power in him of becoming a great dramatist, and this because he was already a great poet. He had shown in them that he was not only capable of writing well on personal topics, but of becoming other than himself in his power of realising objects and persons. He could "become all things, and yet remain the same;" he could "make the changeful god be felt in the river, the lion, and the flame." And thus it is that, in the *Venus and Adonis,* "Shakespeare writes as if he were of another planet, charming you to gaze on the movements of the lovers as you would on the twinkling dances of two vernal butterflies. Finally," the critic proceeds, "in this poem, and the *Rape of Lucrece,* Shakespeare gave ample proof of his possession of a most profound, energetic, and philosophical mind, without which he might have pleased, but could not have been a great *dramatic* poet."

Thus also, in these sonnets, Shakespeare states his proposition dramatically, and portrays a person in whom it might be embodied. His subject is stated as an Object which he may and does apostrophise. Having so stated it, he proceeds logically to its distribution. Its elements are twofold: those that relate to Love, and those that concern Beauty. In treating of Beauty, he does not appropriate the attribute to the opposite sex, but simply as the property of Man. In the 18th, 19th, and 20th sonnets, his theme is Masculine Beauty; in the last, he recognises evidently an aristocratic type, and describes a man with features and manners soft and lovely as a woman's, but furnished with all the forces by which he can command those of his own sex and fascinate the other, and plenarily endowed with all that could administer pleasure to his partner and insure the reproduction of his own image. He paints, in fact, the sensual man in his noblest type. But he does not stop here. . . . [He] passes out of the dramatist into the poet, and invests the object of his apostrophe—as he invariably did even his most dramatic characters—with the gifts of his rich imagination and copious affections. His type-man becomes an ideal, and is furnished out of his own mind and heart with the requisite attributes. (pp. 56-7)

This *quasi* identification of the subject and object doubtless suggested to the German critic the notion on which he has proceeded, that the poet throughout addressed himself. The error is very pardonable, but easily corrected. It was not his *ego,* but his *alter-ego,* in the ideal personality, in the universal humanity, that the poet apostrophised. We shall see presently how he takes the Platonic side of the Baconian philosophy, and ascends to an intuition little short of the theological one, and only avoiding it by the shade of a degree. Man becomes all but the theistic *logos* in the ascending scale of the poet's daring apprehension, and, but for his evident predetermination to keep on this side of the religious aspects of his subject . . . would no doubt have been expressly named as such. By this wise reticence the poet has gained much, and given a classical air to what otherwise would have borne a controversial one. . . . And thus we have in this series of sonnets one entire poem, containing a protest against an expiring superstition, philosophically conducted, but conveyed in the language of poetry,—a diction divested of technical terms; and this was the method of the Italian poets in treating religious or political subjects, which they disguised in mystical or erotic verses. Love is made the cover of much heterodox sentiment, the object of which is sometimes painted as a mistress, in others as a friend. And thus the danger which might have followed on plain speaking was avoided. (pp. 57-8)

His foot once on the steps of the "intellectual ladder," Shakespeare mounts with equal rapidity and daring. He is occupied with his work day and night: the subject is ever present with him. Shakespeare, like another Prometheus, is the Friend of Man, and in turn regards Man as his friend. Ever, even in darkness, his "soul's imaginary sight presents the shadow" of that collective Object "to his sightless view" [Sonnet 27]. He is filled with its beauty, *i.e.* the beauty of Man. . . . Addressing it as an imaginary object, he says, in his 28th sonnet,

> I tell the day, to please him, thou art bright,
>   And dost him grace, when clouds do blot the
>   heaven.
> So flatter I the swart-complexioned night:
>   When sparkling stars twire not, thou gild'st the
>   even.

And in the next he thus disposes of his personal relation therewith—how beautifully, how tenderly, how grandly!

> When in disgrace with fortune and men's eyes,
>   I all alone beweep my outcast state,
> And trouble deaf heaven with my bootless cries,
>   And look upon myself, and curse my fate,
> Wishing me like to one more rich in hope,
>   Featured like him, like him with friends pos-
>   sessed,
> Desiring this man's art, and that man's scope,
>   With what I most enjoy contented least;
> Yet in these thoughts myself almost despising,
>   Haply I think on thee—and then my state
> Like to the lark at break of day arising
>   From sullen earth) sings hymns at heaven's gate;
> For thy sweet love remembered, such wealth
>   brings,
> That then I scorn to change my state with kings.

In this fine sonnet I read the biography thoroughly of the actor and the poet. The whole life of Shakespeare is essentialised in it. In all his sorrows and disappointments, the thought of the ideal man, as he tells us in the next three sonnets, is his great comfort; his hopes, his aspirations, his shortcomings, have all their bourn and limit therein. It is his "*sun of the world;*" nevertheless, as is the case with all ideals, he has been betrayed by it. The morning opened fair enough, and he was tempted to "travel forth without his cloak" [Son-

net 34], but he finds a sufficient excuse in the fact, that he was accessory himself to the illusion. After all, the individual is not the ideal; and he thus makes allowance for the necessary disparity:

> Let me confess that we *two must be twain,*
>   Although our undivided loves are one;
> So shall those blots that do with me remain
>   Without thy help by me be borne alone. . . .
>   [Sonnet 36]
>   (pp. 58-9)

Yes, it is fit that the ideal should be the poet's inspirer. Yet how shall it be distinguished from himself?

> What can mine own praise to mine own self bring?
>   And what is't but mine own when I praise thee?

Yet distinction *is* made, and the implied *separation* is assumed as similar to what "absence" is to a lover. Pursuing the thought, the verse becomes burdened with amorous complaints, allied with many conceits that sometimes claim a license in these days of literal accuracy but grudgingly allowed.

And here the poet, weary of illustrating the theme of Masculine Beauty, turns gradually to the consideration of the second element in the distribution of the subject; namely, Love. Mention is suddenly made of a Woman beloved by the Man, of whom the sonneteer lovingly feigns himself to be jealous. His jealousy is twofold; both on account of her love for the ideal object, and of his for her. And this must needs be so; for as a portion of the universal humanity, the Woman is as ideal as the Man, and as dear to his apostrophiser. The poet is even fond of making a sort of riddle of the necessary correlations, playing with them thus:

> That thou hast her, it is not all my grief,
>   And yet it may be said, I loved her dearly;
> That she hath thee, is of my wailing chief,
>   A loss in love that touches me more nearly.
> Loving offenders, thus I will excuse ye:
>   Thou dost love her, because thou know'st I love
>   her,
> And for my sake even so she doth abuse me,
>   Suffering my friend for my sake to approve her;
> If I lose thee, my loss is my love's gain,
>   And losing her, my friend hath found that loss;
> Both find each other, and I lose both twain,
>   And both for my sake *lay on me this cross;*
> But here's the joy: *my friend and I are one.*
>   Sweet flattery!—then she loves but me alone.
>   [Sonnet 42]

This sonnet might go far to prove the truth of the German's subjective theory. For does not the poet himself declare, that the Ideal Man, the Friend, whom he has addressed, has all along been identified with himself—has simply been his Objective Self? And verily, in some sort, this "Self Love and Social *are* the same." It is the love of the One for the Many; but the Many, how multitudinous soever, are yet properly but the reflex of the One, and the sum of both is the Universe. That Shakespeare saw this as clearly as any German sage of later times is to me manifest; but he had not theorised it. He deals with it in the Italian manner, as a tissue of conceits, with which the poetic mind delights to sport, and which demonstrates its indefinite activity of thought, as instanced in a variety of associations almost infinite, even condescending to a mere play of words, sometimes even to the perpetration of the poorest puns.

I feel that I have now given the reader the key-note to the interpretation of these sonnets for himself; therefore shall hasten over the remainder, only touching on such points as imperatively demand attention.

We find the necessity that the poet felt, of considering the ideal humanity as bisexual, removes the object to a farther distance from the merely subjective feeling that he would indulge, and strengthens the sense of "absence" under which he had formerly imaged their distinction or separation. In the 50th sonnet, he declares his reluctance to realise this new condition. But it is needful, under the second branch of his subject, Love, that the relations of male and female should be acknowledged, and not alone those between man and man. Hence the state which he designates "absence" must be; nor is it barren of benefit to the complaining poet. . . . (pp. 59-60)

[Sonnet 50] is unparalleled for the beauty and appropriateness of imagery, as well as for subtlety of thought. In the next sonnet [Shakespeare] as finely paints his human ideal in the persons of the two sexes—expressly.

> What is your substance, whereof are *you* made,
>   That millions of strange shadows on *you* tend?
> Since every one hath, every one, one shade,
>   And *you,* but one, can every shadow lend.
> Describe Adonis, and the counterfeit
>   Is poorly imitated after *you;*
> On Helen's cheek all art of beauty set,
>   And *you* in Grecian tires are painted new.
> Speak of the spring and foison of the year;
>   The one doth shadow of *your* beauty show,
> The other as *your* bounty doth appear;
>   And *you* in every blessed shape we know.
> In all external grace *you* have some part,
> But *you* like none, none *you,* for constant
>   heart. . . .
>
>   [Sonnet 51]

What is said in [this] sonnet cannot be meant of any individual;—it is only true of the ideal humanity, which, being but one, is nevertheless manifested in all men and women and nature, as its shadows and appearances. It is, too, the source of virtue and truth in all its human representatives. And the poet proceeds to illustrate these essential attributes of its moral character, which are at once the basis and the evidence of its inevitable Immortality. (p. 61)

He now recognises this universal humanity as his sovran, and makes his submission to its supremacy, while lamenting his distance from it. He would seek compensation, moreover, by finding its

>   image in some antique book,
> Since mind at first in character was done.
>
>   [Sonnet 59]

In a word, he would compare the heroes of ancient and modern times, that he may form a better conception of its nature (sonnets 57-59). In a subsequent sonnet (61), the sovran becomes a sacred Power that can send forth its "spirit," "so far from home, into *his* deeds to pry;" adding,

> For thee watch I, while thou dost wake elsewhere,
> From me far off, *with others all too near.*
>
>   [Sonnet 61]

During this metaphysical "absence," the *Adonis* and the *Helen,* in which the ideal had developed, are supposed to

disport in some mystic but amorous seclusion, leaving the poet meanwhile to melancholy self-contemplation. The sonnet in which this is expressed again almost justifies the German's theory. It perhaps is entitled to be esteemed the pivot-sonnet of the series.

> Sin of self-love possesseth all mine eye,
>   And all my soul, and all my every part;
> And for this sin there is no remedy,
>   It is so grounded inward in my heart.
> Methinks no face so gracious is as mine,
>   No shape so true, no truth of such account,
> And for myself my own worth do define,
>   As I all other in all worths surmount.
> But when my glass shows me myself indeed,
>   Bated and chopped with tanned antiquity,
> Mine own self-love quite contrary I read,—
>   Self so self-loving were iniquity.
> 'Tis thee (*myself*) that for myself I praise,
> Painting my age with beauty of thy days.
>
>   [Sonnet 62]

Shakespeare's course, we have said, is upward. The Ideal has already approached the Divine. Its immortality has been declared; but there is also a mortality confessed: the former of the soul, the latter of the body. On the latter, as equally the condition of every man, the poet sorrowfully mediates, and at some length. But the poet's verses will preserve in everlasting memory himself, or his friend, or both, according to the sense in which we may read them. For death itself, he gives many reasons why we should desire it. And here he hints that he has a rival in another poet, who is equally in favour with his Friend. What between a second acquaintance and a mistress, the sonneteer has to combat both with envy and jealousy. But he is fain to own that his murmurs at these natural dispensations are eminently irrational. He justifies his wronger even, for reasons as subtle as they are numerous, even though he imputes to him many faults, as if he rejoiced that the Removed Object of his addresses, however exalted, should have a fellow-feeling of his own infirmity, derived from personal experience. (pp. 61-2)

But soon he calls on his Muse indignantly to withdraw all show of blame, and to occupy herself exclusively in praise of the beloved, whose truth we are now told is as indisputable as his beauty. Indeed, the poet Platonises and identifies truth and beauty in the mysterious Person for whom he cherishes so deep a love. Beauty thus at one with Truth is immortal and ever young:

> To me, fair friend, you never can be old,
>   For as you were, when first your eye I eyed,
> Such seems your beauty still.
>
>   [Sonnet 104]

Yet he fears, unreasonably, that unsuspected decay may somehow inhere; notwithstanding he exclaims:

> Let not my love be called idolatry,
>   Nor my beloved as an idol show,
> Since all alike my songs and praises be,
>   To one, of one, still such, and ever so.
>
>   [Sonnet 105]

And thus he pursues the contradictions and antinomies which perplex philosophy and try the faith of love, growing up in the soil—the heart—that they infest. It is the old contest between the carnal and moral, erotically expressed. Familiar terms are preferred; thus, the "fair friend who never can be old;" that immortal youth whose absence he deplores the poet now addresses as "sweet boy," and boasts of his "eternal love;" and then, excusing his own wanderings, of which before he had said nothing, by his repentings and returnings, exclaims enthusiastically,

> For nothing this wide universe I call,
> Save thou, my rose; in it thou art my all.
>
> [Sonnet 109]

In the next sonnet he arrives at the climax; he speaks it out plainly. This "fair friend," this "sweet boy," this "rose" selected from the "wide universe," is—"a God in love". . . . (pp. 62-3)

The method adopted by the poet in the composition of these serial sonnets is abundantly manifest. They are built up after the fashion, and on the platform, as it were, of a Platonic dialogue. The argument begins with the earthly and animal; but passes, through the intellectual and rational, to the heavenly and divine. (pp. 63-4)

[Shakespeare] had carried his subject as far as Plato could help him,—and he was now proceeding to carry it farther, by means of an illumination which Plato wanted. He had opened the Book, and borrowed from it what remains of his argument.

This Celestial Friend he now finds to be mystically represented in all objects, whether of earth or heaven. The meanest are as privileged as the highest to be his symbols. At this the poet wonders, and demands,

> Or whether doth my mind, being crowned with
>   you,
>   Drink up the monarch's plague, this flattery,
> Or whether shall I say mine eye saith true,
>   And that your love taught it this alchymy,
> To make of monsters and things indigest
>   Such *cherubims* as your sweet self resemble,
> Creating every bad a perfect best,
>   As fast as objects to his beams assemble?
>
> [Sonnet 114]

Yes, yes; not only the kingdoms of nature animate and inanimate, . . . but the *cherubims* themselves resemble the marvellous object of his "idolatry." It is evident that words and phrases from the Sacred Oracles may now be expected; for Shakespeare has unclasped the Volume, and is poring on its pages. . . . Note, too, how he elevates his conception of Love.

> Love is not love
> Which alters when it alteration finds;
>   Or bends with the remover to remove:
> Oh, no! it is an ever-fixed mark,
>   That looks on tempests, and is never shaken.
>
> [Sonnet 116]

It is "not Time's fool;" it changes not "to the *edge of doom.*" We can see that the poet has adopted the biblical sentiment of a "perfect love that casts out fear." Nay, further, he had even discovered the

> Benefit of ill!—now I find true
> That *better is by evil still made better;*
> And *ruined love, when it is built anew,*
>   *Grows fairer than at first, more strong, far great-*
>   *er.*
>
> [Sonnet 119]

Surely it is not necessary to point out the theological meaning of these lines; if it be, let the reader turn for himself to, and read thoughtfully, the seven next sonnets (120-126); after which commences a new theme.

And what a theme! It is the Woman who had gained from the humble friend the affections of the Ideal Man. And here matters have become reversed;—the Woman is portrayed in far other colours. Was the man fair? She is black! Love certainly delighteth in contrasts, and here is an extraordinary one. Desdemona the Moor, and not Othello! Methinks, there is here some riddle to read.

There is—but it is one easily read. The lady is black in two senses, morally and physically, in her deeds as well as in her features. She, like the poet's Ideal Friend, has been "foresworn;" and the poet has in her case likewise to remonstrate, and then to absolve. The like resolution of differences and contradictions is necessary. But, as we have said, the poet has *the* Book open before him. He is in fact reading the Canticles; and there he finds the Bride who is "black but comely"—at once the bride of his Celestial Friend and his own. These confused relations afford the poet an abundant source for quibbles, many of them remarkably pretty, all lovingly playful. . . . [He] begins to pun on his Christian name, and to charge all the perjuries at which Jove laughs on his dark beauty, speaking all ill of her, and then recanting; and all this because he does not "love her with his eyes," but with his "heart, that loves what they despise" [Sonnet 141]. As it was with Adam in relation to Eve, so with Shakespeare in relation to his "darke ladye."

> Love is my sin, and thy dear virtue hate,
> Hate of my sin, grounded on sinful loving.
>
> [Sonnet 142]

In all this, perhaps, Shakespeare carries his fancies rather too far. Yet let us not judge him harshly. The terrestrial embodiment of this mysterious woman was self-contradictory, and her appearance at least very equivocal. Hence he wrote:

> Two loves I have of comfort and despair,
>   Which like two spirits do suggest me still;
> The better angel is a man right fair,
>   The worser spirit, a woman, coloured ill.
> To win me soon to hell my female evil
>   Tempteth my better angel from my side,
> And would corrupt my saint to be a devil,
>   Wooing his purity with her foul pride.
>
> [Sonnet 144]

Shakespeare found himself between two loves,—the Celibate Church on the one hand, that deified herself; and the Reformed Church on the other, that eschewed Mariolatry, and restored worship to its proper object. Such was his position at the beginning of his argument, which having now exhausted, the circle completes itself, and he finds himself again on the earth, which for a while he had transcended. At once he lowers his tone, and brings the series to an end by some fanciful sonnets, which serve no other purpose than to veil his meaning from the incompetent reader.

This interpretation, which is the pure result of induction, effectually relieves Shakespeare from [the] charge of having praised the personal beauty and accomplishments of a youthful friend in a manner "far too ardent to be pleasing." The unclean suggestion belongs alone to the pseudo critic, and leaves the "withers" of the poet "unwrung." The characteristics attributed to this Ideal Friend befit nothing but the Ideal; they never were proper to any actual mortal man. It was common, as I have already said, for poets in his and the previous age so to veil their meaning; signifying religion or government by the term 'love,' and treating them by analogues borrowed from the tender passion. The danger sought to be avoided was not entirely at an end even in Queen Elizabeth's day. The Monarch, as understood by her and her successors down to James II., still clung to the past, though looking forward to the future, and represented *transition* rather than progress. The literary mind, however, was in advance, and instinctively held rather by the coming age, of which it was alike prophetic and productive. It was expedient, therefore, for Shakespeare, while writing a series of sonnets expressive of the spirit of that transition, to adopt the usual safeguards. Love, too, and its rights were properly the argument of the Reformation itself, as projected by Luther. It was eminently the emancipation of the natural appetites, within rational limits, from spiritual prohibition,—substituting a possible moderation for an impossible abstinence. (pp. 64-6)

John A. Heraud, *"A New View of Shakespeare's Sonnets: An Inductive Critique," in* Temple Bar, *Vol. V, April, 1862, pp. 53-66.*

SONNETS.

Or layd great bafes for eternity,
Which proues more fhort then waft or ruining?
Haue I not feene dwellers on forme and fauor
Lofe all,and more by paying too much rent
For compound fweet;Forgoing fimple fauor,
Pittifull thriuors in their gazing fpent,
Noe,let me be obfequious in thy heart,
And take thou my oblacion,poore but free,
Which is not mixt with feconds,knows no art,
But mutuall render onely me for thee.
    Hence,thou fubbornd *Informer*, a trew foule
    When moft impeacht,ftands leaft in thy controule.

126

O Thou my louely Boy who in thy power,
    Doeft hould times fickle glaffe,his fickle,hower:
Who haft by wayning growne,and therein fhou'ft,
Thy louers withering,as thy fweet felfe grow'ft.
If Nature(foueraine mifteres ouer wrack)
As thou goeft onwards ftill will plucke thee backe,
She keepes thee to this purpofe,that her skill.
May time difgrace,and wretched mynuit kill.
Yet feare her O thou minnion of her pleafure,
Si. may detaine,but not ftill keepe her trefure!
Her *Audite*(though delayd)anfwer'd muft be,
And her *Quietus* is to render thee.
    (   )
    (   )

127

IN the ould age blacke was not counted faire,
    Or if it weare it bore not beauties name:
But now is blacke beauties fucceffiue heire,
And Beautie flanderd with a baftard fhame,
For fince each hand hath put on Natures power,
Fairing the foule with Arts faufe borrow'd face,
Sweet beauty hath no name no holy boure,
But is prophan'd,if not liues in difgrace.
        H 3   Therefore

Page H3 of the 1609 edition of Shakespeare's Sonnets, *showing break indication between Sonnets 126 and 127.*

[GERALD MASSEY]   (essay date 1864)

[The following excerpt is from an anonymously published essay attributed to Gerald Massey by Hyder Edward Rollins, editor of the New Variorum edition of the sonnets. Massey comments on the autobiographical or personal view of Sonnets 1-126. Although he regards some of them as personal, he considers most of those in which Shakespeare is the spokesman or speaker to be "dramatic," written by Shakespeare in obligation to Henry Wriothesley, Earl of Southampton and presenting various important events in the earl's life. According to Massey, through certain assumed characters we can make sense of the obvious contradictions in the natures of the speakers, the allusions to events unrelated to Shakespeare, and the amatory language in many of the poems. Massey identifies Christopher Marlowe as the Rival Poet, basing his argument on various biographical facts.]

The sonnets of Shakespeare afford us, if we can but understand them aright, the most certain means whereby we can get at the man. Nothing else except the two prose dedications [to *Venus and Adonis* and *The Rape of Lucrece*] speaks to us so assuredly with his own voice, or tells us so unmistakeably what were his own feelings and thoughts under various interesting circumstances of his own life. And this voice of the man Shakspeare has all the changing tones of his temperament, ranging from the grace of buoyant youth to the sober sadness of that early autumn of his age. Some of these sonnets are majestic as those of Milton, but clothed in a richer vesture of imagination.

Our difficulty is to get the right interpretation of the sonnets, and know when Shakspeare is really speaking in his own person, and where he gives utterance to the thoughts and feelings of another. We often hear the voice of Shakspeare; we *know* the voice, and yet we do not get at the man. It is as though he were speaking in the next room; there is a partition-wall between us. We follow the voice, according to some theory of interpreting the sonnets, but when we get into the next room Shakspeare is not there. Still, the voice, like that of the ghost of Hamlet's father, keeps breaking in, compelling us to follow it. The chief cause of this intangibility, and the main reason why so many of these sonnets, seemingly personal, do not strike straight home to us with the full force that is coiled up in their lines, must be sought for in the conditions under which they were written. Shakspeare is not always communicating directly with us. He was not the man to miss his mark, whatever that may have been, only we are not exactly the objects of his aim. We must stand in the right position to judge of what is going on; we must get the relations of the writer and the reader rightly adjusted before we shall hear the voice of Shakspeare with any certainty, or find out one-half the hidden meanings lurking in these sonnets. What, then, are the conditions under which the sonnets were written? (pp. 437-38)

[Thorpe's] inscription is the sole ground on which the sonnets and the loving friendship of Shakspeare have been awarded to William Herbert [see excerpt above, 1609]. And yet he was not 'Mr. W. H.' when the book was printed, in 1609. He had been Earl of Pembroke for eight years, and had previously been Lord Herbert. So that if Thorpe was aware of the real facts of the case, and became one of the connivers at an intended mystery, it was just as easy to reverse the initials of Henry Wriothesley as to print those of William Herbert, and there is no gain to the Herbert hypothesis. Either Thorpe did *not* know all, and so he may have leaped to a wrong conclusion, or he *did* know and may have hidden the Earl of Southampton as cleverly as though it had been the Earl of Pembroke. Shakspeare had then left London. In the year of publication the Earl of Pembroke was governor of Portsmouth. Where Southampton was we do not clearly trace. He may have been in Holland. The thing was *darkly* done. Possibly William Herbert may have collected the Sonnets, and Thorpe may have inferred that he was their 'only begetter.' Be this as it may, we have Shakspeare's sonnets and Thorpe's inscription, to read them as we are able, and interpret them as we best can. But it is capable of positive, absolute, and overwhelming proof that William Herbert could not in any sense have been the sole begetter of those sonnets. No word was ever publicly addressed to him by Shakspeare. We have no knowledge of any intimate acquaintanceship recorded during Shakspeare's lifetime, and *William Herbert did not come to London till the summer of* 1599. . . . And all we hear of him at that time is that, when he was not ill, he devoted himself to the practice of arms. Whereas Shakspeare's 'sugred sonnets among his private friends' were known to Meres, and spoken of by him in 1598 [see excerpt above, 1598]—spoken of, too, as being of sufficient extent and importance to warrant public recognition by a writer remarkable at times for his compressed brevity. This notice shows us Shakspeare's friends *already* acquired, his sonnets written and known to a circle of admirers. That they were well known, which takes time when poetry is in MS., we should gather from his 'witness,' and his classing them with the published poems.

One upholder of the Herbert hypothesis maintains that the Sonnets referred to by Meres must have been lost! Still, it is *the* Sonnets of Shakspeare, *never before imprinted,* that we hear of again in Thorpe's collection, and the advertisement implies an understanding on the subject. Readers had heard of them in MS., but the only public mention of them that we hear of is this by Meres. But there is further evidence that these *are* the Sonnets known to Meres. Mr. C. Knight has shown that a certain sonnet (the 94th), and consequently the group to which it belongs—by no means one of the earliest written—must have been composed before the year 1596, because this last line of it—

> Lilies that fester smell far worse than weeds,

is quoted in 'Edward the Third,' a play which has been attributed to Shakspeare. This play was entered on the register of the Stationers' Company, December 1st, 1595, after it had been performed 'sundry times' at different theatres. So that we may fairly assume it to have been composed in 1594, when *William Herbert was fourteen years of age, and five years before he came to London!* He was then a student at New College, Oxford. But we have further proof. In the 27th Sonnet there is a beautiful image which has been transferred to the play of 'Romeo and Juliet,' and more richly wrought out in the well-known lines—

> Her beauty hangs upon the cheek of night
> Like a rich jewel in an Ethiop's ear.
> [*Romeo and Juliet,* I.v. 45-6]

In the 127th Sonnet we read this singular defence of a lady's dark complexion and dark eyes:—

> In the old age black was not counted fair,
> Or, if it were, it bore not beauty's name;
> But now is black beauty's successive heir,
> And beauty slandered with a bastard shame;
> For *since each hand hath put on nature's power,*
> *Fairing the foul with art's false borrowed face,*

> Sweet beauty hath no name, no holy bower,
> But is profaned, if not lives in disgrace:
> *Therefore my Mistress' eyes are raven black,*
> Her eyes so suited; and they *mourners* seem
> At such.

And this sentiment of the eyes mourning, and a pale face being your only purity, in a time when so many ladies paint, is reproduced in 'Love's Labour Lost,' which was produced not later than in 1592. . . .

> O, if *in black* my lady's brows be decked,
> It *mourns that painting, and usurping hair,*
> Should ravish doters with a false aspect;
> And therefore is she born to make black fair.
> [*Love's Labour's Lost,* IV. iii. 254-57]

Another repetition so curiously complete we shall scarcely find in all Shakspeare! How, then, could the Earl of Pembroke be the 'sole begetter' or the *object* of Shakspeare's Sonnets? (pp. 439-42)

But it is time we had done with this dedication of the Sonnets. Readers have already been kept too long on the outside of the subject. If Shakspeare had written it, that would have given to it a very different value, and any amount of time and trouble would have been justly spent in trying to fathom its purport. But he did not write it, and there is nothing left for us to do except to study what he did write, and let the facts of the inner life shape the external theory. It is of the highest importance to solve the puzzling question, Who was the 'begetter' of the Sonnets? And, without venturing to speak with certainty upon so difficult a point, we propose to submit to our readers some of the grounds upon which this character may very plausibly be ascribed to Southampton. Whatever may be thought of this interpretation, assuredly no other has yet been suggested which will bear a moment's examination. (pp. 442-43)

Amongst the few precious personal relics of our poet are the short prose epistles in which he inscribes his two poems to the Earl of Southampton. They are remarkable revelations of his feeling towards the Earl. The first—the 'Venus and Adonis'—is shaded with a delicate reserve, and addressed to the *patron;* the 'Lucrece,' printed one year afterwards, glows out full-hearted in a dedication of personal love for the *friend.* The difference is so great and the growth of the friendship so rapid, as to indicate that the 'Venus and Adonis' was sent to the Earl a long time before it was printed. Any way we have it recorded, in 1594, by Shakspeare himself, that the relationship of poet and patron was so close, the friendship had so far ripened, that Shakspeare could dedicate *'love without end,'* and he uses these never-to-be forgotten words:—

> *What I have done is yours.*
> *What I have to do is yours; being part in all I have*
> devoted yours.

Which we read as implying an understanding between them of work then in hand. Southampton, he says emphatically, is a part in all that he has *devoted* his. What work in hand should this be, *devoted to* Southampton, save the Sonnets which he was then composing? It seems probable that the first group of Sonnets was sent to the Earl before the 'Venus and Adonis' was dedicated to him, and that the Sonnets led to the looking up of the poem, which had been written some time before, and the giving of it to the press now a patron had been secured. In Sonnet 16 the poet speaks of his *'pupil'* pen; and in Sonnet 26 he sends a *'written embassage'* to the Earl, and, to our thinking, distinctly *promises something in print.* Take this meanwhile, he says,—

> Till whatsoever star that guides my moving,
> Points on me graciously with fair aspect,
> And *puts apparel* on my tattered loving,
> To *show me worthy* of thy sweet respect;
> *Then* may I *dare to boast* how *I do love thee,*
> Till then, not show my head where thou may'st prove
>   me.

That is a positive allusion to the poet's public appearance *for the first time*: the putting on of apparel in print—the daring to boast in public—the showing of his head where he may be proved—all illustrate this view. This may be as much a private dedication of the 'Venus and Adonis' as the 'epistle' afterwards was a public one. It is curious to notice that the shade of personal feeling in the earliest Sonnets is exactly like to that of the *first* dedication: it is reticent and noticeably modest. There is no large profession of love—no great gratitude. The writer stands at gaze on the picture he paints. He chiefly praises his patron's youth and beauty, and urges him to marry. His freshness of colouring has all the tenderness of spring-tints. And there is as *rathe* a tenderness in the writer's feeling as in the picture's youthfulness. Moreover, we have the young man's age precisely reckoned up in Sonnet 16—

> *Now stand you on the top of happy hours:*

—which shows us that the youth has sprung lightly up the ladder of his life, and now stands on the last golden round of boyhood. He is, we should say, eighteen or nineteen. The Earl of Southampton was born October 6, 1573, which would give the year 1591-2 for this Sonnet to have been written in, and Shakspeare's first public proclamation of Southampton's patronage [the Dedication of 'Venus and Adonis']—in which he vows 'to take advantage of all idle hours' till he has 'honoured him with some graver labour'—was in the next year. There is an expression in the Dedication remarkably like to that of the opening Sonnet. In the one, Shakspeare hopes the young Earl may answer to the *world's 'hopeful expectation;'* in the other he calls him the '*world's fresh ornament,*' and 'only herald to the gaudy spring.' Both are stamped with the same date; both point out the Earl as the 'expectancy and rose of the fair state.'

In this, the earliest group of Sonnets, the poet uses many arguments which all circle round the one idea that this comely noble of Nature should not be so niggardly and unthrifty as not to leave the world some copies of his beauty when he dies. But underneath the surface of these Sonnets, with their quaint play of conceit and sparkle of wit, there seems to us a quiet depth of wisdom. Either Shakspeare was engaged to write them by those who sought to see the young Earl married, or else he felt a most fond and fatherly anxiety that the youth should not linger in the garden of Armida; for the distant admiration, the innocent flattery, the far-fetched comparisons, all play into the hands of a grave purpose. The writer knows there is nothing like true marriage, a worthy wife, the tie of children, and a happy home, to bring the young wild life into keeping of the highest law.

There are two points we would here notice more particularly. One is the distance at which Shakspeare pays his respects. There is no talk of favours, and but little of friendship; he speaks of 'merit' on the one side, and 'duty' on the other. This shows that these Sonnets were written *very early* in the intercourse. It also proves that the person who printed the Sonnets, however ignorant of details, had sufficient guidance to put the first group in its right place. Next—and here we feel an endearing touch of Shakspeare's nature—the youth is so evidently *fatherless,* that it seems strange the fact should have been hitherto overlooked. In Sonnet 10 he is charged with not inclining his ear to the advice given to him that he should marry. Thus—

> Seeking that *beauteous roof to ruinate,*
> Which to *repair should be thy chief desire.* . . .

We find the same use made of the verb 'to ruinate' in *Henry VI.,* Part iii., Act 5—

> I will not *ruinate* my father's house.

Of course the roof would not need repairing if it were not going to decay. Accordingly we find that Southampton's father—head of the house—died in 1581, ere the young Earl was quite eight years old, and within four years of that time his elder brother died. Again in Sonnet 13 the poet urges—

> Who *lets so fair a house fall to decay,*
> Which *husbandry in honour might uphold.*

And—although aware that the lines may not be confined to the literal reading—we cannot avoid thinking that the underlying fact was in the poet's mind when, in the same Sonnet, he wrote—

> Dear my love, you know
> You *had* a father; let your son say so.

Also, in Sonnet 3, he tells the Earl—

> Thou art thy Mother's glass.

There is no mention of his *having* a father living. This, we believe, made the poet express himself in a more paternal manner. (pp. 443-46)

[In] our opinion, nothing but the blindest belief in the Herbert hypothesis, which, of necessity, shifts the date at which the greater portion of [Shakspeare's] Sonnets were written, could possibly have obscured the fact, so patent to us, that Marlowe *was* the [rival] poet. There is circumstantial evidence of this in every line and touch of Shakspeare's description. Marlowe was a dramatic celebrity before Shakspeare, and we have no doubt there was a time when Shakspeare looked up to him and was somewhat led captive by his lofty, flamboyant style. He would fully appreciate the sensuous bodily beauty, so to speak, of many of Marlowe's lines. He would give him full credit for having struck out a new spring of the English Helicon, with the impatient pawing hoof of his fiery Pegasus, in his use of blank verse. He prized his genius, if he could not respect the man. . . . But his finer ear and truer taste would soon detect a good deal of bombast in the 'mighty line,' and he would see that the great glow of Marlowe's imagination had in it a swarthy smoke, and his poetry never attained the true *regulus* of colour, or came from the furnace pure gold. All this and more we discover in Shakspeare's description of the rival poet:—

> Was it *the proud full sail of his great verse,*
> Bound for the prize of all-too-precious you,
> That did my ripe thoughts in my brain inhearse?
> Was it his spirit, *by spirits taught to write*
> *Above a mortal pitch,* that struck me dead?
> No: neither he, nor *his compeers by night*
> *Giving him aid,* my verse astonished,—
> He, nor *that affable familiar ghost*

Which nightly gulls him with intelligence,
As victors of my silence cannot boast;
I was not sick of any fear from thence.
But when *your countenance filed up his line,*
Then lacked I matter; *that* enfeebled mine.

[Sonnet 86]

No other English poet could have sat for that portrait so well as Marlowe:—

He of tall building and of goodly pride.

[Sonnet 80]

The proud full sail of his great verse gives the very picture, the *viva effigies* of Marlowe's poetry—the characteristic that is foremost in the minds of all who are acquainted with his King Cambyses' vein. Who does not recognise 'Faustus,' his necromancy, and his boasts of what he will have the spirits do for him? Who does not see that Shakspeare, thinking dramatically, has identified Marlowe with 'Faustus' and thrown him on the stage, where, in vision—if it be not an actual fact that the play was running at the Curtain Theatre while Shakspeare was composing that Sonnet—he sees his familiar Mephistophiles 'gulling him *nightly*' with such intelligence as that 'in Hell are all manner of delights;' and the drama of Dr. Faustus is played once again in Shakspeare's Sonnet. In other hints and signs we recognise Marlowe, and no other, as the man whom Shakspeare meant where he speaks of the 'strained touches of his rhetoric,' and his 'gross painting' when the rival has, no doubt, laid the flattery on very coarsely. In all probability the Earl [Southampton] had looked over Marlowe's 'Faustus' in MS., making some suggestions, of which the poet would be proud and make ample boast. This it was, Shakspeare confesses, that probed his infirmity—made him feel jealous, and keep silence. That there is a touch of jealousy and a good deal of rivalry in these Sonnets relating to the 'other poet,' is apparent and generally admitted. And in this aspect there is no poet who could make such an appeal so justly to Shakspeare's feelings as Marlowe. Marlowe *was* the rival poet at the opposition theatre in Shoreditch. He was then in the full flush and high tide of his brief and brilliant success. 'Tamberlaine the Great,' 'Faustus,' the 'Jew of Malta,' 'Edward II.,' had come crowding on the stage one after the other, with Alleyne playing his best in the principal characters. Heywood, writing forty years afterwards, celebrates Marlowe as the best of poets, and Alleyne as the best of players. But there was a nobler element in Shakspeare's jealousy of Marlowe. It stands revealed in these Sonnets that he felt more than Southampton's 'filing up his line' or his being drawn to the other theatre. Shakspeare shuddered at what he saw and heard of Marlowe behind the scenes. He felt a most fatherly fear for his youthful friend, and he cries,—

Ah! wherefore with infection should he live,
And with his presence grace *impiety?*

[Sonnet 67]

Whose character does that hit as it does Marlowe's, according to the tenor of all contemporary testimony?

Other poets and writers besides Marlowe and Shakspeare were patronised by the Earl of Southampton. Nash dedicated his 'Life of Jack Wilton' to the Earl (1594), and he says, 'A dear lover and cherisher you are as well of lovers and poetrie as of poets themselves.' Florio, in dedicating his 'World of Words' (1598) to the same nobleman, says, 'In truth I acknowledge an entire debt, not only of my best knowledge, but of all; yea, of more than I know or can, to your bounteous

Lordship, in whose pay and patronage I have lived some years, to whom I owe and vowe the years I have to live. But, as to me and many more, the glorious and gracious sunshine of your honour hath infused light and life.' Chapman, in a dedicatory Sonnet, calls the Earl 'the choice of all our country's noble spirits.' Braithwayt inscribes his 'Scholar's Medley' (1614), to him, as 'Learning's best favourite.' And Minsheu also attests the Earl's munificence to literary men. But of all who dedicated to him, or were familiar with him, Marlowe is the man described by Shakspeare. And, as he died in June, 1593, at least two groups of the Sonnets must have been written before that date, neither of which could possibly have been 'begotten' by the Earl of Pembroke.

It has been asked by supporters of the Herbert hypothesis how it is, if Southampton was the begetter of the Sonnets, that Shakspeare has not celebrated the Earl's exploits—not offered him any comforting words in his misfortunes, or congratulations on his release from prison. The answer is, Shakspeare has done all this, in his own way, in these very Sonnets. The heroic part of the Earl's nature was, no doubt, carefully treasured up in Shakspeare's dramatic works. But his character and career, and his love for the 'faire Mistress Vernon,' through all its touching history, are bound up with the Sonnets. Speaking of these he says,—

Oh let my Books be then the eloquence
And *dumb* presagers of my speaking breast.

[Sonnet 23]

And so they are. How could any one suppose that our greathearted poet would ever forget all about such a friend who had held out the hand of help to him when he was struggling in deep waters, and found for him a firmer bit of foot-hold than he had ever before attained; or imagine that he could lose sight of his promise made in public when he proclaimed his love to be 'without end'? We might depend upon it, even if we failed to prove it, that Shakspeare's soul was not of that shallow, sonnetteering kind, and that his promises were all fulfilled.

Up to the present time it has been generally, though not universally, maintained that the first 120 Sonnets were all addressed to a male friend of Shakspeare, and that our poet outdid all his contemporaries in flattering his patron after the sonnetteering fashion—whilst men like Hallam could scarcely swallow the difficulty of believing that Shakspeare should so prostrate himself at the feet of an Earl to fear his frown and call himself the 'slave'—the 'sad slave'—of a boy, and have wished they had never been written [see excerpt above, 1837-39]. But, upon a very close examination of the Sonnets, *we find the assumption to be perfectly unwarranted.* In the first twenty Sonnets, for example, where Shakspeare speaks to his friend directly, we *are not left in any doubt as to the sex:* there are sixteen distinct allusions to his being a man. Elsewhere, when the poet speaks in person, we frequently find the '*him*' and '*his,*' which (when not used in a proverbial saying) tell the sex. But passing on from those Sonnets to which the 26th is natural L'Envoy, we come upon a series, numbering at least sixteen, and *through the whole of them there is no allusion to a man.* The feeling expressed is more passionate, and the phrase has become more movingly tender; far closer relationship is sung, and yet the object to whom these Sonnets are written never appears in person. There is neither 'man' nor 'boy,' 'him' nor 'his.' How is this? Surely it is not the wont of a stronger feeling and greater warmth of affection to fuse down all individuality and lose sight of sex. That is not the way of Nature's or of Shakspeare's working. With further looking-on we must believe that these said Sonnets . . . were not addressed to a man, but to a woman. All the negative evidence shows it was not a man, and all the positive evidence indicates a woman. Not that Shakspeare is here wooing a woman in person. We do not suppose that he would write so many Sonnets to a woman, and leave out the sex. May we not read them as written on the subject of Southampton's courtship? When we remember Shakspeare's own words [in his dedication of *Lucrece* to Southampton]—'being a part of all I have *devoted* yours,' and 'you and love are still my argument'—there is nothing very startling in the supposition that Shakspeare should have devoted Sonnets to his friend's love for Elizabeth Vernon. . . . It may be maintained that the story of Southampton's courtship is partly told in these sixteen Sonnets. It is not Shakspeare who speaks, but Southampton to his lady. This will account for the passion and tenderness, and, at the same time, for the absence of all mention of the sex of the person addressed, which would naturally result *from the poet's delicacy of feeling*. Again and again we may see how he was fettered in expression on this account. For illustrative evidence let the reader begin with the 50th Sonnet. There we find the lover on a journey, the end of which lies far from his beloved, and he is so heavy-hearted that the horse he rides is 'tired with his woe,' and plods dully on. In the next Sonnet he says if he were only coming back to her he should 'spur,' even though mounted on the wind. Note also the use he makes of the word 'desire' and the horse neighing. Then comes the thought (Sonnet 48), how careful he was, before leaving home, to lock up each little trifle for safety; but she who is his dearest jewel, his 'best of dearest' and his 'only care,' is left out:—

Thee have I not locked up in any chest.

Sonnet 44 implies that the lover is across sea, as we know the Earl of Southampton was several times; but have no reason to think that Shakspeare ever was—still, his thoughts will fly to her in 'tender embassy of love,' and come back to him assured of her *'fair health'* (Sonnet 45), and, in absence, he has her portrait—

With *my love's picture* then my eye doth feast
And to the *painted* banquet bids my heart.

And he rejoices richly in possession. Various expressions point to a woman as the object of address. In Sonnet 57 he is her 'slave,' and she his 'sovereign;' her *'servant,'* which implies the *mistress;* only the poet was fettered in expression. And in the next Sonnet he says:—

That god forbid that made me first your slave.
[Sonnet 58]

What god? if not Cupid, god of love, as the whole Sonnet illustrates, which would be meaningless if addressed from man to man. More feminine still, if possible, is the illustration in Sonnet 61. He cannot sleep at night for seeing her image, and he asks—

Is it thy spirit that thou send'st from thee
So far from home, into *my deeds to pry;*
To *find out* shames and idle hours in me,
The scope and tenor of *thy jealousy?*

In all these Sonnets it is the *speaker* who is so far away. (pp. 446-51)

To take one of Southampton's journeys, we learn that he left

London February 8th, 1598. . . . It was proposed by his friends that he should marry [Elizabeth] before he left, so bitterly did she take to heart the thought of his going. Circumstances prevented this, and his Lordship departed. . . . He came back in the November of the same year. And it is curious to connect herewith the three sonnets, 97, 98, 99, commencing—

How like a winter hath my absence been!
[Sonnet 97]

and yet he tells us it was spring, summer, and autumn all the while; and he gives us this rich bit of love-poetry, which would seem strangely out of place if sent to a man:—

Nor did I wonder at the lilies white,
Nor praise the deep vermilion of the rose;
They were but sweet, but figures of delight,
Drawn after you, you pattern of all those.
The forward violet thus did I chide;
Sweet thief, whence didst thou steal thy sweet that smells,
If not from my love's breath? The purple pride
Which on thy soft cheek for complexion dwells,
In my love's veins thou hast too grossly dyed.
The lily I condemned for thy hand,
And buds of marjoram had stolen thy hair.
More flowers I noted, yet I none could see
But sweet or colour it had stolen from thee.
[Sonnets 98 and 99]

Would Shakspeare have written thus to a man? Luckily, we can make him answer for himself. It often happens that we are enabled to prove a sonnet not personal by the aid of those which are personal. And in Sonnet 21 he says—

So is it NOT with me as with that Muse
Stirred by a *painted beauty* to his verse,
Who heaven itself for ornament doth use
And every fair with his fair doth rehearse,
Making a complement of proud compare
With sun and moon, with earth and sea's rich gems,
With April's first-born flowers, and all things rare.

After which he would not be likely to compare his friend to that same 'painted beauty' by doing the very thing he had denounced.

Such lines, we submit, were never written to any man as from Shakspeare himself, but they might well arise from the poet taking Southampton's courtship for his theme. Coleridge was not without grounds for thinking Shakspeare's Sonnets were addressed to a woman [see excerpt above, 1833]. Poet-like, he felt that there were such gusts of passionate fragrance in the feeling, and such 'subtle-shining secresies' in the expression of some of them, as a woman only could have called forth. The flowery tenderness, the playing with all beauties of external nature as the beloved's shadow, and looking on the flowers as 'figures of delight' drawn after her pattern; the affectionate endearment of epithet, the fondling of the miniature, the almost epicurean sense of possessing the treasure which he will not look at often for fear of 'blunting the fine point of pleasure' (Sonnet 52), the love-sickness in absence, and the rapture of return, are all essentially amatory; all tell of a pure passion for a pure, beautiful woman. Shakspeare's dramatic instinct was too keen for him to have violated the natural fitness of imagery, as he is made to do, by our reading all these Sonnets as addressed to a man. For example, a woman might be likened to Adonis, because of his youthful, beardless beauty and his modesty (Sonnet 53); but it would hardly do to liken a man who was a soldier and a famous fighter to Helen,

> Painted newly in Grecian tires!
>
> [Sonnet 53]

Or take the imagery in Sonnet 114, where the speaker says his love hath the alchemic power—

> To make of monsters and things indigest
> *Such Cherubins* as *your sweet self* resemble.

Then there is Sonnet 93. . . . It is quick with the fears of a lover trembling into suspicions lest his mistress should not prove true—

> How like Eve's Apple doth thy beauty grow,
> If thy sweet virtue answer not thy show!

In the previous Sonnet he says:—

> Thou mayst be *false* and yet I know it not.
>
> [Sonnet 92]

In Sonnet 88 he alludes to a possible contingency, and there says:—

> Against myself I'll fight,
> And prove thee *virtuous* tho' thou art *forsworn*.

In Sonnet 125 the love is a 'mutual render, only me for thee.' Sonnet 87 looks like a lover's quarrel and a possible parting. The lover says:—

> Farewell! thou art too dear for my possessing.

And this is followed by three other pathetic Sonnets on the same subject:—

> Say that thou didst forsake me for some fault, . . .
> Thou canst not, love, disgrace me half so ill,
> To set a form upon *desired change*,
> As I'll myself disgrace; knowing thy will,
> I will *acquaintance strangle*, and *look strange;*
> *Be absent from thy walks:*
>
> [Sonnet 89]

which hardly applies to Shakspeare at the theatre, but is applicable to Southampton about the Court! He continues:—

> Then hate me when thou wilt; if ever, now;
> Now while the world is bent *my deeds* to cross,
> Join with the *spite* of *fortune, make me bow.*

What this can have to do with Shakspeare personally has never been shown. He was not a man of *deeds.* What it may have to do with the Earl we shall see, if we call to mind how he returned to England in October, 1597, and the Queen frowned on him—she being 'on tiff' with Essex—because, while in command of the 'Garland,' he had dared to pursue and sink a vessel of the enemy without Monson's orders. And here he challenges his love to do what the Queen or Fortune, with her injustice, cannot do—make his proud spirit bow. This Sonnet is quick with the feeling of a wronged heroic soul, written in the very life-blood that ran from wounds unfairly given, and a most perfect representation in motive, time, circumstance, when applied to the Earl. In this connection let us look at Sonnet 36, and we shall perceive a meaning never before discovered:—

> Let me confess that we two must be twain,
> Altho' our *undivided* loves are one:
> So shall *those blots that do with me remain,*

Without thy help, by me be *borne alone.*
In our *two loves* there is but *one* respect,
Tho' in our lives a *separable spite;*
Which *tho' it alter not love's sole effect,*
Yet doth it steal sweet hours from love's delight.
I may not evermore acknowledge thee,
Lest my *bewailed guilt* should do thee shame;
Nor thou with *public kindness honour me,*
Unless thou take that honour from thy name:
But do not so; I love thee in such sort,
As, though being mine, *mine is thy good report.*

Apply that to Shakspeare, and you can make nothing of it. It will not even fit in with the supposed affair of the two friends and one mistress, as the poet is not made to call himself the guilty one in that! Apply it to Southampton, and you have the two lovers and the parting enforced by the Queen. He has been forbidden to see his mistress, or she him; and were he to do so, or were she to notice him for others to see, it would injure her good report. They must to all appearance be 'twain,' although one in love, so that she may not be a sharer in his 'blots.' There is but one respect in their love, but a *separable spite* in their lives. The 'separable spite' of Southampton's and Mistress Vernon's lives was the spite of Elizabeth. (pp. 452-55)

We have only internal evidence whereby we can judge whether the Sonnets are or are not personal; and where the internal evidence fits some outer fact which we can identify, we have a right to adopt the reading that is compatible with both. In this respect, our reading will make the Sonnets alive with realities where no meanings have hitherto been found. We will now ask the reader to turn back with us to Sonnet 30, the subject of which is the loss of friends—'precious friends'—very nearly related, who died long ago:—

> When to the sessions of sweet silent thought
> I summon up remembrance of things past,
> I sigh the lack of many a thing I sought,
> And with *old woes* new-wail my *dear time's waste:*
> Then can I drown an eye *(unused to flow)*
> For *precious friends* hid in Death's dateless night,
> And weep *afresh Love's long-since cancelled* woe,
> And moan the expense of many a vanisht sight.
> Then can I grieve at *grievances foregone,*
> And heavily, from *woe to woe,* tell o'er
> The *sad account* of *fore-bemoaned* moan,
> Which I *new-pay* as if not paid before.
> But if the while I think on thee, dear friend,
> All losses are restored, and sorrows end.

We cannot attach this to Shakspeare himself by any known facts of his life; yet it is something very special. The lost friends were most dear—'precious friends'—friends, we should say, in the closest relationship. The next Sonnet says:—

> How many a *holy* and *obsequious* tear
> Hath *dear religious* love stolen from mine eye,
> As interest of the dead!
>
> [Sonnet 31]

The loss is the sorrow of a life-time; the relationship one of the nearest to nature; and the deaths occurred years ago. If we suppose Shakspeare to be speaking, we simply do not know what he is talking about, as so often occurs through the personal theory. The first loss that Shakspeare had up to the time of writing, and the only one, so far as we know, was the loss of his boy. Indeed, this could not have occurred; for if the Sonnets were personal, they would be amongst the earliest written, because they indicate that it is a *newly-found* friend, who is to fill the empty place of those old ones who are gone. . . . Shakspeare's son died in August 1596, but clearly that loss will not bear the description in any way. If we turn to Southampton's life, we shall find the very loss of these 'precious friends,' and the precise lapse of time also. His father had died . . . when Henry Wriothesley wanted two days of being eight years old; and about four years afterwards his elder brother died. That phrase 'lacking' has in it a touch of parental relationship. And as we read the Sonnet, this new love of the Earl for Elizabeth Vernon has come to him to replace the old, and restore to him all he had lost; that which death hid away he has found in her. (pp. 456-57)

When we read these as a portion of Shakspeare's *'sugred Sonnets among his private friends'* it adds a novel significance to the words of Meres. These are *love-Sonnets*, which was what Meres meant by his epithet; but love-Sonnets in so peculiar a fashion that if their true nature was such as we have been supposing, and he had any inkling of it, he would be compelled to generalise. He does not say sonnets *to* his friend or friends, but *among* his private friends. This was in 1598, the year in which the Earl of Southampton and Elizabeth Vernon were married; therefore these sonnets, which are ante-nuptial, if written on the subject of the Earl's love, must have been amongst those mentioned by Meres, for they have the essence of his meaning. And who were Shakspeare's 'private friends'? We have his own positive evidence that Southampton was one, and a very dear one. No amount of negative evidence will alter that or dethrone the Earl to whom he dedicated. The sole evidence on behalf of the Earl of Pembroke is that of the players, or rather of the writer of the dedication to the first folio edition of Shakspeare's plays, whose gratitude was probably quite as much a lively sense of future favours to himself as it was a sense of any past favours to Shakspeare. Southampton, we know, was a private friend of our great poet. And it is only the most natural thing in the world that Elizabeth Vernon should be his friend also. (pp. 457-58)

We now come to a series of Sonnets which are nearly grouped together, and which include Nos. 109, 110, 111, 112, 117, 118, 119, 120, 121, 122, 123, 124, and 125. These Sonnets tell a far different story; the dramatic interest deepens. They are pathetic, with a most passionate pleading; they are defiant of some opposition and slander; they are filled with personal confessions; they are self-criminating, and quick with repentance; they are intensely personal, and one or two touches of literal likeness in external facts have caused them to be taken for the most actual and authentic representation that we have of Shakspeare himself. But *there is no likeness in the inner character. They do not agree with what we know of Shakspeare.* They do not accord with those Sonnets which are personal. These Sonnets look very like replies to expostulations on the subject of personal conduct and character. Yet, we repeat, they do not express either the conduct or character of Shakspeare himself. It is remarkable, however, that they most startlingly represent the character of Southampton. The young Earl, as is well known, was a brave, comely, munificent noble, of Nature's own making. He was ardent and true in friendship, when to be so was injurious to his own best interests; chivalric, and full of warlike fire. But he was one of those who have the occasional flash and outbreak of the fiery mind. . . . His mounting valour was of the restless irrepressive kind that if it could not find vent in battles abroad it was apt to break out in brawls at home. The very man whose vices

Shakspeare would feel to be more amiable than some people's virtues. His generous and self-forgetting nature was irritated and made reckless by the cruelty of Elizabeth, the Queen, in so wantonly opposing his marriage with Elizabeth, his love. His daring was at times turned into dare-devilry; his hardihood into fool-hardihood. At which sorry sight the 'fair Mistress Vernon,' and other friends of the Earl, would mourn, and bewail his getting into such bad courses and lamentable scrapes, or *scapes,* as Shakspeare would have called them.

These Sonnets may well have been written when the Earl had slidden deeper than ever into disgrace, and the fair Elizabeth had heard of his doings with averted eyes. The personal relationship here imaged is altogether different from that of Shakspeare and his patron or friend, Southampton.

> Oh, never say that I was false of heart,
> Tho' *absence* seemed my *flame to qualify.*
>
> [Sonnet 109]

'If I have *rang'd,'* he pleads, 'I return again,' and 'bring water for my stain' [Sonnet 109]. How grossly improbable is it that Shakspeare should have written to his friend and patron thus:

> For if you were by *my unkindness* shaken
> As I by yours, *you've passed a hell of time:*
> And I, a tyrant, have no leisure taken
> To weigh how once I suffered in your crime.
> Oh that our night of woe might have remembered
> My deepest sense, how hard true sorrow hits,
> And *soon to you, as you to me,* then tendered
> The *humble* salve which wounded bosom fits!
>
> [Sonnet 120]

Our poet was one of the most modest of men, therefore one of the last to have presumed on his friend's kindness, and have placed himself on an equality in that way!

The arguments of Sonnets 117 and 118 would be puerile if Shakspeare's own; worthy of a flirting coxcomb. 'Accuse me thus,' he would say, 'that I have scanted all wherein I should repay your great deserts; forgot to call upon your dearest love, whereto all bonds do tie me day to day. Say that I have *hoisted sail to all the winds* that would transport me farthest from you; given to others that which belongs to you, and was so dearly purchased. Say the worst of me that you can; accumulate all my *wilfulness* and errors, and then I shall plead in answer that it was *all done merely to prove the constancy and virtue of your love!'* And this to the person whose frown he is supposed to have feared! If we take Southampton to be the speaker in Sonnet 117, we shall see how appropriate it all is—

> That I have frequent been, with *unknown minds,*
> And *given to time* your own *dear-purchased* right;
> That I *have hoisted sail to all the winds*
> Which should transport me farthest from your sight.

He had been abroad three years running, after he first began to woo Mistress Vernon. He had been in various foreign countries, Spain, France, Ireland; and in doing this he had hoisted sail to those winds that would blow him the farthest from her. Thus he had given to time that which was her own by right, for she had dearly purchased it by her sufferings on his account. In another Sonnet he has come home for good, and he only wants now to be forgiven once for all, and he will not again give way to that lust for action, which has been one of his sins. The excuse of the 118th Sonnet, if used by Shakspeare to his friend, would be still more absurd were it not more insulting. The Sonnets we are now speaking of include the two which have generally been thought to denote the poet's disgust at his player's life. But surely they are more true to the life and character of Southampton than of Shakspeare. 'Alas! 'tis true (I admit all you say) that I have gone *here* and *there,* and made myself a motley to the view [Sonnet 110]. The image may be drawn from the stage; but we do not see how it fits the relation of the poet to his patron. With what propriety could Shakspeare speak of making a fool of himself on the stage which had been their first meeting-place, and which was the fount of Shakspeare's honour; the delight of Southampton's leisure? Besides which we know that Shakspeare's life was no tossing to and fro, going *here* and *there* to make a fool of himself. His life was too steadily anchored in a steadfastness of character. Far more significantly does the image figure the young Earl's public follies to the very life. (pp. 458-61)

If we apply the language of [Sonnets 110, 111, and 112] to Southampton, we shall find a far more satisfactory solution. It was perfectly true, and we know it, that *he* had gone here and there and made a fool of himself; done it publicly 'to the view.' And in doing these things, after meeting with Elizabeth Vernon, he must have 'looked on truth askance and strangely,' and made old offences of *'affections-new.'* Fortune, he says, was the *guilty* goddess of his harmful deeds, in making him a public man, which begets public manners. (p. 462)

We do not know much of Shakspeare's life, but we have no reason to think that he ever uttered one personal complaint against Fortune, nor had he any cause that we know of. His career in life appears to have been one of steady prosperity. When he speaks on this subject in person, it is with a very quiet modesty. He does not accredit Fortune with any spite towards him, and shows none himself. He speaks of his 'well-contented day' (Sonnet 32); and once he alludes to the fact that he is debarred by Fortune from such triumph as results through 'proud titles' and 'public honours' (Sonnet 25); but that is all. The exclamations against Fortune occur in the Sonnets which we have supposed *devoted,* according to the theory which we are stating, to Southampton. In Sonnet 29 he is in 'disgrace with Fortune.' In Sonnet 37 he is 'made lame,' that is, *disabled* by Fortune's excessive 'spite.' Again, in Sonnet 90, it is the 'spite of Fortune.' And, in Sonnet 111, he asks that for his sake the person addressed should chide 'Fortune' rather than him, for she is the 'guilty goddess' of his 'harmful' doings. In Southampton's case the excuse is appropriate. Fortune was against him in the person of the Queen, and her opposition to his marriage; and but for his being a *public* man and so much in the power of the Court for appointment and preferment, he would not have had so long and trying a fight with Fortune. He could have carried off his love and lived a calmer life; he would have escaped many a scar that he received in the struggle with such an untoward Fortune as at length landed him by the side of Essex at the scaffold foot, although he had not to mount the steps.

These Sonnets . . . may be considered as making what defence Shakspeare can on behalf of the Earl. They explain much that he has done; they offer excuses, apologies, contrite feelings, and repentant expressions of all kinds. They reply to what has been said of him, and, while admitting the worst that is true, they denounce indignantly much that is scandal:—

No! I am that I am; and they that level at my abuses
reckon up their own.

[Sonnet 121]
(pp. 464-65)

The passionate feeling at times intensifies, and various signs indicate that they are addressed to a woman:—

For nothing this wide universe I call
Save thou, *my rose!* in it thou art my all.

[Sonnet 109]

What potions have I drunk of Syren tears.

[Sonnet 119]

And

Why should others false adulterate eyes,
Give salutation to my sportive blood?

[Sonnet 121]

Then, in conclusion of the quarrelling and unkindness, we have the voice of Shakspeare himself coming in with a summing-up of the whole matter:—

Let me not to the marriage of true minds
Admit impediments. Love is not *love*
Which *alters* when it *alteration* finds,
Or bends with the remover to remove:
Oh no; it is an *ever fixed mark,*
That *looks on tempests and is never shaken;*
It is the *star* to every *wandering* bark,
Whose worth's unknown, altho' his height be taken.
Love's *not Time's fool,* tho' rosy lips and cheeks
Within his bending sickle's compass come;
Love *alters not* with his brief hours and weeks
But *bears it out even to the edge of doom,*
If this be error, and upon me proved,
I never writ nor no man ever loved.

[Sonnet 116]

A most perfectly apposite discourse on the loves of Southampton and Elizabeth Vernon! Their love did not run smooth. His wandering bark required the stedfast star of her goodness and beauty. Both needed the word of cordial cheer to 'bear it out to the end of doom.' (pp. 465-66)

It may be seen that a large number of the Sonnets *devoted to* Southampton are written during the Earl's absence from England. Sonnets 44, 45, 46, 47, 48, 49, 50, 51, and 52 imply absence at a distance—'injurious distance'—'limits far remote,' on the part of the speaker. Again, there has been an absence in Sonnet 56 and in Sonnets 97, 98, and 99, which is curiously corroborated in the 100th Sonnet. Another journey is indicated in Sonnet 113. And it appears to us that the 39th Sonnet, which is a personal one (we take it that Shakspeare never confuses the characters, and that where he speaks of writing or singing, the Sonnet is personal), tells us quite plainly how the Poet first began to write dramatically for the Patron. It looks like an answer to a request. He feels unworthy to sing of him, and he is glad to make the *absence,* the *separation,* an excuse for doing so. The 'sour leisure' of the Earl's absence is to give him 'sweet leave' to 'entertain the time with thoughts of love.' The separation shall teach him 'how to make one twain,' by 'praising [writing about] him *here* who doth *hence* remain.' This Sonnet occurs at the time of the Earl's first absence, as shown by the Sonnets relating thereto; and so Shakspeare began to write Sonnets on the subject of Southampton's love, his character, and his fortunes; his absence offering the strongest motive; and in this way he 'entertained the time with thoughts of love.'

It may also be urged that if the 77th Sonnet be properly inter-
rogated, it will tell the reader *how* a large number of the Sonnets were written *for* Southampton. The commentators have
hitherto assumed that Shakspeare made his friend a present
of a 'tablebook' with this Sonnet; and added, helplessly
enough, that the friend must have done the same in Sonnet
122; but it is *not* written on making a gift. The subject is the
old one of making a fight with Time. The writer is at the time
writing in *the* book, from which he draws one of a series of
reflections bearing upon his subject. The mirror, he says, will
tell him how his 'beauties wear;' and the dial will show him
Time's stealthy progress to eternity. '*This* book' will also
teach its lesson. Its vacant leaves will take the mind's imprint;
and he advises his friend to write down his own thoughts in
these '*waste blanks*,' and they will be a living memory of the
past, one day—just as the mirror is a reminder to-day. If he
will do this, the habit—'these offices'—will profit him mentally, and much enrich the book. Evidently this is a book for
writing in, and as evidently Shakspeare is *then* writing in it.
Moreover it has 'vacant leaves'—'waste blanks;' therefore it
will have pages that have been filled. It has already been enriched, but if the owner of it—Southampton—would also
write in it, the book would be much richer than it is now.
'*This book*' shows it in Shakspeare's hand, and '*thy book*' tells
us it belonged to the Earl. Into this book, then, we think
many of the Sonnets may have been written, as contributions
are made to an album. In this particular Sonnet we see the
poet actually writing in the book. We may see likewise how
naturally he would thus come to write upon Southampton's
affairs through the medium of this book, which would pass
from poet to patron, and afford matters of peculiar interest
when Mistress Vernon and the Earl looked over it together.
Nor is it wholly inconceivable that this book was a present
from Mistress Vernon to the Earl, and that it is the very one
which we find he has parted with in Sonnet 122. That was a
'*record*' of her, but his mind and memory, he says, retain a
far deeper record. . . . Here the book is for the purpose of
keeping count, as it were, of his love. It has been devoted to
her, but the 'poor retention could not so much hold' [Sonnet
122]; and he has given it away. We suspect also that this book
contained the Sonnets mentioned by Meres; and after it was
given away by Southampton, it ultimately drifted into the
hands of Thomas Thorpe, and formed the nucleus of his collection.

It is demonstrable that *the poet did not contemplate being
known to the world as the writer of these Sonnets.* The work
was a cherished love-secret on his part, all the dearer for the
privacy. He thought of doing it, and he believed it would live,
and that his friend and all the love between them should live
on in it, but *he himself was to steal off unidentified.* In Sonnet
81, he says:—

> Your name from hence immortal life shall have,
> Tho' I, *once gone, to all the world must die:*
> The earth can yield me *but a common grave,*
> *When you entombed in men's eyes shall lie.*
> *Your monument shall be my gentle verse.*

Clearly the Sonnets were to be *nameless,* so far as the author
was concerned, or Shakspeare must have been a sharer with
his friend in both the immortal life and monument! Again,
he says, when he is dead—

> Do not so much as my poor *name* rehearse,
> My *name* be buried where my body is.
>
> [Sonnet 71]

And in Sonnet 76, there is a kind of 'hush!' He speaks of his
friend so plainly, that 'every word doth almost tell *my* name,'
and from whom the Sonnets proceeded, as if that were self-
forbidden. He assures his friend of immortality, he speaks of
having an interest in the verses, for they contain the 'better
part' of himself consecrated to his friend, but he does not contemplate living in them by name.

This view of the subject will explain what has always appeared so great an anomaly in the poet's character. Readers
never could reconcile his carelessness about fame with his
many boasts respecting immortality. It appears to us that
Shakspeare's Sonnetteering for Southampton was nearly
done when the Earl did at length marry late in 1598 or early
in 1599. And from this we assume that the Sonnets which
were begun by the poet, advising the young Earl to marry, and
continued from time to time all through the long, unquiet
course of his wooing, were concluded by the marriage. There
is one exception in Sonnet 107, and it will worthily crown our
illustrations:—

> Not *mine own fears,* nor the *prophetic* soul
> Of the wide world *dreaming on things to come,*
> Can yet the lease of my true love controul,
> *Supposed as forfeit to a confined doom.*
> The *mortal Moon* hath her *eclipse endured,*
> And the sad augurs mock their own presage,
> *Incertainties* now crown themselves *assured,*
> And peace proclaims Olives of endless age.
> Now with the drops of this most balmy time
> My love looks fresh and *Death to me subscribes,*
> Since spite of him I'll live in this poor rhyme,
> While he insults o'er dull and speechless tribes.
> And thou in this shalt find thy monument,
> When *tyrant's crests* and tombs of brass are spent.

There can be no misgiving or mistake here. That Sonnet was
written on the death of Elizabeth, and the consequent release
of Southampton from prison.

The Earl had been condemned to die for his part in Essex's
mad attempt. He was left in prison many weeks, expecting
death. His sentence was at length remitted, but he was kept
in confinement until the 'mortal moon' had 'her eclipse endured.' And it tells us of Shakspeare's fears for his friend—
how he had trembled, the outer world had prophesied, and
the Augurs had foreboded the worst. How he had supposed
the lease of his love forfeited by that 'confined doom!' But all
the uncertainty is over now. His love looks 'fresh with the
drops of this most balmy time.' The new king calls him from
a prison to a seat of honour; and the poet can crow over
Death this time, and his friend shall find a monument in his
verse, when the 'crests' and 'tombs of brass' of all such tyrants as Elizabeth have passed away. (pp. 467-70)

This Sonnet, then, must have been written as late as 1603.
And there is the most curious proof that it was one of those
odd Sonnets which the printer did not know where to place.
The 104th Sonnet tells us that Shakspeare has then known
his friend three years; therefore it was not written later than
1594. The 108th is also one of the earliest, and in it the writer
calls his friend 'Sweet Boy.' And this 107th Sonnet is stuck
between the two. There are but two Sonnets between the Sonnet of 1594 and that of 1603. We could not give a more forcible illustration of the way in which the Sonnets were sent to
press. And this fact alone proves that the printer made no attempt to re-arrange them according to any secret knowledge

of their begettal. As he received them so has he given them to us.

We have now claimed and reclaimed nearly 120 of the Sonnets as addressed to Southampton, or *devoted to* his affairs. We feel so certain that at least the whole of the first 126 are bound up with Southampton, that we ought to be able to account for the remainder of them. Sonnets 40, 41, and 42 have been held to tell a story very damaging to our Poet's moral character. We shall show that at least another reading is possible. If the Earl of Southampton had been allured from the side of his mistress for awhile by some friend of hers, these three sonnets would very fitly express her feelings. She would have the right to speak of 'those pretty wrongs that liberty commits when *I am sometime absent from thy heart*' [Sonnet 41], but Shakspeare could not. Mistress Vernon might chide the Earl for breaking a 'twofold truth'—

> *Hers* by thy beauty tempting her to thee,
> *Thine* by thy beauty being *false to me.*
>
> [Sonnet 41]

But Shakspeare was not in any sense free to reproach the Earl in such an affair as is commonly supposed. What of the truth that he would be breaking? According to one very possible reading, then, the 41st and 42nd represent Mistress Vernon as speaking to the Earl; but the 40th would be addressed to the woman who had stolen, or been supposed to steal, the Earl. The 41st Sonnet tells us it was the *woman* that *wooed*, and here the '*gentle thief*' is reproached in person! We presume that Sonnets 33, 34, and 35 are connected with this part of the subject. The face in tears (Sonnet 34), and the expression 'all men make faults,' are both more womanly than manly. So is the travelling forth '*without my cloak;*' also, the 'loss in love that touches me *more nearly;*' and 'such civil war is in my *love* and *hate.*' The expression 'to him,' we take it, is merely by way of a general and proverbial illustration. Well, then, in the 35th Sonnet we have the 'sweet thief' again spoken of in a way which shows that she must be addressed in person in Sonnet 40. According to the personal reading of these Sonnets, the speaker must address the thief in person here—

> *Lascivious grace!* in whom all ill well shows,
> *Kill me with spites,* yet we must not be foes!
>
> [Sonnet 40]

There is more meaning, however, if Mistress Vernon be the speaker, and Penelope Rich, for example, should be the friend. She and Elizabeth Vernon were cousins, and very intimate. The description 'lascivious grace!' is very appropriate, and, if this be the lady, there were reasons why the two should *not be foes.* (pp. 471-72)

The latter Sonnets, beginning with the 127th, can scarcely have been procured from the same source. For, had they been so, we should not find them massed together at the end. Some of them were certainly written *as early* as those first printed— the 127th for example,—and if held in the same hands they would have come in earlier. But that they were in different and *looser* hands we may infer from the fact that a piratical publisher could obtain two of them for printing in 1599 [in *The Passionate Pilgrim*]. Southampton could not have been the begetter of these unless there was a 'Rosaline' before 'Juliet.' And if Thorpe did really dedicate to 'William Herbert,' then it would be probable that some of these latter Sonnets were written for that young nobleman; and Thorpe concluded that he was the 'only begetter' of Shakspeare's Sonnets.

But we have no space to discuss the subject here, and we only profess to deal with those Sonnets which have the appearance of being connected, in the ways we have shown, with the Earl of Southampton.

It must not be thought that we are losing sight of Shakspeare's personality whilst eliminating the impersonal Sonnets. We are drawing all the more closely to himself. In our reading we lose the phantom Shakspeare who could ungraciously forget his early friend, to whom he had made public promises, given hostages for the future, and dedicated love without end; who could sing of his friend's eternal truth, after passionately denouncing his falsehood, and talk of locking up his jewel lest it should be stolen after it had been filched from him; who could slavishly prostrate himself at the feet of a boy; who could hypocritically reprove his friend for his loose conduct and lament his immoralities, whilst he himself, a married man of ripe age, was partner with the boy in an intrigue with some married woman; who could accuse himself of all sorts of inconsistent things, grow querulous at the slightest cause, and ask pity on all kinds of false pretences; who could write sonnets on his own and his friend's disgraceful amours, and supply copies to their friends for the purpose of raising a laugh at their mutual frailty—for *such, in defiance of dates, facts, and all that we know of our Poet's life and character, or gather from his works,* is the Shakspeare of Messrs. Boaden and Brown's theory of the Sonnets [see excerpts above by Boaden, 1837, and Brown, 1838]—and we have found the real man as he once lived, and loved his friend Southampton, and showed an interest in his passion for Elizabeth Vernon; took sides with them when they were thwarted by the caprice of the Queen, and resented it very strongly; made the most ingenious defence, in play and in earnest, for his friend; fought for him against 'old Time,' and evil 'Fortune,' and 'all-oblivious enmity;' laboured to polish his virtues when they rusted, and lifted them up shiningly in the eyes of his beloved, and strove to shield them from the tarnishing breath of scandal; probably seeing many sad things and having many sad thoughts, but holding on to him faithful and loving to the end. (pp. 473-74)

[Gerald Massey], "Shakspeare and His Sonnets," in *The Quarterly Review, Vol. 115, No. 230, April, 1864, pp. 430-81.*

RICHARD SIMPSON (essay date 1868)

[*Simpson was a prolific nineteenth-century English essayist. In the following excerpt, he contends that a Platonic philosophy of love and beauty, as modified by Italian and English Renaissance sonneteers, informs and unifies Shakespeare's sonnets. Simpson identifies the six stages of love—from the lowest level of passion and awareness of beauty based on physical perception to the highest founded on the lover's recognition of truth in the beloved—in Sonnets 1-126. According to the critic, although this philosophy "is often concealed by the variety and splendour of the jewels that are struck upon it," beneath "all this wealth the main outline of the pre-existing idea which was part of the current Platonism of the epoch may be traced." Simpson is the first critic to examine fully the evidence of Platonism in Shakespeare's sonnets. He also discusses the arrangement of the 1609 Quarto, finding it legitimate, not haphazard.*]

The first edition of Shakespeare's Sonnets, though it carries no positive evidence of being issued under the author's superintendence, yet on the other hand bears none of the marks of surreptitious and unauthorized publication which are so conspicuous in the original quarto edition of the several plays. The printing is exceptionally correct for the time, and the book is dedicated by the publisher to Mr. W. H., the "only begetter" of the Sonnets, who is apparently identified as the man for whom the poet made all the promises of immortality which they contain. For him they had been written or arranged in definite series, intended to illustrate the progress of a known philosophy. There is no reason to suppose that, in delivering them to the printer, he would have broken their continuity and confounded their order; and we ought therefore to suppose, till the contrary is demonstrated, that the order in which they stand is that which was intended by their author.

It is true that most of those who have written on the Sonnets have taken it for granted that their order is merely accidental, and have therefore taken the liberty of arranging them in new groups according to supposed internal similarities, or external relationships to persons and events. But none of those writers who have thus rearranged them seem to have given themselves the trouble to enquire whether it might not be possible to explain them as a series in their present order. They have first of all assumed some theory—that the Sonnets are historical, or that they are mere versifications of separate sentiments—and have thereupon proceeded to group them afresh, according to the persons or events they are supposed to touch, or according to the sentiment each may appear chiefly to enunciate.

And yet, if these poems are examined in the light of the common sonnet-philosophy—of that poetical Platonism which had inspired compositions of this kind ever since their rise—their sequence is quite natural, and they need no new grouping to make them into a single orderly poem. Indeed, examined in this light, they appear to be articulated and arranged with rare subtlety and care. The most superficial examination makes it appear that the 154 Sonnets are divided into two series. The first, consisting of 126, is addressed to a fair youth; the second, consisting of the remaining 28, is addressed to a black-haired, black-eyed, and dark-featured woman. It further appears that the love depicted in the first series is a force ever growing, triumphing over obstacles, and becoming ever purer and brighter; while the love sung in the second series is bad in its origin, interrupted but not destroyed by fits of remorse, and growing worse and worse with time. Such is the general construction of the book of Sonnets. And Shakespeare tells us that his intention was to exhibit two such loves. The opening quatrain of the 144th Sonnet is as follows:—

> Two loves I have, of comfort and despair,
> Which, like two spirits, do suggest me still:
> The better angel is a man right fair,
> The worser spirit a woman coloured ill.

The two loves answer to friendship and concupiscence, the *amor amicitioe* and *amor concupiscentioe* of the schools. The former love has its revolutions, but each time it returns to itself with renewed strength: it is the true infinite—the circular motion which is both perfect and endless. The other love is the false infinite—the eternal alternation of yes and no, without any true progress or any attempt at perfection. . . . In the two series of Sonnets these two kinds of love are put through their trials. The higher love undergoes its probation of absence, suspicion, jealousy, and error, and proves "that better is by evil still made better" [Sonnet 119]. The lower love undergoes also its probation. It also triumphs over jealousy, triumphs over the disenchantments of experience, tri-

umphs over the principles of morals [Sonnet 129], over the unsustained struggles of good resolution [Sonnet 146], and over the stings of conscience, which it finally perverts and blinds [Sonnet 151]. Although these two kinds of progress are treated in a form which is perfectly abstract and impersonal, nothing prevents our supposing that many of the illustrations may be historical—that real persons and real events may be often used as the materials for the philosophic edifice. The only postulate which the theory of the Sonnets here advocated makes is that they are in the first intention philosophical, devoted to the exposition of the received sonnet philosophy, and only in the second intention biographical or historical, and therefore using real events in complete subordination to the philosophical ideas.

This theory both requires and discovers that in both series of sonnets the same cyclic character is found; that the progress in both is similar; that sonnet answers to sonnet; and that the similar sonnets occur in the equivalent phases of each series. This relationship may be traced throughout; and it distinctly proves that the order of the sonnets in the two series is right, or at least that both series are arranged on one principle, striking "each in each by mutual ordering" [Sonnet 8], so that one becomes the counterpart of the other, just as in the dramas the subordinate plots are counterparts of the main plot, which they imitate either directly, or ironically, or by contradiction. It is not unnatural that Shakespeare should employ this method both in his sonnets and in his dramas. The importance of such a double structure for the interpretation of the poems is scarcely to be exaggerated. By means of it the author in a great measure explains himself. He gives us a number of points at which the two series are in contact, thereby marking the main divisions of each series, its salient and significant points of transition, and its parallelism with the other. This parallelism can be readily shown.

As the first series begins with the desire of love to see beauty immortalize itself in its offspring, so the second begins with the confession that beauty is profaned and disgraced, and its offspring bastard. One begins with hope, the other with accents of despair, for the future of beauty. For the *amor amicitioe* looks forward to eternity, the *amor concupiscentioe* looks only to present pleasure, and is reckless of the future. This contrast is found in the two musical sonnets, No. 8 of the first series and No. 128 of the second. . . . The "expense of spirit in a waste of shame" which the 129th Sonnet declares the *amor concupiscentioe* to be, is parallel with the waste of beauty, the ruin, the cold decay, the wastes of Time, the unthriftiness which in Sonnets 9-14 the poet charges on Beauty which is unwilling to fulfil the duty of self-preservation. . . . The next point where the two series approach each other is in Sonnets 21 and 130. The two are perfect counterparts; both turn on the same thought of the folly of racking invention to find comparisons for the object of love, and of turning heaven itself into mere paint to colour it. A person may be worthy of the highest love, or may deeply stir the lowest passion, and yet be nothing like sun, moon, or stars. The two following sonnets of the second series give this thought a development which it lacks in the first. (pp. 36-9)

The next point of contact is in Sonnets 40-42 of the first series, and 133, 134 of the second. These so evidently refer to the same real or imaginary incident, that in all rearrangements of the sonnets they are put together. The earlier set is, however, clearly addressed to the "better angel," the later to the "worser spirit." The *amor amicitioe* dies if it is not reciprocal.

But the baser love asks for no such return. At least it demands no exclusive fidelity, but only so much compassion as will afford consolation to the lover's passion. Hence, the laxity of Sonnets 133, 134, which, however superficially resembling the earlier set (40-42), differ in this, that while friendship needs not be jealous of the friend who seeks not another friend, but only a mistress, the vulgar love may still have reason to quarrel with the mistress who is not only unfaithful to her lover, but also robs him of his friend. (pp. 39-40)

The next place where the two series touch is Sonnet 57 with Sonnets 135 and 136. The two latter are superficially distinguished by the puns upon the name of "Will." In the original edition the final couplet of 57 is distinguished by the same character. Love is such a true fool in the heart of your *Will,* that whatever you do, he thinks no ill of it. In both places the lover expresses absolute humility, which dares not rise to jealousy. "Nor dare I question with my jealous thought where you may be," he says to his friend. Let none of your desires, no wish, be violently suppressed, he says to his mistress. Think them all one, merge them all in the unity of your will; and then let me, who am also a *Will,* approach you as an integral part of the whole. (p. 40)

Proceeding onwards, the 137th Sonnet, though materially corresponding with two sets of sonnets in the first series—43-47, and 113, 114, all of which refer to the violence which love puts upon the eyes, so as to make them false, yet formally has much more real relationship with Sonnet 62. The "sin of self-love" blinds the eye in one case, and the sin of vulgar love blinds both eyes and heart in the other. The 138th Sonnet deals with false seeming and pretence in vulgar love in a contrary way to that in which Sonnets 67-70 deal with false seeming and false surmise in the love of friendship. The 139th and 140th Sonnets are the indubitable counterparts of Sonnets 88-90. In the earlier numbers the lover justifies his friend for wronging him, and invites him, if he intends to be faithless, to be so at once, and to put him out of his misery. He promises, however, to justify his friend's conduct, whatever it may be. In the later numbers the lover warns his mistress not to call upon him to justify the wrongs her unkindness lays upon him; he will do nothing of the sort, but will go mad, and slander her, if she does not at least pretend to be faithful to him. Sonnets 141-143 develope the two ideas of the falsehood of the senses and the madness of the judgment. The lover's fondness is a voluntary madness . . . , and it makes him pursue his mistress as she pursues others, asking only to be accepted as others are, and to experience her kindness only in the intervals which she can spare from them. In the same spirit the lover, in the former series of Sonnets 92-94, wishes to be spared the knowledge of his friend's falsity, if he is false, wishes to live deceived, to enjoy a kind face if he cannot have all the heart, but at the same time warns his friend that his beauty is like Eve's apple, his lilies worse than weeds, if his virtue is not what it seems to be. Sonnet 144 has already been quoted as the key to both series. Its burden, in the latter part, is this—If the absent friend is playing false with the lover's mistress, she will "fire him out." The counterpart to this, in the first series, is found in Sonnets 109, 110. . . . After a brief and lyrical reconciliation with his mistress in Sonnet 145, and a new quarrel with himself, with a half promise of amendment, in Sonnet 146, the votary of the *amor concupiscentioe* in Sonnets 147 and 148 recognizes afresh the feverish delirium and false seeing of his passion, in terms which are the very counterparts of Sonnets 113, 114, where the analogous false vision of the better love is discussed, and Sonnets 118 and

119, where the "sickness" and "madding fever" of passion, which have been a temporary barrier between the lover and his friend, are bewailed and excused. Then while in Sonnet 149 the baser love balances the unkindness of the mistress with the corresponding unkindness and self-torment of the lover, in Sonnet 120 the nobler love balances the unkindness of the friend with that of the lover, and proves the depth of the love by the torments mutually inflicted and endured. . . . It is necessary to bring together the two parallel Sonnets, 121 of the first series and 150 of the second, in order to understand the former, and bring it within the moral code of the higher love.

> 'Tis better to be vile than vile esteemed
> When not to be receives reproach of being.
>
> [Sonnet 121]

In Sonnet 150 the lover complains that it is his mistress's very vileness and insufficiency that has enthralled him. So the lines quoted will mean, it is better in love to be really vile, for vileness itself will sometimes command affection, than to be esteemed vile and thereby lose all love. Lastly, a comparison between the concluding Sonnets of each series, 124, 125, and 151, 152 (for 126 is merely a tag or appendix to the first series, as 153 and 154 are to the second), will show how the higher love in its last development becomes sublimated into a religion, while the lower love perverts conscience and truth, the corner-stones of religion. In this unsatisfactory manner the poem of the love of despair closes. It has a bad end. Shakespeare was too good a philosopher to exhibit all paths as leading alike to bliss; but he shows how of the two kinds of love which he sings, one toils steadily upwards in spite of occasional lapses, the other rapidly descends in spite of occasional halts. One ends in independence of all the powers of change, that is, in immortality; the other in a slough of despair, in the self-condemnation of one whose intellect knows that his choice is evil, but whose will is too weak to revise it.

Thus a comparison of the two series of sonnets shows that they run parallel to each other; the first comprises all that the second possesses, and much more besides; for the love of friendship is treated more fully than the love of desire. To the first 125 sonnets are dedicated, to the second only 26. But these 26 are found to correspond with a proportionate number in the first series; and, so far as the parallelism extends, precisely the same order is found in both series. This is surely a great argument to prove that the sonnets remain in the order in which their author intended them to be read. (pp. 40-3)

• • • • •

When Shakespeare [in his Sonnets] had formed the design of exhibiting the gradual ascent of Love through each degree of its scale, from the first conception of fancy in the eyes to the final possession of the whole heart and intellect by ideal love, he naturally began with a definition of the force whose progress he was about to describe. Every word in this definition is accurate:—

> From fairest creatures we desire increase,
> That thereby beauty's rose might never die.
>
> [Sonnet 1]

"Fairest," he says, because the lover attaches himself not to the fair in the abstract, but to the one fair which approves itself to him as the highest: "creatures," because love, defined as the "desire of generation in the beautiful," applies only to creatures subject to change and death. But this desire of generation is founded on another desire still more general; its roots lie in a still deeper ground, the desire "that beauty's rose might never die." The word "rose" here is full of import. . . . The aspiration for the immortality of the "rose of beauty" is the root of love. The aspiration, when kindled by the beauty of fading creatures, produces the desire of increase from the fairest of them. And the desire, when the lovers are man and woman, is the root of domestic love; and when they are both men, causes the lover to wish to produce an excellent mind in the beautiful body of the beloved youth. But this Platonic creation hardly satisfies the aspiration for immortality, for the mind disappears when the youth dies. Hence before Shakespeare's days there had arisen a current commonplace of friendship, by which one friend would urge another to marry and to transmit his likeness to posterity. . . . [The] advice of Cecropia to her niece Philoclea, in Sidney's novel of *Arcadia*, contains not only the general sentiments of Shakespeare's first batch of Sonnets, but several of the arguments on which they are based. "As Nature made you child of a mother, so do your best to be mother of a child," is, *mutatis mutandis,* the last line of Sonnet 13. "You had a father; let your son say so." Sidney's simile of rose-water in a crystal glass is adopted by Shakespeare in Sonnet 5; his remark about the monotony of one string seems to have suggested Sonnet 8. But Sidney, like Shakespeare, was in this only an echo of his time. (pp. 47-8)

In accordance, then, with the feeling of his age, Shakespeare makes this the first aspiration of the friend who has just been struck with the beauty of the youth he is destined to love. One of the Egyptian gods was armed with a whip with which he excited the Moon to scatter the seeds of fertility upon the earth. Of like kind is the first step in Shakespeare's friendship. In the first nine Sonnets he urges his friend to marry on general grounds; his neglect is wasteful, shameful, unjust, a malversation of trust, and a wilful dilapidation of an estate in which he has only a life-interest. Then with the 5th Sonnet begins a series of rhetorical arguments for marriage. First comes Sidney's crystal; then the same thought, coupled with others which we find in Marlowe's *Hero and Leander,* and which Parolles reproduces in Shakespeare's own drama of *All's Well that Ends Well.* The 7th Sonnet is founded on the converse of a proverb which was often in Queen Elizabeth's mouth when she refused to name her successor—"Men use to worship the rising sun." On the other hand, says Shakespeare, men turn their backs on the setting sun, and the only way to retain their homage is to receive it in the person of a son and successor. . . . From this point the arguments become less rhetorical, and appeal more directly to the feelings. Do you keep single for fear of wetting a widow's eye? But the whole world will be a widow and weep if you leave no copy of yourself. You cannot love others when you commit this murder on yourself. In Sonnet 10, the poet first ventures to introduce his own personality; if you will not marry on other grounds, at least "make thee another self for love of me." In the 13th Sonnet he advances still farther. Now he calls his friend "Dear my love," and affectionately entreats him to reproduce himself; and in the 14th he declares himself prophet enough to know that truth and beauty shall thrive together if he will do so, but that if he will not, his end "is truth's and beauty's doom and date." Then come five Sonnets in which the poet, seeming to despair of being able to influence his friend's conduct, declares that he himself, by his verses, will confer immortality upon him. He will war with Time—"as he takes from you I will graft you new" [Sonnet 15]. You

might make war on Time, he says, "a mightier way" and by "means more blessed than my barren rhyme," by begetting living pictures, "drawn by your own sweet skill" [Sonnet 16]. Without such witness of its truth, he says, my description of you will not be believed; with such witness "you should live twice, in it and in my rhyme" [Sonnet 17]. But, finally, casting away all hope of persuading him, he triumphantly announces his own power of immortalizing him—

> So long as men can breathe, or eyes can see,
> So long lives this, and this gives life to thee— . . .
> —Do thy worst, old Time: despite thy wrong
> My love shall in my verse ever live young.
>
> [Sonnet 18]

This was a common-place of sonnet writers. . . . They considered that Love, as Aristotle says, consists rather in loving than in being loved—that it is action rather than passive receptivity—that it gives rather than receives. The lover gives himself, and does so in order to confer immortality on the beloved. The soul, taken with the beauty of its friend, is seized with melancholy when it reflects that this beauty is only lent, not given, to the world; and its first aspiration is that such grace may never die. At first, while friendship is more in the wish than in the will, the incipient lover, with a kind of distant respect, only urges his friend to immortalize himself; failing in this, he proceeds, timidly at first, to associate himself with his friend, to express a more direct and personal interest in his existence, and to undertake something that shall immortalize him.

The highest expression of this friendship is doubtless self-sacrifice. . . . In the first sonnet of the *Vita Nuova,* Love appears to Dante, carrying Beatrice sleeping in his arms, and holding the poet's heart in his hand. He wakes her, and feeds her with the burning heart, and then departs in tears. The poet asks his friends to interpret the fearful vision. Guido Cavalcanti alone solves it:—

> Your heart he bore away, for he perceived
> That to your lady Death was laying claim,
> And fearing this, sustained her with your heart.

To die for one's friend is the highest expression of friendship; but it does not satisfy the aspiration of love. A brief remainder of life cannot purchase more than it spends. The problem of love, as it proposed itself to the sonnet writers, was to find some surer means of giving immortality. Cicero says that of two friends, both live while one survives; for the dead still lives while his memory is preserved with veneration and tender regret in the bosom of the survivor. Sometimes the survivor can rescue his friend from evil report; and then it becomes his duty to live. Thus Hamlet says to Horatio, who was about to drink the remains of the poison—

> O God, Horatio, what a wounded name,
> Things standing thus unknown, shall live behind
> me!
> If thou didst ever hold me in thy heart,
> Absent thee from felicity awhile,
> And in this harsh world draw thy breath in pain
> To tell my story. . . .
>
> [*Hamlet,* V. ii. 344-49]

Dante begins the *Vita Nuova* by offering his heart to preserve Beatrice; and he ends it with the resolve "to say that of her which was never said of any woman"—a resolve which gave birth to the *Divina Commedia,* in which her memory was embalmed and made eternal. (pp. 48-51)

The 20th Sonnet reverts once more, and for the last time, to the idea of corporeal reproduction. The poems which were to immortalize the beloved youth were in some sense his off-spring, for they were inspired by his eyes—"from thine eyes my knowledge I derive." But yet the poet, in spite of the confidence which he expresses, feels diffident of his powers, and says, in effect—"You are so like a woman, that it is a pity you are not one. Nature, making you a man, deprived me of you. You should be my mistress; as that cannot be, your love may be mine, whether you devote yourself to women or not." This sonnet is a transition. Its familiarity marks a great advance in friendly intercourse, while the light way in which the friend's relation to women is treated in it marks both the abandonment of the persuasions to marriage, and the deficiency of moral depth in this early stage of friendship, which is at present a mere "fancy," bred in the eyes, and dependent on corporeal beauty, and the desire of immortalizing it. Behind the materialism of this love we see here and there a new element arising, the "gentle heart" unacquainted with "shifting change;" but this new element has not yet acquired any moral force.

From this time the love of the two friends becomes a reciprocal passion. In the 21st Sonnet the poet, having the reality of his friend's beauty before his eyes, refuses to compare it with sun, or moon, or gems, or flowers, but simply says that it is as fair as that of any mother's child, though not so bright as the stars. Shakespeare's own practice in Sonnet 98 seems contrary to the theory of this Sonnet, and of the similar one, 130, in the second series, till we remember the different positions occupied in the scale of love by this Sonnet and by No. 98. It is one thing, in the very presence of the beloved, to withdraw attention from his beauty, and frigidly drag in that of the sun and moon and flowers; and another thing, in his absence, to make all beautiful things in nature mere types and memorials of his beauty. (pp. 51-2)

The next Sonnet (22) turns upon another common-place of sonnet philosophy:—

> All that beauty that doth cover thee
> Is but the seemly raiment of my heart,
> Which in thy breast doth live, as thine in me.

This Sonnet must be taken in connection with the 24th: together they show that in this stage of love the heart is only enamoured of beauty's external form. The reciprocal admiration of each lover for the other's beauty, though it seems to effect that interchange of heart which is only fully possible in perfected love, yet does it in a very superficial way. "Fancy" is still in its cradle; it has not yet been delivered from the thraldom of the eyes. . . . The intermediate Sonnet (23) turns upon another commonplace of the philosophy—the awe and trouble which possesses the lover and makes him tongue-tied in the presence of his friend. This trembling . . . is spoken of in the 4th, 5th, 6th, and 7th Sonnets of Dante's *Vita Nuova,* and in several of Petrarch's, as Sonnet 34, where he says that in Laura's presence he can neither speak, nor cry, nor sigh; and that when his tongue would ask recompense, it is frozen, and its words are imperfect, like a dreamer's. Similarly Shakespeare says that the friend is not to believe his ears, but his eyes are to read "what silent love hath writ;" for "to hear with eyes belongs to love's fine wit." These Sonnets are clearly descriptive of the various phases of love entering by the eyes. The 25th Sonnet sums up the happiness of this love: court favourites live in the royal eye, and die of a frown.

It is only the perpetual and present smile of fortune that maintains the warrior's fame. But

> Happy I, that love and am beloved
> Where I may not remove, nor be removed.

With the 26th Sonnet we enter the second degree of the scale of love. Love now learns through absence to be independent of the eyes. . . . [Sonnet 26] is the introduction to the poems of absence. The lover will not venture to show himself in his friend's presence till his "bare" verses are clothed with his friend's loving favour—

> Then may I dare to boast how I do love thee:
> Till then, not show my head where thou may'st
>   prove me.

In its reference to the imperfect utterance of the poet's pen, this Sonnet clearly refers back to Sonnet 23. There he said that his verses expressed his thoughts better than his words could do; here, that these verses are bare till the friend takes them and meditates on them alone, and by his favour "puts apparel" on their tattered love. The 27th and 28th Sonnets depict the first miseries of absence; but through this wretchedness the "shadow" of the friend shines, brightening the day, and gilding the night—for already the first effect of absence upon the imagination is to mitigate the realism of Sonnet 21, which abjures all hyperbole. In Sonnet 29, perhaps the most exquisite of the series, the remembrance of the friend's sweet love is made the one antidote for all the sorrows of life; in Sonnets 30 and 31, again, it becomes the substitute for all past and vanished loves—a kind of new life in which "all losses are restored," and the images of dead friends revivified. Sonnet 32 closes this little series, which begins with Sonnet 26, with a kind of repetition and enlargement of the opening motive. In one place the poet says to his friend, "think over my verses in my absence;" in the other, "think over them when I am dead, and supply their defects by your kind thoughts." In the gradual progress of love we shall find that the poet once more reverts to this thought (in Sonnet 71), and begs his friend to forget him and his poetry alike after death, if the remembrance brings pain. Another little series of Sonnets begins with the 33rd, when the unkind thoughts which besiege the absent begin to make their appearance. . . . In the 34th the lover endures some disgrace at his friend's hands. But in the 35th he declares that no doubts or disgraces can touch his love, and that he even makes himself an accessory to his friend's misdeeds by excusing them. Then, from the notion that the accessory is equally worthy of blame with the principal, he concludes, in Sonnet 36, that absence must be perpetual; he cannot ask his friend to return to one whose bad name he would have to share. As his friend is identified with him, so also his friend's good report becomes his personal concern; and this, with his unworthiness, can only be maintained by separation. And separation has its own consolations. Even the report of his friend's glory, the shadow of his beauty, birth, wealth, and wit, gives him substantial comfort (Sonnet 37). He feels himself blessed when he knows his friend is blessed—

> Look, what is best, that best I wish in thee,
> This wish I have; then ten times happy me!
>   [Sonnet 37]

It is characteristic of this early stage in the ladder of love that all the qualities on which it dwells are such as are more or less external. In the first stage, love is taken in through the eyes, and is kindled only by beauty; in the second, it enters through the sensible imagination, and is kindled by the qualities which affect this imagination—not only beauty, but rank, wealth, and wit.

The third stage in the scale begins with Sonnet 38. Like the 26th, it is a dedicatory and introductory sonnet. The poet declares that whatever excellence appears in his poems is all due to the inspiration they derive from his friend, who is the tenth Muse—

> O give thyself the thanks if aught in me
> Worthy perusal stand against thy sight.

The third stage of love idealizes the data of imagination, and gathers them all up in the friend, in whom the lover lives a second life. . . . With this idea Shakespeare, in Sonnet 39, moralizes on the benefits of absence, which teaches "how to make one twain," to dissolve one life into two, as well as to combine two into one. Then follow three Sonnets which have been a stumbling-block to all interpreters. Taken in connection with Sonnets 133, 134, the Sonnets 40-42 clearly tell a disgraceful story. The lover has some mistress, a married woman, with whom he has a guilty intimacy. He uses his friend as a go-between, and his friend supplants him. Interpreted biographically of the poet and his friend, the story is shocking. It is also improbable in the highest degree that the man who maintains so dignified a silence about himself, or who, when he does speak, as in Sonnet 121, asserts so clearly his own superiority to vulgar scandal, should have only lifted the veil to let us behold such a disgrace as this. . . . But in our theory [these Sonnets] fall most naturally into place. The love of the friends has to be tried by jealousy, but in this stage of love the jealousy which suspects a preference for another friend would be premature; its place is found in the stage of ideal love. Here we require the more superficial jealousy, which would keep to itself those special gifts of the friend which kindle the lover's fancy. Now the lover could not be jealous of his friend's wife; he has devoted seventeen sonnets to one theme, an invitation to him to marry. He could not be jealous of his friend's mistress; in Sonnet 20 he has expressly left him free in his relations with women;—"Mine be thy love, and thy love's use their treasure." He could not be jealous of his friend's friend; for this jealousy belongs to a higher stage of love, that ideal love which admits of no plurality in affection, and which, as Sonnet 119 shows, cancels also the freedom with respect to women which Sonnet 20 grants. The poet must, therefore, devise some real cause for jealousy, and this he has done in the manner we have indicated. In Sonnets 33, 34 he merely alludes to this theft, to blame it, to forgive it, and to excuse it. He owns in Sonnet 35 that the excuse he makes for it is disgraceful in itself, and in Sonnet 36 that it is quite reason enough why his friend should remain separate from him. In Sonnet 40 he refers more explicitly to the transaction, and declares that it must not make him and his friend into foes; in Sonnet 41 he again excuses it, and in Sonnet 42 he even finds in it a fresh symptom of love—

> But here's the joy—my friend and I are one;
> Sweet flattery! then she loves but me alone.

The conclusion is not moral; but the imaginative stage of love is not yet moral. It is as yet but a sentimental fancy; and the scale of love shows by what stages this sentimental fancy is gradually transformed from a non-moral into a moral affection. (pp. 54-8)

This stage of love ends with a short series of three Sonnets, 43-45, which bring to light the unsatisfactory nature of this

merely imaginary love. It is shadowy and unsubstantial. It does not attain to the deep recesses of the soul; it lives rather in the imagination and senses, which are tied to the four material elements of which the body is composed, than in the nimble thought to which distance is nothing, and bodily presence or absence is all one. With this transitional reflection the first division of the first great series of Sonnets is brought to a close. Shakespeare has shown us the three steps of love, conceived in the eyes, generalized in the imagination, and again concentrated in the judgment, but not yet idealized—not yet possessing the whole heart.

To recapitulate. The first stage of love is represented in Sonnets 1 to 25. In the first twenty the lover is represented gradually coming nearer to his object, beginning with a distant respect, and ending with a close intimacy. Then Sonnets 21 to 25 express the first unity of love's simple apprehension, in which it confounds the two lovers into one. The second stage is shown in Sonnets 26 to 37. Here this unity is put through its trials. . . . The third stage is exhibited in Sonnets 38 to 45. Love not only ceases to be troubled by the trials which it surmounts in the second stage; it even assimilates them, and turns them into its own essence. . . . [But] the very insufficiency of the materialistic elements of these first stages of love becomes a force which suggests and helps to carry out the transformation of an imaginative into an ideal love. . . . (pp. 58-9)

Imaginative love occupies the three lower grades in the scale, and ideal love the three higher. Ideal love begins with the substitution of intellectual for sensible beauty; for if love is born in the eyes, its life is in the mind. This change is indicated by Shakespeare in Sonnets 46 and 47. What the eye has been to the prior stages of love, the heart is now to be for the later. . . . To know another man, says Hamlet, is to know one's self. Love therefore when transferred from the beauty of form to that of the mind depends upon the knowledge of one's self; for this knowledge is our grammar and dictionary whereby we may interpret the tokens which reveal to us the hearts and minds of others. Shakespeare then, after introducing the subject in Sonnets 46, 47, has to show how love acquires, of itself, this self-knowledge. First he recurs to the general topic of absence, which leads the lover to fear that absence only typifies the entire loss of his friend [Sonnet 48]. Then he asks himself—"but what claim have I to keep him?" This leads him to a "knowledge of his own desert," and to the confession that he "can allege no cause" why he should be loved [Sonnet 49]. . . . The intention [of Sonnets 50 and 51] is to show how much ideal love transcends the animal powers. The "dull flesh," "the beast that bears" the man, appears in its slowness to sympathize with him in the pains of absence; but in the ardour of desire, and in the triumph of return, the soul must be its own vehicle; no flesh can keep abreast of the mind in its "fiery race," and therefore all such weak auxiliaries have "leave to go." Sonnet 52 carries this asceticism of love even further, and dispenses, except on rare occasions, even with the imagination of the friend's shape. Every object reminds the lover of his friend's beauty [Sonnet 53], but nothing can represent his "constant heart." And yet [Sonnet 54] it is not the visible beauty, but the constant heart or invisible truth, which gives a man his worth. This truth, therefore, and no longer the mere outward form, as in Sonnet 5, the poet's verse is henceforth to distil, to make its memory live for ever [Sonnet 55] and "dwell in lovers' eyes."

With Sonnet 56 a new vein of feeling comes in. The poet finds that the abstention and asceticism of the last few sonnets only "kills the spirit of love by a perpetual dulness." He once more therefore gives play to his imagination. He thinks of the bodily presence of his friend; he wonders where he is and what he is doing, and checks his rising suspicions by the deepest self-humiliation. Being his friend's slave, how can he demand an account of what he is doing? [Sonnets 57 and 58] He finds it much more to the purpose to search old records to find his friend's "image in some antique book," written "since mind at first in character was done" [Sonnet 59]. Thus love retires into itself, chews the cud of meditation, and bears again "the second burden of a former child" by remodelling its old thoughts, and giving new birth to pre-existing ideas. Such new birth is altogether of a higher character than natural nativity, which "crawls to maturity" and is eclipsed. The new life which the poet promises to confer on his friend is one that "shall stand to times in hope" [Sonnet 60].

In Sonnet 61 the poet asks whether his friend's image which visits him so often is sent by him, or is conjured up by his own love. It is, he replies, his own love. But if he creates the image, what must be his own worth that is capable of casting such a shadow? All former self-inspection ended in self-abasement; this ends in a very different self-appreciation [Sonnet 62]:

> Methinks no face so gracious is as mine,
>   No shape so true, no truth of such account;
> And for myself mine own worth do define,
>   As I all other in all worths surmount.

And though he refers all this excellence to his friend, his second self, yet it remains true that he must have all its elements in his own person, or he would not be able to comprehend it. (pp. 60-2)

The main features of this stage of ideal love are the three self-inspections whereby the lover comes to the knowledge of his own heart. First, he recognizes its absolute worthlessness by its defects; secondly, he determines its relation to the friend, whose slave and vassal he feels himself to be; and thirdly, he recognizes its real nobility when he finds in it those principles of superlative excellence which his modesty will not allow him to attribute to himself. Henceforth the self-conscious heart, and not the sensuous imagination, becomes the true interpreter of love.

When once, through self-inspection, the lover has become acquainted with his own soul, and therein with souls in general, he is perforce obliged to substitute a spiritual beauty for the material beauty which he has hitherto worshipped. And this substitution indicates an advance of the understanding from the concrete to the abstract. The lover, says Plato, has now no eyes for gold or colours or outward beauties, but only for the beauty of souls, of arts, of sciences, and of institutions. He is no longer distressed by the waning of fair faces, or the fading of flowers, but by the soul which does not fulfil its high promises, by art which misses its aim, by science which babbles, by political institutions which are turned to purposes of oppression and revolutionary destruction, and by a religion which forswears its faith. To this new phase of love Sonnet 66 is an introduction as beautiful as it is appropriate. In common with Hamlet's famous soliloquy, and indeed in harmony with all Shakespeare's later tragedies, it expresses the poet's deep disgust with the world, and society as he saw them, and declares that his ideal love was the only thing which made life tolerable to him. . . . Sonnet 70 goes far to prove the purely philosophical character of the whole series. While the love was simply imaginative, and contemplated only an outward beauty, it was possible to attribute all kinds of "sensual faults" [Sonnet 35] to the "lascivious grace" of the friend. Now, however, that the friend has become a type of ideal beauty, it is necessary to say of him—

> —Thou present'st a pure unstained prime;
> Thou hast pass'd by the ambush of young days,
> Either not assailed, or victor being charged.

In the two next Sonnets (71, 72) the lover with most intense feeling begs the friend to forget him and his verses after death, "if thinking on me then should make you woe." And in the two next he dwells on the short space yet left to him, which at once makes his friend's love more strong "To love that well which thou must leave ere long," and urges the poet to pour out his whole spirit into the verses which he consecrates to his friend's immortality. . . . In these Sonnets [Shakespeare] really seems to feel himself to be the last minstrel and only herald of a beauty that was already out of date. But he has a supreme confidence in his cause, and a confidence mingled with diffidence in his own powers. Hence his unwillingness to link his love so indissolubly to himself as to make it perish with him. Hence too, mingled with his yearnings for death and oblivion, his confidence that his cause will be immortalized in his verse. He seems to feel that he is destined to a temporary oblivion, but that afterwards his memory will revive, and his writings will become a power to perpetuate the ideals which they embody.

The next two Sonnets, 75, 76, record his single attachment to his ideal love. Absent or present, it is the sole food of his thoughts, and the only topic of his monotonous verse. In Sonnet 77 he gives his friend a note book, and entreats him to commit his thoughts, the children of his brain, to its waste blanks. As imaginative love began with beseeching the friend to marry and leave children like himself, so ideal love looks for offspring—not, however, of the body, but of the mind. The poet felt that the life of the world was changing. He held up a mirror to the old life, that it might paint itself and put itself upon record. In this record the old life lies not dead, but as it were in a nurse's arms, in order once more to rise, and "to take a new acquaintance" of the mind of man. (pp. 62-4)

After this, the purport of the next nine Sonnets, on jealousy, will be clear. Whether any other poet, Marlowe, or Drayton, or Daniel, or Spenser, really usurped Shakespeare's place in the affections of W. H. cannot be determined from them. The course of the argument requires here that ideal love should be tried by an ideal and intellectual jealousy, as imaginative love was tried by an imaginative jealousy in Sonnets 40-42. The poet, fresh from lamenting the transient stay of the beauty he loved, and from proposing it as the model for future ages, to be preserved in the truth-telling records of unaffected verse, naturally is indignant that the subject should be appropriated by men of the affected school whose "gross painting" and "strained touches of rhetoric" [Sonnet 82] only distort the truth they pretend to describe. The lover's object is to think true thoughts, not to speak fine words. To him, the presence of the ideal love in the heart and mind supplies for all lack of education and skill. He has not to ransack the universe for comparisons, but has only to copy what he sees in his ideal love—none can say more

> Than this rich praise, that you alone are you.
>
> [Sonnet 84]

Such creation is the highest aim of art. It gives to its object an individuality which serves to make it for ever unique.

In the next series of Sonnets, 87-96, Love seems to yield to jealousy. The rival has prevailed, and the lover relinquishes his claims on his friend's heart. As in a previous Sonnet, he attributes this breach to his own unworthiness. Yet the self-depreciation here has an additional element. In Sonnet 49 it was simply a result of a comparison of himself, as known by self-reflection, to his ideal love. Jealousy gives rise in the lover to a self-depreciation in comparison with a third person. The first was a mere act of self-apprehension; the second is an act of self-judgment. Such self-judgment the lover practises in Sonnets 87-96. The legal phraseology of Sonnet 87 is itself suggestive of the process of judgment. In the next, the poet excuses his friend's lack of love by a confession of his own secret faults, like that which Hamlet makes to Ophelia. . . . Then the lover almost accepts the hypothesis of the friend's falsehood. His rose has not only colour to please the eyes, but the spiritual fragrance which captivates the mind; but what if this sweetness "with base infection meet"? . . . So he concludes by warning his friend that though his beauty covers every blot, yet in time "the hardest knife loses its edge" [Sonnet 95]. Thus the second stage of ideal love ends with a negative operation of the judgment, which seems to threaten the very existence of love. It is to be noticed that Sonnet 96, the last in the second stage of ideal love, ends with the same couplet as Sonnet 36, the last but one in the second stage of imaginative love. For the same situations recur, but ever in a higher significance.

In the third stage of ideal love all the negations of the judgment are rectified, and its scattered premisses drawn up into one conclusion. The universal soul, the "sacred universal love," which is the final object of ideal love, contains in itself, in a transcendant sense, all that was found in the lower grades of love. Hence this stage is fitly introduced with three beautiful Sonnets, which, in thorough contradiction with Sonnet 21, disparage all the bright lamps of the universe in comparison with the beauty of the friend. For though it is folly to compare a handsome face to sun, and moon, and stars, it is, on the other hand, true that a soul is, in its own nature, better than all the inanimate world, and a spiritual beauty above all possible corporeal beauty. . . . Then, in Sonnets 100, 101, the poet rebukes his muse for her silence. Though her song cannot improve beauty, it can immortalize it. In the next two Sonnets, 102, 103, he excuses silence. It is not becoming to merchandize love in the hubbub of the world's mart, and his verse only mars that which it cannot mend. In Sonnet 104 he declares that his love has passed through its three great seasons, and in 105 that it has united the three elements of love—beauty, goodness, and truth—into a single whole—"one, still such, and ever so."

> Fair, kind, and true have often lived alone,
> Which three till now never kept seat in one.

For the final stage of love is the synthesis of all its elements. (pp. 64-6)

The lover's suspicions and apparent falseness, the fickleness of his affections, the misfortunes of his life, and the scandal which surrounds his name, are all made into fuel for all-consuming, all-embracing love in Sonnets 109-112. The two next sonnets describe the idealizing of the imagination—turning the eye into mind, and the mind into an eye that creates out of chaotic masses images of ideal beauty. In Sonnet 115 the poet corrects former sonnets, such as 76, 105, 107, which seem to say "now I love you best," as if the lover feared for the future of his love, instead of remembering that love is a babe that grows continually, and that growth is the condition of love as it is of life. In the next Sonnet, 116, he celebrates love as the marriage of true minds, a union far above alteration or motion, guiding life, like a star in the heavens. In the next series of four sonnets [Sonnets 117-20] all the moral aberrations of both the lover and friend are first condemned and then consumed in the furnace of love, in order to make its flame the hotter. Better is made still better even by evil; when once the tide turns, and the flow of improvement sets in, everything works with it, and even contradictions and aberrations contribute to the one great conclusion—for all discords are resolved in the final concord. The true nature of evil is, however, distinctly allowed, and the soul of goodness which it contains is made to consist not in anything intrinsic to evil, but in the reaction which it causes. Evil is a kind of analytic power, which prepares for the great synthetic process of perfected love. After the touching confession of evil and its uses, the lover proceeds to state the paradox [Sonnet 121] that it is better to be evil than to be thought so. The reaction from evil produces good under the organizing and healing influence of love. But the evil report chases away love, and with it the hope of perfection. . . . In Sonnet 123 he defies Time and his registers; his love has the character of eternity, and is not helped by any temporal records. In Sonnet 124 he enlarges on the eternal character of his love. It is not the child of state, varying with fortune. It depends not on the accidents of smiling pomp or thralled discontent. It fears not the heretic policy which prefers the temporal to the eternal, but proves itself altogether politic by showing itself invincible and unchangeable. . . . Sonnet 126 is imperfect in form, and though belonging to the series in its general tone, has no special place therein, and hence is appended as a mere tag to it. That it was placed here, and not at the end of all the Sonnets, is a farther proof that the whole first series down to this place have for their object the "lovely boy" . . . so rarely alluded to distinctly after Sonnet 27. . . . [The] reason why sex is not mentioned is that in the gradual elevation of love, and in its transformations through successive stages, its object becomes more and more generalized, more spiritual, with less definite sex, or definite human personality. This consideration does not absolutely preclude reference to the "sweet boy," even in so late and religiously toned a sonnet as 108. But it is quite reason enough to account for the sudden cessation of the continuous reference to the manhood and personality of the beloved object after Sonnet 27, when it will be remembered imaginative love is just entering on its second phase of abstraction and analysis.

In this brief sketch of the connection of these sonnets, and of their agreement with the acknowledged philosophy of other sonnet writers, it has been manifestly impossible to do more than trace their leading ideas, the thread of connection which binds them together, and makes them into a consistent series. This thread is often concealed by the variety and splendour of the jewels that are strung upon it; the philosophic poet covers the bare skeleton which we have traced with the most exuberant tissues, with a profusion of thought and images which is simply astonishing. But under all this wealth the main outline of the pre-existing idea which was part of the current Platonism of the epoch may be traced, if not easily, at least with precision and certainty. (pp. 67-9)

Richard Simpson, in his An Introduction to the Philosophy of Shakespeare's Sonnets, *1868. Reprint by AMS Press, 1973, 82 p.*

A Louers complaint.

BY

WILLIAM SHAKE-SPEARE.

FRom off a hill whofe concaue wombe reworded,
A plaintfull ftory from a fiftring vale
My fpirrits t'attend this doble voyce accorded,
And downe I laid to lift the fad tun'd tale,
Ere long efpied a fickle maid full pale
Tearing of papers breaking rings a twaine,
Storming her world with forrowes, wind and raine.

Vpon her head a plattid hiue of ftraw,
Which fortified her vifage from the Sunne,
Whereon the thought might thinke fometime it faw
The catkas of a beauty fpent and donne,
Time had not fithed all that youth begun,
Nor youth all quit, but fpight of heauens fell rage,
Some beauty peept, through lettice of fear'd age.

Oft did fhe heaue her Napkin to her eyne,
Which on it had conceited charecters:
Laundring the filken figures in the brine,
That feafoned woe had pelleted in teares,
And often reading what contents it beares:
As often fhriking vndiftinguifht wo,
In clamours of all fize both high and low,

Some-times her leueld eyes their carriage ride,
As they did battry to the fpheres intend;
Sometime diuerted their poore balls are tide,
To th'orbed earth; fometimes they do extend,
Their view right on, anon their gafes lend,

                                                          To

Facsimile of the title page of A Lover's Complaint *printed with the 1609 edition of Shakespeare's* Sonnets.

ROBERT BROWNING   (poem date 1876)

[*An English poet and playwright, Browning is considered one of the outstanding literary talents of the nineteenth century. Much of his poetry treats the nature of and relationship between love, knowledge, and faith. In the following excerpt from the tenth stanza of his 1876 poem "House," Browning alludes to William Wordsworth's comment on the autobiographical importance of Shakespeare's sonnets (see excerpt above, 1827), asserting "the less Shakespeare he!" if these verses are truly autobiographical.*]

            "With this same key
Shakespeare unlocked his heart," once more!
Did Shakespeare? If so, the less Shakespeare he!

                                            (p. 530)

Robert Browning, "House," in his The Poetical Works of Robert Browning, *Oxford University Press, 1940, pp. 529-30.*

F. J. FURNIVALL   (essay date 1877)

[*One of the leading philologists of the nineteenth century, Fur-*

nivall founded the New Shakspere Society and was among the first scholars to apply the principles of scientific investigation to the study of Shakespeare's work. The New Shakspere Society set out to measure Shakespeare's poetic and dramatic growth by means of "verse tests"—detailed examinations of variations in the metrical features of Shakespeare's dramatic verse. Furnivall's work is indicative of the influence which nineteenth-century scientism exerted in the field of literary scholarship. In the following excerpt, Furnivall asserts that Shakespeare's sonnets are indeed autobiographical. He further argues that while accepting this view means that we recognize sensual errors on the poet's part, this does not undermine his genius. Furnivall also notes, in defense of Shakespeare's conduct, that adultery and sexual intimacy were considered differently in Shakespeare's day than in Victorian times.]

[Do] Shakspere's Sonnets speak his own heart and thoughts or not? [Were] it not for the fact that many critics really deserving the name of Shakspere students, and not Shakspere fools, have held the Sonnets to be merely dramatic, I could not have conceived that poems so intensely and evidently autobiographic and self-revealing, poems so one with the spirit and inner meaning of Shakspere's growth and life, could ever have been conceived to be other than what they are, the records of his own loves and fears. And I believe that if the acceptance of them as such had not involved the consequence of Shakespere's intrigue with a married woman, all readers would have taken the Sonnets as speaking of Shakspere's own life. But his admirers are so anxious to remove every stain from him, that they contend for a non-natural interpretation of his poems. They forget the difference in opinion between Elizabethan and Victorian times as to those sweet sins of the flesh, where what is said to be stolen is so willingly given. They forget the cuckoo cry rising from nearly all Elizabethan literature, and that the intimacy now thought criminal was then in certain circles nearly as common as handshaking is with us. They forget Shakespere's impulsive nature, and his long absence from his home. They will not face the probabilities of the case, or recollect that David was still God's friend though Bathsheba lived. The Sonnets are, in one sense, Shakspere's Psalms. Spiritual struggles underlie both poets' work. For myself, I'd accept any number of "slips in sensual mire" on Shakspere's part, to have the "bursts of (loving) heart" given us in the Sonnets.

The true motto for the first group of Shakspere's Sonnets is to be seen in David's words, "I am distresst for thee, my brother Jonathan; very pleasant hast thou been unto me. Thy love to me was wonderful, passing the love of woman." We have had them reproduced for us Victorians, without their stain of sin and shame, in Mr. Tennyson's *In Memoriam*. We have had them again to some extent in Mrs. Browning's glorious Sonnets to her husband, with their iterance, "Say over again, and yet once over again, that thou dost love me." We may look upon the Sonnets as a piece of music, or as Shakspere's pathetic sonata, each melody introduced, dropt again, brought in again with variations, but one full strain of undying love and friendship through the whole. (pp. lxiii-lxiv)

With regard to the second group of Sonnets, we must always keep Shakspere's own words in No. 121 before us:—

            I am that I am; and they that level
At my abuses, reckon up their own:
I may be straight, though they themselves be bevel;
By their rank thoughts my deeds must not be shown;
      Unless this general evil they maintain,—

All men are bad, and in their badness reign.

Still I think it is plain that Shakspere had become involved in an intrigue with a married woman who threw him over for his friend Will. She was dark, had beautiful eyes, and was a fine musician, but false. The most repulsive of the Sonnets is no doubt No. 129. But that and the others plainly show that Shakspere knew that his love was his sin (142), and that in his supposed heaven he found hell. Adultery in those days was no new thing, was treated with an indifference that we wonder at now. What was new, is that which Shakspere shows us, his deep repentance for the sin committed. Sad as it may be to us to be forced to conclude that shame has to be cast on the noble name we reverence, yet let us remember that it is but for a temporary stain on his career, and that through the knowledge of the human heart he gained by his own trials we get the intensest and most valuable records of his genius. It is only those who have been through the mill themselves, that know how hard God's stones and the devil's grind. (p. lxvi)

I wish to say with all the emphasis I can, that in my belief no one can understand Shakspere who does not hold that his Sonnets are autobiographical, and that they explain the depths of the soul of the Shakspere who wrote the plays. I know that Mr. Browning is against this view, and holds that if Shakspere *did* "unlock his heart in his Sonnets," then "the less Shakspere he" [see excerpt above, 1876]. But I'd rather take, on this question, the witness of the greatest poetess of our Victorian, nay of all time yet, and ask whether she was the less, or the greater and truer, Elizabeth Barrett Browning, or poet, because she unlockt *her* heart in *her* Sonnets, or because she "went forward and confessed to her critics that her poems had her *heart and life* in them, they were not empty shells!" (pp. lxvi-lxvii)

> *F. J. Furnivall, in an introduction to* The Leopold Shakspere, Cassell, Petter & Galpin, 1877, pp. vii-cxxvi.

HERMANN CONRAD   (essay date 1879)

[*In the following excerpt from an essay originally published in German in 1879, Conrad notes how Shakespeare impressed his own "distinct character" on the sonnet form, arguing that in Shakespeare's sonnets "there is nothing contradictory between form and matter." Indeed, according to Conrad, the sonnet form in this instance is "peculiarly adapted" to the "powerful substance" of Shakespeare's thought, becoming a "solid structure . . . .that defies transitoriness."*]

[By reading other Elizabethan sonnets one can see how far] Shakspere in these poems soars above his most distinguished contemporaries as a lyricist; how with sovereign power he here impresses upon the form an entirely distinct character, *his own*. In other poets the form is feeble and weak even to weariness; in him it becomes the expression of highly concentrated force. One might almost think that the powerful substance in this form must itself produce an effect of comic contrast. But, as a matter of fact, there is nothing contradictory between form and matter. Precisely here we learn that the form has greater merit than has usually been allowed it. It is peculiarly adapted to this poetic power productivity, and no other form could with equal success replace it. Filled with such weighty matter, it has in its solid structure something that defies transitoriness, something bronze. The sonnets stamp themselves in indelible lines upon the receptive mind.

Once comprehended, they can no more be forgotten than can the sight of those very ancient, colossal monuments that seem to be the work of a long since vanished titanic force. But they are more than that: from the esthetic point of view they are *classic*. Without all temporal accessories, in them is revealed the ideal truth of an all-embracing genius. There was never a poet to draw more perfectly lust in all its frightful traits, never a poet to find better expression for a confirmed, healthy pessimism.

> *Hermann Conrad, in an extract in* A New Variorum Edition of Shakespeare: The Sonnets, Vol. II, *edited by Hyder Edward Rollins, J. B. Lippincott Company, 1944, p. 405.*

JAMES ASHCROFT NOBLE   (essay date 1880)

[*The following excerpt is from Noble's essay on the development and present state of the English sonnet. Here, the critic contends that the principal quality of attraction in Shakespeare's sonnets is "their pervading Shakespearianism," which Noble describes as "an unmistakable amplitude of treatment, a large utterance," and "a more impressive spiritual present." The critic also modifies Coleridge's claim (see excerpt above, 1833) that the sonnets display a "condensation of thought," asserting that "the thing which gives to them their specific gravity is not what is usually understood by thought, but what may rather be described as intellectualized emotion."*]

The remarkable, and in many respects pre-eminent, series of fourteen-line poems known as the sonnets of Shakspeare, present a dilemma on one horn of which the writer of an article like the present must be impaled. They fill such a space and hold such a rank in the sonnet literature of England, that to ignore them is impossible, and to treat them adequately is not one whit less so. Numberless volumes, the outcome of long and loving study, have been devoted to a theme which we must needs dismiss in a few brief and necessarily unsatisfactory sentences. True, most of these volumes have been occupied with matters which are irrelevant to our main purpose. Wordsworth, whose briefest criticisms are generally full of insight, surely erred when he said that in these poems Shakspeare unlocked his heart [see excerpt above, 1827], for the precious collection is still, like the book in the Apocalypse, "sealed with seven seals." We know by whom the poems were written, but we can hardly say without uncertainty that we know to whom they were addressed; and, with regard to their true significance, speculation has followed speculation, and theory has set itself against theory. Perhaps it is impossible to repress the desire to penetrate those occult mysteries of literature of which the Shakspeare sonnet problem is among the most fascinating; but it is certainly unfortunate that perplexing questions concerning the genesis and final cause of these poems should so largely have diverted attention from those positive qualities which give them their main value and interest.

The first of these qualities—or rather that quality in which all others are included—is what must be called, for want of another word, their pervading Shakspearianism. We smile at the "Correggiosity of Correggio," and we may smile at the Shakspearianism of Shakspeare; but, after all, how can the bringer-in of a unique type be defined in the terms of an established nomenclature? Shakspeare has this and that quality which belonged to his predecessors—the insight of one, the imagination of another, the expressional felicity of a third; but he unites them all in a new synthesis, and for the product of this synthesis we are bound to make a new definition. Until Shakspeare has a compeer he is a class by himself, and as the world seems to have decided that the compeer has not yet arrived, he remains above all else Shakspearian. And in his poems, notably in these so-called sonnets, which are the richest and completest of them, this unique personal note is as clearly discernible as in the noblest of the plays, and much more discernible than in some of those earlier dramatic efforts which mark the tentative stage of his development. If we could imagine the existence of a person of cultivated taste who was still ignorant of the recognised place of Shakspeare in literature, he could not pass from the sonnet work of Shakspeare's contemporaries to that of the master himself without an instant sense of an enlarged outlook, of a freer, clearer air, of a more impressive spiritual presence. There is the recognition of an unmistakable amplitude of treatment, a large utterance, and ensuing upon this a feeling of fellowship with a soul wealthy enough to disdain the smaller economics of the intellect. In these sonnets there is no sense of strain; we do not feel . . . that the poet has touched his possibilities, but that even in his farthest reaches they are still long ahead of him. Even when the intellectual level attained by an author is not absolutely high, as it is here, there is always a felt charm in his work if it leave such an impression as this; a charm like that which belongs to the feats of some trained athlete who performs what seem muscular miracles with the graceful ease of effortless strength.

Coleridge has spoken of the "condensation of thought" in these sonnets [see excerpt above, 1833] . . . ; but, if we mistake not, the thing which gives to them their specific gravity is not what is usually understood by thought, but what may rather be described as intellectualized emotion—that is, the incarnation of pure emotion, which is itself too rare and attenuated an essence to be adequately and at the same time sustainedly expressed, in a body of symbol or situation which is supplied by the intellect. The simple pouring out of passion is apt to become tiresome to all save the lover and the beloved; but in reading Shakespeare's sonnets we are sensible of no loss of gusto; the last is as piquant as the first; and this because the mere passion, which is in itself an ordinary thing,—though the passion of a Titan must needs be Titanesque,—is supplemented by the tremendous intellectual force which lies behind and beneath it, and bears it up as the foam-bell is borne on the bosom of the great sea. (pp. 457-58)

James Ashcroft Noble, "The Sonnet in England," in Contemporary Review, *Vol. XXXVIII, September, 1880, pp. 446-71.*

EDWARD DOWDEN (essay date 1881)

[*Dowden was an Irish critic and biographer. His* Shakspere: A Critical Study of His Mind and Art, *first published in 1875 and revised in 1881, is the leading example of late nineteenth-century biographical criticism of Shakespeare. Biographical critics sought a record of Shakespeare's personal development in the plays and poems. As that approach gave way in the twentieth century to aesthetic theories with greater emphasis on the constructed, formal nature of literary words, the biographical analysis of Dowden and other critics came to be regarded as limited and often misleading. In the following excerpt, Dowden assesses the autobiographical content of Shakespeare's sonnets, claiming that in these poems we can discern the poet's tender sensitivity, his capacity for forgiveness, and his "measureless personal devotion." Dowden also emphasizes that the sonnets demonstrate that while Shakespeare was not free from*

moral faults, his errors are traceable to his sensitive, imaginative nature.]

If the *Sonnets* of Shakspere, written many years before the close of Shakspere's career as dramatist, be autobiographical, we may perhaps discover the sorrow which first roused his heart and imagination to their long inquisition of evil and grief, and which, sinking down into his great soul, and remaining there until all bitterness had passed away, bore fruit in the most mature of Shakspere's writings, distinguished as these are by serene pathetic strength and stern yet tender beauty. (p. 350)

In the *Sonnets* we recognize three things: that Shakspere was capable of measureless personal devotion; that he was tenderly sensitive—sensitive, above all, to every diminution or alteration of that love his heart so eagerly craved; and that when wronged, although he suffered anguish, he transcended his private injury, and learned to forgive. There are lovers of Shakspere so jealous of his honor that they are unable to suppose that any grave moral flaw could have impaired the nobility of his life and manhood. Shakspere, as he is discovered in his poems and his plays, appears rather to have been a man who, by strenuous effort, and with the aid of the good powers of the world, was saved, so as by fire. Before Shakspere zealots demand our attention to ingenious theories which help us credit the immaculateness of Shakspere's life, let them prove to us that his writings never offend. (pp. 351-52)

Assuredly, the inference from Shakspere's writings is not that he held himself, with virginal strength and pride, remote from the blameful pleasures of the world. What no reader will find anywhere in the plays or poems of Shakspere is a cold-blooded, hard, or selfish line; all is warm, sensitive, vital, radiant with delight, or a thrill with pain. And what we may dare to affirm of Shakspere's life is, that whatever its sins may have been, they were not hard, selfish, deliberate, cold-blooded sins. The errors of his heart originated in his sensitiveness, in his imagination (not at first inured to the hardness of fidelity to the fact), in his quick consciousness of existence, and in the self-abandoning devotion of his heart. (p. 352)

The Shakspere whom we discern in the *Sonnets* had certainly not attained the broad mastery of life which the Stratford bust asserts to have been Shakspere's in his closing years. . . . When the greater number of these *Sonnets* were written, Shakspere could have understood Romeo; he could have understood Hamlet; he could not have conceived Duke Prospero. Under the joyous exterior of those days lay a craving, sensitive, unsatisfied heart, which had not entire possession of itself, which could misplace its affections, and resort to all those pathetic frauds by which misplaced affections strive to conceal an error from themselves. The friend in whose personality Shakspere found a source of measureless delight—high-born, beautiful, young, clever, accomplished, ardent—wronged him. The woman from whom Shakspere for a time received a joyous quickening of his life, which was half pain—a woman of stained character, and the reverse of beautiful, but a strong nature, intellectual, a lover of art, and possessed of curious magnetic attraction, with her dark eyes, which illuminated a pale face—wronged him also. Shakspere bitterly felt the wrong—felt most bitterly the wrong which was least to be expected, that of his friend. It has been held to be an additional baseness that Shakspere could forgive, that he could rescue himself from indignant resentment, and adjust his nature to the altered circumstances. Possibly Shakspere may not have subscribed to all the items in the code of honor; he may not have regarded as inviolable the prohibited degrees of forgiveness. He may have seen that the wrong done to him was human, natural, almost inevitable. He certainly saw that the chief wrong was not that done to him, but committed by his friend against his own better nature. Delivering his heart from the prepossessions of wounded personal feeling, and looking at the circumstances as they actually were, he may have found it very natural and necessary not to banish from his heart the man he loved. However this may have been, his own sanity and strength, and the purity of his work as artist, depended on his ultimately delivering his soul from all bitterness. Besides, life was not exhausted. The ship righted itself, and went ploughing forward across a broad sea. Shakspere found ever more and more in life to afford adequate sustenance for man's highest needs of intellect and of heart. Life became ever more encircled with presences of beauty, of goodness, and of terror; and Shakspere's fortitude of heart increased. Nevertheless, such experiences as those recorded in the *Sonnets* could not pass out of his life, and in the imaginative recurrence of past moods might at any subsequent time become motives of his art. Passion had been purified; and at last the truth of things stood out clear and calm.

The *Sonnets* tell more of Shakspere's sensitiveness than of Shakspere's strength. In the earlier poems of the collection, his delight in human beauty, intellect, grace, expresses itself with endless variation. Nothing seems to him more admirable than manhood. But this joy is controlled and saddened by a sense of the transitoriness of all things, the ruin of time, the inevitable progress of decay. The love expressed in the early *Sonnets* is love which has known no sorrow, no change, no wrong; it is an ecstasy which the sensitive heart is as yet unable to control:

> As an unperfect actor on the stage
> Who with his fear is put beside his part,
> Or some fierce thing replete with too much rage,
> Whose strength's abundance weakens his own
>   heart,
> So I, for fear of trust, forget to say
> The perfect ceremony of love's rite,
> And in mine own love's strength seem to decay,
> O'ercharged with burden of mine own love's might.
>
> [Sonnet 23]

The prudent and sober Shakspere—was it he who bore this burden of too much love, he whose heart was made weak by the abundance of its strength? He cannot sleep; he lies awake, haunted in the darkness by the face that is dear to him. He falls into sudden moods of despondency, when his own gifts seem narrow and of little worth; when his poems, which yield him his keenest enjoyment, seem wretchedly remote from what he had dreamed, and, in the midst of his depression, he almost despises himself because he is depressed:

> Wishing me like to one more rich in hope,
> Featured like him, like him with friends possess'd,
> Desiring this man's art and that man's scope,
> With what I most enjoy contented least.
>
> [Sonnet 29]

He weeps for the loss of precious friends, for "love's long-since-cancelled woe" [Sonnet 30]; but out of all these clouds and damps the thought of one human soul, which he believes beautiful, can deliver him:

> Haply I think on thee, and then my state,
> Like to the lark at break of day arising
> From sullen earth, sings hymns at heaven's gate.
>
> [Sonnet 29]

Then comes the bitter discovery—a change in love that had seemed to be made for eternity; coldness, estrangement, wrongs upon both sides; and, at the same time, external trials and troubles arise, and the injurious life of actor and playwright—injurious to the delicate harmony and purity of the poet's nature—becomes more irksome:

> And almost thence my nature is subdued
> To what it works in, like the dyer's hand.
>
> [Sonnet 111]

He pathetically begs, not now for love, but for pity. Yet at the worst, and through all suffering, he believes in love:

> Let me not to the marriage of true minds
> Admit impediments. Love is not love
> Which alters when it alteration finds.
>
> [Sonnet 116]

It can accept its object even though imperfect, and still love on. It is not, in the common acceptation of the word, prudential—but the *infinite* prudence of the heart is indeed no other than love. . . . He has learned his lesson; his romantic attachment, which attributed an impossible perfection to his friend, has become the stronger love which accepts his friend and knows the fact; knows the fact of frailty and imperfection; knows also the greater and infinitely precious fact of central and surviving loyalty and goodness: and this new love is better than the old, because more real:

> O benefit of ill! now I find true
> That better is by evil still made better;
> And ruin'd love, when it is built anew,
> Grows fairer than at first, more strong, far greater.
>
> [Sonnet 119]

And thus he possesses his soul once more; he "returns to his content" [Sonnet 119].

Such, briefly and imperfectly hinted, is the spirit of Shakspere's *Sonnets*. A great living poet, who has dedicated to the subject of friendship one division of his collected works, has written these words . . . :

> Here the frailest leaves of me, and yet my strongest-
>   lasting:
> Here I shade and hide my thoughts—I myself do
>   not expose them,
> And yet they expose me more than all my other
>   poems.

These words of Whitman may be taken as a motto of the *Sonnets* of Shakspere. In these poems Shakspere has hidden himself, and is exposed. (pp. 353-58)

> *Edward Dowden, "Shakspere's Last Plays," in his* Shakspere: A Critical Study of His Mind and Art, *third edition, Harper & Brothers Publishers, 1881, pp. 336-82.*

W. A. HARRISON   (essay date 1884)

[*Harrison offers evidence that Mary Fitton, a maid of honor to Queen Elizabeth, had connections with Shakespeare's company—the Lord Chamberlain's Men—and thus could very well be the Dark Lady referred to in Shakespeare's sonnets. The critic cites evidence that Fitton was on friendly terms with Will Kempe, the famous "clown" of Shakespeare's troupe, and that she was dramatically inclined herself. Harrison's reference to*

Tyler's remarks on the relationship of William Herbert and Fitton applies to an earlier course of lectures which Tyler revised and included in an introduction to his 1890 edition of the sonnets (see excerpt below, 1890).]

Mr. Tyler's recent [remarks on the Sonnets] . . . furnish tolerably conclusive proof as to the relations which existed between William Herbert, afterwards Earl of Pembroke, and Mary Fitton, maid of honour to Queen Elizabeth [see excerpt below, 1890]. Thus far, however, we have had no direct evidence serving to connect Mrs. Fitton with Shakspere, though such a connexion has been surmised. Will you allow me to bring before the notice of your readers an interesting fact which undoubtedly tends in this direction, proving, as it does, that a close intimacy existed between the lady in question and a very notorious member of Shakspere's dramatic company?

In the spring of 1599, William Kemp started from London on a journey to Norwich which has become historical, dancing the morris in the towns through which he passed. In the following year he published a remarkable pamphlet, giving a detailed account of his adventures. This was entered on the registers of the Stationers' Company, April 22, 1600, as "Kemp's Morris to Norwiche." It is generally called—from the first line in the title-page—Kemp's *Nine daies Wonder.* He tells us that "it was written by himself to satisfy his friends," and "to reprove the slanders spread of him." It is dedicated as follows:—"To the true Ennobled Lady, and his most bountiful Mistris, Mistris Anne Fitton, Mayde of Honour to the most sacred Mayde, Royall Queene Elizabeth." The Christian name, as given here, is clearly a mistake. It may possibly have arisen from a misreading of the MS., or more likely still from a confusing of the names of the two sisters. Mistress *Anne* Fitton was the elder sister of Mary Fitton; but, as she became the wife of Sir John Newdigate, of Arbury, in or before 1597, she could not, of course, be "maid of honour to Queen Elizabeth" at the date of this dedication. Neither is there any evidence to show that she ever had held such a position in the royal household. On the other hand, Mary Fitton was then, and had been for some time previously, one of the maids of honour. (pp. 9-10)

Kemp thus gives his reasons for dedicating his book to Mistress Fitton:—

> In the waine of my little wit I am forst to desire your protection, else euery Ballad-singer will proclaime me bankrupt of honesty . . . Three reasons moove me to make publik this iourney: one to reproue lying fooles I never knew; the other to comend louing friends which by the way I daily found; the third to shew my duety to your honorable self, whose favuor (among other bountiful friends) makes me (dispight of this sad world) iudge my hart Corke and my heeles feathers.

Here, then, we have a fact which seems to me to have an important bearing upon Mr. Tyler's theory as to the identity of Mrs. Fitton with the dark lady of the Sonnets. She is evidently well acquainted with the members of the Lord Chamberlain's company, since the clown and "jig-maker" of the company can speak of the favours he has received from her, and gladly places his book under the "protection" of her name. That she herself possessed dramatic talent we infer from what is said in Whyte's letter to Sidney. Writing a description of the masque acted before the Queen on the occasion of the marriage of Lady Ann Russell, who had been one of the maids of honour, he says that "Mrs. Fitton leade." She

took the leading character in the masque, personating *Affection.* . . . Mrs. Fitton's dramatic talent also stood her in some stead, "when" (as Brooke writes to Dudley Carleton) "she was in favour and a maid of honour; and, when the Earl of Pembroke favoured her," she would at that time assume a disguise "and march out of court like a man to meet him."

What more likely, then, than that she should establish friendly relationships with the members of the Royal Company of Comedians? And if one in the position of Will Kemp could write to her as he does, and could dedicate to her a book of such a character as the *Nine daies Wonder,* how much more probable is it that Shakspere, who held a very superior position in every way to that occupied by Kemp, should be received by her to a still closer degree of intimacy. (p. 10)

W. A. Harrison, "The Dark Lady of Shakespere's Sonnets and Mistress Mary Fitton," in The Academy, *Vol. XXVI, No. 635, July 5, 1884, pp. 9-10.*

J. O. HALLIWELL-PHILLIPPS   (essay date 1887)

[*A nineteenth-century English bibliophile and scholar, Halliwell-Phillipps was the first to make extensive use of town records from Stratford in the study of Shakespeare's life and work. In the excerpt below, he explores the question of whether the sonnets are markedly autobiographical, concluding that the poems are not self-revelatory. There are "abundant difficulties arising from the reception of" an autobiographical theory, he remarks, most notably that "the victim of spiritual emotions that involve criminatory reflections does not usually protrude them voluntarily on the consideration of society." With regard to the composition date, Halliwell-Phillipps suggests that some of the sonnets were written "in clusters," while others were "separate exercises," written for his friends' albums. He further states that "Mr. W. H." of Thomas Thorpe's 1609 Quarto dedication was the person who helped Thorpe acquire the sonnets manuscript.*]

It is in the *Palladis Tamia,* 1598, that we first hear of those remarkable productions, the Sonnets [see excerpt above, 1598]. "As the soul of Euphorbus," observes Meres in that quaint collection of similitudes, "was thought to live in Pythagoras, so the sweet witty soul of Ovid lives in mellifluous and honey-tongued Shakespeare; witness his *Venus and Adonis,* his *Lucrece,* his sugared Sonnets among his private friends, &c." These last-mentioned dainty poems were clearly not then intended for general circulation, and even transcripts of a few were obtainable with difficulty. A publisher named Jaggard who, in the following year, 1599, attempted to form a collection of new Shakespearean poems, did not manage to obtain more than two of the Sonnets. The words of Meres, and the insignificant result of Jaggard's efforts, when viewed in connexion with the nature of these strange poems, lead to the inference that some of them were written in clusters, and others as separate exercises, either being contributions made by their writer to the albums of his friends, probably no two of the latter being favoured with identical compositions. There was no tradition adverse to a belief in their fragmentary character in the generation immediately following the author's death, as may be gathered from the arrangement found in Benson's edition of 1640; and this concludes the little real evidence on the subject that has descended to us. It was reserved for the students of the present century, who have ascertained so much respecting Shakespeare that was unsuspected by his own friends and contemporaries, to discover that his innermost earnest thoughts, his mental conflicts, and so on, are revealed in what would then be the most powerful lyrics yet given to the world. But the victim of spiritual emotions that involve criminatory reflections does not usually protrude them voluntarily on the consideration of society; and, if the personal theory be accepted, we must concede the possibility of our national dramatist gratuitously confessing his sins and revealing those of others, proclaiming his disgrace and avowing his repentance, in poetical circulars distributed by the delinquent himself amongst his most intimate friends.

There are no external testimonies of any description in favour of a personal application of the Sonnets, while there are abundant difficulties arising from the reception of such a theory. Amongst the latter is one deserving of special notice, for its investigation will tend to remove the displeasing interpretation all but universally given of two of the poems, those in which reference is supposed to be made to a bitter feeling of personal degradation allowed by Shakespeare to result from his connection with the stage. Is it conceivable that a man who encouraged a sentiment of this nature, one which must have been accompanied with a distaste and contempt for his profession, would have remained an actor years and years after any real necessity for such a course had expired? By the spring of 1602 at the latest, if not previously, he had acquired a secure and definite competence independently of his emoluments as a dramatist, and yet, eight years afterwards, in 1610, he is discovered playing in company with Burbage and Hemmings at the Blackfriars Theatre. When, in addition to this voluntary long continuance on the boards, we bear in mind the vivid interest in the stage, and in the purity of the acted drama, which is exhibited in the well-known dialogue in *Hamlet,* and that the poet's last wishes included affectionate recollections of three of his fellow-players, it is difficult to believe that he could have nourished a real antipathy to his lower vocation. It is, on the contrary, to be inferred that, however greatly he may have deplored the unfortunate estimation in which the stage was held by the immense majority of his countrymen, he himself entertained a love for it that was too sincere to be repressed by contemporary disdain. If there is, amongst the defective records of the poet's life, one feature demanding special respect, it is the unflinching courage with which, notwithstanding his desire for social position, he braved public opinion in favour of a continued adherence to that which he felt was in itself a noble profession, and this at a time when it was not merely despised, but surrounded by an aggressive fanaticism that prohibited its exercise even in his own native town.

These considerations may suffice to eliminate a personal application from the two sonnets above mentioned, and as to the remainder, if the only safe method, that of discarding all mere assumptions, be strictly followed, the clearer the ideality of most of them, and the futility of arguments resting on any other basis, will be perceived. It will be observed that all the hypotheses, which aim at a complete biographical exposition of the Sonnets, necessitate the acceptance of interpretations that are too subtle for dispassionate reasoners. Even in the few instances where there is a reasonable possibility that Shakespeare was thinking of living individuals, as when he refers to an unknown poetical rival or quibbles on his own Christian name, scarcely any, if any, light is thrown on his personal feelings or character. In the latter case, it is a mere assumption that the second Will is the youth of the opening series, or, at least, that position cannot be sustained without tortuous interpretations of much which is found in the interval. With respect to other suggested personal revelations,

such as those which are thought to be chronicled in Shakespeare's addresses to the dark-eyed beauty of more than questionable reputation,—unless, with a criminal indifference to the risk of the scandal travelling to the ears of his family, he had desired to proclaim to his acquaintances his own infidelity and folly,—he might, perhaps, have repeated the words of the author of *Licia,* who published his own sonnets in the year 1593, and thus writes of their probable effects,—"for the matter of love, it may bee I am so devoted to some one, into whose hands these may light by chance, that she may say, which thou nowe saiest, that surelie he is in love, which if she doe, then have I the full recompence of my labour, and the poems have dealt sufficientlie for the discharge of their owne duetie." The disguise of the ideal under the personal was then, indeed, an ordinary expedient. (pp. 173-76)

· · · · ·

The spring of the year 1609 is remarkable in literary history for the appearance of one of the most singular volumes that ever issued from the press. It was entered at Stationers' Hall on May the 20th, and published by one Thomas Thorpe under the title of—"Shake-speares Sonnets, neuer before imprinted,"—the first two words being given in large capitals, so that they might attract their full share of public notice. This little book, a very small quarto of forty leaves, was sold at what would now be considered the trifling price of five-pence. The exact manner in which these sonnets were acquired for publication remains a mystery, but it is most probable that they obtained from one of the poet's intimate friends, who alone would be likely to have copies, not only of so many of those pieces but also one of the *Lover's Complaint.* However that may be, Thorpe,—the well-wishing *adventurer,*—was so elated with the opportunity of entering into the speculation that he dedicated the work to the factor in the acquisition, one Mr. W. H., in language of hyperbolical gratitude, wishing him every happiness and an eternity, the latter in terms which are altogether inexplicable. The surname of the addressee, which has not been recorded, has been the subject of numerous futile conjectures; but the use of initials in the place of names, especially if they referred to private individuals, was then so extremely common that it is not necessary to assume that there was an intentional reservation. (pp. 226-27)

J. O. Halliwell-Phillipps, in an excerpt in his Outlines of the Life of Shakespeare, Vol. I, *seventh edition, Longmans, Green, and Co., 1887, pp. 173-76, 226-27.*

OSCAR WILDE (essay date 1889)

[Perhaps more than any other author of his time, Wilde is identified with the nineteenth-century "art for art's sake" movement, which defied the contemporary trend that subordinated art to ethical instruction. This credo of aestheticism, however, indicates only one facet of a man notorious for resisting any public institution—artistic, social, or political—that attempted to downplay individual will and imagination. In opposition to the traditional cult of nature, Wilde posed a cult of art in his critical essays and reviews. To socialism's cult of the masses, he proposed a cult of the individual in "The Soul of Man under Socialism" and other works; and in opposition to what he perceived as a middle-class facade of false respectability, he encouraged a struggle to realize one's true nature. In the following excerpt from an essay generally regarded as an important contribution to the study of Shakespeare's sonnets, Wilde considers the identity of the Friend. By way of a fictional sketch,

he proposes the theory that "W. H." is William Hughes, a boy-actor in Shakespeare's company during the years of the sonnets who, because of his appealing youth and beauty and his compelling acting ability, became a supreme source of inspiration for Shakespeare and an embodiment of the poet's dramatic ideals. After encountering this theory through a friend, who himself no longer believes in it, Wilde's narrator attempts to verify its accuracy. After an initial period of optimism, the narrator, too, abandons the hypothesis as absurd. Although the correlation of Mr. W. H. with William Hughes or "Hewes" had been suggested as early as 1780 by Edmond Malone, Wilde was the first to propose that the Friend was a boy-actor in Shakespeare's employment and the earliest to interpret many of the sonnets in the light of this possibility.]

I had been dining with Erskine in his pretty little house in Birdcage Walk, and we were sitting in the library over our coffee and cigarettes, when the question of literary forgeries happened to turn up in conversation. I cannot at present remember how it was that we struck upon this somewhat curious topic, as it was at that time, but I know we had a long discussion about Macpherson, Ireland, and Chatterton, and that with regard to the last I insisted that his so-called forgeries were merely the result of an artistic desire for perfect representation; that we had no right to quarrel with an artist for the conditions under which he chooses to present his work; and that all Art being to a certain degree a mode of acting, an attempt to realise one's own personality on some imaginative plane out of reach of the trammelling accidents and limitations of real life, to censure an artist for a forgery was to confuse an ethical with an aesthetical problem.

Erskine, who was a good deal older than I was, and had been listening to me with the amused deference of a man of forty, suddenly put his hand upon my shoulder and said to me, "What would you say about a young man who had a strange theory about a certain work of art, believed in his theory, and committed a forgery in order to prove it?"

"Ah! that is quite a different matter," I answered.

Erskine remained silent for a few moments, looking at the thin grey threads of smoke that were rising from his cigarette. "Yes," he said, after a pause, "quite different."

There was something in the tone of his voice, a slight touch of bitterness perhaps, that excited my curiosity. "Did you ever know anybody who did that ?" I cried.

"Yes," he answered, throwing his cigarette into the fire—"a great friend of mine, Cyril Graham. He was very fascinating, and very foolish, and very heartless. However, he left me the only legacy I ever received in my life."

"What was that?" I exclaimed. Erskine rose from his seat, and going over to a tall inlaid cabinet that stood between the two windows, unlocked it, and came back to where I was sitting, holding in his hand a small panel picture set in an old and somewhat tarnished Elizabethan frame.

It was a full-length portrait of a young man in late sixteenth-century costume, standing by a table, with his right hand resting on an open book. He seemed about seventeen years of age, and was of quite extraordinary personal beauty, though evidently somewhat effeminate. Indeed, had it not been for the dress and the closely cropped hair, one would have said that the face, with its dreamy, wistful eyes and its delicate scarlet lips, was the face of a girl. In manner, and especially in the treatment of the hands, the picture reminded one of François Clouet's later work. The black velvet doublet with its fantastically gilded points, and the peacock-blue background against which it showed up so pleasantly, and from which it gained such luminous value of colour, were quite in Clouet's style; and the two masks of Tragedy and Comedy that hung somewhat formally from the marble pedestal had that hard severity of touch—so different from the facile grace of the Italians—which even at the Court of France the great Flemish master never completely lost, and which in itself has always been a characteristic of the northern temper.

"It is a charming thing," I cried, "but who is this wonderful young man whose beauty Art has so happily preserved for us?"

"This is the portrait of Mr W. H.," said Erskine, with a sad smile. It might have been a chance effect of light, but it seemed to me that his eyes were quite bright with tears.

"Mr W. H.!" I exclaimed; "who was Mr W. H.?"

"Don't you remember?" he answered; "look at the book on which his hand is resting."

"I see there is some writing there, but I cannot make it out," I replied.

"Take this magnifying-glass and try," said Erskine, with the same sad smile still playing about his mouth.

I took the glass, and moving the lamp a little nearer, I began to spell out the crabbed sixteenth-century handwriting. "To The Onlie Begetter Of These Insuing Sonnets." . . . "Good heavens!" I cried, "is this Shakespeare's Mr W. H.?"

"Cyril Graham used to say so," muttered Erskine.

"But it is not a bit like Lord Pembroke," I answered. "I know the Penshurst portraits very well. I was staying near there a few weeks ago."

"Do you really believe then that the Sonnets are addressed to Lord Pembroke?" he asked.

"I am sure of it," I answered. "Pembroke, Shakespeare, and Mrs. Mary Fitton are the three personages of the Sonnets; there is no doubt at all about it."

"Well, I agree with you," said Erskine, "but I did not always think so. I used to believe—well, I supposed I used to believe in Cyril Graham and his theory."

"And what was that?" I asked, looking at the wonderful portrait, which had already begun to have a strange fascination for me.

"It is a long story," said Erskine, taking the picture away from me—rather abruptly I thought at the time—"a very long story; but if you care to hear it, I will tell it to you."

"I love theories about the Sonnets," I cried; "but I don't think I am likely to be converted to any new idea. The matter has ceased to be a mystery to any one. Indeed, I wonder that it ever was a mystery."

"As I don't believe in the theory, I am not likely to convert you to it," said Erskine, laughing; "but it may interest you."

"Tell it to me, of course," I answered. "If it is half as delightful as the picture, I shall be more than satisfied."

"Well," said Erskine, lighting a cigarette, "I must begin by telling you about Cyril Graham himself. He and I were at the same house at Eton. I was a year or two older than he was, but we were immense friends, and did all our work and all our play together. There was, of course, a good deal more play than work, but I cannot say that I am sorry for that. . . . I should tell you that Cyril's father and mother were both dead. They had been drowned in a horrible yachting accident off the Isle of Wight. His father had been in the diplomatic service, and had married a daughter, the only daughter, in fact, of old Lord Crediton, who became Cyril's guardian after the death of his parents. I don't think that Lord Crediton cared very much for Cyril. He had never really forgiven his daughter for marrying a man who had no title. He was an extraordinary old aristocrat, who swore like a costermonger, and had the manners of a farmer. . . . Cyril had very little affection for him, and was only too glad to spend most of his holidays with us in Scotland. They never really got on together at all. Cyril thought him a bear, and he thought Cyril effeminate. He was effeminate, I suppose, in some things, though he was a very good rider and a capital fencer. In fact he got the foils before he left Eton. . . . [But the] two things that really gave him pleasure were poetry and acting. At Eton he was always dressing up and reciting Shakespeare, and when we went up to Trinity he became a member of the A.D.C. his first term. I remember I was always very jealous of his acting. I was absurdly devoted to him; I suppose because we were so different in some things. . . . I think he was the most splendid creature I ever saw, and nothing could exceed the grace of his movements, the charm of his manner. He fascinated everybody who was worth fascinating, and a great many people who were not. He was often wilful and petulant, and I used to think him dreadfully insincere. It was due, I think, chiefly to his inordinate desire to please. Poor Cyril! I told him once that he was contented with very cheap triumphs, but he only laughed. He was horribly spoiled. All charming people, I fancy, are spoiled. It is the secret of their attraction. (pp. 1-4)

"Well, to come to the real point of the story, one day I got a letter from Cyril asking me to come round to his rooms that evening. He had charming chambers in Piccadilly overlooking the Green Park, and as I used to go to see him almost every day, I was rather surprised at his taking the trouble to write. Of course I went, and when I arrived I found him in a state of great excitement. He told me that he had at last discovered the true secret of Shakespeare's Sonnets; that all the scholars and critics had been entirely on the wrong tack; and that he was the first who, working purely by internal evidence, had found out who Mr W. H. really was. He was perfectly wild with delight, and for a long time would not tell me his theory. Finally, he produced a bundle of notes, took his copy of the Sonnets off the mantelpiece, and sat down and gave me a long lecture on the whole subject.

"He began by pointing out that the young man to whom Shakespeare addressed these strangely passionate poems must have been somebody who was a really vital factor in the development of his dramatic art, and that this could not be said of either Lord Pembroke or Lord Southampton. Indeed, whoever he was, he could not have been anybody of high birth, as was shown very clearly by the 25th Sonnet, in which Shakespeare contrasts himself with those who are 'great princes' favourites'; says quite frankly—

> Let those who are in favour with their stars
> Of public honour and proud titles boast,
> Whilst I, whom fortune of such triumph bars,

> Unlooked for joy in that I honour most;

and ends the sonnet by congratulating himself on the mean state of him he so adored:

> Then happy I, that love and am beloved
> Where I may not remove nor be removed

This sonnet Cyril declared would be quite unintelligible if we fancied that it was addressed to either the Earl of Pembroke or the Earl of Southampton, both of whom were men of the highest position in England and fully entitled to be called 'great princes'; and he in corroboration of his view read me Sonnets CXXIV and CXXV, in which Shakespeare tells us that his love is not 'the child of state,' that it 'suffers not in smiling pomp,' but is 'builded far from accident.' I listened with a good deal of interest, for I don't think the point had ever been made before; but what followed was still more curious, and seemed to me at the time to entirely dispose of Pembroke's claim. We know from Meres that the Sonnets had been written before 1598, and Sonnet CIV informs us that Shakespeare's friendship for Mr W. H. had been already in existence for three years. Now Lord Pembroke, who was born in 1580, did not come to London till he was eighteen years of age, that is to say till 1598, and Shakespeare's acquaintance with Mr W. H. must have begun in 1594, or at the latest in 1595. Shakespeare, accordingly, could not have known Lord Pembroke until after the Sonnets had been written.

"Cyril pointed out also that Pembroke's father did not die until 1601; whereas it was evident from the line,

> You had a father, let your son say so,
>
> [Sonnet 13]

that the father of Mr W. H. was dead in 1598. Besides it was absurd to imagine that any publisher of the time, and the preface is from the publisher's hand, would have ventured to address William Herbert, Earl of Pembroke, as Mr W. H. . . . So far for Lord Pembroke, whose supposed claims Cyril easily demolished while I sat by in wonder. With Lord Southampton Cyril had even less difficulty. Southampton became at a very early age the lover of Elizabeth Vernon, so he needed no entreaties to marry; he was not beautiful; he did not resemble his mother, as Mr W. H. did—

> Thou art thy mother's glass, and she in thee
> Calls back the lovely April of her prime;
>
> [Sonnet 3]

and, above all, his Christian name was Henry, whereas the punning sonnets (CXXXV and CXLIII) show that the Christian name of Shakespeare's friend was the same as his own—*Will.*

"As for the other suggestions of unfortunate commentators, that Mr W. H. is a misprint of Mr W. S., meaning Mr William Shakespeare; that 'Mr W. H. all' should be read 'Mr W. Hall'; that Mr W. H. is Mr William Hathaway; and that a full stop should be placed after 'wisheth,' making Mr W. H. the writer and not the subject of the dedication,—Cyril got rid of them in a very short time; and it is not worth while to mention his reasons, though I remember he sent me off into a fit of laughter by reading to me, I am glad to say not in the original, some extracts from a German commentator called Barnstorff, who insisted that Mr W. H. was no less a person than 'Mr William Himself' [see excerpt above, 1860]. Nor would he allow for a moment that the Sonnets are mere satires on the work of Drayton and John Davies of Hereford. To him, as indeed to me, they were poems of serious and tragic import, wrung out of the bitterness of Shakespeare's heart, and made sweet by the honey of his lips. Still less would he admit that they were merely a philosophical allegory, and that in them Shakespeare is addressing his Ideal Self, or Ideal Manhood, or the Spirit of Beauty, or the Reason, or the Divine Logos, or the Catholic Church. He felt, as indeed I think we all must feel, that the Sonnets are addressed to an individual,—to a particular young man whose personality for some reason seems to have filled the soul of Shakespeare with terrible joy and no less terrible despair.

"Having in this manner cleared the way, as it were, Cyril asked me to dismiss from my mind any preconceived ideas I might have formed on the subject, and to give a fair and unbiased hearing to his own theory. The problem he pointed out was this: Who was that young man of Shakespeare's day who, without being of noble birth or even of noble nature, was addressed by him in terms of such passionate adoration that we can but wonder at the strange worship, and are almost afraid to turn the key that unlocks the mystery of the poet's heart? Who was he whose physical beauty was such that it became the very corner-stone of Shakespeare's art; the very source of Shakespeare's inspiration; the very incarnation of Shakespeare's dreams? To look upon him as simply the object of certain love-poems was to miss the whole meaning of the poems: for the art of which Shakespeare talks in the Sonnets is not the art of the Sonnets themselves, which indeed were to him but slight and secret things—it is the art of the dramatist to which he is always alluding; and he to whom Shakespeare said—

> Thou art all my art, and dost advance
> As high as learning my rude ignorance,—
>
> [Sonnet 78]

he to whom he promised immortality,

> Where breath most breathes, even in the mouths of
>   men,—
>
> [Sonnet 81]

was surely none other than the boy-actor for whom he created Viola and Imogen, Juliet and Rosalind, Portia and Desdemona, and Cleopatra herself." This was Cyril Graham's theory, evolved as you see purely from the Sonnets themselves, and depending for its acceptance not so much on demonstrable proof or formal evidence, but on a kind of spiritual and artistic sense, by which alone he claimed could the true meaning of the poems be discerned. (pp. 4-6)

"It is of course evident that there must have been in Shakespeare's company some wonderful boy-actor of great beauty, to whom he intrusted the presentation of his noble heroines; for Shakespeare was a practical theatrical manager as well as an imaginative poet; and Cyril Graham had actually discovered the boy-actor's name. He was Will, or, as he preferred to call him, Willie Hughes. The Christian name he found of course in the punning sonnets, CXXXV and CXLIII; the surname was, according to him, hidden in the seventh line of Sonnet XX, where Mr W. H. is described as—

> A man in hew, all *Hews* in his controwling.

"In the original edition of the Sonnets 'Hews' is printed with a capital letter and in italics, and this, he claimed, showed clearly that a play on words was intended, his view receiving a good deal of corroboration from those sonnets in which curious puns are made on the words 'use' and 'usury'. Of course I was converted at once, and Willie Hughes became to me as

real a person as Shakespeare. The only objection I made to the theory was that the name of Willie Hughes does not occur in the list of the actors of Shakespeare's company as it is printed in the first folio. Cyril, however, pointed out that the absence of Willie Hughes' name from this list really corroborated the theory, as it was evident from Sonnet LXXXVI, that Willie Hughes had abandoned Shakespeare's company to play at a rival theatre, probably in some of Chapman's plays. It was in reference to this that in the great sonnet on Chapman Shakespeare said to Willie Hughes—

> But when your countenance filled up his line,
> Then lacked I matter; that enfeebled mine—

the expression 'when your countenance filled up his line' referring obviously to the beauty of the young actor giving life and reality and added charm to Chapman's verse, the same idea being also put forward in the 79th Sonnet—

> Whilst I alone did call upon thy aid,
> My verse alone had all thy gentle grace,
> But now my gracious numbers are decayed,
> And my sick Muse doth give another place. . . .
>
> (p. 7)

"It was a wonderful evening, and we sat up almost till dawn reading and re-reading the Sonnets. After some time, however, I began to see that before the theory could be placed before the world in a really perfected form, it was necessary to get some independent evidence about the existence of this young actor, Willie Hughes. If this could be once established, there could be no possible doubt about his identity with Mr W. H.; but otherwise the theory would fall to the ground. I put this forward very strongly to Cyril, who was a good deal annoyed at what he called my philistine tone of mind, and indeed was rather bitter upon the subject. However, I made him promise that in his own interest he would not publish his discovery till he had put the whole matter beyond the reach of doubt; and for weeks and weeks we searched the registers of City churches, the Alleyn MSS. at Dulwich, the Record Office, the papers of the Lord Chamberlain—everything, in fact, that we thought might contain some allusion to Willie Hughes. We discovered nothing, of course, and every day the existence of Willie Hughes seemed to me to become more problematical. Cyril was in a dreadful state, and used to go over the whole question day after day, entreating me to believe; but I saw the one flaw in the theory, and I refused to be convinced till the actual existence of Willie Hughes, a boy-actor of Elizabethan days, had been placed beyond the reach of doubt or cavil.

"One day Cyril left town to stay with his grandfather, I thought at the time, but I afterwards heard from Lord Crediton that this was not the case; and about a fortnight afterwards I received a telegram from him, handed in at Warwick, asking me to be sure to come and dine with him that evening at eight o'clock. When I arrived, he said to me, 'The only apostle who did not deserve proof was S. Thomas, and S. Thomas was the only apostle who got it.' I asked him what he meant. He answered that he had not merely been able to establish the existence in the sixteenth century of a boy-actor of the name of Willie Hughes, but to prove by the most conclusive evidence that he was the Mr W. H. of the Sonnets. He would not tell me anything more at the time; but after dinner he solemnly produced the picture I showed you, and told me that he had discovered it by the merest chance nailed to the side of an old chest that he had bought at a farmhouse in Warwickshire. The chest itself, which was a very fine example of Elizabethan work, he had, of course, brought with him, and in the centre of the front panel the initials W. H. were undoubtedly carved. It was this monogram that had attracted his attention, and he told me that it was not till he had had the chest in his possession for several days that he had thought of making any careful examination of the inside. One morning, however, he saw that one of the sides of the chest was much thicker than the other, and looking more closely, he discovered that a framed picture was clamped against it. On taking it out, he found it was the picture that is now lying on the sofa. It was very dirty, and covered with mould; but he managed to clean it, and, to his great joy, saw that he had fallen by mere chance on the one thing for which he had been looking. Here was an authentic portrait of Mr W. H. with his hand resting on the dedicatory page of the Sonnets, and on the frame itself could be faintly seen the name of the young man written in black uncial letters on a faded gold ground, 'Master Will. Hews.'

"Well, what was I to say? It never occurred to me for a moment that Cyril Graham was playing a trick on me, or that he was trying to prove his theory by means of a forgery."

"But is it a forgery?" I asked.

"Of course it is," said Erskine. "It is a very good forgery; but it is a forgery none the less. I thought at the time that Cyril was rather calm about the whole matter; but I remember he more than once told me that he himself required no proof of the kind, and that he thought the theory complete without it. I laughed at him, and told him that without it the theory would fall to the ground, and I warmly congratulated him on the marvellous discovery. We then arranged that the picture should be etched or facsimiled, and placed as the frontispiece to Cyril's edition of the Sonnets; and for three months we did nothing but go over each poem line by line, till we had settled every difficulty of text or meaning. One unlucky day I was in a print-shop in Holborn, when I saw upon the counter some extremely beautiful drawings in silver-point. I was so attracted by them that I bought them; and the proprietor of the place, a man called Rawlings, told me that they were done by a young painter of the name of Edward Merton, who was very clever, but as poor as a church mouse. I went to see Merton some days afterwards, having got his address from the print-seller, and found a pale, interesting young man, with a rather common-looking wife,—his model, as I subsequently learned. I told him how much I admired his drawings, at which he seemed very pleased, and I asked him if he would show me some of his other work. As we were looking over a portfolio, full of really very lovely things,—for Merton had a most delicate and delightful touch,—I suddenly caught sight of a drawing of the picture of Mr W. H. There was no doubt whatever about it. It was almost a facsimile,—the only difference being that the two masks of Tragedy and Comedy were not suspended from the marble table as they are in the picture but were lying on the floor at the young man's feet. 'Where on earth did you get that?' I said. He grew rather confused, and said,—'Oh, that is nothing. I did not know it was in this portfolio. It is not a thing of any value.' 'It is what you did for Mr Cyril Graham,' exclaimed his wife; 'and if this gentleman wishes to buy it, let him have it.' 'For Mr Cyril Graham?' I repeated. 'Did you paint the picture of Mr W. H.?' 'I don't understand what you mean,' he answered growing very red. Well, the whole thing was quite dreadful. The wife let it all out. I gave her five pounds when I was going away. I can't bear to think of it, now; but of course I was furious. I went off at once to Cyril's chambers, waited there for

three hours before he came in, with that horrid lie staring me in the face, and told him I had discovered his forgery. He grew very pale, and said,—'I did it purely for your sake. You would not be convinced in any other way. It does not affect the truth of the theory.' 'The truth of the theory!' I exclaimed; 'the less we talk about that the better. You never even believed in it yourself. If you had, you would not have committed a forgery to prove it.' High words passed between us; we had a fearful quarrel. I daresay I was unjust, and the next morning he was dead.'

"Dead!" I cried.

"Yes, he shot himself with a revolver. Some of the blood splashed upon the frame of the picture, just where the name had been painted. By the time I arrived,—his servant had sent for me at once,—the police were already there. He had left a letter for me, evidently written in the greatest agitation and distress of mind."

"What was in it?" I asked.

"Oh, that he believed absolutely in Willie Hughes; that the forgery of the picture had been done simply as a concession to me, and did not in the slightest degree invalidate the truth of the theory; and that in order to show me how firm and flawless his faith in the whole thing was, he was going to offer his life as a sacrifice to the secret of the Sonnets. It was a foolish, mad letter. I remember he ended by saying that he intrusted to me the Willie Hughes theory, and that it was for me to present it to the world, and to unlock the secret of Shakespeare's heart."

"It is a most tragic story," I cried, "but why have you not carried out his wishes?"

Erskine shrugged his shoulders. "Because it is a perfectly unsound theory from beginning to end," he answered.

"My dear Erskine," I said, getting up from my seat, "you are entirely wrong about the whole matter. It is the only perfect key to Shakespeare's Sonnets that has ever been made. It is complete in every detail. I believe in Willie Hughes."

"Don't say that," said Erskine, gravely; "I believe there is something fatal about the idea, and intellectually there is nothing to be said for it. I have gone into the whole matter, and I assure you the theory is entirely fallacious. It is plausible up to a certain point. Then it stops. For heaven's sake, my dear boy, don't take up the subject of Willie Hughes. You will break your heart over it."

"Erskine," I answered, "it is your duty to give this theory to the world. If you will not do it, I will. By keeping it back you wrong the memory of Cyril Graham, the youngest and the most splendid of all the martyrs of literature. I entreat you to do him justice. He died for this thing,—don't let his death be in vain."

Erskine looked at me in amazement. "You are carried away by the sentiment of the whole story," he said. "You forget that a thing is not necessarily true because a man dies for it. I was devoted to Cyril Graham. His death was a horrible blow to me. I did not recover it for years. I don't think I have ever recovered it. But Willie Hughes! There is nothing in the idea of Willie Hughes. No such person ever existed. As for bringing the whole thing before the world,—the world thinks that Cyril Graham shot himself by accident. The only proof of his suicide was contained in the letter to me, and of this letter the public never heard anything. To the present day Lord Crediton thinks that the whole thing was accidental."

"Cyril Graham sacrificed his life to a great idea," I answered; "and if you will not tell of his martyrdom, tell at least of his faith."

"His faith," said Erskine, "was fixed in a thing that was false, in a thing that was unsound, in a thing that no Shakespearian scholar would accept for a moment. The theory would be laughed at. Don't make a fool of yourself, and don't follow a trail that leads nowhere. You start by assuming the existence of the very person whose existence is the thing to be proved. Besides, everybody knows that the Sonnets were addressed to Lord Pembroke. The matter is settled once for all."

"The matter is not settled," I exclaimed. "I will take up the theory where Cyril Graham left it, and I will prove to the world that he was right."

"Silly boy!" said Erskine. "Go home, it is after two, and don't think about Willie Hughes any more. I am sorry I told you anything about it, and very sorry indeed that I should have converted you to a thing in which I don't believe."

"You have given me the key to the greatest mystery of modern literature," I answered; "and I shall not rest till I have made you recognise, till I have made everybody recognise, that Cyril Graham was the most subtle Shakespearian critic of our day."

As I walked home through St. James's Park, the dawn was just breaking over London. The swans were lying asleep on the smooth surface of the polished lake, like white feathers fallen upon a mirror of black steel. The gaunt Palace looked purple against the pale green sky, and in the garden of Stafford House the birds were just beginning to sing. I thought of Cyril Graham, and my eyes filled with tears.

It was past twelve o'clock when I awoke, and the sun was streaming in through the curtains of my room in long slanting beams of dusty gold. I told my servant that I would be at home to no one; and after I had had a cup of chocolate and a *petit-pain,* I took down from the book-shelf my copy of Shakespeare's Sonnets, and began to go carefully through them. Every poem seemed to me to corroborate Cyril Graham's theory. I felt as if I had my hand upon Shakespeare's heart, and was counting each separate throb and pulse of passion. I thought of the wonderful boy-actor, and saw his face in every line.

Two sonnets, I remember, struck me particularly: they were the 53rd and the 67th. In the first of these, Shakespeare, complimenting Willie Hughes on the versatility of his acting, on his wide range of parts, a range extending from Rosalind to Juliet, and from Beatrice to Ophelia, says to him:—

> What is your substance, whereof are you made?
> That millions of strange shadows on you tend?
> Since everyone hath, every one, one shade,
> And you, but one, can every shadow lend—

lines that would be unintelligible if they were not addressed to an actor, for the word "shadow" had in Shakespeare's day a technical meaning connected with the stage. . . . These sonnets evidently belonged to the series in which Shakespeare discusses the nature of the actor's art, and of the strange and rare temperament that is essential to the perfect stage-player. "How is it," says Shakespeare to Willie Hughes, "that you

have so many personalities?" and then he goes on to point out that his beauty is such that it seems to realise every form and phase of fancy, to embody each dream of the creative imagination,—an idea that is still further expanded in the sonnet that immediately follows, where, beginning with the fine thought,

> O, how much more doth beauty beauteous seem
> By that sweet ornament which *truth* doth give!
>
> [Sonnet 54]

Shakespeare invites us to notice how the truth of acting, the truth of visible presentation on the stage, adds to the wonder of poetry, giving life to its loveliness, and actual reality to its ideal form. And yet, in the 67th Sonnet, Shakespeare calls upon Willie Hughes to abandon the stage with its artificiality, its false mimic life of painted face and unreal costume, its immoral influences and suggestions, its remoteness from the true world of noble action and sincere utterance. . . . It may seem strange that so great a dramatist as Shakespeare, who realised his own perfection as an artist and his humanity as a man on the ideal plane of stage-writing and stage-playing, should have written in these terms about the theatre; but we must remember that in Sonnets CX and CXI, Shakespeare shows us that he too was wearied of the world of puppets, and full of shame at having made himself "a motley to the view." (pp. 8-12)

One point puzzled me immensely as I read the Sonnets, and it was days before I struck on the true interpretation, which indeed Cyril Graham himself seems to have missed. I could not understand how it was that Shakespeare set so high a value on his young friend marrying. He himself had married young and the result had been unhappiness, and it was not likely that he would have asked Willie Hughes to commit the same error. The boy-player of Rosalind had nothing to gain from marriage, or from the passions of real life. The early sonnets with their strange entreaties to have children seemed to be a jarring note.

The explanation of the mystery came on me quite suddenly and I found it in the curious dedication. (p. 12)

Some scholars have supposed that the word "begetter" in this dedication means simply the procurer of the Sonnets for Thomas Thorpe the publisher; but this view is now generally abandoned, and the highest authorities are quite agreed that it is to be taken in the sense of inspirer, the metaphor being drawn from the analogy of physical life. Now I saw that the same metaphor was used by Shakespeare himself all through the poems, and this set me on the right track. Finally I made my great discovery. The marriage that Shakespeare proposes for Willie Hughes is the "marriage with his Muse," an expression which is definitely put forward in the 82d Sonnet, where, in the bitterness of his heart at the defection of the boy-actor for whom he had written his greatest parts, and whose beauty had indeed suggested them, he opens his complaint by saying—

> I grant thou wert not married to my Muse.

The children he begs him to beget are no children of flesh and blood, but more immortal children of undying fame. The whole cycle of the early sonnets is simply Shakespeare's invitation to Willie Hughes to go upon the stage and become a player. (p. 13)

I collected together all the passages that seemed to me to corroborate this view, and they produced a strong impression on me, and showed me how complete Cyril Graham's theory really was. I also saw that it was quite easy to separate those lines in which he speaks of the Sonnets themselves from those in which he speaks of his great dramatic work. This was a point that had been entirely overlooked by all critics up to Cyril Graham's day. And yet it was one of the most important points in the whole series of poems. To the Sonnets Shakespeare was more or less indifferent. He did not wish to rest his fame on them. They were to him his "slight Muse," as he calls them, and intended, as Meres tells us, for private circulation only among a few, a very few, friends. Upon the other hand he was extremely conscious of the high artistic value of his plays, and shows a noble self-reliance upon his dramatic genius. When he says to Willie Hughes:

> But thy eternal summer shall not fade,
> Nor lose possession of that fair thou owest;
> Nor shall Death brag thou wander'st in his shade,
> When in *eternal lines* to time thou growest:
> So long as men can breathe or eyes can see,
> So long lives this and this gives life to thee;—
>
> [Sonnet 18]

the expression "eternal lines" clearly alludes to one of his plays that he was sending him at the time, just as the concluding couplet points to his confidence in the probability of his plays being always acted. . . . It is, however, perhaps in the 55th Sonnet that Shakespeare gives to this idea its fullest expression. To imagine that the "powerful rhyme" of the second line refers to the sonnet itself is to entirely mistake Shakespeare's meaning. It seemed to me that it was extremely likely, from the general character of the sonnet, that a particular play was meant, and that the play was none other but "Romeo and Juliet."

> Not marble, nor the gilded monuments
> Of princes shall outlive this powerful rhyme;
> But you shall shine more bright in these contents
> Than unswept stone besmeared with sluttish time.
> When wasteful war shall statues overturn,
> And broils root out the work of masonry,
> Not Mars his sword nor war's quick fire shall burn
> The living record of your memory
> 'Gainst death and all-oblivious enmity
> Shall you pace forth; your praise shall still find
>   room
> Even in the eyes of all posterity
> That wear this world out to the ending doom.
> So, till the judgment that yourself arise,
> You live in this, and dwell in lovers' eyes.

It was also extremely suggestive to note how here as elsewhere Shakespeare promised Willie Hughes immortality in a form that appealed to men's eyes—that is to say, in a spectacular form, in a play that is to be looked at.

For two weeks I worked hard at the Sonnets, hardly ever going out, and refusing all invitations. Every day I seemed to be discovering something new, and Willie Hughes became to me a kind of spiritual presence, an ever-dominant personality. I could almost fancy that I saw him standing in the shadow of my room, so well had Shakespeare drawn him, with his golden hair, his tender flower-like grace, his dreamy deep-sunken eyes, his delicate mobile limbs, and his white lily hands. His very name fascinated me. Willie Hughes! Willie Hughes! How musically it sounded! Yes; who else but he could have been the master-mistress of Shakespeare's passion, the lord of his love to whom he was bound in vassalage,

the delicate minion of pleasure, the rose of the whole world, the herald of the spring, decked in the proud livery of youth, the lovely boy whom it was sweet music to hear, and whose beauty was the very raiment of Shakespeare's heart, as it was the keystone of his dramatic power? (pp. 13-15)

After three weeks had elapsed, I determined to make a strong appeal to Erskine to do justice to the memory of Cyril Graham, and to give to the world his marvellous interpretation of the Sonnets—the only interpretation that thoroughly explained the problem. I have not any copy of my letter, I regret to say, nor have I been able to lay my hand upon the original; but I remember that I went over the whole ground, and covered sheets of paper with passionate reiteration of the arguments and proofs that my study had suggested to me. It seemed to me that I was not merely restoring Cyril Graham to his proper place in literary history, but rescuing the honour of Shakespeare himself from the tedious memory of a common-place intrigue. I put into the letter all my enthusiasm. I put into the letter all my faith.

No sooner, in fact, had I sent it off than a curious reaction came over me. It seemed to me that I had given away my capacity for belief in the Willie Hughes theory of the Sonnets, that something had gone out of me, as it were, and that I was perfectly indifferent to the whole subject. What was it that had happened? It is difficult to say. Perhaps, by finding perfect expression for a passion, I had exhausted the passion itself. . . . Perhaps I was simply tired of the whole thing, and, my enthusiasm having burnt out, my reason was left to its own unimpassioned judgment. However it came about, and I cannot pretend to explain it, there was no doubt that Willie Hughes suddenly became to me a mere myth, an idle dream, the boyish fancy of a young man who, like most ardent spirits, was more anxious to convince others than to be himself convinced.

As I had said some very unjust and bitter things to Erskine in my letter, I determined to go and see him at once, and to make my apologies to him for my behaviour. Accordingly, the next morning I drove down to Birdcage Walk, and found Erskine sitting in his library, with the forged picture of Willie Hughes in front of him.

"My dear Erskine!" I cried, "I have come to apologise to you."

"To apologise to me?" he said. "What for?"

"For my letter," I answered.

"You have nothing to regret in your letter," he said. "On the contrary, you have done me the greatest service in your power. You have shown me that Cyril Graham's theory is perfectly sound."

"You don't mean to say that you believe in Willie Hughes?" I exclaimed.

"Why not?" he rejoined. "You have proved the thing to me. Do you think I cannot estimate the value of evidence?"

"But there is no evidence at all," I groaned, sinking into a chair. "When I wrote to you I was under the influence of a perfectly silly enthusiasm. I had been touched by the story of Cyril Graham's death, fascinated by his artistic theory, enthralled by the wonder and novelty of the whole idea. I see now that the theory is based on a delusion. The only evidence for the existence of Willie Hughes is that picture in front of you, and the picture is a forgery. Don't be carried away by mere sentiment in this matter. Whatever romance may have to say about the Willie Hughes theory, reason is dead against it."

"I don't understand you," said Erskine, looking at me in amazement. "Why, you yourself have convinced me by your letter that Willie Hughes is an absolute reality. Why have you changed your mind? Or is all that you have been saying to me merely a joke?"

"I cannot explain it to you," I rejoined, "but I see now that there is really nothing to be said in favour of Cyril Graham's interpretation. The Sonnets are addressed to Lord Pembroke. For heaven's sake don't waste your time in a foolish attempt to discover a young Elizabethan actor who never existed, and to make a phantom puppet the centre of the great cycle of Shakespeare's Sonnets."

"I see that you don't understand the theory," he replied.

"My dear Erskine," I cried, "not understand it! Why, I feel as if I had invented it. Surely my letter shows you that I not merely went into the whole matter, but that I contributed proofs of every kind. The one flaw in the theory is that it pre-supposes the existence of the person whose existence is the subject of dispute. If we grant that there was in Shakespeare's company a young actor of the name of Willie Hughes, it is not difficult to make him the object of the Sonnets. But as we know that there was no actor of this name in the company of the Globe Theatre, it is idle to pursue the investigation fur-ther."

"But that is exactly what we don't know," said Erskine. "It is quite true that his name does not occur in the list given in the first folio; but, as Cyril pointed out, that is rather a proof in favour of the existence of Willie Hughes than against it, if we remember his treacherous desertion of Shakespeare for a rival dramatist."

We argued the matter over for hours, but nothing that I could say could make Erskine surrender his faith in Cyril Graham's interpretation. He told me that he intended to devote his life to proving the theory, and that he was determined to do jus-tice to Cyril Graham's memory. I entreated him, laughed at him, begged of him, but it was of no use. Finally we parted, not exactly in anger, but certainly with a shadow between us. He thought me shallow, I thought him foolish. When I called on him again, his servant told me that he had gone to Germa-ny.

Two years afterwards, as I was going into my club, the hall porter handed me a letter with a foreign postmark. It was from Erskine, and written at the Hôtel d'Angleterre, Cannes. When I had read it, I was filled with horror, though I did not quite believe that he would be so mad as to carry his resolve into execution. The gist of the letter was that he had tried in every way to verify the Willie Hughes theory, and had failed, and that as Cyril Graham had given his life for this theory, he himself had determined to give his own life also to the same cause. The concluding words of the letter were these: "I still believe in Willie Hughes; and by the time you receive this I shall have died by my own hand for Willie Hughes' sake: for his sake, and for the sake of Cyril Graham, whom I drove to his death by my shallow scepticism and ignorant lack of faith. The truth was once revealed to you, and you re-jected it. It comes to you now, stained with the blood of two lives.—do not turn away from it."

It was a horrible moment. I felt sick with misery, and yet I could not believe it. To die for one's theological beliefs is the worst use a man can make of his life; but to die for a literary theory! It seemed impossible.

I looked at the date. The letter was a week old. Some unfortu-nate chance had prevented my going to the club for several days, or I might have got it in time to save him. Perhaps it was not too late. I drove off to my rooms, packed up my things, and started by the night mail from Charing Cross. The journey was intolerable. I thought I would never arrive.

As soon as I did, I drove to the Hôtel d'Angleterre. It was quite true. Erskine was dead. They told me that Erskine had been buried two days before in the English cemetery. There was something horribly grotesque about the whole tragedy. I said all kinds of wild things, and the people in the hall looked curiously at me.

Suddenly Lady Erskine, in deep mourning, passed across the vestibule. When she saw me she came up to me, murmured something about her poor son, and burst into tears. I led her into her sitting room. An elderly gentleman was there, read-ing a newspaper. It was the English doctor.

We talked a great deal about Erskine, but I said nothing about his motive for committing suicide. It was evident that he had not told his mother anything about the reason that had driven him to so fatal, so mad an act. Finally Lady Er-skine rose and said, "George left you something as a memen-to. It was a thing he prized very much. I will get it for you."

As soon as she had left the room I turned to the doctor and said, "What a dreadful shock it must have been for Lady Er-skine! I wonder that she bears it as well as she does."

"Oh, she knew for months past that it was coming," he an-swered.

"Knew it for months past!" I cried. "But why didn't she stop him? Why didn't she have him watched? He must have been mad."

The doctor stared at me. "I don't know what you mean," he said.

"Well," I cried, "if a mother knows that her son is going to commit suicide—"

"Suicide!" he answered. "Poor Erskine did not commit sui-cide. He died of consumption. He came here to die. The mo-ment I saw him I knew that there was no hope. One lung was almost gone, and the other was very much affected. Three days before he died he asked me was there any hope. I told him frankly that there was none, and that he had only a few days to live. He wrote some letters, and was quite resigned, retaining his senses to the last."

At that moment Lady Erskine returned to the room carrying the fatal portrait of Willie Hughes. "When George was dying, he begged me to give you this," she said. As I took it from her, her tears fell on my hand.

The picture hangs now in my library, where it is very much admired by my artistic friends. They have decided that it is not a Clouet, but an Ouvry. I have never cared to tell them its true history, but sometimes, when I look at it, I think there is really a great deal to be said for the Willie Hughes theory of Shakespeare's Sonnets. (pp. 18-21)

Oscar Wilde, "The Portrait of Mr. W. H.," in Blackwood's Edinburgh Magazine, *Vol. CXLVI, No. 885, July 19, 1889. pp. 1-21.*

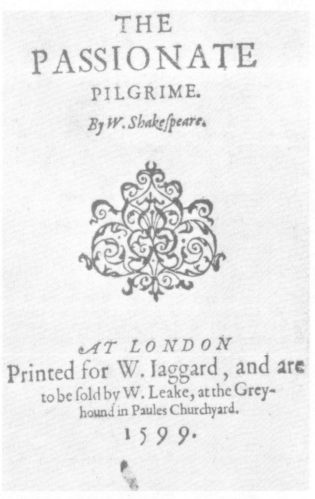

THE PASSIONATE PILGRIME.

By W. Shakespeare.

AT LONDON
Printed for W. Iaggard, and are to be fold by W. Leake, at the Greyhound in Paules Churchyard.
1599.

Title page of William Jaggard's collection, The Passionate Pilgrim *(1599).*

THOMAS TYLER   (essay date 1890)

[Tyler was a nineteenth-century English Shakespearean scholar who is credited with being the first to develop at length the theory that the Dark Lady of the sonnets is Mary Fitton. In the following excerpt, he treats four discrete topics. He begins by considering the arrangement of the 1609 Quarto, pointing to the thematic integrity of various groups of sonnets and concluding that the Quarto order is legitimate. Next, Tyler comments on the autobiographical basis of the poems. maintaining that the sonnets are grounded on fact and asserting that "the incidents alluded to cannot be conceived as fictions." Thirdly, Tyler raises the issue of the identity of the Friend, judging against Henry Wriothesley, Earl of Southampton. Instead, he supports William Herbert, Earl of Pembroke, as the most likely candidate, citing numerous correspondences between recorded events in Herbert's life and allusions in the sonnets. Lastly, Tyler proposes his theory identifying Mary Fitton, a maid of honor in Queen Elizabeth's Court, as the Dark Lady of the sonnets. He cites as evidence Fitton's documented scandalous affair with Pembroke, her physical attributes—which closely correspond with Shakespeare's description of his mistress in Son-

nets 127-52—and her known acquaintances with members of Shakespeare's dramatic troupe, especially Will Kempe.]

[Are Shakespeare's] Sonnets, as a whole, arranged in due order and in chronological sequence? In answer to this question it may be said, that if . . . some portions are duly arranged, this will render it to some extent probable that the case is the same with the whole collection. But here it should be observed that the Sonnets are to be divided into two, or, perhaps still better, into three series. By far the larger proportion, 1 to 126, are addressed to an intimate male friend of the poet, a youth high-born, and wealthy, and beautiful. 127 to 152 are concerned mainly with a certain lady of dark complexion, the poet's mistress. Then there remain the last two Sonnets in the collection, 153 and 154, which have a character of their own. The question as to the order of arrangement is, however, chiefly of importance with respect to the first series, 1 to 126. . . . [It] may be observed that the collection begins with seventeen Sonnets urging on the poet's friend the duty and desirableness of perpetuating his beauty in offspring. The Sonnets concerned with this subject are found together, not scattered promiscuously throughout the entire number—a fact which at once suggests the idea of arrangement. Then we observe that, although in one of these first Sonnets the poet, complying with old custom, addresses his friend as "love" (13), yet, on the whole, the language employed does not express an affection so warm and intimate as that which manifests itself in some of the Sonnets which follow. We remark, also, that, even in these first Sonnets, there are traces of a melancholic view of the world. Youth and beauty are fleeting. Life's golden summer must give place to "hideous winter." Old age creeps on with stealthy tread, disfiguring the glory of manhood with bareness and with wrinkles. Time's remorseless scythe will level all. But melancholy thus expressed appears but mild when compared with what is to follow. By and by the gloom will deepen into pessimistic darkness. The poet, wearied with the world and its perversities, will cry out for "restful death" (66). Manifestly, when this occurs, an exhortation to marry and beget offspring will have become incongruous. Further evidence of due order and arrangement is furnished by a number of Sonnets relating to another poet, a rival, or supposed rival, for the friend's favour. The apprehension of rivalry is at first ambiguously expressed [Sonnet 75], then . . . more and more openly adverted to, till in 86 there is a scarcely doubtful designation of the person intended. In 87, Shakespeare, not having succeeded in ousting his rival, bids his friend farewell. Thus, that the Sonnets relating to the rival poet are in the right order seems scarcely open to question. And considering that we have to do with poetical epistles, no valid objection is furnished by the fact that in 77 and 81 the poet glances aside for a moment from this subject. Such divergence would be quite suitable in a letter. There is a somewhat similar series, though not unbroken, concerned with an offence against the poet committed by his friend. Here again there appears no reason to conclude that the order in which the Sonnets are found is not the order of composition. But in connection with this . . . view it is unnecessary to adduce further evidence. The burden of proof lies on those who object to the order in which the Sonnets were first printed. It is for them to show that the order thus given is not the right order. (pp. 5-7)

• • • • •

[It] is neither from beauty and sweetness, nor majestic strength, that the Sonnets derive their chief attractiveness.

Rather . . . must we attribute the keen interest with which they are investigated to the hope of gaining some additional knowledge with regard to Shakespeare and his surroundings, or of making a nearer approach to the poet's personality. But are the Sonnets concerned with actual facts? Are they not rather to be regarded as mere exercises in verse? If this question could be answered in the affirmative, still the interest and value of the Sonnets would be great, as showing the themes on which Shakespeare elected to discourse. But that any competent critic should have looked on the Sonnets as mere exercises in verse can scarcely be other than surprising. The intensity of feeling which they display is not to be mistaken, and the incidents alluded to cannot be conceived of as fictions. Are we to suppose Shakespeare urging in seventeen Sonnets an ideal youth to beget ideal offspring? Then, as to the incident alluded to in the 40th and various other Sonnets, is it in the least degree probable that the poet speaks of a purely imaginary offence and grievance? Or, if this be thought not incredible, take the Sonnets relating to the rival poet. . . . Fortunately it has become possible to indicate the person actually intended. But if this had not been the case, the evidence of jealous feeling would have been sufficiently clear. It has been suggested, however, that though in relation to the first series of Sonnets the evidence of fact and reality is not to be denied, yet the case is otherwise with the later Sonnets concerned with the dark lady (127 to 152). In all probability this suggestion had its origin in the wish to free Shakespeare's moral character from certain possible imputations. But however commendable the motive, such a view must be rejected. The impress of reality is stamped on these Sonnets with unmistakable clearness; and besides, several of them are linked indissolubly to the first series (as 40 to 144). We must therefore maintain—whatever may be the consequences resulting from this position—that the Sonnets as a whole are concerned with actual fact. At the same time we must beware of treating them as though they were mere prosaic history. Their language is the language of poetry, sometimes of compliment, and as such it should certainly be interpreted. (pp. 10-11)

• • • • •

THE suggestion has been made that Shakespeare's friend in the Sonnets, Mr. W. H., was the Earl of Southampton, the patron to whom the poet had dedicated his *Venus and Adonis* and *Lucrece*. But the difficulties which stand in the way of our accepting this suggestion are altogether insuperable. It is scarcely to be doubted that the W. of W. H. represents William. The evidence of the punning Sonnets, 135, 136, 143, is not easily to be set aside: the "Will" of these Sonnets is too emphatic. Southampton's name, however, was not William, but Henry. If, however, we could pass by this not inconsiderable difficulty, and could go so far as to suppose that, for the purpose of disguise, the order of the initials was inverted, and that W. H. really represents H. W., that is, Henry Wriothesley, Earl of Southampton, still the [chronology of the sonnets] will compel us altogether to reject the suggestion. Shakespeare's acquaintance with Lord Southampton dates, not from 1598, but at least from 1593, the date of the *Venus and Adonis*, when Southampton was nineteen. Then in 1601, our date for Sonnets 100 to 126, Southampton would be quite past the age when he could be addressed as "lovely boy" (126), or when he would feel complimented by being told that his "sweet self" resembled "cherubins" (114). It would be superfluous, therefore, to attempt to show the inapplicability to Southampton of the first seventeen Sonnets and of various other particulars, including that personal beauty which Shakespeare so highly extolled. We must conclude, then, that Mr. W. H. was certainly not the Earl of Southampton. (pp. 28-9)

[But then who] was "Mr. W. H."? The only answer, of any probability on other grounds, which has been given to this question identifies Mr. W. H. with William Herbert, who became Earl of Pembroke on the death of his father in the January of 1601 (according to our reckoning). To William Herbert, together with his brother Philip, "the most noble and incomparable paire of brethren," was dedicated the First Folio edition of Shakespeare's Plays in 1623, by Shakespeare's friends and fellows, Heminge and Condell. The personal acquaintance with Shakespeare of the noblemen just mentioned is clearly implied when it is said that they had "prosequnted" [prosecuted] both the Plays "and their Authour liuing with so much fauour." (p. 44)

William Herbert was born on April 8, 1580, and thus he completed his eighteenth year in 1598. It was in the spring of the year just named that, according to Rowland Whyte, William Herbert was to commence residing permanently in London. Here, however, it must be observed that a fact in Herbert's history of great importance with regard to the Sonnets was discovered in 1884 by the Rev. W. A. Harrison [see excerpt above, 1884]. The fact to which I allude removes pretty completely the difficulty with regard to Shakespeare's urging marriage so strongly on a youth of eighteen (Sonnets 1 to 17). From letters preserved in the Record Office it appears that in 1597 the parents of William Herbert were engaged in negotiations for his marriage to Bridget Vere, daughter of the Earl of Oxford, and granddaughter of the great Lord Burleigh. . . . Both the Earl and Countess of Pembroke wrote to Lord Burleigh on August 16, 1597, expressing their satisfaction at the intended match. William Herbert, it would seem, had an agreeable meeting with the young lady (a damsel of thirteen); and the Countess finds that her son's feelings accord with her own wishes. . . . On September 8 the Earl of Oxford, the father of the young lady, expresses his approval of the match, and says that the young gentleman has good parts, and has been well brought up. He thinks that Lord Pembroke, on account of his state of health, is anxious to see his son suitably married. Why the match was broken off does not appear. Probably William Herbert backed out of it after all. This view accords with what is said in Sonnet 40, line 8, of Mr. W. H.'s "refusing:"—

> By wilful taste of what thyself refusest.

But, whatever view may be taken of this allusion, with the facts just adverted to before us, there can be no difficulty in the exhortations of Sonnets 1 to 17, as addressed to a youth only eighteen years old. And the idea that the Countess, William Herbert's mother, had something to do with these Sonnets being written gains increased credibility from the correspondence. Whether William Herbert came up to London in the October of 1597, or whether . . . he began to reside in town in the spring of 1598, there are apparently no adequate grounds for deciding. It is sufficient for our argument if the spring of 1598 was the time when he first saw Shakespeare. In accordance with what has been already said, he would then be eighteen, an age entirely suitable to his being spoken of as in the "April" of his life (3, line 10), and to such expressions being used concerning him as those which are to be found in the first Sonnet (lines 9 to 12), "the world's *fresh* ornament," "herald to the gaudy *spring*," "thine own *bud*," "*tender* churl." On coming to London, Herbert would no doubt live at Baynard's Castle, south of St. Paul's, and on the bank of the Thames. Now Baynard's Castle was very near indeed to the Blackfriars Theatre, and there is at least a possibility that in some way in connection with this theatre Herbert might have become acquainted with Shakespeare. The intervention of the Countess of Pembroke seems, however, more probable, especially if the allusions in the 3rd Sonnet are considered, allusions agreeing with the well-known personal beauty of the Countess:—

> Thou art thy mother's glass, and she in thee
> Calls back the lovely April of her prime.

Anxious that her son should marry, and the trouble she had taken in 1597 having been . . . resultless, she may in consequence have suggested to Shakespeare the writing of the first seventeen Sonnets. That she should extend her patronage to Shakespeare is likely enough. The sister of Sir Philip Sidney, and herself a lady of literary taste, she may well have been an admirer of the great genius now approaching its fullest maturity. . . . The Countess would probably come to London with her son; but, having regard to the fact that her husband the Earl was suffering from serious disease, it may very well have occurred that he remained in the country, and that Shakespeare was not brought into personal contact with him. . . . Thus, in Shakespeare's being personally unacquainted with Herbert's father some explanation is given of the words of [Sonnet] 13, "You had a father;" and it certainly becomes more easy to understand that these words do not imply, as some have thought, that the father of the person addressed was dead. This sense would be here tame and out of place. It is safe to assert that the words in question must be interpreted in accordance with the drift and scope of these first Sonnets. The person addressed is exhorted to do as his father did, namely, beget a son:—

> Dear my love, you know
> You had a father; let your son say so.

And it may be seen on reflection that, with reference to the sense intended, it would have been less suitable for Shakespeare to write, "You *have* a father; let your son say so." We are not left, however, to follow merely an inference of this kind. Shakespeare has used elsewhere [*The Merry Wives of Windsor*, III. iv. 36-7] a strictly analogous expression, "She's coming; to her, coz: O boy, *thou hadst a father*." Shallow thus urges Slender to woo Anne Page in manly fashion. Slender, however, misunderstands the meaning, and in consequence makes himself ridiculous:—"I had a father, Mistress Anne; my uncle can tell you good jests of him" [III. iv. 38-9]. But, in misunderstanding the words in question, he gives them precisely the sense some have contended for in the Sonnet. In both cases, however, the intention is to exhort to manly conduct, though with an obvious difference of detail.

There [is no evidence] to tell us what William Herbert was doing in the year 1598. According to our chronology, however, it was in all probability during this year that he was concerned in the affair to which the 40th and other Sonnets relate. Herbert's part therein is quite in accordance with the picture drawn of him by Lord Clarendon in his *History of the Rebellion:*—"He was immoderately given up to women. But therein he retained such a power and jurisdiction over his very appetite, that he was not so much transported with beauty and outward allurements, as with those advantages of the mind as manifested an extraordinary wit, and spirit, and

knowledge, and administered great pleasure in the conversation. To these he sacrificed himself, his precious time, and much of his fortune." What is here said refers, no doubt, wholly or chiefly to Herbert's more mature years, but his being fascinated in the fair sex by other endowments rather than personal attractions would accord completely with his becoming enamoured of Shakespeare's dark mistress, if what Shakespeare himself says concerning this lady is to be regarded. (pp. 44-51)

With regard to the personal beauty of William Herbert, such portraits as we possess would scarcely justify those exceedingly warm eulogies in which Shakespeare indulged. But these portraits, so far as I am aware, represent Herbert in mature life, of the age probably of forty or more, when the beauty of youth would have passed away. We should remember the prediction of Shakespeare himself:—

> When forty winters shall besiege thy brow,
> And dig deep trenches in thy beauty's field,
> Thy youth's proud livery, so gaz'd on now,
> Will be a tatter'd weed, of small worth held.
>
> [Sonnet 2]

William Herbert's mother was certainly beautiful; and it is probable enough that this beauty would be inherited by her son. . . . There need not, thus, be any difficulty in admitting the probability that William Herbert was as a youth exceedingly handsome, though, under any circumstances, the poetical and complimentary character of the Sonnets would have to be borne in mind.

The social position of William Herbert and the high rank of his family would suit well the allusions to "so fair a house" in [Sonnet] 13, to his "birth" and "wealth" in [Sonnet] 37, and to the great difference between the station of the poet and that of his friend; a difference preventing public recognition of the acquaintance:—

> I may not ever-more acknowledge thee,
> Lest my bewailed guilt should do thee shame,
> Nor thou with public kindness honour me,
> Unless thou take that honour from thy name.
>
> [Sonnet 36]

The amiability of Shakespeare's friend is not only expressly stated, but is implied also in the poet's deep love. Of Pembroke, Clarendon asserts that he "was the most universally beloved and esteemed of any man of that age." (pp. 70-1)

A much smaller amount of evidence than that which has been adduced would raise a probability that William Herbert was the favoured friend of Shakespeare. But if, keeping always in view the Dedication of 1623, the reader takes into account the multitude of accordant particulars which have been indicated, he can scarcely avoid the conclusion that probability has become changed into certainty. (p. 72)

• • • • •

As the first series of [Shakespeare's] Sonnets (1 to 126) is mainly occupied with a young male friend . . . , and with the relations subsisting between this friend and the poet, so the second series (127 to 152) is chiefly concerned with a certain dark lady, between whom and Shakespeare there was evidently a very close intimacy. This lady was a brunette of strongly marked type, destitute of the characteristics of beauty most highly valued in Shakespeare's time. The poet could note in her "a thousand errors:"—

My mistress' eyes are nothing like the sun;
Coral is far more red than her lips' red:
If snow be white, why then her breasts are dun;
If hairs be wires, black wires grow on her head.
I have seen roses damask'd, red and white,
But no such roses see I in her cheeks.

She had not even—so it would seem—the charm of a soft and melodious voice:—

I love to hear her speak,—yet well I know
That music hath a far more pleasing sound.

[Sonnet 130]

She was, moreover, of blemished character. She could not be satisfied with the attentions of the poet, though she professed fidelity (137, 138, 152). Yet to Shakespeare her looks were "pretty looks" (139); and he could disregard even the blackness of her deeds (131). Though she was abhorred by others (150), her attraction was to him so irresistible as to overpower both his eyes and his reason. He became mad with love:—

My thoughts and my discourse as mad men's are
At random from the truth vainly express'd;
For I have sworn thee fair, and thought thee bright,
Who art as black as hell, as dark as night.

[Sonnet 147]

What, then, was the cause of her thus dominating over Shakespeare's soul? . . . Some answer is afforded by the repeated mention of the lady's raven-black, quick-glancing eyes (127, 139). Shakespeare loved those eyes:—

Thine eyes I love, and they, as pitying me,
Knowing thy heart torments me with disdain,
Have put on black, and loving mourners be,
Looking with pretty ruth upon my pain.
And truly not the morning sun of heaven
Better becomes the gray cheeks of the east,
Nor that full star that ushers in the even,
Doth half that glory to the sober west,
As those two mourning eyes become thy face.

[Sonnet 132]

Then, again, Shakespeare evidently loved music; and she was skilled in touching the virginal. He was spell-bound as he listened to "the wiry concord," and saw the "jacks" dance and leap, swayed by her gentle fingers (128). She was a woman of quick wit, and she had full command of her powers. She could woo without causing disgust, or so use disdain as to quicken desire. Thus, such was her tact and "warrantise of skill" (150), that she knew well, not only how to ensnare, but how to retain the prize she had won. Probably to such endowments she added superior social rank. This may be implied in her skill as a player on the virginal. It is not at all likely that such an accomplishment, in the time of Elizabeth, would be so common as the pianoforte-playing of our own days. A conclusion similar to that drawn from her musical skill may be inferred also from her soft and tender hands (128). And it is in accordance with other indications that Shakespeare speaks of her as his "triumphant prize" and himself as "proud of this pride" (151).

Here, however, the question may suggest itself, Is it possible to identify the dark lady of the Sonnets with any person otherwise known? Identifying Shakespeare's friend Mr. W. H. with William Herbert, we must come to the conclusion that William Herbert had amatory relations with the dark lady. Contemporary notices . . . show that he had amatory rela-

tions with Mrs. Mary Fitton. This fact may make it not incredible that the one is to be identified with the other. There is certainly a remarkable similarity of characteristics. In both we may see strong passions conjoined with an imperious, masterful will. The dark lady of the Sonnets has been compared with Cleopatra. Thus Professor Dowden:—"May we dare to conjecture that Cleopatra, queen and courtesan, black from 'Phoebus' amorous pinches,' a 'lass unparalleled,' has some kinship through the imagination with the dark lady of the virginal?" And the queenly, commanding qualities of Mrs. Fitton are not to be mistaken. Her character, in its "strength," (150, line 7) resembles that of her royal mistress [Queen Elizabeth], who declared, "I have the heart of a king, and of a king of England too." . . . That a lady endowed with characteristics such as those of Mrs. Fitton should become notorious is what we might expect. . . . This [impression] . . . is entirely in accordance with what is said in the Sonnets concerning the dark lady's conduct to both the poet and his young friend. With regard to the latter, she is described as "wooing" him (41, 144), and as "running after him." "So run'st thou after that which flies from thee" (143, line 9). And Shakespeare tells the dark lady that it would be unwise for her to say anything about his "amiss" lest he should be tempted to show that her "sweet self" was guilty of his "faults," and that she had betrayed him into sin (151). Shakespeare's "amiss" and his being "forsworn" (152) resulted, we may presume, from his having already a wife, who was living probably at Stratford-on-Avon.

We are not able to connect Mrs. Fitton personally with Shakespeare by proof as direct as that which, in the case of Herbert, is furnished by the Dedication of the First Folio. The Rev. W. A. Harrison, however, some time ago called attention to evidence which brings Mrs. Fitton into connection with a member of Shakespeare's company, that is, the Lord Chamberlain's company, leaving it to be easily inferred that she must have been acquainted with the members of the company generally, and especially with such as were more prominent [see excerpt above, 1884]. In 1600 William Kemp, the clown in the company, dedicated his *Nine daies wonder* to "Mistris Anne Fitton, Mayde of Honour to most sacred Mayde, Royal Queene Elizabeth." The book gives an account of a journey which Kemp had performed, morris-dancing, from London to Norwich. . . . Mrs. Fitton's Christian name was given erroneously as "Anne." The error may have originated from Kemp not being well acquainted with Mrs. Fitton's Christian name. Perhaps, however, it is more probable that he wrote "Marie," a name which might be so written as to be easily mistaken for "Anne." But, however this may be, Elizabeth certainly had no maid of honour *Anne* Fitton in 1599 or 1600. It follows that the person intended by Kemp was the Mrs. Mary Fitton with whom we are at present concerned; and a good deal of light is thus thrown on her character. That one of the Queen's maids of honour should be chosen as the patroness of a publication of so comparatively frivolous a character as this of Kemp's might well seem surprising. But facts already adduced make this much less wonderful. Kemp, moreover, adopts a style of address which under ordinary circumstances might seem most unsuitable in writing publicly to a distinguished lady of the Court. . . . [He] gives as one of the objects he had in view in the publication, "To shew my duety to your honourable selfe, whose fauours (among other bountifull friends) make me (dispight this sad world) iudge my hert Corke and my heeles feathers, so that me thinkes I could fly to Rome (at least hop to Rome, as the olde Prouerb is) with a Morter on my head." These facts are interesting and important, and, even taken alone, they would go far towards removing the difficulty which might otherwise be felt about Shakespeare's forming a connection with a lady of so high rank as one of the Queen's maids of honour. (pp. 73-7)

What has just been said about Kemp and his dedication may easily suggest that, on Shakespeare's company performing at Court, Mrs. Fitton may have become interested in Shakespeare, either as the author of the play or otherwise, and so have introduced herself to him. A woman such as she was would scarcely find much difficulty about the introduction. This hypothesis agrees well with what is said in 151 about the dark lady being the cause of Shakespeare's fault. And then, with respect to Shakespeare's performing before the ladies of the Court, a very interesting and important piece of evidence must be adduced.

That there is a close analogy between a part of *Love's Labour's Lost* [IV. iii. 243ff.] and some lines in the Sonnets has been for a long while known. Mr. Gerald Massey alluded to the fact, though without satisfactorily accounting for it [see excerpt above, 1864]. Perhaps the best illustration may be given by placing together four lines from Sonnet 127 and four lines from the play:—

> Therefore my mistress' eyes are raven-black,
> Her eyes so suited, and they mourners seem,
> At such who, not born fair, no beauty lack,
> Slandering creation with a false esteem.
>
> [Sonnet 127]

> O, if in black my lady's brows be decked,
> It mourns that painting [and] usurping hair
> Should ravish doters with a false aspect,
> And therefore is she born to make black fair.
>
> [*Love's Labour's Lost*, IV. iii. 254-57]

Recently (1884) in the *Jahrbuch* of the German Shakespeare Society, Hermann Isaac asserted, with regard to the correspondences just adverted to, that the opinion "that the poet wrote the play a little after 1590, and then, towards the end of the century, took Sonnet 127 therefrom, is quite inconceivable. The only natural explanation is, that he at a certain time was inspired with so passionate a devotion to his brunette lady-love, that he not only celebrated her in his Sonnets, but also introduced her into his play as Rosaline, and had her praise expressed by Biron, his own dramatic representative. The passage in the play must have been written very soon after the Sonnet; but, possibly, the question might arise whether the Sonnet and the passage in the play belong to the time of the first composition of *Love's Labour's Lost*, 1591 or 1592, or to that of the re-editing of the play, about 1596." (pp. 78-9)

Now, since the title [of *Love's Labour's Lost*] bears the date 1598, it may be inferred with probability that the re-editing took place either in this year or in that next preceding. Moreover, it is very important that the play is given "as it was presented before her Highnes this last Christmas." "Her Highness" was the Queen, who would see the play, accompanied by the ladies of the Court. Mrs. Fitton would thus probably be one of the spectators; and, if she was the lady celebrated in the second series of Sonnets, it is not difficult to account for the remarkable agreement between the Sonnets and the Play. Shakespeare, we may infer, designed a special allusion to her in the description of Rosaline, just as, in what is said

of the Princess, there are probably some things which he intended specially for the Queen. . . . (p. 80)

The numerous particulars in the Sonnets which thus agree with what we know from other sources concerning Mrs. Fitton make the argument identifying her with the "dark lady" very cogent indeed, even if we have not—what the Dedication to the First Folio gives us in the case of Herbert—direct external testimony to the existence of personal relations between Mrs. Fitton and Shakespeare. On the whole, however, the evidence concerning Mrs. Fitton can scarcely be looked upon as less decisive. (p. 92)

> *Thomas Tyler, in an introduction to* Shakespeare's Sonnets, *edited by Thomas Tyler, David Nutt, 1890, pp. 1-156.*

ROBERT SHINDLER   (essay date 1897)

[*Shindler disagrees with the assumption that Shakespeare's sonnets as presented in Thomas Thorpe's 1609 Quarto "form one organic whole, divisible into two distinct and coherent series," maintaining that this edition is undoubtedly illegitimate, published without Shakespeare's knowledge or authority. He cites in support of this claim the careless printing of the text of the Quarto; the rather embarrassing content of these poems, which Shakespeare never intended for public view; the internal evidence that the present collection is incomplete; and the even stronger evidence that the order of many of the sonnets is incorrect.*]

[I wish] to point out as briefly as may be a certain obliquity of vision which is common to most even of the sanest and soundest writers on the subject [of Shakespeare's Sonnets]. This is the assumption that the Sonnets as we have them form one organic whole, divisible into two distinct and coherent series. This assumption, tacit or expressed, underlies most of the interpretation of the Sonnets. (p. 73)

It is this view that I wish most distinctly to contravene. There is no external evidence for it whatever, and it stands, in my opinion, strongly in opposition to the indications of the Sonnets themselves. Certainly, no unprejudiced person will deny that there is a continuous story to be discovered in the book. Many of the Sonnets are plainly and evidently connected, and they tell their tale clearly enough. That Shakespeare had an enthusiastic friendship for some handsome youth of lofty lineage, that he cherished also some more earth-born kind of passion for a dark lady of doubtful character, and that both friend and mistress were faithless to the man who loved them—this tragedy of the affections is written down so plainly in some of the Sonnets that nothing but obdurate and wilful blindness can refuse to see it. This is clear enough; the error which most writers . . . fall into is to find some stage of this story everywhere, and to refer every single Sonnet either to the fair friend or the dark lady. Many Sonnets are certainly addressed either to the one or the other of this pair, others indubitably are not, and there are a great many whose reference is altogether uncertain.

The views which I am advocating may be briefly stated thus: The theory of two connected series of Sonnets arranged in chronological order must be abandoned, and each Sonnet left to tell its own story, irrespective of the number of its position in the Quarto of 1609. This was probably a pirated edition made during Shakespeare's absence from London, and without his consent or co-operation. The order of arrangement, though not purely at haphazard, is in no way authoritative.

The book may contain Sonnets not by Shakespeare, and it certainly does not include all that the poet had written prior to its publication.

Let us briefly examine what evidence can be adduced in support of these assertions.

First, then, we know that literary piracy was an art which had been discovered before the year 1609. The example of "The Passionate Pilgrim" shows that a publisher of the tribe of Barabbas could be found in London even in the seventeenth century, and the fact that Jaggard foisted all his stolen wares upon the public under Shakespeare's name makes it clear that, in the opinion of one publisher at least, Shakespeare's poems would find a ready sale. There is nothing at all improbable in the supposition that the "well-wishing adventurer," Thomas Thorpe, was, like Jaggard, a purveyor of stolen goods.

And we may, in the first place, point to the state of the text as evidence that the case was really so, or at least as evidence that Shakespeare gave no assistance in the production. The Quarto of 1609 is very carelessly printed, the punctuation is very irregular, and the bad spelling goes beyond even the large limits of Elizabethan license. In these respects it contrasts very unfavourably with "Venus and Adonis," which, as we know, was printed with the author's sanction. And besides the many typographical infelicities which might be pointed out, there are one or two places where the perverseness of the text goes deeper than those printer's errors which an author's careless eye might overlook, and points to an imperfect or undecipherable manuscript. (pp. 73-5)

But a stronger argument still for this view of unauthorised and unassisted publication is to be found in the character of many of the Sonnets. One can hardly read some of them, even cursorily, without feeling sure that Shakespeare never would have permitted their appearance, or have failed to prevent it had it been in his power.

For the story of these poems is not a pleasant one. Even at the present day the Sonnets are read with some misgiving—even now, when the name of Shakespeare has become too majestic and too dear for censure. "It is impossible," Hallam wrote, "not to wish that Shakespeare had never written them" [see excerpt above, 1837-39]. The vagaries of many of the commentators on the Sonnets are due to their wish to save the memory of Shakespeare from the scandal which these verses disclose. And if, at the present day, the Sonnets are spoken of with some hesitation, as if they needed apology or excuse, what could their effect have been on Shakespeare's contemporaries, who saw the great poet through no kindly mist of reverence? Would any prudent man have permitted the publication of what would inevitably damage his character? Would any sensible husband allow so plain a confession of unfaithfulness to appear in his wife's lifetime? And it must be remembered that the blame for his breach of morality is only part of what Shakespeare would have to face. We may take this first, because, though it might have been small enough with most men, with him it might have cut more deeply. The bitter tone of Sonnet 126 is evidence of how intensely the poet was pained by some floating accusations extant against him, accusations which he seems to have been too proud either to admit or deny. Again, Sonnet 146 comes out of the very deepest depths of remorse, and if we refer it to the "dark lady" series, it shows how very poignant Shakespeare's regret over this bad business actually was. And if this

were so, would he, a few years later, have brought, without any satisfactory motive, upon himself a certain amount of public obloquy about the same affair? (pp. 75-6)

I don't want to press this too far, for, as I have said, the condemnation of these moralists would only be a part of the business. Perhaps not many of his contemporaries would think much worse of him for a breach of his marriage vow. But I am afraid that to the great mass of them who bought and read the Quarto of 1609, Shakespeare must have appeared, if not criminal, ridiculous. A man whose friend has robbed him of his mistress does not generally want to announce the fact. Shakespeare showed sufficient common sense in all practical matters, and I don't think he would have held himself up to the derision even of stupid people. To all such it would seem a most evident sign of moral weakness that the offence against the poet moved him to grief, but stirred no longing for revenge, and that his love for his friend was stronger and deeper than his passion for his mistress. The distress of a noble nature is always an amusing spectacle to dull, commonplace people, whose troubles are of another order, and, when Thorpe published the Sonnets there were, no doubt, plenty of Philistines to make merry over their poor, pitiful story. But I cannot think that Shakespeare had any share in helping them to this ignoble pleasure. (pp. 76-7)

Taking all these considerations together, we may then, I think, safely conclude that all the Sonnets were published without Shakespeare's co-operation or consent, and that the Quarto of 1609 was a literary piracy to be classed with these "diverse, stolen, and surreptitious copies, maimed and deformed by the frauds and stealthes of injurious impostors that exposed them"—of which Heminge and Condell complain in the preface to the first Folio.

Let us, then, take this unauthorised publication as practically proved, and see what inferences naturally follow.

In the first place, there is the probability that we have a part, and perhaps only a small part, of all the Sonnets that Shakespeare wrote. As far back as 1598, Meres made his often quoted reference to Shakespeare's "sugared Sonnets among his private friends," and it is not at all likely that Thorpe managed to lay his thievish hands on all of them. One or two passages themselves may be cited which make it clear that he did not. Sonnet 115 begins—

> Those lines that I before have writ do lie,
> Even those that said I could not love thee dearer;

where we have a clear reference to some Sonnet (or other poem) not extant in our collection.

Again, in Sonnet 105 the poet admits that there is a monotony in his themes, that he has rung the changes too often on the three ideas of "fair, kind, and true." Now these complaints cannot be brought against the Sonnets of our collection, which are certainly not occupied with praising either the affection or fidelity of the person or persons addressed. We have, therefore, a clear indication that we have lost, not one Sonnet only, but a considerable number.

Then, on the other hand, it is possible that many of the Sonnets we have are not Shakespeare's. Jaggard had ten years before published a lot of miscellaneous poetry by various authors under Shakespeare's name; Thorpe may have supplied any deficiency of matter by giving the work of some other poet. The Quarto contains just eighty pages, which looks as if the amount of matter was adjusted for the convenience of the printer, so as not to extend or fall below an exact number of sheets. But though there is nothing at all improbable in supposing that Thorpe attributed to Shakespeare what was not Shakespeare's, yet I do not think there are many Sonnets which internal evidence would lead us to reject. Perhaps Sonnet 145 is the one we should condemn most readily, the metre being inferior and the workmanship inferior. And certainly one might be very glad to dissociate No. 151 from Shakespeare's name; it is not only obscene but sickly and nauseous, and may well have come from some other hand. The few other Sonnets which would have to be expelled from a Bowdlerised edition are not really repulsive in the same way, and their double meanings can be matched in the plays. But though it would be going too far to infer that Shakespeare did not write these Sonnets, it is hardly likely he would have wished to see them in print, and their presence in Thorpe's edition is another argument against Shakespeare's having had anything to do with its publication. (pp. 77-8)

[This] view of piratical publication is still more important in its bearing upon the order in which the Sonnets stand, and the question as to whether we may divide them into two series addressed each to one particular individual. On the latter point this much may be said.

Shakespeare wrote Sonnets to several people. This is clear from the evidence of Meres, for his words "Sonnets among his private friends" could hardly be referred to two individuals, one of whom was a woman. If the poet had published the Sonnets himself he might possibly have restricted his selection to the Sonnets addressed to one or other of these two people. But if Thorpe brought out the edition on his own account, it is not at all likely that he would limit his choice in the same way; he probably was glad to publish all he could lay hands on. And in fact, if we once accept the idea that the edition of 1609 was made without authority, we shall have no difficulty in seeing that there are several Sonnets which clearly do not belong to what we may call the main body, and more which probably do not. For example, Sonnets 26 and 116, different in themselves, are still more different from those which we can certainly refer to the "lovely boy," or the "dark lady." Sonnets 129 and 146, two of the finest we have, are not addressed to any person at all. The latter is a religious Sonnet, a kind of Lenten meditation which can hardly be connected in idea with the faithless mistress or the false friend.

And so with regard to the order in which the Sonnets stand; this hypothesis of piratical publication accounts for the confused arrangement which is perceptible even to the casual reader of the Sonnets. This disorder is not absolute chaos; there are signs of continuity, there are numbers which clearly stand together, but the breaks and gaps, the omissions and the wrong arrangements, are just as clear. And on the hypothesis I am maintaining the reason of this muddled state of things is obvious enough. Thorpe, left without any help from the author, could only print the Sonnets just as they stood on his MS. Those that, either in books or on sheets of paper, stood together he printed together, and so produced those traces of orderly arrangement which we see. The confusion which is equally evident was probably due, not only to his want of literary capacity, but also to the fact that he did not get possession of anything like all the Sonnets, and probably, too, to his ignorance as to the persons to whom the different numbers were addressed.

That there is plenty of confusion in the present order of the

Sonnets it will not be difficult to show, and the inquiry is all the more necessary because such an immense amount of ingenuity has been expended in trying to find some connection of ideas between them as they now stand. I will just cite from Professor Dowden a passage which will serve to show on what scanty and insufficient grounds the existing arrangement has been accepted. . . . "That the Sonnets are not printed in the Quarto, 1609, at haphazard is evident from the facts that the 'Envoy' (126) is rightly placed; that poems addressed to a mistress follow those addressed to a friend, and that the two Cupid and Dian Sonnets stand together at the close" [see Additional Bibliography].

Now, in reply to this it may be remarked, firstly, that the question is not one of absolute "haphazard." In whatever way the Sonnets were published, it would be very strange if there were no traces of consecutive arrangement. There is a very wide margin between complete chaos and an authoritative order. As to the "Envoy," it is sufficient to say that there are half a dozen Sonnets which might with equal fitness have stood in that place, and that Sonnet 126 itself might have come earlier without any inappropriateness. Neither is one certain of absolute correctness in saying that the "poems addressed to a mistress follow those addressed to a friend"; it is clear that after 126 there are no Sonnets to the friend, but not at all clear that among the earlier Sonnets there are none in honour of the mistress.

The two Cupid and Dian Sonnets are probably not by Shakespeare, but were thrown in to supply a deficiency of "copy" and fill up an exact number of sheets.

Now let me briefly point out some few instances of confused arrangement. One example might suffice; for the confusion of Sonnets 33-35 and 40-42 with 69, 70 ought to be enough of itself to show that the hypothesis of a single series chronologically arranged is altogether untenable.

In the earlier sequence the poet complains of the great outrage on friendship his friend has been guilty of, and further attempts to excuse the young man's general wantonness of disposition, concluding with a very fanciful and far-fetched apology for the especial and particular wrong which Shakespeare himself had suffered at his hands. On the contrary, the man to whom Nos. 69 and 70 are addressed is praised for his chaste character, and defended from the aspersion of misjudging slanderers.

> For canker vice the sweetest buds doth love,
>   And thou present'st a pure unstained prime.
> Thou hast pass'd by the ambush of young days,
>   Either not assail'd, or victor being charged;
> Yet this thy praise cannot be so thy praise,
>   To tie up envy evermore enlarged.
>
> [Sonnet 70]

It seems inconceivable that Shakespeare should write in this way to a man who had robbed him of his mistress. It is curious to notice that the first line I have quoted above is almost repeated from 35, "And loathsome canker lives in sweetest bud," though with an entire difference of meaning.

But it is perhaps in the interrupted sequences that we see the most striking instances of the want of proper arrangement. Thus the numbers referred to above, 33-35 and 40-42, form a closely connected sequence, but are separated by Sonnets entirely irrelevant.

Again, 39 probably, and certainly 26 and 27, belong to the

series of Absence Sonnets, which begins with 43 and con-cludes with 52, and the right position of the two latter is probably after 51. And this sequence, from 43 to 52, is rudely interrupted by 49, which is manifestly out of place. Sonnet 61, which is now isolated, seems to belong to this series and to be specially connected with 26 and 27.

Again, from 76 to 86 we have in the main what may be called the Rival Poet series. But in this sequence there are two irrelevant intrusions—77, which accompanied a present, evidently to some more distant friend than the "lovely boy," and 81, which is equally out of place.

When we come to the second division of the Sonnets—those which follow 126—the traces of order are fewer and we have almost utter chaos. The position of 129 is perhaps the most striking instance of the publisher's carelessness or inability; the tragic terror of this tremendous poem coming with the most absolute incongruity between two light and playful Sonnets might be enough of itself to mark the arbitrary character of the present arrangement. Again, in this latter series Nos. 143, 144 are plainly anterior to the sequence 133-135, which, chronologically, are the last of the Sonnets addressed to the "dark lady." For all the others are clearly prior to the discovery of her infidelity.

These arguments might be multiplied, but enough has, I think, been said to convince the unprejudiced that the arrangement of the Sonnets in the Quarto is unsatisfactory and unauthoritative. And this result is in exact agreement with the hypothesis of piratical publication which appears for other reasons so highly probable.

The practical outcome of these considerations is to discourage dogmatism and a too elaborate theorising. The materials at our disposal are too scanty; we shall have to be largely satisfied with negative results. Because, for example, we cannot accept the present order of the Sonnets, we shall not, therefore, feel called upon to propound a new one. For the same cause which makes the arrangement wrong, will prevent us from ever putting it right. Thorpe's collection was a stolen and surreptitious one, and it was therefore incomplete; and because it was incomplete, we cannot do much to mend its defects of arrangement. And as to the reference of particular Sonnets, the facts of Shakespeare's life are so little known that we can never be quite sure of anything, and in most cases even the more ingenious conjectures can hardly show a decent appearance of probability. The wisest course would seem to be to accept the Sonnets as they stand, and definitely to abandon a problem for the solution of which there are no sufficient data. (pp. 79-82)

> *Robert Shindler, "The Stolen Key," in* The Gentleman's Magazine, *Vol. CCLXXII, No. 1933, January, 1897, pp. 70-84.*

SIDNEY LEE (essay date 1898)

[*Lee was an English biographer, Elizabethan scholar, and editor of* The Dictionary of National Biography. *His works on Shakespeare include* Stratford-on-Avon from the Earliest Times to the Death of Shakespeare (*1885*), *the highly successful* Life of William Shakespeare (*1898*), *a facsimile edition of the* First Folio (*1905*), Shakespeare and the Modern Stage (*1906*), *and* Shakespeare in the Italian Renaissance (*1915*). *In the excerpt below, he disputes the notion that Shakespeare's sonnets are autobiographical throughout, arguing instead that they are decidedly conventional and that Shakespeare was here*

concerned not with conveying personal experiences but with adapting the sonnet form to his own talents. Lee identifies the various conventions apparent throughout the sonnets, noting similar themes and conceits in the poetry of Sir Philip Sidney, Thomas Watson, Barnabe Barnes, and Samuel Daniel. He does claim, however, that one group of sonnets (Nos. 40, 41, 42, 133, 134, and 144) treats an unconventional theme and appears autobiographical in emotional intensity. But even this group, Lee adds, lacks "seriousness." In an unexcerpted portion of his commentary on Shakespeare's sonnets, Lee identifies Henry Wriothesley, Earl of Southampton as the young patron behind the writing of these poems and Barnabe Barnes as the Rival Poet. He asserts, however, that though this sole biographical inference can be rather confidently deduced from this collection, the emotions and events described therein are conventional and by no means true to those in Shakespeare's life.]

At a first glance a far larger proportion of Shakespeare's sonnets give the reader the illusion of personal confessions than those of any contemporary, but when allowance has been made for the current conventions of Elizabethan sonnetteering, as well as for Shakespeare's unapproached affluence in dramatic instinct and invention—an affluence which enabled him to identify himself with every phase of human emotion—the autobiographic element in his sonnets, although it may not be dismissed altogether, is seen to shrink to slender proportions. As soon as the collection is studied comparatively with the many thousand sonnets that the printing presses of England, France, and Italy poured forth during the last years of the sixteenth century, a vast number of Shakespeare's performances prove to be little more than professional trials of skill, often of superlative merit, to which he deemed himself challenged by the efforts of contemporary practitioners. The thoughts and words of the sonnets of Daniel, Drayton, Watson, Barnabe Barnes, Constable, and Sidney were assimilated by Shakespeare in his poems as consciously and with as little compunction as the plays and novels of contemporaries in his dramatic work. To Drayton he was especially indebted. Such resemblances as are visible between Shakespeare's sonnets and those of Petrarch or Desportes seem due to his study of the English imitators of those sonnetteers. Most of Ronsard's nine hundred sonnets and many of his numerous odes were accessible to Shakespeare in English adaptations, but there are a few signs that Shakespeare had recourse to Ronsard direct.

Adapted or imitated conceits are scattered over the whole of Shakespeare's collection. They are usually manipulated with consummate skill, but Shakespeare's indebtedness is not thereby obscured. Shakespeare in many beautiful sonnets describes spring and summer, night and sleep and their influence on amorous emotion. Such topics are common themes of the poetry of the Renaissance, and they figure in Shakespeare's pages clad in the identical livery that clothed them in the sonnets of Petrarch, Ronsard, De Baïf, and Desportes, or of English disciples of the Italian and French masters. In Sonnet xxiv. Shakespeare develops Ronsard's conceit that his love's portrait is painted on his heart; and in Sonnet cxxii. he repeats something of Ronsard's phraseology in describing how his friend, who has just made him a gift of 'tables,' is 'character'd' in his brain. Sonnet xcix., which reproaches the flowers with stealing their charms from the features of his love, is adapted from Constable's sonnet to Diana (No. ix.), and may be matched in other collections. Elsewhere Shakespeare meditates on the theory that man is an amalgam of the four elements, earth, water, air, and fire [Sonnets 40-45]. In all these he reproduces, with such embellishments as his genius dictated, phrases and sentiments of Daniel, Drayton, Barnes, and Watson, who imported them direct from France and Italy. In two or three instances Shakespeare showed his reader that he was engaged in a mere literary exercise by offering him alternative renderings of the same conventional conceit. In [Sonnets 46 and 47] he paraphrases twice over—appropriating many of Watson's words—the unexhilarating notion that the eye and heart are in perpetual dispute as to which has the greater influence on lovers. In the concluding sonnets, [153 and 154], he gives alternative versions of an apologue illustrating the potency of love which first figured in the Greek anthology, had been translated into Latin, and subsequently won the notice of English, French, and Italian sonnetteers.

In the numerous sonnets in which Shakespeare boasted that his verse was so certain of immortality that it was capable of immortalising the person to whom it was addressed, he gave voice to no conviction that was peculiar to his mental constitution, to no involuntary exaltation of spirit, or spontaneous ebullition of feeling. He was merely proving that he could at will, and with superior effect, handle a theme that Ronsard and Desportes, emulating Pindar, Horace, Ovid, and other classical poets, had lately made a commonplace of the poetry of Europe. Sir Philip Sidney, in his 'Apologie for Poetrie' (1595), wrote that it was the common habit of poets 'to tell you that they will make you immortal by their verses.' 'Men of great calling,' Nash wrote in his 'Pierce Pennilesse,' 1593, 'take it of merit to have their names eternised by poets.' In the hands of Elizabethan sonnetteers the 'eternising' faculty of their verse became a staple and indeed an inevitable topic. (pp. 109-15)

Shakespeare, in his references to his 'eternal lines' [Sonnet 18] and in the assurances that he gives the subject of his addresses that the sonnets are, in Daniel's exact phrase, his 'monument' [Sonnets 81 and 107], was merely accommodating himself to the prevailing taste. Characteristically in [Sonnet 55] he invested the topic with a splendour that was not approached by any other poet:

> Not marble, nor the gilded monuments
> Of princes, shall outlive this powerful rhyme;
> But you shall shine more bright in these contents
> Than unswept stone besmear'd with sluttish time.
> When wasteful war shall statues overturn,
> And broils root out the work of masonry,
> Nor Mars his sword nor war's quick fire shall burn
> The living record of your memory.
> 'Gainst death and all-oblivious enmity
> Shall you pace forth; your praise shall still find
>   room
> Even in the eyes of all posterity
> That wear this world out to the ending doom.
>   So, till the judgement that yourself arise,
>   You live in this, and dwell in lovers' eyes.

The imitative element is no less conspicuous in the sonnets that Shakespeare distinctively addresses to a woman. In two of the latter [Sonnets 135 and 136], where he quibbles over the fact of the identity of his own name of Will with a lady's 'will' (the synonym in Elizabethan English of both 'lust' and 'obstinacy'), he derisively challenges comparison with wire-drawn conceits of rival sonnetteers, especially of Barnabe Barnes, who had enlarged on his disdainful mistress's 'wills,' and had turned the word 'grace' to the same punning account as Shakespeare turned the word 'will.' Similarly in [Sonnet 130] beginning

> My mistress' eyes are nothing like the sun;
> Coral is far more red than her lips' red . . .
> If hairs be wires, black wires grow on her head,

he satirises the conventional lists of precious stones, metals, and flowers, to which the sonnetteers likened their mistresses' features.

In two sonnets (cxxvii. and cxxxii.) Shakespeare amiably notices the black complexion, hair, and eyes of his mistress, and expresses a preference for features of that hue over those of the fair hue which was, he tells us, more often associated in poetry with beauty. He commends the 'dark lady' for refusing to practise those arts by which other women of the day gave their hair and faces colours denied them by Nature. Here Shakespeare repeats almost verbatim his own lines in 'Love's Labour's Lost' [IV. iii. 243-61], where the heroine Rosaline is described as 'black as ebony,' with 'brows decked in black,' and in 'mourning' for her fashionable sisters' indulgence in the disguising arts of the toilet. . . . But neither in the sonnets nor in the play can Shakespeare's praise of 'blackness' claim the merit of being his own invention. Sir Philip Sidney, in sonnet vii. of his 'Astrophel and Stella,' had anticipated it. The 'beams' of the eyes of Sidney's mistress were 'wrapt in colour black' and wore 'this mourning weed,' so

> That whereas black seems beauty's contrary,
> She even in black doth make all beauties flow.

To his praise of 'blackness' in 'Love's Labour's Lost' Shakespeare appends a playful but caustic comment on the paradox that he detects in the conceit. Similarly, the sonnets, in which a dark complexion is pronounced to be a mark of beauty, are followed by others in which the poet argues in self-confutation that blackness of feature is hideous in a woman, and invariably indicates moral turpitude or blackness of heart. Twice, in much the same language as had already served a like purpose in the play, does he mock his 'dark lady' with this uncomplimentary interpretation of dark-coloured hair and eyes.

The two sonnets, in which this view of 'blackness' is developed, form part of a series of twelve, which belongs to a special category of sonnetteering effort. In them Shakespeare abandons the sugared sentiment which characterises most of his hundred and forty-two remaining sonnets. He grows vituperative and pours a volley of passionate abuse upon a woman whom he represents as disdaining his advances. The genuine anguish of a rejected lover often expresses itself in curses both loud and deep, but the mood of blinding wrath which the rejection of a lovesuit may rouse in a passionate nature does not seem from the internal evidence to be reflected genuinely in Shakespeare's sonnets of vituperation. It was inherent in Shakespeare's genius that he should import more dramatic intensity than any other poet into sonnets of a vituperative type; but there is also in his vituperative sonnets a declamatory parade of figurative extravagance which suggests that the emotion is feigned and that the poet is striking an attitude. He cannot have been in earnest in seeking to conciliate his disdainful mistress—a result at which the vituperative sonnets purport to aim—when he tells her that she is 'black as hell, as dark as night,' and with 'so foul a face' is 'the bay where all men ride' [Sonnets 147 and 137].

But external evidence is more conclusive as to the artificial construction of the vituperative sonnets. Again a comparison of this series with the efforts of the modish sonnetteers assigns to it its true character. Every sonnetteer of the sixteenth century, at some point in his career, devoted his energies to vituperation of a cruel siren. Ronsard in his sonnets celebrated in language quite as furious as Shakespeare's a 'fierce tigress,' a 'murderess,' a 'Medusa.' Barnabe Barnes affected to contend in his sonnets with a female 'tyrant,' a 'Medusa,' a 'rock.' 'Women' (Barnes laments) 'are by nature proud as devils.' The monotonous and artificial regularity with which the sonnetteers sounded the vituperative stop, whenever they had exhausted their notes of adulation, excited ridicule in both England and France. In Shakespeare's early life the convention was wittily parodied by Gabriel Harvey in 'An Amorous Odious sonnet intituled The Student's Loove or Hatrid, or both or neither, or what shall please the looving or hating reader, either in sport or earnest, to make of such contrary passions as are here discoursed.' (pp. 115-21)

The dark lady of Shakespeare's 'sonnets' may therefore be relegated to the ranks of the creatures of his fancy. It is quite possible that he may have met in real life a dark-complexioned siren, and it is possible that he may have fared ill at her disdainful hands. But no such incident is needed to account for the presence of 'the dark lady' in the sonnets. It was the exacting conventions of the sonnetteering contagion, and not his personal experiences or emotions, that impelled Shakespeare to give 'the dark lady' of his sonnets a poetic being. She has been compared, not very justly, with Shakespeare's splendid creation of Cleopatra in his play of 'Antony and Cleopatra.' From one point of view the same criticism may be passed on both. There is no greater and no less ground for seeking in Shakespeare's personal environment the original of 'the dark lady' of his sonnets than for seeking there the original of his Queen of Egypt. (pp. 122-24)

It is hardly possible to doubt that had Shakespeare, who was more prolific in invention than any other poet, poured out in his sonnets his personal passions and emotions, he would have been carried by his imagination, at every stage, far beyond the beaten tracks of the conventional sonnetteers of his day. The imitative element in his sonnets is large enough to refute the assertion that in them as a whole he sought to 'unlock his heart.' . . . Very few of Shakespeare's 'sugared sonnets' have a substantial right to be regarded as untutored cries of the soul. It is true that the sonnets in which the writer reproaches himself with sin, or gives expression to a sense of melancholy, offer at times a convincing illusion of autobiographic confessions; and it is just possible that they stand apart from the rest, and reveal the writer's inner consciousness, in which case they are not to be matched in any other of Shakespeare's literary compositions. But they may be, on the other hand, merely literary meditations, conceived by the greatest of dramatists, on infirmities incident to all human nature, and only attempted after the cue had been given by rival sonnetteers. At any rate, their energetic lines are often adapted from the less forcible and less coherent utterances of contemporary poets, and the themes are common to almost all Elizabethan collections of sonnets. (pp. 151-52)

Only in one group, composed of six sonnets scattered through the collection, is there traceable a strand of wholly original sentiment, not to be readily defined and boldly projecting from the web into which it is wrought. This series of six sonnets deals with a love adventure of no normal type. [Sonnet 144] opens with the lines:

> Two loves I have of comfort and despair
> Which like two angels do suggest (*i.e.* tempt) me
> still:

The better angel is a man right fair,
The worser spirit a woman colour'd ill.

The woman, the sonnetteer continues, has corrupted the man and has drawn him from his 'side.' Five other sonnets treat the same theme. In three addressed to the man [Sonnets 40, 41, and 42] the poet mildly reproaches his youthful friend for having sought and won the favours of a woman whom he himself loved 'dearly,' but the trespass is forgiven on account of the friend's youth and beauty. In the two remaining sonnets Shakespeare addresses the woman [Sonnets 133 and 134], and he rebukes her for having enslaved not only himself but 'his next self'—his friend. Shakespeare, in his denunciation elsewhere of a mistress's disdain of his advances, assigns her blindness, like all the professional sonnetteers, to no better defined cause than the perversity and depravity of womankind. In these six sonnets alone does he categorically assign his mistress's alienation to the fascinations of a dear friend or hint at such a cause for his mistress's infidelity. The definite element of intrigue that is developed here is not found anywhere else in the range of Elizabethan sonnet-literature. The character of the innovation and its treatment seem only capable of explanation by regarding the topic as a reflection of Shakespeare's personal experience. But how far he is sincere in his accounts of his sorrow in yielding his mistress to his friend in order to retain the friendship of the latter must be decided by each reader for himself. If all the words be taken literally, there is disclosed an act of self-sacrifice that it is difficult to parallel or explain. But it remains very doubtful if the affair does not rightly belong to the annals of gallantry. (pp. 153-54)

The processes of construction which are discernible in Shakespeare's sonnets are thus seen to be identical with those that are discernible in the rest of his literary work. They present one more proof of his punctilious regard for the demands of public taste, and of his marvellous genius and skill in adapting and transmuting for his own purposes the labours of other workers in the field that for the moment engaged his attention. Most of Shakespeare's sonnets were produced in 1594 under the incitement of that freakish rage for sonnetteering which, taking its rise in Italy and sweeping over France on its way to England, absorbed for some half-dozen years in this country a greater volume of literary energy than has been applied to sonnetteering within the same space of time here or elsewhere before or since. The thousands of sonnets that were circulated in England between 1591 and 1597 were of every literary quality, from sublimity to inanity, and they illustrated in form and topic every known phase of sonnetteering activity. Shakespeare's collection, which was put together at haphazard and published surreptitiously many years after the poems were written, was a medley, at times reaching heights of literary excellence that none other scaled, but as a whole reflecting the varied features of the sonnetteering vogue. Apostrophes to metaphysical abstractions, vivid picturings of the beauties of nature, adulation of a patron, idealisation of a *protégé*'s regard for a nobleman in the figurative language of amorous passion, amiable compliments on a woman's hair or touch on the virginals, and vehement denunciation of the falseness and frailty of womankind—all appear as frequently in contemporary collections of sonnets as in Shakespeare's. He borrows very many of his competitors' words and thoughts, but he so fused them with his fancy as often to transfigure them. Genuine emotion or the writer's personal experience very rarely inspired the Elizabethan sonnet, and Shakespeare's sonnets proved no exception to the rule. A personal note may have escaped him involuntarily in the sonnets in which he gives voice to a sense of melancholy and self-remorse, but his dramatic instinct never slept, and there is no proof that he is doing more in those sonnets than produce dramatically the illusion of a personal confession. Only in one scattered series of six sonnets, where he introduced a topic, unknown to other sonneteers, of a lover's supersession by his friend in a mistress's graces, does he seem to show independence of his comrades and draw directly on an incident in his own life, but even there the emotion is wanting in seriousness. (pp. 158-59)

> *Sidney Lee, "The Borrowed Conceits of the Sonnets" and "The Supposed Story of Intrigue in the Sonnets," in his* A Life of William Shakespeare, *Smith, Elder, & Co., 1898, pp. 109-24, 151-60.*

GEORGE WYNDHAM (essay date 1898)

[*A late nineteenth- and early twentieth-century English politician and man of letters, Wyndham was an outstanding letter writer and the author of such critical works as* Shakespeare's Poems (*1898*) *and* Essays in Romantic Literature (*1919*). *Here, he treats the order of the 1609 Quarto, contending like most critics that Shakespeare's sonnets as presented in Thomas Thorpe's edition can be divided into two series—Numbers 1-126, addressed to the Friend, and Numbers 127-54, concerned with "the author's mistress." He also argues that the first series can be broken down into "seven main groups, each with its own principal theme" and "divided by gaps of silence from the sonnets that succeed them." Some of the themes Wyndham identifies are: Beauty and Delay, absence, infidelity, immortality, and time. Wyndham further maintains that the second series of sonnets "shows fewer traces of design in its sequence than the First."*]

Had Shakespeare's Sonnets suffered the fate of Sappho's lyrics, their few surviving fragments would have won him an equal glory, and we should have been damnified in the amount only of a priceless bequest. But our heritage is almost certainly intact: the Sonnets, as we find them in the Quarto of 1609, whether or not they were edited by Shakespeare, must so far have commanded his approval as to arouse no protest against the form in which they appeared. It would have been as easy for him to re-shuffle and re-publish as it is impossible to believe that he could so re-shuffle and re-publish, and no record of his action survive. Taking the Sonnets, then, as published in their author's lifetime, you discover their obvious division into two Series:—in the First, one hundred and twenty-five, closed by an Envoy of six couplets, are addressed to a youth; in the Second, seventeen out of twenty-eight are addressed to the author's mistress, and the others comment, more or less directly, on her infidelity and on his infatuation. Most critics—indeed all not quixotically compelled to reject a reasonable view—are agreed that the order in the First Series can scarce be bettered; and that within that Series certain Groups may be discerned of sonnets written at the same time, each with the same theme and divided by gaps of silence from the sonnets that succeed them. There is also substantial agreement as to the confines of the principal Groups; but between these there are shorter sequences and even isolated numbers, among which different critics have succeeded in tracing a greater or lesser degree of connexion. The analogy of a correspondence, carried on over years between friends, offers perhaps the best clue to the varying continuity of the First Series. There, too, you have silences which attest the very frequency of meetings, with silences born of long absence and absorption in diverse pursuits; there, too, you have spells of voluminous writing on intimate themes, led up to and followed by sparser communications on matters of a less dear importance. The numbers seem to have been chronologically arranged; and, that being so, the alternation of continuous with intermittent production shows naturally in a collection of poems addressed by one person to another at intervals over a period of more than three years.

There are seven main Groups in the First Series:—

Group A, I.-XIX.:—The several numbers echo the arguments in *Venus and Adonis,* Stanzas XXVII.-XXIX. They are written ostensibly, to urge marriage on a beautiful youth, but, essentially, they constitute a continuous poem on Beauty and Decay. That is the subject, varied by the introduction of two subsidiary themes; the one, philosophic, on immortality conferred by breed:—

> From fairest creatures, we desire increase
> That thereby beauty's *Rose* might never die:—
> [Sonnet 1]

the other, literary, on immortality conferred by verse:—

> My love shall in my verse ever live young.
> [Sonnet 19]

This line is the last of the sonnet which serves as an envoy to the Group. Here follow Sonnets XX.-XXI., XXII., XXIII.-XXIV., XXV.: occasional verses written, playfully or affectionately, to the youth who is now dear to their author. In giving the occasional sonnets I bracket only those which are obviously connected and obviously written at the same time.

Group B, XXVI.-XXXII.:—A continuous poem on absence, dispatched, it may be, in a single letter, since it opens with a formal address and ends in a full close. In this group there are variations on the disgust of separation and the solace of remembered love; but it is a poem and not a letter—turning each succeeding emotion to its full artistic account.

Group C, XXXIII.-XLII.:—The first of the more immediately personal garlands. The writer's friend has wronged him by stealing his mistress's love. The counterpart to this group, evidently written on the same theme and at the same time, will be found in the Second Series (CXXXIII.-CXLIV.), addressed in complaint to the writer's mistress, or written in comment on her complicity in this wrong. The biographical interest of this Group has won it an undeserved attention at the expense of others. Many suppose that all the Sonnets turn on this theme, or, at least, that the loudest note of passion is here sounded. But this is not so. Of all ten three at the most can be called tragic. These are [XXXIV, XXXVI, AND XL]. . . . XXXIII. is indeed beautiful, but the others return to the early theme of mere immortalising, or are expressed in abstruse or playful conceits which make it impossible to believe they mirror a soul in pain. They might be taken for designed interpolations, did they not refer, by the way, to a sorrow, or misfortune, not to be distinguished from the theme of their fellows. Knowing what Shakespeare can do to express anguish and passion, are we not absurd to find the evidence of either in these Sonnets, written, as they are, on a private sorrow, but in the spirit of conscious art?

> If my slight Muse do please these curious days
> The pain be mine, but thine shall be the praise.
> [Sonnet 38]

Here follow XLIII., XLIV.-XLV., XLVI.-XLVII.-XLVIII., XLIX., L.-LI., LII., connected or occasional pieces on mere absence. Then LIII.-LIV., and LV. return to the theme of immortalising. (pp. cviii-cxi)

Group D, LVI.-LXXIV.:—The Poet writes again after silence:—'Sweet love, renew thy force' [Sonnet 56]. The first three are occasioned by a voluntary absence of his friend; but that absence, unexpectedly prolonged, inspires a mood of contemplation which, becoming ever more and more metaphysical, is by much removed from the spirit of the earlier poem on absence (*Group B,* XXVI.-XXXII.) with its realistic handling of the same theme. In LIX. the poet dwells on the illusion of repeated experience, and speculates on the truth of the philosophy of cycles:—

> If there be nothing new, but that which is
> Hath been before, how are our brains beguiled.

In LX. he watches the changing toil of Time:—

> Like as the waves make towards the pebbled shore
> So do our minutes hasten to their end.

In LXI. he gazes into the night at the phantasm of his absent friend, and thus leads up to a poem in three parts (LXII.-LXV., LXVI.-LXX., LXXI.-LXXIV.) on Beauty that Time must ruin, on the disgust of Life, and on Death. These nineteen numbers, conceived in a vein of melancholy contemplation, are among the most beautiful of all, and are more subtly metaphysical than any, save only CXXIII., CXXIV., CXXV. There follow LXXV., LXXVI., LXVII.

Group E, LXXVIII.-LXXXVI., is the second of a more immediate personal interest. It deals with rival poets and their meretricious art—especially with one Poet who by 'the proud full sail of his great verse' [Sonnet 86] has bereft the writer of his friend's admiration. The nine are written in unbroken sequence and are playful throughout, suggesting no tragedy.

But in *Group F,* LXXXVII.-XCVI., the spirit of the verse suddenly changes: the music becomes plangent, and the theme of utter estrangement is handled with a complete command over dramatic yet sweetly modulated discourse. The Group is, indeed, a single speech of tragic intensity, written in elegiac verse more exquisite than Ovid's own. Here the First Series is most obviously broken, and XCVII. XCVIII.-XCIX. emphasise the break. They tell of two absences, the first in late summer (XCVI.), the second in the spring. They are isolated from the Group which precedes, and the Group which follows them, and they embrace an absence extending, at least, from early autumn in one year to April in the next. The first is of great elegiac beauty, the second of curious metaphysical significance; the third seems an inferior, perhaps a rejected, version of the second.

Group G, C.-CXXV., opens after a great silence:—'Where art thou, Muse, that thou forget'st so long' [Sonnet 100]:—and the poet develops in it a single sustained attack on the Law of Change, minimising the importance of both outward chances and inward moods. . . . In this Group, as in earlier resumptions, the music is at first imperfect. But it soon changes, and in CII. the apology for past silence is sung in accents sweet as the nightingale's described. There are marked irregularities in the poetic excellence of the Sonnets: which ever climbs to its highest pitch in the longer and more closely connected sequences. This is the longest of all: a poem of re-

trospect over a space of three years to the time when 'love was new, and then but in the spring' [Sonnet 102]. In its survey it goes over the old themes with a soft and silvery touch: Beauty and Decay, Love, Constancy, the Immortalising of the Friend's beauty conceived as an incarnation of Ideal Beauty viewed from imaginary standpoints in Time. And interwoven with this re-handling, chiefly of the themes in the First and Fourth Groups, is an apology (CIX.-CXII., CXVII.-CXX., CXXII.) for a negligence on the Poet's part of the rites of friendship, which he sets off (CXX.) against his Friend's earlier unkindness:—'*That you were once unkind, befriends me now.*' This apology offers the third, and only other, immediate reference to Shakespeare's personal experience; and, on these sonnets, as on those which treat of the Dark Lady and the Rival Poet, attention has been unduly concentrated. They seem founded on episodes and moods necessarily incidental to the life which we know Shakespeare must have led. (pp. cxi-cxiv)

In CXXI. there is a natural digression from this personal apology to reflexions cast on Shakespeare's good name. In CXXII. the apology is resumed with particular reference to certain tablets, the gift of the Friend, but which the Poet has bestowed on another. He takes this occasion to resume the main theme of the whole group by pouring contempt on '*dates*' and '*records*' and '*tallies* to *score* his dear love': the tablets, though in fact given away, are still 'within his brain, full charactered, beyond all date even to Eternity.' Thus does he lead directly to the last three sonnets (CXXIII., CXXIV., CXXV.), which close this 'Satire to Decay,' and with it the whole series (I.-CXXV.). They are pieces of mingled splendour and obscurity in which Shakespeare presses home his metaphysical attack on the reality of Time; and the difficulty, inherent in an argument so transcendental, is further deepened by passing allusions to contemporary events and persons, which many have sought to explain, with little success. Here follows an Envoy of six couplets to the whole Series.

The Second Series shows fewer traces of design in its sequence than the First. The magnificent CXXIX. on 'lust in action' is wedged between two: one addressed to Shakespeare's mistress and one descriptive of her charm; both playful in their fancy. CXLVI. to his soul, with its grave pathos and beauty, follows on a foolish verbal conceit, written in octosyllabic verse; while CLIII. and CLIV. are contrived in the worst manner of the French Renaissance on the theme of a Greek Epigram. But the rest are, all of them, addressed to a Dark Lady whom Shakespeare loved in spite of her infidelity, or they comment on the wrong she does him. It cannot be doubted that they were written at the same time and on the same subject as the sonnets in Group C, XXXIII.-XLII., or that they were excluded from that group on any ground except that of their being written to another than the Youth to whom the whole First Series is addressed. Like the numbers in Group C, they are alternately playful and pathetic; their diction is often as exquisite, their discourse often as eloquent. But sometimes they are sardonic and even fierce:—

> For I have sworn thee fair and thought thee bright,
> Who art as black as hell, as dark as night.
> [Sonnet 147] (pp. cxiv-cxvi)

George Wyndham, in an introduction to The Poems of Shakespeare, *edited by George Wyndham, Methuen and Co., 1898, pp. vii-cxlvii.*

A. C. BRADLEY   (lecture date 1904)

[*Bradley was a major Shakespearean critic whose work culminated the method of character analysis initiated in the Romantic era. He is best known for his* Shakespearean Tragedy (1904), *an examination of* Hamlet, Othello, King Lear, *and* Macbeth. *Bradley was a pivotal figure in the transition in Shakespearean studies from the nineteenth to the twentieth century. He has been a major target for critics reacting against Romantic criticism, but he has continued to be widely read to the present day. Bradley's commentary on the Sonnets, excerpted below, was originally presented in a lecture at Oxford in 1904. Bradley believes that the sonnets are autobiographical and provide clear impressions of Shakespeare's personality. "No capable poet," he claims, "much less a Shakespeare, . . . would dream of inventing a story like that of these sonnets, or, even if he did, of treating it as they treat it." Bradley asserts that these verses demonstrate that the poet was especially sensitive to the charms of physical beauty and that, at least at one period of his life, his love for the young man verged on adoration. The critic also sees strong evidence here of Shakespeare's forgiving nature. Shakespeare was "probably incapable of fierce or prolonged resentment," Bradley concludes, particularly toward someone, like his young friend, of whom he was so enamored.*]

Such phrases as 'Shakespeare the man' or 'Shakespeare's personality' are, no doubt, open to objection. They seem to suggest that, if we could subtract from Shakespeare the mind that produced his works, the residue would be the man himself; and that his mind was some pure impersonal essence unaffected by the accidents of physique, temperament, and character. If this were so, one could but echo Tennyson's thanksgiving that we know so little of Shakespeare. But as it is assuredly not so, and as 'Shakespeare the man' really means the one indivisible Shakespeare, regarded for the time from a particular point of view, the natural desire to know whatever can be known of him is not to be repressed merely because there are people so foolish as to be careless about his works and yet curious about his private life. For my own part I confess that, though I should care nothing about the man if he had not written the works, yet, since we possess them, I would rather see and hear him for five minutes in his proper person than discover a new one. And though we may be content to die without knowing his income or even the surname of Mr. W. H., we cannot so easily resign the wish to find the man in his writings, and to form some idea of the disposition, the likes and dislikes, the character and the attitude towards life, of the human being who seems to us to have understood best our common human nature.

The answer of course will be that our biographical knowledge of Shakespeare is so small, and his writings are so completely dramatic, that this wish, however natural, is idle. But I cannot think so. Doubtless, in trying to form an idea of Shakespeare, we soon reach the limits of reasonable certainty; and it is also true that the idea we can form without exceeding them is far from being as individual as we could desire. But it is more distinct than is often supposed, and it *is* reasonably certain; and although we can add to its distinctness only by more or less probable conjectures, they are not mere guesses, they really have probability in various degrees. On this whole subject there is a tendency at the present time to an extreme scepticism, which appears to me to be justified neither by the circumstances of the particular case nor by our knowledge of human nature in general.

This scepticism is due in part to the interest excited by Mr. Lee's discussion of the Sonnets in his *Life* of Shakespeare [see

excerpt above, 1898], and to the importance rightly attached to that discussion. The Sonnets are lyrical poems of friendship and love. In them the poet ostensibly speaks in his own person and expresses his own feelings. Many critics, no doubt, had denied that he really did so; but they had not Mr. Lee's knowledge, nor had they examined the matter so narrowly as he; and therefore they had not much weakened the general belief that the Sonnets, however conventional or exaggerated their language may sometimes be, do tell us a good deal about their author. Mr. Lee, however, showed far more fully than any previous writer that many of the themes, many even of the ideas, of these poems are commonplaces of Renaissance sonnet-writing; and he came to the conclusion that in the Sonnets Shakespeare 'unlocked,' not 'his heart,' but a very different kind of armoury, and that the sole biographical inference deducible from them is that 'at one time in his career Shakespeare disdained no weapon of flattery in an endeavour to monopolise the bountiful patronage of a young man of rank.' Now, if that inference is correct, it certainly tells us something about Shakespeare the man; but it also forbids us to take seriously what the Sonnets profess to tell us of his passionate affection, with its hopes and fears, its pain and joy; of his pride and his humility, his self-reproach and self-defence, his weariness of life and his consciousness of immortal genius. And as, according to Mr. Lee's statement, the Sonnets alone of Shakespeare's works 'can be held to throw any illumination on a personal trait,' it seems to follow that, so far as the works are concerned (for Mr. Lee is not specially sceptical as to the external testimony), the only idea we can form of the man is contained in that single inference.

Now, I venture to surmise that Mr. Lee's words go rather beyond his meaning. But that is not our business here, nor could a brief discussion do justice to a theory to which those who disagree with it are still greatly indebted. What I wish to deny is the presupposition which seems to be frequently accepted as an obvious truth. Even if Mr. Lee's view of the Sonnets were indisputably correct, nay, if even, to go much further, the persons and the story in the Sonnets were as purely fictitious as those of *Twelfth Night,* they might and would still tell us something of the personality of their author. For however free a poet may be from the emotions which he simulates, and however little involved in the conditions which he imagines, he cannot (unless he is a mere copyist) write a hundred and fifty lyrics expressive of those simulated emotions without disclosing something of himself, something of the way in which he in particular *would* feel and behave under the imagined conditions. (pp. 311-13)

The remarks I am going to make can have an interest only for those who share the position I have tried to indicate; who believe that the most dramatic of writers must reveal in his writings something of himself, but who recognise that in Shakespeare's case we can expect a reasonable certainty only within narrow limits, while beyond them we have to trust to impressions, the value of which must depend on familiarity with his writings, on freedom from prejudice and the desire to reach any particular result, and on the amount of perception we may happen to possess. I offer my own impressions, insecure and utterly unprovable as I know them to be, simply because those of other readers have an interest for me; and I offer them for the most part without argument, because even where argument might be useful it requires more time than a lecture can afford. (p. 316)

I intend only to state the main reason why I believe the sonnets to be, substantially, what they purport to be, and then to touch upon one or two of the points where they seem to throw light on Shakespeare's personality.

The sonnets to the friend are, so far as we know, unique in Renaissance sonnet literature in being a prolonged and varied record of the intense affection of an older friend for a younger, and of other feelings arising from their relations. They have no real parallel in any series imitative of Virgil's second Eclogue, or in occasional sonnets to patrons or patron-friends couched in the high-flown language of the time. The intensity of the feelings expressed, however, ought not, by itself, to convince us that they are personal. The author of the plays could, I make no doubt, have written the most intimate of these poems to a mere creature of his imagination and without ever having felt them except in imagination. Nor is there any but an aesthetic reason why he should not have done so if he had wished. But an aesthetic reason there is; and this is the decisive point. No capable poet, much less a Shakespeare, intending to produce a merely 'dramatic' series of poems, would dream of inventing a story like that of these sonnets, or, even if he did, of treating it as they treat it. The story is very odd and unattractive. Such capacities as it has are but slightly developed. It is left obscure, and some of the poems are unintelligible to us because they contain allusions of which we can make nothing. Now all this is perfectly natural if the story is substantially a real story of Shakespeare himself and of certain other persons; if the sonnets were written from time to time as the relations of the persons changed, and sometimes in reference to particular incidents; and if they were written *for* one or more of these persons (far the greater number for only one), and perhaps in a few cases for other friends,—written, that is to say, for people who knew the details and incidents of which we are ignorant. But it is all unnatural, well-nigh incredibly unnatural, if, with the most sceptical critics, we regard the sonnets as a free product of mere imagination.

Assuming, then, that the persons of the story, with their relations, are real, I would add only two remarks about the friend. In the first place, Mr. Beeching seems to me right in denying that there is sufficient evidence of his standing to Shakespeare and the 'rival' poet or poets in the position of a literary patron [see Additional Bibliography]; while, even if he did, it appears to me quite impossible to take the language of many of the sonnets as that of interested flattery. And in the second place I should be inclined to push even further Mr. Beeching's view on another point. It is clear that the young man was considerably superior to the actor-dramatist in social position; but any gentleman would be so, and there is nothing to prove that he was more than a gentleman of some note, more than plain 'Mr. W. H.' (for these, on the obvious though not compulsory interpretation of the dedication, seem to have been his initials). It is remarkable besides that, while the earlier sonnets show much deference, the later show very little, so little that, when the writer, finding that he has pained his young friend by neglecting him, begs to be forgiven, he writes almost, if not quite, as an equal. Read, for example, sonnets 109, 110, 120, and ask whether it is probable that Shakespeare is addressing here a great nobleman. It seems therefore most likely (though the question is not of much importance) that the sonnets are, to quote Meres's phrase [see excerpt above, 1598], his 'sonnets among his private friends.'

If then there is, as it appears, no obstacle of any magnitude to our taking the sonnets as substantially what they purport

to be, we may naturally look in them for personal traits (and, indeed, to repeat a remark made earlier, we might still expect to find such traits even if we knew the sonnets to be purely dramatic). But in drawing inferences we have to bear in mind what is implied by the qualification 'substantially.' We have to remember that *some* of these poems may be mere exercises of art; that all of them are poems, and not letters, much less *affidavits;* that they are Elizabethan poems; that the Elizabethan language of deference, and also of affection, is to our minds habitually extravagant and fantastic; and that in Elizabethan plays friends openly express their love for one another as Englishmen now rarely do. Allowance being made, however, on account of these facts, the sonnets will still leave two strong impressions—that the poet was exceedingly sensitive to the charm of beauty, and that his love for his friend was, at least at one time, a feeling amounting almost to adoration, and so intense as to be absorbing. Those who are surprised by the first of these traits must have read Shakespeare's dramas with very inactive minds, and I must add that they seem to be somewhat ignorant of human nature. We do not necessarily love best those of our relatives, friends, and acquaintances who please our eyes most; and we should look askance on anyone who regulated his behaviour chiefly by the standard of beauty; but most of us, I suppose, love any human being, of either sex and of any age, the better for being beautiful, and are not the least ashamed of the fact. It is further the case that men who are beginning, like the writer of the sonnets, to feel tired and old, are apt to feel an increased and special pleasure in the beauty of the young. If we remember, in addition, what some critics appear constantly to forget, that Shakespeare was a particularly poetical being, we shall hardly be surprised that the beginning of this friendship seems to have been something like a falling in love; and, if we must needs praise and blame, we should also remember that it became a 'marriage of true minds' [Sonnet 116]. And as to the intensity of the feeling expressed in the sonnets, we can easily believe it to be characteristic of the man who made Valentine and Proteus [in *Two Gentlemen of Verona*], Brutus and Cassius [in *Julius Caesar*], Horatio and Hamlet; who painted that strangely moving portrait of Antonio, middle-aged, sad, and almost indifferent between life and death, but devoted to the young, brilliant spendthrift Bassanio [in *The Merchant of Venice*]; and who portrayed the sudden compelling enchantment exercised by the young Sebastian over the Antonio of *Twelfth Night*. 'If you will not murder me for your love, let me be your servant' [II.i. 35-6]. Antonio is accused of piracy: he may lose his life if he is identified:

> I have many enemies in Orsino's court,
> But, come what may, I do adore thee so
> That danger shall seem sport, and I will go.
>
> [II. i. 45-7]

The adoration, the 'prostration,' of the writer of the sonnets is of one kind with this.

I do not remember what critic uses the word 'prostration.' It applies to Shakespeare's attitude only in some of the sonnets, but there it does apply, unless it is taken to suggest humiliation. *That* is the term used by Hallam [see excerpt above, 1837-39], but chiefly in view of a particular point, namely the failure of the poet to 'resent,' though he 'felt and bewailed,' the injury done him in 'the seduction of his mistress.' Though I think we should substitute 'resent more strongly' for the mere 'resent,' I do not deny that the poet's attitude in this matter strikes us at first as surprising as well as unpleasant to contemplate. But Hallam's explanation of it as perhaps due to the exalted position of the friend, would make it much more than unpleasant; and his language seems to show that he, like many critics, did not fully imagine the situation. It is not easy to speak of it in public with the requisite frankness; but it is necessary to realise that, whatever the friend's rank might be, he and the poet were intimate friends; that, manifestly, it was rather the mistress who seduced the friend than the friend the mistress; and that she was apparently a woman not merely of no reputation, but of such a nature that she might readily be expected to be mistress to two men at one and the same time. Anyone who realises this may call the situation 'humiliating' in one sense, and I cannot quarrel with him; but he will not call it 'humiliating' in respect of Shakespeare's relation to his friend; nor will he wonder much that the poet felt more pain than resentment at his friend's treatment of him. There is something infinitely stranger in a play of Shakespeare's, and it may be symptomatic. Then Brink called attention to it. Proteus actually offers violence to Sylvia, a spotless lady and the true love of his friend Valentine; and Valentine not only forgives him at once when he professes repentance, but offers to resign Sylvia to him! The incident is to us so utterly preposterous that we find it hard to imagine how the audience stood it; but, even if we conjecture that Shakespeare adopted it from the story he was using, we can hardly suppose that it was so absurd to him as it is to us. And it is not the Sonnets alone which lead us to surmise that forgiveness was particularly attractive to him, and the forgiveness of a friend much easier than resentment. From the Sonnets we gather—and there is nothing in the plays or elsewhere to contradict the impression—that he would not be slow to resent the criticisms, slanders, or injuries of strangers or the world, and that he bore himself towards them with a proud, if silent, self-sufficiency. But, we surmise, for anyone whom he loved

> He carried anger as a flint bears fire;
> Who, much enforced, shows a hasty spark
> And straight is cold again;
> [*Julius Caesar*, IV. iii. 111-13]

and towards anyone so fondly loved as the friend of the Sonnets he was probably incapable of fierce or prolonged resentment. (pp. 330-35)

> *A. C. Bradley, "Shakespeare the Man," in his* Oxford Lectures on Poetry, *second edition, Macmillan and Co., Limited, 1909, pp. 311-57.*

FRANK HARRIS (essay date 1909)

[*Harris was a British-American journalist, editor, playwright, and short story writer whose most significant achievement was serving as editor of several London journals, including the* Saturday Review *from 1894 to 1898, and employing such writers as Bernard Shaw, H. G. Wells, and Max Beerbohm. In* The Man Shakespeare and His Tragic Life Story (1909) *and* The Women of Shakespeare (1911), *Harris offered a psychological study of the dramatist, searching through the plays for evidence of Shakespeare's biography. The first of these received high praise from several of his contemporaries, but his Shakespearean criticism has received no commendation and little attention from modern scholars. In the following excerpt from* The Man Shakespeare, *he argues that although Shakespeare revealed his nature more fully in his plays than in his lyrics, the sonnets are indeed autobiographical, conveying "the story, the whole terrible, sinful, magical story of Shakespeare's passion." On related matters, Harris also identifies the Friend as William Herbert and the Dark Lady as Mary Fitton.*]

Ever since Wordsworth wrote that the sonnets were the key to Shakespeare's heart [see excerpt above, 1827], it has been taken for granted (save by those who regard even the sonnets as mere poetical exercises) that Shakespeare's real nature is discovered in the sonnets more easily and more surely than in the plays. . . . I do not agree with this assumption. The author whose personality is rich and complex enough to create and vitalize a dozen characters, reveals himself more fully in his creations than he can in his proper person. It was natural enough that Wordsworth, a great lyric poet, should catch Shakespeare's accent better in his sonnets than in his dramas; but that is owing to Wordsworth's limitations. And if the majority of later English critics have agreed with Wordsworth, it only shows that Englishmen in general are better judges of lyric than of dramatic work. (p. 202)

Whether the reader agrees with me or not on this point, it may be accepted that Shakespeare revealed himself far more completely in his plays than as a lyric poet. Just as he chose his dramatic subjects with some felicity to reveal his many-sided nature, so he used the sonnets with equal artistry to discover that part of himself which could hardly be rendered objectively. Whatever is masculine in a man can be depicted superbly on the stage, but his feminine qualities—passionate self-abandonment, facile forgivingness, self-pity—do not show well in the dramatic struggle. What sort of a drama would that be in which the hero would have to confess that when in the vale of years he had fallen desperately in love with a girl, and that he had been foolish enough to send a friend, a young noble, to plead his cause, with the result that the girl won the friend and gave herself to him? The protagonist would earn mocking laughter and not sympathy, and this Shakespeare no doubt foresaw. Besides, to Shakespeare, this story, which is in brief the story of the sonnets, was terribly real and intimate, and he felt instinctively that he could not treat it objectively; it was too near him, too exquisitely painful for that.

At some time or other life overpowers the strongest of us, and that defeat we all treat lyrically; when the deepest depth in us is stirred we cannot feign, or depict ourselves from the outside dispassionately; we can only cry our passion, our pain and our despair; this once we use no art, simple truth is all we seek to reach. The crisis of Shakespeare's life, the hour of agony and bloody sweat when his weakness found him out and life's handicap proved too heavy even for his strength— that is the subject of the sonnets.

Now what was Shakespeare's weakness? his besetting temptation? "Love is my sin" [Sonnet 142], he says; "Love of love and her soft hours" [*Antony and Cleopatra*, I. i. 44] was his weakness: passion the snare that meshed his soul. No wonder Antony cries:

> Whither hast thou led me, Egypt?
> [*Antony and Cleopatra*, III. xi. 51]

for his gipsy led Shakespeare from shame to shame, to the verge of madness. The sonnets give us the story, the whole terrible, sinful, magical story of Shakespeare's passion.

As might have been expected, Englishmen like Wordsworth, with an intense appreciation of lyric poetry, have done good work in criticism of the sonnets, and one Englishman has read them with extraordinary understanding. Mr. Tyler's work on the sonnets ranks higher than that of Coleridge on the plays. I do not mean to say that it is on the same intellectual level with the work of Coleridge, though it shows wide reading, astonishing acuteness, and much skill in the marshalling of argument. But Mr. Tyler had the good fortune to be the first to give to the personages of the sonnets a local habitation and a name, and that unique achievement puts him in a place by himself far above the mass of commentators. Before his book appeared in 1890 the sonnets lay in the dim light of guess-work. It is true that Hallam had adopted the hypothesis of Boaden and Bright, and had identified William Herbert, Earl of Pembroke, with the high-born, handsome youth for whom Shakespeare, in the sonnets, expressed such passionate affection [see excerpts above, 1832 and 1827-39], but still, there were people who thought that the Earl of Southampton filled the requirements even better than William Herbert, and as I say, the whole subject lay in the twilight of surmise and supposition.

Mr. Tyler, working on a hint of the Rev. W. A. Harrison, identified Shakespeare's high-born mistress, the "dark lady" of the sonnets, with Mistress Mary Fitton, a maid of honour to Queen Elizabeth [see excerpts above, 1884 and 1890].

These, then, are the personages of the drama, and the story is very simple: Shakespeare loved Mistress Fitton and sent his friend, the young Lord Herbert, to her on some pretext, but with the design that he should commend Shakespeare to the lady. Mistress Fitton fell in love with William Herbert, wooed and won him, and Shakespeare had to mourn the loss of both friend and mistress. (pp. 203-05)

I bring to this theory fresh corroboration from the plays. Strange to say, Mr. Tyler has hardly used the plays, yet, as regards the story told in the sonnets, the proof that it is a real and not an imaginary story can be drawn from the plays. I may have to point out, incidentally, what I regard as mistakes and oversights in Mr. Tyler's work; but in the main it stands four-square, imposing itself on the reason and satisfying at the same time instinct and sympathy.

Let us first see how far the story told in the sonnets is borne out by the plays. For a great many critics, even to-day, reject the story altogether, and believe that the sonnets were nothing but poetic exercises.

The sonnets fall naturally into two parts: from 1 to 126 they tell how Shakespeare loved a youth of high rank and great personal beauty; sonnet 127 is an *envoi;* from 128 to 152 they tell of Shakespeare's love for a "dark lady." What binds the two series together is the story told in both, or at least told in one and corroborated in the other, that Shakespeare first sent his friend to the lady, most probably to plead his cause, and that she wooed his friend and gave herself to him. Now this is not a common or easily invented story. No one would guess that Shakespeare could be so foolish as to send his friend to plead his love for him. That's a mistake that no man who knows women would be likely to make: but the unlikelihood of the story is part of the evidence of its truth—*credo quia incredibile* [I believe it because it is impossible] has an element of persuasion in it.

No one has yet noticed that the story of the sonnets is treated three times in Shakespeare's plays. The first time the story appears it is handled so lightly that it looks to me as if he had not then lived through the incidents which he narrates. In the "Two Gentlemen of Verona" Proteus is asked by the Duke to plead Thurio's cause with Silvia, and he promises to do so; but instead, presses his own suit and is rejected. The incident is handled so carelessly (Proteus not being Thurio's friend) that it seems to me to have no importance save as a mere coin-

cidence. When the scene between Proteus and Silvia was written Shakespeare had not yet been deceived by his friend. Still in "The Two Gentlemen of Verona" there is one speech which certainly betrays personal passion. It is in the last scene of the fifth act, when Valentine surprises Proteus offering violence to Silvia.

> *Val. (coming forward)* Ruffian, let go that rude uncivil touch,—
> Thou friend of an ill fashion!
> *Pro.*   Valentine!
> *Val. Thou common friend, that's without faith or love,—*
> *For such is a friend now;*—treacherous man!
> Thou hast beguiled my hopes: nought but mine eye
> Could have persuaded me. Now I dare not say
> I have one friend alive: thou would'st disprove me.
> Who should be trusted when one's own right hand
> Is perjured to the bosom? Proteus,
> I am sorry I must never trust thee more,
> But count the world a stranger for thy sake.
> *The private wound is deepest: time most accurst*
> *'Mongst all foes that a friend should be the worst!*
> [*The Two Gentlemen of Verona,* V. iv. 60-72]

The first lines which I have italicised are too plain to be misread; when they were written Shakespeare had just been cheated by his friend; they are his passionate comment on the occurrence—"For such is a friend now"—can hardly be otherwise explained. The last couplet, too, which I have also put in italics, is manifestly a reflection on his betrayal: it is a twin rendering of the feeling expressed in sonnet 40:

> And yet love knows it is a greater grief
> To bear love's wrong than hate's known injury.

It contrasts "foe and friend," just as the sonnet contrasts "love and hate." (pp. 205-08)

[This] scene is certainly later than the rest of the play. The truth probably is that after his friend had deceived him, "The Two Gentlemen of Verona" was played again, and that Shakespeare rewrote this last scene under the influence of personal feeling. The 170 lines of it are full of phrases which might be taken direct from the sonnets. (p. 208)

The whole scene tells the story a little more frankly than we find it in the sonnets, as might be expected, seeing that Shakespeare's rival was a great noble and not to be criticised freely. This fact explains to me Valentine's unmotived renunciation of Silvia; explains, too, why he is reconciled to his friend with such unseemly haste. Valentine's last words in the scene are illuminating:

> 'Twere pity two such friends should be long foes.
> [*The Two Gentlemen of Verona,* V. iv. 118]

The way this scene in "The Two Gentlemen of Verona" is told throws more light on Shakespeare's feelings at the moment of his betrayal than the sonnets themselves. Under the cover of fictitious names Shakespeare ventured to show the disgust and contempt he felt for Lord Herbert's betrayal more plainly than he cared, or perhaps dared, to do when speaking in his own person.

There is another play where the same incident is handled in such fashion as to put the truth of the sonnet-story beyond all doubt.

In "Much Ado about Nothing" the incident is dragged in by the ears, and the whole treatment is most remarkable. Every one will remember how Claudio tells the Prince that he loves Hero, and asks his friend's assistance: "your highness now may do me good" [*Much Ado about Nothing*, I. i. 290]. There's no reason for Claudio's shyness: no reason why he should call upon the Prince for help in a case where most men prefer to use their own tongues; but Claudio is young, and so we glide over the inherent improbability of the incident. (pp. 208-09)

Now comes the peculiar handling of the incident. Claudio knows the Prince is wooing Hero for him, therefore when Don John tells him that the Prince "is enamoured on Hero" [*Much Ado about Nothing*, II. i. 164], he should at once infer that Don John is mistaken through ignorance of this fact; but instead of that he falls suspicious, and questions:

> How know you he loves her?
> *D. John.* I heard him swear his affection.
> *Bor.* So did I too, and he swore he would marry her
>   to-night.
>   [*Much Ado about Nothing*, II. i. 167-70]

There is absolutely nothing even in this corroboration by Borachio to shake Claudio's trust in the Prince: neither Don John nor Borachio knows what he knows, that the Prince is wooing for him (Claudio) and at his request. He should therefore smile at the futile attempt to excite his jealousy. But at once he is persuaded of the worst, as a man would be who had already experienced such disloyalty. . . . And then we should expect to hear him curse the prince as a traitorous friend, and dwell on his own loyal service by way of contrast, and so keep turning the dagger in the wound with the thought that no one but himself was ever so repaid for such honesty of love. But, no! Claudio has no bitterness in him, no re-proachings; he speaks of the whole matter as if it had happened months and months before, as indeed it had; for "Much Ado about Nothing" was written about 1599. Reflection had already shown Shakespeare the unreason of revolt, and he puts his own thought in the mouth of Claudio:

> 'Tis certain so; the prince woos for himself.
> Friendship is constant in all other things
> Save in the office and affairs of love:
> Therefore all hearts in love use their own tongues;
> Let every eye negotiate for itself,
> And trust no agent; for beauty is a witch,
> Against whose charms faith melteth into blood.
> *This is an accident of hourly proof,*
> *Which I mistrusted not.* Farewell, therefore, Hero.
>   [*Much Ado about Nothing*, II. i. 174-82]

The Claudio who spoke like this in the first madness of love lost and friendship cheated would be a monster. Here we have Shakespeare speaking in all calmness of something that happened to himself a considerable time before. The lines I have put in italics admit no other interpretation: they show Shakespeare's philosophic acceptance of things as they are; what has happened to him is not to be assumed as singular but is the common lot of man—"an accident of hourly proof"—which he blames himself for not foreseeing. In fact, Claudio's temper here is as detached and impartial as Benedick's. Benedick declares that Claudio should be whipped. . . . That is the view of the realist who knows life and men, and plays the game according to the rules accepted. Shakespeare understood this side of life as well as most men. But Don Pedro is a prince—a Shakespearean prince at that—full of all loyalties and ideal sentiments; he answers Benedick from Shakespeare's own heart:

> Wilt thou make a trust a transgression?
> The transgression is in the stealer.
>   [*Much Ado about Nothing*, II. i. 225-26]

It is curious that Shakespeare doesn't see that Claudio must feel this truth a thousand times more keenly than the Prince. As I have said, Claudio's calm acceptance of the fact is a reve-lation of Shakespeare's own attitude, an attitude just modi-fied by the moral reprobation put in the mouth of the Prince. The recital itself shows that the incident was a personal expe-rience of Shakespeare, and as one might expect in this case it does not accelerate but retard the action of the drama; it is, indeed, altogether foreign to the drama, an excrescence upon it and not an improvement but a blemish. Moreover, the reflective, disillusioned, slightly pessimistic tone of the narra-tive is alien and strange to the optimistic temper of the play; finally, this garb of patient sadness does not suit Claudio, who should be all love and eagerness, and diminishes instead of increasing our sympathy with his later actions. Whoever con-siders these facts will admit that we have here Shakespeare telling us what happened to himself, and what he really thought of his friend's betrayal.

> The transgression is in the stealer.

That is Shakespeare's mature judgement of Lord Herbert's betrayal.

The third mention of this sonnet-story in a play is later still: it is in "Twelfth Night." . . . In the fourth scene of the first act [the Duke] sends Viola to plead his cause for him with Olivia, much in the same way, no doubt, as Shakespeare sent Pembroke to Miss Fitton. The whole scene deserves careful reading.

> Cesario,
> Thou know'st no less but all; I have unclasp'd
> To thee the book even of my secret soul:
> Therefore, good youth, address thy gait unto her
> Be not denied access, stand at her doors,
> And tell them, there thy fixed foot shall grow
> Till thou have audience.
>
> *Vio.*   Sure, my noble lord,
> If she be so abandon'd to her sorrow
> As it is spoke, she never will admit me.
>
> *Duke.* Be clamorous and leap all civil bounds
> Rather than make unprofited return.
>
> *Vio.* Say I do speak with her, my lord, what then?
>
> *Duke.* O, then unfold the passion of my love,
> Surprise her with discourse of my dear faith:
> It shall become thee well to act my woes;
> *She will attend it better in thy youth*
> *Than in a nuncio's of more grave aspect.*
>
> *Vio.* I think not so, my lord.
>
> *Duke.*   Dear lad, believe it;
> For they shall yet belie thy happy years,
> That say thou art a man: Diana's lip
> Is not more smooth and rubious; thy small pipe
> Is as the maiden's organ, shrill and sound;
> And all is semblative a woman's part.
> I know thy constellation is right apt
> For this affair. Some four or five attend him;
> All if you will; for I myself am best
> When least in company.
>   [*Twelfth Night*, I. iv. 12-38]

I do not want to find more here than is in the text: the passage simply shows that this idea of sending some one to plead his love was constantly in Shakespeare's mind in these years. The curious part of the matter is that he should pick a youth as ambassador, and a youth who is merely his page. He can discover no reason for choosing such a boy as Viola, and so simply asserts that youth will be better attended to, which is certainly not the fact. Lord Herbert's youth was in his mind: but he could not put the truth in the play that when he chose his ambassador he chose him for his high position and personal beauty and charm, and not because of his youth. The whole incident is treated lightly as something of small import; the bitterness in "Much Ado" has died out: "Twelfth Night" was written about 1601, a year or so later than "Much Ado."

I do not want to labour the conclusion I have reached; but it must be admitted that I have found in the plays, and especially in "The Two Gentlemen of Verona" and "Much Ado," the same story which is told in the sonnets; a story lugged into the plays, where, indeed, its introduction is a grave fault in art and its treatment too peculiar to be anything but personal. Here in the plays we have, so to speak, three views of the sonnet-story; the first in "The Two Gentlemen of Verona," when the betrayal is fresh in Shakespeare's memory and his words are embittered with angry feeling:

> Thou common friend that's without faith or love.

The second view is taken in "Much Ado About Nothing" when the pain of the betrayal has been a little salved by time. Shakespeare now moralizes the occurrence. He shows us how it would be looked upon by a philosopher (for that is what the lover, Claudio, is in regard to his betrayal) and by a soldier and man of the world, Benedick, and by a Prince. Shakespeare selects the prince to give effect to the view that the fault is in the transgressor and not in the man who trusts. The many-sided treatment of the story shows all the stages through which Shakespeare's mind moved, and the result is to me a more complete confession than is to be found in the sonnets. Finally the story is touched upon in "Twelfth Night," when the betrayal has faded into oblivion, but the poet lets out the fact that his ambassador was a youth, and the reason he gives for this is plainly insufficient. If after these three recitals any one can still believe that the sonnet-story is imaginary, he is beyond persuasion by argument. (pp. 209-15)

> *Frank Harris, "Shakespeare's Love-Story: The Sonnets, Part I," in his* The Man Shakespeare and His Tragic Life Story, *Frank Palmer, 1909, pp. 202-15.*

J. W. MACKAIL (essay date 1912)

[*Mackail was an English critic, biographer, and educator. His critical works, which are primarily devoted to the study of Greek and English poetry, display his scholarly approach to literature and his belief that the development of poetry is an organic process. In the following excerpt, he examines the "vocabulary, syntax, and style" of* A Lover's Complaint*, contending that much in the poem, especially the mannered speech and forced verse, suggests that it was not written by Shakespeare. Mackail also speculates that this poem was written by the Rival Poet referred to in the sonnets, who imitated Shakespeare's style and, at some points, even alluded to events in the sonnets. The manuscript of the poem, he further theorizes, possibly was "copied into the same blank book as the Sonnets" and*

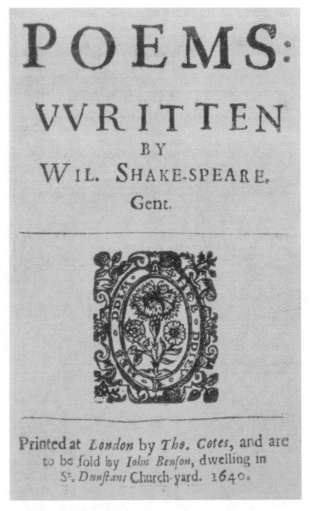

Title page of the 1640 edition of Shakespeare's Sonnets.

then delivered to Thomas Thorpe, who mistakenly ascribed it to Shakespeare.]

The poem entitled *A Lover's Complaint,* printed at the end of the volume of Shakespeare's Sonnets when they were published in 1609, is interesting enough on its own account to have received more attention than has hitherto been paid to it. In most modern editions of the Sonnets it is ignored, or only mentioned casually. Nor has it received any very careful study in editions of Shakespeare's Poems. . . .

This comparative neglect is the more strange, because the piece is expressly ascribed to Shakespeare, and was published as an appendix to the Sonnets, upon which, as much as or more than on any of the plays, comment and interpretation have for many years been concentrated. It obviously cannot be ignored in considering the problem of the Sonnets, and more particularly, that part of the problem which deals with the way in which they reached Thorpe's hands, the MSS. from which they were printed, and the circumstances of their publication. Nor can it be neglected in any general consideration of Shakespeare's poems taken apart from the plays, whether we regard it as an authentic work of Shakespeare or not. (p. 51)

I do not know how far Sir Sidney Lee would still hold by an

obiter dictum in his *Life of Shakespeare,* that 'if, as is possible, [*A Lover's Complaint*] be by Shakespeare, it must have been written in very early days.' Careful study leaves its authorship doubtful, but makes one thing pretty nearly certain, that whether it be by Shakespeare or not, it is not a work of Shakespeare's youth. This will appear on a more detailed consideration of its vocabulary, syntax, and style. (pp. 53-4)

The poem itself consists of 47 stanzas (329 lines) in rhyme royal. The management of the verse is not distinguishable from that of the *Lucrece* of 1594; but this verse was a settled form, in which we find but little metrical variation between one artificer of the period and another. The language, however, presents peculiarities which distinguish it sharply from Shakespeare's other poetry. These may be taken now under the three heads mentioned: (1) Vocabulary, (2) Syntax, (3) Phrasing; the last of which leads up to further consideration of the more subtle and imponderable element which we call style.

I. VOCABULARY.

Almost the first thing which strikes one on reading the poem is that this is highly mannered, and that the mannerism is not daring or even inventive, but rather laboured and tortuous. It does not, as Shakespeare habitually does, 'keep invention in a noted weed' [Sonnet 76], so that even strange words sound natural and right where they occur. Going into it more particularly, we find:

(1) Words which do not occur elsewhere in Shakespeare. Of these there are twenty-three: *plaintful* (l. 2), *untuck'd, sheav'd* (l. 31), *maund* (l. 36), *affectedly* (l. 48), *enswath'd* (l. 49), *fluxive* (l. 50), *fastly* (l. 61), *browny* (l. 85), *termless* (l. 94), *habitude* (l. 114), *weepingly* (l. 207), *annexions* (l. 208), *invis'd* (l. 212), *pensiv'd* (l. 219), *enpatron* (l. 224), *phraseless* (l. 225), *congest* (l. 258), *supplicant* (l. 276), *extincture* (l. 294), *plenitude* (l. 302), *unexperient* (l. 318), *lover'd* (l. 320).

In this list we may particularly notice the large number of Latinisms. . . . (pp. 54-5)

To these twenty-three non-Shakespearian words should perhaps be added seven more:

sistering (l. 2): *sister* as a verb occurs in one of the prologues in *Pericles,* which are generally held to be wholly non-Shakespearian.

forbod (l. 164)—forbidden.

acture (l. 185): but *enacture* occurs in *Hamlet.*

paled (l. 198), meaning not, as in Shakespeare, fenced, but pale; it may be merely a variant spelling of *pallid.*

encrimson'd (l. 201): but *crimson'd* occurs in *Julius Caesar.*

impleach'd (l. 205): but *pleached* occurs in *Much Ado.*

blend (l. 215)—parti-coloured: *blended* in an analogous sense occurs in *Troilus and Cressida.* . . . (p. 55)

(2) Words used in a different sense from their Shakespearian use. Of these there are sixteen, as follows:

fickle (l. 5), meaning delicate or 'nesh'.

storming (l. 7), with the sense of raising a storm over: 'storming her world'.

occasion (l. 86), in the sense of impact.

parcels (l. 87), meaning locks of hair.

phoenix (l. 93), used as an adjective, and apparently meaning newly-sprouting.

cost (l. 96), apparently in the sense of coat (*coste, côte*). It is curious that there is the converse doubt in l. 236, where *coat* seems to mean *cost,* though it may perhaps bear its ordinary meaning.

charmed (l. 146), in the sense of exercising charm.

mood (l. 201), in the sense of tint or colour.

talents (l. 204), meaning locks of (ruddy or golden) hair, like *parcels* already cited.

radiance (l. 214), used in a highly technical sense—power of vision, in accordance with one particular theory as to the nature of the sense of sight.

similes (l. 227), apparently meaning, or substituted through confusion for, symbols: a most curious usage. *Simile* in its ordinary sense is fairly common in Shakespeare.

distract (l. 231), as an adjective—separate.

suit (l. 234), used collectively and—body of suitors.

caged (l. 249), in the sense of cage-like or encaging.

impress (l. 267), in the sense of strike against or attack.

suffering (l. 272), with the meaning of painful.

In this list we have to note the recurrence of two characteristic features in the vocabulary of the poem which have already appeared in list (1) above: namely, the partiality of the author for Latinisms (*occasion, distract, impress*); and for participial neologisms (*storming* and *suffering,* analogously to *sistering; and charm'd* and *caged,* analogously to *sheav'd, pensiv'd, lover'd*).

This mass of *prima-facie* non-Shakespearian words or usages of words in a poem of only 329 lines raises of itself the question of Shakespearian authorship, though it falls short of pointing distinctly to an adverse conclusion. But, taken together with the list next following, it points distinctly to this, that if the poem is by Shakespeare, it belongs not to his early youth, but to his fully developed middle (or later) period. Some of the words already cited have, as we have seen, analogies in *Hamlet, Troilus and Cressida,* and *Julius Caesar.* But there is a further set of words which arrest attention by their strangeness, and which only occur in the Shakespearian plays of that middle or later period.

I now give a list (3) of these: there are twelve of them.
    reword (l. 1), also in *Hamlet.*
    concave (l. 1), also in *Julius Caesar.*
    pelleted (l. 18), also in *Antony and Cleopatra.*
    orbed (earth) (l. 25), also in *Hamlet* (orbed ground).
    commix (l. 28), also in *Cymbeline.*
    grained (bat) (l. 64), also in *Coriolanus* (grained ash).
    (nature's) outwards (l. 80), also in *Troilus and Cressida*
        (beauty's outward).
    pieced (—enhanced) (l. 119), also in *Antony and Cleopatra,*
        Coriolanus, Winter's Tale.
    dialogue (as verb) (l. 132), also in *Timon of Athens.*
    brokers (l. 173), also in *Hamlet.*
    amplify (l. 209), also in *Coriolanus, King Lear, Cymbeline.*
    cautel (l. 303), also in *Hamlet.* (pp. 55-7)

II. Syntax.

Under this head three notable peculiarities are to be observed, all alien from Shakespeare's ordinary usage, though instances of them are to be found in his undoubted work.

(1) Ellipsis of subject:
   l. 5. Ere long [I] espied a fickle maid full pale.
   l. 272. And [it] sweetens, in the suffering pangs it bears.
   l. 312. And, veil'd in them, [he] did win whom he would maim.

(2) Ellipsis of verb:
   l. 8. Upon her head [was] a platted hive of straw.
   l. 190. Among the many that mine eyes have seen, [was] Not one whose flame my heart so much as warm'd.

(3) Asyndeton: this is so largely used as to give a distinct colour to the style. The most striking instances are:
   ll. 44-7. gave the flood . . . cracked . . . found.
   ll. 51, 52. 'gan to tear; cried, O false blood!
   ll. 170-4. And knew . . . heard . . . saw . . . thought.

The influence of such distinctive points in vocabulary and grammatical construction on our judgement as regards the authorship of this or any other work depends on their cumulative effect. Singly, or in small proportion, they count for nothing. If, for example, we take *Lucrece,* a poem of undoubted authorship and known date, we can find in it a few instances of all or nearly all the linguistic points I have taken. . . . But it is obvious that these rare instances in a poem of nearly 2,000 lines present no effective parallel to the mass of peculiarities in *A Lover's Complaint* of little over 300 lines. This is so large that it cannot be ignored.

So far we have been dealing with definite facts, but with facts which prove nothing; at most they only point on the whole in a certain direction and suggest a possible inference. We may pass on now from purely verbal or grammatical points to another investigation, which is subtler, and requires more judgement in handling, but the conclusions of which, if any conclusions can be established, are more convincing; for it deals with matters which come closer to the vital essence of literary workmanship.

III. Phrasing and Style.

'Phrasing', for this purpose, is a part of style, covering characteristic usages in collocation of words and methods of expression. It is an element in style, but when we speak of style we look at the poet's language more largely, and with regard to his whole method and practice in the rhetorical evolution of thought or emotion through language. The word 'rhetorical' is here used in its technical, not in its popular sense; rhetoric meaning the science and art of language used so as to produce what is, in the full sense of the term, literature.

In *A Lover's Complaint* there are a noticeable number of phrases which, in a certain stiffness, tortuousness, or cumbrousness, are equally unlike the habitual ease and fluency of Shakespeare's earlier writing and the habitual full-chargedness (often passing into overchargedness) of his later writing. In the latter, phrasing is often clogged by excess of imagination; this moves quicker than the language can follow it, and the result is a sort of shorthand notation in which the words actually used suggest rather than express the thought which is behind them. . . . In this power of transformation Shakespeare stands alone. We do not find it, or find it very rarely, in this poem. What we do find habitually is a forcing of phrase, which follows a fashion of the period, but follows it as a servant, does not sway it as a master. Sometimes this forcing of phrase appears due to pedantry, to the artificiality of a contracted and ill-digested scholarship; sometimes to mere clumsiness, what Lee aptly calls incapacity of expression. It is needless to say that both these, and the latter even more than the former, are very un-Shakespearian qualities. A few instances will be sufficient to cite. 'The thought might think' (l. 10), and 'to do will aptly find'—'will be apt to find means of doing' (l. 88), are pieces of artificiality. 'A careless hand of pride'—'a hand careless of pride' (l. 30), 'noble by the sway'—'ennobled by submitting himself to government' (l. 108), and 'O, then, advance (of yours) that phraseless hand' (l. 225). . . . A more curious instance is l. 91, 'What largeness thinks in Paradise was sawn'. This is probably the most distorted phrase in the whole poem; but it is not un-Shakespearian; it is a real case of what I called the shorthand notation of Shakespeare's later manner. But of course the point is that (1) Shakespeare does not use this highly compressed shorthand in his poems; and (2) where he does use it, his use of it is masterly.

On the larger matter of style as it bears on the question of authorship the following considerations have to be weighed.

(1) *A Lover's Complaint* is not the work of a beginner. Its style, alike in its good and its bad points, is formed and even matured. After all allowance has been made for Shakespeare's power of imitating the style of other writers, and of anticipating his own later style in his earlier work, it seems to me impossible to think of this poem as a work of his youth, belonging to the period of *Lucrece.* It is either a work of his later and matured period, or not a work of his at all. And what points towards its being not a work of his, is that the formed style is combined with an intellectual weakness leading here and there to feeblenesses and flatnesses. (pp. 58-61)

(2) There are passages in *A Lover's Complaint* which, while quite Shakespearian in their quality, might have been written by any clever versifier who had studied Shakespeare, and learned the trick so far as it is a trick; such as ll. 155-6:

> But ah! who ever shunn'd by precedent
> The destined ill she must herself assay?

or ll. 183-4:

> All my offences that abroad you see
> Are errors of the blood, none of the mind.

And there are others which distinctly give the impression of imitations of Shakespeare by an inferior artist, like l. 21:

> In clamours of all size both high and low;

or ll. 104-5:

> His rudeness so with his authoriz'd youth
> Did livery falseness in a pride of truth;

or the whole of the stanza about horsemanship (ll. 106-12), if compared with the well-known passage in *Venus and Adonis,* stanzas 44-50:

> Well could he ride, and often men would say
> That horse his mettle from his rider takes:
> Proud of subjection, noble by the sway,
> What rounds, what bounds, what course, what stop
>   he makes!
> And controversy hence a question takes,
> Whether the horse by him became his deed,

Or he his manage by the well-doing steed.

Not only is the first line of this stanza incredibly flat, but the whole stanza is poor and ragged.

(3) On the other hand there are more than a few passages in the poem which are like Shakespeare at his best, and of which one would say at first sight that no one but Shakespeare could have written them, so wonderfully do they combine his effortless power and his incomparable sweetness. I need only cite three or four instances (ll. 14, 146-7, 237-8, 288-9):

Some beauty peep'd through lattice of sear'd age.

Threw my affections in his charmed power,
Reserv'd the stalk, and gave him all my flower.

But kept cold distance, and did thence remove,
To spend her living in eternal love.

O father, what a hell of witchcraft lies
In the small orb of one particular tear!

This last passage, as Shakespearian in its concentrated weight of passion as in its exquisiteness of rhythm and phrasing, contains a striking verbal likeness to a phrase in Sonnet 120; and this is only one out of several. . . . (pp. 61-3)

Yet on a large view the style and evolution of *A Lover's Complaint* must be set down as not characteristically Shakespearian, and as in some respects characteristically un-Shakespearian. A certain labouriousness, a certain cramped, gritty, discontinuous quality, affects it subtly but vitally throughout. (p. 63)

One criterion of the work of a really great poet is the way in which he starts a poem. To fumble at the beginning, to strike the first notes uncertainly, to open stiffly or languidly, is the sign of an inferior artist. Shakespeare meets this test from the first. The wonderful speed and certainty with which he sets his plays going has often been commented on. And the same thing is true of his poems. . . .

A Lover's Complaint hardly bears this test. Its opening,

From off a hill whose concave womb re-worded
A plaintful story from a sistering vale,

bears a strong superficial likeness to the opening of *Lucrece*. In both there is the same grammatical and rhetorical evolution. In both the single epithet in the first line is followed and as it were reduplicated by the pair of epithets in the second; in both the middle epithet of the group of three, *trustless, plaintful,* has the same sort of preciousness in its quality. But one cannot but feel that the opening couplet in *A Lover's Complaint* drags and is over-worded. (pp. 64-5)

We may now go back to the volume of 1609 and the circumstances of its production. It is generally held to have been printed from a surreptitiously obtained MS. Analysis of the printed text of the Sonnets shows that their MS. was not all in the same hand. It is a probable inference that what reached Thorpe's printers was a bundle of copied MS., and that together with the rest there was a copied MS. of *A Lover's Complaint.* But there is no need to suppose that either this or any part of the MS. bore on it an express attribution of authorship. We do not know, and presumably never shall know, how the MS. reached Thorpe's hands. The simplest and likeliest way would be that it reached him, directly or indirectly, from the person to whom the Sonnets were addressed. It is not necessary to touch here on the vexed question how far the

Sonnets embody or reflect Shakespeare's personal experience. In any event, the 'boy' of the Sonnets was an actual person; he was one who had poems addressed or dedicated to him by another poet besides Shakespeare; he was one who might very likely, a few years later, lose all the interest that he ever had in either set of poems, and toss them away, or give them to any one who wanted to have them. Thorpe's MS. was most likely a 'blank book' such as is mentioned in Sonnet 77, and may very well have been that actual book into which the contents of the printed volume of 1609 had been transcribed, either by the recipient of the poems, or by some one else for him, or partly by one and partly by the other.

The rival poet of the Sonnets is also admittedly an actual person. Let us put together what the Sonnets themselves tell us about him; this is the only clue we have to his identity.

In Sonnet 78, he had 'got my use': he could write like Shakespeare, or at least so like him as to be thought by others a poet of not inferior quality. That Shakespeare himself knew the difference, we may judge from the compressed bitterness of the single haughty line in Sonnet 86, 'I was not sick of any fear from thence'. From Sonnet 78 we gather also that he was 'learned', that he had 'grace' and 'arts'. In Sonnet 80 he is a 'better spirit'—here again there is an accent of sarcasm—a ship 'of tall building and of goodly pride'. In Sonnet 82 his poetry is called a 'fresher stamp of the time-bettering days'. This has the note of bitterness again: it is what now a painter of the orthodox tradition might say of a post-impressionist or futurist. What Shakespeare really thought of this fresher stamp comes out pretty clearly where, in the same sonnet, he speaks of 'what strained touches rhetoric can lend'. In Sonnet 85, his work is 'richly compiled': its 'character' is 'reserved with golden quill and precious phrase by all the Muses filed'. He is an 'able spirit', who writes 'in polish'd form of well-refined pen'. Lastly, in Sonnet 86, his work, 'the proud full sail of his great verse', is described as ambitious and tumid: his compeers by night (whoever they may be) teach him 'to write above a mortal pitch': he fancies that his own poetry 'astonishes' Shakespeare's, eclipses and outdoes it.

Much of this applies curiously well to *A Lover's Complaint,* with its preciosity, its strained rhetoric, its parade of learned words. . . . [Yet],—notwithstanding, there are bits of the poem in which the poet writes like Shakespeare—in which, we may even venture to say, he writes like Shakespeare at his best. It looks very like as if we had here either the rival poet imitating Shakespeare, or Shakespeare imitating the rival poet.

Shakespeare's power of assimilating almost any style he chose may be conceded. It is, if we think, just the formal or stylistic side of his wonderful dramatic gift; for he was as sensitive to language as he was to character. . . . Yet in this as in other respects he was an Elizabethan, though the greatest of the Elizabethans: in many of his contemporaries we can see, though in varying and inferior degree, something of the same power of what may be called stylistic impersonation. But if we have to choose, it seems easier to believe that a rival poet could catch, here and there, some reflection of Shakespeare's genius, than to believe that Shakespeare would deliberately and with no visible reason write down to the level of a rival's style. Where he does so write down to a style inferior to his own, it is either with a distinct accent of parody, or for a practical purpose—for the production, that is, of a play in which the style of the joint authors should not be too discrepant. He did so in *Henry VIII,* if he wrote the parts of *Henry VIII* which are usually attributed to him. But this latter condition does not arise here: and the former does not apply, for *A Lover's Complaint* is, both where it is good and where it is bad, perfectly serious.

Another point may be noted, though I do not press it. When we speak of a rival poet, we must remember that rivalry is mutual. In *A Lover's Complaint* there is a phrase about the 'deep-brain'd sonnets' received by Bel-Ami from other sources, which might almost be taken to be an oblique reflection on Shakespeare's Sonnets. And, more generally, the portraiture of this hero of the piece, if we may so call him, bears no small resemblance to that of the 'boy' of the Sonnets, seen from a different point of view. The resemblance even goes into particular detail. I would not lay much stress on this, for in both cases it may be mere Elizabethan common-form, the sort of touches 'whereto the inviting time our fashion calls' [Sonnet 124]. But when, for instance, we read of Bel-Ami in *A Lover's Complaint* that 'his browny locks did hang in crooked curls', we are inevitably reminded of the 'buds of marjoram' in Sonnet 99. (pp. 65-9)

Without having come to any certain conclusion, this discussion may have suggested lines of inquiry: and I could wish that some scholar would pursue the inquiry further, starting from the provisional working hypothesis I have sketched: namely, that *A Lover's Complaint* is a composition by the unknown rival poet of the Sonnets; that it got copied into the same blank book as the Sonnets; that this MS. book came into Thorpe's hands, with all its imperfections on its head; that he printed from it the quarto of 1609; that Shakespeare, as usual, took no interest in the matter; that the original recipient of the Sonnets either had likewise become unconcerned in them, or (which is also possible) was a person whose concern did not matter; and that, at a time when the vogue of the Sonnet was already over, the volume consequently attracted little contemporary notice. Even if this hypothesis or conjecture has on fuller investigation to be abandoned, the investigation itself will not be uninteresting, and perhaps may not be fruitless. (pp. 69-70)

J. W. Mackail, " 'A Lover's Complaint'," in Essays and Studies, *Vol. III, 1912, pp. 51-70.*

RAYMOND MACDONALD ALDEN (essay date 1922)

[*Alden was an American philologist and classicist who wrote widely on Shakespearean issues and edited the 1916 variorum edition of the sonnets. In the following excerpt, he discusses several themes that recur in Shakespeare's sonnets, such as the transiency of love and beauty. Alden also argues that while many of these verses are imitative or conventional, others apparently reflect "intimate experiences" of the poet and his friends. Taken as a whole, he judges, the sonnets convey a "reality of experience" and "the effect of sincerity."*]

It is highly probable . . . that Shakespeare first studied the art of the English sonnet in the sequences of Sidney and Daniel. The former poet, we may suppose, interested him in the traditional uses of the conceit in sonnet form, and in the possibility of expressing personal feeling in melodies derived from those of Italian verse; at any rate, Sidney had done both these things in a manner rarely surpassed to this day. But Shakespeare found both the mood and the style of Daniel's sonnets rather more consonant with his own. The same seriousness of tone which he had apparently found suggestive in *The Complaint of Rosamond* for his treatment of the story of

Lucrece, he also adopted in the sonnet. Sidney's most characteristic work in the *Astrophel and Stella* is playful,—profoundly playful, if one may say so, and with plenty of feeling underneath, but marked especially by the enormously clever use of charming dramatic conceits. Shakespeare never produced a sonnet of this type so good as the best of Sidney's, or, for that matter, so good as Drayton's famous "Since there's no help, come let us kiss and part." On the other hand he easily caught, and excelled, the expression of rich, gloomy moodiness, and of moral earnestness, as practiced by Daniel.

He also followed Daniel in adopting the "English" type of sonnet form, which had seemingly been invented by Surrey as a modification of the Italian type, and which most of the Elizabethans, despite Sidney's influence to the contrary, preferred. This form, consisting of three separately rimed quatrains, plus a final couplet, commonly produces a wholly different effect from that of the more intricately composed lines of the Petrarchans; it is rather more colloquial in tendency, more fluent, more suggestive of spontaneous utterance. On the other hand it rarely produces the exquisite sense of highly wrought perfection, as of an ivory carving, which the best specimens of the Italian type attain. It makes an impression of movement, of thought and feeling in evolution, as distinguished from that of thought and feeling recollected and made permanent "in tranquillity." At its best the three quatrains seem like incoming waves of imagery, each following upon its predecessor and rising a little higher; then there is a pause, when the couplet more quietly sums up or comments on the meaning of the three. . . . Perhaps the weakness of this form of sonnet lies chiefly in the possibility that the three quatrains may sufficiently carry out the poet's thought, and leave the final couplet as a mere appendix or anti-climax. This tendency Shakespeare did not wholly escape; even so fine a sonnet as the 116th . . . may seem to many readers to be at its best with the closing pair of lines forgotten.

It has been hinted that Shakespeare's sonnets are unlike Sidney's in making relatively little use, of a characteristic sort, of the conceit. This does not mean that he avoided conceits of any of the conventional kinds; but it is not for them that we remember the poems. Many of Sidney's best sonnets are wholly animated by the conceits that gave rise to them: the poet's ingenious imagery or reasoning is the soul of the composition, often forming a kind of miniature narrative or drama, based on some captivating personification or allegory. It follows that in such cases the charm of the sonnet can be represented in a prose paraphrase, which will bring out clearly the significance of the conceit. With Shakespeare none of these things is true. His conceits are commonly the conventional ones; they are not characteristic of the finest of his sonnets; and the charm of his compositions will almost always disappear when the verbal and metrical body which he gave them is taken away. It is also a quality of his sonnet style—as readers familiar with the plays would expect—that he passes swiftly from one image to another, more often letting a number of conceits represent kaleidoscopically the mood of the poem than building it consistently upon a single one. For example take the interesting 125th sonnet, on the subject of love as concerned not with externals but with realities. It opens with the metaphor of an attendant bearing a canopy over some great personage, but passes swiftly to that of a building on an insecure foundation; then we change from the image of tenants who pay too much rent to that of gluttons who give up simple food for too much sweetness,—thence to an oblation of flour unmixed with inferior grades. And the final couplet, instead of recapitulating any of these, takes still another flight into the figure of an "impeached soul." This, to be sure, is an extreme instance; and on the other hand certain of the sonnets are composed on beautifully unified imagery. Of these one of the noblest is the 106th, on the familiar conceit that when ancient writers set forth the praises of beauty, they were really foreseeing, like prophets, the loveliness of the poet's beloved. Every line is here true to the controlling image, whose evolution is completed by the couplet at the close. (pp. 125-29)

Coming now to look more closely at the real content of the sonnets, we shall doubtless do best to begin with those which are primarily to be viewed as exercises in the conventions of Renaissance lyric, and to pass to those which seem more individual than imitative. It is a natural assumption that in doing so we are also following, on the whole, the order of composition, though special circumstances might make this untrue in a number of cases. At the outset we observe a few sonnets whose only interest lies in the playful ingenuity of the poet's treatment of typical themes: the 128th, which toys with the fingers of a lady playing on the virginal; the 135th and 136th, which pun on the poet's name "Will," in connection with various Elizabethan meanings of the word; the 145th, another bit of word-play, so trifling in content that a number of critics refuse to believe it Shakespeare's; and the 153rd and 154th, parallel exercises in the re-working of a conceit, based on a classic myth, which came down to Shakespeare from an old Greek epigram. All these might have been the work of any of a hundred sonneteers for whom the form was a recreation of the lightest character. Of similar tone and style, but of somewhat more significance for its theme, is Sonnet 20, which sketches lightly, in the Italian manner, the portrait of a youth of such beauty and gentleness that he seems almost a lovely hermaphrodite, a mistake of Nature, whom the poet scarcely knows whether to call master or mistress of his love. For the Italians, as has already been noticed, such a poem would have seemed conventional enough, and Shakespeare treats it not with any suggestion of unnatural affection, but as a jest. Yet the theme was an exotic one, not naturalized in the English sonnet; and the presence in the collection of so many other sonnets having to do with a beautiful youth makes it natural to assume that its origin was personal as well as literary. So, for that matter, may have been the origin of almost any of the sonnets of these conventional types.

Chief, of course, among the themes common to all the sonneteers of the Renaissance, are those of Beauty and Love. . . . [Although] most of the English love poets made but slight use of platonism, in the stricter sense of the term, save for occasional decorative purposes, they nevertheless maintained its general point of view toward the relationship of love and beauty. They also followed the Italians in being concerned with these themes in both sexes, not alone (though no doubt far more largely) with reference to woman. The word love, among the Elizabethans, was as naturally used between men as between man and woman; conversely, the word friend was common between lovers. When, therefore, in the collection of Shakespeare's sonnets we find the sex of the person addressed to be sometimes ambiguous and disputed, it is a matter of difficulty for his biographers but for literary interpretation normal enough. Call it, then, love or friendship,—the sonnets play on all the conventional aspects and conceits of devotion. In the 22nd the heart of the poet has taken up its abode in the beloved's breast, and he bears with him the other's heart instead. In the 24th the beauty of the beloved

has been drawn on his heart, framed in his body, and hung in the shop of his bosom. In the 37th he views all the beauty, wealth, and wit of the beloved as his own by proxy. In the 46th his eye and heart dispute which is the more rightful owner of the beloved's image. In the 53rd he finds all other beauties to be but shadows or imitations (here perhaps is a touch of platonism) of the beauty of the beloved. In the 59th he wishes that the image of the beloved might in some way be transferred to a former age, that he might "see what the old world could say" of such a wonder. In the 68th, conversely, he views the beloved's beauty as an heirloom from better days, preserved by Nature in an age when artificial beauty prevails. In the 91st he finds all the glories which other men boast, according to their various tastes, bettered in "the one general best" of possessing the beloved. In the 99th he condemns the flowers for having stolen their color and perfume from the beloved's cheek and breath. In the 108th he reflects that he can find no new expression for his love, but, as in a liturgy, "hallows" the beloved's name in identical words day after day. In the 114th his eye, by a strange alchemy, changes the forms of even the worst objects presented to it into the "perfect best" of the beloved's image. It would be hazardous to try to say just which of these conceits were borrowed from Shakespeare's predecessors, and which of them he devised, in their present form, anew. But in poetic method they are all conventional.

This, however, is not the whole story. For in some cases the formal ingenuity of the composition is the principal thing, and the personal feeling which it professes to illustrate is rather assumed than felt; whereas in the greater number of the sonnets, even of this group, the poet has so saturated even the conventional imagery with lyric beauty and feeling that an impression of reality of experience dominates the whole. Whether this means more of "sincerity," as we often phrase it, than in the more awkward and merely formal sonnets, one cannot be sure; a lover inexpert in composition is not therefore less a lover. But the *effect* of sincerity is attained when the intellectual effort is submerged in the language of the heart. Nor are the conceits, even in themselves, of equal poetic value: some, like that of the exchange of hearts, or the warfare of eye and heart, are so superficial in character, so far from identifying themselves with any spiritual experience, that one naturally puts them in the same class with the protestations of one's correspondents on St. Valentine's Day. But others faithfully represent a significant reality. For example of this, take the notion that a great love seems to gather into itself all previous affections in the lover's experience, and to fuse in the beloved the identities of dear friends who have been lost awhile: this may be called a conceit, if elaborated formally, but it is a spiritual reality too. Shakespeare knew it as such, and glorified it in the 31st Sonnet:

Thy bosom is endeared with all hearts
Which I by lacking have supposed dead:
And there reigns love and all love's loving parts,
And all those friends which I thought buried.
How many a holy and obsequious tear
Hath dear religious love stolen from mine eye
As interest of the dead, which now appear
But things remov'd that hidden in thee lie!
Thou art the grave where buried love doth live,
Hung with the trophies of my lovers gone,
Who all their parts of me to thee did give;
That due of many now is thine alone.
　　Their images I loved I view in thee,
　　And thou, all they, hast all the all of me.

Over against the sonnets of devotion we must set two or three in what has sometimes been called the "anti-Petrarchan" manner, well known in Italian and French poetry of the sixteenth century. Here the poet, either playfully or satirically, rejects the artifices of the sonneteers of love, though elsewhere abundantly practicing them. . . . Shakespeare's chief examples are the 21st, satirizing the professional maker of similes, who "every fair with his fair doth rehearse," and the 130th, in which the poet renounces, for his mistress, all claim to the beauties wherewith ladies are conventionally adorned. Going a step further, we come to the sonnets of "vituperation," in which a mistress is not merely refused the expected compliments but actually reviled. This type also had become familiar in Italy and France, and some find it represented in a few of Shakespeare's sonnets, the most disagreeable, on the whole, of any in the Elizabethan collections (see especially the 137th, 138th, the 141st, and the 150th). But these go so much further, in apparent realism and seriousness of tone, than any of the models that have been recalled as parallels, that to most readers they seem to belong not in the conventional but in the more personal class.

The evanescence of beauty is another of the dominant themes of the Renaissance sonnet, which brings it in tune with the elegiac element in the love poetry of every age. That youth should fade, that a lovely face "among the wastes of time must go" [Sonnet 12], is the perpetual tragedy that touches us all, but poets most of all. For reasons of which we know nothing, Shakespeare found this theme particularly appealing. One might say that it gives more of unity to the body of his sonnets than any other, and suggests that a great part of them were written when he felt with special keenness the transiency of the precious things that go with youth. This has been made a means of argument, naturally enough, for one date or another, yet we know that the sense of growing old has little to do with the facts of the calendar. The grim autocracy of Time was a familiar subject of the poets, and Lucrece had devoted many lines to it in Shakespeare's version of her story; but in the Sonnets we have not only this shadowing, inexorable figure of Time, but a constant disposition on the part of the poet to count every wrinkle on his own face and every sign of fading bloom on the faces of his friends. Something, too, of a dramatic struggle intervenes, in which we become conscious of the figures of love and poetry contending against Time, now with less of hope, now with more. In the platonic philosophy this notion of the evanescence of beauty was connected with the interpretation of the reproductive instinct: love seeks propagation in order to perpetuate or renew the beauty of the beloved; and the protestations of lovers, throughout Renaissance literature, had made much of this material. . . . In a series of seventeen sonnets, which stand at the opening of the collection, Shakespeare restudied this theme with more of variety and beauty than any other poet of the age, but in a new application,—not, as commonly, in the appeal of a passionate lover to the object of his desire, but in an appeal to a friend whose beauty the poet cannot endure to see fade without renewal. Doubtless the theme was suggested by an interest in some actual youth of marriageable age, but with what degree of personal feeling each reader must judge for himself.

Another means of defeating Time's designs against beauty was to invoke the powers of poetry, the art supremely capable of eternizing worthy things in fadeless lines. Almost every sonneteer of the age took up this story, finding the subject a means of combining the praises of love with the classical theme of the poet's work as "a monument more lasting than bronze"; and Shakespeare, as with other themes, took it up to give it something like final expression in his 55th and 65th sonnets.

> O fearful meditation! where, alack,
> Shall Time's best jewel from Time's chest lie hid?
> Or what strong hand can hold his swift foot back?
> Or who his spoil of beauty can forbid?
>
> [Sonnet 65]

The answer is found in "black ink," in "powerful rhyme":

> 'Gainst death and all-oblivious enmity
> Shall you pace forth; your praise shall still find
>   room
> Even in the eyes of all posterity
> That wear this world out to the ending doom.
>
> [Sonnet 55] (pp. 129-36)

But there is a conflict more important than that of Time with Beauty; it is that of Time with Love. The peril is that Time, in defeating Beauty, may defeat Love also; and poetry can do nothing to forestall this. The platonists had also their answer for this problem: it was that, though love is born of beauty, it properly tends to pass from the beauty of the outer to that of the inner world, and rises eventually to be a thing of the spirit. . . . Shakespeare was not a platonist. He seems sometimes to make allusive use of concepts or phrases which the members of that school had contributed to current poetry, but he was not interested in symbolism, nor in transcendental interpretations of common experience. Yet he could not avoid the problem for which no answer save that of the inner life has ever been found. The deepest of his sonnets of love or friendship, then, are those which represent it as an inner experience triumphant over circumstance. In the 29th it triumphs over ill fortune and defeated ambition:

> When, in disgrace with Fortune and men's eyes,
> I all alone beweep my outcast state,
> And trouble deaf heaven with my bootless cries,
> And look upon myself and curse my fate;
> Wishing me like to one more rich in hope,
> Featur'd like him, like him with friends possess'd,
> Desiring this man's art, and that man's scope,
> With what I most enjoy contented least;
> Yet in these thoughts myself almost despising,
> Haply I think on thee: and then my state,
> Like to the lark at break of day arising
> From sullen earth, sings hymns at heaven's gate.
>   For thy sweet love remember'd such wealth
>   brings
>   That then I scorn to change my state with kings.

In the 30th it triumphs over loss and sorrow. In the 123rd it triumphs over the ravages of Time, and again, in the 124th, over the accidents of Time's love or Time's hate. In the 116th all these triumphs are summed up in a solemn affirmation or credo, which might well stand at the close of the series, were the sonnets arranged in topical order. . . . Each of the sonnets in this group is, of course, a carefully wrought work of art, with a place in the traditions of the form. But none of them is conspicuously conventional, and their very lack of the common formulae of the platonists, the Petrarchans, or the rest, seems to bring us to hear in them the authentic lyric voice of Shakespeare.

We have by no means exhausted the themes of the sonnets of love, but must note the remainder more rapidly. A considerable group concerns the subject of love in absence, including those based on familiar conceits already associated with that theme, such as the 27th or the 43rd, with others of deeper and more individual quality, like the beautiful 52nd, in which the time of separation is viewed

> as the wardrobe which the robe doth hide,
> To make some special instant special blest
> By new unfolding his imprison'd pride.

Wholly of this deeper sort are three or four sonnets on love in contemplation of death: the 66th, which enumerates, in Hamlet-like mood, all the ills which make life easy to renounce; the 71st, in which the poet begs to be forgotten, lest "thinking on me then should make you woe"; the 73rd, perhaps supreme in workmanship . . . , and the 74th, wherein the poet's "better part" is promised to remain with his friend, when "the dregs of life" have been lost. Of quite another character are certain sonnets, some twenty in all, which represent love in estrangement. Here the conventional element is almost wholly wanting, and the personal note very strong; in particular, these poems are marked by an extraordinary spirit of self-submission, far exceeding mere forgiveness, despite the fact that in most of them it is implied that the cause of the estrangement lies wholly in the friend addressed. The poet, we are told (as in the 88th), will take sides against himself on behalf of the one he loves; whatever is alleged against him (in the 89th) he will not merely not deny, but will actually bring proof to support it. The sonnet immediately following these is the poetic climax of the group in question,—perhaps the most beautiful lyric of injured love in all literature:

> Then hate me when thou wilt; if ever, now,
> Now, while the world is bent my deeds to cross,
> Join with the spite of Fortune, make me bow,
> And do not drop in for an after-loss;
> Ah, do not, when my heart hath scap'd this sorrow,
> Come in the rearward of a conquer'd woe;
> Give not a windy night a rainy morrow,
> To linger out a purpos'd overthrow.
> If thou wilt leave me, do not leave me last,
> When other petty griefs have done their spite,
> But in the onset come; so shall I taste
> At first the very worst of Fortune's might;
>   And other strains of woe, which now seem woe,
>   Compar'd with loss of thee will not seem so.

[Sonnet 90]

Clearly we have now passed very largely out of the field of conventionalism in the sonnets, into that of individual lyric art; and there are several other groups or classes which seem even more conspicuously to represent the personal side of the collection. For example, we find a number of sonnets, related in a puzzling way to those just discussed, which imply fault, infidelity, or ill reputation on the part of the poet,—some of them sad yet relatively light of tone, like the 109th and 112th, others deeply serious, and saved from tragedy only by a note of reconciliation, like the 119th and 120th. Certain other groups resemble these sonnets in being not wholly intelligible without some knowledge of the circumstances that gave rise to them. Such are the sonnets on the dark woman, at once fascinating and repellent, those which apparently involve a story of the theft of the poet's friend by a false mistress, and those which concern a rivalry with one or more other poets in the graces of a patron. . . . For all these poems, to be sure, interesting parallels have been found. The Italians had written on women whose beauty was unconventional and whose character was unadmirable, on rival poets and fickle patrons,

on men who depreciated themselves to honor their friends, and who freely forgave their friends for stealing their sweethearts. Thus, if Shakespeare knew intimately the poetry of his continental predecessors and contemporaries, it is true that he had no need to invent a single theme for his sonnets, even of the less usual kinds. But, aside from the doubtful probability of his having any such intimate knowledge, the sonnets we are now considering present little evidence of imitation and much of direct personal utterance. They are not among the best of the collection; they are not so lucid, so skilfully wrought, or so beautiful, as their author could easily have made them, had he been interested in them primarily as works of art. Their power consists in intensity of feeling and ironic realism, rather than in either intellectual or verbal charm. To most readers, then, they seem to show that a lyric form which Shakespeare originally practiced by way of imitative experiment, and later for the most finished expression of the great themes of poetry, he also came to use, purely for private satisfaction, in comment or correspondence on intimate experiences of himself and his friends.

Many of the sonnets have been omitted altogether from the foregoing survey, and cannot be recalled for consideration here. But there are two, standing quite in isolation from all the themes that have been noticed, that we must not altogether let slip. Each is a moral epigram in sonnet form,—mature, compact, and of powerful expressiveness,—which Shakespeare would seem to have composed in some moment of reflection, quite apart from the sonneteering habit. The 129th is on Lust, and might be viewed as a study akin to the verses on that theme in *The Rape of Lucrece.* It sums up all human experience on the subject, in fourteen lines which sternly say all that could be said in forty or four hundred. It would serve as motto for *Measure for Measure,* or epitaph for Edmund in *King Lear.* The 146th sonnet is an equally serious, but less impersonal and more lyrical, study of the soul imprisoned and starved by a sinful body. Again we are reminded of *Lucrece,* and the scene where Tarquin's soul has been captured and enthralled by the rebel subjects, the senses. Shakespeare, striking here a note not of the Renaissance but of Christian renunciation and faith, bids his soul rally her powers, starve the rebels that herself may be fed, and so in the end triumph even over Death, whose dominion is of the body. . . . (pp. 137-43)

It is evident why it has been possible for critics to write so much of the sonnets of Shakespeare, and to quarrel with one another at every point. They have disputed about the date of composition as a single problem, whereas much may be said for indications of many periods of Shakespeare's development. They have debated whether the sonnets were personal or impersonal, and again have discovered proof on both sides. In some cases they have emphasized the conventional conceits in the sonnets, until one would suppose there was nothing else to find there; in others the essential originality of the poet has caused the elements of imitative art to be ignored. Even in the realm of appreciation there have been equally divergent views, ranging all the way from George Steevens's declaration that an act of Parliament could not compel readers for the sonnets, and Hallam's, that "it is impossible not to wish that Shakespeare had never written them," to Wordsworth's judgment that "in no part of the writings of this poet is found, in an equal compass, a greater number of exquisite feelings felicitously expressed [see excerpts above, 1793, 1837-39, and 1815]. . . . For certain of the sonnets every one of these things is true. If all of them are really Shakespeare's, they show us every stage of development, and every mode of application, of his lyric art. Some are purely, even crudely, imitative of the affectations of the Renaissance. Some are powerfully expressive of individual feeling, but too largely the creation of special circumstances to stand by themselves as lastingly significant poems. But the best (and these no meagre handful, such as one culls from among the numerous commonplaces of the Elizabethan sonnet sequences as a whole) combine, like all great lyrics, personal feeling with content of wide and permanent significance; they challenge the affection of one generation after another, both by beauty of form and truth of thought. (pp. 143-44)

> *Raymond Macdonald Alden, "The Poems," in his* Shakespeare, *Duffield & Company, 1922, pp. 105-46.*

L. C. KNIGHTS (essay date 1934)

[*A renowned English Shakespearean scholar, Knights followed the precepts of I. A. Richards and F. R. Leavis as he attempted to identify an underlying pattern in all of Shakespeare's work. His* How Many Children Had Lady Macbeth? *(1933)—a milestone study in twentieth-century reaction to the Shakespearean criticism of the previous century—takes issue with the traditional emphasis on "character" as an approach to Shakespeare's plays. In the following excerpt from one of the earliest analyses of the language and imagery in Shakespeare's sonnets, Knights disparages the biographical approach to the sonnets, arguing that the "most profitable" analysis is to examine their technical elements and "to consider them in relation to the development of Shakespeare's blank verse." He posits that although the language and imagery in the poems are not as complex or encompassing as in Shakespeare's later plays, they demonstrate nonetheless a significant advance from the ornamental verse of the earlier works and, even, the poetry of Edmund Spenser. This is so, according to Knights, because the language of the sonnets plays a crucial part in conveying the meaning of the poems; the vocabulary, imagery, and diction are not mere ornamentation, but are inseparable from the various themes and motifs within each poem. Knights also discusses the autobiographical basis of the sonnets contending that the biographical critics typically fail to recognize that much in these verses is conventional and that Shakespeare, rather than being "completely enthralled" by his feelings for his friend or lover, is often detached, critical of events and figures in these poems. Knights's principal point is, even if we could prove that Shakespeare's sonnets are autobiographical, "the only importance they could have for us would be as poetry, as something made out of experience."*]

That there is so little genuine criticism in the terrifying number of books and essays on Shakespeare's Sonnets can only be partly accounted for by the superior attractiveness of gossip. A more radical explanation is to be found in certain widespread, more or less unconscious assumptions. In the first place, although consciously we may not believe that the Sonnets—even the first hundred and twenty-six—form a continuous and ordered collection, we tend to assume that the collection is more homogeneous than in fact it is, and we tend, therefore, to make rather sweeping generalizations about 'The Sonnets' as a whole. A second assumption was made amusingly explicit in the words which John Benson, the publisher of the 1640 edition—who had an eye on changing taste—addressed to the Reader: 'In your perusall you shall finde them SEREN, cleere and eligantly plaine, such gentle straines as shall recreate and not perplex your braine, no intricate or cloudy stuffe to puzzell intellect, but perfect eloquence' [see excerpt above, 1640]. Many of the sonnets were

written about the time of *A Midsummer Night's Dream* and *Romeo and Juliet;* the verse is therefore essentially unlike the verse of *King Lear*—it is incapable of subtleties; the meaning is on the surface. No doubt this is an exaggeration, but the effects of an assumption not very dissimilar to this can be seen in such essays as keep decently clear of William Hughes, the Sea Cook, and the rest, and which attempt to approach the sonnets directly, as poetry. (p. 133)

If we can rid ourselves of these two presuppositions we shall have gone some way towards a revaluation of the Sonnets. 'Shakespeare's Sonnets' is a miscellaneous collection of poems, written at different times, for different purposes, and with very different degrees of poetic intensity. (Gildon's edition had the appropriate title, *Poems on Several Occasions.*) The first necessity of criticism is to assess each poem independently, on its merits as poetry, and to abandon all attempts to find an ordered sequence. The second necessity is to know what kind of *development* to look for—which is a different matter. (p. 134)

[The] popular view that the Sonnets are in some way 'autobiographical' demands some notice. The eloquent chapters in which Frank Harris melts out Shakespeare's personal history from the poetic alloy ('The Sonnets give us the story, the whole terrible, sinful, magical story of Shakespeare's passion.' [see excerpt above, 1909]) are merely an exotic development of a kind of writing that is common among more eminent critics. 'No capable poet,' says Dr. Bradley, 'much less a Shakespeare, intending to produce a merely "dramatic" series of poems, would dream of inventing *a story like that of the Sonnets,* or, even if he did, of treating it as they treat it.' Now the first point that I wish to make against the common forms of biographical excursion (leaving aside for the moment more important considerations) is that the foundations on which they are built have not, to say the least, been the subject of any very discriminating attention. Those who are unwilling to accept the particular validity of Mr. Eliot's remark that 'the more perfect the artist, the more completely separate in him will be the man who suffers and the mind which creates; the more perfectly will the mind digest and transmute the passions which are its material,' backed though it is by the authority of Coleridge . . . , have only to turn to the Sonnets of supposedly highest biographical significance and consider them as examples of personal poetry: that is, as expressions by a powerful mind of reactions to a situation in which the man himself is deeply concerned. (pp. 135-36)

Sonnet 42 runs:

> That thou hast her it is not all my griefe,
> And yet it may be said I lov'd her deerely,
> That she hath thee is of my wayling cheefe,
> A losse in love that touches me more neerely.

Since the obvious is sometimes necessary, we may say that if Shakespeare had suffered the experience indicated by a prose paraphrase (for some of the biographical school the Sonnets might as well have been in prose) it would have affected him very differently from *this.* The banal movement, the loose texture of the verse, the vague gestures that stand for emotion, are sufficient index that his interests are not very deeply involved. (Contrast the run and ring of the verse, even in minor sonnets, when Shakespeare is absorbed by his subject— 'Devouring time blunt thou the Lyons pawes . . .' [Sonnet

19].) His sole interest is in the display of wit, the working out of the syllogism:

> Loving offendors thus I will excuse yee,
> Thou doost love her, because thou knowst I love
>   her,
> And for my sake even so doth she abuse me,
> Suffering my friend for my sake to approove
>   her, . . .
> But here's the joy, my friend and I are one,
> Sweete flattery, then she loves but me alone.
>
>   [Sonnet 42]

This, I admit, is a particularly glaring example, though it has its parallels amongst the False Friend and Faithless Mistress sonnets of 'Group B' (Numbers 127-152) to which the notes commonly refer us at this point, and the complete insipidity of one 'autobiographical' sonnet is enough to cause some honest doubt. Sonnets 78 to 86, dealing with the rival poets, are superior as poetry, but here also it is plain that Shakespeare derived a good deal of pleasure from the neatness of the argument:

> I grant (sweet love) thy lovely argument
> Deserves the travaile of a worthier pen,
> Yet what of thee thy Poet doth invent,
> He robs thee of, and payes it thee againe.
>
>   [Sonnet 79]

Wyndham remarked that these nine sonnets are 'playful throughout, suggesting no tragedy' [see excerpt above, 1898]—though 'playful' hardly does them justice. They are rather fine examples of an unusual mode of compliment and complaint, at once courtly and ironic. Those who picture Shakespeare as completely enthralled by his love for a particular friend or patron, and therefore deeply wounded by neglect, can hardly have noticed the tone of critical, and sometimes amused, detachment adopted towards himself ('Cleane starved for a looke' [Sonnet 75]), the rival ('He of tall building and of goodly pride' [Sonnet 80]), and the recipient of his verses ('You to your beautious blessings adde a curse, Being fond on praise, which makes your praises worse' [Sonnet 84]).

Of course I do not mean to imply that Shakespeare had never felt love or friendship or exasperation, or that his personal experiences had no effect on his poetry.—One can hardly say of the Sonnets, as Johnson said of Cowley's *Mistress,* that 'the compositions are such as might have been written for penance by a hermit, or for hire by a philosophical rhymer who had only heard of another sex.'—I am merely insisting that those who are attracted by biographical speculation should be quite sure of what Shakespeare is doing, of the direction and quality of his interests, before they make a flat translation into terms of actual life: that is, even the biographers must be literary critics. Some of the most interesting and successful sonnets may well have had their context in a personal relationship; but whenever we analyse their interest . . . we find that it lies, not in the general theme or situation, which is all that is relevant to a biographical interpretation, but in various accretions of thought and feeling, . . . in the exploration of a mood or discrimination of emotion. If this is so, the attempt to isolate the original stimulus (which in any case *may* have been an imagined situation . . .) is not only hazardous, it is irrelevant. After all, even if Shakespeare had assured us that the Sonnets were written under the stress of a friendship broken and restored and an intrigue with Mary Fitton, the only importance they could have for us would be as poetry, as something *made out of* experience.

With this criterion of importance we can see in proper perspective a second argument—commonly offered as the only alternative to the biographical theory—that the sonnets are exercises on conventional themes, embellished with conventional ornaments. The argument has a definite place in criticism, and we should be grateful to Sir Sidney Lee for his exhaustive collection of parallels [see excerpt above, 1898]. When we read

> Not marble, nor the guilded monument,
> Of Princes shall out-live this powrefull rime
>
>   [Sonnet 55]

it is perhaps as well that we should know that the lines have an ancestry reaching back at least as far as Horace; it is as well that we should be familiar with the theme of mutability and the various forms of diluted Platonism that were common when Shakespeare wrote. But a convention is a general thought, a general attitude, or a general mode of presentation, and a discussion of Shakespeare's Sonnets in terms of the 'typical' Elizabethan sonnet sequence tells us no more about them than an account of the Revenge Play tells us about *Hamlet.*

The most profitable approach to the Sonnets is, it seems to me, to consider them in relation to the development of Shakespeare's blank verse. There are certain obvious difficulties: the Sonnets take their start from something that can, for convenience, be called the Spenserian mode, whereas the influence of Spenser on the early plays is both slighter and more indirect; and the dramatic verse naturally contains a good many elements that are not to be found in any of the sonnets. But it is only by making what may seem an unnecessarily roundabout approach—even then at the risk of oversimplification—that one can hope to shift the stress to those aspects of the sonnets that it is most profitable to explore.

No account of the development of Shakespeare's blank verse in general terms can be very satisfactory. A comparison will help to point my few necessary generalizations. Richard's lament at Pomfret is a fairly typical example of the early set speeches:

> And here have I the daintiness of ear
> To check time broke in a disorder'd string;
> But for the concord of my state and time
> Had not an ear to hear my true time broke.
> I wasted time, and now doth time waste me;
> For now hath time made me his numbering clock:
> My thoughts are minutes; and with sighs they jar
> Their watches on unto mine eyes, the outward
>   watch,
> Whereto my finger, like a dial's point,
> Is pointing still, in cleansing them from tears.
> Now sir, the sound that tells what hour it is
> Are clamorous groans, which strike upon my heart,
> Which is the bell: so sighs and tears and groans
> Show minutes, times, and hours: but my time
> Runs posting on in Bolingbroke's proud joy,
> While I stand fooling here, his Jack o' the clock.
>
>   [*Richard II,* V. v. 45-60]

The only line that could possibly be mistaken for an extract from a later play is the last, in which the concentrated bitterness ('Jack o' the clock' has a wide range of relevant associations, and the tone introduces a significant variation in the rhythm) serves to emphasize the previous diffuseness. It is not merely that the imagery is elaborated out of all proportion to any complexity of thought or feeling, the emotion is suspended whilst the conceit is developed, as it were, in its own right. Similarly the sound and movement of the verse, the alliteration, repetition and assonance, seem to exist as objects of attention in themselves rather than as the medium of a compulsive force working from within. Such emotion as is communicated is both vague and remote.

Set beside this the well known speech of Ulysses:

> Time hath, my lord, a wallet at his back,
> Wherein he puts alms for oblivion,
> A great-siz'd monster of ingratitudes:
> Those scraps are good deeds past; which are de-
> vour'd
> As fast as they are made, forgot as soon
> As done: perseverance, dear my lord,
> Keeps honour bright: to have done is to hang
> Quite out of fashion, like a rusty mail
> In monumental mockery. Take the instant way;
> For honour travels in a strait so narrow
> Where one but goes abreast: keep then the path;
> For emulation hath a thousand sons
> That one by one pursue: if you give way,
> Or hedge aside from the direct forthright,
> Like to an enter'd tide they all rush by
> And leave you hindmost.
>
> [*Troilus and Cressida,* III. iii. 145-60]

The verse of course is much more free, and the underlying speech movement gives a far greater range of rhythmic subtlety. The sound is more closely linked with—is, in fact, an intimate part of—the meaning. The imagery changes more swiftly. But these factors are only important as contributing to a major development: the main difference lies in the greater immediacy and concreteness of the verse. In reading the second passage more of the mind is involved, and it is involved in more ways. It does not contemplate a general emotion, it *lives* a particular experience. Crudely, the reader is not told that there is a constant need for action, he experiences a particular urgency. (pp. 136-41)

This line of development (continued in the plays of complete maturity) is central. Primarily it is a matter of technique—the words have a higher potency, they release and control a far more complex response than in the earlier plays—but it is much more than that. The kind of immediacy that I have indicated allows the greatest subtlety in particular presentment . . . , whilst 'the quick flow and the rapid change of the images,' as Coleridge noted, require a 'perpetual activity of attention on the part of the reader,' generate, we may say, a form of activity in which thought and feeling are fused in a new mode of apprehension. That is, the technical development implies—is dependent on—the development and unification of sensibility. It is this kind of development (in advance of the dramatic verse of the same period in some respects and obviously behind it in others) that we find in the Sonnets, and which makes it imperative that discussion should start from considerations of technique. (p. 141)

After 1579 the most pervasive influence on Elizabethan lyric poetry was that of Spenser. *Astrophel and Stella* may have been the immediate cause of the numerous sonnet cycles, but it was from Spenser that the sonneteers derived most of their common characteristics—the slow movement and melody, the use of imagery predominantly visual and decorative, the romantic glamour, the tendency towards a gently elegiac note. In the Spenserian mode no object is sharply forced upon the consciousness. . . . Now there is in Shakespeare's Sonnets a quality that, at a first reading, seems very near to this:

Sonnets 98 and 102, for example, are successful as fairly direct developments of the Spenserian mode. But if we turn to Sonnet 35 we see the conjunction of that mode with something entirely new.

> No more bee greev'd at that which thou hast done,
> Roses have thornes, and silver fountaines mud,
> Cloudes and eclipses staine both Moone and Sunne,
> And loathsome canker lives in sweetest bud.
> All men make faults, and even I in this,
> Authorizing thy trespas with compare,
> My selfe corrupting salving thy amisse,
> Excusing thy sins more then thy sins are:
> For to thy sensuall fault I bring in sence,
> Thy adverse party is thy Advocate,
> And gainst my selfe a lawfull plea commence,
> Such civill war is in my love and hate,
>   That I an accessary needs must be,
>   To that sweet theefe which sourely robs from me.

The first four lines we may say, both in movement and imagery, are typically Spenserian and straightforward. The fifth line begins by continuing the excuses, 'All men make faults,' but with an abrupt change of rhythm Shakespeare turns the generalization against himself: 'All men make faults, and even I in this,' *i.e.* in wasting my time finding romantic parallels for your sins, as though intellectual analogies ('sence') were relevant to your sensual fault. The painful complexity of feeling (Shakespeare is at the same time tender towards the sinner and infuriated by his own tenderness) is evident in the seventh line which means both, 'I corrupt myself when I find excuses for you' (or 'when I comfort myself in this way'), and, 'I'm afraid I myself make you worse by excusing your faults'; and although there is a fresh change of tone towards the end (The twelfth line is virtually a sigh as he gives up hope of resolving the conflict), the equivocal 'needs must' and the sweet-sour opposition show the continued civil war of the emotions.

Some such comment as this was unavoidable, but it is upon the simplest and most obvious of technical devices that I wish to direct attention. In the first quatrain the play upon the letters *s* and *l* is mainly musical and decorative, but with the change of tone and direction the alliterative *s* becomes a hiss of half-impotent venom:

> All men make faults, and even I in thi*s*,
> Authorizing thy trespa*s* with compare,
> My *s*elfe corrupting *s*alving thy ami*ss*e,
> Excusing thy *s*ins more then thy *s*ins are:
> For to thy *s*en*s*uall fault I bring in *s*ence . . .

The scorn is moderated here, but it is still heard in the slightly rasping note of the last line,

> To that sweet theefe which sourely robs from me.

From the fifth line, then, the alliteration is functional: by playing off against the comparative regularity of the rhythm it expresses an important part of the meaning, and helps to carry the experience alive into the mind of the reader. With Spenser or Tennyson in mind we should say that both alliteration and assonance were primarily musical devices, as indeed they are in many of the sonnets:

> Noe longer mourne for me when I am dead,
> Than you shall heare the surly sullen bell
> Give warning to the world that I am fled
> From this vile world with vildest wormes to dwell.
>
> [Sonnet 71]

Here, for example, the sound, if not independent of the meaning, usurps a kind of attention that is incompatible with a full and sharp awareness. But that which links the sonnets, in this respect, with the later plays is the use of assonance and alliteration to secure a heightened awareness, an increase of life and power. . . . (pp. 142-44)

A slight shift of attention brings into focus a second aspect of development connected with the first. If we open any of the great plays almost at random we find effects comparable in kind to this, from *Lear:*

> Crown'd with rank fumiter and furrow-weeds,
> With hor-docks, hemlocks, nettles, cuckoo-flowers,
> Darnel, and all the idle weeds that grow
> In our sustaining corn.
>
> [*King Lear,* IV. iv. 3-6]

The rank and bristling profusion of the weeds is there, in the clogged movement of the first two lines, whilst the unimpeded sweep of the verse that follows contributes powerfully to the image of never-failing fertility. In many of the sonnets we can see Shakespeare working towards this use of his medium, learning to use a subtly varied play of the speech rhythm and movement against the formal pattern of the verse:

> Ah yet doth beauty like a Dyall hand,
> Steale from his figure, and no pace perceiv'd.
>
> [Sonnet 104]

> And on just proofe surmise, accumilate.
>
> [Sonnet 117]

> Then hate me when thou wilt, if ever, now,
> Now while the world is bent my deeds to
> crosse . . .
>
> [Sonnet 90]

> That it could so preposterouslie be stain'd . . .
>
> [Sonnet 109]

In the steady movement of the first extract, in the slightly impeded progress of the second, in the impetuous movement of the third, and the rising incredulity of the fourth, the verse (if I may borrow the phrase) 'enacts the meaning.' Perhaps one can hardly miss this kind of effect, but a development connected with it—the use of speech movement and idiom in the sonnets to obtain a firmer command of tone (a matter of some importance in determining their meaning)—seems to have been fairly consistently overlooked. The sonnet form is a convention in which it is only too easy to adopt a special 'poetic' attitude, and to the four 'strong promises of the strength of Shakespeare's genius' which Coleridge found in the early poems might well be added a fifth: the way in which, in his sonnets, he broke away from the formal and incantatory mode (convention and precedent being what they were) to make the verse a more flexible and transparent medium. Sonnet 7 has a typically stylized opening:

> Loe in the Orient when the gracious light,
> Lifts up his burning head, each under eye
> Doth homage to his new appearing sight,
> Serving with lookes his sacred majesty.

Contrast, say, Sonnet 82:

> I grant thou wert not married to my Muse,
> And therefore maiest without attaint ore-looke
> The dedicated words which writers use

> Of their faire subject, blessing every booke.

In the first line we hear the inflexion of the speaking voice, and it is the conversational movement that contributes the equivocal note of amused irony, directed towards the fulsome dedications and their—inevitably—fair subject. (Compare the 'precious phrase by all the Muses filed' of Sonnet 85). Sometimes a similar effect is used for deliberate contrast, as in

> Thus have I had thee as a dreame doth flatter,
> In sleepe a King, but waking no such matter
>
> [Sonnet 87]

where after a line and a half of yearning the offhand colloquialism shows us Shakespeare detached and critical. It is of course only by exploiting speech movement that any kind of delicacy of statement is possible . . . , but it is the fairly frequent use of various ironic inflexions that it seems particularly important to stress:

> He nor that affable familiar ghost
> Which nightly gulls him with intelligence . . .
>
> [Sonnet 86]

> Farewell thou art too deare for my possessing,
> And like enough thou knowst thy estimate . . .
>
> [Sonnet 87]

—and there are other examples more or less immediately apparent. To be alive to modulations of this kind is to recognize—which is what one would expect—that the *intelligence* that created, say, *Troilus and Cressida,* is also at work in the sonnets. (pp. 144-47)

In [Shakespeare's] later plays a wide range of relevant associations, both of thought and feeling ('relevant' is clearly a matter for concrete illustration), are compressed into the single image ('The bank and shoal of time' [*Macbeth,* I. vii. 6]). Images of sight, touch, muscular adjustment and so on follow in rapid succession (No catalogue of 'visual,' 'tactile,' etc., is sufficient to cover the variety), and different modes may be combined in our response at any one point. And there are those unexpected and startling juxtapositions of contrasted images:

> The *crown* o' the earth doth *melt.*
> [*Antony and Cleopatra,* IV. xv. 63]

> This sensible warm *motion* to become
> A kneaded *clod.*
> [*Measure for Measure,* III. i. 119-20]

Now in the sonnets not all of these characteristic uses of imagery are developed. . . . Such lines as

> Gor'd mine own thoughts . . .
>
> [Sonnet 110]

and

> To bitter sawces did I frame my feeding
> [Sonnet 118]

indicate an important line of development, but there is little of the intensely physical impact that we find in *Macbeth* ('The blanket of the dark' 'We'd jump the life to come' [I. v. 53; I. vii. 7]). Most of the images—even when finely effective—arouse only one set of vibrations in the mind (pp. 148-49)

But even when we have made these qualifications the stress remains on the positive achievement; there is a clear advance on the early plays. In the sonnets no image is *merely* decorative, as in Romeo's 'Two of the fairest stars in all heaven . . .' [*Romeo and Juliet,* II. ii. 15]. Few are excessively developed, as in the laments of Richard II or even as in the Bastard's 'Commodity, the bias of the world . . .' [*King John,* II. i. 574]. There is indeed a constant succession of varied images, which, because they are concrete and because they are drawn from the world of familiar experience, give precise expression to emotion:

> Beated and chopt with tand antiquitie.
>
> [Sonnet 62]

> Incertenties now crowne them-selves assur'de.
>
> [Sonnet 107]

> But makes antiquitie for aye his page.
>
> [Sonnet 108]

> And captive-good attending Captaine ill.
>
> [Sonnet 66]

What it comes to is this: in the sonnets, as in the later plays, the imagery gives immediacy and precision, and it demands and fosters an alert attention. But the range of emotions liberated by any one image is narrower, though not always less intense. We have not yet reached the stage in which 'the *maximum* amount of apparent incongruity is resolved simultaneously.' That is, the creating mind has not yet achieved that co-ordination of widely diverse (and, in the ordinary mind, often conflicting) experiences, which is expressed in the imagery no less than in the total structure of the great tragedies. (pp. 149-50)

A complete account of technical development in the sonnets would include a detailed discussion of ambiguity. . . . But the argument would raise fundamental issues with which I do not feel competent to deal, and all that I have to offer— after a very brief indication of the way in which the language of the sonnets is 'charged' by means of overlaying meanings—is some caution.

There is a clear difference between the kind of compression that we find in 'The steepe up heavenly hill' [Sonnet 7], 'The world without end houre' [Sonnet 57], or 'Th'imprison'd absence of your libertie' [Sonnet 58], and in such lines as 'So thou, thy selfe out-going in thy noon' [Sonnet 7], or 'That I have frequent binne with unknown mindes' [Sonnet 117]. The first three are forms of elliptical construction requiring no unusual agility in the mind accustomed to English idiom. In the last two the context demands that we shall keep two or more meanings in mind simultaneously: 'thy selfe outgoing' means both 'over-reaching yourself' and 'you yourself going further on'; 'unknown minds' are 'strangers,' 'nonentities,' and perhaps 'such minds as I am ashamed to mention'. . . . In the same way as two or more meanings are fused in one word, different constructions may be run together, as in

> None else to me, nor I to none alive,
> That my steel'd sence or changes right or wrong.
>
> [Sonnet 112]

or they may be overlaid:

> My selfe corrupting salving thy amisse
>
> [Sonnet 35]

There can, I think, be no doubt that Shakespeare deliberately (though 'deliberately' may be too strong a word) avails himself of the resources of the language in this way; I have chosen

what seem to be the most incontrovertible examples, and they are clearly in line with his later development. In Sonnet 40 and one or two others we have something very like conscious experimenting with simple forms of ambiguous statement.

Now the important point is this: that when ambiguity occurs in successful verse it is valuable in much the same way as successful imagery is valuable, as representing a heightened, more inclusive and more unified form of consciousness. One need hardly say that the mere presence of ambiguities is not necessarily an indication of poetic value—they may equally represent unresolved contradictions in the poet's mind—or that the estimate of success is a more delicate matter (concerned with the whole poetic effect) than the working-out of alternative meanings. There is no need for me to praise Mr. Empson, though I may say that he is the only critic I know of who has detected the equivocal attitude which Shakespeare sometimes expresses towards his subject, and that some of his analyses (of Sonnet 58, for example) [in his *Seven Types of Ambiguity* (see Additional Bibliography)] seem to me immediately convincing. But in perhaps the majority of cases (I am confining my attention entirely to the pages he devotes to the Sonnets) his lists of meanings seem to me to be obtained by focussing upon a part of the poem (almost one might say by forgetting the poem) and considering the various grammatical possibilities of the part so isolated. His analysis of Sonnet 83, for example, is valuable as suggesting the conscious and subliminal meanings that may well have been in Shakespeare's mind at the time of writing, but only a few of them are there, in the poem. It is very unfair to make this charge without substantiating it in detail, but to do so would add many pages to the already excessive length of this essay; I can only hope that the reader will look up the analysis for himself. . . . Mr. Eliot has remarked [in his essay "Hamlet and His Problems"] that the sonnets are 'full of some stuff that the writer could not drag to light, contemplate, or manipulate into art'. The sentence might be taken by the biographers to refer to an especially painful personal experience lying behind the sonnets. But it suggests more profitable speculation if we interpret it that Shakespeare had not yet fully mastered the technique of complex expression.

These imperfect considerations of technique will perhaps have been sufficient to establish the main point, that in the sonnets Shakespeare is (within the limitations of the sonnet form) working towards the maturity of expression of the great plays. But having said this we need to remind ourselves of two things. . . . The first is that the kind of technical development that we have been discussing is in itself an attempt to become more fully conscious (just as Spenser's technique is a method of exclusion), an attempt to secure more delicate discrimination and adjustment. The second is that technique does not function in a vacuum, it can only develop as the servant of an inner impulse. (pp. 150-52)

> *L. C. Knights, "Shakespeare's Sonnets," in* Scrutiny, *Vol. III, No. 2, September, 1934, pp. 133-60.*

GEORGE RYLANDS (essay date 1934)

[Rylands offers a brief and general discussion of the sonnets. He remarks on the diversity of natural imagery in these verses, ranks Shakespeare with John Donne as a love poet, and notes Shakespeare's expressions in the sonnets of truths "frequently particular and extremely personal." Ryland also comments on the nature and function of the concluding couplet of the Shake-

spearean sonnet, claiming that it is "employed sometimes as climax, sometimes as comment, sometimes as a dying fall, sometimes—it must be confessed—as a lame and impotent conclusion."]

The *Sonnets* have this in common with the *Venus and Adonis,* that artificial and natural imagery are felicitously combined, but actual imagery predominates and is more diverse than in the poem. It is drawn from husbandry, medicine, navigation; from the court, from music and painting, from usury and law; from the stage, military life, astronomy and alchemy. Analogies from the seasons are very frequent and these are more realistically expressed than in the poetry of Spenser and his school. Euphuism also is becoming naturalised. The diversity of imagery is only to be paralleled in Donne, and Dr Johnson's objection to the use of technical words in poetry, which is disproved by most Elizabethan poets, is completely exploded by such a sonnet as Shakespeare's fourth. It is of Donne that we think when we seek for Shakespeare's peer as a love-poet. These two poets before all others have expressed the many different shades of feeling, the varied and complex experiences and attitudes of the lover; the idealism and realism, the *Odi et Amo* [I hate and I love], the constancy and jealousy, the daydreams and disillusion, the selfless dedication and the torments of lust. In the *Sonnets* there are direct statements, 'moral ideas', in Arnold's words, such as

> Love is not love
> Which alters when it alteration finds,
>
> [Sonnet 116]

or

> They that have power to hurt, and will do none,
> They do not do the thing they most do show,
>
> [Sonnet 94]

or

> til action, lust
> Is perjur'd, murd'rous, bloody, full of blame.
>
> [Sonnet 129]

In the plays general truths abound. In the *Sonnets* the truths are more frequently particular and extremely personal in expression, the fruit of individual experience. But, as Gibbon remarked, a love-tale is much the same in Babylon and Putney, and Shakespeare's experiences and intense feelings find an echo in the heart. We read them with all the pleasure of recognition. Our whole being is reorganised. What was faint, confused and half-realised becomes precise, acute, ordered, permanent. Our five senses, and our five wits, our own actions and sufferings approve the evidence, and in the *Sonnets* a personality is revealed as real and as admirable as in the *Letters* of Keats. For the style also they can be read innumerable times and never without fresh shocks of surprise. The imagery is as rich as in the narrative poems and richer; but style and content are no longer separable. The metaphors are no longer decorative; like the conceits of Donne, they are the poem. Only in *A Lover's Complaint* is there something of the same maturity and intelligence. And besides a use of metaphor now concentrated, now extended, which is so happy that we seem to see the English tongue as we know it forming and evolving itself before our eyes, there is a *curiosa felicitas* [felicity of expression] in single words and short phrases; as, for example, 'Siren tears', 'adder's sense', 'ambush of young days', 'tender inward of the hand', 'Nature beggar'd of blood', 'affable familiar ghost', 'sin lace itself with his society', 'what freezings have I felt', 'chopp'd with tann'd antiquity',

'I have frequent been with unknown minds' [Sonnets 119, 112, 70, 128, 67, 86, 67, 97, 62, 117].

The opening sonnets are in a sense exercises on an Elizabethan theme, and throughout the sequence we light from time to time upon a phrase or image which can be paralleled in other Elizabethan sequences, or in Ronsard and du Bellay, whose pockets the sonneteers picked so dexterously. Towards the end of the collection we find sonnets more powerful and more austere than the 'sugred sonnets' referred to by Meres in 1598 [see excerpt above, 1598], sonnets in which imagery is more rare, the expression more intellectual than sensual and the vocabulary, as Beeching indicated, more Latinised. These are to be associated with *Hamlet* and *Troilus and Cressida* rather than with *Romeo and Juliet* and *Love's Labour's Lost.* Sir Philip Sidney alone among the sonneteers is comparable in power of expression and in the value of the experiences communicated; he, like Shakespeare, is at once personal and permanent, and in him there is, although to a less degree, the necessary separation between 'the man who suffers and the mind which creates'.

One word about form. Shakespeare, like his fellows, departs from the Italian pattern; but behind the three quatrains and the couplet which is variously employed sometimes as climax, sometimes as comment, sometimes as a dying fall, sometimes—it must be confessed—as a lame and impotent conclusion, there may frequently be discerned the double movement, the octave and sestet division of the true Petrarchan form. Shakespeare's experience as a sonneteer had some effect on the versification and paragraphing in the earlier plays. The influence of the form is to be detected in parts of *Love's Labour's Lost, The Two Gentlemen of Verona,* and *Romeo and Juliet.* (pp. 109-11)

> George Rylands, "Shakespeare the Poet," in A Companion to Shakespeare Studies, *edited by Harley Granville-Barker and G. B. Harrison, Cambridge at the University Press, 1934, pp. 89-116.*

WILLIAM EMPSON (essay date 1935)

[*An English poet, critic, and scholar, Empson is considered one of the most influential theorists of modern criticism. In two important studies,* Seven Types of Ambiguity (1930) *and* The Structure of Complex Words (1951), *Empson argued that the value of poetic discourse resides not in any ultimate critical evaluation, but in the correspondences and contradictions of the creative structure itself. In short, Empson was more interested in the manner in which poetic elements work together in a literary piece than in assessing the final value of a creative work as a whole. As a Shakespearean critic, he focused on the emotive and connotative aspects of Shakespeare's language, as well as on the ambiguity present in much of the playwright's verse. In the excerpt below, Empson examines the multiple, ironic meanings of Sonnet 94. The basis of the poem's ambivalence, he suggests, "is that W. H. is loved as an arriviste, for an impudent worldliness that Shakespeare finds shocking and delightful." Empson maintains that "W. H." is presented as at once coldly hard but sensitive, vulnerable and impulsive, egotistic and inscrutable. These qualities, the critic continues, are the sources of the highly suggestive linking of "W. H." with flowers and flower imagery, a linking that gives Shakespeare a way of extolling the young man in spite of his essential egotism. Empson also calls attention to Christian parables operating in this sonnet, demonstrating how these fables depicting the wise use of talents and the power of beauty contribute to the central opposition of egocentricity and self-sacrifice.*]

It is agreed that *They that have power to hurt and will do none* [Sonnet 94] is a piece of grave irony, but there the matter is generally left; you can work through all the notes in the Variorum without finding out whether flower, lily, 'owner,' and person addressed are alike or opposed. One would like to say that the poem has all possible such meanings, digested into some order, and then try to show how this is done, but the mere number of possible interpretations is amusingly too great. Taking the simplest view (that any two may be alike in some one property) any one of the four either is or is not and either should or should not be like each of the others; this yields 4096 possible movements of thought, with other possibilities. The niggler is routed here; one has honestly to consider what seems important.

'The best people are indifferent to temptation and detached from the world; nor is this state selfish, because they do good by unconscious influence, like the flower. You must be like them; you are quite like them already. But even the best people must be continually on their guard, because they become the worst, just as the pure and detached lily smells worst, once they fall from their perfection'—('one's prejudice against them is only one's consciousness of this fact'—the hint of irony in the poem might be covered by this). It is a coherent enough Confucian sentiment, and there is no very clear hint as to irony in the words. No doubt *as stone* goes intentionally too far for sympathy, and there is a suggestive gap in the argument between octet and sestet, but one would not feel this if it was Shakespeare's only surviving work.

There is no reason why the subtlety of the irony in so complex a material must be capable of being pegged out into verbal explanations. The vague and generalised language of the descriptions, which might be talking about so many sorts of people as well as feeling so many things about them, somehow makes a unity like a crossroads, which analysis does not deal with by exploring down the roads; makes a solid flute on which you can play a multitude of tunes, whose solidity no list of all possible tunes would go far to explain. The balance of feeling is both very complex and very fertile; experiences are recorded, and metaphors invented, in the Sonnets, which he went on 'applying' as a dramatist, taking particular cases of them as if they were wide generalisations, for the rest of his life. One can't expect, in writing about such a process, to say anything very tidy and complete.

But one does not start interpreting out of the void, even though the poem once partly interpreted seems to stand on its own. If this was Shakespeare's only surviving work it would still be clear, supposing one knew about the other Elizabethans, that it involves somehow their feelings about the Machiavellian, the wicked plotter who is exciting and civilised and in some way right about life; which seems an important though rather secret element in the romance that Shakespeare extracted from his patron. In any case one has only to look at the sonnets before and after it to be sure that it has some kind of irony. The one before is full of fear and horror at the hypocrisy he is so soon to recommend; and yet it is already somehow cuddled, as if in fascination or out of a refusal to admit that it was there.

> So shall I liue, supposing thou art true,
> Like a deceiued husband, . . .
> For ther can liue no hatred in thine eye
> Therefore in that I cannot know thy change, . . .
> How like *Eaues* apple doth thy beauty grow,
> If thy sweet vertue answere not thy show.
>
> 　　　　　　　　　　　　　　　　[Sonnet 93]

So the *summer's flower* may be its apple-blossom. His virtue is still sweet, whether he has any or not; the clash of fact with platonic idealism is too fearful to be faced directly. In the sonnet after, with a blank and exhausted humility, it has been faced; there remains for the expression of his love, in the least flaunting of poetry, the voice of caution.

> How sweet and louely dost thou make the
> 　　shame, . . .
> Take heed (deare heart) of this large privilege.
>
> 　　　　　　　　　　　　　　　　[Sonnet 95]

The praise of hypocrisy is in a crucial and precarious condition of balance between these two states of mind.

The root of the ambivalence, I think, is that W. H. is loved as an arriviste, for an impudent worldliness that Shakespeare finds shocking and delightful. The reasons why he treated his poet badly are the same as the reasons why he was fascinating, which gives its immediate point to the profound ambivalence about the selfishness of the flower. Perhaps he is like the cold person in his hardness and worldly judgment, not in his sensuality and generosity of occasional impulse; like the flower in its beauty, vulnerability, tendency to excite thoughts about the shortness of life, self-centredness, and power in spite of it to give pleasure, not in its innocence and fertility; but the irony may make any of these change over. Both owner and flower seem self-centred and inscrutable, and the cold person is at least like the lily in that it is symbolically chaste, but the summer's flower, unlike the lily, seems to stand for the full life of instinct. It is not certain that the owner is liable to fester as the lily is—Angelo [in *Measure for Measure*] did, but W. H. is usually urged to acquire the virtues of Angelo. Clearly there is a jump from octet to sestet; the flower is not like the owner in its solitude and its incapacity to hurt or simulate; it might be because of this that it is of a summer only and may fester; yet we seem chiefly meant to hold W. H. in mind and take them as parallel. As for punctuation, the only full stop is at the end; all lines have commas after them except the fourth, eighth, and twelfth, which have colons.

> They that haue powre to hurt, and will doe none,
> That doe not do the thing, they most do showe,
> Who mouing others, are themselves as stone,
> Vnmoued, could, and to temptation slow:
>
> 　　　　　　　　　　　　　　　　[Sonnet 94]

They may *show*, while hiding the alternative, for the first couplet, the power to hurt or the determination not to hurt—cruelty or mercy, for the second, the strength due to chastity or to sensual experience, for either, a reckless or cautious will, and the desire for love or for control; all whether they are stealers of hearts or of public power. They are a very widespread group; we are only sure at the end that some kind of hypocrisy has been advised and threatened.

> They rightly do inherit heavens graces,
> And husband natures ritches from expence,
>
> 　　　　　　　　　　　　　　　　[Sonnet 94]

Either 'inherit, they alone, by right' or 'inherit what all men inherit and use it rightly'; these correspond to the opposed views of W. H. as aristocrat and vulgar careerist. There is a similar range of idea, half hidden by the pretence of easy filling of the form, in the pun on *graces* and shift to *riches*. Heaven's *graces* may be prevenient grace (strength from God to do well), personal graces which seem to imply heavenly virtues (the charm by which you deceive people), or merely God's gracious gift of *nature's riches;* which again may be the personal graces, or the strength and taste which make him capable either of 'upholding his house' or of taking his pleasure, or merely the actual wealth of which he is an *owner.* Clearly this gives plenty of room for irony in the statement that the cold people, with their fine claims, do well all round; it also conveys 'I am seeing you as a whole; I am seeing these things as necessary rather than as your fault.'

> They are the Lords and owners of their faces,
> Others, but stewards of their excellence:
>
> [Sonnet 94]

It may be their beauty they put to their own uses, high or low, or they may just have poker-faces; this gives the same range of statement. The capital which tends to isolate *lords* from its phrase suggests 'they are the only true aristocrats; if you are not like them you should not pretend to be one.' *Others* may be stewards of their own excellence (in contrast with *faces*—'though they are enslaved they may be better and less superficial than the cold people') or of the cold people's excellence (with a suggestion of 'Their Excellencies'); the less plausible sense is insisted on by the comma after *others.* This repeats the doubt about how far the cold people are really excellent, and there may be a hint of a doubt about how far the individual is isolated, which anticipates the metaphor of the flower. And 'stewards of their own excellence' may be like 'stewards of the buttery' or like 'stewards of a certain lord'; either 'the good things they have do good to others, not to them' (they are too generous; I cannot ask you to aim so high in virtue, because I desire your welfare, not other people's, and indeed because you wouldn't do it anyway) or 'they are under the power of their own impulses, which are good things so long as they are not in power' (they are deceived; acts caused by weakness are not really generous at all). Yet this may be the condition of the flower and the condition for fullness of life; you cannot know beforehand what life will bring you if you open yourself to it, and certainly the flower does not; it is because they are unnatural and unlike flowers that the cold people rule nature, and the cost may be too great. Or the flower and the cold person may be two unlike examples of the limitation necessary to success, one experienced in its own nature, the other in the world; both, the irony would imply, are in fact *stewards.*

There is a Christian parable at work in both octet and sestet; in the octet that of the talents. You will not be forgiven for hoarding your talents; some sort of success is demanded; you must at least use your powers to the full even if for your own squalid purpose. The pain and wit and solemnity of *rightly,* its air of summing up a long argument, depend on the fact that these metaphors have been used to recommend things to W. H. before.

> Natures bequest giues nothing but doth lend,
> And being franck she lends to those are free:
>
> [Sonnet 4]

> Who lets so faire a house fall to decay,
> Which husbandry in honour might uphold,
>
> [Sonnet 13]

Rightly to be free with yourself, in the first simple paradox, was the best saving of yourself (you should put your money into marriage and a son); it is too late now to advise that, or to say it without being sure to be understood wrongly (this is 94; the first sonnet about his taking Shakespeare's mistress

is 40); the advice to be generous as natural has become the richer but more contorted advice to be like the flower. Rightly to husband nature's riches, earlier in the sequence, was to accept the fact that one is only steward of them;

> Thou that art now the worlds fresh ornament,
> And only herauld to the gaudy spring,
> Within thine owne bud buriest thy content,
> And tender chorle makst waste in niggarding:
>
> [Sonnet 1]

the flower was wrong to live to itself alone, and would become a tottered weed (2) whether it met with infection or not.

Though indeed *husbandry* is still recommended; it is not the change of opinion that has so much effect but the use of the same metaphors with a shift of feeling in them. The legal metaphors (debts to nature and so forth) used for the loving complaint that the man's chastity was selfish are still used when he becomes selfish in his debauchery; Shakespeare's own notation here seems to teach him; the more curiously because the metaphors were used so flatly in the earliest sonnets (1, 2, 4, 6, then 13; not again till now), only formally urging marriage, and perhaps written to order. It is like using a mathematical identity which implies a proof about a particular curve and then finding that it has a quite new meaning if you take the old constants as variables. It is these metaphors that have grown, till they involve relations between a man's powers and their use, his nature and his will, the individual and the society, which could be applied afterwards to all human circumstances.

> The sommers flowre is to the sommer sweet,
> Though to it selfe, it onely liue and die,
>
> [Sonnet 94]

The use of *the* summer's flower about a human being is enough to put it at us that the flower will die by the end of summer, that the man's life is not much longer, and that the pleasures of the creature therefore cannot be despised for what they are. *Sweet to the summer* (said of the flower), since the summer is omnipresent and in a way Nature herself, may mean 'sweet to God' (said of the man); or may mean 'adding to the general sweetness; sweet to everybody that comes across it in its time.' It may do good to others though not by effort or may simply be a good end in itself (or combining these, may only be able to do good by concentrating on itself as an end); a preparatory evasion of the central issue about egotism.

Either 'though it lives only for itself' or 'though, in its own opinion, so far as it can see, it does no more than live and die.' In the first it is a rose, extravagant and doing good because the public likes to see it flaunting; in the second a violet, humble and doing good in private through an odour of sanctity. It is the less plausible sense which is insisted on by the comma after *itself.* Or you may well say that the flower is neither, but the final lily; the whole passage is hinting at the lilies of the field like whom Solomon was not arrayed.

This parable itself combines what the poem so ingeniously keeps on combining; the personal power of beauty and the political power of wisdom; so as to imply that the political power has in itself a sort of beauty and the personal beauty, however hollow it may be, a sort of moral grandeur through power. But in England 'consider the lilies of the field,' were we not at once told of their glory, would suggest lilies-of-the-valley; that name indeed occurs in the Song of Solomon, in surprising correspondence to the obviously grandiose Rose of Sharon. Shakespeare, I think, had done what the inventor of the name must have done, had read into the random flower-names of the Bible the same rich clash of suggestion—an implied mutual comparison that elevates both parties—as he makes here between the garden flower and the wild flower. The first sense (the rose) gives the root idea—'a brilliant aristocrat like you gives great pleasure by living as he likes; for such a person the issue of selfishness does not arise'; this makes W. H. a Renaissance Magnificent Man, combining all the virtues with a manysidedness like that of these phrases about him. The unlikeness of the cold people and the flowers, if you accept them as like, then implies 'man is not placed like flowers and though he had best imitate them may be misled in doing so; the Machiavellian is much more really like the flower than the Swain is.' And yet there is a suggestion in the comparison to the flower (since only beauty is demanded of it—Sonnet 54 made an odd and impermanent attempt at quelling this doubt by equating truth with scent) that W. H. has only power to keep up an air of reconciling in himself the inconsistent virtues, or even of being a Machiavellian about the matter, and that it is this that puts him in danger like the flower. Or however genuine he may be he is pathetic; such a man is all too 'natural'; there is no need to prop up our ideas about him with an aristocratic 'artificial' flower. So this class-centred praise is then careful half to hide itself by adding the second sense and the humble flower, and this leads it to a generalisation: 'all men do most good to others by fulfilling their own natures.' Full as they are of Christian echoes, the Sonnets are concerned with an idea strong enough to be balanced against Christianity; they state the opposite to the idea of self-sacrifice.

But the machinery of the statement is peculiar; its clash of admiration and contempt seems dependent on a clash of feeling about the classes. One might connect it with that curious trick of pastoral which for extreme courtly flattery—perhaps to give self-respect to both poet and patron, to show that the poet is not ignorantly easy to impress, nor the patron to flatter—writes about the poorest people; and with those jazz songs which give an intense effect of luxury and silk underwear by pretending to be about slaves naked in the fields. To those who care chiefly about biography this trick must seem monstrously tantalising; Wilde built the paradox of his essay on it [see excerpt above, 1889], and it is true that Shakespeare might have set the whole thing to work from the other end about a highly trained mudlark brought in to act his princesses. But it is the very queerness of the trick that makes it so often useful in building models of the human mind; and yet the power no less than the universality of this poem depends on generalising the trick so completely as to seem independent of it.

> But if that flowre with base infection meete,
> The basest weed out-braues his dignity:
>> For sweetest things turn sowrest by their deedes,
>> Lilies that fester, smell far worse than weeds.

[Sonnet 94]

It is not clear how the metaphor from 'meet' acts; it may be like 'meet with disaster'—'if it catches infection, which would be bad luck,' or like meeting someone in the street, as most men do safely—'*any* contact with infection is fatal to so peculiarly placed a creature.' The first applies to the natural and unprotected flower, the second to the lily that has the hubris and fate of greatness. They are not of course firmly separated, but *lilies* are separated from the *flower* by a colon and an in-

tervening generalisation, whereas the flower is only separated from the cold people (not all of whom need be lilies) by a colon; certainly the flower as well as the lily is in danger, but this does not make them identical and equal to W. H. The neighbouring sonnets continually say that his deeds can do nothing to destroy his sweetness, and this seems to make the terrible last line point at him somewhat less directly. One may indeed take it as 'Though so debauched, you keep your looks. Only mean people who never give themselves heartily to anything can do that. But the best hypocrite is found out in the end, and shown as the worst.' But Shakespeare may also be congratulating W. H. on an imperfection which acts as a preservative; he is a son of the world and can protect himself, like the cold people, or a spontaneous and therefore fresh sinner, like the flower; he may safely stain, as heaven's sun, the kisser of carrion, staineth. At any rate it is not of virginity, at this stage, that he can be accused. The smell of a big lily is so lush and insolent, suggests so powerfully both incense and pampered flesh—the traditional metaphor about it is so perfect—that its festering can only be that due to the hubris of spirituality; it is ironically generous to apply it to the careerist to whom hypocrisy is recommended; and yet in the fact that we seem meant to apply it to him there is a glance backwards, as if to justify him, at the ambition involved in even the most genuine attempt on heaven. You may say that Shakespeare dragged in the last line as a quotation from [Marlowe's] *Edward III* that doesn't quite fit; it is also possible that (as often happens to poets, who tend to make in their lives a situation they have already written about) he did not till now see the full width of its application.

In a sense the total effect is an evasion of Shakespeare's problem; it gives him a way of praising W. H. in spite of anything. In the flower the oppositions are transcended; it is because it is self-concentrated that it has so much to give and because it is undesigning that it is more grandiose in beauty than Solomon. But it is held in mind chiefly for comfort; none of the people suggested to us are able to imitate it very successfully; nor if they could would they be safe. Yet if W. H. has festered, that at least makes him a lily, and at least not a stone; if he is not a lily, he is in the less danger of festering.

I must try to sum up the effect of so complex an irony, half by trying to follow it through a gradation. 'I am praising to you the contemptible things you admire, you little plotter; this is how the others try to betray you through flattery; yet it is your little generosity, though it show only as lewdness, which will betray you; for it is wise to be cold, both because you are too inflammable and because I have been so much hurt by you who are heartless; yet I can the better forgive you through that argument from our common isolation; I must praise to you your very faults, especially your selfishness, because you can only now be safe by cultivating them further; yet this is the most dangerous of necessities; people are greedy for your fall as for that of any of the great; indeed no one can rise above common life, as you have done so fully, without in the same degree sinking below it; you have made this advice real to me, because I cannot despise it for your sake; I am only sure that you are valuable and in danger.' (pp. 89-101)

William Empson, "They That Have Power," in his Some Versions of Pastoral, *Chatto & Windus, 1935, pp. 89-118.*

Illustration to A Lover's Complaint *in* Cooke's British Poets—Shakespeare's Poems *(1797). By Thomas Kirk.*

JOHN CROWE RANSOM (essay date 1938)

[*Ransom was an American critic, poet, and editor. Generally considered one of the most influential literary theorists of the twentieth century, he was a prominent spokesman for the Fugitive, Agrarian, and New Criticism movements in American literature. In* The New Criticism *(1941), his most important work, Ransom proposed a close reading of poetic texts and insisted that criticism should be based on a study of the structure and text of a given poem, not on its content. In the following excerpt, he evaluates the style and structure of Shakespeare's sonnets. The majority of these verses, he contends, are written in a romantic or associationist vein—that is, a style in which "pretty words have pleasing if indefinite associations" and whose only precision stems from the metrical pattern itself. Ransom asserts that many of the remaining sonnets represent an attempt to develop a poem from a single figure of speech instead of a range of associations, but he judges that Shakespeare's imagination was unequal to the kind of "peculiar and systematic exercises" required to compose superlative metaphysical poetry. He also maintains that the sonnets are generally poorly constructed. Shakespeare frequently fails to meet the requirements of the English sonnet form in terms of logic and coherence, Ransom argues, although through superior craftsmanship he frequently provides at least the appearance of coordinated quatrains and couplets. In 1940, Arthur Mizener published a direct response to Ransom's comments on the sonnets (see excerpt below); and in 1968, Ransom added a postcript to*

his remarks (see Additional Bibliography), acknowledging that further study had led him to discern more instances of internal logic and coherence than he had earlier perceived in the sonnets.]

One may be well disposed to the New Deal, and not relish the attitude of giving comfort to the enemy by criticizing Mr. Roosevelt publicly, yet in a qualified company do it freely. The same thing applies very well in the matter of the poet Shakespeare. It is out of respect to the intelligence of the editors and readers of a serious literary publication that I will not hold back from throwing a few stones at Shakespeare, aiming them as accurately as I can at the vulnerable parts. I have no fear that any group of intellectual critics may succeed beyond their intentions in demolishing Shakespeare, so that he will suffer extinction and be read no more, and I am well aware that if this should happen the public attendance upon poetry in our language would be reduced one-half. But Shakespeare is an institution as well established as the industrial revolution, or the Protestant churches. In the midst of the bombardment he will smile, and smile, and be a villain. (p. 531)

Shakespeare left monument enough behind him, but no face of it is of that precise significance which is attested by a large and assorted volume of minor poems. The truth is that Shakespeare, as compared with writers like Sidney and Spenser, had rare luck as a literary man, and I do not mean to say this out of any regard to whether he was or was not a superior man naturally. It would be impossible to tell how much our poet was determined by the fact that he was not an aristocrat, did not go to the university and develop his technical skill all at once, got into the rather low profession of acting, grew up with the drama, and never had to undergo the torment of that terrible problem: the problem of poetic strategy; or what to do with an intensive literary training. Yet Shakespeare did indulge in one diversion from his natural and happy career as a dramatist. He composed a laborious sonnet sequence. And in the degree that the sonnets are not tied down to "story," to the simple dramatizing of the stages in a human relation, they give us a Shakespeare on the same terms as those on which we are used to having our other poets.

I begin with a most unhappy feature: generally they are ill constructed.

They use the common English metrical pattern, and the metrical work is always admirable, but the logical pattern more often than not fails to fit it. If it be said that you do not need to have a correspondence between a poet's metrical pattern and his logical one, I am forced to observe that Shakespeare thought there was a propriety in it; often he must have gone to the pains of securing it, since it is there and, considering the extreme difficulty of the logical structure in the English sonnet, could not have got in by a happy accident. The metrical pattern of any sonnet is directive. If the English sonnet exhibits the rhyme-scheme ABAB CDCD EFEF GG, it imposes upon the poet the following requirement: that he write three co-ördinate quatrains and then a couplet which will relate to the series collectively.

About a third of the sonnets of Shakespeare are fairly unexceptionable in having just such a logical structure. About half of them might be said to be tolerably workmanlike in this respect; and about half of them are seriously defective.

Already the poet Spenser had calculated very well what sort

of thing could be done successfully in this logical pattern. It was something like the following (*Amoretti,* LVI):

> Fayre be ye sure, but cruell and unkind,
> As is a Tygre, that with greedinesse
> Hunts after bloud; when he by chance doth find
> A feeble beast, doth foully him oppresse.
>
> Fayre be ye sure, but proud and pitilesse,
> As is a storm, that all things doth prostrate;
> Finding a tree alone all comfortlesse,
> Beats on it strongly, it to ruinate.
>
> Fayre be ye sure, but hard and obstinate,
> As is a rocke amidst the raging floods,
> Gaynst which, a ship, of succour desolate,
> Doth suffer wreck both of her selfe and goods.
>
> That ship, that tree, and that same beast, am I,
> Whom ye do wreck, do ruine, and destroy.

Now Spenser's metrical scheme has a special and unnecessary complication, it exhibits rhyme-linkage; the second quatrain begins by echoing the last rhyme of the first quatrain, and the third by echoing the last rhyme of the second. It makes no difference logically. The three quatrains are equal yet sharply distinct. Possibly the linking was Spenser's way of showing off his virtuosity at rhyming, and possibly also he used it as a mnemonic device, to say: The new quatrain must be just like the old one, a logical coördinate, but wait till we come to the couplet, which will not be linked and must not be coördinate. At any rate, his quatrains nearly always are true coördinates. In his architectural design he is superior, I believe, to any other writer of the four-part or English sonnet.

And this means that he carefully attended to the sort of object which might permit this three-and-one division. In the given example each quatrain is a simile which he applies to the lady, and the couplet is a summary comment which is brief, but adequate because the similes are simple and of the same kind. It is not every matter, or logical object, which allows this; and, particularly, the couplet does not give enough room for the comment unless the burden of the quatrains has been severely restricted. If the poet is too full of urgent thoughts, he had better use the two-part or Italian form, which is very much more flexible. The English form, with the more elaborate and repetitive pattern, implies the simpler substance ; in this it would be like other complicated forms, such as the ballade or sestina.

But structurally good also is the following Shakespearean sonnet, the one numbered LXXXVII:

> Farewell! thou art too dear for my possessing,
> And like enough thou know'st thy estimate;
> The charter of thy worth gives thee releasing;
> My bonds in thee are all determinate.
>
> For how do I hold thee but by thy granting?
> And for that riches where is my deserving?
> The cause of this fair gift in me is wanting,
> And so my patent back again is swerving.
>
> Thyself thou gav'st, thy own worth then not knowing,
> Or me, to whom thou gav'st it, else mistaking;
> So thy great gift, upon misprision growing,
> Comes home again, on better judgment making.
>
> Thus have I had thee, as a dream doth flatter,
> In sleep a king, but waking no such matter.

This sonnet is daring and clever. It is legalistic, therefore closely limited in its range, yet the three quatrains all manage to say the same thing differently, and the couplet translates the legal figure back into the terms of a lover's passion.

It is only a large minority of Shakespeare's sonnets in which we can find this perfect adaptation of the logic to the metre. In the others we can find the standard metrical organization, and then some arbitrary logical organization which clashes with it. At least twice we find only fourteen-line poems, with no logical organization at all except that they have little couplet conclusions: in LXVI, "Tir'd with all these, for restful death I cry," and in CXXIX, "The expense of spirit in a waste of shame." Occasionally, as in LXIII, "Against my love shall be, as I am now," the sonnet divides frankly into octave and sextet, so far as the logic goes, though it does not follow that an honest printer has set it up just so. Many modern sonnetwriters, such as my friend, Mr. David Morton, are careful to have their sonnets set up as two-part structures though their rhyme-scheme is four-part. I am afraid some critics will always be wondering whether the poets are unequal, or simply insensitive, to the logical demands made by the English form. I scarcely think that Shakespeare's practice sanctified a procedure.

Possibly the commonest irregularity of logical arrangement with Shakespeare is in sonnets of the following type (LXIV):

> When I have seen by Time's fell hand defac'd
> The rich proud cost of outworn buried age;
> When sometime lofty towers I see down-raz'd,
> And brass eternal slave to mortal rage;
>
> When I have seen the hungry ocean gain
> Advantage on the kingdom of the shore,
> And the firm soil win of the watery main,
> Increasing store with loss and loss with store;
>
> When I have seen such interchange of state,
> Or state itself confounded to decay,
> Ruin hath taught me thus to ruminate,
> That Time will come and take my love away.
>
> This thought is as a death, which cannot choose,
> But weep to have that which it fears to lose.

Here the three quatrains look co-ordinate, but only the first two really are so. The third begins with the same form as the others, but presently shows that it is only summary of their content, and then actually begins to introduce the matter which will be the concern of the couplet. We must believe that Shakespeare found the couplet too small to hold its matter, so that at about Line ten he had to begin anticipating it. But, as I said, this sonnet represents a pattern fairly common with him, and it is possible to argue that he developed it consciously as a neat variant on the ordinary English structure; just as Milton developed a variant from the Italian structure by concluding the logical octet just before or just after the rhyme-ending of the eighth line.

Probably Shakespeare's usual structural difficulty consists about equally in having to pad out his quatrains, if three good co-ördinates do not offer themselves, and in having to squeeze the couplet too flat, or else extend its argument upward into the proper territory of the quatrains. But when both these things happen at once, the obvious remark is that the poet should have reverted to the Italian sonnet.

Structurally, Shakespeare is a careless workman. But probably, with respect to our attention to structure, we are careless readers.

Poetry is an expressive art, we say, and perhaps presently we are explaining that what it expresses is its poet; a dangerous locution, because the public value of the poem would seem to lie theoretically in the competence with which it expresses its object. There is no reason why it should not offer an absolute knowledge of this object, so far as the adjective is ever applicable to a human knowledge, including a scientific knowledge, and a knowledge however "objective." Nevertheless one knowledge will differ from another knowledge in glory, that is, in the purity of intention, and sometimes it is scarcely a knowledge at all; it is rather a self-expression. There is probably a poetry of the feelings just as much as there is a poetry of knowledge; for we may hardly deny to a word its common usage, and poetry is an experience so various as to be entertained by everybody. But the poetry of the feelings is not the one that the critic is compelled to prefer, especially if he can say that it taints us with subjectivism, sentimentality, and self-indulgence. This is the poetry, I think, which we sometimes dispose of a little distastefully as "romantic." It does not pursue its object with much zeal, and it is so common that it involves in a general disrepute all poets, the innocent as well as the guilty, by comparison with those importunate pursuers, the scientists—who may not exactly be expected to fail to make the most of the comparison.

This sort of poetry, I am afraid, is as natural to Shakespeare as language is, and he is a great master in it. In XXXIII we read:

> Full many a glorious morning have I seen
> Flatter the mountain-tops with sovereign eye,
> Kissing with golden face the meadows green,
> Gilding pale streams with heavenly alchemy.

It is pure Shakespeare, it sounds like nobody else; and in it the failure of objectivity, or perhaps "realism" we might prefer to call it, is plain about as soon as we look closely. What the poet intends is simply to have something in the way of a fine-morning quatrain, with an all-ruling fair-weather sun to be the symbol of his false friend, as the sonnet goes on to disclose.

But this sun is weakly imagined; rather, it may be said to be only felt, a loose cluster of images as obscure as they are pleasant, furnished by the half-conscious memories attending the pretty words. (In strict logic: I suppose this sun's eye flatters the mountain-tops in that his look makes them shine; but at once he is kissing the meadows, which is unseemly for a face that contains a sovereign eye; then in the character of an alchemist he is transmuting streams. A mixed and self-defeating figure, and a romantic effect unusually loose; but it does not seem to matter.)

So this is poetry; a poetry that has in mind the subjective satisfactions of the poet, and of reputed millions of readers after him. The cognitive impulse of the participating millions has to be of low grade, yet there is an object, and it is rich and suggestive even while it is vague and cloudy. This is what we might call an associationist poetry. The pretty words have pleasing if indefinite associations; and they are fairly harmonious—that is, the associations tend rather to cohere than to repel each other. And if they do not cohere into a logical or definitive object, at any rate—this is the subtlety of the romantic style—they are arranged externally with great care into a characteristic musical phrase, or at least a metrical one,

which is really (by comparison) objective and absolute. Metric saves this kind of poetry, and its function could not be shown to better advantage than here; a meretricious function, as it lends its objectivity to an act in which the subject does not really propose to lose himself in the object. In other words, it persuades us, unless we are professionally critical, that this is a poetry of wonderful precision, when logically it is a poetry of wonderful imprecision, and the only precision it has is metrical, therefore adventitious. It is not without significance that the age gave to this poet his adjective: sweet. It would be hard to estimate the extent of the influence which Shakespeare's way of writing poetry has exerted upon subsequent English poetry. But Exhibit A would be the actual poems, and Exhibit B, scarcely less significant, would be the critical dictum upon which almost innumerable writers seem to be in perfect agreement, that science if it likes may try to know its object, but that the business of poetry is to express its author's feelings. The Restoration and Eighteenth Century in their poetry resisted Shakespeare's example of sweetness, but the Nineteenth Century did not, and when we are grieving because modern poetry has learned how to furnish such exquisite indulgences to the feelings and yet at the same time so little food for the intellect, there is no reason why we should not remember who is one of its illustrious ancestors.

The image is often conventional, or "literary," which means that it is not really shaped by a genuine observation. In LIII:

> Describe Adonis, and the counterfeit
> Is poorly imitated after you;
> On Helen's cheek all art of beauty set,
> And you in Grecian tires are painted new.

Asseverations like this are the right of a literary lover, but they do more credit to his piety than to his wit. (The medieval lover had a code which obliged him to say, My lady is more beautiful than yours, though I have not seen yours.) The urgency is that of a subject to express his own feelings, not that of an object so individual as to demand expression. But the phrasing is grave and musical; there is great care behind it to get words with the right literary associations, and to make the melody; phrase, in this subjective sense, and regarded as the trick of the poet as workman, receives commonly the particularity that might have gone into the object.

Mr. Santayana says something like this when he remarks, with his usual wisdom, that Shakespeare's poetry is an art like landscaping; for it is pervasive, and tones down every object exposed to it, and is not like architecture, which articulates its objects down to the last constituent stone. Carrying out our figure, Shakespeare's poetry would not be so much the wall, or the temple, as the ivy that clings to it sentimentally, and sometimes may very well even obscure it.

Violence of syntax and of idiom is supposed to express strength of feeling. In the sonnets are many violences. For instance, in XXV,

> The painful warrior famoused for fight,

and in LXIV,

> The rich proud cost of outworn buried age.

In the first of these Shakespeare makes a verb of an adjective, but his coinage could not give it a currency, for it is not that kind of adjective. He also makes a qualitative noun of *fight*, which is less exceptionable, though its present currency seems to lie within the American sporting jargon. Both these forced meanings follow surprisingly upon *painful,* which is exact and even Miltonic. The other bristles with logical difficulties. They attach to the meaning of *cost,* and of the adjective series *rich* and *proud,* and of *outworn* and *buried.* Malone worried over the line and proposed *rich-proud,* but it still strongly resists paraphrase. These phrases will illustrate what is common in romantic poetry: a very great "obscurity," unknown to some "intellectualist" poetry which popularly rates as difficult.

I quote also, and I think not vindictively, from XII:

> When I do count the clock that tells the time,
> And see the brave day sunk in hideous night,
> When I behold the violet past prime,
> And sable curls, all silver'd o'er with white. . . .

The third line of this quatrain interests me as a critic. Shakespeare ordinarily plays safe by electing good substantial conventional objects to carry his feelings, but here his judgment should have come to his aid. The violet, in its exalted context, looks to me like a poet's *ridiculus mus* [absurd mouse], for no instance of floral mortality could well be more insignificant. This little mouse had the merit of being named with three syllables, and a two-minute imaginary tour in the garden does not seem to disclose another one of like syllabic dimensions who would do any better. Shakespeare did not bother; he trusted in the music, and the power of the pleasant associations, to make the line impervious to logical criticism. He trusted also, and not without reason, for the point will generally be conceded by critics who are grateful for any excellence in their difficult art, in the comfortable faith that a poetical passage is unlike a chain in that its true strength is that of its strongest part.

On the other hand, there are certainly sonnets of Shakespeare's in this romantic vein which are without absurdities, structural defects, and great violences, and which are also compact, that is, without excessive dispersion in the matter of the figures; and they are doubtless the best sonnets of the kind there could possibly be. It would be presumptuous to deny this general type of poetry, or Shakespeare's occasional mastery of it.

Those perfect sonnets are not many. It is not a wild generalization, when we look at the sonnets, to say that Shakespeare was not habitually a perfectionist; he was not as Ben Jonson, or Marvell, or Milton, and he was not as Pope.

The sonnets are mixed in effect. Not only the sequence as a whole but the individual sonnet is uneven in execution. But what to the critic is still more interesting than the up and the down in one style is the alternation of two very different styles: the one we have been considering, and the one which we are accustomed to define (following Doctor Johnson) as metaphysical. What is the metaphysical poetry doing there? Apparently at about the time of *Hamlet,* and perhaps recognizably in the plays but much more deliberately and on a more extended scale in the sonnets, Shakespeare goes metaphysical. Not consistently, of course.

So far as I know, Shakespeare has not ordinarily been credited with being one of the metaphysicals, nor have specimen sonnets been included in lists or anthologies of metaphysical poems. But many sonnets certainly belong there; early examples of that style. If it was not then widely practised, had no name, and could hardly yet have been recognized as a distinct style, then I would suppose that the sonnets as a performance

represent Shakespeare seeking such effects as John Donne, a public if still unpublished wonder, by some curious method was achieving. But there was also, on a smaller scale, the example of a genuine pioneer in this field in the person of Sidney, if Shakespeare cared to look there; see his *Astrophel and Stella,* XCIV, "Grief, find the words, for thou hast made my brain."

Certainly Shakespeare's LXXXVII, "Farewell! thou art too dear for my possessing," already quoted as an instance of good structure, is in the style. For its substance is furnished by developing the human relation (that of the renouncing lover) through a figure of speech; a legal one, in which an unequal bond is cancelled for cause. Three times, in as many quatrains, the lover makes an exploration within the field of the figure. The occasions are fairly distinct, though I should think their specifications are hardly respective enough to have satisfied Donne. But the thing which surprises us is to find no evidence anywhere that Shakespeare's imagination is equal to the peculiar and systematic exercises which Donne imposed habitually upon his. None, and it should not really surprise us, if we remember that Donne's skill is of the highest technical expertness in English poetry, and that Shakespeare had no university discipline, and developed poetically along lines of least resistance.

He is metaphysical at times enough, but never so metaphysical as Donne is; nor as later poets, Donne's followers, who were just as bold in intention as their master, though not usually so happy in act.

The impulse to metaphysical poetry, I shall assume, consists in committing the feelings in the case—those of unrequited love for example—to their determination within the elected figure. But Shakespeare was rarely willing to abandon his feelings to this fate, which is another way of saying that he would not quite risk the consequences of his own imagination. He censored these consequences, to give them sweetness, to give them even dignity; he would go a little way with one figure, usually a reputable one, then anticipate the consequences, or the best of them, and take up another figure.

The simplest way to define Shakespeare's metaphysical accomplishment would be by comparison with Donne's, which is standard. I have often tried to find the parallel cases where the two poets developed the same figure of speech. But I have always been forced to conclude that these poets do not even in outline or skeleton treat quite the same things; Shakespeare's things being professionally conventional, and Donne's being generally original. The nearest I can come to this sort of illustration is by comparing Sonnet LV with that Valediction of Donne's which has the subtitle: *of the booke.* It is a "strong" sonnet, not quite intelligent enough to be metaphysical. It begins,

> Not marble, nor the gilded monuments
> Of princes shall outlive this powerful rime,

yet what it develops is not the circumstantial immortality of the rhyme, and of the beloved inhabiting it, but the mortality of the common marbles and monuments, an old story with Shakespeare, and as to the immortality makes this single effort:

> 'Gainst death and all-oblivious enmity
> Shall you pace forth.

The only specific thing here is something about a gait.

The immortality of the rhyme, and of the beloved preserved in it (like a beautiful fly stuck in amber? let poets tell) is as classical, or typical, as anything in European sonnetry; but its specific development is not. It remained for Donne, and hardly anybody or nobody else, really on its own merits to develop it, or an easy variation from it, and that not in a sonnet.

In the Valediction he bids his lady, when he is going on an absence from her, to study his manuscripts, "those Myriades of letters," and write the annals of their love for the sake of posterity. I quote the third stanza, with a little editing of the punctuation:

> This Booke, as long-liv'd as the elements,
> Or as the world's forme, this all-graved tome
> In cypher writ, or new made Idiome
> (We for love's clergie only are instruments),—
> When this booke is made thus,
> Should again the ravenous
> Vandals and Gauls inundate us,
> Learning were safe; in this our universe
> Schooles might learn Sciences, Spheares Musick,
>   Angels Verse.

One understands that he really means what he says: a book. In the three stanzas following he shows respectively what the Divines, the Lawyers, and the Statesmen will learn from this book, and in a final stanza returns to relate to a lover's absence the labor of compiling it. Donne would have performed well within an English sonnet-structure, where he might have gone on three separate little adventures into his image; there are three here, though the stanza is bigger, and perhaps therefore easier, than quatrain. (Structurally, there is no firmer architect of lyric anywhere in English than Donne.) The trick consists, apparently, in guiding the imagination to the right places and then letting it go. To make this controlled yet exuberant use of the imagination is an intellectual feat; though it would not follow that there is no other recipe which will confer upon verse its intellectual distinction. (pp. 533-43)

[In some instances] Shakespeare [too] . . . realizes the metaphysical image, and I shall cite, with some remark, the sonnets in which he seems to me to have the most conspicuous success.

I begin with XXX, "When to the sessions of sweet silent thought"; it is smart work, but only half the sharpness belongs to the strict object; the rest is accidental or mechanical, because it is oral or verbal; it is word-play, and word-play, including punning, originates principally [in] the loose poetry of association. Technically perfect and altogether admirable in its careful modulation is LVII, "Being your slave, what should I do but tend"; and so faithfully does it stick to the object, which is the behavior suitable to the slave kept waiting, that not till the couplet is there any direct expression of the feelings of the actual outraged lover.

Sonnet LX, "Like as the waves make toward the pebbled shore," is ambitious and imperfect. The first quatrain says that our minutes are always toiling forward, like waves. The second quatrain introduces a different and pretentious image of this tendency, and shows its fatal consequence:

> Nativity, once in the main of light,
> Crawls to maturity, wherewith being crown'd,
> Crooked eclipses 'gainst his glory fight,
> And Time that gave doth now his gift confound.

The lines will be impressive to that kind of receptivity whose

critical defenses are helpless against great words in musical phrases. Nativity means the new-born infant, but maturity seems only an object in his path, or at the goal of his path, evidently a crown which he puts on. Thereupon the astrological influences turn against nativity, and Time enters the story to destroy his own gift; this must be the crown that nativity has picked up. We are confused about all these entities. In the third quatrain Shakespeare declines to a trite topic, the destructiveness of Time, and represents him successively as transfixing the flourish set on youth (however he may do that), delving the parallels in beauty's brow (as a small demon with a digging instrument?), feeding on the rarities of nature's truth (as gluttonous monster), and mowing everything with his scythe (as grim reaper). A field of imagery in which the explorer has performed too prodigiously, and lost his chart.

And now LXXIII, with its opening quatrain:

> That time of year thou mayst in me behold
> When yellow leaves, or none, or few, do hang
> Upon those boughs which shake against the cold,
> Bare ruin'd choirs, where late the sweet birds sang.

The structure is good, the three quatrains offering distinct yet equivalent figures for the time of life of the unsuccessful and to-be-pitied lover. But the first quatrain is the boldest, and the effect of the whole is slightly anti-climactic. Within this quatrain I think I detect a thing which often characterizes Shakespeare's work within the metaphysical style: he is unwilling to renounce the benefit of his earlier style, which consisted in the breadth of the associations; that is, he will not quite risk the power of a single figure but compounds the figures. I refer to the two images about the boughs. It is one thing to have the boughs shaking against the cold, and in that capacity they carry very well the fact of the old rejected lover; it is another thing to represent them as ruined choirs where the birds no longer sing. The latter is a just representation of the lover too, and indeed a subtler and richer one, but the two images cannot, in logical rigor, co-exist. Therefore I deprecate *shake against the cold*. And I believe everybody will deprecate *sweet*. This term is not an objective image at all, but a term to be located at the subjective pole of the experience; it expects to satisfy a feeling by naming it (that is, by just having it) and is a pure sentimentalism.

No. LXXXVII, "Farewell! thou art too dear for my possessing," which we have already seen and remarked, needs only the further comment that it is rare and charming among sonnets for the almost complete prevalence of the feminine rhyme.

I cite XCIV, "They that have power to hurt and will do none"; it has proved obscure to commentators, but I think it is clear if taken in context, as an imaginary argument against the friend's relation with the woman, or with any woman, exactly opposite to the argument of the sonnets which open the sequence. And XCVII, "How like a winter hath my absence been," where the logical structure has some nicety though the detail is rather large of scale.

I am interested in CVII, which begins,

> Not mine own fears, nor the prophetic soul
> Of the wide world dreaming on things to come.

The argument is that the auguries of disaster and death to his love need not be trusted; it concludes disappointingly in an old vein, that at any rate this love will endure in the poet's rhyme. I am particularly bothered by the image of the world's prophetic soul; as who is not? The world-soul is a technical concept, I suppose, in the sense that it was of use to Paracelsus and to other theosophists, who knew what they wanted to make of it. It indicates a very fine image for some metaphysical poet who will handle it technically; for Donne, or another university poet. It is not fit for amateurs. The question is whether Shakespeare's theological touch here is not amateurish; elsewhere it sometimes is, as in Hamlet's famous soliloquy beginning, "To be or not to be." It is my impression that our poet is faking, or shall we say improvising; the *wide,* denoting extension, seems to destroy the world's aspect as soul, the *dreaming* is too pretty a form for the prophetic action.

There is evenness in CIX, "O! never say that I was false of heart." In CXXI, ' 'Tis better to be vile than vile esteem'd," the language of the opening quatrain sounds close and technical enough for a passage of Donne's, but the argument is rather obscure; the later quatrains seem to shift the argument. No. CXXV, "Were't aught to me I bore the canopy," is admirable though not unitary enough to be very metaphysical. And finally there is CXLVI, "Poor Soul, the centre of my sinful earth," the most Platonic or "spiritual" sonnet in the entire sequence, a noble revulsion in the progress of the poet's feelings, and the poet might well have employed it to conclude the unhappy history, leaving quite off the eight miscellaneous and indeterminate ones that follow. Perhaps he would have done so if he and not the printer had directed the publication. (pp. 548-51)

> *John Crowe Ransom, "Shakespeare at Sonnets," in* The Southern Review, *Louisiana State University, Vol. 3, No. 3, Winter, 1938, pp. 531-53.*

ARTHUR MIZENER (essay date 1940)

[*Mizener was an American educator, editor, and critic who is chiefly noted for his biographies of F. Scott Fitzgerald and Ford Madox Ford. In the excerpt below, he evaluates the figurative language of Shakespeare's sonnets, disputing John Crowe Ransom's contention that many of them are metaphysical (see excerpt above, 1938). Shakespeare's finest sonnets are characterized by a richness, complexity, and inclusiveness of poetic language that is in sharp contrast to metaphysical poetry, he points out, where "each figurative detail may be examined in isolation" and the verse itself represents "a neatly integrated hierarchy of such details." Mizener closely examines Sonnet 124, calling attention to the many possible implications of its imagery and to the recurring metaphors for the destructive power of time. As in others of his sonnets, Mizener contends, Shakespeare's focus here is intentionally diffuse, and a reader must avoid bringing any one signification of "this complex of interacting metaphors" into greater prominence than the others.*]

Recently Mr. John Crowe Ransom has thrown a few stones at Shakespeare the sonneteer [see excerpt above]; his strategy is to set Shakespeare up as a metaphysical poet and then to assail his metaphysical weaknesses. Mr. Ransom has, I think, been throwing his stones at Blunt or some other gallant knight rather than at Shakespeare; but whether he is right or wrong, he has done the sonnets a good turn by raising in a serious way, for the first time since the eighteenth century, the problem of their figurative language.

In those distant days, some severe strictures were passed on this aspect of Shakespeare. Dr. Johnson remarked that "a quibble was to him the fatal Cleopatra for which he lost the world and was content to lose it"; Warburton laboriously explained that "he took up (as he was hurried on by the torrent of his matter) with the first words that lay in his way; and if, amongst these, there were two mixed modes that had a principal idea in common, it was enough for him"; Steevens roundly declared that "such labored perplexities of language, and such studied deformities of style, prevail throughout these sonnets" that he saw no reason to print them in 1793, since "the strongest act of parliament that could be framed would fail to compel readers into their service" [see excerpt above, 1793]. These eighteenth-century critics were never answered. The usual remarks about this aspect of the sonnets ("An average Shakespeare sonnet comes dancing in, as it were, with the effortless grace of a bird, etc.") are not answers but ways of filling an embarrassing pause.

Here, however, is not Steevens or another of those outspoken and outmoded eighteenth-century gentlemen, but Mr. Ransom, less outspoken and as a consequence in some ways more devastating, and very far indeed from being outmoded. One can of course say that if we distill off the poetry of Shakespeare's sonnets, leaving in the flask only the bare "idea," that "idea" will be found not only familiar but, indeed, trite. Even the most ardent advocate of this view, however, usually gives his case away before he is through with some reference to the mystery of Shakespeare's language. Nor does this view meet Mr. Ransom's argument. The only way that argument can be met is by a description of the structure of the sonnets' figurative language which accounts for that structure without damning Shakespeare as, at his best, a metaphysical poet who lacks the courage of his convictions, and, at his worst, a manufacturer of trifles. If Shakespeare's sonnets are really metaphysical then they are bad in the way and to the extent Mr. Ransom says they are.

Mr. Ransom's argument is that good poetry is always airtight extensively. He is willing to allow it to function intensively only within the limits of a logically airtight statement. A poet, that is, must never be more in earnest about the tenor of his metaphor than about the vehicle, must never be willing to sacrifice the strict logic of his vehicle in order to imply something further about the tenor. This is a seductive definition of good poetry but an arbitrary one, which, if strictly applied, excludes from the category of good poetry all non-metaphysical poetry. In the present state of our knowledge of the way language works, this consideration alone is enough to cast serious doubt on such a definition. It produces, in addition, some curious results. For instance, Mr. Ransom says of the opening quatrain of sonnet LXXIII ("That time of year thou may'st in me behold") that the metaphor here is compounded and that "the two images cannot, in logical rigor, co-exist." It is true that *choirs* can be looked on as a metaphorical extension of *boughs,* but it is only by a pun that this extension can be maintained in the phrase "sweet birds" and Mr. Ransom cannot allow puns. Not even a pun, moreover, will bring "shake against the cold" within the limits of the figure, since by no stretch of the imagination can ruined cathedrals be thought of as shaking against the cold.

But it is plain before one reaches the end of this analysis that the success of Shakespeare's compound metaphor does not depend on the strict logic of its vehicle. His purpose is apparently to relate to his time of life, by some other means than the strictly logical elaboration of vehicle, both the boughs which shake against the cold and the bare ruined choirs. The age of Shakespeare's love, which is his life, is like the autumnal decline of nature, and thus natural, inevitable and, perhaps, only the prelude to a winter sleep rather than death; it is at the same time like the destruction of an artificial and man-made thing by man's wilful violence, and thus not inevitable, save as evil is inevitable, but regrettable as is the destruction of a building beautiful, not only in itself but as a symbol. The fusion of these two meanings brought about by the compound metaphor is richer and finer than the sum of them which would be all the poem could offer if the two metaphors did not coexist. The fact that this fusion gives the vehicle, not logic, but an ingeniously devised air of being logically really deceives no one (least of all, I suspect, Mr. Ransom) into supposing that Shakespeare's lines depend for their power on the rigorous logic of the metaphor's vehicle.

Shakespeare's method is then fundamentally different from the metaphysical method: where Donne, for example, surprises you with an apparently illogical vehicle which can be understood only if its logic is followed, Shakespeare surprises you with an apparently logical vehicle which is understandable only if taken figuratively.

The position taken by critics like Mr. Ransom thus forces them to write down as a blunder one of the most essential features of Shakespeare's kind of poetry. A critic is of course free to dislike Shakespeare's kind of poetry, and I imagine Mr. Ransom is not in his own estimation pulling his punches when he describes it as the kind "which we sometimes dispose of a little distastefully as 'romantic.'" Probably a great many more people than profess to would dislike it were they not bullied into accepting it by Shakespeare's name. But the critic has not the right to treat this poetry as if it were of another kind, as Mr. Ransom does in discussing what he calls Shakespeare's "metaphysical" sonnets.

The characteristic feature of Shakespeare's kind of poetry at its best is a soft focus; a metaphysical poem is in perfect focus, perhaps more than perfect focus (like those paintings in which every detail is drawn with microscopic perfection). In a good metaphysical poem each figurative detail may be examined in isolation and the poem as a whole presents itself to us as a neatly integrated hierarchy of such details. Mr. Ransom suggests that the metaphysical poet shows a special kind of courage in committing his feelings in this way "to their determination within the elected figure"; probably no one will question this claim, or the implication that the special intensity of good metaphysical poetry derives from this self-imposed restriction. But the metaphysical poet shows also a special kind of perversity. He achieves a logical form at the expense of richness and verisimilitude; for the more ingeniously he elaborates his elected figure, the more apparent will it be that it is either distorting or excluding the nonlogical aspects of his awareness of the object.

Mr. Ransom, however, believes that the business of the poem is to express not the poet but the object, and draws a distinction between the poetry of knowledge and the poetry of feelings. This is a useful distinction, particularly in dealing with nineteenth-century poetry of the kind from which Messrs. Ransom and Tate are such experts in selecting horrible examples; but it does not go all the way. For whether or not the object has an existence independent of our awareness of it is for poetry an academic question; so far as poetry is concerned its existence is our awareness of it. Expressing an object, giving to it, in Mr. Ransom's phrase, "public value," consists in "publishing" our awareness of it; and feelings are no less feelings for being a publishable, a communicable, part of that awareness. Mr. Ransom's very proper distaste for a poetry

which presents a gross awareness, one which includes undistinguished or ill-distinguished feelings about the object, seems to have led him to try to eliminate the concept "feeling" from his definition of the best poetry. But to say that the best poetry expresses the object is to use a figure of speech which only apparently allows you to escape the fact that "speech as behavior is a wonderfully complex blend of two pattern systems, the symbolic and the expressive, neither of which could have developed to its present perfection without the interference of the other" [Edward Sapir, in his "Language"].

Since poetry is not the world's body but a verbal construct between which and the world-as-object the poet's awareness mediates, there are bound to be disadvantages to any kind of poetry which requires a definite distortion of that awareness for its intensity. It is this price which Shakespeare's poetry does not have to pay. There is, certainly, much to be said against his kind of poetry too. It is, for one thing, always wantoning on the verge of anarchy; and I think Mr. Ransom is right as to the unhappy effect of Shakespeare's example on such poets as Matthew Arnold, who brought himself to announce of Shakespeare's receding hairline that an assorted collection of painful sensations "find their sole speech in that victorious brow." But whatever may be said against it, much, too, must be said in favor of a poetic method which made possible the richness and verisimilitude of the best of Shakespeare's sonnets.

The only way to particularize this description of Shakespeare's method is to examine one of the sonnets in some detail. I have chosen for this purpose CXXIV:

> If my dear love were but the child of state,
> It might for fortune's bastard be unfathered,
> As subject to time's love, or to time's hate,
> Weeds among weeds, or flowers with flowers gath-
>   ered.
> No it was builded far from accident,
> It suffers not in smiling pomp, nor falls
> Under the blow of thralled discontent,
> Whereto the inviting time our fashion calls:
> It fears not policy that heretic,
> Which works on leases of short numbered hours,
> But all alone stands hugely politic,
> That it nor grows with heat, nor drowns with show-
>   ers.
>   To this I witness call the fools of time,
>   Which die for goodness, who have lived for
>   crime.

This sonnet has at least two advantages in this connection: it is obviously a serious effort and it is not likely therefore that its consequences are unintentional; and it has that "excessive dispersion in the matter of figures" which seems to be characteristic of Shakespeare at his most serious and has annoyed others besides Mr. Ransom.

"If my dear love were but the child of state." The difficulty here is with *state,* which has a very complex meaning. It covers, in its general sense, the condition of those who live in this world and in time; in its specific senses, it includes most of the particular aspects of life which are touched on in the rest of the sonnet. I begin with the general sense. If Shakespeare's love were the product of, had been generated by, the combination of circumstances and attributes belonging to the young man addressed and to the age, it might, as a subject of the kingdom of time and consequently "subject to" the whimsical decrees of Time's perverse rule, at any time be "unfathered." The more specific sense of *state*—the metaphorical father of which Shakespeare's love would risk being deprived—touched on in the rest of the sonnets are: (1) Fortune, the deity who rules worldly affairs; (2) status; (3) wealth; (4) natural endowment (talent, beauty); (5) authority, pomp, display, the more obvious of the secondary characteristics of *state* in the previous senses; (6) the body politic; (7) statesmanship, "policy," the kind of maneuvering by which all earthly results, good or bad, are achieved. Of this complex father Shakespeare's love, were it the child of state, would run the constant risk of being deprived, either as the bastard of state in sense (1) or in order to make way for some other bastard of state as Fortune. In either case, Shakespeare's love, as a child of state, would be a bastard.

Nothing, I think, could show more clearly than these three lines the difference between Shakespeare's figurative language and that of a metaphysical poem. For no single one of the meanings of *state* will they work out completely, nor will the language allow any one of the several emergent figures to usurp our attention; it thus becomes impossible to read the lines at all without making an effort to keep all the meanings of *state*, all the emergent figures, in view at once. That is, the purpose is to make the reader see them all, simultaneously, in soft focus; and the method is to give the reader just enough of each figure for this purpose. The figure of state as Fortune, for example, emerges just far enough to make it possible for the reader to see what this figure would have come to had it been worked out completely; and the figure of state as the body politic within which Shakespeare's love would be subject to Time just far enough to suggest what that figure would have come to. And so of the rest. If any one of these emergent figures had been realized in full, all the rest would necessarily have been excluded. They must then have been developed separately, and Shakespeare would have written a poem in which each of these figures appeared seriatim, perhaps a figure to a stanza, as in Donne's "Valediction; of the booke," which Mr. Ransom offers as an illustration of metaphysical structure.

It is difficult to say how daring a venture "Weeds among weeds, or flowers with flowers gathered" is; it all depends on how familiar in Shakespeare's day the associations of weeds and flowers he is using here were. It is easy enough to show that they were familiar to Shakespeare, but I suspect they were also peculiar to him. Fortunately the line is carefully paralleled with l. 12; indeed, the primary sense-connection of l. 12 is to l. 4. From this parallel I think l. 4 gains enough support so that it will serve simply in its general sense: if Shakespeare's love were the child of state, so long as Fortune favored it, its every aspect would be a flower gathered with all the other flowers blossoming in the sunshine of Time's love; if Fortune ceased to favor it, its every aspect would be a weed, gathered with all the other weeds which rot noisomely in the damp of Time's hate. *Gather'd* carries out the personifications of the first three lines, and hints at a new one, Father Time (cp., the scythe in the final line of CXXIII); the flowers and weeds represent the specific consequences of Time's love and Time's hate.

But the particular value of this line as a summing up of the whole quatrain depends on our familiarity with Shakespeare's usual use of weeds and flowers; and it is not quite fair therefore to say that this value is communicated as well as expressed. In Shakespeare the contrast between weeds and flowers is most frequently applied to court life, society, prob-

lems of state, this-worldly affairs; figures of this kind are frequent in the history plays and in *Hamlet*. Weeds, particularly in their rankness (vigorousness, grossness, rancidity, indecency), are among the strongest of Shakespeare's images for evil. Thus the gardener in *Richard II* ends his elaborate comparison of his garden to a commonwealth by saying:

> I will go root away
> The noisome weeds, which without profit suck
> The soil's fertility from wholesome flowers.
> [*Richard II,* III. iv. 37-9]

Hamlet finds the world

>   an unweeded garden,
> That grows to seed; things rank and gross in nature
> Possess it merely.
>   [*Hamlet,* I. ii. 135-37]

This sense of evil is primarily a result of his mother's sins; these are for Hamlet both weeds on which she is in danger of spreading compost "to make them ranker" and an "ulcerous place," the rank corruption of which may infect all within unseen. But Hamlet's sense of evil is not limited to its immediate cause; it is *all* the uses of this world which seem to him weary, stale, flat, and unprofitable, just as in the present sonnet Shakespeare distrusts Time's love as much as its hate. The "facts" of both the play and the sonnet are the vehicle for a feeling about the world as a whole. It is the essence of Shakespeare's success with this kind of figurative language that he never loses the individual "facts" in the perilously extended feeling.

With the association of rank weeds and spiritual corruption goes quite naturally the association of physical and spiritual decay which appears in Hamlet's "ulcerous place" figure. The ease with which Shakespeare bridged what may seem to the reader the considerable gap between the imagery of flowers and weeds and the imagery of disease can be demonstrated from a simple narrative passage in *Macbeth*:

> CATHNESS: Well, march we on,
> To give obedience where 'tis truly ow'd:
> Meet we the medicine of the sickly weal;
> And with him pour we, in our country's purge,
> Each drop of us.
> LENOX: Or so much as it needs
> To dew the sovereign flower, and drown the weeds.
> [*Macbeth,* V. ii. 25-30]

Here, quite characteristically, their blood, in Cathness's speech a medicine with which to purge the sick society, becomes the dew which makes the sovereign flower grow and drowns the weed. And, precisely as in the present sonnet, the fact that the ultimate referent of weeds is a group of human beings leads Shakespeare to use a verb (*drown*) which is more immediately applicable to persons than to weeds.

The physical decay of this imagery may be either that of disease or that of death. It is the special horror of this aspect of life that the sun's breeding maggots in a dead dog and the son's breeding sinners in that living variety of good kissing carrion, Ophelia, are scarcely distinguishable. Both kinds of physical decay appear frequently in connection with the evils of human life, especially the evils of power and passion. Hamlet's mind is haunted by the smell of rotting flesh as well as by the imposthume that inward breaks. The king will be able to nose the corpse of Polonius as he goes up the stairs into the lobby; and Hamlet's final comment on the humiliating futility of Yorick's life is: "and smelt so? Pah!" [V. i. 200]. But perhaps the most perfect collocation of all these images and their association is the close of sonnet XCIV:

> The summer's flower is to the summer sweet,
> Though to itself, it only live and die,
> But if that flower with base infection meet,
> The basest weed outbraves his dignity,
>   For sweetest things turn sourest by their deeds:
>   Lilies that fester, smell far worse than weeds.

Rain is closely connected with these images of corruption, too, for though it causes flowers as well as weeds to grow (but "sweet flowers are slow and weeds make haste"), it is also the cause of weeds' and flesh's rotting and stinking. The first gravedigger, after observing that "we have many pocky corpses now-a-days, that will scarcely hold the laying in," remarks that a tanner's corpse will last the longest because "'a will keep out water a great while, and your water is a sore decayer of your whoreson dead body" [*Hamlet,* V. i. 166-65, 171-72]. And it is the rankness of nettles which lends the terrible dramatic irony to Cressida's reply to Pandarus.

> PANDARUS: I'll be sworn 'tis true: he will weep you,
>   and 'twere a man born in April
> CRESSIDA: And I'll spring up in his tears, an
>   'twere a nettle against May.
>   [*Troilus and Cressida,* I. ii. 173-76]

It is these associations of weeds and flowers (and of heat and showers too) which give such great force to l. 4.

With the second quatrain Shakespeare starts another of his great metaphors for the destructive power of time, that of a building: "No it was builded far from accident" (where "waterdrops have worn the stones of Troy, / And blind oblivion swallow'd cities up, / And mighty states characterless are grated / To dusty nothing"). This metaphor is then compounded in much the same way that the opening metaphor of sonnet LXXIII is; that is, the building is personified: "It suffers not in smiling pomp, nor falls / Under the blow of thralled discontent." The figurative significances which may be derived from this compounded metaphor, taken in connection with the two metaphors of the first quatrain, are so many and so shaded into each other that a listing of them is neither possible nor desirable. The effect here, as in the first quatrain, depends on our being conscious of as many of these figurative significances as possible without bringing any of them exclusively into focus. They resist any effort to separate them one from the other; if the reader nevertheless insists on trying to force the lines to work for any one meaning alone, they will appear hopelessly defective. If this were not the case, they would be unable to function for all their meanings simultaneously.

The disadvantages of trying to bring any one implication of this complex of interacting metaphors into sharp focus are manifold. If the reader will oversimplify the problem by ignoring the metaphor of a building which intervenes between Shakespeare's love and the personification which suffers in smiling pomp and falls under the blow of thralled discontent, he will discover that there is a variation of meaning in these lines for every variation of meaning to be found in the first quatrain as a result of the multiple signification of *state*. But if he tries to bring each of these possible meanings of the second quatrain successively into focus he will find not only that the lines will not support any one of them alone, but that each of them tends to shade off into every other, till the possibility

of bringing any one into sharp focus becomes remote. There are certainly very real differences between *state* as status, as wealth, and as physical beauty, and it is certain, too, that one can associate a different kind of pomp and a different kind of discontent with each of them. But if the reader attempts to elaborate in detail each of these combinations, he finds in the first place that *suffer* and *fall* range from merely awkward to downright impossible, and in the second that the pomp of the young man's status and the pomp of his wealth begin to fade into each other, that the thralled discontent of status unrecognized, of talent unrealized, of policy unsuccessful begin to merge; and so it is with the rest of these distinctions which are perfectly satisfactory in a general focus.

But the reader cannot afford to ignore the fact that the *it* of l. 6 refers quite as clearly to that which was builded far from accident as to "my dear love." For unless he realize that ll. 6-7 retain the metaphor of the building he will miss the delicacy with which Shakespeare carries out the irony, obvious enough, in a general way, in the implications of the negatives. Shakespeare does not say that the young man is tossed from success to failure and from discontent to satisfaction on the whirligig of time and that, in spite of this, Shakespeare's love remains unchanging. What he does say is that his love is like a building, a building which may be thought of most significantly as not like a courtier riding such a whirligig. The delicacy of the irony thus depends on the fact that this comparison is ostensibly chosen as the perfect description of the building and on the implication that Shakespeare would be surprised and dismayed were he to discover the young man taking it as a reference to himself. Shakespeare, that is, ostensibly and indeed ostentatiously disowns any responsibility for the coincidence of the young man's state and this figurative courtier's.

The insistence of Shakespeare's sonnet on generalizing the focus of the reader's attention will be quite clear, I think, if he will work out the simplest meaning for ll. 6-7 at each of the three levels, without considering either the remoter figurative significances, or the interaction of the various levels of meaning, or the interrelationship of these lines with other lines. A courtier may be said to go about smiling and pompous in the conceit of his success; he may not be said to "suffer smiling and pompous." He may be described as wholly enslaved by discontent but only by some stretching of the figure as falling under the blow of his discontent. A building may be described as rich and elegant; it can scarcely be said to "suffer rich and elegant." It may fall under the blows of rebelling slaves; one blow, however, seems a little inadequate. Finally, Shakespeare's love, not having been generated by anything that dwells in Time's kingdom, is beyond the power of either Time's love or Time's hate, both of which are spoken of in l. 6 as disastrous (the first causing suffering and the second discontent). The language of ll. 6-7 is directed just sufficiently toward each of these meanings to make it impossible for the reader to ignore any one of them. In no instance is it directed toward any one of them sufficiently to make it possible for the reader to contemplate that meaning to the exclusion of the others. The reader is thus forced to try to contemplate them all simultaneously. This procedure obviously permits an immense concentration of meaning within the particular passage. It has the further effect of almost forcing the poet to use the multitude of interrelations between the various passages which suggest themselves. This is, of course, the great danger of Shakespeare's kind of poetry. It is a danger over which Shakespeare at his best always triumphed but which has pretty consistently defeated his imitators.

"Whereto the inviting time our fashion calls." To such an existence this encouraging age calls us to fashion our lives as nobles, our relatively more permanent structures (both physical and social), our lives. But there is another important meaning here. It is impossible to keep this *time* from establishing relations with the *time* that loves and hates in l. 3; thus Time in its local and temporary manifestation, this age, calls upon our fashion to become subject to its love and hate (smiling pomp and thralled discontent being the results of accepting).

In the final quatrain Shakespeare draws together all his metaphorical themes. His love "fears not policy" since it is no child of state but was born in another kingdom than that of Time, in which policy operates. Policy is a heretic by the familiar trick of transferring the vocabulary of the Christian worship of God to the lover's worship of the loved one. But it is also a heretic ("an indifferentist in religion, a wordly-wise man") because it is a child of state, worshipping the god of Time rather than the God of eternity. *Policy* is then said to be able to work only within the limits of human foresight, which is a space of short numbered hours compared to the eternity in terms of which those work who are subjects of God's kingdom. The line in question (10) is another one of those which says several things and works out without defect for none of them alone. That is, policy, personified as a heretic, may be said to work, but scarcely on a lease of any kind; on the other hand this same policy may *have* a lease on life of short numbered hours. A building in Time's world will presumably be held on a short lease, the duration of which is carefully measured; it can hardly, however, be described as *working* on that lease.

"But all alone stands hugely politic." With a slight stretching of "hugely politic" this line will work for the two immediate meanings involved, those of the previous line. That is, Shakespeare's love, as a building, stands all alone, perhaps like New Place with its orchards and gardens rather than like one of those speculative structures in London, crowded between other buildings, which were giving the authorities so much to worry about. It stands "far from accident," incredibly old and wise representing, as it were, the good old certainties of faith rather than the newfangled values of shrewdness and calculation. Shakespeare's love, as person, stands apart from the human world of petty policy, dependent on no earthly devices, politic only in the infinite's craft, learned not in Machiavelli's but in God's book.

Thus Shakespeare's love is unlike the blooming favorites of Time's love and the rank and weedy creatures of Time's hate; it is unlike the worldly courtier who flourishes in the sun of prosperity ("For if the sun breed maggots in a dead dog . . . Let her not walk i' th' sun") and goes down in the floods of adversity ("Pulled the poor wretch from her melodious lay / To muddy death"); it is unlike the house built upon the sand which shows in pomp in the sun and sinks to ruin in storms. "It nor grows with heat, nor drowns with showers."

Shakespeare calls to witness the truth of this statement those people who are made fools of by Time. In general in Shakespeare everyone is in one way or another made a fool of by Time, those who know enough try to escape its tyranny most tragically of all. For these discover, as Troilus did, that their fears are only too well grounded:

> What will it be
> When that the watery palate tastes indeed
> Love's thrice repured nectar! Death, I fear me,
> Sounding destruction, or some joy too fine,
> Too subtle potent, tun'd too sharp in sweetness
> For the capacity of my ruder powers:
> I fear it much; . . .
>
> [*Troilus and Cressida,* III. ii. 20-6]

Troilus, Hamlet, Isabella, all in their ways tried to escape from the life of this world, and all discovered that they could not escape the human consequences of the fact that they were living in it. "Does your worship mean to geld and splay all the youth of the city?" [*Measure for Measure,* II. i. 230-31].

I think these facts are necessary to an understanding of the amazing inclusiveness of Shakespeare's description of the fools of time. At the most obvious level this line (14) makes a distinction between martyrs and worldly-wise men. For though *who* certainly modifies *which,* the change of relatives tends to divide those which die for goodness from those who have lived for crime. And this division is reenforced by the ambiguity of *goodness,* which may mean what Shakespeare takes to be good or what the criminals take to be good. Those who die for goodness in this second, ironic sense may, like "Pitiful thrivers in their gazing spent" [Sonnet CXXV], die physically for the sake of the "compound sweet" which they, "dwellers on form and favour," have devoted their worldly lives to seeking; it may be that they also die eternally, are damned, for lack of goodness in the serious sense and for living sinful lives. Those who die for goodness in the serious sense, who are martyrs, may die physically, because, like Richard, they failed to give enough attention to the worldly-wise man's kind of good, after living lives which, even at their best, were not without sin ("in the course of justice, none of us / Should see salvation" [*The Merchant of Venice,* IV. i. 199-200]) and, at their troubled worst, offended against more than one of the world's canons, to say nothing of the Everlasting's.

The most astonishing consequence of this line is its inclusion among the fools of Time of the author of this sonnet, so that by a terrifying twist of irony Shakespeare offers his own failure—the unavoidable fact that, for all he has been saying about it, his love cannot escape the consequences of his being human and not divine—as part of the evidence for the truth of his contention that his love is not "the child of state."

The pattern which one of Shakespeare's sonnets aims to establish in the reader's mind (using the word in its broadest sense) is not the pattern of logic aimed at by the metaphysical poem; his typical sonnet is rather a formal effort to create in the reader's mind a pattern, externally controlled, very like the pattern of the mind when it contemplates, with full attention but for no immediately practical purpose, an object in nature. Such a pattern is not built simply of logical relations nor does it consist simply of what is in perfect focus; it is built of all the kinds of relations known to the mind, as a result of its verbal conditioning or for other reasons, which can be invoked verbally. The building of a verbal construct calculated to invoke such a pattern requires the use of every resource language as a social instrument possesses, and it involves a structure of figurative language which at least approaches, in its own verbal terms, the richness, the density, the logical incompleteness of the mind.

No one can say how much the effect which a poem may fairly be said to produce can in the ordinary sense have been intended by the poet; apparently a good deal it does is not consciously intended. But unless the best of Shakespeare's sonnets are to be passed off as miraculous accidents, it is difficult to see what grounds there are for supposing that they are the result of following the path of least resistance in contrast to Donne's poems, which Mr. Ransom quite justly claims must be the result of stern intellectual labors. If the structure of figurative language in Shakespeare's sonnets is not an accident, and if its consequences are calculated, in so far as the consequences of any poem may be said to be calculated, then it seems more than probable that their making involved at least as great an effort of the intellect and imagination as the making of Donne's poems.

Mr. Ransom has it that in a formal lyric, "the poetic object is elected by a free choice from all objects in the world, and this object, deliberately elected and worked up by the adult poet, becomes his microcosm. . . . It is as ranging and comprehensive an action as the mind has ever tried." It seems to me that Shakespeare's serious sonnets fail, as they do sometimes fail, not because they do not live up to this admirable description of the formal lyric but because they have tried to live up to it altogether too well. (pp. 730-47)

> Arthur Mizener, "The Structure of Figurative Language in Shakespeare's Sonnets," in The Southern Review, Louisiana State University, Vol. V, No. 2, Spring, 1940, pp. 730-47.

LESLIE HOTSON (essay date 1949)

[Hotson is a Canadian-born scholar and researcher whose comprehensive studies of Elizabethan documents have resulted in important and controversial discoveries about the life of Shakespeare. His published works include The First Night of "Twelfth Night" (1954), an imaginative reconstruction of the first performance of Shakespeare's comedy; Mr. W. H. (1964, see Additional Bibliography); and Shakespeare's Sonnets Dated (1949). In the excerpt below, Hotson proposes a 1589 composition date for Sonnets 107, 123, and 124 on the basis of what he identifies as topical allusions in these verses. Further, the critic claims that Shakespeare completed "the main group of his sonnets"—that is, the first 126—by 1589, and thus his poetic power "had reached maturity by the time he was no more than twenty-five years old." For a response to Hotson's argument, see the excerpt below by F. W. Bateson (1951).]

Even in this age of ours, Science—good luck to it—has no corner in discovery. History, Biography, Literature: these, too, hold important secrets which may still be brought to light. And for the general reader, the processes of discovery in these fields are more interesting than those of science, both because he can more readily follow them, and because their results are more human.

Here we shall look over the shoulder of the master poet of the modern era, Shakespeare, as he views stirring events as they pass, and transmutes them into literature. We shall discover his response to his world's narrow escape from total destruction; to the crucial naval battle of the century; to the most signal triumph of engineering; to the assassination of the King of France.

Stranger still, in doing so we shall uncover something the world has never suspected: the fact that Shakespeare's poetic powers were full-grown when he was no more than twenty-five years old. It will be an adventure of discovery in History, Biography, and Literature rolled into one.

In not a few of the Sonnets we find a supreme beauty and power of emotion clothed in thought; and since in them we feel drawn closer to the heart of Shakespeare than anywhere in his plays, these poems have aroused enormous interest, almost as much as Hamlet has done. But questions about them have also produced volumes of diverse comment, and a perplexing library of conflicting theories. The Sonnets have been called a maze, a labyrinth, the most intricate puzzle in Shakespeare. 'There are many footprints around the cave of this mystery, none of them pointing in the outward direction.' Such is the grim warning of Professor Raleigh.

Just before the War, the danger was pictured for me in a more personal way in Chelsea by Logan Pearsall Smith, whose sane and sensitive judgment is now lost to us. He cautioned me to steer clear of the problem of the Sonnets—a Wandering Wood, he said: an Error's Den. And in his delightful essay On Reading Shakespeare he went farther. Here it is not merely 'the Serbonian sonnet-bog, in which armies whole have sunk,' but a region of inky night where not a soul but feels a fever of the mad:

> For listen! the fanatic followers of no less than five ghostly, resurrected Elizabethan Earls are shouting at each other, the two bands of Pembrokians and Southamptonites, each vociferating that their Lord was the inspirer of the Sonnets, while three other bands proclaim the more glorious boast . . . that Lord Derby, or Lord Rutland, or Lord Oxford, was the author of them. . . . And then, faint and far, as the wind shifts, we hear the ululations of those vaster herds of Baconian believers, as they plunge squeaking down the Gadarene slope of their delusion.

We have been warned! Yet if in the face of all friendly dissuasives we insist on risking our sanity in a fresh attempt, we may draw courage from the remarks of John Benson, on republishing the Sonnets in 1640 [see excerpt above, 1640]. Benson was born in Shakespeare's lifetime, before theories about the Sonnets had been invented. And he told his readers, 'You shall find them serene, clear, and elegantly plain; . . . no intricate or cloudy stuff to puzzle intellect, but perfect eloquence.' We should also remember that Shakespeare was no mystifier. Both he and his audience knew what he was talking about. George Santayana assures us that the comprehensive poet, such as Shakespeare, 'would be a poet of business. He would have a taste for the world in which he lived, and a clean view of it.'

To begin, then, with the first 'mystery': when were the Sonnets written? No agreement has been reached on this primary question. If we could fix that date, we should have a standpoint from which perhaps to decide what (if anything) there is in the rival theories which see in Shakespeare's friend either the Earl of Southampton or the Earl of Pembroke. We might make a better guess at the identity of the Rival Poet. Above all, what is infinitely more important than anything else, by finding out where the Sonnets belong in the story of Shakespeare's development, we might correct and enlarge our understanding of the greatest poet of the modern world.

Shakespeare has not left us without clues to work upon. Two or three of his sonnets are recognized as carrying external or topical references. Under the influence, however, of diverse preconceptions about their date, critics cannot agree on what events Shakespeare is pointing at. This being so, it is curious that no one has carefully compared these references with the news: that is, with the emergent occurrences of the Europe in which Shakespeare lived as the Soul of the Age—to discover to what notable events between 1585 and 1605, grouped fairly closely together in time, the topical sonnets refer. Possibly historians have not been sufficiently interested in Shakespeare. Or perhaps the literary folk have not troubled to go back to the living contemporary history. Whatever the reason, this obligatory job of collation has not been done.

In comparing the facts of his times with the poet's references, we must begin without a theory, and be ready to follow where the evidence leads. 'If you wish to see the meaning of a thing, look directly into it; for if you think about it, it is altogether missed.' To look directly into the years marching to the close of the Sixteenth Century means for us to look into them so far as we can from Shakespeare's point of view, with Elizabethan anxieties, beliefs, and prejudices. Only in this way shall we see his topical references plain.

I. THE MORTALL MOONE

Not mine owne feares, nor the prophetick soule,
Of the wide world, dreaming on things to come,
Can yet the lease of my true loue controule,
Supposde as forfeit to a confin'd doome.
The mortall Moone hath her eclipse indur'de,
And the sad Augurs mock their owne presage,
Incertenties now crowne them-selues assur'de,
And peace proclaimes Oliues of endlesse age.
Now with the drops of this most balmie time,
My loue lookes fresh, and death to me subscribes,
Since spight of him Ile liue in this poore rime,
While he insults ore dull and speachlesse tribes.
    And thou in this shalt finde thy monument,
    When tyrants crests and tombs of brasse are
    spent.

[Sonnet 107]

This is the chief 'dating sonnet,' and it has been called the most difficult of all. And here I think we shall find that the world has been led down a false trail by assuming that *the mortall Moone* means Queen Elizabeth, and that *hath her eclipse indur'de* means either that she is dead, or that she has survived a dangerous crisis in her life.

To read it as 'the Queen is dead' would place this sonnet in 1603. Beyond the unnatural callousness of writing '*the* Moone' instead of '*our* Moone,' there are other serious objections to this interpretation. For the Elizabethan vogue of sonnet-writing, 1603 is too late. It is also too late in Shakespeare's career to suit with the style and tone of his sonnets, in one of which he describes himself as a beginner, wielding a 'pupil pen' [Sonnet 16]. Most critics have therefore taken the second meaning—that *the mortall Moone* is the living Queen.

But this theory will not stand the test of the times. All the English poets write of their beloved Queen in terms approaching adoration. She is a goddess come to earth, a heaven-born Astræa. 'This is that Queen, as writers truly say, That God had marked down to live for aye.' She is Diana. 'Time weares her not . . . Mortalitie belowe her orbe is plaste.' Her word is *Ever the Same.* Her loyal subjects neither wish nor dare to remind her that she is mortal. 'Wee are afraid,' says John Donne, 'to speake to the great men of this world of their death, but nourish in them a vaine imagination of immortality.' Loathing the advances of creeping Time, Elizabeth carries her aversion to the mention of death to strange lengths. Informed by the unwary Lord North that a

certain covered pie is called a 'coffin,' she bursts out in anger, 'And are you such a fool, to give a pie such a name?'

Mortal, moreover, bears a meaning even more hideous, and one equally common in Shakespeare's works: *deadly, death-dealing.* 'Mortal poison,' 'mortal murders,' 'mortal butcher,' 'mortal rage.' To fancy Shakespeare deliberately writing of his 'imperiall Votresse' not only that she is *mortal,* but that she has been obscured by an eclipse, is to imagine him a greater fool than Lord North.

If it cannot be Elizabeth, what then is this *mortall Moone*? For more than three centuries the answer has vainly stared us in the face. It is the *deadly Spanish Armada of 1588*—the mightiest floating army that the world had ever seen—which in its menacing moon-shaped line of battle appeared in the English Channel, only to be shattered by the drum-fire of Elizabeth's heavy guns, and driven northward away before an irresistible gale into ignominy, disaster, and eclipse.

> The Spanish Fleet did flote in narrow Seas
> And bend her ships against the English shore.
>   Theodore Beza, *Ad Serenissimam Eliza-*
> *betham*
>   Angliae Reginam, 1588.

> . . . their fleete was placed in battell araie, after the maner of a Moone cressant, being readie with her horns & hir inward circumference to receiue either all, or so manie of the English nauie, as should giue her the assault.
>   Petruccio Ubaldino, *A Discourse concerninge the Spanish fleete,* 1588.

> . . . a horned Moone of huge and mighty shippes. . . . But all is vaine: for the breath of the Lords mouth hath dimmed the brightnesse of her Moone, and scattered those proud shippes.
>   J[ames] L[ea], *The Birth, Purpose and mortall Wound of the Romish holie League,* 1589.

The *mortall Moone hath her eclipse indur'de.* That Shakespeare, like James Lea in his triumphant political cartoon, is here in Sonnet 107 celebrating the eclipse suffered by the deadly 'Moone of huge and mighty shippes' now appears, as John Benson might say, serene, clear, and elegantly plain.

But if in any mind there lingers a doubt, it is set at rest by Shakespeare himself. For in his dealing with another great sea-fight which likewise marked a turning-point in history, we now discover him repeating his metaphor of an eclipsed moon for a defeated fleet. This was the Battle of Actium on the Ionian Sea, in which the huge heavy galleys of Antony and Cleopatra, crowded with people and not well manned, were beaten by the smaller, nimbler, battle-wise craft of Octavius and Agrippa. Like every Englishman reading his Plutarch, Shakespeare would mark that historic parallel with the Armada fight.

The ranked fleets of beaked galleys faced each other in curving line-abreast. After Agrippa had lured out Antony's left wing from its well-nigh impregnable position and the fierce struggle had been joined, Cleopatra and her Egyptian contingent of sixty huge ships, shamefully followed by her enslaved Antony, 'fled From that great face of Warre, whose seuerall ranges Frighted each other' [*Antony and Cleopatra,* III. xiii. 6]. The brave remnant fought on to defeat.

> *Enobarbus.*   Alacke, alacke.
> *Canidius.*   Our Fortune on the Sea is out of

breath,
And sinkes most lamentably.
[*Antony and Cleopatra,* III. x. 23-5]

This anguished avowal is later echoed by the 'noble ruin', Antony. Plunged in black remorse over their ominous defeat, he cannot hear Cleopatra:

> *Cleo.*   Haue you done yet?
> *Ant.*   Alacke our Terrene Moone is now
>   Eclipst,
>   And it portends alone the fall of *Anthony.*
>   [*Antony and Cleopatra,* III. xiii. 152-54]

Terrene is a short form of *Mediterranean,* favourite with the geographer Ortelius and the dramatist Marlowe: 'not far from Alexandria, Whereas the Terrene and the Red Sea meet.' The mighty battle-crescent of their Mediterranean fleet has suffered eclipse, giving infallible omen of Antony's fall.

The *mortall Moone* sonnet, then, is Shakespeare on the Armada. If this capital fact is now evident, we should also find in the poem some reference to the fatal and wonderful year, 1588: the menacing, long-prophesied Eighty-Eight, ever memorable in the world's mind for the destruction of the Invincible Fleet. For in retrospect the two were inseparable. . . .

> Witness that admirable year eighty-eight. . . . It was a year of strange *expectation,* before it came, and of *admiration,* when it was come. Some designed it to be the end of the world, but were deceived. Others designed it to be the doomsday of England, the ruin of our Church and religion, and the funerals of our prince, people, and kingdom, all on one day: but these also through the great mercy of God were deceived.
> Thomas Taylor, 'Eighty Eight,' a sermon, 1631.

The year of universal apprehension, in which the world expected the day of doom, or at the least miracles full of peril—such was the year 1588. It had loomed for more than a century, ever since that 'most notorious prophesie' of 1475, attributed either to Johann Stoffler or to Johann Müller of Königsberg (Regiomontanus), and taken up and repeated by Melanchthon. . . . These 'Germanical Rhythmes' were expanded into Latin verses, of which the following was one English version:

> When from the Virgin Birth a thousand yeares
> With full five hundred be compleat and told,
> The Eightie Eighth a famous yeare appeares,
> Which brings distresse more fatall then of old.
> If not in this yeare all the wicked world
> Do fall, and land with sea to nothing come;
> Yet Empires must be topsie turvie hurl'd,
> And extream grief shall be the common summe.

As the time foretold inexorably drew near, this was regarded as 'the onely prophesie of the world.' The embattled Protestants worked out 1588 as the world's 'grand climacterical'—the end of ten cycles of sevens—as follows:

> the Captiuitie of Babylon endured 70. yeares, which may be thought too prefigure the Captiuitie of the Gospel in these latter dayes: for from the yeare of our Lord 1518. in the which Martine Luther began truely to preach Gods word, which forthwith became captiue with fire, sworde, and all crueltie, too 1588. are iust .70. yeares, in the

whiche yeare .1588. according as *Iohannes Regiomontanus,* . . . *Schonerus, Leouitius,* and other greate learned men agree, some greater thing shall bee done.

[James Sandford, *Houres of Recreation* (1576)]

Ominous corroboration came from the astronomers. They pointed to 1588's threatening conjunction of the planets Saturn, Jupiter, and Mars; and 'in the selfsame yeere 88 . . . the Sunne shall be eclipsed the 16. day of *February* at the change; and shortly after, at the very next full, namely the second day of *March* there shall follow a Totall Eclipse of the Moone.' On top of this, there would be a second 'vniuersall *Eclipse* of the Moon this 88. to befall the 26. day of August.' Three eclipses in one year! And the renowned Hermes Trismegistus had laid it down that 'there insue manifold mischiefes in the world when the Sun, and Moone are both eclipsed in one moneth.'

Alarm was so deep and general that books had to be written to combat the auguries of dread. John Harvey devised a discourse 'especially in abatement of the terrible threatenings, and menaces, peremptorily denounced against the kingdoms, and states of the world, this present famous yeere, 1588. supposed the *Greatwoonderfull,* and *Fatall* yeere of our Age.' Ministers were preaching repentance before Judgment, as a 'Preparation against the prognosticated dangers of this yeare 1588.' Broadside ballads and books were printed 'Of the end of the world.' For everything clearly pointed to a present fulfilment of the Gospel prophecy of the Last Day:

> And there shalbe signes in the sunne and in the moone, & in the starres: and vpon the earth trouble among the nations, with perplexitie. The sea and the water shall rore.
> And mens heartes shal fayle them for feare, and for loking after these thinges which shall come on the world.
> Luke 21:25, 26.

Leonard Wright sums it up [in his *A Summons for Sleepers* (1589)]:

> who hath not read or hard what wonderful strange eclips of sun & moon, terrible blazing stars, glistering comets, dreadful coniunctions of planets, strange flashing of fire in the elements, & alteration of the heauens, resembling as it were the countenance of the angry Iudge?

Such were the universal fears and auguries of 1588. And the arrogant Spaniards, 'Who by report through all the world, had won The name of conquest ere the fight begun,' assumed that the prophecy would be fulfilled by the fall of England under the blows of their military might. To advertise their purpose, and to strike terror into *los lutheranos,* they painted their England-bound battleships black, and flew great 'pennons tragicall' bearing 'sad ostents of death and dismall feare.' One such displayed a sun and moon, with a menacing legend in Spanish to this effect: *Yesterday the Full, but Today the Wane.*

Now let us read again the beginning of Shakespeare's sonnet:

> Not mine owne feares, nor the prophetick soule,
> Of the wide world, dreaming on things to come,
> Can yet the lease of my true loue controule,
> Supposde as forfeit to a confin'd doome.

His plays amply show Shakespeare as a man of his age, believing in signs and portents. He and the world he lived in had every reason to fear what 1588 might bring. And that the soul in sleep could see into the future was another belief commonly held: 'any person going to his rest . . . his Soule (in sleeping) may fore-see many thinges to come.' The doom prophesied would have put a 'confine,' a limit or end, to the life of the world with everything in it, including the poet's love for his friend.

But Eighty-Eight with all its terrors and eclipses has come— and gone! The apprehensions of doomsday have proved baseless:

> The mortall Moone hath her eclipse indur'de,
> And the sad Augurs mock their owne presage . . .

The Invincible Armada has suffered defeat: an event, writes Professor Trevelyan, 'which all Europe at once recognized as a turning point in history.' Instead of cataclysm, 1588 brought to England, and to all Protestant Europe with her, the rejoicing dawn of certain deliverance. The relief was indescribable. And in his treatise against astrology (1601) John Chamber has the prophets of a black 1588 mocking their own presage:

> It were well that all of that trade had those two figures .88. seared in their foreheads, that when they meet, they might laugh one at another, as did the *Aruspices* in olde time. Howsoeuer they might laugh, it was no laughing matter to the Catholike king, and his inuincible Nauie, who will be famous for that exploit till 88 come againe.

> Incertenties now crowne them-selues assur'de,
> And peace proclaimes Oliues of endless age.

Here is where the modern historian leads us astray. He likes to call the Armada fight the beginning of Elizabeth's formal hostilities with Philip, leaving us to think that Shakespeare's countrymen now knew they were at war. How totally different was the view of the man on the spot! For him, the victory of '88 brought not war, but the certain assurance of *peace* for England. There would be no invasion and butchery, such as the Low Countries suffered under Alva. No savage civil wars of religion, like those torturing France. Throughout her reign, whatever forces she might dispatch to fight her enemies abroad, Elizabeth was incessantly extolled for keeping her land at peace. (pp. 1-17)

Elizabeth's great astrologer, Dr. John Dee, addresses her from Bohemia to thank God for 'this wunderfull triumphant Victorie, against your mortall enemies,' and to thank her Majesty for 'calling me . . . hoame, into your British Earthly Paradise, and Monarchie incomparable.' And Francis Bacon, looking back over Elizabeth's reign, saw the Armada 'first beaten in a battle, and then dispersed and wasted in a miserable flight with many shipwrecks; while on the ground and territories of England, peace remained undisturbed and unshaken' [in his *In Felicem Memoriam Elizabethae*].

> Now with the drops of this most balmie time,
> My loue lookes fresh, and death to me subscribes,
> Since spight of him Ile liue in this poore rime,
> While he insults ore dull and speachlesse tribes.
>   And thou in this shalt finde thy monument,
>   When tyrants crests and tombs of brasse are
>   spent.

The drops of this most balmie time—after the eclipse of the deadly Spanish 'MOONE'—have brought life revived and fresh out of the shadow of doom. Balm is the biblical Balm of Gilead or Balsam of Mecca, the prime life-restoring elixir.

Its source is the Eastern balsam tree, 'out of which issueth a Gumme of excellent swiftnesse.' As Othello says, 'Drops teares as fast as the Arabian Trees Their Medicinable gumme' [*Othello,* V. ii. 350-51].Books were written on the magical healing powers of the drops of blam. Shakespeare often mentions it: 'balme, Earth's soueraigne salue,' 'drop sweet Balme in PRIAMS painted wound,' 'balme to heale their wounds,' 'Balme of hurt Mindes.' It is frequent in his fellow-authors: 'the drops of balsamum, that salueth the most dangerous sores' (Dr. Thomas Lodge). 'The tree of life . . .

> From that first tree forth flowd, as from a well,
> A trickling streame of Balme, most soueraine . . .
> Life and long health that gratious ointment gaue,
> And deadly woundes could heale, and reare againe
> The senselesse corse appointed for the graue.'

> (Spenser)

'*Elizabeth,* who with her English balme, Then much the poysnous biting of that *Spanish* aspe did calme' (Warner). 'The time! O blessed time! Balme to our sorrow!' (Dekker).

Now that the Elizabethans have given us the indispensable background, we are better equipped to attempt a running comment on the thought of Sonnet 107, as follows:

The poet's fear, shared with the whole Protestant world, of the dread cataclysm foretold for 1588, has not been able to put an end to his love. The foe's 'invincible' battle-crescent has, however, met disaster; and the prophets of doom are laughing at their recent fears. Danger of invasion and civil war has vanished as if blown away with the storm that wrecked the beaten Armada. Elizabeth's Englishmen find themselves joyfully gazing down far vistas of assured peace.

To minds hurt by cruel apprehension and suspense, the miraculous passing of 1588 not only in safety but crowned with victory has come as a life-restoring balm. In this blessed time of deliverance love has renewed its youth. Death, shorn of his terrors, now submits to the poet, whose verse is his passport to immortality. The poet's friend, the subject of his lines, will be remembered when the blazoned crests and tombs of the defeated tyrants Philip and Sixtus are long gone into oblivion.

It is deeply satisfying to find that long before he sang the glory of Agincourt, Shakespeare had begun by recording with his 'pupil pen' the overthrow of the Invincible Armada, the eclipse of the Spanish dream of world dominion. To the insatiable monarch—whose inflated motto *The Whole World is Not Enough* Drake found so amusing—Shakespeare gave England's answer, quiet and conclusive:

> The mortall Moone hath her eclipse indur'de.

The naval historian may now see Shakespeare's line great with meaning: an utterance proclaiming the death of the old order and the birth of the new. For he tells us that the Armada fight spelled the eclipse of the ancient naval tactics. The Spaniards' fleet was still ranged line-abreast in the *falange,* 'a battle like a halfe Moone,' like the warships at Actium. Their classic aim was to fight ship against ship, grapple, board, and settle the issue hand to hand. But the nimbler English never gave them the chance. Howard and Drake, coming down a-weather on them in line-ahead, 'crossing their T,' concentrating crushing broadsides of heavy metal on a selected target, brought not only the eclipse of the 'Moone,' but also the dawn of the modern era at sea.

As soon as we locate the spiritual landscape—the passing of

1588—in which it was written, Shakespeare's 'most difficult' sonnet becomes clear and plain. We see what events he has turned into ideas; and, for the first time, we understand. May not other sonnets that still seem puzzling or obscure behave in the same way?

II. THE RIDDLE OF THE NEW-OLD PYRAMIDS

No! Time, thou shalt not bost that I doe change,
Thy pyramyds buylt vp with newer might
To me are nothing nouell, nothing strange,
They are but dressings of a former sight:
Our dates are breefe, and therefor we admire,
What thou dost foyst vpon vs that is ould,
And rather make them borne to our desire,
Then thinke that we before haue heard them tould:
Thy registers and thee I both defie,
Not wondring at the present, nor the past,
For thy records, and what we see doth lye,
Made more or les by thy continuall hast:
    This I doe vow and this shall euer be,
    I will be true dispight thy syeth and thee.

In this sonnet addressed to Time, Shakespeare nonchalantly declares, 'Thy pyramids built up with newer might to me are nothing novel.' By these ostensibly novel pyramids of old Time he obviously cannot mean structures as stupendous as the Great Pyramid of Gizeh. No monsters like that were set up in his age. But what then *does* he mean? His 'pyramids' is certainly a poser.

Now when a concrete term in Shakespeare offers a puzzle, the most promising method of attacking it has two steps. First, to find out what the word meant to his contemporaries. Second, to acquire some notion of its specific application here by studying any contemporaneous events involving the thing referred to.

If we ask what other Elizabethans meant by 'pyramids,' we are told at once. They habitually broadened its sense to include *slim spires,* and particularly *obelisks.* . . . [Were] you to show Shakespeare Cleopatra's Needle and the Washington Monument today, he would naturally call them both 'pyramids.'

If we now substitute the word *obelisk* in Shakespeare's line—*Thy obelisks built up with newer might*—and at the same time recall Elizabethan news about building, at once a flood of light breaks in. For the mightiest builder in all the world in Shakespeare's time was the enterprising, tenacious, and severe Pope Sixtus V, who reigned from 1585 to 1590. So many were his notable constructions that under his hand Rome rose from its ruins and 'forthwith doubled itself.' His most spectacular and world-famous achievement, however, was the re-erection, as 'monuments of religious magnificence,' of four age-old obelisks. These had been brought from Egypt to Imperial Rome by the Caesars and—all but one—were long since thrown down, broken, and even lost many feet underground.

Mighty Sixtus, who regarded himself as one of the two most powerful temporal kings in the world, set up a great Egyptian obelisk in each of the years 1586, 1587, 1588, and 1589. They stand today where he stationed them. The hugest one in existence, which in 1588 he erected by S. Giovanni in Laterano, had been discovered the year before buried in the Circus Maximus, broken into three pieces. This giant of red granite had therefore to be 'born'—extracted from Mother Earth—and then literally 'built,' requiring in its broken state more

'building' than the placing of an entire monolith on a pedestal.

But first in priority, as well as alone in its glory of having survived the centuries unbroken and erect, was the Vatican obelisk, familiarly known as St. Peter's Needle—*la guglia di San Pietro,* 'the largest entire obelisk out of Egypt, and the second in size in the world.' Weighing some 320 tons, it stood near the Basilica, deep in the mud and rubbish of what had once been the *spina* of the racetrack of Nero's Circus. The work of taking it down, moving it to its present commanding site, and re-erecting it on a splendid pedestal in 1586, was the first and most dramatic feat to bring universal fame to the Pope's brilliant engineer, Domenico Fontana.

Flocks of important persons hastened to Rome from the corners of Europe to witness the marvellous operation. As the biographer of Sixtus [J. A. de Hübner] tells us [in his *Sixte-Quint*],

> Contemporary letters, reports of the diplomats, the stage-plays—that precious source of history when it is a matter not of establishing facts but of appreciating the trend of opinion,—numberless verses celebrating the event, and even views of the city of Rome published for visitors, by the exaggerated size they give to the obelisk, all witness to the sympathetic interest Europe took in the successful accomplishment of an enterprise which the leading authorities of art and engineering (Michael Angelo and Antonio de Sangallo) had pronounced impossible. Strangers just off the ship ran to see the Needle.

Among the numberless Latin verses flattering the Pope on this superhuman achievement, the ones most amusing to Englishmen watching Philip building his Armada were doubtless those by a certain Bucovius, a Pole—in English as follows:

> Since an immovable mass, O excellent Father, obeys thy will, and is now shifted by thy commands . . . since moreover it is wicked for it not to follow thy orders; when even stones go under thy yoke, *may I doubt that the unruly Britons are about to bow their necks?*

If the rhetorical Pole wanted the authentic answer, he would get it from those same unruly British necks in a wicked chorus of 'You may, Bucovius, you may!'

The re-discovery in the following year of the tallest obelisk ever quarried, together with its excavation and its building in 1588 as the *Obelisco Lateranense,* was a fresh 'sensation.' And in 1589 Pope Sixtus was once more in the news with a fourth obelisk, likewise dug up out of the Circus Maximus, which he erected in the Piazza della Madonna del Popolo. This was his last: he died in August 1590.

The topical force of Shakespeare's 'pyramids' for the period about 1589 is now evident. On re-reading the sonnet with our eyes opened to the background of the world news, we can now offer a comprehensible summary, somewhat as follows:

Standing firm himself, the poet scorns the tricks of Time. He declines to join the childish world in its admiration over a nine days' wonder which it regards as a 'strange novelty.' Everybody's talking about the pyramids brought forth—as if produced for their special delight—from the womb of earth by the autocrat of Rome and his engineer. The poet is not impressed. After all, these obelisks, while newly set up, consecrated, and dressed with his armorial bearings and Christian crosses by Sixtus, are in fact no new invention, but some 3000 years old, and we had heard about them from historians. Though now palmed off as a novelty on an ignorant world gaping for curiosities, their austere shafts, bearing Time's registers in royal hieroglyphs, were common sights ages ago.

But the poet puts no trust either in Time or in his deceptive memorials. Time's restless pace often destroys his own records, thus making them less. Just now, on the other hand, he has had some lost and forgotten ones dug up, thus making them more. Fickle and unreliable as he thus shows himself, who will believe him? The poet will remain unchanged and a true friend in spite of all that Time the deceiver and destroyer can do.

Notorious events as reported to the Elizabethan world have shown us approximately how Shakespeare's contemporaries would understand the allusions in this sonnet. So far from being metaphorical, intricate, and cloudy (as they seemed to our modern ignorance), they were clear, concrete, and topical. We can easily see now what was conveyed by *pyramids, newer might, novel, dressings of a former sight, admire what thou dost foist upon us that is old,* and *thy registers.*

As for the date of this sonnet, I place it in 1589. Since *pyramids* is in the plural, it cannot have been written before 1587, when the *second* obelisk (S. Maria Maggiore) was set up. The topicality of the term *novel,* meaning new, the latest thing; the phrase *not wondering at the present;* the admired 'birth' of the excavated pyramids of 1588 and 1589 to the satisfaction of a sensation-hungry age in which (as Tom Nashe writes in 1589) 'men hast vnto nouelties, and runne to see new things'; and the present tense of *what thou dost foist upon us*—all these indicate that the sonnet was written while the obelisks were still being set up: while, in short, they were 'news.' After the death of Sixtus in August 1590, the *newer might* of that powerful figure was a thing of the past, and the Roman pyramids were no longer either novel or news.

III. THE BLOW OF THRALLED DISCONTENT

Having found that the topicalities of Sonnet 107—*the mortall Moone,* and of Sonnet 123—the *pyramyds,* lead us to refer them both pretty closely to the year 1589, let us now turn to scrutinize the political allusions in the sonnet which immediately follows the *pyramyds:*

> Yf my deare loue were but the childe of state,
> It might for fortunes basterd be vnfathered,
> As subiect to times loue, or to times hate,
> Weeds among weeds, or flowers with flowers gathered.
> No it was buylded far from accident,
> It suffers not in smilinge pomp, nor falls
> Vnder the blow of thralled discontent,
> Whereto th'inuiting time our fashion calls:
> It feares not policy that *Heriticke,*
> Which workes on leases of short numbered howers,
> But all alone stands hugely pollitick,
> That it nor growes with heat, nor drownes with showres.
>   To this I witnes call the foles of time,
>   Which die for goodnes, who haue liu'd for crime.
>
> [Sonnet 124]

Here we find Shakespeare contrasting the strong, sure structure of his love for his friend with the pitiful insecurity of some prince, some 'child of state' subject to 'accident,' who

'suffers in smiling pomp' and 'falls under the blow of thralled discontent.'

Very little familiarity with the momentous events of Shakespeare's times is required to recognize the ruler he is thinking of. A prince who, suffering shameful deprivation of his royal power, had with smiles dissembled his fierce resentment. A prince who, after waiting his time, deftly murdering his two capital enemies and reporting his deliverance to his politic Queen Mother, himself fell under the blow of an assassin who thought him a tyrant. This 'fortune's bastard,' this victim of 'time's hate,' is Henry of Valois, King Henri III of France, favourite child of Catherine de' Medici, and sometime suitor for Elizabeth's hand.

The first great 'accident' or misfortune that befell him was Paris's famous Day of Barricades, May 12, 1588, which the Venetian ambassador in Madrid called *'l' accidente di Francia contra quel povero Re'*—the accident of France against that poor King. On that day the people of Paris rose against their King in support of his enemies the Duke of Guise and the Holy Leaguers, who already had strong foreign backing in Pope Sixtus and Philip of Spain. Escaping immediate deposition by a hair's breadth, Henry managed to get away. He was obliged, however, to convoke the hostile States General, which sat throughout the autumn scorning him as a do-nothing king, and preparing to make their 'Caesar,' the Duke of Guise, master of the throne.

Elizabeth's ambassador to Henry, Sir Edward Stafford, describes for his Queen how her former suitor suffered in smiling pomp and hid his hate in affability. Stafford writes that though Henry 'was enforced to sett a faire face on the matter, and wisely to dissemble,' he 'laye hoovering in the winde to take the Duke and his fellow-conspirators at an advantage, when he might safelie . . . be revenged upon their cursed bodies.' Hearing that Guise intended to kill him on the approaching Christmas Eve, 1588, 'yett did the King make outward semblance as if he had suspected nothing,' but sat up all night scheming how to end his suffering by taking arms against a sea of troubles. Morning found him resolved to prevent his own murder 'if he could, by hazarding to kill the Duke the next daie.'

In an earlier dispatch Stafford had sent off the first news of Henry's successful murder of the Duke, with his belief—later confirmed—that Guise's brother, the Cardinal of Lorraine, was also killed: Guise, he reports,

> was slaine by 8 of the *quarante cinq* who were there appointed for the same purpose; who executed theire charge so promptly as after he was entred into the said antechamber, hee neuer spake word vntill he was dead. The King beeing assured that hee was dead, and hauing seene him on the ground, hee went to his mother and told her, Madame I am now come to tell you that I am King without companion, and that the Duke of Guise, th'enemy of all my proceedinges, is dispatched.

For his English theatre audience, Christopher Marlowe developed this scene [in his *The Massacre at Paris*] of Henry viewing his dead enemy:

> *Captaine.* My Lord, see where the Guise is slaine.
> *King.* Ah this sweet sight is phisick to my soule . . .
>   I nere was King of France vntill this

houre:
This is the traitor that hath spent my
golde
In making forraine warres and ciuile
broiles.

Duke of Guise and the Cardinal of Lorraine. Now we hear
that a disgruntled friar, a partisan of the League, has murdered the King. 'Slaying is the word; it is a deed in fashion.'
It makes us wonder whether English traitors may not take
to king-killing in the French style, *whereto th'inuiting time
our fashion calls.*

Shakespeare's theme in this sonnet is the grand impregnabili-
ty of his love. Like some great and wise monarch of the forest,
it fears no attack. Its growth is neither cheered by warmth
nor checked by floods. But the contrasting image with which
he began—some insecure prince such as the wretched fallen
Henry of France, lightly plucked from life like a weed or
flower—inevitably conjures up as its opposite the strong majestic figure of his English Queen, untouched by the many attempts on her life. He fuses the thought of her with the poetic
image of his love. Any crafty assaults upon his love are to be
scorned: they are as futile and fatuous as the short-laid, Jesu-
it-inspired plots to cut down Elizabeth. *To this I witnes call
the foles of time, Which die for goodnes, who haue liu'd for
crime.* These fools of time, who on the scaffold say they committed treason for religion's or conscience's sake, recall the
young gentlemen of the recent Babington Plot to kill the
Queen. Their folly and crime are repeatedly censured in contemporary books:

> . . . him they schoole,
> And then transport to *England,* thear to play the
> dangerous Foole:
> Seducingly insisting on performance of their vow,
> That doth Rebellion, Regicide, and breach of Othes
> allow.
> William Warner, *Albions England,* Bk. ix.

Barnwell . . . died an obstinate Papist and for his
treason made conscience his best excuse. He had
had but a rotten conscience that was infected with
the murther of a vertuous Queene.
George Whetstone, *The Censure of a Loyall
Subiect upon . . . those 14 notable Traitors,
1587.*

But these fond youthes (as wayward Children) did
Despise the counsell of their carefull Nurse,
And for the same they seeke her death . . .
These moued were for sacred *Conscience* sake
To do these deedes (a *Deuill* sure they were).
James Aske, *Elizabetha Triumphans,* 1588.

IV. CONCLUSIONS

So much for the more obvious allusions we have discovered
in Sonnets 107, 123, and 124. Against the modern subjective
criticism which treats these sonnets as difficult or obscure,
John Benson's opinion in 1640 that they will be found clear
and plain stands vindicated by the simple expedient of looking into the leading events of Shakespeare's Europe.

'The great poet,' remarks Mr. T. S. Eliot, 'in writing himself,
writes his time.' If Shakespeare, the Soul of the Age, writes
his time, his meanings are not hidden from his contemporaries. To them, his *Moone* is more than a poetic figure: it is
an accurate and familiar description of the Armada's battle-
formation. And this *Moone* was literally *mortall* or deadly.

Chandos portrait of Shakespeare.

It killed a hundred Englishmen, and it meant to kill thousands more. To them, again, *pyramyds* is not metaphor for
'any modern marvels of architecture,' but the common name
for certain particular and world-famous obelisks being set up
by Pope Sixtus in Rome. Finally, for them there is no vagueness or generality about *the childe of state* who *suffers in smil-
inge pomp* and *falls Vnder the blow of thralled discontent.*
This is plainly and exclusively the murdered Henry of Valois,
King of France.

As for the date of these sonnets, we have seen that the *mortall
Moone* was written in 1589, after the close of the Wonderful
Year. The *pyramyds* sonnet, 1587-9, most probably in 1589.
The blow of thralled discontent puts Sonnet 124 in 1589, after
the beginning of August.

What do these discoveries reveal about the date of the rest of
the Sonnets? In the 1609 arrangement as printed by Thomas
Thorpe, these three all stand near the close of the 'first series'
of 126 sonnets. And most of the proposed rearrangements
likewise regard them as belonging near the end of the group.

Here is a fact of cardinal importance. It indicates that *Shakespeare completed this main group of his sonnets by 1589.*

The evidence has led us to a revolutionary conclusion. Heretofore, theory has put the completion of the Sonnets anywhere from 1596 to 1603—from Shakespeare's thirty-third to
his fortieth year. To realize the implications of placing his
later sonnets as early as 1589—this will demand heroic efforts
in casting off notions of Shakespeare long and fondly held.

The grand point which now rises to dwarf all else is the new knowledge—since the Sonnets unquestionably embody some of his highest poetry—that *Shakespeare's power had reached maturity by the time he was no more than twenty-five years old.* Yet strictly speaking he was still a beginner. Now at length we see that he is quite literal in writing in Sonnet 16 of his 'pupil pen.' Like Keats, Shakespeare sprang to maturity in his youth. Had Logan Pearsall Smith known the true date of the Sonnets, he would never have been forced by the mannered narrative poems to conclude that 'of all that wealth of poetic emotion seeking to find expression, that mass of brooding thought we are aware of in young poets like Shelley and Keats, there is no trace.' He would certainly have discovered a profusion of it in the Sonnets, which we may now study as an eloquent portrait of the artist as a young man: a young man expressing in his own person the very movements of the soul and the height of feeling which were later to appear in his plays.

We have long imagined that Shakespeare 'followed the vogue of sonnet-writing.' Rounding out a series of sonnets as a young man in 1589, we find him on the contrary setting rather than following the fashion; and outdoing the lamented leader, Sir Philip Sidney.

Other carefully fabricated structures of theory about Shakespeare's development as a poet must now be drastically altered. For example, *Venus and Adonis* and *Lucrece* were published in 1593 and 1594, and one of the articles of Shakespearean faith has been that they are 'more youthful work' than the Sonnets. What shall we say now?

One need not adopt Hazlitt's description of these two narrative poems as a 'couple of ice-houses' to recognize their striking inferiority to the profound and masterly work Shakespeare had already achieved four or five years earlier in his unpublished 'Sonnets among his private friends.' But how to account for it? The answer must lie in the sort of market for which they were prepared. *Venus* and *Lucrece* were the very stuff required to please the sophisticated taste of the wealthy patron to whom they were offered: that vain, fantastical, amorous, and hare-brained young sprout of the New Nobility, Southampton. As such they were a notable success; for the enthusiastic Gullios of the age exclaimed, 'Let this duncified worlde esteeme of Spencer and Chaucer, I'le worshipp sweet Mr. Shakespeare, and to honoure him will lay his Venus and Adonis under my pillowe.' But to peer into them for guideposts to Shakespeare's 'development' is to look for what is not there.

And the poet's fair friend? What have our discoveries done with him? In Sonnet 104 Shakespeare tells us that he has known him for three years. If that disclosure belongs to 1589, the acquaintance was formed in 1586, when the poet was twenty-two. We may now assume that he had already begun his stage career by that date. And the marvellous poetic accomplishment growing out of the young player's friendship with 'W. H.' at last gives us work of the highest importance to put into the so-called 'lost years' of his life between 1585 and 1592.

As for the Dark Lady, we can now put her back where she belongs—with the mistresses of Jack Donne—in the poet's youth.

What must we now say of the noble candidates who have so long been pushed forward for the role of the young friend, 'Mr. W. H.'—the Earls of Pembroke and of Southampton? In 1586 Pembroke was, alas, but six years old. Under the cir-

cumstances he may be allowed to withdraw. And as for Southampton, late in the same year he began his second academic year at Cambridge and achieved his thirteenth birthday. This would make him all of sixteen when Shakespeare was finishing his Sonnets. Hardly as yet a man who has 'pass'd by the ambush of young days,' or one who at the outset of the Sonnets must be urged to marry and beget a son before it is too late. It looks as though we should have to give up Southampton too.

This is a welcome relief. How could anyone seriously expect us to believe that the publisher's dedication of 1609 to 'the onlie begetter of these insuing sonnets' as '*Mr. W.H.*' could possibly be taken as addressed to a right honourable peer of the realm? Not even a left-wing publisher of today would be guilty of so glaring a breach of manners. And for a Jacobean publisher, seeking a gift of money from the dedicatee,—utterly unthinkable. It is high time to lay away the Cinderella story about Shakespeare's imaginary intimacies with the nobility. To tell the truth, it was an ignorant fancy gotten by Bardolater out of Snobbery.

With the earls cleared away, we perhaps begin to see that if 'Mr. W. H.' means anything, it means what it undoubtedly meant in 1609: a gentleman or an esquire with those initials, generally known as the friend of Shakespeare who as a youth some twenty-odd years earlier inspired the writing of the Sonnets. Need I add that I am grooming a candidate for this position? But to propose him here would be premature and would make a tale too long for these pages. (pp. 1-36)

Leslie Hotson, "Shakespeare's Sonnets Dated," in his Shakespeare's Sonnets Dated and Other Essays, *Rupert Hart-Davis, 1949, pp. 1-36.*

F. W. BATESON (essay date 1951)

[*Bateson was an English scholar, critic, and editor. In his* English Poetry and the English Language *(1934) and* English Poetry: A Critical Introduction *(1950), he explored the relationship between history and criticism, which he considered complementary disciplines. Bateson also wrote* Wordsworth: A Re-Interpretation *(1950) and* The Scholar-Critic: An Introduction to Literary Research *(1972); edited the works of Congreve, Pope, and Blake; and founded and edited* Essays in Criticism: A Quarterly Journal of Literary Criticism. *In the following excerpt, Bateson rejects Leslie Hotson's interpretation of the phrase "mortall Moone" in Sonnet 107, charging that Hotson's assessment detracts from the structural unity of this poem. According to Bateson, Shakespeare designed Sonnet 107 around the parallels and contrasts between his "private world and the public Elizabethan world of which he was a member." The critic demonstrates that the poem presents the "mortall Moone" as a public figure or object of Shakespeare's veneration, comparable to the personal friend the poet loved; thus, he notes, Hotson's identification of the Spanish Armada as the reference undermines the intended parallelism. Bateson also declares that the style of the sonnets is indisputable evidence they could not have been written as early as 1588-89 as Hotson claims.*]

Dr. Leslie Hotson's identification of Shakespeare's 'mortall Moone' (sonnet cvii, line 5) with the crescent formation popularly believed to have been adopted by the Spanish ships in the Armada has, as he has himself noted [in the 2 June 1950 issue of the *Times Literary Supplement*], 'met with very general acceptance'. For example, the reviewer in the *Times Literary Supplement* of Hotson's book *Shakespeare's Sonnets Dated and Other Essays* (in which the suggestion was originally elaborated [see excerpt above, 1949]) found the particular argument 'convincing', and the essay as a whole perhaps 'the most significant contribution to Shakespeare studies of recent years'. And the notice by Dr. J. G. McManaway in [Volume 3 (1950) of] *Shakespeare Survey,* an even more august and responsible organ, was to the same effect, if more temperately expressed ('I think he is right'). The incident provides a nice example of the limitations of pure scholarship. As long as sonnet cvii is considered merely as a historical document, the phrase can no doubt bear the sense that Hotson attributes to it. Although the Armada did not in fact assume a crescent formation, the references collected by Hotson and others make it clear that it was thought to have done so at the time. And the general illusion may well have been shared by Shakespeare. But, of course, the sonnet is only *incidentally* a historical document. Primarily it is a poem, a very beautiful poem by the greatest of all poets, and the final criterion in a disputed passage in such a poem ought never to be the plausibility of a historical allusion. The criterion must be a literary one. Does the proposed interpretation make good poetry or bad poetry? Or, to put it more precisely, does the meaning now assigned to the particular phrase or passage reinforce or contradict the poetic argument of the work as a whole? It must be said that by this test the Hotson interpretation, ingenious though it is, hasn't a leg to stand on.

As printed in the first edition of 1609 the sonnet reads as follows:

> Not mine owne feares, nor the prophetick soule,
> Of the wide world, dreaming on things to come,
> Can yet the lease of my true loue controule,
> Supposde as forfeit to a confin'd doome.
> The mortall Moone hath her eclipse indur'de,
> And the sad Augurs mock their owne presage,
> Incertenties now crowne them-selues assur'de,
> And peace proclaimes Oliues of endlesse age.
> Now with the drops of this most balmie time,
> My loue lookes fresh, and death to me subscribes,
> Since spight of him Ile liue in this poore rime,
> While he insults ore dull and speachlesse tribes.
>   And thou in this shalt finde thy monument,
>   When tyrants crests and tombs of brasse are
>   spent.

[Sonnet 107]

Although there are local obscurities, the sonnet's general meaning is clear enough. The framework round which it is organized is a *parallel,* terminating in the final couplet in a *contrast,* between Shakespeare's private world and the public Elizabethan world of which he was a member. The first quatrain describes the private world. Shakespeare's 'true love'— i.e. either Mr. W. H., or Shakespeare's feelings for Mr. W. H., or perhaps an amalgam of both meanings—has survived the 'doome' prophesied for it. The second quatrain is concerned with the contemporary public world. Here too the prophesies of woe have proved groundless. The third quatrain establishes a connection between the public and the private worlds. The 'balmie time' coincides with the revival of Shakespeare's 'love', and instead of death threatening his private world (Mr. W. H. and Shakespeare's feelings for him) death now 'subscribes' to Shakespeare, because he is a poet and poetry is immortal; that is, because of the *public status* of poetry. The final couplet then asserts the superiority of the private world to the public world. This sonnet, which is essentially a private statement of Shakespeare's feelings for Mr. W. H., will in fact prove a better memorial of him, when he does eventually die, than the 'crests and tombs' provided by the public world.

The internal analogies and interconnections are so close throughout the sonnet that it can be taken for granted that the parallelism between the private situation described in the first quatrain and its public equivalent in the second extends beyond the general notion of unfulfilled prophecy. To deny this is to deny the sonnet's poetic coherence. Now it is to be noted that in the first quatrain, though the *object* threatened—'my true love'—is specified, the *source* of the threat is left undefined. Something disastrous was about to bring the love-affair to an end, but the quarter from which the disaster was to come is left obscure. There is, however, a hint as to the *nature* of the disaster. The references to death later in the sonnet suggest that what Shakespeare's 'owne feares' and the professional soothsayers—presumably this or something like it, is what 'the prophetick soule Of the wide world' means in prose terms—had both expected was Mr. W. H.'s death. But the kind of death that had been feared—in battle, from the plague or some other disease, or on the block—is as indefinite as the source from which it might have emanated.

On the assumption, then, that the second quatrain reproduces the general situation described in the first quatrain in terms of a public world, we may expect to find in it a national object of Shakespeare's affections whose destruction had been feared. In addition, the beloved object will be specified, the source and nature of the threat to it being left undefined. Finally, if the parallelism is complete, the nature of the danger that had threatened the object of Shakespeare's public affections will be at least hinted. (As in the first quatrain, the danger may prove to be that of death.) These presumptions derive their strength from the logic of the sonnet's poetic evolution. Clearly the structural pattern of the poem as a whole demands at any rate the appearance of parallelism between the first two quatrains. Unless the reader can be made to recognize that the second quatrain does in fact reproduce the basic elements—the plot-formula, as it were—of the first quatrain, though of course in a very different social context, the sonnet's last six lines lose all their force. The whole point of the sestet is the concurrence of Shakespeare's private and public worlds. There can be the same happy ending at each level of experience *because* the crisis he had undergone as a lover had been similar to the national crisis. The individual and the citizen have coalesced.

It follows that whatever Shakespeare did or did not mean by the words 'mortall Moone', he cannot conceivably have intended the phrase to refer to the Spanish Armada. The second quatrain *must* introduce, in fairly specific terms, an object of Shakespeare's public affections that his reader can mentally set by the side of Mr. W. H. As the 'mortall Moone' is the only phrase in the quatrain that can possibly bear this sense, there must be a metaphoric reference here to some national institution that Shakespeare loved and revered *qua* citizen. The allusion might be to England or to the Church, but the traditional identification of the 'Moone' as Queen Elizabeth is clearly the most plausible one. Elizabeth was often compared by her subjects to Diana, the virgin goddess of the moon, and she was a *mortal* moon, unlike either Diana or the physical moon, because she was a human being who must sooner or later die. I imagine the sonnet was written on the Queen's recovery from a serious illness. The metaphor of a lunar eclipse had been used by Thomas Cecil, in a letter to Robert Cecil, written July 9th, 1595, which appears to refer to Elizabeth's illnesses that year: 'I left the moon in the wane at my last being at the Court; I hear now it is a half moon again, yet I think it will never be at the full, though I hope it will never be eclipsed.' It is just possible that Shakespeare's sonnet may have been written in the winter of 1595-96, when the Queen's health had been completely restored. Or the reference may be to the rumour of a similar crisis in 1599.

The object, however, of this note is not to date this particular historical allusion, but to exemplify the literary conditions that any allusion imbedded in a poem or play must satisfy. The real objection to the Hotson interpretation of sonnet cvii is that it turns a good poem into a less good poem. It *must* be wrong, because it denies by implication the structural parallel on which the poem hinges. On his view not only is there no *object threatened* in the second quatrain to provide the parallel to Mr. W. H., but the *source of the threat,* to which the first quatrain offers nothing comparable, is described with all the emphasis of Shakespearian metaphor at its most magnificent. In other words, even if the sonnet is concerned, as Hotson suggests, with the position in England in 1588, the Armada is still a poetic irrelevance in line 5. It might have been implied—Samuel Butler, who also dated the sonnet 1588, thought that it was; it could not have been stated. Are there *any* valid reasons for positing a breach in the parallelism of the first two quatrains? If there are I am not aware of them. They have certainly not been propounded by Hotson. But until they can be produced the verdict of literary criticism must be that his interpretation is improbable *a priori,* because it is poetically indefensible.

A not less serious objection is Hotson's assumption that the 'mortall Moone' was necessarily a crescent moon. If Shakespeare had wanted the word to bear this sense he would certainly have qualified it with some such epithet as *horned.* . . . Used without qualification the word, then as now, was as likely to imply a circle as a crescent. In Shakespeare's plays, indeed, in so far as any shape at all is implied, it is apparently *always* a circle, when the word is used without a qualifying epithet. In *Midsummer Night's Dream* [III. i. 203]; *Othello* [IV. ii. 77]; and *Antony and Cleopatra* [V. ii. 80], the human *eye* is compared to the moon (or *vice versa*). In *Richard II* [II. iv. 10] and *Henry IV* [I. iii. 202] it is the human *face.* Eyes and faces certainly suggest a full moon. The one exception is *Macbeth* [III. v. 23-4], where Hecate speaks of 'a vap'rous drop' hanging on 'the Corner of the Moone'. This does no doubt imply a crescent or halfmoon shape. But the exception really proves the rule—and disproves Hotson's assumption—because *Macbeth* III, v is almost certainly an interpolated scene and not by Shakespeare. In any case the metaphor of an eclipse rules out the possibility of a crescent shape. A lunar eclipse can only occur when the moon is full. It is just possible, of course, that Shakespeare may not have known this, but the importance that was attached to eclipses at the Renaissance makes it most unlikely. If this *is* Hotson's contention—he has not discussed the point, as far as I am aware—the *onus* of proof is surely on him. Unless it can be shown that an Elizabethan dramatist would be unlikely to know that a lunar eclipse necessarily involves a full moon, we are entitled to assume that both in sonnet cvii and in the parallel passage in *Antony and Cleopatra* ('Alacke! our terrene moone Is now exclips'd' [III. xiii. 153-54]) the metaphor is *not* that of a crescent.

On the internal literary evidence, then, the Hotson interpretation can be safely dismissed. If Shakespeare had wished to introduce an allusion to the Armada's crescent formation, he would certainly not have done it in the particular context of sonnet cvii. Nor would he have called such a formation *tout*

court a *moon.* And if he had done so it is most improbable that he would have spoilt his metaphor by introducing the notion of an *eclipse.*

The literary *consequences* of the Hotson interpretation are not less fatal to it. The present tenses in lines 5-8 of the sonnet make it clear that the public event referred to is contemporary or almost contemporary with its composition. If there is, as Hotson argues, an allusion to the Armada, sonnet cvii *must* have been written in 1588 or 1589. And this is in fact the desperate conclusion that Hotson reaches. It *is* a desperate conclusion, because it assigns sonnet cvii—and by implication most at any rate of the rest of Shakespeare's sonnets—to a period several years before either *Venus and Adonis,* which is usually dated 1592-93, or *Lucrece,* which cannot possibly have been written before 1593, since it is clearly the 'graver labour' referred to in the dedication to Southampton prefixed to the first edition of *Venus and Adonis.* But the style of this sonnet is more mature, not less mature, than that of either *Venus and Adonis* or *Lucrece.* In other words, it is easy to see how the writer of the narrative poems will in process of time become the writer of the sonnet. But the reverse process posited by Hotson—from writing poetry like Donne, as it were, to writing like Spenser (that is what it amounts to)—is just incomprehensible. The point could be established in a dozen different ways. One argument that seems to me decisive is the absence from the sonnet of the rash of verbal antitheses that characterizes Shakespeare's early manner. I have not been able to find four consecutive lines in *Venus and Adonis* and *Lucrece* without one or more verbal antitheses. A passage of fourteen consecutive lines with only a single verbal antithesis (*Incertenties-assur'de*) can only be described as a stylistic impossibility for the Shakespeare of the early 1590s. Hotson is therefore committed to the hypothesis that the mastery of sentence-structure and verbal phrase evident in almost every line of sonnet cvii represents a style that Shakespeare had achieved in 1588-89 and then lost for a number of years, only to regain it about 1595 in such plays as *Midsummer Night's Dream. Quod est absurdum* [Which is absurd].

No, literary detection is a harmless avocation—'immeasurably more humane than cock-fighting', as E. E. Kellett once, not unreasonably, put it [in his "The Literary Detective"]. But the game has certain elementary rules. One of them is that in the assessment of clues the primacy must always be accorded to the literary fact. (pp. 81-8.)

F. W. Bateson, "Elementary, My Dear Hotson!: A Caveat for Literary Detectives," in Essays in Criticism, *Vol. I, No. 1, January, 1951, pp. 81-8.*

EDWARD HUBLER (essay date 1952)

[*Hubler discusses the evolution of Shakespeare's attitude toward his young friend throughout the sequence of Sonnets 1-126. The critic argues that although the opening sonnets celebrate the young man's physical beauty, subsequent ones hint at his lack of integrity and constancy. Noting the poet's reproofs of the young man in the later sonnets, Hubler claims that these rebukes suggest "a certain arrogance in the young man . . . and tell of his growing self-importance." According to the critic, the later sonnets reveal a somewhat disillusioned Shakespeare, a man who has recognized in his young friend an inadequate "capacity for mature and responsible relationships with his fellow men."*]

The sonnets which Shakespeare addressed to the young man were apparently written over a period of four or five years. At least the story they glance at covers some such time, for a sonnet which does not belong with either the first or the last celebrates the third anniversary of the friendship. The precise duration of the story is neither demonstrable nor, for the purposes of this study, important. One need only think of it as occupying enough time for the development of the shifts in attitude which it discloses. In the later poems the poet's attitude toward the young man is a very different matter from the almost unqualified admiration of the opening sequence. There one reads of his beauty, his sweetness, his obstinate bachelorhood which forbids the immortality which children can bestow, and of the poet's resolution to immortalize the young man in poetry. For all their excellence, none of these seventeen sonnets is one of Shakespeare's best. However, the sequence is immediately followed by a sonnet which has become the possession of all English-speaking peoples. Although the primary purpose of the poem is to promise the friend an immortality in verse, it has won its fame through the sweetness with which the poet employs natural imagery to convey his early impressions of the young man.

"Sweet" and "sweetness" are nowadays terms of derogation, used only in the sense of "sugared" or "sugary." The older senses of the word—"fresh," "unspoiled," and "unseasoned"—are now restricted to the kitchen, as in "sweet cream" and "sweet [that is, unsalted] butter." "The sweet young thing" of not so long ago has disappeared as a type, and it would be quite rude to use the phrase for the few sports, biologically speaking, which now and then crop up. But it was different with Shakespeare. "Sweet" was his favorite epithet, and it is easy to see why. It describes a quality he admired and a state which recurs in his verse from the beginning to the end of his career. It is a quality which the early sonnets admire in the young man, and it is the quality of the opening lines of the eighteenth sonnet:

> Shall I compare thee to a summer's day?
> Thou art more lovely and more temperate:
> Rough winds do shake the darling buds of
>   May . . .
>
> [Sonnet 18]

This is the aspect of Shakespeare's writing which, considered alone, has won him the reputation for unconscious artistry. It is assumed that no poet would have made so ready a comparison in such commonplace terms ("summer's day," "lovely," and "darling") if he had had his craftsman's wits about him. Still less would he have been completely successful. Simple and natural it is, but it is only the beginning of the poem. The next line employs legal terminology with reference to nature, a usage which must have been startling at the time the poem was written:

> And summer's lease hath all too short a date.

He continues with a quatrain of notable artistry:

> Sometime too hot the eye of heaven shines,
> And often is his gold complexion dimm'd;
> And every fair from fair sometime declines,
> By chance or nature's changing course
>   untrimm'd . . .

He then returns to the opening image in verse of comparable simplicity but fuller tone and deeper feeling, and concludes with a promise of immortality which, for the first time in the sonnets, is fully realized:

> But thy eternal summer shall not fade,
> Nor lose possession of that fair thou ow'st;
> Nor shall death brag thou wander'st in his shade,
> When in eternal lines to time thou grow'st:
>   So long as men can breathe, or eyes can see,
>   So long lives this, and this gives life to thee.

It is a poem celebrating three things: the poet's power, the young man's beauty, and his unspoiled nature. Although it is not one of Shakespeare's greatest poems, it approaches perfection. The thing to be noticed is the sonnet's skillful and varied presentation of its subject matter; and we should notice in passing that with the poet's celebration of his friend there is the concomitant disclosure of himself. The more one studies the sonnets in search of the young man, the more one learns of Shakespeare.

The qualities of the young friend which the opening sonnets insist upon are his beauty and temperateness. The temperateness was soon to change, but the beauty remained to the end. It is surely only a captious reader who will suppose that the "wrinkles" referred to in the seventy-seventh sonnet are anything more than such signs of maturity as a man in his early twenties may wear, for the reference is found in a quatrain insisting on the almost imperceptible advance of time—"the dial's shady stealth," "time's thievish progress to eternity" [Sonnet 77]. Still, the wrinkles have won their celebrants among Shakespeare's critics. A sentence of Dr. Johnson's will be sufficient answer: "Why sir, we must allow for some exaggeration." Once in the sonnets Shakespeare described himself as "beated and chopp'd with tann'd antiquity" [Sonnet 62], although he does not even look that old in the Droeshout portrait. Deeply aware of mutability, he knew intellectually that there must be a change in the friend, though he could not see it:

> Ah, yet doth beauty, like a dial hand,
> Steal from his figure, and no pace perceiv'd;
> So your sweet hue, which methinks still doth stand,
> Hath motion, and mine eye may be deceiv'd. . . .
>
> [Sonnet 104]

Physically the young man is represented as the embodiment of nature's best, excelling all contemporary excellence and recalling only the departed glories of the past. "All this," as Shakespeare remarked in another connection, "the world well knows."

What is not so often noticed is that from the very beginning the poet is concerned with more than the physical, and that the concern increases as the poems proceed. There is a growing emphasis on what it was once common to call "moral beauty." That we no longer do so is, I take it, another instance of our tendency to dissociate matters formerly thought related. It is not that as Shakespeare progressed he abandoned his concern with physical beauty, but rather that beauty was not taken to be exclusively physical. And it is abundantly demonstrated that Shakespeare did not take inward and outward beauty to be identical. Although it was fashionable in his time to talk about the coincidence of inward and outward beauty, to believe that the physically beautiful must be good, Shakespeare never took the notion seriously. It bubbles to the surface of the dialogue now and then. In *The Tempest* it helps to characterize Shakespeare's most innocent heroine, who exclaims, on first seeing Ferdinand, that "nothing ill can dwell in such a temple" [I. ii. 459]. But the idea had been demonstrably false since the time of Helen of Troy, and Shakespeare was much too sensible to do more than toy with it. On the desperate morning after her violation the no-tion occurred to Lucrece, but she recalled the disparity be-tween Tarquin's appearance and his heart and quickly reject-ed it. Shakespeare's characteristic insistence is upon the dif-ference between appearance and reality, between the realms of the eye and the mind, the eye and the heart.

It is equally characteristic of him to find that the discrepancy between appearance and reality is the more horrible in pro-portion as the appearance promises values the reality does not disclose. He assumed that one could expect much from a young man as handsomely endowed as his friend. So it hap-pened that as qualities which Shakespeare did not admire emerged with the young man's maturing, the poet's admira-tion became qualified—in different ways and for different rea-sons, but always reluctantly. He seems to have been the sort of person who wanted to think well of those he liked, and whenever possible to return to a good opinion formerly held. In the middle sonnets the young man is praised for mildness and temperance without, it appears, always good reason. The poet's responses to change in the young friend are varied, but perhaps if we look closely at them they will conform to some sort of pattern.

From the poet's point of view the youth's affair with the dark lady was clearly an instance of both inconstancy and intem-perance, yet it seems to have mattered less than other things. The greatest threats to the friendship were offences of the spirit. I trust that no one will suppose me to assert that an illicit affair, adulterous on the woman's part, is by its nature purely a physical matter. It is simply that Shakespeare at first viewed it, or chose to view it, as of relatively minor impor-tance to him. It is often said that Shakespeare introduced the young woman to his friend, who seduced her. This interpreta-tion is a credit to our chivalry and does little harm as long as we remember that it is a way of speaking, but it does not represent the situation depicted in the sonnets and seems to have little to do with the view of life presented in the plays. In all of Shakespeare's plays the virtuous woman is very little endangered and, by standards of later literature, very little re-strained. She normally does the proposing, especially if she finds the lover's reticence to be motivated by some circum-stance of honor or a condition considerable only to the male mind. Desdemona gave Othello the "hint" on which he spoke, and on the night of their first meeting Juliet leaned over the balcony and said to Romeo,

> Three words, dear Romeo, and good night indeed.
> If that thy bent of love be honourable,
> Thy purpose marriage, send me word
>   to-morrow. . . .
>
> [*Romeo and Juliet,* II. ii. 142-44]

The dark lady is presented as already married and altogether unrestrained. She wooed the young man and won him. Shakespeare found the situation difficult but not surprising:

> Gentle thou art, and therefore to be won,
> Beauteous thou art, therefore to be assail'd;
> And when a woman woos, what woman's son
> Will sourly leave her till she have prevail'd?
>
> [Sonnet 41]

The willing seduction of the youth is looked upon as the inev-itable consequence of her attractive wantonness and of his youth and beauty. The "truth" that is broken is the woman's to the poet, and what is threatened is the friendship between

the two men. It is the latter which troubles Shakespeare the more, as the forty-second sonnet discloses:

> That thou hast her, it is not all my grief,
> And yet it may be said I lov'd her dearly;
> That she hath thee is of my wailing chief,
> A loss in love that touches me more nearly. . . .

The attitude disclosed by these lines is consistent with Shake-speare's overall treatment of friendship and the sins of the flesh. He sometimes regards sexual indulgence as an evil ex-cess of something which is good in itself. He is most stern with libertinism in which habit has worn away the sense of transgression, or in which there is no indication that it ever existed—Lucio in *Measure for Measure,* Paris and Helen, [in *Troilus and Cressida*], and, in the sonnets, the dark lady. He is not very tolerant of sexual freedom erected into a principle, nor is he generally cordial to unprincipled transgressors, un-less they are people of whom not much could be expected, and such characters—Doll Tearsheet, [in 2 Henry IV], for ex-ample—are at last overtaken by their past. In the sixty-sixth sonnet's list of disheartening things he places "maiden virtue rudely strumpeted." We should notice that it is not the loss of virginity. Soiled virtue, he keeps saying, may reassert itself, may, through experience, become stronger than before. The line refers to the destruction not of virginity but of virtue. His attitude is not that our acts do not matter or that we can es-cape their consequences (he is, of course, too honest an ob-server to be diagrammatic in his recreations of life) but that all commissions of the same act are not equally culpable. His greatest sympathy is for the intelligent man who cannot in spite of himself "Shun the heaven that leads men to this hell" [Sonnet 129]. The most striking instance of this is Antony. (pp. 78-84)

The young and handsome friend, tempted, is less culpable than the temptress, less culpable than the poet in his relations with her, for the poet was older and, like the woman, bound by vows of truth. On the young man's part the connection was not adulterous, but the difference in the depicted guilt of each party is not simply the difference between adultery and fornication. Shakespeare does not view behavior in so ab-stract a way. Categories of behavior, no matter how necessary to the institutionalization of ethics, were not often adequate to his exposition of specific instances. The poet's tendency was to forgive the young man's sexual transgression to a de-gree to which he did not forgive himself or the dark lady, and to which he did not forgive the young man in other matters.

Much has been written on Shakespeare's admiration for the young man and the indulgence he showed him. Very little has been written on the critical aspects of the poet's attitude to-ward him. Let us turn to that. The reproaches to the youth are sometimes tentative, sometimes, in the way of friendship, softened with compliments. In the forty-first sonnet the young man's wrongs are "petty wrongs." He is told [in Son-net 84] that he is justly praised, but that, "being fond on praise" (that is, fond of praise), he reduces the value of it, and that the world which praises his "outward" (that is, his physi-cal appearance and bearing) can see the beauty of his mind only in his deeds. He is warned [in Sonnet 69] that his mis-deeds are not unnoticed, that men look at his appearance, "thy fair flower," and "add the rank smell of weeds."

> But why thy odour matcheth not thy show,
> The soil is this, that thou dost common grow.

He is reminded [in Sonnet 93] that when inner reality does

not square with appearance, beauty is like Eve's apple, and that although for the moment he lends a kind of beauty to his vices, good reputation will in time be destroyed by unworthy acts [Sonnet 95]. These attempts at paraphrase in the interest of brevity are necessarily inadequate; a paraphrase of poetic irony would be worse than useless. Some of the ironical reproaches are:

> Farewell, thou art too dear for my possessing,
> And like enough thou know'st thy estimate. . . .
>
> [Sonnet 87]

> When love, converted from the thing it was,
> Shall reasons find of settled gravity. . . .
>
> [Sonnet 49]

> I found, or thought I found, you did exceed
> The barren tender of a poet's debt. . . .
>
> [Sonnet 83]

There is no need to exhaust the store of reproaches, and it would be idle to try to indicate most of the occasions which called them forth. Many of the reproaches, such as the one on his growing common, could have been provoked by a number of actions. The only ones with a knowable basis are those arising from the affair with the dark lady. Other references to offenses of a like sort may possibly glance at other women, as in,

> How many lambs might the stern wolf betray,
> If like a lamb he could his looks translate!
> How many gazers mightst thou lead away,
> If thou wouldst use the strength of all thy state.
>
> [Sonnet 96]

There are other reproaches for which the cause cannot even be guessed, the poems disclosing no more than that the young man had not fulfilled his promise.

The reproaches to which Shakespeare attached the greatest importance are, although abstracted from events, clear enough. They hint at a certain arrogance in the young man and tell of his growing self-importance, a fault which at one time threatened the existence of the friendship. In one of the sonnets Shakespeare suggested that perhaps the friend might have given his friendship before he knew his own worth, or that he had mistaken Shakespeare's. In any case, mutuality destroyed, the young man's gift of friendship is returned to him:

> Farewell, thou art too dear for my possessing,
> And like enough thou know'st thy estimate:
> The charter of thy worth gives thee releasing;
> My bonds in thee are all determinate.
> For how do I hold thee but by thy granting?
> And for that riches where is my deserving?
> The cause of this fair gift in me is wanting,
> And so my patent back again is swerving.
> Thyself thou gav'st, thy own worth then not knowing,
> Or me, to whom thou gav'st it else mistaking;
> So thy great gift, upon misprision growing,
> Comes home again, on better judgment making.
>   Thus have I had thee, as a dream doth flatter,
>   In sleep a king, but waking no such matter.
>
> [Sonnet 87]

Throughout the poem the genuine regret is stated with gentle irony. The reader is always aware of the poet's belief in his own worth. In other sonnets the poet's worthiness is insisted upon. Although he realizes that he has not done all he could

to keep the friendship in repair, his protestations of the constancy and disinterestedness of his affection have the stamp of truth. It might appear, he seems to say, that I cultivate your friendship for prudential reasons, but it is not so. There are those who glory in birth, skill, wealth, strength, possessions, and outward show, but "these particulars are not my measure,"

> Thy love is better than high birth to me,
> Richer than wealth, prouder than garments'
>   cost. . . .
>
> [Sonnet 91]

And this, too, is consistent with the point of view disclosed by the works as a whole.

Shakespeare nowhere either says or implies that birth and wealth are unimportant. Quite the contrary! They are admired for certain values, but they are never admired for themselves alone. His is a world in which all things have their uses and do not readily divide themselves into the sacred and the profane. It is apparent that he places a high value on beauty, birth, wealth, and wit, but he insists that though the friend might have "any of these all, or all, or more" [Sonnet 37], his friendship is "engrafted to" the young man's truth and worth. "Builded far from accident,"

> It suffers not in smiling pomp, nor falls
> Under the blow of thralled discontent. . . .
>
> [Sonnet 124]

It is an attitude consistent with his awareness of the transient glory of "great princes' favorites" [Sonnet 25] and his insistence on the prior value of the things of the mind and spirit. In sonnet number one hundred twenty-five he dissociates himself from the "dwellers on form and favor," the "pitiful thrivers" who "lose all and more by paying too much rent."

This is a point of view often forgotten by those who attempt to base their concept of Shakespeare on the external records of his career, which show quite plainly that he was a good businessman. But we ought to remember that the records are only a partial disclosure of the man. His plays, which also show a respect for wealth and position, do not regard them . . . as ends in themselves, and in the sonnets he never accords them a primary value. . . . Every sensible person will regard economic security and the respect of his fellow men as good things, and he will be pleased at Shakespeare's failure to sentimentalize poverty and low birth. Perhaps at first he will be troubled a bit by Shakespeare's insistence on his own worthiness, but further study should put him at ease. Let us look for a moment at the many-sidedness of Shakespeare's self-view.

"The web of life is of a mingled yarn, good and ill together," remarks a character in *All's Well,* who then continues, "our virtues would be proud if our faults whipped them not . . ." [IV. iii. 71-3].

It was Shakespeare's way to be aware of his virtues and to whip them with his faults. Further, he was constantly aware . . . of the faults of virtue. So it happens that in the self-view which the sonnets present, there is self-knowledge without self-satisfaction. He proclaims his worth as a poet in many sonnets, and quite as often he acknowledges his faults. On both scores he was quite right. The contempt he expresses for the rival poet is saved from arrogance by his admiration for the rival's technical excellence. He asserts the worth of the friendship with the young man while fearing its dissolution.

The fear has many sources: that "thou may'st take all this away" [Sonnet 91], that "the filching age will steal his treasure" [Sonnet 75], and his own actions. He confesses that, full of the friend's "ne'er-cloying sweetness," he turned to "bitter sauces" [Sonnet 118], as a healthy person turns to medicine to prevent sickness. There is a good deal in this "bitter sauces" vein, and it looks at first like rationalization. It may be that it is. The point here is the existence of self-admitted follies. The most revealing thing about the apprehensions is the regret which almost always accompanies or follows them. There are times when he regards his apprehensions as a kind of—could we say?—hypochondria of the spirit, and he apologizes for it, recognizing it as a sin against friendship, which, Ellen Terry supposed [in her *Four Lectures on Shakespeare* (1932)], was to him "the most sacred of all human relations."

It was Shakespeare's way, and it increased as he matured, to notice the obverse sides of things, of even his own devotion. . . . He is, of course, saved from inaction by his gusto and his conviction. I should not like to suggest a considerable alloy of Prufrock in him. For the moment we are taking his vigor for granted while we point out that action, while never evaded, is not always clear. His self-awareness, like his outward view, is always multiple. While he protests that his own friendship is "not mix'd with seconds" and "knows no art" [Sonnet 125], he is not always sure that the friend can meet him on terms of a personal equality transcending all other considerations; in short, he is not always certain that his friendship is returned in kind. In the twenty-third sonnet, his first apology for neglecting the friend, he gives as the reason for his silence "fear of trust." There is the recurrent fear that the love given openly is not fully returned and might be misconstrued. (pp. 85-91)

With Shakespeare the essence of friendship, as of love, is mutuality; and in the sonnets there is the recurrent fear that the basis of moral equality which mutuality demands does not exist. In one of his greatest sonnets the ideal friendship is described as "the marriage of true minds," a state which he refuses to consider unattainable:

> Let me not to the marriage of true minds
> Admit impediments.
>
> [Sonnet 116]

Friendship is not true friendship which wavers because of a change in one of the friends, or which succumbs to the machinations of an outsider:

> Love is not love
> Which alters when it alteration finds,
> Or bends with the remover to remove.

Its worth, like that of the star by which the mariner steers his course, is beyond estimation; yet like the mariner who knows the star is fixed in its place, we know the friendship, being true, is fixed, and that we can guide our course by it:

> . . . it is an ever-fixed mark,
> That looks on tempests and is never shaken;
> It is the star to every wandering bark,
> Whose worth's unknown, although his height be
>   taken.

It does not, like physical beauty, fade with time. If this is not true, there is no truth, no reality, Shakespeare himself has never written, and no man has ever loved. This is his standard of friendship. He hopes to be equal to it. Could the friend attain it? Not, it would appear, if the reproach made tentatively

in the early sonnets should, after all, turn out to have been justified:

> For shame, deny that thou bear'st love to any,
> Who for thyself art so unprovident.
> Grant, if thou wilt, thou art belov'd of many,
> But that thou none lov'st is most evident.
>
> [Sonnet 10]

Shakespeare came in time to fear that his friend's estimate of him would have a prudential basis, and that, the friendship failing, the friend would reject him and rationalize the rejection:

> Against that time, if ever that time come,
> When I shall see thee frown on my defects,
> When as thy love has cast his utmost sum,
> Call'd to that audit by advis'd respects;
> Against that time when thou shalt strangely pass,
> And scarcely greet me with that sun, thine eye,
> When love, converted from the thing it was,
> Shall reasons find of settled gravity. . . .
>
> [Sonnet 49]

In the sonnets the assumption of the need for mutuality (it is this assumption which justifies the identity metaphor) is strong enough to motivate the further assumption that when mutuality is known not to exist, the end is in sight and might better be anticipated:

> Then hate me when thou wilt; if ever, now;
> Now while the world is bent my deeds to cross,
> Join with the spite of fortune, make me bow,
> And do not drop in for an afterloss:
> Ah, do not, when my heart hath 'scap'd this sorrow,
> Come in the rearward of a conquer'd woe;
> Give not a windy night a rainy morrow,
> To linger out a purpos'd overthrow. . . .
>
> [Sonnet 90]

The sonnets to the young man begin with celebrations of his beauty, but they move in time to realms in which physical beauty is overshadowed by things of greater importance, the young friend's integrity, for instance, and his capacity for mature and responsible relationships with his fellow men. These are the matters which come to be insisted upon. The sonnets declare that if the promise shown by the young man early in the sonnets is not fulfilled, his outward appearance is of little worth. (pp. 92-4)

> *Edward Hubler, in his* The Sense of Shakespeare's Sonnets, *Princeton University Press, 1952, 169 p.*

G. K. HUNTER   (essay date 1953)

[*Hunter examines the techniques Shakespeare uses to transform the conventional themes and tones of Petrarchan sonneteers and to create verse that is so dramatic and expressive it evokes in readers "an overwhelmingly biographical reaction." The poet conveys individual emotional states within the context of brilliantly vivid language, the critic demonstrates, and with a minimum of characterization leads us to believe we have become involved with real personalities. Hunter notes that in contrast to the detachment and intellectualizing of other Elizabethan sonneteers, Shakespeare gives us in these verses "immediate contact with the suffering mind" and, as in his dramas, the opportunity to become directly involved "in the lives and fates of the persons depicted."*]

Though most modern critics would accept the fact that

Shakespeare's sonnet-sequence has a pervasive poetry with an excellence recognizably Shakespearean, the peculiar quality of this excellence remains undefined. This may be because criticism of the sonnets has been overshadowed by biographical speculation. There have been few aesthetic critics and these have confined themselves to *minutiae,* and have disregarded or noticed only with condemnation the reactions of their biographically-minded fellows. No one seems to have attempted to explain by what means Shakespeare presents traditional materials so that an overwhelmingly biographical reaction is set up in the reader. Neither the accepted categories of lyric or narrative nor the contemporary verse-fashions—Petrarchan, Anti-Petrarchan, Metaphysical, etc.—will account for this unique flavour in the sequence as a whole and for the concentratedly 'Shakespearean' effect of such sonnets as XV, XVIII, XXX, CXXIX. It is not perhaps a coincidence that the critics who accept these categories tend to find Shakespeare's sonnet-technique in some way misdirected, from Keats with his 'full of fine things said unintentionally—in the intensity of working out conceits' [see excerpt above, 1817] to John Crowe Ransom, 'Shakespeare had no University discipline and developed poetically along lines of least resistance' [see excerpt above, 1938].

I wish to suggest here that it is rather the approach to the Sonnets as lyric, narrative, or metaphysical exercises that is misdirected. Critics who ignore the biographical approach miss a valuable clue to the bias of Shakespeare's technique—a bias which twists the normal Petrarchan line towards the characteristically Shakespearean flavour of

> When not to be receives reproach of being . . .
>
> [CXXI]

> Oh that our nights of woe might have remembered
> . . .
>
> [CXX]

> Never believe that in my nature reigneth. . . .
>
> [CIX]

I contend that when Shakespeare writes like this he is not misdirecting his talent, not being a quaint and elaborate lyrist, a failed and soured Petrarchan, a Metaphysical *manqué,* or a passionate autobiographical poet whose confessions are cut short by his conceits, so much as—what one would expect—a *dramatist.*

Let us consider in this light two sonnets which, without being masterpieces, seem to me to sound the authentic Shakespearean note:

> Say that thou didst forsake me for some fault,
> And I will comment upon that offence:
> Speak of my lameness, and I straight will halt,
> Against thy reasons making no defence.
> Thou canst not, love, disgrace me half so ill,
> To set a form upon desired change,
> As I'll myself disgrace; knowing thy will,
> I will acquaintance strangle and look strange;
> Be absent from thy walks; and in my tongue
> Thy sweet beloved name no more shall dwell,
> Lest I, too much profane, should do it wrong,
> And haply of our old acquaintance tell.
>   For thee, against myself I'll vow debate,
>   For I must ne'er love him whom thou dost hate.
>
> [LXXXIX]

> Was it the proud full sail of his great verse,

> Bound for the prize of all too precious you,
> That did my ripe thoughts in my brain inhearse,
> Making their tomb the womb wherein they grew?
> Was it his spirit, by spirits taught to write
> Above a mortal pitch, that struck me dead?
> No, neither he, nor his compeers by night
> Giving him aid, my verse astonished. [etc.]
>
> [LXXXVI]

The power of these poems does not reside in lyrical utterance; the vision they present is an individual's, and to that extent like lyric, but in them the reader is not concerned with solitary imaginings presented as of universal significance (as in the Odes of Keats and Shelley), but with the relation of one human heart to others. By setting up a system of tensions between forces presented as persons Shakespeare's sonnets engage the reader's interest in a manner akin to the dramatic. Sonnet LXXXIX is presented as a 'still' from a love-drama, a picture in which the gestures not only make up a present harmony, but hint (with subtle economy of means, which reveals the dramatist) at a psychological background, so that a powerful reaction is built up, as if to a history of love. In Sonnet LXXXVI the number of characters involved is greater, but the technique is the same. An emotional state (estrangement) is expressed by means of a pattern of human figures; as a result of the hints at characterization we become involved as if with personalities, and so experience the dramatic impact. The reaction of the commentator who finds in the 'lameness' of LXXXIX proof of a physical defect in the author is an indication of the force of this impact, and the number of 'keys' to the 'sonnet-story' would seem to show that it is fairly constant throughout the sequence.

At this point the reader might object that the dramatic vividness in Shakespeare's sonnets is only a heightened form of a commonplace Elizabethan quality and that the biographical reaction is not produced by technique so much as by natural curiosity about the greatest and most enigmatic of our poets. Comparisons with other Elizabethan poets show, however, that the Sonnets are not only supreme in dramatic effectiveness, but almost unique in the methods by which this effect is obtained. Many of the sonneteers in Sir Sidney Lee's collection are good dramatic 'plotters' i.e. they can organize a set scene so that the figures contrast effectively and carry well the emotional charge that the author has imparted to them. For example:

> Oft with true sighs, oft with uncalled tears,
> Now with slow words, now with dumb eloquence;
> I Stella's eyes assailed, invade her ears:
> But this, at last, is her sweet breathed defence.
> 'That who indeed infelt affection bears,
> So captives to his saint both soul and sense;
> That wholly hers, all selfness he forbears: [etc.]
>
> [SIDNEY, *Astrophel and Stella,* LXI]

But such scenes are set at a middle-distance from the reader; the effect that is almost unique in Shakespeare is that of immediate contact with the suffering mind. We learn what it felt like to be the lover in such-and-such a situation, and the figures are arranged to increase the poignant immediacy of our apprehension—so that if the beloved is young the lover is represented as old, if the lover is poor the beloved must be highborn, etc. The brilliance of the language makes the context of these emotions so vivid that the reader naturally supplies from his imagination a complete dramatic situation.

Shakespeare's 'plots' differ from those of contemporary sonneteers in that we are seldom given visual descriptions of the persons involved. This difference does not involve him in a modern 'psychological' presentation: when the lover appears before the reader there is no self-dramatization in the sense that he is presented as a significant and interesting individual. When we hear of him

> Beated and chopped with tanned antiquity
>
> [LXII]

> Desiring this man's art and that man's scope
>
> [XXIX]

> As an unperfect actor on the stage
>
> [XXIII]

we are no nearer any conception of his personality. The dramatic power of conveying personal tensions is achieved by patterning the persons, not by analysing them.

Shakespeare uses the conventions of the sonnet *genre* in such a way that he conjures before us the tone and accent of the traditional personages. Thus like other sonnet-heroes Shakespeare's lover suffers from the tyranny of the beloved while welcoming this slavery as a blessed condition:

> Being your slave, what should I do but tend
> Upon the hours and times of your desire?
> I have no precious time at all to spend,
> Nor services to do, till you require.
> Nor dare I chide the world-without-end hour
> Whilst I, my sovereign, watch the clock for you,
> [etc.]
>
> [LVII]

The verse is charged here with that heartfelt simplicity which gives the utterance of Shakespeare's greatest dramatic creations their full force. We fully share the feelings of this slave, seeing the objects described as coloured by his predominating emotion. Sidney, whose treatment of the Petrarchan situations can often be compared with Shakespeare's in artistic worth, gives charm to a parallel description:

> . . . now, like slave-born Muscovite,
> I call it praise to suffer tyranny:
>   And now employ the remnant of my wit
> To make myself believe that all is well;
> While with a feeling skill, I paint my hell.
>
> [II]

But the effect here is different in kind from Shakespeare's; the intellect is more analytical, and the simile has the objective quality of a rational self-criticism, which Shakespeare's lacks. In Sidney there seems to be a greater distance between speaker and reader and consequently the reader tends to take a less implicated and so less biographical view of the situation.

The tradition in which the Sonnets are written did not always provide material entirely suitable for Shakespeare's dramatic technique; but even in his treatments of the more mechanically ingenious themes something of the same quality of imagination emerges. Sonnet XLVI deals with the traditional theme of a war between the heart and eye; a more commonplace treatment of the same theme may be seen in Thomas Watson's *Tears of Fancy:*

> My hart accus'd mine eies and was offended,
> Vowing the cause was in mine eies aspiring:
> Mine eies affirmd my hart might well amend it,
> If he at first had banisht loues desiring.
> Hart said that loue did enter at the eies,

> And from the eies descended to the hart:
> Eies said that in the hart did sparkes arise,
> Which kindled flame that wrought the inward smart,
> Hart said eies tears might soone haue quencht that fl[ame]
> Eies said . . . [etc.]
>
> [XX]

Compare Shakespeare:

> Mine eye and heart are at a mortal war,
> How to divide the conquest of thy sight;
> Mine eye my heart thy picture's sight would bar,
> My heart mine eye the freedom of that right.
> My heart doth plead that thou in him dost lie,
> A closet never pierced with crystal eyes,
> But the defendant doth that plea deny,
> And says in him thy fair appearance lies.
> To 'cide this title is impanneled
> A quest of thoughts, all tenants to the heart;
> And by their verdict is determined
> The clear eye's moiety and the dear heart's part:
>   As thus; mine eye's due is thine outward part,
>   And my heart's right thine inward love of heart.
>
> [XLVI]

Shakespeare's poem is not simply a better example of a conceited sonnet, it is a more affecting poem, and this is because he makes the conceit serve a felt human situation. Watson concentrates on the antithetical litigants to such an extent that he loses sight of the human 'I' and 'thou'. Shakespeare, in spite of the frigidity of many of the images ('conquest', 'picture', 'closet'), manages to animate the legal imagery with a sense of the lover's craving. He never forgets that the poem is a lover's confession, and accordingly it is directed throughout towards the figure of the beloved.

The same pressure of desire in the speaking voice shapes Shakespeare's treatment of another stock theme—the vision of the beloved in a dream—in such a way that the conceits employed are subordinated to the expression of personal emotion:

> When most I wink, then do mine eyes best see,
> For all the day they view things unrespected;
> But when I sleep, in dreams they look on thee,
> And, darkly bright, are bright in dark directed.
> Then thou, whose shadow shadows doth make bright,
> How would thy shadow's form form happy show
> To the clear day with thy much clearer light,
> When to unseeing eyes thy shade shines so! [etc.]
>
> [XLIII]

Here 'darkly bright, are bright in dark directed' is not merely a piece of wordplay but also a triumphant dance of words expressing the lover's delight. The emphatic 'thee' in line three and 'thou' in line five impress on us the fact that the poem, for all its conceits, is a love poem directed towards a beloved object. The contrasts between the radiance of dream and the drabness of reality, the brightness of the beloved and the brightness of the sun, remain expressive of an emotional situation. Shakespeare does not pursue the paradox into areas where it is liberated from this dramatic use and acquires the 'metaphysical' interest of seeming to comment on the nature of experience in general. This is the effect of Sidney's treatment of the same theme:

> I start! look! hark! but what in closed up sense
> Was held, in open sense it flies away;

Leaving me nought but wailing eloquence.
  I, seeing better sights in sight's decay;
  Called it anew, and wooed sleep again:
  But him her host, that unkind guest had slain.

[XXXVIII]

Here the subsidiary antitheses between closed sleep and open sight, between sight and eloquence, between sleep and Stella as host and guest seem concerned to pursue the mystery in the experience rather than to convey the emotional tension involved. The last line has a degree of detachment common in Sidney but rare in Shakespeare. Other treatments of this theme further sharpen our sense of Shakespeare's individual bias. Linche's version (*Diella* XXIV) and Griffin's (*Fidessa* XIV) are dramatically 'plotted', but raise no emotion. These poets are content to bombast out their fourteen lines with vapid repetitions, whereas Shakespeare's words are for ever creating in the mind of the reader *new* relationships.

At the same time he avoids the enlargement of intellectual interest, the refinement of perception, which accompanies the elaboration of similar material in the poems of Donne. Some critics have claimed that 'the . . . sonnets as a performance represent Shakespeare seeking such effects as John Donne . . . was achieving' [see excerpt above by Ransom, 1938]. I think this is an error. Donne's poem 'The Dreame' (though not Petrarchan and not a sonnet) obviously springs from the convention we have discussed above. Here however we find not the stock contrast between the cruelty of the real lady and the kindness of the phantom, but a more philosophical distinction: the phantom is banished by the coming of the real mistress, but her going again makes the lover question the nature of that reality (in a way not found in any of the previous treatments). The subsidiary antitheses reason/phantasy, fable/history, etc., show us that Donne is not concerned to build up a poignant image of a loving mind; the figure of the beloved in Donne is not the goal of the whole poem, but rather a symbol for the deeper mystery of the things that lovers experience:

  Coming and staying show'd thee, thee,
  But rising makes me doubt, that now,
    Thou art not thou.

It is the whole problem of identity that is raised by lines like these.

The bias of Shakespeare's style is no less evident in his handling of details of technique than in the general effect of his treatment of stock themes. He uses the rhetorical tricks which were the common property of the sonneteers but in a way which is mainly expressive of an individual's emotion. For example, the paradoxes in the Sonnets are used less to present the piquantly paradoxical quality of the objective Petrarchan situation and more to communicate a paradoxical quality in the lover's emotion. Of course, lines like

  Still losing when I saw myself to win

[CXIX]

can easily be paralleled from other sonneteers—e.g. Drayton's

  Where most I lost, there most of all I wan

[*Idea* 62]

but where Drayton and others tend to use such paradoxes to pattern a situation, Shakespeare's are usually expressive—we feel what it is to endure such situations:

Thou blind fool, Love, what dost thou to mine eyes,
That they behold, and see not what they see?
They know what beauty is, see where it lies,
Yet what the best is take the worst to be.

[CXXXVII]

  My love is as a fever, longing still
  For that which longer nurseth the disease;
  Feeding on that which doth preserve the ill,
  The uncertain sickly appetite to please.

[CXLVII]

O, from what power hast thou this powerful might
With insufficiency my heart to sway?
To make me give the lie to my true sight,
And swear that brightness doth not grace the day?

[CL]

In such cases it is not the situation that is paradoxical; it is the condition of the lover's being.

Again, this does not mean that the figure has become 'Metaphysical' in Shakespeare, i.e. that it has become a speculative comment on the human condition. When Donne says

  I must confess, it could not chuse but bee
  Prophane, to think thee any thing but thee.
                      [*The Dreame*]

or

  Since thou and I sigh one anothers breath,
  Who e'r sighes most, is cruellest, and hastes the
    others death.
                  [*A Valediction: of Weeping*]

he uses a paradoxical playfulness to indicate a state of loving but detached emotion; any difficulty in understanding the meaning seems to mirror the intellectual effort of the poet to bring into focus (and almost within comprehension) a truly human but hitherto undescribed situation. Donne's analysis of the state of loving enlarges our appreciation of human richness by its bizarre re-association of elements plucked out of their normal contexts; here, we feel, is a mind thinking its way through an emotional situation; Shakespeare's world is still recognizably a world of 'normal contexts'; the vision is unhackneyed only because he records the intense immediacy of individuals caught in the stock situation:

  Only my plague thus far I count my gain,
  That she that makes me sin awards me pain.

[CXLI]

Here, as in the dramas, the individual voice transcends and transforms the convention Shakespeare accepted.

In simile, as in paradox, Shakespeare's bias is towards expressiveness. In most of the Sonnets in Sir Sidney Lee's collection the simile is a device either to describe the physical charms of the beloved or to indicate general conditions in the Petrarchan situation:

  Like as a ship, that through the ocean wide,
  By conduct of some star, doth make her way . . .
  So I, whose star, that wont with her bright ray
  Me to direct, with clouds is over-cast,
  Do wander now, in darkness and dismay . . .
                          [SPENSER, XXXIV]

  As in some countries, far remote from hence,
  The wretched creature destined to die;
  Having the judgment due to his offence

By Surgeons begged, their Art on him to try . .
Even so my Mistress works upon my ill . . .

[DRAYTON, 50]

These (and the many like them) give clarity and force to the poems they adorn, but do not impart that sense of immediate emotional contact which a majority of Shakespeare's similes, drawn from the familiar experience of simple humanity, do give:

Lo, as a careful housewife runs to catch
One of her feather'd creatures broke away,
Sets down her babe, and makes all swift
    dispatch . . .
So runn'st thou after that which flies from thee,
Whilst I thy babe chase thee afar behind . . .

[CXLIII]

So am I as the rich, whose blessed key
Can bring him to his sweet up-locked treasure . . .

[LII]

In CXLIII the emotional relationships are defined and made immediate by the simile; in LII it is the human emotion implicit in the comparison which makes the chief effect.

Treatments of the same theme—absence—in poems of merit which use simile as the main feature of their construction may be compared, to show in an extended fashion Shakespeare's individual use of this figure.

How like a winter hath my absence been
From thee, the pleasure of the fleeting year!
What freezings have I felt, what dark days seen!
What old December's bareness every where!
    And yet this time removed was summer's time;
The teeming autumn, big with rich increase,
Bearing the wanton burthen of the prime,
Like widowed wombs after their lords' decease:
Yet this abundant issue seem'd to me
But hope of orphans and unfather'd fruit;
For summer and his pleasures wait on thee,
And, thou away, the very birds are mute;
    Or, if they sing, 'tis with so dull a cheer
    That leaves look pale, dreading the winter's near.

[XCVII]

Like as the Culver, on the bared bough,
Sits mourning for the absence of her mate;
And, in her songs, sends many a wishful vow
For his return that seems to linger late:
So I alone, now left disconsolate,
Mourn to myself the absence of my love;
And, wandering here and there all desolate,
Seek with my plaints to match that mournful dove.
No joy of aught that under heaven doth hove
Can comfort me, but her own joyous sight:
Whose sweet aspect both God and man can move,
In her unspotted pleasance to delight.
    Dark is my day, while her fair light I miss,
    And dead my life that wants such lively bliss.

[SPENSER, LXXXVIII]

Spenser's simile is a graceful one and conveys the gentle melancholy of the poem, but it does not make the lover's feelings vivid by conveying them in images universally charged with these emotions. Shakespeare's 'December's bareness' and 'dark days' are stripped back to their bare function as objective correlatives of the emotion between lover and beloved; they do not intrude at all between the reader and this emotion. Spenser's culver on the other hand is intruded deliberately as a symbol to indicate the mood of the poem (rather

than the mood of the persons in the poem). Accordingly, Spenser's image has the charm of an idyll; Shakespeare's generates in the reader a reaction more proper to drama.

Further details of Shakespeare's subject-matter and style could be analysed, but enough has no doubt been said to show how far from the fashions of which they were born Shakespeare's sonnets are taken by his dramatically expressive way of writing. The subject-matter and the rhetoric may be that of the Petrarchan tradition, the effect may sometimes seem Metaphysical, but the uniquely Shakespearean quality of the sequence is not to be explained by either of these labels. We have here what we might expect: a dramatist describes a series of emotional situations between persons (real or fictitious) in a series of separate short poems; the Petrarchan instruments turn in his hands into means of expressing and concentrating the great human emotions, desire, jealousy, fear, hope and despair, and of raising in the reader the dramatic reactions of pity and terror by his implication in the lives and fates of the persons depicted. (pp. 152-64)

> *G. K. Hunter, "The Dramatic Technique of Shakespeare's Sonnets," in* Essays in Criticism, *Vol. III, No. 2, April, 1953, pp. 152-64.*

C. S. LEWIS   (essay date 1954)

[*An English literary critic and novelist, Lewis was also a distinguished Renaissance scholar whose writing was strongly influenced by his Christian beliefs. As a Shakespearean critic, he argued that those commentators who pay too much attention to character analysis are apt to overlook the intention of the plays, particularly their moral and ethical impact. Instead, Lewis suggested that the critic should surrender him or herself to "the poetry and the situation" in all of Shakespeare's dramas. In the following excerpt, he discusses several aspects of Shakespeare's sonnets, particularly addressing questions relating to style and to the sequence's presentation of human love. Shakespeare's depiction of love in these verses resists easy classification, Lewis remarks, because it moves from particularity in the early sonnets to universality in the later ones, ultimately encompassing "all loves whether erotic, parental, filial, amicable, or feudal." The critic also evaluates the poet's language and metrics, calling attention to such elements as rhythm, vocabulary, alliteration, and rhetorical patterns of "theme and variations" within individual sonnets.*]

Shakespeare would be a considerable non-dramatic poet if he had written only the *Lucrece:* but it sinks almost to nothing in comparison with his sonnets. The sonnets are the very heart of the Golden Age, the highest and purest achievement of the Golden way of writing. We do not know when they were composed. They were published in 1609 'by G. Eld for T. T.' together with 'A Lover's Complaint' (a still-born *chanson d'aventure* in rhyme royal, corrupt in text, poetically inconsiderable, and dialectally unlike Shakespeare). But at least two of them (CXXXVIII and CXLIV) existed as early as 1599, for these two were included in the poetical miscellany which William Jaggard published in that year under the title of *The Passionate Pilgrim.* A year earlier, in 1598, Meres had referred to 'sugred sonnets' by Shakespeare [see excerpt above, 1598]: how far these coincided with the sonnets we now have can only be conjectured. External evidence thus failing us, we look for internal, and find ourselves in a world of doubts. Even if an individual sonnet can be dated (and I think it much more likely that CVII refers to the queen's death or her climacteric than to the Spanish Armada) this would not enable us to date the collection as a whole. Many sonnets, such as LXVI, LXXI, XCVII, and CVI, would be appropriate to any lover at any time and might, so far as their matter goes, be divided by years from other sonnets in the same collection. The evidence from style produces strong convictions in all readers, but not always the same convictions. On my own view it helps us much more to a *terminus post quem* than to a *terminus ante quem:* that is, I can hardly conceive a poet moving from the style of the best sonnets (which means in effect nearly all the sonnets) to that of *Venus and Adonis,* but can easily conceive one who had achieved Shakespeare's mature dramatic technique still writing some of the sonnets we have. For in all ages, and especially in that, form affects style. If Shakespeare had taken an hour off from the composition of *Lear* to write a sonnet, the sonnet might not have been in the style of *Lear.* We cannot even be certain that Shakespeare wrote his sonnets when sonneteering was the vogue: there are expressions in XXXII, LXXVI, and LXXXII which can (though they need not) be interpreted to mean that he knew he was adopting a form no longer fashionable. But I am not arguing that the sonnets were later than is usually supposed. I am arguing for agnosticism. We do not know when, or at what different times, they were written.

Shakespeare's sequence differs in character as well as in excellence from those of the other Elizabethans. It is indeed the peculiarity of these sonnets which has led to a misreading of all the rest. For here at last we have a sequence which really hints a story, and so odd a story that we find a difficulty in regarding it as fiction. It is the story of a man torn between passionate affection for another man and reluctant passion for a woman whom he neither trusts nor respects. No reading of the sonnets can obscure that amount of 'plot' or 'situation'. Yet even this sequence is far from offering us the pleasure we expect from a good novel or a good autobiography. Treated that way, it becomes a mass of problems. I do not mean those problems which (rightly) attract students of Shakespeare's life. With those the literary historian has no concern; he would not give a farthing to know the identity of the 'man right fair' or the 'woman colour'd ill' [CXLIV]. The difficulty which faces us if we try to read the sequence like a novel is that the precise mode of love which the poet declares for the Man remains obscure. His language is too lover-like for that of ordinary male friendship; and though the claims of friendship are sometimes put very high in, say, the *Arcadia,* I have found no real parallel to such language between friends in sixteenth-century literature. Yet, on the other hand, this does not seem to be the poetry of full-blown pederasty. Shakespeare, and indeed Shakespeare's age, did nothing by halves. If he had intended in these sonnets to be the poet of pederasty, I think he would have left us in no doubt; the lovely παιδικά [favorite], attended by a whole train of mythological perversities, would have blazed across the pages. The incessant demand that the Man should marry and found a family would seem to be inconsistent (or so I suppose—it is a question for psychologists) with a real homosexual passion. It is not even very obviously consistent with normal friendship. It is indeed hard to think of any real situation in which it would be natural. What man in the whole world, except a father or a potential father-in-law, cares whether any other man gets married? Thus the emotion expressed in the *Sonnets* refuses to fit into our pigeonholes. And this, for two reasons, makes singularly little difference to our delight.

In the first place many individual sonnets, and some of the most prized, are very lightly attached to the theme of the sequence as a whole. CXLVI ('Poor soul, the centre of my sin-ful earth') is not attached at all; it is concerned with the tension between the temporal and the eternal and would be appropriate in the mouth of any Christian at any moment. XXX ('When to the sessions of sweet silent thought'), LXVI ('Tired with all these, for restful death I cry'), LXXIII ('That time of year thou mayst in me behold') are meditations respectively on bereavement, *taedium vitae* [weariness of life], and age, hooked on to the theme of love only by their concluding couplets. The effect of this 'hook' is twofold. On the one hand it makes richer and more poignant the emotion expressed in the preceding twelve lines, but not until that emotion has been allowed to develop itself fully; it converts retrospectively into a mode of love what nevertheless could be felt (and has been felt until we reach the couplet) on its own account. And, on the other hand, there is a formal or structural pleasure in watching each sonnet wind back through unexpected ways to its appointed goal, as if it said at the end *vos plaudite* [give us your applause]. Even where the theme of love reaches farther back into the body of the sonnet it is often as universal, as suitable to every lover, as in a sonnet by Daniel or Lodge. Thus XXV ('Let those who are in favour with their stars') or XXIX ('When in disgrace with fortune and men's eyes') are poems that any man can walk into and make his own. And those must be few and fortunate who cannot do the same with XXXIII ('Full many a glorious morning have I seen') and XXXIV ('Why didst thou promise such a beauteous day').

Such is the effect of many individual sonnets. But when we read the whole sequence through at a sitting (as we ought sometimes to do) we have a different experience. From its total plot, however ambiguous, however particular, there emerges something not indeed common or general like the love expressed in many individual sonnets but yet, in a higher way, universal. The main contrast in the *Sonnets* is between the two loves, that 'of comfort' and that 'of despair'. The love 'of despair' demands all: the love 'of comfort' asks, and perhaps receives, nothing. Thus the whole sequence becomes an expanded version of Blake's 'The Clod and the Pebble'. And so it comes about that, however the thing began—in perversion, in convention, even (who knows?) in fiction—Shakespeare, celebrating the 'Clod' as no man has celebrated it before or since, ends by expressing simply love, the quintessence of all loves whether erotic, parental, filial, amicable, or feudal. Thus from extreme particularity there is a road to the highest universality. The love is, in the end, so simply and entirely love that our *cadres* are thrown away and we cease to ask what kind. However it may have been with Shakespeare in his daily life, the greatest of the sonnets are written from a region in which love abandons all claims and flowers into charity: after that it makes little odds what the root was like. They open a new world of love poetry; as new as Dante's and Petrarch's had been in their day. These had of course expressed humility, but it had been the humility of Eros, hungry to receive: kneeling, but kneeling to ask. They and their great successor Patmore sing a dutiful and submissive, but hardly a giving, love. They could have written, almost too easily, 'Being your slave, what should I do but tend?': they could hardly have written, 'I may not evermore acknowledge thee', or 'No longer mourn' or 'Although thou steal thee all my poverty' [LVI, XXXVI, LXXI, XL]. The self-abnegation, the 'naughting', in the *Sonnets* never rings false. This patience, this anxiety (more like a parent's than a lover's) to find excuses for the beloved, this clear-sighted and wholly unembittered resignation, this transference of the whole self into another self without the demand for a return, have hardly a precedent in profane literature. In certain senses of the word 'love', Shakespeare is not so much our best as our only love poet.

This content is mediated to us through a masterpiece of Golden technique. On the metrical side all those wide departures from the norm which make the life of Donne's or Milton's work, or of Shakespeare's own later blank verse, are excluded. That sacrifice was essential to his *cantabile*. He has to avoid the stunning regularity of Drab, yet to avoid it only by a hair's breadth. There is a high percentage of lines in which every second syllable is not merely stressed but also long: 'So I, for fear of trust, forget to say', 'So you in Grecian tires are painted new', 'When beauty lived and died as flowers do now' [XXIII, XIII, LXVIII]. Most of the rhymes are strong and many of them rest on monosyllables. There is a great use of alliteration both in its obvious and its less obtrusive forms. Thus in XV we have plain alliteration, 'Cheered and check'd' (6) and 'Sets' and 'sight' (10); gentler alliteration on unstressed syllables in 11 ('debateth with decay'); consonant groups linked with simple consonants, where one is unstressed (as 'perceive' and 'plants' in 5) or both (as 'perfection' and 'presenteth', 2, 3). In XII we have the heavy alliteration 'Born', 'bier', 'bristly', 'beard' side by side with the much more artful pattern *s, gr, g, sh* in the previous line—groups linked with simples and arranged chiasmically. CXVI opens with a wonderful fantasia on the consonant *m:* full alliteration of initial stressed syllables in 'marriage' and 'minds', a stressed but not initial syllable in 'admit', and the unstressed 'me' and 'ments' in 'impediments'. Then follow 'love' and 'love', no less an alliteration to the ear because they are the same word, and in the next line, a device Shakespeare used well, the play upon kindred words, 'alters' and 'alteration' (compare 'beauty making beautiful' in CVI, 'the wardrobe which the robe doth hide' in LII). Most of these devices are as sweet to us as they were to our ancestors. But Shakespeare does not share our modern dislike of sibilants (he will 'summon' remembrance to 'sessions of sweet silent thought') and in XLV we find the Simpsonian rhyme of 'to thée' with 'melanchóly'.

In most of the sonnets there is a frank and innocent reliance on words which invite emotion and sensuous imagination. Thus in XII we have *time, day, night, violet, sable, silver, trees, leaves, summer, green, bier, wastes*: in XVIII, *summer* again, *day* again, *buds, winds, sun, gold, death, shades;* in XXI, *heaven, sun* again, *moon, earth, sea, gems, April, flowers, mother;* in XXX, *remembrance, past, waste* again, *death* again, *night* again, *moan;* in LXVIII *cheek, flowers* again, *brow, golden* again, *sepulchres, fleece, hours, summer* again, *green* again, and *Nature*. This differentia of the Golden style becomes tolerably clear if we notice, for contrast, the keywords in the first stanza of Herbert's 'Confession'; *quest, grief, heart, closets, chest, trade, boxes, a till.*

The rhetorical structure is often that of theme and variations, as in *Lucrece*. The variations more often than not precede the theme, and there is usually an application which connects the theme of the particular sonnet with what may be called the 'running' theme of that part of the sequence to which it belongs. There are exceptions to this. In CXLIV, for example, we have something like a continuous progression in which each line adds to the thought. CXXIX ('The expense of spirit') starts as if it were going to develop in that way, but progression almost ends with line 5, 'Enjoy'd no sooner but despised straight'. The next seven lines are largely, though not

entirely, variations on the fifth. To see the typical Shakespearian structure at its simplest we may turn to LXVI ('Tired with all these'). The theme occupies the first line, the application, the final couplet: in between we have eleven instances of the things which produce weariness of life. This numerical equality between the different variations is very uncommon, and chosen, no doubt, to give a special effect of cumulative bitterness. More often it is contrived that the variations should be either unequal simply, or, if they begin by being equal, that they should presently grow longer. Thus XII ('When I do count the clock') is built on the pattern variations—theme—application. The theme ('You too will pass') occupies the four lines beginning 'then of thy beauty do I question make', and the application is in the final couplet. The preceding variations have the numerical pattern I, I, I, I, 2, 2; a line each for the clock, the nightfall, the violet, and the curls, then two lines each for the trees and the harvest. The effect on the reader is one of liberation just at the moment when the one-line *exempla* were about to produce a feeling of constraint. In XXXIII ('Full many a glorious morning') we have only one variation in the form of a continuous simile filling the first eight lines. But then this simile contains its own pattern: one line announcing the morning, three which catch each one aspect of its beauty, and four to tell the sequel. XVIII ('Shall I compare thee to a summer's day?') is exquisitely elaborated. As often, the theme begins at line 9 ('But thy eternal summer shall not fade'), occupying four lines, and the application is in the couplet. Line 1 proposes a simile. Line 2 corrects it. Then we have two one-line *exempla* justifying the correction: then a two-line *exemplum* about the sun: then two more lines ('And every fair') which do not, as we had expected, add a fourth *exemplum* but generalize. Equality of length in the two last variations is thus played off against difference of function. The same transition from variation by examples to variation by generalizing is found in LXIV ('When I have seen by Time's fell hand defaced'); theme in lines 1-2, first *exemplum* in line 3, second *exemplum* in line 4, the third *exemplum* triumphantly expanding to fill lines 5-8, generalization (9-10) passing into Application which occupies the last four lines. To some, I am afraid, such analysis will seem trifling, and it is not contended that no man can enjoy the *Sonnets* without it any more than that no man can enjoy a tune without knowing its musical grammar. But unless we are content to talk simply about the 'magic' of Shakespeare's poetry (forgetting that magic was a highly formal art) something of the kind is inevitable. It serves at least to remind us what sort of excellence, and how different from some other poetic excellences, the *Sonnets* possess. They very seldom present or even feign to present passionate thought growing and changing in the heat of a situation; they are not dramatic. The end of each is clearly in view from the beginning, the theme already chosen. Instead of a single developing thought we get what musicians call an 'arrangement', what we might call a pattern or minuet, of thoughts and images. There are arithmetical elements in the beauty of this pattern as in all formal beauty, and its basic principle is *idem in alio* [similarity in differences]. Of course it affects those who have no notion what is affecting them. It is partly responsible for that immense pleasurableness which we find in the *Sonnets* even where their matter is most painful: and also for their curious stillness or tranquillity. Shakespeare is always standing back a little from the emotions he treats. He left it to his created persons, his Lears and Othellos, to pour out raw experience, scalding hot. In his own person he does not do so. He sings (always sings, never talks) of shame and degradation

and the divided will, but it is as if he sang from above, moved
and yet not moved; a Golden, Olympian poet. (pp. 502-08)

C. S. Lewis, "Verse in the 'Golden' Period," in his
English Literature in the Sixteenth Century, Excluding Drama, Oxford at the Clarendon Press,
1954, pp. 464-535.

G. WILSON KNIGHT   (essay date 1955)

[*Knight was one of the most influential Shakespearean critics
of the twentieth century. He helped shape a new interpretive approach to Shakespeare's work and promoted a greater appreciation of many of the plays. In his studies* The Wheel of Fire
(1930) and The Shakespearian Tempest *(1932), Knight rejected criticism that emphasizes sources, character analysis, psychology, and ethics and outlined his principles of interpretation. The latter, he claimed, would "replace that chaos by
drawing attention to the true Shakespearian unity." Knight argued that this unity lay in Shakespeare's use of images and
symbols—particularly in the opposition of "tempests" and
"music." In the following excerpt from* The Mutual Flame
*(1955), he provides an overview of Shakespeare's use of poetic
symbolism in the sonnets. The principal associations Shakespeare uses, Knight claims, are "on the natural plane, flowers,
especially the rose; on the human plane, kingship, with gold;
on the universal, the Sun, with gold; on the spiritual, "jewels."
Using "spatial" analysis—that is, viewing the symbols as independent of their context, yet in harmony with it—Knight comments on the way in which symbolic language enhances the
theme of love in the sonnets to the Friend. He determines that
it is the idealized Friend, "the distilled truth of the boy, the
eternal 'idea,' in Plato's sense, that [the poet] loves rather than
the boy himself."*]

[Certain] supposed 'conceits' or 'fancies' may be in reality attempts to grapple with some superthought which baffles expression. The most usual medium for such intuitions is poetic
symbolism, and the Sonnets show a rich use of it. Indeed, the
weighty realisation of these imaginative solidities sets them
apart from the poetry of Donne and Marvell. True, both
Donne and Marvell have their imagery and symbols, and
some of Donne's recall Shakespeare's. But with the more
metaphysical poets the symbol is, as it were, subdued to—in
Donne it is often there to be mocked by—the thinking; it
grows from a matrix of metaphysical speculation and intellectual gymnastics. In the best Sonnets the thinking is put at
the service of the symbol, and sometimes appears, as we shall
see, to lag behind it. The result is that whatever 'eternity'
Shakespeare succeeds in establishing is far more than a concept, or web of concepts: it flowers from close physical perception, and holds all the colour and perfume of spring.

One feels that it is only with the greatest reluctance, and perhaps even a sense of guilt, that the poet is forced to admit,
if he ever does admit, that it is the distilled truth of the boy,
the eternal 'idea', in Plato's sense, that he loves rather than
the boy himself; and in so far as he writes of the 'idea' rather
than of the thing itself, his writing becomes philosophic rather than strictly poetic; at the best, 'metaphysical poetry', as
with Donne and Marvell. Those are concerned with, and brilliantly transmit, their own experience of love, but they have
nothing much to say of the loved-one: in Marvell's *Definition
of Love* we cannot even be sure of his or her sex. Since they
never realise a personality outside themselves, we are not
forced to join with them in adoration. But when in Shakespeare we read:

Why should poor beauty indirectly seek

Roses of shadow, since his rose is true?

(67)

we cannot avoid being half-in-love with the youth ourselves.
There is a more vivid realisation of the loved person in that
one little word 'his', which might well be italicised, than in
all Donne's love-poetry. Nor does Shakespeare confine himself, as, on the whole, you might say that Michelangelo does,
to a few archetypal thoughts. Such thoughts he has, but they
are part only of a closely realised drama, showing all the variety, and hinting the physical detail, of an actual experience.
Sense-perception is vivid. We enjoy a rich physical apprehension, the flush and bloom of a young life, with all the perfumes of spring in company, rather as when we read Chaucer's description of his young Squire. We are aware of nature
before we proceed to metaphysics: if 'this composed wonder
of your frame' (59) is a miracle, it is a miracle born less from
our minds than from the 'great creating Nature' of *The Winter's Tale* [IV. iv. 88]. At their greatest moments the Sonnets
are really less love-poetry than an almost religious adoration
before one of 'the rarities of Nature's truth' (60); that is, one
of the splendours of human creation. So, though nothing but
poetry can meet his problem, yet Shakespeare's move from
love to the great poetry of the plays might yet be called, paradoxically, a fall, a second-best: 'for these dead birds sigh a
prayer' [*The Phoenix and Turtle*].

We shall now list the main associations used by the poet to
establish verbal contact with the miracle which is his theme.
About these there is nothing very abstruse or learned. They
are, on the natural plane, flowers, especially the rose; on the
human plane, kingship, with gold; on the universal, the Sun,
with gold; on the spiritual, jewels. Rose, King, Sun, Gold,
Jewels. Our examination need pay slight regard to the Sonnets' order: we shall use our usual practice of 'spatial' analysis, seeing the symbols as existent powers in their own right
irrespective of, though of course never contradicting, their
particular contexts.

Our first sonnet has 'beauty's rose' (1). One of our finest end-
couplets runs:

For nothing this wide universe I call
Save thou, my rose; in it thou art my all.

(109)

The rose as truth is contrasted with shams and vices. The
youth's 'true' rose of beauty, in the exquisite passage recently
quoted, is contrasted with the false beautifyings of society
(67). If faults be present in him, 'roses have thorns, and silver
fountains mud' (35). His beauty encloses 'sins' as the rose
contains a 'canker' (95). But 'canker' may also mean wild
roses, as when 'canker-blooms' are said to have colour without 'the perfumed tincture' of 'sweet roses', which survive
death in distillation, even as the inmost truth of the boy's
beauty is distilled by poetry (54). With the rose we may group
the lily: 'Lilies that fester smell far worse than weeds' (94).
The youth is the 'pattern' of both 'the lily's white' and 'the
deep vermilion in the rose' (98). In one sonnet the poet relates, point by point, violet, lily, marjoram and roses, red and
white, together with the 'vengeful canker' of destruction, to
the separate excellences of his love's beauty (99). In contrast
his mistress' cheeks have nothing of 'roses damask'd, red and
white' in them (130). It is easy to understand the intense poetic appeal made by the Wars of the Roses to Shakespeare in
the three parts of *Henry VI*, so rich in impressions of human
loveliness and pathos caught in the shambles of meaningless

destruction, all summed by the line, 'The red rose and the white are on his face' [*3 Henry VI*, II. v. 97] .

Next, kingship. Royal images recur, as in the love-poetry of Donne, some of them holding similar connotations. The poet addresses the youth as 'lord of my love', to whom he sends a 'written ambassage' (26); he is 'my sovereign' and the poet his 'servant' or 'slave' (57). Love-passages in the dramas offer parallels. There is Bassanio's

> There is such confusion in my powers,
> As, after some oration fairly spoke
> By a beloved prince, there doth appear
> Among the buzzing pleased multitude . . .
>   [*The Merchant of Venice*, III. ii. 177-80]

and Troilus'

> My heart beats thicker than a fev'rous pulse;
> And all my powers do their bestowing lose,
> Like vassalage at unawares encountering
> The eye of majesty.
>   [*Troilus and Cressida*, III .ii. 36-9]

The lover is abased before a blazing power.

The loved one is royal, and so compared to 'a throned queen' (96). He is 'crowned' with various gifts of nature and fortune (37), especially 'all those beauties whereof now he's king' (63). Like a sovereign, he radiates worth, his eyes lending 'a double majesty' to the rival poets' 'grace' (78); if it were not for certain suspicions, he would be owning 'kingdoms of hearts' (70). This royalty is somehow shared by the lover; having found his own king, he regards all other, more commonplace, grandeurs as poor stuff in comparison. His astronomy, learned from those 'constant stars', his love's eyes, cannot, and clearly has no desire to, busy itself with the fortunes of 'princes'; it is a different 'art', prophesying 'truth and beauty' (14). After all, 'great princes' favourites' enjoy an insecure glory in comparison (25); time changes the 'decrees of kings', but his love is lasting (115); it is in no sense 'the child of state', and is independent of 'smiling pomp' (124); bearing 'the canopy' means nothing to him, nor does any such external 'honouring' (125). The result is that the poet, through accepted love, becomes himself royal. His mind is 'crown'd' with the wondrous youth, and is accordingly 'kingly' (114); when he is sure of him, he is a 'king', but when disillusioned, 'no such matter' (87). However depressed he may be in other ways, in so far as his love is assured, it brings such wealth, well-being and power, 'that then I scorn to change my state with kings' (29).

Such symbols act variously as contrasts or comparisons, and apply to either partner of the love-association. Our final impression is of love itself as king, of some super-personality, the Sun of Sonnet 24, made of, or liberated by, the love of two human beings, as when Donne in *The Ecstasy* writes 'else a great Prince in prison lies'. Love liberates this mysterious sovereign, allows him to realise himself in human terms. This sovereign reality it is which is indicated by the word 'love' of our phrase 'in love with', Nerissa's 'lord love' of *The Merchant of Venice* [II. ix. 101]. It is something, or someone, experienced immediately, 'crowning the present' (115); either that, or known beyond death, as in Romeo's 'I reviv'd and was an emperor' in *Romeo and Juliet* [V. i. 9], and Cleopatra's 'I dream'd there was an emperor Antony', in *Antony and Cleopatra* [V. ii. 76]. The associations are just, since the king, properly understood, holds within society precisely this super-personal and supernal function. In more obviously religious terms we have Henry VI's:

> My crown is in my heart, not on my head;
> Not deck'd with diamonds and Indian stones,
> Nor to be seen.
>   [*3 Henry VI*, III. i. 62-4]

But the Sonnets never engage too far in mysticism, and perhaps our finest example of all, warm with meanings both physical and heraldic, is the line, 'Then in the blazon of sweet beauty's best' (106), where kings are not specifically mentioned at all.

Kingship is naturally golden, and golden impressions recur with similar variations in use. 'Gilded honour' may be 'shamefully misplac'd' (66); poets flatter the youth with 'golden quill' (85); his hair is contrasted with false 'golden tresses' (68); Shakespeare's poetry can make him outlive 'a gilded tomb' (101). More important is his eye 'gilding' the object on which it gazes (20)—eyes in Shakespeare's are active powers, not just passive reflections (p. 37)—and the lovely phrase characterising youth as 'this thy golden time' (3). Stars are 'gold candles' (21).

The Sun is nature's king, and also pre-eminently golden. Throughout Shakespeare king and sun are compared. The Dark Lady's eyes are 'nothing like the Sun' (130); they are 'mourning', because dark, eyes, and may at the best be compared to the 'morning sun' in a grey dawn, or the evening star (132). With the Fair Youth, the association 'that sun, thine eye' (49) comes easily enough. The successful lover compares himself to the morning 'lark' singing 'hymns at Heaven's gate' (29), though, when things go wrong, 'basest clouds' obscure the Sun, who now rides 'with ugly rack on his celestial face', and steals to the west disfigured (33); for 'clouds and eclipses stain both Moon and Sun' (35). In our 'transparency' sonnet (24) the Sun functions as the supernal love corresponding to Donne's prince. The Sun, 'daily new and old' (76), is visualised in all positions of his diurnal course, with close reference to age. Youth is a 'day' ready to decline (15), and the poet's age just such an hour 'as after sunset fadeth in the west' (73).

We have various clusters of king, gold, and sun. King and gold come together in 'the gilded monuments of princes' (55); and sun and gold, when the Sun's 'gold complexion' is dimmed in the sonnet, 'Shall I compare thee to a summer's day?' (18), or the young man graces 'the day' and 'gilds' the evening in place of stars (28). We may have all three. So 'great princes' favourites' are compared to the mari*gold* opening to the Sun's 'eye' (25). Man's life resembles the diurnal progress of the Sun, who first 'lifts up his burning head' from the orient, everything beneath him doing 'homage' to his 'sacred majesty' as he makes his 'golden pilgrimage', till finally he 'reeleth' to his setting (7). Love resembles a 'glorious morning' seen to 'flatter the mountain tops with sovereign eye', kissing meadows with his 'golden face', and 'gilding' streams with his 'heavenly alchemy' (33).

These impressions are not just decoration. They are attempts to realize in 'black ink' (65) the wonder of youthful beauty at 'this thy golden time' (3); and beyond that, to make real and visible, without relying on abstract terms, that supernal and authoritative Love of which lovers are part only, expressions, voices.

Nor is all this so simple and obvious as it sounds. The Sun

is not a necessary, nor even a natural, accompaniment to Shakespearian romance: the Moon is more usual. Shakespeare's heterosexual love-themes are usually moonlit, as with the Balcony scene of *Romeo and Juliet,* the central scenes of *A Midsummer Night's Dream,* and the fifth act of *The Merchant of Venice,* though Portia has 'sunny' locks [I. i. 169]. Much of *As You Like It* shows us a shadowed, dappled, world, and in *Twelfth Night* the Sun never dominates until Sebastian's, 'This is the air, that is the glorious sun' [IV. iii. 1]. *Antony and Cleopatra* has 'gaudy' *nights* [III. xiii. 182]. and Enobarbus' moonlit death, the Sun itself acting rather as a background power than as a present witness, until Cleopatra's dream. Certainly in *Love's Labour's Lost* the Sun is lyrically vivid as a love-accompaniment. But this early play is made on a pattern of its own; it ends with winter; it is full of sonnet-material; and it is exactly this sort of love-poetry that is not repeated. Our first really convincingly sun-impregnated love-scene is the sheep-shearing festival of *The Winter's Tale.*

The Sun is male, the Moon female; the one suggests the intellectual consciousness, the other emotion, the twilit world of romance. When Shelley's Hermaphrodite (=poetry) in *The Witch of Atlas* is fully *awakened,* then we may expect the Sun. When sensual love, whose natural medium, as D. H. Lawrence insisted, is the dark world below consciousness, is our theme, the Sun may, as in Donne's *The Sun Rising,* be an intruder, though, in so far as such a love is vividly and directly lived by day, with a strong physical awareness fully accepted, as in *The Winter's Tale,* it may be in place. Normally, we can say that it is far from easy to blend it with a heterosexual love. As an extreme example of a natural tendency, we have the 'woman wailing for her demon-lover' under a 'waning moon' in *Kubla Khan;* and we must remember Lorenzo's and Jessica's list of famous moonlit love-incidents in their 'In such a night . . .' duet [*The Merchant of Venice,* V. i. 1-24]. That last act is, in its way, a recovery and a retreat—yet how wonderful a retreat—from the stern compulsions of the greater action.

But it is precisely among those 'stern compulsions' that the Sun is likely to assume poetic centrality. So Theseus, man of power, efficiency, chivalrous courtesy and common-sense, enters with the dawn on the moonstruck world of *A Midsummer Night's Dream;* the heroic idealism of *Julius Caesar* is marked by important passages of sunrise and sunset, before and after the assassination [II. i. 101-11; V. iii. 60-3]; and in *Cymbeline* the royal boys are sun-worshippers [III. iii. 1-9] and Cymbeline himself 'radiant' [V. v. 475]. Shakespeare's kings, in so far as they carry, or claim, true, that is magical, royalty, are regularly given sun-correspondences, as with Richard's comparison of himself to a rising sun:

> But when, from under this terrestrial ball,
> He fires the proud tops of the eastern pines,
> And darts his light through every guilty hole . . .
>   [*Richard II,* III. ii. 41-3]

Henry VIII is a 'sun' [III. ii. 415], and so on. All this is fairly clear. But, with the waning of the royalistic and aristocratic valuations, there is less of it in English poetry than you might expect. Milton's Samson-like figure of power-with-virtue at the close of the *Areopagitica* is as a sun-gazing eagle; Keats offers some notable splendours in *Hyperion,* and Coleridge's *Zapolya,* with its youthful hero Andreas, is a complete work constructed from this particular area of the imagination (*The Starlit Dome,* IV, 284-7; II, 160-78). Byron, perhaps our subtlest sun-poet of all, offers many variations, serious and amusing (*The Burning Oracle,* VI, 256-9, 284). The sombre Tennyson is happiest with the setting sun: you have to be empowered with an innate, virile, humanistic faith to use the sun-symbol with power. Wordsworth once crashed badly (*The Excursion,* IV, 232; *The Starlit Dome,* I, 55).

The Sun tends to assume poetic centrality when our concern is: (i) any fully-*conscious,* or victorious, love, as defined in Biron's great speech in *Love's Labour's Lost* [IV. iii. 287-362]; with love-as-power, love virile and victorious; or, (ii) royal power felt magically, almost, we might say, erotically. We may say, more generally, that it fits any strong conviction of power or sexual virility fused with virtue, and it is true that in the Renaissance period it can accompany any love in so far as that love is, as in Spenser's *Hymns,* felt as a sovereign power. But it is clear that a male love lends itself most readily to the symbol, and indeed we cannot always be sure how far our Renaissance love-lyrists are using heterosexual terms for a homosexual engagement. In such engagements, being as they are denied sexual consummation, sex is forced into consciousness, so that it becomes . . . a matter of 'eyes', of burning, over-flooding, apprehension; all is strongly idealistic; while the loved object, being male, inevitably assumes the power-properties of male action, aristocracy, and royalty. In his adoration for the loved youth, the two main positive directions of Shakespeare's work are accordingly implicit.

The various natural and cosmic symbolisms of the Sonnets grow from a soil of normal Shakespearian imagery: flowers crops, and seasons; moon and stars; effects of winter, cloud, storm and tempests; inundation (64); and wrecks (80). The love-quest is a sea-voyage (80, 86), as in *Troilus and Cressida.* . . . Stars may be important, sometimes holding astrological significance (14, 15, 26, 116); they may be more directly descriptive or symbolic (21, 132); they are symbols of constancy (14, 116).

We have already reviewed certain impressions of 'gold'. 'Gold' naturally accompanies 'sun' and 'king'; the king's crown, and indeed gold in general, might be called 'solid sunlight'. Gold has for centuries exerted magical radiations and its value, worth and power, its 'virtue' in the old sense, need no emphasis. These properties make it an apt symbol for any high value, or worth.

Love is such a value, and it is regularly in Shakespeare compared to rich metals or merchandise. . . . Throughout poetry precious stones symbolise what may be called 'spiritual value'. . . . All this is powerful in the Sonnets.

The 'rich gems' of 'earth and sea' are regarded as a natural love-comparison (21); though cruel, the Dark Lady is 'the fairest and most precious jewel' (131); and the youth's image by night hangs 'like a jewel' before the poet's soul (27), recalling Romeo's 'It seems she hangs upon the cheek of night like a rich jewel in an Ethiop's ear' [*Romeo and Juliet,* I. v. 45-6]. Compared with 'a prize so dear', the poet's 'jewels' are as 'trifles' (48); even the youth's faults are to be prized as a poor 'jewel' may be on the figure of 'a throned queen' (96); his tears are as 'pearl', and called 'rich' (34); he is himself costly, a matter of 'riches' (87). One sonnet is packed with suggestions of 'rich', 'treasure', 'stones of worth', 'chest', and 'robe', and contains the grand line, 'captain jewels in the carcanet' (52). Most striking of all is:

> Where, alack,
> Shall Time's best jewel from Time's chest lie hid?
>
>   (65)

As elsewhere throughout Shakespeare, such symbols blend with rich merchandise and sea-voyages. Love, it is true, is too rich to be 'merchandis'd' (102), but symbolically the thought may act serenely enough:

> Was it the proud full sail of his great verse
> Bound for the prize of all too precious you . . .
>
> (86)

Poetry is itself a quest. Apart from all flattery and advantage, it is a spiritual penetration and achievement, in some deep sense a possession, of the mysterious splendour. But the poet is, of course, jealous in a human fashion too: he is like a 'miser' so intent on 'the prize of you', that he varies between pride of possession and horrible doubts lest 'the filching age' may 'steal his treasure' (75).

Shakespeare's bitter comments on the youth's risking 'infection' from a sinful society (67), with the cutting conclusion 'thou dost common grow' (69), may in fact arise from a questionable jealousy and possessiveness. We need not assume that the young man, who is once specifically said to have survived the temptations of youth victoriously (70), was naturally vicious. In certain moods Shakespeare would, clearly, regard all society as too base for a youth of so infinite and mysterious a worth. His love was to him the inmost centre and furthest aim of all things, its value lying beyond human assessment:

> It is the star to every wandering bark,
> Whose worth's unknown although his height be
>   taken.
>
> (116)

It was the crowning glory of creation, and more than that. 'Jewels', as we have said, suggest spiritual values, and this love is also religious.

Our theme (31) is 'dear, religious, love' ('dear' meaning 'of highest value'). It is not 'idolatry' (105)—compare Hector's aspersions on idolatry at *Troilus and Cressida* [II. ii. 56]—because it and its object are constant (105). Even though faults be found, even though there be no objective 'image', to quote Hector, 'of the affected merit' [*Troilus and Cressida*, II. ii. 60], 'Heaven' has somehow decreed in the youth's 'creation that only 'sweet love' can dwell in his 'face'; he cannot *look* faithless or bad (93). Such beauty, with its 'heavenly touches' (17), exists in its own right; it is itself 'sacred' (115); and the poet complains that, since artifice became the fashion, 'sweet beauty' has no 'holy bower' (127). As it is, the youth's presence is said to 'grace impiety' when he mixes with sinful people (67). Shakespeare's love-poetry, his own 'better part', is 'consecrate to thee' (74); he has 'hallow'd' his 'fair name' in verses which are as 'prayers divine' (108); and his own love is offered as an 'oblation' (125). The idealised boy is even called 'a god in love', and 'next my heaven the best' (110). He is the poet's 'better angel'. Adoration can go no further.

Such is the experience, or phenomenon, straining the sweetest and grandest symbols, natural, human, and divine, to do justice to 'this composed wonder of your frame' (59). It is preeminently an incarnate mystery or miracle, not unlike that symbolised by Dante's Gryphon in the *Purgatorio* (XXXI). The poetry gives us a close-up of the thing itself, not merely, as does Donne, of the supervening and enclosing experience. It is a marvel here and now, 'crowning the present', even though leaving us 'doubting of the rest' (115). For there can

be no permanence. That is our problem: the problem of *Troilus and Cressida, Hamlet, Othello, Timon of Athens, Antony and Cleopatra*. And yet, somehow, we feel that it should, indeed must, be permanent. The poet must say, and we applaud him for saying it, 'Love's not Time's fool' (116), but he fears, and so do we, that it may be. He starts a sonnet with 'To me, fair friend, you never can be old', but continues:

> Ah, yet doth beauty, like a dial-hand,
> Steal from his figure and no pace perceiv'd.
>
> (104)

Can both be true? One way or another, we shall surely come up against the agony of Troilus: 'This is, and is not, Cressid' [*Troilus and Cressida*, V. ii. 146]. On this torturing antithesis, the greatest passages of the Sonnets converge. (pp. 58-68)

> *G. Wilson Knight, "Symbolism," in his* The Mutual Flame: On Shakespeare's 'Sonnets' and 'The Phoenix and the Turtle', *Methuen & Co. Ltd., 1955, pp. 58-68.*

J. W. LEVER   (essay date 1956)

[*Lever closely examines Sonnets 127 to 152, arguing that this series is governed by satire. The satire, he demonstrates, moves in a "vicious descending spiral," beginning with parodies of pseudo-Petrarchan versifiers, but soon turning to cynicism, nihilism, and even "deliberate obscenity," as the poet struggles to extricate himself from the "emotional dilemma" of loving a woman who has neither virtue nor beauty. Although Lever views these poems as a "fierce diatribe against sexual infatuation," he notes that they describe only one aspect of Shakespeare's estimation of human nature. To achieve a complete*

Southampton in his captivity in the Tower of London, 1601-03.

and accurate perspective on the poet's attitude toward sensual, rational, and divine love, he argues, we must be cognizant of the "dual interpretation" operative throughout the entire sequence of Shakespeare's sonnets.]

[Sonnets CXXVII to CLII in the 1609 Quarto] are an extremely disordered group. Clearly CXXIX ('The expense of spirit') wastes its passions on the desert air between such dwarf shrubs as CXXVIII and CXXX ('How oft when thou, my music', and 'My mistress' eyes'). Nor has the painful self-probing of CXLII ('Love is my sin') much in common with the farmyard conceit and the 'Will' quibble of CXLIII ('Lo, as a careful housewife'). Even the integrity of the series is doubtful. In style, imagery and content, CXXXIX and CXL are more closely related to the group in the main series on the Friend's Fault; while XXI continues the argument of CXXX and is best understood as part of the Mistress series. Since rearrangement cannot be helped, I shall take the lighter eulogies of the Mistress as beginning the series, and proceed by way of the 'Will' conceits to the sonnets of remorse and atonement which seem the only possible ending to the story.

Satire governs the whole course of the series. Sometimes it has a swift, rapier-like thrust; more commonly, it operates like the heavy, old-English broadsword. Satire charged with emotion brings together obscenity and earnestness, savage invective and cynical humour; so that often the assailant is liable to be injured as much as his antagonist. While the opening sonnets show a surface elegance, there is a rapid descent to deeper and murkier levels. In outline the story is broadly reminiscent of [Sir Philip Sidney's] *Astrophel and Stella,* describing an infatuation that is lightly entered upon, but leads to an ever sharper cleavage between conscience and desire, until the affair is dissolved on a note of profound remorse. But Sidney was reinterpreting the romance experience through contemporary life and ideas; Shakespeare consciously aimed at negating all its values. Therefore the resemblance of the Mistress series to *Astrophel and Stella* was rather like that of a parody to its original, and the more nearly Shakespeare's sonnets came to suggesting Sidney's, the more sharply their essential differences stood out.

Tradition required that the sonnet sequence should open with a panegyric to the lady's beauty. In the sonnets describing the Mistress, each item in the usual catalogue of charms was coupled with a negative. Her eyes were nothing like the sun, her lips were not as red as coral, her cheeks had no roses, and her breath was not perfumed. Occasional burlesques of the Petrarchan heroine were nothing new; even Sidney, imitating Berni, included one in the *Arcadia.* But for Shakespeare the real target was the fashionable minor sonneteer, Barnes or Lodge or Constable, not the Mistress herself, who was hardly to blame for their hyperbolical praises. Of course she was no Diana, or any other 'goddess' walking the sky: when *she* walked she trod the ground, as was merely natural. Sonnet CXXX ended with a deliberate paradox:

> And yet by heaven, I think my love as rare
> As any she belied with false compare.

Calling the Mistress as rare as anyone else was an Irishism, the Elizabethan equivalent of declarations that all animals are equal, but some more equal than others. Romance was democratized as never before—yet again the satire was directed at sham-Petrarchanism rather than at the Mistress. The lesson was driven home in XXI ('So is it not with me as with that Muse') and again in CXXVII ('In the old age black was not counted fair'). Constable's *Diana* certainly used

heaven itself for ornament, and in their wider implication these sonnets damned the whole tribe of late-Elizabethan sonneteers. Shakespeare would not praise because he purposed not to sell: the word 'praise' having a secondary meaning of valuing or fixing a price: as much as to say that the conventional sonnet-writer was acting as a procurer for his painted beauty. In contrast to such ladies with their cosmetic charms the natural black colouring of the Mistress was a badge of mourning at the falsehood of the times. Sidney too had scoffed, though less cruelly, at the euphuists of the previous decade who 'with strange similes enrich each line'; but this had only demonstrated the supreme power of Stella, who was so direct an inspiration that no conscious art was needed:

> . . . in *Stellas* face I read
> What Love and Beautie be, then all my deed
> But copying is, what in her Nature writes.

Shakespeare's conclusion to XXI made an instructive contrast:

> O let me, true in love, but truly write,
> And then believe me, my love is as fair
> As any mother's child, though not so bright
> As those gold candles fix'd in heaven's air.

His mistress was no 'poem', nor was she star-like—as Stella's name signified. Her beauty was a general earthly phenomenon, and his truthful description of it was also 'natural', since it made no claim to inspiration.

It is strange that the Mistress is frequently thought of as a painted courtesan, black as sin, but daubed and dyed with cosmetics, exercising an irresistible sensual appeal. This is surely an absurdity. The sonnets describing her all stress her unostentatious appearance and her contempt for artificial aids to beauty. Her main appeal for the Poet was indeed her 'naturalness'. She was as fair as any mother's child; no more, and also no less. It was the heroines encumbered with the attributes of ideal beauty who really depended on false adornment, as did the versifiers with their sham-Platonic claims to inspiration. Such is the initial case made out for the Mistress. Unfortunately for the Poet, this refreshing 'naturalness' has a deeper and more sinister meaning, and the satire against artificiality will prove to be double-edged.

The troubles begin as soon as the Poet turns from physical to moral considerations. The second pillar of the traditional sequence was always the lady's virtue, whether it was deemed transcendental or, as more often in England, judged empirically by effects. Here the premise of virtue itself is denied. Berowne's description of the dark lady he loved may be recalled:

> A wightly wanton with a velvet brow,
> With two pitch balls stuck in her face for eyes;
> Ay, and by heaven, one that will do the deed
> Though Argus were her eunuch and her guard.
>   [*Love's Labour's Lost,* III. i. 196-99]

This was slanderously inappropriate to the Rosaline of *Love's Labour's Lost,* but oddly relevant to the Mistress of the series. The transition from black eyes to black heart was made in CXXXI ('Thou art as tyrannous'). Sidney's Stella had shown 'how virtue may best lodg'd in beauty be', and 'all minds', drawn by her beauty, had been moved that way. In contrast, Shakespeare's Mistress only seemed fair to the poet's 'dear doting heart': for others, her face had not the power to make love groan. The Poet's defence of his own love was equivocal. A thousand groans bore witness that her black was fairest in his 'judgment's place'. Yet as everyone knew, the heart was not the place for true judgement. It was the seat of affections, actual or imaginary; it did not decide matters of fact. The argument was entirely subjective and fallible, pointing to a condition where reason had absconded before passion; and the couplet stated the objective truth:

> In nothing art thou black save in thy deeds,
> And thence this slander, as I think, proceeds.

This sting in the tail, while leaving the Mistress's beauty for the heart to judge, admitted that her evil deeds were self-evident.

The satire now moves in a vicious descending spiral. The Poet's love for a mistress without beauty or virtue persists, though consciously based upon illusion. She does not even afford him sensuous pleasure: neither sight, nor any other of the five senses, receives any satisfaction from her presence (CXLI). Yet his heart is enslaved, leaving him behind as the mere 'likeness of a man'. Here the traditional eyes-heart imagery serves to describe a hopeless state of inner conflict. The eyes deceive themselves; the heart's promptings run contrary to the heart's knowledge.

> If eyes corrupt by over-partial looks
> Be anchor'd in the bay where all men ride,
> Why of eyes' falsehood hast thou forged hooks,
> Whereto the judgment of my heart is tied?
> Why should my heart think that a several plot
> Which my heart knows the wide world's common
>   place?
>
> [Sonnet CXXXVII]

When Shakespeare is caught in an emotional dilemma, his images become a medley of undisciplined associations. The archetypal female image of the bay represents the Mistress. While all men 'ride' there, coming and going freely (the verb has an obvious sexual innuendo), the Poet's eyes are anchored and he cannot float out to sea. His heart, submerged beneath the waters, is caught on hooks like a fish; finally the bay itself becomes dry land, a common which his heart had thought to be private ground. The main concern now is not the Mistress's beauty or virtue, but the Poet's awareness of his own psychical disruption.

With this awareness, a certain cool cynicism appears. Committed to 'nature', the Poet rationalizes his relationship at its lowest level.

> When my love swears that she is made of truth,
> I do believe her, though I know she lies . . .
>
> [Sonnet CXXXVIII]

She protests too much: he knows that she is lying; and she knows he knows. But he too has a secret fear. He is ageing, and his days are 'past the best'. Therefore he will act the ingenuous youth and pretend to believe her; while she, who can readily see through his pretence, will let herself be so deceived. On this new basis of mutual mistrust the idyll is resumed, and with tongue in cheek the Poet commends it as an example to others:

> Therefore I lie with her, and she with me,
> And in our faults by lies we flattered be.

The pun drives to the core of the whole affair. One lies and is thus lain with: falsehood and the act of love, described by one word, are made synonymous.

Moral nihilism passes over into deliberate obscenity in CLI where the Poet answers a reproach from the Mistress that he lacks 'conscience'. He chooses to give the word its special amoral connotation of 'knowing', and explains how this is bound up with the sexual act:

> My soul doth tell my body that he may
> Triumph in love: flesh stays no further reason . . .

The 'insurrection of the flesh', theme of many moral diatribes, here takes on an entirely forthright, priapic quality. Sidney's personified categories of the soul are transposed to the physiology of sex. According to this view of 'conscience', the function of intellect and soul is to act as bawds to the flesh.

To the nadir of the spiral belongs the masochistic satire of the 'Will' sonnets, CXXXV and CXXXVI. Courtship has become a joyless mating of human animals in rut. The Poet pleads with the Mistress: having had so many men, why not add one more? His name is Will, which means lust—why not accept him for his name's sake? The word is repeated like an obsessive formula that serves to obliterate personality. Both Poet and Mistress are reduced to featureless sex-partners, the forerunners of Apeneck Sweeney and the Lady in the Cape. Again the sea image appears, to suggest the primordial female, passive and undiscriminating.

> The sea, all water, yet receives rain still . . .
>
> [Sonnet CXXXV]

There is no question of being jealous of rivals, so long as the Poet is received with all the rest.

But in CXLIV there is a major development. From the mass of unidentified sharers of the Mistress emerges one figure whose moral welfare is endangered.

> Two loves I have of comfort and despair,
> Which like two spirits do suggest me still:
> The better angel is a man right fair,
> The worser spirit a woman colour'd ill.

It is evidently the Friend, and his appearance in this sonnet, as well as in CXXXIII and CXXXIV, provides the thematic link with the main series. The moral issues that the Poet had thrust out of sight in his own case at once present themselves when the Friend is involved. Instead of ambiguities there are clearcut distinctions: the man is fair, the woman dark, in deeds as well as appearance; and between his purity and her 'pride' is the difference between saint and devil. The Poet's suppressed self-hatred is now turned against the woman for corrupting the Friend to whom his better nature is committed:

> Beshrew that heart that makes my heart to groan
> For that deep wound it gives my friend and me!
> Is't not enough to torture me alone
> But slave to slavery my sweet'st friend must be?
>
> [Sonnet CXXXIII]

Here and in CXXXIV there is an intrusion of dramatic conceits. The Poet asks to go bail for his Friend and be imprisoned himself in the Mistress's 'steel bosom's ward'; he claims that the Friend merely stood as surety for the bond with which, like a usurer, she now binds him. These conceits recall actual plot situations in *The Merchant of Venice,* and the analogy is hardly a coincidence. . . . (pp. 174-80)

With this extension of the theme and its clarification of moral issues comes a painful return to normality. Desire is seen as a wasting fever, consuming both body and mind. The conventional image only serves to mark an essentially different approach. While the romance lover, sick for his lady, considered her the only doctor who could cure him, for Shakespeare's poet Reason is the true physician:

> My reason, the physician to my love,
> Angry that his prescriptions are not kept,
> Hath left me, and I desperate now approve
> Desire is death which physic did except.
>
> [Sonnet CXLVII]

Actually the lucid diagnosis of his 'frantic mad' condition is a hopeful symptom, leading to a recovery of spiritual health.

The series ends with familiar palinodes. 'Desire is death'; and in a fury of invective the Poet purges himself of its bitter fruits:

> The expense of spirit in a waste of shame
> Is lust in action . . .
>
> [Sonnet CXXIX]

Perjured, murderous, bloody, savage, rude—the epithets are flung out in a torrent, sweeping away the logic of the quatrain structure and shaping a new course in the verse paragraph. CXXIX is a dramatic monologue rather than a sonnet, with its rhetorical patterning of internal pauses and run-over lines, and its structure of assonance. The Christian antinomies, saint-devil, heaven-hell, spirit-flesh, have progressively asserted themselves in these last sonnets. In conclusion—for it is the one possible finale to the series—the Poet addresses his soul, 'the centre of my sinful earth', and bids it subdue his body:

> Then soul, live thou upon thy servant's loss,
> And let that pine to aggravate thy store:
> Buy terms divine in selling hours of dross;
> Within be fed, without be rich no more:
>   So shalt thou feed on Death, that feeds on men,
>   And Death once dead, there's no more dying
>   then.
>
> [Sonnet CXLVI]

In content, in form, and in their relation to the series, CXXIX and CXLVI are clearly analogous to Sidney's 'Thou blind mans mark' and 'Leaue me, ô Loue'. Desire is castigated in similar terms, and the contrast between sensual and divine love marked out with the same antithetical phrases. Yet the subordinate images of loss and store, buying and selling, with the final, Hamlet-like conceit urging the soul to feed on death (and so cheat the politic worm of its supper), are typically Shakespearean. They maintain the critical and satirical tone of the series to the last.

No ordinarily sensitive reader can doubt that these sonnets have roots in a real and painful experience. But it is by their poetic fruits that we must judge them; by their articulation of the mind of their age, and by their contribution to its outlook. The fierce diatribe against sexual infatuation only brought within the compass of the sonnet ideas which the Neoplatonists of the sixteenth century, notably Bembo and Castiglione, had already expressed in prose concerning *l'amor sensuale,* as compared with the higher relationships of love rational and love divine. Spenser, it might be claimed, had partly anticipated Shakespeare's approach in the sonnets to a Medusa-like mistress which were intermingled with the *Amoretti,* and which stood in much the same relationship to

his sequence as these sonnets do to Shakespeare's main series. For Spenser as well as Shakespeare, the opposition of spirit and flesh, with its deep appeal to the English mind, lay below the stratum of contemporary ideas. It was easier for each poet in his own way to break from the romance tradition of the sonnet than it was for the Italians, who for all their Platonist theorizing, continued to write sequences essentially in the Petrarchan mould. Yet the conscious motivation of Shakespeare's Mistress series was neither Platonic doctrine nor Christian beliefs, but a contemporary empiricism that rejected ideal premises, and through the greater part of the sonnets was content to interpret love as a lust of the blood and a permission of the will. Nature, unadorned and unashamed, was the true force that instigated this courtship.

Nevertheless in Shakespeare's view of life two conceptions of nature were equally valid, and one of them was creative and benevolent. The nihilistic, descending spiral was not the only possible course for love to follow: had it been so, his greatest dramas could never have been written. We shall not fully understand the Mistress sonnets unless we read them in association with the main series to the Friend, and it will . . . be wise to avoid too schematic a contrast between the abstractions of 'love sensual' and 'love rational'. The love for the Mistress, sensual as it may be, contains a large admixture of cold intellectualism. Nor . . . is the friendship wholly rational in its essence. Rather should we prepare to find a dual interpretation of nature and human nature operative throughout the *Sonnets,* giving rise to contradictory and changing responses, and deeply involving Shakespeare's total attitude to life. (pp. 180-82)

> *J. W. Lever, "Shakespeare," in his* The Elizabethan
> Love Sonnet, *Methuen & Co. Ltd., 1956, pp. 162-
> 272.*

M. M. MAHOOD   (essay date 1957)

[*Mahood evaluates the wordplay in a selection of the sonnets, contending that Shakespeare's verbal wit is most effective when he is writing "at a satisfying dramatic distance" from "the experience behind the poem," and when he is able to link the wordplay directly to the sonnet's structure. In most of the verses addressed to the youth, the critic maintains, Shakespeare's conflicting feelings deter him from ordering his experiences into a well-constructed work of art. Mahood finds the sonnets about the Rival Poet and those addressed to the Dark Lady much more "formally satisfying." In many of these, she points out, the irony is fully developed, and a subtle use of wordplay allows Shakespeare to control the counter-movement of thought from the quatrains to the final couplet.*]

The nature of the wordplay in the Sonnets varies according to whether Shakespeare is too remote or too near the experience behind the poem or whether he is at a satisfying dramatic distance from it. When he is detached, the wordplay is a consciously used, hard-worked rhetorical device. When his complexity of feeling upon the occasion of a sonnet is not fully realised by him, the wordplay often reveals an emotional undercurrent which was perhaps hidden from the poet himself. But in the best sonnets the wordplay is neither involuntary nor wilful; it is a skilfully handled means whereby Shakespeare makes explicit both his conflict of feelings and his resolution of the conflict.

Since the publication of [Sir Philip Sydney's] *Astrophel and Stella,* readers had expected a fair measure of deliberately witty puns in a sonnet sequence, and many of Shakespeare's are this kind of embellishment. The first quatrain of the first Sonnet ends with a pretty paronomasia:

> From fairest creatures we desire increase,
> That thereby beauties Rose might neuer die,
> But as the riper should by time decease,
> His *tender heire* might *beare* his memory,

where the learned might spot a concealed Latin pun in *tender heir;* it was a bad one, but could be found in Holinshed, and Shakespeare was to use it later himself in *Cymbeline:*

> The peece of tender Ayre, thy vertuous Daughter
> Which we call Mollis Aer, and Mollis Aer
> We terme it Mulier; which Mulier I diuine
> Is this most constant Wife.
>
>   [V. v. 446-49]

A similar pun on *husbandry* helps Shakespeare to ring rhetorical changes in the first seventeen sonnets on his advice to the young man to marry and have children. In many of these, Shakespeare's feelings are to some degree engaged, and the wordplay is structural and effective. But in less happy 'conceited' sonnets, the puns propel the thought instead of expressing it;

> Mine eye hath play'd the painter and hath steeld
> Thy beauties forme in *table* of my heart,
> My body is the *frame* wherein 'tis held,
> And *perspectiue* it is best Painters art. . . .
>
>   (24)

After such an ill-knit beginning it is not surprising that the poet gets into a hopeless tangle in the second quatrain:

> For through the Painter must you see his skill,
> To finde where your true Image pictur'd lies,
> Which in my bosomes shop is hanging stil,
> That hath his windowes glazed with thine eyes.

Are the windows of this last line the poet's eyes through which the friend looks into his heart? If so, they cannot also belong to the Painter busy inside the shop. But if they are the eyes of the image which the poet carries in his heart, the friend must be looking into his own inside. Whatever sense we try to make of the passage, the resultant image is pure Bosch, an anatomical horror; and while it must be allowed that the best images are often the least picturable, it is difficult not to visualise an image taken from the visual arts. In other unsuccessful sonnets, Shakespeare's habit of hoisting himself up by a word's double meaning when his poetic élan fails him results, not in confusion as here, but in a mechanical consistency. Sonnet 46 begins with the most conventional of poetic themes:

> Mine eye and heart are at a mortall warre,
> How to deuide the *conquest* of thy sight.

In a dogged attempt to give novelty to the theme, Shakespeare seizes upon the legal meaning of *conquest*—'the personal acquisition of real property otherwise than by inheritance', and turns the poem into an elaborate forensic allegory with the help of further puns on *side,* meaning 'to decide' and also 'to assign to one of two sides or parties', and on *quest* in its chivalric meaning of adventurous search and its legal sense of 'inquiry upon the oaths of an empanelled jury'. Love as a lawsuit can never have had, even for the litigious Elizabethans, any of the poetic force of love conceived as war, and this conceit upon a conceit palls long before we have reached the end of the sonnet.

In the first of these examples the image was enforcedly pictorial, and in the second it was elaborately consistent. But Shakespeare's most telling imagery is scarcely ever visual; and it is nearly always made complex by such a fusion of ideas as occurs in Lady Macbeth's 'Was the hope drunke Wherein you drest your selfe?' [*Macbeth,* I. vii. 35-6]. Such imagery as this abounds in the finest of the sonnets, where the wordplay, instead of serving to multiply unrealised images, gives verbal cohesion to images which are already fused in the heat of Shakespeare's imagination. The opening of Sonnet 2 is an illustration:

> When fortie Winters shall beseige thy brow,
> And digge deep trenches in thy beauties *field,*
> Thy youthes proud liuery so gaz'd on now,
> Wil be a totter'd *weed* of smal worth held.

Three senses of *field,* a battlefield, an agricultural field, and the surface of a shield, together with *weed* as both tare and dress, serve to bring the figure of Time the Warrior into association with the more powerful and traditional personification of Time the Reaper, and so prepare us for the sestet of the sonnet. Time reaps, but he also sows; by begetting children the youth can be new made when he is old. The same figure of the Reaper enters Sonnet 116, and here the function of the second, inadmissible meaning of *compass* together with the wordplay of *bear out* (which might mean 'steer a course') is to keep before us in the sestet the octave's powerful navigation image, which might otherwise be effaced by the double personification of Love and Time:

> Let me not to the marriage of true mindes
> Admit impediments, loue is not loue
> Which alters when it alteration findes,
> Or bends with the remouer to remoue.
> O no, it is an euer fixed marke
> That lookes on tempests and is neuer shaken;
> It is the star to euery wandring barke,
> Whose worths vnknowne, although his higth be
>   taken.
> Loue's not Times foole, though rosie lips and
>   cheeks
> Within his bending sickles *compasse* come,
> Loue alters not with his breefe houres and weekes,
> But *beares it out* euen to the edge of doome:
>   If this be error and vpon me proued,
>   I neuer writ, nor no man euer loued.

The same cluster of images recurs in Sonnet 60, and here again the wordplay helps to fuse the metaphors into an imaginative whole:

> Like as the waues make towards the pibled shore,
> So do our minuites hasten to their end,
> Each changing place with that which goes before,
> In sequent toile all forwards do contend.
> *Natiuity* once in the *maine* of light,
> Crawles to maturity, wherewith being *crown'd,*
> *Crooked* eclipses gainst his *glory* fight,
> And time that gaue, doth now his gift confound.
> Time doth transfixe the *florish* set on youth,
> And delues the *paralels* in beauties brow,
> Feedes on the rarities of natures truth,
> And nothing stands but for his sieth to mow.
>   And yet to times in hope, my verse shall *stand*
>   Praising thy worth, dispight his cruell *hand.*

By contrast with the awkward huddle of images at the beginning of Sonnet 24, the start of this is controlled and steady; the first image of minutes as waves is displayed slowly, as if to reassure the reader and win his co-operation for the complex movements of thought which follow in the second and third quatrains. In the fifth line, the word *main* connects the opening image of the sea with the shining sphere of light into which a planet is launched at its ascendant, while *crawls* reflects back on nativity a second meaning of 'child'. In the double image of the infant on the floor and the sun mounting the heavens there is just that blend of the mundane and the cosmic which constitutes the *feliciter audax* [happy valiancy] of Shakespeare's mature style—we meet it everywhere in *Antony and Cleopatra*—and the unity of the images is kept by the double meaning of *glory* which is both an aureole and the pride of manhood. *Crooked,* in its figurative sense of 'malignant' belongs to the astrological figure, while its literal sense evokes the pictorial image of the sliver of an eclipsed sun, curved like a scythe, and so leads us inevitably to the figure of Time the Reaper in the third quatrain. Conversely, *parallels* (in line 10), by recalling the lines of latitude on a celestial globe, harks back to the astrological image. *Flourish* may retain its original meaning of the blossom on a fruit tree, which would give a subsidiary sense to *crown'd* (the crown is the leafy part of a tree); the dominant meaning of *flourish* is probably the figurative one of vigour, prime, perfection, but the calligraphic sense—'a decoration or ornament achieved with a sweep of the pen'—prepares us for the poet's defiance of Time's *hand* in the last couplet; and here the dead metaphor in *stand* is resuscitated to suggest that Shakespeare's praise of his friend is one thing too tough for Time's scythe.

Sonnet 49 will furnish a vivid example of wordplay which reveals an unresolved and painful tension in Shakespeare's feelings for his friend:

> Against that time (if euer that time come)
> When I shall see thee frowne on my defects,
> When as thy loue hath *cast* his vtmost *summe,*
> Cauld to that audite by *aduis'd respects,*
> Against that time when thou shalt *strangely* passe,
> And scarcely greete me with that sunne thine eye,
> When loue conuerted from the thing it was
> Shall reasons finde of setled grauitie.
> Against that time do I insconce me here
> Within the knowledge of mine owne *desart,*
> And this my *hand,* against my selfe vpreare,
> To guard the lawfull reasons on thy part,
>   To leaue *poore* me, thou hast the strength of lawes,
>   Since why to loue, I can alledge no cause.

The second quatrain of this is the rejection of Falstaff in little. The parallel is strengthened by the sun image (as in Hal's 'Yet heerein will I imitate the Sunne' [*1 Henry IV,* I. ii. 197]) and by the way *gravity* calls to mind the Lord Chief Justice's reproach to Falstaff: 'There is not a white haire on your face, but shold haue his effect of grauity [*2 Henry IV,* I. ii. 160-61]. And our divided feelings towards Hal in his premeditated rejection of his old companion are exactly matched by the divided feelings in the wordplay of this sonnet. What distresses the poet about his friend and what distresses us about Hal is not the inevitable gesture of repudiation, but the cold deliberation with which it is prepared. The image of the third line is one of calculation, if we take the words to mean: 'reckoned up your expenditure of affection'. But there's beggary in the love that can be uttered; and the phrase *cast his utmost sum* can also suggest a love that is poured out without counting upon any return, a love such as the poet has lavished on the youth. *Advised respects* in the next line is glossed by Palgrave 'considerations formed by reflection', and, taken in this sense, the words imply a kind of rueful admiration; but they can

also mean 'a prompted, or suggested, consideration of our respective social positions', which would be something far less admirable although, in the late sixteenth century, not easy to evade. While the unemotive meaning of *strangely*—'as a stranger'—represents Shakespeare's effort to understand and justify his friend's coldness, the emotive meaning of the word voices his hurt bewilderment. At the same time, the ambiguity of *deserts* (compare 'As to behold desert a begger borne', in Sonnet 66, with Hamlet's 'Vse euerie man after his desart, and who should scape whipping?' [*Hamlet,* II. ii. 529-30]) shows that the poet's self-abasement has its reservations. In the penultimate line some critical bitterness blends with the abject tone if we read *poor* as cause rather than effect of the writer being abandoned. Finally, the grammatical uncertainty of the last line, taken together with the various meanings of *cause,* sums up all Shakespeare's turmoil of feelings towards his friend. 'I cannot produce any assertible claim for your love. But my love for you is generous, uncalculating, unrestrained, for who can give a lover any law? And if I do not meet with an equally strong love in you, if you are as cold and calculating as I sometimes fear, my love will be without justification.'

This fear that his friend is not worth all the affection that he has spent upon him finds an outlet in unconscious puns in other sonnets: in, for example, the phrase: 'Thou best of *deerest,* and mine onely *care*' in Sonnet 48, or in the opening of Sonnet 67: 'Ah wherefore with infection should he liue', where the implication that the friend is indeed a lily that has festered is not quite effaced by the next line: 'And with his presence grace impietie?' 'Th' expence of Spirit in a waste of shame' [Sonnet 129] is to Shakespeare a less painful, because a more clearly understood, experience than this expenditure of love upon someone whom we, with him, suspect to be a brilliant, prudent, calculating egotist. In the plays some of the anguish of this situation is reflected in Antonio's devotion to Bassanio in *The Merchant of Venice* or that of another Antonio (the identity of names is telling) for Sebastian in *Twelfth Night.* The bitterness which underlies the submerged wordplay of many sonnets invades and nearly shatters the comic mood of *Twelfth Night* when Antonio, mistaking Viola for Sebastian, thinks he has been abandoned by his friend:

> Let me speake a little. This youth that you see heere,
> I snatch'd one halfe out of the iawes of death,
> Releeued him with such sanctitie of loue;
> And to his image, which me thought did promise
> Most venerable worth, did I deuotion.
>   . . . . .
> But oh, how vilde an idoll proues this God:
> Thou hast Sebastian done good feature, shame.
> In Nature, there's no blemish but the minde:
> None can be call'd deform'd, but the vnkinde.
> Vertue is beauty, but the beauteous euill
> Are empty trunkes, ore-flourish'd by the deuill.
>   [III. iv. 359-70]

A fear such as this, that the friend he has entertained for a Horatio because he seems not to be passion's slave, may in fact be an Angelo, makes Sonnet 94 one of the most involved and difficult in the sequence:

> They that haue powre to hurt, and will doe none,
> That doe not do the thing, they most do showe,
> Who mouing others, are themselues as stone,
> Vnmooued, could, and to temptation slow:
> They rightly do inherrit heauens graces,

And husband natures ritches from expence,
They are the Lords and owners of their faces,
Others, but stewards of their excellence:
The sommers flowre is to the sommer sweet,
Though to it selfe, it onely liue and die,
But if that flowre with base infection meete,
The basest weed out-braues his dignity:
    For sweetest things turne sowrest by their
      deedes,
    Lillies that fester, smell far worse then weeds.

If this is praise, it is the most back-handed of compliments, for there is doubtful merit in being cold like a stone and in the narcissic self-enjoyment of living and dying to oneself. The antithesis of lord and steward is another teasing image, for it suggests that the paragon who is the object of all this praise has appropriated talents which are lent and not given. There is here an undercurrent of warning: such a warning as the Duke speaks to Angelo at the beginning of *Measure for Measure:*

                Thy selfe, and thy belongings,
Are not thine own so proper, as to waste
Thy selfe vpon thy vertues; they on thee
Heauen doth with vs, as we, with Torches doe,
Not light them for themselues: For if our vertues
Did not goe forth of vs, 'twere all alike
As if we had them not: Spirits are not finely
    touch'd,
But to fine issues: nor nature neuer lends
The smallest scruple of her excellence,
But like a thrifty goddesse, she determines
Her selfe the glory of a creditour,
Both thanks, and vse.

                            [I. i. 29-40]

Measure for Measure seems to me a great but unsatisfactory play for the same reason that Sonnet 94 is, on its own scale, a great but unsatisfactory poem: in each case Shakespeare is emotionally too involved in the situation to achieve a dramatic clarification of its issues. He was perhaps drawn to the existing versions of the *Measure for Measure* story by the dramatic potentialities in the character he calls Angelo: the self-centred, self-sufficient man who makes a tragic discovery of his own weakness. The story, however, compelled Shakespeare to make the centre of interest the clash between Angelo's hypocrisy and Isabella's integrity whereas the play's fundamental conflict is less a moral than a psychic one, and is summed up in the confrontation of the Duke's Innocent-the-Third asceticism in the 'Be absolute for death' speech with the affirmation of life in Claudio's outcry: 'I, but to die, and go we know not where!' [*Measure for Measure,* III. i. 5-41, 117] A play can quite well embody a psychic alongside a moral conflict, but here the two issues do not correspond. Shakespeare is on Isabella's side in the moral conflict, since he and his audience believe the soul matters more than the body; but he cannot side with her in the psychic conflict because virginity could never seem to him the positive good it appeared to Spenser and Milton. For Shakespeare there could be no doubt that it was better to live and give life than to die, or to live in a way that amounted to a refusal of life. Right at the end of the play, Shakespeare manages to identify Isabella with the affirmative principle by having her ask pardon and life for Angelo. But until then, that principle has to make itself felt in other ways; in, for instance, the nearly silent figure of Juliet serenely carrying Claudio's child, or in the tolerant treatment of Pompey—'a poore fellow that would liue' [*Measure for Measure,* II. i. 223].

Sonnet 94, like several others in the series, originates from a similar confusion of feelings. Shakespeare, who has himself been a motley to the view, is torn between admiration for those who are able to keep themselves detached and seemingly unspotted from the world, and the misgiving that such people may be incapable of the good passions as well as the bad. The equipoise of admiration and distrust is especially delicate in the first seventeen sonnets, written, if we can trust the chronology of the sequence, while the youth's self-sufficiency still appeared wholly virtuous and the poet had not yet discovered that 'suns of the world may stain' [Sonnet 33]. There is repeated play in these first sonnets upon the word *use,* because its three main senses—'employment', 'wear and tear' and 'usury'—suggest a contemporary moral dilemma which acts as a vivid metaphor of Shakespeare's divided feelings towards his friend. It had long been forbidden by the Church, on the authority of Scripture, to make money breed by taking interest for it; but changing economic conditions were driving the Elizabethans to find scriptural warrant for the practice in such passages as the Parable of the Talents. That story, echoed in the speech already quoted from *Measure for Measure,* and in Sonnet 94, is also recalled in Sonnet 11:

    Looke whom she [that is, nature] best indow'd, she
      gaue the more;
    Which bountious guift thou shouldst in bounty
      cherrish.

Repeatedly, through these first seventeen sonnets, Shakespeare thus makes use of the contemporary bewilderment over the ethics of usury to define his own torn emotions about his friend. Fear of the other's inherent selfish coldness makes him urge the youth to put his gifts to use by marrying and begetting children:

    Profitles *vserer* why doost thou *vse*
    So great a summe of summes yet can'st not liue? (4)

    That *vse* is not forbidden vsery,
    Which happies those that pay the willing lone. (6)

    Looke what a vnthrift in the world doth spend
    Shifts but his place, for still the world inioyes it
    But beauties waste hath in the world an end,
    And kept *vnvsde* the *vser* so destroyes it. (9)

Another powerful pun through which Shakespeare conveys, on the one hand, his grudging admiration for his friend's self-sufficiency and, on the other, his longing that he may show some readiness to give himself, is that on *husband* and *husbandry.* In what sense was it meritorious to 'husband natures riches from expence'? *Husbandry* can mean saving, economy, as in Banquo's 'There's Husbandry in Heauen, Their Candles are all out' [*Macbeth,* II. i. 4], or it can mean the outlay of cost and labour that brings forth the fruits of the earth. An association through metaphor of this last meaning with the theme of marriage—as in Enobarbus's 'He plough'd her and she cropp'd' [*Antony and Cleopatra,* II. i. 4] —strengthens the association of ideas through wordplay:

    Who lets so faire a house fall to decay
    Which *husbandry* in honour might vphold? (13)

The paradox that only by spending can we save, which underlies Shakespeare's use of *husbandry* and *usury,* is expressed in yet another image in Sonnet 5:

    Then were not summers distillation left
    A liquid prisoner pent in walls of glasse,
    Beauties effect with beautie were bereft,

Nor it nor noe remembrance what it was.
But flowers distil'd though they with winter meete,
Leese but their show, their substance still liues sweet.

The same metaphor is to be met with in *A Midsummer Night's Dream,* where Theseus warns Hermia that if she does not concur with her father's wishes she must live as a vestal virgin:

Chanting faint hymnes to the cold fruitlesse Moone,
Thrice blessed they that master so their blood,
To vndergo such maiden pilgrimage,
But earthlier happie is the Rose distil'd,
Than that which withering on the virgin thorne,
Growes, liues, and dies, in single blessednesse.

[I. i. 73-8]

The image here suggests the same conflict between traditional moral or religious ideas and strong personal feelings grounded on experience which is found in *Measure for Measure.* Traditionally, the rose plucked stood for present pleasure, and we should expect the rose distilled to stand (as in Herbert's *The Nose-gay*) for the treasure laid up in heaven. The vital opposition for Shakespeare, however, is not between earthly and heavenly, but between the selfish and the generous; and he identifies procreative love with the rose distilled. The meanings given to the word *virtue* in the Sonnets accord with the same distinction. Virtue is not the cold disinclination to passion such as is seen in those who are lords and owners of their faces; it is an active principle, like the *virtue* or healing property of plants and precious stones. The final couplet of Sonnet 93, immediately preceding 'They that have power', makes full play with these meanings:

How like Eaues apple doth thy beauty grow
If thy sweet *virtue* answere not thy show.

At the worst, as Shakespeare here implies, the youth's cool self-possession masks a corrupt heart. And at the best it makes him no better than the canker-roses of which he writes in Sonnet 54:

But for their *virtue* only is their show,
They liue vnwoo'd, and vnrespected fade,
Die to themselues. Sweet Roses doe not so,
Of their sweet deathes, are sweetest odors made.

Shakespeare's feelings about his friend are for the most part too confused to make a shapely sonnet. The interplay of mixed feelings in the sonnets on the woman, on time and poetry, and on the rival poet, are conflicts understood and expressed with a confident wit. But the complex relationship of the poet and the youth is further involved with other relationships: that of player to rich patron and, since the youth represents many things Shakespeare lacks and craves in his own personality, Shakespeare's quarrel with himself. When Shakespeare thus unlocks his heart, it is to reveal its stores in disarray. In only a few of the poems addressed to the youth are these stored experiences ordered into a work of art.

The difficulty confronting us at this point is that any separation of the successful from the unsuccessful sonnets is bound to seem, at worst, an arbitrary and very personal choice and, at the best, to be based on criteria which are not universally acceptable. Thus John Crowe Ransom distinguishes as goats among the sonnets the 'associationist' ones which provide 'many charming resting-places for the feelings to agitate

themselves', and, as sheep, the 'metaphysical' sonnets which go 'straight through to the completion of the cycle and extinction of the feelings' [see excerpt above, 1938]. For Mr Ransom, wordplay belongs to the poetry of association, and so the punning sonnets are among the unsuccessful ones. This view is, of course, based on a strictly kathartic theory of poetry; but probably the poetic theory more generally acceptable today is nearer to that of the seventeenth-century Aristotelians: the belief that poetry should communicate feeling, but feeling purified by being fully and finally comprehended—in fact, all that is summed up in Herbert's definition of prayer as 'The land of spices; something understood'. If this is our criterion, we shall look first in a sonnet, not for the kind of logic which could be reduced to a prose syllogism, but for a satisfying organisation of sound and sense that conveys the ordered movement of thought into which the emotion has been shaped.

The Shakespearean sonnet is not an easy form to handle. In an Italian form of sonnet, even one which, like Milton's 'On his Blindness', does not keep strictly to the divisions of octave and sestet, there is a marked ebb and flow of thought corresponding to two emotional impulses: in that case, despair and resignation. But the final couplet of the English sonnet is too brief to contain the entire counter-statement to the first three quatrains without giving the impression that the poet is trying to wrench the poem back on its course. If, however, the poet too anxiously anticipates the final turn of thought throughout the first twelve lines, the couplet loses its epigrammatic spring. A subdued sort of wordplay is a useful device to the poet in these circumstances. It allows him to introduce the counter-movement of thought before the reader is aware of its presence, so that the final couplet satisfies both by conscious surprise and by its fulfilment of a subconscious expectation. This is what happens in Sonnet 63:

Against my loue shall be as I am now
With times iniurious *hand* chrusht and ore-worne,
When houres haue dreind his blood and fild his brow
With *lines* and wrincles, when his youthfull morne
Hath *trauaild* on to Ages steepie night,
And all those beauties whereof now he's King
Are vanishing, or vanisht out of sight,
Stealing away the treasure of his Spring.
For such a time do I now fortifie
Against confounding Ages cruell knife,
That he shall neuer *cut* from memory
My sweet loues beauty, though my louers life.
His beautie shall in these blacke lines be seene,
And they shall liue, and he in them still greene.

The turn accomplished by the couplet from the theme of time destroying the youth's beauty to that of its preservation through poetry is skilfully prepared, throughout the preceding quatrains, by an oblique image of Time (or Time-Age, a composite figure) and the poet working in competition one with the other. Time defaces the young man's beauty by scribbling upon it or overscoring it, at the same time as the poet is making of it a speaking picture for posterity. This theme of writing or engraving is implicit in the subsidiary meanings of *hand* in line two, *lines* in line four, and *cut,* which can mean engrave. . . . *Trauaild,* one of Shakespeare's favourite portmanteau words, packed with the two meanings 'travelled' and 'travailed', helps here by introducing the ideas of effort; the poet's toil undoes the result of life's weary journey through time.

In Sonnet 65, the couplet's counter-statement is again carefully prepared in the preceding lines:

> Since brasse, nor stone, nor earth, nor boundlesse
>   sea,
> But sad mortallity ore-swaies their power,
> How with this rage shall beautie hold a plea,
> Whose *action* is no stronger then a flower?
> O how shall summers hunny breath hold out,
> Against the wrackfull siedge of battring dayes,
> When rocks impregnable are not so stoute,
> Nor gates of steele so strong but time decayes?
> O fearefull meditation, where alack,
> Shall times best Iewell *from* times chest lie hid?
> Or what strong hand can hold his swift foot back,
> Or who his *spoile* of beautie can forbid?
>   O none, vnlesse this miracle haue might,
>   That in black inck my loue may still shine bright.

The first four lines of this would be a strong rhetorical question, compelling our assent, were its compulsion not weakened by the double meaning of *action;* for while the action of beauty, taking the word in the sense of 'physical force', cannot compare with the resistance of brass and stone, the legal meaning of 'a process', induced by *plea* in the preceding line, hints that physical strength cannot deflect the course of justice and of the justicers above. There is a sense in which both flowers and summer are stronger than rocks, because they are endlessly renewed while rocks are continually eroded away; and with this in mind, we can read both lines three to four and lines five to eight as exclamations, rather than as rhetorical questions compelling a negative answer. The second quatrain can then be paraphrased: 'How successfully the renewing vitality of summer resists the assaults of time! Unassailable rocks and gates of steel are not as strong as it; on the contrary, time itself wears away.' And once our consent to these rhetorical questions has been weakened in this way, without our being aware of it, there may be some hesitation about our response to the next question:

> O fearefull meditation, where alack,
> Shall times best Iewell *from* times chest lie hid?

The ambiguity of *from* imparts two meanings to this: either 'Where can the best jewel that Time has produced out of his casket be hidden?' or 'Where can Time's jewel be hidden away so that it may not be put back into Time's chest, the grave?' Put in this second form, the question produces the inevitable answer that the youth's soul and body will be preserved by their immortality from Time—'the womb of all things and perhaps their grave'. This undertone is sustained by the quasireligious language of 'fearful meditation' and 'miracle', by the harrowing-of-hell notion in 'gates of steel' and by the opening lines' Apocalyptic imagery. Herbert would have developed this undertone into the poem's counter-statement, but Shakespeare is concerned with the immortality bestowed by art, and uses the religious theme only to make the reader receptive to his final claim. The ambiguity of *spoil* helps. It may mean 'spoiling', the ruination of time; but it suggests also precious plunder—gold and jewels—which is indestructible and in safe keeping. So the whole sonnet subtly prepares us for the claim made in the last couplet.

Another formally satisfying sonnet, the thirtieth, also uses an elaborate play of meaning to anticipate its confident end:

> When to the Sessions of sweet silent thought
> I sommon vp remembrance of things past,
> I sigh the lacke of many a thing I sought,

> And with old woes new waile my *deare* times waste:
> Then can I drowne an eye (vn-vs'd to flow)
> For *precious* friends hid in deaths dateles night,
> And weepe a fresh loues long since *canceld* woe,
> And mone th'*expence* of many a vannisht sight.
> Then can I greeue at greeuances *fore-gon*,
> And heauily from woe to woe *tell* ore
> The sad *account* of fore-bemoned mone,
> Which I new *pay* as if not *payd* before.
>   But if the while I thinke on thee (*deare* friend)
>   All losses are restord, and sorrowes end.

Sweet sets the tone of this in the first line. Shakespeare's melancholy is well-savoured. 'Summon' suggests that he is too judiciously detached from his memories for them to be painful to him, and this detachment is implicit in *dear, precious, cancelled, expense, tell, account, pay.* Besides their strongly felt meanings, these words all have neutral meanings which are as impersonal as book-keeping entries; *expense,* for example, means primarily 'the price paid', whereas in 'Th'expence of spirit' this meaning is subordinate to the emotive one. Even when an emotion is stated, the tone of the verse dissipates the force of the statement. 'Then can I greeue at greeuances foregon' has the suggestion of 'I could upset myself—if I tried'; the verbal jingle robs the line of any solemnity, and grievances *forgone* are repudiated and forgotten as well as simply past. This is not the anguish of a Francesca [in Dante's *La Divina Commedia*] over past happiness in days of misery, but the contemplation of old misfortunes in a happy time. Shakespeare's eye, in fact, is kept on the credit side of the ledger all through the poem, and when the *dear* friend is produced at the last we understand why this reverie over disaster has been far more sweet than bitter.

The sonnets in which Shakespeare's conflict of feelings is most clearly understood and so most poetically organised are the ones about the rival poet and these addressed to the dark woman. The poet is clearly an adversary whose skill Shakespeare respects at the same time as he is convinced of the superior strength and sincerity of his own verse, and these counterpoised feelings dance an ironic set of changes in a sonnet such as the eighty-fifth, which begins:

> My toung-tide Muse in manners holds her *still*,
> While comments of your praise richly compil'd
> Reserue their Character with goulden quill,
> And *precious* phrase by all the Muses fil'd.

According to the meanings we give *still* and *precious,* this says either: 'My Muse keeps silent as becomes her when other poets write so exquisitely well in your praise', or: 'My Muse, by her reticence, remains well-mannered whatever excesses of affectation other poets may commit in their praise of you.' Irony is pushed a stage further in the sonnets to the woman. Whereas the equivoques addressed to the youth are veiled by tact and compassion, those to the mistress are brutally obvious. She is 'rich in *Will'*, 'the wide worlds *common* place', 'the *baye* where all men *ride*' [Sonnets 135, 137]. The only satisfying thing for Shakespeare about this infatuation with a light woman who has not even acknowledged beauty to commend her, is that each perfectly understands and accepts the other's deception and self-deception. The theme of Sonnet 138 might be summed up in the refrain of a recent poet as 'You know I know you know I know you know'. Its insight not only makes it a more coherent poem than most of those addressed to the youth but also, if we allow love poetry more scope than the posy to a ring, one of the finest love poems:

When my loue sweares that she is made of truth,
I do beleeue her though I know she lyes,
That she might think me some vntuterd youth
Vnlearned in the worlds false subtilties.
Thus *vainely* thinking that she thinkes me young,
Although she knowes my dayes are past the best,
Simply I credit her false speaking tongue,
On both sides thus is *simple* truth supprest:
But wherefore sayes she not she is vniust?
And wherefore say not I that I am old?
O loues best *habit* is in seeming trust,
And age in loue, loues not t'haue yeares *told*.
    Therefore I *lye* with her, and she with me,
    And in our *faults* by *lyes* we flattered be.

Faults has a double meaning to enforce the wordplay on *lie;* it means both the lovers' adultery and their deception of each other. As Patrick Cruttwell says [in his "A Reading of the Sonnets"]: 'Of this climactic poem the last couplet, with its pun on "lye" is the very apex; the pun forces together the physical union and its context, as it were, its whole surrounding universe, of moral defilement and falsehood.' Yet the total impression of the sonnet is not one of bitterness, but of acceptance. The lovers need one another in their common weakness.

Only a few of the sonnets to the youth show an irony as fully realised and as moving as this. Sonnet 87, which concludes the Rival Poet sequence, allows a pensive understanding of the youth's calculating temper to show through its seeming self-abasement:

    Farewell thou art too *deare* for my possessing,
    And like enough thou knowst thy *estimate,*
    The Charter of thy *worth* giues thee releasing:
    My *bonds* in thee are all determinate.

Here the play of meaning between 'valuable' and 'beloved' for *dear,* 'your valuation of yourself' and 'the amount of my esteem' for *estimate,* 'value' and 'worthiness' for *worth,* and 'claim' and 'shackle' for *bond,* offers distinct and conflicting readings of the whole passage. Either Shakespeare is saying: 'You are so good and great that you may well end our friendship on the ground that there is no corresponding worth in me', or he means: 'Because of your social advantage over me, you exact too high a price for our friendship, so I have decided to break free.' In addition, there is a strong hint of the meaning: 'I have lavished affection on a creature who is just not worth it.' Shakespeare is in fact recording the terrible moment of apprehension when he means all these at once. A tone of guarded compliment masks his feelings in the following lines of the sonnet, but this profound disillusionment breaks through in the final couplet:

    Thus haue I had thee as a dreame doth flatter,
    In sleepe a King, but waking no such matter.

The irony here is grave and steady; in Sonnet 58, where a compliment is likewise framed in two ironic statements, the tone is one of exasperation: 'That God forbid, that made me first your slaue' evokes the natural protest that the speaker was not created any man's slave, and this sting remains even when we have grasped the fact that this god is Cupid. Its smart is still felt in the final couplet, which may be the voice of a man prostrate with adoration or of one querulous with impatience—'You think this is what I am made for, do you?'

    I am to waite though waiting so be hell,
    Not blame your pleasure be it ill or well.

The hectic tone of this suggests a strong tension of feelings. There is more calmness and deliberation in the preceding sonnet, the fifty-seventh, which will serve as a final example of Shakespeare's verbal precision in defining the interplay of mixed feelings:

    Being your slaue what should I doe but tend,
    Vpon the *houres,* and times of your desire?
    I haue no precious time at al to *spend;*
    Nor *seruices* to doe til you require.
    Nor dare I chide the world without end houre,
    Whilst I (my soueraine) watch the clock for you,
    Nor thinke the bitternesse of absence sowre,
    When you have bid your seruant once adieue.
    Nor dare I question with my idealious thought,
    Where you may be, or you affaires suppose,
    But like a sad slaue stay and thinke of nought
    Saue where you are, how happy you make those.
        So *true* a foole is loue, that in your *Will*
        (Though you doe any thing) he thinkes no ill.

Lines three and four are a little obscure. We might paraphrase: 'I have no strong claims on my time and attention except yours'. But *spend* can have a more forceful meaning of 'expend' or even 'waste' and this insinuates an unexpected note of protest: 'Time is too valuable for me to waste in this fashion'. The ecclesiastical senses of *hours* and *services* and the echo of the doxology in 'world without end' serve to buttress the counterstress set up by this protest; Shakespeare resents the time he has squandered upon a false devotion. And once this note of resentment has been struck, its reverberations are heard in the over-strong protestations of 'Nor dare I chide . . .' and 'Nor dare I question'. The extent to which Shakespeare does chide and question is shown in the last two lines of the sonnet which appear to say: 'Love is so foolishly faithful in your Will Shakespeare that he cannot think ill of you, whatever you do'; but which also say: 'Love is so utterly foolish that, however wilful and perverse you are, it cannot see the wrongness of your behaviour.' In depicting this blend of adulation and contempt, and in all those sonnets where verbal ambiguity is thus used as a deliberate dramatic device, Shakespeare shows that superb insight into states of strangely mixed feelings which enabled him to bring to life a Coriolanus or an Enobarbus. Like Freud, he found the causes of quibbling by studying his own quibbles; and the detachment which such an analysis implies imparts to the best of the Sonnets that objectivity we look for in the finest dramatic poetry. (pp. 91-110)

M. M. Mahood, "The Sonnets," in her Shakespeare's Wordplay, *Methuen & Co. Ltd., 1957, pp. 89-110.*

C. L. BARBER   (essay date 1960)

[*An American scholar, Barber was one of the most important contemporary critics of Shakespearean comedy. His influential study* Shakespeare's Festive Comedy *(1959) examines the parallels between Elizabethan holiday celebrations and Shakespeare's comedies. In the first part of the following excerpt, Barber focuses on the design of Shakespeare's sonnets. Within each sonnet, the critic demonstrates, the momentum from one quatrain to the next is sustained not by the imagery—which frequently changes several times from beginning to end—but by "the patterned movement of discourse." He also remarks that in the absence of a consistent metaphorical scheme, seemingly unconnected "strains of meaning" are frequently held together by the interplay of sound and rhythm. In the second section of the excerpt, Barber examines Shakespeare's expression of love for the Friend, arguing that by virtue of writing verses praising the young man's beauty and worth, the poet is able to realize and fulfill the relationship and to experience "a lover's sense of triumphing over time." The critic further discovers in the poet's verse a "complex, resonant personality"; Shakespeare seemingly possessed an "almost unbearable openness to desire and to life," Barber suggests, as well as an over-eagerness that repeatedly betrayed him into acting out "unworthy parts."]*

To read through the sonnets at a sitting, though it is useful for surveying the topography they present, does violence to them and to the reader—it can produce a sensation of hot-house oppression. Each poem needs to be dwelt on; each requires the kind of concentrated attention which could have been given when they were received singly or in small groups. To read and reread is essential if we are to enjoy the way each moves, the use it makes of the possibilities of the sonnet form, the particular development in it of a design of sounds and images. The sonnets ask for a special sort of attention because in them poetry is, in a special way, an action, something done for and to the beloved. Indeed sometimes the activity of the poetry alone makes endurable the passivity of the attitudes expressed by the poet.

Many of the sonnets are wonderfully generous poems; they *give* meaning and beauty. The generosity is at once personal, a selfless love, and impersonal, the glow upon the world at the golden moment when Shakespeare began to write. The poems create a world resonant with the friend's beauty:

> Thou art thy mother's glass, and she in thee
> Calls back the lovely April of her prime;
> So thou through windows of thine age shalt see,
> Despite of wrinkles, this thy golden time.
>
> [Sonnet 3]

The curious theme of the first seventeen sonnets works because to urge a friend to marry and have children provides occasions for saying simple things beautifully: how lovely April is; how fine it is that age, in spite of wrinkles, has windows through which to see its golden time renewed. The poet's vicarious interest in the young man's sexual fulfillment is not queasy because it is realized by evoking the creative power generally at work in nature:

> Those hours that with gentle work did frame
> The lovely gaze where every eye doth dwell. . . .
>
> [Sonnet 5]

The phrase "gentle work" is typical of the direct cherishing of the processes of life. The feeling about the destructiveness of death is equally direct:

> For never resting time leads summer on
> To hideous winter and confounds him there. . . .
>
> [Sonnet 5]

There is no holding back from obvious words or metaphors: the sun's light is gracious, music is sweet, the buds of May are darling; death is winter, darkness, Time's scythe; beauty is all the usual things, for example a flower. But the meaning of the usual things is renewed:

> Since brass, nor stone, nor earth, nor boundless sea,
> But sad mortality o'ersways their power,
> How with this rage shall beauty hold a plea,
> Whose action is no stronger than a flower.
>
> [Sonnet 65]

That a flower is a fragile thing is familiar enough. But that a flower has its own kind of power too—this comes as a poignant realization. It often happens that the metaphorical vehicle in which Shakespeare conveys the tenor of his love absorbs our chief attention, so that the love itself is left behind or fulfilled in what it is compared to. We dwell on the fact that "summer's lease hath all too short a date" [Sonnet 18], that the earth devours "her own sweet brood" [Sonnet 19], that the morning flatters "the mountain tops with sovereign eye" [Sonnet 33], that black night is "Death's second self," and "seals up all in rest" [Sonnet 73]. Consider, as a summary example, the direct descriptions of the seasons in 97 and 98, "old December's bareness every where," "teeming autumn big with rich increase," "proud-pied April, dress'd in all his trim," and summer when we "wonder at the lily's white" and "praise the deep vermillion of the rose." The world is full of value that can be looked at front-face. Shakespeare could get more of this gold into his poetry than anyone else in the golden age because he had the greatest power of admiration.

To quote isolated phrases or lines from the sonnets is unsatisfying, because every line or phrase is, in the act of reading, part of a single movement: when you know a sonnet well, an individual line, quoted alone, rings with the sound that it has in its proper place. Each sonnet is one utterance. Shakespeare's use of the form is simple and forthright and also delicate and subtle. He never varies from three quatrains followed by a couplet, *abab, cdcd, efef, gg:*

> Why write I still all one, ever the same,
> And keep invention in a noted weed,
> That every word doth almost tell my name . . . ?
>
> [Sonnet 76]

Other Elizabethan sonneteers showed more technical restlessness. Shakespeare not only uses nothing but the Shakespearean form (it *does* tell his name!), but for the most part he uses it straight. He does not run his syntax against the line endings or the rhyme scheme. There are exceptions, but normally the sentences close with the close of each quatrain, or else are balanced symmetrically within the four line unit. Within sentences, grammar and thought typically pause or turn at the end of the line; where they do run over, the enjambment is rarely emphatic. Shakespeare does not exploit the more outward forms of variation because within the pattern he is making astonishingly beautiful designs with sound and syllable and cadence. He is like an accomplished figure skater who sticks to the classical figures because what he cares about is what he can make of each evolution. (Shakespeare had, after all, unlimited opportunities in the plays for free-style improvisations, swoops, spins, leaps.) Each sonnet is different, but the difference is achieved not by changing the framework of form but by moving in fresh ways within it.

It seems clear that Shakespeare wrote by quatrains. In coming to know a sonnet by heart, you find yourself recalling it one quatrain at a time and often getting stuck trying to move to the next, for lack of a tangible link. The imagery does not regularly carry through; what does carry through is the momentum of the discourse. The movement from quatrain to quatrain is usually a shift of some sort, though it can be simply a continuing with fresh impetus. The figure skater starts each evolution by kicking off from an edge, and can move from one evolution to another either by staying on the same edge of the same blade, or changing from inside edge to outside edge, or from left foot inside to right foot outside, and so on—each of these technical moves focusing a whole living gesture of the balancing, moving body. People praise Shakespeare's sonnets because each one is about one thing: one should add that each is *one motion* about one thing, the motion normally being composed of three large sweeps and the shorter couplet. (The very different serial movement of 66 is a revealing exception to prove the rule.)

It is important to recognize that in most of the sonnets the couplet is *not* the emotional climax, or indeed even the musical climax; where it is made so, either by Shakespeare's leaning on it too heavily, or by our giving it unnecessary importance, one feels that two lines are asked to do too much. This let-down or over-reach in the couplet is the most common defect in the sonnets, though with tactful reading it usually can be kept from being troublesome. One needs to attend to the motion and the imaginative expansion which the sonnet achieves in the quatrains, realizing that the couplet is often no more than a turning around at the end to look from a new vantage at what has been expressed.

The main line of the sonnet as Shakespeare writes it is the patterned movement of discourse, not the imagery. The voice rides the undulation of the meter, gaining remarkable power and reaching out in ardent or urgent or solemn gestures defined by rhythmical variations. The criticism of our time has been fascinated by the way poetry can explore experience by carrying out the implications of a metaphor or conceit, as notably in Donne's work. Shakespeare in the sonnets occasionally does something like this—most perfectly in the three paralleled metaphors of 73: "That time of year . . . the twilight of such day . . . the glowing of such fire." But the progression by extending metaphors in 73 is most definitely not typical. He is responsible to rhythmical, not metaphorical consistency. The sonnet often starts with something like a metaphorical program, but usually it is not carried through; metaphors are picked up, changed, mixed, dropped *ad lib* while the sonnet runs its strong course as an utterance. One often finds, as one penetrates the poetic texture of a particular poem, that it holds together by determinate rhythm and sound several almost independent strains of meaning, or a cluster of ambiguities which, worked out logically, are almost mutually exclusive. A case in point, which also will be of interest to us in considering the relationship of Shakespeare to the friend he addresses, comes in 16, where the poet urges that children can provide reproductions of the friend "much liker than your painted counterfeit," and then goes on with an extraordinarily rich use of the word "lines":

> So should the lines of life that life repair,
> Which this Time's pencil, or my pupil pen,
> Neither in inward worth nor outward fair,
> Can make you live yourself in eyes of men.

The suggestiveness of "lines of life" appears in the variety of commentators' paraphrases recorded in the Variorum edition: the "lines of life" can be the lines life etches on a face, or the lines of descent in a genealogy, or the lines of the living pictures presented by children, or the lines of children as living poems (as opposed to the mere written lines of the "pupil pen"), or even, perhaps, as an echo at the back of the mind, what one commentator defends in urging unconvincingly that "lines of life" is a misprint for "loins of life" (compare the sonnet's conclusion: "And you must live, drawn by your own sweet skill" [Sonnet 16]). Shakespeare had a supremely wandering mind! To ravel out such associations can of course be misleading. In an actual, live reading of a sonnet such clustering ideas as these are felt together, not sorted; they are the opening out of mind and heart into the plurality of the world's riches. What keeps us from coming to a standstill in walleyed contemplation is the flow of the poem's movement as it gathers in meaning in the service of the poet's love.

One can instance even more dramatic places where the poetry makes a thick harmony out of woolgathering multiplicity—the most famous is "Bare ruin'd choirs where late the sweet birds sang" [Sonnet 73], thanks to William Empson's discussion at the outset of *Seven Types of Ambiguity* [see Additional Bibliography]. What criticism now needs to stress, I think, is not the interplay of imagery but the interplay of sound. (A case in point is the chord of vowels and of "r's" in "bare ruin'd choirs," sounded in three successive long, slow syllables—the mystery of the line comes from this music as much as from the wonderful complex of metaphors it holds in solution.) We need to consider, not a special case like 73, but the much more common case where there is great richness of metaphor but metaphorical consistency is not regarded:

> O how shall summer's honey breath hold out,
> Against the wrackful siege of battering days,
> When rocks impregnable are not so stout,
> Nor gates of steel so strong but Time decays?
>
> [Sonnet 65]

These are splendid lines—but it is the design of sound that chiefly carries them, the open-breathing *o* and *u* sounds and flowing consonants of "How shall summer's honey breath hold out" followed by the battering lines, with "wrackful" and "rocks impregnable." One can understand summer's honey metaphorically as provision for a siege—but one cannot carry the metaphor further, one cannot "batter" honey! And the summer-winter opposition, as well as the battering, have been lost by the time we get to "Time decays."

Sound and rhythm again and again give life to statements or figures which might otherwise be banal: so in a quatrain selected almost at random from 97:

> How like a winter hath my absence been
> From thee, the pleasure of the fleeting year:
> What freezings have I felt, what dark days seen,
> What old December's bareness everywhere!

A rich use of various *e* sounds emerges: the poignant sense of absence from "thee" is developed as we encounter the same sound in "fleeting" and "freezings"; the open *a* sounds in "What dark days" feel cavernous against the prevailing *e* tones; "December's bareness" includes the three vowel sounds present in "everywhere," so that the bareness seems to spread out "everywhere"—and the meter makes "everywhere" larger than it would be in prose by stressing two of its three syllables. Consonants of course are also put to work reinforcing the meaning, for example by linking "*fl*ee*t*ing and *fr*eezing" to "*f*el*t*," "ol*d*" to "*D*ecember," "Decem*b*er" to "*b*areness." One can go on and on in this fashion, once one starts looking for such tangible patterns—and though it is not always possible to know where to draw the line between cases that really matter and cases that are farfetched, such texture of physical relations among words is clearly fundamental to the beauty *and* the meaning of the poetry. When we shift from quatrain to quatrain, like a skater turning to lean into a new evolution, part of the newness is often the sound of a fresh set of dominant vowels; or again, we sometimes recognize a set of sounds carried all through a sonnet to give it its distinctive tune.

The sonnets often would be "witty" if it were not that the wit in them goes along with sound and cadences that hold feeling—the wit is rarely isolated to be felt separately, as Donne's so often is, but enters into the whole motion. If we read them in isolation, we would be amused by the virtuoso alliteration and assonance in lines like

> And with old woes new wail my dear time's
>   waste. . . .
> And heavily from woe to woe tell o'er
> The sad account of fore-bemoaned moan.
>
> [Sonnet 30]

But when we read them as an integral part of the lovely sonnet "When to the sessions of sweet silent thought" [Sonnet 30], the huddled sounds serve to convey the pressure of the past on the present as a thickening or troubling of speech. Where we feel a twinge of amusement, it is usually in combination with feelings dictated by the underlying rhythm, as with the ruefulness of

> But ah, thought kills me that I am not
>   thought. . . .
>
> [Sonnet 44]

It would be wrong to suppose that the sonnets are without humor. There are places where Shakespeare positively romps, but the fun is almost never unmixed with serious feeling:

> Let not my love be call'd idolatry,
> Nor my beloved as an idol show,
> Since all alike my songs and praises be
> To one, of one, still such, and ever so,
> Kind is my love today, tomorrow kind,
> Still constant with a wondrous excellence;
> Therefore my verse to constancy confin'd,
> One thing expressing, leaves out difference.
> Fair, kind, and true, is all my argument,
> Fair, kind, and true, varying to other words. . . .
>
> [Sonnet 105]

This gay whirl is an extreme example of the repetition common in the sonnets, the same words rolled round, each time with added life because they fall differently each time within the poem's progress. In 105 this sort of fun is indulged in almost by itself, in celebration of a moment's carefree confidence. But even 105, which is as near to a *jeu d'esprit* as we come, has its serious side, for it raises a question about idolatry which it does not settle.

The publisher who pirated the sonnets in 1640 changed the pronouns in 1 to 126 so as to make the poems seem to be addressed to a woman; he was the first of the many editors and commentators who have been troubled by the fact that a man is addressed in these love poems. Whether there was only one young man, or several, cannot be definitely settled: what is clear is that there was one role, of beloved younger friend or "lover," corresponding to a need in the poet to live in and through another person. It is usually in the beauty of a person of the opposite sex that we experience, incarnate, the sum of life's powers and perfections. But here we find that the twenty-five sonnets addressed to a woman, "the dark lady," dwell on her imperfections and falsehoods and the paradox that nevertheless she inspires physical desire; in the poems addressed to a man, by contrast, there is exultant contemplation of the beloved's beauty and cherishing of his whole identity, but nothing of specific bodily prurience. The "higher" love is expressed towards a man and the "lower" towards a woman. Poems to both, moreover, deal with a strange and troubling situation: Shakespeare's friend is lured into an af-

fair by Shakespeare's mistress (40-42, 133, 134, 144); the poet's concern, in the midst of anguished humiliation, is to keep the man's love, not the woman's!

Various explanations have been offered. It has been suggested that the friend and mistress are fictions created in the process of an exercise in conventional sonneteering, but this notion has not stood up. A fiction, especially a fiction by Shakespeare, would satisfy our curiosity where the sonnets frequently baffle us by speaking of things which the person addressed is assumed to know but to which we have no key. And much of what is expressed concerning the friend and the mistress is most definitely *not* conventional sonneteering. The claim that passionate sonnets addressed to men were conventional, with which Sir Henry Lee and others attempted to allay Victorian anxieties, is simply not true. It is true that there was a cult of friendship in the Renaissance, and that writers and stories set ideal friendship between men above love for a woman. Professor Edward Hubler, whose valuable book *The Senses of Shakespeare's Sonnets* judiciously explores this and other problems [see excerpt above, 1952], points out that Elizabethans used the term "lover" between men without embarrassment: thus Menenius, trying to get through to see Coriolanus in the Volscian camp, does not hesitate to say to a guard, "I tell thee, fellow, Thy general was my lover" [V. ii. 13-14]. Mr. Hubler, with others, makes the further point that homosexuality, except for a passing slur about Thersites, is never at issue in the plays, either as a trait of character or, what is more revealing, as a latent motif in the imagery (Marlowe's plays provide a striking contrast). We do get in Shakespeare's comedies a series of places where boy actors play the parts of girls disguised as men; but this playful transvestism, convenient in a theater where boys played the women, is never queasy. We are never shown a man pretending to be a woman. What is dramatized is the fun of young women, Portia, Rosalind, Viola, zestfully acting as youths for a while and then falling back gladly and gracefully into their womanliness. This game reflects, not perversity, but the fundamental Elizabethan security about the roles of the sexes. The same security permitted the dramatist to present the Duke in *Twelfth Night* delighting in the page Cesario's fresh youth and graceful responsiveness, and so falling in love without knowing it with the woman beneath the page's disguise. The sensibility of Shakespeare's age was open to appreciating qualities which youths and women have in common. This openness probably goes with the fact that homosexuality had no place in Elizabethan social life. Because their masculinity never was in doubt, men could wear their hair long, dress in silks and ruffles, pose for portraits "leaning against a tree among roses."

These facts should be kept in mind in reading sonnet 20, where Shakespeare praises "the master-mistress of my passion" for possessing feminine beauty without feminine fickleness. The bawdy joke at the end acknowledges that the friend's sexuality is masculine and directed to women; such a pleasantry could only be pleasant where physical relations of the poet with the friend were out of the question. And yet the fact remains that the relationship expressed is a most unusual one: "Mine be thy love, and thy love's use their [women's] treasure." What Shakespeare's metaphor of capital and interest here proposes is that he should enjoy the whole identity of the friend while women enjoy what this capital yields of specific sexuality. And such is indeed the sort of relationship which the sonnets to the friend express, while those to the mistress present an obverse relationship concerned with the use of her sexuality rather than with her love.

Why then do we read the sonnets if the affections they express are so unusual? In the first place, because the love expressed for the friend *is* love, a most important kind of love which is ordinarily part of a relationship but here becomes the whole and is expressed with an unparalleled fullness and intensity. It is love by *identification* rather than sexual possession. Such cherishing love is a leading part of full sexual love between men and women. And it is central in other relations of life, notably between parents and children: the early sonnet (3) which says "thou art thy mother's glass" is followed by one where the poet is in the mother's place:

> My glass shall not persuade me I am old
> So long as youth and thou are of one date.
>
> [Sonnet 22]

In another place (37) he compares himself to a father who "takes delight / To see his active child do deeds of youth." The strangely special theme of the first seventeen sonnets ("What man," C. S. Lewis asks, "ever really cared whether another man got married or not?" [see excerpt above, 1954]) gives Shakespeare occasion to cherish the friend's identity and, beyond that, to envisage generously, in the idea of having children, a process by which one identity is recreated in another, as the poet throughout the sonnets finds himself renewed in his friend.

The universality of the part of love which here becomes the whole makes it easy for us to "join," as congregation, in all those sonnets, among them the most familiar and most beautiful, where the poet expresses how the friend's being galvanizes his whole consciousness. A lover's experience is the same, whoever the beloved, when absence makes a winter (97), when "thy sweet love remembered such wealth brings" (29), when "descriptions of the fairest wights" in "the chronicles of wasted time" seem all to be prophecies of a present beauty (106). These poems make one very conscious of the active transmutation of experience by passion (e.g. 114), and of the lover's imagination straining at the limitations of physical existence: "If the dull substance of my flesh were thought . . ." (48).

Loving by identifying with the person loved can have a special scope for Shakespeare which it does not have for people who are not poets, because he can realize his friend's beauty and value in words. To realize the relationship by turning it into poetry gives a fulfillment which actually is physical, in that the poem, as utterance, is a physical act. That the writing of a sonnet provides a kind of physical union with the friend explains at least in part, I think, the recurrent emphasis on the sonnets as rescuing the beloved from death. Taken literally, the talk of conferring immortality seems rather empty—the friend, after all, is never named, and he is given no determinate social identity, indeed no personality. (It is because all this area is left so blank that the curious have been free to bemuse themselves with conjectures of every kind about the friend's identity.) But the sustaining reality in the theme of immortality is that the poet, in the act of writing the poem, experiences a lover's sense of triumphing over time by becoming one with great creating nature as embodied in another being. We have dwelt on the comparison made in 16 between different kinds of "lines of life." When the poet turns from urging children on his friend to addressing him directly, he uses the same metaphor to say that Death shall not "brag

thou wand'rest in his shade / When in eternal lines to time thou grow'st" (18).

Such claims for poetry's power are of course a universal commonplace of the Petrarchan tradition—Shakespeare regularly links them with poignant, inclusive reflections on mortality. In reflections on mortality in *carpe diem* poems like Marvell's "Coy Mistress," there is often a suggestion, verging on a kind of metaphysical cruelty, that dissolution will come anyway, so it may as well come, delightfully, in sexual surrender. Shakespeare's sonnets often enhance the beauty of his friend and the mystery of life in him by reflections that he "amongst the wastes of time must go," like "the wide world and all its fading sweets" (19). The sense of helplessness in the face of time is more profound and poignant than in most love poetry, partly because Shakespeare looks to no sexual resolution. A great weight is thrown on resolution in the creative act of poetry—and so on poetry's promise of immortality. Not infrequently, as in 19, claims made in a concluding couplet, after large reflections on devouring Time, have not weight enough to make a satisfying balance. But a massive poem like 55,

> Not marble, nor the gilded monuments
> Of princes, shall outlive this powerful rhyme. . . .

makes us realize anew art's power of survival; in 74 and elsewhere we are made to feel how a man's spirit can be preserved in poetry whereas "the earth can have but earth."

The concern to realize and live in the identity of another is just what we should expect, if we think about it, from the man who, beyond all other men, created other identities. And the difficulties with love expressed in the sonnets are also congruous with the capacities demonstrated in the plays. One difficulty, which grows more and more obvious as one reads and rereads the poems to the friend, is that the action, in such a love as this, is almost all on the poet's side. In 53, Shakespeare asks the arresting question,

> What is your substance, whereof are you made,
> That millions of strange shadows on you tend?

The poet's powers as a dramatist at once come to mind when he goes on to say,

> Describe Adonis, and the counterfeit
> Is poorly imitated after you;
> On Helen's cheek all art of beauty set,
> And you in Grecian tires are painted new.

It is clear that the strange shadows come not from the friend, but from the poet, who costumes him now in one role, now in another. Sonnet 61 recognizes this fact in answering another arresting question,

> Is it thy will thy image should keep open
> My heavy eyelids to the weary night?

The conclusion is a troubled recognition that it is the poet's will, not the friend's:

> For thee watch I, whilst thou dost wake elsewhere,
> From me far off, with others all too near.

One is tempted to answer for the friend that after all, not being a poet, he cannot beguile the long night with a companion composed of images and words!

There are sonnets which recognize, too, if only playfully, that such identification as the poet feels with his friend involves

Elizabeth, Countess of Southampton.

selfishness or self-love. Thus 62 exploits a double-take as to who is who: "Sin of self-love possesseth all mine eye, / . . . Methinks no face so gracious is as mine, / No shape so true, no truth of such account." The turn comes with the third quatrain: "But when my glass shows me myself indeed, / Beated and chopp'd with tann'd antiquity. . . ." The same game is played in 39, this time with "worth" and "self": "What can mine own praise to mine own self bring? / And what is't but mine own when I praise thee?" It is easy to dismiss this sort of reasoning, when we read a sonnet in isolation, as sonneteer's logic. But when we come to understand the sort of relationship Shakespeare is expressing, we realize that these poems mean what they say in making equations. The poet's sense of himself hinges on the identification: elation in realizing himself in the friend's self is matched by desolation when he is left in the lurch of selflessness. There are a number of poems where he proposes to do anything, to set himself utterly at naught or injure himself, if by so doing he can contribute to the friend's wishes and give him meaning: "Upon thy side against myself I'll fight . . . That thou, in losing me, shall win much glory." (88) / "Speak of my lameness, and I straight will halt . . ." (89). Commentators have been silly enough to conclude from this that Shakespeare was literally lame; they have argued from "beated and chopp'd with tann'd antiquity" that he wrote the sonnets when he was old. Of course in both cases what is conveyed is not literal incapacity but the poet's sense that without the younger friend he is nothing. Indeed the action of making himself nothing is,

for him, a way of making love real by making the beloved everything.

With the woman, things go just the other way: Shakespeare makes love to her by telling her she is naught! At the best, he tells her that she attracts him even though she is "black" instead of "fair" (127); more commonly, he asks for favors in the same breath that he tells her he loves her in spite of his five wits and his five senses (141); most commonly, he spells out her falsehood and exclaims at the paradox that "in the very refuse of [her] deeds" she somehow makes him love her more "the more I hear and see just cause of hate" (150). These are outrageous poems: one wonders whether in fact most of them can have been sent to the poor woman— whether many of them were not offstage exercises in hate and despite written from a need to get something out of the poet's system. To tell a woman that since she is promiscuous, she may as well let you put in among the rest, especially since your *name* too is Will (135), does not seem a very likely way to win even a hardened profligate. Several poems, notably 151, present a sequence in which degrading the woman and his relation to her frees the poet for an impudent phallic self-assertion:

> For, thou betraying me, I do betray
> My nobler part to my gross body's treason;
> My soul doth tell my body that he may
> Triumph in love; flesh stays no farther reason. . . .

One cannot avoid the conclusion that, for Shakespeare, in the constellation of relations with which the sonnets are concerned, specific sexual love was disassociated from cherishing and adoring love: sonnet 144 summarizes these "two loves," one of "comfort," the other of "despair," one "a man right fair," the other "a woman colored ill." The psychological implications have of course been variously interpreted, most recently by a Dutch psychoanalyst, Dr. Conrad V. Emde Boas. I understand that his large book, which has not yet been translated, sees in Shakespeare's cherishing of a younger man an identification with the mother's role, and a displaced narcissism which in praising the beloved enjoys the contemplation of an ideal image of the poet himself. Such a theory can only be rightly evaluated by mobilizing the whole system of thought which gives its concepts meaning. But common sense can see, I think, that the sonnets reflect only one patterning of a kaleidoscopic personality: the tenderness which here is attached to a man or several men might well, in other phases of Shakespeare's life, have been felt for women.

And without resort to psychoanalytic formulations, our knowledge of Shakespeare's qualities as an artist can help in understanding the attitudes expressed in the sonnets. James Joyce, in pursuing his own obsession with the artist as a natural cuckold, was much preoccupied with the triangle in the sonnets. In *Ulysses,* Shakespeare emerges as a shadowy double for Bloom and as an omen for Stephen Dedalus: the flickering suggestions about Shakespeare center in the notion that he was betrayed because as an artist he would rather see than do, not asserting himself in actual life but taking the lead in love from others, while fulfilling himself in creating the various persons of his plays. Joyce is riding his own concerns, but he provides a useful perspective on the sonnets which deal with the double infidelity. In 40-42, where Shakespeare struggles to find a way of resolving in words the injury that his friend and mistress have done him in deeds, the idea of his identification with his friend is carried to a bitter *reductio ad absurdum:*

But here's the joy, my friend and I are one;
Sweet flattery, then she loves but me alone.

[Sonnet 42]

These tortured and tortuous sonnets adopt and abandon one strained interpretation after another, including the ironic suggestion that the two others are behaving as they do only to satisfy Shakespeare vicariously:

Loving offenders, thus I will excuse ye,
Thou dost love her, because thou know'st I love
    her,
And for my sake even so doth she abuse me,
Suff'ring my friend for my sake to approve her.

[Sonnet 42]

How much simpler it would be if friend and mistress were both of them in a play! Indeed, bitter as these sonnets are, they express a response to the humiliation life has brought which moves in the direction of art. Most men would bury the event in silence, or else turn injury into anger. Shakespeare turns injury into poetry. The very act of writing about the betrayal is a kind of acceptance of it—which goes with the extraordinary effort to accept the friend even in such circumstances. Thus 41 excuses "Those pretty wrongs that liberty commits, / When I am sometime absent from thy heart," only to exclaim poignantly, "Ay me, but yet thou might'st my seat forbear." In 40 the poet attempts a gesture of total self-abnegation:

I do forgive thy robb'ry, gentle thief,
Although thou steal thee all my poverty;
And yet love knows it is a greater grief
To bear love's wrong than hate's known injury.
    Lascivious grace, in whom all ill well shows,
    Kill me with spites; yet we must not be foes.

The whole metrical force of the sonnet is mobilized in the uttering of "Lascivious grace," a phrase which brings into focus the anguish and enjoyment of Shakespeare's continuing identification with the friend. The poet's artistic sympathy encounters the closed ruthlessness of another living identity and remains open to it.

These are disturbing and unsatisfying poems, despite their great power, because they do not achieve a stable attitude towards the experience. We encounter the same irresolute quality in some of the sonnets where the young man's dissoluteness or vanity are both rebuked and accepted (e.g. 95, 84). The poems are twisted on the rack of a sympathy "beyond good and evil," the sympathy which is organized in the plays, flowing into opposites and antagonists so that, as Eglington phrases it in *Ulysses,* "He is the ghost and the prince. He is all in all." Stephen Dedalus takes up the point:

He is, Stephen said. The boy of act one is the mature man of act five. All in all. In *Cymbeline,* in *Othello* he is bawd and cuckold. He acts and is acted on. . . . His unremitting intellect is the hornmad Iago ceaselessly willing that the moor in him shall suffer.

These are wild and whirling words, describing Shakespeare through Stephen and his preoccupations. But in them Joyce brings out how much Shakespeare needed the drama.

The most satisfying of the sonnets which deal with Shakespeare's difficulties in love are those where he is using the sonnet primarily to confront what love reveals to him about himself. Thus in 35 we get, in the midst of excuses for the friend, a recognition that

All men make faults, and even I in this,
Authorizing thy trespass with compare,
Myself corrupting, salving thy amiss. . . .

The most impressive explorations come in sonnets which are late in the numerical order—poems which have a complexity of texture and tone which sets them apart from most, though not all, of the first one hundred, and so were probably composed later. Among those to the woman, I find most satisfying the ones which, forbearing hymns of hate, define the cheapness of the relation—cheapness being one of the hardest things to get into poetry (or indeed to face up to in any fashion). Symmetrical lies are laid out in 138, hers to him and his to her, tea for two and two for tea:

Therefore I lie with her, and she with me,
And in our faults by lies we flattered be.

A stimulating criticism by Mr. Patrick Cruttwell, which relates these sonnets to the plays of the period of *Hamlet* and *Troilus and Cressida,* sees this sonnet as "perhaps the most terrible of the whole sequence," climaxed in the "grim seriousness" of the pun on lie [see Additional Bibliography]. "Grim" seems to me wrong: I find the poem jaunty as well as devastating, and more honest so. Where the sonnets to the woman do become completely grim, there is usually a certain falsifying simplication in resorting to unmeasured abuse, as in the couplet which ends, but does not resolve, the analysis of love's fever in 147:

For I have sworn thee fair, and thought thee bright,
Who art as black as hell, as dark as night.

In the poems of self-analysis addressed to a man, there is a far deeper facing up to the poet's own moral involvement—and to the paradoxes of passion where morality seems no longer to apply. In 109-112 and 117-121 the poet, acknowledging infidelities on his side, confronts directly the polymorphic responsiveness of his own personality:

Alas, 'tis true, I have gone here and there,
And made myself a motley to the view,
Gor'd mine own thoughts, sold cheap what is most
    dear,
Made old offences of affections new.

[Sonnet 110]

Here "made myself a motley" suggests the actor's impulse and his humiliations, and in 111 Shakespeare explicitly asks his friend to forgive in him the "public manners" which are bred by the "public means" from which he must provide for his livelihood:

Thence comes it that my name receives a brand,
And almost thence my nature is subdu'd
To what it works in, like the dyer's hand.

Commentators have emphasized, indeed exaggerated, the ignominious status of the acting profession in the Elizabethan age, seeing in this outward circumstance the source of Shakespeare's self-disabling humility towards his friend. No doubt it was a factor, just as part of the appeal of the young man or young men was superior birth, a heritage the poet did not have and could enjoy through identification. But the temperament which made Shakespeare an actor and dramatist is more fundamental than the matter of status, as these sonnets make clear: they present a complex, resonant personality which, for most purposes in life, is over-responsive, over-eager, drawn on to act unworthy parts and unable to avoid living out in new relationships what has already been found shameful. His fluidity, his almost unbearable openness to desire and to life, are described in 109 in the course of a moving plea:

> Never believe, though in my nature reign'd
> All frailties that besiege all kinds of blood,
> That it could so preposterously be stain'd
> To leave for nothing all thy sum of good.

The sort of knowledge of the heart and its turnings which finds expression in the plays appears in these sonnets with a special if limited intensity—the intensity involved in seeing, in one's single life, the broken lines made by Eros. In the same moment when he asks forgiveness for making "old offences of affections new," Shakespeare has the courage to recognize that there is value, as well as humiliation, in "selling cheap what is most dear":

> Most true it is, that I have look'd on truth
> Askance and strangely. But by all above,
> These blenches gave my heart another youth,
> And worse essays prov'd thee my best of love.
>
> [Sonnet 110]

There is no set posture in these poems against morality or convention: if they simplified things by adopting a romantic or bohemian rationale, they could not be so serious in exploring the way passion turns corners that it cannot see around and moves in directions contrary to the will. Sonnet 121 confronts in a frightening way the break-down of moral categories in this territory: "'Tis better to be vile than vile esteemed. . . . No, I am that I am." The pressure of experience on received categories is so great in this sonnet (and at places in others of this whole group), that it is impossible entirely to comprehend the meaning—though we can apprehend it obliquely. In the dramatic form, Shakespeare could present directly, in several persons, what here is looked at askance from one vantage.

These poems reckoning with himself are not the greatest sonnets Shakespeare wrote, profound and moving as they are. The poems that gather in life with a lover's delight have more sensuous substance than these inward-turning pieces; and the poems which generalize out from love have more that each reader can make his own. But the sonnets confronting his own nature are an astonishing achievement in self-expression. They grow in meaning and beauty as we set one against another—and as we see the whole group in relation to what Shakespeare did in his plays. Few poems have expressed so close to the heart and nerves as 120 the transformation of suffering into compassion:

> That you were once unkind befriends me now,
> And for that sorrow which I then did feel
> Needs must I under my transgression bow,
> Unless my nerves were brass or hammer'd steel.
> For if you were by my unkindness shaken,
> As I by yours, y'have pass'd a hell of time. . . .
> O that our night of woe might have remember'd
> My deepest sense, how hard true sorrow hits. . . .

Here we see particularly clearly how the capacity for identifying with a person loved, sometimes disabling, perplexing and humiliating, also gives Shakespeare his "deepest sense, how hard true sorrow hits." (pp. 652-72)

C. L. Barber, "Shakespeare in His Sonnets," in The Massachusetts Review, Vol. I, No. 4, Summer, 1960, pp. 648-72.

NORTHROP FRYE (essay date 1962)

[*Frye is considered one of the most important critics of the twentieth century and a leader of the anthropological or mythic approach to literature which gained prominence during the 1950s. As he outlines in his seminal work,* Anatomy of Criticism *(1957), Frye views all literature as ultimately derived from certain myths or archetypes present in all cultures, and he therefore sees literary criticism as an unusual type of science in which the literary critic seeks to decode the mythic structure inherent in a work of art. Frye's intention was to formulate a method of literary interpretation more universal and exact than that suggested in other critical approaches, such as New Criticism, biographical criticism, or historical criticism—all of which he finds valuable, but also limited in application. In the following excerpt, Frye recommends that Shakespeare's sonnets be read not as "transcripts of experience," but as poetry written within the framework of a particular literary convention. He outlines the antecedents of Renaissance courtly love poetry and shows that within this genre, the theme of love is variously depicted in "high" and "low" phases. Shakespeare's Sonnets 1 through 126 represent "a 'high' story of devotion," according to Frye, while the dark lady verses focus on desire and "the 'low' dialectic of bondage and freedom." The critic remarks on several aspects of the first group, including the archetypal characterization of the young friend; the presentation of love as ennobling; the contrasting tones of effusiveness and introspection; the opposition of "winter and summer, age and youth, darkness and light"; and the theme of time as annihilator. The relation between the poet and the youth, Frye maintains, has no element of sexual interest. Pairs of male friends recur throughout the development of the genre in which Shakespeare is writing, he points out, and such relationships are traditionally depicted as a "high" form of courtly love. Frye declares that notwithstanding all the speculation and research that has gone into the effort to discover what these verses may tell us about Shakespeare, "our knowledge of what in the sonnets is direct biographical allegory remains precisely zero."*]

Many readers tend to assume that poetry is a record of a poet's experience. Those who tell us that Shakespeare must have been a lawyer to have known so much about law, or a nobleman in disguise to have known so much about aristocratic psychology, always start with this assumption as their major premise. The assumption is then used in value judgments. First-hand experience in life and second-hand experience derived from books are correlated with good and less good poetry respectively. Poem A is very good; therefore a genuine experience must lie behind it; Poem B is duller, so it must be a "mere literary exercise," where the poet's "real feelings" are not involved. Included in these assumptions, of course, is the view that convention is the opposite of originality, and the mark of inferior writers. (pp. 25-6)

The first point to get clear is that if we read the sonnets as transcripts of experience, we are not reading them realistically but allegorically, as a series of cryptic allusions in which a rival poet may be Chapman, a mortal moon Queen Elizabeth, and a man in hue somebody named Hughes. Now if we approach the sonnets in this crude allegorical way, they become "riddles" of a most peculiar kind. They begin with seventeen appeals to a beautiful youth to beget a son. Rationalizing readers tell us that the poet is urging the youth to marry, but only one of these sonnets—the eighth—has any serious treatment of marriage. True, the youth is urged to marry as the only legal means of producing offspring, but apparently any woman will do: it is not suggested that he should fall in love or that there is any possibility of his producing daughters or even a son who takes after his mother, which seems curious when the youth himself does. In real life, one would think, the only possible reply from the youth would be that of Christ to Satan in *Paradise Regained:* "Why art *thou* solicitous?"

The poet then drops his appeal and falls in love with the youth himself. We next observe that although the poet promises the youth immortality, and clearly has the power to confer it, he does not lift a metrical foot to make the youth a credible or interesting person. He repeats obsessively that the youth is beautiful, and sometimes true and kind, if not overvirtuous; but in real life one would think that a poet who loved him so much would delight in telling us at least about his accomplishments, if he had any. Could he carry on a conversation, make puns, argue about religion, ride to hounds, wear his clothes with a dash, sing in a madrigal? The world's greatest master of characterization will not give him the individualizing touch that he so seldom refuses to the humblest of his dramatic creations. Of course, if we are predetermined to see the Earl of Southampton or some other witty and cultivated person in the youth, we may ascribe qualities to him that the poet does not. But considering him as a real person, and reading only what is there, we are forced to conclude that Shakespeare has lavished a century of the greatest sonnets in the language on an unresponsive oaf as stupid as a doorknob and as selfish as a weasel. (pp. 26-7)

Besides—who exactly is given immortality by the sonnets? Well, there was this Mr. W. H., except that some people think he was H. W. and that he wasn't a Mr. And how do we learn about this Mr. W. H., or this not-Mr. H. W.? Through one floundering and illiterate sentence, to call it that by courtesy, which was not written by Shakespeare, not addressed to us, and no more likely to be an accurate statement of fact than any other commercial plug. We are also referred to a story told in *Willobie his Avisa* about a certain H. W., who, "being suddenly infected with the contagion of a fantastical fit, at the first sight of A(visa), pineth a while in secret grief, at length not able any longer to endure the burning heat of so fervent a humour, bewrayeth the secrecy of his disease unto his familiar friend W. S." In short, a very literary story. As an account of something happening in real life, Polonius might believe it, but hardly Rosalind. We are not told that the youth of the sonnets wanted immortality, but if he did he would have done better to marry and beget a son, as he was advised to do all along. About all that one can get out of the sonnets, considered as transcripts of experience, is the reflection that pederastic infatuations with beautiful and stupid boys are probably very bad for practicing dramatists.

This conclusion is so grotesque that one would expect any critic who reached it to retrace his steps at once. But we often find such critics merely trying to save the face of the ridiculous creature that they have themselves created. Benson, the compiler of the 1640 edition of the sonnets, simply altered pronouns, but this is a trifle robust for the modern conscience. Coleridge disapproved of homosexual sentiments in poetry, and sneered at Virgil as a second-rate poet all his life because Virgil wrote the Second Eclogue; but Coleridge had practically signed a contract to endorse everything that Shakespeare wrote, so what to do? Well: "It seems to me that the sonnets could only have come from a man deeply in love, and in love with a woman; and there is one sonnet which,

from its incongruity, I take to be a purposed blind" [see excerpt above, 1833]. Another critic urges that the sonnets *must* be regarded as Shakespeare's earliest work, written in time for him to have got this affair out of his system, for if they are later, Shakespeare's personality must be considered "unwholesome." And what critic urges this? Samuel Butler, author of *Erewhon Revisited,* that genial spoofing of the eternal human tendency to turn untidy facts into symmetrical myths!

The same fate seems to pursue even the details of the allegorical approach. The line in Sonnet 107, "The mortal moon hath her eclipse endur'd," sounds as though it referred to Queen Elizabeth. If so, it means either that she died or that she didn't die, in which case it was presumably written either in 1603 or some time before 1603. Unless, that is, it is a retrospective allusion, of a kind that dilatory poets are only too apt to make, or unless it doesn't refer to Elizabeth at all, in which case it could have been written at any time between 1603 and its publication in 1609. Once again we feel uneasily that "Shakespeare the man" is slipping out of our grasp.

We should be better advised to start with the assumption that the sonnets are poetry, therefore written within a specific literary tradition and a specific literary genre, both of which were developed for specifically literary reasons. The tradition had developed in the Middle Ages, but would hardly have had so much vitality in Shakespeare's day without a contemporary context. In the Renaissance, anyone who wanted to be a serious poet had to work at it. He was supposed to be what Gabriel Harvey called a "curious universal scholar" as well as a practical expert in every known rhetorical device—and Renaissance writers knew many more rhetorical devices than we do. But learning and expertise would avail him little if he didn't, as we say, "have it." Have what? Have a powerful and disciplined imagination, to use the modern term, which, by struggling with the most tempestuous emotions, had learned to control them like plunging horses and force them into the service of poetry. True, the greatest moments of poetic *furor* [frenzy] and *raptus* [ecstasy] are involuntary, but they never descend on those who are not ready for them. Could one acquire such an imagination if one didn't have it? No, but one could develop it if one did have it. How? Well, the strongest of human emotions, love, was also the most easily available.

The experience of love thus had a peculiarly close relation to the training of the poet, a point of some importance for understanding Shakespeare's sonnets. Love was for the Renaissance poet a kind of creative yoga, and imaginative discipline in which he watched the strongest possible feelings swirling around sexual excitement, jealousy, obsession, melancholy, as he was snubbed, inspired, teased, ennobled, forsaken, or made blissful by his mistress. The Renaissance poet was not expected to drift through life gaining "experience" and writing it up in poetry. He was expected to turn his mind into an emotional laboratory and gain his experience there under high pressure and close observation. Literature provided him with a convention, and the convention supplied the literary categories and forms into which his amorphous emotions were to be poured. Thus his imaginative development and his reading and study of literature advanced together and cross-fertilized one another.

Of course the experience of love is a real experience. It is not assumed that the youth trying to be a poet talks himself into a certain state of mind; it is assumed that, if normal, he will feel the emotion of love at some time or other, and that, if destined to be a poet, he will not fall in love tepidly or realistically but head-over-heels. But the experience of love and the writing of love poetry do not necessarily have any direct connection. One is experience, the other craftsmanship. So if we ask, is there a real mistress or does the poet merely make it all up? the answer is that an either-or way of putting the question is wrong. Modern criticism has developed the term "imagination" precisely to get around this unreal dilemma. Poetry is not reporting on experience, and love is not an uncultivated experience; in both poetry and love, reality is what is created, not the raw material for the creation.

The typical emotions inspired in the poet by love are thus formed into the typical patterns of literary convention. When the conventions of love poetry developed, the model for most of these patterns was the spiritual discipline of Christianity. In Christianity one may, with no apparent cause, become spiritually awakened, conscious of sin and of being under the wrath of God, and bound to a life of unconditional service to God's will. Much courtly love poetry was based on a secular and erotic analogy of Christian love. The poet falls in love at first sight, involuntarily or even with reluctance. The God of Love, angry at being neglected, has walked into his life and taken it over, and is now his "lord." His days of liberty are over, and ahead of him is nothing but unquestioning devotion to Love's commands. The first thing he must do is supplicate his mistress for "grace," and a mistress who did not demand long sieges of complaint, prayers for mercy, and protests against her inflexible cruelty was a conventionally impossible female. (pp. 28-32)

The secular and erotic counterpart of the Madonna and Child was Venus and Eros, or Cupid. Cupid was a little boy shooting arrows, and at the same time he was, like his Christian counterpart, the greatest of the gods and the creator of the universe, which had arisen from chaos by the "attraction" of like particles. The domain of Eros included heat, energy, desire, love, and subjective emotion; Venus had the complementary area of light, form, desirability, beauty, and objective proportion. In a sense all lovers are incarnations of Eros, and all loved ones incarnations of Venus. (p. 32)

The possible scale of themes in courtly love poetry is as broad as love itself, and may have any kind of relationship to its Christian model, from an integral part to a contrast or even a parody. We may divide the scale into "high" and "low" phases, using these terms diagrammatically and not morally. In the "high" phases love is a spiritual education and a discipline of the soul, which leads the lover upward from the sensible to the eternal world. In Dante, the love of Beatrice, announced in the *Vita Nuova,* is a spiritual education of this sort leading straight to its own logical fulfillment in the Christian faith. It not only survives the death of Beatrice, but in the *Commedia* the same love conveys the poet upward from the top of Purgatory into the divine presence itself. Dante's love for Beatrice was the emotional focus of his life, but at no point was it a sexual love or connected with marriage. The philosophy of Plato, where one moves from the body's attraction to the physical reflection of reality upward to the soul's union with the form of reality, provided a convenient framework for later treatments of the "high" version of the convention. We find this Platonized form of love in Michelangelo and in the speech of Cardinal Bembo at the end of Castiglione's *Courtier.*

Next comes what we may call the Petrarchan norm, a conflict of human emotions in which the main theme is still unswerv-

ing devotion and supplications for grace. In Petrarch the human situation in love is far more elaborately analyzed than in Dante, but as in Dante the poet's love survives the death of Laura and does not depend on sexual experience. In Christianity love for God is obviously its own reward, because God is love. The Petrarchan poet similarly often finds that it is love itself, not the female embodiment of it, which fulfills his desire, and such a love could logically survive the death of the beloved, or be content, as Herrick says his is, with a contact of almost unbearable refinement:

> Only to kiss the air
> That lately kissed thee.
>
> ["To Electra"]

In Petrarch, however, there is more emphasis placed on physical frustration than on spiritual fulfillment, and the same is true of most of his followers. At this point the relation between heavenly and earthly love begins to appear as a contrast, as it often does in Petrarch himself. Thus Spenser writes his hymns to Heavenly Love (Christ) and Heavenly Beauty (the Wisdom of the Book of Proverbs) as an alleged palinode to his courtly love hymns to Eros and Venus, and Sidney indicates in his famous "Leave me, O Love" sonnet a "higher" perspective on the story told in *Astrophel and Stella.*

In the middle of the scale comes the mistress as potential wife: this was still a rather rare form in love poetry, though of course normal for drama and romance. It is represented in English literature by Spenser's *Amoretti* sequence. We then move into the "low" area of more concrete and human relations, sometimes called anti-Petrarchan, the centre of gravity of the *Songs and Sonnets* of Donne, who remarks:

> Love's not so pure and abstract, as they use
> To say, which have no mistress but their Muse.
>
> ["Love's Growth"]

Here the poet is less aware of the dialectic of Eros and Agape, and more aware of another kind of dialectic established in the normal opening of the convention, when the poet first falls in love. When the God of Love enters the poet's life, the poet may regret his lost liberty of not having to serve a mistress, or he may contrast the bondage of his passion with the freedom of reason. He finds that in this context his love is inseparable from hatred—not necessarily hatred of the mistress, except in cases of jealousy, but hatred of the emotional damage done to his life by love. The God of Love in this situation is a tyrant, and the poet cannot identify the god's will with his own desire. Such moods of despair are often attached to palinodes, or they may be understood to be necessary early stages, where the poet is still establishing his constancy. But in "lower" phases the poet may get fed up with having so much demanded of him by the code and renounce love altogether; or the mistress may be abused as a monster of frigidity who has brought about her lover's death; or the poet may flit from one mistress to another or plunge into cynical amours with women of easy virtue—in short, parody the convention. Ovid, who as far as Shakespeare was concerned was by long odds the world's greatest poet, had a good deal of influence on these "low" phases of courtly love, as Platonism had on the "higher" ones.

It does not follow that the "lower" one goes, the more realistic the treatment becomes. This happens only to a very limited extent. The mistress normally remains almost equally uncharacterized at all stages: the poet is preoccupied with the emotions in himself which the mistress has caused, and with her only as source and goal of these emotions. Similarly with Shakespeare's youth: he is not characterized, in any realistic sense, because the conventions and genres employed exclude that kind of characterization. It is interesting to contrast the sonnets from this point of view with the narrative poem *A Lover's Complaint,* which, whoever wrote it, follows the sonnets in the 1609 Quarto, and presents three characters roughly parallel to the three major characters of the sonnets. Here what belongs to the genre is not so much characterization as description, which is given in abundance.

It was assumed that the major poet would eventually move on to the major genres, epic and tragedy, and from the expression of his own emotions to the expression of heroic ones. The young professional poet learning his trade, and the amateur too high in social rank to become a professional, both tended to remain within the conventions and genres appropriate to love poetry. The appropriate genres included the love lyric and the pastoral. In the love lyric the source of love was a mistress descended from the line of Laura; in the pastoral, following the example of Virgil's Second Eclogue, the love of two men for one another was more frequent. Here again the influence of Plato, in whose conception of love there are no mistresses, but the love of an older man for a younger one, has to be allowed for. Spenser began his career with the pastoral poetry of *The Shepheardes Calender,* because, according to his editor E. K., he intended to go on to epic, and pastoral was a normal genre in which to serve his apprenticeship. In "January," the first eclogue, Spenser represents himself as the shepherd Colin Clout, in love with one Rosalind, but also dearly attached to another shepherd named Hobbinol. E. K. explains in a note that such an attachment has nothing to do with pederasty (just as love for a mistress has no necessary, or even frequent, connection with adulterous liaisons). Spenser devoted the third book of *The Faerie Queene* to chastity, which for him included both married love and courtly *Frauendienst,* and the fourth book to friendship. In the Temple of Venus, described in the tenth canto of the fourth book, pairs of male friends are given an honored place, as friendship has a disinterested factor in it which for Spenser puts it among the "high" forms of courtly love. Examples include Hercules and Hylas, David and Jonathan, and Damon and Pythias. Such friends are called lovers, and it was conventional for male friends to use the language of love, just as it was conventional for a lover to shed floods of tears when disdained by his mistress. Similarly in Shakespeare the relation of poet to youth is one of love, but it is assumed (in Sonnet 20 and elsewhere) that neither the youth nor the poet has any sexual interest except in women. The "homosexual" view of the sonnets disappears at once as soon as we stop reading them as bad allegory.

After all the research, the speculation, and the guesswork, our knowledge of what in the sonnets is direct biographical allegory remains precisely zero. Anything may be; nothing must be, and what has produced them is not an experience like ours, but a creative imagination very unlike ours. Our ignorance is too complete to be accidental. The establishing of a recognized convention is of enormous benefit to poets, as it enables them to split off personal sincerity from literary sincerity, and personal emotion from communicable emotion. When emotions are made communicable by being conventionalized, the characters on whom they are projected may expand into figures of universal scope and infinitely haunting variety. . . . The same principle applies to characterization. By suppressing realistic characterization, convention devel-

ops another kind, an archetypal character who is not individualized, but becomes a focus of our whole literary experience.

In Shakespeare's sonnets, the beautiful-youth group tells a "high" story of devotion, in the course of which the poet discovers that the reality of his love is the love itself rather than anything he receives from the beloved. Here, as in Petrarch and Sidney, the love proves to be an ennobling discipline although the experience itself is full of suffering and frustration. The dark-lady group is "low" and revolves around the theme of *odi et amo* [I hate and I love]. In the beautiful-youth group Shakespeare has adopted the disturbing and strikingly original device of associating the loved one with Eros rather than Venus, a beautiful boy who, like the regular mistress, is primarily a source of love rather than a responding lover. Other familiar landmarks of the convention can be easily recognized. The poet is the slave of his beloved; he cannot sleep for thinking of him; their souls are in one another's breasts; the poet protests his constancy and alleges that he has no theme for verse except his love; he is struck dumb with shame and bashfulness in the presence of his love; he ascribes all his virtues and talents to his love; his verse will immortalize the beloved; his love is triumphant over death (as the love of Dante and Petrarch survived the death of Beatrice and Laura respectively); yet he continually finds love a compulsory anguish.

It is a reasonable assumption that Sonnets 1 through 126 are in sequence. There is a logic and rightness in their order which is greatly superior to that of any proposed rearrangement (such as Sir Denys Bray's "rhyme-link" scheme), and this order is at least as likely to be the author's as the editor's, for Thorpe, unlike Benson, shows no signs of officious editorial meddling. Sonnet 126, a twelve-line poem in couplets containing a masterly summary of the themes and images of the beautiful-youth group, is inescapably the "envoy" of the series—any interpretation that attempts to remove it from this position must have something wrong with it. The repetition of "render," too, shows that it closely follows on the difficult but crucial Sonnet 125. If, then, Sonnets 1 through 126 are in sequence, the rationale of that sequence would be roughly as follows:

We begin with a prelude which we may call "The Awakening of Narcissus," where the poet urges the youth to beget a son in his own likeness. In Sonnet 17 this theme modulates into the theme of gaining eternal youth through the poet's verse instead of through progeny, and this in turn modulates into the main theme of the poet's own love for the youth. The poet then revolves around the youth in a series of three cycles, each of which apparently lasts for a year (Sonnet 104), and takes him through every aspect of his love, from the most ecstatic to the most woebegone. At the beginning of the first cycle the poet is confident of the youth's love and feels that his genius as a poet is being released by it, and the great roar of triumph in Sonnet 19 is its high point. Gradually the poet's reflections become more melancholy and more independent of his love. In Sonnet 30 the final couplet seems almost deliberately perfunctory, a perceptible tug pulling us back to the main theme. The poet's age begins to haunt him in 22; a sense of the inadequacy of his poetry enters in 32, and his fortunes seem to sink as the cycle progresses, until by 37 he is not only old but lame, poor, and despised. Already in 33 a tone of reproach has begun, and with reproach comes, in 36, a feeling of the necessity of separation. Reproach is renewed in 40, where we learn that the youth has stolen the poet's mistress.

In 50 the poet has wandered far away from the youth, but in this and the following sonnet he is riding back to his friend on horseback.

The phrase "Sweet love, renew thy force" in 56 indicates that we are near the beginning of a second cycle, which starts in 52. The slightly effusive praise of the youth in 17 is repeated in 53; the feeling of confidence in the poet's verse, which we met in 19, returns in 55; and the sense of identification with the youth, glanced at in 22, returns in 62. As before, however, the poet's meditations become increasingly melancholy, as in 65 and 66, where again the final couplets seem to jerk us back with an effort to the theme of love. By 71 the poet is preoccupied with images of old age, winter, and death. His poetry, in 76, again seems to him sterile and barren, and in 78 the theme of the rival poet begins. This theme corresponds to that of the stolen mistress in the first cycle, and the two together form an ironic counterpoint to the theme of the opening sonnets. Instead of acquiring a wife and transferring his beauty to a successor, the youth has acquired the poet's mistress and transferred his patronage to a second poet. A bitter series of reproaches follows, with the theme of separation reappearing in 87. In 92, however, we have a hint of a different perspective on the whole subject:

> I see a better state to me belongs
> Than that, which on thy humour doth depend.

This second cycle ends in 96, and a third cycle abruptly begins in 97, with a great rush of coming-of-spring images. Once again, in 100 with its phrase "Return, forgetful Muse," the poet is restored to confidence in his poetry; once again, in 106, the youth is effusively praised; once again, in 107, the poet promises the youth immortality in his verse. Again more melancholy and introspective reflections succeed, but this time the poet does not go around the cycle. He replaces reproach with self-reproach, or, more accurately, he replaces disillusionment with self-knowledge, and gradually finds the possession of what he has struggled for, not in the youth as a separate person, but in the love that unites him with the youth. In 116 the poet discovers the immortality of love; in 123 his own love achieves immortality; in 124 the phrase "my dear love" refers primarily to the poet's love; in 125 the poet's heart is accepted as an "oblation," and in 126 the youth, now only a lovely mirage, is abandoned to nature and time. Thus the problem stated in the opening sonnets, of how to perpetuate the youth's beauty, has been solved by poetic logic. It is the poet's love, not the youth's marriage, which has created a new youth, and one capable of preserving his loveliness forever. This at any rate is the "argument" of these sonnets whether they are in sequence or not, and we reach the same conclusion if we disregard sequence and simply study the imagery.

If Shakespeare himself had identified a specific person with the beautiful youth of the sonnets, that person would have had much the same relation to the youth that Edward King has to Lycidas. Milton tells us that *Lycidas* was written to commemorate the drowning of a "learned friend." But *Lycidas,* as a poem, is a pastoral elegy about Lycidas, and Lycidas is a literary and mythological figure, whose relatives are the Adonis and Daphnis of classical pastoral elegies. Similarly, the beautiful youth, though human, incarnates a divine beauty, and so is a kind of manifestation of Eros: "A god in love, to whom I am confined" [Sonnet 110]. Just as other love poets were fond of saying that their mistress was a goddess to rival Venus or the Platonic form of beauty that had fallen

by accident into the lower world, so the youth is the "rose" (in its Elizabethan sense of "primate") or "pattern" of beauty, a kind of erotic Messiah to whom all past ages have been leading up (17, 53, and 106, or what we have called the "effusive" sonnets), whose death will be "Truth and Beauty's doom and date" [Sonnet 14]. In short, he is a divine man urged, like other divine men, to set about transferring his divinity to a younger successor as soon as he reaches the height of his own powers. And whether the sonnets are in sequence or not, he is consistently associated with the spring and summer of the natural cycle, and winter and old age are associated with absence from him. His moral character has the same associations: it is spring or summer when he is lovable and winter when he is reproachable.

The poet cannot keep the resolution announced in Sonnet 21 of detaching the youth from nature. A human being is a microcosm of nature, and the most obvious and conspicuous form of nature is the cycle. In the cycle there are two elements of poetic importance. One is the fact that winter and summer, age and youth, darkness and light, are always a contrast. The other is the continual passing of one into the other, or the cycle proper. The first element suggests an ultimate separation of a world of youth, light, and "eternal summer" from its opposite. This can never happen in experience, but it would be nice to live in the paradisal *ver perpetuum* [perpetual spring] that the youth's beauty symbolizes (Sonnet 53), and poetry is based on what might be, not on what is. The second element suggests universal mutability and decay. Thus if a final separation of the two poles of the cycle is conceivable, the lower pole will be identical with the cycle as such, and the world of winter, darkness, and age will be seen as the wheel of time that carries all created things, including the blossoms of spring, away into itself.

Time is the enemy of all things in the sonnets, the universal devourer that reduces everything to nonexistence. It is associated with a great variety of eating metaphors, the canker eating the rose, the festering lily, the earth devouring its brood, and the like, which imply disappearance rather than digestion. Death is only a small aspect of time's power: what is really terrifying about time is its capacity for annihilation. Hence the financial metaphors of "lease," "audit," and similar bargains with time are continually associated with the more sinister images of "expense" and "waste." The phrase "wastes of time" in Sonnet 12 carries the heaviest possible weight of brooding menace. Nature itself, though a force making for life as time makes for death, is capable only of "temporary" or time-bound resistance to time. Behind the daily cycle of the sun, the yearly cycle of the seasons, the generation cycle of human life, are the slower cycles of empires that build up pyramids with newer might, and the cosmological cycles glanced at in Sonnets 60 and 64, with their Ovidian echoes. But though slower, they are making for the same goal.

Nature in the sonnets, as in many of the plays, is closely associated with fortune, and the cycle of nature with fortune's wheel. Those who think of fortune as more substantial than a wheel are the "fools of time," who, whatever they are in Sonnet 124, include the painful warrior who is defeated and forgotten and the makers of "policy, that heretic"—policy, in contrast to justice or statesmanship, being the kind of expediency that merely greases the wheel of fortune. Royal figures are also, in Sonnets 7, 33, and perhaps 107, associated with the cycle of nature: they pass into "eclipse" like the sun and moon turning down from the height of heaven.

The nadir of experience is represented by the terrible Sonnet 129, which, starting from the thematic words "expense" and "waste," describes what a life completely bound to time is like, with the donkey's carrot of passion jerking us along its homeless road, causing an agonizing wrench of remorse at every instant. Directly above is "the heaven that leads men to this hell," and which includes in its many mansions the fool's paradise in which the youth is living in the opening sonnets. Here we must distinguish the poet's tone, which is tender and affectionate, from his imagery, which is disconcertingly sharp. As Sonnet 94 explains in a bitterer context, the youth causes but does not produce love: he is a self-enclosed "bud," contracted to his own bright eyes like Narcissus. As with a child, his self-absorption is part of his charm. He does not need to seek a beauty in women which he already contains (Sonnet 20, where all the rhymes are "feminine"). He lacks nothing, so he is never in search: he merely attracts, even to the point of becoming, in Sonnet 31, a charnel-house of the poet's dead loves. He is therefore not on the side of nature with her interest in "increase," "store," and renewed life, but on the side of time and its devouring "waste." He is his own gradually fading reflection in water, not "A liquid prisoner pent in walls of glass," or a seed which maintains an underground resistance to time. The poet's arguments in Sonnets 1-17 are not intended to be specious, like the similar-sounding arguments of Venus to Adonis. The youth is (by implication at least) "the tomb of his self-love" [Sonnet 3], which is really a hatred turned against himself, and has no future but "folly, age, and cold decay" [Sonnet 11].

It would take a large book to work out in detail the complications of the imagery of eyes and heart, of shadow and substance, of picture and treasure, around which the argument of the beautiful-youth sonnets revolves. We can only try to give the main point of it. Above the self-enclosed narcissistic world of the youth of the opening sonnets, there appear to be three main levels of experience. There is the world of ordinary experience, a physical world of subject and object, a world where lover and beloved are essentially separated. This is the world associated with winter and absence, with the "lower" elements of earth and water (Sonnet 44), with the poet's age and poverty which increase the sense of separateness, with the reproach and scandal that separate them mentally and morally. This is also the world in which the poet is a busy actor-dramatist, with a capacity for subduing his nature to what it works in unrivalled in the history of culture, a career which leaves him not only without a private life but almost without a private personality.

Then there is a world above this of lover and beloved in contact, a quasi-paradisal world associated with the presence and kindness of the youth, with spring and summer, with air and fire in Sonnet 45, with content, ecstasy, forgiveness, and reconciliation. It is in this world that the youth appears like a god of love, associated with the sun and its gift of life, the spirit who appears everywhere in nature (Sonnet 113), the god of the spring flowers (99), all hues in his controlling. But even in this world he is still a separate person, contemplated and adored.

There is still another world above this, a world which is above time itself. This is the world in which lover and beloved are not simply in contact, but are identified. The union symbolized by the "one flesh" of Christian marriage is a sexual union: this is the kind of union expressed in the light-hearted paradoxes of *The Phoenix and the Turtle,* where reason is outraged by the fact that two souls are one and yet remain two. In the sonnets the union is a "marriage of true minds" [Sonnet 116], but the symbolism and the paradoxes are much the same. All through the sonnets we meet metaphors of identification and exchange of souls: these are, of course, the regulation hyperboles of love poetry, and in their context (as in Sonnet 39) are often harshly contradicted by the reality of separation. But in the 116-125 group they begin to take on new significance as a genuine aspect of the experience.

Sonnet 125 begins with adoring the youth's external beauty, expressed in the metaphor of bearing the canopy, and thence moves into the youth's heart, where an "oblation" and an exchange of souls takes place. The final consummation carries with it the expulsion of the "informer" or accuser, the spirit of the winter-and-absence world of separation, with all its scandals and rumors and misunderstandings and reproaches. Thus the lower world is left behind, and the higher paradisal world still remaining is dismissed in its turn in Sonnet 126. Here the "lovely boy" is seen in the role of a mock king, invested with the regalia of time, and the poem ends in a somber warning tone. From our point of view it is not much of a threat: he is merely told that he will grow old and eventually die, like everyone else. But the lovely boy from this perspective has nothing to him but what is temporary: what faces him is the annihilation of his essence.

It is not hard to understand how the selfish youth of the winter-and-absence sonnets, whose beauty is as deceitful as "Eve's apple," can also be the divine and radiant godhead of Sonnet 105, an unexampled trinity of kind, true, and fair. Love and propinquity work this miracle every day in human life, and Sonnet 114 shows it at work in the poet's mind. But what relation does the youth have, if any, to the "marriage of true minds"? There is little enough in the sonnets to show that the youth *had* a mind, much less a true one. We can hardly answer such a question: even Christianity, with all its theological apparatus, cannot clearly express the relation of whatever it is in us that is worth redeeming to what we actually are. And Shakespeare is not turning his theme over to Christianity, as Dante does in the moment at the end of the *Paradiso* when Beatrice gives place to the Virgin Mary. In these sonnets the poet assumes the role of both redeemer and repentant prodigal son. His love enables him to transcend himself, but in the instant of fulfillment the *object* of his love vanishes, because it is no longer an object. A straight Platonic explanation would be that the lover leaves behind the beautiful object as he enters into union with the form or idea of love: this is true enough as far as it goes, but we should not infer that the poet has achieved only a subjective triumph (he is no longer a subject) or that the world he enters is devoid of a beloved personality. However that may be, one thing is made clear to us: the identity of love, immortality, and the poet's genius or essential self. As Chaucer says:

> The lyf so short, the craft so long to lerne,
> Th' assay so hard, so sharp the conquering,
> The dredful joye, that alwey slit so yerne,
> Al this mene I by love.
>
> [*The Parlement of Foules*]

Just as Sonnet 129 is the nadir of experience as the sonnets treat it, so Sonnet 146 is its zenith. Here there is no youth, only the poet's soul, which is told, in the exact imagery of the opening sonnets, not to devote all its attention to its "fading mansion" which only "worms" will inherit, but (in an astonishing reversal of the eating metaphors) to feed on death until death disappears. The poet's soul in this sonnet is a *nobile castello* [lofty citadel] or House of Alma, to outward view a beleaguered fortress, but in itself, like the tower of love in Sonnet 124, "hugely politic," reaching clear of time into a paradise beyond its cycle, as the mountain of purgatory does in Dante. In this sonnet, near the end of the series, Shakespeare takes the perspective that Petrarch adopts in his first sonnet, where he looks down at the time when he was another man, when he fed his heart with error and reaped a harvest of shame. But Shakespeare is not writing a palinode: nothing in the previous sonnets is repudiated, or even regretted. Love is as strong as death: there is no wavering on that point, nor is there any tendency, so far as we can see, to change from Eros to a "higher" type of love in mid-climb.

The second group of sonnets, 127 through 154, though a unity, can hardly be in strict sequence. Two of the finest of them, 129 and 146, have already been discussed: they indicate the total range of the theme of love as Shakespeare handles it, including this group as well as its predecessor. Some seem expendable: the silly octosyllabic jingle of 145 does not gain any significance from its context, nor do the last two, which really do come under the head of "mere literary exercise," and for which the models have been discovered. (pp. 32-49)

Most of these sonnets, of course, revolve around a dark female figure, who, unlike the youth, can be treated with irony and detachment, even playfulness. The basis of the attachment here is sexual, and the slightly ribald tone of 138 and 151 is appropriate for it. This ribald tone never appears in the first group except in the close of Sonnet 20, an exception which clearly proves the rule. In the first group the youth takes over the poet's mistress, and the poet resigns her with a pathetic wistfulness ("And yet it may be said I loved her dearly" [Sonnet 42]) which is not heard in the second group. In the second group the poet has two loves, a fair youth and a dark lady, in which the former has the role of a "better angel"—hardly his role in the other group, though of course he could be called that by hyperbole. It is natural to associate the mistress of Sonnet 42 with the dark lady and the "man right fair" of 144 with the beautiful youth. But it is simpler, and not really in contradiction with this, to think of the two groups, not as telling the same story, but as presenting a contrast of two opposed attitudes to love, a contrast heightened by a number of deliberate resemblances—"Minding true things by what their mockeries be," as the chorus says in *Henry V* [Act IV].

The word "fair" in modern English means both attractive and light-complexioned, and Shakespeare's "black" has a similar double meaning of brunette and ill-favored. . . . The uniting of the two meanings suggests an involuntary attachment: involuntary means against the will, and the theme of the imprisoned will leads to more puns on the poet's name.

The center of gravity of the dark-lady sonnets is Sonnet 130, which corresponds to Sonnet 21 in the other group, where the poet stresses the ordinary humanity of his beloved. As we saw, he could not keep this balance with the youth. The youth is either present or absent: when present he seems divine, when absent he turns almost demonic. In the dark-lady group the poet again cannot keep the human balance, and the tone of affectionate raillery in 130 (and in 128) is not heard again. In striking contrast to the earlier group, the dark lady is both present and sinister. She takes on divine attributes up to a

point, but they are those of a "white goddess" or what Blake would call a female will. Like Blake's Gwendolen or Rahab, she can be fitfully maternal (143) and more than fitfully meretricious (142), but her relation to her love is ultimately destructive. Thus these sonnets deal with what we have called the "low" dialectic of bondage and freedom in its sharpest possible form, where the lover is held by a sexual fascination to a mistress whom he does not like or respect, so that he despises himself for his own fidelity.

The dark lady is an incarnation of desire rather than love; she tantalizes, turning away "To follow that which flies before her face" [Sonnet 143], precisely because she is not loved. The youth's infidelities hurt more than hers, but they do not exasperate: they touch nothing in the poet that wants only to possess. The assertion that her "face hath not the power to make love groan" [Sonnet 131] indicates that she is a projection of something self-destructive in the lover, a death as strong as love, a "becoming of things ill" [Sonnet 150] which ends, not in a romantic *Liebestod,* but in a gradual desiccation of the spirit. It is a very Proustian relation (though the role of the captive is reversed), and it is significant that the imagery is almost entirely sterile, with nothing of the former group's emphasis on store, increase, and rebirth.

What one misses in Shakespeare's sonnets, perhaps, is what we find so abundantly in the plays that it seems to us Shakespeare's outstanding characteristic. This is the sense of human proportion, of the concrete situation in which all passion is, however tragically, farcically, or romantically, spent. If the sonnets were new to us, we should expect Shakespeare to remain on the human middle ground of Sonnets 21 and 130: neither the quasi-religious language of 146 nor the prophetic vision of 129 seems typical of him. Here again we must think of the traditions of the genre he was using. The human middle ground is the area of Ovid, but the courtly love tradition, founded as it was on a "moralized" adaptation of Ovid, was committed to a psychological quest that sought to explore the utmost limits of consciousness and desire. It is this tradition of which Shakespeare's sonnets are the definitive summing-up. They are a poetic realization of the whole range of love in the Western world, from the idealism of Petrarch to the ironic frustrations of Proust. If his great predecessor tells us all we need to know of the art of love, Shakespeare has told us more than we can ever fully understand of its nature. He may not have unlocked his heart in the sonnets, but the sonnets can unlock doors in our minds, and show us that poetry can be something more than a mighty maze of walks without a plan. From the plays alone we get an impression of an inscrutable Shakespeare, Matthew Arnold's sphinx who poses riddles and will not answer them, who merely smiles and sits still. It is a call to mental adventure to find, in the sonnets, the authority of Shakespeare behind the conception of poetry as a marriage of Eros and Psyche, an identity of a genius that outlives time and a soul that feeds on death. (pp. 50-3)

Northrop Frye, "How True a Twain," in The Riddle of Shakespeare's Sonnets, *by Edward Hubler and others, Basic Books, Inc., 1962, pp. 23-53.*

R. P. BLACKMUR (essay date 1962)

[Blackmur was a major American critic and poet known for his acute and exacting attention to diction, metaphor, and symbol. He was frequently linked with the New Critics, who be-

lieved that a literary work constituted an independent object to be closely analyzed for its strictly formal devices and internal meanings. Blackmur distinguished himself from this group, however, by broadening his approach to include an appreciation of the "human or moral value" of a work of art. Language as Gesture (1952) is perhaps his most highly acclaimed, as well as his most characteristic, collection of critical commentary. Among his other critical works are The Double Agent *(1935),* The Expense of Greatness *(1940),* The Lion and the Honeycomb *(1955), and* Anni Mirabiles *(1956). His remarks on Shakespeare's sonnets, excerpted below, first appeared in 1961 in the* Kenyon Review *in a slightly different form. Blackmur maintains that the entire sequence represents the transmutation of the theme of infatuation into a discourse on the principles of poetic composition. The collection "gives to infatuation a theoretic form," he asserts, and depicts "its initiation, cultivation, and history, together with its peaks of triumph and devastation." Blackmur contends that the sonnets illuminate the process through which an artist may contend with reality by creating another to rival it. In these verses, he declares, Shakespeare turns "the problem of infatuation . . . into a problem of poetics." Among the sonnets to which he gives particular attention are Numbers 1-40, 66, 73, 76-86, and 151-52.*]

There will never be, I hope, by some chance of scholarship, any more authoritative order for Shakespeare's sonnets than that so dubiously supplied by the 1609 quarto. It is rather like Pascal's *Pensées,* or, even better, like the *order* of the Psalms, as to matters of date or interest. No one can improve upon the accidentally established order we possess; but everyone can invite himself to feel the constant interflow of new relations, of new reticulations—as if the inner order were always on the move—in the sonnets, the *Pensées,* the Psalms. Thus the vitality of fresh disorder enters the composition and finds room there with every reading, with every use and every abuse we make of them. Each time we look at a set of things together but do not count them, the sum of the impression will be different, though the received and accountable numerical order remains the same. If we complain of other people's perceptions, it is because we feel there is greater vitality in our own; and so on; we had better persist with the received order as a warrant that all of us have at least that point in common.

That point is worth a good deal more with Shakespeare's sonnets than with Pascal or the psalmist. It is thought that the text follows that of original manuscripts or fair copies, and no intuition bids me think otherwise. Furthermore, till private interests rise, the sequence we have seems sensible with respect to their sentiments, and almost a "desirable" sequence with respect to the notion of development. Anyone who feels weak about this should try reading the sonnets backwards all the way; they will turn themselves round again from their own force. At any rate numbers 1 to 17 make a preparatory exercise for the theme which emerges in number 18 and continues through number 126. With number 127 there is a break, not to a new theme but to a new level or phase of the old theme which lasts through number 152. The remaining pair of sonnets sound a light echo on an ancient model, but with fashionable rhetoric, of the devouring general theme.

That theme is infatuation: its initiation, cultivation, and history, together with its peaks of triumph and devastation. The whole collection makes a poetics for infatuation, or to use a slight elaboration of Croce's phrase, it gives to infatuation a theoretic form. The condition of infatuation is a phase of life; not limited to sexual attraction, though usually allied with it, it also modifies or exacerbates many matters besides—especially, it would seem in these sonnets, matters having to

do with the imaginative or poetic powers. The story of Pygmalion is one of several ultimate forms of infatuation, and Pygmalion is a name for sonnet after sonnet because the problem of personal infatuation is turned into a problem in poetics. If I cannot have my love, I will create it, but with never a lessening, always an intensification of the loss, the treachery, the chaos in reality; to say this is to say something about what is over-riding whenever we think either of infatuation or poetics. The maxim was never made overt but it was latent—in the undercurrent of the words—throughout much of the Renaissance: If God is reality, I must contend with him even more than I accept him, whether as lover or as poet. So it is in the sonnets. Like all of Shakespeare, they contain deep grasping notions for poetics; and this is precisely, as we master these notions, how we make most use of his poetry. We beset reality.

Let us see. The first seventeen sonnets are addressed to a beautiful young man who seems unwilling to settle down and have children. They could be used by any institute of family relations, and they must have been a great nuisance to any young man who received them. The most they tell him is that he cannot stop with himself (which is just blooming), that he cannot conquer time and mortality and reach immortality (which do not now concern him), and indeed that he can hardly continue to exist unless he promptly begets him a son. If these sonnets were paintings by Titian they would swarm with naked children—little Eroses, or putti—but Venus would be missing; there is no bride in the marriage. The argument of these first sonnets proceeds with an end in view; the prudent member speaks; but there's no premise, and no subject. There was no real "young man" in these poems—though he could be invited in. As they stand, Shakespeare was addressing not a young man, but one of his unaccomplished selves; the self that wants progeny addressing one of the selves that does not. The voices of the children in the apple trees can be heard whenever this set of the sonnets stops in the mind: a deep strain in us all. Perhaps it is this strain in the feelings that makes Shakespeare the poet address the other fellow as the unwilling father—the chap who never answers. Montaigne's thoughts on the affections of fathers for their children (II-VIII) reach the same sort of points Shakespeare dandles a little, but cannot yet accept, in Sonnets 15 to 17. "And I know not whether I would not rather have brought forth one child perfectly formed by commerce with the Muses than by commerce with my wife." Sonnet 17 goes only so far as to offer both immortalities, the child and the rhyme.

In 18 ("Shall I compare thee to a summer's day?") there is a rise in poetic power and the poetic claim is made absolute. At the same time the "young man" gains in presence and particularity, and the emotion begins to ring. The "other" self has been changed. Where the lover had been using verses around a convention, now the poet is using love both to master a convention and to jack up his self-confidence. This is of course only the blessed illusion of *poiesis:* that what *poiesis* seizes is more certain (as it is more lasting) than any operation of the senses. The couplet illuminates:

> So long as men can breathe or eyes can see,
> So long lives this, and this gives life to thee.
>
> [Sonnet 18]

There is a burst of splendor in the tautology of "this." Every essence is eternal, but Shakespeare wants his eternity in time (which, as Blake says, is the mercy of eternity). He keeps both "thy eternal summer" and his own "eternal lines," and these are the tautology of "this." But the sonnet contains also premonitions of the later Shakespeare, especially in the seventh and eighth lines where *we cannot trim sail to nature's course,* and it is this sentiment which haunts the whole poem, its special presence which we get by heart. Shakespeare hung about not only where words were (as Auden says the poet must) but also where sentiments were to be picked up. A good poem (or bad) is always a little aside from its particular subject; a good (or bad) hope from its object; or fear from its horror. Shakespeare could take the nightmare *in* nature as an aspect of unaccommodated man—whether on the heath in *Lear* or in the waste places of private love. At any rate, in this "this" sonnet there is a change in the theoretic form one makes in order to abide nature, a change from convention to *poiesis.* Poetry seizes the eternal essence and the substance (here the poem) ceases to matter. We *give up* the fertile self; one illusion succeeds another, one self another self. The last illusion would be to create or find the second self of second sight. For this a poem is our nearest substitute and furthest reach.

Sonnet 19 ("Devouring Time, blunt thou the lion's paws") comes, for this argument, as a natural digression, where Shakespeare announces and explicates the doctrine of rival creation (creation not adding to but changing God's creation). If in this sonnet we understand time to be God in Nature, the matter becomes plain. We save what is ours, we save what we have made of it: beauty's *pattern* to succeeding *men.* Only the pattern saves and salves. Even the phoenix burns in the blood; only in "my verse" shall the phoenix of my love "ever live young." Perhaps this is to take this sonnet too seriously, for it may be only an expression of vanity—yet vanity may be as near as we come to expressing our doctrine, and vainglory, in this world of time, as near to glory. Poetry is a kind of vainglory in which we are ever young.

Sonnet 19 is not only a digression, it is a nexus to number 20 ("A woman's face with nature's own hand painted") where the notion of verse—or love—ever young sets up a fright. That in us which is immortal is never free of time's attainder. Nothing in us is free, for there is no necessity with which we can cope. We cope with what passes away, necessity leaves us behind. Whenever immortal longings are felt, one begins to learn dread of the immortal. Who has not seen this in the pupils of his beloved's eyes?—that if the immortal is the ultimate form of paradise, it is the immediate form of hell. *One's firmest decision is only the early form of what transpires as a wrong guess.* In the sonnets Shakespeare deals with the reckless firmness of such untranspired decisions, and I would suppose this sentiment to be in vital analogy to the puzzle-phrase of Sonnet 20—"the master mistress of my passion"—and is a phrase at the very heart of the dialectics of infatuation (which is a lower stage of poetics, as our master Plato shows in his *Phaedrus*). Master-mistress of my passion! It is the woman in me cries out, the smothering cry of *Hysterica Passio,* which Lear would have put down as a climbing sorrow. The notion is worth arresting us. Poetics, hysteria, and love are near together—and the nearer when their mode is infatuation. In Sonnet 20 Shakespeare "found" (we may find) the *fabric* of what we call his sonnets—his second-best bed—the fabric, the Chinese silk or Egyptian cotton or West of England cloth or Scotch voile or some animal fur to your choice—some membrane to your touch. Shakespeare is *il miglior fabbro* [the best artificer] in another sense than either Dante or Eliot had in mind; he found the fabric of raised feeling. But when I say "found" I do not mean that Shakespeare

(or we) thought it up. It was the other side of the lamp post or when you opened the bulkhead of the cellar in your father's house. I cannot speak of the particulars: but I fasten for one moment on the rhyme (lines 10 and 12) of "thee fell a-doting" and "my purpose nothing." What is that aspirate doing there in that completing rhyme? Is it the breath of doting in nothing? It was behind the lamp post and in the cellar; and what did Hamlet say to his father's ghost? If that is not enough to get from a rhyme, let us go back to the distich of lines 7 and 8. Here bawdiness is compounded with metaphysics in the new simple: the master-mistress:

> A man in hue all hues in his controlling,
> Which steals men's eyes and women's souls amazeth.
>
> [Sonnet 20]

There is a rhyme of meaning here if not of sound between "controlling" and "amazeth," and the one confirms the other; it is one of the many places where Dante and Shakespeare rhyme—I do not say they are identical—in what they signify. In Canto XIX of the *Purgatorio* Dante converts a thought into a dream of the Siren, and in that dream things change as he wills, all hues are in his controlling, for the object of attention changes complexion or color—*colors*—as love wills: *come amor vuol, così le colorava.* The second line in Shakespeare's distich is the confirmation. The hues attract, draw, *steal* men's eyes, but penetrate, discombobolate, *amaze* the souls or psyches of women. There are infinite opportunities but no direction. A minotaur lives at the heart of this dream which if it lasted would become bad, but the dream wakes in the last line: "Mine be thy love, and thy love's use their treasure."

If you do not like the minotaur with Theseus and Ariadne, then let us repeat that word which superbly rhymes with itself: Narcissus. If so we must leave Narcissus at once and come again to Pygmalion. Narcissus and Pygmalion are at the two extremes of every infatuation. Of Pygmalion alone we had a hint in Sonnet 9 and again in 15 to 17; but in Sonnet 21 we begin to move toward the poetic Pygmalion making not Galatea but Narcissus. In short we come on Pygmalion and the rival poet, the poet who cannot tell the truth but only its convention. Pygmalion works in private on the making of his Narcissus.

If we follow the rival poet, he can only be the will o' the wisp of another self—in reality the anticipation of this self, and so on. We are among the executive hypocrisies by which we get along. Treachery becomes a fount of insight and a mode of action. Indeed, there is a honey-pot of treachery in every loving mind, and to say so is no more than a mild expansion of these lines:

> And then believe me, my love is as fair
> As any mother's child.
>
> [Sonnet 21]

When there is infatuation of soul or body in it, love is always my child. Sonnet 22 has two examples, one of the child, the other of the treachery. There is:

> For all that beauty that doth cover thee
> Is but the seemly raiment of my heart

where the child exaggerates, perhaps corrects, certainly gets ahead of the father; and, for the treachery,

> O therefore, love, be of thyself so wary

As I, not for myself, but for thee will;

—lines which tell that wonderful, necessary lie without which we could not tolerate the trespass we know that our affections make upon others: I love you on your account, not mine, for yourself not myself: a lie which can be true so far as Pygmalion and Narcissus make it so. When I say love, I speak of Eros and Philia but not of Agape who is with the sun and moon and other stars, and under their influences torn to other shreds. I think, too, of Rilke's Prodigal Son who ran away because he could not abide the love around the house. Shakespeare, however, in the couplet, lets the pride of lions loose—the very first *terribilità* [fearfulness] in the sonnets:

> Presume not on thy heart when mine is slain:
> Thou gav'st me thine, not to give back again.

In short, you are nothing but what I created. Put out that child.

However accidentally it is achieved, the sonnets proceed, at least from Sonnet 23 through Sonnet 40, in an order wholly appropriate to the natural consequences of the position reached in Sonnet 22. If we insist on what we have made ourselves, nothing else can serve us much. As we find this and that unavailable we find ourselves subject to the appropriate disorders that belong to our infatuation and the worse disorders—the order of the contingent or actual world—which seem to attack us because we think we have no part in them. The disorders are all familiar; it is the condition of infatuation that makes it impossible for us to ignore them and undesirable to understand them: our intimacy with them frights us out of sense, or so to speak raises the temperature of sense a little into fever. So we find Shakespeare, in his confrontation of the young man, feeling himself the imperfect actor, inadequate to his role and troubled by himself and the world, and all for fear of trust—of himself or of others.

> So I, for fear of trust, forget to say
> The perfect ceremony of love's rite . . .
>
> [Sonnet 23]

The rival poet is in the twelfth line, "More than that tongue that more hath more express'd"—where "more" becomes an ugly accusation indeed from a man "o'er charg'd with burden of mine own love's might." To self-inadequacy is added, as if it were a double self, a new, and worse, and inextinguishable self-love, which at one moment asserts eternal strength and at the next fears impotence and cries out for fresh "apparel on my totter'd loving" [Sonnet 26]. Infatuation does not fill every moment and would not exist at all if one were not half the time outside it. The *miseria* of infatuation is in the work necessary to preserve it *together* with the work necessary sometimes to escape it; and *ennui* is always around the last and next corner—the last and next turning—of *miseria*. It is *ennui* that gives infatuation its sharpest turn. Sonnet 29 ("When in disgrace with fortune and men's eyes") is a poem of *ennui*, but is also (and perhaps consequently) a true monument of self-pity—of ambition, career, profession, as well as infatuation: all places where one finds oneself "desiring this man's art, and that man's scope." . . . Sonnet 30 ("When to the sessions of sweet silent thought") carries on this theme of self-pity which no writer of the first rank—and I think no composer—has been able to avoid, and makes in the first quatrain a human splendor of it. The splendor was so great that nothing could be done with it; so he made a couplet. One engages in self-pity to secure an action or to preserve a sentiment. The sentiment is in the second quatrain, the action in

the third, but the human splendor is in the first. As for the couplet, its force is much better expressed in the third quatrain of Sonnet 31, which otherwise fits poorly in this set, unless as a digressive generalization.

> Thou art the grave where buried love doth live,
> Hung with the trophies of my lovers gone,
> Who all their parts of me to thee did give;
> That due of many now is thine alone.

It seems an accident of *expertise* that the next sonnet should be a complaint—the special complaint of the lover as poet—that this poet cannot join the decorum of style with the decorum of love. Who knows better than the man aware of his infatuation that style is impossible to his love? The content of infatuate love, while one is in it, is of a violence uncontrollable and changeable by a caprice as deep as nature, like the weather; which one might not have thought of did not the next sonnet deal with violent change in actual weather, the one after that with changes in moral and spiritual weather; and the third, (number 35) making something of both weathers, brings us to the civil war of love and hate, from the sense of which we are hardly again free in the course of the sonnets, whether those to the young man or those to dark lady. It is that civil war of love and hate, no doubt, which inhabits Sonnet 36 ("Let me confess that we two must be twain") but appears in the form of the perennial guilt felt in any unrequited love. This kind of guilt is what happens to the motive for action that cannot be taken.

> I may not evermore acknowledge thee,
> Lest my bewailed guilt should do thee shame.

The next batch of sonnets (37 through 40) make something like a deliberate exercise in poetics on the analogy of substance and shadow, with love (or the young man) as the tenth muse who brings presence to the other nine. But they also show (in 40) the first dubious form of the jealousy that is about to rage at large, quite as if it had been what was being led up to all along. Jealousy is perhaps the tenth muse, and has the advantage that she can be invoked from within, the genie in the jar of conscience, needs no help from outside, and operates equally well on both sides in the civil war of love and hate, outlasting both. Jealous, it should be remembered, was once an active verb in English (as it still is in French) having to do with an intense, usually unsatisfiable, craving, especially in its defeated phase. It is the right verb for infatuation in its later and virile stages when all but the pretence of the original force of love is gone. It is of this sort of thing Thomas Mann is thinking when he speaks (in *The Story of a Novel*) of "the motif of the treacherous wooing" in the sonnets, and of their plot as "the relation of poet, lover, and friend"—a relation made for jealousy.

Indeed from sonnet 41 on there is little left truly of love but infatuation and jealousy in a kind of single distillation, sometimes no more than a flavor and sometimes the grasping substance of a poem. Jealousy becomes a part of clear vision and by the special light it casts alters the object of the vision. The three-fold relation makes jealousy thrive and encourages her to create. There is an intermittence of life as well as of the heart, and it takes place in those moments when jealousy reigns absolutely, which it succeeds in doing more frequently than any other of the emotions under love. But the moments of sovereignty are never long; she never rules except by usurpation, and by pretending to powers and qualities not her own—as truth and necessity. In her bottom reality she is a craving, zeal without proper object, and indeed as sometimes in English the words jealous and zealous have been confused; so have what they signify. In the sonnets the occasional return to the purity of infatuation is almost like becoming whole-souled. Again, as before, the accidental order of the sonnets provides a fresh reticulation. After the jealousy of 41 and 42, there is the invocation of dreams and daydreams in 43 and the invocation of thought in 44 and 45, with, in 46, "a quest of thoughts, all tenants to the heart." These remind us that there is a desperation of condition, deeper than any jealousy.

Dreams are a mode and daydreams are the very process of creation. Nathan Sachs' remark which ought to be famous, that "day-dreams in common are the form of art" can perhaps be amended to read "the form of life"—especially when connected with an infatuation which, as in these sonnets, takes over so much else in life than its asserted object. There is much to be said about daydreams as the poetic agent of what lasts in poetry, but not here; here the point is to emphasize that dreams and daydreams—"darkly bright, are bright in dark directed" [Sonnet 43]—show a deep poetic preference at work; this sonnet does not wish to *change* reality so much as to rival it with another creation. Similarly, addressing ourselves to Sonnet 44 ("If the dull substance of my flesh were thought"), there is a great deal to be said about the way the poetic process illuminates the nature of thought; here the immediate interest, and it should not be pushed much out of its context, is in the ninth line: "But, ah! thought kills me that I am not thought." May not this be pushed just enough to suggest that thought and daydream are in the very closest sort of intimacy? Shakespeare seems to grasp what I assume to be the fact that thought takes place elsewhere than in words, though there may be mutual impregnation between them. I believe there is some support for such a notion in Prospero's phrase: "Come with a thought; I think thee, Ariel: come" [*The Tempest,* IV. i. 164]. This is rival creation triumphant.

The three sonnets 49-51 could be taken to represent that awful *ennui* in infatuation when both thought and daydream fail. The idea—image, not thought—of suicide seems at hand, the only refuge from the *ennui* of the unrequited. The idea lurks between the words, lending a thickness. But the *ennui* itself gets bored into a return to the old actions and the old patterns of action, together with the doubts and stratagems appropriate to each, in the contrary stages—the breathless ups and exhausted downs—in the history of any grasping infatuation. Consider the variety—the disorder pushing into order, every created order dropping away—in Sonnets 53 through 65. The paradox of substance and shadow presides, but is constantly recognizing other speakers. It is essential to infatuation that it cannot feel sure of itself except by assertion, and every assertion carries its own complement of doubt and therefore its need for reassertion. In one's love one makes, or finds, the ideal in the beloved; and at once the ideal draws on, breathes in, everything in the lover's mind; then the beloved, so to speak, is surrounded, attended or ignored as the case may be. It is certain among all uncertainties that when Shakespeare speaks of the constant heart (at the end of Sonnet 53), what is signified is the pulsing shadow of the veritable ideal. But, to repeat: consider the variety of these assertions. There is the poetics of beauty and truth, where my verse distills your truth, and with this belongs the immortality of ink. Then there is the feeling of apathy in perception, that slipping off of infatuation where one *knows* it to be self-sustained if not self-created; but to know this is to feel the

pinch that sets one going again, when we get infatuation fully occupied *and* conscious of itself. This releases the possibility, which Sonnet 57 seizes, that one may so rejoice in jealousy that it becomes a masochistic generosity, a martyrdom for love of the enemy and the self—not God. Surely then there is the need to ad lib at the edge of love, playing with eternal recurrence, with the poetics of time, and risking the assertion of self-love (in argument to the beloved) as a form of objective devotion. Then comes the most familiar recurrent assertion of inky immortality, with the poetics of history and ruin and the mutability of Nature herself (as we might say in the second law of thermodynamics) as new modifiers. Such is a summary account of the variety of pattern and shifting pattern. The next sonnet (66) speaks sharply to the whole procession, what is past and what is to come. It is the center of the sequence.

It is better at the center than it would have been at the end, for as it is now the reader can put it in wherever he arrests a particular reading of the sonnets. It is a center that will hold, I think, wherever it is put. "Tir'd with all these, for restful death I cry" [Sonnet 66]. In form it is not a sonnet, nor is it so as a mode of thought, but it exists formally to the degree that it is among sonnets, and as mode of thought it depends on, and is in answer to, the feelings that inhabit these sonnets: it is like a principle issuing order for their values. It is an advantage that the poem has also an independent existence as a catalogue and a naming of the convertibility of goods and ills in the world that makes us—a convertibility to downright domination. The lines are in the Roman sense classic in their modelling and so familiar in their sentiment that we can nearly ignore them as one more cry: All that's upright's gone! But let us look at the lines not as familiars but as strangers—or if as familiars, as familiars we detest. Each line from the second to the twelfth exhibits clichés for what in any other form we could not tolerate and as clichés can dismiss if we read lightly. But once we bend our attention we see that these are insistent clichés, like the ornamental dagger on the desk which suddenly comes to hand. The cliché insisted on resumes its insights, and perhaps refreshes and refleshes itself as well. To re-expand the cliché, so that it strikes once again upon the particular and the potential experience it once abstracted and generalized, may well be a part of the process of wisdom; it is certainly the business and use of serious poetry—a business and use of which Shakespeare was prime master, a mastery our sense of which only redoubles when we remember what we can of the powerful clichés his work germinated in our language. In the present poem the clichés were not germinated by him but were modified by the order he gave them and by the vocabulary—mastery of the force in words—of the last four in the catalogue.

> And art made tongue-tied by authority,
> And folly doctor-like controlling skill,
> And simple truth miscall'd simplicity,
> And captive good attending captain ill.

Do not these items precipitate us at once from the public life which presses us so much but in which we are actually so little engaged directly into the actual life which absorbs both our private momentum and all our free allegiance? These are lines where our public and private lives meet and illuminate, even judge, each other. They strike our behavior down with all its inadequacies to our every major effort; yet this behavior, and its modes, are how we keep alive from day to day though it is how we should die lifetime to lifetime. The reader may gloss as he will the generals of these lines into the privates of his life; but I think he might well gloss in the light they cast on the secret form of the mastering infatuation we have been tracing in these sonnets. These are the circumstances of any love which makes a mighty effort. Here it seems better to gloss only the apposition of "simple truth miscall'd simplicity." What is truly simple is only so to those who are already equal to it; a simple is a compound, like a compound of herbs, of all that we know which bears, into the nearest we can manage of a single substance. Here, in this line, a truth achieved is miscalled perception not begun. Hence the rightness of Shakespeare's couplet.

> Tired with all these, from these would I be gone,
> Save that, to die, I leave my love alone.

Love is the simple truth achieved, and not to be able to love is to be in hell. This sonnet is a critique of love infatuated.

It is a pity not to arrest these remarks now, but there are other themes, and new developments of old themes in the remainder of the sonnets, both those to the young man and those to the dark lady, which will fatten further into fate the truth of the love and of the infatuation here paused at in "Tir'd with all these." A few will do for comment, and the first will be one of the sonnets (number 73, "That time of year thou may'st in me behold") having to do with the imminence of death. I remember H. Granville-Barker talking at great length about the first quatrain of this sonnet. It illustrated his notion of why we need no scene painting when producing the plays. I do not know if these remarks got printed, or I would send the reader to them. Here are lines two through four:

> When yellow leaves, or none, or few, do hang
> Upon those boughs which shake against the cold,
> Bare ruin'd choirs, where late the sweet birds
>   sang . . .

The reader will remember that the second quatrain is an image of sunset fading into dark and sleep, and that the third develops the notion that the ashes of our youth make our death bed and ends with the trope that haunted Shakespeare throughout his work, the trope that something may be "consum'd with that which it was nourish'd by." These two quatrains have no particularity in their imagery or their syntax, and are indeed vague generally, a sort of loose currency. But these quatrains are lent particularity and the force of relations by the extraordinary particularity (barring perhaps the word "choirs") and syntactical unity of the first quatrain. If the reader cannot see this, and see where he *is,* indefeasibly, let him read the lines over till he does, noting especially the order of "yellow leaves, or none, or few." Perhaps it will help if he remembers an avenue of beech trees with nearly all the leaves dropped, and the rest dropping, on a late November afternoon toward dusk; then even the "bare ruin'd choirs" become enormously particular. These words are the shape of thought reaching into feeling and it is the force of that thought that was able to achieve particularity and order in the words. It is to achieve the eloquence of presence, and it is this presence which interinanimates the whole poem, so that what was merely set side by side cannot now be taken apart. I suggest that this is a model in something near perfection for how the order and particularity are reached in the sum of the sonnets if they are not counted but taken by the eloquence of full presence as one thing.

In support of this, the set of eleven sonnets (numbers 76 through 86), which are frankly on poetics, may be brought into consideration as studies of the interinanimation of poetry and love. One begins to think that one of the things to be said

about poetry is that it makes an infatuation out of life itself: the concerns of the two seem identical. At any rate these sonnets are concerned with style—where "every word doth almost tell my name" [Sonnet 76]—with style whereby we both invoke and control the violent talents of the psyche. Grammar and glamor, as the dictionaries will tell you, are at some point one and the same; the one is the secret art, the other the public show; the one is the Muse, the other the Love. The rival poet—the "other" way of writing—also inhabits these sonnets, and I think his shadowy presence suggests that he never existed save as an aid to Shakespeare's poetics.

He makes possible, this rival poet, along with the mistress shared by the lover and the young man, the seeking of humiliation and hatred and personal falsity, and that very grace of shame (Sonnet 95) which discloses what Dostoevsky's Dmitri Karamazov calls the beauty of Sodom together with the harshness of love in action. But he does not make possible, except as something to turn aside from, as a prompt to a reversal of momentum—the deepest change of tide, yet only possibly its fall—these two sonnets of transumption. . . . I mean Sonnets 105 ("Let not my love be call'd idolatry") and 108 ("What's in the brain that ink may character"). The first sonnet is a Phoenix and Turtle poem, with these last six lines:

> 'Fair, kind, and true,' is all my argument,
> 'Fair, kind, and true,' varying to other words;
> And in this change is my invention spent,
> Three themes in one, which wondrous scope af-
>   fords.
> 'Fair, kind, and true,' have often liv'd alone,
> Which three till now never kept seat in one.

I will not gloss the three words, except that they have to do with belonging and that together they make a mood which does not gainsay or transcend but is a crossing over from other moods by the ritual of repetition. The ritual is necessary and superior to the mere words—like Pascal's unbeliever who if he takes the devout posture may find belief—and when ritual is observed the distinction disappears between the hysterical and the actual. This, in effect, is the commentary Sonnet 108 makes on the text and practice of Sonnet 105.

>   . . . like prayers divine,
> I must each day say o'er the very same.

To cultivate one's hysteria and to cultivate the numen may often turn out to be the same thing, and the ritual for the one may be the observance of the other. (pp. 131-52)

Only one other sonnet (number 116, "Let me not to the marriage of true minds") makes a comparable transumption, and again it comes with a reversal of the tide that has been flowing. That tide was undermining and reductive, subduing the lover's nature to what it worked in, reducing love at last to a babe in the couplet of number 115, as if this were the last form the hovering, transmuting eye of infatuation could show. But from Love is a babe we come in number 116 to "Love's not Time's fool." Like Cleopatra's speeches in acts IV and V of her play, we need the right syntax of feeling to see how this sonnet escapes nonsense: it is a nonsense we would all speak—and many of us have said it *again*—as notably Goethe—at the next epiphany, whether of the same person or another. Such nonsense is the only possible company for the mighty effort to identify the ideal of love in the individual. It is the last accommodation of man alive, its loss its deepest discomfort. The second quatrain knows both:

> O, no! it is an ever-fixed mark,

That looks on tempests and is never shaken;
It is the star to every wandering bark,
Whose worth's unknown, although his height be
    taken.

Some say the star is the North star, but I think it may be any star you can see, and lose, and find again when you use the same way of looking, the very star "whose worth's unknown, although his height be taken." It is only the angle of observation that we have learned of the one thing always there. The pang is in the quick.

Beyond this there is nothing in hope or faith; but in cheated hope and bankrupt faith, there are the sicknesses and nightmares of love infected by the infatuation it had itself bred. So it is with the remaining sonnets addressed to the young man. It is not the sickness of love-longing, it is the sickness when the energy has left the infatuation, though the senses are still alert and vanity still itches, and indifference has not supervened. The nightmare is double: the trespass of the actual beloved upon the lover, and the trespass of the actual lover upon the beloved. These are the trespasses that bring us to ruin—if anything of the ever-fixed mark can still be seen—and the amount of ruin in us is inexhaustible until *we* are exhausted. "O benefit of ill!" [Sonnet 119] Nightmare is how we assess the trespass of one individual upon the other (which is why trespasses in the Lord's Prayer are nearer our condition than debts), and if we have dreams and daydreams in common, as Montaigne and Pascal thought then it may be that in the terminal stages of an infatuation we sometimes have nightmares in common. Then the general becomes our particular. Let the first quatrain of Sonnet 119 stand for these trespasses:

What potions have I drunk of Siren tears,
Distill'd from limbecks foul as hell within,
Applying fears to hopes and hopes to fears,
Still losing when I saw myself to win!

Number 126, the last of the verses to the young man, is not a sonnet but six rhymed couplets. Had it become a sonnet, or even added a couplet, it must have become a curse or even an anathema. Nothing is so mortal as that which has been kept too long in one stage of nature; we have horror even of a beauty that outlasts the stage of nature to which it belonged. Not even an infatuation can be maintained more than one and a half times its natural life. There is no relief so enormous as the surrender of an infatuation, and no pang so keen as the sudden emptiness after. Such is the curse, the anathema, upon Pygmalion and Narcissus these sonnets show; but they would show nothing were it not for the presence among them of the three sonnets—"Tir'd with all these" (66), "Let not my love be call'd idolatory" (105), and "Let me not to the marriage of true minds" (116). The first gives the condition of apprehension, the second the numinous ritual, and the third the limits beyond us in hope and faith for the mighty effort, which in one of our traditions is the highest of which we are capable from the *Symposium* and the *Vita Nuova* through these sonnets, the effort to make something last "fair, kind, and true" between one being and another. There is a trinity here. What wonder then, as we find ourselves short of these powers, if in vain hope we resort to infatuation?

And not once but again, with what we call the dark lady as our object, and this second (second or hundredth) time with a prophetic soul for abortion and no hope of children at all. One knows at once one is among the mistakes of life which, unless we can make something of them, are the terms of our

central failure in human relation. Where with the young man it was a question of building something, if necessary with other means short, by the cultivated hysteria of infatuation, with the dark lady there is a kind of unbuilding going on, the deliberate exchange of pounds of flesh for pounds of spirit. It is like drinking too much; every morning the rewards show as losses, and the more they show so, the more one is bound to the system. One's private degradation is the grandest Sodom. If it were not for the seriousness of the language and its absolute jarring speed, a sonnet such as 129 ("Th'expense of spirit in a waste of shame") could have been written of any evening begun in liquor that did not come off well; but there is the language and its speed, and the apprehensions from the central lonely place that this lover must seek what he must shun. The two sonnets, number 133 ("Beshrew that heart that makes my heart to groan") and number 134 ("So, now I have confess'd that he is thine"), together with 129, make a dread commentary on *philia*. In this lover's triangle, where each pair shares the third, mere sexual force—that treachery which moves like an army with banners—is superior to the mightiest effort *philia* can make alone. Once infatuation is simply sexual, it is the great swallower-up of friendship or love. Sonnet 134 does not exact Shylock's pound of flesh, which he was refused because it would have cost spirit, but is sexuality exacting—and receiving, since it does not harm the body—the pound of spirit.

The statute of thy beauty thou wilt take,
Thou usurer that put'st forth all to use,
And sue a friend came debtor for my sake;
So him I lose through my unkind abuse.

The two sonnets are two maws for over-interpretation. Let us say that sexuality is indeterminate and undeterminable; a force that has too much left over to absorb into its immediate end; or a force of which the sexual is only a part, but which sex raises to its extortionate ability. In the impasse of these sonnets, it would help nothing that the dark lady can be thought a third man, but it would hinder only those who wish to improve Shakespeare's reputation. But I suggest this only to return to the possibility, with which I began this paper, that the poetics of infatuation move among the coils and recoils of the various selves that thrive and batten upon the Psyche. This is the sixth line of number 133: "And my next self thou harder hast engross'd." Add to this only what evidence there may be in the two "Will" sonnets (135 and 136) where, other matters being present by chance, Shakespeare paid attention chiefly to the clenching of his wills in the general field of sexuality. Has no one suggested that this clenching of wills was Shakespeare's way of declaring his uncommitted anonymity? There is Thomas Mann's realm of the anonymous and the communal between us all. "Swear to thy blind soul that I was thy *Will*" [Sonnet 136].

Dark Lady, Third Man, Next Self, or the Anonymous One, there is no question of the sexuality and human infatuation pressing to find form within and under and among the words of the sonnets. In this second set, without the mighty effort to lift us that was in the first set, without Pygmalion and Narcissus and the Immortal Ink, the spirit wrestles in the flesh that engorges it, and the flesh—one's own flesh—is convulsed in the spirit that engulfs it. The two journeys are remarkably the same—as are the tower and the abyss—both in itinerary and target. Deceit, distrust, humiliation, jealousy, the plea for annihilation, and self-pity, with occasional glories in general disaster and with the world of the real senses—like the light and sweet air in Dante's Hell—always at hand; these are the common itinerary, with every other "tender feeling to base touches prone" [Sonnet 141]. The common target is repudiation—repudiation without an ounce of renunciation in it. "I am that I am" [Sonnet 121]. To say it once more, the sonnets illustrate the general or typical as the poetic, but there is a force under the words, and a force drawn from the words, which compels us to apprehend what had been generalized.

With that force in mind, let us look at two sonnets just before the end. Number 151 ("Love is too young to know what conscience is") has perhaps as one of its points that love asserts a special form of conscience by escaping its general form (as we use the word in English) into what we know now as consciousness. . . . I myself think that the two sets of meanings are deeply present here, on the simple rule of thumb that a poet can never know exactly which power or powers in his words he is drawing on, and the clearer the intention (what was to be *put* into words, not what was already there) the greater must be the uncertainty of his knowledge; and besides, the words may modify and even correct his intention, as well as ruin it—else there were no reality in words and no rush of meaning either from or to or among them. When I say the two sets of meanings are present, I do not intend to mark an ambiguity, but to urge that two voices are speaking at once which can be heard at once. This is the compacting power of poetry, which commands us so far as we hear it. Love is too young to know what true consciousness might be, Love is too young to know the pang of judgment as to the good and evil nature of an act or thought or condition, "Love is too young to know what conscience is." The second line, "Yet who knows not conscience is born of love?" suggests that intimate consciousness leads to the pang of judgment, just as the pang illuminates the knowledge one did not know that one had. Children and saints, said Dostoevsky, can believe two contrary things at once; poetry has also that talent. Our common idiom, "I could (or couldn't) in all conscience," keeps the pair alive in what seems a single approach. The phrase "in all conscience" generalizes several sorts of behavior in a convenient singleness of form, so that none of them can be dismissed. (pp. 152-59)

As we go further into this sonnet the voices thicken with tumescence, both of the body and of "the nobler part" as well. Priapus, rising, empties the rest of the body and drains something of the spirit ("tender feeling to base touches prone"); there is a physiological and spiritual disarray for the sake of a momentary concentration where it would be out of order to call for order.

This, then, is the priapic parallel, the comment of consciousness and conscience together, now that Pygmalion and Narcissus are in another limbo, for all the sonnets, whether to the young man or to the dark lady. Pygmalion and Narcissus made human efforts, but Priapus is a god and undoes all efforts not his own. His comments are in his searching actions. We can see this in lines seven and eight:

> My soul doth tell my body that he may
> Triumph in love; flesh stays no farther reason. . . .

The Greeks had a word for the bitterness of things too sweet, but Shakespeare has the verbal power for the sweetness of things too bitter. The soul in these lines cannot be taken as reason (the habit of ratio or proportion), and is unlikely to be the immortal soul which in the end must want another lodging and "deserts the body it has used." I think rather of the "blind worm" in Yeats' very late poems, and of the stub-

bornness of dreams prompting, prompting, prompting—for lines forgotten and stage business impossible. The lines may return to mind and action ensue. Because I think of the blind worm I think the soul here is the Psyche, who is much older than the soul and is so much further back in the abysm that she is prepared to identify life with the blind stubbornness of the worm if necessary. It is the Psyche that gurgles in the words of this sonnet. When the Psyche speaks, and is heard, everything merely personal collapses—all that the Psyche must regard with the disdain owed to the mere artifact. One hunts for a grave that is not an artifact, not even the headstone. It is the Psyche's voice, then, in the couplet, where everything is known together and all is pang, all consciousness and conscience, but as a condition, not a commitment, of life.

> No want of conscience hold it that I call
> Her "love" for whose dear love I rise and fall.

The labor of the Psyche is always toward the recovery of the animal life, since there can be none without.

But there is another voice than the Psyche's which makes another labor and another prayer. This is the labor and prayer of all we have made human in us, the prayer of the great lie—noble or ignoble—by which alone all that we create in ourselves or in society can survive. Consider Sonnet 152 ("In loving thee thou knows't I am forsworn"); it is a repudiation, but also a reassertion.

> I am perjur'd most;
> For all my vows are oaths but to misuse thee,
> And all my honest faith in thee is lost:
> For I have sworn deep oaths of thy deep kindness,
> Oaths of thy love, thy truth, thy constancy.

Our oaths and promises are our best lies, if only because we know that the roughage of life will mar if not break them, but more because we know that they make our truth. We lie in search of truth: to build truth: and our great cities and monuments and poems are proof of our powers. They make us meaningful because they are that part of us which survives, what we admire in ourselves even to infatuation, whence our promises come.

> Tir'd with all these, from these I would be gone,
> Save that to die, I leave my love alone.
> (pp. 159-61)

R. P. Blackmur, "A Poetics for Infatuation," in The Riddle of Shakespeare's Sonnets, *by Edward Hubler and others, Basic Books, Inc., Publishers, 1962, pp. 129-62.*

J. B. BROADBENT (essay date 1964)

[*Broadbent discusses the themes of mutability, corruption, and "undivided but separable love" in Shakespeare's sonnets. Throughout the sequence, he claims, a "general mutability of things is observed and enacted," but an antidote is also presented: the procreation of children or art, which preserves intact the substance of beauty or the essence of love. Broadbent also remarks on "the impersonal density" of these verses, arguing that this impersonality is, paradoxically, the very reason the sonnets are "so private."*]

Reading Shakespeare's sonnets, one is often baffled by the heavy Tudor air of public intimacy. They communicate across a breach of rank which we no longer regard, or between two men in terms too rich for newspaper experience of homosexual love:

> I may not ever more acknowledge thee,
> Lest my bewailèd guilt should do thee shame,
> Nor thou with public kindness honour me,
> Unless thou take that honour from thy name.
>
> [Sonnet xxxvi]

Yet in the same poem one can have sudden insight:

> Let me confess that we two must be twain,
> Although our undivided loves are one:
>
> . . . . .
>
> In our two loves there is but one respect,
> Though in our lives a separable spite
> Which, though it alter not love's sole effect,
> Yet doth it steal sweet hours from love's delight.
>
> . . . . .
>
> But do not so: I love thee in such sort
> As, thou being mine, mine is thy good report.

We know what is meant by a love which is undivided, though the lovers are; we know the "one respect" of love, the common goal, the mutual esteem; we know that a lover feels reflected onto him the excellence of the beloved. So we see into the love, though it is strange—but only if we have experienced something like it ourselves. Even then, the literary characteristics of Shakespeare's sonnets may baffle: the slow weightiness, with sudden acceleration; the abrasion of word on word ("loves . . . loves . . . lives") to define them, or make them exchange meanings; the exploding rhymes; the insistence on a felt unity of being which makes the whole poem dense; the pushing argument, with its propositions, its logical qualifiers ("Though . . . though . . . Yet . . . But") and puns.

Although we may have insight, the sonnets are so much working models of what they are about that they remain deeply private. They are about the metaphysics of love—the meaning of erotic words, erotic situations; but they are much more impersonal than Metaphysical poems. It is because they have this Eliotic impersonality that they are, paradoxically, so private. They can be placed in relation to Metaphysical poetry by a glance at *The Phoenix and the Turtle:* there we have the same topic—undivided but separable love—treated with both Metaphysical imagery, and the impersonal density of the sonnets:

> So they loved, as love in twain
> Had the essence but in one;
> Two distincts, division none:
> Number there in love was slain.
>
> [ll.25-8]

In the sonnets, though, we can trace some more public themes. The first group is addressed to a Noble Friend whom the sonneteer loves with a sort of courtly homosexuality (xx and liii are pederastic). The Friend is his patron, the mirror of his own virtues and vices (lxii), and, as in [Plato's] *Symposium* and *Phaedrus,* his inspirer, his muse.

To the Noble Friend the poet addresses a number of sonnets on the threat of mutability and ways of meeting it. The threat is conventional enough, whether presented as a fact of nature arguing for supernature, as in Spenser's Garden of Adonis,

and Mutability Cantos; or as a fact of nature arguing for seduction:

> Ripest apples soon does a-rotten
> Young woman's beauty does agey.

Or presented as the brevity of ecstasy, the decay of love:

> You pick a flower all in the morning
> Until at night it withers away.

Or as a sermon:

> Here nocht abidis, here stands no thing stable,
>   For this fals world aye flittis to and fro;
> Now day up bricht, now nicht as black as sable
>   Now ebb, now flood, now friend, now cruel foe;
>   Now glad, now sad, now weal, now into woe;
> Now clad in gold, dissolvit now in ass;
>   So dois this world transitory go:
> *Vanitas Vanitatum, et omnia Vanitas*
>
> (DUNBAR, *O Wretch, beware*)

But another of Dunbar's mutability poems takes us closer to Shakespeare:

> Our plesance here is all vain glory,
> This fals world is but transitory,
> The flesh is bruckle, the Feynd is slee—
> *Timor Mortis conturbat me.*

This is from the *Lament for the Makaris.* Shakespeare's mutability too is partly the loss of poetic genius—a genius which is a special manifestation of vital power, and depends on love. Correspondingly, its remedy is poetic, in the same way as the reviving power of Cordelia or Perdita is poetic—a ritual assertion of love and poetry against death.

Sonnet lx is central. . . . It is not, as in Sidney, a theatrical colloquy, or as in Donne a logical soliloquy. An impersonal dynamic impels the poem. It moves from the statement of a fact of experience (1-4), through a complex catastrophe (5-8), and draws the sestet into acceptance (9-12)—but then throws the choric couplet up in defiant hope. It is a characteristically active, pragmatic mode, which fully enacts the threat in a series of controlling verbs ("make . . . hasten . . . contend . . . crawls . . . fight . . ."). But the sonnet as a whole transcends the threat, by formalising it. It is this formalisation that gives Shakespeare's sonnets their density. It is achieved largely by series of assonant and alliterative words which grip the elements together ("crawls . . . crowned . . . crooked eclipses . . . confound; stands . . . stand; times in hope . . . despite his cruel hand"). It is a linguistic grappling with experience; and it implies that salvation is in the power to grapple.

To put the implication another way: the experience of mutability, presented so forcefully as a fact of nature, is to be accepted as natural, however threatening; and nature also provides an antidote. This is clearest in Sonnet xv. . . . The first two lines present mutable perfection at a distance, theoretically; but the lines hinge on the natural, heavily stressed rhyme-word, "grows". The next two lines present the world as a stage, on which men "Vaunt" their "brave state"; but these words are often used of flowers, so the actors are still like plants which grow. Life is an "inconstant stay", "eterne in mutabilitie" (Garden of Adonis); and here is the solution for the individual case in the sestet: as each plant grows and falls, only to be followed by another which it has seeded, so the poet will renew the Noble Friend's youth with love and poetry.

The antidote to natural death then is natural life. This doctrine is attractive to us: in an age of mechanical threats and psychic impotence we are fascinated by fertility rites, and we demand in poetry the sensuous richness that the tarmac jungle lacks. But Shakespeare does not present all "life" as redemptive: Cordelia makes the distinction when she describes Lear as

> mad as the vext sea; singing aloud;
> Crowned with rank fumiter and furrow-weeds,
> With burdocks, hemlock, nettles, cuckoo-flowers,
> Darnel, and all the idle weeds that grow
> In our sustaining corn.
>
> [IV. iv. 2-6]

So with the injunctions to the Noble Friend to marry: it is the *essence* of living *beauty* which must be preserved. . . . In the same way, Viola, Cordelia, Guiderius and Arviragus, Perdita, are more "natural" than other characters, and some of them live in a special state of nature; yet they preserve a grace and formality which distinguishes them from the promiscuously "natural"—from Maria and Toby, Edmund, Iachimo, Caliban.

One can't of course tease a philosophy out of Shakespeare's sonnets; but in offering so natural and poetic a remedy against natural threats, they formulate a secular doctrine of incarnation:

> All flesh in grass, and all the goodliness thereof is
> as the flower of the field: the grass withereth, the
> flower fadeth: because the spirit of the Lord blo-
> weth upon it: surely the people is grass. The grass
> withereth, the flower fadeth: but the word of our
> God shall stand for ever.
>
> [Isaiah 40:6-8]

Isaiah's assertion that "to times in hope my verse shall stand", despite Time's scythe, is read as an Advent lesson. Medieval carols often used the contrary springtime metaphors of *Isaiah:*

> there shall come forth a rod out of the stem of Jesse,
> and a Branch shall grow out of his roots . . . the
> desert shall rejoice and blossom as the rose . . . the
> parched ground shall become a pool. . . .
>
> [Isaiah 11:1, 35:1, 7]

Until the rationalism and sentimentality of the 18th Century spoilt it, the incarnation was celebrated as the primal case of winter's conquest by spring, the enlivening of flesh by spirit, the arrival of "more abundant life"; the "increase of thy kingdom":

> A spotless Rose is blowing
>   Sprung from a tender root,
> Of ancient seers' foreshowing,
>   Of Jesse promised fruit;
> Its fairest bud unfolds to light
>   Amid the cold, cold winter,
>   And in the dark midnight.

This is the context of *The Winter's Tale* and of the "increase" sonnets.

Other sonnets, though, examine the ways in which natural power and love may be corrupted. The chief corruptions are selfishness, deception and waste.

Sonnet vi recognises the possibility of beauty going rotten, being "self-killed", if it is not used. Sonnet xciv elaborates such selfishness; its terms are applicable to Angelo and Isabella in *Measure for Measure,* as well as to the conventionally cruel mistress. . . . The middle lines depend on the two parables of the stewards: the one showing that men are but stewards of their excellence, the other that talents must be put to use. The sestet, reverting to flower imagery, shows that the sonnet is part of the "increase" theme; but it leads us from the corruption of natural power by selfishness to Sonnet lxix, about deception:

> But those same tongues, that give thee so thine
>   own,
> In other accents do this praise confound
> By seeing farther than the eye hath shown.
> They look into the beauty of thy mind,
> And that, in guess, they measure by thy deeds;
> Then—churls—their thoughts, although their eyes
>   were kind,
> To thy fair flower add the rank smell of weeds;
> But why thy odour matcheth not thy show,
> The soil is this, that thou dost common grow.

Here the flower imagery takes up what is latent in Sonnet xv, that the "brave state" may be only a show, incapable of love and procreation, bound to rot. Neither lonely self-love, nor promiscuity, can distil sweetness: both turn into weeds. The eyes, the weed, and the commonness of this sonnet recur in a horror of deceiving infidelity:

> Why should my heart think that a several plot
> Which my heart knows the wide world's common
>   place?
> Or mine eyes, seeing this, say this is not,
> To put fair truth upon so foul a face?
>
> [Sonnet cxxxvii]

This horror is shared by the plays. It is Macbeth's and Troilus' that "nothing is But what is not" [*Macbeth*, I. iii. 141], "This is, and is not, Cressid" [*Troilus and Cressida*, V. ii. 146]. It is difficult to reach into this agony unless one has betrayed or been betrayed. Shakespeare presents it—whether the traitor is oneself or another—as a shock that "Shakes so my single state of man, that function is smothered in surmise" [*Macbeth*, I. iii. 140-41]. (pp. 143-50)

Beauty and love may be selfishly, deceptively or wastefully corrupt. Deceptive love and beauty are special cases of the general mutability. They are important because on the lover's ability to trust in the intimate "truth" of his beloved depends his ability to recognise coherent, objective "public" truth—truths of fact, value, belief. Love which is "false" falsifies its entire environment. The only remedy for this is ironic self-knowledge of the kind in Sonnet cxxxviii. . . . The self-knowledge of cxxxviii and other Dark Lady sonnets is unusually complete, and complicated. The puns on "simply"—foolishly dishonest with oneself, and "simple"—pure, are a criticism of language. "Therefore I lie with her, and she with me", where "lie"—sleep with, deceive myself, and deceives me, is a criticism of sexual behaviour, maturer than the "knowing" quality one often finds in ironic love poems. (pp. 151-52)

Shakespeare's insights are peculiarly literary in the sense that he gets at them by playing with dramatic relationships and the meanings of words. A general mutability of things is observed and enacted. The remedy for this is some kind of procreative activity itself springing from natural resources like a graft: it may be the begetting of children, or art—generation and genius fall together; but either way, what is preserved intact is an essence of beauty, or "The spirit of love" (lvi). This remedy is a secular version of the Christian doctrine of the Word made flesh. So in Sonnet lxxxi Shakespeare refines the commonplace of poetic fame into an everlasting life which occurs naturally, "in the mouths of men" inspired by the poet's genius:

> Or shall I live your epitaph to make,
> Or you survive when I in earth am rotten;
> From hence your memory death cannot take,
> Although in me each part will be forgotten.
> Your name from hence immortal life shall have,
> Though I, once gone, to all the world must die;
> The earth can yield me but a common grave,
> When you entombed in men's eyes shall lie.
> Your monument shall be my gentle verse,
> Which eyes not yet created shall o'er-read;
> And tongues to be your being shall rehearse,
> When all the breathers of this world are dead;
>   You still shall live, such virtue hath my pen,
>   Where breath most breathes, even in the mouths
>   of men.
>
> (p. 156)

J. B. Broadbent, "Shakespeare's Sonnets," in his Poetic Love, *1964. Reprint by Barnes & Noble, Inc., 1965, pp. 143-58.*

William Herbert, Earl of Pembroke. Engraving from a painting by Van Dyck.

W. H. AUDEN   (essay date 1964)

[*Auden, an Anglo-American poet, essayist, and critic, is generally regarded as one of the most prominent literary figures of the twentieth century. His early poetry and criticism are informed by the psychological and political theories of Freud and Marx, while his later work is heavily influenced by his conversion to Christianity. Some critics charge that the radical change in Auden's aesthetic philosophy is inconsistent and contradictory, but Auden believed that an artist's work is by its nature evolutionary and responsive to the changing moral and ideological climate of the age. Among his best-known critical works are* The Enchàfed Flood *(1950),* The Dyer's Hand *(1962), and* Forewords and Afterwords *(1973). In the following excerpt, Auden addresses several issues, including the style of Shakespeare's sonnets and the genesis of their composition. The principal experience out of which Sonnets 1-126 arose was, he proposes, a mystical "Vision of Eros," a quasi-religious episode in which the beloved is "revealed to the subject as being of infinite sacred importance." Auden declares that the sonnets depict Shakespeare's tortured endeavor to preserve this vision "in a relationship lasting at least three years, with a person who seemed intent by his actions upon covering the vision with dirt." Shakespeare wrote the sonnets for himself, the critic asserts, and never intended that they be published. Auden also discusses the Shakespearean sonnet form, with particular attention to the problematical concluding couplet, and he notes that melodiousness and "a mastery of every possible rhetorical device" are the most striking stylistic features of these poems.*]

Probably, more nonsense has been talked and written, more intellectual and emotional energy expended in vain, on the sonnets of Shakespeare than on any other literary work in the world. Indeed, they have become the best touchstone I know of for distinguishing the sheep from the goats, those, that is, who love poetry for its own sake and understand its nature, from those who only value poems either as historical documents or because they express feelings or beliefs of which the reader happens to approve. (p. xvii)

Considered in the abstract, as if they were Platonic Ideas, the Petrarchan sonnet seems to be a more esthetically satisfying form than the Shakespearean. Having only two different rhymes in the octave and two in the sestet, each is bound by rhyme into a closed unity, and the asymmetrical relation of 8 to 6 is pleasing. The Shakespearean form, on the other hand, with its seven different rhymes, almost inevitably becomes a lyric of three symmetrical quatrains, finished off with an epigrammatic couplet. As a rule Shakespeare shapes his rhetorical argument in conformity with this, that is to say, there is usually a major pause after the fourth, the eighth, and the twelfth line. Only in one case, Sonnet 86, "Was it the proud full sail of his great verse," does the main pause occur in the middle of the second quatrain, so that the sonnet divides into 6.6.2.

It is the concluding couplet in particular which, in the Shakespearean form, can be a snare. The poet is tempted to use it, either to make a summary of the preceding twelve lines which is unnecessary, or to draw a moral which is too glib and trite. In the case of Shakespeare himself, though there are some wonderful couplets, for example the conclusion of 61,

> For thee watch I, whilst thou dost wake elsewhere,
> From me far off, with others all too near,

or 87,

> Thus have I had thee as a dream doth flatter,
> In sleep a king, but waking no such matter,

all too often, even in some of the best, the couplet lines are the weakest and dullest in the sonnet, and, coming where they do at the end, the reader has the sense of a disappointing anti-climax.

Despite all this, it seems to me wise of Shakespeare to have chosen the form he did rather than the Petrarchan. Compared with Italian, English is so poor in rhymes that it is almost impossible to write a Petrarchan sonnet in it that sounds effortless throughout. In even the best examples from Milton, Wordsworth, Rossetti, for example, one is almost sure to find at least one line the concluding word of which does not seem inevitable, the only word which could accurately express the poet's meaning; one feels it is only there because the rhyme demanded it.

In addition, there are certain things which can be done in the Shakespearean form which the Petrarchan, with its sharp division between octave and sestet, cannot do. In Sonnet 66, "Tired with all these, for restful death I cry," and 129, "Th' expense of spirit in a waste of shame," Shakespeare is able to give twelve single-line *exempla* of the wretchedness of this world and the horrors of lust, with an accumulative effect of great power.

In their style, two characteristics of the sonnets stand out. Firstly, their *cantabile*. They are the work of someone whose ear is unerring. In his later blank verse, Shakespeare became a master of highly complicated effects of sound and rhythm, and the counterpointing of these with the sense, but in the sonnets he is intent upon making his verse as melodious, in the simplest and most obvious sense of the word, as possible, and there is scarcely a line, even in the dull ones, which sounds harsh or awkward. Occasionally, there are lines which foreshadow the freedom of his later verse. For example:

> Not mine own fears nor the prophetic soul
> Of the wide world dreaming on things to come.
> (107)

But, as a rule, he keeps the rhythm pretty close to the metrical base. Inversion, except in the first foot, is rare, and so is trisyllabic substitution. The commonest musical devices are alliteration—

> Then were not summer's distillation left,
> A liquid prisoner pent in walls of glass (5)

> Let me not to the marriage of true minds
> Admit impediments . . . (116)

and the careful patterning of long and short vowels—

> How many a holy and obsequious tear (31)

> Nor think the bitterness of absence sour (57)

> So far from home into my deeds to pry. (61)

The second characteristic they display is a mastery of every possible rhetorical device. The reiteration, for example, of words with either an identical or a different meaning—

> love is not love
> Which alters when it alteration finds,
> Or bends with the remover to remove. (116)

Or the avoidance of monotony by an artful arithmetical variation of theme or illustration.

Here, I cannot do better than to quote (interpolating lines where appropriate) Professor C. S. Lewis on Sonnet 18 [see excerpt above, 1954]. "As often," he says, "the theme begins at line 9,

> But thy eternal summer shall not fade,

occupying four lines, and the application is in the couplet:

> So long as men can breathe or eyes can see,
> So long lives this, and this gives life to thee.

Line 1

> Shall I compare thee to a summer's day

proposes a simile. Line 2

> Thou art more lovely and more temperate

corrects it. Then we have two one-line *exempla* justifying the correction

> Rough winds do shake the darling buds of May,
> And summer's lease hath all too short a date:

then a two-line *exemplum* about the sun

> Sometime too hot the eye of heaven shines,
> And often is his gold complexion dimmed:

then two more lines

> And every fair from fair sometime declines,
> By   chance,   or   nature's   changing   course,
> untrimmed

which do not, as we had expected, add a fourth *exemplum* but generalize. Equality of length in the two last variations is thus played off against difference of function."

The visual imagery is usually drawn from the most obviously beautiful natural objects, but, in a number, a single metaphorical conceit is methodically worked out, as in 87,

> Farewell, thou art too dear for my possessing,

where the character of an emotional relationship is worked out in terms of a legal contract.

In the inferior sonnets, such artifices may strike the reader as artificial, but he must reflect that, without the artifice, they might be much worse than they are. The worst one can say, I think, is that rhetorical skill enables a poet to write a poem for which genuine inspiration is lacking which, had he lacked such skill, he would not have written at all.

On the other hand those sonnets which express passionate emotions, whether of adoration or anger or grief or disgust, owe a very great deal of their effect precisely to Shakespeare's artifice, for without the restraint and distancing which the rhetorical devices provide, the intensity and immediacy of the emotion might have produced, not a poem, but an embarrassing "human document." Wordsworth defined poetry as emotion recollected in tranquility. It seems highly unlikely that Shakespeare wrote many of these sonnets out of recollected emotion. In his case, it is the artifice that makes up for the lack of tranquility.

If the vagueness of the historical circumstances under which the sonnets were written has encouraged the goats of idle curiosity, their matter has given the goats of ideology a wonderful opportunity to display their love of simplification at the expense of truth. Confronted with the extremely odd story they tell, with the fact that, in so many of them, Shakespeare addresses a young man in terms of passionate devotion, the sound and sensible citizen, alarmed at the thought that our Top-Bard could have had any experience with which he is unfamiliar, has either been shocked and wished that Shakespeare had never written them, or, in defiance of common sense, tried to persuade himself that Shakespeare was merely expressing in somewhat hyperbolic terms, such as an Elizabethan poet might be expected to use, what any normal man feels for a friend of his own sex. The homosexual reader, on the other hand, determined to secure our Top-Bard as a patron saint of the Homintern, has been uncritically enthusiastic about the first one hundred and twenty-six of the sonnets, and preferred to ignore those to the Dark Lady in which the relationship is unequivocally sexual, and the fact that Shakespeare was a married man and a father.

Dag Hammerskjöld, in a diary found after his death and just recently published in Sweden, makes an observation to which both the above types would do well to listen.

> How easy Psychology has made it for us to dismiss
> the perplexing mystery with a label which assigns
> it a place in the list of common aberrations.

That we are confronted in the sonnets by a mystery rather than by an aberration is evidenced for me by the fact that men and women whose sexual tastes are perfectly normal, but who enjoy and understand poetry, have always been able to read them as expressions of what they understand by the word *love,* without finding the masculine pronoun an obstacle.

I think that the *primary* experience—complicated as it became later—out of which the sonnets to the friend spring was a mystical one.

All experiences which may be called mystical have certain characteristics in common.

1. The experience is "given." That is to say, it cannot be induced or prolonged by an effort of will, though the openness of any individual to receive it is partly determined by his age, his psychophysical make-up, and his cultural milieu.

2. Whatever the contents of the experience, the subject is absolutely convinced that it is a revelation of reality. When it is over, he does not say, as one says when one awakes from a dream: "Now I am awake and conscious again of the real world." He says, rather: "For a while the veil was lifted and a reality revealed which in my 'normal' state is hidden from me."

3. With whatever the vision is concerned, things, human beings, or God, they are experienced as numinous, clothed in glory, charged with an intense being-thereness.

4. Confronted by the vision, the attention of the subject, in awe, joy, dread, is absolutely absorbed in contemplation and, while the vision lasts, his self, its desires and needs, are completely forgotten.

Natural mystical experiences, visions that is to say, concerned with created beings, not with a creator God, and without overt religious content, are of two kinds, which one might call the Vision of Dame Kind and the Vision of Eros.

The classic descriptions of the first are to be found, of course, in certain of Wordsworth's poems, like *The Prelude,* the Im-

mortality Ode, "Tintern Abbey," and "The Ruined Cottage." It is concerned with a multiplicity of creatures, inanimate and animate, but not with persons, though it may include human artifacts. If human beings do appear in it, they are always, I believe, total strangers to the subject, so that, so far as he is concerned, they are not persons. It would seem that, in our culture, this vision is not uncommon in childhood, but rare in adults.

The Vision of Eros, on the other hand, is concerned with a single person, who is revealed to the subject as being of infinite sacred importance. The classic descriptions of it are to be found in Plato's *Symposium,* Dante's *La Vita Nuova,* and some of these sonnets by Shakespeare.

It can, it seems, be experienced before puberty. If it occurs later, though the subject is aware of its erotic nature, his own desire is always completely subordinate to the sacredness of the beloved person who is felt to be infinitely superior to the lover. Before anything else, the lover desires the happiness of the beloved.

The Vision of Eros is probably a much rarer experience than most people in our culture suppose, but, when it is genuine, I do not think it makes any sense to apply to it terms like heterosexual or homosexual. Such terms can only be legitimately applied to the profane erotic experiences with which we are all familiar, to lust, for example, an interest in another solely as a sexual object, and that combination of sexual desire and *philia,* affection based upon mutual interests, values, and shared experiences which is the securest basis for a happy marriage.

That, in the Vision of Eros, the erotic is the medium, not the cause, is proved, I think, by the fact, on which all who have written about it with authority agree, that it cannot long survive an actual sexual relationship. Indeed, it is very doubtful if the Vision can ever be mutual: the story of Tristan and Isolde is a myth, not an instance of what can historically occur. To be receptive to it, it would seem that the subject must be exceptionally imaginative. Class feelings also seem to play a role; no one, apparently, can have such a vision about an individual who belongs to a social group which he has been brought up to regard as inferior to his own, so that its members are not, for him, fully persons.

The medium of the Vision is, however, undoubtedly erotic. Nobody who was unconscious of an erotic interest on his part would use the frank, if not brutal, sexual image which Shakespeare employs in speaking of his friend's exclusive interest in women.

> But since she pricked thee out for women's plea-
>   sure,
> Mine be thy love, and thy love's use their treasure.
>   (20)

The beloved is always beautiful in the impersonal sense of the word as well as the personal. (pp. xxiv-xxxi)

The Petrarchan distinction, employed by Shakespeare in a number of his sonnets, between the love of the eye and the love of the heart, is an attempt, I think, to express the difference between these two kinds of beauty and our response to them.

In the Vision of Eros, both are always present. The beloved is always beautiful in both the public and the personal sense. But, to the lover, the second is the more important. Dante certainly thought that Beatrice was a girl whose beauty everybody would admire, but it wouldn't have entered his head to compare her for beauty with other Florentine girls of the same age.

Both Plato and Dante attempt to give a religious explanation of the Vision. Both, that is to say, regard the love inspired by a created human being as intended to lead the lover towards the love of the uncreated source of all beauty. The difference between them is that Plato is without any notion of what we mean by a person, whether human or Divine; he can only think in terms of the individual and the universal, and beauty, for him, is always beauty in the impersonal sense. Consequently, on the Platonic ladder, the love of an individual must be forgotten in the love of the universal; what we should call infidelity becomes a moral duty. How different is Dante's interpretation. Neither he nor Beatrice tells us exactly what he had done which had led him to the brink of perdition, but both speak of it as a lack of fidelity on Dante's part to his love for Beatrice. In Paradise, she is with him up until the final moment when he turns from her towards "The Eternal Fountain" and, even then, he knows that her eyes are turned in the same direction. Instead of the many rungs of the Platonic ladder, there is only one step for the lover to take, from the person of the beloved creature to the Person of their common Creator.

It is consistent with Shakespeare's cast of mind as we meet it in the plays, where it is impossible to be certain what his personal beliefs were on any subject, that the sonnets should contain no theory of love: Shakespeare contents himself with simply describing the experience.

Though the primary experience from which they started was, I believe, the Vision of Eros, that is, of course, not all they are about. For the vision to remain undimmed, it is probably necessary that the lover have very little contact with the beloved, however nice a person she (or he) may be. Dante, after all, only saw Beatrice once or twice, and she probably knew little about him. The story of the sonnets seems to me to be the story of an agonized struggle by Shakespeare to preserve the glory of the vision he had been granted in a relationship, lasting at least three years, with a person who seemed intent by his actions upon covering the vision with dirt.

As outsiders, the impression we get of his friend is one of a young man who was not really very nice, very conscious of his good looks, able to switch on the charm at any moment, but essentially frivolous, cold-hearted, and self-centered, aware, probably, that he had some power over Shakespeare—if he thought about it at all, no doubt he gave it a cynical explanation—but with no conception of the intensity of the feelings he had, unwittingly, aroused. Somebody, in fact, rather like Bassanio in *The Merchant of Venice*.

The sonnets addressed to the Dark Lady are concerned with that most humiliating of all erotic experiences, sexual infatuation—*Vénus toute entière à sa proie attachée* [Venus bound completely to her prey].

Simple lust is impersonal, that is to say the pursuer regards himself as a person but the object of his pursuit as a thing, to whose personal qualities, if she has any, he is indifferent, and, if he succeeds, he expects to be able to make a safe getaway as soon as he becomes bored. Sometimes, however, he gets trapped. Instead of becoming bored, he becomes sexually obsessed, and the girl, instead of conveniently remaining an object, becomes a real person to him, but a person whom he not only does not love, but actively dislikes.

No other poet, not even Catullus, has described the anguish, self-contempt, and rage produced by this unfortunate condition so well as Shakespeare in some of these sonnets, 141, for example, "In faith I do not love thee with my eyes," or 151, "Love is too young to know what conscience is."

Aside from the opening sixteen sonnets urging his friend to marry—which may well, as some scholars have suggested, have been written at the suggestion of some member of the young man's family—aside from these, and half a dozen elegant trifles, what is astonishing about the sonnets, especially when one remembers the age in which they were written, is the impression they make of naked autobiographical confession. The Elizabethans were not given to writing their autobiographies or to "unlocking their hearts." Donne's love poems were no doubt inspired by a personal passion, but this is hidden behind the public performance. It is not until Rousseau and the age of *Sturm und Drang* that confession becomes a literary genre. After the sonnets, I cannot think of anything in English poetry so seemingly autobiographical until Meredith's *Modern Love,* and even then, the personal events seem to be very carefully "posed."

It is impossible to believe either that Shakespeare wished them to be published or that he can have shown most of them to the young man and woman, whoever they were, to whom they are addressed. Suppose you had written Sonnet 57,

> Being your slave, what should I do but tend
> Upon the hours and times of your desire?

Can you imagine showing it to the person you were thinking of? Vice versa, what on earth would you feel, supposing someone you knew handed you the sonnet and said: "This is about you"?

Though Shakespeare may have shown the sonnets to one or two intimate literary friends—it would appear that he must have—he wrote them, I am quite certain, as one writes a diary, for himself alone, with no thought of a public.

When the sonnets are really obscure, they are obscure in the way that a diary can be, in which the writer does not bother to explain references which are obvious to him, but an outsider cannot know. For example, in the opening lines of Sonnet 125,

> Were't aught to me I bore the canopy,
> With my extern the outward honoring.

It is impossible for the reader to know whether Shakespeare is simply being figurative or whether he is referring to some ceremony in which he actually took part, or, if he is, what that ceremony can have been. Again, the concluding couplet of 124 remains impenetrable.

> To this I witness call the fools of Time,
> Which die for goodness, who have lived for crime.

Some critics have suggested that this is a cryptic reference to the Jesuits who were executed on charges of high treason. This may be so, but there is nothing in the text to prove it, and even if it is so, I fail to understand their relevance as witnesses to Shakespeare's love which no disaster or self-interest can affect.

How the sonnets came to be published—whether Shakespeare gave copies to some friend who then betrayed him, or whether some enemy stole them—we shall probably never know. Of one thing I am certain: Shakespeare must have been horrified when they were published.

The Elizabethan age was certainly as worldly-wise and no more tolerant, perhaps less, than our own. After all, sodomy was still a capital offense. The poets of the period, like Marlowe and Barnfield, whom we know to have been homosexual, were very careful not to express their feelings in the first person, but in terms of classical mythology. Renaissance Italy had the reputation for being tolerant on this subject, yet, when Michelangelo's nephew published his sonnets to Tomasso de Cavalieri, which are much more restrained than Shakespeare's, for the sake of his uncle's reputation he altered the sex, just as Benson was to do with Shakespeare in 1640.

Shakespeare must have known that his sonnets would be read by many readers in 1609 as they are read by many today—with raised eyebrows. Though I believe such a reaction to be due to a misunderstanding, one cannot say that it is not understandable.

In our culture, we have good reason to be skeptical when anyone claims to have experienced the Vision of Eros, and even to doubt if it ever occurs, because half our literature, popular and highbrow, ever since the Provençal poets made the disastrous mistake of trying to turn a mystical experience into a social cult, is based on the assumption that what is, probably, a rare experience, is one which almost everybody has or ought to have; if they don't, then there must be something wrong with them. We know only too well how often, when a person speaks of having "fallen in love" with X, what he or she really feels could be described in much cruder terms. As La Rochefoucauld observed:

> True love is like seeing ghosts: we all talk about it,
> but few of us have ever seen one.

It does not follow, however, that true love or ghosts cannot exist. Perhaps poets are more likely to experience it than others, or become poets because they have. Perhaps Hannah Arendt is right: "Poets are the only people to whom love is not only a crucial but an indispensable experience, which entitles them to mistake it for a universal one." In Shakespeare's case, what happened to his relations with his friend and his mistress, whether they were abruptly broken off in a quarrel, or slowly faded into indifference, is anybody's guess. Did Shakespeare later feel that the anguish at the end was not too great a price to pay for the glory of the initial vision? I hope so and believe so. Anyway, poets are tough and can profit from the most dreadful experiences. (pp. xxxii-xxxvii)

> *W. H. Auden, in an introduction to* The Sonnets *by William Shakespeare, edited by William Burto, New American Library, 1964, pp. xvii-xxxviii.*

MURRAY KRIEGER   (essay date 1964)

[*Krieger explores Shakespeare's depiction of state, property, and the "politics of reason" in a selection of the sonnets. These verses demonstrate, he claims, that to destroy the hold of the "loveless politic world," one must not be politic at all. Instead, it is necessary to "stand alone outside state, fortune, time, accident, pomp, discontent, heat and showers." Krieger declares that this theme colors a number of these poems, and that the sonnets on reason "stand as an effective case for the operation*

of love's unreasonable reason." For Krieger's postscript to the present study, see the Additional Bibliography.]

[The] vile, wise world of worms is a politic world; and Shakespeare is not likely to overlook the possibilities of metaphorical extension in this direction. His Sonnet 124 realizes them magnificently:

> If my dear love were but the child of state,
> It might for Fortune's bastard be unfather'd,
> As subject to Time's love or to Time's hate,
> Weeds among weeds, or flowers with flowers gather'd.
> No, it was builded far from accident;
> It suffers not in smiling pomp, nor falls
> Under the blow of thralled discontent,
> Whereto th' inviting time our fashion calls.
> It fears not Policy, that heretic
> Which works on leases of short-number'd hours,
> But all alone stands hugely politic,
> That it nor grows with heat nor drowns with show'rs.
>   To this I witness call the fools of time,
>   Which die for goodness, who have liv'd for crime.

The word "state," central object of the poet's disdain, controls the divergent levels that are rooted in the union of its multiple capacities. Primarily, of course, it functions in the majestic world of sovereignty, the summit of the political hierarchy. But it is a transient "state" which, if sovereign in its day, is still "subject" to (which is to say a subject of) time. And its "child" could be "unfather'd" by "Fortune's bastard," that is, by the unlooked for "natural" son, upstart without lineage or history that chance thrusts upward even as it thrusts downward (see "falls under," lines 6-7) the majestic parent "state," which is now proved to be just as accidental, as unsanctioned, in its earlier ascension. The "child of state," then, is "unfather'd" not only in that it is deprived of "state" (its high estate) as its parent but in that state's permanent claim to legitimate fatherhood is shown as false and presumptuous: it also must have been a bastard of fortune after all, as are all who partake of the political realm in which all is vicissitude and there is no true, uncontingent "state."

But the meaning of "state" is thus spreading out to envelop the contingencies of the human condition, the generic "accident" of line 5. The political language continues, but we see politics as the pure, microcosmic reflection of worldly human life, the distillate of its worldly, wormy nature. The word "state" permits us to join the narrowest political notions in the poem to the broadest sense of worldly life as the politic enterprise: state as majesty and as political entity, state as rank or status, state as condition of being (or rather, for time-bound humanity, condition of becoming). In effect, Shakespeare is demonstrating the sweep of the world's semantic history. He proves the justness of his political metaphor by allowing his language to establish the essential oneness of the several political levels of living. Once again the metaphor is earned totally by moving from similarity to substantive identity: the human condition *is* the political condition. "State" and "accident" are finally one, so that the instabilities of the political condition may be read back into the human state at large—or at least the human state without love, the human state in its narcissistic self-enclosure, the self-interest that exposes it to politics as a universal force.

Of course, the broad universality has been indicated earlier by the shift in lines 3-4 to the unaltering natural process at once capricious and all-inclusive: "Time's love," "Time's hate," "Weeds among weeds or flowers with flowers"—but all equally "gather'd" (with the sickle image clearly implied). Still even this universality must allow the exemption of the poet's "dear love." For this love is not "subject to" the capricious sameness of time. And it is not a "child of state" and is thus free from the consequences of "accident" which universal political bastardy otherwise imposes. Nor is it the victim of "Policy," which as "heretic" is another form of the earlier "bastard," unauthorized violator of wholeness and orderly plan since its very existence denies both. But, as a mystic celebrant of love, the poet has been defining love negatively, in terms of what it is *not.* For the only terms available are those of the world, those antagonistic to love that are mentioned only to have their relations to love denied. When finally in line 11 he makes his sole attempt at a positive definition—completed with more negatives in the following line—he again borrows his crucial term from the antagonistic, loveless world. Indeed, the crowning characteristic he bestows upon love, that it "all alone stands hugely politic," gathers its paradoxical power from the juxtaposition of "hugely politic" to its etymological brother, the despised heretic "Policy" just two lines earlier.

It is a brilliant maneuver. The seeming contradiction is finally persuasive: the only way to be successfully politic is to reject policy altogether, not to be politic at all, to stand alone outside state, fortune, time, accident, pomp, discontent, heat and showers. This only is the way to be totally, absolutely, permanently—"hugely"—politic, the way to destroy the hold of the loveless politic world. Master or slave, the user of policy is finally subject. But to stand like love, all alone and hugely politic, is to evade the domain of master and slave, to be by oneself and sovereign, with absolute power, but only over oneself. Indeed, there is yet another likely meaning to the word "politic": to be "hugely politic" is to constitute oneself as a body politic. And so the self-containedness of love, in all its disdain of and inaccessibility to the terms of the world, constitutes itself a body politic distinct and indissoluble, untouchable by all others and subject to none—finally beyond the "state" of man (in all its senses) whose child it is not.

Love's sovereign aloneness is enhanced by its contrast with the undiscriminating inclusiveness of the dominion of time which it excludes. We have already seen in line 4 the sudden absorption of man's unelevated political state within the universal state of nature—a nature seen without the immortalizing circularity and thus as time's subject, in its dying cycle only. But as man's state is shown to be the same as that of *all* creation of which he is but a part, so this universal state under time is shown as totally indifferent to that "all" which share in it. "Time's love" or "Time's hate," "weeds" or "flowers," "smiling pomp" or "thralled discontent," "grows with heat" or "drowns with showers"—all is one and it just does not matter, for accident in the time-ridden state makes the alternatives interchangeable and therefore meaningless, as they all come to the same thing. The alternatives (note the use of "or" and "nor") are meant to be polar and exhaustive. There is no other possibility, except for the irrational one of love's transcendence. As the poet has been able to define love only by using the terms of the loveless world, so he can call to witness the truth of his definition only the members of that inadequate world, "the fools of time." This suggests all people but the lovers, so that he must classify these too in polar alternatives, exhaustive and yet utterly futile, as futile as state. Hence the final line, with its opposing pairs and incon-

gruous clauses of cross-purposes: "die" or "have liv'd," "for goodness" or "for crime"; but, ironically, even cynically, "Which die for goodness," or "who have liv'd for crime." There can be no further witnesses of the extent and foolishness of the time-server and, by negation, of the transcendent power of love.

In Sonnet 64 we have a universalizing of the "accidental" nature of "state" that is more complete and perhaps even more powerful.

> When I have seen by Time's fell hand defaced
> The rich proud cost of outworn buried age;
> When sometime lofty towers I see down rased,
> And brass eternal slave to mortal rage;
> When I have seen the hungry ocean gain
> Advantage on the kingdom of the shore,
> And the firm soil win of the wat'ry main,
> Increasing store with loss, and loss with store;
> When I have seen such interchange of state,
> Or state itself confounded, to decay;
> Ruin hath taught me thus to ruminate,
> That Time will come and take my love away.
>> This thought is as a death, which cannot choose
>> But weep to have that which it fears to lose.

In moving from the first to the second quatrain, we move from the world of man to the world of nature, from the succession of states to the succession of unending cycles in the rhythmic heart of the universe. Shakespeare begins by observing the destruction of the noblest and most ambitious of human productions, with the ironic use of "eternal" (line 4) the clue to his scornful view of human claims to immortality. Even more insulting to the "eternal" is its being at the mercy of that which is itself "mortal." This word "mortal" is the perfect word: first, its juxtaposition to "eternal" inverts the proper relation of master and slave between them; secondly, its implication that the wielders of the rage that destroys the "eternal" are themselves to be destroyed makes them no less the victims of time than are *their* victims; and thirdly, it makes possible the contrast between these "mortal" agents in the first quatrain and the natural, seemingly immortal agents in the second.

But as if to prove the claim that the human political state is a microcosmic reflection of the universal state of time, the antagonists of the second quatrain, the ocean and the shore, are rendered totally in human terms, as they act in accordance with political motives. Thus the apparent distinction between the human and the natural in the two quatrains is methodically blurred. As we have seen in Sonnet 124, all the realms of "state" have been identified and reduced to the extreme consequences of the narrowest meaning, that of human politics. As in Sonnet 124, the one word, despite its range of meanings, from narrow to broad, is shown to be a single reductive entity that can contain and unite them all even within its narrowest confines. For these can be extended unlimitedly without losing their most precise limitations—just the test of the sound metaphor. In Sonnet 64 the extension into nature is even more remarkable.

The ocean, seen as "hungry" for acquisition of another's, is at once the greedy state and the insatiable worm. But it reduces "the kingdom of the shore" only later to be forced to give back what it has gained along with some of its own. He who feeds like a worm shall be fed upon by another. Like Matthew Arnold's "ignorant armies" on Dover Beach several centuries later, these clash futilely and endlessly with none but temporary victories that give way to later defeats, just as temporary. Thus the inconclusive "interchange of state" (line 9) or, in terms that suggest the first quatrain, "state itself confounded to decay" (line 10), as the political sense of state achieves its universal sway under time, incorporating the other senses. The many politic antagonists can only interchange their states, as his metaphor enables Shakespeare's human and natural antagonists to interchange *their* states. And all are on their way to eventual destruction. Thus, in the first two lines of the sequel, Sonnet 65, which summarize these two quatrains of Sonnet 64,

> Since brass, nor stone, nor earth, nor boundless sea,
> But sad mortality o'ersways their power,

Shakespeare can join all the forces, the results of human and natural agents, and characterize them all as subject to "mortality." So none should have any more pretension to being "eternal" than did the brass (Sonnet 64, line 4) and all, by implication, are equally victims of one or another sort of "mortal rage." The human term "mortality" succeeds in reducing the entire material universe, as a struggling, politic, loveless state, to the state of being time's fool.

The fool of time appears again in Sonnet 116, and, as in Sonnet 124, love is exempt from this state.

> Let me not to the marriage of true minds
> Admit impediments. Love is not love
> Which alters when it alteration finds
> Or bends with the remover to remove.
> O, no! it is an ever-fixed mark
> That looks on tempests and is never shaken;
> It is the star to every wand'ring bark,
> Whose worth's unknown, although his highth be
>   taken
> Love's not Time's fool, though rosy lips and cheeks
> Within his bending sickle's compass come.
> Love alters not with his brief hours and weeks,
> But bears it out even to the edge of doom.
>   If this be error, and upon me proved,
>   I never writ, nor no man ever loved.

Love as "the marriage of true minds" reminds us that we are in the world of troth. Thus there must be no "impediments" to this marriage since only a subject of time can be forced to cooperate with time to produce an impediment. The cooperation with time is verbally enforced by the effective repetition that has time's fool following upon the aging action ("alters when it alteration finds") and the destructive action ("bends with the remover to remove") of time and his sickle. The seconding action this repetition suggests is especially persuasive in contrast to the use of repetition, joined by "not," in order to negate—even expunge—in the preceding line ("Love is not love"). There is the further repetition of forms of "bend" and "alter" in lines 10 and 11, giving a reverse or mirror-image of lines 3 and 4 (and, among other things, reinforcing the sickle image of line 4). The third quatrain, as an intensified echo of the first, presses the negative definition of love, of which we have seen a more sustained instance in Sonnet 124. Love will not add its destruction to that of the "rosy lips and cheeks," but rather asserts its eternal fixity. Here in the third quatrain, as in the echoes of lines 3 and 4, we are once more in the world of Sonnet 71 (and the line, "But let your love even with my life decay"). This reminds us of the opposition between truth and troth, time's truth and love's. . . . [Love] is outside the world of Narcissus and his linear time, since to be inside is to become its subject and agent as are the worms. So it is not surprising that, when Shakespeare does introduce

a positive definition in the second quatrain, he insists on a value for the star beyond the futile measurability of fact: "Whose worth's unknown, although his highth be taken." His extravagance—anti-scientific, may we call it?—is of course beyond logic as well as fact. Yet, as if in defiance of logic and fact, the unreasonable reason of love asserts its own version of logic and fact in the pseudo-syllogism of the couplet. The fact is the existence of this very sonnet, which is to prove that the poet has indeed "writ." The tactic here may remind us of the argumentative factuality of the "this" in Sonnet 74, lines 5-6 ("When thou reviewest this, thou dost review / The very part was consecrate to thee") and the couplet ("The worth of that is that which it contains, / And that is this, and this with thee remains"). . . . The logic there is similar too: the fact of this poem is guarantor of the poet's faith ("the very part was consecrate to thee"), of the immaterial "spirit," and of his true (that is, trothful) "worth."

Here, in Sonnet 116, the fact of his having written is the proof of his having loved. Love's faith is constituted by the poem, the one mirror-window testifying to the other. The testament of love is the embassy of poetry. As an aesthetically successful mirror-window, the sovereign entity which is the poem is "hugely politic," the body politic of Sonnet 124, which becomes the material proof as it is the domain, the physical realm, of love. Yet, together with love, it is exempt from man's "state" so that it too is no fool of time. Thus in Sonnet 116, as in Sonnet 74 and elsewhere, Shakespeare does more than borrow the Petrarchan convention of defying mortality through verse: by using the fact of this poem he matches the materialism of mortality and its truth with the materialism of immortality and its troth, with verse—the spirit made word and thing—the incarnation and thus the living proof of the immaterial world. The confident, absolute tone of the couplet is further ensured by the unqualified opposites of eternity, "never" and "ever," especially as these repeat the earlier opposition between them in lines 5 and 6. But nothing less absolute can do for the pure logic of love's reason, with its total identity of faith and the word, of faith *in* the word.

Shakespeare dedicated one of his most brilliant poems to the celebration of love's unreasonable reason. I refer, of course, to *The Phoenix and Turtle*. (pp. 140-50)

[In this poem] reason denies itself and yields to love, while acting as the chorus to love's death from the now fallen world, the death that ensures the continued reign of reason even as it corroborates reason's derogation of itself by showing reason to be master only of apparent truth and imitative beauty. The miracle of love's union, even in its withdrawal from the common world, still towers above reason, accessible to love's mystic. Among many places in the *Sonnets* in which Shakespeare struggles to earn his claim to the miracle's presence is the curious and unique group of Sonnets 33-39. In the implied narrative sequence in these poems, the poet shows himself most impolitic, the antithesis of what he urges his friend to be in Sonnet 71 ("No longer mourn for me"), as he fights to destroy apparent truth, even the truth about the commission of sin. The group traces a circular dialectic. The poet starts with a most disappointed awareness of the friend's crime, then tries to excuse it, sees this attempt as a greater crime of his own, thus takes the guilt upon himself, and ends this inversion by pleading with the now guiltless friend to avoid so darkened a creature as the poet. As reward, his sacrifice has earned an essential union with the friend that allows the poet to share his glory as his own.

Sonnet 33 begins the sequence by acknowledging the moral darkening of his glorious friend, rendered—and in part justified—by the image of the sovereign sun . . . disgracefully eclipsed by "basest clouds." Using the darkening of "heaven's sun" as his excuse, the poet urges the constancy of his love despite the darkening of *his* sun, the friend. It is his constant love that authorizes what he does for the friend in the sequel.

Sonnet 34 has the quality of dialectic that characterizes this entire sequence. The poet first rebukes the friend for surprising and disappointing him, still using the analogy of sun and clouds from Sonnet 33. Nor can the friend's repentant attempt to "dry the rain" on the poet's face cure "the disgrace." But the poet finally joins him in search for a way out of the consequences of the sin. One metaphor is tried after another to dissolve the offense. From the rain as "salve" to heal the "wound," to "shame" as "physic" for "grief," to repentance as relief for the poet's burden. But the last may open the way for the poet to find an escape:

> Th' offender's sorrow lends but weak relief
> To him that bears the strong offence's cross.

The final word, "cross," promises more than we should have expected from the negative force of these lines which in this seem to resemble those that preceded it. With this word we have not only the prospect of the poet, as innocent, taking the sin upon himself, but also the introduction of hope, of the chance for ransom, for redemption. We are ready for the couplet which fulfills that hope, if recklessly so:

> Ah, but those tears are pearl which thy love sheeds,
> And they are rich and ransom all ill deeds.

Finally this metaphor works the trick, if only by fiat. The "Ah" suggests the sudden, surprising discovery of the specious opening that the metaphor in the couplet offers him. The poet leaps to grasp the unearned transfer from "tears" to "pearl" to "ransom" which appears to solve his problem only at an unsubstantive level of language. Are we to see him as permitting himself to be deceived by his language in his desperation to exonerate his friend? And may this not be part of the poet's sin that he makes explicit in the second quatrain of the following sonnet? Still there is the sense in which "ransom" does fulfill the expectations of "cross." It may rather be that the very unearned conclusion of this metaphor is in keeping with the miraculous nature of the "ransom" in the wake of the "cross."

But is it not finally the poet who, as bearer of the "cross" still, is finally to pay the cost of this ransom, empowered as he is by the friend's love indicated by his tears? So there is no miracle in that no absolution is without price. Neither the poet's burden nor his sorrow is actually relieved, despite the verbal satisfaction of the couplet. The following sonnets prove it. The very next opens with the plea that the friend no longer be burdened by his sin, for this sonnet is the very process of the poet's ransoming him at the cost of his own innocence.

> No more be griev'd at that which thou hast done:
> Roses have thorns, and silver fountains mud;
> Clouds and eclipses stain both moon and sun,
> And loathsome canker lives in sweetest bud.
> All men make faults, and even I in this,
> Authorizing thy trespass with compare,
> Myself corrupting, salving thy amiss,
> Excusing thy sins more than thy sins are;
> For to thy sensual fault I bring in sense—

> Thy adverse party is thy advocate—
> And 'gainst myself a lawful plea commence.
> Such civil war is in my love and hate
> That I an accessary needs must be
> To that sweet thief which sourly robs from me.
> [Sonnet 35]

> Let me confess that we two must be twain,
> Although our undivided loves are one.
> So shall those blots that do with me remain,
> Without thy help by me be borne alone.
> In our two loves there is but one respect,
> Though in our lives a separable spite,
> Which though it alter not love's sole effect,
> Yet doth it steal sweet hours from love's delight.
> I may not evermore acknowledge thee,
> Lest my bewailed guilt should do thee shame;
> Nor thou with public kindness honour me,
> Unless thou take that honour from thy name.
> But do not so. I love thee in such sort
> As, thou being mine, mine is thy good report.
> [Sonnet 36]

The comparison in the first quatrain of Sonnet 35 recalls us to the poet's analogical excuse for his friend in the first of this group, Sonnet 33, with line 3 echoing the sun-cloud image on which Sonnet 33 was based. But by now, having taken us through the desperate search for the metaphorical ransom in Sonnet 34, and having gotten us there by way of the "cross," the poet must draw moral conclusions about what his love for his friend has caused him to do. Thus the second quatrain and all that follows it: the very comparisons, in authorizing the "trespass," testify to the poet's "fault."

The tactic of self-accusation is brilliant: first he shows the friend's fault to be like the necessary imperfections in nature; then he claims it shows a fallibility common to all men; then he applies this general proposition about human fallibility to himself as a man, proving his claim by pointing to this very sonnet and his attempt in it to justify his friend's fault "with compare"; finally, he gets lost in the contemplation of his own complicity in sin, even though the poem's rhetoric originally had him offering himself as a mere example of human imperfection. He allows the dialectic to carry him on finally (in Sonnet 36) to the total exoneration of the friend and the total condemnation of himself. Line 7 of Sonnet 35 ends by having quite literal consequences. The poet *has* corrupted himself in "salving" the friend's "amiss." He is now seriously infected as the friend's "amiss" is completely cured. The "physic" worked for the moral patient, and the too anxious physician is left with the moral ailment, stricken by this very physic, and beyond help.

After the grammatical and textual confusions of line 8 (although there seems to be no doubt about its general meaning), line 9 strikes profoundly: "To thy sensual fault I bring in sense." The play on "sense" here is as serious and as significant as Donne's play on it in relation to "absence" in . . . *A Valediction Forbidding Mourning*. . . . The poet has been using "sense" (as reasonable argument, good sense) to transform the friend's "sensual fault" into something else. This is, in effect, like reason playing "the bawd to lust's abuse" in . . . *Venus and Adonis*. . . . This perversion of Lord Reason's proper function is sin enough, for it changes reason into a changeling, into a subordinate and renegade form of lust. But Shakespeare's language forces the opposition between right reason and lust to fade into something close to identity between them. "Sensual fault" and "sense," the same or opposite?—especially when "sense" cannot help but have its other meaning, related to desire, rub off on its intellectual, more austere meaning. Or is it more austere? Can it be when the very word has an ambivalence that can hardly be accidental, in view of how this sonnet is proving it? This phonetic echo ("sensual," "sense") that threatens, in becoming substantive, to destroy opposition, leads to other echoes and to the unhappy identity the poem earns between "adverse" and "advocate" and "sweet" and "sourly" (as well as, without echo, "love" and "hate"), made one by the crucial "accessary," the word that tells us the explicit nature of the charge against the poet.

By Sonnet 36 the transfer of guilt has worked. It has become so concentrated in the poet it corrupted that it seems to be only in him. As bearer of "the strong offence's cross," he has taken it all on himself, leaving the friend with "honour" (line 12), "worth and truth" (Sonnet 37, line 4), and even "glory" (Sonnet 37, line 12). For "those blots that do with me remain," he faithfully promises, "without thy help by me be borne alone." And so it is, thanks to his "bewailed guilt." Now it is the friend who must avoid the poet, to keep his newly purified self uncorrupted by the transferred, corrupting guilt. Of course, by Sonnet 36 it is the reputation of sin in the eyes of the world, rather than sin itself, that is at stake—although the poet, in his selfless generosity, never suggests that the moral reputation and true moral worth are unjustly paired. For he accepts the friend's absolution and never questions the justness of his own dishonor. So the language of Sonnet 36, as later of Sonnet 39, is that of *The Phoenix and Turtle,* with the paradoxical simultaneity of oneness and duality, union and division. By Sonnet 39, this leads to the separation theme (begun with the "separable spite" of Sonnet 36) that is in many ways parallel to Donne's handling of physical separation in *A Valediction Forbidding Mourning.* The seeming duality of the poet and his friend is accentuated by the vastness of the ground separating their moral positions, especially in the eyes of the world. For the sake of the friend's honor the "two must be twain." Indeed, it is their twain-ness that enabled the poet to assume the guilt alone and to permit his friend his "good report." But as in *The Phoenix and Turtle,* the two are essentially one and "undivided" despite whatever separates them. The proof is in these poems: the poet can totally assume the guilt, though it began as the friend's, and he—though lowly and dishonored—can thoroughly share the glory that is the friend's, thanks to his sacrifice. So again Shakespeare has it both ways: he exploits their separateness to allow the poet to absolve the friend of guilt that started as his alone, and he exploits their union to allow the poet to be one with the friend in the glory that has been secured for him. As reward for his sacrifice, the poet—through the oneness he has earned by taking another's sin as his own—gains back all he has given up and more. His assumption of guilt has destroyed this otherness, and all the friend's advantages become his too. The world's "spite" is small price for this victory over its truth and niggardly distinctions. Once more the opening mirror—the mirror-window—has triumphed over the closed mirror of Narcissus.

It is through this sacrifice and winning back, through this assumption of guilt that ends by being an assumption of glory, that this sequence of poems comes to stand as an effective case for the operation of love's unreasonable reason, as it is asserted in *The Phoenix and Turtle.* The affirmation of the effects of union starts mildly enough in the couplet of Sonnet 36: "But do not so. I love thee in such sort / As, thou being

mine, mine is thy good report." Sonnet 37 strengthens the claim:

> As a decrepit father takes delight
> To see his active child do deeds of youth,
> So I, made lame by Fortune's dearest spite,
> Take all my comfort of thy worth and truth . . .

The simile is specially relevant in more than one way. The poet, in making himself "decrepit," *has* fathered the friend, has created him afresh and innocent as his "active child," in whose worth he can share. The early "breed" sonnets should remind us that we cannot take the simile of parentage lightly. . . . [The] son, as mirror-window, is a second coming of the father and one in essence with him. It is thus an ideal vehicle for that other mirror-window created in the beloved, and gives flesh to it.

When, later in this sonnet, Shakespeare introduces the shadow-substance conceit, he is using other terms for the mirror-window—and terms less successful in lending themselves to consistent development.

> For whether beauty, birth, or wealth, or wit,
> Or any of these all, or all, or more,
> Entitled in thy parts do crowned sit,
> I make my love engrafted to this store.
> So then I am not lame, poor, nor despis'd
> Whilst that this shadow doth such substance give
> That I in thy abundance am suffic'd
> And by a part of all thy glory live.
>
> [Sonnet 37]

Here is surely another version of the mirror-window paradox. The lamed poet finds his consoling joy by living in the shadow of his friend's glory, but finds that he is fully part of that glory, so that what seems shadow is finally substance too. He is literally "engrafted" to the friend's "store," can share his living substance and his growth. The poet is richer than he could have been without his sacrifice, since he has allowed the more lordly of this unified pair to remain pure. It is in this sense that he has gained more than he gave away, for the poet now shares in attributes of the friend, related to his high birth, to which he could never have laid claim, except for the fruits of the miraculous union which his sacrifice has produced. So by this point in the sequence of sonnets the poet has considerably strengthened his claim to the extensive consequences of the lovers' union ("That I in thy abundance am suffic'd / And by a part of all thy glory live").

To the two mirror-windows of union—in and through procreation and in and through love—that Shakespeare joined in the first quatrain of Sonnet 37, he adds a third, poetry, as their further reflection in Sonnets 38 and 39. The union is extended even more. For the very value of the friend, achieved through the devaluing of the poet and enhanced by their separation, is one with the value of the poetry ("While thou dost breathe, that pour'st into my verse / Thine own sweet argument" [Sonnet 38]). The internal phonetic pattern of the last line of Sonnet 38 reflects the union of the absent subject and the present poem, of his heights and the poet's depths:

> If my slight Muse do please these curious days,
> The pain be mine, but thine shall be the praise.

The alliteration and assonance between "pain" and "praise," as combined with the "mine"—"thine" internal rhyme, achieve both the polarity and identity of the two. But it is Sonnet 39 which develops the present-absent, worthless-worthy themes to their completion, as the poet's repayment for his sacrifice is made in full, thanks to the Phoenix paradox which the sacrifice has made operative in the world:

> O, how thy worth with manners may I sing
> When thou art all the better part of me?
> What can mine own praise to mine own self bring?
> And what is't but mine own when I praise thee?
> Even for this let us divided live
> And our dear love lose name of single one,
> That by this separation I may give
> That due to thee which thou deserv'st alone.
> O absence, what a torment wouldst thou prove,
> Were it not thy sour leisure gave sweet leave
> To entertain the time with thoughts of love,
> Which time and thoughts so sweetly doth deceive,
>   And that thou teachest how to make one twain—
>   By praising him here who doth hence remain!

The strongest affirmation of union is made in the couplet, because it is affirmed in the presence of duality, a duality that has been proved to be both specious and tactically useful. It fools the world of appearance in order to persuade it of the higher truth of the friend's value. Thus, after the assertion of union in the first quatrain (especially lines 2 and 4), the poet reveals his scheme: the seeming separation before the world will permit me to praise you as I could not in propriety praise myself; and, for all its sorrow, your absence is both a joy and a blessing to my poetry and its estimate of your worth. That worth is finally one with the poet's, as the existence of the poem proves, despite the surface deception that suggests a separation between the poet and his subject ("By praising him here who doth hence remain!"). Lo, there is no absence after all for love's (and poetry's) unreasonable reason—no more here than in Donne's *A Valediction Forbidding Mourning.* And in the sequence beginning with Sonnet 33, Shakespeare's dialectic of sin, ransom, sacrifice, and reward through union has earned the heights of his Platonic denial of the apparent distinctness of entities.

The fruits that this union has entitled the poet to claim appear in many places, with Sonnet 62 a splendid example:

> Sin of self-love possesseth all mine eye
> And all my soul and all my every part;
> And for this sin there is no remedy,
> It is so grounded inward in my heart.
> Methinks no face so gracious is as mine,
> No shape so true, no truth of such account,
> And for myself mine own worth do define
> As I all other in all worths surmount.
> But when my glass shows me myself indeed,
> Beated and chopt with tann'd antiquity,
> Mine own self-love quite contrary I read;
> Self so self-loving were iniquity.
>   'Tis thee (myself) that for myself I praise,
>   Painting my age with beauty of thy days.

Here, in the self-praise which is other-praise, we have the triumph of union over separation in accordance with the tactics indicated in Sonnet 39. In Sonnets 67-68 . . . , Shakespeare condemns the "bastard signs of fair," that come from using another's beauty to enhance one's own. For these constitute imitative beauty, mere "roses of shadow." But this condemnation cannot extend to the poet in Sonnet 62, though he admittedly paints his age with the friend's beauty, since his use—springing from love's union—is not imitative. For the two are one. The high opinion that the poet has of himself in the octave he has in spite of his unmagical mirror; the high opinion is justified in the couplet through the magical mirror

of his friend who, in their union, is both another and the poet himself. With the transforming cosmetic of the younger friend, we see the simile of Sonnet 37 as surely applicable here: the poet is a "decrepit father" rejuvenated by his "active child," as again the two mirror-windows created by affection and parenthood are seen as one. Love here does for the aging, "beated and chopt" poet precisely what we have seen "breed" do in the earliest sonnets. In opening the mirror outward, it has destroyed his limited identity for an enlarged and renewed identity that transcends, as it "confounds," the human state, its property, and its politic reason. (pp. 154-64)

> *Murray Krieger, in his* A Window to Criticism: Shakespeare's "Sonnets" and Modern Poetics, *Princeton University Press, 1964, 224 p.*

JOHN DOVER WILSON   (essay date 1966)

[*Wilson was a highly regarded Shakespearean scholar who was involved in several aspects of Shakespeare studies. As an editor of the* New Cambridge Shakespeare, *he made numerous contributions to twentieth-century textual criticism of Shakespeare, applying the scientific bibliography developed by W. W. Greg and Charlton Hinman. As an aesthetic critic, Wilson does not fit easily into any one critical "school." He was concerned with character analysis in the tradition of A. C. Bradley; delved into Elizabethan culture, but without the emphasis often placed by historical critics on the importance of the concepts of hierarchy and the Great Chain of Being; and, like Harley Granville-Barker, visualized possible dramatic performances of the plays. In the excerpt below, Dover Wilson suggests that the Rival Poet sonnets constitute a satire on the early work of George Chapman. According to the critic, Sonnets 76, 78-80, and 82-6 appear to mock Chapman, "the absurd, abstruse, pedantic author of* The Shadow of the Night" *1593). Yet it also appears, he declares, that Chapman had received the approbation of Shakespeare's Friend and patron, most likely for his continuation of Marlowe's* Hero and Leander *and for his brilliant translation of Homer's* Iliad, *both published in 1598.*]

Shakespeare . . . was a common player, by statute classed with rogues and vagabonds, and it is impossible for us to imagine the social gulf that separated him from anyone of noble rank. A nobleman might honour a famous player with his acquaintance, or even his friendship, Burbadge was so honoured. But neither party would or could ever forget that the one was conferring an honour upon the other; the difference of rank was so absolute that nothing could bridge it. One cannot read the *Sonnets* attentively without realising that the friendship between player and nobleman was nevertheless very real, came indeed to be very intimate. Yet Shakespeare is always aware of the social gulf and not infrequently bewails it, reminds himself of it or is even reminded of it by the Friend. (pp. li-lii)

No situation, then, would more naturally give rise to such utterances as we find in these sonnets than . . . humble adoration of an Elizabethan player for a handsome boy of high rank. Yet the adoration is assuredly even humbler than this situation demanded. One cannot imagine the boisterous Burbadge, for instance, assuming, still less genuinely possessing, that selflessness, self-abnegation, self-effacement, call it what you will, which both J. W. Lever [in his The Elizabethan Love Sonnet] and C. S. Lewis [in his *English Literature in the Sixteenth Century Excluding Drama*] find as the unique quality of Shakespeare's *Sonnets* [see excerpts above, 1956 and 1954]. (pp. liii-liv)

How far does Shakespeare's self-effacement and self-abasement help us to solve the Rival Poet puzzle? I reckon the sonnets clearly relating to this matter to be 76, 78, 79, 80 and 82-86, a virtually unbroken series which suggests that they belong to the authorised framework. In the first four, Shakespeare seems to grieve that he lags behind the fashion in verse-making, that the Friend who had previously taught his 'ignorance aloft to fly' was now adding 'feathers to the learned's wing', that his 'sick Muse doth give another place', and so on. In all this he seems to be voicing the same humility as before, and Lever, quoting 85.5 ('I think good thoughts, whilst others write good words') and 76.1 ('Why is my verse so barren of new pride'), interprets the lines as confessions of *artistic* failure. But perhaps the humblest of the series, number 80, which begins:

> O how I faint when I of you do write,
> Knowing a better spirit doth use your name,

is a confession rather of inferiority than of failure to live up to his own standards. And critics have searched in vain among his contemporaries for a poet whom Shakespeare could possibly have feared as a rival. That he felt him more learned than himself (87.7) is not surprising, since he must have been keenly conscious of that 'small Latin, and less Greek' which was all the learning a curtailed grammar school education had furnished him with. But to what Elizabethan poet, they ask, was the compliment to the 'proud full sail of his great verse' (86.1) appropriate except to Marlowe—and he had been stabbed in a Deptford tavern on 30 May 1593 and is therefore out of question unless the majority of students are altogether astray in their dating of the *Sonnets*. Was Shakespeare then so unconscious of the value of his own work as to be prepared to eat humble pie to poets like Chapman, or Daniel, or Constable, or any other of the various candidates suggested for the position of Rival Poet? Or so uncritical of their work as to credit them with verse like Marlowe's?

There is really only one escape from this dilemma. Suppose the whole Rival Poet group was meant to be satirical?

In 1960, shortly before I set my hand to this edition, Mr Gittings, who had made notable additions to our knowledge of Keats's life, published a little book in which he claimed that the Rival Poet sonnets are satirical and proposed a candidate for the rivalry whom I was inclined for long to accept as the most probable yet put forward [see Additional Bibliography]. He began by noting that the sonnets in question form a progressive sequence which tell 'a remarkably coherent and understandable story without our trying to identify any character in it'. For example: the first two or three sonnets show a half-playful awareness that new fashions in poetic technique are abroad which Shakespeare finds he cannot imitate by changing his style because he cannot do that without changing his subject—the beloved Friend. It is in sonnet 79 that he first begins to speak of a particular rival in whom the Friend is becoming interested; in 80 he calls him a 'better spirit', yet protests that there is room for both his tall ship and Shakespeare's 'saucy bark' in the boundless ocean of the patron's favour. Sonnet 81 reiterates once again that the Friend's surest hopes of immortality lie in the immortality of the Poet's 'gentle verse'. Sonnets 82, 83, 84, 85 develop the theme of the Friend's limitless 'worth', while at the same time slyly criticising the rival's pen by hinting how far it came short of its subject, and more than hinting that if the Friend were not so greedy for praise he would not receive it in such bad verse.

The author of the bad verse that Gittings selects is Gervase Markham, a well-known member of the Essex entourage, a prolific writer of books on horsemanship and country pursuits generally and also of two bombastic epical poems in execrable verse, one dealing with Sir Richard Grenville's fight in the *Revenge,* and the other with the expedition by Essex and his brother to Normandy in 1591.

Gittings works out his thesis persuasively as far as the first eight sonnets are concerned, since it is not difficult to discover lines apparently satirising or ridiculing characteristic passages in Markham. But the evidence altogether breaks down when he comes to sonnet 86. So far Shakespeare had been mildly ridiculing the general characteristics of his rival's style. But in 86 the button is off the foil. He now turns upon the man directly and begins satirising his personal pretensions and way of life, outstanding features which one supposes would have been recognizable not only by the Friend addressed but by other contemporary readers. Yet Gittings was unable to relate any of these features to Markham. The rival must be a poet who was known or at least supposed to have dealings with spirits at night. The author of *Dr Faustus* might have been made to fit this, or Thomas Nashe who wrote *The Terrors of the Night.* But not a suspicion of this kind of thing seems to hang about Markham. Chapman had been the rival generally favoured by critics hitherto. Could it be George Chapman after all? I asked myself. I turned back to see what William Minto had written on the matter in 1874 when he first put forward Chapman's name [in his *Characteristics of English Poetry from Chaucer to Shirley* (1874)].

His theory had fallen into some discredit because it was later taken up and exaggerated by Arthur Acheson [see Additional Bibliography] and others. But I recollected that the identification was mainly based on a passage in Chapman about familiar spirits, and when I looked at it I found the argument more cogent than I had remembered. After rejecting Marlowe, who had previously been conjectured but had died too early, Minto points out that the first line in the sonnet

> Was it the proud full sail of his great verse
>   [Sonnet 86]

which seemed to point directly to Marlowe, 'applies with almost too literal exactness to the Alexandrines of Chapman's Homer' which, though none of it appeared before 1598, must have been known of and generally talked about in literary circles long before. Minto also noted that Chapman's chief patron was Sir Francis Walsingham whose daughter Sir Philip Sidney had married; and suggested that nothing could have been more natural than for Walsingham to have introduced his favourite to the Countess of Pembroke or her son. But what struck many good critics when Minto first published his book was his quotation from the dedicatory epistle to Chapman's *Shadow of Night* (1594) which claims that the true poet cannot succeed 'but with invocation, fasting, watching; yea, not without having drops of their souls like an heavenly familiar'. It is all very obscure, as Chapman usually is, but it does imply a claim to inspiration from a 'heavenly familiar'—whatever that might mean.

Having got so far, I remembered further that my friend the late J. A. K. Thomson, who gave us that admirable book called *Shakespeare and the Classics,* had devoted many paragraphs therein to the relations between Shakespeare and George Chapman—relations which he confessed can only be inferred from their writings, since Shakespeare never mentions Chapman by name nor Chapman Shakespeare [see Additional Bibliography]. A good deal of the argument is concerned with Chapman's persuasion that his spirit and the spirit of Homer were connected in a manner more intimate than can be described as inspiration—after the manner, in fact, that a Greek felt himself associated with his *daemon,* or a Roman with his *genius.* The chief evidence for this belief is to be found in a poem by Chapman entitled *The Tears of Peace,* not printed until 1609 and therefore neglected by previous theorists, but describing something like a vision the young Chapman had received before coming to London—a vision in which the spirit of Homer appeared to him and spoke as follows:

> 'I am', said he 'that spirit Elysian,
> That (in thy native air, and on the hill
> Next Hitchin's left hand) did thy bosom fill
> With such a flood of soul, that thou wert fain
> (With acclamations of her rapture then)
>
> To vent it to the echoes of the vale;
> When (meditating of me) a sweet gale
> Brought me upon thee, and thou didst inherit
> My true sense, for the time then, in my spirit;
> And I, invisibly, went prompting thee
> To those fair greens where thou didst English me.

Upon this Thomson comments:

> I cannot attach any other meaning to these words than this—that Chapman claims to have been directly inspired in his translation of Homer's poems by Homer himself or (what amounts to the same thing) Homer's *anima* which came to him from Elysium. . . . Have we not got now a very probable explanation of the famous couplet in sonnet 86?
>
> He nor that affable familiar ghost
> Which nightly gulls him with intelligence.

Among other things Chapman affected was to be a Stoic and Thomson aptly quotes the following from Burton's *Anatomy of Melancholy* (Pt. 1, sec. 11, mem. 1, subs. 2):

> Cardan . . . out of the doctrine of Stoics, will have some of these genii (for so he calls them) to be desirous of men's company, very affable and familiar with them.

Jerome Cardan, one of the greatest and most widely read 'philosophers' of the age, was undoubtedly known to Shakespeare, so that the correspondence between his words and Burton's is no accident. Both are quoting as from Cardan a demonological cliché of the age. But Shakespeare is of course slyly suggesting, as Thomson observes, that Chapman's visitant, so far from being his good 'angel' or 'heavenly familiar', is a lying spirit, a devil, who 'gulls' his dupe.

In face of all this it looks as if we need have no further doubts about the identity of the Rival Poet. Nevertheless, as so often with Shakespearean biography, there is no documentary evidence to support the circumstantial. If Chapman courted the Friend in verse, no such verses have survived, while, as stated above, Shakespeare never mentions Chapman or Chapman Shakespeare.

Is there anything in the *Sonnets* which might throw light upon this? I think there is if we now round off the case for Chapman as the Rival Poet. First of all notice that if Shakespeare wrote sonnet 86 in mockery, as I believe he did, he had two reasons for deliberately recalling Marlowe when he

spoke of 'the proud full sail of his great verse'. First, he knew that, as Minto says, the words might in Chapman's imagination seem to apply 'with almost too literal exactness' to the Alexandrines of his Homer; and second, by the publication of his continuation of Marlowe's *Hero and Leander,* entered in the Stationer's Register on 2 March 1598, Chapman had just proclaimed himself the heir of Marlowe's genius. Indeed, I incline to think that the appearance of this book together with that of *Seven Books of the Iliad,* the first instalment of Chapman's Homer which was entered in the Register a month later, on 10 April, accounts for the Rival Poet sonnets as a whole. In any case these can hardly have been written until Shakespeare read them. Before the spring of 1598, all he knew of Chapman were the early poems, and he was poking fun at them in sonnet 21. But the new *Hero* and the Homer translation revealed the absurd, abstruse, pedantic author of *The Shadow of Night* as capable of really great poetry in whose presence Shakespeare's 'tongue-tied muse in manners holds her still'.

Further, though in view of the relations between the two men it is not likely that Shakespeare can have read the new Chapman before the publication of his two latest books, potential patrons like Herbert or Southampton may well have received advance copies which, as the custom was in such cases, would be beautifully written manuscript copies, prefaced by dedicatory poems, probably sonnets. And if so, may it not be that Shakespeare is referring to these copies when he alludes in 82 to

> The dedicated words which writers use
> Of their fair subject, blessing every book

or more pointedly in 85, when after declaring in mock-humility to be tongue-tied, he goes on:

> While comments of your praise richly compiled,
> Reserve their character with golden quill,
> And precious phrase by all the Muses filed.

And if no poems by Chapman which can be traced as addressed to Shakespeare's Friend have come down to us, may they not have been those 'dedicated words' which were inscribed with 'golden quill' upon the manuscripts presented to him?

But neither Shakespeare nor, I think, Thomson, fully understood Chapman. For the lines quoted above come from a long dedicatory Induction to Prince Henry which reveal the poet as a mystic, much as Wordsworth was, though of course of a very different variety. In any case one cannot read them without allowing that the vision of Homer vouchsafed to the young scholar Chapman at his native Hitchin was as real to him as was the 'serene and blessed mood' which as a young man often came to Wordsworth and enabled him to 'see into the life of things'.

Shakespeare might laugh at Chapman, but in this affair the rival laughed last, for the couplet that concludes sonnet 86—

> But when your countenance filled up his line,
> Then lacked I matter, that enfeebled mine—

may be paraphrased: When you showed that you liked his verse I was left with nothing to say, was left speechless. We must suppose therefore that the Friend had given some indication that he was willing to extend his patronage to Chapman. This did not, or did not need to, imply a break with

Shakespeare. Indeed, sonnets 92 and 93 seem to say that he remained to all appearances 'gracious and kind', which is what one might expect of a great gentleman. (pp. lxiii-lxxi)

John Dover Wilson, in an introduction to The Sonnets *by William Shakespeare, edited by John Dover Wilson, Cambridge at the University Press, 1966, pp. xiii-cxxii.*

JAMES WINNY   (essay date 1968)

[*Winny discovers "two distinct characters" in the narrator of Shakespeare's sonnets, but he denies that either one of them represents a self-portrait. In the sonnets on Time, he remarks, the narrator is superbly self-assured, but generally the speaker presents himself as "a minor poet whose unadventurous verse makes no impression on fashionable taste." Winny points out that these two distinct characterizations follow the pattern of antithesis which is a basic structural element in Shakespeare's sonnets. The critic also calls attention to Sonnets 109-12, in which the speaker acknowledges that he has been negligent toward both his Friend and his own aesthetic standards. Soon after this, Winny argues, the narrator relinquishes his habitual self-effacement and demonstrates his growing appreciation of "man's divided nature." In this respect, the critic declares, although the sonnets yield nothing about the circumstances of Shakespeare's life, they do provide an account of the development of their author's moral perspective.*]

To those who read the Sonnets as a story involving actual people, the identity of the poet presents no problems. The friend, the rival poet, and the 'woman coloured ill' are all cryptic figures who have aroused curiosity and prompted speculation since the Sonnets were first held to be a work of autobiography. Attempts to identify them still continue. The figure of the poet has excited no such inquiry. To the literalists it has always been self-evident that the poet who narrates the story of his two loves is the same poet who wrote the Sonnets, and that when he speaks of himself he is speaking about Shakespeare. There is in fact no *prima facie* reason for making this assumption; and it is not easy to understand how such a belief has been able to establish itself. That the story is told in the first person proves nothing; but commentators continue to write as though this narrative mode were exclusive to autobiography, and forbidden to fiction. To argue that the self-portrait is unmistakable in 'the generous instincts, the susceptibility to beauty, the moral discrimination, the enthusiasm' which the Sonnets display, amounts only to supposing that Shakespeare possessed the attractive human qualities which seem appropriate to a great poet. His admirers would find the same qualities in the plays; but criticism has developed beyond the level of reading Shakespeare into his dramatic characters, or of attributing to Shakespeare personally the human attributes of his more appealing figures. If he is Hamlet, he is also Pompey and Caliban. However much we know about the character of Shakespeare's work, the personal identity of its author remains in the dark to us; and it is impossible to demonstrate a link between that unknown being and the poet whose enigmatic experiences are described in the Sonnets. Without some independent knowledge of Shakespeare's personal qualities, we have no means of showing that the Sonnets reflect his temperament and outlook; and no grounds for supposing that Shakespeare is speaking of himself in their narrator.

However, we possess some factual information about the general course of Shakespeare's life and career; and if the Sonnets were indeed autobiographical we might expect them to refer to events and circumstances in the poet's life known to us from other sources. There would then be some reason to regard the speaker of the Sonnets as Shakespeare, and to find a reflection of his personal character in their commentary. In this respect the Sonnets are unhelpful. The speaker nowhere refers unambiguously to an event or experience which we know Shakespeare to have undergone. Few happenings of any kind are mentioned, and those in such vague terms that their meaning is in dispute. There are no unmistakable references to Shakespeare's work as a dramatist; and although the speaker repeatedly alludes to his writing of poetry, it does not appear that he has published two narrative poems with considerable success. To the contrary, he describes himself as an ungifted and outdated poet whose work is largely disregarded, and which could appeal to his patron only through its simple sincerity. He complains of suffering misfortune and public disgrace, and while Shakespeare's life is too poorly chronicled for its exigencies to be known, no contemporary allusion suggests that he encountered difficulties of this kind; and likelihoods seem against it. Not only do the Sonnets disclose a chapter of the poet's life whose events are unrelated to anything we know of Shakespeare: they depict a writer whose comments about himself, and whose seeming exclusion from the world of affairs in which Shakespeare actually moved, must suggest that some other person is their narrator.

The belief that Shakespeare himself is the speaker throughout the sequence has been encouraged by some of the narrator's references to his art as a poet; in particular by those sonnets challenging time and promising the young man eternal fame through the poet's 'powerful rhyme.' These promises are a development of the poet's concern that the young man shall himself reproduce his beauty by marrying. If he will not beget a child, the poet will frustrate time in his own creative fashion; preserving in verse an image of the beauty which the young man might renew in his own substance. It is in the course of this proposal that the speaker first reveals, in Sonnet 15, that he possesses such a creative power; without yet revealing that he is a poet:

> As he takes from you, I engraft you new.

He refers to his profession more explicitly in all but one of the six ensuing sonnets, speaking of 'my verse', 'my rhyme', and modestly of 'my pupil pen.' A long run of poems then substantially ignores the subject; but of the first hundred and twenty sonnets, thirty-two make some clear allusion to his writing. These include the bold assertions of creative talent that close some of the great sonnets on Time,

> My love shall in my verse ever live young
> > [Sonnet 19]

and

> His beauty shall in these black lines be seen;
> > [Sonnet 63]

which do most to uphold the belief that Shakespeare himself is speaking. The poet's boldness is seen to have been justified: his work has outlasted tyrants' monuments, and the young man's beauty lives on as he declared it would. The poetry which is still read, eternalising a long-dead friend, is incontestably Shakespeare's; and the implication that he must be the speaker of the Sonnets generally seems impossible to resist. But two considerations make the position less simple than it appears. If Shakespeare were writing in the character of another poet, he would not deliberately degrade the quality of his verse to make it appear the work of a less gifted man. Other sonnets, in which the poet bemoans the limited scope of his abilities, have endured just as capably despite their supposed mediocrity. The valuation which the poet sets on his work is not always to be taken seriously. This point brings in the second consideration, for most of the speaker's references to his poetry admit a sense of inferiority and incompetence that are incompatible with Shakespeare's admitted greatness among his contemporaries. If nothing were known of the respect which Shakespeare's fellow-poets expressed towards him, there would remain the open disparity between the speaker's depressed admissions of being untalented and ignored, and the superbly confident spirit of his prediction in Sonnet 55,

> Not marble, nor the gilded monuments
> Of princes shall outlive this powerful rhyme.

This is the voice we might expect of Shakespeare, announcing awareness of his creative power in language matching its heroic vigour. Such a gift finds part of its natural idiom in the calmly assured forecast of Sonnet 81,

> Your name from hence immortal life shall have;

which fails in its promise only because it omits to name the friend; and which is implausibly associated with the inadequate being who harps on his discontent,

> Desiring this man's art, and that man's scope.
>   [Sonnet 29]

The Sonnets could be a work of collaboration between two poets; one proudly grandiloquent though never merely boastful, the other claiming little for himself though not always to be taken at his word when he seems most self-effacing. To suppose that this second speaker is identical with the poet who promises immortality to the friend seems to be ruled out by his own admission that his writing lacks power to impress itself upon time. One might argue that Shakespeare was not always as confident of his power as Sonnet 55 suggests, but the disparity between these two voices raises doubts whether either represents him. The poet presents himself in two distinct characters; and unless the disparity is consciously noticed it may be easy to extend the sense of Shakespearian presence that is so marked in the sonnets on Time to the whole sequence, despite the much quieter tone of most of its poems.

The richly orchestrated writing of these challenges to Time, in which the poet displays the power that will make good his predictions, embodies a creative energy which the narrator of the more intimate sonnets might well envy. This minor poet, who repeatedly laments that his invention has dried up, knows himself overshadowed by rivals who, if not much more gifted, are much less reluctant to advertise themselves. Unable to compete for attention with the flamboyant style which these younger poets have made fashionable, he can only hope to secure a hearing by offering simple compliments whose true affection the friend will recognise. Sonnet 32 describes his writing in typically self-depreciatory terms, 'poor rude lines . . . outstripped by every pen', and asks the friend to

> Reserve them for my love, not for their rhyme,
> Exceeded by the height of happier men.

He acknowledges that his range of expression is sadly limited, and that while other poets experiment with new and exciting modes of writing, he continues 'still all one, ever the same'; repeating himself in the uninspired process of

> dressing old words new.
> Spending again what is already spent.
>   [Sonnet 76]

This might be accepted as a just comment on the Sonnets' persistent re-working of a restricted area of experience, but the poet is not making this point: he complains that his praise of the young man introduces no fresh form of argument. In fact he does vary the reasons which he gives for repeating himself. The friend is 'still constant in a wondrous excellence,' he explains in Sonnet 105; and it follows that his poetry, 'to constancy confined,' shall adopt the same character. He has no new ideas to express, Sonnet 108 admits, and 'must each day say o'er the very same'; but the words which he addressed to the friend at the beginning of their acquaintance remain still fresh, and are not to be accounted old in repetition. Sonnet 76 offers the simpler explanation that since the poet has only one unvarying subject, he has no need to 'glance aside to new-found methods' which the age thinks fashionable. The worried self-questioning of the octet,

> Why write I still all one, ever the same,
> And keep invention in a noted weed,
> That every word doth almost tell my name?

gives way to reassurance in the sestet as the poet acknowledges that his preoccupation with the friend gives him no reason to change his style, or to devise such 'compounds strange' as other poets have brought in.

This allusion to contemporary literary style has parallels in other sonnets, which show a similar indifference or even hostility towards the kinds of florid and strenuously inventive writing which the poet finds most alien to his own plain truthfulness. He recognises that his poetry is out-dated and commonplace, but refuses to conform with a vogue for extravagant compliment whose showiness declares it insincere. In Sonnet 21 he announces his contempt for those who follow so artificial a fashion:

> So is it not with me as with that Muse,
> Stirred by a painted beauty to his verse,
> Who heaven itself for ornament doth use.

This sense of his moral superiority over poets better-esteemed than himself is absent in Sonnet 85, where the speaker stands respectfully tongue-tied while more gifted poets put his own thoughts with much greater refinement and polish:

> comments of your praise richly compiled
> Reserve their character with golden quill,
> And precious phrase by all the Muses filed.

Here the poet compares himself to an 'unlettered clerk' who can only assent with opinions far more ably expressed than his own meagre gifts would allow. There is some possiblity that he is already speaking with the irony that colours the more famous sonnet that follows; but the self-depreciation of Sonnet 85 characterises the poet, whether he is referring to his literary abilities or to his qualities as a man. Outside the grandly assured statements of the sonnets on Time, little suggests that the poet supposes his work or himself to possess any virtue beyond simple truth of emotion.

The conflict between this simplicity and the poetry of hyperbolic compliment which he condemns provides the theme of the sonnets on the rival poet, who enters the sequence at Sonnet 79. It does not immediately appear that the rival follows the extravagant fashion already condemned by the poet, who tries to resist his influence by arguing that, although the friend deserves the tribute 'of a worthier pen', when the rival praises him he merely reflects the qualities of beauty and virtue he has found in the friend. In Sonnet 80 he admits his inferiority to the 'better spirit' whose more vociferous praises have silenced his own modest utterance;

> I am a worthless boat,
> He of tall building, and of goodly pride.

Here again it is possible to read an ironic purpose into the poet's underlining of his own inadequacy: the humility is a little too deliberate, and his respect for the rival's effortless superiority rather too deferential for these valuations to be taken at face value. (pp. 60-7)

No Elizabethan poet of consequence wrote by ignoring the disciplines of formal rhetoric; least of all Shakespeare. In their systematic development of idea and argument, as in their patterns of language, the Sonnets reveal a continuous and absorbed concern with literary artifice. If the 'strained touches' of the rival's rhetoric imply a use of bombastic and unnaturally forced images, we may agree that in this respect he and Shakespeare adopt different criteria; but this does not mean that Shakespeare writes as simply as the poet of the Sonnets suggests. The poems on Time, which most clearly refute the speaker's picture of himself as ill-assured and ungifted, employ a boldly rhetorical idiom in keeping with their storming energy and confidence. To assert in the face of such monumental writing that he was 'a worthless boat' daunted by a rival's towering magnificence, the poet must either have his tongue in his cheek or be dissociating himself from the companion figure who makes his poetry a challenge to Time. The language of the Sonnets, generally considered, is certainly not plain; nor are the poet's compliments always as unpretentiously direct as he suggests when he discusses his writing. His praise of the friend in Sonnet 53,

> Describe Adonis, and the counterfeit
> Is poorly counterfeited after you;

or his rebuke to the forward violet in a later poem,

> Sweet thief, whence didst thou steal thy sweet that
>　smells,
> If not from my love's breath?
>
> [Sonnet 99]

exemplify the kind of lavish and elaborate personal eulogy that might be written to display virtuosity or to win favour, but not to express simple feeling. In point of style, both poems are condemned by the poet's own censuring of extravagant comparison in Sonnet 21, directed against a rival who 'heaven itself for ornament doth use'. But this poem itself seems equivocal in its condemnation of a poetic practice which the speaker is certainly well-qualified to follow. (pp. 68-9)

The circle of friends who first saw the Sonnets, and who knew Shakespeare's standing among the poets of his day, could not have supposed him to be speaking of himself. Perhaps the best means of refuting the possibility that Shakespeare could have been serious when he wrote as a poet outdated and eclipsed during this productive opening phase of his career, is to compare his work with the attempts of other Elizabethan poets to master the same wittily inventive style. What in them is laboured, in him is instinctive and effortless. The wit and inventiveness which Shakespeare was about to display in the

narrative poems were already attracting attention in 1592, when Chettle spoke of the poet's 'facetious grace in writing'; and the early plays demonstrated these abilities in still more striking manner. In the field in which most Elizabethan poets of note before Jonson wished to distinguish themselves, Shakespeare was the outstanding figure; as the Sonnets themselves help to show in the versatility of their wit. Modern taste does not care for verbal ingenuity, whether it juggles expertly with different senses of the same word—

> How would thy shadow's form form happy show?
>
> [Sonnet 43]

uses alliteration as a decorative figure,

> But day doth daily draw my sorrows longer,
>
> [Sonnet 28]

or doubles word-sounds in phrases whose plain sense is confused by their noise; as in 'when first your eye I eyed' [Sonnet 104]. What most modern readers condemn as a trivial mannerism, Elizabethans were ready to accept as proof of inventive ability; which was for them an immediate criterion of the talent which surpasses nature in her own characteristic activity. The speaker of the Sonnets who complains of his 'blunt invention,' who admits that his writing is repetitive and unvaried, and that he is confined to a single subject, is a poet whose limitations would have appeared still more disabling in Elizabethan eyes than modern readers may appreciate. To believe that Shakespeare could have uttered such complaints on his own behalf might be possible if his apologies for drab and monotonous writing were borne out in the Sonnets; but the reverse is true.

When he speaks of himself, the poet continues to be apologetic and self-depreciating. Very little emerges with any definiteness. He makes no attempt to fill in the background of his commentary, and does not refer to any specific places or to the setting of events. It might be interesting to know where, if at all, the poet saw morning flatter mountain-tops, and waves making towards a pebbled shore. Of his references to his own condition, perhaps the clearest are those alluding to his lack of youth. The advice to marry and have children seems to be offered by an adviser older than the young man; and in Sonnet 22 the poet reveals the disparity of years between himself and the friend by trying to conceal it in a conceit:

> How can I then be elder than thou art?

Sonnet 37 implies that the poet is considerably older than his friend, who stands in the relation of 'active child' to the poet, his 'decrepit father.' The comparison is evidently playful, but consistent with other suggestions of the poet's seniority. In Sonnet 62 these are particularised by an unexpectedly graphic image of the face reflected by the poet's mirror,

> Beaten and chopped with tanned antiquity.

The image remains with the poet in the next sonnet, in which he contemplates the time when his friend will have reached the same wretched state as himself;

> With Time's injurious hand crushed and o'erworn.
>
> [Sonnet 63]

Old age takes a long step towards the poet in Sonnet 73, where he describes himself in terms of a wintry bough, a dying fire, and a day about to be swallowed by night; and warns the friend that he must expect to be parted from him soon. He may still be able to satisfy a mistress, however; though to keep relations even between them each must credit the other's lie, the mistress pretending

> that she thinks me young,
> Although she knows my days are past the best.
>
> [Sonnet 138]

This modifies the picture of 'tanned antiquity' which the poet presents as a self-portrait earlier in the sequence, but still calls for a factual corrective. Shakespeare reached the age of thirty in 1596, when many of the sonnets had probably been written. It is a reasonable assumption that when Sonnets 138 and 144 were published in 1599 the sequence was complete; for the latter of them reads like a commentary on the whole matter of the Sonnets. The furthest likelihood, then, is that Shakespeare was at most thirty-three when he wrote the last of the sonnets, and appreciably younger when he began the series. Elizabethans, we may be reminded, aged more rapidly than ourselves; but if Shakespeare was indeed as time-worn in his early thirties as some of the poet's allusions imply, it might be difficult to explain how he contrived to live for another twenty years. As a dramatist, Shakespeare's creative maturity began with the new century. His energies as a poet had not revealed themselves fully when Meres made the famous reference to Shakespeare's 'sugred sonnets' [see excerpt above, 1598]; and he was hardly to be described as 'crushed and outworn' when he was about to enter the phase of his greatest achievements. To interpret the remark literally would be absurdly credulous. Either Shakespeare is speaking facetiously, exaggerating a modest difference in years and condition, or he is giving a voice to the unimposing counterpart who tells the story of the Sonnets and presents its poems as his own. Even without the knowledge that Shakespeare was much younger than the lined and wasted figure whom the Sonnets describe, we might suspect him of arranging an antithesis between the friend's youthful beauty and the aged and disfigured poet. (pp. 71-4)

Whether we take the speaker to be Shakespeare or not, the inconsistency and sometimes the improbability of his allusions to his age should make us wary of giving literal regard to his remarks about his personal circumstances. Because the poet's comments are so indefinite, they can very easily be made to corroborate interpretations which begin by assuming that the Sonnets contain allusions to Shakespeare's personal and professional life. Although the speaker never claims any connection with the playhouse, critics continue to find references to his association with acting and drama in every sonnet which hints at the poet's means of livelihood. To any dispassionate scrutiny such imparticular allusions reveal nothing, and their very indefiniteness invites the reader to make of them whatever he likes. In the absence of any clear directive, it is better to fall back upon the critical axiom that the poems themselves lay down the terms on which they are to be understood, and not to expect the circumstances of Shakespeare's life to explain them. Instead of assuming that the speaker's allusions to his background can only refer to Shakespeare's social status and professional career, we should question all such remarks very closely; seeking to understand them primarily within the context of ideas which the sequence develops, and of which they form part.

It begins to appear early in the sequence that the poet is dogged by misfortune, which conspires with other disabilities to thwart his hopes. Others, better favoured than himself, may boast of 'public honours and proud titles' [Sonnet 25]:

he is denied such happiness, and must draw a compensating pleasure from the friendship which he has found unlooked-for. . . . In describing himself as one 'whom fortune of such triumph bars' [Sonnet 25], the poet does not explain what prevents him from becoming distinguished; but those who read the Sonnets as autobiography recognise here the first of several allusions to the stigma which Shakespeare incurred by following the calling of common player. A more sceptical reader may suspect that the poet inflicts this arbitrary disqualification upon himself for the sake of antithesis with those who are 'in favour with their stars.' The argument of the sonnet invites such a playing of one against the other. Those who have secured a place in the public eye are not to be envied, for they may suddenly lose it; whereas the poet, although unknown and ungifted, enjoys the happiness of a mutual love too firm ever to be lost. There is no critical justification for putting any more particular construction on the 'public honours and proud titles' which an unkind fate denies the speaker. Shakespeare's status as an actor may have debarred him from certain privileges, though it is not altogether clear what deprivation he suffered as a member of the acting company which, in Chambers' words [in his *William Shakespeare, A Study of Facts and Problems*], 'had practically become an official part of the royal household with a privileged and remunerative position'; but he could not well have complained, as the poet does here, that he was unknown and disregarded. The remark becomes intelligible only if we suppose the speaker to be adopting his habitual character of minor poet whose unadventurous verse makes no impression on fashionable taste; though this is not one of the sonnets in which the speaker refers to himself as a poet. Nor is it—*pace* Dowden, whose 'penetrating note' Dover Wilson quotes with approval [see excerpt above, 1966]—the sonnet in which 'Shakespeare makes his first complaint . . . against his low condition.' The speaker nowhere mentions his social standing.

Four sonnets later his personal difficulties have become more acute. The poet now speaks of himself 'in disgrace with fortune and men's eyes', an aggravated form of the distress alluded to previously. The second line,

> I all alone beweep my outcast state,
>
> [Sonnet 29]

offers the convinced more evidence of the stigma attached to Shakespeare's calling; but the ideas of this poem are shaped by its formal structure, which like Sonnet 25 is directed by antithesis. When the poet describes himself 'with what I most enjoy contented least', he does not invite us to take him quite literally, but to admire the neatness of his reversed figure. The whole sonnet is organised on the same principle; and in this respect as in its vague suggestion of personal misfortune the poem represents a stronger version of Sonnet 25. The octet is taken up with the poet's account of the frustrations that make him curse his fate:

> Wishing me like to one more rich in hope,
> Featured like him, like him with friends possessed;
> Desiring this man's art, and that man's scope.
>
> [Sonnet 29]

The third of these lines contains the speaker's first admission of his lameness as a writer. Those whose art and scope he envies here are presumably related, in the development of Shakespeare's ideas, with those who have acquired public honour and proud titles in the earlier sonnet; and thus the germinal concept to be seen full-grown in Sonnets 79-86 has been implanted in the sequence. By balancing 'this man's art' against 'that man's scope', and reversing the form of 'featured like him' in a matching phrase, the poet continues to show the concern with antithesis which gives the sonnet its shape. (pp. 75-8)

To read [Sonnet 111] as Shakespeare's lament over his shameful association with the stage requires some determination. The greatest writing in our literature was not produced by a poet ashamed of being a dramatist, but by a man whose superlative gift found its fullest expression in supplying the needs of the most distinguished acting company of his age. Nothing suggests that his work brought him into disgrace. To the contrary, we know that it gave him popularity, modest affluence and contemporary fame which the ill-starred poet of the Sonnets does not hope to achieve. If there were reason to suppose that some body of Elizabethan readers or *cognoscenti* held Shakespeare in contempt for his association with the playhouse, the poem might be read in this sense; but evidently it and Sonnet 110 together provide the whole basis of the assumption. A critic who supposes that Shakespeare is speaking must believe that the poet had just dissociated himself from the stage in disgust and self-reproach, and that in Sonnet 111 he is asking the friend to devise a ritual of purification after his exposure to the mob. We need only ask when this sudden abandonment of the playhouse and his fellow-sharers occurred to reveal the absurdity of a reading which makes Shakespeare its speaker.

Sonnet 110 seems to encourage this reading by using the term 'motley', which most critics have taken in a theatrical sense. A more detached appreciation of the poem will recognise another admission of the inconstancy for which the speaker had already rebuked himself in Sonnet 100, coupled with an assurance that he has profited by his mistake, and a plea for a renewal of the friend's affection. Here again the notion that Shakespeare is admitting what shame he has incurred by joining the Lord Chamberlain's Men does not match the terms of the experience outlined in the sonnet; for unlike the speaker, Shakespeare did not—if he discovered that he had committed himself to an ignominious course of life—withdraw from it in disgust. The opening lines of the poem leave us in no doubt of the poet's self-contemptuous feelings:

> Alas, 'tis true, I have gone here and there,
> And made myself a motley to the view;
> Gored mine own thoughts, sold cheap what is most
>   dear,
> Made old offences of affections new.
> Most true it is that I have looked on truth
> Askance and strangely.

> [Sonnet 110]

His mortification seems centred upon the recognition that he has acted without respect for the truth which the friend embodies, and which his own writing has hitherto reflected. Previously the poet has been able to claim an honest sincerity for his writing which made amends for its lack of fashionable polish: the friend might value him for this simple truth of feeling, although other poets put him to shame by their greater fluency and eloquence. Sonnet 100 marks a change of behavior, whose consequences are indicated or hinted at in two groups of poems which follow. The first group deals with the poet's silence towards the friend. . . . [This group contains] a suggestion that the poet has found a new and less distinguished patron, on whom he has been squandering his talent.

This idea lies dormant until Sonnet 109, which opens a group of poems apologising and begging forgiveness for an act never clearly defined, but which is half-identified with the suggested disloyalty of Sonnet 100. The poems of this group, Sonnets 109-112, develop a situation seemingly drawn from this idea thrown out earlier; and present a state of affairs appreciably more serious than the previous group of sonnets outlines, though still related to it. Both show the poet on the defensive, and trying to persuade either himself or the friend that his love is unaffected by the aberrations of behavior that have plainly indicated a weakening of regard for the friend. This is the background of 'story' against which Sonnets 109-112 are to be read.

'Alas, 'tis true', is part of the aftermath of the poet's negligence and disloyalty. He has betrayed the standards that made him unselfishly constant despite the friend's ill-treatment. Still more astonishing, the friend has undergone as complete a metamorphosis. He is now—and to judge from the terms of the poet's self-reproach, has always been—as staunch in affection as the poet was earlier: 'a god in love' [Sonnet 110]. The poet confesses shame at having neglected such a proved friendship for the sake of general esteem, won at the cost of his personal reputation for loyalty. His fickleness has been noted. His next remark, 'Gored mine own thoughts', appears to renew this admission; 'thoughts' being the good opinion in which he had previously been held, and which he himself has injured. It is not an isolated lapse for which he condemns himself: 'Made old offences of affections new' admits that he has persisted in his fault and become habituated to inconstancy. Most true it is, he continues with an ironic play on words, that he has wrenched himself away from the well-tried truth of the friend, to whom he now appeals abjectly for pardon. The reading of Sonnet 110 followed by the autobiographists, who take 'motley' as a keyword referring to Shakespeare's professional life, fails to offer any coherent explanation of the poet's self-accusing remarks. (pp. 82-5)

The poet renews his apology and his appeal in Sonnet 117; an unexpected sequel to the fine poem on 'the marriage of true minds' [Sonnet 116], which although not referring to the friend, suggests that their shaken relationship has been stabilised. Perhaps Sonnet 117 should stand with the previous group of poems, for its self-condemnation

> that I have scanted all
> Wherein I should your great deserts repay,

is closely related in manner to the speaker's listing of his faults in Sonnet 110; but its position suggests rather that Shakespeare revived this theme a little later. The second half of the octet contains a clear indictment of the wrongs done to the poet by his friend, and fills out the previously incomplete picture of the 'harmful deeds' mentioned but not specified in Sonnet 111:

> That I have frequent been with unknown minds,
> And given to time your own dear-purchased right;
> That I have hoisted sail to all the winds
> Which should transport me farthest from your
>   sight.

With the figurative expression of hoisting sail the accusations begin to yield to the indefiniteness which has promoted such oddly literal readings of other sonnets; and one almost expects to see these lines adduced as evidence that Shakespeare made a voyage overseas, callously ignoring his obligation to a noble patron. Whether in plain or figurative language, familiar accusations are being repeated as Shakespeare continues to work and reshape the limited material he has elected to make his subject. The speaker has repaid his friend's kindness with negligence and deliberate disregard; deserting the friend at every opportunity, and slighting his constant affection by spending his time in other company, where he has squandered the friend's rights in him. The 'unknown minds' with whom the poet has been intimate have appeared before; in the 'base subjects' of Sonnet 100, and by inference in the shallow associates who have encountered the poet to make himself a motley. The persistence of these ideas, and the renewal of the poet's appeal through a new explanation of his motives, shows this poem to be another variation on the theme developed earlier; and invites us to use it as a means of elucidating the more puzzling features of Sonnets 109-112. As there is no reference to actual events in these poems, we cannot expect to tie down their meaning very firmly; and if Shakespeare is writing variations on a theme which is itself not entirely constant, there will be still less reason for expecting a single, definite picture to emerge from this group of sonnets. But they treat a kindred subject, and in Sonnet 117 Shakespeare seems to have revealed more clearly the kind of situation to which all five poems refer. Here, in speaking more plainly about his disloyalty and unkindness, the poet makes it much harder to suppose that he is expressing shame about his life as a common player; for none of his expressions contain any certain allusion to the stage. By regarding this poem as the key to the controversial subject behind the earlier apologies, rather than as a postscript to the series, we may reach a truer appreciation of the character in which Shakespeare is presenting his speaker.

This figure appears in two main aspects. In his earlier personal allusions, the speaker describes himself as a man unkindly treated by fortune, which has denied him the advantages showered on the friend. To offset and outweigh these disabling circumstances, he has the friend's intimate companionship, which makes amends even for the meagreness of his poetic talent. His complaint against fortune is echoed in the later group of sonnets, where the speaker tries to shift the blame for his shabby behavior from himself to the fate that made him dependent upon patronage; but this link with his earlier attitude is not maintained. The speaker now appears predominantly as a man who has betrayed a close friendship, either wilfully or because he saw easy popularity and acclaim offered him elsewhere. From the self-pitying postures of his complaints against fortune, cancelled when he recalls the happiness of his intimacy with the friend, the poet moves later in the sequence to self-accusation and apology; blaming himself for his misconduct and trying earnestly to repair the trust he has damaged. There is no likelihood that Shakespeare himself voiced such complaints against the fortune that obliged him to find his living as sharer in the leading dramatic company of his age; and nothing associates him with the speaker's self-accusing admissions of having 'gone here and there' in an undignified search for favour and quick returns. If these sonnets have some special application to Shakespeare, their significance is more likely to lie in the fuller understanding of human character which they disclose. The speaker who is at first content to blame the stars for his personal shortcomings comes to know himself better, and recognises impulses within himself entirely alien to the rational being he has hitherto supposed himself to be. In a final group of sonnets forming a sequel to the poet's self-injuring perver-

sity, the speaker makes a horrified acknowledgement of the idiot purposes that have assumed control of him:

> What wretched errors hath my heart committed
> Whilst it hath thought itself so blessed never?
> How have mine eyes out of their spheres been fitted
> In the distraction of this madding fever?
>
> [Sonnet 119]

At this point of the sequence the sonnets begin to reflect an awareness of man's divided nature not even faintly adumbrated in its opening phase. The poet begins by regarding the friend as an embodiment of beauty and truth, and comes by degrees to perceive that charm and good looks have misled him. Where the poet becomes aware of moral hypocrisy in the friend, the story changes direction: the friend regains the integrity which has previously been impugned, and is injured by the poet to whom his weaknesses are transferred. This exchange of roles allows the speaker to examine from within the kind of vicious impulse which, in the friend, he knew only from the outside; and to bring himself imaginatively to terms with the nature of the impulsive being which acts in man independently of his moral consciousness, and in defiance of it. Such an awareness seems not to have come within reach of the younger Shakespeare, who gave his speaker a grudge against fortune, but no disposition to look into his private weaknesses. This sharper appreciation of man's hidden self appears to have been acquired during the writing of the Sonnets, which are in this respect a record of the development of Shakespeare's moral outlook. After the two linked poems in which the speaker tries to understand what perverse impulse induced him to act against all better counsel and inclination, the relationship of poet and friend seems to have offered Shakespeare no further means of pursuing an imaginatively dominant theme. The story could only be continued through some basic change of circumstance which involved the narrator in a different form of personal relationship; and accordingly with Sonnet 127 a new and unlovely friend enters the story. (pp. 85-9)

> *James Winny, in his* The Master-Mistress: A Study of Shakespeare's Sonnets, *Chatto & Windus, 1968, 216 p.*

PHILIP EDWARDS   (essay date 1968)

[*Edwards views the Dark Lady sonnets as a coherent, highly self-conscious portrayal not only of the degradations of sexual desire, but also of "the driving need of the poet to use his art . . . to make sense of his condition." Sonnets 127-54, he maintains, attempt to show how lust impels a man to self-betrayal, but ultimately, he asserts, they are descriptive rather than explanatory. Edwards argues that although the order of the poems in this sequence may appear random, the irregular, sometimes halting, movement toward resolution successfully reflects the poet's uneven progress toward understanding the complexities of the human heart.*]

Shakespeare's sonnets to the Dark Woman are a triumph of art built on a persistent demonstration of the weakness of art. What we get from these later sonnets, however, depends on the order in which we read them. A convincing order for the sequence (numbers 127-54) is extremely difficult to establish. Many critics who thought that they could make a pattern out of the sonnets to the young man have given up the task for the dark woman. [Edward Dowden wrote in *Shakspere's Sonnets* (1883)]: 'I do not here attempt to trace a continuous sequence in the Sonnets addressed to the dark-haired

George Chapman.

woman . . . ; I doubt whether such continuous sequence is to be found in them.' Most readers, in the end, are content to greet the acknowledged great poems as they come: 'My mistress' eyes are nothing like the sun' (130); 'Th' expense of spirit in a waste of shame' (129); 'Two loves I have of comfort and despair' (144); 'Poor soul the centre of my sinful earth' (146). They can claim with reason that the poetry is not suffering in their eyes through the absence of a settled order.

But the belief that there *is* a correct order is hard to subdue. Brents Stirling [in an essay in *Shakespeare 1564-1964,* ed. E. A. Bloom] has made a new attempt, based upon a theory of the way in which the printer might have disarranged the sheets of an ordered collection. In his view, the sequence ends with the great sonnets on lust and on mortification (129 and 146), and three sonnets are independent (128, 138, 145). I shall show why I disagree with such an ending, and why I find the three 'independent' sonnets necessary to the sequence, but first we have to ask what kind of an order we are looking for. We may mean the order in which they were written, an unplanned 'biographical' order. We should then have to ask whether we suppose the sonnets to have been written for and sent to a woman as a liaison progressed or whether we suppose them to be a deliberate record of an affair. The former seems very unlikely. As Auden has reminded us, it is most improbable that the sonnets of the later sequence were ever sent to the woman herself [see excerpt above, 1964]. If you send sonnets to a woman in which you talk of 'the very refuse of thy deeds', and describe her as 'black as hell, as dark as night' and as 'the bay where all men ride' [Sonnets 150, 147, 137], then sooner or later she either refuses to receive the sonnets or refuses to receive the poet. The sonnets themselves show that the intended audience must have been close friends who play a game of overhearing a poet talking to his mistress;

it is *they* who are meant to appreciate the pervading irony which the ostensible recipient is supposed not to discern.

Even if we regard the poems as a self-conscious record of a liaison rather than as 'spontaneous' occasional poems sent to a woman, we are still faced with a big difficulty implicit in the search for an autobiographical order. It is unlikely that autobiography will yield order; it is unlikely that a 'real-life' sequence will have the tidiness of a self-explanatory order, with a beginning, middle and end. If we are looking for a history or a diary we may expect it to look as confused as the sonnets now look, left in the order in which they were first printed.

If we turn now to look for a planned sequence, belonging only partly (if at all) to the events of Shakespeare's life, we are at once baulked, as we begin to shuffle the 1609 order, by the interference of our own expectations—the kind of interference which made critics wish to close Sidney's *Astrophil and Stella* with 'Leave me O love which reachest but to dust.' Unless the closest chronological continuity can be established (and it cannot), we can only impose what we wish to find. In a set of sonnets like that which we have before us, we cannot, by re-arranging them, do more than give a personal guess at the pattern of love's progress which we think Shakespeare intended to set out.

All the same, it is my opinion that the Dark Woman sonnets were put forward by Shakespeare as a coherent sequence, a sequence which is as much imaginative as historical, as much thought out as lived out. Although I find it inconceivable that the sonnets were not born out of the deepest personal experience, what Shakespeare gave—to his friends if not to the world—seems to me a very long way from a personal diary. How much revising, re-arranging, new writing was needed in the progress from personal experience no one will ever know, but perhaps Yeats is the poet to think of in analogy.

Where is the sequence to be found? I suggest it is in the order in which the sonnets were first printed in 1609: the order in which they are still printed because no one can find a better. In *The Shakespearean Moment* (1954), Patrick Cruttwell said, 'These sonnets which deal with the lady . . . contain most of the greatness and most of the maturity of the whole sequence; they can be taken as a single poem, in the way in which (for instance) Donne's nineteen *Holy Sonnets* are a single poem' [see Additional Bibliography]. It is possible to go further than this comparison takes us and argue that the sonnets are a single poem only if they are read in the 1609 order. (pp. 17-19)

The first face of love is described in the long sequence of poems to the young man, the second in the appended sequence to the dark woman. The first love is non-physical, a mingling of the two selves or souls into one soul; the second love is a mingling of the bodies of man and woman—will with will—without the marriage of the minds. On the one hand is love without physical intercourse; on the other is lust without spiritual intercourse. Shakespeare makes it clear that love and lust (each directed towards a different person) are intertwined in the lover. The story of the dark woman takes place *within* the narrative of the love for the youth; the fact of lust is included in the history of love. That the two experiences are meant to be seen as simultaneous can be inferred from the rather forced insertion, at the centre of each sequence, of the 'triangle' sonnets, 40-2 and 133-4, in which the poet tells us of the sexual relations between the woman and the youth. In these sonnets it is clear that the poet is 'in love' with both the youth and the woman at the same time. They describe how the woman has deserted his bed for the young man's, they voice his feeling of being betrayed by both of them, and they attempt (more or less ironically) various kinds of consolation. The most profound explanation of the predicament is in sonnet 144. . . . At one level, the poem expresses by means of puns the fear that the mistress and the beloved youth are committing fornication and that the youth will be infected with venereal disease. There is also the fear that the young man's lust will corrupt him spiritually as well as physically. If the youth *is* corrupted, then the salvation offered to the poet in loving him disappears. At another level, the complicated story of what is happening to three people can be seen as an image of what is happening to one human soul. The poet shows himself as a man swinging between salvation and damnation as he obeys the desires of his body and of his body and of his spirit. Ultimately, the living-together which the poet describes is the living-together in his own heart of the purity of love and the impurity of lust. The final fear is that his own lust will contaminate and disfigure his capacity to love, and win him soon to hell.

If the two faces of love are to be shown as present at the same time, it has also to be made clear that in essence they are distinct and separate; each kind of affection has its own sequence. It seems right that the lust-sequence should come last. Slowly, after 'all that pain', the sequence of sonnets to the fair youth reaches an equilibrium in the mutual forgiveness of faults when true minds are married (116 and 120 especially). The appending of the second sequence shows how impermanent this equilibrium is, how it is always threatened by the grosser sexual needs. The victory in the first sequence is subdued enough but even so Shakespeare questions it. By adding the Dark Woman sonnets he shows a distrust of the resounding final chord which we shall find again and again in the plays.

The characteristic of the Dark Woman sonnets is that the suggestion of a 'real' relationship is created, running beneath poems which, sometimes ostentatiously, show their failure to crystallize and comprehend this relationship. It is the impression of failure which provides the evidence of the 'real' relationship. It is like defining God by negatives, showing the inability of language to describe Him. We may often enough indulge our fancy about the real relationship which lay behind some love poem and imagine that in life things were not quite as the poet has put it. But love poems do not usually make the effort to hint at a discrepancy; the sense of life is what most of them try to give. I suggest that the most profitable way to read the Dark Woman sonnets is to think of Shakespeare watching his creature-poet at work. The sonnets, strung along a thin line of narrative about wooing, conquest and disgust, are a poet's ordering of his own life, his answering 'the daily necessity of getting the world right'; and Shakespeare is observing his grim failure. As the affair intensifies from courtship to consummation to bitterness, Shakespeare's ironic detachment from his creature becomes less and less, but a distance is maintained throughout.

Each of the first four sonnets is a posture; each introduces a particular kind of artistic ordering which is to be followed up later. Sonnet 127, 'In the old age black was not counted fair', proves that the dark woman is beautiful and is the first of a number of courtship poems in which the sonneteer, delighting in his own poetic wit, denies the distinction between ugliness and beauty, and hence, by traditional symbolism, denies the distinction between evil and good. The second poem, 'How oft when thou, my music, music play'st' [Sonnet 128], is one of those classed as 'independent' by Professor Stirling. It seems to me the very necessary introduction of the purely conventional wooing-poem. The humble lover watches his mistress at her music, envies the keys which touch her hand and pleads for the gratification of a kiss. To explode this world of sighing poetry-love, there follows the great sonnet on lust (129). . . . Magnificent though this sonnet is, taken by itself, it gains a special force from its position. The early sonnets in this sequence, before the reversal in 137, provide a study in self-deception, and the evidence for this is sonnet 129. Here the poet has a momentary vision of himself as a madman, here he sees his courtship as the longings of lust for its reward of self-loathing. Every wooing-poem which follows this is coloured by it; the poet who has had this vision of what he is doing in seeking the favours of the dark woman goes on writing poems which 'convince' him that he is in no danger, poems in which he is able to smother his moral sense in his delight in his own poetic skill. Far from being an ending to the sequence, the sonnet on lust finds its proper place near the beginning. It poses the question to which the sequence as a whole finds that there is no answer; why does a man willingly poison himself?

In the fourth sonnet, 'My mistress' eyes are nothing like the sun' [Sonnet 130], the poet explores the possibilities of the common antipetrarchan convention. . . . At first, this sonnet seems to be a direct attempt to cut through the nonsense of 128 and to come to a 'real' relationship. Rejecting idiotic comparisons, it seems a sane and human acceptance of a woman for what she is. The poet's love seems truer and warmer in its independence of poetic flattery. For the reader to see the poem only in this way, however, is to slip into the very trap which Shakespeare wants to show his poet falling into. Who is the woman who is contemplated so humanly, so warmly, so confidently? The Dark Woman, who is shortly to be shown as an agent of damnation. When we read this poem in its proper context, we can see that the final couplet conveys a double impression. First we congratulate the poet on the honesty of his love which needs no lying comparisons to assist it. Then we reflect on the continuous play in these sonnets between fairness-beauty-virtue and darkness-ugliness-vice, and we wonder whether a sophistical confusion between these two poles is not at work here too. Because all women, however beautiful, are 'belied' by being compared with goddesses, are all women equally beautiful and equally worthy of love? The poet has a right to love whom he will, and to accept a plain woman is no crime, but in so far as the ground of his acceptance is the equality of women as non-goddesses, he shows himself insensitive to the distinction (symbol of a moral distinction) between ugliness and beauty. Shakespeare does not say outright that the woman is ugly; students are taught that 'reeks' does not imply halitosis or garlic. But no one can read the poem without a sense of considerable unattractiveness in the dun breasts, black hair, pallid cheeks and breath which, if it is not sour, is not exactly sweet. The sonnet may be seen as a parody of the usual anti-petrarchan sonnet in which the poet rejects ornamental comparisons because true beauty needs no such aids. While showing that a woman gains nothing from false flattery the poet implies that physical demerits (the emblems of spiritual demerits) are of no account with him. With the gallantry of his wit, he once more confounds all distinction between women. To understand what the lover really achieves in this sonnet, we can turn to any of the later poems, sonnet 150 for example:

> To make me give the lie to my true sight
> And swear that brightness doth not grace the day.

The ugliness of the woman is made obvious in the subtle poem which follows (131). The poet jokes that in spite of her unpromising face, his mistress must be a conventional beauty because she tyrannizes over his heart like the heroine of any ordinary sonnet-sequence. He again denies distinction ('Thy black is fairest in my judgement's place') and tells us outright, for the first time, of the woman's viciousness:

> In nothing art thou black save in thy deeds,
> And thence this slander, as I think, proceeds.

What a great joke it is for him to be in love (if that's the word) with an ugly woman of dubious character and to be able to prove her as fair as the fairest—and, by means of the proof, insult her.

Sonnet 132 carries the jesting on and deepens the sense of ugliness. Conventional comparisons, rejected in 130, are trotted out with an accent which cleverly degrades the woman as they seem to praise her.

> And truly not the morning sun of heaven
> Better becomes the grey cheeks of the east,
> Nor that full star that ushers in the even
> Doth half that glory to the sober west
> As those two mourning eyes become thy face.

The denial in this poem is emphatic, 'Then will I swear beauty herself is black', and the denial is promised as a consequence of her granting him 'pity'. The denial of value is a price he is willing to pay for the satisfaction of his lust.

The 'triangle' sonnets, which follow, are important in reminding us at this stage of the existence of the other kind of love and of the contamination of the higher by the lower kind. The two poems make the woman's 'black deeds' more real as they describe her promiscuity and draw her as a demon whose loathsome magnetism enslaves her victims. The extraordinary 'will' sonnets, 135 and 136, show what wit can do to turn what is dreadful into amusement; the lover's plea for pity is advanced in a crudely physical way. His arguments for being admitted to her favours are at the level of mutual sexual satisfaction; he equates his whole being with his carnal desire and his virility:

> Make but my name thy love, and love that still
> And then thou lovest me, for my name is Will.
>   [Sonnet 136]

He is still laughing at the joke as he unites with the woman he knows the worst of in a congress whose emotional and spiritual consequences he has already foreseen in sonnet 129. The climax of the sequence—the 'kiss' sonnet of discreeter series—is sonnet 137. At the moment of fruition, there is immediate and overpowering revulsion. . . . The question, why does a man betray himself and swallow the bait?, continues for the rest of the sequence, but in the end there is no answer to give beyond the simple statement that it has happened.

The sequence continues with a series of sonnets written in bed. The rapid alterations of mood, the contradictions in viewpoint, may seem bewildering, but they are by no means an indication that the order is haphazard. The mood as a whole is of restless conflict in the single attempt to write the poem that makes the unbearable look bearable. Sonnet 138 ('When my love swears that she is made of truth / I do believe her though I know she lies') tries to follow the pattern of con-

ciliation used in the sequence to the young man—not to insult and despise but to recognize and accept one's own imperfections as well as those of one's partner. But the resolution has a very hollow sound; they will lie to each other and each will pretend to believe the other, for 'love's best habit is in seeming trust'. On this thin surface they will try to build, but all that they have with which to build is sexual pleasure:

> Therefore I lie with her and she with me,
> And in our faults by lies we flattered be.

In 139, he shows himself afraid of his own facility for consoling himself by writing down specious excuses for the woman. The mood is very similar to the mood of sonnet 35 in which the poet begins to pour out tired exculpatory analogies on his friend's behalf, and then pulls himself up in disgust at his own lack of moral courage. In sonnets 141 and 142, the word 'sin' enters for the first time, and the poet sees his suffering as condign punishment. Orthodox moral judgement of himself and his mistress as adulterers brings a new perspective into the sequence.

Sonnets 143, 144, 145, 146 seem to me to be of central importance. Two of them are very weak, the other two are very powerful. Indeed, in 145 ("Those lips that Love's own hand did make") we have one of the worst of all the sonnets, and in 146 ('Poor soul the centre of my sinful earth') one of the best. But when he is writing badly, Shakespeare does so intentionally, not for the first or the only time (we may think of the sonnets given to the young nobles in *Love's Labour's Lost*). In each of these sonnets, Shakespeare—or rather his poet—tries to make the peculiarly unhappy fact of his predicament conform to a different poetic 'idea'; he tries out different objectifications of the intolerable position he finds himself in—and none of them 'works'. Sonnet 143, a study in whimsical self-derision, turns the lover into a neglected baby crying for the mother who is chasing a hen. If this ludicrous image for deserted lover and predatory female lowers the poet, the poem yet provides in the rounded movement of its own logic the promise of consolation:

> But if thou catch thy hope, turn back to me
> *And play the mother's part,* kiss me, be kind.

The next sonnet in the group is 'Two loves I have of comfort and despair' [Sonnet 144], which we have already discussed. Like the lust-sonnet, it gains extra depth from its position, rudely cancelling out the propositions of a weak preceding sonnet. It is followed in its turn by a remarkable song (145). A characteristic and understandable note on this appears in the Harbage and Bush 'Pelican' edition of the Sonnets: 'The authenticity of this sonnet, in tetrameters and rudimentary diction, has been questioned, with considerable show of reason; in any case, it is not in context with the adjacent sonnets.' The Ingram and Redpath edition says:

> These trivial octosyllabics scarcely deserve reprinting. Some editors have considered the poem spurious on account of its feeble childishness. It would seem arbitrary, however, to rule out the possibility that one of Shakespeare's trivia should have found its way into a collection not approved by him. . . .

It can surely be argued that this absurd song *does* fit the place it is given. The idea of the woman's hate, as opposed to coldness or indifference, was first introduced in 142 and is continued here and in later sonnets. The metaphor of heaven and hell makes a direct link with the preceding 'two loves' sonnet and with the mortification-sonnet which follows next. I suggest that this despised poem should be taken as a satirical picture of a poet smoothing out life's problems, whistling to keep his spirits up. All's well that ends well; the fiend flies out of the window. The feebleness of the poem is an exaggerated comment on the weakness of poetry as a means of arranging one's life or even portraying it. Yet, exaggerated as it is, it does make a comment on poetry as a whole. It uses a magic which is quite patently ineffectual, but it draws our attention to poetry as a kind of magic which may or may not work. The poem which follows [Sonnet 146] is a particularly powerful poem. Although, as with two earlier poems I have mentioned, it gains extra force from exploding a namby-pamby predecessor, I believe we must also say that it is coloured by its predecessor. The mortification-sonnet is akin to the song in being a poet's attempt to relieve the pressures on his life through the perspective of art. . . . That mortification of the pride of the flesh and a life turned towards God can be an answer to the attack of the female devil ('there's no more dying then') is ruled out by the next sonnet—

> My love is as a fever longing *still*
> For that which longer nurseth the disease.
>
> [Sonnet 147]

('still' is at least as likely to have here its modern meaning as the older meaning of 'always'.) Death is not dead: 'I desperate now approve / Desire is death.' Sonnet 146 does not put the claims of religion any the less nobly because it does not serve the poet as more than a transient insight into what might be. It may seem a greater poem because of its hint of tragedy in that a man should know what this poem knows and yet be unable to avail himself of what the poem offers. And I certainly do not think that its value is lessened if we see it as one of a series of poems in a *dramatic* sequence in which the hero, a poet, restlessly turns to different poetic images of his own troubles.

The wild music of the few remaining sonnets puts them among the greatest writing of Shakespeare. There is never a last word. The poet accepts his incurable condition as a madness in 147, but then he goes on to degrade himself in anger (149 and 150), blaming *her* for entangling him:

> If thy unworthiness raised love in me,
> More worthy I to be belov'd of thee.
>
> [Sonnet 150]

The obscene sonnet 151 tries vainly to find refuge in the idea that there being nothing nobler in man than his sexual desire, he might find contentment in simply being the woman's drudge. Sonnet 152 ends with yet another repetition of the inexplicable:

> And, to enlighten thee, gave eyes to blindness,
> Or made them swear against the thing they see;
> For I have sworn thee fair; more perjured eye,
> To swear against the truth so foul a lie.

After this, the sequence evaporates in two perfunctory sonnets on the theme of Cupid's brand heating a well.

> Past reason hunted, and no sooner had,
> Past reason hated as a swallowed bait
> On purpose laid to make the taker mad.
>
> [Sonnet 129]

The story of the poet and the dark woman is not some isolated adventure. Shakespeare is writing about sexual desire, and he portrays it as a degradation that a man cannot withstand.

What is perhaps not improperly called the fear of desire is partly submerged in Shakespeare's earlier plays but it reappears at the turn of the century and in almost every play from *Measure for Measure* onwards there is an acknowledgement of the supposed disjunction between the marriage of minds and the union of bodies. In the last plays there is much that is perplexing on this subject. What we have read in the Sonnets helps to explain the chiaroscuro of Marina in the brothel, Polixenes' vision of childhood innocence and the anxiety of Prospero's spirits to keep Venus out of the wedding masque. Auden was right to conclude his essay on the sonnets with the address to all-enslaving Venus from Shakespeare's last offering, *The Two Noble Kinsmen.*

At the moment what concerns us is not Shakespeare's 'attitude to sex' but his attitude towards art. The drama of the Dark Woman sequence is not alone the drama of the curse of the granted wish, but the drama of the poet groping to materialize his emotions in verse. Shakespeare sets poetry the task of describing a certain kind of hopelessness and he shows poetry pulling like a tidal current away from hopelessness towards resolution of one kind or another. Although individual poems, however brilliant, may be 'failures' in that they are shown to be separated from the life they pretend to record, the cumulative effect of the sequence is success of the highest order, not failure. By accretion and implication, the condition is described. It will be found in some of the earlier comedies that a triumph of art can lie in a partial repudiation of art. Winning a victory by allowing a series of defeats resembles what Eliot was doing in *Four Quartets,* for there too the poetry moves round and about, trying every sort of key and tempo, cancelling out its rhetoric, defying heroics, trying to find the poetry for

> A condition of complete simplicity
> (Costing not less than everything).

Another poet than Shakespeare might have made the lust-sonnet and the mortification-sonnet the culmination of his sequence; at the end of the affair the poet-lover is made to recognize the madness of desire and to turn his back on all earthly things. In his very ingenious and persuasive study, Brents Stirling writes that his hypothesis 'accounts for seemingly random displacement—the appearance of a grim sonnet on lust (129) between the dainty, affected 128 and 130, and the sequential absurdity of a pretty sonnet like 145 followed by the *de profundis* note of 146'. I have tried to show that 129 and 146 have a quite special importance in irrupting into the narrative just where they do in 1609, and in not coming at the end. Shakespeare is dealing with great complexities of the mind and the heart, on to which is added the driving need of the poet to use his art, with all *its* complexities, to make sense of his condition. The course of knowledge will not be a symmetrical graph. (pp. 19-31)

> *Philip Edwards, "The Sonnets to the Dark Woman," in his* Shakespeare and the Confines of Art, *Methuen & Co. Ltd., 1968, pp. 17-32.*

DAVID PARKER (essay date 1969)

[*Parker evaluates verbal forms in Shakespeare's sonnets, contending that although the imperative mood predominaes, it is generally elaborately disguised in other forms. At the heart of Shakespeare's eloquence, the critic asserts, is the intent to persuade—either himself or another. Parker offers an extended reading of Sonnet 3, declaring that it "aptly illustrates the vari-*

*ety and subtlety of Shakespeare's verbal moods," the essentially
persuasive nature of the sonnets, and the extreme tension created by alternating verbal forms.]*

The poetic life of Shakespeare's sonnets is essentially a dramatic life. The temptation to discover for every piece of literature a "subject," something that it is "about," is understandable. Literature, like the sentences it is composed of, consists
of words, and there seems to be no reason why we should not
look for the subjects of literary works in the way we look for
the subjects (logical rather than grammatical) of sentences.
Most sentences, that is. It is easy to forget that it is only the
majority of sentences, whose main verbs are in the indicative
mood, that assert, that can be logically broken down into subject and predicate. Sentences whose main verbs are in the subjunctive mood, that are either imperative or interrogative,
rarely assert; and when they do, they do so in odd ways. The
imperative mood is particularly difficult. The sentence "Go
away!" cannot be analyzed into subject and predicate, and to
ask what it is about is strangely nonsensical.

It is profitable, at least temporarily, to consider Shakespeare's
sonnets as other than statements. The way I recommend they
be considered suggests that their mood is imperative, in much
the same way as did the old Elizabethan judgment of the sonnets as great specimens of eloquence, conceived not simply
as good arguing, but as the effective use of a rhetoric that persuades by means of logic, verbal trickery, melody, the expression and deployment of strong feelings—in fact, the whole
range of mental experience and literary technique the poet
can muster. The heart of eloquence is not assertion, the expression of fact, but demand, the expression of will in such
a way that the person addressed responds, or at least feels
guilty about not responding.

To forestall objections from those who doubt whether the
sonnets were sent to the person or persons addressed, I ought
to observe that it is not necessary for a specimen of eloquence
to be directly uttered at the person it is hoped will be affected,
as any politician knows. Publication or circulation is enough.
The obscurity of allusion that characterizes the sonnets
points to a state of affairs in which the target of the eloquence
and the shrewd reader would have caught the precise meaning, others less shrewd would have grasped a more generalized meaning together with the impression that there was a
specific reference intended, and the multitude would have
sensed that the poet at least had cause to write what he did.
Even the persons addressed in the more abusive and ambivalent of the sonnets would have acknowledged the poet's eloquence, at the very least by squirming.

Nearly all the sonnets can be seen as elaborate disguises of
the imperative mood; and some, in the way they mix, balance,
and play off against one another the different verbal moods,
demonstrate Shakespeare's sensitivity to the intricate relations of these moods. The concept of the rhetorical question
suggests that these moods are more flexible in their uses than
might at first appear, and the logical positivists of the 1930's,
whether or not we agree with all their conclusions, certainly
demonstrated that statements, especially ones about value,
may perform more than an indicative function.

Sonnet 3 illustrates particularly well the flexibility of verbal
mood and Shakespeare's sensitivity to it.

> Look in thy glass and tell the face thou viewest,
> Now is the time that face should form another,
> Whose fresh repair if now thou not renewest,

Thou dost beguile the world, unbless some mother.
For where is she so fair whose uneared womb
Disdains the tillage of thy husbandry?
Or who is he so fond will be the tomb,
Of this self-love to stop posterity?
Thou art thy mother's glass and she in thee
Calls back the lovely April of her prime,
So thou through windows of thine age shalt see,
Despite of wrinkles this thy golden time.
  But if thou live remembered not to be,
  Die single and thine image dies with thee.

The first quatrain, a single sentence, has two main verbs in
the imperative mood: "*Look* in thy glass and *tell.* . . ." The
poet is boldly making demands on the young man. But these
demands are softened and disguised by the shape and evasive
circumlocution of the sentence. The poet's imperatives are
got out of the way right at the beginning of the sentence and
of the poem, and they are made acceptable by their insistence
only on preliminary emblems of, or steps toward, what the
poet wants: the boy has only to stand before a mirror and talk
to himself. The demand is carried off with the sort of tactful
daring that allows a man to bully his superior into doing
something he knows he will not refuse.

The next important verb, "that face *should* form another,"
is in the subjunctive mood in order to express exhortation.
Should, however, is such a common form that we hardly realize it is other than indicative. Used as a synonym of *ought,*
it purports to be a straightforward statement about the established rules of behavior. Borrowing from Kant, we can term
it a hypothetical imperative, suggesting as it does complicated justifications there is no time to detail. It is analogous to
the "value words" of the philosophers, in that it appears to
belong to simple factual statement, but actually prescribes behavior. As such, it is a little stronger than the mild and evasive imperatives in the first line; and it is much more direct.
"That face should form another" is only the most perfunc tory of circumlocutions. But both strength and directness are
rendered innocuous because the words are part of what, in
indirect speech, the young man is supposed to say. This device disarmingly suggests that it is what any reasonable
young man might say.

In the following two lines there are three verbs:

> Whose fresh repair if now thou not *renewest,*
> Thou *dost beguile* the world, *unbless* some mother.

The conditional clause would justify the subjunctive, a distinct form of which existed for the second person singular in
Elizabethan English (*renew, do beguile, do unbless*). It would
be pedantic to make the propriety of using the subjunctive
into an important issue here, but its neglect, combined with
the bold use of the present tense, shifts these clauses from the
department of hypothesis into that of prophecy. Tact is maintained only if the words are supposed to be those of the young
man.

Two rhetorical questions, apparently parallel, make up the
second quatrain. Though interrogative in form, the first functions as a complimentary statement:

> For where is she so fair whose uneared womb
> Disdains the tillage of thy husbandry?

The roundabout form stops the flattery being too gross. The
second question, however, behaves as a reproach, an accusatory statement:

> Or who is he so fond will be the tomb,
> Of this self-love to stop posterity?

It is the apparent parallel that makes it gentler. The young man, the poet hopes, will be too happy basking in the praise of rhetorical question one to notice the different intention of rhetorical question two other than by modifying, almost without noticing it, his attitudes and behavior, so as to avoid the implied charge. Question two, we may say, functions not only as a statement, but as a very attentuated imperative.

The third quatrain is full of direct indicatives that strike the reader as bold and optimistic. The one in line 11 is the most compelling:

> So thou through windows of thine age *shalt* see,
> Despite of wrinkles this thy golden time.

The use of the emphatic *shalt* rather than *wilt* reinforces the neglect of the subjunctive more suitable in such a hypothesis, to produce with the imagery the blissful confidence of the quatrain. The young man is virtually challenged not to fulfill such a sunny prophecy.

The couplet contains an unusual and intriguing ambiguity of mood:

> But if thou live remembered not to be,
> Die single and thine image dies with thee.

In Elizabethan English *live* would have stood out as a strict subjunctive (contrast it with *viewest, renewest, dost beguile*). Its clause therefore is not merely conditional in the grammatical sense; there is a suggestion of genuine struggle to comprehend the possibility of such an unlikely eventuality.

Die is the oddity. Without the previous conditional clause (which it is easy temporarily to forget, since it is isolated in its own line), the final line of the poem would read as a version of the not unfamiliar construction in which a verb in the subjunctive mood is co-ordinated with a clause whose verb is in the present indicative, to express a feeling of impersonal inevitability. The construction is often used to give an effect of proverbial wisdom ("Laugh and the world laughs with you") or to make a threat ("Move a muscle and you're a dead man"). In either case it functions as an encouragement or dare, advising the listener, genuinely or ironically, to test the universal law being invoked and disclaiming any instrumentality or responsibility on the speaker's behalf.

One possible explanation of the line, then, is that Shakespeare is pointing out a universal law, disclaiming responsibility, and daring the young man to face up to the consequences of not raising a family. For this interpretation the reader would have to understand something like "then all I can say is . . ." coming after "But if thou live remembered not to be," and would have to treat "Die single and thine image dies with thee" as a ruthless and uncompromising piece of advice. Such an interpretation, I believe, figures as one of the alternatives held in the reader's mind, but it is too strong to be more than hinted at in this tactful and coaxing sonnet.

The suggestion of this meaning is softened by an alternative, grammatically less eccentric. In the alternative, the subjunctive *live* in line 13 would be justified by its reference not to unlikely future possibilities, but to the possible, though scarcely believable, intentions of the young man (as in "live to eat"). *Die single* would then follow closely on the previous line—rhythmically, grammatically, and logically—as a piece of bad advice couched in the imperative mood and offered

with gently despairing irony. The caesura after *single* would be very heavy indeed—a deep sigh of dejection, as it were—and the final words, "and thine image dies with thee," an afterthought uttered with relentless, heartbreaking logic. This final melancholy contemplation of the evaporation of the young man's beauty as an achieved fact—the verb is in the present indicative—acts only as the gentlest of warnings, and its static brooding quality is the last disguise assumed by the continuous series of imperatives the poem covertly presses.

Sonnet 3 is perhaps not among the finest of the sonnets, but it aptly illustrates the variety and subtlety of Shakespeare's use of verbal moods and the essentially suasive quality of the sonnets. The early group on "breed" are often seen, with their clearly stated aim, as a special category, but among the 154 sonnets there are scarcely any that could be conclusively denied a suasive intention.

The terrible "lust in action" sonnet (129) is usually understood as a piece of self-hatred. The verbs are all outraged, dogmatic indicatives. But in the exhausted, embittered, and moralizing couplet, an intention emerges.

> All this the world well knows yet none knows well,
> To shun the heaven that leads men to this hell.

General statements about human weakness rarely lack prescriptive force, and this is no exception. After the frenzy of the first twelve lines, the jogtrot rhythm and truistic sentiment of the couplet establish it as a maxim, the self-evident truth and neglect of which make it the cause of disenchantment that is itself instructive. Whether Shakespeare is trying to instruct himself or another is hardly important.

Sonnet 146 ("Poor soul the centre of my sinful earth") is unusual, anticipating as it does the meditative quality of sonnets by most later poets. It is perhaps best examined in isolation as a piece of devotional verse. If the sonnets are to be taken as a coherent group, it can be seen as Shakespeare setting an example to the young man; if not, there can be no objection to admitting an exception.

Sonnet 144 ("Two loves I have of comfort and despair") is probably meant to serve a double function: to make the woman writhe, the young man blush and reform. Sonnet 130 ("My mistress' eyes are nothing like the sun") pretends to be an announcement of disillusionment, but turns into a compliment, changing its tone rather sooner than is usually realized, at the third quatrain:

> I love to hear her speak, yet well I know,
> That music hath a far more pleasing sound:
> I grant I never saw a goddess go,
> My mistress when she walks treads on the ground.
>   And yet by heaven I think my love as rare,
>   As any she belied with false compare.

With "I love to hear her speak," Shakespeare allows the reader to glimpse his hand. The qualification reveals only sturdy common sense, music being admired chiefly because its sound is more pleasing than that of speech. His impatience with nonsense is continued in line 11, "I grant I never saw a goddess go," which issues a challenge to the hyperbolists to state what basis in experience their similes have. The next line is effectively ambivalent. Compared to the means of locomotion we imagine for goddesses, walking on the ground may seem a disadvantage, but having "both feet on the ground" is a virtue that befits the mistress of a poet who will stand no nonsense. The couplet dispenses with the apparatus of hyperbolic rhetoric at the same time that it compliments the woman by denying its adequacy to do her justice.

The sonnet, in fact, operates as a cathartic compliment, exploiting the relief felt in starting afresh by discarding the lumber of tradition, propriety, and tact. As a compliment it is a statement about value; consequently, under cover of the indicative mood, it demands a response—in this case a change or intensification of attitudes toward the speaker.

Although the richest and the most gratifyingly ironical of the sonnets do not always display the variety of verbal mood found in Sonnet 3, they nevertheless display the same acute tensions between the conditions of statement, question, and demand, the same ambiguities between fact, hypothesis, wish, prophecy, and threat. Consider Sonnet 121:

> 'Tis better to be vile than vile esteemed,
> When not to be, receives reproach of being,
> And the just pleasure lost, which is so deemed,
> Not by our feeling, but by others' seeing.
> For why should others' false adulterate eyes
> Give salutation to my sportive blood?
> Or on my frailties why are frailer spies,
> Which in their wills count bad what I think good?
> No, I am that I am, and they that level
> At my abuses, reckon up their own,
> I may be straight though they themselves be bevel;
> By their rank thoughts, my deeds must not be
> shown
>   Unless this general evil they maintain,
>   All men are bad and in their badness reign.

The disguised imperative in this is, of course, a demand that the young man stop listening to scandal about the poet. It is backed up by the moral rule, containing the usual prescriptive force, that people ought to be true to themselves. The verbs in the first quatrain are in the indicative mood. But the first quatrain is a value judgment, an iconoclastic one, moreover, so that it is quickened by even more tensions than usual, and the reader is barely conscious of any impulse toward factual statement. The quatrain, in fact, functions as a piece of sublimated nagging, containing suggestions of threat ("If you keep listening to scandal, I shall really misbehave") and demand ("Stop listening to scandal and attend to the truth!"). The second quatrain (two rhetorical questions as in Sonnet 3) serves a similar purpose, but is more plaintive in quality, without losing any of the first quatrain's robustness. The rhetorical questions can be paraphrased either as moral statements or as demands: "Imperfect critics have no right to rally my supposed faults or to make clumsy judgments on what I see fit to do"; or "Let all imperfect critics stop criticizing!" The tensions between indicative, interrogative, and imperative produce a quatrain bursting with feeling.

As is normal in a sonnet, the third quatrain changes the tone and feeling. There is an immensely welcome sense of freshness and openness about it, and the reader is relieved to see the grumbling of the first eight lines revealed as rhetorical posture. But the very candor of these lines, together with the gloomy hypothesis of the couplet, turns a simple statement into a subtle invitation. The young man is invited not to identify himself with the open-ended *they* of line 13, who maintain "All men are bad and in their badness reign," but instead to be as fair to the poet as the poet is being to himself. The sestet in fact operates as a covert plea.

The sense of extreme tension, of delicate but ambiguous judgment and impassioned casuistry, that characterizes nearly all

the sonnets derives very largely from the enormous effort put into staying tactful, an effort simply to disguise the imperative mood, an effort that is the heart of eloquence.

That Shakespeare was intrigued and delighted by the art of eloquence, an art clearly important to the drama, concerned not with abstract thought but with the influence of one human being on others, is evident from the most cursory consideration of the plays. Demonstrations of the art that spring directly to mind include Richard's eloquence to the Lady Anne in *Richard III,* Portia's in *The Merchant of Venice,* Mark Antony's to the mob in *Julius Caesar,* and Isabella's to Angelo in *Measure for Measure.* An exhaustive list would doubtless include several examples from each play. As we might expect, Shakespeare adopts no special consistent moral attitude toward artists in eloquence, but, at least at one level, he examines them dispassionately as human beings in the act of influencing their fellows; the influencing is as important to the playwright as the quality of the ideas and arguments, often logically and morally bad, that assist it.

When we realize that the same is true of Shakespeare the sonneteer, we are in a better position to appreciate the poetic nature of the sonnets. Shakespeare may or may not have been committed to one of the varieties of Platonism; he may or may not have attached much importance to the great Elizabethan commonplaces about Mutability. These are questions the answers to which may prove valuable in Shakespeare studies, but it is possible at one level of interpretation to be content with assuming that he adopted the postures such beliefs entailed in order to influence those to whom his sonnets were addressed. Shakespeare was certainly in some sense a poet of ideas and theories, but he was no less a poet of men and women, and it is difficult not to believe that the relationships suggested in the sonnets were as vivid and active as those shown in the plays.

It is a characteristic of many of the best English lyrics and shorter poems that they strive toward a dramatic life. One need only think of the ballads, of Donne's *Songs and Sonets,* and of Keats's great odes. It is not then surprising that the sonnets of a great dramatist should be distinguished by their dramatic qualities. Important developments have taken place in Shakespeare studies during recent years in replacing clumsier critical conceptions with interpretations of the sonnets that see them as rendering precise and complex states of mind. We need still to remind ourselves from time to time that the sonnets render not merely states, but movements of mind, precise, complex, and alive. Far from static, the sonnets are above all dynamic poems. (pp. 331-39)

> David Parker, "Verbal Moods in Shakespeare's Sonnets," in Modern Language Quarterly, *Vol. XXX, 1969, pp. 331-39.*

STEPHEN BOOTH (essay date 1969)

[*Booth explores what he terms the "paradoxical style" of Sonnet 53. He calls attention to the conflicts between syntactical and logical patterns, remarking that nonparallel constructions help achieve a style aptly suited to the essential contrariness of the poem. Patterns of rhyme scheme, phonetics, and syntax "coexist within the formal pattern 4, 4, 4, 2," Booth claims, and these patterns reinforce the paradox evident in, for example, the nonparallel construction of the Adonis/Helen quatrain. Thus, unity and division exist simultaneously in both the poem's theme and structure, offering the reader a "comforting" statement of a condition "opposed to common sense."*]

[Sonnet 53 has] no perceptible octave. That is to say, the reader does not sense, as he finishes line 8 and begins line 9, that he is moving from a unified and clearly defined logical or rhetorical stage in the poem to another. In sonnet 53 there is a pattern of syntactical units that goes 2, 2, 2, 2, 4, 2. Expressed numerically as it is here, the break between the four two-line units and the syntactically unified third quatrain suggests that a distinction between the first two quatrains and the third might be perceptible as the poem is read. A reading of the poem belies the suggestion:

> What is your substance, whereof are you made,
> That millions of strange shadows on you tend?
> Since every one hath, every one, one shade,
> And you, but one, can every shadow lend.
> Describe Adonis, and the counterfeit
> Is poorly imitated after you.
> On Helen's cheek all art of beauty set,
> And you in Grecian tires are painted new.
> Speak of the spring and foison of the year:
> The one doth shadow of your beauty show,
> The other as your bounty doth appear,
> And you in every blessèd shape we know.
>   In all external grace you have some part,
>   But you like none, none you, for constant heart.

The reader has no sense of the first two quatrains as a self-contained unit and, for simple mechanical reasons, can have none. For one thing, there is nothing until he is well into quatrain 3 to show the reader that the pattern of two-line units will not continue. On the contrary, the grammatical parallel between *Speak of the spring and foison*—the imperative with which line 9 begins—and the two imperatives in line 5 and 7 is an apparent signal that, as the spring and foison of the year are in substantial apposition to Adonis and Helen, the syntactical pattern of examples in two-line units will be continued along with the giving of the examples themselves.

The numerical pattern 2, 2, 2, 2, 4, 2 does, however, function in the effect of the poem. The rhythm of the syntactical pattern gives rhetorical conviction to the logical pattern, which, for the first eight lines, is this: a two-line sentence stating the problem in a question (lines 1-2), a two-line sentence justifying puzzlement (lines 3-4), a two-line sentence exemplifying the puzzling nature of the beloved (lines 5-6), another two-line sentence with another example of the same thing (lines 7-8). Lines 9 through 12 are a single sentence. Like the previous two sentences, it provides exemplification of the problem, and, like them, it is a command. Unlike the preceding pair of sentences, the imperative in this sentence has two objects: *the spring and foison*—lumped together in line 9, given a line each in the next two lines, and forgotten in the broad generalization *And you in every blessèd shape we know* (line 12). The progress of the three quatrains is from one element in the initial paradox to the other, from *your substance* to *millions of strange shadows*—from the individual to the universal. Adonis and Helen, the first two examples, are particular individuals other than the beloved. The next example is larger not only in that *spring* and *foison* are seasons and thus big, general, and vague, but also in that the simple mechanics of expression are also larger: *spring* and *foison*, taken together in line 9, are grammatically double the size of *Adonis* in line 5 and of *Helen* in line 7. At the same time, the expansion of the syntactical unit from two lines in the first two quatrains to four in the third sustains the growing expansiveness of the exam-

ples by which in line 12 the reader is brought to accept the syntactical appendage *And you in every blessèd shape we know* as a demonstrated fact, capable of being further summarized and commented on in the couplet.

The 2, 2, 2, 2, 4, 2 pattern is all but unnoticeable. It does its job, but it is completely unobtrusive. This is not, I think, simply because a reader is unlikely to take conscious notice of sentence lengths, but because the syntactical pattern is only one of several that . . . emerge and vanish as the reader moves through the poem. One of the commonest is an effective sense of the separate identity of the first two lines, by which . . . a 2, 12 or 2, 10, 2 pattern is superimposed on the 4, 4, 4, 2 pattern of the formal structure and on whatever other patterns are also in the poem. . . . [The] separate unity of the first two lines may be logical, rhythmic, phonetic, or metaphoric; it may also result from a combination of those factors. In sonnet 53 the first two lines are a question to which the next ten lines are not an answer but a demonstration of the validity of the lover's puzzlement. The couplet, formally separated by its rhymes from the body of the poem, accepts the demonstrated situation and goes on to an additional statement. As the couplet is cut off by rhyme and antimetabole in *you like none, none you* from the poem at the end, so the first two lines are less firmly and by subtler means cut off at the beginning:

> What is your substance, whereof are you made,
> That millions of strange shadows on you tend?

These lines do not, of course, rhyme, but they are given a separable identity both by the traditional pairing of *shadows* and *substance* and by assonance. The fifth syllable of line 2, *strange*, is a mutation with additions of the sounds of *stance*, the fifth syllable of line 1. The last unaccented syllable of each line is the same word, *you*, giving a rhymelike unity to the rhythmically identical *whereof are you made* and *shadows on you tend*.

If the separate identity of the first two lines were a unique characteristic of sonnet 53, the trouble I take about it here would hardly be justified outside of an elaborate dissection of this particular sonnet. The phenomenon, however, is common in the sonnets. . . . The pattern of the rhyme scheme, by which the first two lines of an English sonnet are pulled apart, is countered by unifying phonetic parallels in the first two lines of 53. That conflict is a small and unimportant manifestation of the simultaneous unification and division that is inherent in the sonnet form itself and in the simultaneous existence in many of Shakespeare's sonnets of an octave and the three-quatrain pattern. Moreover, the separate identity of lines 1 and 2 is . . . a temporary identity and demands that the reader see the lines first as a unit, then as half of the first quatrain, and ultimately as an element of the unified and undivided whole that the summary effect of the couplet makes of the first twelve lines. Thus the temporary identity of the first two lines makes one more demand for redefinition of the units of the poem; it is one more demand for intellectual commitment from the reader; it is one more strange shadow to keep the reader's mind in motion.

There are many poems that have phonetically unified, final-sounding opening lines. . . . Although the phonetic patterns . . . [of this kind] are not found exclusively in the first two lines, they are more common in the first two lines than elsewhere. They are also more important there than elsewhere because they provide a phonetic unit before the formal poetic unit, the quatrain, is established. This "pre-rhyme" effect gives one more kind of pattern, one more fleeting structural unit, to poems that, as has been and will be demonstrated, are peculiarly crowded with conflicting patterns otherwise.

In addition to the 4, 4, 4, 2 pattern of the rhyme scheme, the 2, 2, 2, 2, 4, 2 pattern of syntactical units, and the 2, 10, 2 pattern suggested by the phonetic unity of the first two lines, there is also a 4, 8, 2 pattern in sonnet 53. The second and third quatrains are three imperative sentences, and in their grammatical likeness they come together into a unit which, as one reads through the poem, sets the first quatrain and the couplet apart from them. The three imperatives evoke a sense of what could be called an internal octave in much the same way that in 22, 23, 24, and 27 the first two quatrains are set apart from the third by a change in line 9 from declarative to imperative.

All of these patterns coexist with the formal pattern 4, 4, 4, 2. My description might suggest that the identity of the quatrains is obliterated by the other patterns. Obviously it is not. A rhyme scheme is a powerful thing, particularly in a poem like this, where syntactical units do not cross the lines of formal division. In this case, moreover, the quatrain pattern is reinforced by anaphora in *And you,* the phrase with which the fourth line of each quatrain begins. The second line of the couplet continues the pattern in a modified form: *But you like none, none you, for constant heart.* Where the pattern of repeated words emphasizes the formal pattern in the quatrains, the echo of that pattern in the couplet tends to diminish the reader's sense of the overall formal pattern by suggesting equality between the couplet and each of the three quatrains. Wherever one looks in this sonnet, unifying elements balance dividing elements: likeness and differences coexist.

The four lines that begin in a conjunction plus *you* are to that extent similar one to another, but Shakespeare makes no effort to heighten that similarity syntactically. Throughout the sonnets Shakespeare regularly avoids opportunities to add syntactical parallelism to lines or phrases that are similar in some other respect. Sonnet 53 is not unusually conspicuous among the sonnets for the numerousness of its partially parallel constructions, but its second quatrain is particularly well suited as a basis for a discussion of the effective significance of the phenomenon and of its relation to a style that is a vehicle for paradoxes:

> Describe Adonis, and the counterfeit
> Is poorly imitated after you.
> On Helen's cheek all art of beauty set,
> And you in Grecian tires are painted new.

An easy explanation for the nonparallel construction of *Describe Adonis, and the counterfeit* and *On Helen's cheek all art of beauty set* is that the change in construction puts *set* at the end of the line, where it will satisfy the poet's need of a rhyme for *counterfeit.* That explanation appeals strongly to common sense and I see no need to reject it. I am not, after all, attempting to say that Shakespeare purposefully set out to counter the parallel elements in his poems with nonparallel elements. I mean only to point out the presence of such simultaneously parallel and nonparallel verses as these and to comment on their contribution to the overall effect of the finished product. Although it would be preposterous to suggest that Shakespeare set out to undercut parallelism in the sonnets, he went to no trouble to perfect it. In the present lines, even if we say

that Shakespeare lacked sufficient ingenuity to find another rhyme for *counterfeit,* that he had to put his second imperative verb at the end of the sentence, and that he was thus prevented by the nature of the verb *set* from making *Helen* the direct object of the second imperative as *Adonis* is of the first, we must still admit that, had Shakespeare cared at all for the easy rhetorical value of syntactical parallelism, he had no need to introduce *Helen's cheek.* He could, if he had valued parallelism, have written some such line as "On Helen all the art of beauty set," and salvaged some grammatical parallelism between *Adonis* and *Helen* by making *Helen* the object, although indirect, of *set.*

Whatever the reason that this quatrain is as it is, there is an aesthetic value in the lines as they are that is superior to whatever surface glitter might have been had from either a simple or a chiasmic balancing of the two sentences. As they are, these lines draw the reader's attention not to themselves but to their substance. The two lines on Helen are in substantial apposition to the two lines on Adonis; Helen and Adonis are two examples of the same thing. The lines on Helen, however, cannot be read blandly through as more of the same. One cannot read these lines as, for example, one reads classical or medieval lists of trees, listening to the sounds, admiring the pictures, casually picking up the substance, but with as little intellectual commitment as one might make in walking across a real orchard. The unostentatious and regular absence of easy parallelism throughout the sonnets prevents a reader from being lulled or from relaxing. The change in the Helen lines of every grammatical construction in the Adonis lines gives some small part of the urgency of the first quatrain to the second, which might otherwise have relaxed into the simple hyperbole of courtly compliment. The small complication that a change of grammatical construction provides brings with it from the first quatrain genuine bewilderment at the miraculous nature of the beloved. That small complication also makes a demand on the reader. Like the demand that the reader make small but constant redefinitions of the nature of the units of the poems, the lack of grammatical parallelism in the Adonis-Helen quatrain is an unnoticeable, unimportant, but definite demand for the commitment of the reader's intellect to the substance of the poem before him.

One point more, and that the most obvious, is still to be made about the simultaneous parallelism and nonparallelism of this quatrain. The likeness between Adonis and Helen is immediately apparent. They are both figures of perfect beauty and, in a sequence where mythological references are notably rare, they are both from classical mythology. The difference between them is equally obvious: Adonis is male and Helen is female. Here, in a moderated form and incidental to the substance of the poem as a whole, is the essence of the master-mistress paradox from which the bawdy fun of sonnet 20 is contrived. The likeness between the open, self-conscious paradox central to sonnet 20 and the subdued, barely noticeable paradox in the equation of Adonis and Helen provides sorely needed assistance in making a point that probably cannot be made with scientific clarity and is hard to make at all: that, as the substance of the sonnets is paradox, so the style is paradoxical. . . . (pp. 96-104)

Clearly, what I mean by a paradoxical style is central to this essay, but it is difficult to make that meaning clear without either overstating it and thus distorting the essay into an explanation of its author's ingenuity, or understating it and having "paradoxical style" give no more to the essay than the dubious ornament of a vaguely pleasing but generally hollow catch phrase. Clarification of the phrase depends, I think, upon the distinction between a paradox and the situation that evoked it. There is the same difference between the paradox of sonnet 20 and the experience of reading the Adonis-Helen quatrain. A paradox is comforting. It is the *statement* of a condition opposed to common sense; it is that condition codified, given form, brought back into the grasp of common sense, where it delights us not just because of its oddness and contrariness but also because, in the act of stating it, its oddness and contrariness is absorbed, albeit as an alien, into the world of common sense. A paradox is a miniature dilemma labeled and caged in a zoo. Recognizing a paradoxical condition alleviates the dismay we feel when things do not correspond to the patterns we assume for them or to the names we have for them, but before the paradox is stated our dilemma is real. The dilemma can be of any size, from that of Oedipus to that of a person working his way to the realization that the English horn is a French woodwind. A paradoxical situation makes us uneasy about our competence to deal with matters in which we expect no difficulties. It puts us off balance.

I take the time to labor the distinction between our response to a paradox and our response to a paradoxical situation, because I think it is the essential distinction between Shakespeare's sonnets and other poems of similar substance. If I were to say that sonnet 53 is a tissue of paradoxes, I doubt that any reader of the poem would object. Even granting that an audience conditioned to modern criticism is likely to assent blandly to any statement with the phrase *tissue of* in it, it is strange that the truth of this statement should be so easy to accept and so hard to demonstrate. Except for the second sentence (*Since every one hath, every one, one shade, / And you, but one, can every shadow lend*), there is no paradox in the poem that can be satisfactorily restated in prose, and even that exception is doubtful.

As a paraphrase of the second sentence, the following statement is more satisfying than it should be: "one person can have only one shadow; you have many shadows." The paraphrase is a paradox, a paradoxical situation described, pinned down, understood as inexplicable. My paraphrase, like most paradoxes, gives solidity to the situation it describes by means of extralogical form: the verb *have* is repeated in the contrasting clauses; *one,* repeated in the first clause, is set against *many* in the second; *shadows,* the last word of the second clause, balances *shadow,* the last word of the first, and, paired as they are, the singular form and the plural form of the same word capsule the paradoxical situation so that it is an acceptably defined exception within the pale of human logic.

The lines themselves, on the other hand, haven't the simplicity of form or the simplicity of meaning of the paraphrase. To take meaning first, here is an explication of lines 2 through 4 given in 1918 by C. K. Pooler in his Arden edition of the sonnets: the lines, he says, are

> based on a pun: shadow (shade 1.3) is (1) the silhouette formed by a body that intercepts the sun's rays; (2) a picture, reflection, or symbol. 'Tend' means Attend, follow as a servant, and is strictly appropriate to 'shadow' only in the first sense, though shadow is here used in the second. . . . All men have one shadow each, in the first sense; you being only one can yet cast many shadows, in the second sense; for everything good and beautiful is either a representation of you or a symbol of your merits.

Pooler achieves the comfort of mastery over these lines not by composing their substance into a paradox but by analyzing them into submission to human understanding. He, too, oversimplifies: a third meaning of *shade* and *shadow* also functions in the first quatrain. Where the substance of a being is in doubt, there is a strong probability that that being is supernatural. The very idea of millions of strange shadows sounds supernatural, and the idea that these shadows tend, "follow as a servant," the being whose nature is under consideration brings with it suggestions of occult practices in which spirits dance attendance on a witch or magician. Line 3, of course, puts to rest any such suggestions by implying that *shadows* in line 2 meant not spirits but "silhouettes formed by a body that intercepts the sun's rays." However, the word *shadow* is replaced by the word *shade,* the most sinister of its synonyms and the one best calculated to reinforce the occult suggestions that the rest of the line has suppressed. Pooler's paraphrase is a satisfying critical performance, but once add my suggestions about ghosts to it and the paraphrase becomes so complicated that it defeats its own purpose. One is again in doubt what it is that these lines say and how it is that that is said.

Pooler's explication is formally reinforced by the carefully numbered meanings of *shadow.* My statement of lines 3 and 4 as a paradox (which, by the way, is valid even though Pooler's equally valid paraphrase explains it away) has a similar formal substance from its repetition of key words and its parallel clause structure. Both Pooler's analysis and my paradox have a formal solidity that makes them mentally graspable. They are defined, static; their internal dynamics are fixed; they are like physical things. What about the lines themselves?

> What is your substance, whereof are you made,
> That millions of strange shadows on you tend?
> Since every one hath, every one, one shade,
> And you, but one, can every shadow lend.

Obviously, the quatrain has formal integrity in its completed rhyme pattern, but there is something else about the quatrain that gives it the firmness of a paradox or an analysis. The words *one* and *every* are repeated much as *shadow* is in my paradox, but, although they present a complication and define it, that complication is gratuitous. The lines as they are sound like a paradox; the play on *every* and *one* gives a paradox-like solidity of form to "everybody, each person, hath one shade and you, a single individual, can every shadow lend." But the machinery of formal paradox is not applied to the paradoxical condition. The lines sound like a paradox, a petrified dilemma, but they are not. The dilemma is still active. There are three meanings of *shadow* in the quatrain, and as the reader moves from word to word, his mind jumps from one pattern of understanding to another; the jumps are small ones, but there are many of them. The reader's mind is in the state of constant motion appropriate not to paradoxes or poems but to the actual experience of a paradoxical situation.

Look at the syntactical structure of the quatrain: two two-line sentences. The first is a question, the second a statement. The word *since* indicates a logical relationship between them; but what is that relationship, and how many mental steps are required to complete it? It takes a fraction of a second to see that the logical function of *since* is to introduce a justification for asking the question, but all the work of filling in the gap is done by the reader. When he comes to *shade* at the end of line 3, the reader, presented with the rhyme word—emotionally incontrovertible evidence of appropriateness—

has to cast off the suggestions of ghosts and spirits and select for himself the one meaning for *shade* that line 3 can admit.

At the end of line 4, *lend* certainly sounds meaningful; it completes the sentence and the rhyme pattern, but what does it mean? No reader who isn't under an obligation to produce an explication is likely to stop and wonder what *lend* means; its meaning is clear enough, but what is it? Schmidt's *Shakespeare-Lexicon* defines the present use of *lend* as a variation on "to afford, to grant, to admit to use for another's benefit," and says, "*Peculiarly* = to cast: *the mild glance that sly Ulysses lent*, [*The Rape of Lucrece*, l. 1399], *you, but one, can every shadow lend.* Sonn. 53, 4 (forming the rhyme in both passages)." Schmidt is perfectly right. The only thing one can reasonably expect the possessor of a shadow to do with it is to cast it. His implied further argument is also valid enough as far as it goes. Because *lend* is the rhyme word, two different schemes of organization sustain its appropriateness: the meaning, "cast," is put upon it by the reader's expectation that the missing verb in the syntactical pattern "you . . . a shadow" will be "cast"; the sound, "lend," is appropriate to the formal phonetic pattern of the quatrain. In combination, the two organizations make the word *lend* into a synonym for "cast" that rhymes with *tend.*

If Schmidt was right in 1875, why in his edition of 1881 should Dowden have glossed line 4 thus: "You, although but one person, can give off all manner of shadowy images?" Dowden's "give off" does not completely contradict Schmidt's "cast," but the Dowden paraphrase does omit the suggested description of the physical relationship between the "body that intercepts the sun's rays" and the silhouette that it forms. Dowden's "shadowy images" carry occult suggestions appropriate to the preceding lines, and "images" makes line 4 a fitting antecedent to the quatrain on portrait drawing that follows, but since it denies the pertinence of the simple process of casting a shadow, it does not properly describe what line 4 says to a reader immediately after he reads line 3 and before he reads line 5.

The same kind of objection applies to a new and eminently reasonable reading of *And you, but one, can every shadow lend*, offered in a gloss by Alfred Harbage in The Pelican Shakespeare edition of the sonnets: "each 'shadow' can reflect but one of your excellences (with 'you' the object of 'lend')." The substitution in this gloss of *reflect* for *lend* makes line 4 a logically fitting antecedent to the next eight lines, in which it is the shadows who are the actors. The difficulty in taking the syntax of line 4 as inverted is that a reading that makes *shadow* the lender also inverts the reader's probable view of the relationship in the first three lines between an object and its shadow. There are two reasonable ways of thinking about the relationship of an object and its shadow: either one thinks of the object as the doer and its action as casting the shadow, or else one thinks of the shadow as the doer and its action as imitating the shape of the object. Lines 5 through 12 are concerned with the nature and potential of shadows, but lines 1 through 3 are concerned with the nature and potential of the object upon which the strange shadows tend. It is hard to deny the validity of the impression common to earlier editors that, as he reads the first three lines, a reader thinks of the person to whom the poem speaks as a man with a great many shadows—that is, of a great many silhouettes formed by a single body that intercepts the sun's rays. A reader who does not know what the second quatrain will say cannot, I think, be expected to take *you* at the beginning of line

4 as the object of the verb that is still to come. Only when he reaches *lend* does he know that the syntactical pattern suitable to the equally appropriate "you can shadows cast" does not make clear sense when the verb is *lend.* By glossing line 4 as he does, Harbage, who in addition glosses *strange shadows* as "foreign shades (Venus, Adonis, etc.)," restricts the sense of the first quatrain to the terms of the last two.

Actually, all the glosses I have cited are right. What happens as the reader moves through the poem is that the lines that follow quatrain 1 change its terms. A given word in the sonnet is likely to be sharply separated from one scheme of coherence and integral to another: *lend,* for example, breaks from the scheme in which the reader expected "cast," is integral to the rhyme scheme, and comes to cohere with the terms of the following quatrains. . . . [Words] that are simultaneously appropriate to one frame of reference and inappropriate to another provide additional manifestations of simultaneous unity and division in the sonnets. (pp. 104-10)

Stephen Booth, in his An Essay on Shakespeare's Sonnets, *Yale University Press, 1969, 218 p.*

THOMAS P. ROCHE　(essay date 1970)

[*Roche is a distinguished American authority on English Renaissance literature. In the excerpt below, he considers the nature of the sonnet sequence as Shakespeare himself apparently viewed it. Roche begins by rejecting the validity of autobiographical reading for his purposes: "I do not wish to argue from internal evidence. The autobiographical fallacy clouds our reading too much for us to be able to read freshly." Rather, Roche discusses the sonnets in the context of "a fully recognizable tradition of Renaissance poetry, that began with Dante and Petrarch." Shakespeare's sequence, he claims, is a reversal of the conventional sequence. As such, the order in which the sonnets appear in the 1609 Quarto offers a "sense of satisfying richness and diversity," both formally and thematically. Moreover, "A Lover's Complaint" is "an integral part of the sequence," for it complements the story told in the sonnets themselves. Roche also comments on the sonnets individually, noting: "What we respond to is art, our infatuation with poetics, and the only means we have to deliver us from infatuation is the observation of poetic form as it shapes and envelops our experience, without the selfishness of the purely private." Roche concludes his essay with detailed examinations of Sonnets 73, 129, and 146 as examples of Shakespeare's poetic art, which is, he determines, "logical, moral, impersonal, traditional, and indispensable."*]

'With this key, Shakespeare unlocked his heart', said Wordsworth [see excerpt above, 1827], commenting on the sonnets, and thus provided one hundred and fifty-four skeleton keys for generations yet unborn to make off with the treasure of our greatest poet. The only trouble with these keys is that they do not work, and we are forced to agree with C. K. Pooler that 'No theory or discovery has increased our enjoyment of any line in the Sonnets or cleared up any difficulty.' This essay will concern itself with problems of reading Shakespeare's sonnets both as sequence and as individual poems. It will not provide keys; it will not clear up difficulties; it will suggest ways in which I have come to enjoy reading Shakespeare's sonnets. (p. 101)

[The sonnets tell] of two people, a young man of high station and great beauty (sonnets 1-126) and a dark lady (sonnets 127-52). Shakespeare contrasts them as his good and bad angels (sonnet 144). He begins by telling the young man to marry in order to gain immortality through his children (sonnets 1-17) and continues with the promise of immortality through his poetry. His love for the young man's virtues continues to grow, and he becomes worried over the attentions to the young man from a rival poet (sonnets 78-86). At some point Shakespeare starts an affair with the dark lady, who is married to a man named William (sonnets 135-6) to whom she is apparently gladly unfaithful not only with Shakespeare but with the young man as well. Shakespeare is morally revolted but physically attracted (sonnets 127-52).

The story does not end, and even my inadequate summary shows it to be a pretty poor thing as story. It is somewhat surprising that a dramatist who relied so heavily on plot should make such a botch. It is even more surprising that he should have chosen the sonnet sequence to tell any story. Nevertheless one can construct such a story from a reading of the sonnets, and it remains one of the more useful fictions surrounding the sequence, even if we are not assigning the correct values to the people addressed. On the other hand, it leaves us with many uncertainties and not a few unpleasant problems. Disregarding the problem of the identities of these people, we are faced with the question of why Shakespeare should have written sonnets to any young man, a question that Shakespeare answered better than most of his critics in sonnet 20. I think that its sophisticated bawdry indicates quite clearly that Shakespeare realized he was violating the conventions by addressing a young man. But I do not wish to argue from internal evidence. The autobiographical fallacy clouds our reading too much for us to be able to read freshly.

Let us turn from autobiography to tradition, for Shakespeare's sonnets belong to a fully recognizable tradition of Renaissance poetry, that began with Dante and Petrarch. The formal excellence of their sonnets made it virtually impossible for later poets to ignore the conventions of the sonnet sequence, and Dante in *La Vita Nuova* and Petrarch in his *Canzoniere,* or *Rime,* established once and for all the conventions by which the sonnet sequence lived. There is first of all the poet-lover in virtuous and agonized pursuit of an elusive female figure, whose beauty to attract is matched by her virtue to repel the ardour of the poet-lover. Her beauty is usually associated with a blonde woman, and her virtue is so great that it continues to exercise influence on the poet-lover even after her death. The names of Dante's Beatrice and Petrarch's Laura have become the type of the unattainable loved one and have all but been absorbed in nineteenth-century theories of dark and smouldering unrequited passions. As in the case of Shakespeare historical researches have failed to turn up the real Beatrice and Laura, and neither Dante nor Petrarch is at all specific about the kind of reality enjoyed by their loved ones. The fact that contemporaries of Petrarch could question the existence of Laura has not deterred the efforts of critics to continue their biographical researches and to attempt to restrict the meaning of these female figures to specific human beings. . . . If these female figures are not at least partially allegorical, it would be hard to explain why so many poets in so many countries should have had such misfortunes in their love for ladies with the improbable names of Idea, Pandora, Diana, Cynthia, Fidessa, Castara.

The vitality of the sonnet sequence comes not from real life but from the multiple significances inherent in these female figures who symbolize all that is desirable and unobtainable in human life. We need not refer to outmoded theories of courtly love to explain the intensity and endurance of the tradition; we need only consider the later sequences, derived

from Dante and Petrarch, to see that most of them emphasize only one half of the story these poets tell, and that half-story stresses again and again the unhappiness attendant on the poet's not obtaining his lady's love. In both Dante and Petrarch this unhappiness leads to the greater happiness of suffering—through to wisdom and virtue, but in all of the sonnet sequences I have read, with the exception of Spenser's *Amoretti,* the poet is enslaved by despair at the end, trapped by his unobtainable passion. There can be no doubt that the Renaissance reader would have felt some pity for the self-pity of the poet, but I do not think that he would have granted him its inevitability or his ensuing despair. Most of the sonnet sequences seem not merely to depict but to comment on the love: Go and do not likewise. The themes of devouring time and beauty destroyed, no matter how plangently expressed in the voice of the poet-lover, argue the same point of desires not to be fulfilled in this life.

Seen in this light Shakespeare's sequence becomes a dramatic reversal of the conventional sequence. No other sonnet sequence gives marriage counsel, and Shakespeare's sequence opens with seventeen sonnets advising a young man to get married. The loved one becomes genuinely unobtainable because he is a man, and the dark lady, whose physical appearance is the reverse of the conventional lady, in becoming obtainable also becomes, if not undesirable, at least not satisfying. We do not burden Shakespeare with 'Platonic' overtones by insisting that the young man, his 'better angel', is his Beatrice, that the love is 'better' precisely because it does not depend on the flesh. That is why the sequence ends with the dark lady sonnets. We see Shakespeare not in the conventionalized despair of the poet-lover but, as one might expect, in the more realistic morass of a human involvement that will not satisfy all of him.

The tradition of the sonnet sequence will also help us in other ways to turn to more fruitful questions about Shakespeare's sequence. In the first place the sequences seem to be following a principle of ordering not based on the alleged narrative. The thirty-one poems in Dante's *La Vita Nuova* are arranged in an intricate pattern of threes, nines and ones that reflect the numerical symbolism associated with Beatrice and anticipate the numerical symbolism of the *Commedia*. . . . We know from Petrarch's manuscript notations that he spent years putting poems and groups of poems 'in ordine.' There is not time in an article of this length to describe the order, but order there is, and that order includes the placement of poems other than sonnets so that the sequences have not only a temporal but a spatial order as well. It has become increasingly clear to scholars that the interspersed songs in Sidney's *Astrophel and Stella* are grouped and placed in an order that gives meaning to the sonnets and to the sequence as a whole. The subject is complicated and, I believe, deeply involved in the theories of numerological composition recently advanced in studies of Spenser.

We should also take into account those other poems, often narrative, that were published at the end of the sequence proper. We have long been accustomed to accept Spencer's *Epithalamion* as the proper conclusion of the *Amoretti* sequence. It has been less common to think of Daniel's *Complaint of Rosamond* as a complementary poem to the *Delia* sequence, even though the sequence was always printed with the *Complaint,* which begins and ends with references to Delia. The poet-lover in despair at the loss of his Delia is paralleled by the complaint of a young woman who succumbed to the ardour of a lover. Delia, if she had any sense of life at all, would have been flattered by the poet-lover's attentions and been warned away by Rosamond's fate, which it must be remembered was also written by the same man. The tradition began with Petrarch's inclusion of the *Trionfi* with the *Canzoniere,* which must have led later writers to feel that the agonies of the *Canzoniere* were subsumed, or at least spiritually cauterized, in the progressive triumphs of love, chastity, death, fame, time and eternity, which provide a vast moral context in which to judge the poet-lover's agony.

Another kind of proof that poets thought of sequences as something more than a collection of imploring sonnets is Barnabe Barnes's *Parthenophil and Parthenope, Sonnettes, Madrigals, Elegies and Odes.* The volume is divided into three parts: 104 sonnets, 21 elegies, and 20 odes. Each of these sections has other kinds of poems interspersed, and each of the first two sections ends with 'finis'. We might accept the work as three separate groups of poems except for the continuity of the subject matter and for the fact that all the various kinds of poems are numbered consecutively, with the result that ode 20 is followed by sonnet 105, which in turn is followed by sestina 5. Apparently Barnes thought of the three sections as compromising one whole work and numbered the poems accordingly. These are, of course, only tentative suggestions. I offer them to the reader only as possible new ways of considering Shakespeare's sequence as sequence.

The order in which the sonnets appear in Thorpe's edition has been subjected to much criticism, to much rearrangement, from Benson's edition of 1640 to the present day—as Rollins's edition makes clear. Most of these rearrangements have been carried out on the grounds of narrative clarity or thematic continuity. None of the rearrangements I have read gives the same sense of satisfying richness and diversity as Thorpe's. They seem merely to bring together all those poems that are alike in one way or another. They ignore the simple fact that one must have difference as well as similarity to make any pattern apparent to the reader. Thorpe's arrangement, if it is Thorpe's and not Shakespeare's, provides an amazingly large number of imagistic or thematic links between sonnets and sonnet groups. Where a sonnet does seem out of place, it may not be so much a case of intrusion or misplacement as an essential part of a pattern that we no longer recognize. With a poet as complex as Shakespeare it would be dangerous to suggest that there is no design in the sequence, for there are many indications that the order is less than accidental, even though a clear pattern does not emerge for us.

There are first of all the formal considerations. Shakespeare's sequence is different from the majority of sequences in its almost unswerving allegiance to the pentameter fourteen-line form of the sonnet. There are three deviations from this pattern. 99 is a fifteen-line sonnet. 126 is a poem of six couplets. 145 is an octosyllabic sonnet. The question is whether these formal differences are significant or accidental. I am not sure, but it seems more than accidental to end the major division of the sequence (1-126) with a poem that is not quite a sonnet. All references to time or the seasons or the months cease with 126, as do references to the muse and to the glass that the young man is for Shakespeare. This may account for the 'extra' line in 99, for with sonnet 100 Shakespeare reinvokes his muse and urges himself back to the task he had originally set for himself. It may also be significant that this exploded sonnet comes just before 100, the perfect number, for again

in sonnets 100-5 all the major themes of the earlier sonnets are repeated and intensified. What I am suggesting, of course, is that the sonnets may be numerologically organized and that sonnet 100 is both conclusion and beginning.

Two other formal aspects of the sequence should be mentioned. Sonnets 153-4 have always given trouble to the critics. They are clearly set apart from the others in tone and quality. But these two elements relate them unmistakably to the sixteenth-century Greek Anthology and in particular to the kind of poem supposedly written by Anacreon, recently popularized by Ronsard, who is probably responsible for its entry into sonnet literature. Shakespeare is not the only sonneteer to use 'Anacreontics'. Slipped unobtrusively between the last sonnet of the *Amoretti* and the *Epithalamion* are several short 'Anacreontic' verses. They too differ markedly in tone from Spenser's sonnets and marriage hymn and have similarly been dismissed from critical consideration. Nevertheless, if one is willing to give up a lugubriously sentimental approach to the reading of sonnets, one can see in these almost flippant Anacreontics a universalization of the love theme, a comic theogony, that tends to set the subject of love in a new perspective in much the same way that Marlowe's myth of Mercury redirects our moral apprehension of the love in *Hero and Leander.*

My second point is that *A Lover's Complaint* is an integral part of the sequence. Northrop Frye has pointed out the rough parallel between the characters in the poem and in the sequence [see excerpt above, 1962], but there is more to suggest that his poem, like the Anacreontics, is meant to give our moral apprehension another twist. The poem begins:

> From off a hill whose concave womb re-worded
> A plaintful story from a sist'ring vale,
> My spirits t'attend this double voice accorded,
> And down I laid to list the sad-tuned tale.

I do not think it too much to read these lines not only as a description of an echo but as a literal rewording of the 'story' that has already been told in the sonnets themselves. We should not look for direct correspondences, but the young seducer in the poem is described in terms that would suit the young man in the sonnets. The complaint of the young seduced woman bears the same relation to the sonnets that the *Complaint of Rosamond* bears to the *Delia* sonnets. It tells the story of love deceived:

> Ay me! I fell, and yet do question make
> What I should do again for such a sake.
>
> 'O, that infected moisture of his eye,
> O, that false fire which in his cheek so glowed,
> O, that forced thunder from his heart did fly,
> O, that sad breath his spongy lungs bestowed,
> O, all that borrowed motion seeming owed,
> Would yet again betray the fore-betrayed
> And new pervert a reconciled maid!'

It is the same old story, and 'all's to do again'. What the sonnets and *A Lover's Complaint* have in common is a highly realistic view of the torments produced by the passion of love, a view that exists somewhere between the happy marriages of the comedies and the tragic apotheoses of *Romeo and Juliet* and *Antony and Cleopatra.* The sonnets, it seems to me, take a middle path between the joyously acceptable conventionality of the comedies and the dreamlike suppositiousness of the romantic tragedies. They seem closer to that most analytic of plays, *Troilus and Cressida,* and bear the impress of that play's irony-vivified poignancy. Love can be both a glory and a destruction, and the story that the sonnets tell is not so different from the jealousies and rivalries of Chaucer's *Knight's Tale* for us to eschew the providential moral of that tale as a likely comparison. As the sequence exists for us today, Shakespeare's poet-lover turns from the powerful and unfleshly love of the young man to the more immediate and ultimately unconsoling intimacies of the dark lady and ends his sequence with the contradictory clarities of sonnets 153 and 154, which tell us an even older version of Eliot's couplet:

> We only live, only suspire
> Consumed by either fire or fire.
>
> [*Little Gidding*]

These formal considerations of Shakespeare's sequence have not delivered any easy answers, nor were they meant to. They seem to me more fruitful than the biographical approach, for they enable us to see Shakespeare's sequence more clearly in the tradition of Western morality and poetic convention shared by Shakespeare and his contemporaries as well.

But we read sonnet sequences less often than we read sonnets, and we must now turn our attention to the particular excellences of particular sonnets. As the rhyme scheme (ababcdc-defefgg) would indicate, most of Shakespeare's sonnets fall into the pattern of three quatrains and a couplet, with a strong logical break between the second and third quatrains. This form of the sonnet offers innumerable possibilities of rhythm, syntax, and logic, a logic integrating form and the inexorable theme of time.

In turning from the idea of the sequence as a whole to the individual sonnets we find the remorseless logic of our own experience of love—its anxieties, frustrations, momentary anticipations and delights, which is why R. P. Blackmur called the sonnets a 'poetics for infatuation' [see excerpt above, 1962]. His phrase is a deeply penetrating insight into the primary paradox of the sonneteer: love gives life to poetry and poetry will give eternal life to love. The paradox has been generally accepted as truth, but no poem is as warm as a woman, and no woman has so long a life as a poem. I think we find ourselves more often in agreement with Pound's youthful irony:

> When I behold how black, immortal ink
> Drips from my deathless pen,—ah, well-away!
> Why should we stop at all for what I think?
> There is enough in what I chance to say.
>
> It is enough that once we came together
> What is the use of setting it to rime?
> When it is autumn do we get spring weather,
> Or gather may of harsh northwindish time?
>
> It is enough that we once came together;
> What if the wind have turned against the rain?
> It is enough that we once came together;
> Time has seen this, and will not turn again;
> And who are we, who know that last intent,
> To plague tomorrow with a testament!

Our infatuation with our own experience makes us see 'beauty making beautiful old rime / In praise of ladies dead and lovely knights' [Sonnet 106], but we do not believe it except as an act of reading, a prefiguration in poetry but without warmth. The issue is complex, but we should not fail to observe that the poet-lover in the throes of poetic creation is as much in love with the form of the sonnet as with his mistress, a point made by C. S. Lewis many years ago [see excerpt

above, 1954]. What we respond to is art, our infatuation with poetics, and the only means we have to deliver us from infatuation is the observation of poetic form as it shapes and envelops our experience, without the selfishness of the purely private.

Critics of the sonnets have dealt well with the relation of poetry and love as theme, and I shall not burden the reader with a repetition of their work. Fewer have dealt with the logic of the structure, and I shall now address myself to that problem in a few sonnets. One of the most common types is the when-when-then sonnet, a logical structure integrating verbal form and the theme of devouring time. We find it in sonnet 12 in which the octave is really four two-line 'when' clauses, completed by the 'then' clause introducing the sestet. The division does not always coincide with the break of octave and sestet. The 'then' can come early in the octave (as in 30) or late in the sestet (as in 64). The extreme example of this type is 138, which withholds the conclusion until the couplet where the sudden turn of the pun on 'lies' and 'Lying' is strong enough to reverse and rectify our reading of the first twelve lines:

> Therefore I lie with her, and she with me,
> And in our faults by lies we flattered be.

Even a cursory reading of this type of sonnet should make us aware of the extreme dependence of Shakespeare's sonnets on logical patterns and structure to determine the meaning of the poems.

We can do the same kind of analysis with the 'catalogue' poems: 18, 66, 129, 130. They follow the pattern of three connected quatrains and a strong resolving couplet. Sonnet 18 is most interesting from this point of view. It opens with a question about the propriety of the simile that the poet has chosen: 'Shall I compare thee to a summer's day?' the answer, 'Thou art more lovely and more temperate,' denies the propriety and then proceeds to use the simile. If we pay attention to the shifts in the relation of tenor (loved one) and vehicle (summer's day), we shall see that the rest of the octave is a splendid expansion of the vehicle, quite rightly admired. The third quatrain shifts to the loved one, described in terms of summer, but emphasizing the differences between tenor and vehicle. The artful opening question sets up the logic by which the poem will develop. The simile works by insisting on the dissimilarities in the similitude, while at the same time transferring to the loved one all those lovely summer qualities the poet is so busily disavowing.

The kinds of pattern I have been discussing can also be helpful in solving one of the most vexing textual problems of the sonnets. The first two lines of sonnet 146 read: 'Poor soul, the centre of my sinful earth / My sinful earth these rebel powers that thee array.' The hypermetric twelve syllables of line two and the duplication of 'my sinful earth' suggest that the compositor made a slip and thus lost for posterity two syllables of Shakespeare's poetry. Clearly the line needs to be emended, and over one hundred amateur Shakespeares have made suggestions to win this do-it-yourself Shakespeare game. A study of the pattern of the poem will help us at least to the meaning of those two syllables, if not to the precise word. The sonnet breaks down into the octave, a quatrain and a couplet. The octave can be divided into four two-line units, each of which uses a dominant metaphor that unifies the disparate metaphorical elements. The first two lines combine a cosmological image (centre of my sinful earth) with war imagery (rebel powers) and clothing imagery (array). Lines three and four pick up the clothing imagery and transfer it to a building (Painting thy outward walls so costly gay) and introduce words of deprivation (pine, dearth). In lines five and six the metaphor continues the building imagery (walls, fading mansion) and the financial imagery (costly, cost, lease, spend). Lines seven and eight introduce the imagery of worms and eating. If one now proceeds to the third quatrain, one will see that the dominant image of each two-line unit is picked up in the corresponding single line. It will be easier to show this by juxtaposing the appropriate lines.

> Poor soul the centre of my sinful earth,
> *** *** these rebel powers that thee array . . .
>
> Then soul live thou upon thy servant's loss . . .
> Why dost thou pine within and suffer dearth
> Painting thy outward walls so costly gay?
>
> And let that pine to aggravate thy store . . .
>
> Why so large cost having so short a lease,
> Dost thou upon thy fading mansion spend?
>
> Buy terms divine in selling hours of dross . . .
>
> Shall worms inheritors of this excess
> Eat up thy charge? Is this thy body's end?
>
> Within be fed, without be rich no more . . .

The relation of the two sets of lines would indicate a number of possibilities for the missing syllables. If we want to emphasize the primacy of the soul over the body, we may choose an image of lordship (Lord of ?). If we want to emphasize the subjection of the soul, we may choose an image of servitude (slave to, thrall to?). If we want to emphasize the soul's deception, we may choose an image of deception (Fool'd by?). The pattern of the sonnet has not brought us to an answer, but it will allow us to disavow a number of contending phrases that do not conform to the imagery of the sonnet as a whole.

One other sonnet deserves some comment to show the intricate balance between structure and imagery. It is the very famous 73.

> That time of year thou mayst in me behold,
> When yellow leaves, or none, or few, do hang
> Upon those boughs which shake against the cold,
> Bare ruined choirs, where late the sweet birds sang.
> In me thou see'st the twilight of such day,
> As after sunset fadeth in the west,
> Which by and by black night doth take away,
> Death's second self that seals up all in rest.
> In me thou seest the glowing of such fire,
> That on the ashes of his youth doth lie,
> As the death-bed, whereon it must expire,
> Consumed with that which it was nourished by.
> > This thou perceiv'st, which makes thy love more
> > strong,
> > To love that well, which thou must leave ere
> > long.

In many ways this is the quintessential Shakespearean sonnet. The structure is marked very clearly by the skilfully varied repetitions in lines 1, 5, 9, and 13, and each quatrain develops a new metaphor. The vehicles of the metaphors gradually tighten round the reader, moving from a season to a day to a fire, all unified by the element of fire that through the sun regulates the seasons and days.

In the first quatrain the speaker compares himself to a 'time

of year', unspecified by name but vividly described in lines 2-3 by the autumnal attributes of the trees, which in turn become the tenor of a second metaphor: 'Bare ruined choirs', admirably analysed by Mr. Empson in *Seven Types of Ambiguity* [see Additional Bibliography]. It should be pointed out, however, that this metaphor reverts to the first metaphor of trees in the conclusion of the line where we might expect 'boys' rather than 'birds'. The implications of Shakespeare's superb play of metaphor become clear only in the couplet, but he seems to be arresting the very seasonal process he is invoking.

The second quatrain is less complex, less energetic, in keeping with the decorum of the passage. Here again a second metaphor, 'Death's second self', is introduced, but the metaphorical linking of death and night is so common that we are hardly aware of it. The introduction of death and the word 'rest' in this last line of the quatrain cuts off any possibility of invoking the day-night process and ends the quatrain on a note of quiet finality.

The third quatrain compares the speaker's life to the glowing of embers, in which the physiology of fire determines both the meaning and the mood. To nourish fire, fuel must be consumed. In each of the first two quatrains Shakespeare has had to control his metaphor with great care so as not to suggest the cyclical processes of which autumn and night are a part; here the image of embers works admirably to suggest the finality he has been working for and the close link and interdependence of life and death. Some readers have seen in this fire metaphor a hint of the phoenix rising from its own ashes. For me this would destroy the mood of no-spring-after-autumn and no-dawn-after-night. The subtle arrangement of the words achieves a perfect balance between the ultimate finality of death and the subdued fire of the speaker's moribund mood. Ashes—deathbed—consumed are opposed to Lie—expire—nourished.

The three quatrains present an unusually poignant picture of man caught in annual, daily and physiological processes over which he has no control. Despite the poignancy it must be admitted that the first twelve lines of the poem are sentimental. They ask pity for a man who if he were writing from his own experience, could not have been forty-five. They are the *schmerz* [pangs] of middle age. But the couplet puts all in perspective. The whole preceding twelve lines are reduced to the naked simplicity of the pronouns 'This', and the enigmatic 'that' of the last line, 'which THOU must leave ere long.'

> This thou perceiv'st, which makes thy love more
> > strong,
> To love that well which thou must leave ere long.

I do not think that one should read 'leave' as 'forgo'. The brilliance of the shift from the speaker to the loved ones moves the poem from a particularized despair of an individual to a generalized statement about all of human life that includes the speaker and the loved one and the reader. The 'that' is both the speaker and life itself, and in the context of sonnets 71-4 it also means Shakespeare's poetry. Sonnet 71 sets up the situation: 'No longer mourn for me when I am dead . . . / Lest the wise world should look into your moan / And mock you with me after I am gone.' Sonnet 72 develops the theme further, including the poetry as well as the person: 'For I am shamed by *that* which I bring forth, / And so should you, to love things nothing worth.' The irony of the situation is resolved by the couplet in 73 and all of 74, which insists 'but be contented when that fell arrest / Without all bail shall carry me away.' His body will be gone, but his spirit will remain, and

> The worth of that, is that which it contains,
> And that is this, and this with thee remains.

The rightness of the boast needs no further proof but redirects our understanding of that basic paradox, of which I spoke earlier.

Sonnet 73 seems to me the richest, the most evocative of one kind of Shakespearean sonnet, one kind of perfection. It elicits our emotional response before our intellectual. We are taken into the worlds of 'Bare ruined choirs', and night and embers long before we think about the problem of what *that* means. Others of the sonnets hit the intellect before they can become part of our literary lives. The particularized poignancy has been drained from them in the act of composition. Sonnet 94, one of the most perplexing of all the sonnets, is a good example. I have never found a satisfactory explanation of its meaning. Its intellectual abstraction makes it almost a paradigm devoid of meaning—except for the pattern its words make. One cannot refer with any certainty to moral or intellectual situations to which these words apply. One of its main difficulties is the abstractness of the diction, which does not specify its meaning precisely or draw the disparate elements of the poem together unless we resort to imposed ironies or tonal differences. This may be either its glory or its fault. Sonnet 116 has the same kind of abstract diction but avoids the difficulties of 94. The first line and a half specifies the area within which the poem operates by picking up an associative word, 'impediments'.

> Let me not to the marriage of true minds
> Admit impediments . . .

Because of this word the poem must carry almost as an epigraph the line from the marriage service: 'If any of you know cause or just impediment why these persons should not be joined together . . .' The rest of the poem, except for the couplet, is a series of statements about love, which attempt to define it. The poem is justly celebrated but cannot compare with sonnet 129, one of the truly great poems, in which so much happens linguistically that we can hardly take it in.

> Th' expense of spirit in a waste of shame
> Is lust in action, and till action, lust
> Is perjured, murd'rous, bloody full of blame,
> Savage, extreme, rude, cruel, not to trust,
> Enjoyed no sooner but despised straight,
> Past reason hunted, and no sooner had
> Past reason hated as a swallowed bait
> On purpose laid to make the taker mad.
> Mad in pursuit and in possession so,
> Had, having, and in quest, to have extreme,
> A bliss in proof and proved, a very woe,
> Before a joy proposed behind a dream.
>   All this the world well knows yet none knows
>   well,
>   To shun the heaven that leads men to this hell.

This poem is really a syncopated catalogue in which the first two lines and the couplet make statements, and everything between is an intellectual analysis of lust, composed of adjectival forms completing the verb *is* in line 3. The usual form of the sonnet, so scrupulously observed, is neglected here. Syntax and alliterative patterns take over. The poem is a controlled series of balances that view lust grammatically through tenses (had, having and in quest to have) and the possible relationships of the words chosen. In this sonnet

more than in any other Shakespeare seems to rely on the elements of language to sustain his fury. Line one seems to be a simple evocation of the old soul—body dichotomy in terms of an arid desert (waste of shame)—very much like the 'Poor soul' of 146, but the words are more incisive and bear the burden of the physiological meaning of spirit as seminal fluid, and we are given a very powerful statement and definition of the act of love, which is why Shakespeare adds 'in action'. The definition is concise and inclusive. Coupled to it is the other half of line 2 that suggests quite rightly that lust is prior to act. The list of adjectives in lines 3 and 4 is exquisite. From the legalism of 'Perjured' (lust has told something untrue and been convicted of it) we progress to 'murderous' (from act of mind to act) to 'bloody' (result of act) to the culpability of 'full of blame'. 'Extreme' in line 4 seems out of place but is picked up again in line 10 and acts as a link between the earlier and later series of adjectives. 'Not to trust' is superb because it introduces the whole world of social and personal backing off from the implications of the act. The rest of the poem should be clear; it justifies in terms of before and after an all too readily identifiable fact of life, which if you want goes back to the shame of line 1. The couplet rounds out the antithetical development of the first 12 lines with its opposition of heaven and hell and the inversion of 'well knows'.

These few observations on the logical patterns of the sonnets are not intended, as I suggested at the beginning of this essay, to be a key to unlock the heart of Shakespeare or even one of his sonnets. They are intended to direct attention to Shakespeare's art, which is logical, moral, impersonal, traditional, and indispensable for us no matter how we read it. The intensity of his sonnets does not invite comparison to our modern liberated fixations but to the deeply moral assurances of what human love can and cannot accomplish. Most important of all, his sonnets are indispensible for us in determining values, moral and aesthetic, that would abide our question, if we could only decide what questions to ask them. (pp. 101-16)

> *Thomas P. Roche, "Shakespeare and the Sonnet Sequence," in* English Poetry and Prose: 1540-1674, *edited by Christopher Ricks, Barrie & Jenkins, 1970, pp. 102-16.*

ANDREW GURR (essay date 1971)

[*Gurr suggests that Sonnet 145, "arguably the worst of all" in Shakespeare's sequence, is the first sonnet the poet attempted. The thirteenth line of this sonnet contains an apparent pun on the surname of Anne Hathaway, he remarks, and thus would seem to have been written in 1582, when Shakespeare was courting his future wife. Gurr acknowledges that this is "an anaemic poem," with none of the subtleties of language evident in Shakespeare's other sonnets. Yet it is significant, he proposes, as the poet's earliest exploration of the genre.*]

Sonnet 145 is arguably the worst of all the Shakespeare sonnets. In the days when what wasn't *magnifique* wasn't Shakespeare it invariably joined *1 Henry VI* and the other early plays in the limbo reserved for Shakespeare's inferiors. Critics have passed it by on the other side, and so have missed the one really curious feature about it.

It certainly looks like an anomaly among the sonnets, at first sight. It is the only one in octosyllabics. It is located deep in the jumble of Dark Lady sonnets, before the one beginning 'Poore soule the center of my sinfull earth', and after the one about the poet's 'two loves'. The two-loves sonnet, one of the two printed in 1599 in *The Passionate Pilgrim,* belongs in the group written to or about the Dark Lady, though in biographical time it belongs with sonnets 40-42, in which Shakespeare complains to the Young Man of the Young Man's and the Lady's preference of each other to him. The 'Poore soule' sonnet is not concerned with love at all, and as such is unique among the 154 sonnets. J. W. Lever considers it the only possible finale to the series [see excerpt above, 1956].

Sonnet 145 has no link with either of its neighbours. It is addressed to a woman, but there is no evidence that it is a Dark Lady poem. It is a lyric, fairly conventionally complimenting the woman who is its subject, speaking of the poet as languishing for his beloved, who is 'gentle', has a 'sweet' tongue, and whose lips were made by 'Loves owne hand'. It has none of the subtlety which Shakespeare usually gave to the sonnets expressing conventional themes, and it doesn't seem to have any of the intricate word-play which was the chief instrument of his subtlety. Not only is it in the less flexible octosyllabic metre, but it lacks the customary division of syntax and sense into quatrains.

The first twelve lines run straight on:

> Those lips that Loves owne hand did make,
> Breath'd forth the sound that said I hate,
> To me that languisht for her sake:
> But when she saw my wofull state,
> Straight in her heart did mercie come,
> Chiding that tongue that ever sweet,
> Was usde in giving gentle dome:
> And tought it thus a new to greete:
> I hate she altered with an end,
> That follow'd it as gentle day,
> Doth follow night who like a fiend
> From heaven to hell is flowne away.

The day—night simile of lines 10-12 is surely padding. The repetition of 'gentle' in lines seven and ten is clumsy, too, and the closeness of the rhymes in the first four lines is less than euphonous. It is an anaemic poem.

The purists who rejected the sonnet on stylistic grounds appear therefore to have a point. These twelve lines, however, were designed as the build-up to the final couplet, which rounds off the play on 'I hate' in line two, and it is there that I think we can find a hint of authorship. The beloved's tongue has spoken the words 'I hate'; her heart has reproved her tongue for it, so the lady alters her words 'with an end' which is the inevitable continuation of 'I hate'. So the final couplet of the sonnet says

> I hate, from hate away she threw,
> And sav'd my life saying not you.

There is a sort of word-play here, awkward and obscure though it is. The whole sonnet is too contrived to be justified by any lesser ending. The only explanation which makes much sense is that the play on 'hate' and throwing 'hate away' by adding an ending was meant to be read by a lady whose surname was Hathaway. Shakespeare's future wife, so the poet says, took the meaning out of 'hate' by adding its proper ending, and by so doing made it clear that she did not dislike the poet. Hate - away.

According to the spelling of Mistress Ann Hathaway's name, Joyce's pun ('If others have their will, Ann hath a way') is a better fit than Shakespeare's. The testament of Thomas Whittington in 1601 gives the spelling as either Hathaway or Hathway; the bond of sureties for Shakespeare's marriage to

Ann, signed 28 November 1582, spells it Hathway. Nor does E. J. Dobson's monumental work on pronunciation help much. We don't really know what the Stratford pronunciation of the highly variable vowels in 'hath' and 'hate' was. Fairfax did rhyme 'hath' with 'faith', which suggests that a reconciliation between the two vowel-sounds was possible. All we can say is that it is not impossible for Shakespeare to have contorted them into a homonymic pun. The *t* and *th* sounds need not have been a major difficulty. Some proper names accepted either ('Catherine' is recorded in the alternative spellings 'Cattern' and 'Cathern'), and the modern surname Hattaway is a common variant of Hathaway. The number of possible forms of the name in spelling (Shakespeare's name is spelt eighty-three different ways in the Stratford records) may indicate a similar or nearly similar flexibility in pronunciation. Like Shakespeare's own, it is a name which invites puns, and although to modern ears the Joycean reading is the less forced, the putative Shakespearean one cannot be ruled out. The chief support for accepting the pun remains the fact that it is difficult to find another form of word-play in the sonnet which makes it intelligible.

The use of puns on proper names goes back at least to Petrarch's 'l'aure'. Shakespeare made play with his own 'will' in sonnets 135, 136 and 143, and perhaps on 'hews' in sonnets 20 and 67. (We have to remember Wilde's Willie Hughes, however, and exercise a proper degree of caution [see excerpt above, 1889]).

Shakespeare made the twenty-five-year-old Ann Hathaway's waist of shame respectable by marriage late in November 1582, rather less than six months before their first child was born. We can therefore deduce with biological confidence that he was wooing her in the summer of 1582, when he was eighteen. That the sonnet should be relatively crude and elaborately contrived is understandable, and even forgiveable, if it came from an eighteen-year-old poet.

A sonnet dated 1582 would in itself not be extraordinary. Tottel's Miscellany of 1557 has nearly fifty. The miscellanies of the decades following Tottel, and Gascoigne's *A Hundreth Sundry Flowers* (1573), contain individual sonnets in various forms. Surrey's fifteen sonnets in Tottel use the rhyme-scheme found in all of Shakespeare's sonnets *abab cdcd efef gg*. Several variants of the sonnet form beside what Thomas Watson in 1582 called the *quatorzain* managed to get into print, including Watson's own eighteen-line form of three *Venus and Adonis* stanzas.

Despite all the variants there was enough standardisation by 1575 to allow Gascoigne to formulate the first definition of what we now think of as the sonnet. In his distinguished little treatise on rhyme he wrote

> I can beste allowe to call those Sonets whiche are
> of fouretene lynes, every line conteyning tenne syl-
> lables. The firste twelve do ryme in staves of foure
> lines by crosse meetre, and the last twoo rhyming
> togither do conclude the whole.

Shakespeare's sonnet conforms exactly to this definition except that its line-length is eight and not ten syllables. It is not surprising that in a form as tightly-bound as the sonnet the longer and therefore more flexible decasyllabic line should have been preferred to the octosyllabic. In fact I have not been able to find a single example in the period up to 1582 of an octosyllabic sonnet (nor, for that matter, any after that), though a twelve-syllable line appeared occasionally. Lyly in

Alexander and Campaspe (1584) wrote a fourteen-line lyric in octosyllabics, but it was in couplet-rhyme. Poets did use cross-rhymed octosyllabics, of course—Gascoigne himself, in stanzas rhyming *ababccdd,* and Humphrey Gifford in 1580, in quatrains rhyming *abab,* for instance—but normally in ballad forms. Tottel popularised an octosyllabic ballad form rhyming *ababcc.* It does seem to be a fact, extraordinary though it is for an age unrivalled in its metrical inventiveness, that no poet besides Shakespeare in this one curious poem wrote an octosyllabic sonnet. Even if anyone did, and there was an enormous body of manuscript verse which never reached print, it is not likely that Shakespeare at eighteen and in Stratford would have seen it.

If we accept a date of 1582 for Shakespeare's poem we are left, as in so many of the other fields where Shakespeare travelled, with the conclusion that he was the first explorer and innovator of his genre, an original here as everywhere else. No wonder, in fact, that in sonnet 76 he should call his sonnet-making Muse 'barren of new pride'. Source-hunting in the sonnet field becomes yet another vain Shakespearean pursuit. We might note, on a great-minds-thinking-alike presumption, that Sidney launched his great sequence at about the same time as we think this poem was written. Osmosis, however, is a peculiarly unsatisfactory explanation for any such coincidence. One might look for a common stimulus for both sonneteers in Thomas Watson's *Hecatompathia,* entered on the Stationers' Register 31 March 1582, which has some claim to be regarded as an Ur-sequence in the sonneteering tradition. Watson's own *quatorzain* sonnet, a preface to his sequence of eighteen-line poems, is an adroit example of its kind. Sonnets LIII, LXVII, and LXXXIII use elaborate Alexandrian conceits of the kind found in Shakespeare's sonnets 153 and 154.

Just possibly *Hecatompathia* might have reached Shakespeare through the good offices of Richard Field, whose father was a friend of Shakespeare's father and who left Stratford for London in 1579 to become an apprentice printer. He was later to publish *Venus and Adonis.* Watson's book, incidentally, anti-Stratfordians may wish to note, was dedicated to the Earl of Oxford.

Accepting the ascription of the sonnet as written to Ann Hathaway in 1582 would lay a few biographical ghosts. The mysterious Anne Whateley recedes further into the darkness, for instance, and the implication that the poet was still firmly resident at Stratford diminishes the chances of his being identified with the actor William Shakeshafte mentioned in the will of Alexander Houghton of Lea in Lancashire, dated 3 August 1581.

What is really extraordinary in this surmise about sonnet 145 is the implication that a sonnet written to woo Mistress Hathaway by the eighteen-year-old poet survived in the author's possession through twenty-five years of travel and change, until it joined the hundred and twenty-six to the Young Man and the twenty or so to the Dark Lady in Thorpe's publication of 1609. Perhaps Shakespeare kept it for sentimental reasons. (pp. 221-26)

Andrew Gurr, "Shakespeare's First Poem: Sonnet 145," in Essays in Criticism, *Vol. XXI, No. 3, July, 1971, pp. 221-26.*

WILLIAM BOWMAN PIPER   (essay date 1976)

[*Piper evaluates the theme of time in several of Shakespeare's sonnets, arguing that in these verses the poet "enacts upon his readers a process of poetic shift and change that relates directly to the impression of temporal process he is simultaneously rendering discursively." The critic traces this "poetic process," which aims to make visible the invisible encroachments of time, in the syntax, diction, grammatical construction, and metrical organization of the sonnets. In an extensive analysis of Sonnet 104, Piper calls attention to the instability of the rhetorical and metrical patterns, the change of discourse from descriptive to figurative in the third quatrain, and, especially, to the couplet, with its abrupt and shocking withdrawal of the assurance that the young man's beauty will survive the attacks of time. Piper also discusses at some length Sonnets 12, 64, and 73.*]

The consummate greatness of Sonnet 104 has been clouded by an apparent failure of poetic tact in its second line; but it is, nevertheless, the most complete and the most intense representation of temporal process in all of Shakespeare's *Sonnets.*

> To me, fair friend, you never can be old,
> For as you were when first your eye I eyed,
> Such seems your beauty still. Three winters cold
> Have from the forests shook three summers' pride,
> Three beauteous springs to yellow autumn turned
> In process of the seasons have I seen,
> Three April perfumes in three hot Junes burned,
> Since first I saw you fresh, which yet are green.
> Ah, yet doth beauty, like a dial hand,
> Steal from his figure, and no pace perceived!
> So your sweet hue, which methinks still doth stand,
> Hath motion, and mine eye may be deceived:
>   For fear of which, hear this, thou age unbred:
>   Ere you were born was beauty's summer dead.

The poet begins by addressing his young friend with a personal assurance; and he perseveres in this vein not just *to,* but *into* the couplet. Then in line 13, with the exclamatory "hear this," he suddenly abandons it; that is to say, he suddenly abandons the friend: the movement of time, from which he originally declared this young man exempt, has so penetrated his imagination that he can no longer even think of him as alive. And in the last line of the poem he makes a public proclamation informing future generations what they have lost in the friend's long-forgotten death.

This disruption in tone, in address, and in expression is no doubt foreshadowed in the third quatrain. The poet has been concerned throughout 104 with both the visual beauty of the friend and his own visual capacity: "when first your eye I eyed" enforces this persistent duality of attention. However, in the third quatrain his emphasis shifts from the first of these concerns, with which he both opened and closed the octave, to the second: the friend's beauty is mentioned only after two lines on the problem of perceiving the deterioration of beauty in general; and it is finally subsumed in the poet's admission that "mine eye may be deceived." This shift is not merely a wandering of interest from one eye to another, but, rather, a modulation of concern from one particular manifestation of natural beauty to a general awareness of all natural beauty; and it properly broadens the sensibilities of Shakespeare's readers. Moreover, since it arouses a "fear" about the acuteness of the vision on which the original assurance was based, it prepares us for some refinement of that. Nevertheless, the enormous expansion of the audience within line 13, especially since we find ourselves suddenly included, is shocking. And

Mary Fytton, maid of honor to Queen Elizabeth.

the pronouncement addressed to us in line 14 across a great and increasing gulf of time is tremendously strange.

To explain the impact of the couplet further, we may notice that "hear this," which announces the break in the poet's address, reverberates with the accented sounds, "fear . . . which," that immediately precede it; and that "dead," which destroys the claim made in the first line, has been suspended to the poem's final, rhymed position. The whole last line defines a "born . . . dead" antithesis, which the poet pointedly attributes to temporal process. And this line has been isolated, in syntax as well as rhetoric, so that it presents us with a stability, a finality, strikingly in contrast with the erratic, shifting nature of line 13 and, indeed, of all the rest of the poem. The contrast is heightened, moreover, by the integration of the couplet as a whole with the rest of the poem. There are a few other sonnets, notably 71 and 90, into which Shakespeare integrated his couplet as deeply, or almost as deeply, as he has done in 104; and there are quite a number in which he has employed it to define some reversal of sense or feeling. But in no other poem has he so deeply integrated his couplet and, at the same time, used it to illuminate so profound and shattering a contradiction.

The literary practice that allowed Shakespeare to achieve such an effect in the narrow bounds of this sonnet has been explored recently by Stephen Booth [in his *An Essay on Shakespeare's Sonnets* (1969)]. Its essence, broadly speaking, is a shiftiness, a slipperiness, in the handling of diction, rhetoric, syntax, meter, and, indeed, all aspects of poetic composition. Booth has suggested in passing how the poetic style resulting from such a practice might relate especially to a poetic concern with temporal process. The first quatrain of 73, as he has pointed out, "makes the reader participate in little in a mutability in the lines themselves." Again and again, throughout the *Sonnets,* to generalize this observation, Shakespeare enacts upon his readers a process of poetic shift and change that relates directly to the impression of temporal process he is simultaneously rendering discursively.

Consider, for example, the first two quatrains of Sonnet 64:

> When I have seen by Time's fell hand defaced
> The rich proud cost of outworn buried age;
> When sometime lofty towers I see down-rased
> And brass eternal slave to mortal rage;
> When I have seen the hungry ocean gain
> Advantage on the kingdom of the shore,
> And the firm soil win of the wat'ry main,
> Increasing store with loss and loss with store . . .

The adjective "defaced," at the end of line 1, seems first to modify "I," which furnishes the only substantival support for it; and, then, as the reader pushes into line 2, to modify "cost." "Sometime" and "lofty" are more volatile still. The latter of these terms is, as we come to see, a falsehood, not an aspect of the seen evidence at all, but a product of the poet's retrospective supposition. He has sometime seen, not *lofty* towers, but, rather, *down-rased* towers, the sometime loftiness of which he merely imagines. "Eternal" in line 4 strains its syntactic moorings even more forcefully than "sometime," pulling free from "brass"—a tie the apparent caesura strengthens—and docking, as the onward sweep of reading requires, with "slave." This shiftiness in "eternal" augments the paradox between "eternal" and "mortal." When we reach the latter term and struggle with the contrary meanings it raises, we find that Shakespeare has enunciated a shimmering tangle of meanings in this line, this predicate,

that carries us way beyond what the poet or his readers could possibly "see."

The second quatrain of 64 represents the force of time in the natural world and impresses it on the human mind in a fashion which the verb "see" is still less adequate to encompass. The scope of its sense and the scope of its poetic shiftiness are greater; and in the abstract conundrum of its last line Shakespeare has swirled them together into a statement of dizzying intensity. "Increasing," which opens this line, equally modifies "firm soil" in line 7 and "hungry ocean" in line 5, thus involving the whole quatrain in the complications it introduces. Because of its duplicity of connection, this term is self-contradictory, since an increasing ocean means a diminishing shore and vice versa. The idea of increasing "store with loss" is thus doubly contradictory—in its contrary references to "soil" and "ocean" and, of course, in itself. We must recognize, however, as we try to sort out these contradictory meanings, that every one represents some truth about the observed situation, some actual motion or condition in the ocean's address to the land. "Increasing . . . loss with store" further involves us. Once again, although we cannot at the same time both read and untangle the entire tissue of contrarieties within this phrase nor those connecting it to the preceding one, each possible sense and all combinations have, not only an abstract sharpness in themselves, but a convincing relevance, as we must come to feel, to the concrete instance, the ceaseless surge of the shoreline, from which they have been educed. The self-destructive writhing of the words and phrases that Shakespeare has yoked into combination to accommodate his experience forces us to endure in the strains and shudders of our own minds the grinding complexities of temporal process as it creates and destroys the natural world.

The third quatrain of 64, with its repetition "of state, / Or state," using "state" first in one sense and then, in the next iambic beat, in a different sense, and with the less demanding "Ruin . . . ruminate" echo of its last line, maintains something of the pertinent shiftiness of style, but at a sharply reduced level of representative intensity.

> When I have seen such interchange of state,
> Or state itself confounded to decay;
> Ruin hath taught me thus to ruminate,
> That Time will come and take my love away.

Here Shakespeare is actually imposing an intellectual stability upon his representation of natural process, just as his assertions declare, countering the mindless crush of temporal circumstances with a firm lesson, a lasting truth, "That Time will come and take my love away," which his rumination on these circumstances has produced. Since no mention of the poet's beloved was made before line 12, however, this truth, this particularity of focus, is fortuitous. And the emotional response described in the couplet,

> This thought is as a death, which cannot choose
> But weep to have that which it fears to lose,

is both inadequate and improper. But after the experience of the first two quatrains, what could be said?

The rumination that becomes predominant in the third quatrain of 64 permeates a number of Shakespeare's sonnets on time: the famous 73, "That time of year thou mayst in me behold," is one of these. Consider its second line:

> When yellow leaves, or none, or few, do hang . . .

The poet has here rearranged the natural sequence of events, transposing "none" and "few," but not, I believe, contrary to Mr. Booth (for once), at random. This transposition disguises the apparent impropriety of "hang," an impropriety rather like "lofty" in 64: if there were no leaves on the tree, the poet could hardly be justified in using the word "hang" in describing what one may "behold." Of course, using this word, even if it describes no present action, has great value of a kind: it reminds us of the innumerable leafy hangings, recently beheld, of which the winter has deprived us, and makes the lack of any hanging leaves at this moment not merely an observed fact, but a felt loss, a deprivation that time has worked upon us. There is, however, a second and more profound explanation of the transposition of "few" and "none," an explanation, running somewhat counter to the first, that fits the whole intention of the poem, the poet's intention, that is, to teach a valuable lesson. The transposition of "none" and "few" implies a second look at the landscape, a closer scrutiny of these figuratively relevant boughs; and suggests the presence of a mind devoted to the most exact observation and the most precise articulation of things that is possible. The first look informed the poet, we infer, of the final and fatal shudder of the last yellow leaves of fall and filled him with a sense of desolation. But he forces himself to look again, to attend more closely, and thus descries here and there a few yellow leaves still hanging in place. With this transposition of "few" and "none," with this modification of the natural sequence of things, the poet interposes his mind between the object and the viewer, presenting himself to his addressee as a man of intellectual integrity and refinement and thus preparing this addressee to honor the advice he will soon present to him. The conclusion of this quatrain, "where late the sweet birds sang," also reorders the process of time, winding up the image of encroaching winter with a vivid recollection of summer.

Sonnet 73 entire reveals the poet in command of his natural materials, of the images that are relevant to the lesson toward which he is gradually leading us. The poem presents us with three figuratively relevant situations, each one conceived as stationary, as firm enough to provide some foundation for a lasting truth. The obvious interconnections of the three, their ever-narrowing temporal focus, and the increase from one to the next of references to human life all fit the poet's purpose to establish his intellectual command and, by inescapable extension, the reliability of his lesson. He acknowledges the processes leading to and from the three ultimate moments which he has chosen; but, with the aid of verbal repetition and stanzaic definition, he establishes them as separate items of persistent and reliable intellectual relevance.

Sonnet 73 is, in fact, a case of poetic overkill. The lesson, for the sake of which Shakespeare held such a tight control over his materials, is, after all, meager and, despite the reverse English of its articulation, simple-minded. It hardly required the remarkable attention Shakespeare has brought to bear on it. The best praise we can give 73 is this, that it bestows upon us one magnificent quatrain, two excellent ones—each of the three isolable from the other with little loss in descriptive or figurative force—and a couplet that demonstrates chiefly how little is to be gained from taking the three quatrains together.

Shakespeare did not provide the argument of 104 with any philosophic or didactic insulation such as he raised around 64, 73, and, indeed, most of his essays on time. The position he takes up in this poem, that his youthful friend is exempt from time, he submits directly to signs of temporal process that demonstrate the power of time to ruin everything. These signs, moreover, although stylistically similar to those we have discerned working in other sonnets, pervade 104 with special persistence and profundity.

Let us begin with the three parallel exemplifications of seasonal change in the first two quatrains. In each case, two periods of time—every single period being represented by a noun-adjective phrase—are opposed to one another; in each case the earlier period is described as giving way to the later period; and everyone of the three cases, as the recurring term "three" asserts, covers the same three-year span of poetic observation. Such emphatic patterning obviously implies an effective control of the material, an active, ordering intelligence. But the patterning and hence the impression of control are, as the process of reading reveals, ineffective.

In the second of the three exemplary parallels, the two seasonal terms are nouns—although one is plural and one singular; in the third, although "Junes" is a noun, "April" is adjectival. In the first parallel, significantly, we cannot be sure of the syntax. "Winters" first seems, by its position, to modify "cold"; but we find in line 4 that "cold," being a singular noun, cannot govern "Have . . . shook," so that "winters" must be a plural noun in the nominative case, "cold" being an adjective. But "summers' pride" which concludes line 4, just as "winters cold" concluded line 3; partly because of this consonance in position but chiefly because of the substantial consonance of winter and summer, reactivates the first and disallowed option. We may notice, however, that "pride," which obviously fails to balance "winters" in substance, does not correspond to "cold" either. Whether the necessities of rhyme completely block from the reader's mind the fact that winter could be characterized as humble or humbling and that summer could be described as warm I am not sure; but the eminence rhyme gives to "cold" and to "pride" surely illuminates the fact that these terms, here placed in rhetorical balance, belong to quite different realms of human intelligence.

We may notice, more briefly, that "beauteous" and "yellow," the balancing descriptive terms in the second example, are incommensurable with one another; and that each of them, furthermore, stands in an oblique relationship with its rhetorical correspondents in both the exemplary systems surrounding this one. "Hot," although it is obviously out of phase with "perfumes" inside the third system, does reflect "cold" in the first. But the reader who sees this must recognize a further oddity in Shakespeare's three parallel systems: that the later time, the time of destruction, came first in the first system whereas it was placed second in the other two. The time words in the third, moreover, are the names of months rather than the names of seasons. The apparent balancing of noun-adjective pairs, then, and the apparent ordering of parallel examples has resulted not in a marvellously ordered system of discursive evidence, but, rather, in a marvellously illuminated process of discursive slippage.

The first seasonal example, to continue our exposition of this process, is presented as a sufficient fact: winter has deprived the forest of its leaves. But the second example changes before our advancing eyes from the same kind of a fact to one of a quite different kind, to an example of the poet's seeing. Consider the term "have" in line 6. It seems first to echo the strongly emphasized "Have" in line 4—those springs *have* turned to autumn—and, although redundant, to validate the "have" that we ourselves, in order to complete the indicated parallel, supplied between "springs" and "to" in the line above. But this "have," as we are immediately shown, has a quite different use; and the "have" that we supplied, more-over, we must now cancel. On the basis of the adjustments this second example has forced on us, we prepare to endure alternative readings of the third: we may take it to say, "I have seen three April perfumes etc." or "Three April per-fumes have etc." But the chance of preserving the parallel be-tween all three has been destroyed: the realm of general na-ture and the realm of personal observation have become hopelessly confounded.

To underscore the unsteadiness we have already described in the rhetoric and in the realms of meaning of 104, consider as a contrast the first two quatrains of Sonnet 12:

> When I do count the clock that tells the time
> And see the brave day sunk in hideous night,
> When I behold the violet past prime
> And sable curls all silvered o'er with white,
> When lofty trees I see barren of leaves,
> Which erst from heat did canopy the herd,
> And summer's green all girded up in sheaves
> Borne on the bier with white and bristly beard . . .

The passage is, as Stephen Booth has demonstrated, complex and demanding; but its syntax, meter, and rhetoric neverthe-less convey the impression of a firm poetic command, a suffi-cient intellectual comprehension. The poet counts, sees, be-holds, and sees the exemplary evidence of this poem. This syntactic consistency, this maintenance of the speaker in an attitude of active observation, presents his materials to us in a neatly wrapped intellectual package, in a package, further-more, which he is perfectly competent to manage.

The metrical organization, although we may notice some stresses within and between separate lines, enforces this im-pression. The first quatrain presents four evidences of time, defining each one within the bounds of one line. Every line-end thus marks a point of reliable rest. The third line, despite the fact that its verb, "behold," will eventually be seen to gov-ern "curls" in the next line, makes within itself, like 1 and 2, a complete, satisfying statement. And the fourth line (al-though its beginning, "And s . . . ," which apparently re-flects "And s . . ." in line 2, requires a slight adjustment) also provides us with a comforting integrity.

Each of the four line-defined cases properly accommodates the full process it describes. Not only is the separateness, the isolated singularity, of each tick properly represented; but day is shown giving way, with chronological propriety, to night; the violet, which the term "violet" naturally awakens in our minds in its perfect form, is described, after having been so mentioned, in its decay; and the "curls" are presented first as "sable," that is, of course in what we no doubt think of as their true nature, and, thereafter, as silver and white— just as nature presents them. The poet is not slavish, however, in his recognition of these processes. He considers the inter-mediate stage of the curls, for example, as the participle "sil-vered" suggests, not as a condition, like "sable," but as a de-velopment; and the "white" "with" which the curls are final-ly covered, he clearly thinks of as an alien quality imposed upon the real and natural color. The poet, then, has observed the natural sequence that works in each of these cases and yet isolated each one as a separate object of his understanding. The impression of intellectual comprehension and control is augmented further by Shakespeare's having preserved an order among the four items, starting with the narrowest tem-poral span, the tick-tock of the diurnal chronometer, and ad-vancing by degrees to the broadest. We may recall in passing the order of the seasons in 104: winter; summer; spring; au-tumn; April; June.

The second quatrain of 12, although conceived on a grander scale than the first, maintains the impression of poetic com-mand and comprehension. In these four lines, Shakespeare presents us with two complementary items from his observa-tion, parallel predicates of the verb "see," each worked out in two lines, the one describing a pasture and the other a culti-vated field, which convey, finally, when they are taken togeth-er, an image of agrarian autumn. These materials, although differently handled from those in the first quatrain, further demonstrate the poet's command, his comprehension. Both line-pairs open broadly, with "lofty trees" and "summer's green," and, then, at the close of their first lines, are sharply reduced. The trees are focused at the moment when they are "barren of leaves"; and the whole verdant realm of summer is narrowed, in the first place, to the green fields of grain and, in the second, to the time of harvest. The first line of the first pair describes the autumnal present, the second line, the sum-mer past; the pattern is reversed in the second pair, the poet beginning with the departed summer, although he gives that only half a line, and then emphatically returning to the au-tumnal now. This chiasmic patterning of material places the poet's emphasis on autumn, but it does so, we should notice, not in connection with the overwhelming impress upon his mind of temporal process, but, rather, in accord with his dis-cursive, didactic intentions.

We may notice, to enforce this point, that the line he has com-posed by consulting his memory, "Which erst from heat did canopy the herd," rivals in vividness and suggestive power his descriptions of the immediate present. The poet's total expe-rience, the various contents of his mind, as this indicates, are equally subject to his understanding. We may also notice the phrase "with white," which appears in the last lines of both quatrains, cementing the metaphorical image of human old age in the second with the more direct reference to it in the first. There is, finally, the virtuosity of line 8, a final flourish, by which Shakespeare signals his poetical detachment from the images of time that he has here presented and his intellec-tual command of these images.

The transcendent competence that radiates from the entire octave of Sonnet 12 is, of course, perfectly appropriate to the poet's didactic intention, that is, his wish to give his young friend the most impressive possible statement of advice. It must be recognized, however, that in 12 Shakespeare has made, not time, but his own intellectual command of time, impressive: the young man should accept the advice to marry and to procreate, we infer, because it has been offered by so wise a friend.

In 104, on the other hand, the poet's intelligence, although it has been powerfully asserted, is presented only to suffer, like everything within the poet's view and his imagination, from inexorable process. Let us consider now the metrical or-ganization of the octave, which conveyed in 12, as we have just seen, the poet's marvellous control of his subject matter. Its opening assertion takes a full line, thus enjoying a metrical emphasis that begins things on a rather complacent, comfort-able note. But the general explanation of this assertion takes neither a balancing line (like 60, 87, 109, and others) nor the rest of the first quatrain (like 33, 35 and others) but a line-

and-a-half; and the interruptive line break, moreover, empha-sizes not the sense, the intellectual force, of this explanation, but its dubious reliance on the seeing eye of the poet and, again, on the way it "seems" to him. The three examples of seasonal shift, which are metrically queered by this two-and-a-half line opening, continue queer.

The first example, deployed in a single independent clause, covers a line-and-a-half; and the line pause, which especially stresses the noun/adjective "cold" (an emphasis that sits strangely with the poet's avowed determination to assert the friend's exemption from seasonal rigors), separates its nomi-native element from its predicate. The second example takes up first one line, by which it seems to be completed, and then, as Shakespeare's more extensive awareness of "process" as-serts itself, two lines. It never looks like falling into a balanc-ing line-and-a-half. The eventual fit of this example into a pair of lines does not work like the two-line systems in the second quatrain of 12: its finally settling into phase with this formal division illuminates the fact, rather, that it is out of phase with its immediate rhetorical coeval. The third example fills yet a different metrical segment, a complete line. Its formal stability is as deeply compromised, however, as the two-line example just above: first, because it differs in metrical scope from both the first two, although it echoes the first line of the second example; second, because, being dependent syntacti-cally on the syntactically slippery material above, this line must be augmented—but how: by "have"? by "have I seen"? by "In process of the seasons have I seen"? We might notice the false lead given with the term "in" in the middle of the line, which seems briefly, perhaps, to echo the "In" that opened the line above. These three examples entire take up four-and-a-half lines, ending at line seven; and the octave is completed with a line, "Since first I saw you fresh, which yet are green," which reasserts the poet's original position.

This line also, although regular and shapely in itself, presents us with a further metrical strain since it echoes, not one line above, but the statement, "when first your eye I eyed, / Such seems your beauty still," which covers the end of line 2 and the beginning of line 3. The term "first" receives the first met-rical accent in both these statements; the synonymous terms, "when" and "Since," commence both; and the synonymous "still" and "yet" reinforce the second half-line of each. The effect of this echo, coming as it does on the far side of the sea-sonal process from which the friend has been declared ex-empt, is hard to calculate. We may notice, however, that the line definition makes the second statement more emphatic than the first; and that the change from "seems" to "are" ap-parently fits this emphasis. On the other hand, this line defini-tion illuminates a troubling criss-cross rhetorical pattern, the upward movement from "saw" to "are" being countered, perhaps, by the downward slope from "fresh," the meaning of which is firm, to the equivocal "green." We will be better able to weigh this line after discussing the sense and the scope of that climactic term.

In the context of such metrical and rhetorical instability as that which pervades the first two quatrains of this poem, sep-arate terms and phrases also slip and spread, losing old usages and meanings or acquiring new—"Increasing store with loss and loss with store." We have sufficiently acknowledged the shifts Shakespeare's contexts inflict on the different appear-ances of "have" in the first two quatrains, and the syntactic slippage of "winters" and "cold." "Springs" in line 5 is simi-larly stretched, between nominative and accusative, between

turning and being seen. "Perfumes," again, must be under-stood both as a subject governing "[have] burned" and as the object of "[have seen]"; or, rather, as we advance, we super-impose upon its nominative function an accusative function.

The term "turned" in line 5 means "changed" or "become transformed" when understood in the context of the line it completes: the beauteous verdure of spring has changed to autumnal yellow. But as we pursue the poet's understanding of things into the next line, "turned" acquires what is really its more basic meaning, "to go around": the leaves have not simply changed hues; rather, they have become transformed by being caught up in the great seasonal circulation of earth and sun. This new meaning, which emerges from the general statement about the "process of the seasons," is strengthened by the poet's assertion of his presence, that is, by his new in-sistence on the presence of a mind actively concerned with seasonal phenomena, actively engaged in generalizing its ob-servations of them.

The term "yet," used at the end of line 8, is repeated at the beginning of line 9; but, because of the exclamation that pre-cedes this repetition and because of its position at the logical-ly important beginning of the third quatrain, it shifts meaning completely, losing the sense "still" and acquiring the sense "nevertheless." We have in this practice, as in the case of "turned" above (and "state" in 64), not a pun, a pair of tem-porally concurrent meanings, be it noticed, but a slippage, a transformation, and, thus, another example in diction of the erosive power of discursive process. Nor does this power stop at meaning: here in line 9 "yet" also pulls strongly on its syn-tactic moorings, becoming briefly, not the adverb it was in line 8, but a noun: the fact of *yetness*—and that now includes the very slippage in the meaning of this term—"doth . . . Steal . . . beauty . . . from his figure." It is the placing of "yet" in the normal nominative position that inaugurates this syntactic possibility; and the problem of finding an object for "beauty" to steal, a problem that is only overcome when "Steal" begins to flicker, sustains it. In thus withdrawing its comforting meaning from "yet" and in thus endangering its syntactic stability, Shakespeare foreshadows his impending withdrawal of the assurance he originally bestowed upon his young friend.

The recurrence of "still" in line 11, which does have a pun-ning significance, allows us to measure this process. Here "still" means both "continually" or better, perhaps, "yet"— the "yet" of line 8; and also "firmly" or "without motion." But its proximity to "methinks" and its participation in the analogy between the "sweet hue" of the friend and beauty in general, which, like a dial hand, steals imperceptibly away from its figure, render both its meanings suspect, so that it en-forces our sense of the actual erosion of all things. As we rec-ognize the shiftiness of "yet" and the decay of both the origi-nal and the newly acquired meanings of "still," we see that the very terms we use to declare stability are themselves sub-ject to the pervasive processes of time.

Consider now the word "Steal." In *Henry V,* Pistol played on the two meanings that are relevant to 104 when he vowed, "To England will I steal, and there I'll steal" [V. i. 87]— except that these meanings present themselves in 104 in re-verse order. Here the term first represents the action of a hand—we may recall Hamlet's "pickers and stealers" [III. ii. 336]. Beauty, as a pure form, strips its physical manifestation, its "figure." But here is a problem, a mystery: of what does the thief, Beauty, strip this figure? The presence of the option, "yet . . . like a dial hand . . . doth . . . Steal . . . beauty," although obviously problematical in another way, may distract the reader and leave him suspended briefly between two problems, especially since each of them may seem to solve the other. As we proceed through line 10, of which "Steal" is the first word, however, we are reminded of the first action that Pistol planned, an action of legs and feet that normally reveals some "pace"; and this, which frees us from the need of an object for "doth . . . Steal," prompts us to take "beauty" as its subject: beauty itself will steal away from its physical representation, its "figure," as the ambulatory dial hand steals from its. But one mystery is supplanted by another: for this departure of beauty from its natural embodiments, although it happens before our eyes, is accomplished with "no pace perceived." The word "pace," which allowed us to resolve the problem of subject and object that we faced through line 9 and into line 10, has been cancelled in being presented; and we are left with a nondescription of beauty's departure from the natural world.

In the first two quatrains Shakespeare presented a spectacular motion picture of temporal process, forcing his readers to endure both sensible and discursive evidence of its working. But with the third, in which he swerves from a descriptive to a figurative mode of discourse and stoops from broadly divided years to the subatomic ooze of immeasurably tiny seconds, he reveals a further and more frightening aspect of it, that it lies not only beyond our effective resistance and control, but even beyond our powers of detection. The meter of the third quatrain, we may notice, is relatively regular: its first two lines define a general assertion about beauty, and its second two, which are introduced with the appropriate logical term, punctuate a particular application to the poet's present concern, the beauty of his young friend; every line and every mid-line pause, moreover, illuminates some syntactic, rhetorical, or figurative unit of discourse. Thus the mystery of process, which emerges from the explicit statement of the quatrain and inhabits its terms and its figures, is rendered with tremendous poetic emphasis. The invisible encroachments of time are thus vividly present for all to see. After such a demonstration, we should have no trouble understanding and sharing the "fear of which" that motivates Shakespeare's remarkable conduct in the couplet.

The young friend, however, has not shown any signs in the three years since the poet first saw him that natural process, either spectacular or imperceptible, has had any effect on him. Even at the end of the third quatrain, Shakespeare can say no more about the friend's vulnerability but that his eye "may be deceived." How then can we justify the dreadful proclamation with which the poem ends?

Describing the young man's continued freshness as a lasting "green" obviously asserts an essential consonance between him and the verdant world. The first eight lines explicitly draw a distinction between this world, throughout which the power of time has just been demonstrated, and the young man, who has been declared invulnerable; but the term "green" links him with the summer, whose leaves have been thrice destroyed, with the spring, whose fresh foliage has thrice yellowed, and with the savory burgeonings of April, which have been incinerated again and again. Thus the repetition of the assurance to the young man, with which the octave ends, acknowledges in its climactic term its own falsity. "Green," like other words in this poem, flickers before our eyes; actually, even before our eyes reach it, it has turned

from "fresh" to "vulnerable." And the young man's impending death is thus assured. This is the effect, that is to say, if Shakespeare has really earned this use of "green."

Shakespeare was always quick to perceive a similarity, especially in organic development, between men and plants, both of which, as he remarked in 15, being "Cheerèd and checked even by the selfsame sky," were wont to "Vaunt in their youthful sap, at height decrease, / And wear their brave state out of memory." We may no doubt bolster Shakespeare's application of "green" in 104 by recalling such practice, along with its poetic validations, in other of the *Sonnets*. He has actually established his employment of this crucial term in 104, however, within the confines of this poem. In the first place, he has humanized the seasons even while developing their apparent difference from the one human being about whom he is here concerned. Spring is described, for example, by a form of the same word, "beauty," which the poet has already affixed to the friend; summer is characterized with the human quality of "pride"; and the scent of April's blossoming is called perfume, a term which equally indicates a natural and a manufactured fragrance. Thus when Shakespeare calls the youth "fresh," we comprehend this term in the full range of its applications, taking it at once to describe both a wholesome natural, and a healthy human, condition. And the double sense of "green," which has been fit into a rhetorical balance with "fresh," follows in course. Shakespeare has strengthened the present use of this term, moreover, by foreshadowing it in one unmistakably verdant occasion after another in the first two quatrains and yet witholding it from us until the very last.

The expression "sweet hue" in the third quatrain, which obviously refers to "green," enhances the equation between vulnerable vegetal, and vulnerable human, life. "Hue" is, like "beauty" and "fresh," a term that easily canopies both human and vegetal appearances; and the term "sweet," likewise, can describe both a delicate fragrance and a delicate youth. The entire expression is odd, however, since one cannot see sweetness nor smell a hue; and this oddness, which augments the mysteriousness Shakespeare has infused throughout the third quatrain, recalls "April perfumes" in the quatrain above. When the reader considered the option between "Have . . . burned" and "have I seen" to govern that expression, he was likewise faced with the problem of seeing odors; and he must originally have resisted it. But the word "burned," coming at the end of line 7, rekindles the option: the one time when we can see perfumes—or fumes of any kind—the moment at which we do receive visual warrant of their existence is the moment when they ignite. By affixing "sweet hue" to the youth in the third quatrain, then, Shakespeare recalls his earlier application of "green" and reinforces its indications of natural vulnerability.

The final representation of the friend as "beauty's summer," linking him explicitly with "summers' pride" and "beauteous spring," from which he had formerly been distinguished, has thus been fully earned. By the time the poet announces his death, the fair friend has been encompassed by the multifarious workings—fast and slow, hot and cold, visible and unseen—by which every natural thing must eventually be destroyed.

In the course of this essay I have considered the best of Shakespeare's attacks on time and, indeed, the best poetry of this kind in English literature. I have belabored those poems that stand below 104, in the power with which they confront temporal process, in order to illuminate the transcendent greatness of this poem. Sonnet 104, despite its famous "eye I eyed" flaw, is the one sonnet confronting time that maintains its intensity to the end. Some of Shakespeare's best poems on time, among them 12 and 73, actually represent its processes only in their details; others, which endure process more directly—60 and 64 are good examples—collapse after the second quatrain, or earlier. But the discrepancy the poet defined in the first two quatrains of 104, that discrepancy between the observed omnipotence of temporal process and the apparent exemption of his friend, drove him to augment the spectacular manifestations of time described and enacted in the first two quatrains with a recognition in the third of its pervasive mystery. The literary consequence of this extended understanding of time, a consequence that is asserted by the shift in tone and in address within the couplet, is a poem that succeeding generations of readers should find persistently challenging in its development and shattering in its final impact:

> hear this, thou age unbred:
> Ere you were born was beauty's summer dead.
>
> (pp. 444-59)

William Bowman Piper, "A Poem Turned in Process," in ELH, *Vol. 43, No. 4, Winter, 1976, pp. 444-60.*

HEATHER DUBROW (essay date 1981)

[*Dubrow believes that the lyrical rather than narrative or dramatic mode of most of Shakespeare's sonnets facilitates the expression of "his speaker's painful inaction" and is best suited to evoke "the dominant mood of . . . fearful anticipation and suspicion." According to the critic, the principal effect of the lyrical mode in these verses is to heighten our emotional response to the speaker. Our identification is further intensified, Dubrow contends, by the lack of specificity about the persons, situations, and circumstances alluded to in the sonnets. She points out, further, that the world of the sonnets is tumultuous; just as the speaker frequently searches for simplistic answers to moral chaos, so we reach out for explanations that will resolve the uncertainties and ambiguities evoked so vividly in these poems. Dubrow also demonstrates how uncharacteristic Shakespeare's sonnets are when compared to those of other Renaissance poets, and she examines closely how Shakespeare's exploitation of the formal characteristics of the conventional sonnet underscores the moral confusion that exists in the mind of the speaker.*]

We assume that the non-dramatic poetry of a great playwright will in fact be dramatic in many senses of that complex term. And we assume that when a writer who, among his manifold gifts, is a skilled storyteller chooses to write sonnets, at least some of them will be narrative. Those presuppositions help to explain why, despite all the other controversies about Shakespeare's *Sonnets,* certain concepts are so repeatedly and so uncritically brought to bear on interpretations of these poems. We are regularly informed, for example, that they are "dramas" or "stories," a view reflected in the frequency with which critics of the *Sonnets* include the word "dramatic" in the titles of their studies and then proceed to comment on the "plots" and the "characters" that they find in the sequence. But in literary criticism, as in so many other human activities, we are prone to see what we expect to see, and nothing else. While Shakespeare's *Sonnets* evidently do include certain dramatic and narrative elements, in focusing on that aspect of them we have overlooked a more revealing and more sur-

prising fact: that many of the characteristics central to other dramatic and narrative poetry, including other Renaissance sonnet sequences, are signally absent from Shakespeare's *Sonnets.*

A comparison of Shakespeare's Sonnet 87 with two other works that also concern a leavetaking will highlight his approach to the genre. The famous lines of Drayton's *Idea* 61 demonstrate how a poem in what is essentially a lyric mode can become dramatic:

> Since ther's no helpe, Come let us kisse and part.
> Nay, I have done: you get no more of Me,
> And I am glad, yea glad with all my heart,
> That thus so cleanly, I my Selfe can free,
> Shake hands for ever, Cancell all our Vowes,
> And when We meet at any time againe,
> Be it not seene in either of our Browes,
> That We one jot of former Love reteyne;
> Now at the last gaspe, of Loves latest Breath,
> When his Pulse fayling, Passion speechlesse lies,
> When Faith is kneeling by his bed of Death,
> And Innocence is closing up his Eyes,
>   Now if thou would'st, when all have given him over,
>   From Death to Life, thou might'st him yet recover.

Rather than describing the episode in which the lovers part, Drayton enacts it. We are asked to believe (and, thanks to his skill, the illusion is persuasive) that we are actually witnessing the speaker bidding farewell to his lady. We are as conscious of her implicit but powerful presence as that speaker is himself. And we are conscious, too, that what the poem claims to enact is a specified and unique moment in time. To be sure, Drayton briefly uses allegory to distance us from that moment—but his main reason for establishing such a distance is to create a foil against which his final appeal to the woman will seem all the more immediate.

Though Petrarch's *Canzonière* CXC is primarily concerned with rendering certain states of mind—the poet's joy at the beauty of Laura and his intense sorrow at her loss—he evokes those states by telling a story. . . . Petrarch's poem may be visionary and mystical, but like other narratives it is firmly anchored in time. It has a clear beginning, middle, and end: at the opening of the poem the speaker sees the deer, then he admires her, and then he loses her.

Shakespeare wears his rue with a difference:

> Farewell, thou art too dear for my possessing,
> And like enough thou know'st thy estimate.
> The charter of thy worth gives thee releasing;
> My bonds in thee are all determinate.
> For how do I hold thee but by thy granting,
> And for that riches where is my deserving?
> The cause of this fair gift in me is wanting,
> And so my patience back again is swerving.
> Thyself thou gav'st, thy own worth then not knowing,
> Or me, to whom thou gav'st, else mistaking;
> So thy great gift, upon misprision growing,
> Comes home again, on better judgment making.
>   Thus have I had thee as a dream doth flatter,
>   In sleep a king, but waking no such matter.
>
> (Sonnet 87)

The opening word, "Farewell," suggests that this sonnet is going to enact a parting in much the same way that Drayton's does; and the third quatrain does in a sense tell a story. Yet

Shakespeare's poem is not necessarily a rendition of a particular event that takes place at a particular moment: one cannot tell whether the parting is in the process of happening or has already occurred. For Shakespeare's primary concern is not to imitate an incident in which a lover says farewell but rather to evoke the lover's reflections on the process of parting. And Shakespeare's sonnet differs from Drayton's in another and no less significant way: while most of the assertions in Drayton's sonnet are addressed to the beloved, most of those in Shakespeare's are not. In the couplet, for example, Shakespeare's speaker seems to be brooding on his experiences rather than either enacting them or announcing their significance to the person he has loved.

The characteristics of that couplet and of the sonnet in which it figures recur throughout Shakespeare's sonnet sequence. The narrative, dramatic, and lyrical are not, of course, necessarily exclusive of each other, either in general or in Shakespeare's sonnets in particular. In his sequence as a whole, and not infrequently within a single sonnet, we do encounter instances of all three modes. Sonnets 153 and 154, for example, are certainly narrative according to virtually any definition of that term; the entire sequence is indubitably dramatic in the sense that it vividly bodies forth the speaker himself, developing and drawing attention to the nuances of his character. Nevertheless, it is not the presence of certain narrative and dramatic elements but rather the absence of others that is most striking when we read Shakespeare's sequence and most telling when we juxtapose it with the sonnets composed by many other Renaissance poets.

One of the clearest and most important indications that the majority of the *Sonnets* are in certain senses neither narrative nor dramatic is that they do not include a temporal sequence of events, as does, for example, Petrarch's "Una candida cerva sopra l'erba." As we read Shakespeare's *Sonnets,* we witness tortuous shifts in the speaker's emotions and judgments, but very seldom do we encounter a chronological progression of occurrences. Instead, his monologues take place in the kind of eternal present that is usually a mark of lyric poetry. Characteristically, they generalize about an event that recurs frequently rather than focusing on one instance of it: "When I consider everything that grows" (Sonnet 15, line 1); "When to the sessions of sweet silent thought / I summon up remembrance of things past" (Sonnet 30, lines 1-2). In another sense, too, the sonnet sequence that so vividly evokes the horrors of time is not itself rooted in time: Shakespeare's poems seldom refer to datable real incidents or even to incidents that occur at a specific, though symbolic, moment. Petrarch alludes to the date of his meeting with the real woman who was transformed into Laura and the date of her death, and his sequence may also have complex symbolic relationships to the calendar. Spenser's sonnets are apparently keyed to the seasons. One of Daniel's refers to a trip to Italy. But in Shakespeare we find very few such references. To be sure, in one poem the speaker does suggest that he met his beloved three years before; but nowhere else does he allude to time in so specific a way. And Shakespeare is no more specific about place. We know that Sidney's Stella takes a ride on the Thames, while Shakespeare's *Sonnets* never mention a particular locale.

The omission of such allusions to place and time is all the more suggestive in light of Shakespeare's repeated—one is almost tempted to say frenetic—puns on "will." Like Sidney's play on "rich" or his adoption of the pseudonym "As-

trophil," these puns are evidently intended to remind us that the poems in question are closely linked to autobiographical experience. One would presume that the same attitudes that lead a poet to pun on, and hence draw attention to, his own name might well encourage him to refer to specific dates and places. But this Shakespeare chooses not to do.

The lack of temporal perspective in most of the *Sonnets* reflects the absence of anecdotal sonnets. With only a handful of exceptions, Shakespeare's sequence omits not only the mythological stories that so frequently grace the sequences of other sonnet writers but also non-mythological allegories like Spenser's *Amoretti* LXXV ("One day I wrote her name vpon the strand"). Moreover, Shakespeare seldom chooses to narrate an incident that happens to the lovers, as, say, Sidney does in *Astrophil and Stella* 41 ("Having this day my horse, my hand, my launce"). It is as uncharacteristic of Shakespeare to begin a sonnet with "One day" as it is characteristic of Spenser to do so.

A sonnet that does not narrate an anecdote may, of course, be anchored in a specific event or situation nonetheless: it can be the outgrowth of an occurrence which, though not recounted systematically, is referred to frequently and specifically in the course of the poem. Many readers have assumed that the vast majority of Shakespeare's *Sonnets* are "situational" in this sense. But in point of fact comparatively few of them are. In some of Shakespeare's monologues the reflections are inspired not by a particular situation but by a general problem; thus in Sonnet 94 the speaker evokes a certain kind of personality, and Sonnet 129 is an anguished consideration of the nature of lust. Because poems like these rely so heavily on generalizations, critics regularly describe them as interesting exceptions to Shakespeare's approach elsewhere in the sequence. They are, however, merely extreme instances of their author's tendency to detach the speaker's emotions and speculations from an immediate situation.

Some poems in the sequence imply that a specific incident may lie behind the speaker's reactions but omit any discussion of details. We learn little about the "forsaking" to which Sonnet 89 alludes, for example, or the reasons for the parting described in the absence sonnets. As we read Sonnet 35 we do not know what the "sensual fault" to which it refers may be, or even whether "fault" indicates a particular lapse or a general character trait. If we try to enumerate the situations on which Shakespeare's *Sonnets* are based, we find that our list is short and the events on it shadowy. The poet encourages the Friend to marry; there is a period of separation, and there are one or more quarrels; the Friend is praised by another poet; the Friend betrays the speaker with the Dark Lady. By contrast, in *Astrophil and Stella,* a sequence about two-thirds the length of Shakespeare's, the situations include a stolen kiss, Stella's illness, her ride on the Thames, an absence, a quarrel, Astrophil's triumph in a tournament, and many more.

If most of Shakespeare's *Sonnets* do not tell stories, neither do they enact dramas in the way that, say, Drayton's *Idea* 61 does ("Since ther's no helpe, Come let us kisse and part"). And yet the reader becomes involved in these poems. One Shakespearean has attempted to explain why: "By setting up a system of tensions between forces presented as persons, Shakespeare's sonnets engage the reader's interest in a manner akin to the dramatic" [see excerpt above by G. K. Hunter, 1953]. It is true that some of the *Sonnets,* notably the poems addressed to Time, do operate this way. But most do not: Shakespeare's *Sonnets* embody the tension of conflicting forces, but those forces are more often internalized within the speaker than dramatized as characters.

Though the Friend and the Dark Lady dominate the speaker's thoughts, in some important respects they do not function as active participants within the *Sonnets*. The problems engendered by their behavior are frighteningly immediate, but the characters themselves are not. Except for the fact that the young man is attractive and the lady is dark, we do not know what they look like. Unlike the main characters in most sonnet sequences, they are never assigned names, even fictional ones, even in those poems that refer to them in the third rather than the second person. The epithets by which they are addressed serve, if anything, to distance us further from them. When, for example, Shakespeare opens Sonnet 56 on the command, "Sweet love, renew your force," he establishes an unresolved ambiguity about whether the poem concerns his beloved or the abstract quality of love, or both. When he directs an apostrophe to "Lascivious grace" (Sonnet 40, line 13), he initially seems as much to be brooding on the abstraction that the epithet expresses as to be talking to a person who has been reduced (or who has willingly reduced himself) to the state expressed by that oxymoron. Similarly, only once (Sonnet 34, line 13) in 154 sonnets does Shakespeare allude to the movements or gestures of the beloved in a way that suggests that he is physically present and actually listening to the speaker. Contrast *Astrophil and Stella* 31, which so unequivocally sets up the fiction that Astrophil is in the presence of the moon, or *Astrophil and Stella* 47, whose "Soft, but here she comes" (line 13) so effectively signals Stella's arrival.

It is a truth as significant as it is neglected that the Friend and the Dark Lady are not quoted directly within the poems. Despite all his experience in writing plays, Shakespeare chooses not to create the kind of dialogue on which such poems as *Astrophil and Stella* 54 ("Because I breathe not love to everie one") or *Idea* 24 ("I heare some say, this Man is not in love") or even *Amoretti* LXXV ("One day I wrote her name vpon the strand") are based. On those rare occasions when the words of the beloved are recorded, they are presented in a form that distances us from the statements and their speakers: the poet either uses indirect discourse to report what the beloved has said ("When my love swears that she is made of truth" [Sonnet 138, line 1]) or predicts what he or she is likely to say rather than what has actually been said ("O then vouchsafe me but this loving thought: / Had my friend's muse grown with this growing age" [Sonnet 32, lines 9-10]).

If the lovers remain shadowy in the sonnets addressed to them, so too do the other characters who occasionally appear. We know surprisingly little about the Rival Poet himself, though we learn much about his impact on the speaker's emotions. When Shakespeare chooses to refer to society's reactions to his love, he characterizes it vaguely as "all tongues" (Sonnet 69, line 3) rather than evoking specific figures like the nymphs who berate Astrophil. Time is personified, of course, but it generally functions more as a threat looming over the speaker than as an active character. Even in Sonnet 19, the poet only anticipates the effects of "Devouring time" on his beloved, whereas Spenser is engaged in fighting with the waves (and Donne actually invites his "Busie old foole" into his bedroom). It is revealing, moreover, that the kinds of characters who populate other sequences and create miniature dramas by arguing with the speaker are totally ab-

sent from Shakespeare's poems. The ladies who are Laura's companions, the cynical friend who berates Drayton, the court nymphs who criticize Astrophil—no figures like these appear in Shakespeare's *Sonnets*.

Nor is Shakespeare prone to replace them with internalized characters. Though the morality tradition influences his sequence in other ways, only rarely does he depict the conflicts within his speaker as allegorical personages engaged in a confrontation. Many of his sonnets concern a debate between opposing forces such as reason and passion; but very few evoke that debate through allegorical characters like those that figure so prominently in *Astrophil and Stella*.

Most of the sonnets are not narrative, then, in the sense that the speaker is not recounting a story to the reader or to any other implied audience. And they are not dramatic in the sense that we are not witnessing a confrontation that occurs at a specific place and time between a speaker and a particular listener, or even between two clearly distinguished personages within the speaker. Instead, it is the lyric mode that predominates. Some of the poems resemble an internalized meditation, others a letter, others a monologue that the beloved hears but apparently does not respond to.

The soliloquy immediately presents itself as a parallel to and an inspiration for Shakespeare's unusual approach to the sonnet, and in certain respects the comparison is an illuminating one. The speaker in Shakespeare's *Sonnets* often seems to be thinking aloud, to be at once speaking audibly and meditating. But, as the passages that I have cited suggest, in one crucial way the *Sonnets* differ from the soliloquies that are so frequently embedded in their author's plays: the soliloquy normally takes place at a unique moment and is often provoked by a clearly defined event that has preceded it, whereas most of the *Sonnets* are signally lacking in those types of particularization.

Most readers have found the differences between Shakespeare's sonnets and those of his contemporaries puzzling. Several of the most idiosyncratic qualities of Shakespeare's *Sonnets* stem from the poet's decision to shape so many of them as lyrics in the sense of subjective reflections. Thus his couplets, which fail to provide the reassuring summaries we have been told to expect at the end of a "Shakespearean sonnet," can best be understood if we remember the mode in which Shakespeare is generally writing. As long as we think of the *Sonnets* as dramas or stories, we will be conditioned to expect their couplets (like those of many other sonneteers) to be reasoned statements of objective truths: we will expect them to function rather like the chorus's commentary in a play or the narrator's judgments in a novel. When, however, we recognize that so many of the *Sonnets* are internalized monologues, we are in a position to observe that one purpose of Shakespeare's couplets is to reflect the chaos in the speaker's mind, a purpose to which a couplet that merely summarized the preceding twelve lines would prove inadequate.

Some of Shakespeare's couplets resolve difficult problems too neatly, an impression intensified by the tidiness and balance inherent in the couplet form. Thus, for instance, "Pity me then, dear friend, and I assure ye, / Ev'n that your pity is enough to cure me" (Sonnet 111, ll. 13-14) does not persuade the reader that the diseases of the heart chronicled in the previous twelve lines can be cured as readily as the speaker hopes. The jingly rhyme increases our sense that the speaker is whistling in the dark, our sense that the couplet is merely another vain attempt to solve his dilemmas.

Other couplets offer responses that seem inappropriate reactions to what has come before. Once again we are more aware of the stresses that make the speaker seek reassurance than of the reassurance that the couplet, if only by virtue of its innately epigrammatic tone, claims to provide. The quatrains of Sonnet 33, for example, draw attention to the wrongs that the poet has suffered at the hands of his beloved:

> Full many a glorious morning have I seen
> Flatter the mountain tops with sovereign eye.
> Kissing with golden face the meadows green,
> Gilding pale streams with heav'nly alchemy,
> Anon permit the basest clouds to ride
> With ugly rack on his celestial face,
> And from the forlorn world his visage hide,
> Stealing unseen to west with this disgrace.
> Ev'n so my sun one early morn did shine,
> With all triumphant splendor on my brow;
> But out alack, he was but one hour mine,
> The region cloud hath masked him from me now.

Here Shakespeare develops the metaphor of the sun in a way that emphasizes its guilt and hence by implication that of the Friend. Thus "Flatter" (line 2) and "Gilding" (line 4) have connotations that are at the very least ambiguous: flattery can be sycophantic, and gilding can be deceptive. The sort of couplet that these quatrains lead us to expect is something like "I thought our love an everlasting day / And yet my trust thou didst, my love, betray." If we try to read the poem through with this couplet tacked on the end, we find that the uncanonical lines fit the spirit of the poem. If, on the other hand, we read the sonnet through with the couplet that Shakespeare did in fact write—"Yet him for this my love no wit disdaineth; / Suns of the world may stain when heav'n's sun staineth" (ll. 13-14)—we become uneasy. Shakespeare's speaker is trying to fool himself; he takes one conceivable moral from the metaphor (the Friend's betrayal is justified by that of the sun) and neglects the more central one that the reader has been observing (the Friend, like the sun, has been culpably deceptive).

Similarly, the many couplets that offer an unexpectedly pessimistic interpretation of the issues in the poem suggest the impingement of new facts—especially new apprehensions and doubts—on the speaker's troubled consciousness. Sonnet 92, for instance, ends "But what's so blessèd-fair that fears no blot? / Thou mayst be false, and yet I know it not" (ll. 13-14). Just as an unexpected fear enters the speaker's mind and disturbs the peace he has been attempting to achieve, so an unexpected idea enters the couplet and disturbs its potential function as a neat summary of the preceding quatrains.

All of these couplets are a response to the fundamental paradox that confronted Shakespeare as he wrote the *Sonnets*. The sonnet is, as so many of its readers have remarked, one of the most orderly of literary forms; it is tightly structured and compact. Its couplet is the most orderly and ordering of its elements. No matter what the content of the couplet, in contrast to the syntactical and metrical complexities of the preceding quatrains it will often sound like an easily achieved truism. Frequently, too, the convictions expressed in the couplet will be so epigrammatic that they mirror and intensify the impression of assurance that the very form conveys.

The experiences evoked by Shakespeare's *Sonnets* are, however, unusually tumultuous even in a genre that specializes in psychological torment. As we have seen, in a number of ways his sonnets focus our attention on the speaker's chaotic reactions. We would no more expect a man who is wrestling with the kinds of unresolved contradictions plaguing Shakespeare's speaker to express them in the carefully structured and epigrammatically decisive lines of a couplet than the Elizabethans would have expected a madman in a play to speak in verse. Like the poet in Donne's "The Triple Fool," we assume that grief brought to numbers cannot be so fierce.

Rather than ignoring or struggling to overcome these characteristics of his form, Shakespeare exploits them. The reader comes to view the sentiments in many of the couplets not as objective summaries of the problems that the quatrains have been exploring, but rather as yet another symptom of the anguish and confusion that those problems have caused. As we have seen, those couplets that abruptly reverse the ideas in the quatrains and thus disturb the way the sonnet form generally functions reflect the process by which troubling new thoughts disturb the speaker's emotions. Such couplets are the formal equivalent of the turmoil in the lover's heart. Similarly, those couplets that seem deliberately to oversimplify experience effectively mirror the speaker's vain attempts to resolve the conflicts in his own mind: he often appears to turn to the couplet with relief, to find in its easy absolutes of hope or despair (and the straightforward syntax in which these emotions are expressed) a welcome alternative to the torturing ambivalences with which he has been wrestling (and the tortuous syntax in which he has expressed them).

Though Shakespeare's couplets often resemble soliloquies in their evocations of a mind brooding on experience, those that oversimplify complex realities differ from most Elizabethan soliloquies in the unreliability of their reflections: the speaker is lying to himself and hence to us. On first reading we may be confused or even deceived into taking the lines at face value, much as the figure delivering them is himself confused or deceived. That speaker is in a sense compounding his lies by the very act of presenting them through the vehicle of an epigrammatic couplet. For in the sonnets in question that prosodic form itself functions deceptively: we have come to expect from it, not the unreliable and subjective half-truths or untruths that we may in fact encounter, but unexceptional verities. We may therefore be seduced by the very nature of the couplet form into momentarily believing the speaker's assertions.

Shakespeare's couplets explore and often exemplify an issue with which the whole sequence is very concerned: our predilection for deceiving ourselves and others. The Dark Lady uses her artfulness to lie verbally to her lover ("When my love swears that she is made of truth, / I do believe her though I know she lies" [Sonnet 138, ll. 1-2]), while the Friend's physical appearance is itself a kind of visual lie. The behavior of the Friend and the Dark Lady is contagious in this as in so many other regards, for the speaker himself comes to use art (in many senses of that term) to twist or destroy the truth. Some of the speaker's lies are offered in the service of his lovers, for whom he undertakes the process he describes in Sonnet 35: "Myself corrupting salving thy amiss, / Excusing thy sins more than thy sins are" (ll. 7-8). But the most disturbing of the deceptions in the sequence are the speaker's self-deceptions. By shaping so many of the poems as internalized lyrics, Shakespeare provides a forum for his speaker's repeated attempts to lie to himself. Sometimes a whole poem represents his effort to impose a more comforting but fallacious interpretation on a reality that, as the reader uneasily recognizes, demands a different response. At other times the couplet undercuts the neat but false interpretation in the quatrains. Most often, however, it is the couplet itself that contains the lie. The main reason that several of the most complex sonnets in our language end with couplets that are simple or even simplistic is that the pat answers in those lines demonstrate the habits of self-deception that repeatedly lead the speaker, like his companions, to distort his perceptions, his morals, and his language. In sonnets like these, the couplet form itself becomes a symbol of our cursed rage for order, our tendency to simplify and sanitize our experience, even at the expense of truth.

Their emphasis on the lyrical rather than the narrative or dramatic also helps to explain another characteristic of Shakespeare's *Sonnets*: how immediately and how intensely they evoke the speaker's feelings. The reader need channel little or none of his attention to an exposition of a situation or an exploration of the beloved's psyche: he focuses instead on the poet-lover himself. For example, the impact of Sonnet 12, at first glance a comparatively impersonal poem, in fact stems not merely from its vivid depiction of time's ravages but also from its moving evocation of its speaker's sensibility:

> When I do count the clock that tells the time,
> And see the brave day sunk in hideous night,
> When I behold the violet past prime,
> And sable curls all silvered o'er with white,
> When lofty trees I see barren of leaves,
> Which erst from heat did canopy the herd,
> And summer's green all girded up in sheaves
> Borne on the bier with white and bristly beard,
> Then of thy beauty do I question make
> That thou among the wastes of time must go.
> Since sweets and beauties do themselves forsake,
> And die as fast as they see others grow,
>   And nothing 'gainst time's scythe can make defense
>   Save breed to brave him when he takes thee hence.

In one sense this sonnet is a carefully documented argument. The quatrains, which present a series of facts marshaled to support the thesis in the sestet, function as part of a syllogism (all sweets and beauties die; you yourself are a sweet and beauty; therefore you will die). But in presenting this case the poem repeatedly directs our attention to the mind brooding on it: like Marvell's "To His Coy Mistress," this lyric is as much concerned with the speaker's thoughts about death as with ways of combatting that inevitable but unendurable fact. The first five lines contain no fewer than four verbs referring to the speaker's processes of cognition ("do count" . . . "see" . . . "behold" . . . "see"), three of which are preceded by the personal pronoun "I." The anaphora in lines one and three ("When I") further heightens the emphasis on the speaker's sensibility. "Then of thy beauty do I question make" (l. 9), which follows these two quatrains, contains in microcosm the characteristics that we have been noting, for one may gloss those words in two ways: (1) I ask you a question ("thy beauty" functioning as synecdoche in this interpretation) or (2) in my own mind I raise a question about your beauty. Even while communicating with the beloved, then, the speaker also seems to be communing with himself. As he considers the beloved's behavior, therefore, the reader is also led to concentrate on how that behavior affects the speaker.

While a thorough affective study of the *Sonnets* would de-

mand a separate essay, one important truth about the reader's responses is clear: the primary effect of the lyrical mode of these poems is to intensify our identification with the speaker. And one reason our identification becomes so deep is that these sonnets are far more universal than those by any other English poet (with perhaps the interesting exception of Wyatt). As we have observed, they are not linked to particular dates or seasons or places. More important, because the events and situations to which Shakespeare alludes are presented only sketchily, we can readily relate the *Sonnets* to our own lives; we are not conscious of local details that do not conform to our own experiences.

Above all, we identify closely with the speaker because the emotions and reactions we experience when reading the poems are very similar to the emotions and reactions the poems are about. Like the speaker, we are confused by ambiguities in language and in the situations language is exploring. When we read Spenser's *Amoretti* VIII ("More then most faire, full of the liuing fire") we have few doubts about the judgments being passed on the lady; when we read Sonnet 94, however, we have, and I suspect are meant to have, few certainties. We are forced to keep thinking about the issues being raised, to keep re-examining the charged and ambiguous words of the poem.

Like Shakespeare's speaker, his readers try to find oases of order and stability in the tumultuous world of the *Sonnets*. The speaker reaches out for the overly simple answers expressed in his couplets in a way that is not unlike the way we reach out for a reordering of the *Sonnets* that would lessen their complexities and explain their ambiguities. If it is true that the *Sonnets* are the record of meditations, it is equally true that they encourage meditation in their reader far more than most poetry does. Since we are not offered neat answers, we, like the speaker, keep brooding on the questions that have been raised.

The nature of Shakespeare's *Sonnets* reflects the nature of the experience they evoke. Most of them are lyric rather than narrative or dramatic because they concern a world in which narrative and dramatic modes would be inappropriate. One reason so few of these poems reflect a chronological sequence of events is that their speaker is trapped in brooding rather than acting or even being acted on. His mind is tormented with calamities that the future may bring (his beloved will betray him, Time will destroy even this most precious of mortals) or that the present, unbeknownst to him, may already hold (his two friends may have already been unfaithful to him, the beloved may be morally stained). And these calamities are rendered more painful by the fact that the speaker is powerless, whether to prevent those disasters that the future may hold or to be certain that those the present may contain have not in fact come to pass:

> Yet eyes this cunning want to grace their art;
> They draw but what they see, know not the heart.
>   (Sonnet 24, ll. 13-14)

> And even thence thou wilt be stol'n, I fear.
>   (Sonnet 48, l. 13)

In dramas, including the miniature version of drama that a sonnet can embody, characters often commit definite actions; in narratives, even fourteen-line narratives, usually definite events occur. But, as the passages above suggest, the dominant mood of Shakespeare's *Sonnets* is fearful anticipation and troubling suspicion, not clear-cut events. Narrative and dramatic modes would not have been as suited to evoking such a milieu.

Just as Shakespeare's decision to omit certain narrative and dramatic elements from his *Sonnets* aptly expresses his speaker's painful inaction, so it expresses the uncertainties suffered by that speaker and by the reader who is so intimately involved with him. If presented within the intense and concentrated form of the sonnet, both the narrative and the dramatic modes tend to suggest moral and epistemological certainties. When sonnet writers use mythological allegories, for example, they generally do so in order to make some simple but significant point about love; Cupid's tricks may remind us that love is deceptive, and Venus' fickleness that women are untrustworthy. Similarly, in narrating an event involving a lover and his mistress, sonneteers usually establish some important facts about the participants, such as the lady's unremitting and unremorseful chastity. And when sonnets imitate a dialogue between opponents, the two figures generally argue neatly antithetical positions. A victory for one position or the other, or possibly a synthesis of both, is achieved by the end of the sonnet. Even if the poet-lover himself remains trapped in his moral dilemma, a sequence relying extensively on narrative and dramatic modes can establish important verities. Thus *Astrophil and Stella* as a whole documents truths about Neoplatonism that Astrophil can only imperfectly grasp.

In so frequently avoiding the narrative and dramatic in his *Sonnets,* Shakespeare declines to provide the kinds of ethical truths and moral certainties that those modes can generate. He is achieving in formal terms the types of moral confusion he is exploring thematically. Just as the experience of the reader mirrors that of the speaker in these poems, so form mirrors content to an extent unusual in even the greatest art. (pp. 55-68)

> Heather Dubrow, "Shakespeare's Undramatic Monologues: Toward a Reading of the 'Sonnets'," in Shakespeare Quarterly, Vol. 32, No. 1, Spring, 1981, pp. 55-68.

JANETTE DILLON   (essay date 1981)

[*Dillon explores the implications of the repetition of the word "self" in Shakespeare's sonnets. Inwardness and singleness, she remarks, are powerful, controlling concepts throughout the sonnets addressed to the Friend. Dillon argues that the poet becomes increasingly aware of the existence in himself of the very qualities of solitude, self-division, and withdrawal he has disparaged in the young man. The moral perspectives of both men, the poet recognizes, are compromised by virtue of their withdrawal from the judgments of the world into "the prison of the inward self." Dillon further calls attention to the images of mirrors, windows, and shadows in the sonnets, arguing that these emphasize the young man's narcissism and underscore "the weakness, instability, and delusion of the self-lover."*]

One of the most striking characteristics of the Sonnets is their obsessive repetition of the word 'self', which occurs more frequently here than in any other one of Shakespeare's works. It was not until the sixteenth century that 'self' came to be used as an autonomous noun; before then it occurred only as an element of reflexive pronouns. The progress of the word towards autonomy was part of a progress towards increasing autonomy in the actual concept of the self, which was coming to be defined more and more with reference to its own inner world, rather than through its external contexts. The begin-

nings of autonomy can be seen in the repetition of the reflexive in Petrarch's sonnets and Montaigne's essays, although the equivalents of 'self' in their languages did not actually attain grammatical autonomy. Shakespeare's Sonnets, on the other hand, show quite clearly the breaking down of the boundaries between reflexive and autonomous usage from the very first sonnet:

> Thyself thy foe, to thy sweet self too cruel
>
> [Sonnet 1]

> Thou of thyself thy sweet self dost deceive
>
> [Sonnet 4]

> To give away your self keeps your self still
>
> [Sonnet 16]

Variations among modern editors in printing 'thyself' . . . confirm the fluidity of the boundaries.

Almost as characteristic as the repetition of 'self' standing alone or in a pronoun is the prevalence of compound words with 'self': 'self-substantial' [Sonnet 1], 'self-love' [Sonnet 3], 'self-kill'd' [Sonnet 6], 'self-will'd' [Sonnet 6]. The inevitable implications of self-division attaching to such words demonstrate the way the preoccupation with the self in this period was linked almost by definition with a sense of inward division.

From even the small number of lines quoted so far from the Sonnets it is evident that the first sonnet, and by extension the first group of six sonnets, like Richard III's first soliloquy, sets out most of the themes and images of the sequence as a whole. Many of those themes and images are the same as those outlined in Richard's soliloquy. Even the linguistic emblem of the self isolated within its own circularity, Richard's 'myself myself', is transformed in the Sonnets into the patterns of 'thyself thyself' and 'yourself yourself' (see quotations above), and linked with echoes of 'I am myself alone':

> For having traffic with thyself alone,
> Thou of thyself thy sweet self dost deceive.
>
> [Sonnet 4]

The 'thyself alone' and 'thyself thyself' patterns are condemnatory in this instance, where they are followed by an exhortation to exchange this sterile self-enclosure for the satisfaction of breeding other selves:

> That's for thyself to breed an other thee,
> Or ten times happier, be it ten for one;
> Ten times thy self were happier than thou art,
> If ten of thine ten times refigur'd thee.
>
> [Sonnet 6]

Giorgio Melchiori has noted how frequently the second person occurs in Shakespeare's Sonnets, by contrast with other contemporary sonnet sequences, interpreting this to be an indication that Shakespeare's love takes the form of a real dialogue between equals, rather than a distant reverence [see Additional Bibliography]. 'The characteristic feature of Shakespeare's Sonnets', he writes, 'as compared with those of his contemporaries is the balanced predominance of *I* and *thou* rather than the distance between *I* and *she*.' This is true in one sense and distorting in another, for the use of the second person often seems to convey the very distance between the poet and his cold love, particularly when it occurs as part of this pattern of self-loving disengagement on the part of the boy, 'thyself thyself'.

The constant urging of the boy towards marriage, fertility and reproduction in the early sonnets embodies an attempt to dissuade him from the metaphorically sterile life of detachment and self-interest as well as from actual sterility. Other aspects of the language besides this 'thyself thyself' pattern mimic sterility. The reflexive verb *per se,* without repetition, is a potentially 'self-consuming' element, and Shakespeare repeatedly uses it in the Sonnets to show how actions performed within the circle of the self instead of beyond it become thwarted and self-negating. The reversal of an outward action by forcing it inward is self-destructive:

> thou consum'st thyself in single life . . .
> beauty's waste hath in the world an end,
> And kept unus'd, the user so destroys it.
>
> [Sonnet 9]

> Grant, if thou wilt, thou art belov'd of many,
> But that thou none lov'st is most evident;
> For thou art so possess'd with murd'rous hate
> That gainst thyself thou stick'st not to conspire,
> Seeking that beauteous roof to ruinate
> Which to repair should be thy chief desire.
>
> [Sonnet 10]

> to you it doth belong
> Your self to pardon of self-doing crime.
>
> [Sonnet 58]

The only action which could reverse itself to the boy's advantage is the one which would take him outside himself:

> To give away your self keeps your self still.
>
> [Sonnet 16]

Reciprocity, the reverse of the boy's closed inwardness, is the only source of true fulfilment:

> Then happy I, that love and am beloved
> Where I may not remove nor be removed.
>
> [Sonnet 25]

From the first sonnet, the equation between spiritual self-consumption and physical death is explicit:

> Thou that art now the world's fresh ornament
> And only herald to the gaudy spring,
> Within thine own bud buriest thy content,
> And, tender churl, mak'st waste in niggarding.
> Pity the world, or else this glutton be,
> To eat the world's due, by the grave and thee,

anticipating the bitter invective against this same inner rotting in Sonnet 94:

> Lilies that fester smell far worse than weeds.

The flower imagery in both instances is reminiscent of the Narcissus myth. . . . Bacon, referring to the disappointment of early promise in maturity, writes [in his *The Wisdom of the Ancients*]:

> The fact too that this flower is sacred to the infernal deities contains an allusion to the same thing. For men of this disposition turn out utterly useless and good for nothing whatever; and anything that yields no fruit, but like the way of a ship in the sea passes and leaves no trace, was by the ancients held sacred to the shades and infernal gods.

The image of the glass in the Sonnets, as in *Richard III* and *Richard II,* supports the interpretation of the young man as a Narcissus type, Sonnet 3, for example, plays on the double potential of the reflected image to be seen as either the propagation or the imprisonment of the self:

> Look in thy glass, and tell the face thou viewest
> Now is the time that face should form another . . .
> Thou art thy mother's glass, and she in thee
> Calls back the lovely April of her prime;
> So thou through windows of thine age shalt see,
> Despite of wrinkles, this thy golden time.
> But if thou live rememb'red not to be,
> Die single, and thine image dies with thee.

As for Richard II, glass can be looked through as a means of transcending the limits of self, or into, imprisoning the self within those same limits. It can suggest the sense of liberation from the confines of the self, or the claustrophobia within them. The images of glass as mirror and window are extended into the glass vial of Sonnets 5 and 6. The vial, though ostensibly the image of the propagation of self, the 'distillation' of the self's image in the next generation, actually suggests, against the syntactical sense, the closed world of the single boy. The line

> A liquid prisoner pent in walls of glass,
>
> [Sonnet 5]

despite its actual reference to the distilled flower which represents the boy's imagined child, ironically suggests more strongly the imprisonment of the single, uncommitted boy, who is enclosed in a world of mirrors.

The terminology of shadows too, associated with the mirror in *Richard II* and *Richard III,* implies the weakness, insubstantiality and delusion of the self-lover. The young man is 'a weakened being whose activity is crippled' [Louis Vinge, in his *The Narcissus Theme*], a figure stunted inwardly, by contrast with his physical beauty (unlike Richard III, whose inner deformity is given an external image). As in these two plays, Shakespeare does not allow the individual to be defined wholly from within in the way to which he aspires, but measures him against the framework he rejects, a framework which will finally overwhelm him in the shape of time and death. From first to last, the Sonnets warn that the individual's rejection of the world outside him cannot be an absolute. However hard an individual may try to erect himself into his absolute, and define the world as relative only to his inner self, his subjective truth, his mortality will in fact prove that it is he who is the mere relative, and the enclosing framework of the world the absolute. Only a creative act on the part of the individual, an act which moves beyond the self to recognise society, whether it be producing a child or writing poetry, can confer immortality on the individual and enable him to overcome time and death. He transcends the constants of the framework by becoming part of it, not by denying its existence.

The boy's position in relation to society can be summed up by the word 'singleness', to which Shakespeare attributes a widely suggestive semantic range. Most obviously, the word describes the boy's marital status. Being single, he will die without a child, and therefore remain self-contained, single also in that sense:

> Die single, and thine image dies with thee.
>
> [Sonnet 3]

He is single in the sense that he is a part cut off from the whole, a solitary individual without a social context. The vocabulary of 'concord' and 'union' which Shakespeare applies to marriage also suggests the greater social order of which the family was a recognised image:

> If the true concord of well-tuned sounds,
> By unions married, do offend thine ear,
> They do but sweetly chide thee, who confounds
> In singleness the parts that thou shouldst bear.
>
> [Sonnet 8]

'Singleness' suggests too his proud aloofness from other men, the way he holds himself apart from commitment to others, and the preciousness implied by that aloofness. Sonnet 94, despite its bitter denunciation of the rottenness likely to destroy such a one, demonstrates simultaneously an admiration for such self-sufficiency and invulnerability:

> They that have power to hurt and will do none,
> That do not do the thing they most do show,
> Who, moving others, are themselves as stone,
> Unmoved, cold, and to temptation slow—
> They rightly do inherit Heaven's graces,
> And husband nature's riches from expense;
> They are the lords and owners of their faces,
> Others but stewards of their excellence.

Even the flower image, besides evoking the self-consumption of Narcissus, also suggests the fragile and delicate beauty of solipsistic singleness:

> The summer's flow'r is to the summer sweet
> Though to itself it only live and die.
>
> [Sonnet 94]

The quality of singleness, or 'singularity', suggests two kinds of isolation: the voluntary detachment and self-containment described in 'Unmoved, cold, and to temptation slow' and the inherent distinctiveness or superiority implied by the inheritance of 'Heaven's graces'. The boy is singled out from other men not only by his wilful affectation and self-love, but by the distinctive quality which makes him what he is, his 'singularity'. And this singularity, of course, his lover cannot condemn, but can only praise (in another echo of Richard III's phrase):

> Who is it that says most which can say more
> Than this rich praise—that you alone are you?
>
> [Sonnet 84]

Yet this exalts that aspect of nature which distinguishes men and makes them individuals at the expense of the nature which unites them in that they are all men. The boy does not recognise nature in the general sense, the nature that makes him a man like other men, but recognises only his own particular nature, the nature that singles him out from other men. Praise of this second kind of nature was becoming common in the sixteenth century, as individual autonomy was gaining wider recognition. Ralegh, for example, [in his *The History of the World*] praises the nature that separates and distinguishes rather than the nature which unites and identifies:

> But such is the multiplying and extensive vertue of
> dead Earth, and of that breath-giving life which
> GOD hath cast upon Slime and Dust: as that . . .
> every one hath received a severall picture of face,
> and everie one a diverse picture of minde; every one
> a forme apart, every one a fancy and cogitation dif-
> fering, there being nothing wherein Nature so
> much triumpheth, as in dissimilitude.

And just as the emphasis on individual nature characteristically accompanies an emphasis on the inward self, just as the

Portrait of Shakespeare by Gerard Soest.

boy of the Sonnets chooses his own inner world in preference to the outside world, so Ralegh emphasises that distinction and definition are located within, in the mind, not in the external public self or its context: '. . . it is not the visible fashion and shape of plants, and of reasonable Creatures, that makes the difference, of working in the one, and of condition in the other; but the forme internall.'

The most conspicuous point about Shakespeare's reference to the boy as 'single', however, is the irony inherent in the use of such a word to describe one who is fickle and inwardly fragmented. Living entirely within the circle of self, he is in one sense single in his isolation, but in another divided, in that he himself must play the role of both agent and object, must be both active and passive in all his purely self-referential actions. He is divided too on a more superficial level, in exhibiting, like Richard III, a division between face and heart: where Richard's innocent face hides his guilt, the young man's beautiful face hides his treacherous, faithless soul. Even his sexuality bears the marks of division, in that he is physically a man, but has the beauty of a woman and accepts a man as lover. Above all, he is changeable, living, like Richard II, only for the moment, betraying the self he seems or the role he plays from sonnet to sonnet. He is unfaithful to the poet in his acceptance of the dark lady as a lover and in his dallying with the favours of the rival poet; he is unreliable and unstable in his response to the poet even without outside influences:

> Thy self thou gav'st, thy own worth then not know-
> ing,

Or me, to whom thou gav'st it, else mistaking;
So thy great gift, upon misprision growing,
Comes home again, on better judgment making.

[Sonnet 87]

As in *Richard II,* however, where the presentation of Richard's solitude is qualified by comparison with solitude from Bolingbroke's perspective, so the withdrawal and self-division of the boy in the Sonnets do not constitute a single, unchallenged judgement of these qualities. The poet comes progressively to feel the existence in himself of those qualities he has condemned in the boy. In the early poems of the sequence he presents himself as wholly opposed to the boy's detachment and rejection of commitment. He speaks with the voice of society in urging the boy to take a wife and beget a child, thus embracing the values and social bonds of the world to which he belongs. But gradually, as the poet becomes more and more absorbed by the boy who tantalises him, he finds himself increasingly alienated from society, increasingly contained by his own inner world, subjective in his values and judgements, and remote from public concerns. The first person, not even introduced until the tenth sonnet, becomes more prominent and more isolated. Sonnet 29 describes the passing sense of desolation:

When in disgrace with Fortune and men's eyes,
I all alone beweep my outcast state,
And trouble deaf heaven with my bootless cries,
And look upon myself, and curse my fate,

for which he finds comfort in love by retreating from it into a private world. Sonnet 79 recalls fondly the time when he stood alone in the boy's love, glorying in this singularity:

Whilst I alone did call upon thy aid,
My verse alone had all thy gentle grace.

Sonnet 131 echoes Richard III's familiar phrase, the expression of one who sets his own values against those of society, in a context which seems to justify autonomy:

some say that thee behold
Thy face hath not the power to make love groan.
To say they err I dare not be so bold,
Although I swear it to myself alone.

Richard's 'I am I' is also echoed, in a more defiant tone of justification, in Sonnet 121: 'No; I am that I am.' The fact that the poet himself utters the challenge of self-definition, and not the boy, or any character clearly worthy of condemnation, suggests that Shakespeare's response to self-definition is no longer simply one of moral condemnation, and that the feeling of admiring awe which seemed sporadically present in *Richard III* is becoming more dominant than the sense of moral outrage. In this context it brings to mind not only Jehovah's –I AM', but also St Paul's legitimate, because qualified, self-definition: '. . . by the grace of God, I am that I am' [1 Cor. 15:10]. St Paul's statement is compatible with Pico's well-known exaltation of man's capacity for self-definition. God, according to Pico, having made man,

. . . & doubting with what maner of life he shuld adorne this his newe heire, this divine artificer, in the ende determined to make him unto whom hee could not assigne any thing in proper, partaker of al that, which the others enjoyed but in particular, whereupon calling him unto him, he sayd: Live O *Adam,* in what life pleaseth thee best, and take unto thy self those gifts which thou esteemest most deare. From this so liberall a graunt . . . had our

free wil his original, so that it is in our power, to live like a plant, living creature, like a man, & lastly as an Angell: for if a man addict himself only to feeding and nourishment, hee becommeth a Plante, if to things sensuall, he is as a brute beast, if to things reasonable & civil, he groweth a celestial creature: but if he exalt the beautiful gift of his mind, to thinges invisible and divine, hee transfourmeth himselfe into an Angel; and to conclude, becommeth the sonne of God.

[*Oration on the Dignity of Man*]

The Sonnets share with Pico the conception of the individual as fluid, self-defining and preoccupied with the inner world in place of externals. The 'I am that I am' that could be condemned as heresy and a rejection of moral values in Richard III has become transformed into the more morally ambiguous and sympathetic quality of truth to self.

Melchiori considers that the echoing of God's 'I AM' in this phrase in Sonnet 121 implies that 'Shakespeare's God is the man within'. But the increasing emphasis on inwardness in the Sonnets is surely not so unequivocally exalted. As the poet becomes more isolated from the external world he can no longer simply condemn such inner enclosure as he might have done if it had been characteristic only of the boy, but in recognising an increasing inwardness in himself his reaction is not changed to unqualified admiration, since he also feels the torment of his imprisonment. As he becomes more completely identified with his inward self and the love that dominates it, so he can no longer clearly distinguish between himself and the boy, no longer withdraw to judge the boy from the world's perspective. It is the external world from which he has withdrawn to the point where the inner world has become his whole world:

As easy might I from my self depart
As from my soul, which in thy breast doth lie . . .
For nothing this wide universe I call
Save thou, my rose; in it thou art my all

[Sonnet 109]

You are my all the world . . .
You are so strongly in my purpose bred
That all the world besides methinks are dead.

[Sonnet 112]

As for Richard II, the world has become for him a totally subjective experience, a mirror-image of the inner self. Each external impression reflects the perceiving self more clearly than its own essence, as the poet confesses:

Since I left you, mine eye is in my mind;
And that which governs me to go about
Doth part his function, and is partly blind,
Seems seeing, but effectually is out;
For it no form delivers to the heart
Of bird, of flow'r, or shape, which it doth latch . . .
For if it see the rud'st or gentlest sight . . .
              it shapes them to your feature.
Incapable of more, replete with you,
My most true mind thus mak'th mine eye untrue.

[Sonnet 113]

Like the boy, though involuntarily, the poet is becoming increasingly bound in to the prison of the inward self.

The mirror, image of the restrictiveness of such disproportionate subjectivity, becomes important to the poet as well as to the vain boy:

My glass shall not persuade me I am old
So long as youth and thou are of one date;

[Sonnet 22]

Sin of self-love possesseth all mine eye,
And all my soul, and all my every part . . .
But when my glass shows me myself indeed,
Beated and chopt with tann'd antiquity,
Mine own self-love quite contrary I read;
Self so self-loving were iniquity.
'Tis thee, my self, that for myself I praise,
Painting my age with beauty of thy days.

[Sonnet 62]

It is clear that there is a difference in the way the boy and the poet look into their glasses. The boy sees only his own image; the poet sees his own image inextricably bound up with that of the boy, to whom his commitment is total. The boy is so much part of him that he thinks of him as a second self, and this conceit dominates the Sonnets so that self-love and love, in the poet at least, become indistinguishable.

This transformation of self-love into love of another, however, is not really an escape from the solipsistic circle framed by the mirror. The notion of the lover as second self may imply that self-love is transformed into outgoing love; or it may imply the opposite, that all love is really a form of self-love. A peculiarly Elizabethan image, the image of 'looking babies', whereby one lover looks in the other's eyes only to see his or her own reflection in them, is a variation on the image of the glass which makes this ironical observation unmistakable. The irony that love, which would seem to be a way of breaking out of the circle of self-absorption, is in fact another way of reinforcing that circle, is heavily underlined in *Venus and Adonis*. Adonis, like the boy of the Sonnets, seems to be the Narcissist, refusing all love and entirely absorbed in his own image, but it is Venus who sees her own image in Adonis's eyes. Venus speaks an elegy over Adonis's dead body, but can describe his beauty only in terms of its capacity to reflect her. His eyes seem to her to be

Two glasses where herself herself beheld
A thousand times, and now no more reflect,
Their virtue lost wherein they late excell'd,
And every beauty robb'd of his effect.

[ll. 1129-32]

The characteristic 'herself herself' pattern seems to confirm the implication of the 'looking babies' image, that Venus's love for Adonis was in fact as self-absorbed as Adonis's more obvious self-love.

The repeated image of the lover as a second self in the Sonnets performs the same function as the 'looking babies' image, suggesting the poet's doubt about the quality of his own love, his fear that it may be in fact as narcissistic as the boy's frank self-love. He tries to qualify the image of the second self in order to maintain the necessary distinctness between himself and his lover which enables their love to be thought of as a reciprocal rather than a solipsistic experience, and which prevents praise from becoming self-congratulation:

O, how thy worth with manners may I sing,
When thou art all the better part of me?
What can mine own praise to mine own self bring?
And what is't but mine own, when I praise thee?
Even for this let us divided live,
And our dear love lose name of single one,
That by this separation I may give
That due to thee which thou deserv'st alone.

[Sonnet 39]

He wants to keep his love set apart as a unique being, distanced from his own sense of unworthiness:

Let me confess that we two must be twain,
Although our undivided loves are one;
So shall those blots that do with me remain,
Without thy help, by me be borne alone.

[Sonnet 36]

Even the contradictoriness of the poet's feelings, however, his uncertainty as to whether he longs for fusion with or separateness from his love, shows him becoming like the boy in another way, by exhibiting a form of self-division. Just as the boy betrays the image he last presented from moment to moment, so the poet finds himself responding to this fickleness in the boy with a comparable instability. He even offers literally to turn against himself and to frustrate his own actions voluntarily (as the boy's self-love involuntarily frustrates his):

When thou shalt be dispos'd to set me light,
And place my merit in the eye of scorn,
Upon thy side against myself I'll fight,
And prove thee virtuous, though thou art forsworn

[Sonnet 88]

For thee, against myself I'll vow debate,
For I must ne'er love him whom thou dost hate.

[Sonnet 89]

Such inward division comes to resemble the boy's even more strongly when the dark lady enters the sequence and the poet is no longer faithful to one love, but divided between two in his affections.

The self-division of the lover is not, of course, an innovation of Shakespeare's, but familiar in Petrarch and the tradition inspired by him. Yet Shakespeare's emphasis seems to imply that the self-division he explores is perhaps in the nature of self-awareness rather than simply induced by love. The sheer repetition of the word 'self' suggests that his Sonnets are more concerned with the nature of the self than with love *per se*. Sonnet 144, for example, shows the poet divided between his two loves, but the division originating in love is used as a mere starting point to explore a more deeply-rooted division within all men, a division given expression in morality plays by the good and evil angels who accompany every man:

Two loves I have, of comfort and despair,
Which like two spirits do suggest me still;
The better angel is a man right fair,
The worser spirit a woman colour'd ill.

Besides its medieval origins, this division of man between his capacities to be either angel or devil is directly reminiscent of the passage from Pico's *Oration on the Dignity of Man* quoted . . . above, which admires the unique fluidity of man's position in the universe. This passage measures the distance between the classical and the Renaissance conceptions of man: whereas Aristotle conceives of man as occupying a fixed place in the universal hierarchy, and becoming inhuman in behaving like a god or a beast, thus taking a strongly moral stance concerning human action, Pico sees the capacity for self-definition, for autonomous self-creation, as the distinguishing feature of man.

The Sonnets too are characteristic of late sixteenth-century England by virtue of their recognition of this autonomy which the self achieves through becoming aware of its own inward nature and the immense transforming power of subjectivity. The closed inwardness and self-contained quality of each sonnet, the refusal of one sonnet to be bound by the self-images offered by other sonnets, the fluidity of the sequence, in which each sonnet seems to embody a truth which holds true only for the moment in which it is stated, are poetic characteristics which imitate these same qualities within the self. The sonnet, like the individual, asserts its own autonomy in this period, by resolving the paradoxes of experience in the terms of its own self-created world. Like Richard II, the speaker in the Sonnets substitutes the private world for the public, or forces the public world into subservience to the private, so that words themselves come to have a paradoxical relationship with the speaker and his world, in that they both communicate the private experience, yet at the same time isolate the speaker within the subjective nature of that experience. The autonomy of the individual is revealed in his transformation of actual experience through words; where the experience itself is unsatisfactory or unresolved, the poet finds a resolution in the linguistic but arbitrary logic of a conceit:

> But here's the joy: my friend and I are one;
> Sweet flattery! then she loves but me alone.
>
> [Sonnet 42]

> Look what is best, that best I wish in thee;
> This wish I have; then ten times happy me!
>
> [Sonnet 37]

> And all in war with Time for love of you,
> As he takes from you, I engraft you new.
>
> [Sonnet 15]

> So shalt thou feed on Death, that feeds on men,
> And, Death once dead, there's no more dying then.
>
> [Sonnet 146]

The Sonnets show the world of the mind dominating the individual vision of the external world and demonstrating its power over the material world by imposing its own pattern on the experiences it does not resolve to the individual's satisfaction. The sonnet is a perfect form, as the mirror is a perfect image, for expressing the withdrawal of the individual into the inescapable and autonomous solitude of the mind. (pp. 77-91)

> *Janette Dillon, " 'Walls of Glass': The Sonnets," in her* Shakespeare and the Solitary Man, *Rowman and Littlefield, 1981, pp. 77-91.*

A. L. ROWSE (essay date 1984)

[*Rowse is an English historian, poet, and critic who has written extensively on Elizabethan history and literature. In the excerpt below, he offers his views on the identity of the Dark Lady addressed in Sonnets 127-52. She is, Rowse contends, Emilia Lanier, a woman at once "promiscuous and notorious . . . a strong personality, mercurial and fascinating." According to the essayist, the Dark Lady sonnets constitute Shakespeare's retrospective thoughts about their affair, which ended when she grew tired of his attentions. Rowse also asserts that the sonnets are heavily autobiographical; insists that "Mr. W. H. was the publisher's dedicatee, not Shakespeare's"; and identifies the Earl of Southampton as the Friend addressed in Sonnets 1-126.*]

[All the problems of Shakespeare's Sonnets] were solved in my original biography, *William Shakespeare* (1964 [see Additional Bibliography]), except one: the identity of his young

mistress, the Dark Lady. I might never have discovered her, if my original findings—the date when the Sonnets were written, the explanation of the publisher's dedication, the identification of Mr W. H., and the rival poet—had not been correct. Discovering the identity of the Dark Lady (when not looking for her) was a bonus for getting all the other answers right, and also for sticking to my last without giving up, in spite of every kind of obtuseness, obfuscation and obstruction.

I must admit that it *is* very difficult for people to get the story of the Sonnets right, the story is so subtle and complex. (p. ix)

At the very outset there is a stumbling block which has been responsible for a great deal of the confusion: Thomas Thorp, the publisher's, dedication [see excerpt above, 1609]. He had got the manuscript of the Sonnets some fifteen years after Shakespeare had ceased writing them, immersed as he was in the work of the Lord Chamberlain's Company—acting, writing, producing, touring—from 1594 when it was founded. Everybody knows that T. T., Thomas Thorp, wrote the dedication, and scholars know that he was given to writing flowery dedications. He dedicated the Sonnets to Mr W. H., the only person who had got the manuscript—so the crucial point to notice is that *Mr W. H. was the publisher's dedicatee,* not Shakespeare's, who had nothing to do with the publication.

My old friend, Agatha Christie—a good Shakespearean—used to say that everybody misses the significance of the obvious. It is obvious to everybody that Mr W. H. was Thorp's man, and yet almost everybody continues to assume that Mr W. H. was Shakespeare's young man to whom he addressed the Sonnets. How obtuse! when the young lord of the Sonnets is the obvious person, the patron, Southampton. (p. x)

[The] majority of literary scholars, from Malone onwards, have known all along that the addressee of the Sonnets was Southampton, but have not known how to explain the confusion created by Thorp with his 'only begetter, Mr W. H.' Others, especially Victorian and Victorian-minded professors, have been embarrassed and fussed by the tone and language of the Sonnets, and wondered whether they were not homosexual.

This was very naif of them, and really quite anachronistic, showing not much knowledge of Renaissance life and manners, the conventions and decorum of Elizabethan society. It was proper for an Elizabethan poet to address his patron or his love in courtly, flowery language. . . . (p. xii)

It was appropriate decorum that an impecunious actor-poet should address a star in the Elizabethan firmament, a figure coming to the fore at Court and in society, in polite, deferential, flowery language. Also the youth was beautiful, as beautiful as a woman—and Renaissance people had no Victorian impediment in recognising the fragile and passing beauty of youth, whether in women or men. Witness the contemporary Court poets in France, celebrating the young Henri III as combining both masculine and feminine attributes.

Nevertheless, the Sonnets are not homosexual, as some people would like to think—and others, no less absurdly, fear. Shakespeare makes it perfectly clear in Sonnet 20 that he is not interested in the youth sexually—if only he were a woman! Everything in his life and work shows that Shakespeare was an enthusiastic heterosexual, very susceptible, even inflammable where women were concerned. He was utterly infatuated with the dark young woman, driven 'frantic-mad' by her, as a strongly sexed heterosexual well might be—and his language throughout the Plays shows him the sexiest of writers. The more one knows of Elizabethan language the more of it is revealed to one.

Shakespeare's love for his beautiful young lord was real, and in the Sonnets one can watch its growth and progress; its complications and set-backs; concern, anxiety, regret over the entanglement of the youth with the promiscuous Dark Lady, for which Shakespeare felt himself responsible. (p. xiii)

The Sonnets begin in a kind of paradisal innocence, the poet clearly inspired by the society—the world, the power and the glory—opening up for him by the relationship, the opportunity for which his nature yearned and to which it ardently responded. The relationship gets closer, becomes involved, has its strains and disillusionments as is the way in life—it is all very real and recognisable beneath the highly charged, emotional language. No doubt the sensitive poet's heart was touched. He had every reason to be grateful for the fortunate turn his life had taken at last, after the long hard struggle and the discouragements of his earlier life—the Sonnets express again and again his resentment at his lot, that fortune had not done better for him in the lottery. Above all, for a writer, was the inspiration he received from the relationship: 'So are you to my thoughts as food to life' [Sonnet 75], even when regret, reproach, grief come in to play their part, as happens in real life—not in the idealised sequences of Drayton and Daniel.

There are ups and downs in the experiences of these crucial, fateful years, decisive in the life of our greatest writer—and the Sonnets are his inner autobiography. Hence, though a few of the pleasant, non-committal—or not too much committed—ones circulated in the group of friends, they were not for publication, as others' were: too near the bone. After something like a breach comes . . . a new theme. At length comes an exhaustion of themes—after more than a century of Sonnets—and an evident cooling-off in the relationship, with the actor fully employed with the new Company and about the country, new associations and demands, frequenting 'unknown minds'.

The patron has some reason to complain; yet Shakespeare insists that there is no 'alteration' in his mind, he constantly recognises Southampton's 'dear-purchased right' in him and his 'great deserts'. Life goes on; the sequence ends appropriately with Shakespeare's assurance that his mind does not change, the affection remains constant. It had never been that of an external honouring the rank and station of a peer, bearing 'the canopy'. His oblation was 'poor but free . . . but mutual render, me for thee' [Sonnet 125]. Thus the intimacy ends, with a magnificent but courteous—'let me be obsequious in thy heart' [Sonnet 125]—assertion of equality, man to man, no breach of tact.

It does not seem that the young Earl and his busy, hard-working poet were together much—perhaps chiefly at intervals over the performance of plays, *Love's Labour's Lost,* which is a private skit on the group, *A Midsummer Night's Dream,* which was shaped up for the Countess's second marriage, to Sir Thomas Heneage on 2 May 1594. Absence was the normal condition for the busy poet, playing, touring, with family demands upon him at home; while a rich young Earl had plenty of other interests and friends to occupy him, in London or in the country. In reading the outpourings of the poet the silence of the patron can be almost heard and felt.

It is not to be supposed that the young man was so deeply upset, as was the altogether deeper nature of William Shakespeare, by the triangular imbroglio over the Dark Lady.

There was a reason for this. Though Emilia Lanier got hold of the young peer, he was much more able to defend himself than Shakespeare was—for he was not all that attracted by women: he was bisexual. Even after his forced marriage some years later (1598)—a marriage he tried to get out of—we find him enjoying the embraces of braggadoccio Captain Piers Edmonds in his tent in Ireland.

Here is a complete reversal of situation for people who do not know what they are dealing with; it adds a further difficulty for ordinary minds in understanding the Sonnets and their subtle psychological situation. It was not William Shakespeare, for all his emotional language, who was homosexual; it was the young lord who was ambivalent, not attracted to women until seduced by the experienced Emilia. (p. xv)

Shakespeare's affair with this remarkable young lady occupies the last section of the Sonnets in numbering, 127 to 152, though not in time. The affair belongs to 1592-3 contemporaneously with the earlier period of the relationship with Southampton, as Sonnets 34 and 35 show. But the Dark Lady sonnets are different in tone: for one thing they are darker and more upheaved. They are Shakespeare communing with himself about the affair, sometimes light-heartedly, in the end tormentedly, rendered 'frantic-mad' by the young woman, who gives him his dismissal.

All the same the poems were sent to the patron, they were his right. . . . We do not have to exclude the possibility that the young lady herself saw some of the more flattering missives, though that would be mere conjecture. Unlikely, out of the question, that she saw the unflattering, defaming ones; for . . . when Thorp got hold of them and published them, she was furious and reacted vehemently—in keeping with her temperament as Shakespeare describes her.

The patron was the recipient, as of all that his poet was writing at the time, 'since all alike my songs and praises be, To one, of one, still such and ever so' [Sonnet 105]—no-one else. But the difference of tone is very noticeable, in keeping with the difference between the two objects of his affection, two very different spirits and affairs, one of the mind and heart, the other sexual, torment of body, mind and heart:

> Two loves I have, of comfort and despair,
> Which like two spirits do suggest me still:
> The better angel is a man right fair,
> The worser spirit a woman coloured ill.
>
> [Sonnet 144]

Whatever stress Shakespeare incurred in his relationship with his patron, his mind and attitude in the matter are well under control; in the affair of this strongly sexed man with the young woman he loses control of himself, he is infatuated, against what he knows to be her bad character and what other people say about her. For, notice, he tells us that she is a quite well known person, indeed notorious; and everything shows that she was a lady of superior social standing to Shakespeare, if an equivocal one. (pp. xix-xx)

It was always commonsense to realise that, since the Dark Lady was so clearly described as Rosaline in *Love's Labour's Lost*—with Southampton as the King, Shakespeare as Berowne, Antonio Perez as Don Armado, and probably Florio as schoolmaster (he was Southampton's Italian tutor), the young lady was known in the Southampton circle. We learn subsequently, quite independently—from the State Papers and Salisbury Mss—that her husband, Alphonso Lanier, became on friendly terms with Southampton. She was even better known to the Lord Chamberlain, Lord Hunsdon, Patron of Shakespeare's Company, for she had been kept in 'pomp and pride'—so Simon Forman tells us—as mistress of the great man. Hunsdon was first cousin of the Queen herself, owning property in Blackfriars, with which Shakespeare was familiar from these very days; for it was here that his two long poems were printed in 1593 and 1594 by his fellow townsman from Stratford, Richard Field.

The musicality of the young lady, an element in the spell she put upon the most musical of dramatists, is corroborated by her background. She was the orphan daughter of Baptista Bassano, one of the Queen's Italian musicians, brought up in the ambience of the Court by Susan, Countess of Kent. When pregnant by the Lord Chamberlain she was discarded and married off, with a proper dowry and jewels, to another of the Queen's musicians, Alphonso Lanier. After such grandeur, however equivocal, she looked down on her husband and demeaned him to Forman as a mere 'minstrel'. He was, as a matter of fact, a decent fellow, friend of Archbishop Bancroft (whose hobby, and consolation, was music); but she was given to demeaning other people—she demeaned William. She had reason to be resentful, with her talents and intelligence—that she was highly intelligent, we later find evidence—and with her luck in life. She was now down on her luck, cast down from on high. The susceptible poet fell for her at this moment, out of compassion and pity, a vulnerable state of mind for older men, confronted with distressful youth and beauty:

> If thy unworthiness raised love in me,
> More worthy I to be beloved of thee.
>
> [Sonnet 150]

Other emotions entered in, above all sexual passion, though at times Shakespeare—always double- or even treble-minded—was capable of viewing his predicament comically: as in the bawdy 'Will' Sonnets 135 and 136—now for the first time fully interpreted—which gave such a headache to all the Victorian commentators. These offer an emotional let-up in the increasing tension of the affair, and must have made Southampton laugh, as others of them may have provided a salutary warning, particularly against veneral infection, so common among Elizabethans—it would seem from the end-sonnets that the poet had a touch of it. (So had Robert Greene and George Peele; so had Hunsdon's son, also Patron of the Company as Lord Chamberlain, Forman's acquaintance over many years.)

If we were to look at the affair from the young lady's point of view, she may well have become bored with the sexual fixation of an older man pestering her—sometimes she would consent, sometimes not, as the factual Forman corroborates was his experience later. A rich, unmarried young peer nearer her own age—in 1592 she was twenty-three, Southampton nineteen—was a much better bet.

Shakespeare in the candid way of his 'open and free' nature—no mystery about him—tells us everything about the lady, character and personality, except her name; and the pinpointing Forman corroborates him in every respect. Promiscuous and notorious; haughty and tyrannical; temperamental and inconstant; a strong personality, mercurial and fascinat-

ing, exerting a powerful spell, as Shakespeare specifically says, and Forman adds that she was psychic—as to which we have her own evidence. Years later, when she published her own long poem—for she proved to be a poet too—she tells us that she dreamed up the title, *Salve Deus Rex Judaeorum*, years before she thought of writing it.

Thorp the publisher got hold of the manuscript of the Sonnets after the old Countess of Southampton's death and the legacy of her household goods and chattels to Sir William Harvey, and published them in 1609. The book was not carefully read in proof, as when Shakespeare corrected his own proofs of *Venus and Adonis* and *Lucrece*. The very next year, 1610, Emilia Lanier announced the publication of her long religious poem—she had undergone a conversion in the intervening years, as such ladies are apt to do with the fading of youth and beauty. (pp. xx-xxiii)

[The] poem, for all its dedications, was not taken up: it fell flat from the press—or something, or somebody, suppressed it. (p. xxiv)

But why should her book have fallen still-born from the press, unremarked, for all the attention she tried so hard to win for it—so that it has remained unknown right up to our own day? Still more, why did not Thorp's, *not* Shakespeare's, publication of the Sonnets not receive a proper second edition until a century afterwards? A few had circulated in manuscript, a few had been printed in *The Passionate Pilgrim*. But Thorp's publication of the Sonnets went more or less underground for a hundred years. It is surely very strange, for Shakespeare was the most popular dramatist of the age, his acknowledged poems going into edition after edition.

It has been suggested that the book was suppressed; and the total silence regarding both it and Emilia's book shortly after, taken in combination, makes this all the more likely. After all both Shakespeare and Southampton were now well known public figures, one the foremost dramatist of the time, the other a leading figure at Court, in politics and public life. Neither of them would want the intimacies of their early relations revealed to the public, any more than Emilia relished the portrait of her which the book gave. That it contained the most remarkable sonnets ever written, the intense autobiography of the world's greatest writer, went for nothing: complete silence.

Here is the real mystery: everything else we now know, firmly and unanswerably: no more pointless conjectures. (pp. xiv-xxv)

A. L. Rowse, in an introduction to Shakespeare's Sonnets, *edited by A. L. Rowse, third edition, Macmillan Press, 1984, pp. ix-xxv.*

JUDITH KEGAN GARDINER (essay date 1985)

[*Gardiner proposes that Shakespeare's sonnets are principally concerned with the inexorability of time and the impossibility of legitimizing male friendship through marriage. These poems reveal, she maintains, Shakespeare's conviction that "a committed and unified love" is the only means of transcending time. Gardiner points out that the poet seeks to assimilate the "anomalous emotions" he experiences in the relationship with his young friend and patron by treating them in terms of the conventions of marriage and the law. Nevertheless, she suggests, Shakespeare's attempts to discover in male friendship "the 'ever-fixed mark' of spiritual 'marriage'" are generally unsuccessful, thus accounting for "the brooding introspection" of these sonnets.*]

Shakespeare's sonnets confront two intractable facts: time will not stop, and men cannot marry one another. Underlying the sonnets and generating many of their paradoxes is the impossible syllogism: if men could only marry one another, time would stop. In his sonnets as in his plays, Shakespeare assumes that romantic love should initiate heterosexual courtship and be consummated in marriage. His own love for an upper-class young man seems to have surprised and unsettled him. He strove to assimilate the anomalous emotions he felt with social conventions about marriage and with literary conventions about sonnets. The impossibility of this task helps account for the brooding introspection of the sonnets and for their frustrated, brilliant obsession with the paradoxes of love and time. This interpretation of Shakespeare's sonnets cuts across the polarized critical categories of lust/love, homosexual/heterosexual, and public/private, and it solves some of the critical problems arising from these polarizations. (p. 328)

At the age of eighteen, Shakespeare married a woman eight years his senior. She was already pregnant with the first of their three children. For most of his adulthood, he lived in London, while his wife and children remained in Stratford. Contemporary anecdotes imply that he was heterosexually active outside of marriage. Thus when he wrote the sonnets—probably in the 1590's—he was already a married man, and any passions he entertained were therefore adulterous ones. The complex emotional texture of the sonnets arises both from the contrast between his ideology of marriage and the difficulties of applying that ideology to an idealized passion between men and from the contrast between that passion and the expected subject matter of a sonnet sequence. (pp. 329-30)

Just by being a sonnet, Shakespeare's first sonnet implies a conventional relationship between a male lover and a female beloved, and the poem's first few lines, with their second-person familiar address, their reference to "fairest creatures," their praise of beautiful eyes, and their injunction to pity, confirm this impression:

> From fairest creatures we desire increase,
> That thereby beauty's rose might never die,
> But as the riper should by time decease
> His tender heir might bear his memory:
> But thou, contracted to thine own bright eyes. . . .

It gradually becomes clear in this sonnet, however, that the poet speaks to a young man, a "tender churl," and the first seventeen sonnets are charged with their special task of trying to persuade a beautiful young man to marry and beget sons.

In this task the seventeen sonnets recall their popular and orthodox humanist source, Erasmus' "An Epistle to perswade a young gentleman to marriage," translated by Thomas Wilson in his *Arte of Rhetoricke* as an example of deliberative oratory. Erasmus addresses his epistle to a young man who is his family's only hope of "stock"; he condemns the youth's stubborn virginity as unnaturally selfish, even suicidal. Shakespeare cites many of Erasmus' arguments in his first seventeen poems. As is perhaps appropriate to urge in the case of an arranged, upper-class marriage where the groom has no choice of selection, he concentrates on justifications for marriage that uphold the patriarchal family lineage: "thou . . . / Unlooked on diest unless thou get a son" (Son-

net 7). Sonnet 13 argues that the young aristocrat must marry and beget boys in order to uphold his father's "house":

> Who lets so fair a house fall to decay,
> Which husbandry in honour might uphold
>
> . . . .
>
> O, none but unthrifts, dear my love you know,
> You had a father, let your son say so.

The apparently solid aristocratic house, like the beautiful aristocratic face, decays; the first seventeen sonnets can answer time only with the injunction to "breed."

The poems' subject at this point clearly is marriage, but the reader may wonder why Shakespeare chose sonnets rather than expository prose to write about it. His stance of man-to-man advice alludes to the Renaissance lore on wife-choosing, and such a stance becomes an older man tactfully scolding a younger one of higher social standing about humanist values. However, many aspects of Shakespeare's rhetoric in the first seventeen sonnets are highly unusual. As the parenthetical "dear my love" of Sonnet 13 hints, the language of the poems continually recalls courtship for oneself rather than vicariously for another, and thus reminds us what we expect from sonnets. Shakespeare's arguments in behalf of marriage are unusual, too, but more for what they omit than for what they say. Of the three conventional Renaissance reasons for marriage—legitimate procreation, sinless sexuality, and marital love—Shakespeare stresses only the first. Erasmus speaks of choosing a good wife; Shakespeare does not. Erasmus claims virginity is bad for the health and that marriage is "as pleasurable as honest" because the husband can confide in his wife as freely as he talks to himself. Married life is both "saufe" and happy. But Shakespeare does not claim marriage will make the young man happy. The woman who will bear his heir exists solely for this function, not as the man's companion or confidante. If the young man does not cooperate with the marriage scheme, he will "beguile the world, unless some mother" (Sonnet 3), that is, cheat the world generally and deprive some particular woman of her only useful function. As reproductive matter, a woman may originate the external beauty that the beloved reflects; he is his "mother's glass" (Sonnet 3). Yet the young man's or his potential wife's emotions are irrelevant. The poet minimizes the private loss that might "wet a widow's eye" (Sonnet 9) and maximizes the beloved's general obligation to procreate: "the world will be thy widow and still weep" if he does not reproduce his form in a child (Sonnet 9).

Although the first seventeen sonnets repeatedly stress the young man's need to "breed," they mention marriage chiefly through imagery, as in the extended musical analogy of Sonnet 8:

> If the true concord of well-tuned sounds,
> By unions married, do offend thine ear,
> They do but sweetly chide thee, who confounds
> In singleness the parts that thou shouldst bear.
> Mark how one string, sweet husband to another,
> Strikes each in each by mutual ordering;
> Resembling sire, and child, and happy
>   mother. . . .

Thus Shakespeare's first seventeen poems superimpose a traditional subject of humanistic man-to-man advice about marriage onto a sonnet form that connotes heterosexual courtship, and they reinforce those connotations by praising the beloved's beauty, railing against his caution and disdain, and urging him to consummation, much as a lover often treats his poetic beloved. Carol Thomas Neely believes that Elizabethan sonnet sequences in general reach an impasse because the Elizabethan exaltation of marriage is hostile to the adulterous attitudes of the Petrarchan sonnet sequence [in her "The Structure of English Renaissance Sonnet Sequences"]. Shakespeare's sequence conquers this impasse at its beginning, with the proper Elizabethan Protestant praise of the married family, of "sire, and child, and happy mother" (Sonnet 8) and with the concomitant simple solution to time through the reproductive cycle. In the poems to the dark lady, the sonnet sequence describes adultery without idealizing it, in fact, while orthodoxly emphasizing its sinfulness. The complex middle sonnets, however, rebuild their impasse on new and astonishing grounds, the aspiration toward a marriage of male minds.

Sonnets 18 through 126 drop the earlier insistence on reproduction of the male bloodline and hence on conquering time through the generational cycle. Instead, they refer to an intense, personal, and ambivalent relationship between the poet and his male beloved for which there is no recognized institutional form. Yet in these sonnets, as in the contemporaneous comedies, marriage provides the ideal model that validates and unifies body and soul, self and other. The vicarious marriage for which the poet sued in the first seventeen poems is inadequate to his own desires. Like many another John Alden, he woos for himself after having been sent to woo for another. His friend is younger than the poet, more beautiful, and of higher social class—all obstacles that marriage could overcome, according to Renaissance marriage doctrine and romantic comedy—but identical to the poet in sex, an insuperable barrier, as *As You Like It* and *Twelfth Night* laughingly demonstrate. (pp. 333-35)

Following the conventions of sonnets and traditional marriage lore, the poet begins by courting his beloved. The lead card of his own suit, Sonnet 18, combines love for the friend's beauty with the poet's traditional answer to time—art's immortality. But very shortly, the contradictions of his peculiar courtship surface. In Sonnet 20, the poet praises his beloved as though he were a lovely woman; courts him, traditionally enough, by telling him he is superior to (other) women; and then admits his maleness:

> A woman's face, with nature's own hand painted,
> Hast thou, the master mistress of my passion
>
> . . . .
>
> And for a woman wert thou first created,
> Till nature as she wrought thee fell a-doting,
> And by addition me of thee defeated,
> By adding one thing to my purpose nothing.
> But since she pricked thee out for women's pleasure,
> Mine be thy love, and thy love's use their treasure.

Because the poet can imagine courtship only as heterosexual, his impulse to court the young man is baffled, and he deduces that the error must be Nature's. His compromise solution is not one that can last. He tries to assure himself that the male beloved will reward him with perfect constancy because the friend is "not acquainted / With shifting change, as is false women's fashion." None of the seventeen poems urging the young man's marriage mentioned that this would produce "women's pleasure." Here he permits a woman the sexual

"use" or interest on his friend's love, so long as he can keep the full undiminished capital on which that use is paid. Thus Shakespeare tries to assimilate sexuality, the purpose of marriage that the male friendship cannot include, into the relationship by using the language of law, property, and natural generation. Such language, repeated throughout Sonnets 18-126, brings the friendship into the orbit of the generative legal, economic, and social institution that was Renaissance marriage.

Although the poet's friendship cannot sinlessly channel his sexuality, he tries to show it can produce children, even if only metaphorical ones. Sometimes, in keeping with the paternal advice of the first seventeen poems, he acts as though the friend were his own child: he rejoices in his beloved "As a decrepit father takes delight / To see his active child do deeds of youth" (Sonnet 37). But more often he refers to a child as the product of their love. Thus in Sonnet 22, the poet denies he can "be elder than thou art" because he carries within himself the beloved's heart, and this pregnancy of love he "will keep so chary / As tender nurse her babe from faring ill."

When the poet thinks of himself as "married" to his friend, then the sonnets become the couple's children, and art's immortality conflates with generational cycle as a bulwark against time. The beloved inspires and the poet begets the poems, which, like children, are named after him: "every word doth almost tell my name, / Showing their birth . . ." (Sonnet 76). When he gives the friend a blank notebook, he urges him, too, to produce "children . . . delivered from thy brain" (Sonnet 77). The most extreme result of the poet's identification between his poetry and a child is Sonnet 72, in which he pleads with the friend to forget him because he is unworthy of his friend's love:

> My name be buried where my body is,
> And live no more to shame nor me nor you.
> For I am shamed by that which I bring forth,
> And so should you, to love things nothing worth.

Here the poet speaks like a seduced and abandoned girl who is ashamed of her bastard child yet proud that it proves she had a gentleman lover. The illegitimate poetry has no name, yet its likeness to its inspiration shows whose it is.

The poet's friendship with his male beloved cannot literally produce children or countenance sexuality. This leaves conjugal devotion as the main function of the marriage he seeks. At times he attempts to foreclose this issue by claiming that his friend and he are already fused into one and the same being: "Tis thee, myself, that for myself I praise" (Sonnet 62). Yet such a merger collapses into unsatisfying isolation, as Shakespeare showed with shallow Adonis. Therefore, in addition to claiming identity with his beloved, the poet repeatedly woos him. Because this courtship can have no consummation, it has no narrative order but must always be renewed.

As the relationship between the two men grows more profound, the poet tries to secure his beloved in a number of ways that recall the language of the Renaissance marriage literature. The friend has "beauty, birth, or wealth, or wit" (Sonnet 37), the qualities that the Renaissance marriage advice literature said a prospective bridegroom should find in his bride. But just as the middle-class courtship books placed companionate love above prudential considerations like family or property, the poet tells his beloved, "Thy love is better than high birth to me, / Richer than wealth, prouder than garments' cost" (Sonnet 91). In courtly love literature, the lover seeks to pluck the rose; his goal is consummation, and achieving that goal provides a closure to his narrative quest. In contrast, the poet's desire in the sonnets has a goal more like that of the English courtship novel, which climaxes at the marriage proposal, than like that of courtly love literature. The poet seeks his beloved's commitment, not consummation: sacred vows provide some of the most intense moments of the sonnet sequence, and they are intimately connected with the poet's attack on time: "No! Time, thou shalt not boast that I do change. . . . This I do vow, and this shall ever be, / I will be true despite thy scythe and thee" (Sonnet 123). When the beloved is "still constant in a wondrous excellence," the poet is so overwhelmed by the miracle that his love approaches "idolatry" (Sonnet 105). But "idolatry," again, undermines that difficult union between self and other for which the poet strives by distancing them from one another. Only a committed and unified love can truly transcend time, being at once always growing and timeless. Sonnet 115, a poem so self-assured of love that it can invalidate poetry's claim to immortality, best expresses this paradox of perpetual growth:

> Those lines that I before have writ do lie,
> Ev'n those that said I could not love you dearer.
>
> . . . .
>
> Love is a babe; then might I not say so,
> To give full growth to that which still doth grow.

"Love is a babe," but resisting time by appealing to natural cycle risks the cycle's restless return to mortality and loss.

Instead, the whole series aims to answer time through the "everfixed mark" of spiritual "marriage." From this perspective, Sonnet 116 conceptually organizes the entire sequence:

> Let me not to the marriage of true minds
> Admit impediments. Love is not love
> Which alters when it alteration finds,
> Or bends with the remover to remove.
> O no, it is an ever-fixed mark
> That looks on tempests and is never shaken;
> It is the star to every wand'ring bark,
> Whose worth's unknown, although his height be
>   taken.
> Love's not time's fool, though rosy lips and cheeks
> Within his bending sickle's compass come.
> Love alters not with his brief hours and weeks,
> But bears it out ev'n to the edge of doom.
> If this be error and upon me proved,
> I never writ, nor no man ever loved.

Stephen Booth calls this poem "the most universally admired" of the sequence, and he glosses it with references to the Elizabethan marriage service [see Additional Bibliography]. In the sequence as a whole, he records eleven other references to the marriage service, especially to *Ephesians* 5, in which man and wife become "one flesh." For example, in Sonnet 109 the poet claims, "As easy might I from myself depart, / As from my soul, which in thy breast doth lie." In Sonnet 25, he swears their reciprocal love is eternal: "Then happy I, that love and am beloved / Where I may not remove, nor be removed," and Sonnet 36 reconciles physical absence with the idea of a permanent union: "Let me confess that we two must be twain, / Although our undivided loves are one." But the finest expression of this union remains Sonnet 116, in which the poet's courtship of his friend culminates in their "marriage." Insofar as such a "marriage of true minds" is impossible, the poet states it only impersonally, abstractly, and

negatively: "let me not"; "love is not love"; "love alters not." (pp. 337-40)

The "marriage of true minds" would freeze time; in it the perfected personhood of both lovers would shine like the stars. Its progeny would be legitimate poems bearing the names of both men, yet such a union would not need poems to be remembered because it would still be there: one needs to remember where the North Star is, but not that it exists. Appropriately, the vehicle for this impossible aspiration is a navigational metaphor. Below the unattainable North Star's "ever-fixed mark," the sonnets' ships go astray in the night: the dark lady is a "bay where all men ride" (Sonnet 137), and the rival poet puffs "the proud full sail of his great verse / Bound for the prize" of the "all too precious" friend (Sonnet 86).

Sonnet 116 states the sequence's central vision, the ideal "mark" at which the poet aims, and we cannot discount its marital metaphor as irrelevant. We may derive from that metaphor a reason for the stasis and confusion of the sequence: the marriage of men cannot take place. The poet's substitutions for legal marriage all lack sanction and stability: even the success of favored patronage or the momentary pleasures of sexuality return the poet to the mutable fortune he tries to flee through commitment to his friend. In the sonnets he tests their real friendship against the model of marriage, and, except in the few remarkable but normative instances like Sonnet 116, finds it wanting.

What does the adultery of minds mean? Although a pledge that is only between minds has no binding force, the poet associates anything that admits change with ideas of bastardy and adultery: "If my dear love were but the child of state, / It might for fortune's bastard be unfathered" (Sonnet 124), he says. When he is himself inconstant, he counterattacks reproof with the question, "For why should others' false adulterate eyes / Give salutation to my sportive blood?" (Sonnet 121). Three relationships in the sonnet evoke the language of adultery. The first is literal and does not involve the fair young man; it is the married poet's affair with the presumably married dark lady. The second, also literally sexual, creates a triangle among the poet, the friend, and the lady. The third and most problematic triangle violates no bodies, only the marriage of the true minds, as the rival poet cuckolds the poet with his friend. Each of these "adulteries" mocks eternal constancy and plunges the poet into mutability and despair, even as the language of adultery validates the model of ideal marriage that it violates. Moreover, by analyzing the poet's reaction to the rival poet, we will see how the paradigm of marriage for the poet's friendship with the young man overlaps its other paradigmatic relationship, that of patronage.

The sonnets frequently represent the psychology of adultery in situations where it does not usually apply. In the literally adulterous situation described by the sonnets to the dark lady (127 through 152), the lady is not the poet's wife, and he describes himself as both betrayed and cuckolder in their affair. In these poems the poet uses the language of adultery but not that of marriage, which is restricted to his union with the fair young man. The poet's differing attitudes toward the two loves underscore the division of the sequence into parts. The language of Sonnet 127, the first poem to the dark lady, echoes and contrasts with the first poem to the young man, Sonnet 1. Sonnet 1 urges the beautiful beloved to beget legitimate heirs. Sonnet 127 also discusses beauty and inheritance, but it stresses "bastard shame" rather than beauty's "tender heir" (Sonnet 1). To complete the structure, the last poem addressed to the dark lady explicitly insists on the adulterous nature of their affair:

> In loving thee thou know'st I am forsworn,
> But thou art twice forsworn to me love swearing,
> In act thy bed-vow broke and new faith torn,
> In vowing new hate after new love bearing.
>
> (Sonnet 152)

Because the poet and his mistress are adulterous, they are forsworn; their words mean nothing; their appearances deceive; and they can produce no heirs, human or poetic, to outlast time, though one might consider the poor anacreontics, Sonnets 153 and 154, as their bastard progeny.

The mistress has "robbed others' beds' revenues of their rents" so that when the poet wheedles, "be it lawful I love thee" (Sonnet 142), he makes sure we know that his love is not lawful. This situation can lead to two extreme solutions: total sensual immersion or total sensual renunciation. These are the choices posed in the two great generalizing sonnets of this part of the sequence, choices that escape time in two, opposing directions. Sonnet 129, "Th'expense of spirit in a waste of shame / Is lust in action," reduces sexual passion to a restless moment that barely exists, the missing blank between anticipation of the future and regret of the past: "Before, a joy proposed, behind, a dream." In contrast, Sonnet 146, "Poor soul, the center of my sinful earth," confronts the ugly mortality of the body's "hours of dross" with a Christian eternity imagined not as a beautiful heaven but only as a self-consuming annihilation: "So shalt thou feed on death, that feeds on men / And death once dead, there's no more dying then." These two sonnets counterpoint the equally abstract Sonnet 116, "the marriage of true minds," in the poems addressed to the young man, although that poem manages to imply the stasis of eternal bliss, not just the end of time.

Although the poet may describe the essence of these ties as a static extreme, his two passions, for the friend and for the dark lady, form their own narrative connection in the triangle in which the poet's mistress becomes the friend's mistress as well. In comparison to undefined transgressions like the friend's dalliance with the rival poet, the triangle between the poet, friend, and lady, as painful as it may be, is also easier to understand: the two men are rivals for a woman's sexual favors. In Sonnet 41, the poet accuses and excuses his beloved for "those pretty wrongs that liberty commits" like a husband who has been betrayed by his wife in his absence. He admits that his friend's susceptibility to heterosexuality is only natural: "And when a woman woos, what woman's son / Will sourly leave her till he have prevailed?" But he continues like a betrayed husband, "Ay me, but yet thou might'st my seat forbear. . . ." In the next linked sonnet, the poet resolves the grief of double betrayal by returning to metaphors associated with the marriage union: "But here's the joy, my friend and I are one: / Sweet flatt'ry, then she loves but me alone."

The situation in Sonnet 144, "Two loves I have of comfort and despair," recalls farces in which a young man attracts an old husband's pretty young wife. The poet suffers a husband's jealousies and doubts, but it is the love of the friend he misses more than that of the lady. He projects all his negative emotions on the wicked woman, the she-"devil" or "female evil." Like a female version of Persephone's ravisher Hades, the dark lady is associated with sexuality, violence, grief, sin, and

death, as she takes the friend from the poet and carries him off to her "hell." In contrast, the poet idealizes the male friend and hopes that he will return to him in the future: "Yet this shall I ne'er know, but live in doubt / Till my bad angel fire my good one out" (Sonnet 144).

In Sonnet 20, the poet bargained with fate that he have his friend's "love" while that love's "use" be paid to women. The triangle between the friend, lady, and poet reactivates this metaphor. "So now I have confess'd that he is thine," the poet writes the lady:

> Thou usurer, that put'st forth all to use,
>
> . . . .
>
> Him have I lost; thou hast both him and me;
> He pays the whole; and yet am I not free.
>
> (Sonnet 134)

Thus the triangle poems about the poet's two loves at first seem to raise traditional, husbandlike complaints against his wife's lover; then they switch their value as we realize the woman is cast as the cuckolder and the young friend as the seduced victim. The tense emotions between the two men are even more pronounced in those poems that treat the all-male triangle of the poet, his friend, and the rival poet.

Recently critics have begun to explore the connections between Elizabethan poetry and patronage. After all, the poet's tie to the fair young man is only metaphorically a marriage; literally it involves a quest for patronage. Perhaps because of modern preoccupations with status and self-esteem, contemporary critics tend to read the sonnets either as Shakespeare's self-reflexive musings or as reflections of his struggles for patronage and power. Louis Adrian Montrose believes that many Renaissance poets disguised their desire for public power in the language of private love [in his " 'Eliza, Queene of Shepheards' and the Pastoral of Power"]. Arthur Marotti applies this view to "Elizabethan Sonnet Sequences and the Social Order." From his perspective, love is in fact "not love," but only a narcissistic striving for advancement: Renaissance love lyrics covertly express their poets' deepest emotions, which are their political frustrations. Thus when Shakespeare claims that thinking about his friend makes his "state / Like to the lark at break of day arising" (Sonnet 29), Marotti discounts the claim as merely a "manic hyperbole," a "disingenous" gesture to compensate for social loss with hollow love talk. According to Marotti [in his " 'Love Is Not Love': Elizabethan Sonnet Sequences and the Social Order"], the frequent Elizabethan demand for "marriage for love" should be read as a "metaphor for advancement by merit." The poet may wield his art to revenge himself against his fickle friend, but his real goal, patronage, goes to the rival poet, who creates the "most serious crisis of the collection."

Certainly it is good to be reminded of the pressured political contexts in which Renaissance sonneteers wrote, but in Shakespeare's sonnets I think "marriage for love" is a metaphor for ranges of unrealizable passion between men as well as for professional advancement. Sonnets 25 and 26 rest on the analogy that the poet's love for the young man is like the tie that binds a courtier to his feudal lord, an analogy also privileged in the courtly love literature and capable of use by either sex. In Sonnet 26, the poet addresses the young man as "Lord of my love" to whom he must show his "duty." But as Sonnet 25 distinguishes, his bond is a secret, private one like courtly love, not the open "public honour" enjoyed by "great princes' favorites." The resolution of this poem speaks the reciprocal language of committed love, the confidence of marriage, not the insecurity of slippery favoritism: "Then happy I that love and am beloved / Where I may not remove, nor be removed."

When the poet must admit that he has no legitimate claim on his beloved, he temporizes, "Let me confess that we two must be twain / Although our undivided loves are one" (Sonnet 36). Then he returns to the language of marriage and adultery to explain his dilemma. Here he assumes the role of an adulterous wife or mistress. Although such a woman is subservient to her husband, her actions have power to destroy the man's honor:

> I may not evermore acknowledge thee,
> Lest my bewailed guilt should do thee shame,
> Nor thou with public kindness honor me,
> Unless thou take that honour from thy name.
>
> (Sonnet 36)

In Sonnet 36, the poet describes himself as an unfaithful spouse, but one whose claims on the beloved are intact. The rival poet threatens the solidity of these mutual obligations. Lacking the authority of legitimate marriage, the poet can make no claims on the beloved that his rival cannot make equally well. In Sonnet 80, the poet wallows in self-pitying language that describes his rival as superior to him in masculine power:

> O, how I faint when I of you do write,
> Knowing a better spirit doth use your name,
>
> . . . .
>
> My saucy bark inferior far to his
> On your broad main doth wilfully appear.
> Your shallowest help will hold me up afloat
> Whilst he upon your soundless deep doth ride;
> Or, being wracked, I am a worthless boat,
> He of tall building and of goodly pride.

The pain of this situation brings the marital metaphor to the surface, and the poet's denial indicates what he had implicitly expected from his beloved: "I grant thou wert not married to my muse" (Sonnet 82). Since the Muse is traditionally female, the poet employs this fiction to revert to a courtship stance like the one he dramatizes in some comedies—that of the outclassed young virgin who quietly adores a man of superior status, like Viola in *Twelfth Night* or Helena in *All's Well That Ends Well*: "My tongue-tied muse in manners holds her still" (Sonnet 85) while hearing the beloved praised by rivals. The poet assimilates the tensions of patronage with those of the "marriage of true minds" so that their union must suffer if another poet begets poems out of wedlock, so to speak, upon his friend. In Sonnet 86, the poet returns to imagery of sexual procreation:

> Was it the proud full sail of his great verse
> Bound for the prize of all too precious you,
> That did my ripe thoughts in my brain inhearse,
> Making their tomb the womb wherein they grew?

If the friend inspires the rival rather than the poet, the rival grows pregnant, the poet falls sterile. He has no control over the friend's favors, no legitimate way of calling him to account, though he tries to assert his claims for a permanent union:

> But do thy worst to steal thyself away,

> For term of life thou art assured mine,
>
> . . . .
>
> O what a happy title do I find.
>
> (Sonnet 92)

Because the "happy title" of lover is not the socially acknowledged one of husband or wife, the poet can only express the urgency of his need for fidelity by threatening to die if his friend ceases to love him: "Thou canst not vex me with inconstant mind, / Since that my life on thy revolt doth lie" (Sonnet 92). It is as though he can make their bonds last "till death do us part" by insisting he will die rather than "divorce" his friend. Even when striking this histrionic pose, however, the poet remains worried, like the jealous husbands of Shakespeare's plays, because infidelity is invisible even though it is powerful enough to destroy a loving union: "But what's so blessed-fair that fears no blot? / Thou mayst be false, and yet I know it not" (Sonnet 92).

This anxiety about faithlessness erupts, again, in an overt conjugal simile in the lines immediately following that anxious couplet: "So shall I live, supposing thou art true, / Like a deceived husband . . ." (Sonnet 93). Because the beloved's fair appearance gives no clue to his fidelity, the frustrated poet retreats to associative misogyny: "How like Eve's apple doth thy beauty grow, / If thy sweet virtue answer not thy show." Sonnet 20 indicates that the poet connects "shifting change" with "false women's fashion." If the friend breaks his ideal male constancy, then the poet sees him as like a woman and associates him with feminine wile, deceit, and evil, and hence with subjection to mortal time and change. Only the "marriage of true minds," male minds, can escape that subjection, and such a marriage is doubly impossible— first, because no men can marry one another, and, second, because his beloved does not have a "true" enough mind—that is, one that is both constant and male enough.

Shakespeare's sonnets revolve around the colliding conventions of marriage and of patronage. As the first seventeen poems remind us, Renaissance marriage was a legal, economic, sexual, and political tie between families. Both marriage and patronage were public institutions in a hierarchical and patriarchal society, but it oversimplifies Renaissance poetry to believe that it collapses its private passions into its public politics or vice versa. It is more likely that our divisions of public and private misrepresent the emotions involved in making one's way in the world as a Renaissance man. My guess is that Elizabethans eroticized class nearly as much as gender and that for them age categories, too, were sexually charged. I believe that Renaissance sonnet readers might expect a lower-class young man to solicit the patronage of an upper-class older woman; they might also expect to enjoy the vicarious transports of sublimated heterosexual courtship. But in Shakespeare's sonnets, a lower-class older man solicits the patronage of an upper-class man enough younger and prettier than he to be the simultaneous object of his protective advice and of his projective identification. Shakespeare's sublimated courtship in the sonnets is homoerotic, whereas his adulterous heterosexual courtship is consummated. The sequence does not drop its opening insistence on the social necessity and natural rightness of marriage. Instead, it translates marriage into an ideal literary coupling, the only union that can withstand mortal time and change. When flattery seduces the patron, the friend's betrayal of their "marriage of true minds" moves the poet far more than the dark lady's adultery. Men cannot marry one another; therefore, time won't stop. (pp. 341-47)

Judith Kegan Gardiner, "The Marriage of Male Minds in Shakespeare's Sonnets," in The Journal of English and Germanic Philology, *Vol. LXXXIV, No. 3, July, 1985, pp. 328-47.*

THOMAS M. GREENE (essay date 1985)

[*Greene argues that Sonnets 1-126 provide evidence of vain efforts to give substance to the axiom of Sonnet 1, "From fairest creatures we desire increase." In Sonnets 1-17, which the critic terms the "procreation sonnets," the Friend's refusal to marry and have children gives rise to a "terrible fear of cosmic destitution." This and other threats to the Friend's worth, Greene continues, suggest that the young man's value "may reside after all in the poet's fancy," and that "the substance of abundance may actually derive from the shadow of projection." Thus, the poetry becomes "an artifact that successfully resists time and death." The Rival Poet group (Numbers 78-80, 82-6), Greene maintains, makes clear the relationship between poetic potency and sexual potency, a relationship further explored in Sonnet 125. In this poem it becomes evident that "to compose poetry is expensive, just as loving is expensive, and . . . that expense is never truly recuperated. The increase we desire from fairest creatures never materializes."*]

Sonnet 125 of Shakespeare's collection ("Wer't ought to me I bore the canopy") is the penultimate poem in the series addressed to the male friend. It is the last complete sonnet in this series, and in comparison with its somewhat slighter successor, 126, it appears to offer a more substantial, dense, and conclusive instrument of retrospection. It opens by distinguishing the poet from those who court his friend's love by means of external gestures, "dwellers on forme and favor," but who see their calculations fail and are condemned to admire the young man from a distance: "Pittifull thrivors in their gazing spent." The poet's own devotion, he claims, consists purely of uncalculated internal gestures and it leads to a genuine, unmediated exchange.

> Noe, let me be obsequious in thy heart,
> And take thou my oblacion, poore but free,
> Which is not mixt with seconds, knows no art,
> But mutuall render onely me for thee.

The couplet dismisses a "subborned *Informer,*" a slanderer who might accuse the poet himself of dwelling on form. But despite this calumny, the affirmation of the "mutuall render" between the two men acquires in the context of the whole collection a peculiar resonance. It can be regarded as a culminating moment in the twisting history of their relationship, and our understanding of the outcome of the "plot" in Sonnets 1-126 depends in part on our interpretation of this phrase. Contrariwise, fully to grasp the implications of the phrase and the sonnet requires consideration of all that precedes, and even to some degree what follows. An informed reading will necessitate a long swing backward before returning to 125.

Within its immediate context, this is the third of three successive sonnets affirming that the poet's love for his friend is untouched by external accidents. This succession (123-5) needs to be read in the light of an earlier group (109-12) alluding to the poet's shameful and scandalous conduct and another group (117-21) alluding to the poet's apparent neglect and betrayal of the friend. Thus, if one attributes validity to the Quarto sequence, the three protests of uncalculating devotion

follow almost directly an experience of partial rupture, and they attempt to cement a reconciliation which has been to some degree in doubt.

But from a wider perspective, Sonnet 125 is responding to problems raised from the very opening of the collection. Its resolution of pure exchange could be said to respond to the anxiety of cosmic and existential economics which haunts the Sonnets and which marks their opening line: "From fairest creatures we desire increase." The paronomasia which links the two nouns translates phonetically the poet's obsessive concern with metaphorical wealth, profit, worth, value, expense, "store," "content." The "pittifull thrivors" of 125 take their place in a line of disappointed or misguided would-be thrivers distributed throughout the work. The "mutuall render," if in fact it is successful, would thus bring to a happy conclusion a quest for an adequate economic system which would avoid the "wast or ruining" and the excessive "rent" which burden those in 125 who vainly spend themselves. Up to the climactic reciprocity at the close of that sonnet, the sequence to the young man has provided very little by way of stable exchange systems.

The first of the pitiful thrivers is the onanistic friend as he appears in the opening 17 "procreation" sonnets. By refusing to marry and to beget children, he "makst wast in niggarding" (1); he becomes a "profitles userer" "having traffike with [him] selfe alone" (4). The procreation sonnets display with particular brilliance Shakespeare's ability to manipulate words which in his language belonged both to the economic and the sexual/biological semantic fields: among others, "increase," "use," "spend," "free," "live," "dear," "house," "usury," "endowed," along with their cognates. The umbrella-pun which covers them all, and which establishes a semantic node for the whole collection, lies in still another word: "husbandry":

> For where is she so faire whose un-eard wombe
> Disdaines the tillage of thy husbandry? (3)

The *ad hoc* meaning "marriage" joins the traditional meanings of "thrift," "estate management," "agriculture," and, by means of a conventional metaphor, coition as ploughing. When the pun returns ten sonnets later, the dominant meaning will emerge as management:

> Who lets so faire a house fall to decay,
> Which husbandry in honour might uphold,
> Against the stormy gusts of winters day
> And barren rage of deaths eternall cold? (13)

"House" means both the friend's body (the *banhus,* "bonehouse," of the Anglo-Saxon kenning) and the family line. The bourgeois poet accuses the aristocratic friend of a dereliction of those responsibilities incumbent on the land-owning class. The apparent implication is that through marriage the friend could "live" (4), could make a profit by perpetuating his family.

But if, in the procreation sonnets, thriving seems ostensibly within the young man's grasp, one must recognize nonetheless the disproportionate force of the thwarting power, the "barren rage of deaths eternall cold." Procreation progressively comes to appear as a desperate defense, a final maneuver against a principle which is ultimately irresistible.

> And nothing gainst Times sieth [scythe] can make defence
> Save breed to brave him, when he takes thee hence. (12)

The recurrent terror of "winters wragged hand" (6), particularly notable in this opening group, comes to cast doubt on the viability of marriage. Or rather, in view of the threatening "barenes everywhere" (5), husbandry emerges as a universal, existential concern that transcends the addressee's marital status. It even becomes a concern of the poetry we are reading, which alternately promises to "ingraft" the friend anew in the war with Time (15) only to describe itself as "barren" in the sequel (16). The friend, "making a famine where aboundance lies" (1), may after all be closer to the governing principle of the world, in which case the poet and his poetry are left in a confusing limbo.

Thus a terrible fear of cosmic destitution overshadows the husbandry of the procreation sonnets, a fear in excess of the announced argument, not easily circumscribed, rendering the bourgeois desire for "store" more urgent, eccentric, and obsessive. In the main body of the sonnets to the young man (18-126), this fear continues to find frequent expression but it is also localized much more explicitly in the poet's feelings about himself. The poetry reflects a sense of inner depletion, emptiness, poverty, which the friend is asked or stated to fill up; elsewhere it reflects a nakedness which the friend is asked to clothe. Sometimes the language evoking the friend's role might suggest literal patronage; elsewhere it might suggest a literal filling up through sex; but each of these literalizations taken alone would reduce the quality of the expressed need. The sense of depletion is more radical and more diffuse, and it is inseparable from feelings of worthlessness and deprivation. Sonnet 29 ("When in disgrace with Fortune . . .") represents the speaker

> Wishing me like to one more rich in hope,
> Featur'd like him, like him with friends possest,
> Desiring this mans art, and that mans skope,
> With what I most inioy contented least. . . .

The language faintly underscores the economic character of this despondency. Friends, if they existed, would be possessed. "Rich in hope" means both "endowed with hope" and "rich in prospect." "Inioy" here means "possess" as well as "take pleasure in" [according to Stephen Booth], thus justifying a secondary reading of "contented least": "poorest in whatever I own of worth." This privation is only relieved by thoughts of the friend: "thy sweet love remembered . . . welth brings," and this transfer is dramatized by the imagistic wealth of the lark simile interrupting the rhetorical bareness of the octave. In the following sonnet, 30 ("When to the Sessions . . ."), the poet laments the deaths of precious friends, moans the expense of many a vanished sight, pays anew "the sad account of fore-bemoned mone," until with remembrance of his friend "all losses are restord, and sorrowes end." In 26 ("Lord of my love . . ."), the poet sends his naked poetry as an offering to his liege lord, hoping that the friend will dress the drab language in "some good conceipt of thine," will "[put] apparell on my tottered loving." Dressing the tottered (tattered) loving might mean making the poet more eloquent or more rich or more accomplished as a lover, but the nakedness seems finally to transcend rhetoric or money or seductiveness. In 38 ("How can my Muse . . ."), the friend is once again filling a void:

> How can my Muse want subiect to invent
> While thou dost breath that poor'st into my verse
> Thine own sweet argument?

The friend plays the masculine role, pouring his worth into the otherwise barren verse, leaving the poet with the travail of giving birth but rightly taking credit for any success: "The paine be mine, but thine shal be the praise" [Sonnet 38]. In this economic system, all value seems to reside in the friend, or in *thoughts* of the friend, and the poet seems to be a leaky vessel constantly in need of replenishing, his personal and linguistic poverty never definitively abolished.

This system, however, rests on a shaky basis. The worth of the friend may reside after all in the poet's own fancy, as at least one passage may be understood to suggest:

> So then I am not lame, poore, nor dispis'd,
> Whilst that this shadow doth such substance give,
> That I in thy abundance am suffic'd. (37)

The substance of abundance may actually derive from the shadow of projection. This doubt becomes more plausible as fears of betrayal mount

> Thou best of deerest, and mine onely care,
> Art left the prey of every vulgar theefe. (48)

and as the fears are realized in the young man's affair with the poet's mistress (40-2): "Both finde each other, and I loose both twaine" (42). In other sonnets apparently free of jealousy, a threat to the friend's worth looms from the cosmic mutability already evoked in the procreation sonnets, and now an alternative economic system situates the source of value in the poetry of the Sonnets. The poetry, elsewhere naked, becomes in these poems an artifact that successfully resists time and death, assures eternal life to the one it celebrates, distills his truth for the ages, acts as a perpetuating force against "mortall rage" (64). In the sonnets which affirm this source of value, the young man is represented as a potential victim, helpless against the cosmic principle of destruction, passive, disarmed, doomed without the saving power of "my verse." Verse preserves, engrafts, refurbishes; it seems informed with a masculine force the friend lacks. He remains in this system the beneficiary of a gift his worth draws to itself, but this worth is not otherwise active. "Where alack, shall times best Iewell from times chest lie hid?" (65). The young man's excellence is a plunderable commodity, as it is elsewhere perishable; inert as a precious stone, it belongs to the world of basic elements in flux, "increasing store with losse, and losse with store" (64). The alleged source of genuine "store" in this class of sonnets is the poetry.

Yet it is noteworthy that the affirmations of this linguistic power tend to appear in the couplets of these sonnets (15, 18, 19, 54, 60, 63, 65; exceptions are 55 and 81). The couplets, moreover, tend to lack the energy of the negative vision in the 12 lines that precede them. The final affirmation in its flaccidity tends to refute itself; the *turn* fails to reverse the rhetorical momentum adequately, as the language loses its wealth and its potency while asserting them.

> His beautie shall in these blacke lines be seene,
> And they shall live, and he in them still greene. (63)

> O none, unlesse this miracle have might,
> That in black inck my love may still shine bright.
> (65)

The turn toward restoration can be read as a desperate bourgeois maneuver, struggling to shore up the cosmic economy against the mutability which instigates true verbal power. The poetry arguably fails to celebrate, refurbish the worth of the young man. The worth remains abstract, faceless, blurred, even when it is not tainted.

Thus we are left with two distinct sources of alleged value, the friend and the poetry, each the basis for a rudimentary economic system, each vulnerable to skepticism. The presence of each system tends to destabilize the other by casting doubt on the kind of value it attempts to establish. To cite the poetic convention behind each system does not adequately deal with its constituent presence in this work. At stake in this conflict of systems is the status and force of the poetic word, which alternately shares its maker's hollowness and serves his (narcissistic?) fantasies of power. The one system, the one relationship which is *not* to be found before the last sonnets to the friend is equal, direct, unmediated reciprocity. Reciprocity is unattainable partly because of the poet's social inferiority and, so to speak, his felt "human" inferiority, because the friend frequently appears in thought, fantasy, or memory rather than in the flesh, because the adulatory style intermittently gives way to suspicion, resentment, fear, anger (33-5, 40-2, 57-8, 67, 69, etc.) which militate negatively against equality, because the friend as an individual remains a "shadow," undescribed, voiceless, hazy, dehumanized by the very superlatives he attracts, and because the poetry, however unclear its status, is repeatedly presented as the binding agent of mediation, an essential go-between. It is not clear whether *any* of the sonnets is to be read as a spoken address, a dramatic monologue, rather than as a written communication. Many of them refer to themselves as written, refer to paper, ink, pens, and to poetic style. They may occasionally affirm a closeness between poet and friend, but their very existence suggests a distance which has to be crossed. We are never allowed to envision unambiguously the poet in the presence of his friend, as we are in love poems by Wyatt, Sidney, Spenser, and Donne.

The conflicting representations of the poetry's power (potent or weak?), its gender (male or female?), its durability (perennial or transient?) together with its mediating function between the two men raise questions about what might be called its rhetorical economics. The poetry is distinguished by its supercharged figurative density, its inexhaustible ramifications of suggestion, its insidious metaphoric multiplications, a superfetation which might have been accumulated to avoid at all cost the alleged danger of nakedness. The poetry could be working to refute its own self-accusations of dearth and repetition.

> Why is my verse so barren of new pride?
> So far from variation or quicke change? . . .
> So all my best is dressing old words new,
> Spending againe what is already spent. (76)

As though to adorn the monotony, every rift is loaded with ore, to the degree that the rhetorical density can be read as an extraordinary effort to exorcize that stylistic poverty the poetry imputes to itself. The poet may feel himself to be depleted, but he evidently owns enough wit to spend it extravagantly. Yet this very supercharging of language tends to heighten a certain impression of linguistic slippage. Metaphors are mixed, replaced by others, recalled, jostled, interfused, inverted, disguised, dangled, eroded, in ways which blur meanings as they are enriched.

> Nativity once in the maine of light,
> Crawles to maturity, wherewith being crown'd,
> Crooked eclipses gainst his glory fight,
> And time that gave, doth now his gift confound.
>
> (60)

Illustration to Sonnet 2, "When forty winters shall besiege thy brow." From a copper engraving by Peter Lipman-Wulf.

The enriching of metaphor, a putative demonstration of the poet's real potency, is indistinguishable from a mutability of metaphor, a fragmentation which might be said to demonstrate instability. By this reading the process of verbal enrichment would coincide with a process of deterioration; indeed the enrichment might be perceived as leading to the slippage, "increasing store with losse, and losse with store." The poetry would then come to resemble a pail of the Danaids, and the questions regarding the poet's potency would remain open.

That poetic potency is related here to sexual potency is made clear beyond cavil by the rival poet group (78-80, 82-6). The other poet is a rival both for patronage and for sexual favors, and his rhetorical brilliance (or bombast) is associated with his glittering seductiveness. Thus the poetic speaker is doubly threatened by "the proud full saile of his great verse, bound for the prize of (al to precious) you" (86). The revealing word here is *proud,* which meant "lecherous" as well as "stately" and "ostentatious." Cognate forms have already appeared in 80, which constitutes a tissue of sexual double meanings and interweaves poetic competition inextricably with erotic:

> O how I faint when I of you do write,
> Knowing a better spirit doth use your name,
> And in the praise thereof spends all his might,
> To make me toung-tide speaking of your fame.
> But since your worth (wide as the Ocean is)
> The humble as the proudest saile doth beare,

My sawsie barke (inferior farre to his)
On your broad maine both wilfully appeare.
Your shallowest helpe will hold me up a floate,
Whilst he upon your soundlesse deepe doth ride,
Or (being wrackt) I am a worthlesse bote,
He of tall building, and of goodly pride.
        Then if he thrive and I be cast away,
        The worst was this, my love was my decay.

So many words have sexual meanings ("use," "spends," "proudest," "saucy," "wilfully," "ride," "pride"—by attraction, "tall building") that the reader is tempted to interpret the sonnet primarily in erotic terms. But it opens with a contrast of the rivals as writers before shifting in ll. 11-12 to a presumptive contrast of physical endowments. It is true that the analogy of the possibly promiscuous love object with the ocean will return more crudely and unambiguously in the dark lady group (134). But if language is presented in 80 as a means to seduction, seduction on the other hand may consist simply of verbal overpowering. "Love" and poetic language are linked so closely that the primary meaning of the final clause would seem to be "my inadequate verse has led to my rejection." The contrast of the rivals underscores what the speaker will shortly call his *penury,* a word which brings together his financial, poetic, and sexual shortcomings but which leaves uncertain what is figure and what ground. At any rate the rival, however we regard his challenge, introduces a complicating factor in the economics of the Sonnets, by appearing to "thrive" (80, l. 13) while the speaker is ruined. In spending more, verbally, sartorially, and sexually, he may get more. Yet in the end he and his new patron will be revealed as devalued, the one by the vulgarity of his praise and the other by the vulgarity of the pleasure he takes in it. They are pitiful thrivers both. So at least the poet suggests, and he follows the rival poet group with a temporary kiss-off, not without sarcasm:

> Farewell thou art too deare for my possessing,
> And like enough thou knowst thy estimate. (87)

Farewell also to the theme of poetry's immortalizing power: with two brief exceptions (100, 107), it will disappear from the collection.

The rival poet group is of interest because it confirms the implicit linkage between monetary, verbal, and sexual "pride," and because it complicates the linkage between these forms of power and deeper, vaguer intrinsic "worth." The group is equally of interest because it throws up, almost incidentally, a revealing formulation of the Sonnets' essential vulnerability, a formulation which will prove useful when we return to our starting point in Sonnet 125:

> Who is it that sayes most, which can say more,
> Then this rich praise, that you alone, are you,
> In whose confine immured is the store,
> Which should example where your equall grew,
> Leane penurie within that Pen doth dwell,
> That to his subiect lends not some small glory,
> But he that writes of you, if he can tell,
> That you are you, so dignifies his story.
> Let him but coppy what in you is writ. (84)

The pen is penurious which cannot add to its subject, but a praiser of the friend is subject to this penury, since in him "are locked up all the qualities needed to provide an equal example." The friend's alleged excellence is such that no metaphors are available, no imagistic equivalent is possible, and the authentic praiser will limit himself to pure representation

("Let him but coppy"). Only by representing accurately, achieving a perfect counterpart of the young man, will the poet overcome penury, "making his stile admired every where." But this last solution, in its context, proves to be unsatisfactory on several grounds. First it fails to escape epideictic drabness, by the poet's own showing. It leaves the poetry "barren of new pride," spending again the respent, "keep[ing] invention in a noted weed" (76). Second, he who is to be copied proves to be less of a Platonic idea than a changeable and fallible human; for that revelation we need go no further than the couplet of this sonnet (84), with its malicious glance at the rival's demeaning flattery.

> You to your beautious blessings adde a curse,
> Being fond on praise, which makes your praises
>   worse.

A certain pathology of praise can infect both parties. But the third and most momentous reason why the copy solution fails is that pure representation in language is not of this world. Poetry depends on figuration, but precise figural adequation is unattainable. What is said with ostensible hyperbole in the opening quatrain—that no "example" can serve as "equall" to the young man—is universally true. To attempt not to add to one's subject may court penury, as Sonnet 84 argues, but the real failure lies in the necessity of accepting addition, of employing "compounds strange" (76), as the Sonnets most decidedly do and as all poetry does. Poetry as representation will always be vulnerable, because in its shifting mass of meanings it can never copy with absolute precision and because that which is copied changes, gains, and loses value. The economics of copying reserves its own pitfalls for aspirant thrivers; the pen is bound to be penurious.

Sonnet 105 betrays a similar vulnerability:

> Let not my love be cal'd Idolatrie,
> Nor my beloved as an Idoll show,
> Since all alike my songs and praises be
> To one, of one, still such, and ever so.
> Kinde is my love to day, to morrow kinde,
> Still constant in a wondrous excellence,
> Therefore my verse to constancie confin'de,
> One thing expressing, leaves out difference.
> Faire, kinde, and true, is all my argument,
> Faire, kinde, and true, varrying to other words,
> And in this change is my invention spent,
> Three theams in one, which wondrous scope affords.
>   Faire, kinde, and true, have often liv'd alone.
>   Which three till now, never kept seate in one.

This appears to be another apology for an allegedly plain style. (I follow Ingram and Redpath in interpreting "since" in l. 3 as introducing the reason for the accusation, not its defense; the latter begins in l. 5.) Although the poet claims to hew singlemindedly to a unique theme with the same constant language, he cannot, he says, be accused of idolatry because the friend, in his inalterable generosity, deserves no less. The poetry "leaves out difference," spending its invention by varying three words in others. One might argue that *some* difference is already present in this variation. But there are differences in the word "difference" itself, as one learns from a glance at Booth's paragraph on the word; among its relevant meanings are "variety," "anything else," "disagreement," "hostility." *Constant* means both "invariable" and "faithful"; *kinde* means both "generous" and "true to his own nature"; *spent,* that ubiquitous word, means both "used" and "exhausted." The Sonnets escape the charge of idolatry, not because the man they celebrate remains correspondingly unchanging (he is nothing if not inconstant, in both senses), but because they fail to express one thing and systematically admit difference. They alternately valorize and deplore a plain stylistic constancy which they cannot achieve.

The problem of "difference," like the related problem of accurate representation, is pertinent to the affirmation of mutuality which concludes the long section of sonnets to the young man. Before we reach that affirmation, we hear of derelictions on both sides, derelictions grave enough to undermine the fragile economic systems in force earlier. The falsity of the friend, a mansion of vices (95), produces a policy of husbandry the precise reverse of that recommended in the procreation sonnets; now it is those who remain aloof from others like a stone who "husband natures ritches from expence" (94). The poet for his part has made himself a motley to the view, "sold cheap what is most deare" (110), blemished himself and his love. We have already noted the waning of poetry's asserted power as an immortalizing agent. As the Sonnets spiral downward in a vortex of betrayal, counter-betrayal, and justifications not untouched with sophistry, we look for an economic alternative to mere self-deception, that "alcumie . . . creating every bad a perfect best" (114). Something like this alternative can be glimpsed briefly in 120, where the mutuality of suffering and dishonor might produce mutual guilt in compassion and lead to an exchange of quasi-Christian redemption:

> But that your trespasse now becomes a fee,
> Mine ransoms yours, and yours must ransome mee.

This glimpse of reciprocity in shared weakness fades, however, and leads to the group of three (123-5) with which we began, a group essentially protesting the poet's freedom from self-interest and the enduring purity of his feelings, which will never flag and can dispense with ostentatious demonstrations. The last of this group culminates in the proffered "mutuall render" between poet and friend, before the very last poem to the friend, 126, returns to the theme of time and anticipates nature's final, mortal settling of accounts: "her *Quietus* is to render thee."

A skeptical reading of these concluding gambits would represent them as repressing artificially the pain and guilt which have already surfaced, and which will surface even more harshly in the dark lady group to follow. In their context these protests of fidelity, which "nor growes with heat, nor drownes with showres" (124), could be regarded as attempts to mask the real bankruptcy of the relationship. The negative stress of 123-5, lingering over that change (123), "policy" (124), form (125) the poet abjures, might well be read as symptomatic of a bad conscience whose spokesman would be the (internal) accusatory informer of 125. This repressive character of the final sonnets could plausibly be linked to their return to a relatively aureate style after the burst of directness earlier (as in 120—"y'have past a hell of Time"). This *suspicion* of the excessive protest does hang over the concluding group, deepened by their conspicuous discontinuity with their context. Yet a purely cynical reading would strain out that element of real wishing which is also present. The reader can recognize the implausibility of the asserted constancy while regarding the struggle to hope, the conative pathos, with respect.

The crucial sonnet in this group is 125, since it seems to offer at last the possibility of a stable existential economics, a defin-

itive end to penury, a compensation for the expense of living and feeling, even though it does this like its predecessors in large part by exclusion:

> Wer't ought to me I bore the canopy,
> With my extern the outward honoring,
> Or layd great bases for eternity,
> Which proves more short then wast or ruining?
> Have I not seene dwellers on forme and favor
> Lose all, and more by paying too much rent
> For compound sweet; Forgoing simple savor,
> Pittifull thrivors in their gazing spent.
> Noe, let me be obsequious in thy heart,
> And take thou my oblacion, poore but free,
> Which is not mixt with seconds, knows no art,
> But mutuall render onely me for thee.
>   Hence, thou subbornd *Informer*, a trew soule
>   When most impeach, stands least in thy controule.

Lines 1-12 are ostensibly responding to the calumny of the unidentified informer of l. 13, a calumny whose content we can determine only through its refutation. This consists in a repudiation of what might be called affective formalism, external gestures of dutifulness like the carrying of a canopy of state over a monarch's head. Suitors who employ such external gestures may believe that they prepare in this way for an everlasting intimacy with him whose favor they court, but the intimacy "paradoxically turns out to be briefer than the time required to run through an estate by extravagance"[according to Ingram and Redpath]. We have still another example of failed husbandry, combining formalism with the kind of decadent sophistication which would prefer cloying elaborate sauces ("compound sweet") to the familiar taste of homely fare. *Forme* (l. 5) brings together the young man's physical figure, the ceremonial of line I, exaggerated courtesy, hollow gestures of servility, and the craft which produces "compound sweet," artificial confections of any sort, but which is allegedly absent from the poet's oblation. "Compound sweet" recalls the poetic "compounds strange" of 76, which the poet there reproached himself for omitting from his own verse. This suggests that dwellers on form are also ambitious poets whose style is overwrought. The image of the projected manor house (l. 3) is faintly sustained by "ruining" (l. 4), "dwellers" (l. 5), "rent" (l. 6), and the possible allusion to compound and simple interest (l. 7). This version of negative formalism ends with the loaded word "spent" (l. 8), in which so much meaning has sedimented throughout the work; here it means "bankrupted," "exhausted," "failed," ironically "summed up" in reliance on visual externals, and doubtless also "drained of semen," as the suitors' sexual designs are reduced to voyeurism. Unsuccessful entrepreneurs, with only the groundworks built of their mansion of love, the failure of their misguided, formalist generosity is symbolized by the suitors' symbolic distance from their prize, observable but not touchable.

Lines 9-12 supply the poet's redemptive version of erotic ceremonial, which substitutes the eucharistic oblation for the canopied court procession. In this secularized sacrament, the dutiful ("obsequious") poet freely makes an offering intended to manifest the inwardness and simplicity of his own devotion, knowing, or thinking that he knows, that his oblation will win him the unmediated, inner reciprocity which is his goal. The oblation which "knows no art," free from the charge of formalism, is that poetry which, as in 105, is confined to constancy, "to one, of one, still such, and ever so." Just as in 105 it "leaves out difference," in 125 it "is not mixt with seconds." Yet ironically and pathetically, the word "ob-lacion" is mixed with a transcendent "second," the deity of the communion service, so that the metaphor can only be re-garded as a very strange, and somewhat ambiguous, com-pound. The use of the sacramental term leaves the reader un-certain just how much weight to accord it, and, by introduc-ing the unbridgeable hierarchy of human and divine, would seem to annul in advance the pure reciprocity of the "mutuall render." To deny the operation of art requires art, and this art will prohibit the reciprocal affective mutuality toward which the whole work has seemed to want to move. To com-pose poetry is expensive, just as loving is expensive, and the unformulated implication of the work as a whole seems to be that expense is never truly recuperated. The increase we de-sire from fairest creatures never materializes. Spending leaves one spent, and it fails to buy immediacy; it places a residue of compound feeling and compound language between lover and beloved. Here in 125 the very word "seconds" is a com-pound. It means primarily "merchandise of inferior quality," but it associates itself with the "compound sweet" and thus with that formalist craft from which the oblation is supposed-ly pure. But banning "seconds" from his poetry, the poet in-troduces a "second," which is to say a metaphor, and one which is complicated with still more implications. Language is condemned to be compound; poetry *is* art; it shapes and forms and distorts; it introduces inequalities, like the inequal-ity between an offering and an exchange, or the inequality be-tween a secular offering and the sacramental body of Christ.

Thus neither a "pure" offering (Booth discerns this "second" meaning in the word "poore") nor a pure mutuality is possi-ble in a relationship which depends on the word; still less is it possible when the word, as here, is always presented as written. In a curious sonnet which immediately precedes the group 123-5, the poet reports that he has given away a gift he had received from the friend. This gift had been a note-book, "tables." It is unclear whether the notebook contained writing by the friend or memorials of the relationship by the poet, or had been so intended by the giver but been allowed to remain blank. The stress in any case falls on the superior retentiveness of the poet's mind and heart, in contrast to the limits of the "tables":

> That poore retention could not so much hold,
> Nor need I tallies thy deare love to skore. (122)

To dispose of the notebook which contained or might have contained a written record suggests a deep dissatisfaction with language as a mediating instrument. The verb "to skore," to keep a tally, is used contemptuously, as though to insinuate that writing involves a petty arithmetic of feeling. What is striking is that the writing before us has done precise-ly that, has supplied us with the tallies of an intimate cost ac-counting. The phrase in 122 may be scornful, and yet both inside and outside the poetic fiction the language of the poet-ry is all we have, keeping the score and keeping an ambiguous distance open between the tarnished lovers. As that space widens, the poet begins to look like the dwellers on form and favor, spent in his gazing across a distance. He and perhaps the friend as well become pitiful thrivers, barred from the ab-solute immediacy at least one of them yearns for, because po-etry can never be idolatrously one and can never find the met-aphor, the "example," which knows no difference. The poet's real enemy is not the "informer" as slanderer, but the voice within himself through whose forming action feeling comes into being.

In the sonnets to the dark lady that follow, poetic language is thematized less prominently; the poet's sense of inner pov-erty modulates to self-contempt; the physiological meanings of such words as "expense" and "will" are foregrounded. The mistress, who has "robd others beds revenues of their rents" (142), is perhaps the one thriver in the work who is not piti-ful. Her role is antithetical to the young man's of the procre-ation sonnets; she is a "usurer that put'st forth all to use" (134) and her wealth is like the ocean's:

> The sea all water, yet receives raine still,
> And in aboundance addeth to his store,
> So thou beeing rich in *Will* adde to thy *Will*,
> One will of mine to make thy large *Will* more. (135)

But this inflationary economy leads to a depreciation of all values, and the only feasible policy apparently lies in a Chris-tian husbandry:

> Why so large cost having so short a lease,
> Dost thou upon thy fading mansion spend? . . .
> Buy tearmes divine in selling houres of drosse:
> Within be fed, without be rich no more. (146)

By the close of the sequence, however, the poet does not seem to have adopted this policy. In his disgust with sexuality and his own revolting entrapment in it, the poet tries systemati-cally to subvert his own authority as poet and his perception of metaphoric congruence:

> O Me! what eyes hath love put in my head,
> Which have no correspondence with true sight.
> (148)

Language is systematically vulgarized, "abhored," and in the last regular sonnet to the mistress (152) the coherence of the poetic consciousness and the integrity of the poetic statement are simultaneously denied, as though the poetry had no legiti-mate source:

> For I have sworne thee faire; more periurde eye,
> To swere against the truth so foule a lie.

The "eye" is perjured, but also the "I" and the "aye," the ca-pacity to affirm. "Loves eye is not so true as all mens: no" (148). It is as though the pitiless obscenity, love-denying and love-blaspheming, had to expose the *pudenda* of language to register the meanness of the seamy loyalties and tawdry bar-gains.

The Sonnets can be read to the end as attempts to cope with progressively powerful and painful forms of cost and expense. The bourgeois desire to balance cosmic and human budgets seems to be thwarted by a radical flaw in the universe, in emo-tion, in value, and in language. This flaw is already acted out at the beginning by the onanistic friend who "feed'st thy lights flame with selfe substantiall fewell"(1). In Sonnet 73, the metaphoric fire lies in its ashes as on a deathbed, "con-sum'd with that which it was nurrisht by." This becomes, in the terrible Sonnet 129, "a blisse in proofe and proud and very wo," a line always, unnecessarily, emended. The vulner-ability of the Sonnets lies in their ceaselessly resistant reflec-tion of this flaw, their stubborn reliance on economies incapa-ble of correcting it, their use of language so wealthy, so charged with "difference," as to be erosive. The vulnerability of the Sonnets might be said to resemble that nameless flaw that afflicts their speaker, but in their case the flaw is not ulti-mately disastrous. They are not consumed by the extravagant husbandry that produced them. Their effort to resist, to com-pensate, to register in spite of slippage, balances their loss with store. They leave us with the awesome cost, and reward, of their conative contention. The vulnerability is inseparable from the striving that leads us to them: the "poet's" expense and Shakespeare's expense. (pp. 230-44)

> *Thomas M. Greene, "Pitiful Thrivers: Failed Husbandry in the Sonnets," in* Shakespeare and the Question of Theory, *edited by Patricia Parker and Geoffrey Hartman, Methuen, 1985, pp. 230-44.*

JOSEPH PEQUIGNEY   (essay date 1985)

[*The excerpt below is from Chapter Three of Pequigney's* Such is My Love: A Study of Shakespeare's Sonnets *(1985), a full-length study of the sonnets as "the grand masterpiece of homoerotic poetry." Here, Pequigney views Sonnet 20 as pivotal in the sequence, claiming that it clearly demonstrates the poet is sexually attracted to the Friend. According to the critic, the person depicted in this sonnet is "the classic figure of homoerotic poetry": a young male who physically resembles a woman and who displays such "feminine" attributes as shyness, modesty, and naiveté. Pequigney maintains, however, that there is no evidence of "seductive intent" in Sonnet 20. Indeed, he points out, the poet acknowledges that the young man has been formed by Nature to gratify women.*]

Because so much depends on Sonnet 20—it is pivotal in the sequence—and because it has become a locus classicus of essays that seek to define the emotional relations between the poet and his young friend, I am according it a full chapter of discussion.

Interpreters can be divided into two groups, very unequal in size. In the smaller one are the few who, sometimes to their discomfort, find sexual attraction revealed toward the friend; in the larger one are the many who reassure themselves and us that such an attraction, far from being affirmed, is in fact denied. Two eighteenth-century annotators, among the very earliest, can illustrate these conflicting views. George Steevens remarked on 20.2: "It is impossible to read this fulsome panegyrick, addressed to a male object, without an equal mixture of disgust and indignation." Some years later Edmund Malone came to Shakespeare's rescue, writing:

> Some part of this indignation might perhaps have been abated, if it had been considered that such addresses to men, however indelicate, were customary in our author's time, and neither imported criminality nor were esteemed indecorous.

No supporting instances of these customary addresses are cited by Malone, but no matter; his position has been the dominant one among editors, scholars, and critics ever since. While less condescending toward the "indelicate" language of a less polite age, they defend the Sonnets against imputations of indecency and abnormality in much the same vein. They have frequent recourse to a cult of male friendship that enjoyed a certain vogue in the Renaissance, when the amicable ideal was more assiduously practiced and consciously esteemed than in later times; but the thing about this friendship that above all appeals to expositors is their conviction that it was free of all traces of eroticism. (p. 30)

[Sonnet 20] begins,

> A woman's face with nature's own hand painted
> Hast thou, the Master Mistress of my passion.

The word "passion" carries in this context its most glaringly obvious sense, that given by Schmidt (who cites this instance) in his *Shakespeare-Lexicon* as 'amorous desire,' and that given by Partridge (who ignores this instance) in his glossary to *Shakespeare's Bawdy* as 'sexual love, physical desire.' Both Shakespearean lexicographers establish this usage with multiple citations from the plays and narrative poems. The "passion" is directed toward a "Mistress"—a 'man's illicit woman, the woman one loves,' again from Partridge, again based on usage in the plays; and he might have cited Sonnets 127.9 and 130.1. That gloss must be modified to fit this case, and Schmidt handles the problem with a separate entry for "Master-mistress," which he defines as 'a male mistress, one loved like a woman, but of the male sex.' The word "Master" is not hyphenated to "Mistress" in the Quarto as it is in Schmidt and most editions. The hyphen makes the two nouns coordinate, in apposition to "thou," the man who serves as the androgynous object of the ardor; but this obliterates other possibilities, such as taking "Master" as an adjective qualifying this "Mistress" as 'preeminent,' or taking "Master" in the titular sense, abbreviated "Mr.," as in "Mr. W. H." in Thorpe's dedication, and hence the "Mr. Mistress." In no way does "Master" desexualize the associated nouns "Mistress" and "passion"; rather, it indicates that the erotic role played by the lady of other sonneteers, even in Shakespeare's own Sonnets 127-54, is here taken by a man.

Although it is difficult to imagine that the speaker could have anything else in mind than the plainest possible disclosure of his sexual attraction to the friend, we have yet to reckon with the evasive ploys of the exegetes. T. G. Tucker, who is more perspicacious than most, comments [in his *The Sonnets of Shakespeare*], "It is of importance for the relation between the men to remember that the word ["passion"] simply = Lat. *passio* '(strong) feeling.' " That the "importance" is moralistic and that the etymology is obedient to that imperative Tucker confirms by adding, "the end of the sonnet is a negation of the worst." The end may turn out not to eliminate the "worst," which, like Malone's "criminality," dares not speak its name. The language of Sonnet 20, as of the rest of Part I of the cycle, Sonnets 1 through 126, is, as C. S. Lewis justly observes, "too lover-like for that of ordinary male friendship," and he further says, "I have found no real parallel to such language between friends in sixteenth-century literature" [see excerpt above, 1954]. This might serve as a corrective to those, such as Malone, who postulate those parallels without adducing any, and to those, such as Tucker, who are all too eager to absolve the diction of its "lover-like" burdens. But Lewis himself declines to draw the obvious inference from his observation.

Some editors, seeking to mute "passion" at 20.2, have turned for help to old Thomas Watson, who uses the word interchangeably with "sonnet" to denote the individual eighteen-line lyrics, a hundred of which compose his *Hekatompathia or Passionate Century of Love* (1582). These poetic "passions" treat of romantic responses to a "mistress"; so if Shakespeare followed this lead—a big if, for the philological evidence is tenuous—he would simply be designating Sonnet 20 as amatory verse. There is, however, no precedent, in his work or anywhere else, for labeling a poem of friendship a "passion." Moreover, the literary sense of the term does not, as Dover Wilson and Stephen Booth [see Additional Bibliography] among others suppose, supplant the libidinal sense but in fact reinforces it. The gloss, first introduced in Edward Dowden's 1881 edition, according to Rollins, is less efficacious than commentators like to imagine for rehabilitating the verse; for even if "my passion" should denote 'my love-lyric,' "Master

Mistress" is not thereby explained—or exorcised. Furthermore, Watson could employ the term *sonnet* synonymously because it too had the meaning, now obsolete, of 'love-lyric' (OED 2) in addition to the surviving one of 'fourteen-line stanza' (OED 1), the OED including, after the first definition, this note: "In many instances between 1580 and 1650 it is not clear which sense [1 or 2] is intended, as the looser use of the word would appear to have been very common." Thus Watson called his own poems "sonnets," not because they approximated this formal norm, for they exceeded it by a quatrain, but because of the topic, and Donne styled his collection *Songs and Sonnets,* although it contains no quatorzain. The title *Shakespeares Sonnets* would have conveyed to Elizabethans the loverly subject matter at least to the same extent as the specific verse form, and they would not have expected to find this form disjoined, as happened increasingly in the seventeenth century, from that subject. Sonnets were generally, in Spenser's word for his own, "amoretti."

Perhaps only retrospectively can one recognize the first two lines of Sonnet 20 as introductory to its bipartite organization. The octave compares the youth with women, to their disadvantage; the sestet offers a fable of his creation. The two sections have parallel movements; each begins by remarking the youth's feminine aspects and closes by distinguishing male from female reactions to his person.

The octave proceeds:

> A woman's gentle heart but not acquainted
> With shifting change as is false woman's fashion;
> An eye more bright than theirs, less false in rolling,
> Gilding the object whereupon it gazeth;
> A man in hue all hues in his controlling,
> Which steals men's eyes and women's souls amazeth.

The superior (or "Master") feminine (as "Mistress") qualities are ascribed not only to the bodily externals of "face" (20.1) and "eye" but also to the psychical and inward "heart." Although elsewhere "My Mistress' eyes are nothing like the sun" (130.1), here the hyperbolical Petrarchan compliment is not withheld, and the eyes of the "Master Mistress" are very much like the sun, having both brightness and powerful rays to send forth for "Gilding . . . objects." "More bright" than women's, his eye surpasses theirs in brilliancy, and, "less false in rolling," it evinces the capacity, lacking in them, of being true. This comparison of 20.5 has both a physical and moral basis; in 20.3-4, where the womanly virtue of gentleness abides in his heart without women's vice of inconstancy, the comparison has a moral basis; and in 20.1 the implicit comparison between his naturally colored face and their artificially colored ones has, primarily, a physical basis, though the hint of rouging would connote imperfection. On either basis, he comes off best.

Out of context, the catalogue of female characteristics in 20.1-6 could almost cast doubt on the sex of the "thou"; but clues to his maleness beyond the multivalent "Master" are present, the first in the fact of his being measured against womankind, the second in the unlikelihood that praise for a lady would fasten on the *womanliness* of her countenance and disposition. But then one might think about what sort of man would find praise such as this pleasing. At any rate, at 20.7 his masculinity is directly confronted with the phrase "a man in hue." "Hue" can hardly denote 'color,' for the color predicated at 20.1 is feminine; so "hue" should denote, instead, 'form' or 'shape' (OED 1). The female head rests upon, and

the female heart is inside, a male bodily form, whose essential feature, its genitals, remains implicit for now but will soon be explicitly remarked. The noun "hue" serves as the antecedent for the two pronouns, "his" (= its) in the same line and "Which" in the next. The plural "hues" that are "in his [the hue's] controlling" can signify 'species' (also at OED 1) as the two subdivisions of the human genus, for the "Master Mistress" subsumes both sexes within his own person, and he also, in 20.8, has a pronounced effect on the members of both. The plural "hues" can also signify 'colors,' his person ruling and harmonizing all the tinctures that invest it. In the latter reading, 20.7 does not jar with 20.1 but complements it with the observation that, in him, feminine facial coloring does not strike a discordant note. His most fair shape "steals men's eyes and women's souls amazeth." The distinction implied may be that of Tucker's annotation, "In women's case the effect goes deeper than the eyes." And yet the men's response can by no means be dismissed as superficial. Not only is their gaze compelled by this rare handsomeness, but, according to the psychological theory of the period, erotic love is born of the visual apprehension of beauty, and the poet's own love has precisely that origin: he has been engaged unremittingly, since Sonnet 1, in contemplating the youth's comeliness. It has stolen his eyes *and* amazed his soul, so that he combines the men's and women's reactions, and he transcends them as well; for he has been more than amazed—he has been aroused to "passion."

Nature, personified, is introduced in 20.1, where hers was the hand that painted the "woman's face." She does not reappear until the third quatrain, where she is depicted not merely as painting but as fabricating her handiwork:

> And for a woman wert thou first created,
> Till nature as she wrought thee fell a-doting,
> And by addition me of thee defeated,
> By adding one thing to my purpose nothing.
>> But since she prick'd thee out for women's pleasure,
>> Mine be thy love and thy love's use their treasure.

In this flattering fable of the youth's creation, Nature is the efficient cause, and her original intention, to fashion a woman—the formal cause—was partially executed, at least to the extent of the face, eyes, and heart, the parts itemized in 20.1-6. Then she "fell a-doting"—rather like Pygmalion, except that, here, maker and made are of one gender—and somewhat revised her plan. The revision entailed no more than the "addition," which the creatress, smitten, had not the heart to withhold, of the "thing" required, and alone required in this conception, to turn the female into a male.

The "thing" that he was "prick'd out" with becomes the focal point of four verses, which not only constitute about 30 percent of the total number but are placed in the culminating position. Such attention in itself might well argue something other than lack of interest in this organ. Yet 20.11-14 are the very lines adduced by most explicators as conclusive evidence that the sonneteer's attachment to his friend is not sexual. Their position, if tenable, at least should be seen as lending the poetic argument a certain paradoxical drollery.

The effect of Nature's gift on the poet is disclosed in 20.11-12. He finds himself "of thee defeated," and the verb, bearing the sense 'disappointed' or 'defrauded' (OED 7), registers regret on his part and protest at the unfair action of a rival. But the regret and the protest are mild. Nature, far from a villain, is represented as a kindred spirit, one with whom the poet identifies or on whom he projects salient aspects of himself. She is a fellow artist; and while she "creates" in fine art as distinct from his literary art, she and he choose the same subject, on whom alike they dote. Her "addition," too, gains approval in being regarded as a good tenderly conferred. Does the poet, however "defeated" by it, wish it away? His "passion" has certainly not been deflected by it; to the contrary, it was initially excited by the "*Master* Mistress." When he goes on to say that the defeat is accomplished "By adding one thing to my purpose nothing," the question that arises is what he might mean by "my purpose." An answer must take the couplet into account.

The couplet offers a practical program for dealing with the situation at hand. This program, based on final causality, respects rather than opposes Nature's intention when she "prick'd . . . out" (= selected and genitally endowed) the youth "for women's pleasure" (20.13). This aim differs from that ascribed to her earlier in the sequence. At 4.3, "Nature's bequest gives nothing but doth lend" for reproductive purposes, and at 11.9 she makes beauteous persons, if not others, "for store." Now the phrase "for women's pleasure" posits something else: a voluptuous rather than a procreative objective. The notion, incidentally, goes counter to the Victorian one, since here sexual enjoyment accures only to the female, not to the male, partner. Then 20.14 proposes a distribution of the friend's favors. "Mine be thy love" is the first proposal, and it has telling implications. The end of the discourse is to solicit for the poet the undivided and exclusive love of the youth, and love is disassociated from sexual activity, which the second proposal concedes to women in the plural, to no one of them in particular: "and thy love's use their treasure." Here "use" = both 'sexual employment' and, in combination with "treasure," = (figuratively) 'monetary investment.' The diction and the financial metaphor echo the rhetoric formerly devoted to "breed." At 6.3-4 "beauty's treasure" alludes to the young man's semen fecundating a womb, and at 2.6-10 the "treasure of thy lusty days" ought to be put to propagative "use." We would be back in familiar territory if Sonnet 20 did conclude by urging a generative utilization of women, whose compensation would consist of "pleasure" and valued progeny but no love. However, "their treasure" in this instance does not allude to their fecundation but to the precious gratification they would derive from "thy love's use." Sonnet 20 deviates from the persuasions to breed in important respects: the biological perpetuation of beauty is neither advocated by the poet nor demanded by Nature, and the entire stress falls on the bestowal of pleasure as the natural function of the virile member.

In 20.12 the speaker cannot be reverting to the "purpose" he had in mind in Sonnets 1-17, which was to urge reproduction, since the genitals, far from being "nothing" to that purpose, are vital to it. Could he then be adverting to the male reproductive "purpose," defined in those earlier sonnets, as applicable to himself? That is very unlikely, for, having made no previous mention of his own obligation to breed, why would he bring it up at this moment? A farfetched reason for doing so might be based on the supposition that the youth has initiated amorous advances that are being delicately declined. But such advances are nowhere intimated, and the idea of declining is in any event clearly at odds with the conceptual and tonal drift of the poem.

I take "my purpose" to be that of the persona, seized by "pas-

sion," and I take 20.12 to be construable in two distinct but compatible ways. The "one thing" donated by Nature is "to my purpose nothing" in the sense 'immaterial to what I have in view,' and, as the slight transposition "nothing to my purpose" makes plainer, in the sense 'immaterial to the purport of my written discourse' (cf. OED 1, 6).

Still, whether held in mind or set down in writing, the poet's "purpose" has not as yet been discerned, and it is never specified positively. There can be no doubt of his intentions to reveal passion and to request love, and the "purpose" must pertain to them; but its expressed stipulation is negative, a negation of designs on the penis.

Then the reason for this abnegation seems to be that given in the couplet, to abide by the will and purpose of Nature, who "prick'd thee out for women's pleasure." This reason in no way precludes carnal yearnings on the part of the confessedly impassioned lover. The reason may be taken at face value, or taken as adduced to reassure the youth that he should not be anxious about sexual overtures, perhaps unwelcomed, or to rationalize the persona's disinclination to act on impulses in himself that are as yet strange and confusing. The argument of the sestet seems to call for "And since" as a more apt opening of the couplet than "But since." The differing nuances are subtle and hard to describe; yet "But since" does lightly hint at some other possibility in the mind of the poet than the one he chooses to state at the close.

To conform to the Renaissance ideal of friendship, Sonnet 20 would have to rule out, on the one hand, seductive intent, which it does, and, on the other, sexual attraction, which it nowhere does and in line 2 avers. Even though Nature's creative "addition" may be represented as an obstacle to fleshly intimacy between the friends, its presence does not divert the poet's "passion" but may, indeed, serve as a principal cause of its arousal.

The figure depicted in Sonnet 20 is, in its simplest outlines, that of a woman with a penis.

That figure was far from unfamiliar to Shakespeare in another sphere, that of his theater, where boys impersonated women. A young male in "hue" (= form) would show a "woman's face," "eye," and, in his speeches, "heart," and everyone recognized that his dress concealed a sex opposite to that of the character he enacted. The playwright, in conceiving every feminine role of his imagination, had to think of it as performed onstage as a boy. He was accustomed to thinking in terms of this dramatic convention, but in Sonnet 20 he portrays a personage who does not, like the boy actors, *play* a woman's part but instead conjoins, within a single self, female characteristics and the primary male differentia.

Strikingly delineated in this poem is the classic figure of homoerotic fantasy. No less an authority than Freud himself writes on the subject as follows [in his *Three Essays on the Theory of Sexuality: I. The Sexual Aberrations*]:

> It is clear that in Greece, where the most masculine men were numbered among the inverts, what excited a man's love was not the *masculine* character of a boy, but his physical resemblance to a woman as well as his feminine mental qualities—his shyness, his modesty and his need for instruction and assistance. . . . In this instance . . . as in many others, the sexual object is not someone of the same sex but someone who combines the characters of both sexes; there is, as it were, a compromise be-

tween an impulse that seeks for a man and one that seeks for a woman, while it remains a paramount condition that the object's body (i.e. genitals) shall be masculine. Thus the sexual object is a kind of reflection of the subject's own bisexual nature.

This passage is as obviously as it is astonishingly apposite to Sonnet 20. Gentleness, the "female mental quality" alluded to by "a woman's gentle heart," is akin to Freud's "shyness" and "modesty," and the youth's "need for instruction and assistance" was undertaken in the earlier instructions to "breed." In this psychological explanation—and its applicability, the context makes clear, is not restricted to the ancient Greeks—the genital "thing" is affirmed to be the "paramount condition" of the attraction, and the poet in no way disallows that possibility when he views this organ as an impediment to overt sexual relations. He rather provides impressive corroboration of Freud's theory in proclaiming a "passion" aroused in himself by one whom he perceives as both a lovely "Mistress" and, genitally, as a "Master," i.e., by a "sexual object" who is "a kind of reflection of the subject's own bisexual nature."

The poet discloses in manifold ways, explicit and implicit, his erotic attachment to the young man. Two of them have already been discussed, the first, and most explicit, being the language of 20.2, and the second, tacit, consisting of the phallic awareness suffusing 20.11-14. Two other components of that attachment are admiration for the feminine aspects of the friend and the poet's bias, in respect to him, against womankind.

The object of the passion was "Created for [= to be] a woman" and is rendered womanly of face, eye, and heart. This detail is descriptive and laudatory. It describes someone hardly of a virile complexion and one who, though young, is past boyhood, for he is likened to a woman, not a girl. He is imagined by the poet, and must be thought of by the reader, as taking satisfaction not only in the praise heaped on him but also in the title "Mistress," though modified, of course, by "Master." The recipient of the praise, having a marked female element in his makeup, inflames the male praiser, and the dynamics of the stimulus and response are those described by Freud.

The proposal that the friend go off to pleasure women, when it is made to one who has feminine attributes and who seems to have been unaffected by so many arguments to breed, might impress us as a bit disingenous. This late access of concern for the opposite sex represents something of a turnabout from the animus earlier entertained against it. Comparison of the friend with women in 20.1-6 was intended to establish at once his resemblance and his superiority to them. That his face is painted "by nature's own hand" carries the implication—confirmed in the very next sonnet, which alludes (21.1-2) to the "painted beauty" of many another "Muse" (= poet)—that their faces need, or undergo, cosmetic coloring by human hands. Further, they are "false"; their hearts, unlike his, are "acquainted / With shifting change"; and their eyes, less bright than his, are "false in rolling." This is an odd preliminary to, if not an actual undermining of, the counsel of 20.14, that he go off to give them orgasmic delight, but it is an apt preparation for the rest of the counsel, that he hold back his love from these creatures.

The poet's attitude toward the other sex is ambivalent, and the favorable side is revealed in a rather oblique manner. The traits that make the friend adorable are in large measure woman-like. But that need not imply effeminacy, which is hardly a basis for compliments and is usually considered unbecoming. A certain feminineness in a young man can exert a powerful appeal on some sensibilities—and the poet has one—that are also responsive to female charms. And Nature is personified, playfully and respectfully, as a slightly comic but also reverenced "she." Aside from the slight chagrin, vented in the verb "defeats," at her phallicizing his inamorato, the persona represents himself, in various respects, as her disciple or else represents her as his alter ego; for each is a maker, and the self-same youth serves both of them at once as subject of art and object of infatuation. The fact that she initially made the youth female does not prevent Nature from falling in love, and, once in love, she cannot doom her unfinished creature to the "deprived" state of womanhood but must add the perfecting touch that will transform "her" into a "him." Thereupon she decrees, in a show of concern for her own gender after all, that the masculine "addition" is to be employed in intercourse with women. All that, of course, is the invention of the poet, as is the corresponding role he assigns to himself. He follows her example by falling in love with one of the same sex as himself and by introducing the penis at the end of his own creative process; he also shows a readiness to abide by her decree in his willingness to keep his distance from that "mastering" organ. However, this threefold conformity to Nature—psychological, artistic, and moral—generates a conflict, a tension within him.

The dramatic tension inherent in the text of Sonnet 20 is between, on the one hand, the attitude embodied in the second line's salutation, "thou, the Master Mistress of my passion," and, on the other, the last line's resolve—but not resolution— "Mine be thy love, and thy love's use *their* treasure." Can the enamored poet be content with "thy love" while giving up "thy love's use"? And how could he develop an erotic passion, and for how long could he sustain it, in the absence of any means whatsoever of giving it sensual expression? It would be a hopeless and tormenting desire that had for its object a "Master Mistress" who responded with affection but bestowed his sexual favors elsewhere.

In sum, in the sonnet that Shakespeare placed in the twentieth position of his sequence the speaker confesses himself impassioned of a "Master Mistress"; a man of salient feminine traits is entreated to grant all his love to another man; the beseecher betrays considerable ambivalence toward the opposite sex; Nature herself sets an example for homoerotic "doting"; and the penis of the beloved is dwelled upon at length. This poem seems a curiously inappropriate one for annotators and critics to single out as the principal prop of their contention that the friendship treated in the Sonnets is innocent of erotic content. But on second thought it is not so surprising that Sonnet 20 figures so prominently in their efforts at whitewashing, for it confronts so openly the question of eroticism in the relations between the friends that until, or unless, it can somehow be rendered innocuous, their efforts are doomed to failure. (pp. 31-40)

Joseph Pequigney, in his Such Is My Love: A Study of Shakespeare's Sonnets, *The University of Chicago Press, 1985, 249 p.*

JOHN KERRIGAN (essay date 1986)

[*In the excerpt below, Kerrigan examines the relationship between the Dark Lady sonnets and those addressed to the*

Friend, arguing that while the latter "unfold sequentially," the former are "fragmentary, juxtaposed, oddly modern in effect." He maintains that the two groups are "best regarded as foils of each other, like divergent areas of action in a Shakespeare play." Kerrigan also considers the nature of the love depicted in the Dark Lady poems. The woman, he claims, is generally identified with debased love: an infertile, sexually enshrined "hell" that contrasts markedly with the Friend's amplitude. Yet, Kerrigan concludes, even the "lovely boy" is not immune from the same effects of time that worked ill upon the Dark Lady, for in the sonnets, "at the last, Time circumscribes the natural world and the very springs of life, while verse can only make memorials."]

If the sonnets to the youth grow out of comradely affection in the literature of friendship, those to the dark lady extend and degrade the rival attractions of heterosexual passion. While the comedies either accept the humanistic elevation of 'paederastice' over 'gynerastice' reluctantly, as in the last scene of *The Two Gentlemen of Verona,* or test and explicitly reject the claim of comradeship to dominance (as in *The Merchant of Venice*), the Sonnets as a collection come closer to the traditional view so vividly expressed by Montaigne in his essay 'Of Friendship':

> To compare the affection towards women unto [friendship], although it proceed from our own free choice, a man cannot nor may it be placed in this rank: Her fire, I confess it to be more active, more fervent, and more sharp. But it is a rash and wavering fire, waving and diverse: the fire of an ague subject to fits and stints . . .
>
> (translated by Florio)

A stream of lines and images from Sonnets 127-54 pours into the reader's mind: 'My love is as a fever, longing still / For that which longer nurseth the disease' (147.1-2), 'Till my bad angel fire my good one out' (144.14), 'Cupid . . . his love-kindling fire', 'his heart-inflaming brand' (153.1 and 3, 154.2), 'Beshrew that heart that makes my heart to groan / For that deep wound' (133.1-2). But once Sonnet 129, 'Th' expense of spirit', is remembered, it will not budge, as Montaigne's immovable analogue.

It is also, of course, the one poem in the dark lady group to stand entirely above the first person. As an absolute statement about 'the love which enflameth men with lust toward womankind,' an account of lust's 'rash and wavering fire,' it can be compared with 'Let me not to the marriage of true minds' [Sonnet 116] in the primary sequence:

> Th' expense of spirit in a waste of shame
> Is lust in action, and, till action, lust
> Is perjured, murd'rous, bloody, full of blame,
> Savage, extreme, rude, cruel, not to trust,
> Enjoyed no sooner but despisèd straight,
> Past reason hunted, and no sooner had,
> Past reason hated as a swallowed bait
> On purpose laid to make the taker mad . . .
>
> [Sonnet 129]

While 116 deals with Love complexly, however, questioning the absolute which it erects, 129 describes and enacts with single-minded, though cynically quibbling, forcefulness the distemperature of phallocentric lust. Fitful and fretting, such a passion squanders the moral powers along with the semen, committing both to a 'waste of shame' and 'shameful waist'. 'More active, more fervent, and more sharp' than comradeship, it goads men towards satisfaction, yet, once sated in the irrational frenzy of orgasm, it is queasy, woeful, and full of remorse:

> Mad in pursuit, and in possession so,
> Had, having, and in quest to have, extreme,
> A bliss in proof, and proved, a very woe,
> Before, a joy proposed, behind, a dream.
>   All this the world well knows, yet none knows well
>   To shun the heaven that leads men to this hell.

Lust is fixated by the moment: yearning towards emission, it lies sullied and futile in its wake, sourly foretasting hell, with nothing to hope for but further 'pursuit'. Its imaginative field is vorticose, centripetal, obsessive.

In this 129 provides an epitome of its group. While the sonnets to the youth are 'spiralling, uneven, discontinuous', they are nevertheless caught up by the onward drift of time. They move inexorably onward, within, and from, poem to poem. The sub-sequence to the dark lady is, by contrast, disjunctive, wildly various, contained by a matrix of mood not pace, emotion not process. While poems 1-126 ultimately unfold sequentially, like one of those Elizabethan pictures recording an aristocrat's life—that of Sir Henry Unton, for instance—selecting and concentrating parts of the noble young man's life as he ages, the dark lady sonnets are fragmentary, juxtaposed, oddly modernist in effect. There are moments of terrible climactic insight which, outgone, are lost; the poet returns obsessively to anxieties already analysed into hopelessness. These poems do not operate under the aegis of Time—indeed, the word 'Time', so common in 1-126, does not appear in 127-54—but are trapped in a chaos of inescapable passion. And here again, one might add, the reorderers respond wrongly to an urgently apprehended effect. It is precisely the fragmentariness of the dark lady sonnets which is their point, but also that which, making them detachable in ones and twos and threes, allows them, in the hands of reorderers, to ruin the coherence of the collection. To snatch such poems so promptly from emotional turmoil is merely to make innocuous Shakespeare's apposite unordering.

Which is not to say that the two groups are discrete. They are best regarded as foils of each other, like divergent areas of action in a Shakespeare play. As in the drama, links between the diverse threads of 'story' are ultimately complex yet incidentally explicit. There are, for example, the interlinked sonnets 21 and 130 on 'false' and 'proud compare'; there are paired poems on love and musical harmony (8 and 128); and there are several sonnets, verbally connected, on love-deluded eyes. This is 137:

> Thou blind fool, Love, what dost thou to mine eyes
> That they behold and see not what they see?
> They know what beauty is, see where it lies,
> Yet what the best is take the worst to be.
> If eyes corrupt by over-partial looks
> Be anchored in the bay where all men ride,
> Why of eyes' falsehood hast thou forgèd hooks,
> Whereto the judgment of my heart is tied?
> Why should my heart think that a several plot,
> Which my heart knows the wide world's common place?
> Or mine eyes seeing this, say this is not,
> To put fair truth upon so foul a face?
>   In things right true my heart and eyes have erred,
>   And to this false plague are they now transferred.

The sonnet is indicative as well as typical, when compared

with such poems as 113-14, in that by virtue of its theme it is as much opposed to the sonnets written to the youth as it is in itself concerned with opposition: 'best' and 'worst', 'fair' and 'foul', feeling 'heart' against seeing 'eyes'. Indeed, it offers a hideous parody of those poems which seek to magnify the friend. The young man's sexuality includes a world of fruitful 'increase'; the dark lady, a 'bay where all men ride', is a kind of global whore, the 'wide world' of 107's 'common place'. If the sonnets to the lady parallel, they also refract and invert, those written to the youth: they behave like the sub-plot of a Shakespeare play.

Indeed, the two groups of sonnets, to the fair youth and dark lady, interact rather like the meshed 'stories' in *Othello*, where the fair Bianca ('white one') turns out to be a prostitute, though not finally evil, and the Moor can be judged, when heard with sympathy, 'far more fair than black' [I. iii. 290]. In the period, colour prejudice, reinforced by the neo-platonic association between brightness and virtue, blackness and evil, ran so deep that it was impossible to extirpate, and to praise things dark inevitably sounded sophistical. Some writers welcomed this: Barnfield, in the second pastoral of *The Affectionate Shepherd,* for instance, argues at tedious length that 'white compared to black is much condemned'; and Shakespeare, possibly under Barnfield's influence, takes a similar line at *Love's Labour's Lost* [IV. iii. 244-79], where Berowne defends the beauty of his dark lady Rosaline with bewildering ingenuity. The prevailing prejudice might be contested, then, but it remained in control. Hence, for example, Ben Jonson's difficulties when Queen Anne commanded him to present her and her ladies as Blackamoors in *The Masque of Blackness.* The resourceful poet had to argue that the women had grown dark by absorbing too much light—by basking too long, as it were, in virtue—but was careful to add that, if they saw more of King James, his sun-like presence would bleach them white again. In his Sonnets, as in *Othello,* Shakespeare welcomes and exploits the same prejudice to give his material—if not the stuff of life already—the unpredictability of life. The fair young man turns out to be, like Bianca, morally grey; and at first the lady seems to be his opposite. Helped, perhaps, by a shift of taste during the 1590s away from blond to dark hair (Daniel's Delia is fair in 1592, dark in the revised edition of 1601), and supported, certainly, by the convention that black could be sophistically defended, the poet says in 127 that, though ugly to some, the lady is to him 'far more fair than black'. Yet within four sonnets, in 131, he is claiming that, though 'fair', the woman is still 'black'—in her 'deeds'. So the fair friend is found to be less than fair, though forgivable, and the dark lady (like Othello, in the last extremity of anger) decidedly dark in the conduct of her love-life.

Elsewhere in the volume, the same uncertainties impinge. A Lover's Complaint may present its 'fickle maid' as the victim of 'false compare' and sexual charm, but the elaboration of her speech complicates our sense of her predicament. When she calls the young man 'maiden-tongued' though duplicitous, 'pure maid' in preaching but seductive in practice (lines 100 and 315), her own 'pure' and 'maiden' witness falls in doubt—not least because we learn that, seduced, she is no more a 'maid' than the youth. In the complaint as in the Sonnets, blame cannot be fixed on the corrupter alone, and what at first seemed morally fair turns out to have shades of grey. If anything, the complaint makes us more agnostic than the sequence, for it articulates an 'emotional triangle' from a single, turbulent point of view. Judgement is bound to be com-

plex when the 'fickle maid', circumstantially unplaced, is also left unanswered by the poet. The conventions of the genre encourage us to credit the speaker, yet a vehemence so self-undoing (notably at lines 316-29) prompts us to deduce, and then trace back to the underlying plot, deception. As in the dark lady sonnets—and the more surely since the complaint is read and reread after those texts—we sense duplicity doubling. Indeed, the youth's voice blends with the maiden's to the point at which his false words are hers. Especially in the quarto, where Jacobean typography eschews quotation marks round reported speech, their two tongues seem to fuse and his vaunting becomes her 'boast' (line 246). What registers in 1-126 as godlike androgyny here becomes the mastery of a mistress, and 127-52's flattery by lies urges ethical alertness on the reader.

If opposition and symmetry, with intermittent suggestions of moral equivalence, characterize relations between the fair friend poems and those to the dark lady, when these structures converge and become explicit, in 144, the result is one of the strongest sonnets in the volume:

> Two loves I have, of comfort and despair,
> Which like two spirits do suggest me still;
> The better angel is a man right fair,
> The worser spirit a woman coloured ill.
> To win me soon to hell, my female evil
> Tempteth my better angel from my side,
> And would corrupt my saint to be a devil,
> Wooing his purity with her foul pride.
> And whether that my angel be turned fiend
> Suspect I may, yet not directly tell;
> But being both from me, both to each friend,
> I guess one angel in another's hell.
>   Yet this shall I ne'er know, but live in doubt
>   Till my bad angel fire my good one out.

The poet suspects that his friend has become a fiend, seduced by the dark lady, thrall to E. K.'s 'love which enflameth men with lust' and Montaigne's 'rash and wavering fire', and he breaks out in a frenzy of sordid quibbling. Thus, 'I guess one angel in another's hell', while ostensibly extending the idea of suffering found in line 5 ('To win me soon to hell') to mean 'I presume that one angel is making the other miserable', uses a slang sense of 'hell' to clinch its rhyme in a bawdy joke ('I guess the good angel is in the bad one's cunt') while alluding at the same time to the game of barley-break, in which couples tried to run through a home base called 'hell' without being caught. And that last line, apparently meaning 'Until my mistress stops seeing my friend', is darkly fraught with the suggestion that the good angel has become an animal to be smoked out of its burrow, the lady's vagina ('He that parts us shall bring a brand from heaven', Lear cries at [V. iii. 22-3], 'And fire us hence like foxes'), while hectically glancing at the proverb 'One fire drives out another', and touching—via the standard Elizabethan quibble on 'angel' (both 'spirit' and 'gold coin stamped with the figure of Michael')—on a financial apophthegm commonly known as Gresham's Law, 'Bad money drives out good', only to be tortured still further by the sexual implication of 'fire . . . out': 'Till my bad angel gives my good one a dose of the pox (confirming that he has been in her hell)'.

What seems most striking in the polysemy of 144, however, is the ambivalence of 'love' in line 1. Those 'two loves' must register as different modes of feeling—comforting and hopeless—until the second line makes them 'spirits'. Two kinds of loving are summed in two individuals, and the ambiguity . . . in such poems to the youth as 65, 80, and 107 recurs, with 'love' at once emotion and the loved object. But the 'bad angel' represents only the 'dark' side of love; she is 'the love which enflameth men with lust toward womankind'. Once again, 129 clamours for quotation:

> Mad in pursuit, and in possession so,
> Had, having, and in quest to have, extreme,
> A bliss in proof, and proved, a very woe,
> Before, a joy proposed, behind, a dream.
>   All this the world well knows, yet none knows well
>   To shun the heaven that leads men to this hell.

Beyond time, indeed Time, and the process of Love's Growth, the dark lady's 'love' is not imaginatively 'redeemable'; its infertile delusions have no purchase on 'increase'; morally she inhabits, as she sexually enshrines, a 'hell'. Is it any wonder that 127-52 should include, as 1-126 could not, a religious sonnet, the poet's palinode, a Donne-like cry from the heart of corruption, 'Poor soul, the centre of my sinful earth' (146)?

Nowhere is the woman more clearly identified with debased 'love' than in 151, 'Love is too young to know what conscience is'. At the end of a complicated and extravagantly obscene argument, which copes with guilt, deception, and the fall of man *en route,* the poet declares: 'No want of conscience hold it that I call / Her "love" for whose dear love I rise and fall.' So the sonnet equates the lady with 'love'. Yet, oddly, the love involved is Cupid, not his mother, the 'young' god,

Illustration to Sonnet 54, "O how much more doth beauty beauteous seem." From a copper engraving by Peter Lipman-Wulf.

not the Venus who (according to renaissance mythographers) gave birth to Cupid in the Garden of Adonis. At first sight this seems unaccountable; but other poems in the secondary sequence associate the lady with Cupid (137 and 145, for instance), and all these lead to 153-4. In some respects a buffer group, with the function of the anacreontics and epigrams in *Delia,* the *Amoretti, Phillis,* and the rest, these sonnets about Cupid and his brand are also the logical outcome of the dark lady sonnets, since they make visible the erotic principle at work in them. Not 'obviously linked' with what precedes them, they are nevertheless inseparable from 127-52, and essential to those poems' effect. Shakespeare has taken the Danielesque convention of a three-part structure and, with characteristic revivifying economy, made its central term work twice, separating the sonnets from *A Lover's Complaint* but concluding the dark lady group. Indeed, he has, like Richard Linche, used the fourteen-line form as his textual link to signal his intentions. Nor can there be thought a contradiction between the structure of these texts and their epigrammatic content; nine of Sir John Davies's forty-eight *Epigrams* are in sonnet form, and Shakespeare's 153-4 would have been effortlessly read by early readers as simultaneously sonnet—epigrams.

These poems record, of course, how Cupid's 'heart-inflaming brand' was stolen by a nymph of Dian's train and quenched in 'a cold valley-fountain' or 'cool well by'. In the first, the torch is reignited; in the second, with perhaps greater claims to resolution, it simply makes the water seethe. Yet such a description makes the poems sound naive when they are very knowing. As a number of critics have pointed out, the sonnets contain innuendoes which are not the less blatant for being baroque. The burning 'brand' reignited at 'my mistress' eyes' (the 'eyes' which are 'nothing like the sun' in 130) is patently phallic; it is the 'flesh' which 'rises' and 'falls' for 'love' in Sonnet 151. And the 'cool well' made a healthful bath 'For men diseased' by the 'brand' of 'love' is distinctly reminiscent of the sweating tubs used to cure the pox in Jacobethan London. The sonnets may be deft, but they are sordid too. This 'little Love-god', unlike the 'god in love' of Sonnet 110, inhabits a sterile landscape. Like his bizarre human correlative, the dark lady, the 'boy' Cupid brings sensation, where the poet's 'lovely boy' is a god of 'increase'.

For we are back, finally, with the question of a sub-plot. Just as, in Sonnet 137, the lady offers a ghastly parody of the young man's amplitude, a 'wide world's common place' to his 'spring and foison of the year', so, in the conflation of her 'love' with Cupid, there is an echo of Shakespeare's exaltation of the youth into a 'god in love'. The two final sonnets on Cupid find their lofty equivalent in the last poem to the young man, Sonnet 126:

> O thou, my lovely boy, who in thy power
> Dost hold Time's fickle glass, his sickle hour,
> Who hast by waning grown, and therein show'st
> Thy lovers withering, as they sweet self grow'st;
> If Nature, sovereign mistress over wrack,
> As thou goest onwards, still will pluck thee back,
> She keeps thee to this purpose, that her skill
> May Time disgrace and wretched minutes kill.
> Yet fear her, O thou minion of her pleasure;
> She may detain, but not still keep her treasure.
>   Her audit, though delayed, answered must be,
>   And her quietus is to render thee.

The poem resonates with material from the early sonnets: treasure and the treasury, the audit, skill, the 'sweet self,' and, of course, Time's wrack. But here, the powers of Adonis reach their full height, and the young man grows by waning, increasing in decay. Like Spenser's 'wanton boy' in the Garden of Adonis, Shakespeare's 'lovely boy' dwindles into foison, producing, in the words of his Venus, seeds from seeds, beauty from beauty (*Venus and Adonis* 167). In 107, a 'mortal moon' had been 'eclipsed'; but in 126 Time's 'sickle' is borrowed by 'waning' in line 3, to make the youth a moon that grows when it is shaded. He is 'eterne in mutabilitie', favoured by Nature as Spenser's 'boy' was favoured by Aphrodite Pandemos, the Venus of the natural world. And like that youth, he is apparently above Time: 'O thou, my lovely boy, who in thy power / Dost hold Time's fickle glass, his sickle hour'. Many critics have quoted that, as though it were the end of the matter. But this last poem to the friend includes a reversal quite as violent as Spenser's at *The Faerie Queene* III. vi. 39. Nature is in debt to Time, and, despite, her dotage, she 'must' render the 'lovely boy' to mortality. The youth cannot escape from Time. Beauty cannot save him, nor all the poet's labours, which strive to make the friend a 'god', and try to recoup, by recounting, the clock. In Shakespeare's Sonnets, at the last, Time circumscribes the natural world and the very springs of life, while verse can only make memorials, inscribing what, without art, would always already be gone. (pp. 55-63)

> *John Kerrigan, in an introduction to* The Sonnets and "A Lover's Complaint" *by William Shakespeare, edited by John Kerrigan, Penguin Books, 1986, pp. 7-63.*

ADDITIONAL BIBLIOGRAPHY

Acheson, Arthur. *Shakespeare and the Rival Poet.* London: John Lane, The Bodley Head, 1903, 360 p.

Argues that Shakespeare's sonnets were written over a three-year period between 1594-95 and 1597-98. Acheson disputes the theory that the Friend addressed in Sonnets 1-126 is William Herbert, Earl of Pembroke, instead identifying Henry Wriothesley, Earl of Southampton as the Friend. Drawing on the theory of William Minto, the critic regards George Chapman as the Rival Poet, citing evidence in works of both Chapman and Shakespeare of a bitter rivalry between them, especially during the years 1595-98.

————. *Mistress Davenant: The Dark Lady of Shakespeare's Sonnets.* London: Bernard Quaritch, 1913, 332 p.

A book-length study of the sonnets in which Acheson makes the following claims: 1) Shakespeare wrote his sonnets during a six- or seven-year period between 1592 and 1598-99; 2) the Friend addressed in Sonnets 1-126 is Henry Wriothesley, Earl of Southampton; 3) the Rival Poet is George Chapman; 4) the Dark Lady was a real person—a Mistress Davenant, who was the wife of an innkeeper in Oxford; and 5) Thomas Thorpe's 1609 Quarto is piratical and illegitimate in order. The critic also maintains that Shakespeare's sonnets were issued without his consent by George Chapman as part of an effort to discredit the poet.

Adams, Joseph Quincy. "Period of Non-Dramatic Composition." In his *A Life of William Shakespeare,* pp. 145-83. Boston: Houghton Mifflin Co., 1925.

An overview of the circumstances surrounding Shakespeare's composition of the sonnets. Adams dates the earliest sonnets to the period 1592-94 and divides them into "several well-marked groups": Sonnets 1-99, addressed to a young man and all written soon after first meeting him; Sonnets 100-125, addressed to the same young man but after a lapse of nearly three years; Number 126—"not a sonnet at all"—which serves as the envoy; Numbers 127-52, an "appendix" dealing chiefly with the Dark Lady; and Sonnets 153 and 154, two poems "attached in the end" in celebration of the town of Bath. Adams also comments on *A Lover's Complaint,* noting that Thomas Thorpe's attribution to Shakespeare "carries little authority."

Akrigg, G. P. V. "The First Sonnets" and "The Unfaithful Friend and the Sonnets." In his *Shakespeare and the Earl of Southampton,* pp. 201-6, 228-39. London: Hamish Hamilton, 1968.

Maintains that the earliest of Shakespeare's sonnets were written in 1593 or 1594. Akrigg also notes that the sonnets, "unlike most Elizabethan sonnet collections, do not constitute a 'cycle' for they are not a sequence of poems addressed to one particular person or exploring one particular relationship." The critic also identifies George Chapman as the Rival Poet.

Alden, Raymond Macdonald. Introduction to *The Sonnets of Shakespeare,* by William Shakespeare, edited by Raymond Macdonald Alden, pp. vii-xiv. Boston: Houghton Mifflin Co., 1916.

Identifies the main lines of argument in aesthetic criticism of Shakespeare's sonnets. In an appendix, Alden offers excerpts from selected pre-1916 studies of the poems.

Allen, Michael J. B. "Shakespeare's Man Descending a Staircase: Sonnets 126 to 154." *Shakespeare Survey* 31 (1978): 127-38.

Contends that Shakespeare brought the dramatic techniques of transference, abreaction, shifts in irony, explosive juxtaposition, and anticipation to a climax in the Dark Lady sonnets. Noting Francis Meres's 1598 characterization of Shakespeare as "most passionate among us to bewaile and bemoane the perplexities of love," Allen states: "It is precisely this union of passion and perplexity that accounts for the genre of the . . . Dark Lady sequence. For not only its individual sonnets but its ordering too is the work of a supremely dramatic imagination."

Andrews, Michael Cameron. "Sincerity and Subterfuge in Three Shakespearean Sonnet Groups." *Shakespeare Quarterly* 33, No. 3 (Autumn 1982): 314-27.

Explores the autobiographical element in Shakespeare's sonnets. Noting that "the poetic presentation of the self is in some measure the freeing of the self, the translation of life to art," Andrews views the Shakespeare of the sonnets as a "dramatic character at one remove from his creator." Thus, Andrews suggests, the poet of the sonnets is involved to varying degrees in interplay between self-confusion and self-protection.

Bates, Paul A. "Shakespeare's Sonnets and Pastoral Poetry." *Shakespeare Jahrbuch* 103 (1967): 81-96.

Maintains that "Mr. W. H.," the Rival Poet, and the Dark Lady "existed only as the creations of Shakespeare's imagination." Calling Shakespeare's sonnets "an imitative work" and "a fiction," Bates argues that the sequence was created—"like *King Lear, Henry the Fourth,* part I, and numerous other plays"—by combining two plots, both derived from traditional pastoral poetry. Pastoralism, Bates concludes, is the "key" to Shakespeare's sonnet sequence, for it is, in effect, "a long pastoral without shepherds."

Beeching, H. C. Introduction to *The Sonnets of Shakespeare,* by William Shakespeare, edited by H. C. Beeching, pp. vii-lxvii. Boston: Ginn & Co., 1904.

Argues that Shakespeare's sonnet sequence was written between 1597 and 1601 and, thus, the subject and inspirer could not be Henry Wriothesley, Earl of Southampton. Beeching disputes the claim that much in the sonnets is conventional rather than autobiographical, asserting that while the form and style of the poems are conventional, the emotions they express are likely real. Though Beeching finds the claim for William Herbert, Earl of Pembroke, as the patron and Friend more convincing than the Southampton theory, he remains skeptical of this as well.

Benzon, William L. "Lust in Action: An Abstraction." *Language and Style: An International Quarterly* XIV, No. 4 (Fall 1981): 251-70.

Employs computational linguistics and cognitive network theory to elucidate "lust in action" in Shakespeare's Sonnet 129.

Booth, Stephen, ed. *Shakespeare's Sonnets,* by William Shakespeare. New Haven: Yale University Press, 1977, 578 p.

A parallel-text edition of Shakespeare's sonnets, offering modernized versions of the poems alongside corresponding facsimiles from the 1609 Quarto. Booth reveals his method and purpose in his preface: "Both my text and my commentary are determined by what I think a Renaissance reader would have thought as he moved from line to line and sonnet to sonnet in the Quarto." Booth's commentary focuses on thematic issues while glossing selected words and phrases. In many cases, detailed parallels are drawn between the sonnets and other works by Shakespeare, as well as with the works of a number of Shakespeare's contemporaries.

Brown, Ivor. "Shakespeare's Dark Lady." In his *Dark Ladies,* pp. 253-309. London: Collins, 1957.

An overview of scholarship concerning the identity of the Dark Lady of Shakespeare's sonnets. Noting that the Dark Lady "has not been certainly identified, and perhaps never will be," Brown presents objective cases for three candidates: Mrs. Davenant, Anne Whateley of Temple Grafton, and Mary Fitton. Although he determines that the Dark Lady must be left as "Mistress Anonyma," Brown concedes that he favors the candidacy of Mary Fitton above all others.

Butler, Samuel. *Shakespeare's Sonnets Reconsidered.* London: Jonathan Cape, 1927, 316 p.

A close study, originally published in 1899, of the text, date, and arrangement of Shakespeare's sonnets. Butler dates all the sonnets between Spring 1585 and "probably about November 24," 1588. He also proposes an arrangement different from that in the 1609 Quarto, basing his reordering on his belief that only nine of the Dark Lady sonnets are addressed to a woman, while Sonnet 126 in the Quarto "should be considered not as the last of the first group, but as the first of the second."

Cruttwell, Patrick. "Shakespeare's Sonnets and the 1590's." In his *The Shakespearean Moment,* pp. 1-38. London: Chatto and Windus, 1954.

Approaches Shakespeare's sonnet sequence as the consummate witness of "an intensely sensitive awareness of the currents and cross-currents" of the Elizabethan 1590s. Cruttwell states that the sonnets show "a blending of new and old, the new *in* the old, and the new growing through the old." He adds that they use "a form (the sonnet-sequence) which was above all the chosen form of the old, and in that form they say something completely at odds with the old, and destined to conquer it." The sonnets, Cruttwell concludes, "are a sort of embryo, in which the essential evolution of the whole of Shakespeare is carried out in miniature."

Douglas, Lord Alfred. *The True History of Shakespeare's Sonnets.* London: Martin Secker, 1933, 216 p.

A response to Samuel Butler's 1899 reading of Shakespeare's sonnets (see entry above). Douglas agrees with a number of crucial points made by Butler—for example, that Shakespeare wrote the sonnets at an early age; that "the onlie begetter" cited in the 1609 Quarto dedication was a young fellow actor by the name of William Hughes; and that the placement of the Dark Lady sonnets is incorrect. But he vehemently disagrees with Butler's claim that these verses clearly demonstrate that Shakespeare was a homosexual.

Dowden, Edward. Introduction to *The Son. of William Shakspere,*

by William Shakspere, edited by Edward Dowden, pp. 1-110. London: Kegan Paul, Trench & Co., 1881.

A two-part critical and historical survey of the sonnets. Part I treats the arrangement of the 1609 Quarto, which Dowden finds legitimate for at least Sonnets 1-126; the identity of the Friend, here said to be William Herbert, Earl of Pembroke; and the value of autobiographical interpretation of Shakespeare's works, which Dowden considers especially revealing for the sonnets. Part II provides summaries of major studies of the sonnets up to 1880.

Duncan-Jones, Katherine. "Was the 1609 *Shakespeares Sonnets* Really Unauthorized?" *The Review of English Studies* XXXIV, No. 134 (May 1983): 151-71.

Queries the critical assumption that the 1609 Quarto edition of Shakespeare's sonnets was published without his knowledge, assistance, or consent. Duncan-Jones cites Thomas Thorpe's practice and associations as a publisher—he was, she claims, a man "of some deserved status and prestige, handling works by close associates of Shakespeare, and producing, in many cases, highly authoritative texts"—as evidence that the integrity of the Quarto should not be impugned simply because Thorpe, who has been mislabeled "predatory" and "irresponsible," published it. Further, Duncan-Jones argues, the 1609 text is far more coherent than it is often supposed to be, suggesting Shakespeare's own hand in determining the arrangement of the sonnets. Duncan-Jones concludes: "It seems more than possible that Shakespeare himself sold the [manuscript of the sonnets to] Thorpe entire."

Eckhoff, Lorentz. "Shakespeare's Sonnets in a New Light." *Studia Neophilologica* XXXIX (1967): 3-14.

Determines that the Friend and the Dark Lady of Shakespeare's sonnets are fictitious. Eckhoff states in his conclusion: "Those two figures, the friend and the dark lady, are nothing but objects; the objects of the poet's unselfish love, and created by the poet himself."

Empson, William. *Seven Types of Ambiguity.* New York: New Directions, 1966, 256 p.

A landmark work in the history of English literary criticism. As he analyzes the different kinds of "verbal nuance, however slight, which [give] room for alternative reactions to the same piece of language," Empson frequently cites individual Shakespearean sonnets as examples. He offers an extended evaluation of the emotional complexities of Sonnet 83 and a brief but important explication of the many associations of meaning in "Bare ruined choirs, where late the sweet birds sang" (Sonnet 73). Empson also discusses the ambiguities of grammar and syntax in Sonnets 13, 16, 31, 32, 42, 58, 74, 81, 93, and 95. *Seven Types of Ambiguity* was first published in 1930.

Ferry, Anne. "Shakespeare." In her *All in War with Time: Love Poetry of Shakespeare, Donne, Jonson, Marvell,* pp. 1-63. Cambridge: Harvard University Press, 1975.

Studies the "struggling" speaker in Shakespeare's sonnets, who is, according to Sonnet 15, "all in war with Time" for love of the Friend. Concentrating on the figure of the poet-lover, Ferry notes ways in which Shakespeare shapes the sonnet convention of an eternizing conceit. The critic also comments on the poet's handling of other literary devices, particularly imagery, meter, language, and verbal constructs.

Fineman, Joel. *Shakespeare's Perjured Eye: The Invention of Poetic Subjectivity in the Sonnets.* Berkeley: University of California Press, 1986, 365 p.

Argues that Shakespeare invents "a genuinely new poetic subjectivity" in his sonnets. Moreover, the critic claims, "this poetic subjectivity possesses special force in post-Renaissance or post-Humanist literature because it extends by disrupting what until Shakespeare's sonnets is the normative nature of poetic person and poetic persona." Fineman defends his argument by reference to the theory and practice of epideictic poetry, "for in a very general way," he claims, "the poetics and the poetry of praise together define the literariness through which Shakespeare thinks his sonnets."

Fleissner, Robert F. "That 'Cheek of Night': Toward the Dark Lady." *CLA Journal* XVI, No. 3 (March 1973): 312-23.

Concludes that the Dark Lady of Shakespeare's sonnets was "very likely" black. Fleissner finds textual evidence for his view in Sonnets 127, 130-33, 141, 144, and 147, proposing one Lucy Morgan, known also as Lucy Negro and Black Luce, as the woman to whom Shakespeare addressed the Dark Lady sequence.

Forbis, John F. *The Shakespearean Enigma and an Elizabethan Mania.* New York: American Library Service, 1924, 342 p.

Probes Shakespeare's sonnets for "obscured meanings." Forbis argues that the person addressed in the poems is "none other than Shakespeare himself; and the marriage advised is the espousal of, surrender to, Wine, and the progeny to be begotten are not children of the body, but the products of the mind—poetry."

Forrest, H. T. S. *The Five Authors of 'Shake-Speares Sonnets.'* London: Chapman & Dodd, Ltd., 1923, 271 p.

Speculates that Shakespeare wrote only about one quarter of the 154 sonnets published in Thomas Thorpe's 1609 Quarto. The remaining poems, Forrest asserts, "were contributed in varying proportions by four other poets"—Barnabe Barnes, William Warner, John Donne, and Samuel Daniel—"writing in competition with [Shakespeare] and each other in a series of private sonnet-tournaments, which were fought out some time between 1594 and 1599, under the auspices of the Earl of Southampton."

Fowler, Roger. "Language and the Reader: Shakespeare's Sonnet 73." In *Style and Structure in Literature: Essays in the New Stylistics,* edited by Roger Fowler, pp. 79-122. Ithaca, N. Y.: Cornell University Press, 1975.

Discusses the pros and cons of using applied linguistics in criticism of Shakespeare's sonnets. Fowler focuses on Sonnet 73. Finding metaphors in the poem that are semantically connected and alike in stature, he claims: "If the poem strikes us instantly, and reliably, with its formal symmetry, it also impresses with the concreteness and density of its texture." This concreteness, Fowler suggests, is evident both in physical reference and phonetic texture. Of crucial importance, the critic adds, is the recognition that the order in which metaphoric, rhetorical, and metrical constructs are arranged in the poem bears heavily on thematic concerns.

Giroux, Robert. *The Book Known as Q: A Consideration of Shakespeare's Sonnets.* New York: Atheneum, 1982, 334 p.

A detailed examination of the 1609 Quarto edition of Shakespeare's sonnets. Giroux examines the dichotomy between the apparent early circulation of the poems in manuscript and the preparation of the printed edition well over a decade later. Making much use of historical and biographical evidence, he argues for the early dating of all but one of the poems.

Gittings, Robert. *Shakespeare's Rival: A Study in Three Parts.* London: Heinemann, 1960, 138 p.

Maintains that the Rival Poet in Shakespeare's sonnets is Gervase Markham, a minor English poet who was, like Shakespeare, closely connected to Henry Wriothesley, Earl of Southampton.

Godwin, Parke. *A New Study of the Sonnets of Shakespeare.* New York: G. P. Putnam's Sons, 1900, 306 p.

A book-length study in which Godwin reviews past readings of Shakespeare's sonnets and offers his own theories. The critic maintains that the 1609 Quarto order is illegitimate and states that the sonnets are addressed to various individuals. He also claims that more than half of the poems are imaginary, dealing with Shakespeare's "poetic development," and that Henry Wriothesley, Earl of Southampton was most likely the object

of some of the sonnets, although many of the poems commonly believed to be addressed to him are, he argues, directed to a woman, Anne Hathaway.

Goldstien, Neal L. "Money and Love in Shakespeare's Sonnets." *Bucknell Review* XVII, No. 3 (December 1969): 91-106.

Considers the conjoining of money and love in Shakespeare's sonnets. Goldstien pays particular attention to what he terms the "sacred use" of money imagery in the poem—a view he espouses as illustrating the nondepreciatory effect money may have as a poetic complement of love.

Graves, Robert, and Riding, Laura. "A Study in Original Punctuation and Spelling." In *The Common Asphodel: Collected Essays on Poetry, 1922-1949,* by Robert Graves, pp. 84-95. London: Hamish Hamilton, 1949.

An important and controversial study, originally published as "William Shakespeare and E. E. Cummings" in 1927 and revised for inclusion in the present volume, in which Graves and Riding call into question what they deem the "perversely stupid" habits of modern editors of Sonnet 129. The critics contend that the 1609 Quarto text of the sonnet offers the richest, most open, most polysemous version of the poem yet printed. These virtues, they claim, stem from the complexity of the poem as it originally appeared: punctuated in a manner not readily appreciated by modern readers whose knowledge of Elizabethan pointing is generally very poor.

Graziani, René. "The Numbering of Shakespeare's Sonnets: 12, 60, and 126." *Shakespeare Quarterly* 35, No. 1 (Spring 1984): 79-82.

Discusses apparent correspondences between sonnet numbers and themes or imagery in the 1609 Quarto edition of the poems. Graziani concludes: "In point of fact there is a reason . . . for crediting Shakespeare himself with the numbering of the sonnets. The evidence for this appears in only a very limited number of sonnets, but the conclusion one is led to is that the poet numbered his sonnets as he wrote them and envisaged them as a sequence at a very early stage."

Green, Martin. *The Labyrinth of Shakespeare's Sonnets: An Examination of Sexual Elements in Shakespeare's Language.* London: Charles Skilton Ltd., 1974, 193 p.

A close study of sexual imagery, language, and punning in Shakespeare's sonnets. Contending that a number of the poems are highly charged with revealing, graphic sexual themes, Green argues that Shakespeare "engaged in sexual activities with the fair friend to whom he addressed so many love poems, as a consequence of which Shakespeare contracted a venereal disease and became impotent." Green also notes that the poet "was physically attracted to, and had sexual relations with, more than one woman."

Grivelet, Michel. "Shakespeare's 'War with Time': The Sonnets and *Richard II.*" *Shakespeare Survey* 23 (1970): 69-78.

Considers the plausibility of a close connection between Shakespeare's sonnets and his English history plays. Grivelet focuses on parallels between *Richard II* and the sonnets, arguing that the sonnets are "irradiated with an imaginative energy" drawn from the play.

Grundy, Joan. "Shakespeare's Sonnets and the Elizabethan Sonneteers." *Shakespeare Survey* 15 (1962): 41-9.

Places Shakespeare's sonnets within the context of Elizabethan sonneteering. Grundy determines: "There are . . . sonnets in which [Shakespeare] is merely playing the fashionable game—sonnets XLIII-XLVI, for instance, which employ the fashionable themes of sleeplessness, absence, and the war between eye and heart. . . . But in the core of the sequence—the sonnets concerning the young man—he both re-examined the sonneteer's 'poetic,' and gave it, through his practice, a philosophical and critical depth that it had not possessed before."

Hammond, Gerald. *The Reader and Shakespeare's Young Man Sonnets.* Totowa, N. J.: Barnes & Noble Books, 1981, 247 p.

A multifaceted study of Shakespeare's sonnets to the Friend. Hammond views Sonnets 1-126 as "an organized, coherent, and developing sequence of poems," a "journey" involving "progress and a goal without its having a story's watertight unity." Within this context, the critic examines the poet's depiction of time, immortality, self-containment, and love, focusing on reader response to "the force of individual words."

Hayashi, Tetsumaro. *Shakespeare's Sonnets: A Record of 20th-Century Criticism.* Metuchen, N. J.: The Scarecrow Press, Inc., 1972, 163 p.

A 2,503-entry bibliography of twentieth-century criticism of Shakespeare's sonnets. Hayashi collects his citations under three headings: 1) "Primary Sources"; 2) "Secondary Sources (Criticism of the Sonnets)"; and 3) "Background Sources."

Herbert, T. Walter. "Dramatic Personae in Shakespeare's Sonnets." In *Shakespeare's "More Than Words Can Witness": Essays on Visual and Nonverbal Enactment in the Plays,* edited by Sidney Homan, pp. 77-91. Lewisburg, Pa.: Bucknell University Press, 1980.

Probes Shakespeare's dramas for contexts that illuminate what is said in the sonnets. Herbert finds parallels between Sonnet 71 and *Henry IV* and *Henry V,* arguing that the poem fits Falstaff's state "sometime between his rejection and his death"; between Sonnet 42 and *Twelfth Night,* chiefly in the portrayal of women taking charge of their destinies; between Sonnet 85 and *King Lear,* in both of which the critic detects "a poet painfully conscious of a glib rival"; and between Sonnet 107 and Cleopatra's state just before her death in *Antony and Cleopatra.*

Hotson, Leslie. *Mr. W. H.* New York: Alfred A. Knopf, 1964, 328 p.

Identifies "Mr. W. H." in the dedication of the 1609 Quarto edition of Shakespeare's sonnets as William Hatcliffe of Lincolnshire, "a youth so excellent in beauty, character, and princely parts as to be chosen as 'True Love', Gray's Inn's Christmas King." Hotson contends that "Shakespeare's hyperbolic praise of his loveliness, and its expression in terms of a woman's beauty, are both normal and expected for an Elizabethan prince; that the puzzling sonnets urging marriage and an heir were addressed to him in his role as 'Prince of Purpoole' . . . , and that Shakespeare's *my sovereign* and *Love* are titles proper for this Prince."

Huttar, Charles A. "The Christian Basis of Shakespeare's Sonnet 146." *Shakespeare Quarterly* XIX, No. 4 (Autumn 1968): 355-65.

A close textual and aesthetic reading of Shakespeare's Sonnet 146. Huttar views this poem as markedly Christian in language, phrase, and imagery. Contrary to critics who have labeled Shakespeare's views in the sonnet ironic and satirical, Huttar declares them to be sincere and heartfelt.

Ingram, W. A., and Redpath, Theodore, eds. *Shakespeare's Sonnets,* by William Shakespeare. London: University of London Press, 1964, 382 p.

An important and influential edition of Shakespeare's sonnets, extensively annotated with textual and critical commentary. Ingram and Redpath describe their aims as fourfold: 1) to establish and justify the text; 2) to gloss difficult words; 3) to "tackle all really difficult problems of interpretation"; and 4) to "make some contribution towards a fuller realization of the subtler features which characterize a considerable number of the poems and make for their excellence as artistic works."

Jackson, MacD. P. "Punctuation and the Compositors of Shakespeare's *Sonnets,* 1609." *The Library* 5th ser., XXX, No. 1 (March 1975): 1-24.

A bibliographical analysis of the 1609 Quarto edition of Shakespeare's sonnets, focusing on modifications the manuscript may have undergone in the printing house. Jackson determines that the Quarto was set in type by two compositors, one of whom ("Compositor B") did most of the work while the other ("Compositor A") "helped him out sporadically," setting somewhat less than a third of the text. Further, noting likely differences

in the two compositors' treatment of the text, Jackson contends that "if one compositor reproduced the punctuation of his copy for the *Sonnets,* the other obviously did not; perhaps neither did."

Kott, Jan. "Shakespeare's Bitter Arcadia." In his *Shakespeare Our Contemporary,* translated by Boleslaw Taborski, pp. 237-92. New York: W. W. Norton & Co., 1974.

Argues that the main themes of the sonnets—the impossibility of choice between the Friend and the Dark Lady, the boundary between friendship and love, the power of beauty, the universality of desire—return in *The Two Gentlemen of Verona, Love's Labour's Lost, As You Like It,* and *Twelfth Night.* Kott also notes that a strong propensity among Renaissance men for boys is evident not only in Shakespeare's sonnets but also in the works of Sandro Botticelli, Leonardo da Vinci, Michelangelo, Marsilio Ficino, and others. In praising the ambiguous physical form of the youthful friend, the critic suggests, Shakespeare was very much writing in a tradition that honored the androgynous beauty of boys.

Krieger, Murray. "The Innocent Insinuations of Wit: The Strategy of Language in Shakespeare's *Sonnets.*" In his *The Play and Place of Criticism,* pp. 19-36. Baltimore: The Johns Hopkins Press, 1967.

A postscript to Krieger's 1964 study *A Window to Criticism: Shakespeare's "Sonnets" and Modern Poetics* (see excerpt above, 1964). Here, Krieger proposes to "stand aside from [his] more substantive work" in order to generalize upon the metaphoric method or strategy of Shakespeare's sonnets.

Landry, Hilton. "The Marriage of True Minds: Truth and Error in Sonnet 116." *Shakespeare Studies* III (1967): 98-110.

A line-by-line explication of the language, imagery, and intent of Sonnet 116. Landry argues that the sonnet "begins with an optative definition negatively stated, elaborates on that definition in positive form in the second and third quatrains, and concludes with a desperate paradox in the subjunctive mood." Isolating the nature of true love as the principal theme of the poem, Landry concludes: "I think the most that we can say about the poet's view of true love is that he earnestly hopes it exists here and now in the friend's affection for him."

Lee, Sir Sidney. "Ovid and Shakespeare's Sonnets." In his *Elizabethan and Other Essays,* edited by Frederick S. Boas, pp. 116-39. Oxford: Oxford University Press, 1929.

A 1909 essay, originally published in the *Quarterly Review,* dealing chiefly with the influence of Ovid's philosophy on Shakespeare's sonnets.

Leishman, J. B. *Themes and Variations in Shakespeare's Sonnets.* 2d ed. London: Hutchinson & Co., 1963, 254 p.

Labels speculations about the identity of "Mr. W. H.," the Friend, the Rival Poet, and the Dark Lady "unprofitable" for the purposes of literary criticism. Of greater value, Leishman suggests, is the comparative study of the poems with the sonnets and love poems of other authors. Leishman therefore examines Shakespeare's sonnets within the context of three major themes or literary traditions: "poetry as immortalisation from Pindar to Shakespeare"; "devouring time and fading beauty from the Greek Anthology to Shakespeare"; and " 'hyperbole' and 'religiousness' in Shakespeare's expressions of his love."

Mackenzie, Barbara A. *Shakespeare's Sonnets: Their Relation to His Life.* Cape Town, South Africa: Maskew Miller Ltd., 1946, 82 p.

Discusses Shakespeare's sonnets in the light of the poet's apparent emotional states at the time of their composition. Mackenzie dates the sonnets between late 1591 and the first half of 1596; argues that they are addressed to Henry Wriothesley, Earl of Southampton, as well as to "the enigmatic 'Dark Lady' "; and concludes that "Mr. W. H." was probably "merely the instrument through whom the sonnets achieved initial publication" and in all likelihood should be identified with William Hervey.

Mahony, Patrick. "Shakespeare's Sonnet Number 20: Its Symbolic Gestalt." *American Imago* 36, No. 1 (Spring 1979): 69-79.

Views Sonnet 20 as the expression of "a homosexually motivated castration anxiety giving rise to derivatives of absence and overcompensating excess." Mahony finds evidence in the poem of anal eroticism, phallicism, and bisexually grounded "oxymoronic unification" of nature and culture.

Melchiori, Giorgio. *Shakespeare's Dramatic Meditations: An Experiment in Criticism.* Oxford: Oxford University Press, 1976, 206 p.

A statistical analysis of Shakespeare's sonnets, focusing on Numbers 20, 94, 121, 129, and 146. Melchiori examines formal structure, semantic value, logical structure, and metrical structure in the poems, approaching his subject as "rather an experiment in trying out, perhaps amateurishly, some old and new tools of critical production, in order to test not only their efficiency but their actual usefulness and functionality within the context of today's existential predicament."

Muir, Kenneth. " 'A Lover's Complaint': A Reconsideration." In his *Shakespeare the Professional and Related Studies,* pp. 204-19. Totowa, N. J.: Rowman and Littlefield, 1973.

Marshals evidence that Shakespeare is indeed the author of *A Lover's Complaint.* In presenting his argument, Muir considers parallels of imagery, word usage, syntax, and thematic concerns between the sonnets and *A Lover's Complaint,* noting as well links and correspondences with other works by Shakespeare. Muir determines that while *A Lover's Complaint* suffers from stylistic, generic, and rhetorical faults, the poem is "not without its own special flavour, and it adds something to the total impression we have of Shakespeare as a poet."

——. "The Order of Shakespeare's Sonnets." *College Literature* IV, No. 3 (Fall 1977): 190-96.

Examines links between the Psalms and Shakespeare's sonnets, maintaining that the order of the poems in the 1609 Quarto is very likely Shakespeare's own. Muir bases his conclusion on apparent thematic parallels between the two groups of poems.

——. *Shakespeare's Sonnets.* London: George Allen & Unwin, 1979, 179 p.

A concise overview of major issues in criticism of Shakespeare's sonnets. Muir offers commentary on the date, text, and order of the poems; the vogue of the sonnet in Renaissance England; the peculiarities of Shakespeare's sonnet style; and links between the sonnets and other works by Shakespeare. In addition, in a series of brief appendixes, he treats controversies surrounding the identity of "Mr. W. H.," the Dark Lady, and the "Rival Poets"; the authorship of *A Lover's Complaint;* and textual questions relating to *The Passionate Pilgrim.*

Murry, John Middleton. "The Sonnet Story." In his *Shakespeare,* pp. 91-117. London: Jonathan Cape, 1936.

Addresses a number of issues concerning Shakespeare's sonnets. Murry argues that the poems were published surreptitiously; that the story told in the sonnets to the Friend belongs to the years 1592 to 1594; that the order of the poems in the 1609 Quarto is roughly chronological; and that the Dark Lady was probably a woman of the courtesan type to whom Shakespeare was attracted for sensual reasons only.

Nelson, Lowry, Jr. "The Matter of Rime: Sonnets of Sidney, Daniel, and Shakespeare." In *Poetic Traditions of the English Renaissance,* edited by Maynard Mack and George deForest Lord, pp. 123-42. New Haven: Yale University Press, 1982.

An overview of the rhyming practices of three English sonneteers of the 1590s. Shakespeare is noticed here as a poet adept at using the interrogative mode to avoid platitudinous assertion.

Nisbit, Ulric. *The Onlie Begetter.* London: Longmans, Green and Co., 1936, 112 p.

Contends that "Mr. W. H." in the dedication of the 1609 Quarto edition of the sonnets is William Harbert, a minor poet and nephew of Mary, Countess of Pembroke.

Nowottny, Winifred M. T. "Formal Elements in Shakespeare's Sonnets: Sonnets I-VI." *Essays in Criticism* 2, No. 1 (January 1952): 76-84.

Contends that Shakespeare's sonnets reveal the author's "strong sense of form, and that it is with respect to their form that the peculiar features or striking effects of individual sonnets may best be understood." Focusing on Sonnets 1-6, Nowottny states that Shakespeare made formal aspects of languge his chief consideration in these poems, even to the extent of sacrificing the integration of imagery in individual sonnets. This overriding concern with rhetoric and verbal patterns, the critic concludes, informs all the sonnets in the 1609 Quarto, including several not commonly held to be artistically distinguished.

Partridge, A. C. "Non-Dramatic Poetry: Marlowe and Shakespeare." In his *The Language of Renaissance Poetry: Spenser, Shakespeare, Donne, Milton,* pp. 102-40. London: Andre Deutsch, 1971.

Compares Christopher Marlowe's poetic language with that of Shakespeare in his sonnets. Partridge notes that Shakespeare is relatively moderate in his taste for epithets but, like Marlowe, shows remarkable fluidity of movement in verse. The critic also considers Shakespeare's language from a phonetic point of view, determining that it does not yet have the facility of French or Italian "because of the ruggedness of most consonants and the predominance of Anglo-Saxon monosyllables."

Peterson, Douglas L. "Shakespeare's Sonnets." In his *The English Lyric from Wyatt to Donne: A History of the Plain and Eloquent Styles,* pp. 212-51. Princeton: Princeton University Press, 1967.

Surveys Shakespeare's treatment of love, friendship, Christianity, and courtly tradition in the sonnets. Peterson views the sequence as evidence that Shakespeare was "impatient" with the repetition of Petrarchan themes and "contemptuous" of poetic excesses he perceived in the verse of his contemporaries. The critic thus sees Shakespeare as going beyond the courtly and Petrarchan assumptions and traditions, offering a distinct diction, imagery, cadence, and, most important, "attitude," in his sonnets.

Purdum, Richard. "Shakespeare's Sonnet 128." *Journal of English and Germanic Philology* LXIII (April 1964): 235-39.

Explores Shakespeare's Sonnet 128, which, Purdum notes, has often been discounted by critics from the Shakespeare canon. Arguing that the poem is, in fact, by Shakespeare, the critic claims: "Sonnet 128 seems deliberately constructed to arouse protest . . . against the moral state that it dramatizes. One measure of the effectiveness of this impersonation may be the very disapproval that it has succeeded in evoking."

Ransom, John Crowe. "A Postscript to Shakespeare's Sonnets." *The Kenyon Review* 30, No. 4 (1968): 523-31.

A postscript to Ransom's 1938 essay "Shakespeare at Sonnets" (see excerpt above, 1938). He claims that "More of [the sonnets] than I had thought are innocent of my charge of anticlimax in their descending quatrains; and the final couplets are pithier and more adequate to their arguments." Ransom cites Sonnets 27, 28, and 33 as those to which he did the least justice. He also notes that he "need not have brought Donne" into his essay, "especially on the strength of a mere bit of lyrical verse." Ransom concludes by commenting on the homosexual tone of the sonnets, noting, by way of contrast, that "there is not a single case of homosexuality in all the plays of Shakespeare."

Rendall, Gerald H. *Personal Clues in Shakespeare Poems & Sonnets.* London: John Lane, The Bodley Head, 1934, 199 p.

Aims to demonstrate that the 1609 volume titled *Shakespeares Sonnets* was in fact written by Edward de Vere, Earl of Oxford.

Robertson, J. M. *The Problems of the Shakespeare Sonnets.* London: George Routledge & Sons, Ltd., 1926, 291 p.

Provides a comprehensive survey of commentary on Shakespeare's sonnets up to the early twentieth century. Robertson also offers his own thoughts on some of the principal questions surrounding the 1609 Quarto edition, arguing for a cautious reading of the poems and emphasizing that little can be proved in their behalf. He postulates that William Hervey, stepfather of the young Henry Wriothesley, Earl of Southampton, could well have been the "begetter," in the sense of "instigator," of the sonnets. The critic further contends that many of the verses are impersonal or dramatic; that many are perhaps about various individuals rather than one or two figures; and that many were probably not even written by Shakespeare.

Roche, Thomas P., Jr. "How Petrarchan Is Shakespeare?" In *Shakespeare's Art from a Comparative Perspective,* edited by Wendell M. Aycock, pp. 147-64. Proceedings of the Comparative Literature Symposium, Texas Tech University, Vol. XII. Lubbock: Texas Tech Press, 1981.

> Considers the connection between the sonnets of Petrarch and the sonnets of Shakespeare. Roche claims that "Shakespeare did not unlock his heart in the *Sonnets.* These poems have nothing whatsoever to do with his personal life." These verses stem directly from Petrarchan conventions, the critic maintains: although they are not as explicitly Christian as Petrarch's sonnets, they are similarly insistent "in ironically undercutting the demands of the lover."

Roessner, Jane. "Double Exposure: Shakespeare's Sonnets 100-114." *ELH: Journal of English Literary History,* 46, No. 3 (Fall 1979): 357-78.

> Studies Sonnets 100-114 as Shakespeare's parodic testament about sonnet-writing itself. Roessner views these poems as being "*about* the work the sonnets have done to make [the] false friend seem true." Beginning with Sonnet 100, the commentator argues, "the speaker turns from using poetry to hide or deny or dissuade his friend's untruthfulness to the complex trick of appearing to praise him while in fact exposing just how and why those praises are written."

———. "The Coherence and the Context of Shakespeare's Sonnet 116." *JEGP* LXXXI, No. 3 (July 1982): 331-46.

> Argues that "the pain and, finally, the heroism of Sonnet 116 derive from the speaker's assumption that the work of time is destruction, and that a person's truth deteriorates just as surely as does his beauty." This assumption, Roessner suggests, is the source of the poet's realization that "there is no safe place (and no ordinary language) for love on this earth."

Rollins, Hyder Edward, ed. *The Sonnets,* by William Shakespeare. A New Variorum Edition of Shakespeare, edited by Joseph Quincy Adams. 2 vols. Philadelphia: J. B. Lippincott Co., 1944.

> Widely considered the definitive critical edition of Shakespeare's sonnets. In establishing the text—here based on the 1609 Quarto—Rollins collates over fifty editions of the sonnets, ranging from John Benson's 1640 *Poems* to W. A. Neilson and C. J. Hills's *Complete Plays and Poems* (1942). Volume II is devoted to a redaction of published textual and aesthetic criticism of the poems. Major topics include "The Arrangement," "The Question of Autobiography: General Interpretations," and "Musical Settings."

Rowse, A. L. "The Story of the Sonnets." In his *William Shakespeare: A Biography,* pp. 161-200. New York: Harper & Row, 1963.

> Maintains that historical method is "indispensable" in attempting to solve textual, aesthestic, and contextual problems concerning Shakespeare's sonnets. Rowse offers a detailed biographical reading of the sonnet sequence, identifying Henry Wriothesley, Earl of Southampton as the Friend and Christopher Marlowe as the Rival Poet.

Schaar, Claes. "Conventional and Unconventional in the Descriptions of Scenery in Shakespeare's Sonnets." *English Studies* 45, No. 2 (1964): 142-49.

> Studies descriptions of landscape and natural scenery in Shakespeare's sonnets, attempting to discover which are literary set pieces and which are the product of real observation. Schaar focuses on flower description particularly, which he finds to be largely conventional. Similarly, he argues that the thematic as-

sociations of landscape and season as invoked by Shakespeare—of fertility and decay, of life and death—are also literary commonplaces.

Schoenbaum, Samuel. "His Majesty's Servant." In his *William Shakespeare: A Documentary Life,* pp. 195-227. Oxford: Oxford University Press, 1975.

> Briefly reviews the publication history of Shakespeare's sonnets. "All the riddles of the *Sonnets,*" Schoenbaum states—"date, dedication, sequence, identity of the *dramatis personae*—elude solution, while at the same time teasing speculation." The critic notes that he "takes satisfaction in having no theories of his own to offer."

———. "Shakespeare's Dark Lady: A Question of Identity." In *Shakespeare's Styles: Essays in Honour of Kenneth Muir,* edited by Philip Edwards, Inga-Stina Ewbank, and G. K. Hunter, pp. 221-39. Cambridge: Cambridge University Press, 1980.

> A selective overview of the various claims that have been put forth concerning the identity of the Dark Lady of Shakespeare's sonnets. Schoenbaum reviews the cases of Anne Hathaway, Mary Fitton, Lucy Morgan, Jacqueline Field, Penelope Rich, and Emilia Lanier. Ultimately, Schoenbaum concedes, the identity of the Dark Lady may never be known.

Smith, Barbara Herrnstein, ed. *Sonnets,* by William Shakespeare. New York: New York University Press, 1969, 290 p.

> A glossed critical edition of Shakespeare's sonnets, with an introduction, commentary, and thematic index. Smith dates many of the sonnets before 1600, but adds that it is "improbable that they were composed before 1592." Although she labels the sequence of the 1609 Quarto "dubious" and "not altogether coherent," she judges it not "altogether arbitrary," either. Smith also reviews criticism concerning the identities of "Mr. W. H.," the Rival Poet, and the Dark Lady, and briefly treats thematic and structural problems in the poems.

Smith, Marion Bodwell. "The Poetry of Ambivalence." In her *Dualities in Shakespeare,* pp. 53-78. Toronto: University of Toronto Press, 1966.

> Provides an overview of Shakespeare's sonnets, probing "duality of attitude as reflected in poetic techniques, and especially in ambiguity of language and in the structure and dramatic dialectic of the sequence." Smith pays particular attention to Shakespeare's portrayal of love and sexuality in the poems.

Spalding, T. K. "Shakspere's Sonnets." *The Gentleman's Magazine* CCXLII, No. 1767 (March 1878): 300-18.

> A detailed account of the arrangement of the 1609 Quarto edition of the sonnets. The critic maintains that the order of the sonnets in Thorpe's edition is legitimate and reflects, chronologically, events in Shakespeare's life. Spalding further classifies the individual poems to support this original order, contending that Numbers 1-25, the first class, can be grouped under the heading "From Familiarity to Friendship"; Numbers 26-96 under "Clouds"; and Numbers 97-126 under "Reconciliation."

Stirling, Brents. *The Shakespeare Sonnet Order: Poems and Groups.* Berkeley: University of California Press, 1968, 317 p.

> Offers an arrangement of the sonnets based in part on the 1609 Quarto and in part on logical, structural, and aesthetic claims. In presenting an emended sonnet order, Stirling concludes that "although the sonnets can be praised for narrative art of short extent, they tell no definable continued story."

Theobald, Bertram G. *Shake-speare's Sonnets Unmasked.* London: Cecil Palmer, 1929, 117 p.

> Aims to establish "beyond all reasonable doubt that Francis Bacon was the author of [the volume issued in 1609 bearing the title *Shake-speares Sonnets*], and that he has given us such ample and convincing proof in the book itself, that no unprejudiced person can, in common fairness, deny his authorship."

Thomson, J. A. K. *Shakespeare and the Classics,* pp. 44ff. London: George Allen & Unwin Ltd., 1952.

Contains scattered brief references to Shakespeare's sonnets. Thomson focuses on Shakespeare's apparent literary relationship with George Chapman, who, the critic notes, has often been nominated as the Rival Poet of the sonnets.

Thomson, Walter. Introduction to *The Sonnets of William Shakespeare & Henry Wriothesley, Third Earl of Southampton, Together with "A Lover's Complaint" and "The Phoenix & Turtle."* by William Shakespeare and Henry Wriothesley, Third Earl of Southampton, edited by Walter Thomson, pp. 1-89. Oxford: Basil Blackwell, 1938.

Maintains that Henry Wriothesley, Earl of Southampton is the true author of Sonnets 32, 36, 38-9, 43-5, 47-8, 50-2, 58-9, 61-2, 72, 74, 101, 105, 109, 114, 117-18, 121-22, and 127-54, all of which are generally credited to Shakespeare. In support of his case, Thomson remarks that "A thread of peevish, thwarted querulousness which is the antithesis of Shakespeare's characteristic attitude, runs through the 'Dark Woman' series."

Waddington, Raymond B. "Shakespeare's Sonnet 15 and the Art of Memory." In *The Rhetoric of Renaissance Poetry: From Wyatt to Milton,* edited by Thomas O. Sloan and Raymond B. Waddington, pp. 96-122. Berkeley: University of California Press, 1974.

An extensive examination of Shakespeare's Sonnet 15. In the first quatrain, Waddington notes, the speaker reflects upon the mutability and transience of all life; in the second, he particularizes the reflection of the first couplet to human life and activity; in the third, he "applies the lesson in an expression of fear for the change which the Youth must undergo." The couplet, Waddington suggests, "offers the consolation of immortality through the speaker's love."

Wells, Stanley. Introduction to *Shakespeare's Sonnets and "A Lover's Complaint,"* by William Shakespeare, edited by Stanley Wells, pp. 1-11. Oxford: Oxford University Press, 1985.

Briefly surveys major issues in criticism of Shakespeare's sonnets. Wells dates most of the poems to the late 1580s and early 1590s, and he also comments on the arrangement of the poems in the 1609 Quarto, which he finds as logical and satisfying as any other order yet suggested. He further asserts that the identity of "Mr. W. H." has not been proved conclusively, nor has it been shown whether "W. H." was the inspirer of the sonnets or the procurer of the manuscript. Wells concludes his essay with remarks on *A Lover's Complaint,* suggesting that although the poem lacks the immediacy of Shakespeare's sonnets and is self-conscious in its artifice, it is probably authentic.

Willen, Gerald, and Reed, Victor B., eds. *A Casebook on Shakespeare's Sonnets.* New York: Thomas Y. Crowell Co., 1964, 311 p.

An annotated edition of Shakespeare's sonnets, supplemented with a selection of previously published essays and explications by distinguished Shakespearean commentators. Essayists include Gordon Ross Smith on Sonnet 143, R. M. Lumiansky on Sonnet 73, and Albert S. Gérard on Sonnet 146.

Wilson, Katharine M. *Shakespeare's Sugared Sonnets.* London: George Allen & Unwin, 1974, 382 p.

Studies Shakespeare's use of the sonnet form, including his interpolation of sonnets into his dramatic works. Wilson examines the verses within the framework of late sixteenth-century English sonneteering, noting Shakespeare's departures from traditional modes and subjects. In an appendix, the critic comments on Shakespeare's alleged homosexuality, stating that there is no external evidence, nor any indication in his poems or plays, that Shakespeare was a pedophile.

Winters, Yvor. "Poetic Styles, Old and New." In *Four Poets on Poetry,* edited by Don Cameron Allen, pp. 44-75. Baltimore: The Johns Hopkins Press, 1959.

A response to the poetics of Shakespeare's sonnets by a practicing poet. Although he finds "traces of genius" in all but a few of these verses, Winters declares that "in the past ten years or so" he has found them "more and more disappointing." He traces this disappointment to an attitude of "servile weakness" on the part of the poet in the face of the person addressed; Shakespeare's seldom taking the sonnet form seriously; and the poet's often allowing his "sensitivity to the connotative power of language to blind him to the necessity for sharp denotation, with the result that a line or passage or even a whole poem may disappear behind a veil of uncertainty."

Venus and Adonis

DATE: *Venus and Adonis* was first published in 1593, having been entered in the STATIONERS' REGISTER on 18 April of that year. In his dedication to the Earl of Southampton, Shakespeare describes the work as "the first heire of my inuention," leading some scholars to postulate that this is the poet's earliest literary endeavor. These critics—G. G. Gervinus and Sidney Lee (see Additional Bibliography) among them—cited the dedication and the extensive nature imagery in the poem as evidence that it was composed some years previously, when Shakespeare lived in Stratford. Modern critics, however, have almost unanimously interpreted "the first heire of my inuention" as meaning that this is either Shakespeare's first nondramatic piece or at least his first published work. They argue that although none of the author's plays were printed before 1594, several are believed to have been written and produced before 1593. These scholars agree it is likely that *Venus and Adonis* was composed in the period between August 1592 and the following April. Because of the plague, the London theaters were closed during this period, leaving Shakespeare and other actors and playwrights idle.

TEXT: The first edition of *Venus and Adonis* (1593) was in QUARTO form. Most scholars agree that it is based on some form of FAIR COPY, possibly the author's own manuscript. It was printed and published in London by Richard Field, a Stratford acquaintance of Shakespeare. As the Arden editor F. T. Prince observed (see Additional Bibliography), much care would be taken with this poem, for it was not only the author's first publication, but also a work dedicated to a noble patron. The text of Q1 is exceptionally good, requiring only a minimum of editorial emendation.

Venus and Adonis was immediately and extremely popular. It was reprinted as many as ten times over the next twenty-five years, with an additional five editions published by 1640. Scholars commonly refer to all of these subsequent editions as quartos, although after the Second Quarto (1594) all were actually printed in OCTAVO form. They are all based on one or more of the previous editions and thus, critics concur, have little independent textual authority.

SOURCES: As early as 1595 commentators remarked on the relationship between *Venus and Adonis* and the works of OVID. On the evidence of this poem, FRANCIS MERES declared in his *Palladis Tamia* that Shakespeare possessed the "sweet wittie soule of Ouid." Among modern scholars there is virtually no dispute that the direct source of *Venus and Adonis* is Ovid's tale of the goddess and the young hunter in Book X of his *Metamorphoses.* Critics have long observed, however, Shakespeare's significant modifications of Ovid's myth, particularly his creation of a resistant Adonis. They suggest that for this trait the later poet likely turned to either the portrait of the bashful Hermaphroditus, who in Book IV of the *Metamorphoses* is pursued by Salmacis, or the story in Book III in which Narcissus is sought by the nymph Echo. Whether Shakespeare drew from the Latin original or from Arthur Golding's 1567 English translation is indeterminable. Critics have discerned occasional similarities between *Venus and Adonis* and Golding's translation, but, as Geoffrey Bul-

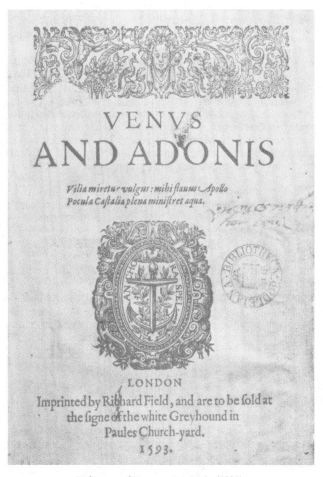

Title page of Venus and Adonis *(1593).*

lough stated (see Additional Bibliography), Shakespeare also "draws on Ovidian pieces of which no translation had been published." Prominent among these latter works is the *Ars Amatoria,* a mock didactic verse from which Shakespeare may have derived his version of Venus's conquest of Mars and Adonis's contention that he is too young to love.

Scholars such as T. W. Baldwin (see Additional Bibliography) have stressed the pervasive influence of Ovid's works on *Venus and Adonis,* and it is a commonplace of criticism to observe that it was a passage from Ovid's *Amores* that Shakespeare selected as the epigraph to his poem; the Roman writer's importance as a direct source, critics concur, is clearly substantial. Perhaps equally significant is the effect on Shakespeare's poem of the Ovidian tradition, a set of stylistic conventions derived from the classical poet's works and used, in Prince's words, for the "witty and sensuous re-telling of mythological stories." Critics underscore Shakespeare's adherence to these conventions and deem the setting, structure, tone, and rhetoric, as well as the story of *Venus and Adonis,* characteristic of the genre. They also cite several English Ovidian poems as possible models for Shakespeare, including Thomas Lodge's *Scilla's Metamorphosis, Interlaced with the Unfortunate Love of Glaucus* (1589), which was later published under the title *Glaucus and Scilla.* This work features a young man being pursued by a maiden, employs the same six-line verse form as Shakespeare's poem, and includes a passage about Venus and Adonis. Less certainly a model for *Venus and Adonis* is Christopher Marlowe's *Hero and Leander,* a work often regarded as one of the finest of the mythological-erotic poems. Marlowe was composing this piece at the time of his death in May 1593, one month after the entry of *Venus and Adonis* in the Stationers' Register. Critics have noted affinities between the two works and postulated that Shakespeare may have seen Marlowe's work in manuscript. However, since it is equally possible that Marlowe was influenced by Shakespeare, "the only safe course," as the Cambridge editor J. C. Maxwell suggests, "is to treat the two as substantially independent and probably simultaneous compositions" (see Additional Bibliography).

While scholars consider Ovid's works and the traditions based on them the predominant influences on Shakespeare's *Venus and Adonis,* a host of analogues and literary parallels have also been identified. Critics have long observed that Edmund Spenser employed the myth of Venus and Adonis in his *The Faerie Queene* (1590, 1596) and in *Astrophel* (1591), his elegy on Sir Philip Sidney that adopts the same verse form as *Venus and Adonis.* Similarly, Marlowe's *Hero and Leander* contains references to the goddess and the hunter, and, as already noted, Lodge's *Scilla's Metamorphosis* includes a passage featuring the pair. The eighteenth-century scholar and editor Edmund Malone posited "The Sheepheards Song of Venus and Adonis" by H. C. (perhaps Henry Chettle or Henry Constable) as a possible precursor, but modern critics consider this poem, first printed in 1600, an imitation rather than a source of Shakespeare's narrative. In 1710, the Neoclassical commentator Charles Gildon compared *Venus and Adonis* to the classical Greek poet Bion's *Lament for Adonis.* Sidney Lee also cited this piece and a host of continental successors as writings Shakespeare may have assimilated. Whether these or any number of other works alluding to Venus and Adonis inspired Shakespeare's poem remains uncertain. As Douglas Bush stressed, "mythological allusions were . . . common property" in Shakespeare's time.

Scholars have also identified a wide variety of other conventions, traditions, and literary parallels, ranging from the rules of rhetoric to flower and color symbolism, that may have affected Shakespeare's conception of *Venus and Adonis.* Significant among these other influences are Platonic concepts of love and the traditional correlation of hunting and lovemaking. Scholars such as Baldwin and A. C. Hamilton have claimed that Shakespeare delineates Venus's pursuit of Adonis in accordance with the Platonic definition of Love as the desire for Beauty. And Don Cameron Allen maintained that much of the action of *Venus and Adonis* is controlled by the contrast traditionally drawn between base and noble kinds of hunting.

CRITICAL HISTORY: *Venus and Adonis* was enormously successful when it was first published. The frequency with which the poem was reprinted and the wide variety of allusions, quotations, imitations, and parodies it stimulated attest to its large and appreciative audience. By the middle of the seventeenth century, however, the poem's popularity had waned and it fell into relative obscurity. For the next century and a half, criticism of the poem was sporadic and cursory. It was not until early in the nineteenth century that the first detailed assessments of *Venus and Adonis* appeared. In the following years, the poem was, with some notable exceptions, often dismissed by commentators who disparaged its elaborate rhetoric and meticulous descriptions and decried what they perceived as the immorality of its subject. The twentieth century, however, has seen a heightened interest and a general rise in critical esteem. Increasingly, modern critics have come to regard *Venus and Adonis* as an accomplished work in which Shakespeare transcends the limitations of the conventions of Renaissance sensual poetry by employing them to address serious philosophical issues.

The early history of *Venus and Adonis* is marked by widespread approbation. Shakespeare's modest appraisal of the piece in his dedication to the Earl of Southampton stands in distinct contrast to the effusions of his contemporaries, who considered it an inspired work. John Weever in 1595 and Francis Meres three years later each applied the epithet "hony-tongued" to Shakespeare, and Richard Barnfield extolled the beauty of the poem's "hony-flowing" verse. Gabriel Harvey's comment, while less enthusiastic, nevertheless confirms the poem's popularity. Though "wiser" readers prefer *Hamlet* or *The Rape of Lucrece,* he observed, "the younger sort" favor *Venus and Adonis.* The frivolousness imputed by Harvey is also suggested by allusions to the poem in two anonymous plays, The First and Second Parts of *The Return from Parnassus,* produced around the turn of the seventeenth century. The First Part presents a foppish character rhapsodizing over a parody of Shakespeare's poem; in the Second Part, the student Judicio praises the verse but disparages the subject of "loues foolish lazy languishment." It is evident from these passages that *Venus and Adonis* had gained a reputation for eroticism, and as the seventeenth century progressed, the poem came under increasing attack for its sensuality. Both John Davies of Hereford in 1610-11 and Richard Brathwait twenty years later condemned the work as lewd and pernicious.

Perhaps it is not surprising, in view of the moral climate reflected in Davies's and Brathwait's comments, that *Venus and Adonis* fell from favor and languished in comparative neglect from the middle of the seventeenth to the beginning of the nineteenth century. During this period, Shakespeare's poems were routinely omitted when editors compiled his collected works; even when they were reprinted, they were generally dismissed as inferior pieces. For example, in 1780, Edmund Malone compiled a supplement to Samuel Johnson and George Steevens's 1778 edition of Shakespeare's plays that included the poems and featured commentary by the earlier editors. Steevens severely censured the style of *Venus and Adonis,* judging the verse labored and the story stretched out in wearisome detail. In addition, according to Steevens, the moral intent was obscure, inasmuch as, he claimed, the behavior of both the goddess and the boy is offensive. Malone here offered only a brief, tentative defense of the poem, but a decade later, when he issued his own edition of Shakespeare's works, he presented a more systematic apology. He urged that *Venus and Adonis* be compared to the works of Shakespeare's contemporaries rather than judged by present-day standards. In this context, the poem's brilliance is readily observable, he claimed, and it can be seen as a work far superior to any other of its kind.

Early in the nineteenth century Samuel Taylor Coleridge and Nathan Drake both produced detailed and favorable assessments of the poem. Coleridge was perhaps the most significant and influential of the pre-modern critics of *Venus and Adonis.* Repeatedly, in lectures, notes, and essays concerning the nature of Shakespeare's poetic genius, Coleridge illustrated his arguments with passages from this work. In notes to his 1811 Shakespeare lectures (see Additional Bibliography), he maintained that the "unpleasing" subject matter of *Venus and Adonis* accentuates the poet's ability to write vividly and convincingly on topics alien to him. He claimed that Shakespeare writes about the goddess and the boy as though he were a man "from another planet" observing the behavior of a pair of butterflies. Coleridge further underscored the poet's aloofness in his *Biographia Literaria* (1817), arguing that although Shakespeare imbues the poem with an intense intellectual passion, he also remains distant, meticulously detailing the images and characters. Readers are also detached from the narrative, according to Coleridge, for Shakespeare dissipates our attention "among the thousand outward images" and prevents close identification with the "animal impulse" depicted in the story. Significantly, Coleridge observed similarities between Shakespeare's dramatic art and the detached mode of presentation in *Venus and Adonis;* as with his plays, the critic noted, "you seem to be told nothing, but to see and hear everything." Drake also praised the poem's imagery, together with its depictions of Adonis's horse, the timid hare, and other "objects of nature." Like Malone, Drake judged aspects of *Venus and Adonis* superior to anything produced by Shakespeare's contemporaries, and, like Coleridge, he observed evidence of the power that is manifest in the author's later works.

High regard for the poem was by no means universal in the nineteenth century. Writing in 1817, William Hazlitt argued that Shakespeare's narrative poems are greatly inferior to his dramatic works. Describing *Venus and Adonis* and *The Rape of Lucrece* as "a couple of icehouses," cold, glittering, and hard, he found their language and imagery forced and the thought labored, as though Shakespeare were more concerned with the "technicalities of art" than with the development of his story and characters. More than thirty years later, G. G. Gervinus was more moderate in his disapproval; he regarded *Venus and Adonis* as very much the work of an inexperienced poet. The luxurious style and sensuous depiction of Venus inadvertently obscure the work's moral content, he claimed, and in this sense, the poem as a whole is "one brilliant error." Gervinus was, however, among the earliest to consider the episode of Adonis's horse and the jennet thematically significant; this scene, Gervinus asserted, emphasizes the purely "animal" nature of Venus's desire. In 1875, Algernon Charles Swinburne declared *Venus and Adonis* "a model of what a young man of genius should not write." In contrast to Malone and Drake who considered this work the finest of its kind, Swinburne judged Marlowe's *Hero and Leander* far superior to Shakespeare's poem. Although he recognized *Venus and Adonis*'s "undeniable charms," Swinburne viewed its "overcrowding beauties of detail" and vaguely offensive subject matter as significant flaws. Edward Dowden, too, faulted the poem's elaborate descriptions. He regarded the minutely drawn pictures as indicative of Shakespeare's detachment and, in opposition to Coleridge, censured this dispassionate quality.

George Wyndham and Walter Raleigh, both writing near the turn of the twentieth century, offered more favorable appraisals of the poem's ornate style. In the introduction to his 1898 edition of Shakespeare's poems, Wyndham celebrated rather than deprecated the complexity of *Venus and Adonis.* He detected the influence of Chaucer as well as Ovid in the poem and admired Shakespeare's fusion of sensuality, realism, and medieval intricacy. In addition, he defended the morality of the poem, claiming that although *Venus and Adonis* affirms Shakespeare's "faith in Beauty as a principle of life," it does not expound a particular ethical view. According to Wyndham, to seek a specific moral message in this work is to willfully misread it. Nine years later, Raleigh echoed many of Wyndham's judgments, but he also stressed the poem's artificiality, deeming it a work designed to allow Shakespeare to demonstrate his facility with rhetoric. The "love of beauty for beauty's sake, and of wit for the exercise of wit" were the poet's primary motives in composing *Venus and Adonis,* Raleigh claimed.

Following Wyndham's lead, twentieth-century scholars have intensely scrutinized the moral, social, philosophical, and literary conventions of Shakespeare's time, attempting to discover the context in which *Venus and Adonis* was composed and thereby arrive at the poet's intention and the work's meaning. On the basis of their findings, critics have proposed a variety of interpretations, which can be grouped into three distinct but often overlapping groups: those focusing on the poem's allegorical elements, those emphasizing its humorous or sensuous aspects, and those stressing its complex or ambivalent perspective. Many critics have expressed an increased respect and admiration for its penetrating analysis of love and for Shakespeare's masterful poetic technique. Not all recent commentators, however, have shared these views.

The commentary of the first half of the century reflects this great diversity of interpretation. Douglas Bush and W. B. C. Watkins found *Venus and Adonis* derivative, merely a collection of literary conventions. John Dover Wilson and G. Wilson Knight, on the other hand, applauded its sensuous depictions of the goddess and the young hunter. And Lu Emily Pearson described the work as a highly moral allegory. In his 1932 study, Bush examined *Venus and Adonis* in light of earlier English mythological tales and compared it to other works featuring the natural settings, elaborate rhetoric, and legendary characters typical of the genre. He concluded that although Shakespeare has in many ways surpassed his predecessors, *Venus and Adonis* remains little more than "a tissue of bookish conventions." Dover Wilson, however, writing in the same year as Bush, praised it as "the supreme example of what may be called the Elizabethan 'fleshly school of poetry'." He lauded the work's celebration of beauty and sensuality, comparing it with Edmund Spenser's poems of temperance and virtue. Another view was offered by Pearson, who judged *Venus and Adonis* perhaps the most didactic work Shakespeare ever composed. According to her allegorical interpretation, Venus represents destructive sensuality and Adonis the rational element of love. When Adonis is killed, she claimed, the world is left in chaos. Like Dover Wilson, Knight admired the vitality of *Venus and Adonis,* particularly noting the sensuous but sympathetic picture of the young hunter. According to Knight, Shakespeare's "vital identification" with his subjects allows a wide range of precise portraits, from that of the young hunter to the dissimilar yet equally vivid description of his horse. In contrast, Watkins echoed Bush's earlier disparagement of *Venus and Adonis.* He maintained that the young poet was "carried out of his own element" as he attempted to imitate the elaborate rhetoric and witty sensuality of Ovidian poetry. Watkins faulted the frigid versification, inconsistent characterization, and ambivalent representation of sexuality, and he further claimed that the poem's strained tone sometimes results in an "unconscious satire" of Ovidian techniques.

Throughout the 1940s and 50s, critics offered an increasing variety of interpretations of *Venus and Adonis* as they broadened the scope of their investigations into the poem's sources to include philosophical and literary traditions outside the conventions of Ovidian poetry. Hereward T. Price was among the first modern critics to approach *Venus and Adonis* as a unified work of art. Writing in 1945, he argued that Shakespeare utilizes the traditional meanings associated with colors, flowers, and other natural objects to construct conflicting patterns of imagery that transform the contention between Venus and Adonis into a microcosm of the strife between the beauty and destructiveness inherent in nature. According to Price, the poem is organized around the theme of "the destruction of something exquisite by what is outrageously vile." The death of Adonis allegorically represents the death of beauty, the critic maintained, and the ensuing "black chaos" mirrors Shakespeare's own "bitter pessimism" about the forces that govern creation. Five years later, T. W. Baldwin (see Additional Bibliography) conducted an exhaustive review of the sources of, and possible influences on, *Venus and Adonis*. He assessed the pervasive impact of Ovid's writings and pointed out elements of Platonic philosophy in the poem. According to Baldwin, "Adonis is Love and Beauty, and when he dies Chaos is come again." Venus urges procreation, the critic remarked, so that Beauty and Love can survive. In 1952, Robert P. Miller also investigated Shakespeare's novel use of traditional symbolism in *Venus and Adonis*. Focusing on the courser and jennet episode, he observed there not only a witty parody of courtly rituals, but an exemplum of Renaissance moral doctrine that offers an elaborate commentary on the main action. In Miller's view, when Venus urges Adonis to follow the courser's example, she is inviting him to reenact Adam's Fall by throwing off the "healthy bridle" of reason and submitting to the "brute aspects" of human nature. In two separate studies, Rufus Putney focused on the erotic and humorous aspects of *Venus and Adonis*, delineating his view of the work as a "sensuous, sophisticated farce." Shakespeare employs a host of comic conventions in the characterization, versification, dialogue, and action of the poem, he maintained. C. S. Lewis, however, was not amused. If Venus is meant to be the alluring subject of an erotic poem, she is a "very ill-conceived" and unattractive temptress, he asserted. If, on the other hand, Shakespeare intends her to be an emblem of lust in a didactic poem, his technique is crude and unsuccessful. In 1957, Franklin M. Dickey offered another allegorical interpretation of *Venus and Adonis*, proposing that the goddess represents "Pandemia," the elemental drive to procreate. In this poem, Dickey argued, Shakespeare vividly illustrates the duality of Renaissance doctrine, which acknowledged this force as essential, but also recognized it as a "violent passion" that must be kept in check by reason. Two years later, Don Cameron Allen observed different sets of conventions operating in the poem, specifically those involving hunting. One tradition likens seduction to a chase, an ignoble "soft hunt" of timid quarry; another regards the "hard hunt" of a prey who turns and stands as proper training for great and noble men. The goddess and the youth are distinguished by these different forms of pursuit, the critic claimed: "Venus hunts Adonis; Adonis

hunts the boar. The first hunt is the soft hunt of love; the second is the hard hunt of life."

A. C. Hamilton, in a pivotal 1961 essay, analyzed Shakespeare's merging of Ovidian conventions and Platonic doctrine in the poem. This fusion, the critic claimed, results in an entirely new version of the Venus and Adonis myth. Reassigning the functions in Baldwin's equation, Hamilton argued that the youth stands for Beauty; the goddess represents Love, the protector of Beauty; and the boar symbolizes the "enemies of Beauty." According to the critic, these modifications shift the story's center from Adonis to Venus, who is developed by Shakespeare into a complex figure evoking ambivalent responses from readers.

Several critics in the 1960s focused on the relation between *Venus and Adonis* and Shakespeare's plays. J. W. Lever (see Additional Bibliography) emphasized the poem's comic and tragic elements and observed themes consonant with motifs in the dramas. Like Hamilton, both Kenneth Muir and Norman Rabkin observed complexity and "ambivalence" in *Venus and Adonis*, and both likened this to the fruitful ambiguity of Shakespeare's dramas. Muir maintained that "almost everything in the poem appears to be ambivalent," including the red and white imagery, the mixture of humorous and erotic elements, and the antithetical moral points of view. The poem thus reveals Shakespeare's "acceptance of conflicting feelings about love" and demonstrates "the essentially dramatic nature of his imagination," Muir stated. Rabkin emphasized that in *Venus and Adonis* Shakespeare "explores reality" as he does in the plays, that is, "by imitating its complexity." According to Rabkin, the poem's irresolvable conflict between sensual and spiritual interpretations of love demonstrates the self-contradiction inherent in this "central human activity" and mirrors the dramas' characteristic opposition of incompatible views. Similarly, Huntington Brown (see Additional Bibliography) detected affinities to drama in the poem's vivid characterizations and vigorous action. In addition, he claimed, the narrator of *Venus and Adonis* functions as an "ideal chorus," offering commentary and opinions but never moralizing on the action.

In the same decade, scholars also began to explore the relationship between Shakespeare's poem and numerous paintings depicting Venus and Adonis. Eugene B. Cantelupe (see Additional Bibliography) compared Shakespeare's poem with other literary and pictorial representations of the pair, noting the iconography or traditional symbolism common to all these works. Erwin Panofsky, in a study focusing on Titian (see Additional Bibliography), claimed that the painter's portrayal of the goddess and the young hunter was the source of Shakespeare's concept of a reluctant Adonis; indeed, he asserted, *Venus and Adonis* sounds "like a poetic paraphrase" of the painting.

Building on the ground work laid by scholars in the 1960s, critics in the following two decades have further explored the intricacies of Shakespeare's intellectual and creative achievement in *Venus and Adonis*. They have assessed the function of the rhetoric, examined the structure of conflict and contradiction, and brought an even wider range of Renaissance cultural and artistic traditions to bear on the poem. Writing in 1970, J. D. Jahn argued that Adonis is a coquette whose sly enticements are comparable to Venus's attempts at overt seduction. The validity of the boy's definition of love is undermined by his behavior, the critic claimed, making his position as untenable as the goddess's. In 1973, Heather Asals, like

Hamilton a dozen years earlier, examined *Venus and Adonis*'s relation to Platonic doctrine. She claimed that Venus's desire progresses from wishing to touch Adonis to appreciating the sight of him, a process that reflects the concept of a "hierarchy of the senses" (see Additional Bibliography). A year later, Lucy Gent (see Additional Bibliography) proposed that in this poem Shakespeare uses rhetorical antitheses to construct a consistent world; she further asserted that the juxtaposition of contradictions produces a paradoxical myth about the ambiguous nature of love. William E. Sheidley argued, however, that the various seemingly contradictory viewpoints comprise a "dialectic" on the imperfect nature of love in an imperfect world (see Additional Bibliography). In 1975, both David N. Beauregard and Barry Pegg (see Additional Bibliography) outlined correspondences between *Venus and Adonis* and Renaissance beliefs. Beauregard contended that the concept of the "concupiscible" and "irascible" aspects of the human soul governs the action of the poem. According to Beauregard, the first produces love, desire, and joy in Venus and hate, aversion, and sorrow in Adonis; the other, he declared, is responsible for Venus's alternating moods of despair and hope, fear and courage. Pegg delineated Shakespeare's use of the significance traditionally associated with the "elements" of fire, air, water, and earth, and with their counterparts in the human body. He asserted that Adonis is trapped between Venus, who represents "generative warmth and moisture," and the boar who represents "corruptive cold death," the two poles between which Adonis, as a human being, is trapped. Like Jahn, Coppélia Kahn focused on the character of Adonis. In her 1976 psychological study of the young hunter, she stressed his lack of a stable identity and his consequent fear that in sexual union the goddess would overwhelm and devour him. To compensate, Kahn asserted, Adonis "projects his anxiety about being devoured by Venus onto the boar, and attempts to destroy the boar so that Venus will not destroy him."

In recent years, several critics have scrutinized the poem's system of oppositions and conflicts. In 1976, Richard A. Lanham (see Additional Bibliography) discerned both an ethical opposition of sexuality and virtue and an aesthetic opposition of eloquence and spare speech. He suggested that as Venus and Adonis employ individual modes of speech and react to each other's language, the poem's rhetoric is dramatized and "made part of the story." William Keach (see Additional Bibliography) demonstrated how Shakespeare's use of antitheses in the rhetoric and imagery helps formulate an "extraordinarily dense artificial order" in *Venus and Adonis*. While this structure of contradictions is "conceptually satisfying," Keach noted, it prevents "complete conceptual clarity" and defeats attempts to determine the meaning of the work. Clark Hulse maintained, however, that by repeatedly constructing new sets of symbols that crystallize the oppositions and contradictions, Shakespeare creates an appearance of unity and cohesion in the poem. The critic likened this process to both the development of myths and the use of iconography in painting. Wayne A. Rebhorn (see Additional Bibliography) claimed that the conflicts in *Venus and Adonis* reflect Renaissance man's fear of women. He argued that the poem's presentation of Venus as maternal and Adonis as infantile, the narrator's ambivalence toward the goddess, and the inversion of customary male-female roles all illuminate "the fear that the temptress's mantrap was nothing less than the mother's smothery embrace." In 1980, Lennet J. Daigle (see Additional Bibliography) addressed the contrarieties of *Venus and Adonis* by further examining the poem's relation to Renais-

sance traditions and beliefs. He detected two value systems at work in the poem: one "a system of human ethics" that condemns lust and praises abstinence, the other a "divinely established order of nature" that stresses the need for procreation and censures "fruitless chastity." Three years later, John Doebler, like Gent, Lanham, and Keach, focused on the rhetoric of *Venus and Adonis*. He underscored Shakespeare's subtle variations of theme and tone from comic to sensual to pathetic. By these means, Doebler argued, the poet creates "a constantly shifting drama of the mind," with complex, multifaceted characters and situations that defy unified interpretations. Nancy Lindheim similarly emphasized *Venus and Adonis*'s "shifts in tone, perspective, and sympathy," judging the work a technical tour de force in which Shakespeare successfully presents intricate characterizations and a profound concept of love within the confines of Ovidian narrative. Lindheim maintained that the multiple perspectives keep the work from becoming an unqualified endorsement of Adonis's simplistic opposition of love and lust.

In the past thirty years critics have rescued *Venus and Adonis* from centuries of disparagement and restored a measure of its early acclaim. Scholars now esteem Shakespeare's intricate interweaving of Renaissance traditions, artistic conventions, philosophy, and myth in a witty and sensuous work that is shaped but not limited by its many elements. Rather than seeing the paradoxes and contradictions within the poem as inadvertent results of overelaboration or Shakespeare's imperfect control of his medium, recent scholars have admired the carefully balanced oppositions and polarities in the poem's themes, imagery, and rhetoric. *Venus and Adonis*, they maintain, provides a detailed analysis of the complexities of love and morality. Many critics would likely agree with Coleridge, who observed more than a century and a half ago that "the power of reducing multitude into unity" was among the many signs of Shakespeare's genius evident in *Venus and Adonis*.

WILLIAM SHAKESPEARE   (essay date 1593)

[*In his dedication of* Venus and Adonis *to the Earl of Southampton, Shakespeare characterizes the work as "the first heire of my invention," leading some critics to conclude that the poem is his earliest artistic endeavor. Others, however, insist that he was speaking figuratively about this, his first published work, and they have maintained that he composed several plays prior to the poem. Scholars have generally concurred that the self-effacing tone and the reference to "unpolisht lines," reflect conventional modesty rather than Shakespeare's true assessment of* Venus and Adonis.]

TO THE RIGHT HONORABLE
Henrie VVriothesley, Earle of Southampton,
and Baron of Titchfield.

Right Honourable, I know not how I shall offend in dedicating my vnpolisht lines to your Lordship, nor how the world vvill censure mee for choosing so strong a proppe to support so vveake a burthen, onelye if your Honour seeme but pleased, I account my selfe highly praised, and vowe to take aduantage of all idle houres, till I haue honoured you vvith some grauer labour. But if the first heire of my inuention proue deformed, I shall be sorie it had so noble a god-father: and neuer after eare so barren a land, for feare it yeeld me still so bad a haruest, I leaue it to your Honourable suruey, and your Honour to your hearts content, vvhich I wish may alvvaies ansvvere your ovvne vvish, and the vvorlds hope full expectation.

Your Honors in all dutie,

William Shakespeare.

> *William Shakespeare, in a dedication to Henrie Wriothesley in 1593, in* Shakespeares Venus and Adonis, *1593. Reprint by Oxford at the Clarendon Press, 1905, p. 1.*

JOHN WEEVER   (poem date 1595)

[*The following poem was first published in Weever's* Epigrammes *(1599), but it is commonly believed to have been written in 1595. It is perhaps one of the earliest surviving references to Shakespeare. Weever here praises "honie-tong'd Shakespeare" for his sublime creation of Venus, Adonis, and other poetic "issue."*]

> Honie-tong'd *Shakespeare* when I saw thine issue
> I swore *Apollo* got them and none other,
> Their rosie-tainted features cloth'd in tissue,
> Some heauen born goddesse said to be their moth-
>   er:
> Rose-checkt *Adonis* with his amber tresses,
> Faire fire-hot *Venus* charming him to loue her,
> Chaste *Lucretia* virgine-like her dresses,
> Prowd lust-stung *Tarquine* seeking still to proue
>   her:
> *Romea Richard;* more whose names I know not,
> Their sugred tongues, and power attractiue beuty
> Say they are Saints althogh that Sts they shew not
> For thousands vowes to them subiectiue dutie:
> They burn in loue thy childrē *Shakespear* het them,
> Go, wo thy Muse more Nymphish brood beget
>   them.

> *John Weever, "Ad Gulielmum Shakespeare," in his* Epigrammes in the Oldest Cut and Newest Fashion, *edited by R. B. McKerrow, 1911. Reprint by Shakespeare Head Press, 1922, p. 75.*

FRANCIS MERES   (essay date 1598)

[*Meres was an English schoolmaster, critic, and clergyman. The following excerpt is taken from his* Palladis Tamia, Wit's Treasury *(1598), a compendium of observations and commentary on a wide range of topics that has played a valuable role in determining the dates of several of Shakespeare's plays and poems. In the section entitled "A Comparative discourse on our English Poets with the Greeke, Latine, and Italian Poets," Meres compares Shakespeare's work favorably with that of Ovid, Plautus, and Seneca, extolling* Venus and Adonis *and other poems of "hony-tongued Shakespeare," who, in his opinion, embodies Ovid's spirit.*]

As the soule of *Euphorbus* was thought to liue in *Pythagoras:* so the sweete wittie soule of *Ovid* liues in mellifluous & hony-tongued *Shakespeare*, witnes his *Venus* and *Adonis*, his *Lucrece*, his sugred Sonnets among his priuate friends, &c. (pp. 281-82)

> *Francis Meres, "A Comparative Discourse of Our English Poets with the Greeke, Latine, and Italian Poets," in his* Palladis Tamia: Wits Treasury, *1598. Reprint by Garland Publishing, Inc., 1973, pp. 279-87.*

RICHARD BARNFIELD   (poem date 1598)

[*The excerpt below is taken from Barnfield's "A Remembrance of some English Poets," first published in 1598 in his* Poems: In divers humors. *This verse, which also praises the work of Spenser, Daniel, and Drayton, concludes with the following apostrophe to Shakespeare, lauding his* Venus and Adonis *and* The Rape of Lucrece.]

> *Shakespeare* thou, whose hony-flowing Vaine,
> (Pleasing the World) thy Praises doth obtaine.
> Whose *Venus*, and whose *Lucrece* (sweete, and
>   chaste)
> Thy Name in fames immortall Booke haue plac't.
>   Liue euer you, at least in Fame liue euer:
>   Well may the Bodye dye, but Fame dies
>   neuer.
>
>   (p. 120)

> *Richard Barnfield, "A Remembrance of Some English Poets," in his* Poems: 1594-1598, *edited by Edward Arber, The English Scholar's Library, 1882, pp. 119-20.*

GABRIEL HARVEY   (essay date 1598?)

[*A friend of Edmund Spenser, Harvey was an English poet, critic, and satirist, as well as a Latin scholar who promoted the use of classical meters in English poetry. He is perhaps best known for his bitter literary fued with Robert Green and Thomas Nashe, involving a prolonged exchange of acrimonious pamphlets. Harvey's marginalia and letters reveal a wide variety of interests and are prized by scholars for the glimpses they provide of his contemporaries, including Sidney and Shakespeare. The brief but often cited comment reprinted below was inscribed by Harvey in his copy of Speght's* Chaucer, *which was printed in 1598. This note reflects the common sixteenth-century view of* Venus and Adonis *as a pleasant but inconsequential work.*]

The younger sort takes much delight in Shakespeares *Venus, & Adonis:* but his *Lucrece*, & his tragedie of *Hamlet, Prince of Denmarke*, haue it in them, to please the wiser sort. (p. 232)

> *Gabriel Harvey, "Appendix II (Marginalia in Speght's 'Chaucer'}," in his* Gabriel Harvey's Marginalia, *edited by G. C. Moore Smith, Shakespeare Head Press, 1913, pp. 225-34.*

ANONYMOUS   (play date 1599-1600)

[*The following excerpt is drawn from The First Part of* The Return from Parnassus, *an anonymous play written by students at Cambridge and first performed during the Christmas season, 1599-1600. In earlier, unexcerpted portions of this scene, the foppish Gullio, who has commissioned the student Ingenioso to compose amorous verses in the styles of various contemporary writers, rejects those written in the manner of Chaucer and Spenser. Now Gullio—who betrays his ignorance by substituting "cattle" for "lion" in the proverb "a lion is known by his claws"—asks to hear some in Shakespeare's style. Ingenioso's comic imitation of* Venus and Adonis *and Gullio's rapturous response have often been cited by critics as evidence of the poem's early popularity and its reputation for frivolous sensuality.*]

> *Gullio*   . . . Let mee heare Mr Shakspears
>   veyne.
> *Ingenioso*   Faire Venus, queene of beutie and of
>   love,
>   Thy red doth stayne the blushinge of the morne,

Thy red doth stayne the blushinge of the morne,
Thy snowie neck shameth the milke white doue,
Thy presence doth this naked worlde adorne;
Gazinge on thee all other nymphes I scorne.
When ere thou dyest slowe shine that Satterday,
Beutie and grace muste sleepe with thee for aye.
Gullio   Noe more, I am one that can iudge ac-
cordinge to the proverbe *bouem ex unguibus*. Ey
marry Sr, these haue some life in them: let this duncified worlde esteeme of Spēcer and Chaucer, Ile
worshipp sweet Mr Shakspeare, and to honoure
him will lay his *Venus and Adonis* vnder my pillowe, as wee reade of one (I do not well remember
his name, but I am sure he was a kinge) slept with
Homer vnder his beds heade.

(pp. 192-93)

*"The First Part of 'The Return from Parnassus',"
in* The Three Parnassus Plays (1598-1601), *edited
by J. B. Leishman, Ivor Nicholson & Watson Ltd.,
1949, pp. 133-214.*

ANONYMOUS   (play date 1601-02)

[*The following excerpt is taken from* The Second Part of The
Return from Parnassus, *an anonymous play written by students at Cambridge University and first performed during the
Christmas season, 1601-02. In an unexcerpted part of this
scene, the student Ingenioso asks his friend Judicio to "censure" various contemporary writers. Here, in his critique of
Shakespeare, Judicio admires the beauty of the verse in* Venus
and Adonis *but laments the triviality of the subject matter.*]

Ingenioso   . . . [What's thy iudgement of] *William Shakespeare.*
Iudicio   Who loues not *Adons* loue or *Lucrece*
rape? His sweeter verse contaynes hart robbing
lines. Could but a grauer subiect him content,
Without loues foolish lazy languishment.

(p. 244)

*"The Second Part of 'The Return from Parnassus',"
in* The Three Parnassus Plays (1598-1601), *edited
by J. B. Leishman, Ivor Nicholson & Watson Ltd.,
1949, pp. 215-367.*

JOHN DAVIES   (poem date 1610-11)

[*The poem from which the following excerpt is drawn,* Papers
Complaint, compild in ruthfull Rimes against the Paper-
spoylers of these Times, *was originally published in 1610-11
as part of Davies's* The Scourge of Folly, *a collection of satirical and miscellaneous verses. He here attacks* Venus and Adonis *as a lewd poem that incites lustful thoughts.*]

What heart so hard that splits not when it heares
What ruthlesse Martyrdome my Body beares
By rude *Barbarians* of these later Times,
Blotting my spotlesse Brest with *Prose* and *Rimes*
That *Impudence*, itselfe, would blush to beare;
It is such shamelesse Stuffe and irkesome
    Geare? . . .

One raies me with course Rimes, and Chips them
    call,
Offals of wit, a fire burne them all. . . .

Another (ah Lord helpe) mee vilifies
With Art of Loue, and how to subtilize,
Making lewd *Venus*, with eternall Lines,
To tye *Adonis* to her loues designes:

Fine wit is shew'n therein: but finer twere
If not attired in such bawdy Geare.
But be it as it will: the coyest Dames,
In priuate read it for their Closset-games:
For, sooth to say, the Lines so draw them on,
To the venerian speculation,
That will they, nill they (if of flesh they bee)
They will thinke of it, sith *loose* Thought is free.

(p. 75)

John Davies, " 'The Scourge of Folly'," in his The
Complete Works of John Davies of Hereford, Vol.
II, *edited by Rev. Alexander B. Grosart, 1878. Reprint by Georg Olms Verlagsbuchhandlung, 1968,
pp. 1-82.*

RICHARD BRATHWAIT   (essay date 1631)

[*The following excerpt originally appeared in Brathwait's* The
English Gentlewoman, *a 1631 treatise on the proper dress,
conduct, and entertainments of a woman of good breeding. He
condemns* Venus and Adonis, *charging it with having a pernicious influence on female readers.*]

Books treating of light subiects, are Nurseries of wanton-
nesse: they instruct the loose Reader to become naught;
whereas before, touching naughtinesse, he knew
naught. . . . *Venus* and *Adonis* are vnfitting Conforts for a
Ladies bosome. Remoue them timely from you, if they euer
had entertainment by you, lest, like the *Snake* in the fable,
they annoy you.

Richard Brathwait, in an extract in The Shakspere
Allusion-Book: A Collection of Allusions to Shak-
spere from 1591 to 1700, Vol. I, *edited by John
Munro, revised edition, 1932. Reprint by Books for
Libraries Press, 1970; distributed by Arno Press,
Inc., p. 354.*

GEORGE STEEVENS   (essay date 1780)

[*Steevens was an English scholar who collaborated with Samuel Johnson on a ten-volume edition of Shakespeare's dramatic
works in 1773. The subsequent revision of this collection, along
with Steevens's own edition of 1793, formed the textual basis
for the first two Variorum editions of Shakespeare's plays. The
following excerpt is taken from* Supplement to the Edition of
Shakespeare's Plays published in 1778 by Samuel Johnson
and George Steevens (1780), *a two-volume work in which the
narrative poems are reprinted along with commentary on them
and on Shakespeare's dramatic works. In his observations on*
Venus and Adonis, *Steevens considers the poem's moral intent
poorly delineated, inasmuch as the youth's "sluggish coldness"
is as offensive as the goddess's "impetuous forwardness." Adonis's rejection of Venus's enticements is not based on any clear
moral principles, he asserts, but rather on the boy's simple preference for the gratifications of hunting to those of love. Steevens
wryly notes that readers will scarcely respect Adonis's judgement in making this choice. The critic also faults the style of
the verse as cold and forced, and he censures Shakespeare for
having "spun out" the tale to an unnecessary length.*]

[*Venus and Adonis*] is received as one of Shakspere's undisputed performances,—a circumstance which recommends it
to the notice it might otherwise have escaped.

There are some excellencies which are less graceful than even
their opposite defects; there are some virtues, which being
merely constitutional, are entitled to very small degrees of

praise. Our poet might design his Adonis to engage our esteem, and yet the sluggish coldness of his disposition is as offensive as the impetuous forwardness of his wanton mistress.
To exhibit a young man insensible to the caresses of transcendent beauty, is to describe a being too rarely seen to be acknowledged as a natural character, and when seen, of too little value to deserve such toil of representation. No elogiums
are due to Shakspeare's hero on the score of mental chastity,
for he does not pretend to have subdued his desires to his
moral obligations. He strives indeed, with Platonick absurdity, to draw that line which was never drawn, to make that
distinction which never can be made, to separate the purer
from the grosser part of love, assigning limits, and ascribing
bounds to each, and calling them by different names; but if
we take his own word, he will be found at last only to prefer
one gratification to another, the sports of the field to the enjoyment of immortal charms. The reader will easily confess
that no great respect is due to the judgment of such a would-
be Hercules, with such a choice before him.—In short, the
story of Joseph and the wife of Potiphar [in Genesis, chapter
39] is the more interesting of the two; for the passions of the
former are repressed by conscious rectitude of mind, and obe-
dience to the highest law. The present narrative only includes
the disappointment of an eager female, and the death of an
unsusceptible boy. The deity, from her language, should seem
to have been educated in the school of Messalina; the youth,
from his backwardness, might be suspected of having felt the
discipline of a Turkish seraglio.

It is not indeed very clear whether Shakspeare meant on this
occasion . . . to recommend continence as a virtue, or to try
his hand . . . on a licentious canvas. If our poet had any
moral design in view, he has been unfortunate in his conduct
of it. The shield which he lifts in defence of chastity, is
wrought with such meretricious imagery as cannot fail to
counteract a moral purpose.—Shakspeare, however, was no
unskilful mythologist, and must have known that Adonis was
the offspring of Cynaras and Myrrha. His judgment therefore
would have prevented him from raising an example of continence out of the produce of an incestuous bed. . . .

If we enquire into the poetical merit of this performance, it
will do no honour to the reputation of its author. The great
excellence of Shakspeare is to be sought in dramatick dialogue, expressing his intimate acquaintance with every passion that sooths or ravages, exalts or debases the human
mind. Dialogue is a form of composition which has been
known to quicken even the genius of those who in mere uninterrupted narrative have sunk to a level with the multitude
of common writers. The smaller pieces of Otway and Rowe
have added nothing to their fame.

Let it be remembered too, that a contemporary author, Dr.
Gabriel Harvey, points out the *Venus and Adonis* as a favourite only with *the young,* while *graver* readers bestowed their
attention on the *Rape of Lucrece* [see excerpt above, 1598].
Here I cannot help observing that the poetry of the Roman
legend is no jot superior to that of the mythological story. A
tale which Ovid has completely and affectingly told in about
one hundred and forty verses, our author has coldly and imperfectly spun out into near two thousand. The attention
therefore of these *graver* personages must have been engaged
by the moral tendency of the piece, rather than by the force
of style in which it is related.

George Steevens, " 'Venus and Adonis'," *in* Supplement to the Edition of Shakspeare's Plays Pub-

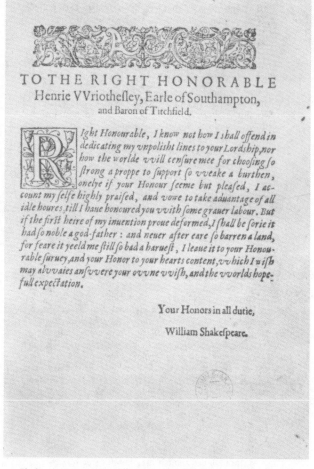

Shakespeare's dedication of Venus and Adonis *to the Earl of Southampton.*

lished in 1788, Vol. I *by Samuel Johnson and George Steevens, edited by E. Malone; C. Bathurst and others, 1780.*

EDMOND MALONE   (essay date 1790)

[*An eighteenth-century Irish literary scholar and editor, Malone was the first critic to establish a chronology of Shakespeare's plays. He was also the first scholar to prepare a critical
edition of Shakespeare's sonnets and the first to write a comprehensive history of the English stage based on extensive research
into original sources. As the major Shakespearean editor of the
eighteenth century, Malone collaborated with George Steevens
on Steevens's second and third editions of Shakespeare's plays
and issued his own edition in 1790. In the following excerpt,
Malone responds to Steevens's negative appraisal of* Venus and
Adonis *(see excerpt above, 1780). He emphasizes the great popularity of Shakespeare's narrative poems in his lifetime and
contends that they are "superior to any pieces of the same
kind" produced by Shakespeare's contemporaries. Regarding
the earlier critic's objection that the moral design of this poem
is obscure, Malone maintains that in his plays as well as his
poems, Shakespeare generally adheres to no fixed moral principles.* Venus and Adonis *is typically Shakespearean, he claims,
in its intent to entertain rather than instruct. Although Malone
agrees with Steevens about the work's wearisome length, he
praises the imagery and style of the verse and observes that it*

*was the fashion of Shakespeare's day to compose "a great num-
ber of verses on a very slight subject."*]

[*Venus and Adonis*] is frequently alluded to by our authour's
contemporaries. "As the soul of Euphorbus (says Meres in
his *Wit's Treasury*, 1598 [see excerpt above]) was thought to
live in Pythagoras, so the sweet, witty soul of Ovid lives in
mellifluous and honey-tongued Shakspeare. Witness his
Venus and Adonis, his *Lucrece*," &c.—In the early part of
Shakspeare's life, his poems seem to have gained him more
reputation than his plays;—at least they are oftener mentioned, or alluded to. Thus the authour of an old comedy
called *The Return from Paranassus*, written about the year
1602 [see excerpt above, 1601-02], in his review of the poets
of the time, says not a word of his dramatick compositions,
but allots him his portion of fame solely on account of the
poems that he had produced. When the name of William
Shakspeare is read, one of the characters pronounces this elo-
gium:

> Who loves Adonis' love, or Lucrece' rape?
> His sweeter verse contains heart-robbing life;
> Could but a graver subject him content,
> Without love's foolish lazy languishment.

This subject was probably suggested to Shakspeare either by
Spenser's description of the hangings in the *Lady of Delight's*
Castle, [in *The Faerie Queene*] . . . , or by a short piece entitled *The Sheepheard's Song of Venus and Adonis*, subscribed
with the letters H. C. (probably Henry Constable,) which, I
believe, was written before Shakspeare's poem; though I have
never seen any earlier copy of it than that which we find in
England's Helicon, 1600. He had also without doubt read the
account of Venus and Adonis in the tenth book of Ovid's
Metamorphoses, translated by Golding, 1567, though he has
chosen to deviate from the classical story, which Ovid and
Spenser had set before him, following probably the model
presented to him by the english poem just mentioned. (p. 67)

This first essay of Shakspeare's Muse does not appear to me
by any means so void of poetical merit as it has been represented [see excerpt above by George Steevens, 1780]. In what
high estimation it was held in our authour's life-time, may be
collected from what has been already observed. . . . (p. 71)

Let us, however, view [*Venus and Adonis* and *The Rape of
Lucrece*], uninfluenced by any authority.—To form a right
judgment of any work, we should always take into our consideration the means by which it was executed, and the contemporary performances of others. The smaller pieces of
Otway and Rowe add nothing to the reputation which they
have acquired by their dramatick works, because preceding
writers had already produced happier compositions; and because there were many poets, during the period in which
Rowe and Otway exhibited their plays, who produced better
poetry, not of the dramatick kind, than theirs: but, if we except Spenser, what poet of Shakspeare's age produced poems
of equal, or nearly equal, excellence to those before us? Did
Turberville? Did Golding? Did Phaer? Did Drant? Did
Googe? Did Churchyard? Did Fleming? Did Fraunce? Did
Whetstone? Did Gascoigne? Did Sidney? Did Marlowe,
Nashe, Kyd, Harrington, Lilly, Peele, Greene, Watson, Breton, Chapman, Daniel, Drayton, Middleton or Jonson? Sackville's *Induction* is the only small piece of that age, that I recollect, which can stand in competition with them. If Marlowe
had lived to finish his *Hero and Leander*, of which he wrote
little more than the first two Sestiads, he too perhaps might
have contested the palm with Shakspeare.

Concerning the length of these pieces, which is, I think, justly
objected to, I shall at present only observe, that it was the
fashion of the day to write a great number of verses on a very
slight subject, and our poet in this as in many other instances
adapted himself to the taste of his own age.

It appears to me in the highest degree improbable that Shakspeare had any *moral view* in writing this poem; Shakspeare,
who, (as Dr. Johnson has justly observed [in the preface to
his 1765 edition of Shakespeare's plays],) generally "sacrifices virtue to convenience, and is so much more careful to
please than to instruct, that he seems to write without any
moral purpose;"—who "carries his persons indifferently
through right and wrong, and at the close dismisses them
without further care, and leaves their examples to operate by
chance." As little probable is it, in my apprehension, that he
departed on any settled principles from the mythological
story of Venus and Adonis. As well might we suppose, that
in the construction of his plays he deliberately deviated from
the rules of Aristotle, (of which after the publication of Sir
Philip Sidney's Treatise he could not be ignorant,) with a
view to produce a more animated and noble exhibition than
Aristotle or his followers ever knew. His method of proceeding was, I apprehend, exactly similar in both cases; and he no
more deviated from the classical representation on any
formed and digested plan, in the one case, than he neglected
the unities in the other. He merely (as I conceive,) in the present instance, as in many others, followed the story as he
found it already treated by preceding English writers. . . .
(pp. 72-3)

[In examining *Venus and Adonis* and *The Rape of Lucrece*]
we should do Shakspeare injustice, were we to try them by
a comparison with more modern and polished productions,
or with our present idea of poetical excellence.

It has been observed, that few authours rise much above the
age in which they live. If their performances reach the standard of perfection established in their own time, or surpass
somewhat the productions of their contemporaries, they seldom aim further; for if their readers are satisfied, it is not
probable that they should be discontented. The poems of
Venus and Adonis, and *The Rape of Lucrece*, whatever opinion may be now entertained of them, were certainly much admired in Shakspeare's life-time. In thirteen years after their
first appearance, six impressions of each of them were printed, while in nearly the same period his *Romeo and Juliet* (one
of his most popular plays) passed only twice through the
press. They appear to me superior to any pieces of the same
kind produced by Daniel or Drayton, the most celebrated
writers in this species of narrative poetry that were then
known. (p. 186)

If it should be asked, how comes it to pass that Shakspeare
in his dramatick productions also, did not content himself
with only doing as well as those play-wrights who had gone
before him, or somewhat surpassing them; how it happened,
that whilst his contemporaries on the stage crept in the most
groveling and contemptible prose, or stalked in ridiculous
and bombastick blank verse, he has penetrated the inmost recesses of the human mind, and, not contented with ranging
through the wide field of nature, has with equal boldness and
felicity often expatiated *extra flammantia moenia mundi* [be-
yond the fiery walls of the world (Lucretius, *De Rerum Natura*)], the answer, I believe, must be, that his disposition was
more inclined to the drama than to the other kinds of poetry;
that his genius for the one appears to have been almost a gift

from heaven, his abilities for the other, of a less splendid and transcendent kind, and approaching nearer to those of other mortals.

Of these two poems *Venus and Adonis* appears to me entitled to superior praise. Their great defect is, the wearisome circumlocution with which the tale in each of them is told, particularly in [*Lucrece*]. When the reader thinks himself almost at his journey's end, he is led through many an intricate path, and after travelling for some hours, finds his inn at a distance: nor are his wanderings always repaid, or his labour alleviated, by the fertility of the country through which he passes; by grotesqueness of scenery or variety of prospect.

Let us, however, never forget the state of poetry when these pieces appeared; and after perusing the productions of the contemporary and preceding writers, Shakspeare will have little to fear from the unprejudiced decision of his judges. . . . [We can see] almost every stanza of these poems fraught with images and expressions that occur also in his plays. To the liquid lapse of his numbers, in his *Venus and Adonis*, his *Lucrece*, his *Sonnets*, his *Lovers Complaint*, and in all the *songs* which are introduced in his dramas, I wish particularly to call the attention of the reader. In this respect he leaves all his contemporaries many paces behind him.— Even the length of his two principal poems will be pardoned, when the practice of his age is adverted to. (p. 187)

Edmond Malone, "'Venus and Adonis'" and "'The Rape of Lucrece'," in The Plays and Poems of William Shakspeare, Vol. X, *edited by Edmond Malone, 1790. Reprint by AMS Press, 1968, pp. 1-78, 79-188.*

S[AMUEL] T[AYLOR] COLERIDGE   (essay date 1817)

[*Coleridge's lectures and writings on Shakespeare constitute a major chapter in the history of English Shakespearean criticism. As an advocate for the critical ideas of the German Romantics and as an original interpreter of Shakespeare in the new spirit of Romanticism, Coleridge played a strategic role in overthrowing the last vestiges of the Neoclassical approach to Shakespeare and in establishing the modern view of the dramatist as a conscious artist and masterful portrayer of human character. Coleridge was one of the few nineteenth-century critics who treated* Venus and Adonis *as a serious work of art rather than merely a youthful display of rhetorical pyrotechnics. In his notes and lectures he often cited passages from this poem to illustrate various aspects of Shakespeare's poetic genius. The following excerpt from Coleridge's* Biographia Literaria *comprises his most sustained examination of* Venus and Adonis *and continues to be regarded as one of the seminal studies of the poem. The critic lauds Shakespeare's ability to infuse the poem with intense passion while at the same time remaining aloof, meticulously detailing the images and characters. Significantly, Coleridge observed close similarities between the detached mode of presentation in* Venus and Adonis *and Shakespeare's dramatic art, claiming that here, as in his plays, "you seem to be told nothing, but to see and hear everything."*]

I have endeavoured to discover what the qualities in a poem are, which may be deemed promises and specific symptoms of poetic power, as distinguished from general talent determined to poetic composition by accidental motives, by an act of the will, rather than by the inspiration of a genial and productive nature. In this investigation, I could not, I thought, do better, than keep before me the earliest work of the greatest genius, that perhaps human nature has yet produced, our *myriad-minded* Shakespeare. I mean the "Venus and Ado-

nis," and the "Lucrece"; works which give at once strong promises of the strength, and yet obvious proofs of the immaturity, of his genius. From these I abstracted the following marks, as characteristics of original poetic genius in general.

In the "Venus and Adonis," the first and most obvious excellence is the perfect sweetness of the versification; its adaptation to the subject; and the power displayed in varying the march of the words without passing into a loftier and more majestic rhythm than was demanded by the thoughts, or permitted by the propriety of preserving a sense of melody predominant. The delight in richness and sweetness of sound, even to a faulty excess, if it be evidently original, and not the result of an easily imitable mechanism, I regard as a highly favourable promise in the compositions of a young man. "The man that hath not music in his soul" [*The Merchant of Venice*, V. i. 83] can indeed never be a genuine poet. Imagery (even taken from nature, much more when transplanted from books, as travels, voyages, and works of natural history); affecting incidents; just thoughts; interesting personal or domestic feelings; and with these the art of their combination or intertexture in the form of a poem; may all by incessant effort be acquired as a trade, by a man of talents and much reading, who . . . has mistaken an intense desire of poetic reputation for a natural poetic genius; the love of the arbitrary end for a possession of the peculiar means. But the sense of musical delight, with the power of producing it, is a gift of imagination; and this together with the power of reducing multitude into unity of effect, and modifying a series of thoughts by some one predominant thought or feeling, may be cultivated and improved, but can never be learned. It is in these that "poeta nascitur non fit" [a poet is born, not made].

A second promise of genius is the choice of subjects very remote from the private interests and circumstances of the writer himself. At least I have found, that where the subject is taken immediately from the author's personal sensations and experiences, the excellence of a particular poem is but an equivocal mark, and often a fallacious pledge, of genuine poetic power. We may perhaps remember the tale of the statuary, who had acquired considerable reputation for the legs of his goddesses, though the rest of the statue accorded but indifferently with ideal beauty; till his wife, elated by her husband's praises, modestly acknowledged that she herself had been his constant model. In the "Venus and Adonis" this proof of poetic power exists even to excess. It is throughout as if a superior spirit more intuitive, more intimately conscious, even than the characters themselves, not only of every outward look and act, but of the flux and reflux of the mind in all its subtlest thoughts and feelings, were placing the whole before our view; himself meanwhile unparticipating in the passions, and actuated only by that pleasurable excitement, which had resulted from the energetic fervor of his own spirit in so vividly exhibiting, what it had so accurately and profoundly contemplated. I think, I should have conjectured from these poems, that even then the great instinct, which impelled the poet to the drama, was secretly working in him, prompting him by a series and never broken chain of imagery, always vivid and, because unbroken, often minute; by the highest effort of the picturesque in words, of which words are capable, higher perhaps than was ever realized by any other poet, even Dante not excepted; to provide a substitute for that visual language, that constant intervention and running comment by tone, look and gesture, which in his dramatic works he was entitled to expect from the players. His "Venus and Adonis" seem at once the characters themselves, and the whole representation of those characters by the most consummate actors. You seem to be told nothing, but to see and hear everything. Hence it is, that from the perpetual activity of attention required on the part of the reader; from the rapid flow, the quick change, and the playful nature of the thoughts and images; and above all from the alienation, and, if I may hazard such an expression, the utter *aloofness* of the poet's own feelings, from those of which he is at once the painter and the analyst; that though the very subject cannot but detract from the pleasure of a delicate mind, yet never was poem less dangerous on a moral account. Instead of doing as Ariosto, and as, still more offensively, Wieland has done, instead of degrading and deforming passion into appetite, the trials of love into the struggles of concupiscence; Shakespeare has here represented the animal impulse itself, so as to preclude all sympathy with it, by dissipating the reader's notice among the thousand outward images, and now beautiful, now fanciful circumstances, which form its dresses and its scenery; or by diverting our attention from the main subject by those frequent witty or profound reflections, which the poet's ever active mind has deduced from, or connected with, the imagery and the incidents. The reader is forced into too much action to sympathize with the merely passive of our nature. As little can a mind thus roused and awakened be brooded on by mean and indistinct emotion, as the low, lazy mist can creep upon the surface of a lake, while a strong gale is driving it onward in waves and billows.

It has been before observed that images, however beautiful, though faithfully copied from nature, and as accurately represented in words, do not of themselves characterize the poet. They become proofs of original genius only as far as they are modified by a predominant passion; or by associated thoughts or images awakened by that passion; or when they have the effect of reducing multitude to unity, or succession to an instant; or lastly, when a human and intellectual life is transferred to them from the poet's own spirit. . . . (pp. 13-16)

[In this regard] Shakespeare even in his earliest, as in his latest, works surpasses all other poets. It is by this, that he still gives a dignity and a passion to the objects which he presents. Unaided by any previous excitement, they burst upon us at once in life and in power. (p. 17)

As of higher worth, so doubtless still more characteristic of poetic genius does the imagery become, when it moulds and colors itself to the circumstances, passion, or character, present and foremost in the mind. (p. 18)

Scarcely less sure, or if a less valuable, not less indispensable mark . . . will the imagery supply, when, with more than the power of the painter, the poet gives us the liveliest image of succession with the feeling of simultaneousness!

> With this, he breaketh from the sweet embrace
> Of those fair arms, that held him to her heart,
> And homeward through the dark lawns runs
>   apace: . . .
> *Look! how a bright star shooteth from the sky,*
> *So glides he in the night from Venus' eye*
>   [ll. 811-13, 815-16]

The last character I shall mention, which would prove indeed but little, except as taken conjointly with the former; yet without which the former could scarce exist in a high degree, and (even if this were possible) would give promises only of transitory flashes and a meteoric power; is DEPTH, and ENERGY of THOUGHT. No man was ever yet a great poet, without

being at the same time a profound philosopher. For poetry is the blossom and the fragrancy of all human knowledge, human thoughts, human passions, emotions, language. In Shakespeare's *poems* the creative power and the intellectual energy wrestle as in a war embrace. Each in its excess of strength seems to threaten the extinction of the other. At length in the DRAMA they were reconciled, and fought each with its shield before the breast of the other. Or like two rapid streams, that, at their first meeting within narrow and rocky banks, mutually strive to repel each other and intermix reluctantly and in tumult; but soon finding a wider channel and more yielding shores blend, and dilate, and flow on in one current and with one voice. The "Venus and Adonis" did not perhaps allow the display of the deeper passions. But the story of Lucretia seems to favor and even demand their intensest workings. And yet we find in *Shakespeare's* management of the tale neither pathos, nor any other *dramatic* quality. There is the same minute and faithful imagery as in the former poem, in the same vivid colors, inspirited by the same impetuous vigor of thought, and diverging and contracting with the same activity of the assimilative and of the modifying faculties; and with a yet larger display, a yet wider range of knowledge and reflection; and lastly, with the same perfect dominion, often *domination,* over the whole world of language. What then shall we say? even this; that Shakespeare, no mere child of nature; no automaton of genius; no passive vehicle of inspiration possessed by the spirit, not possessing it; first studied patiently, meditated deeply, understood minutely, till knowledge, become habitual and intuitive, wedded itself to his habitual feelings, and at length gave birth to that stupendous power, by which he stands alone, with no equal or second in his own class; to that power which seated him on one of the two glory-smitten summits of the poetic mountain, with Milton as his compeer, not rival. While the former darts himself forth, and passes into all the forms of human character and passion, the one Proteus of the fire and the flood; the other attracts all forms and things to himself, into the unity of his own IDEAL. All things and modes of action shape themselves anew in the being of MILTON; while SHAKESPEARE becomes all things, yet for ever remaining himself. (pp. 18-20)

S [amuel] T [aylor] Coleridge, "Chapter XV," in his Biographia Literaria, Vol. II., edited by J. Shawcross, Oxford at the Clarendon Press, 1907, pp. 13-20.

WILLIAM HAZLITT   (essay date 1817)

[*Hazlitt is considered a leading Shakespearean critic of the English Romantic movement. A prolific essayist and commentator on a wide range of subjects, Hazlitt remarked in the preface to his* Characters of Shakespear's Plays, *first published in 1817, that he was inspired by the German critic August Wilhelm Schlegel and was determined to supplant what he considered the pernicious influence of Samuel Johnson's Shakespearean criticism. Hazlitt's commentary is typically Romantic in its emphasis on character studies. In the following excerpt, he describes* Venus and Adonis *and* The Rape of Lucrece *as "a couple of ice-houses": hard, glittering, and cold. Contrasting these works with Shakespeare's drama, Hazlitt contends that the forced language, labored thought, and incongruous imagery of these poems indicate that the author is more concerned with demonstrating his mastery of the "technicalities of art" than with the development of his subject and characters.*]

Our idolatry of Shakespear (not to say our admiration) ceases with his plays. In his other productions, he was a mere author, though not a common author. It was only by representing others, that he became himself. He could go out of himself, and express the soul of Cleopatra; but in his own person, he appeared to be always waiting for the prompter's cue. In expressing the thoughts of others, he seemed inspired; in expressing his own, he was a mechanic. The licence of an assumed character was necessary to restore his genius to the privileges of nature, and to give him courage to break through the tyranny of fashion, the trammels of custom. In his plays, he was "as broad and casing as the general air": in his poems, on the contrary, he appears to be "cooped and cabined in" [*Macbeth,* III. iv. 22-3] by all the technicalities of art, by all the petty intricacies of thought and language, which poetry had learned from the controversial jargon of the schools, where words had been made a substitute for things. There was, if we mistake not, something of modesty, and a painful sense of personal propriety at the bottom of this. Shakespear's imagination, by identifying itself with the strongest characters in the most trying circumstances, grappled at once with nature, and trampled the littleness of art under his feet: the rapid changes of situation, the wide range of the universe, gave him life and spirit, and afforded full scope to his genius; but returned into his closet again, and having assumed the badge of his profession, he could only labour in his vocation, and conform himself to existing models. The thoughts, the passions, the words which the poet's pen, "glancing from heaven to earth, from earth to heaven" [*A Midsummer Night's Dream,* V. i.13], lent to others, shook off the fetters of pedantry and affectation; while his own thoughts and feelings, standing by themselves, were seized upon as lawful prey, and tortured to death according to the established rules and practice of the day. In a word, we do not like Shakespear's poems, because we like his plays: the one, in all their excellencies, are just the reverse of the other. It has been the fashion of late to cry up our author's poems, as equal to his plays: this is the desperate cant of modern criticism. We would ask, was there the slightest comparison between Shakespeare, and either Chaucer or Spenser, as mere poets? Not any.—The two poems of *Venus and Adonis* and of *Tarquin and Lucrece* appear to us like a couple of icehouses. They are about as hard, as glittering, and as cold. The author seems all the time to be thinking of his verses, and not of his subject,—not of what his characters would feel, but of what he shall say; and as it must happen in all such cases, he always puts into their mouths those things which they would be the last to think of, and which it shews the greatest ingenuity in him to find out. The whole is laboured, up-hill work. The poet is perpetually singling out the difficulties of the art to make an exhibition of his strength and skill in wrestling with them. He is making perpetual trials of them as if his mastery over them were doubted. The images, which are often striking, are generally applied to things which they are the least like: so that they do not blend with the poem, but seem stuck upon it, like splendid patch-work, or remain quite distinct from it, like detached substances, painted and varnished over. A beautiful thought is sure to be lost in an endless commentary upon it. The speakers are like persons who have both leisure and inclination to make riddles on their own situation, and to twist and turn every object or incident into acrostics and anagrams. Every thing is spun out into allegory; and a digression is always preferred to the main story. Sentiment is built up upon plays of words; the hero or heroine feels, not from the impulse of passion, but from the force of dialectics. There is besides a strange attempt to substitute the language of paint-

ing for that of poetry, to make us *see* their feelings in the faces of the persons. . . . (pp. 211-13)

The description of the horse in Venus and Adonis has been particularly admired, and not without reason:—

> Round hoof'd, short jointed, fetlocks shag
>   and long,
> Broad breast, full eyes, small head, and nostril
>   wide,
> High crest, short ears, strait legs, and passing
>   strong,
> Thin mane, thick tail, broad buttock, tender hide,
> Look what a horse should have, he did not lack,
> Save a proud rider on so proud a back.
>
> [ll. 295-300]

Now this inventory of perfections shews great knowledge of the horse; and is good matter-of-fact poetry. Let the reader but compare it with a speech in the *Midsummer Night's Dream* where Theseus describes his hounds—

> And their heads are hung
> With ears that sweep away the morning dew—
>
> [IV. i. 120-21]

and he will perceive at once what we mean by the difference between Shakespear's own poetry, and that of his plays. (pp. 213-14)

> *William Hazlitt, "Poems and Sonnets," in his* Characters of Shakespear's Plays & Lectures on the English Poets, *The Macmillan Company, 1903, pp. 211-15.*

NATHAN DRAKE   (essay date 1817)

[*In the excerpt below, Drake concedes that* Venus and Adonis *possesses numerous faults and shortcomings, principally in its "fatiguing circumlocution," overly subtle conceits, and questionable morality. However, he contends, the melody and rhythm of the verse and the power of many images are "worthy of the genius of Shakspeare." In Drake's estimation, the depictions of Adonis's horse, the timid hare, and other "objects of nature," surpass anything in the works of Shakespeare's contemporaries and provide glimpses of the power that was to become manifest in the poet's later works.*]

["Venus and Adonis"], the earliest offspring of our poet's prolific genius, consists of one hundred and ninety-nine stanzas, each stanza including six lines, of which the first four are in alternate rhyme, and the fifth and sixth form a couplet. Its length, indeed, is one of its principal defects; for it has led, not only to a fatiguing circumlocution, in point of language, but it has occasioned the poet frequently to expand his imagery into a diffuseness which sometimes destroys its effect; and often to indulge in a strain of reflection more remarkable for its subtlety of conceit, than for its appropriation to the incidents before him. Two other material objections must be noticed, as arising from the conduct of the poet, which, in the first place, so far as it respects the character of Adonis, is forced and unnatural; and, in the second, has tempted the poet into the adoption of language so meretricious, as entirely to vitiate the result of any moral purpose which he might have had in view.

These deductions being premised, we do not hesitate to assert, that the "Venus and Adonis" contains many passages worthy of the genius of Shakspeare; and that, as a whole, it is superior in poetic fervour to any production of a similar kind by his contemporaries, anterior to 1587. It will be necessary, however, where so much discrepancy of opinion has existed, to substantiate the first of these assertions, by the production of specimens which shall speak for themselves; and as the conduct and moral of the piece have been given up as indefensible, these must, consequently, be confined to a display of its poetical value; of its occasional merit with regard to versification and imagery.

In the management of his stanza, Shakspeare has exhibited a more general attention to accuracy of rhythm and harmony of cadence, than was customary in his age; few metrical imperfections, indeed, are discoverable either in this piece, or in any of his minor poems; but we are not limited to this negative praise, being able to select from his first effort instances of positive excellence in the structure of his verse.

Of the light and airy elegance which occasionally characterises the composition of his "Venus and Adonis," the following will be accepted as no inadequate proofs:—

> Bid me discourse, I will enchant thine ear,
> Or, like a fairy, trip upon the green,
> Or like a nymph, with long dishevel'd hair,
> Dance on the sands, and yet no footing seen.
>
> If love have lent you twenty thousand tongues,
> And every tongue more moving than your own,
> Bewitching like the wanton mermaid's songs,
> Yet from mine ear the tempting tune is blown.
>
> [ll. 145-48, 775-78]

To terminate each stanza with a couplet remarkable for its sweetness, terseness, or strength, is a refinement almost peculiar to modern times, yet Shakspeare has sometimes sought for and obtained this harmony of close: thus Venus, lamenting the beauty of Nature after the death of Adonis, exclaims,

> The flowers are sweet, their colours fresh and trim;
> But true sweet beauty liv'd and died with him;
>
> [ll. 1079-80]

and again, when reproaching the apathy of her companion,—

> O learn to love; the lesson is but plain,
> And, once made perfect, never lost again.
>
> [ll. 407-08]

Nor are there wanting passages in which energy and force are very skilfully combined with melody and rhythm; of the subsequent extracts, which are truly excellent for their vigorous construction, the lines in Italics present us with the point and cadence of the present day. Venus, endeavouring to excite the affection of Adonis, who is represented

> more lovely than a man,
> More white and red than doves or roses are,
>
> [ll. 9-10]

tells him,

> I have been woo'd, as I entreat thee now,
> Even by the stern and direful god of war,
> Whose sinewy neck in battle ne'er did bow . . .
> Over my altars hath he hung his lance,
> His batter'd shield, his uncontrolled crest,
> And for my sake hath learn'd to sport and dance,
> *To coy, to wanton, dally, smile, and jest;*
>
> [ll. 97-99, 103-06]

and, on finding her efforts fruitless, she bursts forth into the following energetic reproach:—

> Fie, lifeless picture, cold and senseless stone,
> Well-painted idol, image, dull and dead,
> Statue contenting but the eye alone,
> *Thing like a man, but of no woman bred.*
>
> [ll. 211-14]

The death of Adonis, however, banishes all vestige of resentment, and, amid numerous exclamations of grief and anguish, gives birth to prophetic intimations of the hapless fate of all succeeding attachments:—

> Since thou art dead, lo! here I prophesy,
> Sorrow on love hereafter shall attend; &c. &c.
>
> [ll. 1135-36]

These passages are not given with the view of impressing upon the mind of the reader, that such is the constant strain of the versification of the "Venus and Adonis"; but merely to show, that, while in narrative poetry he equals his contemporaries in the general structure of his verse, he has produced, even in his earliest attempt, instances of beauty, melody, and force, in the mechanism of his stanzas, which have no parallel in their pages. (pp. 359-60)

It now remains to be proved, that the merits of this mythological story are not solely founded on its occasional felicity of versification; but that in description, in the power of delineating, with a master's hand, the various objects of nature, it possesses more claims to notice than have hitherto been allowed.

After the noble pictures of the horse which we find drawn in the book of Job, and in Virgil, few attempts to sketch this spirited animal can be expected to succeed; yet, among these few, impartial criticism may demand a station for the lines:—

> Imperiously he leaps, he neighs, he bounds,
> And now his woven girts he breaks asunder,
> The bearing earth with his hard hoof he wounds,
> Whose hollow womb resounds like heaven's thunder.—&c. &c.
>
> [ll. 265-68]

Venus, apprehensive for the fate of Adonis, should he attempt to hunt the boar, endeavours to dissuade him from his purpose, by drawing a most formidable description of that savage inmate of the woods, and by painting, on the other hand, the pleasures to be derived from the pursuit of the hare. The danger necessarily incurred from attacking the former, and the various efforts by which the latter tries to escape her pursuers, are presented to us with great fidelity and warmth of colouring.

> Thou had'st been gone, quoth she, sweet boy, ere this,
> But that thou told'st me, thou would'st hunt the boar, &c.
>
> [ll. 613-14]

This poem abounds with similes, many of which include miniature sketches of no small worth and beauty. A few of these shall be given, and they will not fail to impart a favourable impression of the fertility and resources of the rising bard. . . . [The following] especially deserve notice, the former representing a minute piece of natural history, and the latter describing in words adequate to their subject, one of the most terrible convulsions of nature. . . .

> Or, as the snail, whose tender horns being hit,
> Shrinks backward in his shelly cave with pain.

As when the wind, imprison'd in the ground,
Struggling for passage, earth's foundation shakes.
                                    [ll. 1033-34, 1046-47]

We shall close these extracts from the "Venus and Adonis," with two passages which form a striking contrast, and which prove that the author possessed, at the commencement of his career, no small portion of those powers which were afterwards to astonish the world; powers alike unrivalled either in developing the terrible or the beautiful.

And therefore hath she bribed the Destinies,
To cross the curious workmanship of nature,
To mingle beauty with infirmities,
And pure perfection with impure defeature;
      Making it subject to the tyranny
      Of sad mischances and much misery;

As burning fevers, agues pale and faint,
Life-poisoning pestilence, and frenzies wood,
The marrow-eating sickness, whose attaint
Disorder breeds by heating of the blood:
      Surfeits, impostumes, grief, and damn'd
         despair . . .

And not the least of all these maladies,
But in one minute's sight brings beauty under . . .
      As mountain snow melts with the mid–day sun.
      Lo! here the gentle lark, weary of rest,
From his moist cabinet mounts up on high,
And wakes the morning, from whose silver breast
The sun ariseth in his majesty;
      Who doth the world so gloriously behold,
      That cedar tops and hills seem burnish'd gold.

Venus salutes him with this fair good morrow:
O thou clear god, and patron of all light,
From whom each lamp and shining star doth
      borrow
The beauteous influence that makes him bright.
                        [ll. 733-43, 745-46, 750, 853-62]

If we compare the "Venus and Adonis" of Shakspeare with its classical prototypes; with the "Epitaphium Adonidis" of Bion, and the beautiful narrative of Ovid, which terminates the tenth book of his Metamorphoses, we must confess the inferiority of the English poem to the former in pathos, and to the latter in elegance; but if we contrast it with the productions of its own age, it cannot fail of being allowed a large share of relative merit. It has imbibed, indeed, too many of the conceits and puerilities of the period in which it was produced, and it has lost much interest by deviating from tradition; . . . yet the passages which we have quoted, and the general strain of the poem, are such as amply to account for the popularity which it once enjoyed. (pp. 361-62)

Nathan Drake, "Chapter V," in his Shakspeare and His Times, *1817. Reprint by Burt Franklin, 1969, pp. 352-88.*

G. G. GERVINUS (essay date 1849-50)

[*One of the most widely read Shakespearean critics of the latter half of the nineteenth century, the German critic Gervinus was praised by such eminent contemporaries as Edward Dowden, F. J. Furnivall, and James Russell Lowell; however, he is little known in the English-speaking world today. Gervinus wrote in the tradition of the "philosophical criticism" developed in Germany in the mid-nineteenth century. He believed that Shakespeare's work contained a rational ethical system independent of any religion. The following excerpt is reprinted from an En-*

glish translation of his Shakespeare, *first published in Germany in 1849-50. In his discussion of* Venus and Adonis, *Gervinus identifies several aspects of the poem, particularly Shakespeare's "immoderate" depiction of Venus's sensuality, as indications of the poet's youthfulness. The luxurious style betrays the inexperienced poet and inadvertently obscures the moral qualities of the work, he contends; thus, in this sense, the work as a whole is "one brilliant error." Gervinus is the first critic to note a thematic significance in the episode involving Adonis's horse. This scene, he argues, is designed to emphasize the "purely animal" nature of Venus's desire.*]

Of the two narrative or rather descriptive poems which we possess of Shakespeare, the one ('Venus and Adonis') was first printed in the year 1593, the other ('Lucrece') in 1594. Both are dedicated to the Earl of Southampton. The poet himself, in his dedication, calls 'Venus and Adonis' his first work [see excerpt above, 1593], but 'Lucrece' belongs indisputably to the same period. Both poems were certainly revised at publication. Their first conception may place them at a period previous to Shakespeare's settlement in London. Everything betrays that they were written in the first passion of youth.

We at once perceive how completely in matter and treatment they are interwoven with the youthful circumstances and moods of the poet. . . . The subject of 'Venus and Adonis' is the goddess of love wooing the cold yet insensible boy, and her laments upon his sudden death. In the first part the poet has endowed the wooer with all the charms of persuasion, beauty, and passionate vehemence; with all the arts of flattery, entreaty, reproach, tears, and violence; and in so doing he appears a Croesus in poetic ideas, thoughts, and images, a master and victor in the matter of love, a giant in passion and sensual power. From this point of view, the whole piece is one brilliant error, such as young poets so readily commit: immoderate sensual fervour mistaken for poetry. Yet in the opinion of the time this poem alone placed Shakespeare in the rank of admired poets. The very point we mention gave the poem at once its attractive power. All that had at that time been read in similar mythological poems by English and Italian writers upon the nature and effects of love, were elaborate imaginative works, more brilliant in words than profound in truth of feeling. But here love appeared as a 'spirit, all compact of fire' [l. 149], a real paroxysm and passion defying all the artificial bombast of delineation. Thus, by its truth to nature, the poem had a realistic effect beyond any similar mythological and allegorical pictures. Like Goethe's 'Werther,' it was proverbially held as the model of a love-poem; it was frequently reprinted, and called forth a series of imitations; and poets praised it as 'the quintessence of love,' as a talisman and pattern for lovers, from which might be learned the art of successful wooing.

Glowing as are the colours with which Shakespeare has portrayed this passion, his delight in the subject of his picture has never betrayed him into exclusive sensuality. He knows that he is sketching, not the image of human love in which mind and soul have their ennobling share, but the image of a purely sensual desire, which, purely animal, like 'an empty eagle' [l. 55], feeds on its prey. In the passage where he depicts the wooing of Adonis' horse which had broken loose from its rein, his intention is evidently to compare the animal passion in the episode with that of the goddess, not in opposition but in juxtaposition. Rebukingly Adonis tells the loving goddess that she should not call that love, which even he, the poet, names careless lust, 'beating reason back, forgetting shame's pure blush, and honour's wrack' [ll. 557-58]. This purer thought, which more than once occurs in the poem, is yet, it must be admitted, half concealed by the grace of the style and by the poet's lingering on sensual descriptions. (pp. 36-7)

G. G. Gervinus, "Shakespeare's Descriptive Poems," in his Shakespeare Commentaries, *translated by F. E. Bunnètt, revised edition, 1877. Reprint by AMS Press, Inc., 1971, pp. 36-44.*

ALGERNON CHARLES SWINBURNE (essay date 1875)

[*Swinburne was an English poet, dramatist, and critic who devoted much of his literary career to the study of Elizabethan writers. His three books on Shakespeare—*A Study of Shakespeare *(1880),* Shakespeare *(1909), and* Three Plays of Shakespeare *(1909)—all demonstrate his keen interest in the dramatist's poetic talents and, especially, his major tragedies. In the following excerpt, he disparages* Venus and Adonis, *judging it greatly inferior to Marlowe's* Hero and Leander. *Although Shakespeare's poem possesses "undeniable charms," its "overcrowding beauties of detail" and vaguely offensive subject make it, according to Swinburne, a "model of what a young man of genius should not write."*]

The name of Marlowe's poem [*Hero and Leander*] has been often coupled with that of the 'first heir' of Shakespeare's 'invention' [*Venus and Adonis*]; but with all reverence to the highest name in letters be it said, the comparison is hardly less absurd than a comparison of *Tamburlaine* with *Othello.* With all its overcrowding beauties of detail, Shakespeare's first poem is on the whole a model of what a young man of genius should not write on such a subject; Marlowe's is a model of what he should. Scarcely the art of Titian at its highest, and surely not the art of Shakespeare at its dawn, could have made acceptable such an inversion of natural rule as is involved in the attempted violation by a passionate woman of a passionless boy; the part of a Joseph, as no less a moralist than Henri Beyle has observed in his great work on *Love,* has always a suspicion about it of something ridiculous and offensive: but only the wretchedest of artists could wholly fail to give charm to the picture of such a nuptial night as that of Hero and Leander. The style of Shakespeare's first essay is, to speak frankly, for the most part no less vicious than the matter: it is burdened and bedizened with all the heavy and fantastic jewellery of Gongora and Marini. . . . Not one of the faults chargeable on Shakespeare's beautiful but faultful poem can justly be charged on the only not faultless poem of Marlowe. The absence of all cumbrous jewels and ponderous embroideries from the sweet and limpid loveliness of its style is not more noticeable than the absence of such other and possibly such graver flaws as deform and diminish the undeniable charms of *Venus and Adonis.* (pp. lix-lx)

Algernon Charles Swinburne, "Essay on the Poetical and Dramatic Works of George Chapman," in The Works of George Chapman: Poems and Minor Translations, *Vol. 2, Chatto and Windus, 1875, pp. ix-lxxi.*

EDWARD DOWDEN (essay date 1881)

[*Dowden was an Irish critic and biographer whose* Shakspere: A Critical Study of His Mind and Art, *first published in 1875 and revised in 1881, was the leading example of the biographical criticism popular in the English-speaking world near the end of the nineteenth century. Biographical critics sought a re-cord of Shakespeare's personal development in the plays and poems. In the excerpt below, Dowden stresses Shakespeare's detachment from his subject matter in* Venus and Adonis, *a work whose studied elaboration of detail, according to the critic, bespeaks the poet's dispassion.*]

The *Venus and Adonis* is styled by its author, in the dedication to the Earl of Southampton, "the first heir of my invention" [see excerpt above, 1593]. Gervinus believes that the poem may have been written before the poet left Stratford [see excerpt above, 1849-50]. Although possibly separated by a considerable interval from its companion poem, *The Rape of Lucrece* (1594), the two may be regarded as essentially one in kind. The specialty of these poems as portions of Shakspere's art has perhaps not been sufficiently observed. Each is an artistic *study;* and they form, as has been just observed, companion studies—one of female lust and boyish coldness, the other of male lust and womanly chastity. Coleridge noticed "the utter aloofness of the poet's own feelings from those of which he is at once the painter and the analyist" [see excerpt above, 1817]; but it can hardly be admitted that this aloofness of the poet's own feelings proceeds from a dramatic abandonment of self. The subjects of these two poems did not call and choose their poet; they did not possess him and compel him to render them into art. Rather the poet expressly made choice of the subjects, and deliberately set himself down before each to accomplish an exhaustive study of it. (pp. 43-4)

[For] a young writer of the Renascence, the subject of Shakspere's earliest poem was a splendid one—as voluptuous and unspiritual as that of a classical picture by Titian. It included two figures containing inexhaustible pasture for the fleshly eye, and delicacies and dainties for the sensuous imagination of the Renascence—the enamoured Queen of Beauty, and the beautiful, disdainful boy. It afforded occasion for endless exercises and variations on the themes Beauty, Lust, and Death. In holding the subject before his imagination, Shakspere is perfectly cool and collected. He has made choice of the subject, and he is interested in doing his duty by it in the most thorough way a young poet can; but he remains unimpassioned—intent wholly upon getting down the right colors and lines upon his canvas. Observe his determination to put in accurately the details of each object; to omit nothing. Poor Wat, the hare, is described in a dozen stanzas. Another series of stanzas describes the stallion—all his points are enumerated:

> Round-hoof'd, short-jointed, fetlocks shag and
> long,
> Broad breast, full eye, small head and nostril wide,
> High crest, short ears, straight legs and passing
> strong,
> Thin mane, thick tail, broad buttock, tender hide.
> [ll. 295-98]

This passage of poetry has been admired; but is it poetry or a paragraph from an advertisement of a horsesale? It is part of Shakspere's study of an animal, and he does his work thoroughly. In like manner, he does not shrink from faithfully putting down each one of the amorous provocations and urgencies of Venus. The complete series of manoeuvres must be detailed. (pp. 44-5)

It was the same hand that drew the stallion in *Venus and Adonis* which afterwards drew with infallible touch, as though they were alive, the dogs of Theseus:

My hounds are bred out of the Spartan kind
So flew'd, so sanded, and their heads are hung
With ears that sweep away the morning dew;
Crook-kneed, and dew-lapp'd like Thessalian bulls;
Slow in pursuit; but match'd in mouth like bells,
Each under each. A cry more tunable
Was never holla'd to, nor cheer'd with horn,
In Crete, in Sparta, nor in Thessaly.
[*A Midsummer Night's Dream*, IV. i. 119-26]
(pp. 45-6)

Edward Dowden, "The Growth of Shakspere's Mind
and Art," in his Shakspere: A Critical Study of His
Mind and Art, *third edition, Harper & Brothers
Publishers, 1881, pp. 37-83.*

GEORGE WYNDHAM   (essay date 1898)

[*The following commentary, drawn from Wyndham's introduction to his 1898 edition of Shakespeare's non-dramatic
poems, has been called the first modern criticism of* Venus and
Adonis. *Wyndham acknowledges Shakespeare's debt to Ovid
and Chaucer, but he also finds a remarkable blend of medieval
intricacy and startling realism in this poem. He likens the
poet's fusion of elaborate rhetoric, sophisticated alliteration,
classical narrative, and vivid natural imagery in* Venus and
Adonis *to the techniques of brilliant ornamentation characteristically applied by Renaissance painters and artisans. Moreover, this richly decorated poem affirms Shakespeare's "faith
in Beauty as a principle of life," the critic believes, but it does*

First text page of Venus and Adonis *(1593).*

*not expound a particular ethical view; indeed, Wyndham in-
sists, to seek a moral message in this work is to willfully misread it. Significantly, Wyndham further observes that Shakespeare draws from Ovid's depiction of the mythological figure
Hermaphroditus as well as from his portrayal of Adonis in delineating the young hunter of this poem.*]

[*Venus and Adonis* reveals] Shakespeare's loving familiarity
with Ovid whose effects he fuses: taking the reluctance of
Adonis from *Hermaphroditus* [in the *Metamorphosis*]; the
description of the boar from Meleager's encounter . . .; and
other features from the short version of *Venus and Adonis*
which Ovid weaves on to the terrible and beautiful story of
Myrrha. In all Shakespeare's work of this period the same fusion of Ovid's stories and images is obvious. Tarquin and
Myrrha are both delayed, but, not daunted, by lugubrious
forebodings in the dark; and *Titus Andronicus,* played for the
first time in the year which saw the publication of *Venus and
Adonis,* is full of debts and allusions to Ovid. Ovid, with his
power of telling a story and of eloquent discourse, his shining
images, his cadences coloured with assonance and weighted
with alliteration; Chaucer, with his sweet liquidity of diction,
his dialogues and soliloquies—these are the 'only true begetters' of the lyric Shakespeare. In these matters we must allow
poets to have their own way: merely noting that Ovid, in
whom critics see chiefly a brilliant man of the world, has been
a mine of delight for all poets who rejoice in the magic of
sound, from the dawn of the Middle Ages down to our own
incomparable Milton. His effects of alliteration . . . , his
gleaming metaphors, . . . are the very counterpart of Shakespeare's manner in the Poems and the Play which he founded
in part on his early love of the *Metamorphosis.*

But in *Titus Andronicus* and in *Venus and Adonis* there are
effects of the open air which hail, not from Ovid but, from
Arden:—

The birds chant melody on every bush;
The snake lies rolled in the cheerful sun;
The green leaves quiver with the cooling wind,
And make a chequer'd shadow on the ground.
[*Titus Andronicus,* II. iii. 12-15]

Thus the Play (ii. 3), and thus the Poem:—

Even as the wind is hush'd before it raineth . . .
Like many clouds consulting for foul weather.
[ll. 458, 972]

Indeed in the Poem, round and over the sharp portrayal of
every word and gesture of the two who speak and move, you
have brakes and trees, horses and hounds, and the silent
transformations of day and night from the first dawn till eve,
and through darkness to the second dawn so immediately impressed, that, pausing at any of the cxcix, stanzas, you could
almost name the hour. The same express observation of the
day's changes may be observed in *Romeo and Juliet.* It is a
note which has often been echoed by men who never look out
of their windows, and critics, as narrowly immured, have denounced it for an affectation. Yet a month under canvas, or,
better still, without a tent, will convince any one that to speak
of the stars and the moon is as natural as to look at your
watch or an almanack. In the *Venus* even the weather
changes. The Poem opens soon after sunrise with the ceasing
of a shower:—

Even as the sun with purple colour'd face,
Had ta'en his last leave of the weeping morn.

[ll. 1-2]

But by the 89th Stanza, after a burning noon, the clouds close in over the sunset. 'Look,' says Adonis:—

> The world's comforter with weary gate
> His day's hot task hath ended in the west,
> The owl (night's herald) shrieks, 'tis very late,
> The sheep are gone to fold, birds to their nest,
> And coal-black clouds, that shadow heaven's light,
> Do summon us to part and bid good-night.
>
> [ll. 529-34]

The next dawn is cloudless after the night's rain:—

> Lo here the gentle lark, weary of rest,
> From his moist cabinet mounts up on high,
> And wakes the morning, from whose silver breast
> The sun ariseth in his majesty;
> Who doth the world so gloriously behold,
> That cedar tops and hills seem burnisht gold.
>
> [ll. 853-58]

Beneath these atmospheric effects everything is clearly seen and sharply delineated:—

> The studded bridle on a ragged bough
> Nimbly she fastens.
>
> [ll. 37-8]

The illustrations from nature:—

> As the dive-dapper peering through a wave
> Who being lookt on, ducks as quickly in . . .
>
> As the snail whose tender horns being hit
> Shrinks backward in his shelly cave with pain
> [ll. 86-7, 1033-34]

are so vivid as to snatch your attention from the story; and when you read that 'lust' feeding on 'fresh beauty,'

> Starves and soon bereaves
> As caterpillars do the tender leaves,
>
> [ll. 797-98]

the realism of the illustration does violence to its aptness. It is said that such multiplicity of detail and ornament is out of place in a classic myth. But Shakespeare's Poem is not a classic myth. Mr. Swinburne contrasts it unfavourably with Chapman's *Hero and Leander* [in his "Essay on the Poetical and Dramatic Works of George Chapman"], in which he finds 'a small shrine of Parian sculpture amid the rank splendour of a tropical jungle.' Certainly that is the last image which any one could apply to *Venus and Adonis*. Its wealth of realistic detail reminds you rather of the West Porch at Amiens. But alongside of this realism, and again as in Mediaeval Art, there are wilful and half-humorous perversions of nature. When Shakespeare in praise of Adonis' beauty says that

> To see his face, the lion walked along
> *Behind some hedge,* because he would not fear him,
>
> [ll. 1093-94]

or that

> When he beheld his shadow in the brook,
> The fishes spread on it their golden gills,
>
> [ll. 1099-1100]

you feel that you are still in the age which painted St. Jerome's lion and St. Francis preaching to the birds. But you feel that you are half way into another. The poem is not Greek, but neither is it Mediaeval: it belongs to the debatable dawntime which we call the Renaissance. There is much in it of highly charged colour and of curious insistence on strange beauties of detail; yet, dyed and daedal as it is out of all kinship with classical repose, neither its intricacy nor its tinting ever suggests the Aladdin's Cave evoked by Mr. Swinburne's Oriental epithets: rather do they suggest a landscape at sunrise. There, too, the lesser features of trees and bushes and knolls are steeped in the foreground with crimson light, or are set on fire with gold at the horizon; there, too, they leap into momentary significance with prolonged and fantastic shadows; yet overhead, the atmosphere is, not oppressive but, eager and pure and a part of an immense serenity. And so it is in the Poem, for which, if you abandon Mr. Swinburne's illustration, and seek another from painting, you may find a more fitting counterpart in the Florentine treatment of classic myths: in Botticelli's *Venus,* with veritable gold on the goddess's hair and on the boles of the pine trees, or in Piero di Cosima's *Cephalus and Procris,* with its living animals at gaze before a tragedy that tells much of Beauty and nothing of Pain. Shakespeare's Poem is of love, not death; but he handles his theme with just the same regard for Beauty, with just the same disregard for all that disfigures Beauty. He portrays an amorous encounter through its every gesture; yet, unless in some dozen lines where he glances aside, like any Mediaeval, at a gaiety not yet divorced from love, his appeal to Beauty persists from first to last; and nowhere is there an appeal to lust. The laughter and sorrow of the Poem belong wholly to the faery world of vision and romance, where there is no sickness, whether of sentiment or of sense. And both are rendered by images, clean-cut as in antique gems, brilliantly enamelled as in mediaeval chalices, numerous and interwoven as in Moorish arabesques; so that their incision, colour, and rapidity of development, apart even from the intricate melodies of the verbal medium in which they live, tax the faculty of artistic appreciation to a point at which it begins to participate in the asceticism of artistic creation. 'As little can a mind thus roused and awakened be brooded on by mean and indistinct emotion, as the low, lazy mist can creep upon the surface of a lake while a strong gale is driving it onward in waves and billows':—thus does Coleridge resist the application to shift the venue of criticism on this Poem from the court of Beauty to the court of Morals [see excerpt above, 1817], and upon that subject little more need be said. How wilful it is to discuss the moral bearing of an invitation couched by an imaginary Goddess in such imaginative terms as these:—

> Bid me discourse, I will inchant thine eare,
> Or like a Fairie, trip upon the greene,
> Or like a Nymph, with long disheveled heare,
> Daunce on the sands, and yet no footing seene!
>
> [ll. 145-48]

As well essay to launch an ironclad on 'the foam of perilous seas in fairylands forlorn' [John Keats, "Ode to a Nightingale"].

When Venus says, 'Bid me discourse, I will inchant thine ear,' she instances yet another peculiar excellence of Shakespeare's lyrical art, which shows in this Poem, is redoubled in *Lucrece,* and in the Sonnets yields the most perfect examples of human speech:—

> Touch but my lips with those fair lips of thine,
> Though mine be not so fair, yet are they red. . . .
>
> Art thou ashamed to kiss? Then wink again,

And I will wink, so shall the day seem night. . . .
[ll. 115-16, 121-22]

These are the fair words of her soliciting, and Adonis's reply
is of the same silvery quality:—

If love have lent you twenty thousand tongues,
And every tongue more meaning than your own,
Bewitching like the wanton mermaid's songs,
Yet from mine ear the tempting tune is blown. . . .
[ll. 775-78]

And, as he goes on:—

Lest the deceiving harmony should run
Into the quiet closure of my breast:—
[ll. 781-82]

you catch a note prelusive to the pleading altercation of the
Sonnets. It is the discourse in *Venus and Adonis* and *Lucrece*
which renders them discursive. And indeed they are long
poems, on whose first reading Poe's advice, never to begin at
the same place, may wisely be followed. You do well, for instance, to begin at Stanza CXXXVI. [ll. 811-16] in order to
enjoy the narrative of Venus' vain pursuit: with your senses
unwearied by the length and sweetness of her argument. The
passage hence to the end is in the true romantic tradition:
Stanzas CXL. and CXLI. [ll. 835-46] are as clearly the forerunners of Keats, as CXLIV. [ll. 859-64] is the child of Chaucer.
The truth of such art consists in magnifying selected details
until their gigantic shapes, edged with a shadowy iridescence,
fill the whole field of observation. Certain gestures of the
body, certain moods of the mind, are made to tell with the
weight of trifles during awe-stricken pauses of delay. Venus,
when she is baffled by 'the merciless and pitchy night,' halts

amazed as one that unaware
Hath dropt a precious jewel in the flood,
Or stonisht as night wanderers often are,
Their light blown out in some mistrustfull wood.
[ll. 821, 823-26]

She starts like 'one that spies an adder'; 'the timorous yelping
of the hounds appals her senses'; and she stands 'in a trembling extasy' [ll. 878, 881-82, 895].

Besides romantic narrative and sweetly modulated discourse,
there are two rhetorical tirades by Venus—when she 'ex-
claimes on death':—

Grim grinning ghost, earth's-worme, what dost
thou meane
To stifle beautie and to steale his breath, etc.:—
[ll. 930, 933-34]

and when she heaps her anathemas on love:—

It shall be fickle, false and full of fraud,
Bud, and be blasted in a breathing while;
The bottome poyson, and the top ore-strawed
With sweets, that shall the truest sight beguile,
The strongest bodie shall it make most weake,
Strike the voice dumbe, and teach the foole to
speake:—
[ll. 1141-46]

and in both, as also in Adonis's contrast of love and lust:—

Love comforteth, like sunshine after raine,
But lust's effect is tempest after sunne,
Love's gentle spring doth always fresh remaine,
Lust's winter comes ere summer halfe be donne;

Love surfets not, lust like a glutton dies:
Love is all truth, lust full of forged lies:—
[ll. 799-804]

you have rhetoric, packed with antithesis, and rapped out on
alliterated syllables for which the only equivalent in English
is found, but more fully, in the great speech delivered by Lucrece. The seed of these tirades, as of the dialogues and the
gentle soliloquies, seems derived from Chaucer's *Troilus and
Criseyde;* and in his *Knight's Tale* . . . there is also a foreshadowing of their effective alliteration, used—and this is the
point—not as an ornament of verse, but as an instrument of
accent. . . . [This use of alliteration by Shakespeare] does
not consist in collecting the greatest number of words with
the same initial, but in letting the accent fall, as it does naturally in all impassioned speech, upon syllables of cognate
sound. Since in English verse the accent is, and by Shakespeare's contemporaries was understood to be, 'the chief lord
and grave Governour of Numbers' [Samuel Daniel in his *Defense of Ryme*], this aid to its emphasis is no less legitimate,
and is hardly less important, than is that of rhyme to metre
in French verse: we inherit it from the Saxon, as we inherit
rhyme from the Norman; both are essential elements in the
poetry built up by Chaucer out of the ruins of two languages.
But Shakespeare is the supreme master of its employment: in
these impassioned tirades he wields it with a naked strength
that was never approached, in the Sonnets with a veiled and
varied subtilty that defies analysis. There are hints here and
there in the *Venus* of this gathering subtilty:—

These blew-vein'd violets whereon we leane
Never can blab, nor know not what we meane . . .
Even as a dying coale revives with winde . . .
More white and red than doves and roses are.
[ll. 125-26, 338, 10]

But apart from the use of cognate sounds, which makes for
emphasis without marring melody, in many a line there also
lives that more recondite sweetness, which plants so much of
Shakespeare's verse in the memory for no assignable cause:—

Scorning his churlish drum and ensigne red. . . .
Dumbly she passions, frantiekely she doteth. . . .
Showed like two silver doves that sit a billing. . . .
Leading him prisoner in a red-rose chaine. . . .
Were beautie under twentie locks kept fast,
Yet love breaks through and picks them all at
last. . . .
O learne to love, the lesson is but plaine
And once made perfect never lost again.
[ll. 107, 1059, 366, 110, 575-76, 407-08]

Herein a cadence of obvious simplicity gives birth to an inexplicable charm.

I have spoken of Shakespeare's images, blowing fresh from
the memory of his boyhood, so vivid that at times they are
violent, and at others wrought and laboured until they become conceits. You have 'No fisher but the ungrown fry forbears' [l. 526], with its frank reminiscence of a sportsman's
scruple; or, as an obvious illustration, 'Look how a bird lies
tangled in a net' [l. 67]; or, in a flash of intimate recollection:—

Like shrill-tongu'd tapsters answering everie call,
Soothing the humours of fantastique wits:—
[ll. 849-50]

the last, an early sketch of the 'Francis' scene in *Henry IV.*
[*1 Henry IV,* Act II, *Scene* iv], which, in quaint juxtaposition

with 'cedar tops and hills' of 'burnisht gold' [l. 858], seems instinct with memories of John Shakespeare and his friends, who dared not go to church. But, again, you have conceits:—

> But hers (eyes), which through the crystal tears
>   gave light,
> Shone like the Moone in water seen by night;
>
> [ll. 491-92]

'A lilie prison'd in a gaile of snow' [l. 362]; and 'Wishing her cheeks were gardens full of flowers So they were dew'd with such distilling showers' [ll. 65-6]. But, diving deeper than diction, alliteration, and rhythm: deeper than the decoration of blazoned colours and the labyrinthine interweaving of images, now budding as it were from nature, and now beaten as by an artificer out of some precious metal: you discover beneath this general interpretation of Phenomenal Beauty, a gospel of Ideal Beauty, a confession of faith in Beauty as a principle of life. And note—for the coincidence is vital—that these, the esoteric themes of *Venus and Adonis,* are the essential themes of the *Sonnets.* In Stanza XXII.:—

> Fair flowers that are not gathered in their prime
> Rot and consume themselves in little time:—
>
> [ll. 131-32]

and in Stanzas XXVII., XXVIII., XXIX. [ll. 157-74], you have the whole argument of Sonnets I.-XIX. In Stanza CLXXX.:—

> Alas poore world, what treasure hast thou lost,
> What face remains alive that's worth the viewing?
> Whose tongue is musick now? What canst thou
>   boast,
> Of things long since, or any thing insuing?
> The flowers are sweet, their colours fresh, and trim,
> But true sweet beautie liv'd, and di'de with him:—
>
> [ll. 1075-80]

you have that metaphysical gauging of the mystical importance of some one incarnation of Beauty viewed from imaginary standpoints in time, which was afterwards to be elaborated in Sonnets XIV., XIX., LIX., LXVII., LXVIII., CIV., CVI. And in Stanza CLXX.:—

> For he being dead, with him is beautie slaine,
> And beautie dead, blacke Chaos comes again:—
>
> [ll. 1019-20]

you have the succinct *credo* in that incarnation of an Ideal Beauty, of which all other lovely semblances are but 'shadows' and 'counterfeits,' which was to find a fuller declaration in Sonnets XXXI. and LIII., and XCVIII.

But in Shakespeare's Poems the beauty and curiosity of the ceremonial ever obscure the worship of the god; and, perhaps, in the last stanza but one, addressed to the flower born in place of the dead Adonis and let drop into the bosom of the Goddess of Love, you have the most typical expression of those merits and defects which are alike loved and condoned by the slaves of their invincible sweetness:—

> Here was thy father's bed, here in my brest,
> Thou art the next of blood, and 'tis thy right,
> So in this hollow cradle take thy rest,
> My throbbing hart shall rock thee day and night;
> There shall not be one minute in an houre
> Wherein I will not kiss my sweet love's floure.
>
> [ll. 1183-88]

Here are conceits and a strained illustration from the profession of law; but here, with these, are lovely imagery and per-

fect diction and, flowing through every line, a rhythm that rises and falls softly, until, after a hurry of ripples, it expends itself in the three last retarding words. (pp. lxxxi-xcii)

> *George Wyndham, in an introduction to* The Poems of Shakespeare, *edited by George Wyndham, Methuen and Co., 1898, pp. vii-cxlvii.*

WALTER RALEIGH (essay date 1907)

[*Raleigh was a professor of English literature at Oxford and an essayist, literary critic, and biographer who employed a humanistic approach in his work. In addition to biographies of Milton, Wordsworth, Robert Louis Stevenson, and Shakespeare, he published several works on Samuel Johnson and on the English novel. In the excerpt below, Raleigh contends that "the love of beauty for beauty's sake, and of wit for the exercise of wit" were Shakespeare's primary motives in composing* Venus and Adonis. *He considers the poem an intellectual exercise in applying techniques of rhetoric and painting to poetry and finds it typical of the Renaissance in its insistent demonstration of the poet's power and skill.*]

Venus and Adonis and *The Rape of Lucrece,* which were published in 1593 and the following year, are, first of all, works of art. They are poetic exercises by one who has set himself to prove his craftsmenship upon a given subject. If traces of the prentice hand are visible, it is not in any uncertainty of execution, nor in any failure to achieve an absolute beauty, but rather in the very ostentation of artistic skill. There is no remission, at any point, from the sense of conscious art. The poems are as delicate as carved ivory, and as bright as burnished silver. They deal with disappointment, crime, passion, and tragedy, yet are destitute of feeling for the human situation, and are, in effect, painless. This painlessness, which made Hazlitt compare them to a couple of ice-houses [see excerpt above, 1817], is due not to insensibility in the poet, but to his preoccupation with his art. He handles life from a distance, at two removes, and all the emotions awakened by the poems are emotions felt in the presence of art, not those suggested by life. The arts of painting and rhetoric are called upon to lend to poetry their subjects and their methods. From many passages in the plays it may be inferred that Shakespeare loved painting, and was familiar with a whole gallery of Renaissance pictures. Portia's elaborate comparison of Bassanio to

> young Alcides, when he did redeem
> The virgin tribute paid by howling Troy
> To the sea-monster,
>
> [*The Merchant of Venice,* III. ii. 55-7]

is only one of many allusions which can be nothing but reminiscences of pictures; and in the Induction to *The Taming of the Shrew* the servants submit to Christopher Sly a catalogue which is the best possible commentary on Shakespeare's early poems:

> We will fetch thee straight
> Adonis painted by a running brook,
> And Cytherea all in sedges hid,
> Which seem to move and wanton with her breath,
> Even as the waving sedges play with wind.
>   We'll show thee Io as she was a maid,
> And how she was beguiled and surpris'd,
> As lively painted as the deed was done:
>   Or Daphne roaming through a thorny wood,
> Scratching her legs, that one shall swear she bleeds;
> And at that sight shall sad Apollo weep,

So workmanly the blood and tears are drawn.

[Induction ii, 49-60]

Here is the very theme of *Venus and Adonis,* and another theme closely akin to *The Rape of Lucrece.* It would not be rash to say outright that both the poems were suggested by pictures, and must be read and appreciated in the light of that fact. But the truth for criticism remains the same if they took their sole origin from the series of pictures painted in words by the master-hand of Ovid. "So workmanly the blood and tears are drawn."

The rhetorical art of the poems is no less manifest. The tirades and laments of both poems, on Love and Lust, on Night, and Time, and Opportunity, are exquisitely modulated rhetorical diversions; they express rage, sorrow, melancholy, despair; and it is all equally soothing and pleasant, like listening to a dreamy sonata. . . . There is no morality in the general scheme of these poems; the morality is all inlaid, making of the poem a rich mosaic. The plays have to do with a world too real to be included in a simple moral scheme; the poems with a world too artificial to be brought into any vital relation with morality. The main motive prompting the poet is the love of beauty for beauty's sake, and of wit for the exercise of wit.

It is at this point that Shakespeare was touched by the new spirit of the Renaissance. . . . It was an age of new philosophies, new arts, new cults; none of them modest or sober, all full of the spirit of bravado, high-towering but not broad-based, erected as monuments to the skill and prowess of the individual. That arrogance and self-sufficiency of craft which by the men of the Renaissance was called virtue is found in many different guises; and Shakespeare did not wholly escape the prevalent infection. What the love of power was to Marlowe, the love of beauty was to him. In these early poems the Venus of the Renaissance takes him captive,

Leading him prisoner in a red-rose chain.

[l. 110]

The devout religion of the eye and ear is all-in-all to him: his world is a world of gleaming forms and beautiful speech. He exhibits beauty as Marlowe exhibits power, freed from all realistic human conditions. Only here and there in the poems a note of observation, a touch of homely metaphor, remind us that he is not out of reach of the solid earth that is hereafter to be his empire. This passionate cult of beauty was transformed, rather than superseded, by the intrusion of thought and sorrow; so that the much talked of phases, or stages, in Wordsworth's love of nature are paralleled by similar stages in Shakespeare's love of humanity. If the poems were lost, we should know all too little of his apprenticeship, when human life was to him

An appetite, a feeling, and a joy,
That had no need of a remoter charm;

[William Wordsworth, "Lines
composed a few miles above Tintern Abbey"]

when his delight in the shows and exercises of the world left him no leisure for unintelligible problems or unwelcome cares.

His early play of *Titus Andronicus,* which is like the poems, shows how strangely hard-hearted this love of beauty can be, and makes it easy to understand how he was fascinated and dominated, for a time, by Marlowe. Yet even in *Venus and Adonis* there is evidence that he had outgrown Marlowe, and is on the way to a serener and wiser view of things. The protest of Adonis, beginning "Call it not love," is unlike anything in Marlowe, and sounds the knell of violent ambitions and desires.

Love comforteth like sunshine after rain,
But Lust's effect is tempest after sun;
Love's gentle spring doth always fresh remain;
Lust's winter comes ere summer half be done;
  Love surfeits not, Lust like a glutton dies;
  Love is all truth, Lust full of forged lies.

[ll. 793, 799-804]
(pp. 80-5)

Walter Raleigh, "Books and Poetry," in his Shakespeare, *Macmillan and Co., Limited, 1907, pp. 63-93.*

DOUGLAS BUSH   (essay date 1932)

[*In the following excerpt from his influential study of* Venus and Adonis, *Bush places Shakespeare's poem in the context of the English mythological tradition, a set of poetic conventions with roots in the works of Ovid and other classical writers. Tales in this style, which was extremely popular in Shakespeare's day, often feature mythological characters and naturalistic settings described in elaborate rhetorical figures. Bush catalogues the similarities between* Venus and Adonis *and other works of the period and, while conceding that Shakespeare has in some ways bettered his predecessors, judges the poem "a tissue of bookish conventions." The "vain pursuit" of a reluctant youth was a stock situation in both Italian and English pastorals, he notes, and suggestions of a reluctant Adonis—a seemingly unusual feature of Shakespeare's poem—appear in other late sixteenth-century works. Bush concludes that* Venus and Adonis *is an "expansive and empty" exercise in the exploitation of popular rhetorical techniques.*]

Venus and Adonis was entered in April, 1593, and published shortly afterward. There is no need for considering the old theory that the poem had been written years before, since there is no evidence in favor of such a speculation, and very much evidence against it. The obvious facts are that the mythological poem was beginning to be fashionable and that the young playwright, in a theatrical off-season, decided to advance himself by using the new recipe.

There is no reason to think that Shakespeare borrowed from any Italian source. The citations of Sir Sidney Lee [see Additional Bibliography] and others only help to show, what is important enough in itself, that certain motives and methods of treatment were common property among Renaissance poets. It is hardly necessary to ransack continental authors to find a source for the sunny atmosphere of *Venus and Adonis,* or for such a conceit as the boar's wanting merely to kiss the youth, which was a commonplace of sixteenth-century verse. (pp. 139-40)

The chief items in Shakespeare's debt to Ovidian material are set forth in every edition of the poems and may be briefly summarized. From the tenth book of the *Metamorphoses* he takes the central figures and something of the general background; from the eighth book the description of the boar, which reveals verbal echoes of [Golding's translation]. Since the Adonis of Ovid and common tradition is not a reluctant lover, it has generally and reasonably been assumed that Shakespeare partly modeled his characters on the wanton and dominating Salmacis and the shy young Hermaphroditus, as these appear in Ovid's fourth book. The somewhat similar story of Narcissus and Echo may also have been in the poet's mind; but more will be said of Adonis a little later. This rapid outline gives an exaggerated notion of the actual amount of matter taken over from Ovid, for, in proportion to the length of Shakespeare's poem, it is really slight. (p. 140)

The most attractive passage of any length in *Venus and Adonis* is the account of the hunted hare, a very English vignette in this conventional Arcadia. Reading it we may say, with Bagehot, that we know Shakespeare had been after a hare. But recollections of Warwickshire seem to be mixed with recollections of Ovid. Poor Wat in desperation

> sometimes sorteth with a herd of deer;
> Danger deviseth shifts; wit waits on fear.
>
> [ll. 689-90]

Ovid, describing the pursuit of Daphne by Apollo, has an elaborate simile of a hare and hound, which ends with a typical Ovidian line, *Sic deus et virgo est, hic spe celer, illa timore* ["So farde Apollo and the Mayde: hope made Apollo Swift, / And feare did make the Mayden fleete devising how to shift," in Golding's translation]. Shakespeare's phrase is an evident attempt to rival in English the antithetical brevity of the Latin.

This particular example suggests the importance of Ovid as one source of a conspicuous element in the style of *Venus and Adonis,* that is, the antithetical pattern of lines and phrases. Here are some of the more obvious instances in the first fifty lines:

> Hunting he lov'd, but love he laugh'd to scorn.
>
> Saith that the world hath ending with thy life.
>
> But rather famish them amid their plenty.
>
> Ten kisses short as one, one long as twenty.
>
> He red for shame, but frosty in desire.
>
> Backward she push'd him, as she would be thrust,
> And govern'd him in strength, though not in lust.
>
> [ll. 4, 12, 20, 22, 36, 41-2]

It is hardly too much to say that the whole fabric of the poem is woven of antitheses, as if Shakespeare had fallen in love with one of Ovid's tricks and worked it to death. The central antithesis of subject, between the warm goddess and the cold youth, is reflected in line after line that breaks more or less clearly into two parts containing opposed ideas. The use of the antithetical formula is marked enough in narrative and descriptive passages; it is, as one would expect, still more persistent in the speeches. The effect is somewhat as if a clever young writer of prose had resolved to outdo Mr. Chesterton. One must allow of course for the Petrarchan and euphuistic delight in logical and verbal antitheses, but eager first-hand imitation of Ovid evidently counted a good deal. When one compares *Venus and Adonis* with the work of Lodge and Spenser it is plain that, while Shakespeare exploits Italianate conventions, his taut style is different in texture from the smooth velvet of Italianate verse.

To say that *Venus and Adonis* reveals hardly a trace of direct foreign influence is not of course to say that apart from Ovidian elements it is an original poem. Even in the plays Shakespeare was seldom an innovator; his way was to accept the current fashion and excel in it. His first narrative poem, natu-

rally, is almost wholly conventional, an exhaustive collection of traditional motives and devices, though he appropriates them, and plies his nimble wit in embroidering them, with as much zest as if they were his own jerks of invention. Shakespeare breathed the same air as other men, and his scent for popular formulas was unusually keen and prophetic. The luxuriant Italianate manner had been naturalized in England, and no immediate foreign contacts were necessary. Not only was every poetical device at hand, there was also Elizabethan fiction. If in Shakespeare's poems action bears to rhetoric much the same proportion as bread to sack in Falstaff's bill [in *I Henry IV*], we may remember the technique of Pettie, Lyly, and Greene in their prose tales.

Shakespeare's representation of a chaste youth solicited by an amorous woman had precedents not only in Ovid but in the pastoral tradition derived partly from Ovid. The vain pursuit of a woman by a man or of a man by a woman was . . . the stock situation of the Italian pastoral. The conventions had now become familiar in English, and *Venus and Adonis,* like the other mythological poems, makes use of them (though it stands somewhat apart on account of its more direct imitation of Ovidian style). There must be an obstacle somewhere in such stories of love; if Adonis were as willing as Barkis [in Charles Dickens's *David Copperfield*], and Venus equally laconic, what would become of the poem? As for Shakespeare's choice of the more piquant of the two standard situations, it offered some obvious advantages. Since it appears virtually certain that he had read *Hero and Leander,* he might have felt as Rossetti did about *The Raven*—that, as Poe had said all that could be said on one aspect of the theme, *The Blessed Damozel* would take the other side. Anyone who knew Leander's plea could hardly avoid the conviction that the subject must be freshened by reversal of the parts.

For the particular conception of a reluctant Adonis there were suggestions at hand also. There is a faint hint of initial coyness in the Adonis of Spenser:

> Then with what sleights and sweet allurements she
> Entyst the Boy, as well that art she knew,
> And wooed him her Paramoure to be.

Further, Spenser's picture of Venus watching Adonis bathe suggests a mild combination of the story with that of Salmacis and Hermaphroditus. Less vague are two songs of Greene's quoted by all the editors, which show that the notion of a chaste Adonis was current; they appear in *Perimedes the Blacke-smithe* (1588) and *Never Too Late* (1590). Marlowe's allusion to Venus and "proud Adonis" is sufficiently different from Shakespeare's conception to suggest independent use of a nonclassical variant. Thus Shakespeare had only to look about him to find hints for a cold Adonis.

Shakespeare was obviously indebted to Lodge's languidly pretty *Glaucus and Scilla,* both in the central theme and in details, such as the popular sixain stanza and the likewise popular "echo" device. Lodge's purple patch on Venus and Adonis [in his *Glaucus and Scilla*] . . . is enough to indicate not only the degree to which Shakespeare caught the Italianate style, but the extent of his rhetorical originality and vigor. In all points, form as well as detail, Shakespeare greatly bettered his instruction.

Shakespeare doubtless knew at least two treatments of Adonis in Spenser; a few lines from one passage have already been quoted. Spenser's half-symbolic adaptation of the myth in the sixth canto of the third book is quite remote from Shakespeare's, for Shakespeare's attitude toward his material is simply that of a Renaissance Ovid; his Venus and Adonis are symbolic only in the sense that they and everything connected with them are manifestations of physical beauty. The pictorial warmth and richness of Spenser's work in general must have affected Shakespeare, as such qualities affected most poets of the day, but *Venus and Adonis* has a distinct hardness and precision of line which is not Spenserian. Whatever Italian Shakespeare picked up, he does not, even at his most florid, write like Spenser and others to whom the soft fluidity of Italian verse was both more familiar and more congenial.

The influence of Marlowe the dramatist upon Shakespeare was so strong that it affected the structure, characterization, and style of some of the earlier plays. The influence of *Hero and Leander* upon *Venus and Adonis,* however, is both obvious and superficial. Some apparent resemblances are only characteristics of the mythological genre. What seem to be demonstrable borrowings, though numerous, are mainly incidental and external, and Shakespeare, for good or ill, subdues them to his own style and mode of treatment. Many passages in the Marlowesque plays one might assign to Marlow; there are few bits of *Venus and Adonis* that could be mistaken for quotations from *Hero and Leander.*

Conceits of course everyone delighted in, but Shakespeare's, especially those of the myth-making sort, sometimes resemble Marlowe's. Mythological allusions were also common property, and Shakespeare, like his fellows, took them indifferently from Ovid and from modern sources. Since Shakespeare's plays are full of mythological allusions, and since these were a conventional element in the mythological poem as established by Lodge and Marlowe, it may be observed that such allusions in *Venus and Adonis* are relatively scanty and unadorned. If in this respect Shakespeare departed from the convention he was evidently following Lodge and Marlowe—and—Ovid—when he scattered aphorisms and epigrams through an erotic poem. The amorous arguments of Venus recall Leander's and those of the *Sonnets,* where the theme of procreation is decidedly more pertinent than in the mouth of the undomestic goddess.

The differences between Marlowe and Shakespeare are no less obvious, and more important, than the resemblances. Hero and Leander, despite Marlowe's inconsistencies of characterization and excess of decoration, win our sympathy; there is warmth and something of natural passion. Shakespeare, dealing with an unattractive pair who are more remote from humanity, fiddles on the strings of sensuality without feeling or awakening any such sympathy, without even being robustly sensual. Marlowe has too many merely pretty lines, but generally he is strong, masculine, swift; Shakespeare is much more content with prettiness, and the poem, though far from languid, is sicklied o'er with effeminacy. Many lines in *Hero and Leander* glow with a beauty that might be called haunting if the word were not overworn; the reader of *Venus and Adonis* is chiefly impressed by the astonishing skill of phrase and rhythm—

> Which bred more beauty in his angry eyes.

> Leading him prisoner in a red-rose chain.

> Full gently now she takes him by the hand,
> A lily prison'd in a gaol of snow.

> [ll. 70, 110, 361-62]

But when one thinks of "Love's not Time's fool" [Sonnet

116], not to mention the plays, one is made aware of the fatal lack of emotion. Finally it is noteworthy, in a poem which is a tissue of bookish conventions, that Shakespeare's best bits of imagery are fresh pictures of nature. Marlowe's images are almost wholly a fusion of art, literature, and imagination.

Incongruity of costume [was] . . . a normal element of mythological poems as well as other types of Renaissance writing, and Shakespeare of course does not depart from the mode. When Venus approaches Adonis and "heaveth up his hat" [ll. 351], and at other times, we have a suspicion that we are witnessing an Arcadian encounter between a scantily clad Maid of Honor and, say, the Earl of Southampton in a rare moment of satiety. Indeed if one considers the opportunities offered by Shakespeare's subject, and the popularity of voluptuous anatomical catalogues, in which even the sober Sidney and philosophic Chapman indulged, Shakespeare's neglect of "the nude" is somewhat remarkable. In this respect he is less sensuous than Marlowe the pagan or Spenser the moralist. We have here another instance in which Shakespeare is closer to Ovid—the Ovid of the *Metamorphoses,* that is—than to the Italianate fashion.

The Shakespeare of the mature plays is greatest perhaps in his power over words; he uses language as if it were his own creation and he alone understood its infinite capacities. What is missing in these poems—and in the early plays—is just that faculty, that genius for packing a world of meaning into a phrase. In the poems there is hardly a trace of such concentration and suggestion; the words mean what they say, and that is not much. (One remembers that in the fifteenth chapter of *Biographia Literaria* Coleridge, undertaking to elucidate "the specific symptoms of poetic power," strangely chose these poems for "critical analysis" [see excerpt above, 1817].) Only a few times in *Venus and Adonis* is there a slight break in the flat, two-dimensional surface, when the poet works in a natural image from his own observation, the divedapper, the snail, the gentle lark, the dew-bedabbled hare, and such fresh glimpses of something real, welcome as they are, heighten the total effect of artifice. In them, however, we do have a faint promise of the real Shakespeare, the poet who can see and feel and communicate what he sees and feels. On the other hand the auctioneer's description of the horse, which, since Hazlitt [see excerpt above, 1817], has so often been put beside the passage on the hounds in the *Midsummer Night's Dream,* shows the difference between the minute, self-defeating realism of the tyro and the swift, suggestive strokes of the master. The horse embodies all the good points prescribed in Elizabethan treatises on the animal, and remains a catalogue; we see, hear, touch, and smell the hounds.

The living things described in the poem are not all creatures of the English countryside. We know that the man who wrote of the lark ascending, or of "poor Wat," had been in the fields as well as in his study. We know that the same man fully shared the taste of his age when we read this:

> To see his face the lion walk'd along
> Behind some hedge, because he would not fear him;
> To recreate himself when he hath sung,
> The tiger would be tame and gently hear him;
> 　If he had spoke, the wolf would leave his prey,
> 　And never fright the silly lamb that day.

> When he beheld his shadow in the brook,
> The fishes spread on it their golden gills . . .

> [ll. 1093-1100]

Even if such a string of fancies be half humorous—and Venus' lamentation is not especially merry—it reminds us that Shakespeare not only laughed at euphuism but practiced it with some relish. The poem everywhere shows that its author lavished artistic labor upon it, in a sense put himself into it, yet perhaps nothing proves more clearly what a circumscribed self it was than the fact that the creator of this polite lion behind an English hedge was shortly to create another kind of polite lion for Snug the joiner [in *A Midsummer Night's Dream*]. But every age, our own included, has its stylistic tricks which lose their charm for posterity.

The Elizabethans generally anticipated Wilde in believing that nothing succeeds like excess, and if we dislike their rhetorical extravagance it is after all no great price to pay for their unique virtues. Their exuberant excesses were the natural overflow of tremendous energy in an era of uncertain taste and an intoxicated delight in words. In the plays Shakespeare never entirely outgrew his love of rhetoric, though his critical powers ripened with his other faculties and enabled him to satirize flamboyance. In *Venus and Adonis* he seems quite satisfied and happy in seriously exploiting the popular conceits, decoration, rhetorical wooing, rhetorical declamation. In the speeches of Venus we have the arguments of an Ovidian lover combined with the strained fancies of a sonneteer, moral aphorisms, and, even from Adonis when he finds his tongue, some of the paradoxes on the nature of love so dear to Elizabethan writers, all worked out with an inexhaustible ingenuity that compels a kind of admiration. The poem is indeed a bible for lovers. To quote one allusion out of many, a character in a play of 1640 [Pupillus in Lewis Sharpe's *The Noble Stranger*] longs for "the book of *Venus and Adonis* to court my mistress by." And when speaking of rhetoric one must notice Venus' apostrophe to Death. It is thoroughly of the Renaissance; it is also thoroughly medieval.

If *Venus and Adonis* were wholly bookish, a piece of pure tapestry, all would be well, in a limited sense. But for an orgy of the senses it is too unreal, for a decorative pseudo-classic picture it has too much homely realism. We [can observe] somewhat similar discords in *Hero and Leander,* but in the cooler, shallower, more deliberate *Venus and Adonis* the effect of artifice is much greater. *Hero and Leander* exists more fully in a poetic world of its own, and its author's passion for beauty partly reconciles inharmonious elements. With such distinctions Elizabethans were not greatly concerned. Shakespeare was wholly successful in what he set out to do, and it is only a posterity for whom the poem was not written that asks "Was it worth doing?" Since at the moment the poetic shibboleth is a line of Donne, the answer is not in doubt, yet Shakespeare, at the age of twenty-nine and thirty, chose to write not merely one unsatisfactory classical poem but two. At any rate his cultivation of these expansive and empty pieces did not prevent his studying the plays with allusions of often concentrated and suggestive beauty. (pp. 141-49)

Douglas Bush, "Shakespeare: 'Venus and Adonis' and 'The Rape of Lucrece'," in his Mythology and The Renaissance Tradition in English Poetry, *1932. Reprinted by Pageant Book Company, 1957, pp. 139-55.*

J. DOVER WILSON   (essay date 1932)

[*Dover Wilson was a highly regarded Shakespearean scholar who was involved in several aspects of Shakespeare studies. As an editor of the* New Cambridge Shakespeare, *he made numerous contributions to twentieth-century textual criticism of Shakespeare; as a critic, he was concerned with character analysis in the tradition of A. C. Bradley; and his interest in visualizing possible dramatic performances of the plays links him with his contemporary, Harley Granville-Barker. In the comments excerpted below, Dover Wilson describes* Venus and Adonis *as a "supreme example of what may be called the Elizabethan 'fleshly school of poetry'." He also speculates about the sensation created by the publication of this work in 1593 and judges Shakespeare's erotic narrative as a response to Spenser's poems of temperance and virtue.*]

The publication of *Venus and Adonis* must have produced an effect upon London in 1593 not unlike that which the First Series of Swinburne's *Poems and Ballads* created in 1866, except that Shakespeare put himself at the head of a fashion instead of initiating one. When *Poems and Ballads* "fell like a thunderbolt upon Philistia", the youth of England were tired of the "lilies and langours" of Tennyson, and turned with delight to the "roses and raptures" the new poet offered. In the same way, to understand the popularity of *Venus and Adonis,* we must remember that, since the appearance in 1579 of *The Shepheard's Calender,* the puritan Spenser had been the dominant star in the poetic heavens, and that in 1590 he began the publication of *The Faerie Queene,* the ostensible purpose of which, with its Book I on "Holiness", its Book II on "Temperance", and its Book III on "Chastity", was to "fashion a gentleman or noble person in virtuous and gentle disposition". Shakespeare's retort to Spenser's destruction of the Bower of Bliss was *Venus and Adonis,* in which "sweet desire" was given divine honours, and her rites exhibited according to the example of Ovid, a quotation from whom stands on the title-page of the book. The poem is the supreme example of what may be called the Elizabethan "fleshly school of poetry". Yet there is nothing whatever Swinburnian about it. The note of revolt, of craving for forbidden fruit, is entirely absent: the "roses and raptures" are not of vice, but of a frank acceptance of what Rossetti called "the passionate and just delights of the body". It is at times laboured and at others a little stuffy, but in its defects as in its merits, in its pictorial quality and in its loading of every rift with ore, it reminds us more of the young Keats, the Keats of *Endymion,* than of any other poet.

As with Keats too, the passion for Beauty, less explicit than the fleshly passion, is so all-pervading as to remain our abiding impression when the book is closed and the details fade from the memory. It comes out most in those references to country life and animals in which the poem abounds. These glimpses of Stratford are indeed so much happier than the descriptions of the efforts by amorous Venus to awaken passion in her Adonis, that it is not difficult to see where Shakespeare's heart lay. Yet even in the wanton passages his feet often move to such bewitching measures that one is ravished by the witchery into forgetting the wantonness. (pp. 54-6)

J. Dover Wilson, "Enter William Shakespeare with Divers of Worship," in his The Essential Shakespeare: A Biographical Adventure, *Cambridge at the University Press, 1932, pp. 38-67.*

LU EMILY PEARSON   (essay date 1933)

[*In the following excerpt, Pearson describes* Venus and Adonis *as perhaps the most didactic work Shakespeare ever composed.*

She declares that the poem's theme is the contest between rational love, represented by Adonis, and sensual, destructive love, symbolized by Venus. When Adonis is killed, she maintains, "beauty, the soul of matter," is also killed, and the world is left in chaos.]

Shakespeare had to solve the problem of harmonizing physical and rational love, and like a true Petrarchan, he approached this analysis through a study of the soul of woman. But in order to follow him as he worked his way toward a solution, we shall have to . . . consider his early poems and plays about love. In *Venus and Adonis,* he used the sonnet theme of the contest between sensual love and reasonable love, elaborating the whole struggle with all the gorgeous descriptions one might expect from his Renaissance age. He showed Venus, trying all the sweet snares of the flesh, in her effort to win the youth, but Adonis, who loved hunting and the manly sports of wholesome living, "laughed love to scorn" [l. 4]. . . .

Unable to send sensual love from him, Adonis finally said plainly:

> Remove your siege from my unyielding heart;
> To love's alarms it will not open the gate.
>
> [ll. 423-24]

As a last resort, Venus tried her most appealing charm; she fainted, all lovely as beautiful death before the youth's glance of fierce disdain. And when he revived her, and she renewed her entreaties to love, he answered:

> I hate not love, but your device in love
> That lends embracements unto every stranger
>   You do it for increase: O strange excuse!
>   When reason is the bawd to lust's abuse.
>
> [ll. 789-92]

All the pent-up anger of reason in love then burst forth against lust:

> Call it not love, for Love to heaven is fled,
> Since sweating Lust on earth usurp'd his name;
> Under whose simple semblance he hath fed
> Upon fresh beauty, blotting it with blame;
>   Which the hot tyrant stains and soon bereaves,
>   As caterpillars do the tender leaves.
>
> [ll. 793-98]

And like a cooling shower in the heat of summer, came the following words:

> Love comforteth like sunshine after rain,
> But Lust's effect is tempest after sun;
> Love's gentle spring doth always fresh remain,
> Lust's winter comes ere summer half be done.
>   Love surfeits not, Lust like a glutton dies;
>   Love is all truth, Lust full of forged lies.
>
> [ll. 799-804]

So Venus is shown as the destructive agent of sensual love; Adonis, as reason in love. The one sullies whatever it touches; the other honors and makes it beautiful. The one is false and evil; the other is all truth, all good. Reason in love, truth, beauty—these are the weapons with which lust must be met, or the ideals of man must go down in defeat before the appetites. Thus it is that when Adonis is killed, beauty is killed, and the world is left in black chaos, for beauty, the soul of matter, unites all parts of creation with the great God of beauty. This is the teaching of *Venus and Adonis,* as didactic

a piece of work, perhaps, as Shakespeare ever wrote. (pp. 283-85)

> Lu Emily Pearson, "Shakespeare, Petrarchist and Anti-Petrarchist," in her Elizabethan Love Conventions, *University of California Press, 1933, pp. 231-96.*

G. WILSON KNIGHT   (essay date 1939)

[*Knight was one of the most influential Shakespearean critics of the twentieth century; he helped shape a new interpretive approach to Shakespeare's work and promoted a greater appreciation of many of the plays. In his studies* The Wheel of Fire *(1930) and* The Shakespearian Tempest *(1932) Knight outlined principles of interpretation that, he claimed, would replace the "chaos" of criticism by drawing attention to the "true Shakespearian unity" that lay in the author's poetic use of images and symbols. In the following excerpt, Knight praises Shakespeare's vivid descriptions of the characters and animals in* Venus and Adonis, *claiming that the poet's "universal inwardness and sympathy" is revealed in the way he enters into the spirit of each figure. This "vital identification" with his subjects, according to the critic, allows Shakespeare to portray the beauty of the young hunter and the lustfulness of the stallion with equal vigor and sensitivity.*]

[The central thrust of the Shakespearian art-form is] positive

Adonis and Venus. Frontispiece to the Rowe edition (1714).

and creative; indeed, a love. This is both an outward sensu-ousness and an inward sympathy. The sensuousness is not Marlowe's. Marlowe's descriptions of Leander [in *Hero and Leander*] are sensuous to dangerpoint; and the danger will be found to lie in his abstracting tendency. His sensuousness is mental, and therefore limited. In *Venus and Adonis* you get an even stronger sensuousness: and yet it appears, because not so limited, healthy in the sense that Lawrence is, or tried to be, healthy. Marlowe's poem concentrates on Leander's es-pecially beautiful body; the blue sea in which he is swimming; and, when we get to shore, on artificial metalwork. Smooth water may be by itself a too facile way to sensuous descrip-tion; and, for the rest, the poem's territory is both mentalized and narrow; and there are, moreover, touches bordering on the lascivious charged here with poetic approval, yet with ever so faint a sense of sin to increase the delight. Shake-speare's physical descriptions work outside the sin-consciousness altogether; apply equally to nature as to man; and do not expand the superficially desirable, any more than he elsewhere descends to the superficially ugly. The beauty of Adonis, seen through Venus's mind, is indeed most lus-ciously felt; but so also is the horse, restless with hot instincts, his stallion magnificence, buttock and all, finely described. There is an inclusive purity in Shakespeare's sensuousness; and a wide realization of animal vitality, as in the baying hound's lifted head, the snail's withdrawn antlers, the 'chaf-ing' boar. Moreover, everything is inwardly conceived: he even imagines the darkness closing over the frightened snail in his tiny shell-house. Adonis's blood-life is felt through his physique: he is, as it were, a body lighted from within, and you get more of a real physical existence than in Marlowe's description of Leander's nakedness. Shakespeare is inside one object after another: which is, paradoxically, the one condi-tion of being properly outside it, and able to show it in con-vincing action. The famous description of 'poor Wat' the hunted hare shows, even more strongly, this universal in-wardness and sympathy. In *Venus and Adonis* and *Lucrece* Shakespeare gets his main sexual, and general, poles of refer-ence clear; and his later extreme intensities of love and evil are already implicit. The subjectively conceived agony of Venus predicts the later tragedies. Study of this poem alone, therefore, reveals the psychological centre of Shakespeare's work: a love rather than a lust; a vital identification rather than a confined sense-relation whether of eye or touch, as in Marlowe's Leander; and this not limited to the beautiful, and thence by a rebound to the satirically ugly as in Marlowe, but dispassionately universal. Exact differentiation is hard since every one of the opposite qualities is contained: lust, sense-perception, beauty. The difference is one of direction. All is so trusted—as Marlowe seldom trusts—that each object ex-pands, dissolves into a universal particularity where inward and outward are not distinct: which is perhaps what the Gos-pels mean by being pure in heart. Thence everything becomes sacramental. The difference is analogous to that between marriage-love and flirtation; between a dynamic adventure and a static enjoyment. Shakespeare is continually *married* to whatever he is treating, accepting it as itself and as a whole. His animals and people are thus neither ideal nor realistic, but real: the vital principle of each is apprehended and their actions therefore powerful. (pp. 30-2)

G. Wilson Knight, "The Shakespearian Integrity," in his The Burning Oracle: Studies in the Poetry of Action, *1939. Reprint by The Folcroft Press, Inc., 1969, pp. 19-58.*

W. B. C. WATKINS   (essay date 1942)

[*In the excerpt below, Watkins argues that Shakespeare did not have full control of his medium in* Venus and Adonis. *The frigid rhetoric, inconsistent characterization, ambivalent repre-sentation of sexuality, and "strained tone" of the poem, he con-tends, all demonstrate that the young poet failed in his attempt to execute the techniques of Ovidian poetry. An "unconscious satire" of the genre is one result of Shakespeare's straining for effect, he adds. Watkins also contrasts* Venus and Adonis *with Marlowe's* Hero and Leander, *and he concludes that inasmuch as Shakespeare's strength lies in imagery based on "natural ob-servation," he is markedly inferior to Marlowe in creating the "intellectualized, artificial imagery" characteristic of the Ovidian tradition.*]

Shakespeare was not a genius operating in a literary vacuum, and not so untaught as Ben Jonson's "small Latin and less Greek" seemed to indicate. No University wit himself, Shakespeare knew many of that select circle; however diffi-cult it is to demonstrate satisfactorily, he must have been deeply affected by his personal and literary association with them. The safest evidence is in his own works, and that evi-dence is most illuminating which shows the impact of a cur-rent literary mode on Shakespeare's individual poetic temper-ament, insofar as we can deduce that temperament from the constant study of the whole body of his works. Evidence of this kind is the player's speech about Hecuba in *Hamlet:*

> But who, O who had seen the mobléd queen . . .
> Run barefoot up and down, threat'ning the flames
> With bisson rheum; a clout upon that head
> Where late the diadem stood, and for a robe,
> About her lank and all o'erteemed loins,
> A blanket, in the alarm of fear caught up—
> Who this had seen, with tongue in venom steep'd
> 'Gainst fortune's state would treason have pro-
>   nounced.
>
> [II. ii. 502, 505-11]

This speech, significantly based directly on the *Aeneid,* re-duces the player to tears and draws an extraordinary panegy-ric from Hamlet:

> The play, I remember, pleas'd not the million,
> 'twas caviar to the general; but it was (as I received
> it, and others whose judgment in such matters cried
> in the top of mine) an excellent play, well digested
> in the scenes, set down with as much modesty as
> cunning.
>
> [II. ii. 435-40]

Such commendation of an extravagant, bombastic vein by the most intellectual of Shakespeare's characters has bewildered all thoughtful students of the play; the tone of the praise is so personal that it seems to be Shakespeare himself speaking. [In his *Shakespearean Tragedy,* A. C.] Bradley analyzes in some detail many suggested interpretations. More recently Sir Herbert Grierson [in his *Cross Currents in English Litera-ture of the Seventeenth Century*] maintains that the speech represents "Shakespeare's conception of classical tragedy, something that moved on loftier buskins than would suit a play at the Globe Theatre or his own taste for life and reali-ty." That Shakespeare had a taste for life and reality does not necessarily preclude an interest in more formalized "literary" types, or the implication that he may really have wanted to write in this vein; in fact, the genuineness of his desire is at-tested by his two early, self-consciously literary poems, *Venus and Adonis* and the *Rape of Lucrece,* and it can easily be proved that his interest in current literary types never left him, though the types are more perfectly assimilated in his mature work.

In *Venus and Adonis* Venus is so shocked to discover Adonis wounded that she sees double:

> "My tongue cannot express my grief for one.
> And yet" quoth she, "Behold two Adons dead:
> My sighs are blown away, my salt tears gone,
> My eyes are turn'd to fire, my heart to lead.
>   Heavy heart's lead, melt at mine eyes red fire,
>   So shall I die by drops of hot desire."
>
> [ll. 1069-74]

This anticipates the highly-wrought Hecuba vein, and such a line as

> Variable passions throng her constant woe
>
> [l. 967]

is exactly the sort of rhetoric usually deplored in eighteenth-century poetry by the same Romantic critics who have a neat way of blaming "un-Shakespearean" passages in Shakespeare on other men—"This is not Shakespeare; let the chips fall where they may."

We find in *Venus and Adonis* this overelaborate yet beautiful image:

> Or as the snail, whose tender horns being hit,
> Shrinks backward in his shelly cave with pain,
> And there, all smother'd up, in shade doth sit,
> Long after fearing to creep forth again,
>
> [ll. 1033-36]

followed by a couplet which is dubious:

> So at his bloody view her eyes are fled
> Into the deep-dark cabins of her head.
>
> [ll. 1037-38]

An attempt to explain exactly why I find the first four lines successful poetry and the final couplet dubious would require an elaborate analysis, out of place here; for, while it is an essential critical technique, intellectual analysis, unless it is constantly (and somewhat tediously) tested against the poem and one's intuition of it, is liable to become merely a skillful rationalization, a self-indulgence of the intellect at the expense of the poem. I shall merely make a few suggestions.

At this point in the poem Venus instinctively recoils from the realization of her anticipated dread, Adonis' death, shutting her eyes at the sight of his wounds. The snail image, though a daring conceit, shows both emotional and imaginative correspondence with Venus's recoil; if there is any emotion at all in the following couplet, it is a melodramatic violence quite inconsistent (despite the equivalence suggested by *so*) with the emotional tone preceding, while the imagistic correspondence is overliteral and rationalistic. We are led somewhat away from Venus's closing eyes by the snail image, so beautifully delicate and elaborate that it draws attention to itself; even so, the tenderness and timorous shrinking from pain fuse both images, the snail and Venus's eyes, and the incidental correspondence between shell and skull we absorb without too-literal visualization. In his attempt in the couplet to bring us back to Venus, Shakespeare makes unfortunately explicit and visual what the snail-image had subtly suggested; we see with brutal clarity the two eye-sockets of her skull—"the deep-dark cabins of her head"—into which her two now—virtually—personified eyes are fleeing. However ingenious

the conception may be, it is frigid; and the continued elaboration through two more stanzas is strikingly anticipatory of Cowley's cold-blooded, protracted autopsy of a conceit.

The fault in this couplet is not the resort to conceit, which is successful in the snail-image; nor is it the highly-wrought language. All his life Shakespeare indulged in rhetoric from time to time, either for its own sake, or to indicate a certain quality of emotion; but the rhetoric in *Venus and Adonis* is disconcerting because it does not seem to be always intentional or under full control. Much of the poem fails where *Hero and Leander* succeeds. *Venus and Adonis* remains caviar to the general; its partial failure, however, makes it extremely illuminating to the student of Shakespeare.

Shakespeare at this period is immature and over-ambitious, and this must be taken into account. He is straining for effect and consequently ill at ease. One suspects that his head is in the poem but not his heart. He seems carried out of his own element by his great admiration for Ovid and for Marlowe's recapture of the Ovidian spirit in *Hero and Leander*. And Marlowe's Ovidianism, like classic drama, is as much caviar to Shakespeare as to the general, though I think that he would have been reluctant to admit it, just as some ten years later the *Hamlet* passage suggests a reluctance to give up entirely a drama moving "on loftier buskins than would suit a play at the Globe Theatre."

Ovid unquestionably affected Shakespeare profoundly. "The whole character of Shakespeare's mythology," according to Mr. Root [in his *Classical Mythology in Shakespeare*], "is essentially Ovidian." But in *Venus and Adonis* he is at once too close to Ovid and Marlowe and too far removed from them. He could not accept the Ovidian spirit either pure or in Marlowe's Italianate version, and he had not yet learned to transmute it. Marlowe seems to be the immediate cause of the difficulty. Despite Shakespeare's immense debt to him, the minds of the two poets, their imaginations, their emotional quality, their interests are on the whole fundamentally different. Both are passionate and intense, but in different ways and about different aspects of life. Marlowe is the more intellectual; his mind is more single in focus and narrow in range. He is definitely more literary. Literary allusion and imagery have for him and for Milton deeper imaginative meaning than they have for Shakespeare, who is more emotional than intellectual, more interested in people than in books. The Ovidian tradition is essentially literary. Marlowe is completely at home in it; Shakespeare is not, though he tries to be in *Venus and Adonis*.

It has often been remarked that what vitality the poem has is owing to the nature imagery drawn from first-hand observation of the fields and woods. Shakespeare is inferior to Marlowe in intellectualized, artificial imagery; Marlowe is completely incapable of the Shakespearean type. Such are the snail image which I have already quoted, the hare, the hounds, the horses, the divedapper, the shooting star, the caterpillar, the blue-veined violets, and especially

> Lo, here the gentle lark, weary of rest,
> From his moist cabinet mounts up on high
> And wakes the morning, from whose silver breast
> The sun ariseth in his majesty.
>
> [ll. 853-56]

The artifice of the phrase "moist cabinet" is in keeping with the poem, yet it is interesting to observe the more characteristically Shakespearean expression of the same image not long after in *Sonnet 29:*

> . . . the lark, at break of day arising
> From sullen earth, sings hymns at heaven's gate,

and many years later, in *Cymbeline,* another transmutation into the inexplicable magic of

> Hark, hark, the lark at heaven's gate sings,
> And Phoebus 'gins arise.
> His steeds to water at those springs
> On chaliced flowers that lies.
>
> [II. iii. 20-3]

Quite apart from the growth in poetic maturity, this last passage shows perfect assimilation of a literary image with one of natural observation, an assimilation conspicuously absent in many parts of *Venus and Adonis.* In attempting to combine a conservatory atmosphere and the out-of-doors, an ornate style and simplicity of observation, Shakespeare may have had in mind something more than merely another Ovidian poem, or something different, but he failed.

The limitations of Marlowe's *Hero and Leander* are the limitations of its genre, the full imaginative, sensuous and humorous possibilities of which he exploits. The poem embodies, as Mr. Bush says [in his discussion of *Hero and Leander* in *Mythology and the Renaissance Tradition in English Poetry*], "the best qualities of the Italianate Ovidian tradition, along with its vices." This tradition derives as much from the *Amores* as from the *Metamorphoses,* as much from the sensualist as from the excellent story-teller. *Venus and Adonis,* for instance, combines two fables from the *Metamorphoses,* that of Venus and Adonis and of Salmacis and Hermaphrodite, while its motto is taken from the *Amores.* In *Hero and Leander* Marlowe sacrifices characterization and flow of narrative to sensuous elaboration for its own sake and to a kind of contemplative sensuality. He makes little attempt at consistency. Leander is presented as sexually innocent part of the time merely for the piquancy of the situation; at other times he speaks with all the authority of the "Professor of Love." Both lovers, in fact, are hardly presented in individual terms at all; they are primarily instruments for subtle sensuous and sensual impressions. And for this reason Marlowe, unlike Ovid, removes all traces of the unpleasant, so that the purely sensual is presented as unadulterated beauty. (pp. 706-12)

Shakespeare in *Venus and Adonis* is no more elaborate than Marlowe. Superficially, he seems to be trying for the same effect:

> Her two blue windows faintly she upheaveth
>
> [l. 482]

and

> Once more the ruby-colored portal opened
> Which to his speech did honey passage yield.
> Like a red morn, that ever yet betokened
> Wrack to the seaman, tempest to the field.
>
> [ll. 451-54]

Something may be said for the first image, despite the exaggerated conceit and mixed figure; but the second is both more frigid and more cloying than Marlowe's extravagances. As in Marlowe, there is a certain humorous awareness at times in the exaggeration. Desire lends Venus strength—

> Courageously to pluck him from his horse.
>
> [l. 30]

and there is even a Byronic colloquialism and use of pathos—

> "Sweet boy," she says, "this night I'll waste in sorrow,
> For my sick heart commands mine eyes to watch.
> Tell me, love's master, shall we meet tomorrow?
> Say, shall we? Shall we? Wilt thou make the match?"
> He tells her no; to-morrow he intends
> To hunt the boar with certain of his friends.
>
> [ll. 583-88]

Marlowe surpasses Byron in this sort of effect; Shakespeare only equals him. But the important point is that the humor in *Venus and Adonis* is sporadic and incidental rather than interfused throughout. Shakespeare wavers between taking himself too seriously and not seriously enough.

This wavering in tone is symptomatic of his lack of perfect control; whether we attribute this to ignorance of exactly what he was trying to do or to failure to achieve his end makes no real difference. The same wavering is apparent in his handling of the two characters in the story. If the embryonic dramatist intended to dramatize two conflicting points of view, as he does frequently in his plays with complete success, the result is fumbling.

Mr. Wilson Knight, preoccupied with what he calls "infeeling," finds that "Adonis's blood-life is felt through his physique; he is, as it were, a body lighted from within, and you get more of a real, physical existence than in Marlowe's description of Leander's nakedness" [see excerpt above, 1939]. He is right to the extent that Shakespeare recognizes certain more realistic, less preeminently beautiful aspects of physical relationship, though his recognition is not completely Ovidian. As for the "real existence" of Adonis, physical or otherwise, I think the most that can be said is that he is an incomplete sketch of what might, in a less confusing poem, have been a characterization. Shakespeare seems to have begun, like Marlowe, with the idea of frankly exploiting all the possibilities of the innocent young man in a sexual situation. Then, like Leander, Adonis suddenly and unexpectedly becomes a mouthpiece for wise aphorisms on love. This sacrifice of all interest in characterization in Marlowe we ultimately accept because we recognize a clearly perceived purpose; in Shakespeare the imperfect characterization remains confusing to the end, for no clear purpose is apparent and we are left wondering whether at certain critical points the poet is not merely using Adonis as a mask for his own conflicting emotions. I do not think that Mr. Knight clarifies the issue by calling the sensuousness of *Venus and Adonis* healthy "in the sense that Lawrence is, or tried to be, healthy," and completely disagree with his belief that "in *Venus and Adonis* and *Lucrece* Shakespeare gets his main sexual, and general, poles of reference clear." Clarity of pole or reference is precisely what is lacking.

Venus is reminiscent of the seventh elegy of the Third Book of the *Amores* when she protests—

> Fie, liveless picture, cold and senseless stone,
> Well-painted idol, image dull and dead,
> Statue contenting but the eye alone,
> Thing like a man, but of no woman bred!
>
> [ll. 211-14]

And it must be confessed that she is right to an extent that

Shakespeare can hardly have intended; throughout most of the poem Adonis is a "well-painted idol, image dull and dead," and the mere fact that the conditions of the story impose unresponsiveness from him is not sufficient explanation.

Mr. Knight points out that the poem "is written from the woman's view and the sensuous attractiveness is masculine." He suggests a relation to the "heterosexual" sonnets and an explanation akin to Mr. Wyndham Lewis's contention that Shakespeare's "sex organization," "his sentimentality was directed towards other men and not towards women." This literal extension of the conception of the "feminine" nature of genius is over-facile, ignoring on the one hand the limitations of the story, and on the other the nature of the imagination. When the preponderant majority of creative artists since the beginning of time have been masculine, the phenomenon of creative activity is hardly clarified by calling it feminine. When modern psychology is beginning to reveal something of the complexity of the ordinary human organism, little is gained by these over-simplifications, especially where normal complexity is complicated by genius. . . . It is not my purpose to enter the controversy, beyond pointing out that, though as a man of the Renaissance Shakespeare was fully cognizant of homosexuality, there is nothing in *Venus and Adonis* comparable to the Neptune-Leander passage in Marlowe's poem, and nothing in *Richard II* so frank and sympathetic in treatment as the Piers Gaveston portrait in Marlowe's *Edward II.*

The possibility of a revulsion from the physical fact of sex is more germane to the issue and plausible as an explanation of the confused emotional tone of *Venus and Adonis,* though not wholly convincing, especially since not so many years later Shakespeare writes with extraordinary frankness this sonnet to the dark lady:

Love is too young to know what conscience is;
Yet who knows not conscience is born of love?
Then, gentle cheater, urge not my amiss,
Lest guilty of my faults thy sweet self prove.
For, thou betraying me, I do betray
My nobler part to my gross body's treason;
My soul doth tell my body that he may
Triumph in love; flesh stays no farther reason,
But, rising at thy name, doth point out thee
As his triumphant prize. Proud of this pride,
He is contented thy poor drudge to be,
To stand in thy affairs, fall by thy side.
　　No want of conscience hold it that I call
　　Her "love" for whose dear love I rise and fall.
                                                    [Sonnet 151]

And much of the beauty of Juliet's speech on her wedding night comes from her frank recognition of the physical:

Come, civil night,
Thou sober-suited matron, all in black,
And learn me how to lose a winning match,
Play'd for a pair of stainless maidenhoods,
Hood my unmann'd blood, bating in my cheeks,
With thy black mantle till strange love, grown bold,
Think true love acted simple modesty.
                          [*Romeo and Juliet,* III. ii. 10-16]

The answer seems to be not so much a refusal to accept the physical aspects of love, as an inability to accept them entirely in Ovid's or Marlowe's terms.

Shakespeare, who was to become the supreme master of emo-

tional intensity, tries to achieve the intensity of Venus's passion thus:

By this, the lovesick queen began to sweat. . . .
Her face doth reek and smoke, her blood doth boil.
                                              [ll. 175, 555]

Even Adonis has a "sweating palm," his breath is a "steam" on which Venus feeds "as on a prey." She denies that she "lacks juice," and her heaving bosom she compares to an earthquake. All of this suggests the early pantomimic portrayal of passion in the silent cinema and is equally unconvincing. There is nothing wrong with sweat in a love scene; it adds to rather than detracts from Britomart as Spenser portrays her [in *The Faerie Queen*] after her fight with Artegall, her helmet off and her hair loose. Lovers sweat like anybody else, but they do not love by sweat alone. And it is not enough to say that Shakespeare, in moving the Ovidian poem outdoors, is seeking greater realism of expression and merely showing the effect of a beating sun. The whole tone of these passages suggests not intensity of passion, but the savage satire of Donne's

Rank sweaty froth my mistress brow defiles,
                    [*Elegie VIII, The Comparison*]

or Aldous Huxley's

Two lovers quietly sweating palm to palm.
                                      ["Frascati's"]

It is difficult to accept *Venus and Adonis* as conscious satire on the Ovidian tradition; but unconscious satire, probably an accidental result of the strained tone of the poem, is present. There is an opposite view. "Study of this poem alone, therefore, reveals the psychological center of Shakespeare's work," according to Mr. Knight: "a love rather than a lust; a vital identification rather than a confined sense-relation whether of eye or touch, as in Marlowe's Leander; and this not limited to the beautiful, and thence by a rebound to the satirically ugly as in Marlowe, but dispassionately universal." Though love considered as a vital identification rather than a confined sense-relation is characteristic of the later Shakespeare, it is not true of *Venus and Adonis,* taken as a whole; and the rebound from the beautiful to the satirically ugly, despite Mr. Knight, is more characteristic of Shakespeare than of Marlowe. A further comment of his on Shakespeare—that his 'physical descriptions work outside sin-consciousness'—is again not applicable to *Venus and Adonis,* but very descriptive of *Hero and Leander.*

Physical contact, real or mentally contemplated, which forms so much of the substance of the *Amores* and which Marlowe exploits to the full, Shakespeare either makes frenetic or shies away from. Take this passage from the *Amores:*

And don't allow him to place his arms about your neck, don't let your yielding head be on his rigid breast; and don't let your hidden charms submit to his touch; and, more than all, don't let him kiss you—not once . . . Bring not thigh near thigh, nor press with the limb, nor touch rough feet with tender ones . . .

The nearest parallel is not to be found so much in Venus's athletic exertions as in other passages of Shakespeare's, quite different in import, such as Hamlet's speech to Gertrude:

Let the bloat king tempt you again to bed;
Pinch wanton on your cheek; call you his mouse;

And let him, for a pair of reechy kisses,
Or paddling in your neck with his damn'd fingers
Make you to ravel all this matter out.
[*Hamlet,* III. iv. 182-86]

and Iago's account to Othello of Cassio's supposed dream:

And then, sir, would he gripe and wring my hand,
Cry "O sweet creature!" and then kiss me hard,
As if he pluck'd up kisses by the roots
That grew upon my lips; then laid his leg
Over my thigh, and sigh'd, and kiss'd,
Cried "Cursed fate that gave thee to the Moor."
[*Othello,* III. iii. 421-26]

The passage from Ovid portrays eminently natural sexual jealousy, together with a slightly perverse pleasure in that jealousy; the Shakespearean passages are an extreme combination of attraction and repulsion—the repulsion not latent, as in Spenser's description of the Adder Cymocles [in *The Faerie Queene*], but savagely dominant in imagery and emotional tone. In *Hamlet* and *Othello* the tone of these passages is clarified by the context. This tone is extraordinarily close to that of some parts of *Venus and Adonis,* in which it is not completely clarified by the context, and seems to indicate a partially repressed or not completely recognized emotional current.

This current emerges in the most astonishing moment in an Ovidian poem, when Adonis with a passion and eloquence suddenly acquired turns finally on Venus—

Call it not love, for Love to heaven is fled
Since sweating Lust on earth usurp'd his name;
Under whose simple semblance he hath fed
Upon fresh beauty, blotting it with blame;
    Which the hot tyrant stains and soon bereaves
    As caterpillars do the tender leaves.

Love comforteth like sunshine after rain,
But Lust's effect is tempest after sun.
Love's gentle spring doth always fresh remain;
Lust's winter comes ere summer half be done.
    Love surfeits not. Lust like a glutton dies:
    Love is all truth, Lust full of forged lies.
[ll. 793-804]

This is the tune of moral Spenser or of Milton in *Comus,* not of Ovid or Marlowe; and the quality of the poetry shows the depth of feeling behind this speech. Yet the speech does not have the inevitability that it would have had in Milton, who was quite clear from the beginning as to exactly what he was doing in *Comus.* It is hard to believe that the dramatic surprise of this outburst is an effect carefully calculated by the poet, or that Venus is meant to typify lust only.

In the *Rape of Lucrece,* his second poem, Shakespeare is concerned clearly with lust, but in *Venus and Adonis* Venus is not consistently lust; she is fitfully an Ovidian, non-moral embodiment of sexual love. Shakespeare in his dilemma is to some extent merely responding to the currents of his age; of all the poets of the Elizabethan Ovidian School, Marlowe alone accepts and embodies the pure Italianate Ovidian tradition. (pp. 715-21)

Shakespeare in failing to accept unmodified the Ovidian tradition is more typical than Marlowe of his age, though, being early in the field, he had only Marlowe and possibly Spenser to guide him. We should make due allowance for historical considerations, but if we regard this ambitious early poem in the light of his subsequent work I think we shall find in Shakespeare's own poetic temperament an important explanation of these waverings and inconsistencies. He manifestly tries, yet he cannot fully assimilate either the aureate style or the spirit of Ovid beyond a certain point. After Venus emerges from all the sweat and steam as a momentary apotheosis of Lust she becomes in desertion a much more sympathetic figure, despite the fact that the tone of the poem still shifts disconcertingly from frigid conceits to moving pathos. For instance, she is guilty of this extravagance:

'Tis true, 'tis true! thus was Adonis slain:
He ran upon the boar with his sharp spear,
Who did not whet his teeth at him again,
But by a kiss thought to persuade him there;
    And nuzzling in his flank, the loving swine
    Sheath'd unaware the tusk in his soft groin.
[ll. 1111-16]

But she can be more moving—

For he being dead, with him is beauty slain,
And, beauty dead, black chaos comes again.
[ll. 1019-20]

Black chaos comes again is not an Ovidian or Marlowian phrase; it suggests another Shakespearean context which accomplishes with immediate success what these lines try to do:

Excellent wretch! Perdition catch my soul
But I do love thee! And when I love thee not,
Chaos is come again.
[*Othello,* III. iii. 90-2]

In this speech of Othello's Shakespeare has found himself. The intensity of emotion and physical passion which fails of expression in Venus's Ovidian-styled speeches is supreme here:

O thou weed
Who art so lovely fair, and smellst so sweet
That the sense aches at thee.
[*Othello,* IV. ii. 67-9]

And seldom has sheer intensity of the senses been so well expressed as in these lines of Troilus, who is not the Ovidian or Marlowian but the Shakespearean sensualist:

I am giddy; expectation whirls me round.
The imaginary relish is so sweet
That it enchants my sense. What will it be
When that the wat'ry palates taste indeed
Love's thrice-repured nectar? Death I fear me;
Sounding destruction: or some joy too fine,
Too subtle-potent, tun'd too sharp in sweetness
For the capacity of my purer powers.
[*Troilus and Cressida,* III. ii. 18-25]

Shakespeare is no longer trying to master and present something intellectually in a style alien to him, as he was in *Venus and Adonis;* he is writing with perfect control in his own idiom about a sensuality emotionally and imaginatively fully apprehended. (pp. 722-23)

W. B. C. Watkins, "Shakespeare's Banquet of Sense," in The Southern Review, *Louisiana State University, Vol. VII, No. 4, Spring, 1942, pp. 706-34.*

HEREWARD T. PRICE   (essay date 1945)

[Price is among the first modern critics to consider Venus and Adonis a unified and well constructed work of art. In the following excerpt, he maintains that the poem's patterns of nature and color imagery are organized around the theme of "the destruction of something exquisite by what is outrageously vile." In Price's view, the contention between Venus and Adonis, described in terms of a "war" between red and white images, is transformed by the nature imagery into a microcosm of the conflict within nature, which is "with herself at strife." The death of the boy, which symbolizes the death of beauty and the unleashing of "black chaos" upon the world, the critic maintains, discloses Shakespeare's own "bitter pessimism about whatever power may rule the world."]

In *Venus and Adonis* Shakespeare has devised for himself a new technique of imagery. The microcosm, the little world inside man, is carried out into the macrocosm, the great world of Nature at large. By strictly adhering to a special sort of figure Shakespeare has made his poem appear so "objective" or so "external" that most scholars and critics ignore its power of projecting in a chosen form the inner life of man, the only reality for which Shakespeare ever cared.

Nobody has worked this out for *Venus and Adonis* in detail. Coleridge, of course, in a memorable passage, has celebrated the power that Shakespeare displayed in the images of *Venus and Adonis* [see excerpt above, 1817]. J. S. Hart has put Shakespeare's technique into a sentence: "The poem is not marked by stirring action, but by a series of minutely finished pictures" [see Additional Bibliography]. In this paper my purpose is to go beyond Coleridge and Hart in an endeavor to show how a common center of reference links all these images together and so gives them meaning. It is unnecessary to point out that meaning cannot be separated from form. I stress meaning, however, because, so far as I am aware, nobody has given adequate thought to the meaning of *Venus and Adonis* and, as a consequence, the poem has been hugely underrated.

Let us then, at the risk of repeating what has been said too often, make clear what Shakespeare was doing. He was not a Sophocles or a Boccaccio telling a tale that holds us by the faultless development of the action. He has, indeed, a story that gives the poem a beginning, a middle, and an end. But on a superficial view at any rate, his work seems to be flooded by an ocean of superfluous images. The truth is that Shakespeare makes the plot of *Venus and Adonis* as simple as possible in order to enable the reader to follow the intricate imagery more easily. It is important, therefore, to show that Shakespeare's images are interrelated by a general similarity of subject and that they all bear reference to the same central idea. They are full of the open air and the life of man and beast and plant in wild nature, and they are all steeped in the same implication with regard to the nature they symbolize. *Mutatis mutandis,* the technique is not unlike that of T. S. Eliot's *Waste Land.* As in all his works, Shakespeare creates a world existing by its own laws and so powerfully alive that it makes on us the impression of being as real as the world in which we move. It is not a pleasant place. The business both of the scholar and of the critic is to discover what happens in that world to make it a thing of such horror.

I propose to proceed by the historical method and to see the poem in connection with its age. The young Aristotelians of my acquaintance deprecate such methods. They assert that a poem must be considered as a thing apart and that the critic must never explain one work of art by another. A poem, they say, must stand on its own legs; the poet made it the way it is, and we must take it or leave it, just as he gave it to us. But I do not see why we should refuse the aid of history. It is important to point out that there is some resemblance between the work of Shakespeare and of Dürer. In an engraving by Dürer we have a multitude of details, all reinforcing one another, all pointing in the same direction, but they are so numerous that they have prevented critics from seeing what the picture is about. As a consequence, we have had to wait until the present generation for an adequate interpretation of his "Melancolia." Now it is curious that *Venus and Adonis* and *Lucrece* are in the same case as the "Melancolia." I am not accusing Shakespeare of being Dürer, but it is important to note that the art of these two men rises from the same sources. They are both the offspring of Gothic, and the principle of their technique is to convey a great idea not through economy and the clear line, but through a multiplicity of significant detail. A student of the Renaissance who has soaked himself in Dürer and recognized how superb is his achievement will find himself at home in *Venus and Adonis.*

But there is a more intimate aspect of the historical method. It is a sober fact that *Venus and Adonis* does not stand alone in Shakespeare's work. On the contrary, it is more or less contemporary not only with the historical plays like *Henry VI, Richard III,* and *Richard II,* but also with *Romeo and Juliet* and with *Lucrece.* In these works we find the same theme, intermittent in some, overwhelmingly predominant in others— the theme, namely, of the destruction of something exquisite by what is outrageously vile. Man and the cosmic process are at irreconcilable war; the ends of man are denied by the world he lives in. The good life is at the mercy of a blind destructive force. All these works are tragedies, and the fundamental theme of Shakespeare's tragedy is the existence of evil. . . . Whence evil? All these works are concerned with the same problem of why evil should be free to destroy the good. Shakespeare can no more answer the question than any other poet, but in posing it he shows that negative capability of which Keats speaks. What is not clear to him, what he does not know, he excludes; he gives only that aspect of the problem which he sees, without trying to bring in the whole of truth. In these works he is fascinated by the complete irrationality of evil. It is the situation he treats most superbly in *Othello.* . . . Now *Othello* and *Romeo and Juliet* and *Lucrece* and *Venus and Adonis* are all about the same thing— that is to say, the destruction of something good by a force that is not only vile but also so blind that it does not even know what it is destroying. (pp. 275-78)

[*Venus and Adonis*] has had its ups and downs. At first a best seller, it ran to sixteen editions in Shakespeare's lifetime, but from 1655 to 1866 not a single separate edition was published. The general attitude of critics is indicated by the note in Gabriel Harvey's *Marginalia:* "The younger sort takes much delight in Shakespeare's *Venus and Adonis:* but his *Lucrece,* and his tragedie of *Hamlet,* have in them, to please the wiser sort" [see excerpt above, 1598]. A tendency to deprecate Shakespeare's choice of subject has persisted down to the present day. For shame's sake I shall refrain from giving names or references. But one critic speaks of the poem's being "saved from degradation" by airiness and grace. Another rejects it for its sensualism and speaks of its "occasional and tardy morality" but praises its "outdoor poetry." As a rule, the criticism of *Venus and Adonis* reminds us of Tennyson in a black Victorian mood ranting about "art with poisonous honey stolen from France" and the "troughs of Zolaism." Few critics see that Shakespeare is both fascinated and appalled by the evil he is describing; fewer still have penetrated his savage irony.

Scholars and critics have all earned the same reproach. They see the poem as a fortuitous concourse of atoms that have nothing to do with one another. Surely nobody ought to have set pen to paper until he had brought the "sensualism," the "morality," and the "outdoor poetry" into line. Even when critics are not offended by the subject matter, there is no disposition to treat the poem seriously. Coleridge, as one might expect, has dug deepest. He is the only critic who has even attempted to understand the poem properly or whose judgment of it approaches the truth. I propose to show that *Venus and Adonis* is much greater than Coleridge knew or, at any rate, implied. It is a serious attempt to grapple with a problem that gave Shakespeare for the greater part of his career no rest—the problem, that is, of evil.

Philologists who have a way of saying all that can be said about a poem and who yet miss the point have wreaked their wicked will on *Venus and Adonis.* They have pointed out that Shakespeare did not invent the motif of the coy Adonis, that the stanza he uses was not new in narrative, that the poem is permeated with the sweetness of mellifluous Ovid, that Shakespeare in an effort to make poetry do the work of painting blazoned the tale in splendid colors, that for the rest he proceeds by means of an old and almost threadbare technique, employing the debate, elaborate dialogue, long speeches and apostrophes, amplification, and God's plenty of proverbs, wise saws, and gnomic sayings. In his narrative technique Shakespeare is a disciple of Chaucer, starting where Chaucer left off. Scholars add that Shakespeare's use of images observed directly from nature proves that he wrote *Venus and Adonis* in the countryside of Stratford-on-Avon, apparently before he lost contact with nature in the town. It has never occurred to them to ask about the function of such natural imagery in this poem, and until that question has been answered, nothing else matters.

It is important to notice that Shakespeare's scale of images comes to him from Bion's elegy on Adonis. Venus mourns Adonis, whom a boar has slain by a wound in the thigh. She rushes to the body of Adonis, through brake and brier, her clothes torn, and the sharp thorns covering her body with blood. All nature mourns for Adonis, the mountains, the oaks, the rivers, and the flowers. From the ground where he dies two flowers spring up, the rose from his blood, and the anemone from the tears of Venus. Apart from the details of the story, Shakespeare may have learnt from Bion's skill in contrasting color; purple and black robes, blood on snow-white skin, bright eyes and rosy lips fading to pallor, the purple pall on the corpse of Adonis, the two contrasting flowers. But, most significant of all, Bion's elegy is not *about* Venus and Adonis. With a Greek delicacy and subtlety that an English pen finds it hard to convey, it is *about* a process of nature. One might almost say that the spirit of Bion had passed into Shakespeare. At any rate, whether by accident or design, *Venus and Adonis* resembles no poem so closely as it does the elegy of Bion. (pp. 286-87)

Shakespeare read up his story in other classical sources besides Bion. He complicated Bion's simple tale by many inventions. From the thirty-first idyl of Theocritus he brought in the motif of the boar killing Adonis by misadventure, without intention. "I him beheld for love . . . Which made me for-

ward shove His thigh . . . Thinking to kiss, alas." Moreover, Shakespeare obviously knows Ovid's story of Adonis, and he interweaves with it motifs from the fables of the coy Salmacis. Shakespeare takes his boar from Ovid, but he makes significant additions, such as that the boar strikes whatever is in his way, his snout digs sepulchers, and the brambles and bushes are afraid of him.

The red and white flower into which Shakespeare transforms Adonis has a long history. We have seen that in Bion two flowers spring up from the blood of Adonis, a red one and an anemone. Ovid transforms Adonis into a red flower, and in another story tells how Narcissus was transformed into a white and yellow flower. In the Renaissance Ronsard follows Bion closely in his elegy on Adonis. Spenser, in his *Astrophel,* a pastoral elegy on the death of Sidney, tells how his love flung herself upon his dead body, and died of a broken heart. The gods in pity transformed them into a flower "both red and blue." It is certain that the Elizabethans read a meaning into the incident of the flower. George Sandys [in his translation of Ovid's *Metamorphoses* (1632)] says:

> The Boy, *with whom Loue seem'd to dy,* [my italics]
> Bleeds in the fresh Anemony.

And later on:

> The louely Adonis is fained to haue been changed
> into Anemony, a beautifull but no permanent flow-
> er: to expresse the fraile condition and short contin-
> uance of Beautie.   (p. 288)

Thus Shakespeare's red and white flower comes to him through Bion, Ovid, Spenser, and perhaps Ronsard. Sandys sees in this flower a symbol of the frailty of Beauty, of the boy with whom Love seemed to die. It gives one a thrill of pleasure to know that Shakespeare's symbolism was based not only upon tradition but also upon observed fact; the *flos Adonis* was an anemone, and some forms of anemone were "purple . . . checkred with white" [l. 1168].

However, the truth about *Venus and Adonis* is that, while Shakespeare borrows much from established convention, he is at the same time daringly original. In the main the poem is constructed with two series of images, finely articulated and often interlacing, namely, the images from nature, especially from wild animals, on the one hand; on the other, the images of red and white, dark and light. There is little about these images that is bookish, most of them being observed straight from the object. There is probably no other poem in which direct first-hand observation of nature has been used with such brilliant effect to create form. It is important to note how closely nature links *Venus and Adonis* with the *Midsummer Night's Dream* and *Romeo and Juliet.* In these three works nature is shown with subtle and profound significance, not as a backdrop to action but itself as a force, active in human life. The important matter, then, is to consider what sort of force this nature is shown to be.

The other set of symbols, the contrast between red and white, runs through the whole poem. In the use of this image Shakespeare shows as much originality and perhaps even more subtlety than in the images from nature. The technique of intertwining two or more series of images is the same as in *Lucrece,* where . . . the main image is taken from war, while a subsidiary image, that of contrasting red and white, is also used.

Let us consider the nature symbol first. In *Venus and Adonis* nature is first of all a symbol at large. The story is about a boar hunt in a forest; the whole action occurs in the open air, and it might be said that the story is really about this nature in which men live, and move, and have their being. To repeat, nature interpenetrates the story so intimately that one cannot say that nature is the background or scene of events; rather, she is part of the action. Her colors are those of the characters:

> Even as the sunne with purple-coulourd face,
> Had tane his last leaue of the weeping morne,
> Rose-cheekt Adonis hied him to the chace. . . .
>
> [ll. 1-3]

When we say that the poem is about nature, then it is about nature in the widest possible sense. Shakespeare is not giving us a mere study of Stratford woods and fields. The subject is boldly announced in the opening of the poem:

> Nature that made thee *with her selfe at strife,* [my italics]
> Saith that the world hath ending with thy life.
>
> [ll. 11-12]

The poem is about "nature with herself at strife." In these words Shakespeare states the subject of all tragedy, the problem of the dissonances that destroy the harmony in the moral order of the world. Using nature in this sense as the subject of the poem, Shakespeare proceeds to set forth his meaning by a closely related chain of figures drawn entirely from nature in the sense of the world exterior to man. At the same time the system of natural imagery mirrors both the workings of whatever power rules the world and the moral qualities of human beings.

As the story takes place entirely in the open, so the poem vibrates with the movement of the air. Shakespeare fills it with the changes of nature as day passes into night and night again into day or as they are shown in the phenomena of the weather. As one example for many:

> Loue comforteth like sun-shine after raine,
> But lusts effect is tempest after sunne,
> Loues gentle spring doth alwayes fresh remaine,
> Lusts winter comes, ere sommer halfe be donne.
>
> [ll. 799-802]

This image is not simply something that occurred to Shakespeare and that he thought worth putting into his poem. He invents it with cold deliberation, illustrating the division of man's nature into good and bad by a figure showing that nature at large is split in the same way. By strictly limiting his choice of figures to such as accord with his central theme, Shakespeare achieves that unity of impression at which all poets aim, Classical or Romantic.

Since Homer elaborate descriptions of sunrise and sunset have been traditional in epic poetry. In days when there were neither clocks nor watches, time was observed from the progress of the sun or the stars. Shakespeare, following the ancient tradition, marks the passage of events by two descriptions of sunrise [ll. 1-2, 853-58] and one of sunset [ll. 529-34]. In this way he kills two birds with one stone; he plays the game according to the rules, while at the same time making his poem as purely natural as possible. His first sunrise, with which the poem opens, is a red one and thus indicates the disaster to come. The coming of the second day is celebrated at [ll. 853-58]. Venus immediately salutes the sun:

> Oh thou cleare god, and patron of all light . . .
> There liues a sonne that suckt an earthly mother,
> May lend thee light, as thou doest lend to other.
>
> [ll. 860, 863-64]

Adonis . . . is identified with light. The coming of night [ll. 529-34] is heralded by that fatal bellman the owl. Night is one of the most frequent figures in Shakespeare to symbolize Death. Nor is it mere prettiness that makes Shakespeare conclude his picture of nightfall with the line: "Cole-black clouds, that shadow heauens light" [l. 533]. In these passages Shakespeare hints at the division of nature—this time into night and day, death and life, into darkness that swallows up light.

The persons of the poem are placed then in this setting of a world divided against itself. But what about these persons? For them Shakespeare invents a finely linked chain of animal images. Venus and Adonis are the huntress and the hunted. There is one set of figures for Adonis and a much larger and more important group for Venus. The figures invented for Adonis stress, of course, his sensitive delicacy.

> Vpon this promise did he raise his chin,
> Like a diuedopper peering through a waue,
> Who being lookt on, ducks as quickly in.
>
> [ll. 85-7]

His mood is described:

> Like a wild bird being tam'd with too much handling,
> Or as the fleet-foot Roe that's tyr'd with chasing.
>
> [ll. 560-61]

Shakespeare foreshadows his fate in the long figure of the hare, lust's victim, relentlessly pursued to be enjoyed, only to its destruction [ll. 679-708]. Shakespeare did not invent these figures merely because he still happened to be living in the country. They are part of an intricate scheme in which the cruelties practiced in nature symbolize the fate of something too bright and exquisite to live.

Venus is described in a series of figures that represent the various sides of her nature. Her irrepressible desire to possess and to destroy is represented in three figures; she is the eagle [ll. 55-60], the horse [ll. 259-318], the boar [ll. 611-12, 1105-18]. The figures gradually rise in intensity. The eagle's fierce desire is remorseless as it tears its prey to pieces. It is a figure of lust and cruelty joined in destruction, but as Shakespeare is for the present only foreshadowing the climax, he keeps it short. Then comes the figure of the horse, its uncontrollable animal passion a convincing picture of the power of lust in Venus, lust that has taken the bit between its teeth.

> The yron bit he crusheth tweene his teeth,
> Controlling what he was controlled with.
>
> [ll. 269-70]

Then the boar, that kills blindly, not seeing or knowing what it destroys, Venus in her most horrible symbol.

But the boar loves while he blindly slays, and Venus also has her moments of tenderness.

> She wildly breaketh from their [bushes'] strict imbrace,
> Like a milch Doe, whose swelling dugs do ake,
> Hasting to feed her fawne, hid in some brake.
>
> [ll. 874-76]

Henry Wriothesley, Earl of Southampton.

Only the man to whom has been vouchsafed the luck of seeing the milch doe in the forest can realize the wonder of this figure. I have enjoyed it once when a milch doe loped by me with an indescribable grace and bent over a fence to lick its young, a tiny stag calf, and, when I approached, lightly footed away with the same entrancing beauty. This is the most glorious sight that the forest has to show. It would not be easy to imagine any other figure from animal life that should depict so aptly the Queen of Love in her distress for Adonis.

The primary importance of these images is that they are not chosen at random, the idle harvest of a luxurious mind remembering happy hours. Zola is said to have observed that the artist when he begins to write must be as cold as ice. In order, then, to build up his great symbol of life in nature, Shakespeare, in Zola's spirit, puts together these figures with cunning deliberation. The images cohere and form a logical unit. Carefully planned, they lead on from one to another in a rising scale of intensity, with the result that in no other Elizabethan poem is the intellectual interest sustained at such a high level.

When we come to the second series of symbols, the conflict of red and white which is resolved in the flower that springs from the corpse of Adonis, it is difficult at first for the modern reader to find his way. We cannot nowadays recapture the

Elizabethan delight in the symbolism of colors and flowers. But taking probability as our guide, we can say that we shall probably go wrong if we are insensitive to the manifold suggestions of meaning that are implied by the use of colors and flowers in poetry. The difference between Shakespeare and the other Elizabethan poets of the nineties is that his flowers and colors are firmly integrated into a scheme of symbols, so firmly that they are, like his animal pictures, fitted into a tight, logical structure. (pp. 289-93)

"The war of red and white" is one of those figures that Elizabethan poets wore thin. Shakespeare makes fun of it in *The Taming of the Shrew* [IV. v. 30], but in *3 Henry VI* [II. v. 97-101] he uses it to symbolize the tragic mess of the Wars of the Roses. No doubt the bitter memory of these disastrous wars heightened any reference to the "war of red and white." In the same way the union of red and white was seen as a symbol of reconciliation such as was effected by the union of Lancaster and York in the house of Tudor. (p. 293)

The conflict between red and white runs through the poem. It is suggested in the opening lines when the sun "with purple-coloured face" takes his leave of the "weeping morne," and the suggestion is carried to its height in the second stanza:

> More white, and red, then doues, or roses are:
>   Nature that made thee with her selfe at strife,
>   Saith that the world hath ending with thy life.
>
> [ll. 10-12]

At line 21 Venus tells him her kisses will make his lips "red, and pale, with fresh varietie," alternating "sacietie" and "famishing." At line 36 Adonis is "red for shame, but frostie in desier." Frosty-cold, but hoarfrost is white. At line 50 "red for shame" becomes "the maiden burning of his cheekes." At line 76 you have:

> Twixt crimson shame, and anger ashie pale,
>   Being red she loues him best, and being white,
>   Her best is betterd with a more delight.
>
> [ll. 76-8]

In these cases red and white are in conflict; they are the symbols of passions fighting one another. This mingled red and white is the fatal livery of the boar that kills while meaning to be kind:

> Whose frothie mouth bepainted all with red,
> Like milk, & blood, being mingled both togither.
>
> [ll. 901-02]

In Venus herself red wars with white:

> O what a sight it was wistly to view,
> How she came stealing to the wayward boy,
> To note the fighting conflict of her hew,
> How white and red, ech other did destroy:
>   But now her cheeke was pale, and by and by
>   It flasht forth fire, as lightning from the skie.
>
> [ll. 343-48]

The two colors cannot exist together; they are always in conflict. They are mutually contradictory, and they symbolize the conflict and the contradictions that are the subject of the poem. But the two colors are not only at war with one another; each is at war with itself. Red is the color of disaster as in the opening stanza or in [ll. 451-56], where the red of Adonis's lips is likened to a red morn. But it is also the symbol of vigor, richness, and warmth of life; it is the color of the life-giving blood. Again, red is the symbol of shame in Adonis but of passion in Venus. It is the same with white; anger makes Adonis pale, while fear does the same for Venus. Shakespeare even invents a stanza to show white at war with white:

> Full gently now she takes him by the hand,
> A lillie prisond in a gaile of snow,
> Or Ivorie in an allablaster band,
> So white a friend, ingirts so white a fo.
>
> [ll. 361-64]

But after Adonis dies, the red and white are reconciled:

> By this the boy that by her side laie kild,
> Was melted like a vapour from her sight,
> And in his blood that on the ground laie spild,
> A purple floure sproong vp, checkred with white,
>   Resembling well his pale cheekes, and the blood,
>   Which in round drops, vpon their whiteness
>   stood.
>
> She bowes her head, the new-sprong floure to smel,
> Comparing it to her Adonis breath. . . .
>
>   She [Venus] crop's the stalke, and in the breach
>   appeares,
>   Green-dropping sap, which she compares to
>   teares.
>
> [ll. 1165-72, 1175-76]

The flower is to wither in her bosom. Adonis was twice butchered, once in blindness by the boar, and the second time in equal blindness but no less effectively by Venus. I know of no irony in literature so savage as this.

Shakespeare reinforces his tragic imagery by emphatic statement. The curse that Venus pronounces on love cannot be dismissed as mere rhetoric. It reinforces the well-known lines in the *Midsummer Night's Dream* [I. i. 145-49]. . . . It states in so many words the meaning of *Romeo and Juliet* and of *Lucrece.* One must admit that the curse is expressed in conventional terms, but that should not blind us to the bitter passion by which it is inspired. It bears every mark of utter sincerity. The pessimism of the poem is emphasized by two lines that only one scholar has noticed:

> For he being dead, with him is beautie slaine,
> And beautie dead, blacke Chaos comes againe.
>
> [ll. 1019-20]

"When Adonis is killed, beauty is killed, and the world is left in black chaos, for beauty, the soul of matter, unites all parts of creation with the great God of beauty. This is the teaching of *Venus and Adonis,* as didactic a piece of work, perhaps, as Shakespeare ever wrote" [see excerpt above by Lu Emily Pearson, 1933].

To this I might add that in reading Elizabethan poetry we are apt to forget that beauty refers in the first place not to what gives a sensual pleasure but to the principle, Platonic idea or Christian plan, of which the thing seen is but a reflection or a symbol. Adonis is so often described in the poem as "beauty" that there can be no doubt that Shakespeare sees him as a symbol.

> Thrice fairer than my selfe . . .
> The fields chiefe flower, sweet aboue compare,
> Staine to all Nimphs, more louely than a man,
> More white, and red, than doues, or roses are:
>   Nature that made thee with her selfe at strife,
>   Saith that the world hath ending with thy life.
>
> [ll. 7, 8-12]

"The fields chiefe flower"—almost the words with which Capulet [in *Romeo and Juliet*] describes the daughter he believes to be dead:

> Death lies upon her like an untimely frost
> Upon the sweetest flower of all the field.
>
> [IV. iv. 28-9]

"Nature that made thee. . . ." There is the problem of the poem. In *Romeo and Juliet* Shakespeare stresses the perfection of his hero and heroine as children of nature, and yet there is some power in nature to destroy them. Adonis is the darling of nature.

> To see his face the Lion walkt along,
> Behind some hedge, because he would not fear [i.e.
>   terrify] him:
> To recreate himself when he hath song,
> The Tygre would be tame, and gently heare
>   him. . . .
>
> [ll. 1093-96]

When he died:

> No floure was nigh, no grasse, hearb, leaf, or weed,
> But stole his blood, and seemd with him to bleed.
>
> [ll. 1055-56]

Shakespeare states the problem, but he offers no answer. He is content for the time being with presenting it. *Venus and Adonis* displays the dualism of all Shakespeare's work up to *Coriolanus.* No saint ever adored spiritual beauty with Shakespeare's passion, but his bitter pessimism about whatever power may rule the world makes it unlikely that the Church will ever canonize him. However, after *Coriolanus* in his last plays Shakespeare finds his answer, and he becomes, to use a phrase coined for Spinoza, "a God-intoxicated man."

Now you will probably say this paper is off its subject. The object of criticism is to show whether the work under consideration communicates the joy appropriate to poetry. That is just my point. I make the immodest claim that I am the only man of our days to say in print that he has really received from *Venus and Adonis* the joy that Shakespeare intended to communicate. The cause of my enjoyment is simple. I have found the poem full of meaning. It links the images and interrelates all the various parts of the poem in such a way that by meaning alone does *Venus and Adonis* achieve form. The meaning gives to the poem its magnitude, its importance, and its value. Now I will not imitate the vices of the modern school by limiting poetry to just one kind or variety and assert that no poetry has value unless it has meaning or that all poetry must be like *Venus and Adonis.* I cannot tell how many different sorts of poetry are to be found. There may be plenty of good poems that lack meaning. All I say is that Shakespeare has based this one poem at least on a profound conception, held with passionate intensity and conviction, expressed in finely imagined symbols that are combined with subtely and delicate art into a form of such beauty that it thrills the reader with an immense joy. (pp. 294-97)

Hereward T. Price, "Function of Imagery in 'Venus and Adonis'," in Papers of the Michigan Academy of Science, Arts and Letters, *Vol. XXXI, 1945, pp. 275-97.*

ROBERT P. MILLER (essay date 1952)

[*In the following excerpt, Miller suggests that the episode of Adonis's courser and the jennet "may sound the keynote" of* Venus and Adonis. *According to the critic, by careful "manipulations of style and subject," Shakespeare links the behavior of the two horses to that of Venus and Adonis and thereby offers a significant commentary on the main narrative. Not only are the animals' actions a parody of romantic courtship, Miller asserts, they are used to wittily convey a sound moral lesson. By urging the youth to follow the courser's example, Venus is, in terms of Renaissance moral doctrine, inciting him to reenact the Fall of Adam by throwing off the "healthy bridle" of reason and submitting to the impulse of sensual appetite. Miller further calls attention to Shakespeare's emphasis on the jennet's role as a propagator of her breed and to the poet's depiction of Venus as interested only in the immediate pleasures of sexual intercourse.*]

The episode of the Courser and the Jennet in *Venus and Adonis* has received considerable attention as a noteworthy example of the youthful Shakespeare's mastery of descriptive realism, but the few attempts to relate the part thematically to the whole have been unspecific in their application, leaving the poem open to the criticism of lacking organic unity. A critical approach which takes commonplace Renaissance symbols and moral ideas into consideration may offer possibilities for a better understanding of this passage both in its own right and in its relation to the main narrative. If so, a fresh approach to the poem as a whole may be indicated. For if the horses and associated details are considered symbolically, we may view the episode as expressing—through a fairly complex analysis of romantic love—a 'moral dimension' in the poem: the concept of love thus presented being reinforced and heightened by the poet's stylistic treatment of his material. The following study points to a degree of conscious artistry and control of his medium earlier in the career of Shakespeare than is generally assumed. Further, it shows that his seemingly digressive treatment of the horses may be said to form an integral part of the total conception of the poem. Finally, it suggests a mature attitude toward romantic courtship on the part of the early Shakespeare.

The section of *Venus and Adonis* devoted to the horses deserves attention for several reasons. It is by far the most extensive interpolation of material extraneous to the Ovidian source to be found in the poem. Matter of Shakespeare's own invention has here been deliberately inserted into a story well known to the reading audience he was addressing, and would presumably have attracted notice as a significant departure from the traditional account. Although it may have been included as a mere exercise in ingenuity, it is more likely that the episode was intended to emphasize or to clarify Shakespeare's own interpretation of Ovid's tale. In this connection we may note, furthermore, that this is the only place in the poem where the author describes at all extensively, in his own words, something not immediately concerned with Venus and Adonis themselves. (In effect, he has introduced two new characters at this point.) Ideas or attitudes expressed here are therefore presumably his own, as distinguished from those of his characters, and important enough to warrant lengthy digressive treatment. The significant decision to include the digression, as well as the provocative nature of this material, suggest that a thorough examination of the passage should be a fruitful preliminary step for the interpretation of *Venus and Adonis*.

Formal considerations indicate that the episode of the Courser and the Jennet [ll. 259-324] was conceived as a unified whole. It has a beginning, middle and end, artistically organized with relation to each other. The Jennet, who is mentioned only in this section, appears "from forth a copp's that neighbors by" [l. 259], and the two horses, at the end of the digression, disappear back into the thicket. Adonis seeks to take his horse at both beginning and end. The account intervenes between these efforts as though it took no time, or were out of time. If, as such an entity, it is examined from the point of view of stylistic exposition, the episode shows a highly conscious and consistent presentation of its material in a humorously ironic manner. It will be seen that for this purpose Shakespeare takes full advantage of contrasting modes of diction, of the nature of his stanza, and of verbal ambiguity, in order to develop *two* subjects in his interlude; and that, in addition, the artistic effects he attempts to achieve depend upon the recognition of this dual reference: that is, to horses and to men, which are implicitly compared throughout.

As at least a reflection of the main plot, the episode deals with a love-affair. The Jennet tempts the Courser, and the action proceeds according to the artificial conventions of romantic courtship. The Courser becomes a suitor, and tries, in equine fashion, by posturing to impress his lady. He neighs his proposal, only to meet (as lovers always do) with disdain [ll. 307-12], the mistress' cruelty. His resulting melancholy [ll. 313-16] is in due course followed by pity, however, and finally by consent on the part of the "faire breeder." Isolated from its context in the poem, the entire episode is, in its own right, a parody of the game of romantic courtship familiar to the Elizabethan reader—for these are, after all, only horses. In context, the fact that Shakespeare has chosen to parody this concept of courtship is of additional significance.

The particular force of the parody depends upon the style in which it is presented. Reflecting the traditional atmosphere of love, much of the description is conducted in the refined and artificial language associated with romance, but hardly appropriate for realistically conceived horses. The Courser and Jennet are treated in terms conventionally applied to the ideal knight and his lady. Courtly overtones abound; there are echoes of the heroic hyperbole. On the other hand, we are not allowed to forget that these are horses, although no two horses ever acted in exactly this way. An element of realistic wording preserves the duality of reference between lovers and beasts. They are said to "neigh," "snort," "trot," bite flies in fume, and to possess a "melting buttocke" (something the romantic lover never mentions outright). The Courser is described at length as an ideal *horse*. When he and the Jennet elope, a last deflating touch is added to the picture of their flight: in their hasty speed they outstrip no noble bird, but "crowes"—which brings the whole episode, at the last, back to the more naturalistic animal world. The intended contrast between the activities of horses and those of romantic lovers is consciously maintained and utilized for the purpose of irony in the interplay of discordant poetic styles. Further, Shakespeare's handling of stanza structure and his use of the double meaning of certain words aid in presenting an ironic view.

In general, throughout the poem, Shakespeare develops an idea or description slowly in the quatrain of his stanza, and epitomizes it in the couplet where the rhetorical emphasis naturally falls. The nature of the stanza invites this technique. The same form, however, is peculiarly appropriate for the purpose of irony. That is, the development of the quatrain may be *punctured* by the couplet, and the sense of the whole quickly reversed. The concluding line of stanza 50 [ll. 295-300] . . . undercuts both this and the preceding stanza by presenting one "lack" which, especially in the human analogy, may make the entire roll of virtues superfluous; the animal implication of line 312 makes the romantic build-up of stanza 52 [ll. 307-12] ironic; while the concluding line of stanza 54 [ll. 319-24] . . ., in its widest sense, undercuts the whole episode. The intent of this formal technique is obviously to make fun, not of the horses themselves, but of the conventions of romantic courtship insofar as the horses' actions reflect them; just as in style artificial, romantic diction is made fun of, not only by the presence of the horses, but also by its juxtaposition with a more realistic terminology.

The same double reference is maintained, furthermore, in individual words. For instance, stanza 52 is stylistically constructed with this double standard in mind [ll. 307-12].

> He lookes vpon his loue, and neighes vnto her,
> She answers him, as if she knew his minde,
> Being proud as females are, to see him woo her,
> She puts on outward strangenesse, seemes vnkinde:
>   Spurnes at his loue, and scorns the heat he feeles,
>   Beating his kind imbracements with her heeles.

Everything in the quatrain would be much more appropriate to human lovers than to horses, with the exception of the phrase "neighes vnto her" carefully planted in the first line. While the Courser proposes and the Jennet manifests her proud disdain, the reader is not to forget that these are animals. The preliminary illusion, however, of the polite ritual of love-making is effectively dispelled with subtle changes of terminology, and with increasing force. The shift in reference begins with the word "spurnes," which Shakespeare uses in a double sense. The politer sense of contempt or disdain is, by addition of the preposition *at,* given an active, animal force: "to kick (*at* something)." Both meanings are carried in the phrase, though the romantic mistress is not usually said to "spurn at" her lover or "his loue." The implication of this phrase is fully carried out in the last line: she *beats* "his kind imbracements *with her heeles*"—an act undeniably animal. With the context shifted from lovers to horses the polite term "kind imbracements" has been introduced, but the physical picture of the line is perfectly apparent, and the ridiculous affectation of the term is obvious.

"*Kind* imbracements" has itself a dual meaning: in the politer context, *gentle, affectionate, courteous* (as it apparently has in the earlier phrase "seemes vnkind"), and in the animal context, *natural.* In her disdain, then, the Jennet also "seemes" as if she is going to act unnaturally; and later she is said to "grow kinder," upon her acceptance of the Courser's suit [l. 318]. The double possibility in meaning points up a philosophical distinction between man and animal at the heart of the episode. More important for the present point, it takes advantage of the double reference consciously worked out in the stanza.

By a shifting manipulation of style and subject Shakespeare thus plays variations of irony and parody. Basically humorous, his artistic intent is evidently to ridicule an artificial system by exposing its essential nature, using as actors horses, whose motivations cannot be questioned insofar as they are only animals. His handling of the episode implies the criticism that the love game played by the romancers is little more than a polite formula created to disguise the fact that the 'service of Venus' is actually to follow the dictates of natural sexual desire. The carefully chosen terms and effects depend upon this assumption for their force. In [ll. 314-15],

> He vailes his taile that like a falling plume,
> Coole shadow to his melting buttocke lent,

we may see how closely style reflects the burden of the author's attitude. Under the refined language exists the fact that these are but horses: the last three words turn the lines back on themselves in tone. Under the "falling plume" exists the "melting buttocke." The dangerous 'lover's melancholy,' it is suggested, is sexual frustration disguised; the courtly activity of the romantic ritual is a rich caparison for lust.

That the purpose of the episode is to comment by parallelism upon the main narrative is sufficiently evident from the application made by Venus to her own affair [ll. 385-408], in which she praises the horses. The first stanza of the episode itself indicates the existence and nature of this parallelism. As in the case of Venus and Adonis themselves, it is the female who makes the first advances. The Courser, however, unlike Adonis, immediately follows the impulses of his animal nature [ll. 263-64].

> The strong-neckt steed being tied vnto a tree,
> Breaketh his raine, and to her straight goes hee.

His actions therefore contrast forcibly with those of his parallel in the main narrative.

The fact that, although the actors in the episode are horses, their described activities must be interpreted by reference to human as well as equine conduct, suggests the application intended by the author. But if the horses are parallel to Venus and Adonis in a significant number of respects, the technique must yet be termed '*conditional parallelism.*' That is, the Courser does not do what Adonis does; he does what Adonis *would* do *if* he were the kind of man Venus wishes him to be. The episode is conditional in that it indicates what would be the nature of the love affair if Adonis were differently constituted. It also expresses Shakespeare's criticism of this possibility, the particulars of which are implied by his use of certain Renaissance conventions.

If we look at the episode as a conditional parallel of the main action, and take *human* nature into consideration, it is possible to explain the significance of elements which are more meaningful in relation to men than to horses. In selecting a horse as the main actor of the passage Shakespeare was able to expand a very common traditional image: that of the horse, the bridle and the rider. At least as old as the black horse of Plato's *Phaedrus,* this image provides a useful analogy with the faculties of man. The horse, in later convention, symbolizes the lower appetites of the flesh, while the rein and rider stand for the powers of reason which are theoretically supposed to control and direct such lusts. Used in this way, the image may be found frequently in Renaissance literature. Arthur Golding, for example, in the rhymed prefatory epistle to his translation of the *Metamorphoses* (1567), says,

> The man in whom the fyre of furious lust dooth
>   reigne Dooth run to mischeefe like a horse that getteth loose the reyne.

Spenser's Sansjoy [in *The Faerie Queene*] excuses his rash behavior before Lucifera with a reference to the convention:

> Pardon the errour of enraged wight,
> Whom great griefe made forget the raines to hold
> Of reasons rule;

while in *Hero and Leander* (*c.* 1593) Marlowe makes use of the same image to describe a romantic lover.

> For as a hot proud horse highly disdains
> To have his head controll'd, but breaks the reins,
> Spits forth the ringled bit, and with his hooves
> Checks the submissive ground: so he that loves,
> The more he is restrain'd, the worse he fares;
> What is it now but mad Leander dares?

As applied to the nature of man, the horse that has broken his reins represents the appetite no longer in control of the rational faculty, and reflects, in terms of Christian morality, a capitulation to the consequences of Adam's Fall, contrary to the best interests of man and society. For Renaissance moral doctrine the importance of reason can hardly be over-emphasized. Man was considered, most fundamentally, as *duplex:* that is, composed of two parts, soul and body, often called the 'inward' and 'outward' man, after the terminology of the Bible. When originally created, these parts worked in harmonious order, the body serving the mind, as the horse obeys the rider. The Fall of Adam, however, disturbed this ideal order, so that, as a result of original sin, the rational powers were weakened and the appetites of the flesh assumed greater power than before, continually seeking to usurp the control of the will. The reins of reason's rule became weaker, and a less agreeable bondage, since they checked immoderate pleasure of the flesh.

The 'inward man' and the 'outward man,' it was affirmed in Renaissance catechisms and moral treatises, are both equipped with appropriate senses: the senses of the body operating for the perception of material things, and the mental senses which perceive incorporeal and immaterial things. Two types of judgment are accordingly possible, depending on which type of perception is utilized; and the will acts in accordance with the dictates of such judgments. But whereas the reason refers its judgment to ulterior criteria, principally the will of God, the flesh refers only to the immediate satisfaction of itself. When the eye of the mind is blinded and the powers of the *rational* judgment are weakened in man, the will abides by the preferences of the fleshly senses. The 'wilful' (or 'self-willed') man acts without the benefit of wisdom. Fallen man will not abide the healthy bridle that would subject his will to the higher will of God, but, like Adam, acts by his own direction for self-satisfaction only. Like the Courser, he conducts himself according to the untrustworthy judgments of the external senses; in human relationships he seeks with outward show to "captiuate the eye" of the flesh in others. To allow the appetites alone to select the objects of desire, without attention to the more perceptive checks of reason, is a recapitulation of Adam's loss of perfection—a submission to the impulsive, brute aspects of one's nature.

> VVhile Lust is in his pride no exclamation
> Can curbe his heate, or reine his rash desire,
> Till like a Iade, self-will himselfe doth tire.
>   [*The Rape of Lucrece,* ll. 705-07]

Shakespeare works the image of the horse, rein, and rider into the fabric of the courser-jennet episode, using its moral associations to intensify the commentary there. The breaking of the bridle is referred to in the couplets of the two introductory stanzas of the episode—a position of rhetorical importance, the effect of which is to indicate immediately the nature of the activity that follows. The first reference [l. 264] is general and subordinate to the sense of the whole couplet; but

the second picks up the allusion and particularizes it, indicating clearly its metaphorical significance [ll. 269-70].

> The yron bit he crusheth tweene his teeth,
> *Controlling what he was controlled with.*

Later yet, completing the long catalogue of the points of a perfect horse, there is a third reference, this time to the rider [ll. 299-300].

> Looke what a Horse should haue, he did not lack,
> *Saue a proud rider on so proud a back.*

The rhetorical emphasis accorded these statements by position and repetition, is artistically warranted only if they are also considered in relation to human conduct, as a description of man breaking away from reason, thinly disguised in other terms. Although the "proud rider" is an addition to the conventional roll of the points of a good horse, it is Shakespeare himself who says that this horse needs one, and the comment is therefore the more significant. Like references to bit and bridle, it is completely meaningful only in the wider context of psychological analogy.

By allusion this image reinforces the stylistic implications of the episode. Besides presenting the ritual of romantic courtship ironically, and suggesting that beneath it lie the sexual appetites, Shakespeare uses a conventional symbol of lust for this presentation, and stresses a particular criticism: that is, that this procedure is also essentially irrational—that in it the appetites exceed their proper bounds to run wild self-willfully. (pp. 249-59)

The distinction between human and bestial modes of conduct forms the basis for one final important aspect of the comparison between man and animal in the courser-jennet episode. This concerns the problem of propagation, which is the subject also of much of Venus' argument elsewhere in the poem. The implication, emphasized verbally by Shakespeare, reinforces the criticism of artificiality which lies behind his stylistic treatment of the episode.

If Adonis is unlike his Courser in his unwillingness to follow the dictates of his appetites, the Jennet is unlike Venus in one respect not immediately apparent. The mare is mentioned seven times in the episode: three times romantically as the Courser's "loue," once indeterminately as a "female," but the other three times as a "breeder." She is introduced as "a breeding Iennet" [l. 260], the horse calls her a "faire breeder" [l. 282], and as an "vnbackt breeder" she leaves the scene [l. 320]. Significantly, the Jennet is mentioned specifically as an animal only in these terms. Shakespeare is careful to point out that *this* "female" is a *breeder,* and to keep the idea in his reader's mind. Insofar as the actors are to be considered as *animals,* then, the sensual urge to copulate exists for the purpose of propagation, and insures the perpetuation of species lacking rational comprehension of the problem of mortality. The repetition of the word *breeder* is deliberately introduced with regard to the horses, whose "imbracements" are, after all, "kind." But to direct attention to the *use* is to point up the *abuse* when it occurs elsewhere in connection with Venus. The repetition of the word *breeder* is deliberately introduced with reference to the Jennet in order to emphasize the abuse which Venus represents. Where Adonis is unwilling she is too willful. Venus, who would imitate the horses in action, wishes, nevertheless, only to enjoy that which should be used.

Reason clearly explains to the lover in [Chaucer's] *The Romaunt of the Rose* the folly of Venus' position:

Of other thing loue retcheth nought
But setteth her harte and all her thought
More for delectacioun
Than any procreacioun
Of other fruict by engendrure
Which loue to God is nat pleasure.

According to Renaissance morality also, love-making which stresses intercourse for the sake of pleasure only is artificial, a perversion of nature because a misuse of natural functions. This love falls into the old confusion of *utendum* and *fruendum*, use and abuse—a confusion that lies behind much of the persuasive philosophy of the goddess of love throughout *Venus and Adonis.*

Adonis, then, is exhibiting not modern priggishness but sound Renaissance morality when he somewhat coldly chides Venus [ll. 787-92]:

VVhat haue you vrg'd, that I can not reproue?
The path is smooth that leadeth on to danger,
I hate not loue, but your deuise in loue,
That lends imbracements vnto euery stranger,
    You do it for increase, ô straunge excuse!
    VVhen reason is the bawd to lusts abuse.

Venus, by praising the Courser as an example for Adonis to emulate [ll. 385-408], unwittingly makes clear her position in the poem, and also clarifies the relationship which this episode bears to the larger whole. The Courser is developed as a conditional Adonis for Venus to point to as that which she would like Adonis to be. But Shakespeare has developed the portrait of the Courser in such a manner as to leave no doubt in his reader's mind about the poet's own attitude toward the type of love Venus represents. He treats the entire episode with ironic humor, exposing the pretensions in the ritual of romantic courtship as it is acted out by the horses. By indicating their sexual motivation, he stresses the artificiality of romantic conventions. In addition, he includes in his description images and allusions which, by their traditional associations, show his position more precisely to be that of conventional Renaissance morality.

As a result, Venus is depicted exuberantly praising fallen and unregenerate man as the ideal lover, to be emulated by Adonis; and it is evident that her school lesson is intended to teach him the 'wisdom' by which Adam fell. The horse is not only, as a beast, an appropriate symbol of the 'animal man' defined in Renaissance catechisms and moral tracts, but is also *per se* a conventional symbol of lust or of the fleshly appetites. In the world of Venus, too, reason has no place, for reason would control the immoderate enjoyment of such appetites. Therefore it is not surprising to find her attitude toward "the raines of reasons rule" in conflict with the attitude of Shakespeare. For her the "leatherne raine" is a "base thong," a "pettie bondage," by which one is "seruily maisterd"; and she advises breaking it. The bondage she offers is more pleasing—a "red rose chaine" [l. 325]: the *roseae catenae* of temporal delights, as Boethius called them [in his *De consolatione philosophiae*], by which she kept the warlike Mars "seruile." It is clear that what the goddess of love desires is abandonment to the enjoyment of sensual pleasure for its own sake, not for the purpose of propagation. The ritual of romantic courtship—that which Venus stands for—is presented by Shakespeare in an artistically complex and coherent manner as an activity unworthy of the nature of man.

If Shakespeare's attitude embodies the principles of conventionally accepted moral doctrine, the tenor, however, of the courser-jennet episode is far from homiletic. Shakespeare is giving artistic expression to current ideas. The activity he describes was to him apparently an aspect of human folly, and, although its degenerate nature is quite precisely specified, his total presentation of it is delightfully humorous. The delicacy of Shakespeare's treatment is more evident if his use of the horse-bridle image is set beside that of Golding. One is Puritanical, the other is moral. Is it not possible that the episode of the Courser and the Jennet may sound the keynote for *Venus and Adonis* as a whole? (pp. 261-64)

> Robert P. Miller, "Venus, Adonis, and the Horses," in ELH, *Vol. 19, No. 4, December, 1952, pp. 249-64.*

RUFUS PUTNEY (essay date 1953)

[*Several commentators have noted elements of humor, irony, or parody in* Venus and Adonis; *but in a 1941 essay (see Additional Bibliography) and in the following excerpt, Putney maintains that Shakespeare's primary intent in this poem is comic. The characterization, versification, structure, dialogue, and action, he claims, all contribute to the work's tone of "sensuous, sophisticated farce." Putney focuses on Shakespeare's portrayal of Venus, whom he describes as the poet's "first great comic character" and whose depiction he judges "the supreme achievement of the poem."*]

Even a hasty glance at the comments on *Venus and Adonis* reprinted in the Variorum edition of Shakespeare's *Poems* suggests that reading the poem has often proved a dull or a disturbing experience. The failure of readers to see the poem as Shakespeare created it is the most probable explanation for this distress. In this case we have the rare good fortune of receiving some help from Shakespeare himself. A real clue to his spirit and intentions while writing *Venus and Adonis* is provided by Rosaline's description of Berowne in *Love's Labour's Lost,* a play probably written at the same time as the poem and similarly calculated to impress what Shakespeare took to be the literary *avant garde* of the day. Readers need to be better acquainted with the concept advanced here of a lyric comedy, ravishing by its eloquence and humorous through its combination of wit and fancy.

Berowne they call him; but a merrier man,
Within the limit of becoming mirth,
I never spent an hour's talk withal.
His eye begets occasion for his wit;
For every object that the one doth catch
The other turns to a mirth-moving jest,
Which his fair tongue, conceit's expositor,
Delivers in such apt and gracious words,
That aged ears play truant at his tales,
And younger hearings are quite ravished;
So sweet and voluble is his discourse.

[II. i. 66-76]

"Sweet" and "voluble" are adjectives that all will agree describe Shakespeare's discourse in *Venus and Adonis.* To show that the poem also contains enough mirth to have been written by the merry man Berowne is the purpose of this essay.

Coleridge's commentary remains the most illuminating discussion of the poem. He is the only critic, so far as I know, who, viewing the two narratives [*Venus and Adonis* and *The Rape of Lucrece*] as a dramatist's sally into an alien genre, emphasizes their profoundly dramatic nature [see excerpt above, 1817]. But most scholars and critics, after a perfunctory reading of Coleridge, have preferred to let Hazlitt and Swinburne mislead them [see excerpts above, 1817 and 1875].

Now, unhampered by that ethical solemnity that forced Coleridge to add that the poem deals with a subject that "cannot but detract from the pleasure of a delicate mind", we may be struck by the comic nature of the spectacle Shakespeare presents. And once the reader sets out in quest of comedy, the poem that has usually seemed a mellifluously told, richly decorated, erotic story, long-winded, cold, and dull, is completely metamorphosed. All that has been branded lascivious, tedious, or inept is transformed into stuff for laughter. The narrative, instead of appearing an amorphous mass, assumes form, and Shakespeare's vivacity, invigorating every part of the work, reflects the writer's joy in his mastery and power. His control over his verse is almost if not quite complete as he adapts it to narrative, dialogue, description, to farce, comedy, lyric humor, and pure lyricism. In his images are blended Elizabethan literary conventions, rural observations, and the sights, sounds, and smells of the taverns, shops, courts, and streets of London to create the ridiculous, the grotesque, and the charming. Dialogue outweighs description or narration, and the dramatic power of the poem is further enhanced by the diversities of the characters' emotions as well as by vivid pictorial images and intimations of action. Above all, the reader finds himself unexpectedly confronted in Venus with Shakespeare's first great comic character.

In asserting the humorous nature of the poem, one finds it difficult to be sure from precisely what critics one is differing. The enthusiasm or disapproval of Elizabethan and Jacobean readers has been recorded, but in so equivocal a manner that the interpretation of their allusions is more difficult than reading the poem. The work of other contemporary poets yields, however, a kind of circumstantial evidence. . . . Shakespeare, like his predecessors and imitators in the light, pseudo-Ovidian legend, intended to write a sensuous, sophisticated farce. He changed the story as Ovid narrated it, and his alterations are essentially comic. Venus and Adonis, in the Latin version, unite in reciprocal passion, but Shakespeare's wretched goddess cannot with all her divinity, wit, and beauty awaken desire in a youth whose sweating palm was "precedent of pith and livelihood" [l. 26]. Not only was the poem popular with readers; it also set the wits of other poets working, and their bawdy rather than lascivious imitations can be illustrated while disposing of the most common source of error in interpretation. Adonis urges his youth as the reason for rebuffing Venus, and many a critic has sentimentalized over this Elizabethan Joseph. Such lucubrations reveal more ethical nicety than literary acumen, for Shakespeare, one must confess, placed less value on male chastity than the biblical author [in Genesis, chapter 39]. In Sonnet XLI he excused the "pretty wrongs" his friend had committed with the Dark Lady saying:

> Gentle thou art, and therefore to be won,
> Beauteous thou art, therefore to be assail'd;
> And when a woman woos, what woman's son
> Will sourly leave her till she have prevail'd?

The same amoral tolerance was displayed by many contemporaries. The ghost of Narcissus in Thomas Edwards' clever perversion of that legend [*Cephalus and Procis. Narcissus*] invokes Adonis' spirit to bear witness that no good comes of too strict chastity. Most of the other imitators adopted like attitudes. A complete survey of them would require inordinate space since to regain fully the contemporary perspective one has only to read the four sonnets in *The Passionate Pilgrim* that toy with Shakespeare's story. In all of them, the fol-

lowing for example, Venus is made ludicrous and Adonis a fool:

> Scarce had the sun dried up the dewy morn,
> And scarce the herd gone to the hedge for shade,
> When Cytherea, all in love forlorn,
> A longing tarriance for Adonis made
> Under an osier growing by a brook,
> A brook where Adon us'd to cool his spleen:
> Hot was the day; she hotter that did look
> For his approach, that often there had been.
> Anon he comes, and throws his mantle by,
> And stood stark naked on the brook's green brim:
> The sun look'd on the world with glorious eye,
> Yet not so wistly as this queen on him:
>   He spying her, bounc'd in, whereas he stood:
>   'O Jove,' quoth she, 'why was not I a flood!'

This and its companion sonnets represent in miniature the longer narratives of the species. Here in narrow compass are displayed the principal features of the genre: conceits, hyperbole, myth-making, *double-entendre*, wit, and the perception of the comedy inherent in the situation and the characters.

Before proceeding to the narrative and the actors, we may with profit observe the similarity between Berowne's conversational style and Shakespeare's method. Rosaline said of him,

> His eye begets occasion for his wit;
> For every object that the one doth catch
> The other turns to a mirth-moving jest.

Such jests crowd the poem as they do the play. The modern reader may not be prepared at the outset to laugh at the parody in Venus' first greeting to Adonis, where she seeks to gain his immediate acquiesence with the flattery and promises of the male seducer. But when desperate passion compels the goddess to shift from words to action, the result is a kind of farce to which the Elizabethans were always responsive. Even if no pun was intended in the lines

> Being so enrag'd, desire doth lend her force
> Courageously to pluck him from his horse,
>   [ll. 29-30]

the absurd picture that follows of Venus with the flushed, indignant Adonis tucked under one arm, his horse's reins over the other, hastening to the bank that is their destined battleground should acquaint us with Shakespeare's mirth:

> Over one arm the lusty courser's re'n,
> Under her other was the blushing boy,
> Who blush'd and pouted in a dull disdain
> With leaden appetite, unapt to toy;
>   She red and hot as coals of glowing fire,
>   He red for shame, but frosty in desire.
>   [ll. 31-6]

Nor could it ever have been easy to write or read solemnly a poem in which falling is so common an activity. At the start, impatience overcoming Venus' tenderness,

> Backward she push'd him, as she would be thrust,
>   [l. 41]

and, as he falls, she falls beside him. Venus, at line 463, faints and falls. Presently they kiss, and,

> Their lips together glu'd, fall to the earth.
>   [l. 546]

Finally, at line 594, they tumble most comically,

> He on her belly falls, she on her back.

If we may judge from the conversation of Rosaline and her friends, those cheerful girls would not have thought this exceeded "the limits of becoming mirth".

Shakespeare's eye lit constantly upon objects which his pen, in this case "conceit's expositor", could turn into humor. Many instances of his incongruous imagery will appear in this essay. For the present, a few other examples will be cited by way of introduction. Venus is compared to a starving eagle [l. 55], to a glutton [l. 548], and to a vulture [l. 551]. Inflamed by kissing Adonis, she is daintily described:

> Her face doth reek and smoke, her blood doth boil.
>
> [l. 555]

To illuminate her plight when she is briefly denied the solace of speech, Shakespeare employed the following clever but graceless similes:

> An oven that is stopp'd, or river stay'd
> Burneth more hotly, swelleth more with rage;
> So of concealed sorrow may be said:
> Free vent of words love's fire doth assuage,
>   But when the heart's attorney once is mute,
>   The client breaks as desperate of his suit.
>
> [ll. 331-36]

Her disappointment when she cannot accomplish her desire is likened to birds deceived by painted grapes. As she grapples him to her bosom and blurts out her fears should he go boar-hunting, Venus vividly suggests the discomfort of his posture as well as her own distress:

> My boding heart pants, beats, and takes no rest,
> But like an earthquake shakes thee on my breast.
>
> [ll. 647-48]

To these comparisons one might add such witty epigrams as the observation, "O how quick is love" [l. 38], where at least one pun is surely intended, and the Mercutio-like comment,

> Love is a spirit all compact of fire,
> Not gross to sink, but light and will aspire,
>
> [ll. 149-50]

or another pun that makes a joke, since an immortal goddess cannot actually die, of the slight confidence Venus placed in Diana's vow of chastity:

> So do thy lips
> Make modest Dian cloudy and forlorn,
> Lest she should steal a kiss and die forsworn.
>
> [ll. 724-26]

In these and many other places, Shakespeare's jocose tone fumigates the eroticism and belies the critical conviction that he had any serious intention beyond writing a delightful poem.

For the purposes of literary debate, the "argument from the sensitive ear" has often proved an effective and sometimes a valid form of the *argumentum ad hominem* [argument by disparagement of an opponent]. It is no less dear to the New Critics than it was to George Saintsbury, though they are too genteel to snort down the opposition with his charming ferocity. This argument is indispensable to the analysis of Shake-

speare's purpose in *Venus and Adonis* for two reasons. First, the tone and texture of the verse provide the most reliable evidence of the author's intention in a case like this where historical scholarship has postulated an ideology of sober sensuousness to give plausibility to a serious interpretation of the narrative, and, second, it has long been received, though Coleridge would not have assented, that the verse of *Venus and Adonis* is a cloying amalgam of saccharine conceit and honeyed melody. Although enough has already been quoted to dispel this opinion, it is desirable before proceeding to insist that the verse itself is comic. Since I have just cited examples of the realistic and grotesque, the variety of the poem requires illustrations more imaginative and fanciful. The following stanza is one of three in which her desperate passion makes Venus assert that Adonis has charms powerful to enchant her through any one of the five senses:

> Say that the sense of feeling were bereft me,
> And that I could not see, nor hear, nor touch,
> And nothing but the very smell were left me,
> Yet would my love to thee be still as much;
>   For from the stillitory of thy face excelling
>   Comes breath perfum'd that breedeth love by
>   smelling.
>
> [ll. 439-44]

So banal are the first four lines of this stanza, exhibiting even such impoverished rhyming as "bereft me" with "left me", that one must explain their flatness as the result either of ineptitude or of dramatic propriety. Inadequate as lyric verse, these lines neatly convey the folly Venus' passion induces. Similarly, the extravagant handling in the couplet of the convention that the lover's sweet-smelling breath enamours can be the product only of appalling tastelessness or of deliberate burlesque. Perhaps, Shakespeare's comments on his mistress' breath in Sonnet CXXX should not be brought into this argument, but the facile, charmless sound of the couplet,

> For from the stillitory of thy face excelling
> Comes breath perfumed that breedeth love by
> smelling,

as well as the grotesque conceit it contains, indicates burlesque when contrasted with a passage which treats the same convention with genuine, though humorous, loveliness:

> Forc'd to content, but never to obey,
> Panting he lies, and breatheth in her face;
> She feedeth on the steam, as on a prey,
> And calls it heavenly moisture, air of grace;
>   Wishing her cheeks were gardens full of flowers,
>   So they were dew'd with such distilling showers.
>
> [ll. 61-6]

The lyrical rapture of Venus' hyperboles makes this stanza as ravishing as it is amusing. Comic verse of this eloquence is rare, but this example is by no means unique in a poem where the versification constantly matches the writer's intentions.

The supreme achievement of the poem resides in the characterization of Venus, but Shakespeare's success in creating her implies also deft handling of Adonis' rôle and skillful organization of the narrative. A simple, severe structure supports the weight of decoration. Venus' vain attempts throughout one day to fire Adonis' love and his death the following morning, by which the problem is resolved, comprise the plot. It requires only a little more attention than readers usually accord the poem to see that Shakespeare conceived it like a play

Venus. By Sandro Botticelli.

shy, diffident male, but neither the situation nor the characters are developed in precisely the fashion to which we have been accustomed by popular playwrights and novelists. Although the violence of Venus' passion makes her ludicrous, she is beautiful and attractive rather than grotesque or sinister. She provokes both sympathy and laughter. Adonis' naïveté is comic, his priggishness repellent, yet he is far from seeming preposterous.

In developing his characters Shakespeare used the method he employed in the theatre. Having indicated their essential qualities, he hurried them into the dramatic action and set them talking. A pair of lines in the first stanza suffices for Adonis:

> Rose-cheek'd Adonis hies him to the chase,
> Hunting he lov'd, but love he laugh'd to scorn.
>
> [ll. 3-4]

Slightly more scope is needed to introduce Venus since she has the stellar rôle and will do most of the speaking. The fifth stanza not only completes the preliminary sketch of the impatient goddess, but also illustrates the lyrical humor, the mixture of wit and charm, diffused throughout the story:

> With this she seizeth on his sweating palm,
> The precedent of pith and livelihood,
> And trembling in her passion calls it balm,
> Earth's sovereign salve to do a goddess good:
>   Being so enrag'd desire doth lend her force
>   Courageously to pluck him from his horse.
>
> [ll. 25-30]

Adonis is distinctly secondary to Venus and only occasionally appealing. He is rendered comic by the obtuse view he takes of the passion he has inspired in the goddess, but even more by his petulance and self-pity. He writhes and squirms in Venus' arms and, when he finds words, reprehends her:

> 'Fie, fie,' he says, 'you crush me; let me go;
> You have no reason to withold me so.'
>
> [ll. 611-12]

> 'Give me my hand,' he saith, 'why dost thou feel it?'
>
> [l. 374]

> 'You hurt my hand with wringing; let us part.'
>
> [l. 421]

> 'For shame,' he cries, 'let go, and let me go;
> My day's delight is past, my horse is gone,
> And 'tis your fault I am bereft him so;
> I pray you hence, and leave me here alone.'
>
> [ll. 379-82]

He complains, though only scholars believe him, that he is too young for Venus. Finally, he refuses even to listen to her:

> 'Lest the deceiving harmony should run
> Into the quiet closure of my breast;
> And then my little heart were quite undone,
> In his bedchamber to be barred of rest.
>   No, lady, no; my heart longs not to groan,
>   But soundly sleeps while now it sleeps alone.'
>
> [ll. 781-86]

The plaintive tone of the verse even more than the fantastic metaphor reduces Adonis to unheroic and unallegoric absurdity.

The comic nuances in Shakespeare's treatment of such delicately predatory heroines as Juliet, Viola [in *Twelfth Night*],

as a series of dramatic episodes, which may conveniently if not accurately be compared to acts. The first forty-two lines, eighteen of them in dialogue, perform the expository functions of the first act. They set the scene, introduce the characters, and stretch them out side by side on the grassy bank. Venus' courtship makes up the bulk of the narrative and provides the equivalent to acts two and three. Her wooing is interrupted first at line 258, when Adonis escapes from her arms only to be stranded by his stallion's pursuit of the mare. Venus renews her suit and holds him fast until, at line 816, he wrenches himself loose and runs from her into the darkness. To maintain the analogy to conventional dramatic structure, Venus' soliloquies, in which during the remainder of the night and early next morning she bewails her unrequited passion and apostrophizes Death, may be equated with the fourth act; her discovery of Adonis' body and final lament, with the fifth. Stated baldly these divisions seem somewhat arbitrary and obscure too much the diversities of tone within each section, but there is reasonable basis for them, and they emphasize the real simplicity of the structure.

The obvious farce inherent in the representation of the Goddess of Love's failing to arouse passion in a mortal youth is transmuted and heightened by the beauty of the characters and the lyrical humor of the dialogue. Both Venus and Adonis are comic types, the frustrated, voracious woman and the and Desdemona [in *Othello*] suggest his robust mode of presenting Venus. The rôle of wooer, the exorbitance of her passion, and her perplexity when refused render humorous the long harrangues in which she flatters, reasons, rants, shames, chides, pleads, and weeps. Her manner is alternately argumentative, abusive, lyrical, persuasive, and witty, and the tone of the comedy ranges from playfulness to absolute farce.

Since Shakespeare's method of characterizing his frustrated and, presently, perspiring goddess is the same he used with such figures as Falstaff and Juliet's Nurse, it can be studied best by tracing it progressively. With unflagging gusto he invented the amorous dialectic in which, with infinite diversity and verve, Venus pursues her courtship from the first encounter until Adonis' flight. When early in the story he ducks to elude her kiss, the occasion is presented for her first long appeal:

> 'O pity!' gan she cry, 'flint-hearted boy:
> 'Tis but a kiss I beg; why art thou coy?'
>
> [ll. 95-6]

Adonis' disinterest inspires the recital of her conquest of Mars, but her narration of that triumph brings fears lest Adonis pride himself on excelling the god and consequently scorn her. Reprobation of pride, calculated to forestall that disaster, soon gives way to pleading in a stanza of characteristic excellence for its combination of insatiate desire, illogical disputation, and pictorial suggestion:

> 'Touch but my lips with those fair lips of thine,—
> Though mine be not so fair, yet are they red,—
> The kiss shall be thine own as well as mine:
> What seest thou in the ground? hold up thy head:
>   Look in mine eyeballs, there thy beauty lies;
>   Then why not lips on lips, since eyes in eyes?'
>
> [ll. 115-20]

The sharp, peremptory tone of the fourth line—so similar to the hints to actors in the plays—creates a vivid picture and provides here the dramatic variety that Venus' speeches constantly display.

Praise of her own pulchritude comprises much of Venus' early assault. The unsparingly elaborate description of the heroine's beauty, which became a convention of the Ovidian narrative poem, had appeared in the *Arcadia* and elsewhere before Thomas Lodge incorporated an "anatomical catalogue" in the little verse tale that graces his *History of Forbonius and Prisceria* and another in *Scylla's Metamorphosis*. Marlowe in *Hero and Leander* gorgeously surpassed all rivals. In keeping the lush inventory of the lady's charms, Shakespeare made it part of his comic characterization of Venus by transferring the description from the poet or the lover to the goddess herself. He further enhanced its dramatic quality by providing an internal motivation, by breaking into it with Adonis' preposterous complaint that he is suffering from sunburn, by altering Venus' moods during her long speech, and by varying the tone of her self-description from the lyrical to the ridiculous.

Venus' perception of Adonis' youth and beauty provides the motive. She must prove herself a suitable mate for him. Hence she begins:

> 'Were I hard favour'd, foul, or wrinkled-old,
> Ill-nurtur'd, crook'd, churlish, harsh in voice,
> O'erworn, despised, rheumatic, and cold,
> Thick-sighted, barren, lean, and lacking juice

> Then mightst thou pause, for then I were not for
>   thee;
> But having no defects, why dost abhor me?

> 'Thou canst not see one wrinkle in my brow;
> Mine eyes are grey and bright and quick in turning:
> My beauty as the spring doth yearly grow:
> My flesh is soft and plump, my marrow burning;
>   My smooth moist hand, were it with thy hand
>   felt,
>   Would in thy palm dissolve, or seem to melt.'
>
> [ll. 133-44]

After two more intoxicating stanzas have produced no sensible effect, she explores the possibility that self-love is the cause of his indifference and warns him of Narcissus' fate. Then for twelve lines she showers him with the arguments used in the early sonnets to promote reproduction, until, finally out of breath, she is silenced long enough for a brief bit of description and rejoinder:

> By this the love-sick queen began to sweat,
> For where they lay the shadow had forsook them,
> And Titan tired in the midday heat,
> With burning eye did hotly overlook them,
>   Wishing Adonis had his team to guide,
>   So he were like him and by Venus' side.

> And now Adonis with a lazy spright,
> And with a heavy, dark, disliking eye,
> His louring brows o'erwhelming his fair sight,
> Like misty vapours when they blot the sky,
>   Souring his cheeks cries, 'Fie! no more of love:
>   The sun doth burn my face; I must remove.'
>
> [ll. 175-86]

Venus' first answer to this rebuff is the mild, sad chiding of

> 'Ay me,' quoth Venus, 'young and so unkind!
> What bare excuses mak'st thou to be gone!'
>
> [ll. 187-88]

But presently the sense of injury arouses her indignation, and she scornfully upbraids him:

> 'Art thou a woman's son, and canst not feel
> What 'tis to love? how want of love tormenteth?'
>
> [ll. 201-02]

> 'What am I that thou shouldst contemn me thus?
> Or what great danger dwells upon my suit?
> What were thy lips the worse for one poor kiss?'
>
> [ll. 205-07]

> 'Fie! lifeless picture, cold and senseless stone,
> Well-painted idol, image dull and dead,
> Statue contenting but the eye alone,
> Thing like a man, but of no woman bred:
>   Thou art no man, though of a man's complexion,
>   For men will kiss even by their own direction.'
>
> [ll. 211-16]

When Adonis can be neither allured nor shamed into gratifying her, frustration leads her into such absurdities that the concupisence of Lodge and Marlowe evaporates:

> 'Fondling,' she saith, 'since I have hemm'd thee
>   here
> Within the circuit of this ivory pale,
> I'll be a park, and thou shalt be my deer;
> Feed where thou wilt, on mountain or in dale:
>   Graze on my lips, and if those hills be dry,
>   Stray lower where the pleasant fountains lie.'
>
> [ll. 229-34]

Adonis smiles, albeit in disdain, at these conceits, well worthy of Berowne, and in a moment makes his escape from the goddess' arms.

After the entr'acte of the stallion and the jennet, introduced as an object lesson in proper masculine conduct, Venus recaptures Adonis, whom she then manages to control for four hundred and ninety lines. This second stage of her wooing is interlarded with more digressions, notably the description of the boar and the hunting of poor Wat, but there is no slackening in Shakespeare's invention of comic dialogue. Prominent in this section are Venus' assertion that, were their positions reversed, she would suffer even bodily harm to please him, her plea that he learn appropriate behavior from his stallion, and the three stanzas in which she analyzes his charms that enchant each of the five senses. When he agains rebuffs her, she farcically faints. His rough and humorous efforts to restore her culminate in a kiss. The enthusiasm with which Venus responds to the last remedy is funny in itself and leads to two witty stanzas, in which, using imagery derived from commercial law, she begs for prolonged treatment:

> 'Pure lips, sweet seals in my soft lips imprinted,
> What bargains may I make still to be sealing?
> To sell myself I can be well contented,
> So thou wilt buy, and pay, and use good dealing;
>   Which purchase if thou make, for fear of slips
>   Set thy seal manual on my wax red lips.
>
> 'A thousand kisses buys my heart from me;
> And pay them at thy leisure, one by one.
> What is ten hundred touches unto thee?
> Are they not quickly told and quickly gone?
>   Say for non-payment that the debt should double,
>   Is twenty hundred kisses such a trouble?'
>
> [ll. 511-22]

Can we doubt that "younger hearings were quite ravished" by such sweet and voluble discourse?

Gently and more hopefully now Adonis begs her to let him go and promises a kiss in payment. The interlude has no other purpose than to make the transition to new complications:

> Her arms do lend his neck a sweet embrace;
> Incorporate then they seem: face grows to face.
>
> [ll. 539-40]

Kiss follows kiss until Venus out of pity resolves to let him go, but in a superbly dramatic stanza begs an assignation on the morrow:

> 'Sweet boy,' says she, 'this night I'll waste in sorrow,
> For my sick heart commands mine eyes to watch.
> Tell me, love's master, shall we meet tomorrow?
> Say, shall we? shall we? wilt thou make the match?'
>   He tells her no; tomorrow he intends
>   To hunt the boar with certain of his friends.
>
> [ll. 583-88]

Overcome with terror she falls and drags him down on top of her. After she has warned him against the frightful boar and urged him to hunt the timorous hare instead, two stanzas of grotesque dialogue ensue:

> 'Lie quietly and hear a little more;
> Nay, do not struggle, for thou shalt not rise:
> To make thee hate the hunting of the boar,

> Unlike myself thou hear'st me moralize,
>   Applying this to that, and so to so;
>   For love can comment upon every woe.'
>
> 'Where did I leave?' 'No matter where,' quoth he;
> 'Leave me, and then the story aptly ends:
> The night is spent.' 'Why what of that,' quoth she.
> 'I am,' quoth he, 'expected of my friends;
>   And now 'tis dark, and going I shall fall.'
>   'In night,' quoth she, 'desire sees best of all.'
>
> [ll. 709-20]

Her pleading continues in fanciful conceits and wild hyperboles until Adonis interrupts, refuses to listen longer to her, and scolds her with his famous comparison of love and lust. This is the most serious passage in the poem, and we may assume that Shakespeare agreed now as later with much that Adonis says. Nonetheless, it should be noted that in the lines describing Adonis' flight,

> With this he breaketh from the sweet embrace
> Of those fair arms which bound him to her breast,
>
> [ll. 811-12]

Shakespeare still espoused the cause of Venus. It is scarcely effective preaching that leaves the preacher openly infatuated with the temptress.

Shakespeare relied upon Venus' character not only to make the wooing comic, but also to cancel the pathos at the end of the story. After his escape into the darkness, Adonis reappears only as a corpse. The major problem was to suggest Venus' emotions without allowing the reader to feel her pain. Shakespeare accomplished this by making her speeches burlesques of conventional Elizabethan complaints. The elegiac tastes of the late sixteenth century ran to such extravagance that parody was not easy; yet differences are apparent between Venus' exclamations against Death and, for example, Lucrece's apostrophes to Night and Opportunity. Shakespeare, furthermore, gave his readers indications of his intentions. Deserted by Adonis, Venus is overwhelmed with grief:

> And now she beats her heart, whereat it groans,
> That all the neighbour caves, as seeming troubled,
> Make verbal repetition of her moans:
> Passion on passion deeply is redoubled:
>   'Ay me!' she cries, and twenty times, 'Woe, woe!'
>   And twenty echoes twenty times cry so.
>
> [ll. 829-34]

That Shakespeare intended his readers to be amused by the caves that echo Venus' plaints—and have aroused critics'—is clinched by the stanza that rounds out the conceit:

> For who hath she to spend the night withal,
> But idle sounds resembling parasites;
> Like shrill-tongu'd tapsters answering every call,
> Soothing the humour of fantastic wits?
>   She says, ' 'Tis so;' they answer all, ' 'Tis so;'
>   And would say after her if she said, 'No.'
>
> [ll. 847-52]

We have no justification for assuming Shakespeare even in 1593 a poet so maladroit that he would try to heighten Venus' pathos by means of this magnificent simile with its realistic detail of drunken gallants and obsequious tapsters. The imagery here completes the burlesque of the romantic convention.

Dawn finds Venus first cursing then flattering Death as she alternately fears Adonis dead and hopes he is alive. Even though there is nothing shockingly outlandish in her apostrophes, Shakespeare paused, lines 985-990, to remark that these vacillations which love inspires render the lover ridiculous. Suddenly she comes upon Adonis' body. Of the first conceit in the stanza that opens her lament over his corpse, one can say, at least, that it has no parallel elsewhere in Shakespeare's works and that its extravagance is such that genuine emotion is inhibited. Venus has stared so long at Adonis' body before she speaks that her sight is blurred and she sees double:

> 'My tongue cannot express my grief for one,
> And yet,' quoth she, 'behold two Adons dead!'
>
> [ll. 1069-70]

The quality of the conceit may well be questioned, but it enabled Shakespeare to surmount the most difficult point in the story without even inadvertent pathos.

There can be no question of the skill with which he brought the story to its conclusion. The pathetic fallacy, responsible for so much sixteenth century bathos, becomes in Venus' final lament a diverting parody of mourners, zoological, inanimate, and disembodied. With Adonis dead, no one need wear bonnet or veil, for the sun scorns and the wind hisses humanity. But when he was alive, all nature loved and wooed him:

> 'To see his face the lion walked along
> Behind some hedge because he would not fear him.
> To recreate himself when he hath sung,
> The tiger would be tame and gently hear him.'
>
> [ll. 1093-96]

The considerate lion and the music-loving tiger only begin the list. Fish vied to sport in the shadow he cast in their brooks, and the birds fed him berries. As in Bion, the boar sought only to kiss him, and multigenarian Venus, in words that anticipate Falstaff's cry, "They hate us youth" [*I Henry IV*, II. ii. 85], reflects:

> 'Had I been tooth'd like him, I must confess,
> With kissing him I should have killed him first;
> But he is dead, and never did he bless
> My youth with his; the more I am accurst.'
>
> [ll. 1117-20]

With goddess-like egoism she prophecies that love, since it has brought woe to her, shall be bitter to men for evermore. Adonis is metamorphosed into a flower, and the poem ends in the perfection of the last stanza with Venus, all passion temporarily spent in grief, departing for her shrine at Paphos, there to mourn.

Shakespeare, it must be clear, deliberately and deftly avoided the pathos the legend contained. Instead, he maintained the comedy from first to last on a variety of levels. He achieved his diverse effects primarily through his brilliant and dramatic characterization of the suffering goddess. Venus, though she is enchantingly persuasive to readers more susceptible than Adonis, we not only love but laugh at. We see her amorous, tender, violent, lustful, distraught, perplexed, in joy, tears, and frustration. Although she lacks Cleopatra's infinite variety and many of her mature and subtle allurements, Venus is nonetheless the earliest intimation of Shakespeare's power to create his great, tragic wanton queen. Meanwhile, Venus is in her own right a fine and satisfying comic character. (pp. 52-66)

Rufus Putney, "Venus 'Agonistes'," in University of Colorado Studies Series in Language and Literature, *No. 4, 1953, pp. 52-66.*

C. S. LEWIS (essay date 1954)

[*An English literary critic and novelist, Lewis was also a distinguished Renaissance scholar whose writing was strongly influenced by his Christian beliefs. As a Shakespearean critic, he argued that commentators who pay too much attention to character analysis are apt to overlook the intention of the plays, particularly their moral and ethical impact. Instead, Lewis suggested, the critic should surrender him or herself to "the poetry and the situation" in all of Shakespeare's dramas. In the comments excerpted below, Lewis places* Venus and Adonis *in the genre of "epyllion," medium-length narrative poems based on classical sources and often erotic in tone. The critic maintains that if Venus is meant to be the alluring subject of such a poem, she is very crudely depicted. If, on the other hand, Shakespeare intends her to be an emblem of lust in a moral poem, she is "a very ill-conceived temptress," repulsive rather than attractive.*]

Shakespeare's *Venus and Adonis* [may be seen] as an epyllion among epyllions, a successor to *Scylla* and *Hero and Leander*. We notice at once that it has abandoned Lodge's medieval preliminaries and that it does not, like Marlowe's poem, begin with long descriptions. The characters are in action by line 3. This is promising. We get, too, but not so soon nor so often as we might wish, lines of the deliciousness which was expected in this type of poem; 'leading him prisoner in a red-rose chain', 'a lily prisoned in a gaol of snow' [ll. 110, 362]. But in that direction Shakespeare does not rival Marlowe. We get, with surprised pleasure, glimpses of real work-day nature, in the spirited courtship of Adonis's horse or the famous stanza about the hare. The account of Venus's growing uneasiness during the hunt and her meeting with the wounded hounds gives us a fairly strong hint that the poet has powers quite beyond the range which the epyllion requires. What is not so certain is that he has the powers it does require. For as we read on we become more and more doubtful how the work ought to be taken. Is it a poem by a young moralist, a poem against lust? There is a speech given to Adonis [ll. 769-810] which might lend some colour to the idea. But the story does not point the moral at all well, and Shakespeare's Venus is a very ill-conceived temptress. She is made so much larger than her victim that she can throw his horse's reins over one arm and tuck him under the other, and knows her own art so badly that she threatens, almost in her first words, to 'smother' him with kisses. Certain horrible interviews with voluminous female relatives in one's early childhood inevitably recur to the mind. If, on the other hand, the poem is meant to be anything other than a 'cooling card', it fails egregiously. Words and images which, for any other purpose, ought to have been avoided keep on coming in and almost determine the dominant mood of the reader—'satiety', 'sweating', 'leaden appetite', 'gorge', 'stuff'd', 'glutton', 'glutton-like'. Venus's 'face doth reek and smoke, her blood doth boil' [l. 555], and the wretched 'boy' (that word too was dangerous) only gets away 'hot, faint and weary with her hard embracing' [l. 559]. And this flushed, panting, perspiring, suffocating, loquacious creature is supposed to be the goddess of love herself, the golden Aphrodite. It will not do. If the poem is not meant to arouse disgust it was very foolishly written: if it is, then disgust (that barbarian mercenary) is not, either aesthetically or morally, the feeling on which a poet should rely in a moral poem. But of course Shakespeare may well have failed because he was embarrassed by powers, essential for drama, which he could not suspend while writing an epyllion. Perhaps even then he could not help knowing what the wooing of Adonis by Venus, supposing it to be a real event, would have looked like to a spectator. (pp. 498-99)

C. S. Lewis, "Verse in the 'Golden' Period," in his English Literature in the Sixteenth Century, Excluding Drama, Oxford at the Clarendon Press, 1954, pp. 464-535.

FRANKLIN M. DICKEY (essay date 1957)

[In the following excerpt, Dickey offers an allegorical interpretation of Venus and Adonis, arguing that Shakespeare emphasizes the goddess's personification of "Pandemia," the elemental drive of "men and animals to reproduce themselves and perpetuate life on earth." In this poem, the critic states, Shakespeare illustrates the Renaissance doctrine that recognized this force as essential, but also held that sexual love is a "violent passion" to be kept in check by reason. Dickey also demonstrates the interrelationship of the poem's theme of "lust versus love" and its imagery, noting, in particular, the repeated association of lust with gluttony.]

Critics have spent a great many words trying to fit Venus and Adonis to their own ethical and aesthetic predispositions. . . . [There] is a bewildering variety of critical opinion written to show that Shakespeare's poem is either shockingly sensual or really very moral, to show that the poem is passionately Italianate or to show that it is completely cold. Some, pointing to the lavishly sensual descriptions of Venus's lust, think Adonis's reproaches perfunctory and insincere or at best out of place in an erotic poem. To them Venus is much more convincing and more eloquent than Adonis; she urges propagation of physical beauty, and so do Shakespeare's sonnets. How, except subjectively, can we decide whom to listen to, Venus or the boy, lust or chastity?

In a dilemma like this a knowledge of contemporary doctrine, if it cannot show us Shakespeare's intent, can at the very least show us the probable interpretation many of his contemporaries would have put upon the struggle; and unless we are quite sure that everything we think is superior to what Elizabethans thought, we must accept their probable interpretations as valuable.

Venus and Adonis (1593) may be apprentice work on fashionable themes, although it might be added that it probably set the fashion as much as it followed it. One of its central themes, love versus lust, interested Shakespeare almost to the end of his active career, as Troilus and Cressida (1602), Antony and Cleopatra (1606-1608), Pericles (1607-1608), and Cymbeline (1610) preeminently show. The theme occurs in other works as well and at no point in his career did Shakespeare tire of it. The contrast between lust and true love is of course repeated emphatically and with additions in Lucrece (1594). It is important in Two Gentlemen (1592), The Merry Wives (1599-1600), All's Well (1602), and Measure for Measure (1604). It is furthermore one of the motivations of tragedy in Lear (1605), and it threads the later sonnets. Apparently the contrast troubled Shakespeare throughout his life, and if the first two statements of it fall short of greatness, at times, as in Sonnet 129, "Th' expense of spirit," it inspired Shakespeare to some of his most powerful effects.

Anyone familiar with the Ovidian tradition will recognize Venus and Adonis as a member of a special genre related to the medieval mythological tale and the classical epyllion. Imitating the Metamorphoses either closely or at a distance, the Elizabethan erotic poet embroiders stories of mythological lovers in characteristically digressive rather than straightforward narrative. Typically he dramatizes emotional scenes by the use of extensive dialogue and by interior monologues in which the characters' divided souls reveal themselves in a formal psychomachy. His imagery is ornamental, copious, and elaborate, as is his choice of words and rhetorical devices. And like his medieval counterpart, the Elizabethan Ovid, to judge by his prefaces, takes pride in the complexities of his allegory.

Though by no means an allegory in its form, Venus and Adonis remains subject to the allegorical interpretations which its peculiar genre demands. All of Venus's actions and all her arguments accord with what she stands for—Plato's Aphrodite Pandemos or Ficino's amor vulgaria. As the representation or personification of the "mysterious stimulus for propagating offspring," she argues the necessity of continuing the beauty of earthly forms, which would die out unless she continually renewed them. In this function Venus is praiseworthy. Yet here, as elsewhere in Shakespeare, the urge which Pandemia governs is good only within its limits.

All the details of Venus's actions and character accord with this reading of her allegorical signification. The images of consuming fire, of heat, of gluttonous feeding, of the hunt compose a speaking picture of the abstract passion. Moved by the irresistible desire for generation, the goddess is ruthless in her pursuit of her ends. Despite the humor implicit in Shakespeare's picture of an adolescent Adonis, Venus is a tyrannical and cruel goddess. There is something a little frightening in the images and the action of this poem, an unnaturalness even in her frenzied pursuit of the boy.

"Sick-thoughted," "enflam'd," and "enrag'd" with "careless lust," she kisses Adonis with the fierce savagery of "an empty eagle" [l. 55]. Nor can we escape the sacrificial implications of Shakespeare's images of food and fire. Venus is a starved hawk, Adonis a "dabchick" in her power:

Now quick desire hath caught the yielding prey,
And glutton-like she feeds, yet never filleth;
Her lips are conquerors, his lips obey,
Paying what ransom the insulter willeth;
    Whose vulture thought doth pitch the price so
        high
    That she will draw his lips' rich treasure dry.

And having felt the sweetness of the spoil,
With blindfold fury she begins to forage;
Her face doth reek and smoke, her blood doth boil,
And careless lust stirs up a desperate courage;
    Planting oblivion, beating reason back,
    Forgetting shame's pure blush and honour's
        wrack.

[ll. 547-58]

One is continually struck by the consistency with which Shakespeare has handled both imagery and allegory. Unlike "true love" in which, as Renaissance authors define it, the delights of the higher senses take precedence over the lower, Venus revels in smell, touch, and taste. Praising Adonis's beauty, she descants on the pleasures of each sense, saving for the climax her voluptuous cry of hunger,

But, O, what banquet wert thou to the taste. . . .

[l. 445]

Time and again Shakespeare uses images of gluttonous feeding to demonstrate the true nature of her passion. Since the equation between lust and gluttony was common in Renaissance literature, the educated readers to whom this poem was directed could not have mistaken the bias of its imagery.

Unlike the manifestations of true love Venus's passion makes her blood boil and carries her into "blindfold fury" that conquers the dictates of reason, shame, and honor. The "careless lust" with which Venus burns may be equated with the elemental force (Ficino calls it a daemon) that governs the mating of animals but which human love transcends.

If we see the poem in this way, its parts will cohere more closely and amplify each other. The episode of the mating horses in the central section of the poem will not seem an idle digression but a demonstration of the nature of the generative passion. The episode shows the power of Venus and serves to illustrate precisely the sort of love she stands for.

Men and animals share this passion, but the Renaissance God had endowed men with reason, not indeed to spoil them for generation but to keep their passions in check. Renaissance readers could not have confused human love with the lust which inspires the breeding of animals. If men fell into this passion, they were thought to lose the characteristics which distinguished men from beasts. Although the Renaissance moralists were too wise to demand that men lead passionless lives, they demanded that even in love reason must play a part, lest love turn into what Adonis calls "sweating Lust."

But Venus is a goddess and a great one. Throughout the poem she makes her eloquent pleas in the most ornate rhetoric at Shakespeare's command. She preaches the necessity of generation brilliantly, and her arguments are all sound, as Shakespeare's repetition of them in the sonnets implies. For all this there is a flaw in her reasoning, and Shakespeare is careful not to let us miss it. As Adonis reminds us in blunt terms, her arguments do not apply to the situation. Instead Venus has turned logic inside out to make reason, as he says, "the bawd to lust's abuse" [l. 792].

Earthly beauty, Venus pleads, cannot last but is subject to all the accidents of time and chance. Like Duke Theseus [*Midsummer-Night's Dream*, I. i. 67 ff.] she pictures the vanity of celibacy,

> That on the earth would breed a scarcity
> And barren dearth of daughters and of sons. . . .
>
> [ll. 753-54]

Transferring the image of eating from love to death, she calls the body a "swallowing grave," and reminds him that the end of all earthly treasure is "Foul-cank'ring rust" [ll. 757, 767].

Adonis may be a priggish child, but his answer to this siren's song states, rather nobly, the answer the far-from-prudish Renaissance gave those who confused burning lust with lawful love. For three vigorously pointed stanzas he moralizes her actions. Venus's reason is no true guide, being subject to her will and passion. All she has pleaded, he says, may be true, but she has misapplied valid arguments against celibacy as a mere cover for lust:

> I hate not love, but your device in love,
> That lends embracements unto every stranger.
> You do it for increase: O strange excuse,
> When reason is the bawd to lust's abuse!
>
> [ll. 789-92]

Using food imagery once more, Adonis equates the lust which consumes Venus with the destructive gluttony of caterpillars; however we may interpret the poem, these lines picture forcefully and convincingly the difference between true love and lust:

> Call it not love, for Love to heaven is fled,
> Since sweating Lust on earth usurp'd his name;
> Under whose simple semblance he hath fed
> Upon fresh beauty, blotting it with blame;
>   Which the hot tyrant stains and soon bereaves,
>   As caterpillars do the tender leaves.
>
> Love comforteth like sunshine after rain,
> But Lust's effect is tempest after sun;
> Love's gentle spring doth always fresh remain,
> Lust's winter comes ere summer half be done;
>   Love surfeits not, Lust like a glutton dies;
>   Love is all truth, Lust full of forged lies.
>
> [ll. 793-804]

The whole poem gives life to the dried abstractions of moral philosophy by setting them out in moving images. The infection of love is intimately bound up with the vital spirits of the blood, compounded in the heart of air and fire; thus Shakespeare's goddess describes herself as "all compact of fire" [l. 149] and is so light that she does not press down the flowers she lies on. Love heats the blood, and Venus's frenzy makes her "red and hot as coals of glowing fire" [l. 35].

Physicians held that the ardor of love dries the body, and in our poem Venus kisses Adonis as if she would "draw his lips' rich treasure dry" [l. 552]. The heat of love clouds the imagination and causes the lover to vacillate between fear and hope; in Shakespeare's phrasing "Despair and hope" make Venus "ridiculous" [l. 988]. Passionate love runs to extremes, is violent, cannot be checked by reason once it rages, disregards the precepts of morality and common sense—all these Renaissance truisms revive in the action and the images of the poem.

The whole thematic significance of *Venus and Adonis* is reiterated in Adonis's reproach to her advances and in her curse upon love which ends the poem. Both passages define the difference between love and lust, between ideal love and the excessive passion that in the life of man does much mischief. Unlike true love the love which Venus urges is a fleeting pleasure; unlike true love false desire looks fair but weakens the body and sows dissension in the soul. The bitter antitheses with which Venus curses love after the death of Adonis recall Sonnet 129:

> Sorrow on love hereafter shall attend;
> It shall be waited on with jealousy,
> Find sweet beginning, but unsavoury end,
>   Ne'er settled equally, but high or low,
>   That all love's pleasure shall not match his woe.
>
> It shall be fickle, false, and full of fraud,
> Bud and be blasted in a breathing-while;
> The bottom poison, and the top o'erstraw'd
> With sweets that shall the truest sight beguile.
>   The strongest body shall it make most weak,
>   Strike the wise dumb and teach the fool to
>   speak. . . .
>
> [ll. 1136-46]
> (pp. 46-52)

These curt antitheses are more than rhetorical flourishes. By the use of balanced examples Shakespeare contrasts the appearance of violent desire with its reality, its promise with its performance, and we shall see this contrast again in the plays. The poem was of course meant to delight, but it also has something to say. The modern reader who feels that Shakespeare has written a purely decorative poem loses a great deal.

Renaissance poetry was meant to teach by moving the affections with sensuous imagery. Thus it seems to me that Venus's eloquence is designed to convince and that if it did not convince, the poem would not be a good poem. Yet to suppose that Shakespeare made Venus persuasive only in order to tickle our senses underestimates his craftsmanship. As in a good battle poem the enemy must be given his due if the victory is to be meaningful, so in this poem Shakespeare must make Venus plausible. Were Venus not more than ordinarily attractive, Adonis's refusal would not interest us very long. But more important than this, Venus's strength and power and beauty are necessary to the allegory. As *Aphrodite Pandemos* she is the powerful goddess whose charms continually lure men and animals to reproduce themselves and perpetuate life on earth. In this aspect she is fair, and truly fair. However, this Venus, this earthly love, despite her proper function, is a violent passion which disturbs men's lives. In keeping with the allegory lust or desire must be powerful and apparently fair, for lust is enticing.

The reader who finds Venus more convincing than Adonis, when she argues the case of lust, is the man who finds Milton's Satan a more "sympathetic" character than God [in *Paradise Lost*]. Only a predisposition to prize the passionate will for its own sake could blind the reader to the care with which Shakespeare inserts images unflattering to Venus in the height of her passion. Venus is fairest when she argues the natural law of generation to perpetuate the body's beauty. But what are we to think when Shakespeare describes her other aspect, unbridled lust, when we see her as an "empty eagle" devouring "feathers, flesh, and bone" [ll. 55, 56], or when he speaks of her as a gluttonous vulture? (pp. 52-3)

> Franklin M. Dickey, "Attitudes toward Love in 'Venus and Adonis' and 'The Rape of Lucrece'," in his Not Wisely but Too Well: Shakespeare's Love Tragedies, The Huntington Library, 1957, pp. 46-62.

DON CAMERON ALLEN   (essay date 1959)

[*Allen examines* Venus and Adonis *in terms of two literary conventions that are based on classical and medieval philosophies, and both of which employ the terminology of hunting. The first tradition likens seduction to a chase, an ignoble "soft hunt" of timid quarry; the second regards the "hard hunt" of a prey who turns and stands as proper training for great and noble men. The goddess and the youth in this poem, he points out, are distinguished by their different forms of pursuit: "Venus hunts Adonis; Adonis hunts the boar. The first hunt is the soft hunt of love; the second is the hard hunt of life."*]

It is possibly an error to think of Shakespeare's *Venus and Adonis* as a legitimate child of the tenth book of the *Metamorphoses* even though some of its elaborate wit is plainly fathered by twists and turns in the Latin text. When the poem is broadly regarded, it is rather certain that in tone, purpose, and structure the two poems have little to share. To begin with, the true poet of the Latin poem is by artistic pretence not Ovid at all but widower Orpheus, whose personal tragedy quietly informs each one of the songs that he sings on his Thracian hill to an assembly of wild beasts and birds. (p. 100)

In Shakespeare's version none of this pathos comes through, and the Ovidian music that the annotators have heard is ghost music. True enough, the Latin poet's description of Venus in the role of a rustic Diana is the germ of Shake-speare's finished caricature of the frustrate lady, flushed and sweating. Her advice on hunting to the rumpled Adonis, tersely expressed in Latin, becomes a sportsman's lecture in English. But, in the main, the two poets saw the myth differently. Shakespeare's Adonis, contrary to the whole tradition, scorns love. In the sonnets of *The Passionate Pilgrim,* if these be Shakespeare's, the boy is mocked for missing his chance, but the longer poem takes, I think, a different position. The legend of Atalanta and Hippomenes, which Ovid relates as a harmonious part of the central legend, is also omitted by Shakespeare and replaced by an animal diversion between Adonis's stallion and an eager mare. Actually Shakespeare's intent and plan is as different from that of Ovid as his Venus—a forty-year-old countess with a taste for Chapel Royal altos—is from the eternal girl of the Velia.

Venus and Adonis is clearly the work of a young and unfinished artist, but there is no question about his independence. When we read previous poems based on the myth, we see at once that something very new is being ventured. Parabosco [in his *Delle Lettere Amorose*] has the goddess come down from a cloudy reach and exhibit herself naked to the little hunter. Unused to the sensation of passion, he falls at her feet, and the text is then Italianly expanded as a warm prelude to the cold Roman conclusion. Ronsard's 'L'Adonis' is a virtuoso conflation of Ovid's narrative and Bion's lament. The French poet, who was as curiously fearful of women as Shakespeare's Adonis, writes in warning terms. Venus may mourn passionately for Adonis, but almost at once she will find consolation in the young Anchises. For Ronsard the scattering anemone is a symbol of the faith of women. Now no one knew more about the thinness of certain kinds of love-sorrow than Shakespeare; but in this poem, he stresses vagaries of ladies that are beyond the intellectual reach of the French poet; in fact, his goddess is far more seductive—at least to men of the north—than even those conjured up by his Italian predecessors. We must read Shakespeare's poem for its differences from its predecessors to learn what it is about.

Orthodox commentaries have regularly observed that *Venus and Adonis* is an epyllion like *Hero and Leander,* and, consequently, it is possible to point to a few similar poems before it and a good many after. This measurement tells us very little about the poem, under the surface of which one hears the faint murmur of an inverted pastourelle, of a mythological satire, and of a poetic discourse on the nature of the decent Venus. Rising above these mutes are the silver horn calls of an English *cynegeticon* [the art of hunting], for *Venus and Adonis* can be partially explained in terms of a timeless hunt. Venus, the amorous Amazon (both Plautus and Shakespeare say that she manhandled Adonis) hunts with her strong passions; the hunted Adonis lives to hunt the boar; and the boar is death, the eternal hunter. The text, if one is needed, hangs on a common theme, succinctly expressed by an Italian of Shakespeare's generation [V. Belli, in his *Madrigali*]:

> Questo mondo è una caccia, e cacciatrice
> La Morte vincitrice. [This world is a hunt, and
> Death the inexorable hunter.]

The metaphors and epithets that adorn the Shakespearian text come, if I may be permitted a metaphoric pun, from the lexicon of venery. The great goddess is an 'emptie eagle', given to 'vulture' thoughts; whereas the young hunter is a bird 'tangled in a net' [l. 67], a dabchick hiding in the waves, a 'wild bird being tamed' [l. 560], a protected deer in Venus's 'parke', a 'yeelding pray', a roe 'ty'rd with chasing' [l. 561], and an escaped quarry that 'runs apace' homeward 'through the dark lawnd' [l. 813]. The omitted Ovidian parenthesis of Atalanta and Hippomenes reminds us that in the other half of her legend the runner was a huntress and that her lover-conqueror dissolved his first disappointments in love by hunting.

So it is the larger literary scheme of the hunt that controls the first four scenes of this poem, from the sunshine morning of the first day to the dismal grey of the second, and the whole notion was passed on to Shakespeare through the means of a long symbolic tradition. The Middle Ages, for instance, had laid it down that Venus, in her pursuit of Adonis, had proved herself the mistress of the chase. . . . Men who could subscribe to this conclusion naturally agreed that Ovid, arch-priest of Venus, was also a mighty hunter of both beasts of venery and of the chase. The Middle Ages, which stood so close to antiquity as to think of its goods as its own in a way that the Renaissance never could, knew its uncles of Greece and Rome and rightly bestowed this title on him who told Cupid that a good hunter pursued only *fugaces* [the elusive], who put hunting terms in the mouth of amorous Apollo [in his *Metamorphoses*], and who describes women as fit to be hunted, likening the lover to the skilful *retiarius* [gladiator] spreading his nets [in his *Ars Amatoria*]. He who knew Ovid, knew that love was a hunt.

But Ovid did not invent this simile to which he gave so much currency. Plato, who discovered most of what we know, was the first to call Eros 'the mighty hunter' [in his *Symposium*], and to classify the 'lovers' chase' . . . as a subdivision of the great hunt [in his *Sophist*]. In addition to this philosophical metaphor, the lover in antiquity is often a hunter and the hunter often a lover. (pp. 100-03)

But the love-hunt, dangerous and valiant as it may be, does not on the lower venerian level ennoble the soul; hence, the classical pedagogues did not recommend it to young men for whom life had a grander course. Plato [in his *Laws*] much prefers the hunting of the 'sacred hunters' . . . , an assembly of brave youths, similar to those described by Philostratus [in his *Imagines*], who take the great land animals with little aid beyond that of their own physical and mental powers. In the same section, Plato condemns 'the hunters of men', but for many Greeks hunting was the hero's preliminary education. To the grave end of testing and training heroes, Apollo and his sister Diana, the legend runs, taught hunting to Chiron, who, in turn, imparted this wisdom to a great register of demigods and noble men. Both the Middle Ages and the Renaissance had this myth by heart, and so hunting became first the proper preparation for knighthood and, later, for the forming of a gentleman. (p. 105)

But while most knights were skilled hunters and the hunt was widely commended by men of the Middle Ages, it was not for everyone nor for every hunter were all kinds of hunting. 'God', according to the precepts of the *Livre de Chasse du Roy Modus*, 'has given each man different tastes and desires, and so he authorized several hunts accommodated to the nature of one's virtues and station.'

Thanks to poetical texts from antiquity, from the Middle Ages, and from the Renaissance itself, we can . . . sit before Shakespeare's *Venus and Adonis* with something better than a blank understanding. We know that Love is a hunter, that the seduction of the beloved is a kind of chase, and that it is

all the soft hunt, which is essentially improper. On the other hand, the hard hunt, the work of the sacred hunters, is the honest training of those who would be heroes. But there are hunts available to some and not to others, and the best that one can do is to see, as Bruno suggests [in his *Degli Heroici Furori*], that all of life is a hunt and to hope that one has the implements helpful in its conduct. The poem fits this doctrine as well as any poem fits any doctrine. Venus hunts Adonis; Adonis hunts the boar. The first hunt is the soft hunt of love; the second is the hard hunt of life. But in this simple exposition, there are some interesting implications that I should attend to before I return to the nature of the two hunts.

The myth of Atalanta and Hippomenes, which is the centre of Ovid's poem and explains the goddess's hatred and fear of the bitter beasts, is replaced in *Venus and Adonis* by the episode of the horses, which is a love chase on a bottom level. Shakespeare's Venus produces this event as a burning incitement to the adolescent Adonis and as a living text for her sermon on lust to the more mature readers. Actually, it can be interpreted as an animal allegory springing from the race described by Ovid and setting the tone for Venus's wooing. It is at once love among the beasts and a satire on courtly love, for the stallion is a noble earl and the jennet a maid-in-waiting. But before we understand the moral meaning of the episode, we should ponder the reason for Shakespeare's substitution of it for the older legend. Without doubt Shakespeare felt that the lengthy tale of Atalanta and Hippomenes was a dramatic distraction that threw the central story out of focus, and for this reason should be omitted. I also suspect that an associative process led him to add the mating of the horses.

Shakespeare's Adonis is, after all, a remaking of the notoriously chaste Hippolytus. The son of Theseus is on every list of heroic hunters, but his similarity to Shakespeare's Adonis does not end here. His chaste resistance, his death through Venus's agents, his connexion with horses make him a member of Adonis's set. The ancient poets and mythographers sometimes said that a jealous Mars or an avenger Apollo sent the boar that killed Adonis, but Passerat, a French contemporary of Shakespeare's, invented a new and, perhaps, more congenial legend. Diana sent the boar to revenge the killing of Hippolytus. . . . In addition to this, there is a hint in the names. Hippomenes (ιππο-+μεωοδ: passion or strength of a horse) has a connexion with Hippolytus and with Adonis's stallion that one with 'small Greek' would notice. So the episode of the stallion and the jennet slides into the poem by normal associations. But why is it there?

With the exception of Robert Miller [see excerpt above, 1952], no critic has seen much in the episode of the horses beyond a splendid testimony to Shakespeare's knowledge of livestock. It is always pleasant to discover that Shakespeare knew about as much as the average man, but it is possible that on this occasion he knew more. Perhaps the poet who would shortly write

> But you are more intemperate in your blood
> Than Venus, or these pamp'red animals
> That rage in savage sensuality,
>
> [*Much Ado about Nothing,* IV. i. 59-61]

had something else in mind. If one could read with Venus and Shakespeare the book of creatures from which both of them took this animal *exemplum,* one would find some very interesting classical footnotes about the love madness of stallions and the libidinousness of jennets. Of course, any pasture would hold suggestion; but, as Miller observed, this stallion breaks his reins and crushes his bit with his teeth, 'Controlling what he was controlled with' [l. 270]. He is a creature of virtue, but he lacks 'a proud rider on so proud a back' [l. 300]. It is Shakespeare who makes this complaint. When it is the turn of Venus to speak, the horse's rebellion is praised:

> How like a iade he stood tied to the tree,
> Servilly maistred with a leatherne raine,
> But when he saw his love, his youths faire fee,
> He held such pettie bondage in disdaine:
> Throwing the base thong from his bending crest,
> Enfranchising his mouth, his backe, his brest.
>
> [ll. 391-96]

For Venus lust equals freedom, but when we, tutored by a longer tradition than she knew, view the chase and hear these words, we recognize the horse.

Plato, who first supplied us with the doctrine of the hunt, returns to give us [in his *Phaedrus*] the correct annotation on the horse.

> Now when the charioteer sees the vision of Love and his whole soul is warmed throughout by the sight and he is filled with the itchings and prickings of desire, the obedient horse, giving in then as always to the bridle of shame, restrains himself from springing on the loved one; but the other horse pays no attention to the driver's goad or whip, but struggles with uncontrolled leaps, and doing violence to his master and team-mate, forces them to approach the beautiful and speak of carnal love.

Yes, here he is;

> Imperiously he leaps, he neighs, he bounds,
> And now his woven girthes he breaks asunder,
> The bearing earth with his hard hoofe he wounds,
> Whose hollow wombe resounds like heavens thunder,
> The yron bit he crusheth tweene his teeth,
> Controlling what he was controlled with.
>
> [ll. 265-70]

Adonis's stallion is certainly Plato's horse, but Venus's little lesson is sadly blunted by Shakespeare who describes the mare as a 'breeding jennet'. Venus had used her animal parable to argue that Adonis should reproduce himself (a curious obsession of Shakespeare's at this time), but Adonis, a youth learning the hard hunt, spoils her moral.

> You do it for increase, o straunge excuse!
> When reason is the bawd to lusts abuse.
>
> [ll. 791-92]

It is clear that Venus's strategy was first to get Adonis dismounted so that she could demonstrate her powers. Her second task is to make the soft hunt with its meaningful ease so attractive that he will abandon the hard hunt, the preparation for the heroic life. Venus knows that Adonis is not yet ready for her kind of love: 'The tender spring upon thy tempting lip, / Shewes thee unripe' [ll. 127-28]. In spite of this knowledge, Venus, who is rich with experience, tries her blandishments on Adonis; she even translates him into a deer and accords him the luscious grange of her body. But Adonis knows allegory when he hears it, and so he rushes to remount his horse at the exact moment that it smells the jennet, 'sees the vision of Love'. The adolescent hunter, the sullen morning boy of 'lazie sprite', 'heavie, darke, disliking eye' [l. 182] loses his

temper; he is angry with the older woman who has cost him his horse, who has hindered his natural duties. From this anger grows a partial kind of love, but it is not the sort Venus would have. Adonis is a child with her. When she swoons, he fusses over her as a boy might fuss over his mother. He will readily kiss her good-night when it is time for bed. The goddess takes advantage of this filial-maternal relationship which is really all Adonis wants. Then the horse-metaphor returns: 'Now is she in the verie lists of love' [l. 595]. But Adonis will not manage her; he will only hunt the boar. Venus equates the boar with Death, and, as becomes an otiose goddess, returns to the problem in hand and praises the soft hunt.

In Venus's venery, the soft hunt is the pursuit of the *fugaces,* of those timid animals that never turn and stand—the hare, the cony, the fox, and the deer, but especially the hare. . . . Ovid, himself, describes the god Apollo bounding after the flying Daphne like a French hound pursuing a hare in an open meadow. It is, of course, by no artistic accident that Venus who could describe the grazing of the deer so sensuously, now paints the hunting of wet 'wat' so well. The whole section, like that on the horses, has been vastly admired by the Shakespearian lovers of nature, and I do not doubt that Shakespeare like any country lad sent his dog after rabbits. But the landscape over which 'poore wat' tours, the 'farre off' hill upon which he stands erect with 'listning eare', is not too different from Venus's 'parke'; moreover, the creatures among which he seeks to lose himself—'deare', 'sheepe', 'conies'—were not without female counterparts among the Elizabethans. There is no doubt that little Will Shakespeare watched the hare run, but this 'wat' is probably more than a 'deaw-bedabbled wretch'.

It was not unusual for artists to show Venus accompanied by the hare; its unbelievable fecundity, for it was said to conceive while it was gestating, made it a symbolic companion for the generative mother. The ancients thought that hares could exchange sex, and an aggressive masculinity was attributed to the females that suits Shakespeare's impression of Venus. The lubricity of the hare was also long the subject of human comment, but the symbolism of the Shakespearian hare probably goes beyond this. In the *Satiricon* of Petronius, the witch who has undertaken to heal the impotence of the hero, turns at the proper moment and remarks to her assistant: 'You see, my Chrysis, you see; I have raised a hare for others.' The hunting of the hare can probably have only one meaning; but Shakespeare, as only Titian before him, alters Adonis from the soft hunter of hares, who meets death when he turns to the harder hunt, to a youth whose whole intent is on the hunting of the boar.

If the boar meant something to Shakespeare's generation besides the hard hunt, the proper education of the sacred hunter, and, as Venus herself names him, Death, I have not been able to find it. In the legend Adonis always dies at the tusk of the boar, and in the more orthodox accounts of the story, the commentators had no trouble with the meaning. In the medieval annotations, the boar was lechery. Horologgi who explained an Italian translation of the *Metamorphoses* puts the boar down as jealousy, and, interestingly enough, in Shakespeare's account Venus is strangely jealous of the boar. For the more sophisticated Sandys [in his *Metamorphosis Englished*], the ancient weather myth holds valid, so his Adonis is destroyed as the summer is when boarish winter comes. At this time in his poetic life, Shakespeare, one should observe, may have had boars in his head because he had only recently been looking through the life records of Richard III, 'the wretched, bloody, and usurping boar' [*Richard III,* V. ii. 7], and he was also fascinated, as young men often are, by innocent and unmerited death in youth. He needed, I imagine, no goddess to expound any of this to him, but, none the less, he brings Venus back in the later part of the poem to discourse foolishly on love like a fluttery and apprehensive Doll Tearsheet [in *2 Henry* IV] of forty. As for his Adonis—since all Adonises must die—this one, the invention of Shakespeare, gets off with a cleaner biography than any. (pp. 105-11)

> Don Cameron Allen, "On 'Venus and Adonis'," in Elizabethan and Jacobean Studies: Presented to Frank Percy Wilson, *Oxford at the Clarendon Press, 1959, pp. 100-11.*

A. C. HAMILTON   (essay date 1961)

[*In his essay, excerpted below, Hamilton focuses on Shakespeare's adaptation of several myths and traditions in his narrative of Venus and Adonis. By infusing the Ovidian tradition with "the Platonic doctrine that love is the desire for beauty," the critic claims, Shakespeare creates an entirely new version of the story—one in which the youth stands for Beauty, "the sustaining power of creation," the goddess represents Love, the protector of Beauty, and the boar symbolizes "the enemies of Beauty." According to Hamilton, these modifications help to free the myth of Venus and Adonis from its traditional burden of moral signification and allow Shakespeare to create a poem that, in its depiction of Adonis's death and the ensuing chaos, "treats the mystery of creation and the fall."*]

After having been greatly in vogue in its own day, and establishing a tradition of erotic mythological poetry, *Venus and Adonis* was neglected by the later centuries until, in Coleridge's judgment, the poem "gave ample proof of [Shakespeare's] possession of a most profound, energetic, and philosophical mind" [see Additional Bibliography]. This judgment has not been accepted and today, as Hyder Rollins noted in 1938, "scholars and critics seldom mention *Venus* . . . without apologies expressed or implied" [see Additional Bibliography]. (p. 1)

Modern judgment, without apology, is given by C. S. Lewis:

As we read on we become more and more doubtful how the work ought to be taken. Is it a poem by a young moralist, a poem against lust? There is a speech given to Adonis (769 et seq.) which might lend some colour to the idea. But the story does not point the moral at all well, and Shakespeare's Venus is a very ill-conceived temptress. . . . If, on the other hand, the poem is meant to be anything other than a "cooling card," it fails egregiously. Words and images which, for any other purpose, ought to have been avoided keep on coming in and almost determine the dominant mood of the reader—"satiety," "sweating," "leaden appetite," "gorge," "stuff'd," "glutton," "gluttonlike" . . . And this flushed, panting, perspiring, suffocating, loquacious creature is supposed to be the goddess of love herself, the golden Aphrodite. It will not do. If the poem is not meant to arouse disgust it was very foolishly written: if it is, then disgust (that barbarian mercenary) is not, either aesthetically or morally, the feeling on which a poet should rely in a moral poem [see excerpt above, 1954].

But there are several ways in which we can learn something of how the poem is to be taken. Mr. Lewis' "It will not do," was not echoed by Shakespeare's contemporaries, and their praise and imitation offer us an insight, unique among his works, into how he was read and understood by his age. Secondly, there is the treatment of the myth of Venus and Adonis by contemporary poets, and by the allegorical commentators, which may suggest how Shakespeare would read the myth, and how he would expect his audience to read his treatment. At the very least, the first may show us what the poem is not, and the second may suggest what it could be. I shall consider later what, in my judgment, the poem is.

If Shakespeare really wrote his poem against lust, all his contemporaries were deceived. Barnfield, who is entirely representative of their judgment, writes:

And *Shakespeare* thou, whose hony-flowing Vaine,
(Pleasing the World) thy Praises doth containe,
Whose *Venus,* and whose *Lucrece* (sweet, and
    chaste)

Venus and Mars. By Sandro Botticelli.

Thy Name in fames immortall Booke haue plac't
[see excerpt above, 1598].

They may have been deceived, of course, and there is no evidence from their allusions that they read the poem as carefully as the modern apologists have done. Yet the numerous imitators from T. H. in *Oenone and Paris* (1594) to Phineas Fletcher in *Brittain's Ida* (1628), who clearly did read the poem carefully, all reinforce the praise of the "sweet," "wittie," and "honey-tongued" Shakespeare [see excerpt above by Francis Meres, 1598]. "Who loues not *Adons* loue?" Judicio asks in *The Return from Parnassus,* and since everyone did, adds a judgment which became more vocal, that the poem was written *for* lust:

> His sweeter verse contaynes hart robbing lines,
> Could but a grauer subiect him content,
> Without loues foolish lazy languishment
> [see excerpt above, 1601-02].

Of course, imitators rarely clarify a tradition, being content to feed upon crumbs from the banquet, which for the erotic tradition is Venus' banquet. Chapman is the exception, and he illuminates Shakespeare's poem by adapting it to his own purposes. In *The Shadow of Night* (1594) he urges his Muse to sing of Cynthia's glory, but warns:

> Presume not then ye flesh confounded soules,
> That cannot beare the full Castalian bowles,
> Which seuer mounting spirits from the sences,
> To looke in this deepe fount for thy pretenses.

These lines, with their apparent reference to the motto of *Venus and Adonis,* rebuke Shakespeare, so it has been argued, for his eroticism. Yet Chapman does not deny the senses their pleasure, for only through their contentment is the spirit free to mount. Accordingly, his *Ovids Banquet of Sense* (1595) derives from the banquet of the senses which Venus seeks in Adonis, but adds:

> The sence is giuen vs to excite the minde,
> And that can neuer be by sence exited
> But first the sence must her contentment [find],
> We therefore must procure the sence delighted,
> That so the soule may vse her facultie.

Love satisfies sensual desires; lust does not. It follows that when he writes in "A Coronet for his Mistresse Philosophie" to "Mvses that sing loues sensuall Emperie," he helps define the kind of poem that Shakespeare writes. When man is inspired by proper self-love, sensual love is not an end in itself, for he may proceed from the banquet of the senses to the banquet of the mind. Since Shakespeare's poem shows only that first stage when the banquet of the senses is denied, Chapman pleads with him (and his followers) to go beyond love's sensual empery and sing of his mistress Philosophy. Whatever the poem is, its contemporary reputation and the tradition it established show that it is not a poem against lust.

But does the poem itself reveal that it is written against lust in its picture of the "loue-sicke Queene" [l. 175] who so violently rapes Adonis to the limit of her power, and especially in his lecture against her conduct:

> I hate not loue, but your deuise in loue,
> That lends imbracements vnto euery stranger,
> You do it for increase, o straunge excuse!
> When reason is the bawd to lusts abuse.
>
> Call it not loue, for loue to heauen is fled,
> Since sweating lust on earth vsurpt his name,
> Vnder whose simple semblance he hath fed,

Vpon fresh beautie, blotting it with blame;
> Which the hot tyrant staines, & soone bereaues:
> As Caterpillers do the tender leaues.
>
> Loue comforteth like sun-shine after raine,
> But lusts effect is tempest after sunne,
> Loues gentle spring doth alwayes fresh remaine,
> Lusts winter comes, ere sommer halfe be donne:
> Loue surfets not, lust like a glutton dies:
> Loue is all truth, lust full of forged lies.
> [ll. 789-804]

Certainly his argument is powerful enough to prevent our saying that the poem is *for* lust. Mr. Miller comments on these lines that Adonis rightly names Venus' passion as mere lust which seeks pleasure and not love which seeks procreation, and finds support for his distinction in the Church Fathers [see excerpt above, 1952]. But, in fact, Adonis is more rigorous than the compromising Church Fathers: their reason, too, is the bawd to lust's abuse when they allow sexual union for procreation. Adonis' rejection of love is absolute. In the opening lines we are told that "hunting he lou'd, but loue he laught to scorne" [l. 4] as later he maintains:

> I know not loue (quoth he) nor will not know it,
> Vnlesse it be a Boare, and then I chase it,
> Tis much to borrow, and I will not owe it,
> My loue to loue, is loue, but to disgrace it.
> [ll. 409-12]

The distinction which he draws between love and lust *is* valid, but only after his death. In the poem that destroying power which feeds on beauty, which is the tempest after the sun, the destroying winter, the surfeiting glutton, and the forged truth is not Venus but the Boar. As Adonis breaks away "from the sweet embrace, / Of those faire armes" [ll. 811-12] ("sweet" and "fair" mocking his disdain), one line surrounds the whole distinction he has made with the strongest irony. Breaking away, he "leaues loue vpon her backe, deeply distrest" [l. 814]. He has claimed that "loue to heauen is fled, / Since sweating lust on earth vsurpt his name" [ll. 793-94]; but Love has not fled, for she is with him now. Only with his death, as Venus prophesies, will discord, dissension, and hatred—that is, lust—usurp the name of love. And only after his death does Love, that is, Venus, flee to heaven.

Contemporary treatments of the myth of Venus and Adonis suggest what the poem could be. In the *Countess of Pembroke's Iuychurch* (1592), Abraham Fraunce translates certain Ovidian myths and adds philosophical explications, for he believed, in common with his age, that poetry is radically allegorical. . . . He translates Ovid's story of Venus and Adonis in highly erotic terms, and appends, without any sense of incongruity, a highly philosophical explication:

> By *Adonis,* is meant the sunne, by *Venus,* the vpper
> hemisphere of the earth (as by *Proserpina* the
> lower); by the boare, winter: by the death of *Adonis,*
> the absence of the sunne for the sixe wintrie mo-
> neths; all which time, the earth lamenteth: *Adonis*
> is wounded in those parts, which are the instru-
> ments of propagation: for, in winter the son, see-
> meth impotent, and the earth barren: neither that
> being able to get, nor this to beare either fruite or
> flowres: and therefore *Venus* sits, lamentably hang-
> ing downe her head, leaning on her left hand, her
> garments all ouer her face.

To this traditional interpretation, he adds the moral: "*Adonis* was turnd to a fading flowre; bewty decayeth, and lust leaueth the lustfull, if they leaue not it. . . . *Adonis* was borne of *Myrrha; Myrrhe* prouoketh lust: *Adonis* was kilde by a boare, that is, he was spent and weakened by old age: *Venus* lamenteth, lust decayeth". The potentialities of the Venus-Adonis myth, as Shakespeare inherited it, were enormous: possibly, a naive literalism; perhaps, but not likely with this myth, a moral significance; and most likely, what Fraunce calls the "hidden mysteries of naturall . . . philosophie."

If Shakespeare needed to be taught how poetry can realize those potentialities, he could have turned to Spenser, and probably did. Since Adonis resists Venus' love, the first part of his poem centers upon the theme of temptation, as does *The Faerie Queene*, Book II. Acrasia, like Venus, meets a very reluctant Adonis in Guyon, who resists all the seductive persuasions of her garden, what Venus calls her park. In the opening episode of Book III, the walls of Castle Joyeous are decorated by a tapestry which portrays Venus' love for Adonis in all its stages. Her passionate love is manifest in the Lady of Delight who loves Britomart, taking her for a man, but on coming to her bed, finds a very reluctant Adonis. Later in Canto VI, Spenser exploits the myth for its philosophical significance: Venus is the great mother of all creation, *Venus Genetrix*, Adonis who has been preserved from the Boar is "the Father of all formes," and their love in the Garden of Adonis sustains all creation. Spenser's allegory in Book III moves in the area defined by these two versions of the myth, displaying its full poetic potentiality. Shakespeare's poem is somewhere between.

What is so surprising, and the mark of his poetic genius, is his simple, yet profound, change in the myth. Adonis does not yield to Venus. Although he is forced to submit passively to her, she must let him go, and at the end laments that "neuer did he blesse / My youth with his, the more am I accurst" [ll. 1119-20]. In the traditional version, his yielding to Venus brings his death by the Boar. In *Perimedes the Blacke-Smith* (1588), Greene tells the story of Venus and Adonis, and adds the moral:

> The *Syren Venus* nourist in hir lap
> Faire *Adon*, swearing whiles he was a youth
> He might be wanton: Note his after-hap
> The guerdon that such lawlesse lust ensueth,
>   So long he followed flattering *Venus* lore,
>   Till seely Lad, he perisht by a bore.

The Boar signifies concupiscence or (spiritual) Death which results from concupiscence. By his change, Shakespeare frees the myth from that heavy weight of moral meaning, freeing it for the kind of poetic meaning which he wished to supply. Whatever that meaning is, it cannot be simply "moral." Since Adonis does not yield to Venus, the poem's center becomes a mystery. Why was he slain by the Boar? What does the Boar signify? Why does Adonis resist? What is the nature of Venus' love for him? These questions may now be explored in a poetic context, freed from the traditional associations which affirm, and give the poem its reason for existing.

That Shakespeare shared Fraunce's belief that poetry treats the "hidden mysteries of naturall . . . philosophie" is suggested by his choice of the Venus-Adonis myth, and also by the Ovidian motto so daringly placed on the title-page of his poem: "let the crowd admire what is common, for me golden Phoebus ministers full cups from the Muses' well." Upon that level, beyond the moral, where readers "entertaine their heauenly speculation," his poem treats the mystery of creation and the fall. While Venus is traditionally identified with Beauty, and her son Cupid with Love, Shakespeare identifies Venus with Love. Adonis is identified with Beauty: "true sweet beautie liu'd, and di'de with him" [l. 1080]. He represents the perfection of Nature in its unfallen state, for to frame her "best worke," as Venus tells her, Nature stole divine moulds from heaven. His beauty is seen as the sustaining power of creation, the sun, in the opening lines where "the sunne with purple-colour'd face" is aptly compared to the "rose-cheekt Adonis" [ll. 1, 3], and later in Venus' praise of him as the greater sun [ll. 859-64]. His death means an end to the world: "Nature that made thee with her selfe at strife, / Saith that the world hath ending with thy life" [ll. 11-12]. He "must not die," she pleads with Jove,

> Till mutuall ouerthrow of mortall kind.
>   For he being dead, with him is beautie slaine,
>   And beautie dead, blacke Chaos comes againe.
>
>   [ll. 1017, 1018-20]

But his power to sustain creation must be sustained, in turn, by Venus, for only Love seeks to preserve Beauty. She counsels him against the enemies of Beauty who are her enemies: mortality, time, Nature's imperfection, those perversions of love in the self-loving, the love-lacking, and the love-denying, Death, and the Boar. "That his beautie may the better thriue" [ll. 1011], she will even flatter Death. By his own "will" [l. 639], however, he chooses to leave her for the Boar. And when he dies, Beauty dies, Love leaves the world with her place usurped by "lust," Nature lies ruined, creation reverts to original chaos, and there is the "mutuall ouerthrow of mortall kind."

This philosophical level of the poem shown in Adonis' death becomes the framework within which is shown Venus' love. With Shakespeare's change in the myth, the poem's center shifts from Adonis to Venus. Unlike all other poems of temptation in which the one tempted is the subject—Ulysses with Circe, Aeneas with Dido, Troilus with Criseyde, Guyon with Acrasia, or the Lady with Comus—Shakespeare's temptress is the subject through whom we see all the action. First we see her erotic courtship of Adonis, and then her grief on finding him dead. The first part of the poem reaches its erotic climax when Adonis tells Venus that he intends to hunt the boar, and in her anguish she pulls him to the ground. At the beginning he was mounted on his horse: now he is mounted on her; but when he remains "liuelesse" she is frustrated in her desire. The mention of the boar, her violence, and frustration coincide to link the first part with the second where the action is climaxed in the Boar's violent kiss and her final frustration on finding his lifeless body. Tone changes between these two parts. The bawdy, even comic, account of Venus' actions which we see through the witty and dispassionate eye of the poet gives place to a plaintive, even tragic, lament. The change is seen in Venus herself: before Adonis leaves, she is aggressive, domineering, and lustful; afterwards, she becomes humble, submissive, and pathetic. She appeals to her divinity when she is with Adonis; without him, she sees herself as a woman suffering in love. For when he leaves her, like the earth without the sun, all her strength goes: she is left amazed, astonished, her senses appalled and her spirit confounded, lost in a labyrinth of emotions. Over two hundred lines anatomize her "variable passions" [l. 967] until, seeing him dead, she leaves the world in anger, anguish, and despair. Her agony confirms all that Adonis had feared once love had disturbed the quiet heart, and fulfills her own prophecy of how love will bring dissension and grief. Further, all that she had feared once Adonis had refused her for the boar is confirmed through his death. Her violence is now justified by his death, as her suffering now separates her love from that pure lust seen in Tarquin after his rape of Lucrece, or in the withdrawn, self-possessed, and silent Acrasia. Through the pattern set up between the two parts, the poem explores the nature of Venus' love, of Adonis' refusal, and the significance of the Boar.

The basis for Shakespeare's treatment of Venus' love for Adonis is the Platonic doctrine that love is the desire for beauty. For this reason he identifies Venus with Love, and Adonis with Beauty. That doctrine, however, is treated with a sophisticated play of wit through her "deuise in loue" [l. 789] According to Platonic doctrine, Love turns from the enjoyment of the sight and hearing of the beloved to the love of Beauty itself which is not found in the outward show of things. The "Platonist" Spenser asks [in *Hymne in Honour of Beautie*]:

> Hath white and red in it such wondrous powre,
> That it can pierce through th'eyes vnto the hart,
> And therein stirre such rage and restlesse stowre,
> As nought but death can stint his dolours smart?

Yet just this outward show of Adonis' beauty, and specifically the white and red of his cheeks and lips, arouses Venus' passion. She does not distinguish between outer and inner beauty: with ears alone she would love "that inward beautie and inuisible" [l. 434], with eyes alone each part of her would love his outward parts, with touch alone she would be in love, the smell from his face would breed love, but with taste as "nourse, and feeder of the other foure" [l. 446] she seeks to banquet all the senses. Again according to Platonic doctrine, the climax of courtship comes with the kiss which joins the souls of reasonable lovers. In Castiglione's *Courtier,* Bembo says:

> a kisse may be said to be rather a cooplinge together of the soule, then of the bodye, bicause it hath suche force in her, that it draweth her vnto it, and (as it were) seperateth her from the bodye. For this do all chast louers couett a kisse, as the cooplinge of soules together . . . *Salomon* saith in his heauenly boke of *Balattes, Oh that he would kiss me with a kisse of his mouth,* to expresse the desire he had, that hys soule might be rauished through heauenly loue to the behouldinge of heauenly beauty in such maner, that cooplying her self inwardly with it, she might forsake the body.

The poem's witty play upon this doctrine is shown through the action turning upon a kiss. At the beginning when Venus plucks Adonis from his horse to "sit, where neuer serpent hisses, / And being set, Ile smother thee with kisses" [ll. 17-18], hissing herself like a serpent, she begs a kiss. He promises, but refuses. Later his kisses revive her from her swoon. Finally when he leaves, his kiss arouses all her violence:

> Her armes do lend his necke a sweet imbrace,
> Incorporate then they seeme, face growes to
>   face . . .
> Now quicke desire hath caught the yeelding pray,
> And gluttonlike she feeds, yet neuer filleth . . .
> And hauing felt the sweetnesse of the spoile,
> With blind fold furie she begins to forrage,
> Her face doth reeke, & smoke, her blood doth boile,
> And carelesse lust stirs vp a desperat courage.
>   [ll. 539-40, 547-48, 553-56]

The description given here seems almost designed to answer Bembo's description of the conduct of reasonable lovers. Yet the second part of the poem does not allow us to contrast her conduct with theirs. In the world of the poem her kiss is contrasted to the Boar's kiss which brings Adonis' death.

In his morally "innocent" state as one who "know[s] not loue . . . nor will not know it" [l. 409], Adonis sees Venus as lust. But Shakespeare does not, and neither may readers of the poem. Venus' dilemma is precisely that she is Love:

> Looke how he can, she cannot chuse but loue . . .
> Being Iudge in loue, she cannot right her cause.
> Poore Queene of loue, in thine own law
>   forlorne . . .
> She's loue; she loues, and yet she is not lou'd . . .
>   [ll. 79, 220, 251, 610]

The law of which she is judge is illustrated in the jennet episode: Adonis' horse, being all that a horse should be, responds to the breeding jennet as a horse should. The example is used by Venus to urge Adonis to "learne to loue":

> Who sees his true-loue in her naked bed,
> Teaching the sheets a whiter hew then white,
> But when his glutton eye so full hath fed,
> His other agents ayme at like delight? . . .
> Let me excuse thy courser gentle boy,
> And learne of him I heartily beseech thee,
> To take aduantage on presented ioy.
>   [ll. 397-400, 403-05]

Her law is that all creatures must love in return when they are truly loved. (After Adonis' death she inverts that law: love becomes discordant, suspicious, deceiving, and perverse; and "they that loue best, their loues shall not enjoy" [l. 1164]. Though she strives to present herself as his "true-loue," he chooses to remain "vnkind" [l. 187], that is, unnatural and outside the law which she invokes. In her dilemma, she asks: "why doest abhor me?"

> Thou canst not see one wrinckle in my brow,
> Mine eyes are grey, and bright, & quicke in turning:
> My beautie as the spring doth yearelie grow,
> My flesh is soft, and plumpe, my marrow burning,
>   My smooth moist hand, were it with thy hand
>   felt,
>   Would in thy palme dissolue, or seeme to melt.
>   [ll. 138-44]

Just here where we may wish to see her simply as Lust, she continues:

> Bid me discourse, I will inchaunt thine eare,
> Or like a Fairie, trip vpon the greene,
> Or like a Nimph, with long disheueled heare,
> Daunce on the sands, and yet no footing seene.
>   Loue is a spirit all compact of fire,
>   Not grosse to sinke, but light, and will aspire.
>   [ll. 145-50]

Moreover, she offers us visible proof that she is Love in the flowers which support her without bending and in the doves which draw her through the sky. This juxtaposition of flesh and spirit is too deliberate, too much part of the poem's wit to be cancelled out by any reduction of Venus to a moral description as lust opposed to love. The union in Venus of the "marrow burning" and the "spirit all compact of fire" is essential to the poem's argument.

The "marrow burning" is the reason which Adonis finally offers for rejecting Venus. Earlier he had equivocated: he hated love yet didn't know it, he didn't hate love but only Venus' device in love. As we have noted earlier, even his lecture against Venus as lust is undercut by its context. He could be seen as Aristotle's truly temperate man, one lacking all desire, if only he were supported by reason. He cannot be seen as the merely innocent boy too young to love, for Venus, who should know, says that he is old enough to be tasted. Again, that first stage belongs to love, as we see in Longus' romance [*Daphnis and Chloë*] where Daphnis who does not know love is brought to the same erotic position as Venus brings Adonis, only Nature teaches him the way. The poem's Ovidian motto is really Adonis': let the base crowd admire what is vulgar, that is, follow *Venere vulgare,* and being Adonis he may claim the ministrations of the golden-haired Apollo. Yet Shakespeare strips him of all the defence that arms heroes similarly tempted: Guyon is sustained by moral virtue assisted by grace, the Lady in [Milton's] *Comus* by "the Sun-clad power of Chastity," Aeneas by his sacred mission, Ulysses by the need to return to his own home and wife. All other heroes have a way to follow which ends in triumph: Adonis prefers to hunt the Boar which brings his death. He alone resists temptation, only to die. He has one desire, as Venus tells us at the end: "to grow vnto himselfe was his desire" [l. 1180]. Her metaphor is revealing, for Adonis is described throughout the poem as the flower that wishes to grow and not be plucked. In the beginning Venus calls him "the fields chiefe flower" and plucks him from his horse. To make him yield, she argues that "faire flowers that are not gathred in their prime, / Rot, and consume them selues in litle time" [ll. 131-32], to which he replies:

> Who plucks the bud before one leafe put forth? . . .
> The mellow plum doth fall, the greene sticks fast,
> Or being early pluckt, is sower to tast.
>
> [ll. 416, 527-28]

He rejects lust because it feeds on beauty "as Caterpillers do the tender leaues" [l. 798]. "Thou pluckst a flower" [l. 946], Venus accuses Death; then with his death we see the "solemne sympathie" [l. 1057] of all the flowers that seem to bleed with him. At the end he is changed into a flower which Venus plucks. In his conception of Adonis, Shakespeare reverts to that primitive figure in Bion's *Lament,* one who is the god of Nature.

His dilemma is simply that he is Adonis. If he yields to Venus, he will not grow to himself, but be plucked. If he does not yield, he will be plucked by the enemies of Beauty: by mortality and time, by the imperfections in Nature which result from Cynthia's jealousy, disease, Death. His greatest enemy is himself:

> What is thy bodie but a swallowing graue,
> Seeming to burie that posteritie.
> Which by the rights of time thou needs must haue,
> If thou destroy them not in darke obscuritie?
> If so the world will hold thee in disdaine,
> Sith in thy pride, so faire a hope is slaine.
>
> [ll. 757-62]

All these enemies of Beauty are seen ultimately in the ugly Boar. Though Venus warns Adonis, "Beautie hath naught to do with such foule fiends, / Come not within his danger by thy will" [ll. 638-39], he chooses to follow his own will. Yet we cannot name the Boar for what it is, unless we say that it is the violence of Love's desire not to let Adonis grow to himself (as she says: "had I bin tooth'd like him I must confesse, / With kissing him I should haue kild him first" [ll. 1117-18]), and love's jealousy which first projects the image

of Adonis slain by the boar, and Cynthia's shame which causes her to corrupt the works of Nature and hide her light that Adonis might fall (in accord with the tradition that Diana sent the boar that killed Adonis), and Death, and Adonis himself. In short, the Boar expresses all those forces which seek to pluck the flower of Beauty. Accordingly, it functions as a poetic symbol through which Shakespeare explores the mystery of evil.

Against this background that yields Adonis' death, the poem projects the immortal goddess of love. It was inevitable that Shakespeare's first work, one in which he announced himself as a poet, should be dedicated to Venus. For the major poets in the English tradition, Spenser and Chaucer, were poets of love. Both poets display Venus chiefly as a statue to be adored, while Shakespeare's contribution is to show her intense vitality. In her two postures, reclining in the first part and fleeing in the second, she ranges through all moods and passions. For the sake of love she is prepared to do and become all things: at times she is the bustling mother caring for that petulant boy who weeps when the wind blows his hat off, or the coy disdainful woman with Mars, or the predatory female. Her roles are nicely catalogued by Helena in *All's Well,* who is herself an aggressive Venus wooing a reluctant Adonis in Bertram:

> A mother, and a mistress, and a friend,
> A phoenix, captain, and an enemy,
> A guide, a goddess, and a sovereign,
> A counsellor, a traitress, and a dear.
>
> [I. i. 167-70]

Which aspect of her dominates in our total impression becomes a deeply personal question, and indeed that may be Shakespeare's point in centering the myth upon her. Certainly our response to her must remain ambivalent.

The erotic element in the poem is designed to turn the poem towards us: for Venus' temptation is not directed against Adonis—he is no more capable of responding than a flower—but against the reader. How may we answer her frank question:

> What am I that thou shouldst contemne me thus?
> Or what great danger, dwels vpon my sute?
>
> [ll. 205-06]

A simple moral response becomes as irrelevant as it is to Chaucer's Wife of Bath. (Her rambling in her tale to Adonis, "where did I leaue?" [l. 715] seems directly reminiscent of the Wife's "but now, sire, lat me se, what I shal seyn?"). How are we to respond to the girlish tone of "say, shall we, shall we, wilt thou make the match?" [l. 586], or to the poet's tone in telling Adonis' refusal: "the poore foole praies her that he may depart" [l. 578], and Venus' frustration:

> But all in vaine, good Queene, it will not bee,
> She hath assai'd as much as may be prou'd,
> Her pleading hath deseru'd a greater fee.
>
> [ll. 607-09]

For Shakespeare's first readers the context of the poem would include the spiritual pilgrimage where the pilgrim meets Venus; but, of course, she is condemned by the form itself. In De Guileville's *Pilgrimage of the Life of Man,* translated by Lydgate, the pilgrim meets Venus riding on a swine (or boar). She disguises herself, so she reveals, because she is so ugly. She has him bound, fastened to the swine, beaten, and robbed. But the pilgrim may escape, as Grace Dieu has already told him, by flight. In Nicholas Breton's *Pilgrimage to Paradise* (1592), the pilgrim may escape Venus' temptations and keep on the right way by holding his hand before his face. Or in another form, amatory yet still moral, Gower's *Confessio Amantis,* the lover may separate himself from Venus because he is in the time of winter—here Gower is closer to the Venus-Adonis myth than is Shakespeare—and he leaves the earth. For Adonis, however, there is no escape, except to death. Traditionally Venus appears in a moral world where her evil temptations must be resisted in order that man may achieve the perfected virtuous life. Shakespeare translates the action of his poem into the prelapsarian state.

The poem moves from Venus' temptations, to her grief, to her prophecy of what love will become now that she is "accurst": that is, from her role as goddess, to a woman, and ends with her seen suspended as a planet ruling the world:

> Thus weary of the world, away she hies,
> And yokes her siluer doues, by whose swift aide,
> Their mistresse mounted through the emptie skies,
> In her light chariot, quickly is conuaide,
>   Holding their course to Paphos, where their queen,
>   Meanes to immure her selfe, and not be seen.
>
> [ll. 1189-94]

When she prophesies that hereafter love will "bud, and be blasted, in a breathing while" [ll. 1142], she defines the state of mutability—as in Spenser's Garden of Adonis—which succeeds that state where Love strove to enjoy and propagate the divine Beauty seen in Adonis. That this vision of Venus was indeed the "first heire" of the poet's "inuention" is shown in the plays that follow. Venus becomes the presiding goddess of the comedies, and her love for Adonis is their archetype. Adonis' death and her flight prepare for the world of the tragedies. Perhaps Shakespeare was, after all, tempting himself. (pp. 2-15)

> A. C. Hamilton, "Venus and Adonis," in Studies in English Literature, 1500-1900, *Vol. I, No. 1, Winter, 1961, pp. 1-15.*

KENNETH MUIR (essay date 1964)

[*A British critic, educator, and translator, Muir has published numerous volumes of Shakespearean criticism, edited several of Shakespeare's plays, written book-length critical studies of* King Lear *and* Antony and Cleopatra, *and served as the editor of* Shakespeare Survey *from 1965 to 1980. In the excerpt below, Muir asserts that "almost everything" in* Venus and Adonis, *"appears to be ambivalent." According to the critic, the poem's imagery, its mixture of humorous and erotic elements, and its opposing moral points of view all contribute to the atmosphere of uncertainty, revealing Shakespeare's "acceptance of conflicting feelings about love" and demonstrating "the essentially dramatic nature of his imagination."*]

The Elizabethans interpreted the Adonis story in several different ways. In Book III of *The Faerie Queene,* Spenser makes the love of Venus and Adonis sustain all creation. Greene, in *Perimides,* makes the boar symbolize lust, and Adonis is slain because he yields to Venus. Abraham Fraunce, in *The Countess of Pembroke's Ivy-church,* published in the year before Shakespeare's poem, interprets the story as an allegory of the seasons:

> By *Adonis,* is meant the sunne, by *Venus,* the vpper hemisphere of the earth (as by *Proserpina* the

lower) by the boare, winter: by the death of *Adonis,* the absence of the sunne for the six wintrie moneths; all which time, the earth lamenteth: *Adonis* is wounded in those parts, which are the instruments of propagation: for, in winter the son seemeth impotent, and the earth barren: neither that being able to get, nor this to beare either fruite or flowres: and therefore *Venus* sits, lamentably hanging downe her head, leaning on her left hand, her garments all ouer her face.

We can see from these different treatments of the Adonis story that Shakespeare could have used it for various purposes. But there is no sign in his poem that he was following Spenser in making the love of Venus and Adonis sustain all creation, for their love is never consummated, and he makes no reference to the resurrection of Adonis. Although, at the end of his career, perhaps influenced by Leonard Digges who afterwards translated Claudian, Shakespeare seems to have been aware of the allegorical treatment of the Proserpine story, there is no evidence that he regarded the story of Venus and Adonis as a vegetation myth. Nor, surely, could he have intended the Boar to symbolize lust, since Adonis is anything but lustful.

According to . . . L. E. Pearson "Venus is shown as the destructive agent of sensual love; Adonis, as reason in love" [see excerpt above, 1933]. Most critics, indeed, seem to assume that the moral of the poem—if it has a moral—is to be found in the distinction made by Adonis between love and lust:

> Call it not love, for love to heaven is fled,
> Since sweating lust on earth usurp'd his name,
> Under whose simple semblance he hath fed
> Upon fresh beauty, blotting it with blame;
>   Which the hot tyrant stains, and soon bereaves,
>   As caterpillers do the tender leaves.
>
> Love comforteth like sunshine after rain,
> But Lust's effect is tempest after sun;
> Love's gentle spring doth always fresh remain,
> Lust's winter comes ere summer half be done:
>   Love surfeits not, lust like a glutton dies:
>   Love is all truth, lust full of forged lies.
>
> [ll. 793-804]

T. W. Baldwin seems to agree in part with this interpretation, for he suggests that Venus's pretended love is lust because, unlike the true Neoplatonic lover, she wants to touch Adonis [see Additional Bibliography]. He goes on to quote Ficino to the effect that "the lust to touch the body is not a part of love." But Shakespeare's plays are singularly free from such Neoplatonic nonsense. It is difficult to imagine him blaming Romeo because he wanted to touch Juliet, or blaming Juliet because she was anxious to "lose a winning match" [*Romeo and Juliet,* III. ii. 12]. He knew, as well as Donne, "the right, true end of love" [*Elegies,* No. 18. *Love's Progress*]. There are, moreover, other stanzas in the poem which prevent us from accepting Adonis's moral without qualification. Venus compares Adonis to the self-lover, Narcissus, who "died to kiss his shadow in the brook" [l. 162]. She points out the dangers of self-sufficiency:

> Torches are made to light, jewels to wear,
> Dainties to taste, fresh beauty for the use,
> Herbs for their smell, and sappy plants to bear:
> Things growing to themselves are growth's abuse.
>   Seeds spring from seeds, and beauty breedeth beauty;

Thou wast begot—to get it is thy duty.

Upon the earth's increase why shouldst thou feed,
Unless the earth with thy increase be fed?
By law of nature thou art bound to breed,
That thine may live when thou thyself art dead;
    And so in spite of death thou dost survive,
      In that thy likeness still is left alive.

[ll. 163-74]

Later in the poem she asks Adonis:

What is thy body but a swallowing grave,
Seeming to bury that posterity
Which by the rights of time thou needs must have,
If thou destroy them not in dark obscurity?
    If so, the world will hold thee in disdain,
      Sith in thy pride so fair a hope is slain.

[ll. 757-62]

We are inevitably reminded of the first fourteen sonnets in which Shakespeare urges his friend to marry, so as to ensure the survival of his beauty in his children. The theme is repeated over and over again. "From fairest creatures we desire increase" [Sonnet 1], so as to cheat the grave; after the friend has lost his beauty, he will be able to say "This fair child of mine Shall sum my count, and make my old excuse" [Sonnet 2]; his mother, looking at him, "Calls back the lovely April of her prime" [Sonnet 3], and so might the friend do with his son; not to marry is to be guilty of the sin of self-will; and the only protection against the scythe of Time is breed:

Who lets so fair a house fall to decay,
Which husbandry in honour might uphold
Against the stormy gusts of winter's day
And barren rage of death's eternal cold?

[Sonnet 13]

We are reminded, too, of passages in the mature plays in which Shakespeare's spokesmen attack self-sufficiency. Duke Vincentio, for example, in the first scene of *Measure for Measure* tells Angelo:

                 Thyself and thy belongings
Are not thine own so proper as to waste
Thyself upon thy virtues, they on thee.
Heaven doth with us as we with torches do,
Not light them for themselves; for if our virtues
Did not go forth of us, 'twere all alike
As if we had them not.

[I. i. 29-35]

He is preaching on the text of "Let your light so shine before men" [Matthew 5: 16]; and Ulysses in *Troilus and Cressida* has variations on the same theme:

          no man is the lord of anything,
Though in and of him there be much consisting,
Till he communicate his parts to others;
Nor doth he of himself know them for aught. . . .

[III. iii. 115-18]

Of course, we might argue that Shakespeare puts good arguments into Venus's mouth, as Milton puts an eloquent plea into the mouth of Comus. Adonis himself points out that "Reason is the bawd to lust's abuse" [l. 792] as Hamlet was later to declare that "Reason panders will" [III. iv. 88]. But, in fact, there are several reasons why we should not take Adonis's moralizing as an objective statement of the situation. First, it reads too much like an afterthought on his part. In the first half of the poem he is bashful, but he seems to feel

no moral objections to Venus's suit: he merely declares that he is too young and implies that Venus is a "baby-snatcher":

Who wears a garment shapeless and unfinish'd?
Who plucks the bud before one leaf put forth?
If springing things be any joy diminish'd,
They wither in their prime, prove nothing worth.
    The colt that's back'd and burden'd being
        young
    Loseth his pride and never waxeth strong.

[ll. 415-20]

Here he is concerned with the maintenance of his own strength, not with Venus's sensuality; and later he ascribes his reluctance to his youth:

Fair Queen . . . if any love you owe me,
Measure my strangeness with my unripe years;
Before I know myself, seek not to know me;
No fisher but the ungrown fry forbears.
    The mellow plum doth fall, the green sticks
        fast,
    Or being early pluck'd is sour to taste.

[ll. 523-28]

He is implying that he would make an unsatisfactory lover. Between these two passages Adonis had kissed Venus when she fainted, and we may suspect that this was not merely a method of First Aid.

Secondly, as we see everything through Venus's eyes, we cannot help feeling that Adonis is guilty of pride and self-sufficiency. He is a kind of Hippolytus, a follower of Artemis and a scorner of Aphrodite, as he himself admits:

I know not love . . . nor will not know it,
Unless it be a boar, and then I chase it.
'Tis much to borrow, and I will not owe it.
My love to love is love but to disgrace it.

[ll. 409-12]

It is not virtue which makes him repulse Venus, but an unwillingness to give himself. He is like the friend as depicted in the 94th sonnet:

Who, moving others, are themselves as stone,
Unmoved, cold, and to temptation slow—

They rightly do inherit Heaven's graces,
And husband nature's riches from expense;
They are the lords and owners of their faces,
Others but stewards of their excellence.

The boar, loved by Adonis, symbolizes death and mutability. Beauty which refuses Love is doomed to destruction and decay.

Thirdly, Shakespeare's epithets should surely prevent us from adopting a moral attitude to Venus's behaviour. After her final failure to obtain her desire, the poet comments: "But all in vain; *good* queen, it will not be" [l. 607]. And just before this Adonis is called "the poor fool" [l. 578].

Fourthly, at the end of the poem, after Adonis's death, Venus prophecies the corruption of love:

Since thou art dead, lo, here I prophesy
Sorrow on love hereafter shall attend:
It shall be waited on with jealousy,
Find sweet beginning but unsavoury end,
    Ne'er settled equally, but high or low,
    That all love's pleasure shall not match his
      woe.

It shall be fickle, false, and full of fraud,
Bud and be blasted in a breathing while,
The bottom poison, and the top o'erstraw'd
With sweets that shall the truest sight beguile;
    The strongest body shall it make most weak,
    Strike the wise dumb, and teach the fool to
        speak. . . .

[ll. 1135-46]

Compared with this state of affairs, the straightforward sensuality of Venus's love for Adonis represents a state of innocence. Although Adonis claims that love to heaven is fled, Love has not fled, as Mr. A. C. Hamilton points out, for she is with him now:

Only with his death, as Venus prophesies, will discord, dissension, and hatred—that is, lust—usurp the name of love. And only after his death does Love, that is, Venus, flee to heaven [see excerpt above, 1961].

This, however, is not the whole truth about the poem. Although an interpretation that seeks to show that Shakespeare was writing a sermon against lust is clearly impossible, it is equally impossible to assume that the poem is a straightforward eulogy of sexual love. Almost everything in the poem appears to be ambivalent. The famous description of Adonis's stallion pursuing the mare can be taken either as an emblem of the naturalness of desire, as Venus herself points out, or as an emblem of uncontrolled desire, or lust, as it frequently was.

Some modern critics, of whom Mr. Rufus Putney is perhaps the most persuasive [see excerpt above, 1953], have argued that the poem is meant to be comic throughout and that it belongs to the popular *genre* of erotic narratives, mostly derived from Ovid. They had several characteristics in common: they all had elaborate sensuous descriptions; they tended to be realistic in their treatment of mythological love-stories; they used wit to offset the sensuous atmosphere; they introduced, as Ovid had done, sententious generalizations about love; and most of them were steeped in irony. The masterpiece in this kind was Marlowe's *Hero and Leander* which illustrates all the characteristics outlined by Putney. The description of Leander could be given as an example of sensuous description; the pictures in Venus's temple exemplify the grotesque realism of his treatment of mythology, with Jupiter

for his love Europa bellowing loud,
And tumbling with the Rainbow in a cloud;

Marlowe's wit is ubiquitous; and his poem is full of generalizations about love:

Who ever lov'd, that lov'd not at first sight? . . .
Love is not full of pity, as men say,
But deaf and cruel where he means to prey.

Certainly *Venus and Adonis* displays many of the same characteristics. It contains some lovely descriptions. Some stanzas are frankly erotic and Shakespeare provides plenty of realistic touches, so that Venus at times appears to be an amorous country girl in the pastoral tradition. Although she is as beautiful as Titian's painting of her, she sweats, weeps, hurts Adonis's hand by grasping it too hard, and, though she compares herself to a fairy and a nymph and claims that she does not leave footprints on the sand, she is substantial enough to pluck Adonis from his horse. Shakespeare introduces plenty of generalizations about love:

Love is a spirit, all compact of fire. . . .
The sea hath bounds, but deep desire hath
    none. . . .
Foul words and frowns must not repel a lover. . . .

[ll. 149, 389, 573]

And Shakespeare, like Marlowe, qualifies his eroticism with wit.

But, all the same, Putney's account of the poem does not quite fit in with one's own experience of it. Even the total impression of *Hero and Leander* is not primarily comic, but rather of a mingling of wit and sensuousness such as we find in the best of the Metaphysicals; and the dominant impression of *Venus and Adonis* is not really of "jocosity." Putney thinks that the stanzas describing the imprisonment of Adonis by the locking of Venus's lily fingers must have seemed very funny to the Elizabethans:

"Fondling," she saith, "since I have hemm'd thee
    here
Within the circuit of this ivory pale,
I'll be a park, and thou shalt be my deer;
Feed where thou wilt, on mountain or in dale;
    Graze on my lips; and if those hills be dry,
    Stray lower, where the pleasant fountains lie.

"Within this limit is relief enough,
Sweet bottom-grass, and high delightful plain,
Round rising hillocks, brakes obscure and rough,
To shelter thee from tempest and from rain. . . .

[ll. 229-38]

The erotic imagery and the pun on "deer" are not "funny," but rather sensuousness tempered with wit; and the later comparison of the echoes of Venus's laments to

shrill-tong'd tapsters answering every call,
Soothing the humour of fantastic wits,

[ll. 849-50]

although we are reminded of the cruel baiting of Francis by Prince Hal [in *1 Henry IV*], is grotesque rather than funny. Even the comparison of Adonis lying on Venus to a man on a horse is brilliant rather than erotic, grotesque rather than jocose. It is, moreover, difficult to believe with Putney that the lament of Venus at the conclusion of the poem is intended to be "a diverting parody of mourners, zoological, inanimate and disembodied." It seems rather to be the expression of real, if distanced, emotion.

There is, after all, a large amount of imagery in the poem, and many lines and stanzas, which no one could regard as comic:

Leading him prisoner in a red-rose chain . . .
A lily prison'd in a gaol of snow . . .

Hot, faint, and weary, with her hard embracing,
Like a wild bird being tam'd with too much han-
    dling,
Or as the fleet-foot roe that's tir'd with chasing,
Or like the froward infant still'd with
    dandling. . . .

Look how a bright star shooteth from the sky,
So glides he in the night from Venus' eye.

Or as the snail, whose tender horns being hit,
Shrinks backward in his shelly cave with pain,
And there, all smoth'red up, in shade doth sit,
Long after fearing to creep forth again. . . .

[ll. 110, 362, 559-62, 815-16, 1033-36]

Some of the imagery, as in Shakespeare's mature work, is derived from books rather than from nature. The description of the boar, for example, is derived from Golding and Brooke; and even the description of Adonis's stallion is based not merely on observation. But *Venus and Adonis* has more natural imagery than *Lucrece;* and in the description of the hunted hare, which begins as an argument for hunting it, Shakespeare's own sympathies with the hare militate against the argument.

There are traces of iterative imagery in the poem, a year or two before Shakespeare began to use it in his plays. There is, for example, a frequent recurrence of red and white, the colours of love, combined in Adonis's cheeks, and in his lips after they have been kissed, and separate in the red of Adonis's shame and of Venus's desire, and in the white of Adonis's anger and of Venus's fear. There are some thirty references to burning and cooling, used both metaphorically and literally, and symbolizing desire and chastity. Equally important is the iteration of words denoting sweetness—sweet boy, sweet kiss, sweet look, sweet desire, sweet lips, deep-sweet music, honey secrets, honey fee, and nectar. The atmosphere of the poem would be cloying and enervating without the frequent touches of realism.

We are driven to conclude that the poem cannot easily be categorized. It is not straightforwardly didactic, designed, like *Lucrece,* as a warning against lust or in praise of chastity. It is not, on the other hand, a straightforward paean in praise of sexual love or of "breed," since Venus—not merely in the eyes of Adonis, but in the eyes of Shakespeare himself—allows passion to usurp the place of reason. She is compared to a famished eagle and a vulture, sweating, reeking, smoking, boiling,

> beating reason back,
> Forgetting shame's pure blush, and honour's
> wrack.
>
> [ll. 557-58]

Nor, as we have seen, can the poem be regarded as "comic," for its frequent touches of wit are offset by the tragic ending, in which the boar symbolizes death rather than lust.

Shakespeare, we may suppose, set out to write a poem, based on Ovid, with Lodge as his closest model for form, and Marlowe for style. The theme gave him opportunities for rivalling some of the effects of Renaissance painting, and of repudiating the denial of the flesh by puritan moralists and Neoplatonic theorists. At the same time, it enabled him to express through the mouth of Venus the theme of "breed" he was afterwards to develop in the early sonnets—if indeed the sonnets were not written earlier. In accordance with the conventions of the *genre* he was committed to a realistic treatment of mythology, so that Venus, though surpassingly beautiful, has the physiological characteristics of an ordinary woman; and a woman who takes the sexual initiative is apt to seem like a Colette heroine engaged in the seduction of a boy. In Sonnet 41 Shakespeare asks:

> And when a woman woos, what woman's son
> Will sourly leave her till she have prevailed?

Adonis sourly leaves Venus, preferring hunting the boar to being hunted by her. As his objections to her promiscuity are an afterthought, we cannot help thinking that he preserves his virginity more because of his self-centeredness than because of his virtue; and Venus arouses our pity as any woman will whose passion is not reciprocated. As Dr. Bradbrook says, "a lofty form and classic authority is invoked to display the continuity of animal, human and divine passion" [see her second entry in the Additional Bibliography].

The ambivalence of the poem is caused partly by the poet's own acceptance of conflicting feelings about love, and partly by the essentially dramatic nature of his imagination. Just as he had as much delight in depicting an Iago [in *Othello*] as an Imogen [in *Cymbeline*], he had as much delight in depicting a Venus as an Adonis. He sees the situation from both points of view, so that we feel the force of Venus's arguments for love, as well as the reluctance of the unawakened adolescent. Both use reason to justify an irrational position. (pp. 4-13)

Kenneth Muir, " 'Venus and Adonis': Comedy or Tragedy?" in Shakespearean Essays, *edited by Alwin Thaler and Norman Sanders, The University of Tennessee Press, Knoxville, 1964, pp. 4-13.*

NORMAN RABKIN   (essay date 1966)

[*Rabkin stresses the similarity of artistic approach in* Venus and Adonis *and Shakespeare's dramas, remarking that, in both, art "explores reality by imitating its complexity." Just as*

Venus. By Lucas Cranach.

Shakespeare often presents a conflict between incompatible views in his plays, the critic argues, in the poem he presents an irresolvable conflict between sensual and spiritual views of love; thus, for Rabkin, Venus and Adonis *examines the inescapable self-contradiction inherent in this "central human activity."*]

What are we to make of *Venus and Adonis?* Participants in the old debate could argue on the one side that the poem is correct, salable, meaningless poetry written to please the palate of a jaded earl, on the other that it is a glowing fragment of the sunrise landscape of the Renaissance, a verbal counterpart to Botticelli's *Venus* and Piero di Cosimo's *Cephalus and Procris.* But that debate has died, because the view of poetry that underlay it is gone; for or against *Venus and Adonis,* modern critics all assume, as did neither Robertson in attacking it [see Additional Bibliography] nor Wyndham in defending it [see excerpt above, 1898], that a poem by Shakespeare is likely to be a coherent and significant structure. The estimation of its value perhaps remains the critic's goal, but the way to that goal is through the process of understanding. And here our trouble starts all over again, for the disagreements are as sharp between the critics who think they know what the poem means as they once were between critics who thought they knew its worth. To Dover Wilson *Venus and Adonis* is a supreme example of "the fleshly school of poetry," whose theme is "a frank acceptance of what Rossetti called 'the passionate and just delights of the body'" [see excerpt above, 1932]. To Geoffrey Bush [in his *Shakespeare and the Natural Condition*], on the other hand, "the theme" of the poem "is the phrase from one of the sonnets, 'Desire is death' [Sonnet 147], and to Hereward T. Price it is a bitter rejection of physical passion: Venus, as the embodiment of the principle of lust, is a primal force of destruction; the boar that kills the beautiful and innocent Adonis is "Venus in her most horrible symbol" [see excerpt above, 1945]. In [Hallet Smith's] view, Adonis is neither beauty incarnate nor an epicurean feast for the senses, but rather "an adolescent lout . . . from the country and very conscious that he hasn't been around"; not "a creature of a world of myth but . . . a young fellow from Stratford ill at ease in the presence of a court lady" [see Additional Bibliography].

Critical conflicts as serious as this need reduce us neither to skepticism about the ultimate validity of criticism nor to mistrust of the poem in question. They may indicate only that the critics have not learned what kinds of questions to ask. Certainly our experience with *Hamlet* in recent decades should be reassuring: having come closer to a common understanding of the nature of Shakespearean tragedy and the conventions of revenge tragedy, we have learned what to expect, and the best critics comfortingly sound more and more like one another in talking about the play. Approaching the Shakespearean play we know what is important to watch; approaching *Venus and Adonis,* however, critics have behaved often like travellers from an immaterial universe alighting on the earth, unable yet to interpret the signals that should tell them what are mountains and what valleys. Thus for one scholar the fact that *Venus and Adonis* is a version of myth is paramount; for another the fact that it is rich in decorative embellishment; for a third the episode of the horses, a fourth the symbolism of white and red, and a fifth the reflection of Florentine neoplatonism. And all of these views are presented as if they are as mutually exclusive as once were the views of *Hamlet* which have so copiously filled our libraries.

It might be wise, then, simply to remind ourselves first of all of certain undeniable facts: the qualities of the poem. With the entire landscape in view we are less likely to mistake a bush for a bear. Immediately we must note that this romance is funny. Whatever one wants to make of the famous horse episode, for example, in which "Adonis' trampling courser" [l. 261] carries on with "a breeding jennet, lusty, young, and proud" [l. 260], to the delight of Venus and the dismay of Adonis, who refuses to accept the example as useful instruction, one begins by laughing:

> Giue me my hand (saith he,) why dost thou feele
>   it?
> Giue me my heart (saith she,) and thou shalt haue
>   it.
> O giue it me lest thy hard heart do steele it,
> And being steeld, soft sighes can neuer graue it.
>   Then loues deepe grones, I neuer shall regard,
>   Because Adonis heart hath made mine hard.
>
> For shame he cries, let go, and let me go,
> My dayes delight is past, my horse is gone,
> And tis your fault I am bereft him so,
> I pray you hence, and leaue me here alone,
>   For all my mind, my thought, my busie care,
>   Is how to get my palfrey from the mare.
>   [ll. 373-84]

One laughs at the high comedy of the overbearing, lustful Venus and the boy too young and too uninterested to respond; at sudden changes in tone and unexpected disruptions of the placid atmosphere:

> I know not loue (quoth he) nor will not know it,
> Vnlesse it be a Boare, and then I chase it,
> Tis much to borrow, and I will not owe it,
> My loue to loue, is loue, but to disgrace it,
>   For I haue heard, it is a life in death,
>   That laughs and weeps, and all but with a breath.
>
> Who weares a garment shapelesse and vnfinisht?
> Who plucks the bud before one leafe put forth?
> If springing things be anie iot diminisht,
> They wither in their prime, proue nothing worth,
>   The colt that's backt and burthend being yong,
>   Loseth his pride, and neuer waxeth strong.
>
> You hurt my hand with wringing, let vs part,
> And leaue this idle theame, this bootlesse chat,
> Remoue your siege from my vnyeelding hart,
> To loues allarmes it will not ope the gate,
>   Dismisse your vows, your fained tears, your flat-
>   try,
>   For where a heart is hard they make no battry.
>
> What canst thou talke (quoth she) hast thou a tong?
>   [ll. 409-27]

The outcome of *Venus and Adonis* and the issues it raises are serious, but the vehicle is seldom far from comedy.

Moreover, the poem is vivid and sensuously immediate; it is realized. Even a first reading leaves indelible memories of the horses and the boar and poor Wat, the dew-bedabbled hare, of Venus' fainting, of Adonis at the mercy of his enormous and uninvited lady-love:

> The studded bridle on a ragged bough,
> Nimbly she fastens, (ô how quicke is loue!)
> The steed is stalled vp, and euen now,
> To tie the rider she begins to proue:
>   Backward she pusht him, as she would be thrust,
>   And gouernd him in strength though not in lust.
>
> So soone was she along, as he was downe,

Each leaning on their elbowes and their hips:
Now doth she stroke his cheek, now doth he frown,
And gins to chide, but soone she stops his lips,
    And kissing speaks, with lustful language bro-
        ken,
    If thou wilt chide, thy lips shall neuer open.

                                                    [ll. 37-48]

In good part the poem's vividness is the illusion created by
its characters: the illusion, that is, that they *are* characters.
Much of the critics' trouble stems, in fact, from being deceived into seeing the entire poem in terms of its characters
alone and finding on closer examination that the illusion is
undercut by the quality of the language used to create it (thus
C. S. Lewis [see excerpt above, 1954]); yet other trouble, most
notably that of H. T. Price, stems from attempting to deal
with *Venus and Adonis* as if it had no characters in it.

Another immediate impression, apparent even in what I have
been describing, is that Shakespeare maintains a remarkable
control over the responses of his reader. Theories about what
the whole poem adds up to may turn small matters into great,
and vice versa, but no reader fails to note the incongruity of
the horse episode and Venus' and Adonis' reactions to it, or
the delicate shifts in tone from sympathy to laughter as the
poet regards the paradox of the wooing mistress:

Sometime she shakes her head, and then his hand,
Now gazeth she on him, now on the ground;
Sometime her armes infold him like a band,
She would, he will not in her armes be bound:
    And when from thence he struggles to be gone,
    She locks her lillie fingers one in one.

Fondling, she saith, since I haue hemd thee here.
Within the circuit of this iuorie pale,
Ile be a parke, and thou shalt be my deare:
Feed where thou wilt, on mountaine, or in dale;
    Graze on my lips, and if those hils be drie,
    Stray lower, where the pleasant fountaines lie.

Within this limit is reliefe inough,
Sweet bottome grasse, and high delightfull plaine,
Round rising hillocks, brakes obscure, and rough,
To shelter thee from tempest, and from raine:
    Then be my deare, since I am such a parke,
    No dog shal rowze thee, though a thousand bark.

                                                    [ll. 223-40]

The last major element which the critic ignores only at his
own peril is the imagery which for some has seemed to *be* the
poem. The famous arias about the horses and the hare and
the boar are imbedded in a recitative in which motifs recur
and are continually varied; a central element in one's experience of *Venus and Adonis* is the strong sense of clearly defined
groups of images bridging and unifying the poem.

What can such a catalogue of the poem's most obvious qualities tell us? Listen to the most brilliant critic who has ever
written about this work:

Venus and Adonis seem[s] at once the characters
themselves, and the whole representation of those
characters by the most consummate actors. You
seem to be *told* nothing, but to see and hear everything. Hence it is, that from the perpetual activity
of attention required on the part of the reader; from
the rapid flow, the quick change, and the playful
nature of the thoughts and images; and above all
from the alienation, and, if I may hazard such an
expression, the utter *aloofness* of the poet's own

feelings, from those of which he is at once the painter and the analyst; that though the very subject cannot but detract from the pleasure of a delicate
mind, yet never was poem less dangerous on a
moral account . . . Shakespeare has here represented the animal impulse itself, so as to preclude
all sympathy with it, by dissipating the reader's notice among the thousand outward images, and now
beautiful, now fanciful circumstances, which form
its dresses and its scenery [see excerpt above by
Samuel Taylor Coleridge, 1817].

Coleridge is telling us that the poem is best read as one reads
a Shakespearean play. H. T. Price attempts "to show that
Venus and Adonis is much greater than Coleridge knew, or,
at any rate, implied." But if he really understood what Coleridge tells us, he could not make such a statement; and he
could not reduce the poem so deftly to precisely half its statement. To know that we can approach this poem as we might
one of the plays is to know a good deal about it. We need
not—should not—hinge our interpretation on the meaning of
one image; we do not have to turn into iconologists or historians of philosophy and hunt for analogues and obscure
sources, though all of these will help us to refine what we understand about the poem. If it shares, as Coleridge implies it
does, some of the more important qualities of the plays, it is
an aesthetic object which our experience with the plays has
already well equipped us to understand.

One way in which the plays may be useful is in suggesting to
us the kind of theme Shakespeare might conceive. "*Othello*
and *Romeo and Juliet* and *Venus and Adonis*," says Price,
"are all about the same thing—that is to say, the destruction
of something good by a force that is not only vile but also so
blind that it does not even know what it is destroying." The
sense of relationship among these works is as convincing as
the interpretation is wrong. We might recall what Shakespeare tells us about the subject of *Venus and Adonis* in his
plays. From the beginning to the end of his career he works
variations on a constantly evolving theme—and that theme
is presented in his epyllion as a myth that explains what love
is in the fallen world in which we live.

The Shakespearean vision of love is always double. *Romeo
and Juliet* focuses—to the embarrassment of the announced
theme of star-crossed innocence—on the maturing and the
responsibility of its protagonists; and their maturing is a
growth towards a more complex and profound comprehension of love than the jejune Romeo and Juliet feel at the outset. Paradoxically Romeo learns at the same time to salt his
idealism with Mercutio's awareness of the reality of the flesh
and to understand his own love for Juliet as one that can find
its ultimate satisfaction only in death. The play's expressed
judgment is against impetuosity and irrationality as destructive, but the valuation it implies is a judgment in favor of precisely these qualities as the foundation and essence of a transcendent love. Juliet's wedding invocation to the friendly
night and Romeo's love of night and blackness suggest their
growing up to a view of love which simultaneously incorporates and refutes Mercutio's; Romeo's rejection of a chaste interest in Rosaline for a love for Juliet that is of the body as
well as of the soul leads ironically to his fulfillment in a death
which does not merely happen to him, but which he chooses.

In *A Midsummer Night's Dream* the vision is double again:
love is both absurd and magnificent because, like art and
other engagements of the imagination, it is willful, passionate, happily deceived and deceiving, unconditioned by and

virtually irrelevant to reason. In *Much Ado About Nothing* Claudio is wrong when he believes what his eyes tell him about Hero, right when he ultimately agrees to marry her "cousin" about whom he knows absolutely nothing and in whom he agrees to believe faithfully. Beatrice and Benedick are comically wrong when they protect themselves, on rational grounds, against the irrationality of love, right when they forswear the life of wit in order to trust one another and their own feelings. Here Shakespeare seems to identify wit with sterile egotism; yet in his subplot lovers he presents the wit against which the play implies strong criticism as so attractive that the play lived for generations as "Beatrice and Benedick."

In such comedies as *A Midsummer Night's Dream* and *Much Ado* the irrational faith on which love is based is justified by the comic providence which guides and rewards the lovers, but Shakespeare is not always so sanguine, and the dualism of his vision of love produces a variety of somber themes. When, unlike misguided Claudio, Troilus insists on loving Cressida despite the empirical assurance that she isn't worth his love, he destroys himself. The play allows no simple solution to Troilus' predicament. The very qualities that make his love admirable—its basis in commitment and faith—make him ultimately the satirized embodiment of values that the play presents as dangerous and irresponsible. On the other hand, Othello, whose love for Desdemona moves us from the outset because like Troilus' it was based on faith, is a fool when he allows that irrational faith to be shaken by an argument that appears to be based on reason and that is supported by just the sort of "ocular proof" that Troilus, thinking about either Helen or Cressida, would wrongly discredit. Othello is mistaken not in allowing false reason to weaken his trust in his wife, but in conceding even for a moment that his love has more to do with "facts" and with any kind of reason than with his intuitive sense of Desdemona; yet Troilus is mistaken in allowing the faith of the lover to weigh more than the measurable worth of the beloved. In exploring the implications of the various relationships between the value of love and the value of its object, the knowledge of the mind and the knowledge of the heart, Shakespeare presents love in both of these pessimistic plays as hopelessly paradoxical, based on tragic antinomies in the human spirit and the world in which that spirit resides. In both *Othello* and *Troilus and Cressida* love is the noblest of passions for the same reasons that it is ridiculous.

Even in the more optimistic *Antony and Cleopatra* Shakespeare sees love as ennobling and liberating only at the expense of everything else we ordinarily prize in the world, including honor. In other words, Shakespeare presents love, in the play that apotheosizes his vision of it, as preposterously bound to aging flesh, and yet as so far beyond the merely physical that to give it expression the whole world, life itself, must dissolve. As in *Romeo and Juliet,* so in *Antony and Cleopatra:* love is of the flesh, yet only the liberation from flesh and the finality of death can express its full value.

What then of *Venus and Adonis?* The poem begins with a contrast—ironic since Venus will throughout identify herself with the body's cause, Adonis with spiritual longings— between "Rose-cheekt Adonis" and "Sick-thoughted Venus" [ll. 3, 5]; it describes nature in the second stanza as "with her selfe at strife" [l. 11]; its plot consists of the unsuccessful wooing of Adonis, with his notion of what love is all about, by Venus, who has a different notion; it leads to the reconcilia-

tion in death of the opposition between principles that makes the tragic ending inevitable; and it ends in Venus' prophecy that "Sorrow on loue hereafter shall attend": love will be a torturesome mixture of paradoxical qualities, "raging mad, and sillie milde . . . cause of warre, and dire events," "Subject, and servill to all discontents"; yet, while plucking down the rich, it shall "inrich the poore with treasures" [ll. 1136, 1151, 1159, 1161, 1150]. In brief, by reinterpreting the myth of Venus and Adonis, Shakespeare is half-playfully projecting the genesis of all the paradoxical qualities of love he so frequently observes in his plays.

The charms that lead one school of critics to see the poem as an encomium to the life of the senses are demonstrably present. Venus is the apologist for those charms, and in the poem's prelapsarian world we sense unmistakably a nature that is radiantly fresh and appealing, populated by idyllic animals and flowers of brilliant hue and by the magical force of generation. Part of that same world is Adonis, most beautiful of all its creatures; and there's the rub. For, like the world not yet fallen in [Milton's] *Paradise Lost,* the garden of *Venus and Adonis* carries the seeds of its own destruction, and Adonis feels himself cut off by the purity of his ideals from the ability to participate in its life:

> What hau you vrg'd, that I can not reproue?
> The path is smooth that leadeth on to danger,
> I hate not loue, but your deuise in loue,
> That lends imbracements vnto euery stranger,
>   You do it for increase, ô straunge excuse!
>   When reason is the bawd to lusts abuse.
>
> Call it not loue, for loue to heauen is fled,
> Since sweating lust on earth vsurpt his name,
> Vnder whose simple semblance he hath fed,
> Vpon fresh beautie, blotting it with blame;
>   Which the hot tyrant staines, & soone bereaues:
>   As Caterpillers do the tender leaues.
>
>   [ll. 787-98]

If Venus sees love as the delight and fulfillment of the senses, with all the passion and transitoriness that this implies, Adonis sees it as the opposite: immutable, not subject to time, passionless, incapable of being surfeited (while lust "like a glutton dies" [l. 803]). The two argue their opposed positions magnificently, and the end is ruin. What Shakespeare has done is to present simply, embodied in two characters as two separate principles, the two aspects of love that the neoplatonic Renaissance delighted in seeing paradoxically fused: Venus argues for the steps of the ladder with no vision of its uppermost rung; Adonis longs for the spiritual consummation to which sensual love, as Castiglione and the like saw it, claimed to aspire, but hates the way to that consummation. Thus Shakespeare idealizes two incompatible views; and thus simplistic criticism can be led to glorify one at the expense of the other.

The Shakespearean play is the climactic example of the ways in which art explores reality by imitating its complexity. Reading *Venus and Adonis* with the expectations given us by the plays, we find there the same sort of complexity. For its protagonists not only oppose each other: the poem's theme is the self-contradiction implicit in a central human activity, and because they are imitations of human beings, each clinging desperately to his own passionately held but partial view of experience, Venus and Adonis make clear in their own behavior the inadequacy as well as the magnificence of their views. Just so do Antony and Othello and Troilus, Lysander [in *A Midsummer Night's Dream*] and Romeo and Benedick exemplify the paradoxes of love.

The trouble with love, as Venus sees and embodies it, is that it is bound to all that is least noble in life: animality, mortality, lust, egotism. At the beginning of the poem we find no criticism of Adonis, we hear only Venus: yet we know what her limitations are. Time and again her eloquent arguments end in grotesque and risible detail. "Looke in mine ey-bals, there thy beautie lies, / Then why not lips on lips, since eyes in eyes" [ll. 119-20]. In Venus' speech even the Petrarchan cliché about beauty finding its mirror in the beloved's eyes becomes an uncomfortably untranscendent statement. She responds to the magic beauty of Adonis, but her response is flesh-bound. How often her rhetoric carries us only to this sort of awkwardness:

> Here come and sit, where neuer serpent hisses,
> And being set, Ile smother thee with kisses.
>
> And yet not cloy thy lips with loth'd sa[t]ietie,
> But rather famish them amid their plentie,
> Making them red, and pale, with fresh varietie:
> Ten kisses short as one, one long as twentie:
>   A sommers day will seeme an houre but short,
>   Being wasted in such time-beguiling sport.
>
> With this she ceazeth on his sweating palme,
> The president of pith, and liuelyhood,
> And trembling in her passion, calls it balme,
> Earths soueraigne salue, to do a goddesse good,
>   Being so enrag'd, desire doth lend her force,
>   Couragiously to plucke him from his horse.
>   [ll. 17-30]

When she argues that "Loue is a spirit all compact of fire, / Not gross to sink, but light, and will aspire" [ll. 149-50], Venus is almost convincing; when she becomes Venus Genetrix and argues, along with a number of the sonnets, that love is necessary to procreation, she sounds like Shakespeare himself:

> Vpon the earths increase why shouldst thou feed,
> Vnlesse the earth with thy increase be fed?
> By law of nature thou art bound to breed,
> That thine may liue, when thou thy selfe art dead:
>   And so in spite of death thou doest suruiue,
>   In that thy likenesse still is left aliue.
>   [ll. 169-74]

But the next line topples the whole argument: "By this the louesicke Queen began to sweate." Undercutting the simple glorification of physical love as Spenser was doing in his contemporary *Hymn to Love*, Shakespeare makes his Venus catalogue the woes of love: the ugliness of age, of which she and Adonis are ironically free at this moment, "disturbing iealousie," and the threat of mortality; and we know that her view of the world is all too tragically limited. Likewise her appeal to the example of the horses works against itself: no matter how magnificent, they are after all only animals (not even Houyhnhnms), and as R. P. Miller points out Shakespeare emphasizes their inappropriateness to Venus' policy by calling them, three times out of seven, mere "breeders" [see excerpt above, 1952]. Venus, then, embodies the glorification of the senses without the rationale that justifies that glorification in the familiar Renaissance scheme.

The implicit criticism of Adonis is as easy to perceive. Many readers have found in the character of the boy too young to respond to Venus' aggressive wooing a figure of fun; and as soon as Adonis appears comic, the jig is up for the view that he simply represents beauty. But the effect of the comedy at his expense is to lead us to an understanding of what is wrong with his position. If Venus unwittingly overemphasizes the animal element in love, Adonis conversely underestimates its importance, and the significance of his mistake becomes clear in some of the most famous images in the poem. Recall, for example, the stanza in which he is compared to "a wild bird being tam'd with too much hãdling" and to "the fleet-foot Roe that's tyr'd with chasing" [ll. 560, 561]; such detail tells us more than that Venus is a huntress: it suggests also an aspect of Adonis that he never acknowledges. Throughout the poem he is associated with animals: the famous dive-dapper, like the bird tangled in the net, is an analogy to Adonis, and the horse belongs to him. Furthermore his hand sweats, despite his hatred for "sweating lust"; he pants; and he is described repeatedly in physical terms which belie the asceticism of his language and his action.

But even more important is the fact that the love Adonis yearns for, fled to heaven, is to be found not in life—that life which Venus so vigorously espouses and at the prospect of losing which poor Wat the hare so trembles—but only in death. Throughout the poem Adonis turns away from what Venus offers to seek the boar: "I know not loue (quoth he) nor will not know it, / Vnlesse it be a Boare, and then I chase it" [ll. 409-10]. As Adonis knows in his longing for that hunt, as Venus knows in her premonitory dream, and as the language demonstrates when the fatal encounter is consummated, the boar-hunt is the pursuit of a kind of love, significantly parallel to Venus' pursuit of Adonis. As Don Cameron Allen observes, "the boar is death" [see excerpt above, 1959]; ironically Adonis rejects the animal in himself only to be destroyed by the insentient beast he seeks. "And nousling in his flanke the louing swine, / Sheath'd vnware the tuske in his softe groine" [ll. 1115-16].

In this romance of the self-denying Adonis whose definition of love leads him to the search for a purity attainable only in death, and of the earth-bound Venus whose love never reaches beyond apotheosized animality, Shakespeare reflects the hopelessly opposed elements of love as he found it in Renaissance neoplatonism. In the prophecy of Venus and the conclusion of the poem he reshapes a familiar myth, telling us how these elements were fused into the tragicomic hybrid that love is now. *Venus and Adonis* thus is not the merely decorative tapestry its enemies and some of its friends have taken it to be, but rather an immediate and sensuous presentation, in the narrative mode, of the issue that lies at the heart of many of Shakespeare's most intense plays. Like them it is a convincing and searching mirror of a view of life that makes great poetry because it cannot be reduced to critical formula. (pp. 20-32)

Norman Rabkin, "'Venus and Adonis' and the Myth of Love," in Pacific Coast Studies in Shakespeare, *edited by Waldo F. McNeir and Thelma N. Greenfield, University of Oregon, 1966, pp. 20-32.*

J. D. JAHN (essay date 1970)

[*In the following excerpt, Jahn contends that Adonis is a coquette who leads Venus on in the manner of a hunter baiting his prey; moreover, he states, the youth's coy enticements are shown to be similar to the lustful goddess's overt seduction. The poem's imagery and dramatic action present Adonis's diffidence and Venus's aggressive courting as equally flawed re-*

sponses to the need to propagate beauty and perpetuate human life, Jahn maintains. Significantly, in his discussion of the episode of Adonis's courser and the jennet, Jahn argues that Venus, as the pursuer, is identified with the courser and Adonis, as the pursued, with the jennet. The jennet's conduct is, he states, "both an explanation of and a more honest alternative to Adonis' behavior."]

One of the more significant results of modern Shakespeare criticism has been the disclosure of complexity in Shakespeare's moral vision, particularly in the master plays. Even so, his narrative poems have received much less such attention. It is possible, however, to discover in *Venus and Adonis* important traces of what was to become the sophisticated moral conception underlying the great tragedies. Admittedly, this early poem seems to invite no more than a facile reading. Since a "sick-thoughted" heroine appears to dominate the action, the error of her lust has frequently towered in the consideration of critics. Franklin Dickey, for instance, reads the poem as reflecting Renaissance opinion on the dangers of excessive passion [see excerpt above, 1957]; and Robert P. Miller anticipated this view, finding in Adonis' rejection of Venus "not modern priggishness but sound Renaissance morality" [see excerpt above, 1952]. These opinions echo Mrs. Pearson's assertion that "Venus is shown as the destructive agent of sensual love; Adonis, as reason in love" [see excerpt above, 1933]. When read in this way, the poem hinges on a contrast between two kinds of love—the one good, the other evil. A different tack has been taken recently by Muriel C. Bradbrook, who, in arguing that *Venus and Adonis* was Shakespeare's bid for "social dignity," is more tolerant of Venus [see Additional Bibliography]. The poem, she says, portrays a "continuity of animal, human, and divine passion; the 'vulgar' are rejected only in their narrow prejudice, for the natural at all levels is celebrated." The most common reaction to *Venus and Adonis,* nevertheless, has been to see the poem depicting "the destruction of something exquisite by what is outrageously vile" [see excerpt above by Hereward T. Price, 1945]. A contrast between Venus, "red and hot as coals of glowing fire" [l. 35], and Adonis, "red for shame, but frosty in desire" [l. 36], appears too obvious to be ignored.

Yet Shakespeare is seldom esteemed for obvious statements. Something more than his immaturity is needed to explain trite moralizing. . . . Kenneth Muir suggests that Adonis "preserves his virginity more because of his self-centeredness than because of his virtue, and Venus arouses our pity as any woman will whose passion is not reciprocated" [see excerpt above, 1964]. Muir's general perspective is the essential starting point in a proper interpretation of the poem—although the desperate fumbling of Venus seems more comic than he allows. For Adonis is guilty not only of self-centeredness, but of a seductive coquetry as well. The poem is by no means a simple presentation of eroticism versus chastity; it reveals, rather, two kinds of human culpability in the realm of courtship.

A clue to reading Adonis properly can be found in his mythical background. As Geoffrey Bullough has pointed out [see Additional Bibliography], Venus associates him with Narcissus [ll. 157-62], and Shakespeare has altered the Ovidian Adonis so that there is something of Hermaphroditus in him as well. "Both Hermaphroditus and Narcissus are hostile to female blandishments, the one from youthful unreadiness, the other from self-engrossment." As we shall see, these two aspects of Adonis are crucial to understanding his behavior. The connection with Narcissus suggests a personality based

on self-love. And in his actions and speeches, Adonis bears out that charge. On one level, Adonis proves physically vain; on a second, self-righteous.

What is at once a comic and revealing instance of his vanity occurs in the very first lines he utters. Venus has just made her opening appeal to which Adonis answers: "Fie, no more of love! / The sun doth burn my face. I must remove" [ll. 185-86]. That is hardly the rational defense of a Platonic ideal. A similar fastidiousness crops up when Venus "full gently" takes him by the hand [l. 361] and he, as an excuse for leaving pouts, "you hurt my hand with wringing. Let us part" [l. 421]. Such remarks manifest a consciousness of his beauty and a desire to preserve that physical excellence which is his by nature. He argues that he is too young for love, that "the colt that's back'd and burthen'd being young / Loseth his pride and never waxeth strong" [ll. 419-20]. But an excessive love of one's physique may be a sign of moral, not merely physical, immaturity. Like Narcissus, Adonis is in love with his own appearance. And vanity of this kind is symptomatic of other human errors.

If an undue concern for his face is unattractive in a handsome man, so is righteousness distasteful in a moralist. While *Venus and Adonis* does not overtly counter Adonis' drive to remain chaste, it does leave his methods open to question. His response to unwanted attention is, without exception, described fully in line 33 where, tucked under Venus' arm, he "blush'd and pouted in a dull disdain." His reactions to all adversities are of a kind: Venus kisses him, he pouts; his horse runs away, he sulks; he glowers at every imposition upon his will, suggesting a rather childish understanding of the world and of love. Such an attitude might be attributed to mere immaturity were it not for the arrogance with which he presses his case against romance. "I know not love," he insists [ll. 409-10], "nor will not know it, / Unless it be a boar, and then I chase it." Our narrator has prepared us for this attitude at line 4: "Hunting he lov'd, but love he laugh'd to scorn." Clearly, Adonis would substitute the hard hunt for fame for the soft pursuit of love. But the hard hunt has its limitations. It does not allow for the preservation of beauty through propagation. And in that respect it operates in opposition to the forces of nature and time. Adonis in his single-minded search for glory ceases to be exemplary of reason in love. Rather, he is excessive in his denial of it, and therefore, by Renaissance standards, in an indefensible position.

Adonis is not content merely to refuse love (of any kind) a place in his life. He compounds that error with a pride in the power of the hard hunt over love. Listen to the tone of his remarks:

> My love to love is love but to disgrace it. . . .
>
> . . . leave this idle theme, this bootless chat.
> Remove your siege from my unyielding heart;
> To love's alarms it will not ope the gate.
>   Dismiss your vows, your feigned tears, your
>   flatt'ry;
>   For where a heart is hard they make no
>   batt'ry.
>
>   [ll. 412, 422-26]

For Adonis, love is an opponent, a force to be disgraced on the field of valor. There is an imperious contempt in his reception of the advances of Venus. In fact, he is so superior to Love's lures that the goddess can only accuse him of a stoniness of heart, "nay, more than flint, for stone at rain relenteth" [l. 200]. But such is the aloofness of the self-righteous, devoid of all compassion for those less rigorous than themselves. Adonis' brusque disdain of Venus throughout the early scenes, his childishness and physical vanity, ought to dissuade readers from the belief that he is somehow a sacrificial lamb of a lustful goddess.

But there are further evidences in the text which implicate Adonis even more fully in the tragic course of events. On the surface, the narrator (and a good many subsequent critics) condemns Venus for an unwarranted assault upon a defenseless boy. Yet it seems improbable that Love's passion could reach such a pitch without some encouragement. Adonis supplies that encouragement in ways characteristic of all who are "coy." His behavior in that respect is both active and passive. Were he to act more decisively, Venus would find less time for her amorous complaint. As it is, we must imagine an Adonis who indifferently allows himself to be mauled, or else a young man pinned in the vice-like grip of a Herculean Venus. There are comic indications that this latter might be the case: Venus does pull him bodily from his horse, tuck him under her arm, push him backward, entwine him in her lily-white fingers, and pull him into the "very lists of love" [l. 595]. In retaliation, Adonis asks her to let him go once or twice, chides her with a certain lack of conviction (and with no immediate effect), and pouts. Surely, from such a self-proclaimed hunter as Adonis, averse to love and to the lady, we might expect resistance of a more physical nature. Venus is forceful with him; he remains oddly passive.

Take, for example, the curious beginning of the long seduction. She yanks him from his horse, and yet has time to tie that horse to a bough. The narrator assures us that Adonis is "red for shame, but frosty in desire" [l. 36], and that he is governed "in strength, though not in lust" [l. 42]. But these descriptions of Adonis indicate only embarrassment; they say nothing of Reason, nor do they necessarily imply any morality contrasted to that of Venus. Adonis here seems unwilling to defend himself by either word or deed. Unless Venus is considerably bigger than he (which would make the whole of her plan superfluous), there seems little logical explanation why a budding hunter could be "forc'd to content, but never to obey" [l. 61]. His chiding can be stopped with a kiss [l. 46], not only for that moment but for the next one hundred and thirty lines. Venus can stroke his cheek, weep all over him, embrace him, without a sound from the dour boy until the sun gets in his eyes. We must recognize a passivity in Adonis that not only permits this fondling, but engenders it—a passivity that constitutes only a token show of resistance.

Mere inactivity on the part of Adonis becomes more comprehensible in light of the real role he is playing in the seduction. The fact is, he invites Venus' attention, doing as much as he can to arouse her without violating the ground rules of coyness. Adonis is the pool of water and the bough of figs which torment Venus:

> He will not manage her, although he mount her;
> That worse than Tantalus' is her annoy,
> To clip Elysium and to lack her joy.
>
> [ll. 598-600]

He flirts with Venus in the fashion of the coquette, leading her on while denying that which he seems ready to give. The narrative must begin some time after the initiation of his action, for Venus (like Tarquin in *Lucrece*) enters in a state of inexplicable passion. We know Adonis is beautiful, and we know, from his vanity, that he knows it too. What then would be more natural than for such a man, conscious of his prowess in the hard hunt, to urge on his prey? What could be more natural than for Adonis to have sensed Venus' attraction to him and to have encouraged it? (pp. 11-14)

Throughout the seduction scenes, Adonis is careful to maintain the illusion of indifference. We have already observed his strange passivity which, in its total effect, borders on an acceptance of Venus' efforts. And yet it is the particular direction that passivity takes that makes it activity.

> Forc'd to content, but never to obey,
> Panting he lies and breatheth in her face.
> She feedeth on the stream as on a prey
> And calls it heavenly moisture, air of grace.
>
> [ll. 61-4]

From a superficial viewpoint there is little else Adonis can do; possibly he is short of breath from the smothering attentions of Venus. But we are offered no explanation for his failure at least to turn his head, thereby stopping her frenzied feeding. That Adonis can see full well what effect his breath is having, and that it is precisely the effect he had intended, becomes a strong possibility.

When he does take action, it is at a point which is, for Venus, perhaps the most frustrating of her career. He offers to give the kiss she craves, "but when her lips were ready for his pay, / He winks and turns his lips another way" [ll. 89-90]. That action transports Venus into one of her long complaints which begins with a fairly accurate estimation of Adonis' character. " 'O, pity,' gan she cry, 'flint-hearted boy! / 'Tis but a kiss I beg. Why art thou coy?' " [ll. 95-6]. She has grasped the essence of Adonis' deeper nature; he is toying with her in a stone-hearted manner gained from his calculated detachment. He can evoke a lust in her over which he has absolute power, and is not about to quench that fire until he has had the full pleasure of the hunt. He represents, in fact, the "well-painted idol, image dull and dead, / Statue contenting but the eye alone" [ll. 211-12]. He is unresponsive to the passion he stirs in others and is, therefore, as morally reprehensible as Venus, if not more so. For it is in his petty war on love that he is the cruelest.

His eyes are one of his main weapons. The narrator sees the couple's glances as a "war of looks" [l. 355], attributing to the eyes of Adonis a disdain for the pleas in hers. But there are a number of considerations which make the narrator's perception here suspect. Eyes are windows to the soul, and in them man reads the conflicting passions of the heart. . . . [They] are both the catalyst which stirs the love of the suitor and the slayers of that suitor. So, in that double sense, we understand Venus' outburst at line 196: "Thine eye darts forth the fire that burneth me." As we know from *Lucrece,* rejection and a virtuous front can stoke lust. There, Tarquin is roused to greater desire by Lucrece's glance: "For those thine eyes betray thee unto mine" [l. 483]. There too, echoing the image of Adonis' flinty heart, we learn that tears and refusals "harden lust, though marble wear with raining" [l. 560]. Lust is never quenched by a passive rejection of it or of the lust-driven person. Strong and unmistakable action is needed; and Adonis seems unwilling to take that action.

Instead, his behavior is juvenile. Glowering and pouting constitute the extent of his resistance. We are reminded of the coquette's continual pretense at having taken offense. Indeed, perverse behavior as a method of seduction is recommended by the queen of that female art, Cleopatra (see *Antony and Cleopatra,* I. iii). Adonis, as male coquette, exercises the technique to perfection, for his struggle with Venus excites her until she is caught in the snare she once used on Mars: "Yet was he servile to my coy disdain" [l. 112]. Adonis' most cunning stroke comes just after Venus, in complete immodesty (though in marvelous euphemism), has offered him the whole of her "ivory pale." At this moment he has achieved his victory, but since a flat refusal might end the game, Adonis rolls out his heavy artillery. Having reduced Venus to a direct plea, he "smiles as in disdain, / That in each cheek appears a pretty dimple" [ll. 241-42]. Those "lovely caves," those "round enchanting pits," prove a bit too much even for the narrator, who remarks: "struck dead at first, what needs a second striking?" [l. 250]. The narrator's response here forms a fairly reliable guideline for our own judgment. His growing sensitivity to the cruelty in Adonis ought to alert the reader to the distinction Shakespeare makes. Clearly, the passivity of Adonis, his tantalizing breath and temptingly refused kiss, serves only to twist the knife of frustration deeper into Venus' bosom. And now, adding insult to injury, his "pretty" dimples merit more praise than Venus can muster for her whole body; they prove more erotic than her "round rising hillocks" or her "brakes obscure and rough" [l. 237] and force Venus to new heights of passion. Furthermore, there is ambiguity in his smile. We have already seen that coy disdain can stir the lust of a suitor; and Adonis smiles "*as* in disdain" (my italics). The same construction is used again (with the same assonance and metrical pattern) at line 473: Venus lies on the grass "as she were slain." In both cases, the syntax demands we read "as *if.*" There is the suggestion, then, that the disdain is coy, that Adonis has been flirting with Venus all along. She is struck dumb by those dimples, and he "hasteth to his horse" [l. 258], another love-foe successfully lured to his battlements and crushed there. Unfortunately for Adonis, his horse has ideas of its own in the form of a "breeding jennet," and thwarts Adonis' departure from his conquest.

So far—up to the jennet episode which caps the first third of the poem [ll. 1-324]—Shakespeare has presented the pride and flirtation of Adonis through covert details in the poetry. The youth's basic nature has been suggested by what might be termed the iconography of love. For instance, when Venus despairs of her chances of wooing Adonis down from his charger, she "seizeth on his sweating palm, / The precedent of pith and livelihood" [ll. 25-6]. She calls it "balm" and well she might, for as in Chaucer and in *Lucrece* [l. 396], the moist hand is a traditional sign of sexual interest. Venus herself gives us an understanding of how we are to regard that symptom when she describes her own readiness:

> My flesh is soft and plump, my marrow burning;
>   My smooth moist hand, were it with thy hand
>   felt,
>   Would in thy palm dissolve or seem to melt.
>
>   [ll. 142-44]

Shakespeare reinforces the idea at line 175: "By this, the lovesick queen began to sweat." We can assume that Adonis is, in fact, stirred by Venus although effeminately coy with her. When he "sees her coming and begins to glow, / Even as a dying coal revives with wind, / And with his bonnet hides his angry brow" [ll. 337-39], we are rewarded with insight if we pay attention to the imagistic detail. The freshened coal, in connection with his moist palm, indicates that Ado-

nis' anger stems not from disdain alone, but from a consciousness of his sexual arousal as well.

Other imagery throughout the poem yields similar insights into Adonis' character. At line 429, for instance, Venus accuses him of having a "mermaid's voice"—a complaint which he returns [l. 777] as a condemnation of *her* honeyed wooing. Likewise, the image of the glowing coal [l. 337] and of the moist hand picture Adonis in terms reminiscent of the aggressor Venus, "red and hot as coals of glowing fire" [l. 35]. Such similarities weaken the assumed polarity between the two figures; they come to resemble, rather, opposite sides of the same coin. And the war between red and white, which figures prominently in *Lucrece,* need not necessarily signal dichotomized values in *Venus and Adonis.* In Lucrece, as Professor Battenhouse has pointed out [in his *Shakespearean Tragedy: Its Art and Its Christian Premises*], the evident conflict between red and white marks her oscillation between divided aspects of a love of fame. The contending colors enhance the lady's sensuous appeal more than her virtue. H. T. Price interpreted the colors in *Venus and Adonis* as "symbols of passions fighting one another," although he had to admit that each color seems to represent a multiplicity of contradictory emotions. The text itself shows white and red associated with doves and roses [l. 10], with the cheeks of Adonis [l. 3], with passionate variety [l. 21], with passion itself [l. 35], and with shame and anger [l. 36]—all within the first few lines of the poem. Apparently red and white have no pure values; it is a mistake to assign them constant equivalents. Adonis, like Lucrece, can take advantage of the red of his beauty (with its hint of sexuality) and of the white of his anger and disdain (with its element of coquetry), turning them to inflammatory purposes. The very contention of these two colors marks the contradictory nature of Adonis.

But the most significant image of the first third of *Venus and Adonis,* and perhaps the most crucial to an understanding of the whole poem, is that of the river and of rain. It demands our careful attention, for it explains much of what Adonis is doing and, more particularly, what happens to his game in the second third of the poem. It first occurs, full-blown, early in the action and in close conjunction with the important notion of disdain as a lever of love:

> Pure shame and aw'd resistance made him fret,
>   Which bred more beauty in his angry eyes.
>   Rain added to a river that is rank
>   Perforce will force it overflow the bank.
>
>   [ll. 69-72]

Here Adonis is pictured innocently enough. His righteous anger only arouses the love-sick Venus to further desire. Yet the logic of the lines is flawed. The rain, not the river, initiates the action of overflowing, and it is the "pure shame" or the "angry eyes" of Adonis that the poet links with the rain. Coy disdain, then, is here presented as a cause of stimulation. The image recurs later in the poem: "An oven that is stopp'd, or river stay'd / Burneth more hotly, swelleth more with rage" [ll. 331-32]. Here the metaphor follows on the heels of the breeding horses—a section often regarded as the key to the poem—and mixes the idea of the fire of passion with the enormous kinetic energy of a dammed river. The message is clear. Adonis, whether intentionally or out of ignorance, has been adding fuel to the fire of Venus' lust by his behavior. The net effect of his beauty (which he cannot help) and of his bearing and demeanor (which he can) work to incite her passion. The fact that the image of the dammed river is repeated twice—in

Venus and Vulcan. By Jacobo Robusti Tintoretto.

fact, it is used a third time [ll. 959-60] at which point the floodgates actually burst open—ought to direct us to its wider application. One does not urge passion on, even passively, on the one hand, and refuse that passion a vent on the other. But that is precisely the aim of coquetry.

Within the ongoing narrative of *Venus and Adonis,* however, another aspect of the coquette comes into play. Adonis manages the courtship to his liking up to the point at which his horse runs off. Then, his escape route blocked, the Hermaphroditus in his character threatens to take over. No longer can he safely toy with Venus. He has raised her to a fever pitch; now he is trapped alone with her. He becomes the young coquette whose game, suddenly, is up. Instinctively, he falls back upon his old tricks, disdain and contempt [ll. 409-26], to which he adds the excuse of immaturity. As A. C. Hamilton has said, Adonis rejects lust because it feeds on his beauty [see excerpt above, 1961]. And now, without his horse, he must choose either the glutton lust or the slower (but more deadly) appetite of time. He must surrender his beauty to sexuality, or, by rescinding the sexual promise his coquetry implies, sacrifice his beauty to human mortality. Like the Adonis of the first seventeen sonnets, he favors the latter alternative.

Adonis was about to repeat his successes of the earlier encounter when "cunning love did wittily prevent" [l. 471]. His adversary has changed tactics, catching him off guard with

some deception of her own. Her "fainting" brings out the "silly boy" in his nature; he drops his sophisticated disdain to kiss her. Don Cameron Allen regards his action as a spontaneous "filial affection" which Venus subsequently employs to her advantage [see excerpt above, 1959]. But in light of what we have seen previously of his character, Adonis may well be acting out of a double motivation. In the first place, there is, in his psychology, the desire to be deflowered, for coquetry is an invitation at heart. But Adonis is young, and the fear of lust and perhaps of love itself (which he admits he does not know) governs his responses. He had no intention of allowing his affair with Venus to reach culmination. It has been a kind of hunt for him, a means of laughing to scorn what he refuses to acknowledge except on a battlefield of his own choosing. But the game has apparently gone too far, and so, "a thousand ways he seeks / To mend the hurt that his unkindness marr'd" [ll. 477-78]. Finally he kisses her and in that kiss the attraction she holds for him and the fear of having overdone his coy cruelty cause him to drop the mask of disdain. He is at once tricked and revealed. Venus presses her advantage. Raised by Adonis to a "quickness" of desire, she "hath caught the *yielding* prey" ([l. 547]; my italics). His defenses have been undermined; he offers hastily erected barricades: the hour is late, his years are yet "unripe"—perhaps (he hopes) a final kiss will cool her. Finally, only by abrupt, physical retreat, is Adonis able to flee "Love upon her back, deeply distress'd" [l. 814]. He has nearly become a victim of that overflowing river, that stopped-up oven; and the imagery surrounding him in this section focuses on a wild bird, trapped and fondled, on Wat, naked and hounded on a hill. Adonis has not come out of this battle unscathed. Love has all but forced him to a culmination [ll. 593-94]; Love has forced him to kiss her; for the first time Adonis is the quarry and not the hunter. But he himself has precipitated his predicament. We have seen him play the tempter, partly out of pride, partly out of a secret spring of desire. The irony of his position is that of any coy virgin. He has urged Venus on, and, unable to escape, has become the frantic game of his own snare. In the role of coquette, he has disdainfully toyed with the goddess; in the role of frightened virgin, he now runs.

Before looking at the final third of *Venus and Adonis* for a resolution to the poem's thematic issues, we had better consider the two segments most often regarded as keys to the work, Adonis' attack on Venus' "devices in love" and the episode of the "breeding jennet." For the critic who maintains that *Venus and Adonis* depicts a conflict between reason in love and excessive passion, lines 769-810 have to be the mainstay of his argument. There, Adonis answers the repeated urging that he "breed." "You do it for increase. O strange excuse, / When reason is the bawd to lust's abuse!" [ll. 791-92]. This is the "sound Renaissance morality" Miller spoke of, and can only picture for us an Adonis well-grounded in practical ethics. And yet, criticism has not been universal in its applause of Adonis' sentiments. Kenneth Muir, for instance, has argued that "Shakespeare's plays are singularly free from such Neo-platonic nonsense" as this, and that the rebuttal "reads too much like an afterthought . . . in the first half of the poem he is bashful, but he seems to feel no moral objections to Venus's suit: he merely declares that he is too young." Muir is right in questioning the sincerity of Adonis' Neo-platonic stand.

As we have already seen, Adonis has, at this point in the action, become the hunted, his defenses are down, and as is usual under such conditions, his argument for reasoned love is curiously contradictory. Even Adonis seems to sense the weak rationale of his shotgun approach to the issue when, immediately upon its conclusion, he breaks and runs—hardly the response of a man whose morals are sound and whose arguments are irrefutable. In the first stanza of his rebuttal [ll. 769-74], Adonis takes back the kiss he has given Venus, telling her he likes her less than ever (and yet the kiss must make the claim appear a coy lie). In the second and third stanzas [ll. 775-86], Adonis boasts again, as he had before, that no matter what Venus might say, he, like his heart, will "sleep alone." It is ironic that his expressed motives for doing so are not, on close analysis, as noble as he seems to think. His refusal of love is for a purely selfish reason: "lest the deceiving harmony should run / Into the quiet closure of my breast" [ll. 781-82]. He is afraid to risk personal contact. His idea of fun is the hunt, an imposition of his will on the external world, not a reciprocal exchange with it.

From that point, he returns to his boasting. "What have you urg'd that I cannot reprove?" [l. 787]. Up to now, of course, he has offered no convincing argument against Venus' main point—that he must submit to preserve his beauty—and does not seem likely to do so. "The path is smooth that leadeth on to danger" [l. 788] is true enough but has little to do with either his preceding remarks or his subsequent ones. And then, as if in a moment of insight, he observes, "I hate not love, but your device in love" [l. 789]. The statement is directly con-

trary to his earlier remark, "My love to love is love but to disgrace it" [l. 412]. The fact that he contradicts himself suggested to Muir that this attack on Venus is but an afterthought; it has very little relation to his true feelings, except inasmuch as it offers him a new means of escape. His attempted "moral distinction" is really little more than a fortuitous turn of phrase. His accusation happens to be true; nevertheless, he is just as guilty as Venus of making reason "bawd," this time for the abuse of righteousness. Adonis uses the scanty reason and the grain of truth his arguments contain as he would have used his horse, to effect a face-saving escape. His catechism ends with the painfully naive assertion that love's "gentle spring doth always fresh remain" [l. 801], and a return to his stock defense, his age. All in all, we are justified in regarding the whole of Adonis' speech somewhat askance. He is, at this point, in dire straits; still, he is able to muster the tone of disdain and of irreproachable morality, bound up in a dubious logical structure, under cover of which he makes his exit.

The second major key to the poem has often been found in the episode of the horses [ll. 259-324]. Here, as with his attack on lust, critics who view Adonis sympathetically align him with Reason. Robert P. Miller explains the interlude as a contrast to the action taking place on the human level. He sees in the maneuverings of the steed and the jennet an aping of the tradition of romantic courtship, and, in the bolting of the courser, the bit in his teeth, an emblematic presentation of lust controlling reason. Adonis, however, declines to follow the poor example of his horse, saving himself from bestial lust. Even critics who would deny that Adonis is an exemplar of reasoned morality argue that the horse is somehow correct in accepting passion, while Adonis is mistaken in not following his example. Such interpretations rest on the assumption that we are to understand a direct parallel between Venus and the jennet and Adonis and the stallion.

But it is dangerous to assume parallelism solely on the basis of sex. The sixth line of the poem ought to make it clear that Venus is to play the role of the "bold-fac'd suitor"; Adonis correspondingly becomes the woman wooed. This reversal of roles continues throughout the first two-thirds of the work, and results in a pervasive comic effect there. Here, reflections of Adonis in the jennet and of Venus in the stallion are not hard to find. Venus does, in fact, break the reins of reason and modesty for lust—she is like a "well-proportion'd steed" [l. 290]. Rebuffed, her fainting resembles the horse's "melancholy malcontent," and she bounds forward again when she thinks Adonis' kisses signal an invitation to the wood. But more interesting is the behavior of the jennet-Adonis. She rushes forth, "snorts and neighs aloud" [l. 262] in unmistakable invitation. But then, having roused the stallion to a high state of desire, she

> answers him, as if she knew his mind.
> Being proud, as females are, to see him woo her,
> She puts on outward strangeness, seems unkind,
>   Spurns at his love and scorns the heat he feels,
>   Beating his kind embracements with her heels.
>
> [ll. 308-12]

If this episode is something more than ornament, we assume that it reflects upon the principal characters of the poem in some way. And so it does; it gives us, in miniature, a critique of the larger action. It implies the proper response of the kind of person who pours rain into the river of another's passion. The male coquette, like the jennet, ought to come through with his implied promise, otherwise he adds cruelty to his sins. The jennet episode is as much a criticism of Adonis as of the lusty Venus; at least the mare is finally honest with herself and with the stallion—Adonis is not. Thus, Adonis' reasoned attack on lust, while incidentally defining Venus' error, represents merely the argumentative potpourri of a young coquette caught in the passionate embrace of his victim. And in the jennet episode we find both an explanation of and a more honest alternative to Adonis' behavior.

In the final third of *Venus and Adonis* [ll. 823-1194], Shakespeare works out the implications of his *carpe diem* theme. At one extreme is Venus, whose insistence on mere breeding is really nothing more than a veil for her lust. Of course, the destructiveness of lust was established early in the poem. There, love's queen, passionate and sick-thoughted, was a comic figure of the vice itself. And by virtue of the comedy, the weight of ethical judgment was brought to bear on her antics. Now, the issue of lust is joined again in the imagery surrounding the boar. Venus' speculation on the manner of Adonis' death recalls her own sin, for as she recreates that death, she unwittingly implicates herself in it.

> 'Tis true, 'tis true! thus was Adonis slain:
> He ran upon the boar with his sharp spear,
> Who did not whet his teeth at him again,
> But by a kiss thought to persuade him there;
>   And nuzzling in his flank, the loving swine
>   Sheath'd unaware the tusk in his soft groin.
>
> Had I been tooth'd like him, I must confess,
> With kissing him I should have kill'd him first;
> But he is dead, and never did he bless
> My youth with his—the more am I accurst.
>
> [ll. 1111-20]

Clearly, the lust she possessed, if allowed culmination, would have destroyed Adonis as surely as does the boar. But, just as clearly, Venus does not understand that fact. For her, lust is not toothed; her formulation of that possibility is purely fanciful. She does not see that her appetite is as deadly as the boar's.

Furthermore, Venus fails to understand the real nature of her love object. Thinking to praise Adonis, she reminds us of his coquetry. His vanity seems a virtue to her: "But when Adonis liv'd, sun and sharp air / Lurk'd like two thieves, to rob him of his fair; / And therefore would he put his bonnet on" [ll. 1085-87]. As she recalls his rapport with the birds and fish ([l. 1104]: "He fed them with his sight, they him with berries"), we are reminded of the coquette's parasitic nature that feeds on the desires of suitors. And Venus' infatuation with Adonis, while blinding her to the worst in his character, leads her to a final error. Her pronouncement on the love of succeeding generations [ll. 1135-64] projects the qualities of Adonis into the world at large:

> It shall be fickle, false, and full of fraud . . .
> It shall be merciful, and too severe,
> And most deceiving when it seems most just.
>
> [ll. 1141, 1155-56]

The law she lays down perpetuates coquetry and insures the frustration of future lovers as well.

> Sith in his prime death doth my love destroy,
> They that love best their loves shall not enjoy.
>
> [ll. 1163-64]

So that Venus has failed to understand her experience properly. Not only does she ignore the questionable basis of her own attraction to Adonis, but, with a petulance matching his childishness, she denies others what she could not have. In her denouncement of love and her withdrawal to Paphos, Shakespeare provides a mythic sanction for the current state of secular love.

As they do the errors of Venus, the final stages of the drama demonstrate the limitations of Adonis' understanding of courtship. Consistently, he has appealed to his youthful unreadiness. He has asked for time. But time is a double-edged sword that destroys what it has allowed to ripen. In the *carpe diem* tradition, of course, the urgency created by mortality is the basis of the suitor's appeal. Shakespeare's handling of that theme in his first seventeen sonnets illuminates the mistake Adonis makes. There, the propagation of beauty is urged as a way of asserting human dignity in the face of universal mortality. The sonnets do not argue, simply, the garnering of pleasure while it is fresh, but the defiance of death. In that way Shakespeare shifts the emphasis of the *carpe diem* theme away from pure eroticism. Similarly, Adonis' concern with the hard hunt leaves him vulnerable to waste, for he chooses to ignore mortality in much the same way that Venus chooses to ignore the destructiveness of extreme passion. Adonis believes his choice is between chastity and sexuality. As the poem demonstrates, it is not. His quest for adventure, for the excitement of the hard hunt in love, leaves him open to waste; he denies his beauty to the world by refusing to admit propagation as the necessary outcome of courtship. The imagery surrounding the boar suggests the limitations of his coquettish vision. The boar is linked with Death and the grave: "his snout digs sepulchres where'er he goes" [l. 662]. He is a figure who represents more than the danger of the hunt; he reminds us of the mutability of all that is beautiful.

> Alas, he naught esteems that face of thine,
> To which Love's eyes pays tributary gazes;
> Nor thy soft hands, sweet lips, and crystal eyne,
> Whose full perfection all the world amazes;
>   But having thee at vantage (wondrous dread!),
>   Would root these beauties as he roots the
>   mead.
>
> [ll. 631-36]

Beauty and worldly joy are imperfect; Adonis is innocent of that knowledge. Venus is not. Although her motives are questionable, her sense of Adonis' mortality and of the danger of his brand of hunting is justified by the course of events.

> And therefore hath *Cynthia* brib'd the Destinies
> To cross the curious workmanship of Nature,
> To mingle beauty with infirmities
> And pure perfection with impure defeature,
>   Making it subject to the tyranny
>   Of mad mischances and much misery. . . .
>
> And not the least of all these maladies
> But in one minute's fight brings beauty under.
>
> [ll. 733-38, 745-46]

The coquette moves in a realm of fruitless dalliance. And so, because of his imperfect understanding of the human condition Adonis wastes his beauty.

Venus and Adonis, then, presents flawed alternatives that come out of the *carpe diem* tradition. On one hand, the reader cannot endorse mere eroticism. Adonis is perceptive enough to see that Venus makes reason "bawd to lust's abuse." But Adonis' behavior is not an acceptable alternative either. Aside from the fact that his coquetry is cruel, it leads to a limited understanding of man's place in the cycle of life. It leads, finally, to waste. *Venus and Adonis* investigates "love's urgencies, perversities and contrarieties," it is true, but points as well to the failure of the two extremes in a traditional courtship situation. Venus and Adonis are polar opposites, not in terms of relative immorality and morality, but in terms of their basic errors. Neither lust nor coquetry encompasses true human love. *Venus and Adonis* demonstrates through imagery and through dramatic action the shortcomings of each stance. (pp. 16-24)

> J. D. Jahn, "The Lamb of Lust: The Role of Adonis in Shakespeare's 'Venus and Adonis'," in Shakespeare Studies: An Annual Gathering of Research, Criticism, and Reviews, *Vol. VI, 1970, pp. 11-25.*

COPPÉLIA KAHN   (essay date 1976)

[*Kahn proposes a psychological reading of* Venus and Adonis, *suggesting that Adonis is confronted with the choice between "intimacy with Venus, which constitutes entry into manhood, and the emotional isolation of narcissism, which constitutes a denial of growth." According to Kahn, the boy chooses the latter and rejects the goddess's advances because he lacks a stable, inner self and consequently fears that, in sexual union, she will overwhelm and devour him. Adonis metaphorically defends himself, the critic claims, by means of the hunt, in which he "projects his anxiety about being devoured by Venus onto the boar, and attempts to destroy the boar so that Venus will not destroy him." Adonis prefers risking physical death in hunting to risking the loss of his identity in loving.*]

Shakespeare's contemporary Gabriel Harvey dismissed *Venus and Adonis* as a poem which would delight only "the younger sort" [see excerpt above, 1598]. His judgment reflected the moral decorum of Renaissance taste: physical love was a concern proper to hot-blooded youth, and usually matter for comedy. "The wiser sort," Harvey declared, would interest themselves in tragedies like *Lucrece* or *Hamlet,* in dilemmas more profound than how to answer an invitation to erotic pleasure on a summer's day.

Modern critics have taken the poem more seriously, and have explained the central conflict and the narrative action as illustrating a philosophical or moral theme. (p. 351)

In contrast to this prevailing critical tendency, I propose a radically psychological reading of the poem. I see it as a dramatization of narcissism—self-love in the form of withdrawal from others into the self. This theme is richly explored in Shakespeare's source, Ovid's *Metamorphoses*. Brilliantly improvising on several Ovidian tales, Shakespeare portrays the paradox of the narcissist, whose attempt to protect himself against the threat of love actually results in his self-destruction. The conflict between Venus and Adonis is essentially a conflict between eros and death fought within the narcissistic self. The boyish Adonis, whom Venus, the very incarnation of desirable femininity, presents with an enviable chance to prove his manhood, sternly rejects that opportunity, meets death in the boar hunt, and metamorphosed into a flower, ends up as a child again, sheltered in Venus' bosom. A similar conflict is strongly implied in the first seventeen of Shakespeare's sonnets, possibly written about the same time as *Venus and Adonis.* There the speaker urges the beautiful youth contracted to his own bright eyes to love and procreate, as Venus urges Adonis, and warns him that in his refusal to love he will become "the tomb / Of his self-love" [Sonnet 3].

In the *Metamorphoses,* in the sonnets, and in *Venus and Adonis,* narcissism is specifically a crisis of identity which occurs in youth. Ovid's Narcissus and his Shakespearean successors are male adolescents, poised between youth and manhood, forced to confront the emerging imperative of mature sexuality, but reluctant to answer it and define themselves as men by making love to women. In a way, *Venus and Adonis* portrays a *rite de passage* in reverse. As an archetypal event in youth, the *rite de passage* marks "the complete symbolic separation of the male adolescents from the world of their youth, especially from their close attachment to their mothers" [S. N. Eisenstaedt, in his "Archetypal Patterns of Youth"]. At the same time, this separation marks the youth's new sexual and social identity as a man, whose future love-choices will be women not his mother. The Adonis of Shakespeare's poem is caught between the poles of intimacy and isolation: intimacy with Venus, which constitutes entry into manhood, and the emotional isolation of narcissism, which constitutes a denial of growth, change, and the natural fact of mortality which underlies them. But Adonis' self-absorption and claims of autonomy actually mask an intense need for dependency, a wish to escape the risk and conflict involved in having a separate identity, a wish symbolically fulfilled in his metamorphosis into the flower which Venus treats as her child.

Shakespeare's characterization of Venus and Adonis, and the coherence of the narrative, can best be understood in terms of this dilemma. The following interpretation will center on four major questions suggested by the poem. Why does Adonis refuse to love Venus? Why does he choose the boar instead, and what does the boar signify? What does his metamorphosis mean? In answering these questions, I will stress Shakespeare's use of Ovid and the way in which Ovidian myth can be a means of expressing the unconscious needs and conflicts of narcissism.

Before I proceed, I want to distinguish between the context in which I use this concept and other contexts for it. In Shakespeare's day, the story of Narcissus was allegorized in accordance with medieval tradition, the fate of its hero illustrating the folly of trusting in riches, beauty, and the things of this world. The common meaning of the term today arises from the idea that Narcissus loved his own beauty; in most dictionaries, narcissism is defined as self-love, excessive admiration of oneself or interest in all that pertains to oneself.

As a psychoanalytic concept, however, narcissism has subtler and more inclusive reference to the effect of self-love on one's relations with others. Freud first used it in 1910, in discussions of homosexuality, characterizing it as the choice of love objects modelled on the self rather than on the mother. Later he differentiated between this sense of the word and "primary narcissism," normal in infancy and early childhood, when satisfactions experienced in the body itself are the object of libido. Since Freud, an extensive and complicated controversy over the concept has arisen, involving the serious theoretical questions of when and how the ego is formed and the role that object relations play in its formation.

Whatever the theory of its etiology, however, a paradox lies at the center of narcissism: the one who seems to love himself does not really have a self and thus is not really capable of loving himself or others. The narcissist lacks a coherent, stable, realistic image of himself as distinct from others:

he has not become a securely independent person—

not created a core of himself—and unless he becomes an independent person he cannot himself in
turn love. . . . Such separation as the narcissist
achieves will remain uncertain and he will always
be more than willing to put it off [Grace Stuart,
Narcissism: A Psychological Study of Self-Love].

His apparent preference for himself over others, his superior
attitude or claims of autonomy, are actually defensive attempts to keep this inner deficiency secret, even from his conscious self. They enable him to withdraw into himself, to
avoid the risk of opening up to others in the challenge, conflict, and frustration of normal intimacy. In such relationships as he does pursue, the narcissist seeks total, unquestioning reassurance and acceptance, and finds ordinary demands
from others threatening. I refer to "the narcissist" only for
convenience, for narcissism is a component of many neurotic
illnesses, as well as a trait of many healthy people. Not only
in the character of Adonis, but as a narrative and poetic
whole, *Venus and Adonis* reveals its nature.

It has long been known that Shakespeare took the narrative
outline of his poem from Ovid's tale of Venus and Adonis.
But his fidelity to the Ovidian conception of eros as an imperative, an inescapable force which creates and destroys, hurts
and delights, has not been adequately recognized. Nor has
the significance of his alterations to the source material been
noted. He actually created the character of Adonis and the
conflict between him and Venus not from the tale of Venus
and Adonis, but from the stories of Narcissus and of Salmacis
and Hermaphroditus, which are dominated by the figure of
the youth who refuses to love a woman and suffers for it.
Shakespeare worked in fruitful harmony with Ovid, taking
from him the theme of self in conflict with eros which gives
his poem a firm psychological coherence.

The story of Deucalion and Pyrrha in Book I of the *Metamorphoses* is a symbolic statement of Ovid's conception of eros.
Sole survivors of the first iniquitous race of men, which Jove
destroyed in the flood, this innocent and worshipful couple
are advised by the oracle of Themis, goddess of Justice,

> Go hille your heads, and let your garments slake,
> And both of you your Graundames bones behind
>   your shoulders cast.

Horrified at this commandment to desecrate the sacred worship of their ancestors, at last they realize that the earth is
their mother, that the stones of earth are her bones. When
they do as Themis commands, the stones become the men
and women of a new human race. The story insists that our
primary obligation is to the Great Mother; the goddess of justice hands down only one law, the law of generation, which
is conditional on an act of destruction. Born of mothers who
must die, nourished by the fruitful earth, we all in turn must
love, procreate, and die. It is the only norm Ovid recognizes,
and in Shakespeare's poem, it is Venus' most compelling argument for love: "Thou wast begot, to get it is thy duty" [l.
168].

Eros regulates nature, but, paradoxically, eros creates anarchy. Anyone, god or mortal, may be struck with desire for
anyone else, and whatever the cost, even to an innocent victim, that desire must be satisfied. One group of stories emphasizes the inexorable character of sexual passion by treating in-
cest and homosexuality at length. Though Ovid often affects,
usually through the persona of a narrator, a decorous horror
of such perversions, he no doubt does so only to amuse an au-

dience which he assumes to be as sophisticated and unshock-
able as himself. We share the author's knowing smile rather
than the narrator's pious judgment. Ovid as author regards
men and women as creatures of nature, and to him nothing
in nature is unnatural. Thus he relates with a sympathy born
of tolerance the story of Byblis, who loved her brother
Caunus and in her crazed passion was turned into a fountain;
of Iphis, a girl raised as a boy who loved the bride chosen for
her and, in answer to her prayers, was changed into a man;
of Adonis' mother Myrrha who, horrified at her own passion,
slept with her father and was changed to an ever-weeping
tree. No moral scheme governs the dénouements of these stories: a capricious fate either gratifies or denies, legitimates or
punishes the forbidden wishes.

Though eros is the only constant that Ovid recognizes, he is
too much of a realist to believe that it reigns
unchallenged. . . . Lust struggles with love, perversion with
normal affection. Similarly, Shakespeare announces "Nature
with herself at strife" [l. 11] as a theme in the second stanza
of the poem. The idea of a conflict in which neither side is
right, in the sense of being more reasonable, more natural, or
morally more justifiable, is as basic [to] Shakespeare's poem
as it is to Ovid's. The beauteous war of red and white repeatedly reminds us of this conflict. If in nature roses and lilies
have equal claims, do not desire and rejection, blushes and
pallor, Venus and Adonis? Because eros itself is potentially
destructive as well as creative, the human reaction to it is necessarily ambivalent, compounded of joy and fear, loathing
and desire.

Yet in Adonis' rejection of Venus there is something more
than natural. He does not merely shun her as a particular
woman, for she is a goddess and represents love itself, no matter how realistically Shakespeare portrays her. Rather, in repudiating her he repudiates love itself. His reasoned arguments are less convincing than his emotional stance: a cold
and harsh withdrawal from the very idea of sexual union. Impervious to her erotic appeal, he meets all her pleas with withering scorn and sweeping negation. Shakespeare might have
depicted Adonis as experiencing a common adolescent conflict between newly felt desire and a fear of sexual inadequacy
due to inexperience. But though Adonis claims he is too
young to love, what he conveys in deeds as well as in words
is that he *will not* love. What lies behind this adamant refusal?

In Ovid's tale of Venus and Adonis, Adonis is characterized
merely as a handsome youth. He is Venus' lover, and no point
is made of his attitude toward her. He merely ignores her
fond warning against the boar hunt; there is no conflict between them about it. In Shakespeare's poem, that conflict is
the main issue, and in a striking reversal of roles which parallels that in the stories of Narcissus and of Hermaphroditus,
the hero is courted by the heroine, and strenuously rejects her
advances.

Though Shakespeare directly compares Adonis to Narcissus
only once [ll. 1616-20], Ovid's conception of the cold, withdrawn, beautiful youth and his self-destructive resistance to
love permeates the poem. The frequent comparison of Adonis
to a flower, for instance, is more than a merely conventional
compliment because it refers unconventionally to a man, and
thus recalls Narcissus, who was changed into a flower. Insofar as Adonis' beauty is fresh, delicate, and richly hued, the
flower metaphor daintily suggests his physical qualities. It
furnishes arguments for Venus' urgency ("For flowers that
are not gathered in their prime / Rot, and consume them-

selves in little time," [ll. 131-32]), but also for Adonis' stubbornness ("Who plucks the bud before one leaf put forth?" [l. 416]). Poignantly, it hints at an early mortality for the youth but also foreshadows his transformation to a flower after death.

Most significantly, the flower image comments on Adonis' attitude toward himself and others. Flowers grow and die heedless of human existence; they blush unseen on the desert air, sublimely indifferent to admiration or its absence. Capable of inspiring the tenderest feelings, they themselves feel nothing. Such flower-like self-regard and self-sufficiency typifies a number of Ovidian heroes and heroines: Daphne, Syrinx, the nameless heroines of the tales of Jove in Arcady and of the raven; Arethusa, and most notably, Hermaphroditus and Narcissus. All are young and surpassingly beautiful; all flee sexual encounter, perceiving it as an ultimate danger, and find their escape in metamorphosis.

In some stories, the youth's transformation into a natural object represents the power of art to sublimate sexuality: Daphne becomes the laurel, symbol of poetic achievement; Syrinx, the reed through which Pan pipes his songs. But in other stories, the children of earth who begged to be relieved of their bodies as a way of escaping from sex ironically become images for the imprisonment of human consciousness in mere physicality. Whether or not they themselves feel alien to their new non-human forms, Ovid makes us feel their transformations as a pathetic loss of human identity. . . . The flower-children who unconditionally refuse love are trying to assert their separateness from eros, an impossibility in the Ovidian world. They flee the personal imperatives of their own natures, only to end up immured in the terrifyingly impersonal natural world. Though they retain their minds, without their bodies, they no longer have human identities, and are cut off forever from love and community.

These Ovidian stories provided Shakespeare with a broad sense of the role of the body and sexuality in the formation of identity. More specifically, he found the major elements of Adonis' character in Ovid's account of Narcissus, which begins,

> For when yeares three times five and one he fully
> lyved had;
> So that he seemde to stande betweene the state of
> man and Lad,
> The hearts of divers trim yong men his beautie gan
> to move,
> And many a Ladie fresh and faire was taken in his
> love.
> But in that grace of Natures gift such passing pride
> did raigne,
> That to be toucht of man or Mayde he wholy did
> disdaine.

Rarely does Ovid give the precise age of his characters. Here and in the story of Hermaphroditus he notes that the hero is an adolescent, implying a connection between his age and his rejection of love. Significantly, Narcissus is "betweene the state of man and Lad"; since he is already sexually attractive to others, he can define himself as a man if he wishes to. But he would like to remain a boy forever, and repels attempts at sexual intimacy so strenuously that "no one can touch him," hinting at a fear that sexual contact might damage him physically, as it damages Hermaphroditus, who loses his masculinity as a result of Salmacis' embrace.

Ovid stresses Narcissus' self-protective autonomy through a

contrast with Echo, an image of the person wholly dependent on others for the creation and maintenance of a self. Incapable of speaking first, but also unable to remain silent when others talk, she parrots their words but cannot say anything of her own. When Narcissus fails to respond to her ardent wooing, she literally wastes away, becoming only a voice. His stout resistance to bodily contact with her emphasizes his precious dedication to his own body as an object:

> Upon these wordes she left the Wood, and forth she
> yeedeth streit,
> To coll the lovely necke for which she longed had
> so much.
> He runnes his way, and will not be imbraced of no
> such.
> And sayth: I first will die ere thou shalt take of me
> thy pleasure.

Shakespeare's Adonis reveals a similar attitude toward his body in the famous "divedapper" passage when he offers his lips to Venus, then "winks" and turns away. Venus, of course, is the counterpart of Echo, and though she easily manages to do more than get her arms around Adonis, he stalwartly maintains his emotional distance from her: "Still is he sullen, still he lours and frets" [l. 75], despite her tenderest embraces.

Narcissus' rejection of Echo stands for his rejection of all proffered love, and Ovid portrays his death as resulting directly from this rejection. One of his despairing suitors prays that the youth may actually fall in love with himself so that he too will suffer unrequited love, and Nemesis, goddess of vengeance, answers the prayer. Even though Narcissus realizes that his self-love is destroying him, he is helpless to stop it. Burning with love of his own body, he prays to escape from it in order to possess it; but death brings only the ironic retribution of transformation into the object he most resembled in life, a flower.

Shakespeare, following Ovid's tale of Narcissus, centers his poem on a conflict between the ardent pursuing female and the retreating, rejecting male. In both heroes, the preference for the self is revealed only by pressure to give the self to another. While the exceptional beauty of both heroes leads others to love them, that is not why they love themselves. Their primary need is to defend against sexual involvement in order to protect the fragile inner self. This defense is ironically self-destructive, as Narcissus' death (in Ovid's version, he wastes away gradually, literally consumed by love of himself) and Adonis' in the boar hunt, as I shall show, make clear. Shakespeare suggests that Adonis' fate will resemble Narcissus', because he is similarly unable to nourish and develop the self by intimacy. In the striking phrase,

> Narcissus so himself himself forsook,
> And died to kiss his shadow in the brook.
>
> [ll. 161-62]

the repetition of "himself" imitates Narcissus' intense need to fasten on himself as an object to the exclusion of others. To forsake one-self means to lose consciousness of oneself in relation to others and to external reality, as in the expression "to forget oneself"; in the context of the legend, it means to die, symbolizing the utter annihilation of self. When Venus reproaches Adonis with failing a duty to reproduce his kind, she calls his body "A swallowing grave" [l. 757] which buries his posterity, and phrases the idea much as in the earlier passage, commenting "So in thyself thyself art made away" [l.

763]. The second "thyself" means both Adonis' potential off-spring and his sense of himself, which he makes away or destroys by rejecting Venus. In Adonis, Shakespeare depicts a narcissistic character who regards eros sexual encounter—as the most serious threat to his self. But the real threat is internal, and comes from that very urge to defend against eros.

Adonis would be threatened by any kind of intimacy, because it might force him to reveal his secret—that he has no core, nothing to offer from within, only an enormous need to be reassured. It is precisely Venus' kind of love, however, which mirrors this inner need which Adonis would keep hidden.

First, both by virtue of traditional associations invoked in the poem and through Shakespeare's characterization of her, Venus is something of a mother figure. When she bases her arguments for love on procreation as the law of nature, she is *Venus genetrix,* and she presides over a lush natural ambiance which suggests omnipresent fecundity, especially in the coupling of the horses and the rabbit hunt. Her oft-repeated plea for a kiss is an invitation to physical fusion which suggests a parallel with the infant's relation to the mother at the breast, before he has begun to differentiate between self and others—precisely the stage at which Adonis exists psychologically. In this sense, Venus offers the only kind of relationship with another that Adonis is capable of—one in which he is totally dependent on a nurturing figure who offers him unending oral gratification.

But the kiss is also an act of sexual intimacy, so that to kiss willingly would in a crucial way define Adonis as a man. And Venus is the queen of love, the supreme object of desire for any man, whose manliness is defined by his desire for a woman; thus Venus asks,

> Art thou a woman's son and canst not feel
> What 'tis to love, how want of love tormenteth?
>
> [ll. 201-02]

Furthermore, at certain moments she embodies lust as a blind impersonal force in the Ovidian sense, desire for the opposite sex which overwhelms man or woman and momentarily obliterates self-consciousness. It is this aspect of her that mirrors the narcissist's basic fear: that he who has such a slender sense of self will lose it all if he allows himself to be loved.

All these aspects of Venus—mother, woman, eros itself—are depicted in oral imagery, the imagery of kissing or eating. At the crises of her passion, the two kinds of imagery merge, in the kiss that devours its object. Thus Venus bears a highly ambivalent quality; union with her would both confer manly identity and obliterate the self. The kiss she pleads for evokes conflicting reactions from the reader, in effect putting us in Adonis' place. The oral contact she seeks bears, despite her good intentions and the naturalness of her desire, an aggressive and even murderous quality. As she begins, trying to be gently seductive, she unwittingly conveys an insatiable eagerness:

> Here come and sit, where never serpent hisses.
> And being set, I'll smother thee with kisses.
>
> And yet not cloy thy lips with loathed satiety,
> But rather famish them amid their plenty. . . .
>
> [ll. 17-20]

After she "plucks" Adonis from his horse and pushes him to the ground, she "stops his lips" [l. 46] with kisses to keep him

from speaking, and when he protests, "What follows more, she murders with a kiss" [l. 54].

That kiss is described through the comparison of Venus to an eagle devouring its prey, a simile which both repels and awes the reader:

> Even as an empty eagle, sharp by fast,
> Tires with her beak on feathers, flesh, and bone,
> Shaking her wings, devouring all in haste,
> Till either gorge be stuffed or prey be gone:
>   Even so she kiss'd his brow, his cheek, his chin,
>   And where she ends she doth anew begin.
>
> [ll. 55-60]

This all-consuming, never-ending kiss becomes rapaciously impersonal. Yet the stanza also suggests an Ovidian perspective on it as a natural urge. We learn in the first line that the eagle is "empty" and "sharp by fast"; therefore, her ferocious appetite gains a certain legitimacy. In the next stanza, when the panting Adonis breathes in Venus' face,

> She feedeth on the steam as on a prey,
> And calls it heavenly moisture, air of grace. . . .
>
> [ll. 63-4]

The imagery of preying is softened and prettied into a joke: Venus may act like a hungry eagle, but she is forced to content herself with conceits. Finally, in a third stanza, Adonis is no longer being devoured; he is merely "a bird . . . tangled in a net" [l. 67], captured in Venus' loving embrace.

Shakespeare orchestrates this dominant oral motif in various keys. In the following lines, for example, Venus' devouring qualities are balanced by the erotic appeal of her coy preoccupation with "lips":

> Touch but my lips with those fair lips of thine—
> Though mine be not so fair, yet are they red—
> The kiss shall be thine own as well as mine.
> What see'st thou in the ground? Hold up thy head,
>   Look in mine eyeballs, there thy beauty lies:
>   Then why not lips on lips, since eyes on eyes?
>
> [ll. 115-20]

The description of the kiss begins as a "touch" in the first line, and the fusion it involves is pictured as a gain to Adonis in the third line ("The kiss shall be thine own . . ."). But by the fifth line, Adonis, his image reflected in Venus' eyes, has become part of her, and the last line suggests a blurring of boundaries, an anonymous merging of "eyes" and "lips" which echoes the narcissistic fear of losing the self. In the famous passage in which Venus compares her body to a park [ll. 229-40], inviting Adonis to "Feed where thou wilt" [l. 232], her devouring aspect gives way to her nurturing side. Yet later, when Adonis offers her a goodnight kiss (only in order to make his escape), her voracious drive returns, again in the imagery of an animal devouring its food:

> Now quick desire hath caught the yielding prey,
> And glutton-like she feeds, yet never filleth.
> Her lips are conquerors, his lips obey,
> Paying what ransom the insulter willeth;
>   Whose vulture though doth pitch the price so high
>   That she will draw his lips' rich treasure dry.
>
> And having felt the sweetness of the spoil,
> With blindfold fury she begins to forage;
> Her face doth reek and smoke, her blood doth boil,
> And careless lust stirs up a desperate courage,

> Planting oblivion, beating ranson back,
> Forgetting shame's pure blush and honor's
>   wrack
>
>   [ll. 547-58]

In contrast to the earlier eagle image, these lines convey a cruel lust for conquest, rather than hunger. In the first stanza, gluttony has replaced fast; the eagle is now a vulture, and the kiss a kind of rape in which eros seems heartless fury rather than pleasure. These stanzas, in fact, use imagery strikingly similar to that describing Tarquin when he is about to rape Lucrece; in both situations, lust becomes a tyranny of force, likened both to the animal world and the battlefield. In the first stanza, Venus' lips are "conquerors," and the kisses she takes, "ransom" and then (in the first line of the second stanza) "spoil." The dehumanization of Venus is stressed more strongly than that of Adonis, for the reeking, smoking and boiling of the third line make her a personification of the turmoil and destruction of battle itself.

This frightening depersonalization strongly recalls Ovid's tale of Hermaphroditus, in which the amorous woman destroys the sexual and thus the human identities of herself and her reluctant lover. Venus' style of wooing is, in general, inspired by that of Salmacis, who first offers herself to Hermaphroditus boldly, but in carefully controlled rhetoric. Later, her desire inflamed by the sight of his naked body, she cries in the language of conquest, *"Vicimus, et meus est"* ("I win, and he is mine"), as she struggles to clasp him to her. When he resists, she struggles the harder, and her embraces are compared to a snake coiling itself around the eagle which has caught it, to ivy twining itself around tree trunks, and to an octopus' tentacles grasping its prey on every side. When she prays that she and Hermaphroditus may never be separated, the prayer is granted with ironic literalness:

> The members of them mingled were and fastened
>   both together,
> They were not any longer two: but (as it were) a toy
> Of double shape. Ye could not say it was a perfect
>   boy,
> Nor perfect wench; it seemed both and none of both
>   to beene.

Had Hermaphroditus yielded to her, the actual intimacy would have been less injurious than the metamorphosis he suffers. Like Narcissus and Adonis, he is in effect punished for his resistance by being robbed of his individuality and in his case, of his manhood. While Salmacis obtains the eternal union she desires, he suffers a loss and becomes "but halfe a man." The defense brings worse results than the fear threatens; the attempt to protect the self ends in the loss of self.

We know Venus as a character only through the demands she makes on Adonis; the overwhelming impression we have of her is of a mouth, pressing insistently on or toward him. Most of the poem's 1200 lines are hers, in the form of direct speech; in contrast, Adonis speaks only eighty-eight lines. Venus pours forth a flood of words at Adonis and at us. This volubility contributes to the comic situation, of course; the queen of love can only assuage "love's fire" through words, and her oral aggressiveness is humorously at variance with the conventional female role of silent auditor receiving poetic tribute from a male poet-speaker. Adonis' passive silence also becomes a joke when, after speaking only two curt sentences in the first 400 lines, he opens up with three stanzas of high-pressured argument against love. Venus remarks in mock surprise, "What, canst thou talk?" [l. 427], and then, true to

form, launches into another amorous sermon. The more stubbornly a silent Adonis "winks, and turns his lips another way" [l. 90], the thirstier Venus grows for a taste of those lips. For each character, a fundamental need is at stake. The struggle of the open heart against the closed heart is imaged in an oral war.

The needs which impel Adonis to reject Venus are now clear, I hope, and we are ready to ask why he should choose to hunt the boar *instead* of loving her. I propose two kinds of explanation for his strange choice: a general one, in which hunting serves as a defense against eros; a specific one, in which the boar, though it is inimical to all Venus stands for, serves as a projection of Adonis' fears of her.

If Shakespeare had intended hunting to be understood as an acceptable alternative to Venus and a viable mode of releasing Adonis' closed self, he might have presented it as an activity suitable to young men of good birth, valuable in teaching skills and forming character, pleasant in the male camaraderie it affords. He might have sketched a scene of hairbreadth 'scapes and heroic challenge in the hunt. But the hunt appears only in terms of its object, the boar—a powerful creature wholly and blindly destructive. We see it only through Venus' jealous and fearful eye; significantly, we are given no other view. Adonis himself makes no arguments for hunting *per se;* in opposition to Venus, he holds only that he is too young to love, without saying why boar hunting is a better pursuit for one of his age.

In fact, hunting serves Adonis' deepest unconscious need, which is to keep eros out of his life. He acts as though hunting *is* his life; the action begins when Venus accosts him even as he "hies him to the chase" [l. 3], and their encounter consists of her resourceful (but ultimately futile) attempts to stop him from mounting his horse to resume that chase. In his first major speech, Adonis states his opposition to love in a strangely turned phrase which puts the boar in the place of the love object:

> "I know not love," quoth he, "nor will not know
>   it,
> Unless it is a boar, and then I chase it.
> 'Tis much to borrow, and I will not owe it;
> My love to love is love but to disgrace it,
>   For I have heard, it is a life in death,
>   That laughs and weeps, and all but with a
>   breath,"
>
>   [ll. 409-14]

The alliterated double negatives of the first line, "not," "nor," and "not," stress the intensity of his aversion. After its first use, the word "love" is suppressed into the unaccented pronoun "it" and the contraction "'tis" in lines one through three, minimizing its importance. In the fourth line it is the repetition of "love" which serves a similar purpose—to mock it; here Adonis comes close to saying that he hates love. In the last two lines, he seems to ridicule love as it appears in Petrarchan poetry, making its paradoxes and oxymorons sound absurd. But the phrase "life in death" alludes ironically to the boar hunt as well, since it is quite easily a fatal sport, and one to which he devotes his life.

Adonis' use of the word "know" in the first line provides a clue to the nature of his defense against love. In this context, knowing suggests carnal knowledge, and the verb hints at a criticism of the youth on his own grounds. How can he reject something of which he "knows" nothing? Later he plays on "know" again in the sense of carnal knowledge: "Before I know myself seek not to know me" [l. 525], he warns Venus, and again unintentionally raises the question of how he can know what his self is by isolating it from experiences which help to form it. The playful suggestion in the second line that he would rather "know" or love the boar seems a kind of risqué joke at first, a glance at sodomy. But it carries the serious undertone that he is deeply alienated from his own kind, determined not to love even at the expense of being perverse. The boar, as Elizabethans knew, is an ugly creature, and the effect of identifying it with love is to make love not only repulsive but impossible; he could never love a boar. All the poetic devices employed in this stanza combine to reveal Adonis' unconscious intention; to make love nonexistent by denying its existence for him. Clearly, he is using denial as a defense against love.

His conscious objection to love elsewhere is that he is too young for it. He compares himself to an unfinished garment, a leafless bud, an unbroken colt, an undersized fish, and a green plum, with an air of narcissistic pride in his very insufficiency [ll. 415-20, 526-28]. By arguing that he is too young, he uses defenselessness as a defense, and dares Venus to be so heartless as to hurt him.

In a similar sense, it is not hunting which Adonis uses as a defense, but his very self, precarious and incomplete though it is. This is revealed in the imagery of the following stanzas, which is so strongly oriented toward outer threat and resistance from an inner stronghold:

> If love have lent you twenty thousand tongues,
> And every tongue more moving than your own,
> Bewitching like the wanton mermaid's songs,
> Yet from my heart the tempting tune is blown;
>   For know, my heart stands armed in mine ear,
>   And will not let a false sound enter there;
>
> Lest the deceiving harmony should run
> Into the quiet closure of my breast,
> And then my little heart were quite undone,
> In his bedchamber to be barr'd of rest.
>   No, lady, no; my heart longs not to groan,
>   But soundly sleeps, while now it sleeps alone.
>
>   [ll. 775-86]

Adonis begins by hyperbolically evoking Venus' amorous rhetoric ("Twenty thousand tongues") as an oral threat against which his heart "stands armed," oddly perched outside the body, in the ear. But then in the second stanza, the heart turns out to be not only protector and defender but also the thing being protected which ordinarily dwells inside, in a "quiet closure" like the womb. The contradictions in this metaphor are psychological truths. If "heart" is the inmost self, and the capacity for loving, it is Adonis' inmost self which keeps him from loving, in order to protect him from a threatening seductive female (the "wanton mermaid" in the first stanza) who, like the sirens singing to Ulysses, deceptively lures him not to love but to death. The conception of the heart as a static realm of pure rest, dwelling in the solitude and quiet of a bedchamber, is rather preciously emphasized in the repetition of "my" before heart and breast in both stanzas. That his heart is *his* matters to Adonis, and so long as it is his he can remain in a regressive, unchanging state of utter calm.

Edward Hubler's remarks [in his *The Sense of Shakespeare's Sonnets*] on "the closed heart" of the young man in the son-

nets are highly appropriate to Adonis. Commenting on sonnet 94, he says,

> The closed heart may be poor, but it is at ease. Those men are most content who, though they inspire affection in others, have no need of it themselves . . . They are the owners of themselves, whereas throughout Shakespeare's works self-possession in the sense of living without regard for others is intolerable.

Shakespeare's great heroes are men who finally appreciate the supreme value of love and human bonds, no matter how blindly they may have denied it before: Lear, Othello, Macbeth. His great villains are solitary individualists who hate love: Iago [in *Othello*], Edmund [in *King Lear*], Richard III. In *Venus and Adonis* Shakespeare is saying the life apart from eros is death.

Turning now to the specific way in which the boar reflects Adonis' fear of Venus, though from the first stanza hunting is opposed to love, curiously it is Venus who describes the boar at some length, who actually sees it, and who supplies our only vision of the boar killing Adonis. Even more curiously, Shakespeare suggests through imagery associated with these two opposed figures a similarity in their meanings for Adonis. The hero's insistence on an absolute boundary between hunting and love actually masks the way in which, by chasing the boar, he acts out his deeper feelings toward Venus.

What Venus stresses most in her account of the boar is, not surprisingly, his destructiveness; in particular, his tusks. Those are his mortal weapons, and make him, like Venus, the personification of an oral threat:

> Oh be advis'd, thou know'st not what it is,
> With javelin's point a churlish swine to gore,
>   Whose tushes never sheath'd he whetteth still,
>   Like to a mortal butcher, bent to kill.
>
>   [ll. 615-18]

The phrase "bent to kill" refers to the placement of his tusks, pointing downward, and his natural habit of foraging by "rooting the mead" with his snout to earth. Driven by instinct, he seeks food and unintentionally "digs sepulchres," "killing whate'er is in his way" [l. 623]. Just as Venus at the height of her desire turns into an eagle or a vulture blindly seeking the natural needs she is denied, and thus seems to murder what she would enjoy, so does the boar. Both are capable of a purely natural, unreflective, and impersonal kind of aggression. The boar personifies the aspect of Venus most threatening to Adonis: her seemingly unsatiable desire. The more he resists her, the more her ardor increases, and causes him to resist her all the more. In a supremely revealing speech delivered as she gazes at the dead Adonis, the fondly grieving goddess imagines that the boar was as taken with his beauty as she was. The boar becomes the very image of Venus:

> If he did see his face, why then I know
> He thought to kiss him, and hath kill'd him
> so. . . .
>
> Had I been tooth'd like him, I must confess,
> With kissing him I should have kill'd him first.
>
>   [ll. 1109-10, 1117-18]

Then why does Adonis prefer the boar to Venus, when both bear a fatal quality for him? We can look at the hunt as Adonis' attempt to regain mastery over the inner danger of losing

Venus and Adonis. By Paolo Veronese.

his sense of self by mastering an external representative of that danger. In short, he projects his anxiety about being devoured by Venus onto the boar, and attempts to destroy the boar so that Venus will not destroy him. The danger emanating from the boar hunt is physical, and that emanating from Venus is emotional, but insofar as Adonis is narcissistically oriented toward his own body, the physical act of love carries a threat, pointedly suggested in the goddess- vision of the boar emasculating Adonis [ll. 1115-16]. Thus the hunt allows Adonis to "experiment" with an inner danger through confronting an outer danger.

But in a deeper sense, projecting Venus into the boar allows him to establish a rudimentary, provisional kind of "negative identity," a total identification with what he is least supposed to be. Venus argues that a lover "follows the law of nature" [l. 171] and feels desire like every man or woman bred [ll. 214-16]; it would be only normal, she makes us feel, for the youth to love her. The boar, on the other hand, embodies all that is inimical to life, beauty, and love. Adonis scornfully rejects the easier, more overtly pleasurable and normal course for the fatal one. He takes the boar as his object because, like her, it is blindly destructive in an oral way and thus most dangerous and most real to him. Yet it also provides a way of defending his inner self against her; it gives him a substitute self as a hunter, as one who loves a boar instead of a woman. His

readiness to face danger or death in the manly boar hunt conceals his inability to be more than a boy—"not-quite-somebody"—in the love hunt. He would rather pursue death in seeking the boar, than risk the annihilation of self which loving Venus threatens.

In Venus' rage and grief at being cheated by death of her prize, she utters a long prophecy that is part curse. In predicting that "Sorrow on love hereafter shall attend" [l. 1136], she expresses the Ovidian view of eros as a capricious, arbitrary force which levels mankind. All must love, but none shall find perfect satisfaction:

> It shall be sparing, and too full of riot,
> Teaching decrepit age to tread the measures;
> The staring ruffian shall it keep in quiet,
> Pluck down the rich, enrich the poor with treasures;
>   It shall be raging mad, and silly mild,
>   Make the young old, the old become a child.
>   [ll. 1147-52]

Her own aborted love affair is the model for this vision of a world turned upside down by love: the woman aggressively wooing the passive boy, the goddess of love herself denied love. In five stanzas of encyclopedic example, she equates eros with conflict and frustration: "They that love best, their loves shall not enjoy" [l. 1164].

This picture of perpetual struggle then gives rise to Adonis' metamorphosis, the symbolic resolution of his struggle against eros. His transformation to a purple (from Lat. *purpureus,* a variety of red) and white flower represents the ending of the war of white and red mentioned so often. Adonis' pale coldness opposed Venus' fiery ardor; in death, his red blood stained the perfect whiteness of his skin. Now, as a flower, he can "grow unto himself" [l. 1180] as he wanted to in life, and Venus can possess him totally and forever as she could not before. But in order to do so, she must pick the flower—that is, she must kill him.

Thus in one sense, the ending recapitulates the fear of eros which dominated Adonis in life. When Venus picks the flower and puts it in her bosom, sexual fusion is equated with death, and envisioned as her total possession of him, obliterating his identity. But the terms of union are no longer sexual: they are infantile. Venus calls Adonis the father of this flower, and puts the baby in the father's place, at the breast:

> Here was thy father's bed, here in my breast;
> Thou art the next of blood, and 'tis my right.
> Lo in this hollow cradle take thy rest;
> My throbbing heart shall rock thee day and night:
>   There shall not be one minute in an hour
>   Wherein I will not kiss my sweet love's flower.
>   [ll. 1183-88]

The devouring mother whose oral demands constituted a threat to Adonis' very identity has now become the nurturant mother on whom he depends as an infant for survival. Several previous mentions of Adonis as an infant and Venus as a mother have hinted at this relationship. Taunting him for his coldness, Venus asks "Art thou a woman's son. . . . ?" [l. 201] and later describes him as "a son that sucked an earthly mother" [l. 863]. When she searches anxiously for him in the hunt, she is compared to "a milch doe, whose swelling dugs do ache. / Hasting to feed her fawn" [ll. 874-75]. In the stanza quoted above, the fierce oral qualities of Venus' desire are transmuted to an omnipotent maternal tenderness which nevertheless carries disturbing overtones of Adonis' anxieties about sexual fusion: "it is as good / To wither in my breast as in his blood" [ll. 1181-82], says Venus to the flower. Here Shakespeare suggests that this resolution of Adonis' dilemma is but another kind of death, parallel to the murder of the self through narcissistic withdrawal. Venus' apostrophe to the flower concludes with the image which dominates the poem, a kiss—the kind of perpetual oral gratification she sought in the poem. No longer able to deny her, Adonis is now but a gratifying object, lacking mind and will.

The metamorphosis, however, can just as fittingly be seen as the fulfillment of his deepest narcissistic wish: to regress to the state in which he had no separate identity—nothing to fight for and nothing to lose. Paradoxically, though in this state he is wholly dependent on Venus, he also dominates her totally; he is always with her and she kisses him every minute. The metamorphosis is undeniably tender and moving: it appeals to a desire present to some degree in all of us. But it also implies the desperation underlying the narcissist's dominance. Adonis has finally allowed Venus to get close to him, on the only terms he can tolerate: her total subservience to his need for constant reassurance.

Thus the poem's ending is as ambivalent as any narcissist

could wish. Venus loses her lover to the boar, but wins symbolic possession of him as a flower. Adonis successfully fights off Venus' sexual demands, but surrenders to her all-embracing love after death. In his total passivity, he dominates Venus, but she also dominates him. *Venus and Adonis* has long been seen as a young man's poem for relatively superficial reasons: its erotic subject matter and sensuous playfulness. But Shakespeare deserves more credit than he has been given for his understanding of youth's deeper conflicts, of the ways in which eros shapes the growing self. (pp. 352-71)

> *Coppélia Kahn, "Self and Eros in 'Venus and Adonis',"* in The Centennial Review, *Vol. XX, No. 4, Fall, 1976, pp. 351-71.*

CLARK HULSE   (essay date 1978)

[*Hulse examines the relation between* Venus and Adonis *and "mythography," a process in painting and poetry in which a story is told by means of carefully constructed symbols or emblems, each of which represents a particular attribute of character or series of events. The symbol associated with Adonis is the flower, the critic observes, signifying the beauty that must inevitably fade. Venus, however, is identified by many symbols, including the jennet, the milch doe, and the boar, revealing the multiple aspects of love. The poem is structured, Hulse contends, around a series of oppositions in both the imagery and the plot. Although these conflicts are never resolved in the poem, an appearance of unity and cohesion is achieved as Shakespeare, in a process the critic likens to the creation of myths, continually constructs new sets of symbols that represent and reconcile "the paradoxes of experience."*]

Shakespeare alters the myth of Venus and Adonis so casually that the importance of his change is not at first apparent. Instead of being Love's lover, as in ancient literary sources, Adonis leaves her flat on her back and runs off to hunt with the boys. This interpretation had appeared before in the Renaissance, in Titian and in Marlowe, and Shakespeare's treatment may owe something to them, to the stories of Narcissus and of Salmacis and Hermaphroditus, or to the poet's obscure relationship with the Earl of Southampton. Whatever its origin, though, the change threatens to make hash of the poem. Advancing on Adonis in the first lines, Venus seems to become a sweaty, muscular rapist. In the middle, as Adonis resists her, the sweet couple fall into a philosophic bicker over whether Venus or Diana is the author of death. At the end, Venus bursts into a passionate lament over the dead Adonis, which is admirable poetry but is utterly inconsistent with her earlier characterization as a comic seducer and immoral lecher. And why is Adonis killed for what he didn't do or, worse yet, why didn't he do it? The modern reader, as J. W. Lever sums it up, usually takes the poem as "a very funny story which somehow forgets the joke; or as a highly cautionary tale which, in showing the dangers of caution, does not point the moral at all well" [see Additional Bibliography].

A famous poet [Richard Wilbur] has remarked that it is hard to applaud *Venus and Adonis* unless one knows the rules of the game [see Additional Bibliography]. A basic rule of myth, which differentiates it from other stories, is that it has some force, or appeal to the imagination, that overcomes seeming contradictions and improbabilities. It creates chimeras—serpent, goat, and lion held together by unnatural force. Shakespeare draws far more than we have realized on the highly sophisticated tradition of allegorical poetry and painting, so that the various aspects of his Venus portray alternately the comic and serious qualities of physical love, while the death of Adonis suggests the internal contradiction of earthly beauty, whose splendor comes at the price of transience. Yet the poem adds up to no homily on love. In the strife between Venus and Adonis, Shakespeare holds his conflicting attitudes toward earthly love in an esthetic balance through a form that, in the same iconographic tradition, is both narrative and pictorial. This form in itself seems to be one solution to that characteristic Shakespearean ambivalence, the living "in uncertainties, Mysteries, doubts," which, as a systematic way of thinking, resembles primitive myth.

An acceptable general theory of myth is hard to come by. With the passing of the once easy rule of the *Golden Bough* [by Sir James George Frazer], the territory has been reduced to chaos amid the strife of ritualists, psychologists, and structuralists. One might try to reconcile them around the idea of mediation. For Frazer, Cassirer, and the ritualists, myth intervenes between the sacred and the profane; for Freud and Campbell, between the unconscious and the conscious; for Jung, between the individual and the collective; for Lévi-Strauss, between the polarities and contradictions of a social system. But even if one could overcome the vast differences in methodology involved, such a compromise definition can finally be no more than an analogue to esthetic form and can only account for some rudimentary unity that Shakespeare's poem would share with any work based on the same myth. To account for Shakespeare's variations on the story, myth criticism must be joined to literary history, to see how the myth developed in the Renaissance, especially in the mythographic tradition that largely shaped Shakespeare's material.

Most significant for Shakespeare's poem was the development of the attribute system as a way of representing mythic characters in allegorical poetry and painting. A description of a god or goddess in, say, Vincenzo Cartari's *Le imagini de i dei de gli antichi* will show a unitary figure—suitable for a painting, emblem, or medallion—decorated and embellished with various attributes, each the relic of a story about the deity and the symbol of an abstract quality. Venus, for instance, is described with a rose, which recalls how she cut her foot as she ran to the dying Adonis and represents the painful side of love.

The technique is, of course, not restricted to pagan subjects. The archangel Raphael, for instance, is regularly depicted with a youth carrying a fish, recalling the tale of Tobias and signifying Raphael's role as the "affable archangel" who aids and protects men. Tobias is his attribute, as the rose is Venus', or the caduceus is Mercury's. Mythography, then, is not just a content but a *process* of representation, a continual infolding and unfolding of pictorial and narrative forms. It mediates between two modes of conception, between discursive and nondiscursive thinking: the material of the visual world is made into narrative, narrative into argument, and argument into vision.

That Shakespeare uses mythography as a formal constituent of his poetry is amply illustrated by the figure of Adonis. Arthur Golding, Shakespeare's favorite translator of Ovid, wrote in his Dedicatory Epistle to the Earl of Leicester that Book x of the *Metamorphoses* "chiefly doth contain one kind of argument, / Reproving most prodigious lusts." The same argument springs to the lips of Adonis when he rejects Venus. Yet she has a word or two of answer; and anyway, Adonis'

refusal means that the pair will enact no lusts worthy of reproof, so Shakespeare's own position must go beyond Golding's simpleminded moral. Golding's source, the Regius-Micyllus Ovid, indeed offers more varied allegory. Historically, the myth recalls ancient religious festivals in Assyria. Physically interpreted, Adonis represents the crops of the earth, as Micyllus learned from scholia in Theocritus, No. 3. Or, in Boccaccio's version, Adonis is the sun and Venus the earth; their love brings forth lush flowers, leaves, and ripe fruit. But winter is like the boar that slays the beautiful Adonis, for then the sun seems banished from our world, Venus mourns, the earth lies barren.

The most common interpretation, though, is suggested by Ovid himself. When Adonis is changed to a flower at the end of his tale, he writes: . . .

> . . . But short-lived is their flower;
> for the winds from which it takes its name shake off the flower
> so delicately clinging and doomed too easily to fall.

This sense of transience acquires almost proverbial weight as it is repeated by mythographers. Boccaccio writes [in his *Genealogie*]:

> But as to the fact that Adonis is transformed into a flower: by that invention I think is shown to us the brevity of beauty, which in the morning is richly colored, but at a late hour, drooping and pale, grows feeble; and so mankind in the morn, that is, in the time of youth, is blooming and splendid; but in the eve, that is, in the time of old age, we grow pale, and we fall into the shadows of death.

What this philosophical interpretation has in common with the physical is the importance given to flowers. In one case, Adonis *is like* a flower; in the other, he *causes* flowers. Both statements describe the action of Shakespeare's poem. Its opening lines link Adonis to the purple sun:

> Even as the sun with purple-colour'd face
> Had ta'en his last leave of the weeping morn,
> Rose-cheek'd Adonis hied him to the chase.
>
> [ll. 1-3]

At the end, his purple blood begets a flower:

> And in his blood that on the ground lay spill'd,
> A purple flower sprung up, checker'd with white,
> Resembling well his pale cheeks and the blood
> Which in round drops upon their whiteness stood.
>
> [ll. 1167-70]

Throughout, he is linked to flowers, explicitly as a metaphor for his beauty:

> "Thrice fairer than myself," thus she began,
> "The field's chief flower, sweet above compare;
> Stain to all nymphs, more lovely than a man,
> More white and red than doves or roses are."
>
> [ll. 7-10]

The realization that Adonis is Beauty, which fadeth like the flower, explains his peculiar, unmotivated death. Beauty fades, flowers wither, no matter what. His death does not show a doom that awaits lechery, since he will have none, and Venus (who he does think is a lecher) has sought to protect him. Certainly it does not prove that sex is very nice; it proves simply that beauty fades. In short, the sequence of the narrative is not finally a causal or argumentative sequence; rather, it is an unfolding of Adonis' attributes, a making explicit of what is implicit in line 8—"the field's chief flower." Shakespeare can say he *is* a flower, while a painter would show him *with* a flower; the narrative repeats this attribute by showing him *becoming* a flower. Narratively, he must die to become that flower, and what the flower means is that he must die.

If Shakespeare's portrayal of Adonis is deceptive only because it is so simple, the portrait of Venus is a genuine problem. That Venus is Love is axiomatic; that she is earthly love is quickly apparent. Adonis calls her Lust; she herself claims to be fruitful and generative; and her hand is moist, the proper characteristic of a passionate lover. George Wyndham, the first modern critic of the poem, likened her to Botticelli's Venus, rising from the foam [see excerpt above, 1898]. But, if she is born of the sea, it is in Abraham Fraunce's sense [in his *Countesse of Pembrokes Yvychurch*]:

> She is borne of the sea, lovers are inconstant, like
> the troubled waves of the sea: Hereof was she also
> called *Aphrodite*, of the froath of the sea, being like
> to *Sperma*.

Shakespeare's description of her is a metaphoric catalog of the characteristics of physical love. When he wishes to show that love is light, that is, merry and delightful, he says that Venus does not weigh much:

> "Witness this primrose bank whereon I lie:
> These forceless flowers like sturdy trees support
>   me. . . .
> Is love so light, sweet boy, and may it be
> That thou should think it heavy unto thee?"
>
> [ll. 151-52, 155-56]

The pun is outrageous, and the figure contorted, for its literal and metaphoric senses have reversed positions. As Cartari prescribes, the principal characteristics of the god are those that signify the god's nature and effects. We are used to the physical being the literal, but literally Venus is delightful, and so she is figured as if she were light in weight. But, curiously, this reversal changes the impact of the image; instead of seeing a sylph supported on flowers, we see tree trunks, holding aloft an awesome bulk. This is the core of the poem's problem. If one grants that Venus is earthly love, what is the attitude toward earthly love? Is it loathsome, foul lust? Delightful sense? A near-sacred force of natural propagation?

The most casual glance at the sonnets would remind us that Shakespeare is perfectly capable of portraying love in all three ways. *Venus and Adonis* opens in travesty, as if love were something that reduces humans to the grotesque and foolish:

> Over one arm the lusty courser's rein,
> Under her other was the tender boy,
>
> [ll. 31-2]

Backward she push'd him, as she would be thrust,
And govern'd him in strength, though not in lust.

> [ll. 41-2]

> "Were I hard-favour'd, foul, or wrinkled old,
> Ill-nurtur'd, crooked, churlish, harsh in voice,
> O'erworn, despised, rheumatic and cold.
> Thick-sighted, barren, lean, and lacking juice,
>   Then mightst thou pause, for then I were not for
>   thee."
>
> [ll. 133-37]

He wrings her nose, he strikes her on the cheeks,
He bends her fingers, holds her pulses hard.

> [ll. 475-76]

She sinketh down, still hanging by his neck;
He on her belly falls, she on her back.

> [ll. 593-94]

If the moments of direct physical contact are ludicrous, the passages of enticement reveal the sensuality that led Francis Meres to call Shakespeare "Mellifluous & hony-tongued" [see excerpt above, 1598]:

> "Bid me discourse, I will enchant thine ear,
> Or like a fairy trip upon the green,
> Or like a nymph, with long dishevell'd hair,
> Dance on the sands, and yet no footing seen."
>
> [ll. 145-48]

> "Sweet bottom grass and high delightful plain,
> Round rising hillocks, brakes obscure and rough,
> To shelter thee from tempest and from rain:
>   Then be my deer, since I am such a park."
>
> [ll. 236-39]

These two moods have won the poem its reputation for comic sensuousness. But there is another tone, like to that of Sonnet 129—"The expense of spirit in a waste of shame"—in which love is presented as a violent force of destruction:

> Even as an empty eagle, sharp by fast,
> Tires with her beak on feathers, flesh and bone,
> Shaking her wings, devouring all in haste,
> Till either gorge be stuff'd or prey be gone:
>   Even so she kiss'd his brow, his cheek, his chin.
>
> [ll. 55-9]

> And having felt the sweetness of the spoil,
> With blindfold fury she begins to forage;
> Her face doth reek and smoke, her blood doth boil,
> And careless lust stirs up a desperate courage,
>   Planting oblivion, beating reason back,
>   Forgetting shame's pure blush and honour's
>   wrack.
>
> [ll. 553-58]

We have, in effect, not one but three Venuses—comic, sensual, and violent—all embodying earthly love but differently depicted to reveal different aspects. Venus is the empty eagle, the randy jennet, the tender snail, the anguished milch doe, and the timid hare. Even the boar is finally her animal. Traditionally, the boar represents jealousy, because Mars took its shape to eliminate his rival. In Shakespeare's version, Mars has been mastered by Venus, who is herself the jealous one, that is, possessive of Adonis. When first the boar is mentioned, she quakes with fear of loss:

> "For where love reigns, disturbing jealousy
> Doth call himself affection's sentinel; . . .
>   Distemp'ring gentle love in his desire,
>   As air and water do abate the fire."
>
> [ll. 649-50, 653-54]

So, when the boar appears, he possesses Adonis with a firm embrace that Venus can only envy:

> "And nuzzling in his flank, the loving swine
> Sheath'd unaware the tusk in his soft groin.

> "Had I been tooth'd like him, I must confess,
> With kissing him I should have kill'd him first."
>
> [ll. 1115-18]

Venus is a series of images, even of puns, like the strange animal-headed figures who inhabit the pages of Cartari. Contradictory elements require contradictory figures. Cartari depicts Venus five different ways, and once, rather like Shakespeare, groups three different Venuses in the same frame. . . .

Too much can be made of the "character" of Shakespeare's Venus. She is no Lady Macbeth or Prince Hamlet. The idea of character requires a personality continuous over a period of time. But not the allegorical figure, as Dante explained in *La vita nuova:* one "could be puzzled at my speaking of Love as if it were a thing in itself, as if it were not only an intellectual substance, but also a bodily substance. This is patently false, for Love does not exist in itself as a substance, but is an accident in a substance." Shakespeare's mythic goddess is not so much a person as a diverse group of actions inhabiting a single body.

If the characters of Venus and Adonis show the kinship in this instance between poetry and the visual arts, they may also remind us of Lessing's warning [in his *Laöcoon*] about the fundamental difference between the arts. Painting, he says, employs figures and colors in space and imitates bodies; poetry articulates sounds in time and imitates actions. The mythographic depiction of Shakespeare's characters gives them a self-contained unity, a perfect balance of action and physique within each figure. But that very completeness *within* the figures transforms the traditional relationship *between* them: Adonis no longer needs an affair with Venus to define himself. Shakespeare goes further still, making Adonis not just indifferent to Venus but downright disdainful of her. This novel arrangement, we may recall, was devised by Titian, in whose painting we may find mythographic structures that break down Lessing's dichotomy between iconic and discursive forms and offer a model for Shakespeare's handling of the affair.

Titian's *Venus and Adonis* is built around conflict—Adonis pulls away, Venus restrains him. Dogs and boar spear are his attributes; an overturned urn is hers. In the background is an inert, winged figure, his bow and quiver hanging from a nearby tree. Panofsky identifies him as a sleeping Cupid, symbolic of cool passions [see Additional Bibliography]. Ovid and others, though, tell us of the resemblance of Adonis to Cupid; they look so much alike that, unless one had wings and the other his quiver, we could not tell them apart. This figure, equipped with both wings and quiver, lies in the same position as the dying Adonis in illustrated Ovids of the Renaissance, so the dead shepherd may here be fused with the sleeping boy, reminding us of the conclusion of the tale. The allegorical significance of the physical conflict is clear enough: *eros* versus *heros.* But the painting offers no solution to the conflict—its unity is strictly esthetic, achieved through synthetic perspective, a masterful use of color, and a balance of horizontals and verticals accented by the single diagonal of the intertwined figures.

Titian's painting, then, can work as a narrative, much as narratives can work as pictures. He can imply narrative through the depiction of attributes; through gesture, which is itself interrupted action; and through the device of continuous representation, in which the several scenes of a painting depict successive events. He can also use space as an equivalent to logical extension, so that the visual relationship of his figures expresses their conceptual relationship. As each figure is allegorized to become an abstraction, so space is allegorized to become a visual syntax. The introduction of temporal and allegorical sequence, though, threatens to fragment the visual realm of imitation. Pictorial success then depends upon the artist's ability to control the tension between visual and rhetorical schemes through the unifying forces of three-dimensional perspective and two-dimensional symmetry, in order to create a "speaking picture," in which the ocular unity of the scene brings a sense of completeness to the story and argument.

In attaining its narrative unity, Shakespeare's poem, like Titian's painting, seems to operate through a reconciliation of tension, in which visual images hold together the machinery of an incomplete argumentative sequence. Shakespeare's fundamental alteration of the myth, we may recall, was to make Venus and Adonis antagonists instead of lovers. Precisely what this does is to place them physically in a tableau of conflict and to transform this conflict of action into a conflict of ideas, enacted in a formal debate. Why does beauty wither? Venus argues that Diana, goddess of chastity and narcissism, is to blame and that love is the force that preserves:

> "And therefore hath [Diana] brib'd the destinies
> To cross the curious workmanship of nature,
> To mingle beauty with infirmities
> And pure perfection with impure defeature,
>   Making it subject to the tyranny
>   Of mad mischances and much misery."
>
> [ll. 733-38]

Adonis will have none of it. Venus he sees unequivocally as lust—not Venus Genetrix, but Venus Vulgaris. Passion itself, then, is the force of death:

> "Call it not love, for love to heaven is fled,
> Since sweating lust on earth usurp'd his name;
> Under whose simple semblance he hath fed
> Upon fresh beauty, blotting it with blame;
>   Which the hot tyrant stains and soon bereaves,
>   As caterpillars do the tender leaves."
>
> [ll. 793-98]

The debate between Venus and Adonis persistently resolves into the more traditional debate between Venus and Diana, which, in as immediate a source as Book III of [Spenser's] the *Faerie Queene,* represents warring attitudes toward sexual love. Both goddesses are, in their way, hunters, though of different prey. Ovid tells how Venus, . . .

> over mountain ridges, through the woods, over rocky places set with thorns, she ranges with her garments girt up to her knees after the manner of Diana. She also cheers on the hounds and pursues those creatures which are safe to hunt, such as the headlong hares, or the stag with high-branching horns, or the timid doe.

Ovid lightly parodies the passage in Vergil's *Aeneid* where Venus in the guise of Diana helps Aeneas in his epic quest. The choice between the "hard hunt" for the boar and the "soft hunt" for Wat the hare becomes a choice between the heroic and erotic lives, as Titian knew.

Venus tells us how in erotic mastery she subdued the virile Mars:

> "Thus he that overrul'd I oversway'd,
> Leading him prisoner in a red rose chain:
> Strong-temper'd steel his stronger strength obey'd,

Yet was he servile to my coy disdain."

[ll. 109-12]

If Mars here is robbed of heroism, one may recall that to the Neoplatonists the love of Mars and Venus was an allegory of a transcendent concordance of Virtue and Pleasure. Shakespeare too crosses his debate structure with images suggesting a reconciliation between eros and heroism. Adonis' horse is an epic steed, fit for the fields of praise; yet he is also a descendant of Plato's dark horse [in his *Phaedrus*], the emblem of license. The horse simultaneously breaks his servile bondage and unbridles his lust:

> The iron bit he crusheth 'tween his teeth,
> Controlling what he was controlled with.

[ll. 269-70]

Adonis too has been in bondage to Venus:

> Look how a bird lies tangled in a net,
> So fasten'd in her arms Adonis lies.

[ll. 67-8]

Although Venus conquered Mars, Adonis has conquered her, and has a chance to reenact his horse's epic deed:

> Now is she in the very lists of love,
> Her champion mounted for the hot encounter.
> All is imaginary she doth prove;
> He will not manage her, although he mount her.

[ll. 595-98]

The moment of union slips away, love's freedom and bondage still at strife.

The debate structure of the poem permeates not only individual symbols but the syntax of the verse as well, so that images are yoked in warring pairs. At the opening of the poem, red and white appear as a smooth parallel: Adonis' cheek is "more white and red than doves or roses are" [l. 10]. It is a familiar Petrarchist trope for the complexion of the beloved, embodying that blend of opposites which defines beauty and linking this master-mistress with the birds and flowers sacred to Venus.

As Adonis demurs, the conceit is inverted to show his unreadiness for love: "He red for shame, but frosty in desire" [l. 36]. Syntactically the colors are now in opposition, yet metaphorically they again express parallel sentiments—shame and disdain, both aspects of *pudor*. When the figure is transferred to Venus, its tension is heightened, reflecting a clash of emotions:

> . . . the fighting conflict of her hue,
> How white and red each other did destroy!
> But now her cheek was pale, and by and by
> It flash'd forth fire, as lightning from the sky.

[ll. 345-48]

The figure then goes underground, only to make two startling reappearances, one at the first sight of the boar:

> Whose frothy mouth bepainted all with red,
> Like milk and blood being mingled both together.

[ll. 901-02]

Syntactically the colors are in harmony, but, because of its position in the narrative, the conceit is a torturous mockery, death in the garments of love. Then the corpse of Adonis is transformed:

> A purple flower sprung up, checker'd with white,

> Resembling well his pale cheeks and the blood
> Which in round drops upon their whiteness stood.

[ll. 1168-70]

In the dozens of versions of this myth in classical and Renaissance verse and prose, nowhere else is the flower both red and white. Some say Adonis is turned to a rose, some say to an anemone, and some record that the flower formerly was white but now is stained red with the shepherd's blood. Shakespeare's insistence is clear, recalling the antithesis one last time, restored nearly to its original form but applied now to an object that is the negation of the original—a summation of the struggle among Venus, Adonis, and the boar.

The war of red flame and pale frost is echoed by the more elementary strife of fire and water. Ovid, at the opening of the *Metamorphoses,* tells how an unknown god bound in harmony the warring elements. Natali Conti [in his *Mythologia*], meditating on a passage in Euripides, discovers that Harmony is "the offspring of the elements of all things; and that force which is born from the motion of celestial bodies, whether we call it divine or natural, acting so that the elements themselves are led into this mixture, or rather leading them, that force is called Venus." Shakespeare's Venus strives to harmonize the elements, as they appear in various guises: in climatic terms, they are wind, sun, earth, and rain; in emotional terms, sighs, desires, disdain, and tears. As Aphrodite, foam-born, she is already hot and moist . . . :

> "My flesh is soft and plump, my marrow burning.
> My smooth moist hand, were it with thy hand felt,
> Would in thy palm dissolve, or seem to melt."

[ll. 142-44]

While love is, as she tells us, all fire [l. 149], the excess of burning passion will "set the heart on fire" [l. 388] and must be cooled with tears. The hot and dry of fire oppose the cold and moist of water, so that between the two elements there can be either chaotic strife or creative union. In the balance of these elements, as Adonis points out, lies the distinction between sweet love and sour lust:

> "Love comforteth like sunshine after rain,
> But lust's effect is tempest after sun;
> Love's gentle spring doth always fresh remain,
> Lust's winter comes ere summer half be done."

[ll. 799-802]

The union of Mars and Venus is precisely the harmonious blending of heat and moisture. . . . Venus seeks such a union with Adonis, but he is cold and dry, with his eyes and passions fixed on earth [ll. 118, 340], and he can only intermittently supply either heat or moisture:

> Panting he lies and breatheth on her face.
> She feedeth on the steam as on a prey,
> And calls it heavenly moisture.

[ll. 62-4]

> He sees her coming, and begins to glow,
> Even as a dying coal revives with wind.

[ll. 337-38]

Adonis spoke sound doctrine concerning the elements but refuses the act of temperance of which Shakespeare wrote in his Anacreontic sonnets (Nos. 153-54): to cool his torch in her fountain. The strife of elements with which Venus is left makes her subject to a chaos within, the very tempest that Adonis predicted. Her grief at his loss is an earthquake of wind struggling with earth [ll. 1046-47], and she threatens finally to consume herself in a reaction of air, earth, fire, and water that seems like a reverse alchemy:

> "My sighs are blown away, my salt tears gone;
> Mine eyes are turn'd to fire, my heart to lead.
>   Heavy heart's lead melt at mine eyes' red fire!
>   So shall I die by drops of hot desire."
>
> [ll. 1071-74]

The struggle to harmonize the elements, as Pico believed [in his *A Platonic Discourse upon Love*], was the struggle for the *discordia concordans* that sustains love and beauty. The inability of Venus to overcome that strife foreshadows the tragic ending of the poem. The debate structure, operating in individual lines and images as well as in the central action of the poem, becomes a syntactic principle that prepares us for a resolution, in which the unity of the poem would reside in the simultaneous closure of plot and argument. The ending of the poem, indeed, is cast as an etiology, appropriate for the conclusion of a rationalized myth:

> "For he being dead, with him is beauty slain,
> And beauty dead, black Chaos comes again."
>
> [ll. 1019-20]

> "Since thou art dead, lo here I prophesy,
> Sorrow on love hereafter shall attend:
> It shall be waited on with jealousy,
> Find sweet beginning, but unsavoury end."
>
> [ll. 1135-38]

Precisely at the point where we expect logical conclusion, though, the syntax of plot and argument breaks down, for the etiology is false. Black Chaos is already loose in the world in Cynthia's jealousy, in the bristling boar, and in Venus' own passions, which from their sweet beginning were full of gluttony, jealousy, wrath, and anguish. Shakespeare has stretched the sinews of prolepsis, for the action of the poem is as much a result as a cause of its conclusion. As if that were not enough, Shakespeare adds a second conclusion, which demonstrates the opposite point about love. From the blood of Adonis springs a flower, which Venus plucks: so Venus remains faithful to Adonis, and the two are, finally, fruitful:

> "Here was thy father's bed, here in my breast;
> Thou art the next of blood, and 'tis thy right.
> Lo in this hollow cradle take thy rest;
> My throbbing heart shall rock thee day and night:
>   There shall not be one minute in an hour
>   Wherein I will not kiss my sweet love's flower."
>
> [ll. 1183-88]

The debate between Venus and Adonis is never resolved. A series of metaphors mediates between them, each of which generates the same antithesis. Love is life and death, harmony and chaos, bliss and agony, beauty and horror—the paradoxes teeter out of sight on the even feet of oxymoron:

> "Ne'er settled equally, but high or low,
> That all love's pleasure shall not match his woe."
>
> [ll. 1139-40]

The tension of paradox, though, is constantly released by the shifting structures of the poem: by its proleptic narrative, by its double ending. The terms of the debate slide from one set of images to another, joined at innumerable points. The conflict moves from syllogisms to proverbs, to goddesses, to horses and rabbits, to colors and elements. With each set of terms, an abstract dualism is momentarily balanced in a sen-

sible image, generating a kind of "insight," or brief resolution, for, as E. H. Gombrich observes [in his *Symbolic Images: Studies in the Art of the Renaissance*], "the sense of sight provides an analogue to the non-discursive mode of apprehension which must travel from multiplicity to unity." In that pattern of tension and release, of the recurrent dualism momentarily resolved in an image, lies the experience of cohesion that gives unity to the poem.

Shakespeare's literary myth comes surprisingly close to the function that Lévi-Strauss suggested for primary myth [in his *Structural Anthropology*]: to bridge the gap between conflicting values through "a series of mediating devices, each of which generates the next one by a process of opposition and correlation. . . . The kind of logic in mythical thought is as rigorous as that of modern science . . . the difference lies, not in the quality of the intellectual process, but in the nature of the things to which it is applied." Just as primary myth may be an alternative form of logical reasoning indulged in by whole societies, Shakespeare's manner of paradox making has the characteristics of a persistent personal syntax. Indeed, if we once again think of myth as a conceptual form rather than as a content, we might call it Shakespeare's personal myth, a way of perceiving and reconciling the paradoxes of experience.

Venus and Adonis has been compared to the sonnets, the early comedies, even the tragedies. In its handling of paradox, it most closely resembles the mature comedies, or even a problem comedy. What makes a problem comedy problematic is the realization that the tension between opposed values is a permanent condition of life. In *Measure for Measure*, Angelo and Escalus enter into a formal debate between Justice and Mercy in Act II, but the conflict disappears in the final sentencing of all the characters to marriage. High comedy conceals similar difficulties, for its argument, as Northrop Frye tells us [in his essay "The Argument of Comedy], is individual fulfillment and social harmony—admirable values both, but perhaps less easily reconciled than Frye's formula would admit. *As You Like It* is obviously a play working toward both values, and its ending brings them into a *theatrical* balance through the simple technique of a double ending. First Hymen, the embodiment of social harmony, links each couple; then Jaques, the soul of humorous individualism, repeats Hymen's action and nearly his very words, giving to each the fulfillment of his ambition.

Two insightful critics of Shakespeare, Norman Rabkin and Stephen Booth, have examined this obsessive paradox making. In *Hamlet,* Rabkin finds [in his *Shakespeare and the Common Understanding*], "Shakespeare tends to structure his imitations in terms of a pair of polar opposites," between which we must, but cannot, choose. Examining the sonnets [in his *An Essay on Shakespeare's Sonnets*], Booth finds the reverse—that one set of opposites is incommensurate with another—that syntactic paradox leads us one way, imagistic paradox another, prosodic a third, with no release of the tension created. *Venus and Adonis* offers us, I think, something between the two models: by shifting in the manner described by Booth, from one set of terms—one whole structure—to another, a release from paradox is achieved. The style of *Venus and Adonis* might best be epitomized in the metaphors of red and white: a constant shifting of the significance of the images and of the syntactic structures linking them, which are held together as a series simply by the repetition of the image itself.

As Rabkin observes, though, the reconciliation "cannot be reduced to prose paraphrase or statements of theme because the kind of 'statement' a given play makes cannot respectably be made in the logical language of prose." For a work like *Venus and Adonis,* where the serial form of narrative encourages the serial form of logical discourse, the achievement of a purely esthetic resolution is particularly fine. It is done by shifting out of the dialogue of argument into a discourse of images—iconography—thus opening the possibility of an iconic resolution of the same sort that Shakespeare habitually achieved on the stage through the visual image of coupling. Paradox, then, is too neat a word; it suggests a final, balanced position, the *seeming* opposition overcome. Shakespearean paradox, in *Venus and Adonis* at least, is a problem, not of seeing or seeming, but of being. Erotic experience can be described only by combining two ways of thinking, the discursive and the iconic, and shuttling from one to the other when the variety of that experience can be described in no other words and the unity recalled in no other way. (pp. 95-103)

Clark Hulse, "Shakespeare's Myth of Venus and Adonis," in PMLA, Vol. 93, No. 1, January, 1978, pp. 95-105.

JOHN DOEBLER (essay date 1983)

[*Doebler argues in the following excerpt that* Venus and Ado-

nis *is "a constantly shifting drama of the mind," in which Shakespeare evokes a detached, intellectual response from his readers. By carefully varying the poem's theme and tone from comic to sensual to pathetic, the critic claims, Shakespeare creates complex, multifaceted characters and situations that defy definitive interpretation.*]

> Thus weary of the world, away she hies,
> And yokes her silver doves, by whose swift aid
> Their mistress mounted through the empty skies,
> In her light chariot quickly is convey'd,
>   Holding their course to Paphos, where their
>   queen
>   Means to immure herself and not be seen.
>
>   [ll. 1189-94]

This graceful ending to *Venus and Adonis* makes it difficult to believe that so many readers of the poem conclude it with a feeling of exasperation. Perhaps part of the problem is the tendency to force every stanza into a single mold. The range of traditional interpretations includes artistic failure, Neoplatonic allegory, and sexual comedy. Even Freudian ambivalence is now suggested with increasing frequency. I propose a response to the shifting rhetoric of the poem that takes into account the several personalities Venus has in both the philosophy and the mythography of the Renaissance. The poem can not be held to a single tone, nor does only one Venus,

Venus and Adonis. By Titian.

486

however ambivalent, command the attention of Shake-speare's contemporaries. (p. 33)

The most helpful way into the artistry of *Venus and Adonis* may still be Coleridge [see excerpt above, 1817], whose observations on the poem have been cited by Douglas Bush [see excerpt above, 1932] and a number of others.

In his *Biographia Literaria* Coleridge comments on the "aloofness" of Shakespeare from his account, forcing the reader into intellectual stimulation rather than feeling participation and diverting our attention from the possibilities available to the flesh by a thousand shifts in image and tone. We are simply kept too busy in mind, eye, and literary response to focus and thus engage our attention, erotic or moral. If Coleridge is fundamentally correct, it is no wonder that very different conclusions have been reached by those who would pin the poem down to a consistent point of view, including not only those favorable to Renaissance didacticism and allegory but also those who discover modern sexual playfulness or Freudian ambivalence. The buried assumption shared by nearly everyone but Coleridge reaches the surface in an article by W. R. Streitberger: "Unless we are willing to give the poem up as defective, the key to a unified interpretation must lie in a theme which satisfactorily relates all of its elements" [see Additional Bibliography]. The problem of redeeming the poem from defectiveness by the discovery of a single "theme" or "unified interpretation," however complex or "ambivalent," has been the unsolved problem in this century. Coleridge earlier went beyond the problem by not seeing it as one. *Venus and Adonis* does not have the single impetus of either lyrical expression or allegory, the reason why it was disliked by both Samuel Butler [in his *Note-Books*] and C. S. Lewis [see excerpt above, 1954]. Yet C. S. Lewis, who found the poem both confusing and distasteful, did understand its theatrical effect. According to Lewis, Shakespeare "could not help knowing what the wooing of Adonis by Venus . . . would have looked like to a spectator." In Coleridge's phrase, "the utter aloofness" of Shakespeare makes us the "spectator" described by Lewis. *Venus and Adonis* is a constantly shifting drama of the mind, divided into at least two acts and a number of scenes.

The two broad divisions, the attempted seduction of Adonis and the grief of Venus over her slain beloved, have caused no end of scholarly and critical anguish because these divisions seem sharply contrasting in theme and tone. J. W. Lever has put the problem well when he says that most of us take the poem as "a very funny story which somehow forgets the joke" [see Additional Bibliography]. But the Renaissance has no apparent difficulty with sudden conversions and changes of heart when it comes to drama. The change of Leontes in *The Winter's Tale* from insane jealousy to grief-stricken repentance is instant upon the news of his son's death. The conversion is motivated not by rational (or even supernatural) proof of his wife's fidelity but by a feeling response to the death of his only and beloved son. One passion drives out another as one nail drives out another, one of the commonplaces of Renaissance psychology. In *Venus and Adonis* the comic lust of sweaty hands, glued kisses, and steaming breath is rendered in a shifting way in the first section of the poem, but both the lust in the bowels of Venus and our amusement at her expense (as well as at the expense of Adonis to some extent) are driven out by the actual death of her beloved. The poem ends in pathos, if not tragedy, with Adonis suffering an agonizing death and Venus freed from the tyranny of lust and restored to the heavens.

The Renaissance simply had not fixed its dramatic genres in the manner of ancient Greece and Rome, and Shakespeare, through Polonius [in *Hamlet*], clearly ridicules the attempt to find labels for all the different possibilities. *Venus and Adonis*, like a Shakespearean play, should be experienced scene by scene, at times even line by line, in the spirit of both Coleridge's understanding of the poem and recent criticism about the best way of encountering the plays.

This understanding of the poem as drama kept at a distance is perfectly consistent with the diverse personalities of Venus in Renaissance philosophy and mythography.

In an article based upon a knowledge of Renaissance mythography, S. Clark Hulse finds not one but three Venuses—comic, sensual, and violent—borne out by the imagery of the poem [see excerpt above, 1978]. Hulse is right to avoid the usual interpretation of the story by mythography easily accessible to Shakespeare in English. In 1592, one year before *Venus and Adonis*, Abraham Faunce [in his *The Countesse of Pembrokes Yuychurch*] stresses the application of the myth made by the mystery religions of antiquity. Venus is the Earth Mother who revives Adonis in the spring after he has been slain by the boar of winter. If he knew this fertility myth, Shakespeare clearly ignores it for the sake of the literary tradition in which Venus puts all her effort into her lament. The *locus classicus* is Bion's *Epitaphium Adonidis*. Of interest in mythography, however, is the way in which Boccaccio, Natale Conti, and Vincenzo Cartari easily move from the symbol of a vulgar Venus *in malo* to her heavenly role *in bono*, and back again. The careful distinctions made by Plato and Plotinus separating out different Venuses are easily lost in the writings of the medieval and Renaissance interpreters of the classical literary texts in which she makes her appearance. In the speech of Pausanius in *The Symposium* we hear of two Venuses—the one common and the other heavenly—with quite different nativities. In Lynche's translation of Cartari, however, despite references to Plato's *Symposium*, the various goddesses are jumbled together in just the way objected to by Pausanius. The Lynche translation (1599) is typical of the mythographic tradition in which it stands. Setting out to describe the "several natures and conditions understood and signified by her," Lynche lists Venus as "the goddesse of wantonnes and amorous delights"; the patroness of "holie wedlockes"; the "secret and hidden virtue by which all creatures whatsoever are drawne" into "generation"; the image of "inordinat lust, like" that of "beasts, deprived of sence"; and even the inspiration of "manly courages, stoutnesse, and resolutions" in "womans hearts." Shakespeare is not jumbling diverse meanings in *Venus and Adonis*, however, in contrast to the tendency of the mythographers. Rather, he is creating a rich drama in which character evokes tension in the mind of the reader. The largely comic Venus at the beginning of the poem is perceived by the distanced reader as appealing one moment and frightening the next, as Falstaff [in *1 and 2 Henry IV*] is both a fool and a threat to the state without ever losing our measured admiration and his ability to delight the audience. An even better parallel to Venus is Cleopatra, a glamorous tramp with a capacity for both Chaucerian bawdry and transcendent immortality of fame.

The shifting rhetoric of *Venus and Adonis* can be illustrated by a thousand instances of image and tone, as Coleridge understood so well, but several passages from early in the poem, where Shakespeare is alerting his readers to repeated techniques, illustrate my thesis. The first of these passages occurs after Venus plucks Adonis from his horse and tucks him under one arm, while using the other to restrain the horse. Her heroic scale at his expense is turned toward paradox: "Backward she push'd him, as she would be thrust" [l. 41]. Her subsequent frenzy of kissing her captured victim is made the subject of the famous epic simile where Venus is compared to an eagle and Adonis to its prey:

> Even as an empty eagle, sharp by fast,
> Tires with her beak on feathers, flesh and bone,
> Shaking her wings, devouring all in haste,
> Till either gorge be stuff'd or prey be gone:
>   Even so she kiss'd his brow, his cheek, his chin,
>   And where she ends she doth anew begin.
>
> [ll. 55-60]

The pathetic spectacle of a small bird in the beak of a famished predator is followed in the next stanza, however, by a metamorphosis.

> Forc'd to content, but never to obey,
> Panting he lies and breatheth in her face.
> She feedeth on the steam as on a prey,
> And calls it heavenly moisture, air of grace,
>   Wishing her cheeks were gardens full of flowers,
>   So they were dew'd with such distilling showers.
>
> [ll. 61-6]

The word "prey" exactly midway through the stanza is the only recollection of the tone sustained throughout the first four lines of the preceding stanza. The eagle and its victim, which began as a Venus and Adonis, are now converted to the particulars of her face and his breath. The beautiful face and moist breath are then turned back into metaphor, her face a garden and his breath a gentle shower. A savage simile concludes twelve lines later as a submerged and peaceful blazon. The metamorphosis of subject and tone in these two stanzas points toward the conclusion of the poem, where the body of Adonis, pitifully mangled by the tusk of "the loving swine," melts "like a vapour" into a "new-sprung flower," whose scent is compared by Venus "to her Adonis' breath" [ll. 1115, 1166, 1171, 1172]. Thus, at least one passage early in the poem points ahead toward an ending not entirely detached in theme and tone.

The maddening effect of Adonis upon Venus arises in part from the way in which her advances so often meet with near success. Soon after the epic simile of the eagle and its prey, Venus tries to tempt Adonis into compliance by offering to exchange for one willing kiss his release from her stranglehold:

> Upon this promise did he raise his chin,
> Like a dive-dapper peering through a wave,
> Who being look'd on, ducks as quickly in:
> So offers he to give what she did crave,
>   But when her lips were ready for his pay,
>   He winks, and turns his lips another way.
>
> [ll. 85-90]

Her frustrated anger begins with verbal abuse of Adonis, "flint-hearted boy, . . . why art thou coy?" [ll. 95, 96], and then turns to a description of her earlier power over Mars:

> "I have been woo'd as I entreat thee now,
> Even by the stern and direful god of war,
> Whose sinewy neck in battle ne'er did bow,
> Who conquers when he comes in every jar;

> Yet hath he been my captive and my slave,
> And begg'd for that which thou unask'd shalt
>   have.

> "Over my altars hath he hung his lance,
> His batter'd shield, his uncontrolled crest;
> And for my sake hath learn'd to sport and dance,
> To toy, to wanton, dally, smile and jest,
>   Scorning his churlish drum and ensign red,
>   Making my arms his field, his tent my bed.

> "Thus he that overrul'd I oversway'd,
> Leading him prisoner in a red rose chain:
> Strong-temper'd steel his stronger strength obey'd,
> Yet was he servile to my coy disdain."
>
> [ll. 97-112]

Up to "coy disdain" the reader is momentarily drawn by Venus into a respect for the divine power that subdues even the gods. With that single phrase, bringing to mind her earlier description of Adonis' coyness, we suddenly see Venus from a distance in an entirely different way. She is now as much the victim of love as was Mars. The rapacious eagle changes this time into the comic yet pathetic woman: "Poor queen of love, in thine own law forlorn" [l. 251].

The Mars passage quickly shifts from epic description to dramatic irony. Venus is now the victim of the "coy disdain" she earlier inflicted upon Mars. She now wears the "red rose chain" [l. 110], but Venus fails to make the connection. The full import of the reference to "coy disdain" does not alter her consciousness as it does ours. Her sense of power and importance remains curiously intact and her relentless seduction continues unabated.

Another example of the sudden diverting and distancing of the reader is illustrated by the seduction argument where Venus is the author of her own blazon, rendered at first by counterexamples. She is not ugly, sick, or old. Venus finally comes to what she is, rather than what she is not. Then, despite the athletic superiority over Adonis confirmed earlier in the poem, her self-glorification emphasizes lightness and grace:

> Bid me discourse, I will enchant thine ear,
> Or like a fairy trip upon the green,
> Or like a nymph, with long dishevell'd hair,
> Dance on the sands, and yet no footing seen.
>   Love is a spirit all compact of fire,
>   Not gross to sink, but light, and will aspire.

> Witness this primrose bank whereon I lie:
> These forceless flowers like sturdy trees support
>   me.
>
> [ll. 145-52]

The "sturdy trees" suddenly dispel the verbal enchantment created by "dance," "spirit," and "fire." On the surface of meaning, Venus is so buoyant that not even primroses respond to her weight, but the phrase comparing the flowers to "sturdy trees" has the opposite rhetorical effect of making us feel that only a grove of oak would have the stability to bear up the gross size and strength we suddenly remember from earlier in the poem. Yet her very next image restores the goddess to the elements of air and light: "Two strengthless doves will draw me through the sky / From morn till night . . ." [ll. 153-54]. Venus is composed of flesh and bone, but she can also enchant. The earthbound body can briefly manifest a spirit "all compact of fire," suggesting Cleopatra's "I am fire and air; my other elements / I give to baser life . . ." [*Antony and Cleopatra*, V. ii. 289-90].

Shakespeare has seen the many faces of love, "golden"-haired one moment, rapacious "eagle" feeding on "flesh and bone" the next, and finally swept by grief over the fragility of beauty. Rhetorical control allows for the full range of this diversity in the experience of the reader. The "swift aid" of Shakespeare's complex artistry can hold the course to Paphos if we but mount the chariot of his verse. (pp. 36-42)

> *John Doebler, "The Many Faces of Love: Shakespeare's 'Venus and Adonis',"* in Shakespeare *Studies: An Annual Gathering of Research, Criticism, and Reviews, Vol. XVI, 1983, pp. 33-43.*

NANCY LINDHEIM (essay date 1986)

[*Lindheim considers* Venus and Adonis *a technical tour de force in which Shakespeare presents a profound conception of love within the confines of Ovidian narrative. Through the use of subtle "shifts in tone, perspective and sympathy" and the repetition of images and metaphors in changing contexts, she claims, the poet has formed a work of depth and complexity in a genre that typically features a simple action occurring within a brief time span. Lindheim emphasizes the maturity of Shakespeare's intricate characterization of Venus and the portrayal of Adonis as an innocent victim of forces outside himself. In addition, she declares that the poem offers a variety of perspectives and is thus no simple endorsement of the young hunter's reductive opposition of love and lust.*]

Although not a great poem, *Venus and Adonis* is still fully Shakespearean and repays examination as a pivotal work in its author's technical as well as intellectual development. It is from this double perspective that I want to read the poem. My argument is thus composed of two different elements, though they are not rigorously separated: the two aspects, form and content, are so closely linked that I shall view the poem as if it were the consequence of decisions which are basically formal and generic. The paper offers, first, a reading of the poem which emphasizes the conceptual maturity of Shakespeare's new understanding of love. His impetus for examining the subject came, I think, from the decision to write an Elizabethan Ovidian poem—i.e., to write a love poem that would be a poem about love, and that, like Marlowe's *Hero and Leander,* would take the dark underside, the witty salaciousness, and the possibility of pain (all available in Ovid, in one place or another) as simultaneously necessary to a description of love. Intellectually, the new interest in the emotional complexity of love is itself significant for Shakespeare's later work. But the complexity of understanding, combined as it is with the formal narrowness of the Ovidian tale, also calls for new technical resources to realize it. The most interesting and seminal of these is the handling of tonal shifts, an important factor for the first time in Shakespeare's work. A discussion of shifts in tone, perspective, and sympathy forms the second, technical, part of my argument. Both parts are necessary to understanding how *Venus and Adonis* is pivotal in Shakespeare's development, for, in both content and form, *Venus and Adonis* is a "Shakespearean" poem in ways that have not before been appreciated. In attempting to show this, my desire is not to redefine our notion of what is "Shakespearean," but rather to place a seemingly marginal or curious specimen of his work in fruitful relation to the canon.

Venus and Adonis, written in 1592-93, seems to present an especially interesting moment in Shakespeare's development.

The period of "retirement" forced by the closing of the theatres created a hiatus between the plays of his comic apprenticeship (probably *The Comedy of Errors, The Two Gentlemen of Verona,* and *The Taming of the Shrew*) and the plays that are the artistic culmination of the early period (*Love's Labor's Lost, A Midsummer Night's Dream,* and *Romeo and Juliet*). If we accept this chronology, *Venus and Adonis* becomes Shakespeare's earliest poetic or dramatic exploration of the nature of love. Whatever consideration of love appears in the first three comedies is perfunctory compared to its growing richness in *Love's Labor's Lost, A Midsummer Night's Dream,* and *Romeo and Juliet,* and of course in the *Sonnets* as well. Moreover, the problem of conveying that richness within the exceedingly narrow limits of Ovidian narrative asks us to see this period also as one of technical experimentation. In *Venus and Adonis* I think we see the poet's very early attempts to manage considerable tonal complexity: he integrates comedy with tragedy, parody with straight representation, all the while manipulating our response to Venus so that by the time she comes to fear and then know Adonis's death, Shakespeare has moved us from ridicule to sympathy. Again, this sort of complexity and manipulation is not conspicuous in the stage works that probably precede *Venus and Adonis,* but is notable in the ending of *Love's Labor's Lost* and becomes more significant in such plays as *A Midsummer Night's Dream, Romeo and Juliet,* and *Richard II.*

The choice of Ovid as model for the Elizabethan erotic poem was both logical and paradoxical. In substance and style several aspects of his poetry mesh particularly well with late-Elizabethan tastes; technically, however, the choice was paradoxical because the Elizabethans seem to have wanted to write mythological poems that were long and independent or free-standing. The aesthetic ideal of the age reflected Aristotle's approval of "magnitude": "the longer the story, consistently with its being comprehensible as a whole, the finer it is by reason of its magnitude" [*Poetics*]. Yet Ovid's amorous tales are not long (compared to Shakespeare's 1194 lines, Ovid's tale of Venus and Adonis runs only 74 lines, or, including the Atalanta-Hippomenes interpolation, 220 lines). Nor, if we accept Brooks Otis's argument [in his *Ovid as an Epic Poet*] that the stories of the *Metamorphoses* are organized to explore an "amatory system," are they independent. The brevity of Ovid's episodes and their dependence on context for resonance have formal implications, of course: each episode generally contains only a single action, likely even a single incident, and most often is concerned with only two characters. Lacking the dimension of time, each offers little opportunity for change or development, either psychological or thematic. The initial decision to write a long poem on such a brief narrative base might seem curious, but Renaissance rhetoric provided the Elizabethans with the instruments needed to convert these tales into what they desired—i.e., copious poems organized for strongly thematic purposes. Their apparent problem—if we generalize from the poems we have—was to make the conversion while retaining the essential features of Ovidian narrative: namely, single action, few characters, and little extension in time.

Elizabethan techniques for achieving *copia* [magnitude] are readily seen in the first of these Ovidian transformations, Lodge's *Glaucus and Scilla,* where the strategy for achieving length is to make of the poem a compendium of love conventions and practices. Even in this early example, Lodge, led by the strong thematic bias of his amplification, has converted a love story into a story about love. Marlowe's *Hero and Le-*

ander offers a still more suggestive comparison for *Venus and Adonis,* because these two poems correspond in overall conception. The authors of both see the erotic narrative and its Ovidian tradition as an opportunity for exploring within a narrow focus an exceptionally broad and deep range of amatory experience. (pp. 190-92)

Shakespeare's poem shares with Marlowe's the strong thematic concern with love, the sharp divergences of tone, even the paradoxical formula "comic poem, tragic action" [see Additional Bibliography entry for Clifford Leech]. Shakespeare also makes use of a discernible narrative voice for purposes of generalizing, responding sympathetically, and judging behavior; but his narrator is neither so conspicuous nor in such control of the poem as Marlowe's. This may well be because Shakespeare has less need of an authority who can bridge the gap between particular experience and universal meaning. He can be more "dramatic" in his conception of the poem because the choice of Venus as his chief character offers the inherent possibility of generalizing about the nature of love. The kind of universal significance Marlowe must earn by forging a superhuman beauty for his lovers out of invidious comparisons and other commerce with the gods, Shakespeare gains "naturally" by considering Venus the personification of love, though he does not restrict his conception of her to this semi-allegorical dimension. Shifts in focus (from actor to principle, lover to love) occur at several points in the poem, providing much the same effect for the reader as a sudden modal transposition in music. The line "Love is a spirit all compact of fire" [l. 149] is such a revelation: we have been watching a strapping, predatory creature make herself ridiculous both in her physical overtures to an indifferent young man and in her wildly subjective appraisal of the situation, when suddenly we see quite another being, whose "beauty as the spring doth yearly grow" [l. 141], who can

> . . . like a fairy trip upon the green,
> Or like a nymph, with long dishevell'd hair,
> Dance on the sands, and yet no footing seen.
> 　　　　　　　　　　　　　　[ll. 146-48]

This enchanting goddess is certifiably Venus as tradition recognizes her, and since the complex set of characteristics means to represent love itself, we concede the justice of the contradictions. It gives rise to a different sort of wit and comedy. Even the most flat-footed labelling has rich possibilities: "She's love; she loves, and yet she is not lov'd" [l. 610] is a triumphant paradox, just as the line, "Leaves love upon her back deeply distress'd" [l. 814], strikes us as deliciously funny until one's perceptions are altered by the lyric beauty of the rest of the stanza (Coleridge's favorite lines [see excerpt above, 1817]), or even by the assertion made by the two words after the caesura ("deeply distress'd").

The identification of Venus and love lies at the heart of Shakespeare's conception of the poem, though this identification is neither allegorical nor doctrinal. Venus is not "Love" in the abstract way the Neoplatonists conceive it, but in the contradictory way it is experienced. From this grows the emotional complexity that the poem displays. Venus is—by turns and simultaneously—comic, pathetic, ridiculous, humiliated, exulting, self-deceiving, playful, devious, repulsive, aggressive, sensitive to pain, and helpless because all these possibilities are contained in the experience of love. It is both critically and humanly reductive to assume that the poem shares Adonis's simple dichotomies:

> Call it not love, for love to heaven is fled,
> Since sweating lust on earth usurp'd his name;
>
> Love comforteth like sunshine after rain,
> But lust's effect is tempest after sun;
> Love's gentle spring doth always fresh remain,
>
> Love is all truth, lust full of forged lies.
> 　　　　　　　　　　　　[ll. 793-94, 799-801, 804]

Venus is there to tell us that love is love even if it incorporates sexual desire, jealousy, anxiety, and other such negative feelings as the humiliation, cruelty, and frustration of Marlowe's poem, or the powerlessness and self-abasement that Shakespeare will touch again in the sonnets. And love also exhibits tender maternal feelings and qualities of friendship and dependency that leave the lover peculiarly vulnerable to sadness, pain, and loss:

> 　　　　　　　. . . as one on shore
> Gazing upon a late embarked friend,
> Till the wild waves will have him seen no more,
> Whose ridges with the meeting clouds contend:
> 　So did the merciless and pitchy night
> 　Fold in the object that did feed her sight.
>
> Whereat amaz'd, as one that unaware
> Had dropp'd a precious jewel in the flood,
> Or 'stonish'd as night-wand'rers often are,
> Their light blown out in some mistrustful wood:
> 　Even so confounded in the dark she lay,
> 　Having lost the fair discovery of her way.
> 　　　　　　　　　　　　　　　[ll. 817-28]

These stanzas (arrived at through the famous simile of the shooting star) are virtually Venus's response to Adonis's self-righteous pronouncement quoted just above, a response all the more effective because unspoken. The lines express qualities of longing and admiration and suggest a depth of vulnerability which exposes the shallowness of his position. I wish to place this evaluation alongside Adonis's to emphasize the fullness of Shakespeare's conception as a part of the shaping impulse of *Venus and Adonis.* It is an aspect of the conversion of a love poem into a poem about love and then further into a poem that is an "anatomy" of love. Hermann Fränkel [in his *Ovid: A Poet Between Two Worlds*] speaks of the classical tradition that underlies this apparently paradoxical conversion:

> Love, it is true, does not appear at first sight to lend itself easily to systematic discussion, but we remember that in Rome erotic poetry had from the outset a touch of the didactic and the methodical, in that even a collection of disconnected elegies was designed to represent all the main phases and aspects of the passion in their ideal and most satisfactory form.

One aspect of this breadth of conception, the poem's insistence on the maternal element in Venus's feelings, has been recognized, yet even the remarkable simile in which she seeks the wounded Adonis "Like a milch doe, whose swelling dugs do ache, / Hasting to feed her fawn, hid in some brake" [ll. 875-76] has been said to depict Venus "driven by purely animal instinct" [M. C. Bradbrook, in her *Shakespeare and Elizabethan Poetry*]. Animal, yes, but not distinguished here from the fully human bond between mother and nursing child. Yet Shakespeare is not simple even in this. That Venus's wish to protect and cherish is interwoven with other desires is emphasized in her very last words in the poem, spoken to the flower that has sprung from Adonis's blood:

> Here was thy father's bed, here in my breast,
> Thou art the next of blood, and 'tis thy right.
> Lo in this hollow cradle take thy rest;
> My throbbing heart shall rock thee day and night:
>   There shall not be one minute in an hour
>   Wherein I will not kiss my sweet love's flower.
>
>   [ll. 1183-88]

It is characteristic of Venus's self-deception that she should imply Adonis's willingness to lie in such a bed, but if we smile at her words, we nevertheless agree with her comparison of Adonis to a child. (One also notes, however, that associating him with infancy in this way makes the stanza teeter between pathos and humor.) Adonis's youthfulness is stressed throughout the poem, frequently being given expression in gestures and turns of phrase that are downright childish: "Still is he sullen, still he lours and frets" [l. 75], he pulls his "bonnet" down over his eyes and pretends she is not there [ll. 339-42]; he petulantly blames her, " 'For shame,' he cries, 'let go, and let me go: / My day's delight is past, my horse is gone, / And 'tis your fault I am bereft him so . . . ' " [ll. 379-81]. His description of love proves his assertion that "I know not love . . . nor will not know it" [l. 409]:

> 'Tis much to borrow, and I will not owe it:
> My love to love is love but to disgrace it,
> For I have heard, it is a life in death,
> That laughs and weeps, and all but with a breath.
>
>   [ll. 411-14]

The willful ignorance and the refusal to risk (or understand) emotional turbulence affirm for the reader the impression of Adonis's childishness, an impression greatly magnified in Venus's memory of him after his death:

> And therefore would he put his bonnet on,
> Under whose brim the gaudy sun would peep:
> The wind would blow it off, and being gone,
> Play with his locks; then would Adonis weep,
>   And straight, in pity of his tender years,
>   They both would strive who first should dry his
>   tears.
>
>   [ll. 1087-92]

Finally, then, the reader comes to see Adonis's childishness as the complement of Venus's maternal instinct—material available for pathos, but like the image of the baby in its cradle, capable also of evoking a smile. A smile, however, and not a smirk. There is considerable control here over the quality of the erotic joke: the point is not that the object of Venus's passion is a child (i.e., not the hint of sexual perversion), but that the very childlike innocence and vulnerability by which she is attracted make him, because they are linked with childishness, impervious to her womanly persuasions.

For all Adonis's high-minded articulation of the difference between love and lust, the poem does not present him as the embodiment of any spiritual or intellectual position whatever. His governing principle instead is immaturity. He is simply too young to value another experience more highly than his games and his sleep. He recognizes himself to be at a particular stage of growth. He does not assert that he is outside Nature, but merely that he is not yet ready to give himself to Venus:

> Who wears a garment shapeless and unfinish'd?
> Who plucks the bud before one leaf put forth?

> Measure my strangeness with my unripe years.
> Before I know myself, seek not to know me:
> No fisher but the ungrown fry forbears;
>   The mellow plum doth fall, the green sticks fast,
>   Or being early pluck'd, is sour to taste.
>
>   [ll. 415-16, 524-28]

Shakespeare seems to have decided that the way to examine metamorphosis in a comic mode is to reinterpret the implications of the word. The metamorphic paradigm is no longer nymph into laurel tree or white into purple berry, but tadpole into frog or caterpillar into butterfly. This too is an indication of new directions in Shakespeare's thought, for the idea is intrinsic to the comedies that follow: we may well be reminded of the three young men of Navarre [in *Love's Labour's Lost*] who believe themselves to be at a stage where the totally male pursuits of Platonic study are still feasible, but even closer are the connections with another work pervaded by Ovid's *Metamorphoses*, *A Midsummer Night's Dream*. C. L. Barber [in his *Shakespeare's Festive Comedy: A Study of Dramatic Form and Its Relation to Social Custom*] has beautifully demonstrated the way in which the idea of maturation is central to that play: e.g., in the exchange of girlhood ties (growing like two cherries on a stem) for marriage, or in the propriety of the young Indian page's giving up the maternal protection of Titania's band to become a knight in Oberon's train.

Reconceiving Ovid's Adonis (who is explicitly not *puer* [a boy] but *iuvenis*, i.e., a young man in his twenties) so that he is an adolescent may well have been the crucial fact in Shakespeare's transformation of the story. It heightens both the comedy and the pathos of Adonis, depending on whether one views him in relation to Venus or to the boar. With Venus, as we have seen, the disparity between her vigorous sensuality and his standoffish refusal to place himself psychologically at risk gives rise to a spectrum of comedy that runs from tenderness to titillation and frank vulgarity. In terms of the boar, however, this sheltered innocence emphasizes Adonis's vulnerability both to time (the boar is traditionally a figure of winter) and to death. Perhaps paradoxically, his status as Beauty is focused more sharply, certainly more poignantly, when he is pursued by Time than by Love.

Compared to Ovid's, Shakespeare's version seems more firmly rooted in the double tradition of Adonis as ritual figure of vegetative myth and as poetic subject of elegy. Both traditions (the second of course growing from the first) hinge on Adonis's mortality. The pathos of the elegiac tradition depends on the perfection of the creature who has died through no fault of his own and in defiance of what is called "justice" in the universe. Underlying the myth is a fertility ritual that tries to influence the process of vegetative death and rebirth, of seasonal fallowness and harvest, with sexual links clear enough to become the basis of Spenser's Garden of Adonis [in the *Faerie Queene*]. The relations among the elements in the triad of innocence-sexuality-death are not simple or punitive: the elegiac tradition reminds us that Adonis's tragedy inheres not in the loss of innocence but of life. It is possible for Adonis to feel that the boar and Venus are equally his enemies, and it is possible for Venus to see in the boar's nuzzling of Adonis with his tusk an analogue to her own sexual desires, but the reader has learned to see these reductive views as part of a larger complexity. Adonis the dying god is scapegoat, not criminal, and Adonis the dying shepherd-hunter is also innocent of harm; both are victims of "Nature," as is Shakespeare's adolescent. Though it is abstractly possible to see the boar's association with the violence of both sexuality and time (its identification with lust and death) as causally related, it seems to me to destroy the narrative integrity of the poem to do so. Both the logic of the story itself and the most pressing meanings arising from it encourage one to understand the boar as something outside Adonis and not projected from his psyche. "Devouring Time" [Sonnet 19], which "feeds on the rarities of nature's truth" [Sonnet 60] is the force that interests Shakespeare, in 1593 as well as later. Neither the original tradition nor the poem as written provides support for a punitive reading of the story. Adonis is not killed for what he does but for what he is. In Yeats's words, "Man is in love and loves what vanishes, / What more is there to say?" [*Nineteen Hundred and Nineteen*].

That Adonis is locked into nature I take to be of primary importance to the poem; in addition to allowing Shakespeare to escape a narrow punitive moralism, it affords him the setting, metaphors, and digressions for realizing a relation between lover and beloved that will be worked out more intensively in the middle sonnets. Although the obvious parallels between *Venus and Adonis* and the *Sonnets* are with the early "procreative" group, the sonnets on mutability and those exploring the psychological dependence and virtual helplessness of the lover can also be seen as a mature development of the implications of *Venus and Adonis*. In the conception of both Adonis and the Young Man of the *Sonnets,* two things are critical: (1) their beauty, which becomes a sign or symbol for whatever the lover finds valuable and sustaining in the world (clearer in the *Sonnets,* but surely the meaning of Venus's assertion that after Adonis's death "black Chaos comes again" [l. 1020]) and (2) their mortality. As in Keats, this is "Beauty that must die" ["Ode on Melancholy"].

The realization of mutability—its full terror and how man must live in the shadow of inevitable loss—is merely adumbrated in this poem. More fully developed is the *Sonnets'* constant recourse to nature for the pattern and interpretation of experience, as well as for analogies to the value that the poet perceives. Beauty, however moral and spiritual we would make it by extension, is first a material quality for Shakespeare, existing in nature before man creates it in art. His paradigms for the experiences of human love would lie in nature even if Adonis were not by origin a figure from vegetative myth. They are to be seen in the round of the sun, the course of the seasons, the life of a flower, the joyful lark, the stallion's sexual instinct, the isolation and fear of a hunted hare, the destructiveness of a wild boar, the rapacious eagle, the need of a milch doe to feed her fawn, the snail "Shrink[ing] backward in his shelly cave with pain" [l. 1034].

The two long digressions—the episode of the horses and Venus's lecture on Wat the hare—inconceivable in a poem like *Hero and Leander* or *Glaucus and Scilla,* are thus fully consonant with Shakespeare's conception of *Venus and Adonis*. Thematically the function of the horses is easier to understand than that of the hare, in which we are perhaps to feel our powerlessness against the forces that bring death. Adonis, like Wat, will soon be a victim of the hunt; even Venus herself, the goddess tied to a mortal, becomes associated with Wat's plight as she rushes through the forest to confirm her fearful premonition. She too is caught and scratched by bushes in her way [ll. 871-74], she too "treads the path that she untreads again" [l. 908]. Adonis's stallion defiantly asserts control of his actions when he breaks his rein at the urging of sexual instinct, but he is no more master than is the hunted hare. All are within nature's dominion, even Venus insofar as her "life" depends on the mortal Adonis.

I have thus far largely been separating technical from intellectual matters, form from content, but the distinction is of course partly artificial. Concerning the digressions, for example, the thematic function just discussed is only one way of explaining how they work in the poem. They also have a technical function related to narrative or rhetorical "tension," by which I mean that they play a role in shaping the reader's response to the narrative flow. The short Ovidian tale cannot be converted into a long Elizabethan poem merely by multiplying the number of lines required by each action. The intensity of Apollo's pursuit of Daphne or Salamacis's of Hermaphroditus can suitably be maintained for forty or fifty lines, but not for two or three hundred. In Shakespeare's poem the reeking, the sweating, the smothering, the references to rivers swelling their banks, the tortuous ingenuity of Venus's obsessed pleading—all these must take a toll on the reader, who welcomes the emotional release, the change of pace and the feeling of uncomplicated energy that the horses' actions provide. Even the sermon on Wat the hare, again less clear in its working, offers release by shifting the subject away from the hothouse atmosphere of Venus's pleading. Such use as Shakespeare makes of his narrator's voice seems often to have the same rhetorical justification: generalizing, commenting, and judging are all means of offering the reader some possibility of distance from the action of a poem so long confined to an emotional contention between two characters.

However important the psychological respite provided by this "aeration," the genesis of Shakespeare's digressions was more likely aesthetic. Renaissance literature of all sorts displays a preference for plots that are neither simple nor linear in progression. Shakespeare's natural response to the need for magnitude, based either on his experience as a dramatist or as a reader of contemporary narratives—the first three books of *The Faerie Queene* and Sidney's *Arcadia* were both published only a few years earlier—would be to multiply characters and create analogous situations that comment on one another through parallelism and juxtaposition. This method, though worked out with more discrete units, operates in such an "anatomy" as the whole of Ovid's *Metamorphoses*. The challenge presented to Renaissance Ovidian poets is not to invent new techniques for writing narratives, but to find ways of amplifying when the obvious sources of it—multiple actions and extension of time—are formally prohibited. Shakespeare seems especially to have seen the challenge in these terms, perhaps welcoming it as a means of showing off his virtuosity. The dedication to Southampton implies the poet's willingness to stake his literary reputation on *Venus and Adonis,* called "the first heir of my invention" [see excerpt above, 1593]; to this end its aspect as a tour de force, the triumph of difficulty overcome, might well be as significant as the flamboyance of its wit and language.

Perhaps the most interesting—certainly the most seminal—example of virtuosity in the poem can be found in the way Shakespeare handles the tonal shift that occurs with Adonis's death. The tonal change is one of the "givens" of the story of Venus and Adonis, which traditionally depicts the pleasant general tenor of their love as a contrast to the lament of the bereaved goddess. In a short poem, the narrative would be controlled by the action of the second section; for a reader familiar with the myth, the idyll would feel like a prologue. Shakespeare's long version changes all this: the first 800-odd lines are given so much "character" (most of it contrary to the reader's expectations) that it shifts the weight of the poem to the earlier section and makes its mode decidedly comic. The maneuver emphasizes the fact that the poem has a binary form—sequentially it moves from comic themes of wooing and maturation to tragic themes of death, destruction, and grief; it emphasizes as well the paradox or oxymoron at its heart: the work as a comic poem with a tragic action. This last formulation suggests a doubleness which is apposite, for Shakespeare's virtuosity lies in his means of ensuring the double perspective: the very images and metaphors first used to convey Venus's ludicrous desire he now employs in the second part to express some dimension of her suffering and grief. We are perhaps aware enough of these repetitions to be made uncomfortable, and the excessiveness of the language of her grief also contributes a measure of distance, but these factors do not, I think, undermine our sympathy with Venus in the latter part of the poem.

A signal example of the kind of repetition I mean occurs within the ten-stanza span between Adonis's departure and Venus's sight of the boar. Once Adonis has finally left, Venus, "Having lost the fair discovery of her way" [l. 828], wails and groans ("twenty echoes twenty times" redoubling her "Woe, woe" [ll. 834, 833]), and "sings extemporally a woeful ditty" [l. 836] that generalizes about the foolishness of love—moving the narrator in turn to generalize about the tediousness of lovers and their insistence on being humored:

> For who hath she to spend the night withal,
> But idle sounds resembling parasites,
> Like shrill-tongu'd tapsters answering every call,
> Soothing the humour of fantastic wits?
>   She says, " 'Tis so," they answer all, " 'Tis so,"
>   And would say after her, if she said "No."
>
> [ll. 847-52]

These tapsters are undoubtedly the originals of Prince Hal's Francis [in *1 Henry IV*], but the "fantastic wits" here seem as much drunk as high-spirited and arrogant, a suggestion strengthened by reference in the previous stanza to tellers of interminable stories who seem unaware that their audience has vanished or is no longer listening. All this knowing mockery is clearly at Venus's expense. The Venus we meet after she has spied the boar with "frothy mouth bepainted all with red, / Like milk and blood being mingled both together" [ll. 901-02] is no longer so cheerful and complacent; yet in spite of her desperation and near panic, in spite of the irony's deepening tone, she is again likened to a drunkard:

> A thousand spleens bear her a thousand ways,
> She treads the path that she untreads again;
> Her more than haste is mated with delays
> Like the proceedings of a drunken brain,
>   Full of respects, yet naught at all respecting,
>   In hand with all things, naught at all effecting.
>
> [ll. 907-12]

This represents something quite different from the simple unfolding of an action. We are being persuaded to see simultaneously what normally we think about only in sequence: an irrationality comprehending ludicrous self-deception and high-spirited folly, as well as a frustrated desperation whose seriousness does not free it from the taint of ridicule. Venus does not suddenly "change" from one sort of character to another, so that we disapprove of her earlier actions and sympathize with her later ones. The qualities inherent in the nature of love, both positive and negative, have all always been there.

Techniques of doubling motifs and of counterpointing humor against the stark tonal shift demanded by the action allow Shakespeare to insinuate both the unity and the complexity of his conception of love.

Many of the earlier descriptions of Venus are similarly made to do second service in the latter part of the poem as a way of integrating or reinterpreting our experience. Very telling similes comparing her to a bird of prey (the "empty eagle, sharp by fast," of lines 55-60, or the rapacious vulture of lines 547-52) are recalled in the different context of Venus's momentary hope that she has heard Adonis's "merry horn" [l. 1025]. "As falcons to the lure, away she flies; / The grass stoops not, she treads on it so light" ([ll. 1027-28]: even the grass here recapitulates motifs of lines 145-56, where the primrose bank shows "forceless flowers [that] like sturdy trees support [her]," part of love's association with fairy enchantment). That Venus is likened to a falcon must evoke memories of the earlier violence, but the particular image of lines 1027-28 points in a different direction. She is being deceived by a lure (transformed into a sort of victim?) and then redefined in terms of flight, speed, perhaps grace. There is thus apparently no stock or single response to the objective reality called "bird of prey."

While the falcon echo seems a significant attempt to revise the reader's associations, there are other places in the poem where shifting perspectives give rise instead to confusion. Why, for example, should Venus's pleas that Adonis pursue only small game turn into an intensely sympathetic account of poor Wat as a "dew-bedabbled wretch" [l. 703], and then within the stanzas given over to Wat's point of view, why shift yet again to a momentary consideration of the dogs who are "driven to doubt" because they have lost the hare's smell [ll. 690-94]? An extraordinary diffusion of sympathy also seems to underlie a stanza that purports to convey Adonis's victimization by an aggressively unattractive Venus:

> And having felt the sweetness of the spoil,
> With blindfold fury she begins to forage;
> Her face doth reek and smoke, her blood doth boil,
> And careless lust stirs up a desperate courage. . . .
>
> Hot, faint, and weary with her hard embracing,
> Like a wild bird being tam'd with too much handling,
> Or as the fleet-foot roe that's tir'd with chasing,
> Or like the froward infant still'd with dandling:
>   He now obeys, and now no more resisteth. . . .
>
> [ll. 553-56, 559-63]

The first simile [l. 560] may be ambiguous in the light of Elizabethan ideas about the relative value of wild and tame, though by ending on "too much handling," the line gives final weight to our discomfort. In the pivotal second simile we sympathize with the roe's exhaustion, yet note that "tir'd with chasing" may also be ambiguous; I imagine, though, we give greater weight to the meaning "being chased." The third simile allows us to see that cessation of effort has been the point all along. But "too much handling" is now "still'd with dandling" and the ambiguous wild bird has become a "froward child": Adonis's behavior is fretful, erratic, and a patient mother or nurse has soothed him until he calms down—one supposes for their mutual good.

Can one find significance for the confusions arising from this extraordinary diffusion of sympathy, or from the acute discrepancy of judgment between narrator and reader at this

Mars and Venus. By Paolo Veronese.

point when the narrator becomes ecstatic over what he considers Venus's "success" [ll. 565-73]? The problem may stem from Shakespeare's still immature control over his material, but it can also be usefully set in the context of the poem's general concern with complicating judgment. The reason for this concern seems to me here, as often in Shakespeare, more "moral" than epistemological, geared at undermining the reader's assumption that he already has moral categories for dealing with such experience. Further illustrations of the "doubling" or echoed motifs I was listing earlier can demonstrate how Shakespeare prevents conventional moral associations from becoming fixed. The reader's assessment of the catalogue of senses, for example, which the poet uses in the first section for sensuous seduction (with rhetorical excess apparently designed for our amusement) must be readjusted upon its return as a catalogue of loss as Venus studies and touches the dead body of Adonis [ll. 433-50 and 1123-28]. To the recapitulation of maternal and smothering motifs at the very end of the poem already cited, one ought also to add the recurrence of similes of "overflowing" that had previously been attached to passion and the helplessness of the lover. Both are gently alluded to in a stanza controlled by the narrator's admiring sympathy:

> Here overcome, as one full of despair,
> She vail'd her eyelids, who like sluices stopp'd

The crystal tide that from her two cheeks fair
In the sweet channel of her bosom dropp'd;
> But through the flood-gates breaks the silver
>   rain,
> And with his strong course opens them again.
>   [ll. 955-60]

One may well argue that the "sympathy" of this stanza is considerably distanced and its emotion diluted by the prettiness of the diction. But I see the refusal to replace earlier modes of expression because of the different tonal needs of the later action as parallel to Shakespeare's refusal to abandon earlier negative perceptions. If his Venus is a study of the nature of love, then the complexity of the experience demands techniques of incorporation rather than simplification. The similarity between the impassioned, self-deluding, "fantastic" lover still in pursuit of desire and one whose beloved is irretrievably lost is a point worth making because in the unity of the experience lies the basis of its value. The value of love can be affirmed without denying its cruel, animal, ludicrous, or self-asserting underside. The distance afforded by the lavish rhetoric and the overwrought surface guarantees judgment throughout, inducing us to see similarities and complexities rather than (like Adonis) to insist upon discrepancies and simplicity. In its sharpest form, we are asked to apply the same simile twice—once for laughter or to highlight cruelty, and a second time to illuminate pathos. The virtuosity verges on impudence in its assertion that the poet's power lies not in his subservience to reality but in his mastery of it. The handling, the context—in other words, the poet's labor—is what gives meaning to his material, which is neutral in itself, patient of varying and contradictory interpretations. Yet however playful and artificial *Venus and Adonis* may be, I would not consider it "metapoetry": the virtuosity is ultimately at the service of interpreting experience, and the energies, as one would expect of a Renaissance text, are not reflexive but rhetorical in the sense that they turn outward towards shaping the reader's responses. (pp. 192-203)

The ideas underlying these tonally modulated repetitions must have been important to Shakespeare, since he worked with them again and again in the plays that are his first considerable achievements. Beyond the intrinsic merit of *Venus and Adonis,* then, we ought thus to see its relation to Shakespeare's development in the years which followed, past the 1595 plays to the middle sonnets. Its conception of love was one that could be reasserted in even so late a work as *Antony and Cleopatra.* The poem proved an occasion for exploring tendencies that are intrinsic to his way of working, allowing him to crystallize certain problems more sharply than the pressures of dramatic form perhaps permitted at this early stage in his career. The richest connections of the poem are thus not with Ovid (its source) or with Marlowe and Lodge (other examples of the same genre) but with Shakespeare's own works. As I hope I have shown, *Venus and Adonis* is pivotal in the development of some of their concerns and techniques. (p. 203)

> *Nancy Lindheim, "The Shakespearean 'Venus and Adonis'," in* Shakespeare Quarterly, *Vol. 37, No. 2, Summer, 1986, pp. 190-203.*

ADDITIONAL BIBLIOGRAPHY

Asals, Heather. "*Venus and Adonis:* The Education of a Goddess." *Studies in English Literature 1500-1900* XIII, No. 1 (Winter 1973): 31-51.
    Offers a reading of the poem according to the Neoplatonic hierarchy of the senses, noting that Venus's desire progresses from wishing to touch the boy to appreciating the sight of him, a process which "ennobles her passion and, with her passion, herself." This evolution from Lust to Love, Asals contends, further reflects the poem's basis in Neoplatonism, which defines Love as the desire for Beauty, an attribute perceivable only by sight.

Baldwin, T. W. "The Literary Genetics of *Venus and Adonis.*" In his *On the Literary Genetics of Shakspere's Poems & Sonnets,* pp. 1-93. Urbana: University of Illinois Press, 1950.
    An exhaustive assessment of the influence of Ovidian poetic conventions, Platonic concepts of love, and other literary and philosophical traditions on Shakespeare's *Venus and Adonis.*

Beauregard, David N. "*Venus and Adonis:* Shakespeare's Representation of the Passions." *Shakespeare Studies* VIII (1975): 83-98.
    Contends that the Renaissance concept of the "concupiscible" and "irascible" aspects of the human soul governs the action of *Venus and Adonis.* Beauregard argues that the former aspect gives rise to the goddess's love, desire, and joy and the boy's complementary passions of hate, aversion, and sorrow early in the poem, while the latter produces Venus's alternating "hope

and despair, courage and fear, and anger" after Adonis has left her to pursue the boar.

Berry, J. Wilkes. "Loss of Light in 'Venus and Adonis'." *Discourse* XII, No. 1 (Winter 1969): 72-6.
    Correlates the course of Venus's hopes and desires with the progression of the day "from dawn through sunset to black night." It is poignantly ironic, Berry notes, that Adonis's death and thus the goddess's deepest despair occur at dawn; the brilliant sun cannot dispel the "night of sorrow" that envelops her.

Bowers, A. Robin. "'Hard Armours' and 'Delicate Amours' in Shakespeare's *Venus and Adonis.*" *Shakespeare Studies* XII (1979): 1-23.
    Examines the traditional associations of a boar with lust and of a kiss with succumbing to temptation in an effort to reconcile the seemingly contradictory moods of *Venus and Adonis.* Although the poem is initially delightful and amusing, Bowers claims, it progresses from the humorous to the tragic when Adonis, by agreeing to kiss Venus, symbolically fails to resist temptation and must suffer the fatal consequences of surrendering to lust.

Bowers, R. H. "Anagnorisis, or the Shock of Recognition, in Shakespeare's *Venus and Adonis.*" *Renaissance Papers* (1962): 3-8.
    Asserts that Venus's "state of mind is the real subject of the poem" and that Shakespeare's true interest is in presenting and interpreting events from her point of view. According to Bowers, the techniques used in *Venus and Adonis* represent a significant departure from conventional Elizabethan forms of narration. In addition, the critic remarks, the goddess's recognition that her motives are the same as those she attributes to the boar is a marked alteration of sources that reveals the dramatic nature of Shakespeare's imagination.

Bradbrook, M. C. "The Ovidian Romance." In her *Shakespeare and Renaissance Poetry: A Study of his Earlier Work in Relation to the Poetry of the Time,* pp. 51-74. London: Chatto and Windus, 1951.
    Assesses *Venus and Adonis* as a typical Ovidian Romance with its characteristic pastoral background, fusion of the human with the "natural," and use of a metamorphosis to suggest the inherent mutability of the world.

———. "Beasts and Gods: Greene's *Groats-Worth of Witte* and the Social Purpose of *Venus and Adonis.*" *Shakespeare Survey* 15 (1962): 62-72.
    Suggests that *Venus and Adonis* is a response to *Groats-Worth of Witte,* a work in which Robert Greene attacks Shakespeare as an "upstart Crow" and places him among the lowest type of actor, the "antic" who portrayed "grotesque characters with animal heads." This "sumptuous and splendidly assured" poem, Bradbrook states, does not merely disprove Greene's charge, it simultaneously rehabilitates Venus—who was typically treated with contempt in contemporary plays—defends "the natural and instinctive beauty of the animal world against sour moralists" like Greene, and makes "a claim to social dignity for its author."

Brown, Huntington. "*Venus and Adonis:* The Action, the Narrator, and the Critics." *Michigan Academician* II, No. 2 (Fall 1969): 73-87.
    Counters critical assessments of *Venus and Adonis* that either dismiss it as an inferior work or interpret it as a moral allegory by stressing the poem's affinities with drama. Brown lauds the vivid characterizations and vigorous action of the poem, as well as the "dramatic role" played by the narrator, who, according to the critic, functions as an "ideal chorus," offering opinions and commentary but never summarizing or moralizing.

Bullough, Geoffrey. "*Venus and Adonis.*" In his *Narrative and Dramatic Sources of Shakespeare, Volume I: Early Comedies, Poems, "Romeo and Juliet,"* pp. 161-78. London: Routledge and Kegan Paul, 1957.
    Surveys Shakespeare's use of several stories from Ovid's *Metamorphoses* in his *Venus and Adonis,* including those of Her-

maphroditus and Narcissus, and provides extracts of the relevant passages in Ovid. Although the poem is not a Platonic allegory about Beauty, Bullough maintains, neither is it a simple celebration of sexual love; rather, it is "a pictorial and psychological study" of love's "urgencies, perversities and contrarieties."

Butler, Christopher and Fowler, Alistair. "Time-Beguiling Sport: Number Symbolism in Shakespeare's *Venus and Adonis*." In *Shakespeare 1564-1964: A Collection of Modern Essays by Various Hands,* edited by Edward A. Bloom, pp. 124-33. Providence, R. I.: Brown University Press, 1964.

Discovers a complex "numerological structure" in *Venus and Adonis,* in which the number of lines and stanzas, as well as the overt references to quantities by the characters and narrator, possess symbolic significance. Among the numerical patterns Butler and Fowler's calculations reveal is a correlation between the duration of one day in the poem and Adonis's lifespan, suggesting a link between the boy and the sun consistent with astronomical and seasonal myths.

Cantelupe, Eugene B. "An Iconographical Interpretation of *Venus and Adonis,* Shakespeare's Ovidian Comedy." *Shakespeare Quarterly* XIV, No. 2 (Spring 1963): 141-51.

Compares Shakespeare's poem with other literary and pictorial representations of Venus and Adonis and concludes that this work parodies traditional presentations of the two mythical lovers and satirizes Neoplatonic concepts of love. However, Cantelupe observes, despite the lighthearted tone created by the "comic characterization, humorous actions, and witty speeches," the "lust motif" strikes a serious note in the poem that enables Shakespeare to impart a didactic message.

Coleridge, Samuel Taylor. "The Lectures and Notes of 1818: Shakspere as a Poet Generally." In his *Lectures and Notes on Shakspere and Other English Poets,* edited by T. Ashe, pp. 218-23. London: George Bell and Sons, 1897.

A collocation of miscellaneous notes and observations on *Venus and Adonis* assembled after Coleridge's death. Coleridge's admiration of Shakespeare's poetic power is enhanced rather than diminished by the "unpleasing" subject matter of the poem. The author of this poem writes, the critic claims, "as if of another planet," meticulously and dispassionately describing the actions of Venus and Adonis as though they were butterflies or some other creatures alien to him.

Daigle, Lennet J. "*Venus and Adonis:* Some Traditional Contexts." *Shakespeare Studies* XIII (1980): 31-46.

Examines traditional interpretations and representations of the goddess and the young hunter in an attempt to resolve the apparent contradictions in the characters and the uncertain meaning of *Venus and Adonis.* Daigle detects two value systems operating in Shakespeare's poem: one, "a system of human ethics" that condemns lust and praises abstinence; the other, a "divinely established order of nature" that stresses the need to sustain nature through procreation and censures "fruitless chastity."

Dubrow, Heather. " 'Upon misprision growing': *Venus and Adonis.*" In her *Captive Victors: Shakespeare's Narrative Poems and Sonnets,* pp. 21-79. Ithaca, N. Y.: Cornell University Press, 1987.

An extensive analysis of the ways the poem's language and the conventions of the epyllion affect readers' perceptions of and responses to the characters in *Venus and Adonis.* Dubrow observes in this work a typically Shakespearean preoccupation with language and its complex interrelation with psychology and the shaping of experience.

Gent, Lucy. " 'Venus and Adonis': The Triumph of Rhetoric." *The Modern Language Review* 69, No. 4 (October 1974): 721-29.

Proposes that the eloquence and internal consistency of the worlds Venus and Adonis create with their rhetoric are of greater importance than the "truth" of their arguments. Gent maintains that in a similar process, Shakespeare constructs the larger world of the poem and juxtaposes antitheses and contradictions

to construct a paradoxical myth about the ambiguous nature of love.

Griffin, Robert J. " 'These Contraries Such Unity Do Hold': Patterned Imagery in Shakespeare's Narrative Poems." *Studies in English Literature 1500-1900* IV (1964): 43-55.

Detects a "rich substructure" of nature, color, weather, day/night, and other image patterns that supports and unifies the narrative design of *Venus and Adonis.*

Hart, John S. "Shakespeare's Minor Poems." *Sartain's Union Magazine* VI, No. 2 (February 1850): 129-32.

Asserts that although *Venus and Adonis* "is not marked by stirring action, but by a series of minutely finished pictures," these vivid descriptions nevertheless demonstrate Shakespeare's dramatic power. According to Hart, the goddess and the boy seem as alive and powerfully conceived as the characters in Shakespeare's plays, despite the non-dramatic nature of the poem.

Harwood, Ellen April. "*Venus and Adonis:* Shakespeare's Critique of Spenser." *The Journal of the Rutgers University Libraries* XXXIX, No. 1 (June 1977): 44-60.

Contrasts Shakespeare's poem to the Venus and Adonis passages in Edmund Spenser's *The Faerie Queene.* Harwood contends that *Venus and Adonis* exposes the impossibility of Spenser's separation of sexuality into its "life-enhancing" and "sterile" aspects and demonstrates its inherently dual nature.

Hatto, A. T. " 'Venus and Adonis'—And the Boar." *The Modern Language Review* 41, No. 4 (October 1946): 353-61.

Traces the medieval and Germanic "pedigree" of the boar as a symbol of a jealous lover's fear of a rival and its corollary association with usurpation. Hatto claims that the goddess's jealous and fearful reaction to the boar of *Venus and Adonis* is readily understandable in light of such traditional symbolism.

Jackson, Robert Sumner. "Narrative and Imagery in Shakespeare's *Venus and Adonis.*" *Papers of the Michigan Academy of Science, Arts, and Letters* XLIII (1958): 315-20.

Defines the "center of meaning" of *Venus and Adonis* as the uncertain relation between "nature and divinity, earth and heaven, man and god." Jackson contends that the multiple associations of both Venus and Adonis with divinity as well as nature, together with the shifting significance of the poem's red and white imagery, reflect the ambiguity surrounding this crucial issue.

Keach, William. "*Venus and Adonis.*" In his *Elizabethan Erotic Narratives: Irony and Pathos in the Ovidian Poetry of Shakespeare, Marlowe, and their Contemporaries,* pp. 52-84. New Brunswick, N. J.: Rutgers University Press, 1977.

Argues that in *Venus and Adonis,* Shakespeare contructs an "extraordinarily dense artificial order" based on antitheses in both the rhetoric and imagery that reflect the essential conflict between the characters. While this structure is "conceptually satisfying," permitting a wide range of critical interpretations, Keach notes, such complexity resists "complete conceptual clarity" and defeats attempts to determine the work's meaning.

Lake, James H. "Shakespeare's Venus: An Experiment in Tragedy." *Shakespeare Quarterly* XXV, No. 3 (Summer 1974): 351-55.

Proposes reading *Venus and Adonis* as a tragedy in which the goddess steadily rises in dignity until she attains the stature of a tragic figure. In Lake's view, the goddess's speech at the poem's close, where she vows to nurture the plucked flower, represents anagnorisis, or the tragic recognition that she has destroyed rather than nurtured Adonis.

Lanham, Richard A. "The Ovidian Shakespeare: *Venus and Adonis* and *Lucrece.*" In his *The Motives of Eloquence: Literary Rhetoric in the Renaissance,* pp. 82-110. New Haven: Yale University Press, 1976.

Discerns two distinct but interrelated antitheses in *Venus and Adonis:* an ethical opposition of sexuality and virtue, and an aesthetic opposition of the goddess's eloquence and the boy's spare speech. Lanham suggests that as they debate the moral issues, each protagonist employs individual rhetorical strategies and reacts to the other's modes of speech; thus, he claims, the poem's rhetoric is dramatized and "made part of the story."

Lee, Sidney. Introduction to *Shakespeare's "Venus and Adonis": Being a Reproduction in Facsimile of the First Edition, 1593,* edited by Sidney Lee, pp. 1-75. Oxford: At the Clarendon Press, 1905.

Discusses the composition date and the text of *Venus and Adonis* and surveys the myriad versions of the story in English and European literature.

Leech, Clifford. "Venus and Her Nun: Portraits of Women in Love by Shakespeare and Marlowe." *Studies in English Literature 1500-1900* V, No. 2 (Spring 1965): 247-68.

Assesses the relationship between *Venus and Adonis* and Marlowe's *Hero and Leander,* demonstrating the similarities and differences between these contemporaneous poems. Leech judges Shakespeare's work less successful than Marlowe's; the heavy ornamentation of the rhetoric in *Venus and Adonis* "limits the range" of the poem's wit and prevents us from fully sympathizing with Venus, he claims.

Lever, J. W. "Venus and the Second Chance." *Shakespeare Survey* 15 (1962): 81-8.

Suggests that Venus's concept of procreation as the means of transcending death is fully realized in Shakespeare's later dramas. This is most notable in *Antony and Cleopatra,* Lever maintains, where the tragic lovers enact the "union of love and death," and become immortal in the "country of the imagination." This essay also contains Lever's often quoted observation that for many modern readers *Venus and Adonis* seems "a very funny story which somehow forgets the joke."

Maxwell, J. C. Introduction to *The Poems* by William Shakespeare, edited by J. C. Maxwell, pp. ix-xxxvi. Cambridge: At the University Press, 1966.

Provides a balanced survey of modern commentary on *Venus and Adonis.* Maxwell acknowledges the value of a wide variety of approaches to the poem, including those that emphasize its relation to myth, comedy, and the Ovidian tradition.

Miller, Robert P. "The Myth of Mars's Hot Minion in *Venus and Adonis.*" *ELH* 26, No. 4 (December 1959): 470-81.

Argues that Shakespeare consciously manipulates his contemporaries' expectations regarding the well-known story of Venus's escapade with Mars. Miller calls attention to traditional interpretations of the fable as a struggle between the spirit and the flesh and as a "mythological reenactment of man's fall to sin." He further suggests Shakespeare's audience would have been keenly aware of the irony of the goddess's use of this tale which supports the very argument she is attempting to refute.

Panofsky, Erwin. "Titian and Ovid." in his *Problems in Titian: Mostly Iconographic,* pp. 139-71. New York: New York University Press, 1969.

Asserts that Titian invented the character of a reluctant Adonis in his 1554 painting of the goddess and the young hunter. Panofsky maintains that Shakespeare's poem sounds "like a poetic paraphrase of Titian's composition." This painting was in England for many years, he notes, and engravings of it were widely available.

Partridge, A. C. "Non-Dramatic Poetry: Marlowe and Shakespeare." In his *The Language of Renaissance Poetry: Spenser, Shakespeare, Donne, Milton,* pp. 102-40. London: Andre Deutsch, 1971.

Analyzes the versification, syntax, grammar, imagery, and rhetoric of *Venus and Adonis.*

Pegg, Barry. "Generation and Corruption in Shakespeare's *Venus and Adonis.*" *Michigan Academician* VIII, No. 1 (Summer 1975): 105-15.

Examines the "scientific" imagery of *Venus and Adonis,* particularly the elements of fire, air, water, and earth and their corresponding choleric, sanguine, phlegmatic, and melancholy humors in the human body. Pegg contends that Venus represents "generative warmth and moisture" and the boar "corruptive cold death," the two poles between which Adonis, as a human being, is trapped. He must either accede to the goddess's exhortation, the critic notes, or face death by the boar.

Prince, F. T. Introduction to *The Poems* by William Shakespeare, edited by F. T. Prince, pp. xi-xlvi. London: Methuen & Co., 1960.

Reviews the text and composition date of Shakespeare's poem and provides extracts of both the Venus and Adonis and the Hermaphroditus and Salmacis stories from Ovid's *Metamorphoses.* Prince considers *Venus and Adonis* a brilliant work, "a poem which was unique in its own time, and which in its own kind was never to be equalled."

Putney, Rufus. "*Venus and Adonis:* Amour with Humor." *Philological Quarterly* XX, No. IV (October 1941): 533-48.

Contends that *Venus and Adonis* is a "sparkling and sophisticated comedy." Putney claims that the action burlesques Ovid's tale of the two lovers and the goddess's hyperboles and conceits parody the rhetoric of other Elizabethan erotic poems.

Rebhorn, Wayne A. "Mother Venus: Temptation in Shakespeare's *Venus and Adonis.*" *Shakespeare Studies* XI (1978): 1-19.

Maintains that *Venus and Adonis* is the only work of its time to openly confront Renaissance man's fear of women. Rebhorn contends that the poem's presentation of Venus as maternal and Adonis as infantile, the narrator's ambivalent perspective on the goddess, and the inversion of customary male-female roles are all designed to illuminate "the fear that the temptress' mantrap was nothing less than the mother's smothery embrace."

Robertson, John M. "Shakespeare's Culture-Evolution." In his *Montaigne and Shakespeare: And Other Essays on Cognate Questions,* pp. 139-60. London: Adam and Charles Black, 1909.

Attacks *Venus and Adonis* and *The Rape of Lucrece* as "uninspired and pitilessly prolix poems." Robertson contends that they are "manufactured poems, consciously constructed for the market" and devoid of artistic merit.

Rollins, Hyder, ed. *A New Variorum Edition of Shakespeare: The Poems.* Philadelphia: J. B. Lippincott Company, 1938, 667 p.

Discusses the composition date, text, and sources of *Venus and Adonis.* Rollins also extensively reviews the early popularity of this poem and *The Rape of Lucrece* and surveys their critical history from the early nineteenth to the early twentieth century.

Rylands, George. "Shakespeare the Poet." In *A Companion to Shakespeare Studies,* edited by Harley Granville-Barker and G. B. Harrison, pp. 89-115. Cambridge: At the University Press, 1934.

Charges that although *Venus and Adonis* is "a masterpiece of decoration," the poem's elaborate imagery dissipates rather than intensifies the emotion. Ryland concedes that the imagery and versification give the work a measure of unity and form; nevertheless, he concludes, "in the *Venus and Adonis* there is no drama and no characterization."

Sheidley, William E. " 'Unless It Be a Boar' ": Love and Wisdom in Shakespeare's *Venus and Adonis.*" *Modern Language Quarterly* 35, No. 1 (March 1974): 3-15.

Refutes critical theories that *Venus and Adonis* offers an ambivalent perspective on love, countering that the poem intentionally offers a multiplicity of viewpoints. Shakespeare "generates a dialectic" among the various points of view, Sheidley argues, that fosters "ironic detachment, wise empathy, and a compassionate awareness" of the imperfect nature of love in an imperfect world.

Smith, Hallett. "Ovidian Poetry: The Growth and Adaptations of Forms." In his *Elizabethan Poetry: A Study in Conventions, Meaning, and Expression,* pp. 64-130. Cambridge, Mass.: Harvard University Press, 1964.

Considers *Venus and Adonis* a failed attempt to adapt Ovidian poetry to English. The "basic English earthiness" that Shakespeare uses to great effect in such plays as *A Midsummer Night's Dream*, Smith observes, seems rustic and crude amid the sophisticated eroticism of the Ovidian tradition.

Streitberger, W. R. "Ideal Conduct in *Venus and Adonis*." *Shakespeare Quarterly* XXVI, No. 3 (Summer 1975): 285-91.

Suggests that inasmuch as Adonis is too young to love, Venus's temptation, rather than inviting lust, represents a call to abandon duty and "reject everything a young noble must train for." Streitburger underscores the Renaissance belief that hunting savage animals such as the boar is proper training for young gentlemen and that hunting creatures like the hare is ignoble. Thus, he states, the easy hunt that Venus advocates "would destroy his virtues and make him an unfit gentleman."

Swinburne, Algernon Charles. *Shakespeare.* London: Henry Frowd, Oxford University Press, 1909, 83 p.

Includes Swinburne's oft-quoted dismissal of Shakespeare's narrative poems. Although, he declares, there are "touches of inspiration and streaks of beauty" in *Venus and Adonis* and "fits of power and freaks of poetry" in *The Rape of Lucrece,* "good poems they are not."

Watson, Donald G. "The Contrarieties of *Venus and Adonis*." *Studies in Philology* LXXV, No. 1 (January 1978): 32-63.

Applies to *Venus and Adonis* the Renaissance theory dividing human passions into two general groups, "concupiscence" or desire and "irascibility" or anger. Watson proposes that the goddess and the boy "are not characters in any traditional sense," but representatives of these two "passionate dispositions."

Wilbur, Richard. Introduction to *The Narrative Poems and Poems of Doubtful Authenticity* by William Shakespeare, edited by Richard Wilbur and Alfred Harbage, pp. 8-21. Baltimore: Penguin Books, 1974.

Observes in *Venus and Adonis* numerous skillfully drawn passages, but no "depth or intelligible development" of characterization and only obscure moral significance. In Wilbur's estimation, the poem is a "concatenation of virtuoso descriptions, comparisons, apostrophes . . . and what have you."

Williams, Gordon. "The Coming of Age of Shakespeare's Adonis." *The Modern Language Review* 78, Part 4 (October 1983): 769-76.

Argues that Shakespeare exploits the common Elizabethan conflation of death and sex in his presentation of the killing of Adonis by the boar—an animal traditionally associated with both lust and death. Williams scrutinizes the poet's careful construction of this event, which, the critic claims, likens the boy's demise to a sexual awakening.

Yoch, James J. "The Eye of Venus: Shakespeare's Erotic Landscape." *Studies in English Literature 1500-1900* XX, No. 1 (Winter 1980): 59-71.

Contrasts *Venus and Adonis* to similar works by Renaissance Italian writers and emphasizes Shakespeare's technique of refracting the world through Venus's eyes. Yoch claims that the goddess's "power to arrange the world to suit her desires" not only reveals her complex psychology, it also continually reshapes our view of scenes and events in the poem.

Glossary

APOCRYPHA: A term applied to those plays which have, at one time or another, been ascribed to Shakespeare, but which are outside the canon of the thirty-seven dramas generally accepted as authentic. The second issue of the THIRD FOLIO included seven plays not among the other thirty-six of the FIRST FOLIO: *Pericles, The London Prodigal, Thomas Lord Cromwell, Sir John Oldcastle, The Puritan, A Yorkshire Tragedy,* and *Locrine.* These seven were also included in the FOURTH FOLIO, but of them only *Pericles* is judged to be the work of Shakespeare. Four other plays that were entered in the STATIONERS' REGISTER in the seventeenth century listed Shakespeare as either an author or coauthor: *The Two Noble Kinsmen* (1634), *Cardenio* (1653), *Henry I* and *Henry II* (1653), and *The Birth of Merlin* (1662); only *The Two Noble Kinsmen* is thought to be, at least in part, written by Shakespeare, although *Cardenio*—whose text is lost—may also have been by him. Scholars have judged that there is strong internal evidence indicating Shakespeare's hand in two other works, *Sir Thomas More* and *Edward III.* Among other titles that have been ascribed to Shakespeare but are generally regarded as spurious are: *The Troublesome Reign of King John, Arden of Feversham, Fair Em, The Merry Devil of Edmonton, Mucedorus, The Second Maiden's Tragedy,* and *Edmund Ironside.*

ASSEMBLED TEXTS: The theory of assembled texts, first proposed by Edmond Malone in the eighteenth century and later popularized by John Dover Wilson, maintains that some of the plays in the FIRST FOLIO were reconstructed for the COMPOSITOR by integrating each actor's part with the plot or abstract of the play. According to Dover Wilson, this reconstruction was done only for those plays which had not been previously published in QUARTO editions and which had no company PROMPT-BOOKS in existence, a list he limits to three of Shakespeare's works: *The Two Gentlemen of Verona, The Merry Wives of Windsor,* and *The Winter's Tale.*

BAD QUARTOS: A name attributed to a group of early editions of Shakespeare's plays which, because of irregularities, omissions, misspellings, and interpolations not found in later QUARTO or FOLIO versions of the same plays, are considered unauthorized publications of Shakespeare's work. The term was first used by the twentieth-century bibliographical scholar A. W. Pollard and has been applied to as many as ten plays: The First Quartos of *Romeo and Juliet, Hamlet, Henry V,* and *The Merry Wives of Windsor; The First Part of the Contention betwixt the two famous Houses of Yorke and Lancaster* and *The True Tragedy of Richard Duke of Yorke,* originally thought to have been sources for Shakespeare's *2* and *3 Henry VI,* but now generally regarded as bad quartos of those plays; the so-called "Pied Bull" quarto of *King Lear;* the 1609 edition of *Pericles; The Troublesome Reign of King John,* believed to be a bad quarto of *King John,* and *The Taming of a Shrew,* which some critics contend is a bad quarto of Shakespeare's Shrew drama. The primary distinction of the bad quartos is the high degree of TEXTUAL CORRUPTION apparent in the texts, a fact scholars have attributed to either one of two theories: some have argued that each quarto was composed from a stenographer's report, in which an agent for the printer was employed to surreptitiously transcribe the play during a performance; others have held the more popular explanation that the questionable texts were based on MEMORIAL RECONSTRUCTIONS by one or more actors who had performed in the plays.

BANDELLO, MATTEO: (b. 1480? - d. 1561) Italian novelist and poet who was also a churchman, diplomat, and soldier. His literary reputation is principally based on the *Novelle,* a collection of 214 tragic, romantic, and historical tales derived from a variety of material from antiquity to the Renaissance. Many of the stories in the *Novelle* are coarse and lewd in their presentation of love, reflecting Bandello's secular interests rather than his clerical role. Together with the dedications to friends and patrons that accompany the individual stories, the *Novelle* conveys a vivid sense of historical events and personalities of the Renaissance. Several translations and adaptations appeared in the third quarter of the sixteenth century, most notably in French by Francois Belleforest and Pierre Boaistuau and in English by William Painter and Geoffrey Fenton.

BLACKFRIARS THEATRE: The Blackfriars Theatre, so named because it was located in the London precinct of Blackfriars, was originally part of a large monastary leased to Richard Farrant, Master of the Children of Windsor, in 1576 for the purpose of staging children's plays. It was acquired in 1596 by James Burbage, who tried to convert the property into a professional theater, but was thwarted in his attempt by surrounding residents. After Burbage died, the Blackfriars was taken over by his son, Richard, who circumvented the objections of his neighbors and, emulating the tactics of Farrant's children's company, staged both children's and adult plays under the guise of a private house, rather than a public theater. This arrangement lasted for five years until, in 1605, the adult company was suspended by King James I for its performance of the satire *Eastward Ho!* Shortly thereafter, the children's company was also suppressed for performing George Chapman's *Conspiracy and Tragedy of Charles Duke of Byron.* In 1608, Burbage organized a new group of directors consisting of his brother Cuthbert and several leading players of the KING'S MEN, including Shakespeare, John Heminge, Henry Condell, and William Sly. These "housekeepers," as they were called, for they shared no profits accruing to the actors, arranged to have the Blackfriars used by the King's Men alternately with the GLOBE THEATRE, an arrangement that lasted from the autumn of 1609 to 1642. Because it was a private house, and therefore smaller than the public theaters of London at that time, the Blackfriars set a higher price for tickets and, as such, attracted a sophisticated and aristocratic audience. Also, through its years of operation as a children's theater, the Blackfriars developed a certain taste in its patrons—one which appreciated music, dance, and masque in a dramatic piece, as well as elements of suspense, reconciliation, and rebirth. Many critics attribute the nature of Shakespeare's final romances to the possibility that he wrote the plays with this new audience foremost in mind.

BOOKKEEPER: Also considered the bookholder or prompter, the bookkeeper was a member of an Elizabethan acting company who maintained custody of the PROMPT-BOOKS, or texts of the plays. Many scholars believe that the bookkeeper also acted as the prompter during any performances, much as a stage manager would do today; however, other literary historians claim that another official satisfied this function. In addition to the above duties, the bookkeeper obtained a license for each play, deleted from the dramatist's manuscript anything offensive before it was submitted to the government censor, assembled copies of the players' individual parts from the company prompt-book, and drew up the "plot" of each work, that is, an abstract of the action of the play emphasizing stage directions.

COMPOSITOR: The name given to the typesetter in a printing shop. Since the growth of textual criticism in modern Shakespearean scholarship, the habits and idiosyncrasies of the individual compositors of Shakespeare's plays have attracted extensive study, particularly with respect to those works that demonstrate substantial evidence of TEXTUAL CORRUPTION. Elizabethan compositors set their type by hand, one letter at a time, a practice that made it difficult to sustain a sense of the text and which often resulted in a number of meaningless passages in books. Also, the lack of uniform spelling rules prior to the eighteenth century meant that each compositor was free to spell a given word according to his personal predilection. Because of this, scholars have been able to identify an individual compositor's share of a printed text by isolating his spelling habits and idiosyncrasies.

EMENDATION: A term often used in textual criticism, emendation is a conjectural correction of a word or phrase in a Shakespearean text proposed by an editor in an effort to restore a line's original meaning. Because many of Shakespeare's plays were carelessly printed, there exist a large number of errors in the early editions which textual scholars through the centuries have tried to correct. Some of the errors—those based on obvious misprints—have been easily emended, but other more formidable TEXTUAL CORRUPTIONS remain open to dispute and have solicited a variety of corrections. Perhaps the two most famous of these are the lines in *Henry V* (II. iii. 16-17) and *Hamlet* (I. ii. 129).

FAIR COPY: A term often applied by Elizabethan writers and theater professionals to describe the corrected copy of an author's manuscript submitted to an acting company. According to available evidence, a dramatist would presumably produce a rough copy of a play, also known as the author's FOUL PAPERS, which would be corrected and revised either by himself or by a professional scribe at a later date. Eventually, the fair copy of a play would be modified by a BOOKKEEPER or prompter to include notes for properties, stage directions, and so on, and then be transcribed into the company's PROMPT-BOOK.

FIRST FOLIO: The earliest collected edition of Shakespeare's plays, edited by his fellow-actors John Heminge and Henry Condell and published near the end of 1623. The First Folio contains thirty-six plays, exactly half of which had never been previously published. Although this edition is considered authoritative for a number of Shakespeare's plays, recent textual scholarship tends to undermine this authority in calling for a broader consideration of all previous versions of a Shakespearean drama in conjunction with the Folio text.

FOLIO: The name given to a book made up of sheets folded once to form two leaves of equal size, or four pages, typically 11 to 16 inches in height and 8 to 11 inches in width.

FOUL PAPERS: The term given to an author's original, uncorrected manuscript, containing the primary text of a play with the author's insertions and deletions. Presumably, the foul papers would be transcribed onto clean sheets for the use of the acting company which had purchased the play; this transcribed and corrected manuscript was called a FAIR COPY. Available evidence indicates that some of Shakespeare's early QUARTOS were printed directly from his foul papers, a circumstance which would, if true, explain the frequent errors and inconsistencies in these texts. Among the quartos alleged to be derived from Shakespeare's foul papers are the First Quartos of *Much Ado about Nothing, A Midsummer Night's Dream, Love's Labour's Lost, Richard II,* and *1* and *2 Henry IV;* among the FIRST FOLIO editions are *The Comedy of Errors, The Taming of the Shrew,* and *Coriolanus.*

FOURTH FOLIO: The fourth collected edition of Shakespeare's plays, published in 1685. This, the last of the FOLIO editions of Shakespeare's dramas, included a notable amount of TEXTUAL CORRUPTION and modernization—751 editorial changes in all, most designed to make the text easier to read.

GLOBE THEATRE: Constructed in 1599 on Bankside across the Thames from the City of London, the Globe was destroyed by fire in 1613, rebuilt the following year, and finally razed in 1644. Accounts of the fire indicate that it was built of timber with a thatched roof, and sixteenth-century maps of Bankside show it was a polygonal building, but no other evidence exists describing its structure and design. From what is known of similar public theaters of the day, such as the Fortune and the Swan, it is conjectured that the Globe contained a three-tiered gallery along its interior perimeter, that a roof extended over a portion of the three-storied stage and galleries, and that the lowest level of the stage was in the form of an apron extending out among the audience in the yard. Further, there is speculation that the Globe probably included a tiring room or backstage space, that the first two stories contained inner stages that were curtained and recessed, that the third story sometimes served as a musicians' gallery, and that beneath the flat roof, which was also known as "the heavens," machinery was stored for raising and lowering theatrical apparatus. It is generally believed that the interior of the Globe was circular and that it could accommodate an audience of approximately two thousand people, both in its three galleries and the yard. The theater was used solely by the LORD CHAMBERLAIN'S MEN, later known as the KING'S MEN, who performed there throughout the year until 1609, when the company alternated performances at the fully-enclosed BLACKFRIARS THEATRE in months of inclement weather.

HALL (or HALLE), EDWARD: (b. 1498? - d. 1547) English historian whose *The Union of the Noble and Illustre Famelies of Lancastre and York* (1542; enlarged in 1548 and 1550) chronicles the period from the death of Richard II through the reign of Henry VIII. Morally didactic in his approach, Hall shaped his material to demonstrate the disasters that ensue from civil wars and insurrection against monarchs. He traced through the dynastic conflicts during the reigns of Henry VI and Richard III a pattern of cause and effect in which a long chain of crimes and divine retribution was ended by the accession of Henry VII to the English throne. Hall's eye-witness account of the pageantry and festivities of the court of Henry VIII is remarkable for its vivacity and embellished language. His heavy bias on the side of Protestantism and defense of Henry VIII's actions against the Roman Church led to the prohibition of his work by Queen Mary in 1555, but his interpretation of the War of the Roses was adopted by all subsequent Tudor historians. Hall's influence on Shakespeare is most evident in the English history plays.

HOLINSHED, RAPHAEL: (d. 1580?) English writer and editor whose *Chronicles of England, Scotlande, and Irelande* (1577; enlarged in 1587) traced the legends and history of Britain from Noah and the flood to the mid-sixteenth century. The *Chronicles* reveal a Protestant bias and depict the history of the British monarchy in terms of the "Tudor myth," which claimed that Henry

IV's usurpation of the crown from Richard II set off a chain of disasters and civil strife which culminated in the reign of Henry VI and continued until the accession to the throne of Henry VII, who, through his marriage to Elizabeth of York, united the two feuding houses of Lancaster and York and brought harmony and peace to England. Holinshed was the principal author of the *Chronicles,* being responsible for the "Historie of England," but he collaborated with William Harrison—who wrote the "Description of England," a vivid account of six-teenth-century customs and daily life—and Richard Stanyhurst and Edward Campion, who together wrote the "Description of Ireland." "The History and Description of Scotland" and the "History of Ireland" were translations or adaptations of the work of earlier historians and writers. The *Chronicles* were immediately successful, in part because of the easily accessible style in which they were composed and because their patriotic celebration of British history was compatible with the rise of nationalistic fervor in Elizabethan England. As in the case of EDWARD HALL, Holinshed's influence on Shakespeare is most evident in the English history plays.

INNS OF COURT: Four colleges of law located in the City of London—Gray's Inn, the Middle Temple, the Inner Temple, and Lincoln's Inn. In the sixteenth and seventeenth centuries, the Inns were not only academic institutions, but were also regarded as finishing schools for gentlemen, providing their students with instruction in music, dance, and other social accomplishments. Interest in the drama·ran high in these communities; in addition to producing their own plays, masques, and revels, members would occasionally employ professional acting companies, such as the LORD CHAMBERLAIN'S MEN and the KING'S MEN, for private performances at the Inns. Existing evidence indicates that at least two of Shakespeare's plays were first performed at the Inns: *The Comedy of Errors* and *Twelfth Night.*

KING'S MEN: An acting company formerly known as the LORD CHAMBERLAIN'S MEN. On May 19, 1603, shortly after his accession to the English throne, James I granted the company a royal patent, and its name was altered to reflect the King's direct patronage. At that date, members who shared in the profits of the company included Shakespeare, Richard Burbage, John Heminge, Henry Condell, Augustine Phillips, William Sly, and Robert Armin. Records of the Court indicate that this was the most favored acting company in the Jacobean era, averaging a dozen performances there each year during that period. In addition to public performances at the GLOBE THEATRE in the spring and autumn, the King's Men played at the private BLACKFRIARS THEATRE in winter and for evening performances. Because of the recurring plague in London from 1603 onward, theatrical companies like the King's Men spent the summer months touring and giving performances in the provinces. Besides the work of Shakespeare, the King's Men's repertoire included plays by Ben Jonson, Francis Beaumont and John Fletcher, Thomas Dekker, and Cyril Tourneur. The company continued to flourish until 1642, when by Act of Parliament all dramatic performances were suppressed.

LORD ADMIRAL'S MEN: An acting company formed in 1576-77 under the patronage of Charles Howard, Earl of Nottingham. From its inception to 1585 the company was known as the Lord Howard's Men, from 1585 to 1603 as the Lord Admiral's Men, from 1604 to 1612 as Prince Henry's Men, and from 1613 to 1625 as the Palsgrave's Men. They were the principal rivals of the LORD CHAMBERLAIN'S MEN; occasionally, from 1594 to 1612, these two troupes were the only companies authorized to perform in London. The company's chief player was Edward Alleyn, an actor of comparable distinction with Richard Burbage of the Lord Chamberlain's Men. From 1591 the company performed at the ROSE THEATRE, moving to the Fortune Theatre in 1600. The detailed financial records of Philip Henslowe, who acted as the company's landlord and financier from 1594 until his death in 1616, indicate that an extensive list of dramatists wrote for the troupe throughout its existence, including Christopher Marlowe, Ben Jonson,

George Chapman, Anthony Munday, Henry Chettle, Michael Drayton, Thomas Dekker, and William Rowley.

LORD CHAMBERLAIN'S MEN: An acting company formed in 1594 under the patronage of Henry Carey, Lord Hunsdon, who was the Queen's Chamberlain from 1585 until his death in 1596. From 1596 to 1597, the company's benefactor was Lord Hunsdon's son, George Carey, and they were known as Hunsdon's Men until the younger Carey was appointed to his late father's office, when the troupe once again became officially the Lord Chamberlain's Men. The members of the company included Shakespeare, Will Kempe—the famous 'clown' and the most popular actor of his time—, Richard Burbage—the renowned tragedian—, and John Heminge, who served as business manager for the company. In 1594 they began performing at the Theatre and the Cross Key's Inn, moving to the Swan on Bankside in 1596 when the City Corporation banned the public presentation of plays within the limits of the City of London. In 1599 some members of the company financed the building of the GLOBE THEATRE and thus the majority became ''sharers,'' not only in the actors' portion of the profits, but in the theatre owners' allotment as well. This economic independence was an important element in the unusual stability of their association. They became the foremost London company, performing at Court on thirty-two occasions between 1594 and 1603, whereas their chief rivals, the LORD ADMIRAL'S MEN, made twenty appearances at Court during that period. No detailed records exist of the plays that were in their repertoire. Ben Jonson wrote several of his dramas for the Lord Chamberlain's Men, but the company's success is largely attributable to the fact that, after joining them in 1594, Shakespeare wrote for no other company.

MEMORIAL RECONSTRUCTION: One hypothesis used to explain the texts of the so-called BAD-QUARTOS. Scholars have theorized that one or more actors who had appeared in a Shakespearean play attempted to reconstruct from personal memory the text of that drama. Inevitably, there would be lapses of recall with resultant errors and deviations from the original play. Characteristics of these corrupt ''reported texts'' include the transposition of phrases or entire speeches, the substitution of new language, omission of dramatically significant material, and abridgements of extended passages. It has been speculated that memorial reconstructions were produced by companies touring the provinces whose PROMPT-BOOKS remained in London, or by actors who sold the pirated versions to printers. W. W. Greg, in his examination of the bad quarto of *The Merry Wives of Windsor,* was the first scholar to employ the term.

MERES, FRANCIS: (b. 1565 - d. 1647) English cleric and schoolmaster whose *Palladis Tamia, Wit's Treasury* (1598) has played a valuable role in determining the dates of several of Shakespeare's plays and poems. The work is a collection of observations and commentary on a wide range of subjects, including religion, moral philosophy, and the arts. In a section entitled ''A Comparative discourse on our English Poets with the Greeke, Latine, and Italian Poets,'' Meres compared Shakespeare's work favorably with that of OVID, PLAUTUS, and SENECA and listed the titles of six of his tragedies, six comedies, and two poems, thus establishing that these works were composed no later than 1598. Meres also praised Shakespeare as ''the most excellent'' of contemporary writers for the stage and remarked that, in addition to his published poetry, he had written some ''sugred sonnets'' which were circulated among a group of his ''private friends.''

MIRROR FOR MAGISTRATES, A: A collection of dramatic monologues in which the ghosts of eminent historical figures lament the sins or fatal flaws that led to their downfalls. Individually and collectively, the stories depict the evils of rebellion against divinely constituted authority, the obligation of rulers to God and their subjects, and the inconstancy of Fortune's favor. William

Baldwin edited the first edition (1559) and wrote many of the tales, with the collaboration of George Ferrers and six other authors. Subsequently, six editions appeared by 1610, in which a score of contributors presented the first-person narrative complaints of some one hundred heroic personages, from King Albanact of Scotland to Cardinal Wolsey and Queen Elizabeth. The first edition to include Thomas Sackville's *Induction* (1563) is the most notable; Sackville's description of the poet's descent into hell and his encounters with allegorical figures, such as Remorse, Revenge, Famine, and War, is generally considered the most poetically meritorious work in the collection. With respect to Shakespeare, scholars claim that elements from *A Mirror for Magistrates* are most apparent in the history plays on the two Richards and on Henry IV and Henry VI.

OCTAVO: The term applied to a book made up of sheets of paper folded three times to form eight leaves of equal size, or sixteen pages. The dimensions of a folded octavo page may range from 6 to 11 inches in height and 4 to 7½ inches in width.

OVID [PUBLIUS OVIDIUS NASO]: (b. 43 B.C. - d. 18 A.D.) Roman poet who was extremely popular during his lifetime and who greatly affected the subsequent development of Latin poetry; he also deeply influenced European art and literature. Ovid's erotic poetry is molded in elegaic couplets, a highly artificial form which he reshaped by means of a graceful and fluent style. These erotic poems—*Amores, Heroides, Ars amatoria,* and *Remedia amoris*—are concerned with love and amorous intrigue, depicting these themes in an amoral fashion that some critics have considered licentious. Ovid's *Metamorphoses,* written in rapidly flowing hexameters, presents some 250 stories from Greek and Roman legends that depict various kinds of transformations, from the tale of primeval chaos to the apotheosis of Julius Caesar into a celestial body. *Metamorphoses* is a superbly unified work, demonstrating Ovid's supreme skills in narration and description and his ingenuity in linking a wide variety of sources into a masterly presentation of classical myth. His brilliance of invention, fluency of style, and vivid descriptions were highly praised in the Renaissance, and familiarity with his work was considered an essential part of a formal education. Ovid has been cited as a source for many of Shakespeare's plays, including *The Merry Wives of Windsor, A Midsummer Night's Dream, The Tempest, Titus Andronicus, Troilus and Cressida,* and *The Winter's Tale.*

PLAUTUS, TITUS MACCIUS: (b. 254? - d. 184 B.C.) The most prominent Roman dramatist of the Republic and early Empire. The esteem and unrivaled popularity he earned from his contemporaries have been ratified by scholars and dramatists of the past five hundred years. Many playwrights from the sixteenth to the twentieth century have chosen his works, particularly *Amphitruo, Aulularia, Captivi, Menaechmi, Miles Gloriosus, Mostellaria,* and *Trinummus,* as models for their own. Plautus adapted characters, plots, and settings from Greek drama, combined these with elements from Roman farce and satire, and introduced into his plays incongruous contemporary allusions, plays upon words, and colloquial and newly coined language. His dramatic style is further characterized by extensive use of song and music, alliteration and assonance, and variations in metrical language to emphasize differences in character and mood. His employment of stock character types, the intrigues and confusions of his plots, and the exuberance and vigor of his comic spirit were especially celebrated by his English Renaissance audience. The plays of Shakespeare that are most indebted to Plautus include *The Comedy of Errors, The Taming of the Shrew, The Merry Wives of Windsor, The Two Gentlemen of Verona, Romeo and Juliet,* and *All's Well That Ends Well.* His influence can also be noted in such Shakespearean characters as Don Armado (*Love's Labour's Lost*), Parolles (*All's Well That Ends Well*), and Falstaff (*Henry IV* and *The Merry Wives of Windsor*).

PLUTARCH: (b. 46? - d. 120? A.D.) Greek biographer and essayist whose work constitutes a faithful record of the historical tradition, moral views, and ethical judgments of second century A.C.

Graeco-Roman culture. His *Parallel Lives*—translated into English by Sir Thomas North and published in 1579 as *The Lives of the Noble Grecianes and Romans compared together*—was one of the most widely read works of antiquity from the sixteenth to the nineteenth century. In this work, Plutarch was principally concerned with portraying the personal character and individual actions of the statesmen, soldiers, legislators, and orators who were his subjects, and through his warm and lively style with instructing as well as entertaining his readers. His portrayal of these classical figures as exemplars of virtue or vice and his emphasis on the successive turns of Fortune's wheel in the lives of great men were in close harmony with the Elizabethan worldview. His miscellaneous writings on religion, ethics, literature, science, and politics, collected under the general title of *Moralia,* were important models for sixteenth- and seventeenth-century essayists. Plutarch is considered a major source for Shakespeare's *Julius Caesar, Antony and Cleopatra,* and *Coriolanus,* and a minor source for *A Midsummer Night's Dream* and *Timon of Athens.*

PRINTER'S COPY: The manuscript or printed text of a work which the compositor uses to set type pages. The nature of the copy available to the early printers of Shakespeare's plays is important in assessing how closely these editions adhere to the original writings. Bibliographical scholars have identified a number of forms available to printers in Shakespeare's time: the author's FOUL PAPERS; a FAIR COPY prepared either by the author or a scribe; partially annotated foul papers or a fair copy that included prompt notes; private copies, prepared by a scribe for an individual outside the acting company; the company's PROMPT-BOOK; scribal transcripts of a prompt-book; a stenographer's report made by someone who had attended an actual performance; earlier printed editions of the work, with or without additional insertions provided by the author, a scribe, or the preparer of a prompt-book; a transcript of a MEMORIAL RECONSTRUCTION of the work; and an ASSEMBLED TEXT.

PROMPT-BOOK: Acting version of a play, usually transcribed from the playwright's FOUL PAPERS by a scribe or the dramatist himself. This copy, or "book," was then presented to the Master of the Revels, the official censor and authorizer of plays. Upon approving its contents, he would license the play for performance and endorse the text as the "allowed book" of the play. A prompt-book represents an alteration or modification of the dramatist's original manuscript. It generally contains detailed stage directions, including cues for music, off-stage noises, and the entries and exits of principal characters, indications of stage properties to be used, and other annotations to assist the prompter during an actual performance. The prompt-book version was frequently shorter than the original manuscript, for cuts would be made in terms of minor characters or dramatic incidents to suit the resources of the acting company. Printed editions of plays were sometimes based on prompt-books.

QUARTO: The term applies to a book made up of sheets of paper folded twice to form four leaves of equal size, or eight pages. A quarto page may range in size from 8½ inches to 12½ inches in height and 6¾ to 10 inches in width.

ROSE THEATRE: Built in 1587 by Philip Henslowe, the Rose was constructed of timber on a brick foundation, with exterior walls of lath and plaster and a roof of thatch. Its location on Bankside—across the Thames River from the City of London—established this area as a new site for public theaters. Its circular design included a yard, galleries, a tiring house, and "heavens." A half-dozen acting companies played there, the most important being the LORD ADMIRAL'S MEN, the chief rival to the LORD CHAMBERLAIN'S MEN, who performed at the Rose from 1594 to 1600, when they moved to the new Fortune Theatre constructed by Henslowe in Finsbury, north of the City of London. Among the dramatists employed by Henslowe at the Rose were Thomas Kyd, Christopher Marlowe, Shakespeare, Robert Greene, Ben Jonson, Michael Drayton, George Chapman, Thomas Dekker, and John Webster. The building was razed in 1606.

SECOND FOLIO: The second collected edition of Shakespeare's plays, published in 1632. While it is essentially a reprint of the FIRST FOLIO, more than fifteen hundred changes were made to modernize spelling and to correct stage directions and proper names.

SENECA, LUCIUS ANNAEUS: (b. 4? B.C. - d. 65 A.D.) Roman philosopher, statesman, dramatist, and orator who was one of the major writers of the first century A.D. and who had a profound influence on Latin and European literature. His philosophical essays castigating vice and teaching Stoic resignation were esteemed by the medieval Latin Church, whose members regarded him as a great moral teacher. His nine tragedies—*Hercules Furens, Thyestes, Phoenissae, Phaedra, Oedipus, Troades, Medea, Agamemnon,* and *Hercules Oetaeus*—were translated into English in 1581 and exerted a strong influence over sixteenth-century English dramatists. Seneca's plays were composed for reading or reciting rather than for performing on the stage, and they evince little attention to character or motive. Written in a declamatory rhetorical style, their function was to instruct on the disastrous consequences of uncontrolled passion and political tyranny. Distinctive features of Senecan tragedy include sensationalism and intense emotionalism, the depiction of wicked acts and retribution, adultery and unnatural sexuality, murder and revenge, and the representation of supernatural beings. Shakespeare's use of Seneca can be discerned most readily in such plays as *King John,* the histories from *Henry VI* to *Richard III, Antony and Cleopatra, Titus Andronicus, Julius Caesar, Hamlet,* and *Macbeth.*

STATIONERS' REGISTER: A ledger book in which were entered the titles of works to be printed and published. The Register was maintained by the Stationers' Company, an association of those who manufactured and those who sold books. In Tudor England, the Company had a virtual monopoly—aside from the university presses—on printing works written throughout the country. Having obtained a license authorizing the printing of a work, a member of the Company would pay a fee to enter the book in the Register, thereby securing the sole right to print or sell that book. Many registered texts were acquired by questionable means and many plays were published whose titles were not entered in the records of the Company. However, the Stationers' Register is one of the most important documents for scholars investigating the literature of that period.

TEXTUAL CORRUPTION: A phrase signifying the alterations that may occur as an author's original text is transmitted through the subsequent stages of preparation for performance and printing. In cases where the PRINTER'S COPY was not an author's FAIR COPY, the text may contain unintelligible language, mislineations, omissions, repetitious lines, transposed verse and prose speeches, inaccurate speech headings, and defective rhymes. Through their investigation of the nature of the copy from which a COMPOSITOR set his type, textual scholars attempt to restore the text and construct a version that is closest to the author's original manuscript.

THIRD FOLIO: The third collected edition of Shakespeare's plays, published in 1663. Essentially a reprint of the SECOND FOLIO, it contains some corrections to that text and some errors not found in earlier editions. The Third Folio was reprinted in 1664 and included ''seven Playes, never before Printed in Folio.'' One of these seven—*Pericles*—has been accepted as Shakespeare's work, but the other six are considered apocryphal (see APOCRYPHA).

VARIORUM: An edition of a literary work which includes notes and commentary by previous editors and scholars. The First Variorum of Shakespeare's works was published in 1803. Edited by Isaac Reed, it was based on George Steevens's four eighteenth-century editions and includes extensive material from Samuel Johnson's edition of 1765, together with essays by Edmund Malone, George Chalmers, and Richard Farmer. The Second Variorum is a reprint of the First, and it was published in 1813. The Third Variorum is frequently referred to as the Boswell-Malone edition. Containing prefaces from most of the eighteenth-century editions of Shakespeare's work, as well as the poems and sonnets, which Steevens and Reed omitted, the Third Variorum was published in 1821. Edited by James Boswell the younger and based on the scholarship of Malone, it includes such a wealth of material that it is generally regarded as the most important complete edition of the works of Shakespeare. The Fourth Variorum, known as the "New Variorum," was begun by Horace Howard Furness in 1871. Upon his death, his son, Horace Howard Furness, Jr., assumed the editorship, and subsequently—in 1936—a committee of the Modern Language Association of America took on the editorship. The Fourth Variorum is a vast work, containing annotations, textual notes, and excerpts from eminent commentators throughout the history of Shakespearean criticism.

Cumulative Index to Topics

[The Cumulative Index to Topics identifies the principal topics of debate in the criticism of each play and non-dramatic poem. The topics are arranged alphabetically; page references indicate the beginning page number of those excerpts offering innovative or substantial commentary on that topic.]

208

nature of love for Antony: pp. 25, 27, 37, 39, 48, 52, 53, 62, 67, 71, 76, 85, 100, 125, 131, 133, 136, 142, 151, 161, 163, 165, 180, 192

as a subverter of social order: pp. 146, 165

as a superhuman figure: pp. 37, 51, 71, 92, 94, 178, 192

as a tragic heroine: pp. 53, 120, 151, 192, 208

as a voluptuary or courtesan: pp. 21, 22, 25, 41, 43, 52, 53, 62, 64, 67, 76, 146, 161

variety and/or magnetism: pp. 24, 38, 40, 43, 48, 53, 76, 104, 115, 155

comic or realistic elements: pp. 52, 85, 104, 125, 131, 151, 192, 202, 219

contemptus mundi, theme of: pp. 85, 133

Dryden's All for Love, compared with: pp. 20, 21

Egyptian and Roman values, conflict between: pp. 31, 33, 43, 53, 104, 111, 115, 125, 142, 155, 159, 178, 181, 211, 219

Enobarbus: pp. 22, 23, 27, 43, 94, 120, 142

irony or paradox: pp. 53, 136, 146, 151, 159, 161, 189, 192, 211, 224

language and imagery: pp. 21, 25, 39, 64, 80, 85, 92, 94, 100, 104, 142, 146, 155, 159, 161, 165, 189, 192, 202, 211

love or passion, theme of: pp. 51, 64, 71, 80, 85, 100, 115, 159, 165, 180

Octavius: pp. 22, 24, 31, 38, 43, 53, 62, 107, 125, 146, 178, 181, 219

political and social disintegration, theme of: pp. 31, 80, 146

reason and imagination or passion, theme of: pp. 107, 115, 142, 197, 228

reconciliation or regeneration, theme of: pp. 100, 103, 125, 131, 159, 181

religious or supernatural elements: pp. 53, 94, 111, 115, 178, 192, 224

Roman imperialism and political conflict: pp. 43, 53, 60, 71, 80, 100, 107, 111, 180, 197, 219

royalty, theme of: p. 94

Seleucus episode (Act V, Scene ii): pp. 39, 41, 62, 133, 140, 151

Shakespeare's major tragedies, compared with: pp. 25, 53, 60, 71, 120, 181, 189, 202

Shakespeare's moral judgment of the protagonists, question of: pp. 33, 37, 38, 41, 48, 51, 64, 76, 111, 125, 136, 140, 146, 163, 175, 189, 202, 211, 228

sources: pp. 20, 39

unity and/or structure: pp. 20, 21, 22, 24, 25, 32, 33, 39, 43, 53, 60, 67, 111, 125, 146, 151, 165, 208, 211, 219

wheel of fortune, motif of: pp. 25, 178

As You Like It (Vol. 5)

autobiographical elements: pp. 25, 35, 43, 50, 55, 61

characterization: pp. 19, 24, 25, 36, 39, 54, 82, 86, 116, 148

Christian elements: pp. 39, 98, 162

dramatic shortcomings: pp. 19, 42, 52, 61, 65

duration of time: pp. 44, 45

Forest of Arden

as a "bitter" Arcadia: pp. 98, 118, 162

contrast with Duke Frederick's court: pp. 46, 102, 103, 112, 130, 156

pastoral elements: pp. 18, 20, 24, 32, 35, 47, 50, 54, 55, 57, 60, 77, 128, 135, 156

as a patriarchal society: p. 168

as a source of self-knowledge or reconciliation: pp. 98, 102, 103, 128, 130, 135, 148, 158, 162

as a timeless, mythical world: pp. 112, 130, 141

genre, question of: pp. 46, 55, 79

the Hymen episode: pp. 61, 116, 130

irony: pp. 30, 32, 154

Jaques

as a conventional malcontent: pp. 59, 70, 84

melancholy: pp. 20, 28, 32, 36, 39, 43, 50, 59, 63, 68, 77, 82, 86, 135

relation to love-theme: p. 103

relation to pastoral convention: pp. 61, 63, 65, 79, 93, 98, 114, 118

relation to Shakespeare: pp. 35, 50, 154

Seven Ages of Man speech (II. vii. 139-66): pp. 28, 52, 156

as a superficial critic: pp. 28, 30, 43, 54, 55, 63, 65, 68, 75, 77, 82, 86, 88, 98, 138

juxtaposition of opposing perspectives: pp. 86, 93, 98, 141

language and imagery: pp. 19, 21, 35, 52, 75, 82, 92, 138

love, theme of: pp. 24, 44, 46, 57, 79, 88, 103, 116, 122, 138, 141, 162

metadramatic elements: pp. 128, 130, 146

Neoclassical rules: pp. 19, 20

Orlando

hardships as a younger brother: pp. 66, 158

as an ideal man: pp. 32, 36, 39, 162

primogeniture, theme of: pp. 66, 158

psychoanalytic assessment: pp. 146, 158

relation of art and nature, theme of: pp. 128, 130, 148

relation to Elizabethan culture: pp. 21, 59, 66, 68, 70, 158

as a romance: pp. 55, 79

Rosalind

charm: pp. 55, 75

compared to Beatrice in Much Ado about Nothing: pp. 26, 36, 50, 75

disguise, role of: pp. 75, 107, 118, 122, 128, 130, 133, 138, 141, 146, 148, 164, 168

femininity: pp. 26, 36, 52, 75

reconciliation of opposites: pp. 79, 88, 103, 116, 122, 138

relation to love-theme: pp. 79, 88, 103, 116, 122, 138, 141

relation to pastoral convention: pp. 72, 77, 122

rustic characters: pp. 24, 60, 72, 84

as a satire or parody of pastoral conventions: pp. 46, 55, 60, 72, 77, 79, 84, 114, 118, 128, 130, 154

self-control or self-knowledge, theme of: pp. 32, 82, 102, 116, 122, 133, 164

Silvius, Phebe, and Corin

as parodies of pastoral conventions: pp. 54, 57, 72

sources: pp. 18, 32, 54, 59, 66, 84

structure and/or design: pp. 19, 24, 25, 35, 44, 45, 46, 86, 93, 116, 138, 158

time, theme of: pp. 18, 82, 112, 141

Touchstone

callousness: p. 88

as a philosopher-fool: pp. 24, 28, 30, 32, 36, 63, 75, 98

relation to pastoral convention: pp. 54, 61, 63, 72, 75, 77, 79, 84, 86, 93, 98, 114, 118, 135, 138, 166

selflessness: pp. 30, 36, 39, 76

verisimilitude, question of: pp. 18, 23, 28, 30, 32, 39, 125

The Comedy of Errors (Vol. 1)

audience perception: pp. 37, 50, 56

autobiographical elements: pp. 16, 18

characterization: pp. 13, 21, 31, 34, 46, 49, 50, 55, 56

classical influence: pp. 13, 14, 16, 31, 32, 43, 61

comic elements: pp. 43, 46, 55, 56, 59

composition date: pp. 18, 23, 34, 55

dramatic structure: pp. 19, 27, 40, 43, 46, 50

farcical elements: pp. 14, 16, 19, 23, 30, 34, 35, 46, 50, 59, 61

illusion, theme of: pp. 13, 14, 27, 37, 40, 45, 59, 63

language and imagery: pp. 16, 25, 39, 40, 43, 57, 59

mistaken identity, theme of: pp. 13, 14, 27, 37, 40, 45, 49, 55, 57, 61, 63

Plautus's works, compared to: pp. 13, 14, 16, 53, 61

romantic elements: pp. 13, 16, 19, 23, 25, 30, 31, 36, 39, 53

sources: pp. 13, 14, 16, 19, 31, 32, 39

supernatural, role of: pp. 27, 30

tragic elements: pp. 16, 25, 27, 45, 50, 59

Coriolanus (Vol. 9)

Aufidius: pp. 9, 12, 17, 19, 53, 121, 148, 153, 157, 169, 180, 193

butterfly episode (I. iii. 57-69): pp. 19, 45, 62, 65, 73, 100, 125, 153, 157

capitulation scene (Act V, Scene iii): pp. 19, 26, 53, 65, 100, 117, 125, 130, 157, 164, 183

characterization: pp. 9, 11, 12, 15, 78, 84, 130, 148, 193

Cominius's tribute or encomium (II. ii. 82-129): pp. 80, 100. 117, 125, 144, 164, 198

Coriolanus

anger or passion: pp. 19, 26, 45, 80, 92, 157, 164, 177, 189

death scene (Act V, Scene vi): pp. 12, 80, 100, 117, 125, 144, 164, 198

as an epic hero: pp. 130, 164, 177

immaturity or boyishness: pp. 62, 80, 84, 110, 117, 142

inhuman attributes: pp. 65, 73, 139, 157, 164, 169, 189, 198

internal struggle: pp. 31, 43, 45, 53, 72, 117, 121, 130

introspection or self-knowledge, lack of: pp. 53, 80, 84, 112, 117, 130

isolation or autonomy: pp. 53, 65, 142, 144, 153, 157, 164, 180, 183, 189, 198

Topic Index

Topic Index

Cumulative Index to Critics

Abel, Lionel
Hamlet **1:**237

Adams, John F.
All's Well That Ends Well **7:**86

Adams, John Quincy
Othello **4:**408
Romeo and Juliet **5:**426

Adams, Joseph Quincy
The Phoenix and Turtle **10:**16

Adamson, Jane
Othello **4:**591

Addison, Joseph
Hamlet **1:**75
Henry IV, 1 and 2 **1:**287
King Lear **2:**93

Adelman, Janet
Antony and Cleopatra **6:**211
Coriolanus **9:**183

Agate, James
The Two Noble Kinsmen **9:**462

Alden, Raymond Macdonald
Sonnets **10:**247

Alexander, Peter
Henry VIII **2:**43

Allen, Don Cameron
The Rape of Lucrece **10:**89
Venus and Adonis **10:**451

Allen, John A.
A Midsummer Night's Dream **3:**457

Almeida, Barbara Heliodora C. de M. F. de
Troilus and Cressida **3:**604

Altick, Richard D.
Richard II **6:**298

Altieri, Joanne
Henry V **5:**314

Alvarez, A.
The Phoenix and Turtle **10:**31

Amhurst, Nicholas
Henry VIII **2:**15

Anson, John
Julius Caesar **7:**324

Anthony, Earl of Shaftesbury
Hamlet **1:**75

Archer, William
Twelfth Night **1:**558

Arnold, Aerol
Richard III **8:**210

Arthos, John
All's Well That Ends Well **7:**58
Macbeth **3:**250
Othello **4:**541
The Phoenix and Turtle **10:**50
The Two Gentlemen of Verona **6:**532

Auberlen, Eckhard
Henry VIII **2:**78

Auden, W. H.
Henry IV, 1 and 2 **1:**410
Much Ado about Nothing **8:**77
Sonnets **10:**325
Twelfth Night **1:**599

Bacon, Lord Francis
Richard II **6:**250

Bagehot, Walter
Measure for Measure **2:**406

Baildon, H. Bellyse
Titus Andronicus **4:**632

Baker, George Pierce
Romeo and Juliet **5:**448

Baker, Harry T.
Henry IV, 1 and 2 **1:**347

Baldwin, Thomas Whitfield
The Comedy of Errors **1:**21

Barber, C. L.
As You Like It **5:**79
Henry IV, 1 and 2 **1:**414
Love's Labour's Lost **2:**335
The Merchant of Venice **4:**273
A Midsummer Night's Dream **3:**427
Pericles **2:**582
Sonnets **10:**302
Twelfth Night **1:**620
The Winter's Tale **7:**480

Barnet, Sylvan
As You Like It **5:**125
Twelfth Night **1:**588

Barnfield, Richard
Venus and Adonis **10:**410

Barnstorff, D.
Sonnets **10:**190

Barton, Anne
Antony and Cleopatra **6:**208
The Comedy of Errors **1:**61
The Merry Wives of Windsor **5:**400
Twelfth Night **1:**656

Baskervill, Charles Read
The Merchant of Venice **4:**226

Bates, Ronald
The Phoenix and Turtle **10:**27

Bateson, F. W.
Sonnets **10:**277

Battenhouse, Roy W.
Antony and Cleopatra **6:**192
Henry IV, 1 and 2 **1:**434
Henry V **5:**260
Macbeth **3:**269
Measure for Measure **2:**466

Critic Index

Critic Index

Critic Index

Critic Index